WEBSTER'S DICTIONARY

Composite Edition, Especially Compiled for Home, School, and Office Use

Self-Pronouncing—Synonyms and Antonyms—Words Frequently Mispronounced

Based upon the lexicography of

NOAH WEBSTER, LL.D.

and Modern American Authorities

Editor-in-chief,

EDWARD N. TEALL, A.M.

Lexicographer

1989 Edition

PRONUNCIATION

The key to pronunciation in WEBSTER'S NEW CONCISE DICTIONARY (Composite Edition) has been simplified to the utmost. The symbols used do not differ in meaning from those of other dictionaries. The only difference is that there are fewer of them.

Short vowels are not marked, and the difference between stressed and unstressed vowels (that is, between those in accented and unaccented syllables) is not marked, for this distinction takes care of itself in pronunciation; for example, the short unstressed *a* in fi'nal is naturally given its correct value if the first syllable is stressed. Similarly the *a* in afford' is given its correct value as a short unstressed vowel if the last syllable is stressed. The pronunciation of the *e* in nov'el, the two short *i*'s in illu'minate, the second *o* in om'icron and the short *u* in fo'cus is taken care of in the same fashion. The following examples show the difference between stressed and unstressed vowels:

a in *a*bsolute and in *a*bsurd
o in historical and in history
e in *e*ven and in *e*vent
u in m*u*le and in em*u*late

Stress in a sentence makes similar differences, as the student will see by pronouncing these sentences and noting the pronunciation of the vowel in question.

In the word *has*:

He has the book. He has found the book.

In the word *could*:

How could you? I could have gone.

These differences in vowel values are learned by *hearing* English sentences and phrases, not by looking up a single word in the dictionary.

A detailed key to pronunciation follows. A brief key occurs at the bottom of each right-hand page, containing words so chosen and marked as to make constant turning back to the full key unnecessary.

* ENTRIES preceded by a star are words often mispronounced or pronounced in different ways by different authorities.

⁾See Key to Pronunciation on following page.

KEY TO PRONUNCIATION

a
- **ā:** māke, lāte, sāy, abrogate (ab' rō gāt).
- **â:** bâre, pârent, where (hwâr).
- **a:** at, map, fat, afford, elephant, vocal.
- **ä:** färm, fäther, cär, psälm.
- **a̍:** a̍sk, da̍nce, laugh (la̍f).
- **a:** sofa, banana, pajama, Cuba.

c
- **s:** cereal (sē' rē-al).
- **k:** cat (kat), cabbage (kab' ij).

ch
- **ch:** chat, charm, cherub.
- **ch:** loch, ich, Cuchulain.

e
- **ē:** ēqual, feet (fēt), see (sē), mēre, cē' rē al, edition (ē di' shun).
- **e:** let, bend, elect, violent, novel.
- **e:** fingēr, racēr, thē (usually not stressed).

- **f:** fun, phosphorus (fos' fō-rus).

g
- **g:** go, grand.
- **j:** gem (jem), edge (ej).

i
- **ī:** bīte, fīre, mīght.
- **i:** it, pin, him.

- **j:** jelly, jury, judge (juj).

- **k:** cat (kat); quake (kwāk).

- **n:** seance (sā äns).
- **ng:** song, uncle (ung' kl).

o
- **ō:** gō, coat (kōt), vōte, sew (so), sōlarium.
- **ô:** ôrder, all (ôl), hôrse, dôg, gône, lôft, bought (bôt).
- **o:** lot, not, knock, romp, what (hwot), om' i cron.
- **oi:** oil, voice.
- **o͞o:** no͞on, do (do͞o), ro͞ot.
- **oo:** good, foot, could (kood).
- **ou:** out, sound.

s
- **s:** so, sell, silly, ceiling (sēl' ing).
- **sh:** she, nation (nā' shun), sure (sho͞or).
- **z:** is (iz), surprise (sûr prīz'), dogs (dôgz).

th
- **th:** there, breathe.
- **th:** thin, thorough.

u
- **ū:** ūse, mūte, few (fū), execūte.
- **û:** tûrn, her (hûr), cûrse, permanent (usually stressed).
- **u:** up, but, abrupt, under, focus, nation (nā' shun).
- **ü:** menü.

x
- **gs:** exist (egs-ist').
- **ks:** execute (eks' ē cūt).
- **z:** Xenophon (zen-)

- **zh:** usual (ū' zhū al), rouge (ro͞ozh), measure (mezh' ēr).

' : primary accent or stress.

ABBREVIATIONS IN COMMON USE

A. A. A.—Agricultural Adjustment Administration

A1—First Rate (at Lloyd's)

A. B.—Bachelor of Arts; able-bodied seaman

A. C.—Ante Christum (before Christ)

A. D.—Anno Domini

A. D. C.—Aide-de-camp

ad lib.—ad libitum (at discretion)

Advt.—Advertisement

A. E. F.—American Expeditionary Forces

A. F. of L.—American Federation of Labor

A. M.—Ante Meridian (before mid-day); Anno Mundi (in the year of the world); Master of Arts

A. N. A.—Associate National Academician

A. P.—Associated Press

A. R. A.—Associate of the Royal Academy

B. A.—Bachelor of Arts

B. Arch.—Bachelor of Architecture

Bart., Bt.—Baronet

B. C.—Before Christ; British Columbia

B. Litt.—Bachelor of Letters

B. LL.—Bachelor of Laws

B. M. A.—British Medical Association

B. Mus.—Bachelor of Music

Bp.—Bishop

Brig.—Brigade; Brigadier

B. S.—Bachelor of Surgery

B. Sc.—Bachelor of Science

C., Cent.—Centigrade

C. A.—Chartered Accountant

Capt.—Captain

C. B.—Companion of the Bath

C. B. E.—Commander Order of the British Empire

C. E.—Civil Engineer

cf.—Compare

Chem. E.—Chemical Engineer

C. I. O.—Committee for Industrial Organization

C. M. G.—Companion of St. Michael and St. George

C. O.—Commanding Officer

C. O. D.—Cash on Delivery

C. P. A.—Certified Public Accountant

C. V. O.—Commander of the Royal Victorian Order

cwt.—Hundredweight

D. B. E.—Dame Commander Order of the British Empire

D. C. L.—Doctor of Civil Law

D. D.—Doctor of Divinity

D. D. S.—Doctor of Dental Surgery

D. F. C.—Distinguished Flying Cross

D. G.—(Dei Gratia), by the grace of God

Ditto, do.—The same

Dom.—Dominus

dr.—Drachm

D. Sc.—Doctor of Science

D. S. M.—Distinguished Service Medal

D. S. O.—Distinguished Service Order

dwt.—Pennyweight

12mo,—Duodecimo (folded in 12)

e. g.—(L. exempli gratia), for example

F. A. G. S.—Fellow of the American Geographical Society

F. B. A.—Fellow of the British Academy

F. D. I. C.—Federal Deposit Insurance Corporation

F. E. R. A.—Federal Emergency Relief Administration

F. G. S.—Fellow of the Geological Society

F. M.—Field-Marshal

Fo.—Folio (a sheet of paper folded once)

f. o. b.—Free on board

Fr.—French

F. R. A. M.—Fellow of the Royal Academy of Music

F. R. A. S.—Fellow of the Royal Astronomical Society

F. R. C. P.—Fellow of the Royal College of Physicians

F. R. C. S.—Fellow of the Royal College of Surgeons

F. R. G. S.—Fellow of the Royal Geographical Society

F. R. I. B. A.—Fellow of the Royal Institute of British Architects

F. R. S.—Fellow of the Royal Society

F. Z. S.—Fellow of the Zoological Society

G. C. B.—Knight Grand Cross of the Bath

G. C. I. E.—Knight Grand Commander of the Indian Empire

G. C. M. G.—Knight Grand Cross of St. Michael and St. George

G. C. S. I.—Knight Grand Commander of the Star of India

G. C. V. O.—Knight Grand Cross of Royal Victorian Order

H. E.—His Excellency; His Eminence

H. H.—His (or Her) Highness; His Holiness

H. M. S.—His Majesty's Ship

H. O. L. C.—Home Owners Loan Corporation

h. p.—Horse-power

H. Q.—Headquarters

H. R. H.—His (or Her) Royal Highness

H. S. H.—His (or Her) Serene Highness

Ib., Ibid.—Ibidem (in the same place)

i. e.—id est (that is)

ign.—Ignotus (unknown)

I. H. S.—Jesus Hominum Salvator (Jesus the Saviour of Men), more correctly IHS, the first three letters in the name of Jesus in Greek

incog.—Incognito (in secret)

Inst.—Instant; Institute

I O U—I owe you

ital.—Italics

I. W. W.—Industrial Workers of the World

J. P.—Justice of the Peace

K. B. E.—Knight Commander of the British Empire

K. C.—King's Counsel; Knights of Columbus

K. C. B.—Knight Commander of the Bath

K. C. I. E.—Knight Commander of the Indian Empire

ABBREVIATIONS IN COMMON USE

K. C. M. G.—Knight Commander of St. Michael and St. George

K. C. V. O.—Knight Commander of the Royal Victorian Order

K. G.—Knight of the Garter

kil.—Kilometre

kilo.—Kilogramme

K. K. K.—Ku Klux Klan

Kt., Knt.—Knight

Lat.—Latin

lat.—latitude

L. H. D.—(Literarum Humaniorum Doctor) Doctor of Literature

Lit. D.—Doctor of Literature

Litt. D.—Doctor of Letters

LL. B.—Bachelor of Laws

LL. D.—Doctor of Laws

LL. M.—Master of Laws

log.—Logarithm

long.—Longitude

M.—Monsieur; Meridian (noon)

M. A.—Master of Arts

Marq.—Marquis

M. B. A.—Master of Business Administration

M. C.—Military Cross; Member of Congress

M. D.—Doctor of Medicine

mdse.—merchandise

M. E.—Mining Engineer; Mechanical Engineer; Methodist Episcopal

Med.—Medical

Mgr.—Monsignor

Mlle.—Mademoiselle (Miss)

Mme.—Madame

Most Rev.—Most Reverend (of an Archbishop)

M. P.—Member of Parliament

MS., MSS.—Manuscript, Manuscripts

M. Sc.—Master of Science

Mus. B.—Bachelor of Music

Mus. D.—Doctor of Music

N. A.—National Academician

N. B.—Nota Bene, notice

net. nett—(It.) Netto (free from all deductions)

N. L. R. B.—National Labor Relations Board

non seq—Non sequitur (it does not follow)

N. R. A.—National Recovery Administration

obit—obitur (he died)

O. H. M. S.—On His Majesty's Service

oz.—Ounces

8vo—Octavo (folded in eight)

p. c.—per centum (by the hundred); post card

Ph. B.—Bachelor of Philosophy

Ph. D.—Doctor of Philosophy

P. M.—Post Meridiem (after mid-day); Postmaster

P. O.—Post Office; Postal Order

P. P.—Parish Priest

Pp.—Pages

Pro tem.—Pro tempore (for the time being)

Prov.—Provost; Provisional

Prox.—Proximo (next)

P. S.—Postscriptum (postscript) prompt side

pt.—Pint

P. W. A.—Federal Emergency Administration of Public Works

Q. E. D.—Quod erat demonstrandum (which was to be demonstrated), applied to a theorem

Q. E. F.—Quod erat faciendum (which was to be done); applied to a problem

q. v.—quod vide (which see)

R. A.—Royal Academician; Royal Artillery

R. A. F.—Royal Air Force

R. A. S.—Royal Astronomical, or Asiatic, Society

R. B. S.—Royal Society of British Sculptors

R. E.—Royal Engineers

R. F. A.—Royal Field Artillery

R. F. C.—Reconstruction Finance Corporation

R. G. A.—Royal Garrison Artillery

R. H. A.—Royal Horse Artillery

R. H. G.—Royal Horse Guards

R. I.—Royal Institute of Painters in Water Colors

R. I. B. A.—Royal Institute of British Architects

R. I. P.—Requiescat in pace (May he or she rest in peace)

R. M.—Royal Marines; Resident Magistrate

R. N. V. R.—Royal Naval Volunteer Reserve

R. O. T. C.—Reserve Officers Training Corps

R. S. V. P.—Fr. Repondez s'il vous plait (Please answer)

Rt. Hon.—Right Honourable (Member of British Privy Council)

S. A. S.—Fellow of the Society of Antiquaries (U. S.)

Sc. B.—Bachelor of Science

Sc. D.—Doctor of Science

Sc. M.—Master of Science

s. p.—sine prole (without issue)

S. P. C. A.—Society for the Prevention of Cruelty to Animals

S. P. Q. R.—Senatus Populusque Romanus (The Senate and People of Rome)

SS.—Steamship; Saints

St.—Street; Saint

stet.—let it stand

tr.—transpose

T. V. A.—Tennessee Valley Authority

ult.—Ultimo (last)

U. S. P.—United States Pharmacopoeia

v., vid.—Vide (see)

V. C.—Victoria Cross

Vet.—Veterinary

Visc.—Viscount

vis.—videlicet (namely)

Vol.—Volume; Volunteers

vs.—versus (against)

W. P. A.—Works Progress Administration

AN ENGLISH LANGUAGE DICTIONARY

A

A, a (ā) n.; pl. A's, As, a's, as (āz). 1 The first letter of the English alphabet; originally the first letter of the Phoenician alphabet; same as Latin a, Greek a (alpha), Hebrew a (aleph); one of the vowels of the English language. When used as a vowel it is given varying degrees of sound, often indicated by diacritical marks or the phonetic pronunciation of the words in which it occurs. (See KEY TO PRONUNCIATION.) 2 adj. and indef. art. (before words beginning with a consonant): **a** one, any, same, some particular kind of; as, a stone, a dog. **b** each, to, in; as, three times a day. (a, with similar meanings, is changed to an when used before vowels or silent h. See **an.**) **a** prep. in, on, at, to, usually signifying place or condition; as abed (in bed); aboard (on board); afoot; aslant. 3 pfx., signifying action; as, alight (to alight from the train); arise. 4 any object having an A-like shape, such as type. A Roman numeral denoting 50 or 500; with bar (Ā), 5000. In algebra one of the known quantities of an equation. In astronomy one of the bands of the solar spectrum. In chemistry argon. In electricity ampere. In finance denotes the rating of a security, firm or individual. In heraldry argent. In law, reasoning, etc., any one thing or person. In logic a universal affirmative. In medicine (aa), equal parts. In music the 6th note in the diatonic scale of C major, corresponding to la, or the first of the relative minor scale of C. Also, the scale of a composition with A as its keynote. In physics an absolute. **A.** abr. (See List of Abbreviations.)

A1 (ā wun'), adj. 1 of highest quality, grade or degree; first-rate; as, an A1 player, in A1 condition. 2 in shipping registry, the rating of a first-class ship: numerals prefixed to the A indicate iron, steel, or wooden construction, while the 1 denotes first-class equipment.

a' (ā) adv. all. Scot., N. of Eng., and Ir.

aa (ā ä) n. Hawaiian term for rough or broken lava.

Aa (ā), n. a river in Latvia where Russians defeated Germans in 1915; the name of several minor rivers of Europe.

aardvark (ärd' värk), n. a burrowing animal about the size of a pig, native to Africa. Its principal diet is ants which it sucks from nests with its long, slender, slimy tongue. An anteater or ant bear (g. Orycteropus).

Aardvark.

aardwolf (ärd' woolf), n. a hyena-like mammal of South Africa, which feeds upon carrion and insects (g. Proteles cristata).

Aaron (ār' un), n. a masculine name; first high priest of the Jews and brother of Moses.

Aaronic (ā ron' ik), **Aaronical** (i kal), adj. of or pertaining to Aaron, or to one of several high dignitaries of the church.

Aaron's-beard (bērd), n. a low-growing evergreen shrub; a name given to several varieties of plants which bear a bloom resembling a beard.

Aaron's rod (rod), n. name given to several plants like the goldenrod and mullein, that flower on a long stem having a fancied resemblance to a rod; in arch. an ornament resembling a rod, usually with a serpent twined about it, after the fashion of the biblical rod of Aaron.

Ab (ab), n. fifth month of the Hebrew sacred year, and 11th month of the civil year, covering 30 days and corresponding to part of July and August; 12th month of the Syrian year, or last month of summer.

ab (ab), pfx. off, away, apart from; as abnormal; in electricity it denotes an electromagnetic unit, as in abvolt, abampere.

aba (äb' ä), n. 1 a cloth made from camel or goat's hair. 2 a sleeveless garment worn in Arabia and Syria. 3 a nautical instrument used as substitute for sextant, and named after the inventor, Antoine d'Abbadie.

abaca (ä bä kä'), n. Philippine name of a plant and its fiber from which Manila hemp is obtained.

aback (a bak'), adv. backward; pressed back against the mast: taken aback, taken by surprise.

*abacus (ab' a kus), n. a Chinese counting device consisting of beads or balls which slide on wires within a frame; in architecture, a flat block of stone on the top of a column, on which the superstructure rests.

Abacus (1).

abaft (a baft'), adv. and prep. Naut. at, near or toward the stern of a boat; astern; behind.

abalone (ab a lō' ni), n. edible mollusk (g. Haliotis) having an ear-shaped shell from which mother-of-pearl is obtained.

abandon (a ban' dun), n. lack of restraint.

abandon (a ban´ dun), v.t. to give up; to desert; to forsake utterly.

Syn. Abdicate, desert, forego, renounce, surrender. The crew abandoned the sinking ship; a king abdicates his throne; a coward deserts his family; we *forego* pleasures; the monk *renounces* the world; the bereaved often *surrender* to grief.

Ant. Maintain, hold, retain.

abandoned (a ban' dund), *adj.* given up entirely; deserted; also, unrestrained.

Syn. Depraved, discarded, forsaken, uncontrolled. We speak of *depraved* characters; *discarded* ideas; *uncontrolled* laughter.

Ant. Controlled, kept, moderate, scrupulous.

abase (a bās'), *v.t.* to humble or degrade; to dishonor; to reduce.

Syn. Debase, degrade, disgrace, dishonor, mortify, shame. These words are usually applied to persons only. *Debase* and *reduce*, however, have other applications; metal may be *debased;* weight may be *reduced*.

Ant. Advance, dignify, honor, raise.

abash (a bash'), *v.t.* to put to confusion; to make ashamed by consciousness of guilt or error; to overawe.

Syn. Confuse, confound, embarrass.

Ant. Animate, embolden, encourage, exalt, reassure.

abate (a bāt'), *v.t.* to put an end to; to suppress: *v.i.* to decrease; to moderate; to subside.

Syn. Decline, decrease, diminish, lessen, recede, sink, slacken, wane.

Ant. Augment, foment, rage.

abatis (ab' a tis), *n.* in warfare, a fortification made of felled trees with sharpened branches pointing toward the enemy; a similar obstruction composed, in modern military practice, of barbed wire.

abattoir (ab a twär'), *n.* a public slaughterhouse.

abb (ab), *n.* in weaving, the yarn of the warp.

abba (ab' a), *n.* father; a bishop or patriarch of Syriac and Coptic churches.

abbacy (ab' a si), *n.* the office and jurisdiction of an abbot.

abbatial (a bā shal), *adj.* belonging or relating to an abbey or an abbot.

°abbé (a bā'), *n.* an abbot.

abbess (ab' es), *n.* a mother superior.

abbey (ab' i), *n.* [pl. abbeys (-biz)], a monastery or convent; the church connected with a monastery.

abbot (ab' ut), *n.* the head of a monastery.

abbreviate (a brē' vi āt), *v.t.* to shorten, especially words, as we *abbreviate* avenue to ave.

Syn. Reduce, shorten. Distinction is made between abbreviation and contraction of words. Abbreviation is omission of letters at the end of the word; contraction, of letters in the middle, as *coll.* for *college*, *Mr.* for *Mister*.

Ant. Amplify, enlarge, lengthen.

abbreviation (a brē vi ā' shun), *n.* the shortened form of a word.

ABC (ā' bē' sē'). *n.* the essentials or fundamentals of a subject; *pl.* abc's the alphabet as a whole.

abdicate (ab' di kāt), *v.t.* and *v.i.* to renounce, as kingly power; to make a formal surrender or renunciation of authority, privilege, or

responsibility.

°abdomen (ab dō' men), *n.* the part of the body containing the digestive organs and intestines.

abdominal (ab dom' i nal), *adj.* pertaining to the abdomen.

abduce (ab dūs') *v.t.* to draw or wean away from by logic or reasoning.

abduct (ab dukt'), *v.t.* to carry off by stealth or force; to kidnap.

abeam (a bēm'), *adv.* at right angles to the keel of a ship.

abecedarian (ā be se dār' i an), *n.* 1 a learner or teacher of the alphabet; hence, a beginner. *adj.* elementary, rudimentary. 2 nickname given to a member of 16th century German religious sect opposed to learning.

abecedarium (ā be se dār' i um), *n.* [pl. abecedaria] a primer, book of a-b-c's.

abecedary (ā be sē' da rē), *n.* [pl. abecedaries] an a-b-c book; an element or rudiment.

abed (a bed'), *adv.* in bed, to bed.

abele (à bēl'), *n.* the white poplar (g. *Populus alba*), grown as a shade tree.

abelmosk (ā' bel mosk), *n.* a herb, native to the East Indies and southeastern Asia, whose seeds yield a musk used in perfumery (g. *Abelmoschus moschatus*).

°aberrant (ab er' ant), *adj.* departing from the usual path, type or standard.

aberration (ab ēr ā' shun), *n.* departure from the normal, in mental, moral or physical matters; deviation from a correct course of action; nonconformity to an accepted standard; seeming departure of a star or other heavenly body from its normal or proper position, due to conditions of the atmosphere or light; departure of light rays from their proper focus, producing a blurred image after passage through a lens or upon reflection in a mirror.

abet (a bet'), *v.t.* to encourage, incite, aid, especially in connection with wrong action.

Syn. Assist, back, countenance, foment, second, support, sustain, further. The bad official *abets* crime.

Ant. Deter, disapprove, discourage, frustrate, forbid.

abettor (a bet' ēr), *n.* one who aids or abets.

abeyance (a bā' ans), *n.* state of being held, kept back or held over; a state of suspension, as the title to an estate may be in *abeyance* due to nonappearance of a qualified claimant, or an executive decision may be held in *abeyance* pending accumulation of relevant facts.

°abhor (ab hôr'), *v.t.* to be strongly averse to; to loathe; to detest; to view or regard with dislike and repugnance, as I *abhor* your beliefs but cannot dispute your right to hold them.

Syn. Abominate.

Ant. Admire, crave, esteem, love.

abhorrence (ab hor' ens), *n.* a feeling of detestation or repugnance; that which causes such a feeling, as economic slavery is his principal *abhorrence*.

abide (a bīd'), *v.t. and v.i.* to dwell, reside; to wait for something; to endure, tolerate, as *abide* my return, *abide* by your decision, I cannot *abide* delay in the settlement of this case.

Syn. Sojourn, live, inhabit. *Abide* is to make a partial stay. *Sojourn* signifies to pass a certain portion of one's time in a place. *Dwell* implies residence, which is expressed in common discourse by the word *live*. *Reside* conveys the full idea of settling down. *Inhabit* signifies to have or occupy for a permanency.

Ant. Depart, move, reject, resist.

abiding (*a* bīd ´ ing), *p. adj.*, lasting, enduring, continuing, as you have my *abiding* confidence.

abidingly (*a* bīd' ing lē), *adv.* in a constant or enduring manner.

ability (a bil' i ti), *n.* power to perform; possession of enough strength or skill to accomplish a given task.

Syn. Capability, competence, aptitude, faculty. *Ability* means the power of doing in general; *capability* combines the idea of fitness to do with the power to do; *competence* carries the idea of entire fitness to do; *aptitude* implies a natural tendency as well as *ability* to do; a *faculty* is a natural gift or talent.

Ant. Inability, incapability.

abiogenesis (ab i ō jen' e sis), *n.* spontaneous generation; theory of the production of living matter without parent life. **abiogenist** (ab i oj' e nist), *n.* one who subscribes to that theory.

abiogenetic (ab i ō je net' ik), *adj.* pertaining to the belief in doctrines of spontaneous generation.

abiological (ab i ō loj' i kal), *adj.* having no connection with biology; not biological.

abiology (ab i ol' ō ji), *n.* the study of nonliving matter; distinguished from biology, which is the science of animate and growing things.

abiosis (ab i ō' sis), *n.* absence of life, as in inorganic substances.

abirritate (ab ir' i tāt), *v.t.* to soothe; to lessen pain or irritation.

abirritation (ab ir ri tā' shun), *n.* asthenia.

***abject** (ab' jekt), *adj.* fallen to a low estate; cringing; servile; beggarly.

abjure (ab joor'), *v.t.* to renounce upon oath; to forswear allegiance to; to repudiate or recant.

ablation (ab lā' shun), *n.* 1 removal, as by surgical amputation. 2 a wearing away, as of rock.

ablative (ab' la tiv), *n.* in Latin grammar a noun case expressing chiefly separation and agency, used to signify *from, in, by*.

ablaut (ab' lout), *n.* the systematic change in the root vowel of related words, showing a variation in meaning or tense; as, *swim, swam; bear, burden*.

able (ā' bl), *adj.* possessed of power, means or ability; qualified, competent.

-able (á' bl), *adj. sufx.*, denoting capacity, fitness, merit, tendency.

ablegate (ab' le gāt), *n.* papal envoy sent on a special mission.

abluent (ab' loo ent), *n.* a detergent or cleansing agent.

***ablution** (ab lū' shun), *n.* a cleansing of the body by water; the washing of sacred vessels used in religious ceremonies.

abnegate (ab' nē gāt), *v.t.* to refuse or deny; reject.

abnegation (ab nē gā' shun), *n.* self-denial.

abnormal (ab nôr' mal), *adj.* irregular; deformed; unnatural; departing from a type or standard.

abnormality (ab nôr mal' i ti), *n.* 1 an abnormal person, thing or condition; 2 deformity of body, mind or shape; peculiarity; aberration.

abnormity (ab nôr' mi ti), *n.* marked abnormality; a freak or monstrosity.

aboard (a bōrd'), *adv.* on or in a ship or train, as the passengers were all *aboard*.

aboard (a bōrd'), *prep.* on or in a conveyance, as we went *aboard* the airplane.

abode (a bōd'), *n.* a place of continued residence.

abolish (a bol' ish), *v.t.* to do away with entirely; to cancel; to annul.

Syn. Abrogate, cancel, nullify, repeal. *Abolish* refers to the permanent ending of established human institutions, as we *abolished* slavery. *Abrogate* refers to the setting aside of laws or treaties by a high executive. To *cancel* is to set aside written contracts. *Nullify* refers to the making void of a Federal law by a state; *repeal* refers to the recalling of an enactment by the same legislative body that made it.

Ant. Establish, enforce, maintain.

abolition (ab ō lish' un), *n.* the act of abolishing; state of being abolished; in American history, the ending of slavery.

aboma (á bō' ma), *n.* the largest species of boa constrictors, native to tropical America.

abomasum (ab ō mā' sum), *n.* the fourth and main digestive stomach of cud-chewing animals.

abominable (a bom' i na bl), *adj.* hateful; odious; offensive.

abominate (a bom' i nāt), *v.t.* to abhor; regard with disgust or hatred.

abomination (a bom i nā' shun), *n.* detestation; that which causes abhorrence; anything vile.

aboriginal (ab ō rij' i nal), *adj.* original; primitive; dating from earliest history.

***aborigine** (ab ō rij' i nē), *n.* one of the first inhabitants of a region.

abort (a bôrt'), *v.i.* 1 to miscarry as in premature birth. 2 to become arrested in development and remain rudimentary.

aborticide (a bôr' ti sīd), *n. Med.* destruction of the fetus in the womb; an agent which induces abortion.

abortion (a bôr' shun), *n.* 1 the premature expulsion of a fetus; miscarriage. 2 the fetus itself. 3 an act or plan that is halted before completion. 4 an organ of the body which fails to attain its full development or function. -al *adj.*

abortive (a bôr' tiv), *adj.* futile, incomplete.

abound (a bound'), *v.i.* to exist in plenty, as

fish *abound* in a river; to have in generous measure, as the river *abounds* in fish.

about (a bout´), *adv.* around; on all sides, as bushes *about* the house; nearly, as *about* a mile; intending, as I was *about* to do it; in alternation, as *turnabout* is fair play.

about (a bout´), *prep.* concerning: I will tell you all *about* it.

above (a buv´), *adv.* overhead, in the heavens.

above (a buv´), *prep.* over; on top of; higher than.

aboveboard (a buv´ bōrd), *adj. and adv.* in open sight; without trickery.

abracadabra (ab ra ka dab´ ra), *n.* the letters of a mystic word arranged in triangular form as a charm, supposed to have the power of keeping away evil; hocus-pocus; jargon.

abrade (ab rād´), *v.t.* to wear or rub away, to remove as by friction.

Abraham's bosom (booz´ um), *n.* a figurative term for the blissful abode of souls after death.

abrasion (ab rā´ zhun), *n.* the act of rubbing or wearing away; a chafe.

abreast (a brest´), *adv.* side by side; in line with.

abri (a brē´), *n.* [*pl.* abris (-brēz´)] *n.* (*Fr.*) a place of refuge, *esp.* a dugout or cellar; also a hut.

abridge (a brij´), *v.t.* to curtail, shorten, condense, epitomize, as a dictionary.

abridgment (a brij´ ment), *n.* the state of being contracted or curtailed; an epitome.

Syn. Compendium, epitome. An *abridgment* is the reduction of a large work into a smaller compass. A *compendium* is a boiled-down, concise presentation of any whole subject, as geography or astronomy. An *epitome* is a brief summary of all the substantial parts of a subject or treatise.

Ant. Enlargement; expansion.

abroach (a brōch´), *adj. and adv.* ready to be poured or emptied, as a cask that has been tapped. 2 astir; abroad.

abroad (a brōd´), *adv.* far and wide; in foreign lands or beyond customary limits.

abrogate (ab´ rō gāt), *v.t.* to abolish, annul or repeal by official action.

abrupt (ab rupt´), *adj.* precipitous, as a cliff; sudden, jerky, as movements; short, terse, as speech.

abscess (ab´ ses), *n.* [*pl.* abscesses (-ez)] a collection of diseased matter in the body tissues.

abscissa (ab sis´ a), *n. Geom.* in the system of coordinates, the distance of a point from the axis of *y* measured parallel to the horizontal axis of *x*.

abscond (ab skond´), *v.i.* to run away secretly, especially with stolen goods or funds.

absence (ab´ sens), *n.* the state of being absent, period of being absent.

absent (ab´ sent), *adj.* not present, away; wanting; abstracted.

absent (ab sent´), *v.t.* to retire or keep away from.

absentee (ab sen tē´), *n.* one who is not present.

absinthe (ab´ sinth), *n.* a liquor made of brandy and wormwood.

absolute (ab´ sō lūt), *adj.* free as to condition; perfect in itself; unlimited in power.

Syn. Arbitrary, supreme, utter. Anything *absolute* is complete and without qualification or question. *Absolute* power is independent of and superior to all other power. *Arbitrary* power might be despotic; an *arbitrary* judgment might be final and decisive yet unreasonable or based on personal caprice. *Supreme* refers to the highest or utmost of anything. *Utter* means complete or extreme, as *utter* joy.

Ant. Qualified, relative, partial.

absolute scale (ab´ sō lūt skāl), a scale of temperature with its zero at —273.1° C.

absolute temperature (tem´ pēr a tūr), *n.* temperature reckoned from absolute zero, or —273.1°C (—459.6°F).

absolution (ab sō lū´ shun), *n.* the act of freeing or state of being free from the consequences of sin.

absolutism (ab´ sō lū tizm), *n.* in government, freedom from limits to power.

absolve (ab solv´), *v.t.* to free from obligation; to clear of guilt; to forgive or remit.

Syn. Acquit, clear, discharge, exculpate, exempt, exonerate, forgive, free, liberate, pardon, release. To *absolve* is to *set free* from any bond. One may be *absolved* from a promise by a breach of faith on the part of one to whom the promise was made. To *absolve* from sins is formally to remit their condemnation and penalty, regarded as a bond upon the soul. To *acquit* of sin or crime is to *free* from the accusation of it; the innocent are rightfully *acquitted*; the guilty may be mercifully *absolved*.

Ant. Accuse, blame, condemn, impeach.

absorb (ab sôrb´), *v.t.* to drink in, imbibe; to suck or swallow up; to engross or engage wholly.

Syn. Engross, assimilate. The boy was *engrossed* in the examination of the engine. The body *assimilates* food.

Ant. Emit, radiate.

absorbent (ab sôrb´ ent), *adj.* having the capacity for taking up or assimilating, as a blotter is *absorbent*.

absorption (ab sôrp´ shun), *n.* the act or process of absorbing; reduction of power in a radio due to a variety of causes.

abstain (ab stān´), *v.t.* to forbear, refrain; to hold aloof, keep away from.

abstemious (ab stē´ mi us), *adj.* temperate in eating and drinking.

abstergent (ab stûr´ jent), *n.* that which cleanses or purges.

abstergent (ab stûr´ jent), *adj.* possessing cleansing or purging properties.

abstinence (ab´ sti nens), *n.* the act or practice of abstaining; self-denial.

abstinent (ab´ sti nent), *adj.* refraining from indulgence, especially of any appetite; temperate.

abstract (ab´ strakt), *n.* an epitome; a summary comprising the essence or principal parts of a larger work.

abstract (ab' strakt), *adj.* considered or conceived apart from any concrete or material nature; ideal; general.

abstract (ab strakt'), *v.t.* to take or draw away; to separate; to purloin or steal; (ab'-strakt), epitomize.

Syn. Separate. We *abstract* what we wish to regard particularly and individually; we *separate* what we wish not to be united.

Ant. Add, append, combine, expand, restore.

abstracted (ab strak' ted), *adj.* separated; mentally absent.

Syn. Absent-minded, absorbed, inattentive, oblivious, preoccupied. *Absorbed, abstracted* and *preoccupied* refer to lack of attention to the immediate environment; *absent-minded* implies an unintentional wandering of the thoughts but an *absent-minded* man may be *oblivious* of his surroundings because he is *preoccupied* with other thoughts.

Ant. Alert, prompt, thoughtful, wideawake.

abstraction (ab strak' shun), *n.* the act of separating or drawing away; mental state of being abstracted.

*****abstruse** (ab strōōs'), *adj.* difficult to apprehend; obscure.

*****absurd** (ab sûrd'), *adj.* contrary to reason or sense.

Syn. Anomalous, chimerical, foolish, irrational, ludicrous, nonsensical, paradoxical, preposterous, ridiculous, senseless, unreasonable, wild. Anything *absurd* is contrary to the first principles of reasoning; anything *paradoxical* appears at first thought contradictory or *absurd* though it may be really true; *irrational* qualifies that which is clearly contrary to sound reason, *foolish* means contrary to practical good sense, *silly* indicates petty folly, *erroneous* suggests error that vitiates the result, *unreasonable* indicates something so extremely illogical as to be *absurd*. *Monstrous* and *preposterous* refer to what is overwhelmingly *absurd*. The *ridiculous* or the *nonsensical* is worthy only to be laughed at.

Ant. Demonstrable, established, logical, sagacious, sound, true, wise.

abundance (a bun' dans), *n.* plenteousness; an overflowing quantity; affluence.

abundant (a bun' dant), *adj.* plentiful; abounding.

*****abuse** (a būs'), *n.* mistreatment; misuse of anything; revilement.

*****abuse** (a būz'), *v.t.* to illtreat; to address with insulting language.

Syn. Aggrieve, defame, disparage, malign, maltreat, misuse, molest, revile, victimize, vilify, vituperate, wrong. Everything is *abused* which receives any sort of *injury;* it is in *disuse* if not used at all; *misused* if turned to a wrong use. It is possible to *abuse* a man without *harming* him, as when the criminal *vituperates* the judge; or to *harm* a man without *abusing* him, as when the witness tells the truth about the criminal. *Defame, malign, revile, slander, vilify,*

and *vituperate* are used always in a bad sense.

Ant. Applaud, cherish, consider, favor, praise, protect, respect, uphold.

abut (a but'), *v.i.* [*p.t. and p.p.* abutted, *pr.p.* abutting] to border upon; to touch at some point.

abutment (a but' ment), *n.* that which abuts upon something else.

abysm (a bizm'), *n.* an abyss.

abysmal (a biz' mal), *adj.* pertaining to an abyss; bottomless; indeterminably deep.

abyss (a bis'), *n.* a bottomless pit, a chasm; anything immeasurable in space or time.

academic (ak *a* dem' ik) or **academical** ('-i kal), *adj.* having to do with school or college; scholarly; theoretical rather than practical.

*****academician** (a kad e mish' an), *n.* a member of an academy.

*****academy** (a kad' e mi), *n.* a school for higher branches of education, as the Naval Academy of the United States; a high school; an association of learned men to promote literature, science or the arts.

acanthus (a kan' thus), *n.* a plant with sharp-toothed leaves; ornamentation used in the capitals of the Corinthian and Composite orders.

Acanthus

accede (ak sēd), *v.i.* to come or attain; to agree or yield: used with *to.*

*****accelerate** (ak sel' ẽr āt), *v.t.* to cause to move faster.

acceleration (ak sel ẽr ā' shun), *n.* the act of moving faster; the state of going faster; in physics, the ratio of time to increase of velocity.

*****accent** (ak' sent), *n.* stress laid by the voice upon a particular syllable or word; emphasis placed upon certain notes of a bar of music.

accentuate (ak sen' tū āt), *v.t.* to stress, emphasize.

accept (ak sept'), *v.t.* to take or receive with approbation; to agree to; to take as true.

acceptable (ak sep' ta bl), *adj.* fit to be accepted, welcome.

acceptance (ak sep' tans), *n.* the act of accepting; the fact of being accepted; a draft which the seller draws against the buyer and which the buyer endorses with the word *accepted* and his signature.

*****access** (ak' ses), *n.* admittance or approach to a person or place; means of approach or admission.

accessible (ak ses' i bl), *adj.* capable of being reached; attainable.

accession (ak sesh' un), *n.* entrance or attainment; an increase or addition.

accessory (ak ses' ō ri), *n.* [*pl.* accessories (-rēz)] one who without being present agrees to or contributes to an action or enterprise, especially a crime; a small, separate article or part, as automobile *accessories.*

accessory (ak ses' ō ri), *adj.* aiding; contributing to some result or effect.

accident (ak' si dent), *n.* a mishap, commonly

one causing injury, damage or loss.

Syn. Calamity, mishap, misfortune. An *accident* is always an unforeseen or unintentional happening. A *calamity* is a great disaster; a *mishap* is an unlucky accident. Since the unforeseen is often feared, *accident* tends to signify *calamity* or *disaster*, unless the contrary is expressed, as when we say a fortunate or happy *accident*. *Misfortune* is a more general word which embraces all these others.

accidental (ak si den' tal), *adj.* happening by chance.

accidental (ak si den'tal), *n.* a musical symbol, such as a flat, sharp or natural altering the pitch of a single note.

acclaim (a klām'), *n.* a shout of joy or praise.

acclaim (a klām'), *v.i.* to shout applause.

acclamation (ak la mā' shun), *n.* applause with shouts of joy or approval; a vote by voice in an assembly.

*acclimate (a klī' mit), *v.t. and v.i.* to accustom to a foreign climate; to become used to a new climate.

accommodate (a kom' ō dāt), *v.t.* to make fit or suitable; to adjust, as conflicting interests; to do a favor for; to provide quarters for.

accommodation (a kom´ ō dā´ shun), *n.* that by, with or through which one is accommodated: *accommodations*, lodgings.

*accompaniment (a kum' pa ni ment), *n.* something that goes with the principal thing; in music, a supplementary part supporting the main part, vocal or instrumental.

accompanist (a kum' pa nist), *n.* one who renders an accompaniment.

accompany (a kum' pa ni), *v.t.* to keep company with; escort; join in movement or action; play an accompaniment for.

accomplice (a kom' plis), *n.* an associate or companion in crime.

accomplish (a kom' plish), *v.t.* to bring to completion; to achieve an end.

Syn. Achieve, do, effect, execute. To *accomplish* is to *do* or finish something by dint of perseverance or skill. To *effect* is to *do* or finish in spite of resistance. To *achieve* is to *accomplish* something difficult or important. To *execute* is to put into effect formally, as to *execute* a law.

Ant. Leave, neglect.

accomplished (a kom' plisht), *adj.* finished, completed; attained; proficient.

accomplishment (a kom' plish ment), *n.* full performance; achievement; something acquired by study and practice that contributes to social qualification.

accord (a kôrd'), *n.* agreement, harmony.

accord (a kôrd'), *v.t. and v.i.* to be in agreement with; to reconcile; to agree; to give; to grant; to concede.

according (a kôrd' ing), *adj.* agreeing, conforming: *according to*, in agreement with, as *according to* the records.

accordingly (a kôrd' ing li), *adv.* consequently; correspondingly.

accordion (a kôr' di un), *n.* a musical instrument, with bellows, keyboard and metal reeds.

accordion plaits (plĕtz) *n.* folds made in the goods like the creases in the bellows of an accordion.

accost (a kost´), *v.t.* to speak to before being spoken to in an intrusive manner.

account (a kount'), *n.* a record or reckoning.

Accordion

account (a kount'), *v.i. and v.t.* to make a reckoning as of finances; to consider as, as I *account* you my friend; to explain, as to *account* for an absence.

accountable (a kount' a bl), *adj.* answerable; responsible; liable to be called to account.

accountant (a kount' ant), *n.* one whose business it is to check up on accounts kept by others.

accredit (a kred' it), *v.t.* to give credit to; to assign with credentials, as a diplomatic agent to a foreign country.

accretion (a krē' shun), *n.* increase by natural growth; the addition of external parts; that which is added.

*accrue (a krōō'), *v.i.* to come, to happen or result to naturally as an increment, as of profit or loss.

accumulate (a kū' mū lāt), *v.t. and v.i.* to collect or bring together, amass; to heap up, to increase in quantity or number.

accumulation (a kū mū lā' shun), *n.* the process of collecting or amassing; things accumulated, regarded collectively.

accumulator (a kū' mū lā tēr), *n.* one who or that which accumulates; an apparatus for equalizing pressure or storing energy.

accuracy (ak' ū ra si), *n.* detailed correctness; exactness.

*accurate (ak' ū rit), *adj.* exact; without error.

accusation (ak ū zā' shun), *n.* a charge of wrongdoing.

accuse (a kūz'), *v.t.* to charge with wrongdoing or guilt.

Syn. Charge, arraign. We *accuse* a person directly. To *charge* is formally to lay the weight of wrongdoing on someone. We may *accuse* a man of taking money; but we formally *charge* him with theft when the law is called in. To *arraign* means to bring a person before a court or a judge to answer to a *charge*.

accustom (a kus' tum), *v.t.* to habituate or familiarize by usage.

ace (ās), *n.* [*pl.* aces] a unit; a die or domino marked with a single spot; a narrow margin, as within an *ace*; a flier who has brought down five or more enemy planes.

*acerbity (a sûr bi ti), *n.* bitterness; severity.

*acetanilide (as et an' i lid), *n.* a powder used to relieve pain, derived from aniline and acetic acid.

acetate (as' ē tāt), *n.* a salt of acetic acid.

*acetic acid (a sē' tik as' id), a sour-tasting, sharp-odored liquid, the acid constituent of vinegar.

*acetose (as' ē tōs), *adj.* of the nature of vinegar; sour; causing acetification.

*acetylene (a set' i lĕn), *n.* a gas that burns

with an extremely hot flame, used in welding and in cutting metals, as armor plate, structural steel and rails.

ache (āk), *n.* pain, more or less continuous.

ache (āk), *v.i.* to suffer, or be in, pain; as my head *aches*.

achieve (a chēv'), *v.t.* to perform; carry out; accomplish, especially something difficult.

achievement (a chēv' ment), *n.* accomplishment; something achieved.

achromatic (ak rō mat' ik), *adj.* transmitting light without breaking it up, as a prism does, into the colors of the spectrum, as an *achromatic* lens.

acid (as' id), *n.* a sour substance that makes litmus turn red.

acidification (a sid i fi kā' shun), *n.* the process of becoming or changing to acid.

acidify (a sid' i fi), *v.t.* [*p.t. and p.p.* acidified, *pr.p.* acidifying] to make acid.

acidimeter (as i dim' e tēr), *n.* an instrument or a solution for measuring acid strength.

acidity (a sid' i ti), *n.* the quality of being acid or sour.

acidosis (as i dō' sis), *n.* an acid condition of the body.

acid test (as' id test), a specially severe test of a person's merit or quality; probably from the practice of testing gold with acids.

acidulate (a sid' ū lāt), *v.t.* to render slightly acid.

aciform (as' i fôrm), *adj.* needle-shaped.

acknowledge (ak nol' ej), *v.t.* to recognize as true or valid; accept as a fact; to admit receipt of, as a check; confess, as a fault.

acknowledgment (ak nol' ej ment), *n.* admission or recognition of the truth or validity of anything; in law, a certified declaration; in business, a receipt or recognition of an obligation.

acme (ak' mē), *n.* the highest point; perfection.

acne (ak' nē), *n.* a skin disease caused by clogging of oil glands and marked by eruption of pimples.

*acolyte (ak' ō lit), *n.* one holding the highest of the four minor orders in the Roman Catholic Church; a boy who serves a priest at mass.

aconite (ak' ō nit), *n.* the plant wolfsbane or monkshood; a medicine made from this plant, used in reducing fever.

*acorn (ā' kôrn), *n.* the fruit of the oak.

*acoustics (a kōōs' tiks), *n. pl.* the science of sound; the architectural conditions affecting the hearing of sounds throughout a room or hall, as the *acoustics* of a theater.

Acorn

acquaint (a kwänt'), *v.t.* to familiarize, especially through experience, as to *acquaint* oneself with Latin; to inform, as to *acquaint* him with the news.

acquaintance (a kwän' tans), *n.* the state of knowing a person or subject; a person known somewhat less than intimately.

Syn. Association, companionship, familiarity, intimacy, knowledge. *Acquaintance* between persons supposes that each knows the other; there may be *association* in busi-

ness without *intimacy* or *friendship*. *Friendship* includes *acquaintance* with some degree of *intimacy*, and ordinarily *companionship*; *fellowship* involves not merely *acquaintance* and *companionship*, but mutual interests as well.

Ant. Ignorance, unfamiliarity.

acquiesce (ak wi es'), *v.i.* to agree tacitly; to accept, as to *acquiesce* in the plans.

acquiescence (ak wi es' ens), *n.* silent assent.

acquire (a kwir'), *v.t.* to get possession of.

acquisition (ak wi zish' un), *n.* the act of acquiring; that which is attained or secured, as a material possession.

acquit (a kwit'), *v.t.* to declare free of guilt; to discharge or perform; as the singer *acquitted* himself well in the new role.

acquittal (a kwit' al), *n.* a court decision freeing an accused person of the charge of an offense.

acre (ā' kēr), *n.* a surface measure of land containing 4,840 square yards.

acreage (ā' kēr ij), *n.* extent of land measured by the acre; land bought and sold by the acre, not in front-foot lots.

acrid (ak' rid), *adj.* sharp or biting to the taste; pungent; irritating; stinging.

acrimonious (ak ri mō' ni us), *adj.* bitter; caustic; stinging.

acrimony (ak' ri mō ni), *n.* sharpness of temper or language.

Syn. Acerbity, asperity, tartness. *Acrimony* springs from a sharp, satirical temper and is expressed in biting, bitter speech. *Asperity* implies quick irritability and the sudden expression of it. *Acerbity* is the expression of a sour nature. *Tartness* implies acidity of tongue and temper, but carries also the idea of a pleasing sprightliness of speech or idea.

Ant. Amiability, gentleness, mildness.

acrobat (ak' rō bat), *n.* one who does skillful and daring feats of aerial gymnastics or tumbling.

across (a krôs'), *adv.* from one side to the other; over, as to run *across*.

across (a krôs'), *prep.* from one side of anything, as a road or stream, to the other side.

*acrostic (a kros' tik), *n.* a composition, usually in verse, in which the first or last letters of the lines or other letters taken in order form a motto, phrase, name or word.

act (akt), *n.* an action; process of doing; a decree, edict or enactment; the judgment of a court; a statute resulting from passage of a bill.

acting (ak' ting), *n.* performing on the stage, for radio or motion pictures; pretense, as your limp is mere *acting*.

acting (ak' ting), *adj.* performing on the stage; substituting, as an *acting* secretary.

actinic (ak tin' ik), *adj.* chemically effective by reason of radiant or radioactive energy.

actinium (ak tin' i um), *n.* a radioactive element.

action (ak' shun), *n.* doing; something done, a deed; in a play or story, the things done by the characters; a suit at law; the working of mechanical parts; an engagement with the enemy.

actionable (ak' shun ĭ bl), *adj.* giving grounds for an action at law.

active (ak' tĭv), *adj.* endowed with or exercising the power or quality of action; using motion or force to produce an effect; moving quickly; given to working, busy; designating that voice of a verb that represents the subject as the doer of the action: opposite of *passive.*

Syn. Agile, brisk, nimble. Quickness, energy and constancy of action are implied in *active; agile* refers to skillful and easy use of one's body; *brisk* galt; *nimble* implies lightness and great speed of action.

Ant. Dull, idle, inert, lazy, latent.

actor (ak' tēr), *n.* one who acts or performs; one who portrays a character on stage or screen or for radio.

actress (ak' tres), *n.* a woman who acts a part.

*****actual** (ak' tū al), *adj.* real, existing; present.

actuality (ak tū al' ĭ tĭ), *n.* [*pl.* actualities (-tĭz)] the state of being real; a reality.

actuary (ak' tū ẽr ĭ), *n.* [*pl.* actuaries (-rĭz)] a registrar or clerk of a court; an insurance statistician.

actuate (ak' tū ăt), *v.t.* to move or incite to action.

*****acumen** (a kū' men), *n.* quickness of perception; penetration; discrimination.

acute (a kūt'), *adj.* sharp-pointed; intellectually sharp quick of perception; severe, as pain.

Syn. Keen, shrewd. In the original sense sharpness and pointedness are predominant in the word *acute,* and cutting or a fitness for cutting, in the word *keen.* The *shrewd* man is clever in practical affairs. *Keen* means sharp and probing, as a *keen* analysis of a subject.

Ant. Blunt, dull, slow-witted.

acute accent (a kūt' ak' sent), a diacritical mark indicating emphasis.

acute angle (a kūt ang' gl), an angle of less than 90°.

adage (ad' ĭj), *n.* an ancient proverb or pithy saying.

adamant (ad' a mant), *n.* a substance of extreme hardness; formerly, a diamond.

adamant (ad' a mant), *adj.* very hard; unyielding, as an *adamant* decision.

adapt (a dapt'), *v.t.* to make to correspond; to fit by alteration, adjust.

adaptation (ad ap tā' shun), *n.* the act of adjusting; the state of being adjusted.

add (ad), *v.t.* to join, unite, sum up; to increase; to affix.

Syn. Affix, amplify, annex, append, attach, augment, enlarge, extend, increase, subjoin. To *add* is to *increase by adjoining* or *uniting;* to *augment* is to *increase by any means;* but we *enlarge* a house a farm or an empire; *extend* influence or dominion; *augment* riches, power or influence; *attach* or *annex* a building; *affix* a seal or a signature.

Ant. Decrease, deduct, detract, diminish, lessen, remove, subtract.

addendum (a den' dum), *n.* [*pl.* addenda (-da)] something to be added to something else.

adder (ad' ẽr), *n.* a snake, especially a certain viper.

*****addict** (ad' ĭkt), *n.* one who is governed by a habit, as of using drugs.

addict (a ĭkt'), *v.t.* to devote or give oneself up to.

addition (a dĭsh' un), *n.* the act or process of adding together; something added, increase.

addle (ad' l), *v.i. and v.t.* to spoil or become spoiled, as an egg; to confuse or become confused, as a mind.

*****address** (a dres'), *n.* a speech; (ad' res), indication of the place where one lives, city, street, house number.

*****address** (a dres'), *v.t.* to direct speech or writing to; to place an address on, as an envelope.

Syn. Accost, apostrophize, appeal, approach, court, greet, hail, salute. *Address* is slightly more formal than *accost* or *greet;* one may *address* another at considerable length or in writing, he *accosts* orally and briefly; to *accost* is to speak first, to friend or stranger; *greet* and *hail* may imply but a passing word; *greeting* may be altogether silent; to *hail* is to *greet* in a loud-voiced and commonly hearty and joyous way; to *salute* is to *greet* with special token of respect, as a soldier his commander; to *apostrophize* is to solemnly *address* some person or personified attribute; to *appeal* is strictly to call for some form of help or support.

Ant. Avoid, ignore, overlook, shun.

*****adduce** (a dūs'), *v.t.* to bring forward or cite as for proof or substantiation.

adenoids (ad' ē noidz), *n. pl.* a swelling of lymphoid tissues in the nose-to-throat passage.

*****adept** (ad' ept), *n.* one who is highly skilled.

*****adept** (a dept'), *adj.* well skilled.

adequacy (ad' ē kwa sĭ), *n.* sufficiency for a particular purpose.

adequate (ad' ē kwĭt), *adj.* equal to a certain requirement or occasion; fully sufficient.

adhere (ad hēr'), *v.i.* to stick fast, become firmly attached, cling; to be devoted, as to *adhere* to a friend or a faith.

adhesion (ad hē' zhun), *n.* the state or act of sticking fast; something that adheres.

adipose (ad' ĭ pōs), *n.* animal fat; *adj.* pertaining to fat; fatty, as *adipose* tissue.

adit (ad' ĭt), *n.* an entrance or passage; an entrance to a mine more or less horizontal.

adjacent (a jā' sent), *adj.* near, close to, neighboring; bordering.

Syn. Abutting, adjoining, contiguous. *Adjacent* farms may not be connected; if *adjoining,* they meet at the boundary line; *contiguous* means touching along one side; *abutting* implies some point of contact, as a lot *abuts* on a road or one building *abuts* against another.

Ant. Distant, far, remote.

adjective (aj' ek tĭv), *n.* a word used with a substantive or noun to express a quality or attribute of the thing named.

adjoin (a join'), *v.t. and v.i.* to be or be put next to some other thing.

adjourn (a jûrn'), *v.t.* to put off to another day, defer; to dissolve; to close.

adjournment (a jûrn' ment), *n.* the act of postponing.

adjudge (a juj'), *v.t.* to decide according to law; to sentence.

adjunct (aj' ungkt), *n.* something added to another thing, but not an essential part of it.

adjuration (a joo rā' shun), *n.* the solemn charging on oath.

adjure (a joor'), *v.t.* to command on oath; to charge solemnly.

adjust (a just'), *v.t.* to fit or make exact; to make correspondent or accurate; to bring into harmony.

adjutant (aj' oo tant), *n.* a regimental staff officer who assists the commanding officer.

administer (ad min' is tēr), *v.t.* to manage as chief agent or minister, as a king or president; to conduct, as a business; to adjust and settle, as an estate.

administration (ad min is trā' shun), *n.* the act or process of managing; management; the executive department of a government or business; the executive officials; the length of time certain officials are in power.

administrator (ad min is trā' tēr), *n.* one who administers affairs; one who settles an estate.

admirable (ad' mi ra bl), *adj.* worthy of admiration; excellent.

admiral (ad' mi ral), *n.* the commander of a fleet; in most of the world's navies, the highest ranking grade of officer.

admiration (ad mi rā' shun), *n.* a feeling of enjoyment, appreciation, delight, caused by beauty or excellence.

admire (ad mir'), *v.t.* to regard with approval; to honor; to esteem.

Syn. Esteem, honor, revere.

Ant. Abhor, despise, dislike, hate, loathe.

admissible (ad mis' i bl), *adj.* worthy or capable of being admitted, conceded or allowed.

admission (ad mish' un), *n.* the power, permission or right to enter; the price paid for the privilege of entering; confession, as of a fault; concession or granting, as of an argument.

admit (ad mit'), *v.t.* to permit to enter; to acknowledge or concede.

admittance (ad mit' ans), *n.* the power or permission to enter.

Syn. Admission. *Admittance* is used to mean literal entrance, as *admittance* to a building or place. *Admission* implies privilege or rights, as *admission* to citizenship, club membership or a social group.

admix (ad miks'), *v.t.* to add by mixing.

admixture (ad miks' tūr), *n.* that which is added by mixing.

admonish (ad mon' ish), *v.t.* to reprove gently; warn; to command by warning, as to *admonish* obedience.

admonition (ad mō nish' un), *n.* friendly reproof or warning.

admonitory (ad mon' i tō ri), *adj.* conveying reproof or warning.

ado (a dōō'), *n.* bustle, trouble.

adobe (a dō' bi), *n.* unburnt brick dried in the sun, used for building in the southwestern United States, Central America and Mexico.

adolescence (ad ō les' ens), *n.* the period of life between childhood and maturity; youth.

adolescent (ad ō les' ent), *adj.* in process of growing to maturity.

adopt (a dopt'), *v.t.* to choose or take to oneself, as a child, an opinion or a course of action.

adoption (a dop' shun), *n.* the act of adopting; the state of being adopted.

adorable (a dōr' a bl), *adj.* worthy of worship.

adoration (ad ō rā' shun), *n.* act of worship; deep reverence.

adore (a dōr'), *v.t.* to worship as divine; to honor highly; to love intensely.

adorn (a dôrn'), *v.t.* to beautify; trim with ornaments, embellish.

adornment (a dôrn' ment), *n.* decoration.

adrenal (ad rē' nal), *adj.* near, of or from the kidneys.

adrenalin (ad ren' al in), *n.* a drug made from the extract of the suprarenal glands: used to stimulate heart action.

adrift (a drift'), *adj. and adv.* floating at the mercy of wind, tide or circumstances.

adroit (a droit'), *adj.* having skill; dexterous; clever.

adulation (ad ū la' shun), *n.* obsequious praise; flattery.

adult (a dult'), *adj.* grown up to full age, size and strength.

adulterant (a dul' tēr ant), *n.* an inferior ingredient mixed with one of better grade or greater strength.

adulterate (a dul' tēr āt), *v.t.* to corrupt or make poorer by baser admixture.

adulteration (a dul' tēr ā' shun), *n.* the debasing by admixture.

adultery (a dul' tēr i), *n.* [*pl.* adulteries (-iz)] violation of the marriage vow.

adumbrate (ad um' brāt), *v.t.* to represent by mere outline or indicate vaguely; to foreshadow.

advance (ad vàns'), *n.* a forward movement; progress; an improvement.

advance (ad vàns'), *v.i. and v.t.* to go forward; further; make a payment of beforehand.

advancement (ad vàns' ment), *n.* furtherance, progress; promotion.

advantage (ad vàn' tij), *n.* superiority in position, condition or skill, as the enemy has the *advantage;* any condition or opportunity resulting in success or benefit, as the *advantages* of an education.

advantageous (ad van tā' jus), *adj.* beneficial, profitable.

advent (ad' vent), *n.* a coming or arrival.

Advent (ad' vent), *n.* the period including the four Sundays before Christmas.

adventitious (ad ven tish' us), *adj.* happening by chance; casual; fortuitous.

adventure (ad ven' tūr), *n.* an event the issue of which is determined by chance; an unusual or thrilling experience.

adventuresome (ad ven' tūr sum) or **adventur-**

ous (ad ven' tūr us), *adj.* inclined to incur risk; eager for dangerous enterprise.

adverb (ad' vûrb), *n.* a word used to modify a verb, adjective or another adverb.

adversary (ad' vēr ser i), *n.* [*pl.* adversaries (-riz)] an opponent.

***adverse** (ad' vûrs'), *adj.* opposed to; unfavorable.

adversity (ad vûr' si ti), *n.* misfortune, hardship: opposite of *prosperity*.

advert (ad vûrt'), *v.i.* to turn the attention to; to refer, allude, as *advert* to yesterday's testimony.

***advertise** (ad' vēr tīz), *v.t.* to turn the attention of the public to, especially through print, as in newspapers or magazines, by radio and on cards or billboards.

***advertisement** (ad vûr' tiz ment), *n.* a notice of something for sale or something about to happen in public print; any public notice.

advice (ad vīs'), *n.* an opinion given for the practical direction of conduct.

advisable (ad vīz' a bl), *adj.* good to do; expedient, wise or appropriate.

advise (ad vīz'), *v.t.* to give an opinion to; to counsel.

advised (ad vīzd'), *adj.* considered, deliberated, as *well-advised*, *ill-advised*.

advisedly (ad vīz' ed li), *adv.* upon advice; with forethought and judgment.

advisement (ad vīz' ment), *n.* consideration, deliberation, as to take or keep a matter under *advisement*.

advisory (ad vī' zō ri), *adj.* having power to advise.

advocacy (ad' vō ka si), *n.* the act of pleading for or supporting.

advocate (ad' vō kāt), *n.* one who pleads for or defends a cause or a person.

advocate (ad' vō kāt), *v.t.* to plead or argue for; to support, as a policy.

adz or **adze** (adz), *n.* a cutting tool having a curved blade at right angles to the handle; *adz-plane*, a tool for molding and rabbeting.

aegis or **egis** (ē' jis), *n.* 1 a protective shield; any protective power. 2 a shaggy and tasseled accouterment ascribed in Homer to Zeus; a breast ornament decorated with serpents, ascribed to Athena.

***aerate** (ā' ēr āt), *v.i.* to combine or charge with carbonic-acid gas or air; to expose to the air, as water.

***aerial** (ā ē' ri al), *n.* a radio antenna.

***aerial** (ā ē' ri al), *adj.* pertaining to air; of or like air; airy.

aerie (ā' ēr i), *n.* an eagle's nest; a brood of eagles or hawks; eerie.

***aerification** (ā ēr i fi kā' shun), *n.* the state of being made aëriform or being charged with air.

aerobics (âr ō´ biks), *n.* pl. conditioning of the heart and lungs by means of exercise.

aerobatics (ā ēr ō bat' iks), *n.* stunt flying.

aerodynamics (ā ēr ō di nam' iks), *n.* the science that treats of air in motion and its action under force and in producing force.

aerogram (ā' ēr ō gram), *n.* a message conveyed by means of aircraft or radio; airgram.

aerolite (ā' ēr ō līt), *n.* a meteorite.

***aerometer** (ā ēr om' ē tēr), *n.* an instrument for weighing air and other gases or measuring their density.

***aeronaut** (ā' ēr ō nôt), *n.* an aërial navigator in airship or balloon.

aerostatics (ā ēr ō stat' iks), *n.* the science which treats of the equilibrium of bodies sustained in air.

aesthetic or **esthetic** (es thet' ik), *adj.* pertaining to aesthetics.

aesthetics or **esthetics** (es thet' iks), *n.* the science or theory of the beautiful.

afar (a fär'), *adv.* at, to or from a distance.

affair (a fâr'), *n.* that which is done or is to be done, any matter or proceeding: *affairs*, business.

affect (a fekt'), *v.t.* to produce an effect upon; to influence.

affectation (af ek tā' shun), *n.* a manner which is not one's own; artificial speech or mannerism.

affected (a fek' ted), *adj.* unnatural, assumed, artificial.

affection (a fek' shun), *n.* tender attachment; fondness, warm regard.

affectionate (a fek' shun it), *adj.* showing or feeling fondness; loving.

***afferent** (af' ēr ent), *adj.* conveying inward, as a nerve stimulus to the brain: opposite of *efferent*.

affiance (a fī' ans), *n.* trust; a marriage contract.

affiance (a fī' ans), *v.t.* to betroth.

affianced (a fī' anst), *adj.* betrothed; pledged.

affidavit (af i dā' vit), *n.* a sworn statement in writing.

affiliate (a fil' i āt), *v.t. and v.i.* to unite, as to *affiliate* two railroad companies, *affiliate* oneself with a society; to trace, as to *affiliate* French to Latin; to join or become connected, as to affiliate with a political party.

affinity (a fin' i ti), *n.* [*pl.* affinities (-tiz)] close kinship, relationship; close structural connection, as the *affinity* between animals or languages; the special chemical attraction that causes certain atoms to combine with others.

affirm (a fûrm'), *v.t. and v.i.* to assert strongly; in law, to make a declaration for record without oath.

affirmation (af ēr mā' shun), *n.* an averment; a statement before a court but not under oath.

affirmative (a fûr' ma tiv), *n.* that which affirms; in a debate, the side that defends the proposition being argued.

affix (a fiks'), *v.t.* to fix to or attach, as a seal; to add, as a signature.

afflatus (a flā' tus), *n.* inspiration, especially from a supernatural source.

afflict (a flikt'), *v.t.* to cause prolonged pain to body or mind; to distress.

affliction (a flik' shun), *n.* prolonged pain of body or mind; state of distress; that which causes pain or grief.

Syn. Grief, sorrow. *Sorrow* is a general term embracing *grief*, which arises from a definite cause, such as bereavement or remorse, and *affliction,* which is great physical or mental distress arising from loss or disaster.

Ant. Happiness, joy, well-being.

affluence (af' lū ens), *n.* an abundant supply, as of thoughts, words, riches; wealth.

affluent (af' lū ent), *n.* a tributary stream.

affluent (af' lū ent), *adj.* flowing abundantly; wealthy.

afford (a fōrd'), *v.t.* to supply; to produce; to yield; to be capable of bearing the expense of.

affray (a frā'), *n.* the fighting of two or more persons in a public place.

affront (a frunt'), *n.* an insult.

affront (a frunt'), *v.t.* to offend or insult intentionally.

afghan (af' gan), *n.* a crocheted or knitted soft wool blanket or carriage robe.

afraid (a frād'), *adj.* frightened.

afresh (a fresh'), *adv.* again, anew.

aft (äft), *adj. and adv.* toward or at the stern of a ship.

after (äf' tēr), *adj.* next; subsequent; later.

after (äf' tēr), *adv.* behind in time or place.

after (äf' tēr), *prep.* next following; later than; concerning, as to look *after* the house; returning in search of, as to go back *after* supplies; in imitation of, as he takes *after* his father.

aftermath (af' tēr math), *n.* a second mowing or crop; consequences.

afterward (af' tēr wērd) or **afterwards** (-wērdz), *adv.* at a later time; subsequently.

*****again** (a gen'), *adv.* a second time; in return; further; anew.

*****against** (a genst'), *prep.* upon; opposite to; in opposition to; contrary to; in preparation for, as save *against* need or a rainy day.

*****agape** (a gāp'), *adj. and adv.* gaping.

agate (ag' it), *n.* variegated quartz, a variety of chalcedony; 5½ point type.

age (āj), *n.* a particular period of time in life or in history; time.

aged (ā' jed), *adj.* very old; (ā jd), having reached certain year, as *aged* 21.

agency (ā' jen si), *n.* action, as we cook through the *agency* of heat; an office where agents transact business.

agenda (a jen' da), *n.* a program of things to be done, as at a meeting.

agent (ā' jent), *n.* one who acts for another; an active power or cause.

agglomerate (a glom' ēr āt), *v.t.* to gather into a heap; accumulate.

agglomeration (a glom er ā' shun), *n.* a mass or heap.

agglutinate (a glōō' ti nāt), *v.t.* to glue or fasten together.

*****aggrandize** (ag' ran dīz), *v.t.* to make great or greater, as in power or honor.

aggrandizement (a gran' diz ment), *n.* exaltation; advancement.

aggravate (ag' ra vāt), *v.t.* to make worse or increase; to intensify.

aggravation (ag ra vā' shun), *n.* the act of making worse; anything that increases the seriousness of a burden, illness, offense or the like.

aggregate (ag' rē gāt), *n.* the total, a mass or sum: *in the aggregate,* collectively.

aggregate (ag' rē gāt), *adj.* formed into a whole.

aggregate (ag' rē gāt), *v.t.* to bring together; to form into a whole.

aggregation (ag rē gā' shun), *n.* a collection of particulars.

aggression (a gresh' un), *n.* unprovoked attack; any first act of enmity.

aggressive (a gres' iv), *adj.* assuming the offensive without cause; self-assertive, pushing.

aggressor (a gres' ēr), *n.* one who attacks.

aggrieve (a grēv'), *v.t.* to afflict with pain or sorrow; to oppress.

aghast (a gàst'), *adj.* struck with sudden astonishment or terror.

*****agile** (aj' il), *adj.* moving easily; active and nimble in body.

agitate (aj' i tāt), *v.t.* to put or keep in motion, stir violently; to stir up, excite, disturb.

agitation (aj i tā' shun), *n.* the act of agitating; excitement.

agitator (aj' i tā tēr), *n.* one who starts or keeps up a political or other agitation.

aglow (a glō'), *adj.* in a glow; glowing.

*****agnostic** (ag nos' tik), *n.* one who, while he does not deny the existence of God, believes there is no proof of a Supreme Being: sometimes confused with *atheist.*

agog (a gog'), *adj.* in a state of expectancy; eager.

agonize (ag' ō nīz), *v.i.* to suffer anguish; to make desperate efforts.

agony (ag' ō ni), *n.* [*pl.* agonies (-niz)] extreme pain; anguish.

agrarian (a grâr' i an), *adj.* relating to land, or to land tenure.

agree (a grē'), *v.i.* to harmonize physically, mentally or morally; to accord.

Syn. Accede, concur, coincide, acquiesce. To *agree* is the general term and implies formal consent. We *accede* by becoming a party to a thing; those who *accede* yield up an opinion to the point of agreement; one objects to that to which one does not *accede;* we *concur* by expressing a definite agreement in opinion or action; ideas or opinions *coincide* if they are identical; to *acquiesce* is quietly to admit or agree to.

Ant. Differ, disagree, object, refuse.

agreeable (a grē' a bl), *adj.* pleasing to the mind or senses.

agreement (a grē' ment), *n.* harmony of opinions or feelings; in grammar, correspondence of words in number, person, case or gender.

agriculture (ag' ri kul tūr), *n.* the science and art of cultivating the soil or raising livestock; farming.

aground (a ground'), *adj. and adv.* on the ground; of a boat or ship, stranded.

ague (ā' gū), *n.* a malarial fever marked by a chill that alternates with the fever.

ahead (a hed'), *adv.* in the front; forward.

aheap (a hēp'), *adv.* in a heap.

ahoy (a hoi'), *interj.* a call used in hailing, as a vessel.

aid (ād), *n.* help; assistance.

aid (ād), *v.t.* to assist; to support.

aide-de-camp (ād' dĕ kamp), *n.* [*pl.* aides-de-camp (ādz)] an officer who assists a general.

AIDS (ādz), *n.* Acquired Immune Deficiency Syndrome; a deficiency of leukocytes which can lead to cancer, pneumonia, and other diseases.

ail (āl), *v.i. and v.t.* [*p.t. and p.p.* ailed, *pr.p.* ailing] to feel pain; to be afflicted with pain or illness; to cause pain: what *ails* you?

aileron (ā' lēr on), *n.* a small, hinged plane surface operated by the pilot of an airplane as a stabilizer.

*****ailment** (āl' ment), *n.* a slight disorder of the body; sickness.

aim (ām), *v.i.* [*p.t. and p.p.* aimed, *pr.p.* aiming] to strive for; to point or direct at something.

air (âr), *n.* the atmosphere.

air (âr), *v.t.* to expose to the air; to dry, as clothes; to exhibit ostentatiously.

air-conditioned (âr con dish' und), *adj.* having air cleansed and regulated as to humidity.

airfoil (âr' foil), *n.* any surface, as of wing or rudder of an airplane, used to control or direct flight by pressure of the air.

airiness (âr' i nes), *n.* the state of being airy; gaiety.

airing (âr' ing), *n.* exposure to air; a walk, ride or drive in the open air.

airline (âr lin), *n.* a straight line, drawn as if through the air.

airlock (âr' lok'), *n.* an airtight chamber which adjusts the air pressure for astronauts entering or leaving a spacecraft.

air line (âr lin), *n.* a system of transport by aircraft, which are spoken of as *air liners.*

airplane (âr' plān), *n.* a heavier than air, motor-driven form of aircraft, supported by the action of air against the wing planes.

air pocket (âr pok' et), *n.* a condition of the atmosphere that makes an airplane drop suddenly.

airs (ârz), *n.* affectation, pretense, as to put on *airs.*

airtight (âr' tit), *adj.* tight enough to prevent entrance or passage of air.

airworthy (âr' wûr thi), *adj.* in fit condition for flying.

airy (âr' i), *adj.* exposed to, like or composed of air; breezy; unsubstantial, unreal.

*****aisle** (il), *n.* a passageway between blocks of seats in a meeting room or between display counters in a store.

akimbo (a kim' bō), *adv.* with hands on hips and elbows turned outward.

*****alabaster** (al' α bas tēr), *n.* a white, marble-like mineral, a form of gypsum.

alack (a lak'), *interj.* an exclamation of blame, sorrow or surprise.

alacrity (a lak' ri ti), *n.* eager readiness; joyous activity; briskness.

alarm (a lärm'), *n.* sudden fear of danger; a warning signal.

alarm (a lärm'), *v.t.* to arouse to a sense of danger; to give a warning signal.

alarmist (a lärm' ist), *n.* one who is easily

and needlessly excited over public questions and seeks to excite others.

alas (a lás'), *interj.* an exclamation expressive of unhappiness or pity.

albatross (al' ba trôs), *n.* a very large sea bird allied to the petrel.

albeit (ôl bē' it), *conj.* although; even though; notwithstanding.

*****albino** (al bī' nō), *n.* a person or animal with white skin and hair and pink eyes.

album (al' bum), *n.* a blank book for autographs, photographs, stamps.

*****albumen** (al bū'·men), *n.* the white of an egg.

alchemy (al' ke mi), *n.* a science of the Middle Ages that tried to change baser metals into gold and to make a compound that would cure all disease and extend life indefinitely.

alcohol (al' kō hôl), *n.* a colorless and inflammable liquid produced by fermentation and distillation.

alcoholism (al' kō hôl izm), *n.* a diseased condition caused by excessive use of alcoholic liquors.

alcove (al' kōv), *n.* a recess in a room or a garden.

alder (ôl' dēr), *n.* a genus of trees and shrubs growing in moist land and related to the birch.

alderman (ôl' dēr man), *n.* [*pl.* aldermen] a member of a city government who represents a district.

ale (āl), *n.* a liquor made from an infusion of malt by fermentation.

alee (a lē'), *adv. and adj.* on the lee or sheltered side, as of a ship or wall.

alert (a lērt'), *adj.* on the watch, active.

alfalfa (al fal' fa), *n.* a hay and forage plant, deep-rooted, fast-growing and having leaves like those of the clover.

*****algebra** (al' jē bra), *n.* the science of treating the properties of numbers by means of general symbols.

*****algebraic** (al jē brā' ik) or **algebraical** (-i kal), *adj.* occurring in or dealing with algebra.

*****alias** (ā' li as), *n.* [*pl.* aliases] an assumed name.

*****alias** (ā' li as), *adv.* otherwise named.

alibi (al' i bi), *n.* an accused person's plea of or fact of his having been elsewhere when the alleged act was done.

*****alien** (āl' yen), *n.* a foreign-born nonnaturalized resident of a country.

*****alien** (āl' yen), *adj.* foreign; differing from, as ideas *alien* to ours.

alienate (āl' yen āt), *v.t.* to estrange, as the affections; to transfer to another, as property.

alienist (āl' yen ist), *n.* a specialist in mental diseases.

alight (a lit'), *adj.* lighted, kindled; lighted up, as with emotion.

alight (a lit'), *v.i.* to dismount; to descend and settle; to come upon accidentally.

align or **aline** (a lin'), *v.t. and v.i.* to arrange into or fall into line.

alike (a lik'), *adj.* similar, not different.

alike (a lik'), *adv.* in the same way, as to treat all *alike.*

alimentary (al i men' ta ri), *adj.* pertaining to nutrition; nutritious.

alimentary canal (al i men' ta ri ka nal'), the great duct which conveys food to the stomach and carries off waste matter.

alimentation (al i men tā' shun), *n.* the act of giving nourishment or method of being nourished.

alimony (al' i mōn i), *n.* means of living; an allowance made by decree of court to a wife out of her husband's income or to a husband from his wife's income after a divorce or separation.

alive (a līv'), *adj.* having life; in a state of action or existence; sprightly; thronged; as *alive* with people.

alkali (al' ka li), *n.* [*pl.* alkalis or alkalies] one of a class of bases, as soda or potash, that neutralize acids and form salts.

alkanet (al' ka net), *n.* a plant the root of which yields a rich red dye.

all (ôl), *n.* the whole of anything, as I give you my *all.*

all (ôl), *adj.* the whole quantity or number of; as *all* oaks are trees.

all (ôl), *adv.* completely, as *all* gone.

allay (a lā'), *v.t.* to quiet or calm, assuage, appease; to relieve.

Syn. Alleviate, mitigate. To *allay* is to lessen, especially any physical or mental disturbance, as pain, fever or fear; to *alleviate* is to decrease something enough to make it more endurable; to *mitigate* is to make milder or less severe, as punishment or grief.

Ant. Aggravate, arouse, intensify.

allegation (al ē gā' shun), *n.* the act of alleging; something alleged.

allege (a lej'), *v.t.* to state positively, but not under oath and without proof; to affirm.

Syn. Adduce, advance. To *allege* is to state as true or capable of proof, without proving; to *adduce* is to bring forth the evidence of what has been *alleged.* When an *alleged* criminal is brought to trial the counsel *advance* a theory and *adduce* evidence in its support.

*****allegiance** (a lē' jans), *n.* the obligation of a subject or citizen to his sovereign or government; loyalty to a person, principle or organization commanding respect.

allegoric (al ē gor' ik) or **allegorical** ('-i kal), *adj.* in the nature of allegory; figurative.

allegory (al' ē gō ri), *n.* [*pl.* allegories (-riz)] a story in which symbols are used to present moral truths, as in *Pilgrim's Progress.*

allergy (al' ēr ji), *n.* disease resistance as affected by inoculation.

alleviate (a lē' vi āt), *v.t.* to lighten, lessen, make easier, mitigate.

alley (al' i), *n.* [*pl.* alleys (-liz)] a passageway or narrow back street between two rows of buildings; a long, narrow space for bowling.

alliance (a li' ans), *n.* the state of being allied; a group of governments or other units combining for some special purpose, as defense.

alligator (al' i gā tēr), *n.* a large thick-skinned water reptile closely resembling the crocodile but having a shorter and broader nose.

alligator pear (pâr), *n.* a pearlike fruit, the avocado.

alliteration (a lit ēr ā' shun), *n.* the repetition of the same initial letter or the same initial sound in closely succeeding words.

allocate (al' ō kāt), *v.t.* to assign or allot, distribute.

allot (a lot'), *v.t.* [*p.t. and p.p.* allotted, *pr.p.* allotting] to distribute or divide, as by lot; to assign.

allow (a lou'), *v.t.* to grant, yield, admit; to deduct.

allowance (a lou' ans), *n.* admission, concession; a credit given on a purchase.

alloy (a loi'), *n.* a compound or fusion of two or more metals.

alloy (a loi'), *v.t.* to combine with another metal, as to *alloy* tin with copper to make pewter.

allspice (ôl' spīs), *n.* a spice made from the dried berry of a West Indian tree.

allude (a lūd'), *v.i.* to refer to; to mention incidentally.

Syn. Hint, refer, suggest. *Allude* is not quite so direct as *refer* but is more clear and positive than *hint* or *suggest.* We *allude* to something by indirect suggestion; we *refer* to an event by expressly naming it; we *hint* at something by implying a hidden meaning; we *suggest* an idea by leading up to it indirectly-and concluding without positive statement.

allure (a lūr'), *v.t.* to tempt, entice.

allusion (a lū'zhun), *n.* indirect mention; a casual reference.

alluvium (a lū' vi um), *n.* [*pl.* alluvia] a deposit of mud, sand or gravel made by a stream.

*****ally** (a-li'), *n.* [*pl.* allies] a person or nation joined with another by treaty, especially for war against a common foe; any associate or helper.

ally (a li'), *v.t. and v.i.* [*p.t. and p.p.* allied, *pr.p.* allying] to unite for a common purpose.

almanac (ôl'ma nac), *n.* a book containing a calendar for a full year, with facts about the weather, the heavenly bodies, tides.

almighty (ôl mī' ti), *adj.* possessing all power, omnipotent, as the *almighty* God.

*****almond** (ä' mund), *n.* the nut or fruit of the almond tree.

almoner (al' mun ēr), *n.* one who gives out alms to the poor for another.

almost (ôl' mōst), *adv.* nearly, just about, not quite.

alms (ämz), *n.* money given and distributed for relief of the poor and needy.

almshouse (ämz' hous), *n.* a house where charity is dispensed and poor persons are cared for.

aloe (al' ō), *n.* a plant with thickly clumped basal leaves, related to the lily.

aloft (a lôft'), *adv.* on high; in the upper rigging of a ship.

alone (a lōn), *adj. and adv.* without company, escort or associates, as to walk *alone;* only, as that *alone* is the answer; exclusively.

along (a lông'), *prep.* parallel to the length of; lengthwise of; beside, as *along* a wall, *along* a road.

along (a lông'), *adv.* onward, as pass this *along;* together, as to study art *along* with music.

aloof (a loof'), *adv.* at a distance but in sight; apart in interest or feeling.

aloud (a loud'), *adv.* audibly.

alpaca (al pak' a), *n.* a South American wool-bearing animal; cloth made from its wool.

alphabet (al' fa bet), *n.* the letters of a language.

already (ôl red' i), *adv.* previously; before some specified time.

also (ôl' sō), *adv.* too, in addition to.

altar (ôl' tēr), *n.* a raised place for the offering of sacrifices or burning of incense or for worship in churches.

alter (ôl' tēr), *v.t. and v.i.* to effect some change in; to become different.

alteration (ôl tēr ā' shun), *n.* the act of altering or changing; a change or variation.

*altercation (ôl tēr kā' shun), *n.* a dispute, wrangle.

*alternate (ôl' tēr nāt), *v.i. and v.t.* to take turns; to follow in turn, as summer and winter *alternate;* to cause to happen by turns.

alternately (ôl' tēr nit li), *adv.* first one, then the other.

alternation (ôl tēr nā' shun), *n.* the act of alternating; state of being alternate.

*alternative (ôl tûr' na tiv), *n.* a choice between two things; either one of two things between which choice is to be made.

     Syn. Choice, option. *A choice* may be made among many things; an *alternative* is a choice between two; *option* is the right or privilege of choosing.

although (ôl thō'), *conj.* even if, notwithstanding; supposing that.

altimeter (al tim' ē tēr), *n.* an instrument for measuring altitude.

altitude (al' ti tūd), *n.* height.

alto (al' tō), *n.* in music, the lower range of the female voice, a part lower than soprano; also called *contralto;* high, relief carving.

altogether (ôl too geth' ēr), *adv.* completely, entirely, including all or everything.

*altruism (al' trōō izm), *n.* unselfish consideration of others.

alum (al' um), *n.* a mineral salt used in medicine.

*aluminum (a lū' mi num), *n.* a bluish-white, light-weight, durable metal which does not rust.

alumna (a lum' na), *n.* [*pl.* alumnae] a girl or woman graduate of a school or college.

always (ôl' wāz), *adv.* constantly, all the time.

Alzheimer's disease (älts' hi ' merz dizēz '), *n.* a disease of the brain which is increasingly degenerate as to normal functions.

amalgam (a mal' gam), *n.* any metallic mixture or alloy of which mercury is the chief constituent; any mixture or blend.

amalgamate (a mal' ga māt), *v.i.* to mix, combine; to mingle, as one race with another.

amass (a mas'), *v.t. and v.i.* to collect, accumulate in great quantity.

*amateur (am a tūr'), *n.* one who engages in art or sport on a nonprofessional basis.

amatory (am' a tō ri), *adj.* relating to or expressive of love.

amaze (a māz'), *v.t.* to cause fear or astonishment; to surprise, bewilder.

ambassador (am bas' a dēr), *n.* the highest ranking diplomatic representative of one government to another.

amber (am' bēr), *n.* a yellowish fossil resin found chiefly on the shores of the Baltic.

amber (am' bēr), *adj.* made of amber; having the yellowish color of amber.

ambiance (am' bē äns), *n.* the atmosphere or environment of a place that makes it distinctive.

ambidextrous (am bi dek' strus), *adj.* able to use either hand equally well.

ambiguity (am bi gū' i ti), *n.* uncertainty or vagueness of meaning; an expression that can be taken two ways.

ambiguous (am big' ū us), *adj.* capable of more than one interpretation; not clearly stated.

ambition (am bish' un), *n.* desire for advancement, wealth, honor or power.

ambitious (am bish' us), *adj.* eager for success, honor or fame; determined to succeed.

amble (am' bl), *n.* a gentle gait; a slow pace of horses with two legs of one side raised at the same time.

*ambrosia (am brō' zhi a), *n.* the food of the gods; anything exquisitely pleasing to the taste.

ambulation (am bū lā' shun), *n.* the act of walking about.

ambuscade (am bus kād'), *n.* a strategic disposition of troops in ambush.

ambush (am' boosh), *n.* a lying in wait to attack by surprise; the troops lying in wait.

*ameba (a mē' ba), *n.* [*pl.* amebas] a one-celled animal of microscopic size, found in stagnant water; one of the simplest forms of life, also amoeba.

*ameliorate (a mēl' yō rāt), *v.t. and v.i.* to make better or grow better; to improve.

amen (ā men'), *interj.* so be it.

*amenable (a mē' na bl), *adj.* easily led, reasonable, docile.

amend (a mend'), *v.t.* to free from fault; to make better.

     Syn. Emend, mend. To *amend* signifies to improve by removing faults or defects, as to *amend* a law; to *emend* is to make corrections or suggest improvements in a literary work; to *mend* is to repair something broken, torn or otherwise impaired.

     Ant. Impair, spoil.

amendment (a mend' ment), *n.* the removal of faults; the altering of a bill, act or other formal papers.

amends (a mendz'), *n. pl.* reparation for loss or injury; compensation, as he made *amends* for his rudeness.

amenity (a r:en' i ti), *n.* [*pl.* amenities] pleasantness, as of demeanor, geniality: *amenities,* courtesies and civilities of social life.

amerce (a mûrs'), *v.t.* to punish by arbitrary fine.

amethyst (am' a thist), *n.* a violet-purple variety of quartz or rock crystal.

amiability (ā mi a bil' i ti), *n.* good nature, friendliness.

amiable (ā' mi a bl), *adj.* sweet-tempered, kind-hearted, agreeable, as an *amiable* person.

amicable (am' i ka bl), *adj.* from or showing friendliness, as an *amicable* remark.

amid (a mid'), *prep.* in the middle of, among.

amiss (a mis'), *adj.* wrong, faulty.

amiss (a mis'), *adv.* wrongly.

amity (am' i ti), *n.* friendly relations, friendship.

ammeter (am' mē tēr), *n.* an instrument for measuring the intensity of an electric current in units that are known as amperes.

ammonia (a mō' ni a), *n.* a transparent, pungent, volatile gas used in fertilizers and in making ice; this gas dissolved in water, used as a household cleaning fluid.

ammonite (am' mon īt), *n.* any of numerous fossil shells of cephalopods, having form of a sharp spiral; flourished in Mesozoic age.

amnesia (am nē' zi a), *n.* loss of memory.

amnesty (am' nes ti), *n.* a general pardon; an official forgetting, as of a debt.

among (a mung'), *prep.* mixed in with; surrounded by; amidst.

amorous (am' ō rus), *adj.* fond of the opposite sex; loving.

amorphous (a môr' fus), *adj.* shapeless, formless.

amortize (a môr' tīz), *v.t.* to arrange for paying a future debt or obligation by making periodic contributions to a fund that will discharge it when it comes due.

amount (a mount'), *n.* a sum, aggregate, any quantity.

amount (a mount'), *v.i.* to mount up; be equivalent or equal.

amperage (am pēr' ij), *n.* strength of an electric current measured in amperes.

ampere (am pēr'), *n.* the unit for measuring the force of an electric current.

amphibious (am fib' i us), *adj.* able to live either on land or in water, as a frog.

amphitheater (am' fi thē' a tēr), *n.* a round or oval structure with tiers of seats surrounding an arena or stage.

amphora (am' fo ra), *n.* a large earthen jar having two handles.

ample (am' pl), *adj.* large; sufficient.

amplification (am pli fi kā' shun), *n.* the act of amplifying; something enlarged.

amplifier (am' pli fi ēr), *n.* a mechanism to magnify electric impulses and add to the volume of sound.

amplify (am' pli fi), *v.t.* [*p.t. and p.p.* amplified, *pr.p.* amplifying] to enlarge; increase in scope or volume.

amputate (am' pū tāt), *v.t.* to cut off.

amputation (am pū tā' shun), *n.* the operation of cutting off a limb.

amuck (a muk') or **amok** (a mok'), *adv.* in a state of frenzy; as he ran *amuck*.

amulet (am' ū let), *n.* a luck charm, talisman.

amuse (a mūz'), *v.t.* to entertain, divert.

an (an), *indef. art.* one, any: used before words beginning with a vowel or the sound of a vowel, as *an* egg, *an* hour.

anaconda (an a kon' da), *n.* a large nonvenomous snake that crushes its prey.

anaglyph (an' a glif), *n.* a work of art carved in relief, as a cameo.

anagram (an' a gram), *n.* a word or sentence constructed out of another word or sentence by transposing.

analgesia (an al jē' zi a), *n.* insensibility to pain in any part of the body.

analgesic (an al jēs' ik), *adj.* counteracting pain.

*****analogous** (a nal' ō gus), *adj.* resembling, corresponding to another thing on certain points, as a bird's claws are *analogous* to human fingers.

analogue (an' a lôg), *n.* an object which bears analogy to something else.

*****analogy** (a nal' ō ji), *n.* [*pl.* analogies (-jiz)] agreement, resemblance or correspondence in relations between different objects.

analysis (a nal' i sis), *n.* [*pl.* analyses (-sēz)] reduction of anything into its parts; the examination of anything to determine its make-up; a statement of the process or the examination, point by point.

analytic (an a lit' ik) or **analytical** (-i kal), *adj.* relating to or characterized by the method of analysis.

analyze (an' a līz), *v.t.* to separate or resolve into elementary parts.

anapest (an' a pest), *n.* a metrical foot in poetry of two unaccented syllables and one accented syllable.

anaplasty (an' a plas ti), *n.* repairing wounds by transplanting healthy tissue.

*****anarchist** (an' ar kist), *n.* one who believes in or promotes anarchy.

*****anarchy** (an' ar ki), *n.* lack of governmental rule: a chaotic state resulting from the overthrow of government.

anathema (a nath' ē ma), *n.* [*pl.* anathemas (-maz)] the curse accompanying excommunication; any solemn curse; a person or thing distasteful.

anatomic (an a tom' ik), *adj.* relating to anatomy, pertaining to the structure of the body.

anatomist (a nat' ō mist), *n.* one possessing a knowledge of bodily structure, a specialist in anatomy.

anatomy (a nat' ō mi), *n.* [*pl.* anatomies (-miz)] the science of the bodily structure of animals and plants; dissection.

ancestor (an' ses tēr), *n.* a forefather or progenitor.

ancestry (an' ses tri), *n.* the line of one's descent traced from a period more or less remote.

anchor (ang' kēr), *n.* a metal implement that holds a floating vessel in a particular place by connecting it with the bottom. **Sea anchor,** a canvas float that keeps a vessel's head into the wind.

*****anchor** (ang' kēr), *v.i. and v.t.* to make fast with an anchor, as we *anchored* the boat; to cast anchor.

anchorite (ang' kō rīt), *n.* one who voluntarily secludes himself from society and lives a solitary life, a hermit.

*anchovy (an chō' vl), *n.* [pl. anchovies (-viz)] a diminutive fish abounding in Mediterranean waters.

ancient (ān' shent), *adj.* of or pertaining to the early history of the world; of past times or remote ages; very old.

ancillary (an' sl lēr l), *adj.* auxillary, accessory, subservient.

and (and), *conj.* also; in addition to; besides: used between words, phrases, clauses and sentences of equal importance.

anecdote (an' ek dōt), *n.* a brief narrative of an entertaining character, usually about some notable person or event.

*anemia (a nē' mi a), *n.* deficiency or low count of red corpuscles in the blood.

*anemone (a nem' ō nē), *n.* [pl. anemones (-nēz)] a plant of the buttercup family having white, star-shaped blossoms, often with colored sepals; windflower.

aneroid (an' ēr old), *adj.* containing no liquid.

*anesthesia (an es thē' zi a), *n.* a partial or entire loss of sensation.

anesthetic (an es thet' ik), *n.* any substance, usually a gas or drug, that causes partial or entire loss of sensation, as novocaine or ether.

anesthetize (an es' tha tīz), *v.t.* to bring under the influence of an anesthetic.

aneurism (an' ū rizm), *n.* a local swelling or dilation of an artery.

anew (a nū'), *adv.* afresh, over again.

angel (ān' jel), *n.* a messenger of God, a heavenly being.

angelic (an jel' ik) or angelical (-i kal), *adj.* like an angel.

anger (ang' gēr), *n.* strong resentment of injury or wrong, wrath.

Syn. Fury, indignation, ire, rage, wrath. *Anger* is a sudden, keen displeasure aroused by injury or injustice and usually accompanied by desire to punish; *indignation* is intense *anger* awakened by anything unworthy, as cruelty or meanness; both *wrath* and *ire* are literary terms for *anger;* *rage* is a vehement expression of anger; and *fury* is an excess of rage.

Ant. Gladness, pleasure, satisfaction.

angle (ang' gl), *n.* the figure formed by the intersection of two straight lines or planes.

angle (ang' gl), *v.i.* to fish with rod and line; to try to get something indirectly, as a favor.

anglicize (ang' gli sīz), *v.t. and v.i.* to make or to become like English in manner or language.

Angora (ang gō' ra), *n.* cloth made from Angora wool.

Angora cat (kat), a long-haired domestic cat.

Angora goat (gōt), a domestic goat with long, silky hair.

Angora wool (wool), the wool of the Angora goat, mohair.

angostura bark (ang gos tū' ra bärk), a bitter, aromatic bark of a South American tree, used as a tonic.

angry (ang' gri), *adj.* extremely resentful or indignant, provoked; sore and inflamed, as a festering wound.

anguish (ang' gwish), *n.* intense pain or grief.

angular (ang' gū lēr), *adj.* possessing an angle or angles.

anhydrous (an hi' drus), *adj.* lacking water.

*aniline (an' i lin), *n.* a colorless, oily liquid used in dyemaking; obtained from coal tar.

animal (an' i mal), *n.* any living creature different from plants by its capacity for sensation and spontaneous movement. *adj.* of or pertaining to animals.

animate (an' i māt), *v.t.* to impart life to, inspire with energy or action, enliven.

animated (an' i māt ed), *adj.* vivacious, lively.

animation (an i mā' shun), *n.* the act of giving life or spirit; liveliness, vivacity.

animosity (an i mos' i ti), *n.* hostility, hatred, active enmity.

animus (an' i mus), *n.* any actuating spirit or impulse; a hostile spirit or purpose.

anise (an' is), *n.* a plant native to Egypt, yielding the aniseed of commerce.

ankle (ang' kl), *n.* the joint connecting the foot with the leg.

anklet (ang' klet), *n.* an ornament or support for the ankle, a sock.

annalist (an' al ist), *n.* a compiler of annals; a historian.

annals (an' alz), *n. pl.* chronological history of events, each being identified by its year; periodically published records of scientific, historical and other societies.

anneal (a nēl'), *v.t.* to heat or fix by heat.

annex (an' neks), *n.* that which is added; an addition.

annex (a neks'), *v.t.* to add or join one thing to another, especially for use or ownership, as a nation *annexes* territory.

annexation (an eks ā' shun), *n.* the act of annexing; that which is annexed.

*annihilate (a nī' i lāt), *v.t.* to reduce to nothing, destroy.

annihilation (a nī i lā' shun), *n.* obliteration.

anniversary (an i vēr' sa ri), *n.* [pl. anniversaries (-riz)] the yearly recurrence of the date of an event.

annotate (an' ō tāt), *v.t.* to mark or note; to furnish with explanatory notes, as a book.

announce (a nouns'), *v.t.* to proclaim or make publicly known.

Syn. Declare, proclaim. To *announce* is to make known for the first time, as to *announce* an engagement; to *declare* is to make known specifically and formally, as to *declare* one's plans; to *proclaim* is to *announce* to a national or world audience, as to *proclaim* war or peace or the abolition of slavery.

Ant. Conceal, suppress.

announcement (a nouns' ment), *n.* a notice either of something about to happen or that has happened.

annoy (a noi'), *v.t.* [p.t. and p.p. annoyed (-noid), *pr.p.* annoying] to vex or trouble by repeated acts; harass or discompose by petty injury or opposition.

annoyance (a noi' ans), *n.* the state of being vexed; that which vexes.

annual (an' ū al), *adj.* once in twelve months;

yearly; of or belonging to a year.

annuitant (a nū' i tant), *n.* one who receives an annuity.

annuity (a nū' i tĭ), *n.* [*pl.* annuities (-tĭz)] a sum of money to be paid yearly, either in a lump sum or by instalments.

annul (a nul'), *v.t.* [*p.t. and p.p.* annulled, *pr.p.* annulling] to make void, abolish or obliterate.

annular (an' ū lẽr), *adj.* ringlike.

annulment (a nul' ment), *n.* the act of rendering null and void.

anodyne (an' ō dīn), *n.* medicine that relieves pain.

anoint (a noint'), *v.t.* to pour oil upon, as in a religious ceremony.

***anomalous** (a nom' a lus), *adj.* deviating from the common order; abnormal.

anomaly (a nom' a lĭ), *n.* deviation from the natural order; that which deviates.

anon (a non'), *adv.* soon, again.

anonymity (an ō nim' i tĭ), *n.* the state of bearing no name.

anonymous (a non' i mus), *adj.* bearing no name; of unknown authorship.

another (a nuth' ẽr), *adj. and pron.* one more; not the same.

answer (an´ sẽr), *n.* a reply; response, by word or act.

Syn. Reply, rejoinder, response. An *answer* is given to a question; a *reply* is made to an assertion; a *rejoinder* is made in terms of a statement by another. We *answer* either for the purpose of affirmation, information or contradiction; we always *reply* or *rejoin*, in order to explain or confute; *responses* are apt to be made by way of assent or confirmation.

Ant. Charge, question.

answer (an´ sẽr), *v.t. and v.i.* to reply, respond.

answerable (an' sẽr a bl), *adj.* capable of being answered; responsible.

ant (ant), *n.* a small social insect noted for its industrious habits.

antacid (ant as' id), *n.* an alkaline remedy for acidity.

antacid (ant as' id), *adj.* counteracting acidity.

antagonism (an tag' ō nizm), *n.* active opposition or resistance.

antagonist (an tag' ō nist), *n.* an opponent, contender, adversary.

antagonize (an tag' ō nīz), *v.t. and v.i.* to oppose, arouse opposition.

***antarctic** (ant ärk' tik), *n.* the south polar regions.

antarctic (ant ärk' tik), *adj.* pertaining to the south polar regions: opposite of *arctic*.

ant bear (ant bâr), *n.* the great anteater of South America that is like a diminutive bear.

anteater (ant' ēt ẽr), *n.* one of a group of quadrupeds that feed upon ants.

***antecedent** (an tē sēd' ent), *n.* the noun to which a relative or personal pronoun refers; anything that goes before: *antecedents*, one's previous history or ancestry.

antecedent (an tē sēd' ent), *adj.* preceding.

antechamber (an' tē chăm bẽr), *n.* an apartment next the principal room.

antedate (an' tē dāt), *v.t.* to precede in time.

antediluvian (an tē di lū' vi an), *adj.* of or pertaining to the world before the Flood.

antelope (an' tē lōp), *n.* an Old World animal resembling a deer but with hollow horns tilted upward and backward

antemeridian (an tē mē rid' i an), *adj.* preceding noon.

antenna (an ten' a), *n.* [*pl.* antennae (-ē)] the jointed horns or feelers upon the heads of insects and crustaceans; a radio aerial.

***antepenult** (an tē pē' nult), *n.* the syllable third from the end of a word.

anterior (an ter' i ẽr), *adj.* more to the front; former.

anteroom (an' tē rōom), *n.* a room forming an entrance to another.

anthem (an' them), *n.* a composition from the Scriptures or liturgy set to sacred music; a national hymn.

anther (an' thẽr), *n.* the top of the stamen of a flower containing the pollen or fertilizing dust.

***anthology** (an thol' ō jĭ), *n.* a collection of songs, poems or selected prose, generally grouped according to style or period.

anthracite (an' thra sīt), *n.* hard coal.

***anthropoid** (an' thrō poid), *n.* one of the higher apes resembling man.

anthropology (an thrō pol' ō jĭ), *n.* the science that deals with the physical and cultural development of mankind; a book that treats this subject.

antiaircraft (an ti âr' kraft), *adj.* used for protection from enemy aircraft.

antibiotic (an´ ti bī ot´ ik), *n.* any of such substances as penicillin or streptomycin which destroy or arrest microorganisms of infectious diseases.

antichristian (an ti kris' chan), *adj.* opposed to or denying Christ or Christianity.

anticipate (an tis' i pāt), *v.t.* to deal with by previous action, as to *anticipate* an examination with study; to forestall; to expect; to look forward to; to foresee and provide for, as to *anticipate* need.

anticipation (an tis i pā' shun), *n.* the act of anticipating, expectation.

anticlimax (an ti clī' maks), *n.* a weakening of action and interest where a dramatic rise is needed or expected in a play or story; any occurrence in a series that is ludicrously less significant than the one that immediately preceded it.

antics (an' tiks), *n.* clownish pranks.

antidote (an' ti dōt), *n.* a counteractive to the effects of poison or disease; a remedy for anything evil.

antimony (an' ti mō ni), *n.* a white lustrous metal, one of the chemical elements used in making alloys.

***antipathy** (an tip' a thi), *n.* [*pl.* antipathies (-thiz)] a feeling of aversion, intense dislike.

Syn. Aversion, disgust, repugnance. *Antipathy* is an instinctive recoil from connection or association with a person or thing; *aversion* is a deep and permanent *dislike*, usually expressed in avoidance of the disliked person or thing; *repugnance* implies active opposition; *disgust* is the reaction of outraged taste or feeling.

Ant. Fondness.

antiphon (an' ti fon), *n.* a chant or hymn rendered alternately by two choirs.

*antiphonal** (an tif' ō nal), *adj.* characterized by antiphony, responsive.

antiphony (an tif' ō ni), *n.* [*pl.* antiphonies (-niz)] the alternate or responsive rendering of psalms or chants by a dual choir.

antipodes (an tip' ō dēz), *n. pl.* two portions of the earth's surface which are exactly opposite to each other; direct opposites.

antiquary (an' ti kwēr i), *n.* one who collects or deals in objects of great age and rarity; a student of ancient times and objects.

antiquated (an' ti kwāt ed), *p. adj.* long out of date, outmoded.

antique (an tēk'), *n.* something old and rare, especially furniture and glass.

antique (an tēk'), *adj.* of a former age, ancient.

Syn. Antiquated, old-fashioned, superannuated. *Antique* refers to age, *antiquated* to anything outmoded. We speak of *antique* furniture and *antiquated* customs, an *old-fashioned* fireplace, a *superannuated* person, incapacitated by reason of age.

Ant. Modern.

antiquity (an tik' wi ti), *n.* [*pl.* antiquities (-tiz)] great age; early ages.

antiscorbutic (an ti skôr bū' tik), *adj.* counteracting scurvy.

anti-Semitism (an ti sem' i tizm), *n.* antagonism to the Jewish race.

antiseptic (an ti sep' tik), *adj.* destructive to the germs of disease or putrefaction.

antislavery (an ti slā' vēr i), *adj.* opposed to slavery.

antisocial (an ti sō' shal), *adj.* opposed to or destructive of human society.

antithesis (an tith' ē sis), *n.* [*pl.* antitheses (-sēz)] direct opposition, contrast, as of ideas, shown by close, contrasting words.

antithetic (an ti thet' ik) or **antithetical** (-i kal), *adj.* in direct opposition.

*antitoxin** (an ti toks' in), *n.* a substance formed in the blood that neutralizes the disease or poison that produced it; serum thus formed in certain animals, used hypodermically to combat same disease in humans.

antler (ant' lēr), *n.* a deer's horn or one of its branches.

ant lion (ant li' un), an insect whose larva constructs a pitfall for ants and other insects.

antonym (an' tō nim), *n.* a word opposite to another in meaning, as bad is the *antonym* of good.

anvil (an' vil), *n.* an iron block on which metal pieces are shaped by hammering.

anxiety (ang zī' e ti), *n.* [*pl.* anxieties (-tiz)] a condition of mental uneasiness arising from fear, solicitude or apprehension.

Syn. Care, concern, solicitude, trouble, worry. *Anxiety* is great disquiet referring to future uncertainty; *care* implies disquiet because of burden or oppression; *concern* is anxious thought arising from interest; *solicitude* is greater than *concern* and us-

ually implies tender caring; *worry* is unnecessary *anxiety* or *solicitude*.

Ant. Indifference, unconcern.

anxious (angk' shus), *adj.* deeply concerned, desiring earnestly, solicitous, apprehensive.

any (en' i), *adj. and pron.* one, indeterminately, unlimited; some; an indefinite number, quantity or amount.

anybody (en' i bod i), *pron.* any person.

anyhow (en' i hou), *adv.* in any way; haphazard.

anyway (en' i wā), *adv.* in any manner, nevertheless.

*aorta** (ā ôr' ta), *n.* [*pl.* aortae (-tē)] the chief artery or main trunk of the arterial system.

apace (a pās'), *adv.* quickly, at a fast pace, speedily.

apache (a päsh'), *n.* French street ruffian.

apache (e' pachē), *n.* American Indian tribe.

apart (a pärt'), *adv.* separately, aside, asunder.

apartheid (ā pärt' hīt), *n.* racial segregation as practiced in the Republic of South Africa.

apartment (a pärt' ment), *n.* a set or suite of two or more rooms of a house set apart as lodgings.

apathetic (ap *a* thet' ik) or **apathetical** (ap *a* thet' i kal), *adj.* devoid of feeling or emotion.

apathy (ap' *a* thi), *n.* [*pl.* apathies (-thiz)] lack of feeling, want of passion or emotion.

ape (āp), *n.* a tailless monkey.

ape (āp), *v.t.* to imitate.

apeak (a pēk'), *adv.* vertical in position or nearly so.

*aperient** (a pēr' i ent), *n.* a food or medicine with mild laxative effect.

aperient (a pēr' i ent), *adj.* gently laxative.

*aperture** (ap' ēr tūr), *n.* an opening, gap.

*apex** (ā' peks), *n.* [*pl.* apexes (ā' pek sez) and apices (ap' i sēz)] the point, tip or summit of anything.

*aphasia** (a fā' zhi a), *n.* a brain condition involving loss of ability to use or comprehend ordinary speech.

*aphelion** (a fē' li on), *n.* [*pl.* aphelia (-li a)] that point in the orbit of a planet or comet which is farthest from the sun.

*aphid** (ā' fid), *n.* a plant louse.

*aphorism** (af' ō rizm), *n.* a concise statement of a rule or precept; a maxim.

apiary (ā' pi ēr' i), *n.* [*pl.* apiaries (-riz)] a place where bees are kept; a beehouse; a group of hives or bee colonies.

apiculture (ā' pi kul tūr), *n.* beekeeping.

apiece (a pēs'), *adv.* to or for each; severally.

aplomb (a plom'), *n.* self-possession; assurance.

apocalypse (a pok' *a* lips), *n.* a disclosure, revelation; (A-), the last book of the New Testament.

Apocrypha (a pok' ri fa), *n. pl.* certain writings received by some Christians as an authentic part of the holy Scriptures but rejected by others.

apogee (ap' ō jē), *n.* that point in the orbit of the moon or a planet which is most distant from the earth; culmination.

apologetic (a pol ō jet' ik) or **apological**

(-l kal), *adj.* offering an excuse; acknowledging, commonly with regret.

apologetics (a pol ō jet' iks), *n.* the defense and vindication of the principles and laws of the Christian belief.

apologize (a pol' ō jīz), *v.i.* to offer an excuse; to acknowledge a fault or offense with regret.

apologue (ap' ō lôg), *n.* a very short moral fable or allegory.

apology (a pol' ō ji), *n.* [*pl.* apologies (-jīz)] an expression of regret for something said or done; acknowledgment and explanation; a makeshift.

apoplectic (ap ō plek' tik) or **apoplectical** (-l kal), *adj.* caused by apoplexy; afflicted with apoplexy.

apoplexy (ap' ō plek si), *n.* sudden loss of consciousness and motive power due to a ruptured blood vessel or blood clot in the brain.

aport (a pōrt'), *adv.* on or toward the port or left side of a ship.

apostasy (a pos' ta si), *n.* [*pl.* apostasies (-siz)] the forsaking of what one has hitherto professed or adhered to.

apostate (a pos' tāt), *n.* one who has forsaken his faith or party.

*****apostle** (a pos' l), *n.* one charged with a high mission; (A-), one of the twelve persons specially selected by Christ to spread His teachings.

apostolic (ap os tol' ik) or **apostolical** (-l kal), *adj.* of or pertaining to an apostle.

*****apostrophe** (a pos' trō fē), *n.* a breaking off in a speech to address directly a person or thing that may or may not be present; the mark used in writing and print to indicate omission of letters or figures and as the sign of the possessive case.

apostrophize (a pos' trō fīz), *v.t.* to address by a rhetorical aside.

apothecaries' weight (a poth' ē ker iz wāt), the scale of weights used for compounding drugs.

apothecary (a poth' ē ker i), *n.* [*pl.* apothecaries (-riz)] one who prepares and dispenses medicines and drugs for profit.

apothegm (ap' ō them), *n.* a pithy saying embodying a wholesome truth or precept.

*****apotheosis** (ap ō thē' ō sis), *n.* [*pl.* apotheoses (-sēz)] deification, glorification.

appall (a pôl'), *v.t.* [*p.t. and p.p.* appalled, *pr.p.* appalling] to frighten; to horrify.

*****apparatus** (ap a rā' tus), *n.* [*pl.* apparatus] an outfit of tools, utensils or instruments for any kind of work.

apparel (a par' el), *n.* clothing, vesture, garb.

apparel (a par' el), *v.t.* [*p.t. and p.p.* appareled, *pr.p.* appareling] to clothe, supply with clothing.

apparent (a par' ent), *adj.* open to view, capable of being readily perceived or understood; seeming.

   Syn. Clear, evident, obvious, manifest, seeming.

   Ant. Hidden, actual.

apparition (ap pa rish' un), *n.* a ghost, specter.

appeal (a pēl'), *n.* a request for help; a plea;

removal of a law case to a higher court for reconsideration.

appeal (a pēl'), *v.t.* to transfer or refer to a superior court or judge; to request, as help or advice.

appear (a pēr'), *v.i.* to be or become visible; to come before some tribunal, as to plead a cause; seem.

appearance (a pēr' ans), *n.* the act of becoming visible; the object seen; look, aspect; seeming, as the *appearance* of compliance.

appease (a pēz'), *v.t.* to allay, assuage, quiet, satisfy, pacify.

*****appellant** (a pel' ant), *n.* one who appeals to a higher court.

*****appellate** (a pel' at), *adj.* pertaining to appeals.

appellation (ap e lā' shun), *n.* a name or nickname.

append (a pend'), *v.t.* to attach, add, annex or affix.

appendage (a pen' dij), *n.* something attached to a larger thing as a part.

*****appendicitis** (a pen di si' tis), *n.* inflammation of the vermiform appendix.

appendix (a pen' diks), *n.* [pl. appendixes (-dik ses) and appendices (-di sēz)] that which is added as a supplement; a tube admitting gas into a balloon or dirigible. The small worm-shaped tube 3 or 4 inches long (called the *vermiform appendix*) attached to the blind sac of the large intestine.

appertain (ap ēr tān'), *v.i.* to belong or pertain.

appetite (ap' ē tit), *n.* the desire for gratification of some want, craving or passion.

appetizer (ap' ē tī zēr), *n.* something that excites or whets the appetite.

applaud (a plôd'), *v.t.* to praise, express approval loudly, as by hand clapping.

applause (a plôz'), *n.* the expression of approval by hand clapping or cheers.

apple (ap' l), *n.* the round, fleshy fruit of the apple tree.

appliance (a pli' ans), *n.* the act of applying; any small mechanical apparatus designed to perform a particular task.

applicable (ap' li ka bl), *adj.* capable of being applied; suitable, to the point.

applicant (ap' li kant), *n.* one who applies.

application (ap li kā' shun), *n.* the act of applying, putting to or on; something applied, as a poultice.

applied (a plīd'), *adj.* put to concrete use, as *applied* science; opposite of *theoretical*.

*****appliqué** (ap' li kā'), *n.* a method of ornamentation in which cut-out figures of one material are applied on another.

apply (a plī'), *v.i.* to ask for; to have a bearing upon.

apply (a plī), *v.t.* [*p.t. and p.p.* applied, *pr.p.* applying] to place one to another, lay on; to put into practice, as rules.

appoint (a point'), *v.t.* to fix, select; to name for an office.

appointment (a point' ment), *n.* the act of appointing; the assigning to an office or trust; the office to which one is appointed; an engagement, as to meet someone at a certain place and time: *appointments,* equipment, as for a restaurant or dentist's office.

apportion (a pŏr' shun), *v.t.* to distribute in shares or parts, portion out, allot.

***apposite** (ap' ŏ zĭt), *adj.* proper; appropriate.

apposition (ap ŏ zĭsh' un), *n.* the act of placing or state of being placed side by side; relation of one noun or pronoun to another which it explains or characterizes, as God, the Father.

appraisal (a prāz' al), *n.* the act of appraising; an estimate of value or the value estimated.

appraise (a prāz'), *v.t.* to set a price upon; to estimate the value of.

appreciable (a prē shi *a* bl), *adj.* large enough or sufficient to be perceived, recognizable.

appreciate (a prē' shi āt), *v.i. and v.t.*; to grow in value; to value, enjoy with gratitude; have a sensitive understanding of.

appreciation (a prē shi ā' shun), *n.* the just valuation of worth or merit; advance in value.

apprehend (ap rē hend'), *v.t.* to understand; to anticipate fearfully; to seize or arrest.

apprehension (ap rē hen' shun), *n.* the act of seizure or laying hold, arrest; anticipation of something feared, dread; mental conception, understanding.

Syn. Foreboding, misgiving. *Apprehension* is the dread of future evil. *Misgiving* is such great *apprehension* as to affect courage and action; *foreboding* is not only dread but conviction of coming evil.

apprentice (a-pren' tĭs), *n.* one bound by agreement to learn some trade or craft.

approach (a prōch'), *n.* act of drawing near, advance; an approximation.

approach (a prōch'), *v.i.* to draw near; to approximate.

approbation (ap rō bā' shun), *n.* approval, commendation.

appropriate (a prō' prĭ āt), *v.t.* to take for one's own use; to designate and set aside for some special use.

appropriation (a prō prĭ ā' shun), *n.* the act of appropriating, especially to oneself; a sum of money set aside for a specified purpose.

approval (a proov' al), *n.* approbation, sanction.

approve (a proov'), *v.t.* to favor, accept, think favorably of.

***approximate** (a proks' ĭ māt), *v.t.* to come near to, approach, especially in number.

approximate (a proks' ĭ mit), *adj.* nearly but not exactly the same, as *approximate* figures.

approximately (a proks' ĭ mit lĭ), *adv.* very nearly but not absolutely.

approximation (a proks ĭ mā' shun), *n.* a near approach; something almost but not exactly correct.

appurtenance (a pur' tē nans), *n.* that which belongs or relates to something else.

***apricot** (ā' prĭ kot), *n.* the orange-colored fruit of a tree allied to the peach and the plum.

April (ā' prĭl), *n.* the fourth month of the year.

apron (ā' prun), *n.* a garment of cloth, leather or other material, worn in front to protect the clothing; a paved space in front of an airplane hangar.

apse (aps), *n.* [*pl.* apses (-ez)] a polygonal or semicircular recess, usually arched or domed, at the end of a church behind the choir space.

apt (apt), *adj.* suitable, pertinent, appropriate; inclined, as *apt* to stutter; quick, skillful, as an *apt* speller or workman.

aptitude (ap' tĭ tūd), *n.* ability to learn, special fitness.

***aqua** (ak' wa), *n.* a term used in pharmacy in the abbreviated form aq., and denoting water.

***aquamarine** (ak wa ma rēn'), *n.* a bluish-green variety of beryl.

***aquarium** (a kwâr' ĭ um), *n.* [*pl.* aquariums (-umz) and aquaria (-*a*)] a tank or globe for the keeping and cultivation of aquatic plants and creatures.

aquatic (a kwat' ĭk), *adj.* pertaining to water; living in water.

aquatint (ak' wa tint), *n.* a species of etching with aqua fortis resembling a watercolor or India-ink drawing.

***aqua vitae** (vī' tē), unrectified alcohol; brandy and other ardent spirits.

***aqueduct** (ak' wē dukt), *n.* a conduit or artificial channel to bring water from a distance.

***aqueous** (a' kwē us), *adj.* of the nature of water; abounding in water.

aquiline (ak' wĭ lĭn), *adj.* belonging to or resembling an eagle; hooked like an eagle's beak, as an *aquiline* nose.

***Arabic numerals** (ar' *a* bĭk nū' mēr alz), the figures 0, 1, 2, 3, 4, 5, 6, 7, 8, 9.

arable (ar' a bl), *adj.* fit for cultivation, especially with the plow.

arachnid (a rak' nid), *n.* any of a class of arthropods (Arachnida): spiders, scorpions, etc.

arbiter (är' bĭ tēr), *n.* an umpire or judge.

arbitrament (är bĭt' ra ment), *n.* a decision; the right or power to decide.

arbitrary (är' bĭ trer ĭ), *adj.* depending on will or whim; imperious; self-willed.

arbitrate (är' bĭ trāt), *v.i. and v.t.* to act as arbiter; to settle, as a dispute.

arbitration (är bĭ trā' shun), *n.* the settlement of a dispute by a neutral agency; the policy of referring disputed matters to arbitrators.

arbitrator (är' bĭ trā tēr), *n.* a person or court empowered by disputants to give judgment on their claims or contentions.

arbor (är' bēr), *n.* a bower; a shaded nook.

***arboretum** (är bō rē' tum), *n.* [*pl.* arboreta (-ta) and arboretums (-tumz)] a place in which trees are cultivated and exhibited.

arboriculture (är' bō rĭ kul tūr), *n.* the cultivation of trees and shrubs.

***arbor vitae** (är' bēr vī' tē), an evergreen tree extensively cultivated in gardens.

arc (ärk), *n.* a segment of a circle.

arcade (är kād'), *n.* an arched gallery or promenade, usually lined with shops.

arcanum (är kā' num), *n.* [*pl.* arcana ('na)] a secret, a mystery.

arch (ärch), *n.* a curved structure of brick or masonry made of wedge-shaped parts having their joints at right angles to the curved line; any doorway or passage topped by such a construction.

arch (ärch), *adj.* coy and playful; chief, as in *arch*deacon.

archaic (är kā' ĭk) or **archaical** (-ĭ kal), *adj.* antiquated; long out of use.

archangel (ärk ān' jel), *n.* an angel of the highest order.

*****archbishop** (ärch bish' up), *n.* a chief bishop.

archdeacon (ärch dē' kn), *n.* a dignitary ranking next below a bishop.

archduchess (ärch duch' es), *n.* the wife of an archduke.

archduchy (ärch duch' ĭ), *n.* [*pl.* archduchies ('-ĭz)] the territory or rank of an archduke.

archduke (ärch dūk'), *n.* a prince of the former imperial house of Austria.

archeology or **archaeology** (är kē ol' ō jĭ), *n.* scientific study of the relics of ancient civilizations.

archer (är' chēr), *n.* a bowman.

archery (är' chēr ĭ), *n.* the art of using the bow and arrow.

*****archetype** (är' kĕ tīp), *n.* the original type, pattern or model of anything.

*****archipelago** (är kĭ pel' *a* gō), *n.* [*pl.* archipelagoes (-gōz)] any sea or body of salt water interspersed with numerous islands; also the group of islands.

*****architect** (är' kĭ tekt), *n.* one who makes plans for buildings and bridges and supervises their erection.

architecture (ar' kĭ tek chûr), *n.* the science or art of building; a certain method or style of building, as Roman *architecture;* building in general, as fine *architecture.*

archives (är' kĭvz), *n. pl.* public records; the place where public records and documents are stored.

archly (ärch' lĭ), *adv.* roguishly, waggishly, coyly.

arc lamp (ärk lamp), a lamp having a luminous bridge or arc.

arc light (lĭt), *n.* a light produced by a current of electricity passing between two carbon points.

*****arctic** (ärk' tĭk), *adj.* relating to the north polar regions; frigid, polar.

arctic circle (sûr' kl), an imaginary circle parallel to the equator and distant 23° 30' from the north pole.

ardent (är' dent), *adj.* hot, eager.

ardor (är' dēr), *n.* heat, warmth of affection or passion; eagerness, zeal, enthusiasm.

arduous (är' dū us), *adj.* steep, hard to climb, difficult.

*****area** (ā' rē *a*), *n.* [*pl.* areas (-as)] any plane surface having bounds; the extent of such a surface in units of square measure.

arena (a rē' na), *n.* [*pl.* arenas (-naz)] the central inclosed space of a Roman amphitheater; area of combat or competition, as in war or sport.

argent (är' jent), *adj.* silvery; white and shining.

argentiferous (är jen tif' ēr us), *adj.* bearing silver.

argil (är' jĭl), *n.* potter's clay or earth.

argol (är' gol), *n.* crude tartar from which cream of tartar is prepared.

argon (är' gon), *n.* a gaseous element associated with nitrogen and forming one of the constituents of the air.

argosy (är' gō sĭ), *n.* [*pl.* argosies (-sĭz)] a large, richly freighted merchant vessel; a fleet of ships.

argue (är' gū), *v.t. and v.i.* to discuss a proposition, as in a debate; to reason for or against; to reason, dispute.

argument (är' gū ment), *n.* that which is advanced in support or proof, reasoning; discussion.

argumentation (är gū men tā' shun), *n.* the act of arguing; disputation.

argumentative (är gū men' ta tĭv), *adj.* exhibiting or fond of controversy.

argyrol (är' jĭ rōl), *n.* a silver salt used in a water solution as an antiseptic, especially for the eyes and throat.

*****aria** (ä' rĭ *a*), *n.* an air; a melody or tune for single voice with accompaniment.

arid (ar' ĭd), *adj.* dry, parched, barren.

aridity (a rĭd' ĭ tĭ), *n.* dryness, barrenness.

aright (a rīt'), *adv.* rightly; in a right way or form.

arise (a rīz'), *v.i.* [*p.t.* arose, *p.p.* arisen, *pr.p.* arising] to mount up or ascend; to come into existence or to notice; to originate.

aristocracy (ar ĭs tok' ra sĭ), *n.* [*pl.* aristocracies (-sĭz)] the nobility or best persons in a state; any government by a minority supposedly best qualified to rule; any state so governed; those superior in rank, wealth or intellect; a privileged class.

*****aristocrat** (a rĭs' tō krat), *n.* a personage of rank and noble birth; a person who possesses traits supposed to characterize the nobility.

arithmetic (a rith' me tĭk), *n.* the science of numbers.

arithmetical (ar ĭth met' ĭ kal), *adj.* of or pertaining to arithmetic.

ark (ärk), *n.* the repository of the Covenant, or Tables of the Law, in the Jewish tabernacle; the vessel in which Noah and his family were preserved during the deluge; a place of safety.

arm (ärm), *v.i. and v.t.* to arm oneself, prepare for battle; to supply with arms for military service; to fortify mentally.

arm (ärm), *n.* a weapon; a branch of an active army.

arm (ärm), *n.* the limb of the human body that extends from the shoulder to the hand; the forelimb of a quadruped; an inlet of the sea; the armrest of a chair.

*****armada** (är mä' da), *n.* a fleet of armed vessels.

armament (är' ma ment), *n.* a nation's total equipment for war; the act of supplying the means of war.

armature (är' ma tūr), *n.* a piece of soft iron connecting the poles of a magnet; the conductors in a motor that move when an electric current passes through them.

armchair (ärm' chär), *n.* a chair with side pieces on which one may rest his arms.

*****armistice** (är' mĭs tĭs), *n.* a temporary cessation of hostilities; a truce.

armlet (ärm' let), *n.* a bracelet, an elastic or

ornamental band for the upper arm.

armor (är' mẽr), n. any defensive covering; protective plates of steel or other metal for the body of a warrior or the hull of a ship.

armorer (är' mẽr ẽr), n. a maker of arms or armor; one in charge of arms.

armorial (är mō' ri al), adj. pertaining to armor or to the arms or escutcheon of a family.

armory (är' mẽr i), n. [pl. -ries (-riz)] a place where arms are kept, often containing a big space for the assembly of soldiers.

armpit (ärm' pit), n. the hollow beneath the joining of the arm and shoulder.

arms (ärmz), n. pl. weapons of offense or defense; the military service; a design symbolic of a family or nation.

army (är' mi), n. [pl. armies ('-miz)] a body of men trained and equipped for war on land, composed of a headquarters, two or more corps and auxiliary troops.

arnica (är' ni ka), n. a genus of perennial herbs; a remedy for bruises made from the roots.

*****aroma** (a rō' ma), n. [pl. aromas] perfume, fragrance, pleasing odor, scent.

aromatic (ar ō mat' ik), adj. having, giving out or containing an agreeable odor; pungent, spicy, fragrant.

around (a round'), adv. in a circle; on every side; roundabout.

around (a round'), prep. encircling, as run around the house; enveloping, as pull the blanket around you; about, almost, as around the end of the year, it cost around $5.

arouse (a rouz'), v.i. and v.t. to stir to action; to awaken.

*****arraign** (a rān'), v.t. to summon, as a prisoner at the bar of a court to answer to a charge; to call to account.

arraignment (a rān' ment), n. a summons to a prisoner to defend himself in court; an accusation.

arrange (a rānj'), v.t. and v.i. to put in proper order or sequence; to classify; to arrive at an agreement or settlement.

arrangement (a rānj' ment), n. the act of putting in proper form or order; preparation and provision for future happenings; plan, order, disposition.

arrant (ar' ant), adj. confirmed; unmitigated.

arras (ar' as), n. tapestry.

array (a rā'), n. a grouping of men or things in orderly arrangement; rich attire.

array (a rā'), v.t. [p.t. and p.p. -ed, pr. p. -ing] to place or dispose in order, marshal; to deck or dress.

arrear (a rēr'), n. that which is overdue, delinquent in payment; in arrears, in debt.

arrest (a rest'), n. the act of stopping motion or action; seizure by officers of the law.

arrest (a rest'), v.t. to stop or stay; to check or hinder, as action or motion; to seize; to take by legal authority.

arresting (a res' ting), adj. commanding attention; remarkable.

arrival (a ri' val), n. the act of coming to a place; attaining an objective; a person or thing that has arrived, as new arrivals at a

hotel.

arrive (a rīv'), v.i. to come to or reach.

arrogance (ar' ō gans), n. an undue degree of self-importance.

arrogant (ar' ō gant), adj. making exorbitant claims to dignity or estimation; haughty.

arrogate (ar' ō gāt), v.t. to assume or lay claim to unduly; to usurp.

arrow (ar' o), n. a slender, missile weapon shot from a bow, usually feathered and barbed; a mark used to indicate direction.

arsenal (är' se nal), n. a building for the making, repairing and storing of military weapons.

*****arsenic** (är' se nik), n. a metallic element of steel-gray color and brilliant luster and exceedingly brittle; a poisonous salt of this metal, especially arsenic trioxide.

arson (är' sn), n. the malicious burning of another person's property; intentional burning of one's own property.

art (ärt), n. skill in doing obtained from experience or study; the skillful adaptation and application to some human purpose or use of knowledge acquired from nature; creation of beauty in literature, painting, music, dancing.

arterial (är tēr' i al), adj. pertaining to an artery or the arteries: contained in an artery.

artery (är' tēr i), n. [pl. arteries (-iz)] one of a system of tubes or vessels which convey the blood from the heart to all parts of the body.

artesian well (är tē' zhan wel), a well formed by boring to reach stores of water between strata of rock, the water being forced up by pressure from below.

artful (ärt' ful), adj. cunning, crafty.

artichoke (är'ti chōk), n. a plant with thistle-like foliage and bearing large terminal flower heads, eaten as a vegetable.

article (är' ti kl), n. a distinct portion or member; a single clause, item or particular, as in a formal agreement or treaty; a prose composition complete in itself, as in a newspaper or magazine; a part of speech, a word limiting a noun and showing that it is a definite (the is the definite article) or indefinite (a and an are indefinite articles) person or thing.

articulate (är tik' ū lāt), v.t. and v.i. to joint; to form, as words; to utter in distinct syllables; to fit together by means of a joint; to speak.

articulate (är tik' ū lāt), adj. jointed; possessing the power of speech; clear and distinct.

articulation (är tik ū lā' shun), n. the act of jointing; the act of speaking distinctly.

*****artifice** (är' ti fis), n. an artful or crafty device; an ingenious expedient.

artificial (är ti fish' al), adj. made or contrived by art: produced by human skill or labor not by nature; synthetic; unnatural, affected.

artificiality (-fish i al' i ti), n. the quality of being unreal or unnatural; affected manners.

artificially (-fish i al li), adv. by human skill

or contrivance.

artillery (är til′ er l), *n.* cannon; mounted guns; the army service that uses them.

artisan (är′ ti zan), *n.* one skilled in any art or trade.

artist (är′ tist), *n.* one skilled in any fine art.

artistic (är tis′ tik) or **artistical** (-ti kal), *adj.* pertaining to art or to artists; characterized by taste or skill in one of the arts; having esthetic feeling or appreciation.

artless (ärt′ les), *adj.* lacking art; natural; unskillful.

as (az), *adv.* to the same extent or degree, as Tom sings *as* well as Bob; for instance.

as (az), *conj.* in the same manner, as speak *as* I do; while, as run *as* you read; since, as let's not go, *as* it is raining.

*asbestos (as bes′ tos), *n.* a fibrous variety of hornblende, incombustible and a nonconductor of heat, used for fireproofing and insulation.

ascend (a send′), *v.i. and v.t.* to take an upward direction; to mount, go up, rise; to climb, as to *ascend* a hill.

ascendancy (a sen′ dan si) or **ascendency** (′den si), *n.* a governing or controlling power or influence; domination.

ascendant (a sen′ dant), *n.* dominant position; ruling influence.

ascendant (a sen′ dant) or **ascendent** (-dent), *adj.* rising, superior, predominant; above the horizon.

ascension (a sen′ shun), *n.* the act of moving upward, a rising.

ascent (a sent′), *n.* the act of rising, an upward movement or slope.

ascertain (as ĕr tān′), *v.t.* to find out for certain.

*ascetic (a set′ ik), *n.* one who renounces the pursuit of pleasure; a hermit, recluse.

*ascetic (a set′ ik), *adj.* rigid in the exercise of religious duties and mortification of worldly desires; austere.

ascribe (as krib′), *v.t.* to attribute, impute or assign, as to *ascribe* success to hard work.

ascription (a skrip′ shun), *n.* the act of attributing or imputing.

aseptic (a sep′ tik), *adv.* free from germs of disease or putrefaction.

ash (ash), *n.* a tree of the olive family; its tough and elastic wood, suitable for many uses.

ash (ash), *n.* [*pl.* ashes (-ez)] the remains of matter after burning; the color of ashes.

ashamed (a shămd′), *adj.* affected or touched by shame; fearful of reproach.

ashen (ash′ n), *adj.* pertaining to the ash tree; made of ash; of the color of ashes, pale.

aside (a sid′), *n.* a remark not meant to be heard by all present.

aside (a sid), *adv.* at, to or on one side; apart.

asinine (as′ i nīn), *adj.* silly, like an ass, stupid; obstinate.

ask (åsk), *v.t. and v.i.* to request; to question; to inquire; to invite.

Syn. Inquire, interrogate, request, beg. We perform all these actions in order to get information. To *ask* is the general term for to question; to *inquire* is purely to seek

information. People *ask* of one another whatever they wish to know; learners *inquire* the reasons for things which are new to them; a magistrate *interrogates* criminals formally and systematically. To *request* is to ask formally and politely; to *beg* is to ask very respectfully. It is a convention of politeness, as I *beg* your pardon, I *beg* you will come.

askance (a skans′), *adv.* sideways, obliquely, awry; with suspicion or disdain.

askew (a skū′), *adv.* crookedly; awry.

askew (a skū′), *adj.* set to one side, as my hat is blown *askew.*

aslant (a slånt′), *adv. and adj.* obliquely at an angle.

asleep (a slēp′), *adj.* sleeping; numb.

asp (asp), *n.* a small venomous snake of Egypt.

asparagus (as par′ a gus), *n.* a plant having tender edible stalks.

aspect (as′ pekt), *n.* appearance to the eye or mind; look, mien, air; outlook or prospect.

aspen (as′ pen), *n.* a species of poplar tree whose leaves tremble when the air stirs.

asperity (as per′ i ti), *n.* [*pl.* asperities (-tiz)] roughness, harshness; bitterness of temper.

aspersion (as pĕr′ shun), *n.* slander.

asphalt (as′ fôlt), *n.* a compact, brittle variety of native bitumen, used in paving, roofing or cementing.

*asphyxia (as fik′ si *a*), *n.* suffocation, due to lack of oxygen.

asphyxiate (as fik′ si āt), *v.t.* to suffocate.

*aspirant (as pir′ ant *or* as′ pi rant), *n.* one who seeks to attain something, as an office.

aspirate (as′ pi rāt), *v.t.* to pronounce with a full breathing; to pronounce the sound of the letter *h.*

aspiration (as pi rā′ shun), *n.* ambition; an aspirated sound, a breath.

aspire (as pir′), *v.i.* to seek ambitiously; to desire with great longing.

aspirin (as′ pi rin), *n.* a drug derived from salicylic acid used to relieve pain.

ass (ås), *n.* a quadruped resembling the horse but smaller and having longer ears, a shorter mane and a tufted tail.

assail (as sāl′), *v.t.* to fall upon or attack with vehemence.

assassin (a sas′ in), *n.* one who kills treacherously or by covert assault.

assassinate (a sas′ i nāt), *v.t.* to kill by secret or treacherous means.

assault (a sôlt′), *n.* an attack with violence by physical means; an onslaught.

assay (a sā′), *n.* the act or process of determining by analysis the quantity or proportion of any one or more metals in a metallic compound.

assay (a sā′), *v.t. and v.i.* to analyze a compound of metals; to estimate a value by analyzing.

assemblage (a sem′ blij), *n.* the act of meeting or gathering together; a large group.

assemble (a sem′ bl), *v.i. and v.t.* to collect or gather together in one place or body.

assembly (a sem′ bli), *n.* [*pl.* assemblies (-bliz)] a collection or company of persons brought together in one place.

assent (a sent′), *n.* agreement, concurrence.

assent (a sent'), *v.i.* to admit as true; to concede.

Syn. Consent. *Assent* respects the understanding. We *assent* to what we admit to be true. *Consent* respects the will; we *consent* to what we allow to be done.

Ant. Disagree, dissent.

assert (a sûrt'), *v.t.* to maintain, declare positively or with assurance.

Syn. Maintain, vindicate. We *assert* anything to be true; we *maintain* it by adducing proofs, facts or arguments; we *vindicate* our own conduct or that of another when it is called in question.

Ant. Deny.

assertion (a sûr' shun), *n.* the act of asserting; that which is asserted, statement.

assertive (a sûr' tiv), *adj.* positive; dogmatical.

assess (a ses'), *v.t.* to fix or determine, as damages; to appraise for taxation, as property.

assessor (a ses' ẽr), *n.* one appointed to assess property or persons for taxation.

*****assets** (as' ets), *n. pl.* the property or effects of an insolvent debtor; the entire property of an individual, partnership or corporation.

asseverate (a sev' ẽr āt), *v.t.* to affirm or aver positively or with great earnestness.

assiduity (as i dū' i ti), *n.* [*pl.* assiduities (-tiz)] close application or unremitting attention to a task; perseverence.

assiduous (a sid' ū us), *adj.* constant in application, diligent, persistent.

assign (a sīn'), *v.t.* to appoint, mark out, apportion, make over; to fix; to designate for a specific purpose.

*****assignee** (as i nē'), *n.* one to whom an assignment of anything is made.

assignment (a sīn' ment), *n.* a setting apart, allotment or appointment; a transfer of legal title or of an interest in a property or business.

assigner (a sīn' ẽr) or **assignor** (-ôr), *n.* one who assigns or transfers an interest.

assimilate (a sim' i lāt), *v.t.* to bring to conformity or agreement with something else; to digest.

assimilation (a sim i lā' shun), *n.* the absorption of nutritive elements; transformation of food into body tissues.

assist (a sist'), *v.t. and v.i.* to help, aid, give support to.

assistance (a sis' tans), *n.* help, aid.

assistant (a sis' tant), *n.* one who helps; an aid of any kind.

assistant (a sis' tant), *adj.* helping, lending aid.

*****assize** (a sīz'), *n.* [*pl.* assizes (-sī' zez)] a court session for the trial by jury of civil or criminal cases.

associate (a sō' shi āt), *n.* a companion; confederate; ally; colleague.

associate (a sō' shi āt), *v.i. and v.t.* to join; to co-operate; to be intimate; to join or combine, as things or thoughts, as we *associate* the idea of water with swimming.

associate (a sō' shi āt), *adj.* joined with, as in business.

*****association** (a sō si ā' shun), *n.* the act of associating or state of being associated; union.

assort (a sôrt'), *v.t.* to divide or separate into lots according to arrangement.

assorted (a sôr' ted), *adj.* consisting of different varieties.

assortment (a sôrt' ment), *n.* the act of assorting; a collection of different varieties.

*****assuage** (a swāj'), *v.t.* to soften, mitigate.

assume (a sūm'), *v.t.* to take to oneself; to take in or into; to take upon oneself; to take for granted.

assumption (a sump' shun), *n.* the act of assuming; that which is assumed.

assurance (a shoor' ans), *n.* a pledge, promise; confidence, self-reliance; insurance.

assure (a shoor'), *v.t.* to make sure or certain; to inspire confidence by declaration or promise.

aster (as' tẽr), *n.* a genus of flowering plants with rosette-shaped flowers; any plant of the genus aster.

asterisk (as' tẽr isk), *n.* the mark (*) used in printing as a reference to a footnote or to indicate omission of letters or words (***).

astern (a stẽrn'), *adv.* at or toward the hinder part of a ship.

asthma (az' ma), *n.* a respiratory disease, chronically recurrent and attended by difficulty of breathing.

astigmatism (a stig' ma tizm), *n.* a defect in the structure of the eye, causing a blur in parts of the field of vision.

astir (a stûr'), *adj.* on the move, active.

astonish (a ston' ish), *v.t.* to strike with sudden wonder, amaze.

astonishment (a ston' ish ment), *n.* surprise, amazement.

astound (a stound'), *v.t.* to stun or bewilder with amazement.

astray (a strā'), *adv.* out of the right way.

astride (a strīd'), *adv.* with the legs straddling, as to ride *astride*.

astringent (as trin' jent), *adj.* binding, contracting.

astrologer (as trol' ō jẽr), *n.* one who professes to forecast events by means of the stars.

astrology (as trol' ō ji), *n.* the pseudo science of prediction by means of the stars.

astronaut (as' trō nôt), *n.* a person trained to travel in outer space.

astronomer (as tron' ō mẽr), *n.* one who studies or is versed in astronomy.

astronomic (as trō nom' ik) or **astronomical** (-i kal), *adj.* pertaining to astronomy or according to astronomical laws.

astronomy (as tron' ō mi), *n.* the study of the heavenly bodies.

astroturf (as' trō turf), *n.* manmade imitation grass for an indoor stadium.

*****astute** (as tūt'), *adj.* shrewd, keenly penetrating, sagacious, cunning, crafty.

asunder (a sun' dẽr), *adv.* apart; into parts.

asylum (a sī' lum), *n.* [*pl.* asylums (-lumz)] an institution for the care or relief of the aged, destitute, insane or otherwise afflicted; a refuge, protection.

*****asymmetrical** (a si met' ri kal), *adj.* without symmetry.

at (at), *prep.* in, on or near in place or time,

as *at* school, *at* one o'clock; to or toward, as look *at* that, aim *at* a mark; by, as come in *at* the door; in a state of, as *at* war, *at* a disadvantage; for, as to sell *at* $1.; assuming, as *at* best.

*atavism (at' *a* vizm), *n.* the reversion or tendency to revert to a primitive type; the appearance in an individual of the traits of a remote ancestor.

*ataxia (a taks' i *a*), *n.* lack of muscular coordination.

atheism (ā' thē izm), *n.* disbelief in the existence of God.

atheist (ā' thē ist), *n.* one who disbelieves or denies the existence of God.

*athlete (ath' lēt), *n.* a competitor in sports; one trained to great physical skill and strength.

athletic (ath let' ik), *adj.* pertaining to athletes or their performances.

athletics (ath let' iks), *n. pl.* athletic games and sports in general.

athwart (a thwôrt'), *prep.* across, from one side to the other.

atlas (at' las), *n.* [*pl.* atlases (-ez)] a collection of maps in a volume.

atmosphere (at' mos fēr), *n.* the air enveloping the earth; the kind of air prevailing in any place, as a foggy *atmosphere;* the tone of a work of art; any permeating influence, as the *atmosphere* of school life.

atoll (at' ol), *n.* an outer ring of coral surrounding a basin or lagoon.

atom (at' um), *n.* a particle of matter, until recently considered the smallest part into which an element could be divided.

atomic (a tom' ik) or a·tomical (-i kal), *adj.* pertaining to or consisting of atoms.

atomic number (num' bēr), the number of positive electric charges carried by an atom.

atomizer (at' um iz ēr), *n.* an instrument for spraying a liquid, as a gargle or perfume.

atone (a tōn), *v.i.* [*p.t. and p.p.* atoned, *pr.p.* atoning] to make reparation or amends.

atonement (a tōn' ment), *n.* reparation or explation; the recompense for sin typified by the sufferings and death of Christ.

atrocious (a trō' shus), *adj.* wicked in the highest degree, outrageous.

atrocity (a tros' i ti), *n.* [*pl.* atrocities (-tiz)] an act of barbarism or cruelty, as the bombing of a hospital in war.

*atrophy (at' rō fi), *n.* a wasting or withering, as of a part of the body.

*atrophy (at' rō fi), *v.i.* [*p.t. and p.p.* atrophied, *pr.p.* atrophying] to waste away, to dwindle.

attach (a tach'), *v.t.* to fasten or affix.

attachment (a tach' ment), *n.* the act of attaching; something attached, a connection; affection, devotion.

attack (a tak'), *n.* an assault; a hostile act; injurious criticism; seizure, as of disease.

attack (a tak'), *v.t.* to assault; to censure; to start upon, as a task.

attain (a tān'), *v.t.* to achieve, gain, compass.

attainder (a tān' der), *n.* the depriving a criminal of civil rights; disgrace, dishonor.

attainment (a tān' ment), *n.* the act of attain-

ing; accomplishment.

attaint (a tānt'), *v.t.* to taint, corrupt; to judge a person guilty of a crime that forfeits civil rights; to disgrace.

attempt (a tempt'), *n.* a trial, effort.

attempt (a tempt'), *v.t.* to make an effort to accomplish, try, endeavor to perform.

attend (a tend'), *v.t. and v.i.* [*p.t. and p.p.* attended, *pr.p.* attending] to wait upon; to accompany or be present with or at; to take care of, as *attend* a furnace; to pay attention, listen, mind, as *attend* to your own business.

attendance (a ten' dans), *n.* the act of attending; waiting on; presence; the persons present, as at a meeting.

attendant (a ten' dant), *n.* one who accompanies or serves another; that which follows upon or accompanies.

attention (a ten' shun), *n.* the act of applying the mind to anything; consideration or regard for any person or thing.

attenuate (a ten' ū āt), *v.t.* to make thin or slender; to weaken or reduce; to thin out by dilution; to rarefy.

attest (a test'), *v.t.* to bear witness to; to certify as being genuine or true.

attic (at' ik), *n.* the top floor of a house directly under the roof and generally unfinished; a garret.

*attire (a tīr'), *n.* clothing; apparel.

attire (a tīr'), *v.t.* to dress, clothe, array.

attitude (at' i tūd), *n.* bodily position; disposition toward.

*attorney (a tûr' ni), *n.* a lawyer; one empowered to act for another in matters of business.

attract (a tract'), *v.t.* to draw to or toward; to arouse attention and interest.

attraction (a trak' shun), *n.* the act or power of attracting; charm; anything that draws onlookers or an audience.

attribute (at' ri būt), *n.* a characteristic; essential quality.

attribute (a trib' ūt), *v.t.* to ascribe, as to a cause; to give credit for.

attributive (a trib' ū tiv), *n.* a word that denotes a quality or characteristic of something; an adjective or adjectival phrase standing before its noun.

attrition (a trish' un), *n.* a wearing away by rubbing or friction.

attune (a tūn'), *v.t.* to tune; bring into harmony; to adjust.

auburn (ô' bērn), *adj.* reddish brown.

auction (ôk' shun), *n.* a public sale at which the highest bidder becomes the buyer.

auction (ôk' shun), *v.t.* to sell by taking bids.

auctioneer (ôk shun ēr), *n.* a person authorized to sell by taking bids.

audacious (ô dā' shus), *adj.* bold, daring; impudent.

audacity (ô das' i ti), *n.* boldness, daring; impudence.

audible (ô' di bl), *adj.* capable of being heard.

audience (ô' di ens), *n.* an assemblage of persons listening or looking on; an interview.

audio (ô' dē o), *adj.* of or using sound.

audit (ô' dit), *n.* official examination of claims

or accounts.

audit (ô′ dit), *v.t.* to check accounts or claims.

audition (ô dish′ un), *n.* a test hearing of a speaker or musician for professional engagement.

auditor (ô′ di tẽr), *n.* a person whose business it is to check and adjust claims and accounts.

auditorium (ô di tô′ ri um), *n.* a building or hall in which an audience gathers.

auditory (ô′ di tô′ ri), *adj.* having to do with the sense of hearing or the organs of hearing.

auger (ô′ gẽr), *n.* a tool for boring holes.

aught (ôt), *n.* anything; a cipher.

*augment (ôg ment′), *v.i. and v.t.* to enlarge; to increase.

augur (ô′ ger), *n.* an ancient Roman diviner or prophet; a soothsayer.

augur (ô′ gẽr), *v.i. and v.t.* to predict from signs or omens.

augury (ô gū′ ri), *n.* prediction by interpretation of signs; divination.

august (ô gust′), *adj.* impressive; having great dignity; majestic.

August (ô′ gust), *n.* the eighth month of the year.

auk (ôk), *n.* a diving bird of the Arctic regions.

*aunt (änt), *n.* the sister of one's father or mother.

*aura (ô′ ra), *n.* an invisible radiation from the body, supposed to surround it like an atmosphere and to influence others.

aural (ô′ ral), *adj.* having to do with the ear.

*auricle (ô′ ri kl), *n.* the outer part of the ear; one of the upper chambers of the heart that receives blood from the veins.

auriform (ô′ ri fôrm), *adj.* ear-shaped.

aurochs (ô′ roks), *n.* a shaggy-coated breed of bison of which the surviving specimens are carefully protected in Lithuania and the Caucasus.

*auspice (ôs′ pis), *n.* omens or signs, especially those used by ancient Roman augurs; patronage, as under the *auspices* of.

auspicious (ôs pish′ us), *adj.* having promise of success; favorable, propitious.

austere (ôs tẽr′), *adv.* harsh, severe; unadorned.

austerity (ôs ter′ i ti), *n.* severity of manner or of way of living.

authentic (ô then′ tik), *adj.* genuine, as an *authentic* signature; duly authorized, as information; true; trustworthy.

authenticate (ô then′ ti kāt), *v.t.* to show to be genuine; to give authority to.

authenticity (ô then tis′ i ti), *n.* genuineness.

author (ô′ thẽr), *n.* an originator, especially, the writer of a book.

authoritative (ô thôr′ i tā tiv), *n.* having authority; commanding.

authority (ô thôr′ i ti), *n.* the power or right to command; one whose judgment is accepted as decisive; anything cited as proof, as the dictionary is my *authority: the authorities*, those in power or command.

authorize (ô′ thẽr iz), *v.t.* to give authority to; to sanction; to approve.

*autobiography (ô tô bi ôg′ ra fi), *n.* the story of a person's life as told by himself.

*autocracy (ô tŏk′ ra si), *n.* absolute, unlimited power in government; a state having the government vested in one supreme individual.

autogiro (ô tô ji′ rô), *n.* an aircraft moved up or down by horizontal vanes over the fuselage.

autograph (ô′ tô gráf), *n.* a person's own, handwritten signature.

autograph (ô′ tô gráf), *v.t.* to write one's signature in, as a book, or on, as a picture.

autointoxication (ô tô in tok si kā′ shun), *n.* poisoning from matter produced within one's own body.

automat (ô′ tô mat), *n.* a self-operating device, as for service of food in a restaurant.

automatic (ô tô mạt′ ik), *adj.* self-operating.

automaton (ô tom′ a ton), *n.* a self-operating mechanism that moves in imitation of a live body.

autonomous (ô ton′ ô mus), *adj.* self-governing.

autonomy (ô ton′ ô mi), *n.* self-government.

*autopsy (ô′ top si), *n.* a post-mortem examination to determine the cause of death.

*auxiliary (ôg zil′ ya ri), *n.* a helper; anything that helps, as an *auxiliary* engine; a verb used in forming the different moods and tenses of other verbs. *Shall, will, can, must* are some of the *auxiliary* verbs in English.

auxiliary (ôg zil′ ya ri), *adj.* helping; subsidiary.

avail (a vāl′), *v.i. and v.t.* to be of use or service; to help, as subterfuge will not *avail* you.

available (a vāl′ a bl), *adj.* usable; at hand, ready for use.

*avalanche (av′ a länch), *n.* the slide of a mass of loose earth, rock or snow and ice down a mountainside; impact of a sudden crushing weight, as of grief or disaster.

avarice (av′ a ris), *n.* greed; inordinate desire for wealth.

avaricious (av a rish′ us), *adj.* greedy for wealth; mean; grasping.

*avast (a väst′), *v.t. and v.i.* stop: used only in imperative, as *avast* hauling.

*avaunt (a vônt′), *interj.* begone.

avenge (a venj′), *v.t.* to inflict punishment or exact satisfaction for wrong done.

Syn. Punish, retaliate, revenge. To *avenge* is to inflict punishment in order to vindicate the righteous; to *revenge* is to inflict suffering upon another through personal anger and resentment; to *avenge* is unselfish; to *revenge* is selfish; to *retaliate* may be necessary for self-defense.

*avenue (av′ ê nū), *n.* a broad roadway; wide city street; an approach to something desired; means of attainment.

*aver (a vûr′), *v.t.* to affirm positively.

average (av′ ẽr ij), *n.* an arithmetical mean, the result obtained by dividing a sum by the number of its separate constituent parts; an ordinary specimen or type; something between what would be too much and what would be too little, or between very good or large and very bad or small.

average (av′ ẽr ij), *v.t. and v.i.* to find the

average of a number of things; to do or get an average number or amount, as profits *average* $5 per day.

average (av′ ĕr ij), *adj.* typical; medium.

averse (a vûrs′), *adj.* unwilling; not favorable to.

*****aversion** (a vur′ zhun), *n.* dislike; an object of dislike.

avert (a vûrt′), *v.t.* to turn something aside.

*****aviary** (ā′ vi er i), *n.* an enclosure for keeping live birds.

*****avid** (av′ id), *adj.* greedy; very eager.

avigation (av i gā′ shun), *n.* air navigation.

*****avocado** (av ō kä′ dō), *n.* the alligator pear; also, the tree that bears it.

avocation (av ō kā′ shun), *n.* a subordinate or occasional occupation; diversion.

avoid (a void′), *v.t.* to keep away from; to shun.

avoidance (a void′ ans), *n.* tne act of shunning; the act of annulling or making void.

*****avoirdupois** (av ĕr du poiz′), *n.* a system of weights based on a 16-ounce pound.

avouch (a vouch′), *v.t.* to affirm openly; to vouch for.

avow (a vou′), *v.t.* to declare openly; to acknowledge.

avowal (a vou′ al), *n.* an open declaration.

await (a wāt′), *v.t.* to wait for; to look for or expect.

awake (a wāk′), *v.i.* to arouse from sleep.

awake (a wāk′), *adj.* not sleeping.

awaken (a wāk′ en), *v.t. and v.i.* to arouse from sleep.

award (a wôrd′), *n.* a decision between contestants; a prize of honor given as the result of such a decision.

award (a wôrd′), *v.t.* to assign to one of two or more contestants, as a prize or an honor.

aware (a wâr′), *adj.* conscious; informed.

away (a wā′), *adv.* absent; at a distance; apart from.

awe (ô), *n.* reverential fear; the emotion inspired by contemplation of the sublime.

awesome (ô′ sum), *adj.* colloquialism used to denote something spectacular or very special.

awful (ô′ fool), *adj.* arousing deep fear or fearful reverence; appalling.

awhile (a hwīl′), *adv.* for a short time.

awkward (ôk′ wĕrd), *adj.* clumsy; unskillful; puzzling; embarrassing.

awl (ôl), *n.* a tool to make holes, as in heavy cloth or leather.

awning (ôn′ ing), *n.* a covering, as of canvas, stretched over a frame to provide shade, as at a window or door.

awry (a rī′), *adj. and adv.* twisted; turned to one side.

ax (aks), *n.* a steel head on a long handle, with a wedgelike cutting edge, for chopping wood.

*****axiom** (ak′ si om), *n.* a self-evident truth.

axis (ak′sis), *n.* the straight line, real or imaginary, passing through a body and upon which it revolves or is imagined to revolve.

axle (ak′ sl), *n.* the bar on which a wheel hub turns.

aye (ā), *adv.* always; ever.

aye (ī), *adv.* yes.

*****azalea** (a zāl′ ya), *n.* a flowering plant of the rhododendron family.

*****azure** (azh′ ĕr), *n.* the clear blue of the sky.

azure (azh′ ĕr), *adj.* blue, like the clear sky.

B

babble (bab′ l), *n.* chatter; prattle; a confusion of gentle, meaningless sounds.

babble (bab′ l), *v.i.* to produce indistinct sounds; to prattle.

babe (bāb), *n.* an infant; baby.

baboon (ba bōōn′), *n.* an African and Asiatic ape with a face somewhat resembling that of a dog.

baby (bā′ bi), *n.* an infant; a very young child.

baby (bā′ bi), *v.t.* to treat like a baby.

baccalaureate (bak a lô′ rē ăt), *adj.* relating to the degree of bachelor: *baccalaureate sermon,* an address to a graduating class.

*****baccarat** (bak a rä′), *n.* a French gambling game played with cards.

bachelor (bach′ e lĕr), *n.* a man who is not and has not been married; a college graduate with a bachelor's degree.

*****bacillus** (ba sil′ us), *n.* a microscopic, rod-shaped organism, one of a class of bacteria found in hay, soil, water or milk and often producing disease.

back (bak), *n.* the hinder part of the body in man; in quadrupeds, the upper part of the body from neck to rump; the rear part of anything.

back (bak), *v.t.* to furnish with a back or backing; to finance; to support; to move something backward, as a car.

back (bak), *adj.* located at the rear, as a *back* door; overdue or out of date, as *back* pay, *back* numbers of a magazine.

back (bak), *adv.* toward the rear; in reverse direction, as to be held *back*, to look *back;* in return, as to expect a letter *back;* hidden, as to keep the news *back*.

backbite (bak′ bīt), *v.t.* to say mean things about a person who is not present.

backbone (bak′ bōn′), *n.* the spine; courage; firmness; spunk.

backfire (bak′ fīr), *n.* a blaze started in the path of a forest fire or grass fire to check its advance; a reverse explosion of gas in an automobile engine or of powder in a gun.

background (bak′ ground), *n.* the setting against which a picture is made; the further part of a landscape; a person's past experience and training.

backhand (bak′ hand), *n.* writing that slopes to the left instead of the right.

backhanded (bak′ han ded), *adj.* made or done with the hand in a reversed position, as a *backhanded* stroke in tennis.

backing (bak' ing), *n.* something placed behind to strengthen; financial support; aid given to a person or cause; encouragement.

backslide (bak slid'), *v.i.* to slide back; fail to keep a resolution, slip from virtue or religion.

backward (bak' wĕrd), *adj.* turned toward the back; reluctant; undeveloped, retarded.

backward (bak' wĕrd), *adv.* toward the rear or on the back, as to fall *backward;* in reverse direction.

backwash (bak' wosh), *n.* water thrown back, as by the paddles of a moving steamboat.

backwater (bak wô' tĕr), *n.* slack water at the side of a stream, apart from the main current.

*****bacteria** (bak tēr' i a), *n.* microscopic, one-celled vegetable bodies, found in and causing fermentation, soil fertilization, decay of organic matter and many diseases.

*****bacteriology** (bak tēr' i ol' ō ji), *n.* the scientific investigation or study of bacteria, especially in relation to disease.

bacterium (bak tēr' i um), *n.* singular of *bacteria.*

bad (bad), *adj.* evil; wicked; wrong: the opposite of *good.*

badge (baj), *n.* a token of membership in some organization, commonly pinned to one's clothing.

badger (baj' ēr), *n.* an animal, about 2 feet long, thick-bodied, strong and aggressive, that burrows, eats flesh, prowls at night, and has coarse hair used in making brushes.

badger (baj' er), *v.t.* to tease; torment; harry with questions.

badinage (bad' i naj), *n.* teasing; banter.

baffle (baf' l), *v.t.* to foil; to balk; to confuse and hinder.

bag (bag), *n.* a pouch; sack; valise; a day's take of game.

bag (bag), *v.t. and v.i.* to place in a bag; to take by shooting or trapping, as game; to swell or bulge.

baggage (bag' ij), *n.* a traveler's bags, trunks; luggage.

bagging (bag' ing), *n.* coarse cloth used in making bags.

baggy (bag' i), *adj.* loose; flabby; ill-fitting.

bagpipe (bag' pipe), *n.* a primitive musical instrument, of shrill tone, consisting of a leather windbag, a tube with stops and several pipes.

bail (bāl), *n.* money deposited or property pledged as security for the appearance of a prisoner for trial; a scoop used in bailing a boat; the semicircular handle of a pail.

bailiff (bāl' if), *n.* a sheriff's assistant, who serves papers; a court attendant.

bait (bāt), *n.* anything used to lure fish to the hook or animals to the trap; anything used to lure that which is to be caught.

bait (bāt), *v.t.* to put bait in or on, as a trap or hook; to harass, provoke.

baize (bāz), *n.* a coarse woolen material with a nap on one side, used to cover pool tables.

bake (bāk), *v.t.* to cook in an oven with dry heat.

bakelite (bā' ke lit), *n.* a synthetic resin used as a substitute for hard rubber or celluloid.

baker (bāk' ēr), *n.* one whose business it is to make and often to sell bread, cake, etc.

bakery (bāk' ēr i), *n.* a place where baking is done; a baker's shop.

balance (bal' ans), *n.* equilibrium; evenness of disposition; poise; a pair of scales for weighing; the amount by which one side of an account exceeds the other or which it would require to make them balance evenly.

balance (bal' ans), *v.t. and v.i.* to bring into equilibrium; to set one thing off against another; to make equal; to be equal in weight, amount or value, as scales *balance,* gains and losses *balance.*

*****balcony** (bal' kō ni), *n.* a platform projecting from a wall and enclosed with a balustrade; in a theater, an upper section of seats overlooking the pit and with a railing across the front.

bald (bôld), *adj.* lacking hair on the head; bare.

bale (bāl), *n.* a bundle of goods bound with cord or wire ready for shipping, especially hay or cotton.

bale (bāl), *n.* woe; evil.

bale (bāl), *v.t.* to make up into a bale or bales.

baleful (bāl' ful), *adj.* woeful; of deadly or malign influence.

balk (bôk), *n.* a heavy squared timber; a strip or ridge of land left unplowed; in baseball, a false motion in delivering the ball; a check or hindrance.

balk (bôk), *v.i. and v.t.* to shy at a jump; to refuse to go; to baffle; to hinder, obstruct, thwart.

ball (bôl), *n.* a round body; a game played with a ball; in baseball, a pitched ball that does not pass over the plate at the required height; a formal dance.

ball (bôl), *v.i. and v.t.* to form into a ball.

ballad (bal' ad), *n.* a sentimental song; a short narrative poem.

ballast (bal' ast), *n.* heavy materials carried by a ship or a balloon to insure stability; broken stone between the rails of a railroad.

ball bearing, a bearing in which friction is reduced by means of metal balls.

*****ballet** (bal' ā), *n.* a dance performed by a group on the stage, generally one that tells a story or presents a theme; the group of dancers performing a ballet.

ballistics (ba lis' tiks), *n.* the science of designing projectiles for maximum flight performance.

balloon (ba lōōn'), *n.* a bag inflated with gas lighter than air, having a basket attached in which aëronauts go aloft; a small, similar bag used as a toy.

ballot (bal' ut), *n.* a printed form which a voter fills in to express his choice between candidates in an election.

balm (bäm), *n.* the aromatic sap of certain trees, used for healing or soothing.

*****balsam** (bôl' sam), *n.* a certain flowering plant; an oily, aromatic, resinous substance yielded by certain trees and used in medicine and perfume making.

baluster (bal' us tẽr), *n.* a post that supports a handrail.

*****balustrade** (bal' us trãd), *n.* a handrail with balusters on a stairway or balcony.

bamboo (bam bōō'), *n.* a tropical tree with a hollow stem that grows in jointed sections, used in making furniture, walking sticks and fishing rods.

ban (ban), *n.* a decree of excommunication; a curse; an order forbidding an action.

ban (ban), *v.t.* to forbid; to put under a curse.

*****banal** (bã' nal), *adj.* commonplace; trite.

banana (ba nan' a), *n.* a tropical fruit, growing in heavy clusters on a plant resembling a palm tree.

band (band), *n.* that which binds together; a strip of binding material; a company of musicians; a group of persons united by a common purpose.

band (band), *v.i. and v.t.* to unite; to fasten with a band.

bandage (ban' dij), *n.* a strip of soft cloth for dressing wounds.

bandage (ban' dij), *v.t.* to cover and protect a wound with a strip of soft cloth.

bandbox (band' boks), *n.* a small box or case to hold articles of clothing or hats.

bandit (ban' dit), *n.* an outlaw; highwayman.

bandoleer (ban dō lēr'), *n.* a cartridge belt worn over shoulder and across breast.

band wagon (band wa' gun), *n.* the high, gaudy wagon on which the musicians ride in a circus parade; an imaginary wagon supposedly carrying the leaders of a popular cause.

band saw (band sô), *n.* a saw constructed on an endless belt that runs on pulleys.

bandy (ban' di), *v.t.* to toss back and forth; to give and take, as to *bandy* words.

bandy-legged (ban' di-leg ed), *adj.* bowlegged.

bane (bãn), *n.* a cause of ruin, especially poison.

baneful (bãn' fool), *adj.* poisonous; ruinous.

bang (bang), *n.* a sudden, explosive noise, as of a sharp blow or explosion; a sharp blow or whack.

bang (bang), *v.i. and v.t.* to make a noise like that of a heavy blow; to strike such a blow.

bangs (bangz), *n.* hair cut straight across the forehead so as to form a fringe.

banish (ban' ish), *v.t.* to send into exile.

    Syn. Exile, expatriate, expel. One may be *banished, exiled* or *expatriated* from a country, but *expatriated* only from his own. One may *expatriate* himself; he is *banished* by others. One may *banish* disturbing thoughts; care may *banish* sleep. To *expel* is to drive out with violence or rudeness.

banister (ban' is tẽr), *n.* a baluster: *banisters,* a balustrade.

banjo (ban' jō), *n.* a musical instrument resembling a guitar, with strings and a circular body covered with tightly stretched parchment.

bank (bangk), *n.* a ridge of earth; the land at the edge of a stream; a rise in the bottom of a stream or the sea, making shoal water, as a *sandbank,* the *banks* of Newfoundland;

a mass, as of snow or clouds; an establishment where money is kept or loaned.

bank (bangk), *v.i. and v.t.* to engage in the business of banking; to place money in a bank; to heap up in a mound or ridge like a bank; to build or drive as if on the side of a bank of earth, incline, as to *bank* a road or an airplane; to cover a fire with ashes to make it burn more slowly.

bankbook (bangk' bŏŏk), *n.* a small book in which a record of deposits and withdrawals of money is kept.

banknote (bangk' nōt), *n.* a bank's promise to pay, which circulates as money.

bankrupt (bangk' rupt), *n.* one legally declared insolvent, unable to meet his debts.

bankrupt (bangk' rupt), *adj.* having liabilities in excess of assets and subject to legal action as an insolvent debtor; stripped of resources.

bankruptcy (bangk' rupt si), *n.* legal insolvency; an utter lack of any specified quality.

banner (ban' ẽr), *n.* an ensign, standard or flag of a country, state or organization.

banner (ban' ẽr), *adj.* worthy to carry the standard; leading, surpassing, as a *banner* year.

banns (banz), *n.* the proclamation in church of an intended marriage.

*****banquet** (bang' kwet), *n.* an elaborate, formal dinner; sumptuous entertainment or feast.

bantam (ban' tam), *n.* a diminutive breed of domestic fowl; a small, active person.

bantam weight (-wãt), *n.* a boxer or wrestler weighing not more than 118 pounds.

banter (ban' tẽr), *n.* good-natured teasing.

banyan (ban' yun), *n.* fig tree of India with spreading branches that send down shoots which take root and produce new trees.

baptism (bap' tizm), *n.* a ceremony in which water is used as a symbol of purification, initiating a person into the visible church of Christ.

baptize (bap tīz'), *v.t.* to administer the rite of baptism; to christen; to consecrate.

bar (bär), *n.* a piece of wood or metal, long in relation to its thickness; a barrier; a sandbank at the entrance to a harbor; a counter where drinks are sold; a place of justice; the legal profession; a vertical line dividing the musical staff into measures or the space between two such lines.

bar (bär), *v.t.* to fasten with a bar; to obstruct; to exclude; to prohibit.

barb (bärb), *n.* a sharp point projecting backward, as on an arrowhead or fishhook.

barbarian (bär bãr' i an), *n.* an uncivilized person.

barbaric (bär bar' ik), *adj.* pertaining to or like primitive peoples, as *barbaric* customs, *barbaric* ornaments.

barbarism (bär' ba rizm), *n.* an uncivilized condition of life; in grammar, an expression not in good use.

barbarity (bär bar' i ti), *n.* savageness; cruelty.

barbarous (bär' ba rus), *adj.* not pure, as language; merciless, cruel.

barbecue (bär´ bĕ kū), *n.* a metal grill over hot coals where food is cooked outdoors.

barbed wire (bär´ bd wīr), wire for fences with barbs at regular intervals.

barber (bär´ bĕr), *n.* one whose business it is to cut hair and shave beards.

bare (bâr), *adj.* uncovered; naked; nude; unadorned.

bare (bâr), *v.t.* to uncover; to expose; to reveal.

barely (bâr´ lĭ), *adv.* hardly, scarcely, as *barely* enough to eat.

*bargain (bär´ gĭn), *n.* an agreement for a transaction in business; something bought at low price.

bargain (bär´ gĭn), *v.i.* to make an agreement; to discuss the terms of a purchase or sale; to haggle.

barge (bärj), *n.* a large, flat-bottomed boat.

*baritone or **barytone** (bar´ ĭ tŏn), *n.* a male voice between tenor and bass; a man having such a voice.

bark (bärk), *n.* the outside layer of woody stems or tree trunks; the sharp, sudden sound made by a dog; a three-masted ship, square-rigged on fore and main masts, fore-and-aft rigged on the mizzenmast: also spelled *barque.*

bark (bärk), *v.i. and v.t.* to utter the sound of a bark; to take the bark off a tree or log; to scrape the skin, as to *bark* one's shins.

barley (bär´ lĭ), *n.* a grain used as a cereal and for making malt liquors.

barnacle (bär´ na kl), *n.* a small shellfish which fastens onto rocks, hulls of ships and timbers under water; a hanger-on; an unwelcome dependent.

barometer (ba rom´ e tĕr), *n.* an instrument that measures the pressure of the atmosphere.

baron (bar´ un), *n.* the title of an English peer of the lowest rank; in early English history, one who held an estate conferred on him by the king for military services; an American industrial magnate, as a coal *baron.*

baronet (bar´ ŏ net), *n.* an English title below a baron and above a knight; one who holds this title.

baronetcy (bar´ on et sĭ), *n.* the rank and honors of a baronet.

baronial (ba rō´ ni al), *adj.* relating to a baron or barony.

barony (bar´ ŏ nĭ), *n.* the rank and honors of a baron; a baron's estate or domain.

barracks (bar´ raks), *n.* buildings in which soldiers are housed at an army post or cantonment.

barrage (ba räzh´), *n.* a screen of gunfire covering the advance of troops.

barrel (bar´ el), *n.* a bulging cylindrical container made of wooden staves bound together by hoops; the tube of a firearm through which the bullet passes; the case containing the mainspring of a watch.

barren (bar´ en), *n.* sterile; unable to reproduce its kind; unproductive, as land or plans.

barricade (bar ĭ kād´), *n.* a barrier set up to block a hostile advance.

barricade (bar ĭ kād´), *v.t.* to block a passageway with barriers.

barrier (bar´ ĭ ĕr), *n.* anything that prevents or obstructs passage or advance.

barrow (bar´ ō), *n.* a frame covered with boards and having handles at one end or both ends, as in a wheel*barrow;* a mound of earth or stones over a grave.

barter (bär´ tĕr), *n.* exchange of goods; trading without use of money.

basal metabolism (bā´ sal me tab´ ō lism), *n.* the energy turnover of the body when it is in a state of rest.

*basalt (ba sôlt´), *n.* a greenish-black rock of volcanic origin.

base (bās), *n.* the part of an object on which it stands or rests; a foundation; a center of operations or supplies, as for a military unit; in chemistry, that which combines with an acid to form a salt.

base (bās), *v.i. and v.t.* to rest upon a base; to provide a base for; to found, establish.

baseball (bās´ bôl´), *n.* a game played by teams of nine players each, in which runs are scored by a player making his way around a diamond formed by three bases and a home plate; the ball used.

baseless (bās´ les), *adj.* unfounded; not supported by facts.

basement (bās´ ment), *n.* the lowest floor of a building next below the ground floor.

bashful (bash´ fool), *adj.* diffident, shy.

basic (bā´ sik), *adj.* relating to a base; fundamental.

basin (bā´ sn), *n.* a shallow vessel for holding a liquid; the region drained by a river.

basis (bā´ sis), *n.* the groundwork or fundamental principle of anything; the statement or assumption on which an argument rests.

bask (båsk), *v.i.* to lie in warmth; to enjoy or revel in pleasant conditions.

basket (bås´ ket), *n.* a container made of interwoven splints; the amount a basket will hold, as two *baskets* of apples.

bas-relief (bä rē lēf´), *n.* a kind of sculpture in which the design projects (is raised) only slightly—in low relief.

bass (bas), *n.* an American gamefish.

bass (bās), *n.* the deepest-toned part of a musical score; a male voice of the deepest range.

bass (bās), *adj.* in music, deep in tone.

bast (bast), *n.* the inner fiber of certain trees; a cord or matting made from its fibers.

baste (bāst), *v.t.* to drip some of its own grease on meat while it is roasting; to fasten temporarily with long stitches.

bastille (bas tēl´), *n.* a prison; especially a fortress used as a prison by a government.

*bastion (bas´ chun), *n.* an angular projection from a fortification, affording crossfire on attackers.

bat (bat), *n.* a heavy stick or club, such as is used in baseball; a night-flying, insect-eating mammal with arms and legs connected by a membrane and used as wings.

bat (bat), *v.i. and v.t.* to use a bat; to strike something with a bat.

batch (batch), *n.* a quantity of anything produced or handled at one time or by one operation, as a *batch* of dough, a *batch* of papers.

bate (bāt), *v.t.* to lessen; to moderate; to deduct something, as from a bill.

bath (bàth), *n.* the act of washing the body by immersion; immersion of anything; a tub or tank filled with water for bathing; a solution in which a photographic film is immersed.

bathe (bā*th*), *v.i. and v.t.* to take or give a bath.

bath tub (bàth ˌtᴜb), any tub used for bathing, but especially a body-length tub of porcelain or metal, with faucets for hot and cold water.

batiste (ba tēst'), *n.* a fine fabric of cotton.

***baton** (ba tôn'), *n.* a staff used as a badge of office or to beat time for an orchestra.

battalion (ba tal' yun), *n.* a military unit composed of a headquarters and two or more companies; any large portion of an army acting together.

batten (bat' n), *n.* a strip of wood for fastening edges, as of a tarpaulin to a deck.

batten (bat' n), *v.i. and v.t.* to make or become fat; to thrive, usually at someone else's cost; to fasten down with battens.

batter (bat' ēr), *n.* a mixture of ingredients beaten together, as for making cake; one who uses a bat.

batter (bat' ēr), *v.i. and v.t.* to strike with blow after blow; to beat, pound.

battery (bat' ēr i), *n.* the act of beating, as in assault and *battery;* a group of guns, with men and equipment; a group of machines, as a *battery* of linotype machines; a group of cells converting chemical energy into electric current; in baseball, the pitcher and catcher.

batting (bat' ing), *n.* wool or cotton prepared in sheets.

battle (bat' l), *n.* combat between armed forces in the field of war; fighting.

battlement (bat' l ment), *n.* a parapet with openings through which defenders fire.

battleplane (bat' l plān), *n.* an airplane carrying guns.

battleship (bat' l ship), *n.* the heaviest and most heavily armed kind of warship.

bauble (bô' bl), *n.* a trifling piece of finery; worthless trinket.

bauxite (bôks' ît), *n.* a sort of clay from which aluminum is obtained.

bawl (bôl), *v.i.* to cry loud and long.

bay (bā), *n.* a body of water partly enclosed by land; the long, deep cry of a hunting dog; the state of a hunted creature when it turns on its pursuers, as at *bay.*

bay (bā), *v.i.* to utter a deep-toned, prolonged bark, as that of a hound in the chase.

bayonet (bā' ō net), *n.* a thrusting weapon fixed to the barrel of a rifle.

***bayou** (bī' ŏŏ), *n.* a sluggish inlet from a gulf, lake or river, especially in the southern states.

bazaar (bà zär'), *n.* an Eastern market place; a sale of foods or handwork to aid a charity.

be (bē), *v.i.* [*p.t.* was, *p.p.* been, *pr. p.* being],

to exist, as there *is* a time for all things, there *are* no ghosts; to equal, as 2 and 2 *are* 4; to occupy a certain place, as a coat *is* on a hook, France *is* in Europe; to belong in a certain category, as an ant *is* an insect; to experience a certain condition, as to *be* at war, I *am* happy; to represent, as let's *be* Romeo and Juliet. As an auxiliary verb to *be* is used to form the passive voice of other verbs, as we *were* attacked; and the progressive form, as I *am* reading.

beach (bēch), *n.* a sandy shore; a strand.

beach (bēch), *v.t.* to run, as a boat, up on a beach.

beacon (bē' kun), *n.* a signal fire or light.

bead (bēd), *n.* a little ball with a hole through it, for stringing; a knob or notched plate at the end of a gun barrel, for use in aiming.

beagle (bē' gl), *n.* a small breed of hound used in hunting rabbits.

beak (bēk), *n.* a bird's bill; anything shaped like a beak, as the lip of a pitcher.

beam (bēm), *n.* a long timber; a ray of light; a radio ray; the greatest width of a ship.

beam (bēm), *v.i.* to send out rays of light; to glow, as with pleasure.

bean (bēn), *n.* the smooth, kidney-shaped seed of many leguminous plants.

bear (bâr), *n.* a large animal with heavy fur: the brown *bear,* grizzly *bear,* polar *bear;* a dealer in stocks who tries to send market prices down for his own profit.

bear (bâr), *v.i. and v.t.* to be in a productive state, as the orchards are *bearing* well this year; to support, as this beam *bears* great weight; to bring forth, as to *bear* a child; to follow a certain direction, as *bear* to the east.

beard (bērd), *n.* the hair that grows on the chin.

beard (bērd), *v.t.* to confront; to defy.

bearing (bâr' ing), *n.* 1 carriage, behavior; meaning, point, as the *bearing* of an argument. 2 those parts of a mechanical device which bear the friction, on which a shaft or axle turns.

beast (bēst), *n.* a quadruped; a vile person.

beat (bēt), *n.* a recurring stroke; pulsation or throb; a route repeatedly traversed, as a policeman's *beat.*

beat (bēt), *v.i. and v.t.* to throb; to pulsate; to strike repeatedly; to thrash; to defeat in a contest; to range over, as woods, in quest of game; to mix by striking many times in swift succession, as with a spoon.

beatnik (bēt ´ nik), *n.* the Bohemian unconventional devotee of the arts in the late 1950's and early '60's.

beauty (bū' ti), *n.* a combination of graces and charms pleasing to the eye or gratifying to the esthetic sense; physical or mental loveliness.

beaver (bē' vēr), *n.* a fur-bearing animal with flat oval tail and webbed feet that lives in and beside ponds and builds dams.

becalmed (bē kämd'), *adj.* prevented from sailing by lack of wind.

beckon (bek' un), *v.ˌ. and v.t.* to summon by a nod or gesture, signal.

become (bĕ kum'), *v.i. and v.t.* to pass from one state to another, as warm things *become* cool; to befit; accord with, as his manner *becomes* a king.

bed (bed), *n.* an article of furniture on which to sleep, usually a wooden frame containing springs and mattress; a portion of ground prepared for plants, as a strawberry *bed;* the bottom of something, as the *bed* of a river; a layer, as of rock.

bedeck (bĕ dek'), *v.t.* to decorate, adorn.

bedlam (bed' lum), *n.* a lunatic asylum; any scene of confusion.

bedridden (bed' rid n), *adj.* confined to bed.

bee (bē), *n.* a four-winged insect that lives in colonies and gathers honey; a gathering of persons to help in some kind of work, such as building a house, or to compete in a test, as a spelling *bee.*

beech (bēch), *n.* a tree related to the oak, with smooth gray bark and triangular, edible nuts.

beef (bēf), *n.* the meat of cattle.

beeline (bē' līn), *n.* a straight course from one point to another, such as a bee follows when flying with honey to its hive.

beer (bēr), *n.* a beverage made from malt, barley and hops.

beet (bēt), *n.* a plant with a thick edible root; the beet root, used as a vegetable and in making sugar.

beetle (bē' tl), *n.* an insect having four wings, the inner pair being protected by the outer pair, which are hard like thin horn; a mallet, used to drive wedges.

beetle (bē' tl), *v.i.* to project; overhang, as a cliff.

befall (bĕ fôl'), *v.i. and v.t.* to happen; to come to pass.

befit (bĕ fit'), *v.t.* to be worthy of or suitable to, as conduct that *befits* a king.

befog (bĕ fog'), *v.t.* to bewilder.

before (bĕ fōr'), *adv.* in front, as go *before;* formerly, as you said that *before.*

before (bĕ fōr'), *prep.* in front of, as to bow *before* an idol; preceding in time, as March comes *before* April; preceding in rank or worth, as a captain comes *before* a lieutenant, value happiness *before* wealth.

before (bĕ fōr'), *conj.* previous to the moment when, as think *before* you speak; rather than, as I'd die *before* I'd betray him.

befriend (bĕ frend'), *v.t.* to be a friend to; to help.

beg (beg), *v.i. and v.t.* to beseech; ask for.

beget (bĕ get'), *v.t.* to procreate, to father; to cause, as one lie *begets* another.

beggar (beg' ẽr), *n.* one who begs; one who lives by asking alms.

begin (bĕ gin'), *v.i. and v.t.* to start; to come into being; to commence, found.

beginning (bĕ gin' ing), *n.* the start of anything; time or place of origin.

*****begonia** (bĕ gō' ni a), *n.* a house plant with ornamental leaves and small flowers, pink, red or white.

begrudge (bĕ gruj'), *v.t.* to envy; to wish to withhold.

beguile (bĕ gīl'), *v.t.* to deceive by guile; to tempt; to delude; to charm.

behalf (bĕ hȧf'), *n.* help; defense; interest: used with prepositions, as *in behalf* of the poor, *on behalf* of the owner.

behave (bĕ hāv'), *v.t. and v.i.* to conduct or comport (oneself), as the child *behaved* herself at the table; to conduct oneself or itself, act, as the horse *behaves* well on the road.

behavior (bĕ hāv' yẽr), *n.* manner of behaving; conduct.

behead (bĕ hed'), *v.t.* to cut off the head of.

behest (bĕ hest'), *n.* a command.

behind (bĕ hīnd'), *adv.* to or at the rear, as left *behind.*

behind (bĕ hīnd'), *prep.* at the back of, as *behind* the lines.

behold (bĕ hōld'), *v.t.* to look at; to see.

behold (bĕ hōld'), *interj.* look! see!

beholden (bĕ hōl' dn), *adj.* indebted.

behoof (bĕ hōōf'), *n.* advantage, interest, as in your *behoof.*

*****behoove** (bĕ hōōv'), *v.t.* to be necessary or right for, as it *behooves* you to go.

being (bē' ing), *n.* existence; life; a living person.

belabor (bĕ lā' bẽr), *v.t.* to beat soundly.

belated (bĕ lā' ted), *adj.* tardy, delayed.

belch (belch), *v.i. and v.t.* to bring up violently, as gas from the stomach, ashes from a volcano, smoke from a chimney.

belfry (bel' fri), *n.* a bell tower.

belie (bĕ lī'), *v.t.* to give the lie to, misrepresent; to be false to.

belief (bĕ lēf'), *n.* intellectual acceptance of anything as true; the act of believing.

believe (bĕ lēv'), *v.t.* to accept as true; to have faith in, trust.

belittle (bĕ lit' l), *v.t.* to underestimate; to depreciate; to make seem smaller.

bell (bel), *n.* a hollow metal cup-shaped instrument that gives forth a clear resonant note when struck by a clapper.

bell (bel), *v.t.* to put a bell on.

belle (bel), *n.* a beautiful girl or woman.

bellicose (bel' i kōs), *adj.* warlike; pugnacious.

*****belligerence** (be lij' ẽr ens), *n.* the act of making war or state of being at war.

belligerent (be lij' ẽr ent), *n.* a nation engaged in a war.

bellow (bel' ō), *n.* a bull's roar; a sound similar to that call.

bellows (bel' ōz), *n.* an instrument that folds like an accordion, taking in air and expelling it with force, used to fan a fire or supply a current of air for a pipe organ.

belly (bel' i), *n.* [*pl.* bellies (-liz)] part of the body between the ribs and the hips; the abdomen; in quadrupeds, the under part of the body.

belong (bĕ lông'), *v.i.* to be part of, owned by, or proper to, as it *belongs* to me, I *belong* to the club.

belonging (bĕ lông' ing), *n.* a possession.

below (bĕ lō'), *adv.* in a lower place; further down, beneath.

below (bĕ lō'), *prep.* lower than, as on the shelf *below* the top one; unbefitting, as such conduct is *below* your station.

belt (belt), *n.* a band, as of leather, worn around the waist; a leather strip running over wheels in machinery; a zone or region, as the corn *belt*.

belt (belt), *v.t.* to encircle; to put a belt on.

belted (belt' ed), *adj.* wearing a belt indicative of rank; having its coat of fur or feathers marked by a stripe like a belt.

belting (belt' ing), *n.* material from which belts are made; a system of belts, as in a machine shop.

bench (bench), *n.* a long seat, which may or may not have a back; the judges' seat in a court; judges collectively; a ledge in a formation of rock; a raised level river bank.

bend (bend), *n.* a curve, as in a road or stream.

bend (bend), *v.i. and v.t.* to curve in its course, as a road or stream; to force something straight into a curved line.

beneath (bē nēth'), *adv.* in a lower position.

beneath (bē nēth'), *prep.* below; under (something else); unworthy of.

benediction (ben ē dik' shun), *n.* a blessing.

benefaction (ben ē fak' shun), *n.* the conferring of a benefit; a benefit conferred.

benefactor (ben' ē fak tēr), *n.* one who confers a benefit, renders a service, does a favor; a kindly helper.

beneficence (bē nef' i sens), *n.* active goodness; charity.

beneficent (bē nef' i sent), *adj.* actively good.

beneficiary (ben' ē fish' i er i), *n.* one who benefits by something; the one to whom insurance is payable.

benefit (ben' ē fit), *n.* advantage or profit; a public entertainment of which the proceeds are pledged to charity.

benefit (ben' ē fit), *v.i. and v.t.* to profit by; to be helpful to.

benevolence (bē nev' ō lens), *n.* the disposition to do good; charitableness.

benighted (bē nī' ted), *n.* lost in darkness; in the darkness of ignorance.

*__benign__ (bē nīn´), *adj.* of kind or gentle disposition; not malignant.

*__benignant__ (bē nig' nant), *adj.* kind; gracious.

benignity (bē nig' ni ti), *n.* graciousness.

bent (bent), *n.* tendency; a strong liking, as a *bent* for music.

benzene (ben' zēn), *n.* a volatile, highly inflammable liquid distilled from coal tar and used in the manufacture of dyes, for illuminating and as a motor fuel.

*__benzine__ (ben' zēn), *n.* a liquid derived from petroleum, used in cleaning textiles.

*__benzoin__ (ben' zō in), *n.* sap of an aromatic tree of the Malay lands, used in making perfumes and as a remedy for bronchitis.

*__bequeath__ (bē kwēth'), *v.t.* to bestow by will.

bequest (bē kwest'), *n.* a legacy.

berate (bē rāt'), *v.t.* to scold, chide.

bereave (bē rēv'), *v.t.* to deprive; to make desolate by loss, especially death.

bereavement (bē rēv' ment), *n.* loss, especially of a loved one by death.

bereft (bē reft'), [*p.t. and p.p.* of *bereave*] deprived, robbed, as *bereft* of joy or faith.

berry (ber' i), *n.* a small juicy fruit such as the blackberry; a fruit with pulpy flesh containing seeds, as the tomato, cranberry and grape.

berth (bûrth), *n.* a sleeping bunk on a ship or railroad car; a ship's mooring place: *give a wide berth,* pass at sufficient distance to allow to swing at anchor, hence, avoid.

beryl (ber' il), *n.* a precious stone of various colors but commonly green or greenish blue.

beseech (bē sēch'), *v.i. and v.t.* to entreat, implore earnestly.

beseem (bē sēm'), *v.t.* to be suitable to, as the act does not *beseem* a king.

beset (bē set'), *v.t.* to attack, besiege; to stud, as with gems.

beside (bē sīd'), *prep.* at the side of, as *beside* the hearth; compared with, as he seems cowardly *beside* you; wide of, as *beside* the point.

besides (bē sīdz'), *adv.* in addition, also.

besiege (bē sēj'), *v.t.* to surround with armed forces, beset; to harass.

besmirch (bē smûrch'), *v.t.* to soil; to smear with slander.

bespeak (bē spēk'), *v.t.* to ask for in advance; to foretell.

bespoken (bē spōk' en), *adj.* previously claimed or promised.

best (best), *adj. and adv.* good in the highest degree; in the most desirable manner.

*__bestial__ (best' yal), *adj.* like a beast.

bestow (bē stō'), *v.t.* to confer, give.

bet (bet), *n.* a wager or stake given; that which is wagered on, as a fast horse is a good *bet*.

bet (bet), *v.i. and v.t.* to wager; to stake, as money, on a contention or contingency.

betide (bē tīd'), *v.t.* to happen to.

betimes (bē tīmz'), *adv.* in good season; speedily.

betoken (bē tō' ken), *v.t.* to indicate by signs, portend.

betray (bē trā'), *v.t.* to make a breach of trust, deliver over to an enemy, through treachery; to deceive and lead into evil.

*__betrothal__ (bē troth' al), *n.* a marriage engagement.

better (bet' ēr), *adj. and adv.* more good or desirable; in a more excellent manner.

between (bē twēn'), *prep.* in the interval of time or space separating, as *between* the chair and the table, *between* Monday and Tuesday; from one to another, joining, as love *between* brothers; by the interaction of, as they caught 10 fish *between* them, war *between* tribes.

bevel (bev' el), *n.* a tool for setting surfaces at an angle; any angle not a right angle between planes or lines.

*__bevel__ (bev' el), *v.t. and v.i.* to impart a sloping edge to; to have a sloping edge, slant.

beverage (bev' ēr ij), *n.* any prepared drink.

bevy (bev' i), *n.* a flock of birds, as quail; a group of girls.

bewail (bē wāl'), *v.i. and v.t.* to lament; to weep for.

beware (bē wâr'), *v.i. and v.t.* to be on guard, to guard against.

bewilder (bē wil' dēr), *v.t.* to disturb and confuse.

bewitch (bē wich'), *v.t.* to cast a spell upon; to charm.

beyond (bē yond'), *adv.* further along.

beyond (bē yond'), *prep.* on the other side of; past some given mark or measure.

biannual (bī an' ū al), *adj.* occurring twice a year.

bias (bī' as), *n.* a cut or seam oblique to the texture of a fabric; prejudice.

bias (bī' as), *v.t.* to foster prejudice.

biased (bī' ast), *adj.* prejudiced.

bib (bib), *n.* a cloth placed under a child's chin; an upper section added to an apron.

bibliography (bib li og' ra fi), *n.* the history of books with their dates, authors, editions, printings, manufacture; a list of books by one author or of books on a given subject.

*bibliophile** (bib' li ō fil), *n.* one who loves books.

biceps (bī' seps), *n.* the front muscle of the upper arm.

bicker (bik' ēr), *v.i.* to wrangle, quarrel.

biconcave (bī kon' kāv), *adj.* curving in on both surfaces.

bicuspid (bī kus' pid), *n.* a two-pointed tooth.

bicycle (bī' sik l), *n.* a two-wheeled vehicle propelled by pedals working on a crank shaft.

bid (bid), *n.* an offer to give a certain price; the price named; an invitation.

bid (bid), *v.i. and v.t.* to make an offer; to name a price in competition with other bidders, for privilege, goods or work; to invite; to command.

bide (bīd), *v.t.* to wait, as *bide* your time.

biennial (bī en' i al), *adj.* happening once in two years.

bifurcation (bī fēr kā' shun), *n.* division into two branches.

big (big), *adj* large, of great size.

bigamy (big' a mi), *n.* the crime of contracting a marriage while a previous marriage is still legally in effect.

bight (bīt), *n.* a loop or bend of a rope; a bend in a shore line forming a bay.

bigot (big' ut), *n.* one who is blindly attached to a particular creed and intolerant of the beliefs and practices of others.

bilateral (bī lat' ēr al), *adj.* having two sides.

bile (bīl), *n.* a yellowish-green fluid secreted by the liver.

bilge (bilj), *n.* the broadest part of a ship's bottom; the bulge of a cask.

bilge water (bilj wō' tēr), water that collects in the bottom of a ship.

*bilious** (bil' yus), *adj.* having too much bile; bad-tempered.

bilk (bilk), *v.* to swindle or defraud.

bill (bil), *n.* a statement of money owed and request for payment; a banknote or government promise to pay, as a dollar *bill;* a list of available items, as a *bill* of fare; a proposed act of legislation, as a labor *bill;* a bird's beak; a kind of hatchet with a hook-shaped blade, also called *billhook.* **Note:** The noun *bill* is used in the sense of *certificate, document,* as *bill of entry, bill of exchange, bill of health, bill of lading, bill of sale.*

bill (bil), *v.t.* to state an account and request payment; to charge, as to *bill* a man for a

hat; to advertise or announce by posters.

billboard (bil' bōrd),*n.* a structure on which posters are displayed.

billet (bil' et), *n.* a written notice to a householder that he must provide lodgings for soldiers; lodgings for soldiers in private houses; a stick of firewood.

billet (bil' et), *v.t.* to lodge, as the army *billeted* soldiers on the townspeople.

billiards (bil' yērdz), *n.* a game played with ivory balls and a cue on an oblong, cloth-covered table.

billion (bil' yun), *n.* in the U. S., a thousand millions (1,000,000,000); in Great Britain, a million millions (1,000,000,000,000).

billow (bil' ō), *n.* a great rolling wave of water.

billposter (bil' pōs tēr), *n.* one whose occupation is pasting posters on billboards.

bimanual (bī man' ū al), *adj.* done with both hands.

bimonthly (bī munth' li), *adj.* occurring once in two months.

bin (bin), *n.* a box or compartment used for storing such things as flour or coal.

binary language (bī ´ na rē lan´ gwiz), *n.* the first language used by programmers to give orders to computers.

bind (bīnd), *v.t. and v.i.* to fasten together with or as with a cord; to confine or restrain, hold together; to cause to cohere; to bandage, as to *bind* up a cut; to fasten together and put a cover on, as to *bind* a book; to protect or strengthen with a band, as to *bind* a hem; to hold by force of duty, love or law, as a promise or a contract *binds;* to cohere.

bindery (bīn' dēr i), *n.* a place where books are bound.

binding (bīn' ding), *n.* that which binds; the cover of a book.

binding (bīn' ding), *adj.* having obligatory force.

binnacle (bin' a kl), *n.* a box containing a ship's compass and a night light.

*binocular** (bin ok' ū lēr), *n.* a glass, as a fieldglass or telescope having lenses for both eyes.

*binomial** (bī nō' mi al), *n.* an algebraic expression of two terms, connected by a plus or minus sign.

biodegradable (bī ´ ō di grā da bl), *adj.* can be broken down by natural processes, such as bacterial action.

*biography** (bī og' ra fi), *n.* the written story of a person's life.

biology (bī ol' ō ji), *n.* the science of life in its various forms.

bipartite (bī pär' tit), *adj.* divided into two parts.

biped (bī' ped), *n.* a two-footed animal.

biplane (bī' plān'), *n.* an airplane with two pairs of wings, one above the other.

birch (bûrch), *n.* a tree having valuable hardwood and sometimes bark that can be stripped off in thin layers.

bird (bûrd), *n.* a warm-blooded, feathered vertebrate that flies.

birdlime (bûrd' lĭm), *n.* sticky stuff prepared from holly and smeared on twigs to catch birds.

bird's-eye (bûrdz' ĭ), *adj.* seen from above, as if by a flying bird; so marked as to resemble the eye of a bird, as *bird's-eye* maple.

birth (bûrth), *n.* the act of being born or coming into existence; origin; descent, as a man of noble *birth*.

birthright (bûrth' rĭt'), *n.* any privilege to which one is entitled by birth.

biscuit (bĭs' kĭt), *n.* a small baked unsweetened cake of raised dough; a small baked cake of unleavened dough, a cracker.

bisect (bĭ sekt'), *v.t.* to cut or divide into two parts, usually two equal parts.

bishop (bĭsh' ŭp), *n.* a church officer having charge of a diocese or other church district.

bismuth (bĭz' muth), *n.* a metallic element used in alloys, medicine and the manufacture of cosmetics.

*•bison** (bī' sn), *n.* the buffalo of the North American plains.

bit (bĭt), *n.* a removable drilling tool; the metal mouthpiece of a bridle; a small piece of anything; used in connection with computers a single, basic unit of information.

bite (bīt), *n.* a mouthful bitten off a piece of food; a nibble by a fish; the sting of an insect; a wound made with the teeth; a stinging sensation; the grip of a tool on the substance being worked.

bite (bīt), *v.i. and v.t.* to seize with the teeth; to sting or cause a smarting sensation; to eat into, as acid; to take hold, as a boring tool.

bitingly (bīt' ĭng lĭ), *adv.* in a sarcastic manner, sharply.

bitt (bĭt), *n.* a wooden or iron post aboard ship to which cables are made fast.

bitter (bĭt' ẽr), *adj.* having a sharp, generally disagreeable taste; painful, as a *bitter* experience; severe, as *bitter* cold; cruel, stinging, as *bitter* words.

bittern (bĭt' ẽrn), *n.* a wading bird of the heron family.

bitters (bĭt' ẽrz), *n.* liquor in which bitter herbs or roots have been steeped.

bitumen (bĭ tū' men), *n.* mineral pitch, asphalt; any of various other inflammable mineral substances, as petroleum or naphtha.

bituminous coal (bĭ tu mĭ nus kōl), soft coal.

bivalve (bī' valv), *n.* any shellfish, such as the oyster, having two sections of shell hinged together.

*•bivouac** (bĭv' oo ak), *n.* an encampment of soldiers in the open for one night or a very short time.

biweekly (bī wēk' lĭ), *adj.* occurring once in two weeks.

biyearly (bī yēr' lĭ), *adj.* occurring twice in one year.

bizarre (bĭ zär'), *adj.* grotesque, odd or incongruous.

blab (blab), *v.i. and v.t.* to reveal or give away, as a secret; to tattle.

black (blak), *n.* complete lack of light or color or the darkest of all colors: opposite of *white;* a person belonging to a dark-skinned race.

black (blak), *adj.* of the darkest possible hue; without light, very dark, as a *black* night; gloomy, discouraging, as a *black* view of things; dressed in black, as the *Black* Prince; having a dark skin, as a Negro; sullen, inimical, as a *black* look.

blackball (blak' bôl), *v.t.* to vote against a candidate for membership in an organization.

blacken (blak' en), *v.t.* to make black.

*•blackguard** (blag' ärd), *n.* a fellow of low character, a scoundrel.

blackguard (blag' ärd), *v.t.* to revile in coarse terms.

blacking (blak' ĭng), *n.* a black polish for shoes or stoves.

blackjack (blak' jak'), *n.* a small, leather-covered club with a weighted head and a flexible handle.

blacklist (blak' lĭst), *n.* a list of persons under suspicion, in disfavor or to be punished.

blacklist (blak' lĭst), *v.t.* to place on a black-list.

blackmail (blak'māl), *n.* extortion by means of intimidation.

blackmail (blak' māl), *v.t.* to force a person to pay money to avoid scandal.

blacksmith (blak' smith), *n.* one whose calling is to hammer iron into various shapes on an anvil.

bladder (blad' ẽr), *n.* a thin, elastic, membranous sac in animals, in which a fluid is collected.

blade (blād), *n.* the cutting part of an edged tool or weapon; a leaf of a grass or cereal plant; anything resembling a leaf or blade, as the *blade* of a paddle.

blame (blām), *n.* censure; responsibility for error or wrongdoing.

blame (blām), *v.t.* to censure; to reproach; to hold responsible.

Syn. Censure, reprove, reproach, upbraid. To *blame* is simply to ascribe a fault to; to *censure* is to express disapprobation; the former is less personal than the latter. The thing more than the person is *blamed;* the person more than the thing is *censured*. A person may be *blamed* for his good nature, and *censured* for his negligence; *reprove* is even more personal than *censure*. A *reproof* passes from one individual to another, or to a certain number of individuals; *reproaching* and *upbraiding* are as much the acts of individuals as *reproving*, but the former denotes the expression of personal feelings and may be just or unjust; the latter is presumed to be divested of all personal feeling.

Ant. Approve, commend, praise.

blanch (blânch), *v.t. and v.i.* to whiten by taking out color; to turn pale with emotion.

bland (bland), *adj.* mild, soft, gentle.

blandishment (blan' dĭsh ment), *n.* flattering, persuasive expressions or actions; artful caresses.

blank (blangk), *n.* a paper on which there is

blank (blangk), *adj.* without writing or print; an empty space, a void.

blank (blangk), *adj.* without writing or print; empty; confused, bewildered, as a *blank* answer; lacking variety or incident.

blanket (blang' ket), *n.* a soft, loosely woven woolen bed cover; a heavy covering, as of snow.

blare (blâr), *v.i.* to give forth a loud sound like that of a trumpet.

*blaspheme (blas fēm'), *v.t.* to speak irreverently of God or sacred things; to curse.

blasphemy (blas' fē mi), *n.* impious speech.

blast (blåst), *n.* a sudden gust of wind; an explosion.

blast (blåst), *v.t.* to break up by means of an explosion, as rock.

blast furnace (blåst fûr' nis), a furnace in which the heat is intensified by air currents, used for reducing oil and melting metal.

blast-off (blast ´ ôf), *n.* the launching of a space vehicle or rocket.

blaze (blāz), *n.* a body of flame; intense light and heat; an outburst of passion; a mark made on a tree by cutting off a piece of the bark.

blaze (blāz), *v.i. and v.t.* to burst into flame; to shine; to mark, as a trail, with blazes.

bleach (blēch), *v.t.* to whiten by removing color.

bleak (blēk), *adj.* bare and desolate; piercing, as a wind; cheerless, as a *bleak* point of view.

bleat (blēt), *n.* the cry of a sheep or goat.

bleed (blēd), *v.i. and v.t.* to lose blood; to lose sap, as a tree; to experience sorrow or pity, as one's heart *bleeds* for the poor; to shed blood, as to *bleed* a patient.

blemish (blem' ish), *n.* a defect, flaw, any disfigurement, as a spot or scar.

Syn. Defect, flaw. A *blemish* is superficial and mars the appearance of something; a *defect* is a lack of something necessary or expected in a perfect thing; a *flaw* is an imperfection, as a crack or a fissure, in the essential texture of something, as a *flaw* in a diamond.

blemish (blem' ish), *v.t.* to mar, injure.

blench (blench), *v.i.* to flinch, quail, grow pale.

blend (blend), *n.* a mixture; a product of mixing, as a *blend* of coffee.

blend (blend), *v.t.* to mix into a new entity.

bless (bles), *v.t.* to make happy; to consecrate.

blessing (bles' ing), *n.* an invocation of happiness; a benediction.

blight (blīt), *n.* a disease in plants that causes them to stop growing and wither; an insect that causes plant disease; anything that destroys or ruins hopes or aims.

blight (blīt), *v.t.* to cause to wither and decay.

blimp (blimp) *n.* a small dirigible airship.

blind (blīnd), *n.* anything intended to obstruct sight, as a window shade or a screen; anything intended to mislead or deceive; a ruse; a decoy.

blind (blīnd), *v.t.* to make sightless, as the accident *blinded* him; to dazzle, as the sun *blinds* me; to darken the mind, as prejudice *blinds* him.

blind (blīnd), *adj.* without sight; unreasoning, rash, as a *blind* choice; lacking understanding, undiscerning, as *blind* to beauty; hidden, as a *blind* seam; closed at one end, leading nowhere, as a *blind* alley, a *blind* chase; done without seeing, as *blind* flying.

blink (blingk), *v.i.* to wink repeatedly and fast; to half-shut one's eyes to, as to *blink* against the sun; to overlook an offense.

blinker (blingk' ẽr), *n.* a leather flap on a bridle, to prevent a horse from seeing in any direction but straight ahead; a traffic light that goes on and off at short, regular intervals.

bliss (blis), *n.* a continuing state of extreme happiness.

blister (blis' ter), *n.* a thin sac containing water, on the skin of the body, or a painted surface.

*blithe (blīth), *adj.* joyous, gay, mirthful.

blitz (blits), *v.* a term used in football to describe a sudden and overwhelming attack on the quarterback.

blizzard (bliz' erd), *n.* a furious, sustained wind with light, fine, drifting snow.

bloat (blōt), *v.t. and v.i.* to cause to puff up; to cure or dry, as a herring, in smoke; to swell.

bloater (blōt' ẽr), *n.* a herring smoked, salted and half-dried.

block (blok), *n.* a solid mass of wood or metal; a set of pulleys in a frame; the distance from one street intersection to the next; a square of streets.

block (blok), *v.t.* to obstruct; to impede passage.

blockade (blok ād'), *n.* the closing of a port by enemy forces.

blockhouse (blok' hous), *n.* a log fort.

blond (blond), *adj.* fair-skinned, with light-colored hair.

blood (blud), *n.* the red fluid circulating in the arteries and veins.

blood pressure (blud presh' ẽr), the pressure of blood in the arteries, varying with body conditions and with age.

blood vessel (blud ves' l), any tube in which blood circulates in an animal body.

bloom (blōōm), *n.* the state of flowering; a blossom; a flourishing condition, as when knighthood was in *bloom*.

bloom (blōōm), *v.i.* to flower; to be bright with health.

blossom (blos' um), *n.* a flower.

blossom (blos' um), *v.i.* to bloom or flower; to flourish.

blot (blot), *n.* a spot or stain, as of ink; blemish.

blot (blot), *v.t.* to spot with ink; to dry a wet blot with soft paper.

blotch (bloch), *n.* a large, irregular spot or stain.

blotter (blot' ẽr), *n.* a sheet of soft absorbent paper, to take up wet ink.

*blouse (blous), *n.* a light, loose overgarment; the jacket of a uniform.

blow (blō), *n.* a hard stroke, as with the hand, fist or a club; a sudden affliction or misfortune; a gale; a shock.

blow (blō), *v.i.* to move, as air; to force a current of air, as from the mouth; to brag; to blossom.

blowfly (blō' flī), *n.* any species of fly that deposits eggs upon animal flesh.

blowout (blō' out), *n.* the bursting of a pneumatic tire; the hole thus made in the tire.

blowpipe (blo' pīp), *n.* a tube through which a current of air or gas is blown upon a flame.

blubber (blub' ēr), *n.* the layer of fat under a whale's hide.

bludgeon (bluj' un), *n.* a short club with one thick heavy end.

bludgeon (bluj' un), *v.t.* to strike with a club.

blue (blōō), *n.* the color of the clear sky.

blueblood (blōō' blud), a person of aristocratic lineage.

bluebottle (blōō' bot l), *n.* any of several steel-blue flies that buzz; a blowfly.

bluegrass (blōō' grås), *n.* a grass bearing a small blue flower, common in Kentucky and typical of that state.

blueprint (blōō' print), *n.* a print in white lines on blue paper used for maps and architectural plans.

bluff (bluf), *n.* a high, steep bank.

bluff (bluf), *v.i.* to try to deceive through a bold manner.

bluff (bluf), *adj.* rising steeply, as a cliff; blunt and hearty in manner.

bluing (blōō' ing), *n.* a preparation of indigo used in washing clothes.

blunder (blun' dēr), *n.* a gross mistake or error.

blunder (blun' dēr), *v.i.* to make stupid mistakes; to bungle.

blunt (blunt), *adj.* thick-edged, not sharp; plain-spoken.

blur (blûr), *n.* a smudge or smear; indistinct appearance; dimmed vision.

blur (blûr), *v.i. and v.t.* to appear indistinctly; to make obscure or indistinct.

blurt (blûrt), *v.t.* to speak without reflection; to divulge unadvisedly.

blush (blush), *n.* a reddening of the face as from shame, embarrassment or confusion.

bluster (blus' tēr), *v.i.* to blow noisily and violently; to talk windily or threateningly.

*****boa** (bō' a), *n.* a huge serpent of South America; neck wrap of fur or feathers.

boar (bōr), *n.* the male of swine.

board (bōrd), *n.* a piece of timber long and wide in proportion to its thickness; regular supply of meals, for pay.

board (bōrd), *v.t.* to buy meals by the day or week; to go upon, as a ship or train.

boardwalk (bōrd' wôk'), *n.* a promenade along a beach.

boast (bōst), *v.i.* to speak vaingloriously, brag.

boat (bōt), *n.* a small open vessel propelled either by oars or sail.

*****boatswain** (bō' sn), *n.* a petty officer of a ship.

bob (bob), *n.* a jerky movement; a float on a fishline; a short haircut for a woman.

bob (bob), *v.i. and v.t.* to move up and down jerkily; to cut short.

bobbin (bob' in), *n.* the spool that holds the thread in a sewing machine.

bobolink (bob' o lingk), *n.* an American songbird.

bobsled (bob' sled), *n.* a short sled joined to another by a long plank; the conveyance thus formed.

bobtail (bob' tāl), *adj.* having the tail cut short.

bode (bōd), *v.i. and v.t.* to portend, foreshow by signs.

bodice (bod' is), *n,* a close-fitting waist.

bodkin (bod' kin), *n.* a pointed instrument for punching holes, as in cloth.

body (bod' i), *n.* the physical structure of a human being or other animal; matter in a unit mass, as a heavenly *body*, a *body* of water; the main part, as the *body* of a car.

Syn. Carcass, clay, corpse, dust, form, frame, remains, system, trunk. *Body* denotes the structure considered as a whole; *form* looks upon it as a thing of shape and outline; *frame* regards it as supported by its framework; *system* views it as an assemblage of many related and harmonious organs. *Body, form, frame* and *system* may be either dead or living, *clay* and *dust* are sometimes figuratively so used, *corpse* and *remains* are used only of the dead, *carcass* applies only to the *body* of an animal.

Ant. Mind, soul, spirit.

bog (bog), *n.* a stretch of wet, spongy ground.

bog (bog), *v.i. and v.t.* to sink or cause to stick in a bog.

bogus (bō' gus), *adj.* false.

bohemian (bō hē' mi an), *n.* a person of free and easy life, generally literary or artistic.

*****boil** (boil), *n.* the state of boiling, as to bring to a *boil;* an inflamed, festering sore on the skin.

boil (boil), *v.i. and v.t.* to bubble with heat; to be agitated, as with anger; to cook in boiling water.

boiler (boil' er), *n.* a vessel in which water is boiled for cooking or washing; a tank in which water is boiled to make steam for heating.

boisterous (bois' tēr us), *adj.* noisy, rough.

bold (bōld), *adj.* venturesome; prominent, as a headland; impudent; requiring or evincing daring, as a *bold* deed.

Syn. Fearless, intrepid, undaunted. *Boldness* is a positive characteristic of the spirit; *fearlessness* is a negative state of the mind, that is, simply an absence of fear. A person may be *bold* through *fearlessness*, but he may be *fearless* without being *bold;* he may be *fearless* where there is no apprehension of danger or no cause for apprehension, but he is *bold* only when he is conscious or apprehensive of danger, and prepared to encounter it. A man is *intrepid* who has no fear where the most *fearless* might tremble; he is *undaunted* whose spirit is unabated by that which would make the stoutest heart yield.

Ant. Cowardly, dastardly, fearful.

bole (bōl), *n.* the trunk of a tree.

*****boll** (bōl), *n.* a round pod or capsule of a plant containing seeds, as of cotton.

*****boll weevil** (bōl wē' vl), an insect pest that feeds on cotton bolls.

bologna (bŏ-lō' nya), *n.* a type of sausage.

bolster (bōl' stēr), *n.* a long pillow.

bolster (bol' stēr), *v.t.* to prop up.

bolt (bōlt), *n.* a sliding bar to fasten a door; a metal pin, generally threaded at one end, to hold a nut for fastening metal parts together; a discharge of lightning; a sudden break into speed; a roll of cloth.

bolt (bōlt), *v.i. and v.t.* to fasten with a bolt; to run away; to swallow food fast without chewing; to sift flour from bran.

bomb (bom), *n.* a hollow shell filled with explosive, set off by a time fuse or by impact from being hurled.

bombard (bom' bärd), *v.t.* to attack with cannon fire.

bombast (bom' bast), *n.* pompous, extravagant talk.

bomber (bom' ēr), *n.* an aircraft used to drop bombs.

bona fide (bō' na fī' dē), in good faith.

bonanza (bŏ nan' za), *n.* a rich strike of ore, especially silver; any lucky strike.

bond (bond), *n.* anything that binds; a pledge under seal by which one binds himself to an obligation; an interest-bearing certificate of debt issued by a corporation or government: *bonds,* fetters.

bondage (bon' dij), *n.* slavery; any enforced subjugation.

bondsman (bondz' man), *n.* one who binds himself as security for another.

bone (bōn), *n.* one of the pieces of an animal's skeleton, the framework of the body; something made of bone, as dice.

bone (bōn), *v.t.* to take the bones from; to put bones in, as a corset.

bonfire (bon' fīr), *n.* a fire built in the open.

bonnet (bon' et), *n.* a piece of headgear for women and children, generally brimless and having strings.

bonus (bō' nus), *n.* a sum paid in excess of what is actually due for service rendered.

booby (bōō' bi), *n.* a dunce; stupid person.

book (book), *n.* blank, written or printed sheets of paper bound together inside a cover; a volume containing a literary or musical composition or a series of compositions.

bookish (book' ish), *adj.* fond of reading; pedantic.

bookkeeping (book' kēp ing), *n.* the business of making accurate records of transactions.

bookworm (book' wûrm), *n.* an insect larva that eats holes in books; a person devoted to study.

boom (bōōm), *n.* a deep, reverberating sound; a spar at the bottom of a fore-and-aft sail; a string of floating logs; a sudden outburst of business activity and prosperity.

boon (bōōn), *n.* a gift; favor; great benefit.

boon (bōōn), *adj.* convivial, cheerful, merry.

boor (boor), *n.* a rough, rustic person.

boost (bōōst), *v.t.* to push or lift from underneath; to raise, as prices.

boot (bōōt), *n.* high-topped footgear, covering the calf of the leg and sometimes the thighs; something additional, offered as an inducement to a buyer or trader, as *to boot.*

booth (bōōth), *n.* a rough house or shelter; a stall, as a telephone *booth,* a sound *booth.*

bootleg (bōōt' leg), *v.i. and v.t.* to make, transport or sell liquor illegally.

booty (bōō' ti), *n.* plunder, especially supplies taken from an enemy.

boracic (bŏ ras' ik), *adj.* of or containing boron.

borax (bō' raks), *n.* a salt compounded of sodium, boron and oxygen.

border (bôr' dēr), *n.* an edge; boundary; a strip along the edge, as of a garden.

border (bôr' dēr), *v.t. and v.i.* to put a border on; to lie along the edge or boundary of.

bore (bōr), *n.* a hole made by boring; a long tunnel or tube; a tiresome person or thing.

bore (bōr), *v.t.* to make a hole through; to weary others by dullness.

boric acid, any acid obtained from boron trioxide, used as an antiseptic: also called *boracic acid.*

born (bôrn), *adj.* brought into life by birth or as if by birth; naturally gifted, as a *born* horseman, a *born* singer.

boron (bō' ron), *n.* a nonmetallic element occurring in borax.

borrow (bor' ō), *v.t.* to procure in the form of a loan with promise of return to the owner.

bosom (booz' um), *n.* the breast; the part of a garment that covers the breast.

bosom (booz' um), *adj.* cherished, intimate.

boss (bos), *n.* a circular knob; a superintendent; foreman; one who gives orders.

botany (bot' a ni), *n.* the science of plants, dealing with their structure, growth and varieties.

botch (boch), *v.t.* to mend or patch in a clumsy manner, to bungle or mar.

both (bōth), *pron. and adj.* each of two.

bother (both' ēr), *n.* fuss, annoyance, inconvenience.

bother (both' ēr), *v.i. and v.t.* to concern oneself; pester, tease, annoy.

bothersome (both' ēr sum), *adj.* annoying, troublesome.

bottle (bot'l), *n.* a glass container for liquids, with a neck and closed with a cork.

bottom (bot' um), *n.* the lowest part; the earth under a body of water.

bottom line (bot um lin), *n.* the final figures, the ultimate result or consideration.

boudoir (bōō' dwär), *n.* a small room elegantly furnished for a lady's use.

bough (bou), *n.* a branch of a tree.

bouillon (bōō yong'), *n.* beef tea; any clear soup made by boiling and straining stock.

boulder (bōl' dēr), *n.* a big stone worn by the action of water or weather.

boulevard (bōō' le värd), *n.* a wide avenue in a city, usually lined with trees; a wide, main highway.

bounce (bouns), *n.* a rebound, as of a ball striking some hard surface when thrown or dropped.

bound (bound), *n.* a limit; boundary.

bound (bound), *v.t.* to limit; to enclose in boundaries.

bound (bound), *v.i.* to leap easily, spring.

bound (bound), *adj.* determined; headed for, destined.

boundary (boun' da ri), *n.* the limiting line about a surface.

boundless (bound' les), *adj.* unlimited.

bounteous (boun' tē us), *adj.* giving generously; plenteous.

bounty (boun' ti), *n.* liberality in bestowing gifts; a grant from a government to encourage business.

*** bouquet** (bō kā'), *n.* a bunch of flowers; the aroma of wine.

bourgeois (boor zhwä'), *adj.* pertaining to the middle class.

*** bourgeoisie** (bōor zhwä zē'), *n.* the middle class.

*** bourse** (boors), *n.* an exchange; money market.

bout (bout), *n.* a contest, as in boxing.

*** bovine** (bō' vīn), *adj.* pertaining to the ox or cattle in general.

bow (bou), *n.* a forward and downward movement of the head and shoulders; the forward part of a boat or ship.

bow (bō), *n.* a bend or curve; something curved; a weapon for shooting arrows; a looped knot, as of ribbon; the staff, strung with horsehair, used in playing the violin.

bowel (bou' el), *n.* an intestine.

bower (bou' ẽr), *n.* a shady shelter; arbor; an anchor carried at the bow of a ship.

*** bowie** (bōō' i), *n.* a long strong knife for cutting and stabbing.

bowl (bōl), *n.* a circular vessel, bigger than a cup, of wood, china or other material and generally without handles, for holding liquids, much used in kitchen work; the ball used in bowling.

bowl (bōl), *v.i. and v.t.* to hit with a rolling ball; to take part in a game of bowling; to roll the ball down an alley or over a bowling green.

bowling (bōl' ing), *n.* a game played on a wooden alley or a smooth bit of turf in which the object is to knock over wooden pins.

*** bowsprit** (bou' sprit), *n.* a spar running out from the stem of a sailingship, to which rigging is attached.

box (boks), *n.* a case, generally of wood or metal, for holding things; a compartment in a theater; a little wooden house in which a sentry finds shelter; the oblong space in which a baseball pitcher, batter or coach stands; a slap on the ear; a small evergreen shrub used in making hedges.

box (boks), *v.i. and v.t.* to place in a box; to spar.

boy (boi), *n.* a male child.

*** boycott** (boi' kot), *v.t.* to refuse to buy goods from or trade with.

brace (brās), *n.* a support; a pair; a handle for a boring tool.

brace (brās), *v.t.* to furnish with supports; to strengthen; make firm and secure.

bracelet (brās' let), *n.* an ornamental band or chain worn on the wrist.

bracing (brās' ing), *adj.* invigorating, stimulating.

bracket (brak' et), *n.* a projecting piece to support something, as a shelf; a square-cornered parenthesis mark.

bracket (brak' et), *v.t.* to enclose in brackets; to pair.

brackish (brak' ish), *adj.* salty, as water.

brad (brad) *n.* a thin nail with a very small head.

brag (brag), *v.i.* to boast.

braggart (brag' ẽrt), *n.* a boaster.

braid (brād), *n.* a narrow strip or plaited band used for trimming or edging on fabrics or garments.

Braille (brāl), *n.* an alphabet for the blind, consisting of combinations of raised dots.

brain (brān), *n.* the nerve tissue within the skull: *brains,* intelligence.

*** braise** (brāz), *v.t.* to stew meat in a covered pan.

brake (brāk), *n.* a device for curbing the speed of a moving vehicle or slowing down a machine; a thicket; an instrument for separating the fiber of flax or hemp from the stem.

bramble (bram' bi), *n.* the English blackberry bush; any tangle of prickly vines or bushes.

bran (bran), *n.* the coarse husks of grain separated from the flour by bolting.

branch (branch), *n.* a limb of a tree; any offshoot from a main stem, as the *branch* of a stream, a family, or a bank.

brand (brand), *n.* a burning piece of wood; a trademark; a certain make of anything; an identifying mark burned in, as the *brand* of the ranch was Cross and Star.

brand (brand), *v.t.* to put a trademark on; to mark with a hot iron, as range cattle; to mark, as to *brand* one as a traitor.

brandish (bran' dish), *v.t.* to wave or flourish, as a flag or a club.

brandy (bran' di), *n.* an ardent alcoholic liquor distilled from wine.

brass (bras), *n.* an alloy made of copper and of zinc.

*** bravado** (bra vä' dō), *n.* make-believe courage; defiance.

brave (brāv), *n.* a North American Indian warrior.

brave (brāv), *adj.* courageous, daring, valiant, dauntless.

bravery (brāv' ẽr i), *n.* courage, intrepidity, fortitude.

Syn. Courage, boldness, gallantry, valor, heroism. *Courage* is a general term implying fearlessness in the presence of danger; *bravery* implies daring and defiance often in spite of fear. *Boldness* is the opposite of timidity; gallantry is spectacular, adventurous *courage; valor* is the lack of personal caution in the presence of danger; *heroism* is completely selfless and implies a scorn of danger inspired by devotion.

Ant. Cowardice, fear.

*** bravo** (brä' vō), *interj.* well done!

brawl (brôl), *n.* a disorderly quarrel; a small riot.

brawl (brôl), *v.i.* to quarrel noisily and violently.

brawn (brôn), *n.* muscle, strength; boar's flesh.

brawny (brôn' ĭ), *adj.* big and strong, husky.

bray (brā), *v.i. and v.t.* to beat or pound fine and small; to utter a harsh cry, as of a jackass or make a noise resembling it.

braze (brāz), *v.t.* to cover with brass; solder with brass.

brazen (brā' zn), *v.t.* to face a situation or meet a charge with impudent swagger.

brazen (brā' zn), *adj.* made of brass or resembling brass; impudent, shameless.

brazier (brā' zhēr), *n.* a pan in which charcoal is burned.

breach (brēch), *n.* a break, as in a wall; violation of a law, contract or other agreement, as a *breach* of faith.
    Syn. Cleft, chasm, gap; infringement; quarrel, dispute.

breach (brēch), *v.t.* to break an opening through, as a wall.

bread (brĕd), *n.* a staple food made from ground grain, especially wheat or rye flour.

bread (brĕd), *v.t.* to cover, as a chop or cutlet, with bread crumbs before cooking.

breadth (brĕdth), *n.* distance across, from side to side; width; liberality of thought.

break (brāk), *n.* a breach; rupture; interruption; a sudden drop in prices, as in the stock market; a lucky change in the tide of battle, as a *break* in a ball game; an untimely remark or action, as to make a bad *break*.

break (brāk), *v.i. and v.t.* to separate with violence; to fail to honor, as a law or a promise; to tame or train, as a horse or dog; to begin suddenly, as a storm.
    Syn. Burst, crack, split. To *break* does not specify any particular manner or form of action; what is *broken* may be *broken* in two or more pieces, *broken* short or lengthwise, and the like; to *burst* is to break suddenly and with violence, frequently also with noise. To *crack* and *split* are modes of breaking lengthwise, the former in application to hard or brittle objects, as clay, or the things made of clay; the latter in application to wood. [See *breach.*]
    Ant. Attach, bind, join, mend, unite.

breakage (brāk' ĭj), *n.* loss due to breaking.

breakdown (brāk' doun), *n.* a collapse; failure.

breaker (brāk' ĕr), *n.* a wave that breaks on a beach; anything that breaks things up.

breakfast (brĕk' fast), *n.* the first meal of the day, breaking the night's fast.

breakneck (brāk' nek), *adj.* involving danger of a broken neck, as *breakneck* speed.

breakwater (brāk' wô tēr), *n.* a structure protecting a shore or harbor from the pounding of waves.

breast (brest), *n.* the fore part of the human body, between neck and abdomen; a gland in women that secretes milk for the young.

breastplate (brest' plāt), *n.* that part of a suit of armor which covers the upper front section of the body.

breastwork (brest' wûrk), *n.* a low defensive wall of earth or stone, often temporary.

breath (breth), *n.* air drawn into the lungs and expelled.

breathe (brēth), *v.i. and v.t.* to inhale and exhale; to let out, as a secret: don't *breathe* it to anyone.

breathless (breth' les), *adj.* out of breath, as from exercise or emotion; lifeless.

*breech** (brēch), *n.* the buttocks; the hind end of anything; the rear end of the barrel of a gun or bore of a cannon, of which the other end is the muzzle.

*breeches** (brich' ez), *n.* trousers, a garment worn by men, covering the legs and hips.

breechloader (brēch' lōd' ēr), *n.* a gun loaded at the breech, not the muzzle.

breed (brĕd), *n.* a race or strain of animals or fowl.

breed (brĕd), *v.i. and v.t.* [*p.t.* and *p.p.* bred, *p.pr.* breeding] to engender or produce young, as rabbits *breed* fast; to raise, as he *breeds* white Leghorns; to bring up, train, foster, as a well-*bred* child.

breeding (brĕd' ing), *n.* the raising of plants or animals; bringing up, education; knowledge of or training in the social niceties.

breeze (brēz), *n.* a gentle wind; waste ashes and coke dust, used in baking brick.

breezy (brēz' ĭ), *adj.* moderately windy; lively in manner.

*brevet** (bre vet'), *n.* an advancement in rank in the army without change of duties or increase in pay.

*breviary** (brē' vĭ er ĭ), *n.* a book containing the daily prayers of the Roman Catholic Church.

brevity (brev' ĭ tĭ), *n.* shortness of time; conciseness of speech.

brew (broō), *n.* the action, process or product of brewing.

brew (broō), *v.i. and v.t.* to make liquors from malt; to make by infusion, as tea; to grow in force, as a storm is *brewing;* to bring about, as to *brew* mischief.

brewer (broō' ēr), *n.* one whose business it is to make beer or ale.

brewery (broō' ēr ĭ), *n.* a building where beer or ale is made commercially.

bribe (brīb), *n.* money or other reward offered as inducement to betray a trust, as of public office.

bribery (brīb' ēr ĭ), *n.* the giving or taking of money or gifts in return for betrayal of trust.

*bric-a-brac** (brik' a brak'), *n.* small objects of art, in a collection; knickknacks.

brick (brik), *n.* a block of baked clay, used in building and paving; anything shaped like a brick.

brick kiln (brik' kil), *n.* a furnace in which brick is baked.

bricklayer (brik' lā ēr), *n.* one whose occupation is to pave or build with bricks.

bridal (brīd' al), *n.* a wedding.

bridal (brīd' al), *adj.* pertaining to a bride or to a wedding.

bride (brīd), *n.* a woman being or about to be married; one recently married.

bridegroom (brīd' groōm'), *n.* a man being or about to be married or one newly married.

bridesmaid (brĭdz' mād), *n.* a woman who acts as attendant to bride at wedding.

bridge (brĭj), *n.* a structure that carries a roadway across a river, a railroad or another road; a structure above the deck of a ship for the navigating officer; any of various things resembling a bridge, as the arched part of the nose; certain games of cards, as *bridge* whist, auction *bridge*.

bridge (brĭj), *v.t.* to build a bridge over or across; span, as the brook was *bridged* by a log; fill, as to *bridge* a gap in the argument; surmount, as the problem was quickly *bridged*.

bridging (brĭj' ĭng), *n.* a system of wooden cross-bars holding beams in place, as under a floor; the material used in such construction.

bridle (brī' dl), *n.* the part of a horse's harness that fits on the head and to which the bit and reins are attached.

bridle path (brī' dl path), *n.* a narrow track for horseback riding.

brief (brēf), *n.* a synopsis of a law case.

brief (brēf), *adj.* short; concise.

brief case (brēf kās), *n.* a flat leather bag in which loose papers are carried.

brier or briar (brī' ẽr), *n.* a thorn; a thorny shrub; a smoking pipe made from brier root.

brig (brĭg), *n.* a sailing vessel with two square-rigged masts; the quarters, aboard ship, in which members of the crew are confined as punishment for offenses against discipline.

brigade (brĭ gād'), *n.* a military unit composed of a headquarters and two to four regiments, itself a unit in a corps or division.

brigade (brĭ gād'), *v.i. and v.t.* to form as a brigade; organize in brigades.

*brigadier** (brĭg *a* dẽr'), *n.* an officer commanding a brigade, a brigadier general, ranking between colonel and major general.

*brigand** (brĭg' and), *n.* a bandit, especially one who travels in bands.

*brigantine** (brĭg' an tēn), *n.* a two-masted sailing vessel, square-rigged on the foremast and mainmast, except for a fore-and-aft mainsail.

bright (brīt), *adj.* shining, sunny, as a *bright* day; lively, gay; clever, as a *bright* child.

brighten (brīt' n), *v.i. and v.t.* to grow bright; to make bright.

brilliant (brĭl' yant), *adj.* sparkling; witty; talented.

brilliant (brĭl' yant), *n.* a small size of type; a gem cut with many facets so as to bring out its sparkle.

brim (brĭm), *n.* the rim of a cup; the flat rim of a hat; the edge of anything.

brim (brĭm), *v.i. and v.t.* to fill or be filled to the brim.

brimstone (brĭm' stōn), *n.* sulphur.

brindled (brĭn' dld), *adj.* streaked with black or brown against a tawny background.

brine (brīn), *n.* the salt water of the sea; water strongly salted, for use in pickling.

bring (brĭng), *v.t.* [*p.t.* and *p.p.* brought,

p.pr. bringing], to come, convey (a person or thing) from one place to another by carrying or leading, as *bring* me a book, *bring* Tom to the party; to persuade, as your plea *brought* him to relent; to sell for, as a rare object *brings* a high price; to cause, as wrongdoing *brings* grief; to win or attract, as an orator *brings* cheers from the crowd.

Syn. Fetch. To *bring* usually indicates to come or carry with; to *fetch* implies to go and get and come back with.

brink (brĭngk), *n.* the edge, margin, brim, the very edge.

brisk (brĭsk), *adj.* lively, active, swift, vivacious.

brisket (brĭs' ket), *n.* that part of an animal's breast where the ribs join the breastbone; meat from that part.

*bristle** (brĭs' l), *n.* a short, stiff, coarse hair, especially of swine; such a hair used in a brush.

bristle (brĭs' l), *v.i. and v.t.* to cause to stand up like bristles; to furnish with bristles; to show anger, as if by raising bristles.

brittle (brĭt' l), *adj.* easily broken, as by snapping.

broach (brōch), *n.* a boring tool; reamer.

broach (brōch), *v.t.* to make public; to bring up for discussion; to open a keg of wine.

broad (brôd), *adj.* wide; spacious, as the *broad* heavens; coarse, as a *broad* joke; liberal, tolerant, as a *broad* view of something; clear, as *broad* daylight, a *broad* hint; said with the throat open, as the a in father is *broad* a.

broadcast (brôd' kást), *n.* anything transmitted by radio, as news or a musical program.

broadcast (brôd' kást), *v.t.* to send by radio over the air, as news or programs.

broadcloth (brôd' klôth), *n.* a fine woolen, cotton or silk cloth with a smooth-finished surface.

broaden (brôd' n), *v.* to make broad or comprehensive.

broad jump (brôd jump), a jump for distance, not height.

broadside (brôd' sīd), *n.* a volley from all the guns on one side of a ship; a large sheet of paper with print on one side only.

brocade (brō kād'), *n.* a silk fabric with raised figures.

*brochure** (brō shūr'), *n.* a pamphlet.

*brogue** (brōg), *n.* a dialect of English, especially with an Irish pronunciation; a heavy shoe.

broil (broil), *n.* a noisy quarrel; a brawl.

broil (broil), *v.t.* to cook on a gridiron.

broken (brō' ken), *adj.* in pieces, fractured; of language, incorrectly spoken; of land, hilly; of ground, plowed; of health, impaired; of a promise, not kept.

broker (brō' kẽr), *n.* one whose business it is to buy for another, on commission, as a stock *broker*, real estate *broker*.

brokerage (brō' kẽr ij), *n.* the business of a broker; his percentage on a transaction.

*bromide** (brō' mīd), *n.* a compound of bromine, used to induce sleep.

*bromine (brō' mĭn), n. a nonmetallic element.

bronchial tubes (brong' kĭ al tūbz), the tubes that carry air from the windpipe to the lungs.

*bronchitis (brong kī' tis), n. inflammation of the bronchial tubes.

broncho (brong' kō), n. a small, hardy horse widely used in herding cattle.

bronze (bronz), n. an alloy of copper and tin; a statue or medal made of that metal.

*brooch (brōch), n. an ornamental dress clasp; breastpin.

brood (brōod), n. the young birds hatched at one time; one mother's offspring.

brood (brōod), v.i. and v.t. to sit on eggs or hover over young birds, as the mother bird does, covering them with her wings; to incubate or hatch, as eggs; to dwell upon, sorrowfully or with regret.

brook (brook), n. a small stream.

brook (brook), v.t. to put up with, stand for.

*broom (brōom), n. a brush with a long handle used in sweeping; a flowering shrub.

broomstick (brōom' stik), n. a broom handle.

broth (brôth), n. a thin soup.

brother (brŭth' ēr), n. a male person having the same parents as another.

brotherhood (brŭth' ēr hood), n. the state of being a brother; a group or society of men united by common interest; a fraternity.

brow (brou'), n. the arch of hair over the eye; edge of a cliff or hill.

browbeat (brou' bēt), v.t. [p.t. browbeat, p.p. browbeaten, pr.p. browbeating], to bully.

brown (broun), n. a dark color, which may lean toward red or yellow.

brown (broun), v.i. and v.t. to become brown; make brown.

brown (broun), adj. having brown coloring.

browse (brouz), v.i. to graze; to read at random.

bruin (brōo' in), n. a bear.

bruise (brōoz), n. a flesh injury; contusion.

bruise (brōoz), v.t. to inflict a hurt upon without breaking the skin or surface.

bruit (brōot), v.t. to noise abroad, start rumors.

brunet or brunette (brōo net'), adj. having a dark complexion and dark hair and eyes.

brunt (brunt), n. the shock of an onslaught; the heaviest or hardest part, as the brunt of battle.

brush (brush), n. a bristled implement for cleaning clothes, furniture, for shining shoes and stoves or for applying paint; undergrowth in the woods; a fox's tail; a collection of thin plates or rods of metal that connect with a commutator, collector or slip ring and conduct electric current.

brush (brush), v.t. to go over an object with a brush, to clean it, apply paint or smooth it.

*brusque (brusk), adj. blunt, brisk, abrupt in manner.

brutal (brōo' tal), adj. like a brute, savage, cruel.

brutality (brōo tal' i ti), n. cruelty; a cruel act.

brute (brōot), n. any animal not a human

being; a person who acts without reason; a cruel person.

brutish (brōo' tish), adj. like a brute, stupid, gross.

bubble (bub' l), n. a small globule filled with air or gas in a liquid; anything unreal or delusive.

bubble (bub' l), v.i. to form bubbles, foam.

*buccaneer (buk a nēr'), n. a pirate.

buck (buk), n. the male of the deer, goat or rabbit; a gay fellow; a support for wood to be sawed; a sudden spring of a horse from the ground in trying to throw off a rider; in football, a short, sharp play straight at the opposing line.

buck (buk), v.i. and v.t. to leap suddenly into the air, as a horse in trying to dismount a rider; to aim a play straight at the opposing line in football.

buckboard (buk' bōrd), n. a light four-wheeled wagon with long limber boards set on the axles instead of springs.

bucket (buk' et), n. a pail; the scoop of a dredging machine; as much as a bucket will hold, as a bucket of water.

buckeye (buk' ī), n. a tree related to the horsechestnut tree.

buckle (buk' l), n. a metal clasp, as on a belt, with a movable tongue or catch; a bend or warp.

buckle (buk' l), v.i. and v.t. to fasten with a buckle; to apply oneself to work; to become bent or warped; to sag, crumple.

bucksaw (buk' sô), n. a saw set in a frame and worked with both hands.

buckshot (buk' shot), n. shot of a large size used in hunting game.

buckwheat (buk' hwēt), n. a plant cultivated for its seeds, which are ground into meal and used for food.

bud (bud), n. a little swelling on the stem of a plant or on a branch of a tree, which opens into leaf or flower.

budge (buj), v.i. and v.t. to move or cause to move from one's position.

budget (buj' et), n. an estimated schedule for expenditure of money in proportion to income; a collection of news items.

budget (buj' et), v.t. to make an itemized and proportioned plan for spending, as to budget one's income; to allocate resources.

buff (buf), n. a soft, thick leather; its color, a brownish yellow; a stick covered with soft leather for polishing.

buff (buf), v.t. to polish with a buff.

buffalo (buf' a lō), n. any of several wild oxen of India and Africa; the North American bison.

buffer (buf' ēr), n. any contrivance serving to deaden the shock when two bodies come violently together.

buffet (buf' et), n. a blow with the open hand, a slap.

*buffet (boo fā'), n. a sideboard; a counter for refreshments.

buffet (buf' et), v.t. and v.i. to strike, fight; to strive as if by fighting, as to buffet one's way through life.

*buffoon (bu fōon'), n. a clown; a professional

jester.

buffoonery (bu foon' ēr ĭ), *n.* clownish fooling; prank-playing.

bug (bug), *n.* loosely, any crawling insect; especially certain flat crawling insects with sucking mouths, as bedbugs or lice.

bug (bug), *n.* a mistake whether accidental or not in a computer program.

buggy (bug' ĭ), *n.* a light four-wheeled carriage.

bugle (bū' gl), *n.* a military wind instrument; a huntsman's horn.

bugloss (bū' glŏs), *n.* a hairy-stemmed European herb that grows in America as a weed, sometimes used in making medicine: also called *oxtongue*.

build (bĭld), *v.i. and v.t.* [*p.t.* and *p.p.* built, builded, *p.pr.* building] to construct; to form by putting parts and materials together according to a plan; to be a builder.

building (bĭld' ing), *n.* the act or business of constructing; a structure; edifice, as a house, office *building*.

bulb (bulb), *n.* a thick root formed of layers of thick leaflike pieces, from which grow plants like the onion, dahlia or lily; anything shaped like a bulb, as an electric light bulb.

bulbous (bulb' us), *adj.* shaped like a bulb, as a *bulbous* tumor; growing from a bulb, as certain plants.

bulge (bulj), *n.* an outward swell as in the side of a keg or ship.

bulge (bulj), *v.i.* to swell outward.

bulk (bulk), *n.* volume; cubic size; the main mass of an object.

bulk (bulk), *v.i. and v.t.* to assume volume; to form solidly; have size and mass, or importance in an aggregation.

bulkhead (bulk' hed), *n.* a partition, in a ship, separating spaces, as watertight compartments; in mining, a wall to hold back water or landslides.

bulky (bul' kĭ), *adj.* big, massive.

bull (bool), *n.* the male of any kind of cattle; a dealer in stocks who rides with a rising market; a papal decree bearing a leaden seal, the bulla; a ludicrous inconsistency in language.

bullet (bool' et), *n.* a lead ball fired from a gun.

bulletin (bool' e tin), *n.* an official report; a pamphlet published periodically reporting the activities of a society; a brief statement issued to the public, as by doctors reporting on illness of a prominent person.

bullfinch (bool' finch), *n.* a songbird.

*****bullion** (bool' yun), *n.* gold or silver to be coined.

bullock (bool' uk), *n.* an ox or steer.

bull's-eye (boolz' ĭ), *n.* the center of a target; a shot that hits it.

bully (bool' ĭ), *n.* a cowardly brow beating ruffian.

bully (bool' ĭ), *v.t.* to threaten and torment a weaker person.

bulrush (bool' rush), *n.* a tall waterside weed.

*****bulwark** (bool' wērk), *n.* a rampart; the side of a ship projecting above the deck.

bumblebee (bum' bl bē), *n.* a big bee that hums as it flies.

bump (bump), *n.* a collision; a swelling caused by a blow.

bump (bump), *v.t. and v.i.* to hit against something, collide with or cause to collide, as to *bump* one's head, two cars *bump*.

bumper (bump' ēr), *n.* something to absorb the shock of a bump, as on an automobile.

bumpy (bump' ĭ), *adj.* characterized by bumps; causing jerks or jolts, as a *bumpy* road.

bun (bun), *n.* a small sweet cake, sometimes with icing or with nuts or raisins mixed in the dough, and often spiced.

bunch (bunch), *n.* a group or collection of like things collected as a new unit, as a *bunch* of flowers, a *bunch* of grapes.

*****buncombe** or **bunkum** (bung' kum), *n.* idle or showy speech; empty promises of a politician seeking votes.

bundle (bun' dl), *n.* a number of things bound together; a roll or package.

bundle (bun' dl), *v.t.* to put together or tie in a bundle.

bung (bung), *n.* a wooden stopper for the hole in a keg.

bungalow (bung' ga lō), *n.* a one-story cottage.

bungle (bung' gl), *v.i. and v.t.* to do clumsily; botch.

bunion (bun' yun), *n.* a sore swelling at the base of the big toe.

bunk (bungk), *n.* a bed built against a wall; a berth in a ship or car.

bunker (bungk' ēr), *n.* a large stowing space, as for coal aboard ship.

bunt (bunt), *n.* a grain fungus; in baseball, a ball hit lightly, inside the diamond.

bunt (bunt), *v.t. and v.i.* to butt with horns, as a goat; to hit a ball lightly.

bunting (bunt' ing), *n.* a small bird of the finch family; a light woolen fabric used for flags.

*****buoy** (boo' ĭ), *n.* a floating object moored in shallow water as a warning or guide to navigators.

buoy (boo' ĭ), *v.t.* to support, sustain: generally with *up*, as to *buoy* one up; to place buoys in a channel.

buoyancy (boo' yan-sĭ), *n.* ability to stay afloat; lightness on the water; elasticity of spirits.

bur (būr), *n.* the rough, prickly seed case of certain weeds; a throaty rendering of the sound of *r*.

burden (būr' dn), *n.* a heavy load; a weight of trouble.

burdensome (būr' dn sum), *adj.* oppressive, heavy.

burdock (būr' dok), *n.* a large, coarse weed with broad leaves and burlike flowers.

*****bureau** (bū' rō), *n.* [*pl.* bureaus or bureaux] a chest of drawers in which light clothing is kept; a writing table with drawers; an office, as of a governmental agency.

*****bureaucracy** (bū rō' kra sĭ), *n.* a system of government with many subdivisions and a large staff of bureau chiefs.

*burglar (bûr' glẽr), *n.* one who breaks in to rob.

burglary (bûr' gla rĭ), *n.* the crime of breaking into a building to rob or commit a felony.

Burgundy (bûr' gun dĭ), *n.* a wine made in Burgundy, or a wine of the same type made elsewhere.

*burial (ber' ĭ al), *n.* the act of placing a body underground; interment.

burlap (bûr' lap), *n.* a coarse fabric of jute or hemp, used in making bags or wrapping bales.

burlesque (bûr lesk'), *n.* coarse or ridiculous caricature; a cheap, vulgar show.

burley (bûr' lĭ), *n.* a kind of tobacco grown in Kentucky.

burn (bûrn), *n.* an injury caused by burning; Scotch word for brook or stream.

burn (bûrn), *v.i. and v.t.* [*p.t. and p.p.* burned or burnt, *pr.p* burning] to consume or injure, be consumed or injured, by fire; to be on fire; to set afire.

burner (bûrn' ẽr), *n.* the part of a lamp or gas jet where the flame emerges: *oil burner,* a furnace in which oil is used as fuel.

burnish (bûr' nish), *v.t.* to polish by friction.

burn-out (burn' out), *n.* when mission fuel is burned up and missile enters free flight; emotional exhaustion from mental stress.

burro (bûr' o), *n.* a small donkey.

burrow (bûr' ō), *n.* a hole or passageway dug in the ground by an animal, as a fox or rabbit, for shelter or to live in.

burst (bûrst), *n.* a sudden outburst or spurt of something, as a *burst* of applause or speed, a *burst* of flame.

burst (bûrst), *v.i. and v.t.* to break open with violence; yield to internal force or pressure.

*bury (ber' ĭ), *v.t.* to place in the ground.

bus (bus), *n.* [*pl.* busses or buses] a vehicle for public passenger transportation, usually a large automobile with seats on either side of a central aisle.

bush (boosh), *n.* a thick shrub; uncleared woodland.

bushel (boosh' el), *n.* a unit of dry measure; 4 pecks, 32 quarts.

bushing (boosh' ing), *n.* a removable metal lining to reduce friction.

business (biz' nes), *n.* employment; trade; profession; something to be transacted.

buskin (bus' kin), *n.* a laced high boot worn by actors in old Greek tragedy.

bust (bust), *n.* the chest; the head, neck, shoulders and breast, represented in sculpture.

bustard (bus' tẽrd), *n.* a cranelike European game bird.

*bustle (bus' l), *n.* haste; commotion, confused movement.

Syn. Tumult, uproar. *Bustle* has most of hurry in it; *tumult* most of disorder and confusion; *uproar* most of noise; the hurried movements of one or many cause a *bustle;* the disorderly struggles of many constitute a *tumult;* the loud elevation of many opposing voices produces an *uproar; uproar* is the consequence either of general anger or mirth.

Ant. Calm, peace, quiet.

busy (biz' ĭ), *n.* actively employed.

busybody (biz' ĭ bod ĭ), *n.* a meddling, officious person.

but (but) *prep.* except, as we are all here but Tom.

but (but) *conj.* on the contrary, yet, as willing *but* unable; that not, as not so sick *but* he can eat; except, as he would have drowned *but* for you; that, as there is no question *but* war will come.

but (but), *adv.* only, as *but* a child; to stay *but* a minute; no more or no less than, as she can *but* say no.

*butcher (booch' ẽr), *n.* one who kills animals for food; one who sells meat.

butcher (booch' ẽr), *v.t.* to kill animals for food; to kill men brutally; to botch.

butchery (booch' er ĭ), *n.* the business of a butcher; wanton killing; slaughter.

butler (but' lẽr), *n.* a manservant who has charge of the dining room and is usually head of the house servants.

butt (but), *n.* a push with the head; the thick end, as of a rifle or billiard cue; a large cask; an embankment behind a target or a pit in front of a target to shelter those checking hits.

butt (but), *v.t.* to push with the head.

butte (būt), *n.* an abrupt isolated height in the midst of a level region.

butter (but' ẽr), *n.* a solid, fatty substance obtained from cream or milk by churning; anything having the texture of butter, as apple *butter,* peanut *butter.*

buttercup (but' ẽr kup), *n.* a plant with yellow flowers shaped like a shallow cup.

butterfly (but' ẽr flī), *n.* an insect with wide, colored wings, differing from moths in several respects and by being diurnal instead of nocturnal.

buttermilk (but' ẽr milk), *n.* the liquid remaining after the butter has been separated from the cream or milk in churning.

butternut (but' ẽr nut), *n.* the North American white walnut tree, bearing sweet, oily nuts.

buttery (but' ẽr ĭ), *n.* a pantry.

button (but' n), *n.* a small disk used to fasten a garment; a similar fastener for a door.

button (but' n), *v.t.* to fasten with buttons.

buttonwood (but' n wood), *n.* the plane tree.

buttress (but' res), *n.* masonry or brickwork built against a wall to strengthen it; any support.

buttress (but' res), *v.t.* to supply with buttresses; to support, strengthen.

buxom (buk' sum), *n.* plump, healthy, jolly.

buy (bī), *v.t.* to purchase, get for a price; bribe, as to buy a lawyer.

buzz (buz), *v.i.* to make a continuous humming noise.

buzzard (buz' ẽrd), *n.* an American vulture.

buzz saw (buz sô), a circular saw.

by (bī), *prep.* near, alongside of, as a tree *by* a brook; along, through or over, as come *by* the lower road, travel *by* sea; not later than, as she will be here *by* noon; during, as work *by* day, sleep *by* night; through the means of, as cook *by* gas, cured *by* a new treatment; concerning, regarding, as to do right *by* a friend.

bylaw (bī lô), *n.* a secondary law or rule.

by-product (bī prod' ukt), *n.* an incidental product in manufacture.

byte (bīt), *n.* a unit of information representing a letter or number used in computers. There are eight bits in a byte.

C

cab (kab), *n.* a closed public vehicle; the covered space for the engineer in a locomotive.

*cabal** (ka bal'), *n.* a combination of persons for carrying out some secret design; intrigue.

cabalistic (kab' a lis' tik), *adj.* pertaining to the cabala, a secret Jewish doctrine.

*cabaret** (kab a rā'), *n.* a restaurant where customers are entertained with dancing and vaudeville acts.

cabbage (kab' ij), *n.* a vegetable plant with closely folded succulent leaves.

cabin (ka´ bin), *n.* a small, crude house; a sleeping room aboard ship for officers or passengers.

cabinet (kab' i net), *n.* a group of official advisers to a nation's chief executive; a piece of furniture with shelves and drawers.

cabinetmaker (kab' i net māk' ēr), *n.* one whose occupation is the making of fine furniture.

cable (kā' bl), *n.* a large, strong rope or chain, for mooring ships, towing or hanging suspension bridges; an insulated bundle of wires enclosing an electric line; a cabled message, cablegram.

cable (kā' bl), *v.i. and v.t.* to send a message by cable or submarine telegraph.

cablegram (kā' bl gram), *n.* a message sent by submarine telegraph.

caboose (ka boos'), *n.* a little car for trainmen's use, at the end of a freight train.

*cacao** (ka kā' ō), *n.* a tropical tree from the seeds of which cocoa and chocolate are made.

*cache** (kash), *n.* a hiding place for food and supplies for future use, used by explorers; anything hidden in such a place.

cackle (kak' l), *n.* the cry of a hen after laying an egg.

cactus (kak' tus), *n.* a fleshy desert plant with spines in place of leaves.

cad (kad), *n.* a vulgar, ill-bred fellow.

*cadaver** (ka dā' vēr), *n.* a corpse.

cadaverous (ka dav' ēr us), *adj.* resembling a corpse, pale, haggard.

caddie (kad' i), *n.* one who carries a golf player's clubs.

caddy (kad' i), *n.* a can in which tea is kept.

cadence (kā' dens), *n.* rhythm in music; the rise and fall of the human voice in speech.

cadet (ka det'), *n.* a student in a military school.

cafe (ka fā'), *n.* a coffeehouse or restaurant; a barroom.

cafeteria (caf e tēr' i a), *n.* a restaurant where patrons serve themselves.

cage (kāj), *n.* a structure with bars where birds or animals are kept.

*caisson** (kā' sun), *n.* an ammunition wagon; a box in which workmen work under water.

*cajole** (ka jōl'), *v.t.* to coax or persuade with flattery.

cake (kāk), *n.* a small mass of dough, sweetened and baked on all surfaces; a small amount of batter or other materials fried on both sides, as pan*cakes*, fish*cakes;* any substance molded into small flattened form, as a *cake* of soap.

cake (kāk), *v.i. and v.t.* to form into a small, flattened mass.

*calabash** (kal' a bash), *n.* a large gourd.

calamity (ka lam' i ti), *n.* a great misfortune, ruin.

Syn. Disaster. A *calamity* is a great misfortune with far-reaching personal or public consequences; a *disaster* is an unforeseen misfortune bringing ruin, sometimes but not always brought about through one's own fault.

calcium (kal' si um), *n.* a soft white metal found combined with lime, marble, bone and other substances.

calculate (kal' cū lāt), *v.t.* to compute; to design or plan.

Syn. Reckon. To *calculate* denotes any numerical operation in general, but is particularly applicable to the abstract science of figures; the astronomer *calculates* the motions of the heavenly bodies; the mathematician makes algebraic *calculations;* to *reckon* is to enumerate and set down things in detail; tradesmen keep their accounts by *reckoning;* children learn to *reckon* by various simple processes. *Calculation* is therefore the science, *reckoning* the practical use of numbers.

calculation (kal cū lā shun), *n.* reckoning by numbers; computing.

calculator (kal´ kū lā ter), *n.* a special purpose machine which works with numbers and is controlled by a computer chip.

*caldron** (kôl' drun), *n.* a kettle, boiler.

calendar (kal' en dēr), *n.* a register of the days, weeks and months of the year.

calender (kal' en dēr), *n.* a machine with rollers in which cloth or paper is pressed.

calf (käf), *n.* the young of cattle and certain other animals, as the elephant or whale.

caliber (kal' i bēr), *n.* the diameter of a tube, especially of a gun barrel.

calico (kal' i kō), *n.* [*pl.* calicoes] cotton cloth with a design printed on one side.

calipers (kal' i pērz), *n.* compasses for measuring degrees on a circle.

*caliph** (kā' lif), *n.* a Mohammedan ruler; a

sultan of Turkey.

*__calisthenics__ (kal is then' iks), *n.* physical exercises.

__calk__ (kôk), *n.* the projecting piece at the ends of a horseshoe; a plate with projections on the sole of a shoe to prevent slipping on icy walks.

__calk__ (kôk), *v.t.* to fill the seams of a boat with something like tarred hemp to make them watertight.

__call__ (kôl), *n.* a cry for attention, a shout; a summons; a telephone ring; a formal visit.

__call__ (kôl), *v.t. and v.i.* to summon, as to *call* someone to breakfast; to name, as *call* the pup Rover; to announce or command, as to *call* a meeting or a strike; to communicate with by telephone; to make formal demand for payment of, as to *call* a loan; to consider as, as we *call* it a daisy; to cry aloud or shout; to pay a short visit.

__calling__ (kôl' ing), *n.* an occupation, profession; an invitation or summons.

*__callous__ (kal' us), *adj.* thickened and hardened, as skin; hard-hearted, indifferent to the sufferings of others.

__callow__ (kal' ō), *adj.* of a bird, unfledged; of a person, young, inexperienced.

__callus__ (kal' us), *n.* a growth of thick, hard, dry skin, as on the palms of the hand.

__calm__ (käm), *n.* stillness; tranquillity.

__calm__ (käm), *v.t.* to soothe; to pacify; to make still, peaceful, quiet.

__calm__ (käm), *adj.* peaceful; quiet; undisturbed.
    Syn. Tranquil, serene, placid. *Calm* refers usually to weather and means the opposite of *stormy*, hence the opposite of any kind of agitation; *tranquil* implies a calm that never is or was disturbed, as convent life is *tranquil*; *serene* denotes a calm too great to be discomposed, as a mind *serene* in spite of trouble; *placid* implies a contentment apparent in the appearance or temper, as a *placid* face, a *placid* remark.

*__calomel__ (kal' ō mel), *n.* a compound of chlorine and mercury used in medicine.

*__caloric__ (ka lor' ik), *adj.* relating to heat.

*__calorie__ (kal' ō ri), *n.* a unit for measuring the heat-value of food.

*__calumet__ (kal' ū met), *n.* the North American Indian peace pipe or ceremonial pipe.

__calumniate__ (ka lum' ni āt), *v.t.* to bring false, malicious accusation against; to slander.

__calumny__ (kal' um ni), *n.* slander.

__calve__ (käv), *v.i.* to bring forth a calf.

*__calyx__ (kā' liks), *n.* the cuplike collection of sepals that sheathe the petals of a flower.

__cam__ (kam), *n.* a projecting part on a wheel or shaft to govern the motion of a roller, pin or valve with which it comes in contact.

__cambric__ (käm' brik), *n.* a fine thin white linen, or a cotton imitation of it.

__camel__ (kam' el), *n.* a large cud-chewing animal native to Asia and Africa, used as a beast of burden.

*__camellia__ (ka mel' ia), *n.* a tropical shrub with red or white flowers.

__camelopard__ (ka mel' ō pärd), *n.* the giraffe.

__cameo__ (kam' ē ō), *n.* a stone such as onyx or agate on which designs are carved in relief,

for use as personal ornament in rings or brooches.

*__camera__ (kam' ĕr a), *n.* an apparatus for taking pictures by means of a lens through which rays of light pass to a sensitive plate or film inside a lightproof box.

__camion__ (ka' myôn), *n.* a motor truck used to transport cannon.

__camomile__ (kam' ō mīl), *n.* an herb of which the leaves are used in medicine.

__camouflage__ (kam' oo fläzh), *n.* the art of concealing a military position or disguising a ship or airplane; pretense; false appearance.

__camp__ (kamp), *n.* a group of tents or shelters for troops or hunters; the ground on which these shelters stand.

__camp__ (kamp), *v.i.* to make or live in a camp; encamp.

__campaign__ (kam pān'), *n.* a series of military operations with a single, final objective; a series of political speeches, meetings and appeals for votes preliminary to an election; a planned series of business operations for a stated purpose.

*__campanile__ (kam pa nē' lē), *n.* a bell tower.

__camphor__ (kam' fēr), *n.* the aromatic resin of an Asiatic evergreen, whitish in color, translucent, crystalline, used in medicine and in the manufacture of celluloid.

__camphorate__ (kam' fō rāt), *v.t.* to saturate or impregnate with camphor.

__camp meeting__ (kamp mēt ing), an outdoor religious gathering, generally extending over several days.

__campstool__ (kamp' stool), *n.* a portable folding seat for use outdoors or in a tent.

__campus__ (kam' pus), *n.* the grounds of a school or college.

__can__ (kan), *n.* a small, generally cylindrical metal container for liquids, as oil, milk, soup or for preserving solid foods, as meat.

__can__ (kan), *v.t.* to put up or preserve in cans, as to *can* vegetables, *can* fruit.

__can__ (kan), *auxiliary verb* [*p.t.* could], to be able or have the power to, as he *can* read, he *can* overcome difficulties.

__canal__ (ka nal'), *n.* a made waterway for navigation or irrigation; any tube in an animal body through which food or fluids pass, as the alimentary *canal*; any channel.

__canalize__ (ka nal' iz *or* kan' al iz), *v.t.* to equip with canals, make a canal through, as to *canalize* an isthmus.

__canard__ (ka närd'), *n.* an absurd or false story or report intended to deceive the public.

__canary__ (ka nâr' i), *n.* a yellow songbird; a light yellow color; wine from the Canary Islands.

__cancel__ (kan' sel), *v.t.* to cross off, put a line through, as to *cancel* a word or passage of a composition; to nullify, as a legal document; to revoke or recall, as an order or meeting.

__cancer__ (kan' sēr), *n.* a malignant tumor; an evil likened to a poisonous sore, as the illegal drug trade is a social *cancer*.

*__candelabrum__ (kan de lä' brum), *n.* a branching candlestick.

__candent__ (kan' dent), *adj.* white-hot; glowing

or shining with heat.

candid (kan' did), *adj.* sincere, frank; unreserved, straightforward; unbiased, impartial.

Syn. Frank, open, plain. *Candid* refers specifically to a lack of prejudice or partiality; we can have *candid* friends, give a *candid* account of something or express a *candid* opinion. *Frank* refers to a lack of reserve in stating opinions or expressing feelings; *open* refers to a lack of concealment; *plain* describes a manner of speaking or a temperament free from affectation.

candidacy (kan' di da si), *n.* the condition of presenting oneself as an applicant or contestant for an office, appointment, or honor.

candidate (kan' di dāt), *n.* one who seeks office; one nominated for office; a contestant for any public honor.

candied (kan' did), *adj.* preserved in sugar; coated with sugar in cooking.

candle (kan' dl), *n.* a cylindrical piece of tallow or wax with a wick running through it that can be burned to give light.

candle (kan' dl), *v.t.* to test by the light of a candle, as eggs for freshness.

candle foot (kan' dl foot), the amount of light given by a standard candle at a distance of 12 inches: used as a unit in measuring light.

candle power (kan' dl pou' ẽr), illuminating power, measured with the light of one candle as the base unit.

candlestick (kan' dl stik), *n.* a holder for a candle, generally with a traylike base to catch the melted grease.

candor (kan' dẽr), *n.* fairness, impartiality; frankness, sincerity of speech.

candy (kan' di), *n.* confectionery; sweetmeats.

candy (kan' di), *v.i. and v.t.* to crystallize; cause to turn into a crystalline substance resembling candy; to incrust with sugar.

candy pull (kan' di pool), a social gathering at which molasses taffy is made and worked from syrupy into firm state by being drawn back and forth by the hands.

cane (kān), *n.* a walking stick; the stem of certain palms and grasses as rattan, sugar-*cane* or bamboo.

canebrake (kān brāk), *n.* a thicket of cane.

cane sugar (kān shoog' ẽr), sugar made from cane, not beets.

***canine** (kā' nin), *n.* a dog; a pointed tooth.

canine (kā' nin), *adj.* of or pertaining to dogs or the dog family; like a dog.

canister (kan' is tẽr), *n.* a metal case holding tea or spice; a case filled with bullets, that breaks open when fired from a cannon.

***canker** (kang' kẽr), *n.* an ulcerous sore; a cankerworm.

canna (kan' a), *n.* a large-leaved plant with red or yellow flowers.

canned (kand), *adj.* preserved in sealed tins.

cannel coal (kan' el kōl), bituminous coal containing much gas and burning with a candle-like flame.

cannery (kan' ẽr ĭ), *n.* an establishment where foods are canned.

cannibal (kan' i bal), *n.* a human being who eats human flesh.

cannon (kan' un), *n.* a piece of artillery; a large gun, mounted either on a fixed base or on wheels.

canny (kan' i), *adj.* knowing; shrewd, especially in practical matters.

canoe (ka nōō'), *n.* a small light boat propelled by paddles.

***canon** (kan' un), *n.* a rule or law, as of a church; a standard for judgment, as the *canons* of art; the authorized books of the Bible; a bishop's assistant.

canonize (kan' un iz), *v.t.* to enroll in the list of saints.

***canopy** (kan' o pi), *n.* a covering usually framed, over a bed or throne; an overhead shelter in front of buildings; any overhead covering, as, a *canopy* of stars.

cant (kant), *n.* hypocritical speech; the terms used by some particular group or class of people; a slope, as of a roof.

cant (kant), *v.t.* to cause to slope, as a roof.

***cantaloupe** (kan' ta lōp), *n.* a kind of muskmelon, with an especially delicate flavor.

cantankerous (kan tang' kẽr us), *adj.* ill-natured; contentious.

***cantata** (kan tä' ta), *n.* a choral composition in dramatic form.

canteen (kan tēn'), *n.* a drinking flask used by troops on the march; a shop at a military post.

canter (kan' tẽr), *n.* an easy gallop.

cant hook (kant hook), a movable hook at the end of a long handle, used to turn over floating logs.

***cantilever** (kan' ti lē' vẽr), *n.* one of the long trusses used in building a cantilever bridge.

cantle (kan' tl), *n.* the raised part at the back of a saddle.

canto (kan' to), *n.* a chief division of a long poem.

canton (kan' ton), *n.* one of the districts into which Switzerland is divided; the rectangular section in a corner of a coat of arms or a flag.

***cantonment** (kan ton' ment), *n.* the quarters of troops in training, or of an army not in active service.

canvas (kan' vas), *n.* a coarse, heavy cloth of hemp or flax, used for making tents, sails or awnings.

canvasback (kan' vas bak), *n.* a North American wild duck.

canvass (kan' vas), *n.* a call upon all persons of a certain district for votes or orders for goods.

canvass (kan' vas), *v.i. and v.t.* to go through a district with some request to each person in it, as for votes.

canyon (kan' yun), *n.* a deep gorge with almost perpendicular sides.

***caoutchouc** (kōō' chook), *n.* the sap of certain tropical trees, as the rubber tree; raw rubber.

cap (kap), *n.* a covering, as for the head or a bottle; a pinch of gunpowder wrapped in paper; a size of paper.

cap (kap), *v.t.* to cover with a cap; to mark

the peak of, as a column; to match or outdo, as to *cap* the climax.

capable (kā′ pa bl), *adj.* having the power, skill or ability to do something.

capacious (ka pā′ shus), *adj.* roomy; spacious.

capacity (ka pas′ i ti), *n.* the power of receiving or containing; the amount that can be received or contained, content, as the *capacity* of a barrel; mental ability, knowledge; position, as in the *capacity* of manager.

*caparison** (ka par′ i sun), *n.* ornamental trappings, as for a horse.

cape (kāp), *n.* a headland; a covering for the shoulders.

caper (kā′ pēr), *n.* to skip and leap about, like a goat.

caper (kā′ pēr), *n.* a prancing leap, a skip; a prank, as to cut *capers*.

*capillary** (kap′ i ler i), *n.* a very small blood vessel.

capillary (kap′ i ler i), *adj.* like a hair, slender.

capital (kap′ i tal), *n.* a chief city, as the *capital* of a state; principal for investment; a large letter used to begin a proper name or a sentence; the top of a pillar or column.

capital (kap′ i tal), *adj.* principal; excellent.

capitalism (kap′ i tal izm), *n.* a system of economics in which private ownership of resources is permitted, along with the right to transact business for personal profit: opposite of socialism.

capitalize (kap′ i tal īz), *v.t.* to start with a capital letter; to convert into capital or supply with capital.

capital punishment (kap′ i tal pun′ ish ment), the death penalty for crime.

capitulate (ka pit′ ū lat), *v.i. and v.t.* to surrender on fixed terms.

*caprice** (ka prēs′), *n.* a whim.

*capricious** (ka prish′ us), *adj.* ruled by whim.

capsicum (kap′ si cum), *n.* a pepper-producing plant.

capsize (kap sīz′), *v.i. and v.t.* to overturn, as a boat.

capstan (kap′ stan), *n.* an upright drum or cylinder worked by bars or levers, to raise an anchor or wind a cable.

capsule (kap′ sūl), *n.* a case enclosing a seed; a case made of gelatin enclosing a dose of medicine.

capsule (kap′ syool), *n.* a separate compartment which holds men or instruments in a rocket.

captain (kap′ tin), *n.* a commander or leader, as of an athletic team; an army officer ranking next below a major; the commanding officer of a ship.

caption (kap′ shun), *n.* a heading over an article, a chapter or other section of a book; subtitle in a movie.

captious (kap′ shus), *adj.* ready to criticize, find fault or take offense.

captivate (kap′ ti vāt), *v.t.* to charm, fascinate.

captive (kap′ tiv), *n.* one captured; a prisoner.

captive (kap′ tiv), *adj.* made prisoner; held in duress, as a *captive* animal, a *captive* balloon.

captivity (kap tiv′ i ti), *n.* the state of being held in bondage or confinement.

captor (kap′ tēr), *n.* one who captures.

capture (′kap′ tūr), *n.* the act of capturing; the thing or person captured.

capture (kap′ tūr), *v.t.* to take as a prisoner; to seize by force.

car (kär), *n.* any wheeled vehicle, as a carriage, railroad car or automobile.

caracal (kar′ a kal), *n.* a lynx or wild cat of Asia and Africa, larger than a fox, reddish brown with black tipped ears.

caramel (kar′ a mel), *n.* burnt sugar, used in cooking for coloring and flavoring; candy made of sugar, butter and other ingredients.

carat (kar′ at), *n.* the unit of weight, 3.086 grains troy measure, used in weighing diamonds and other precious stones.

caravan (kar′ a van), *n.* a company of travellers, merchants or pilgrims, associated together for safety on the road.

*caravansary** (kar a van′ sa ri), *n.* an Eastern inn with a yard in which caravans may put up for the night.

caraway (kar′ a wā), *n.* a biennial plant with pleasantly flavored seeds, which are used for flavoring.

*carbide** (kär′ bīd), *n.* a compound of carbon with other elements, as *calcium carbide* which is used in making acetylene gas.

carbohydrate (kär′ bō hi′ drāt), *n.* a compound of carbon with hydrogen and oxygen, such as sugar, starch, cellulose.

carbon (kär′ bon), *n.* an elementary substance found in all organic compounds and in some minerals; an identical copy of written or typewritten matter made with carbon paper; a piece of hard carbon used in an electric arc light.

carbonic acid (kär bon′ ik as′ id), an acid composed of hydrogen, oxygen and carbon.

carbon monoxide (kär′ bon mon ok′ sīd), a colorless, odorless, deadly gas formed from incompletely consumed carbon and occurring in the exhaust of an automobile engine.

carborundum (kär bō run′ dum), *n.* a certain compound of carbon with silicon, extremely hard, and used for sharpening edged tools.

carboy (kär′ boi), *n.* a large bottle, generally protected with an outside case as of wickerwork, for holding acids.

carbuncle (kär′ bung kl), *n.* a gem of deep red color; an inflamed sore of the skin and neighboring flesh, with pus.

*carburetor** (kär′ bū ret ēr), *n.* a device for combining air with the vapor of liquid fuel to explode it.

carcass (kär′ kas), *n.* the dead body of an animal.

card (kärd), *n.* a piece of pasteboard printed or engraved with the name and address of an individual or a business firm, with an invitation, greeting or picture, as a calling *card*, a post card; one with symbols used in games of cards; a wire brush for cleaning wool, cotton or hair.

card (kärd), *v.t.* to comb and clean wool with a card.

cardiac (kär' di ak), *adj.* having to do with the heart.

cardinal (kär' di nal), *n.* a prince of the Roman Catholic Church next in rank and dignity to the Pope.

cardinal (kär' di nal), *adj.* of chief importance; chief, as *cardinal numbers, cardinal points* of the compass, *cardinal signs* of the zodiac, *cardinal virtues.*

care (kâr), *n.* anxiety, concern, trouble or a cause of trouble; charge, oversight, as the *care* of a child; caution, as take *care* on the stairs.

care (kâr), *v.i.* to feel anxiety or concern; to look after; to be fond of; to mind, as *he* doesn't *care* if he falls.

careen (ka rēn'), *v.i. and v.t.* to heel over, as a ship; to tip over on one side or incline, as to *careen* a ship so as to scrape it.

career (ka rēr'), *n.* a free course, full speed; a life's work and achievement; success in some certain profession.

carefree (kâr' frē), *adj.* without responsibilities; happy.

careful (kâr' fool), *adj.* acting with care; done with care.
Syn. Cautious, discreet, wary. *Careful* means taking pains or being alert under any circumstances, not necessarily in the presence of danger; *cautious* means being alert or on guard against danger; *wary* implies expectation of danger; *discreet* means careful in speech and conduct.
Ant. Careless, negligent.

careless (kâr' les), *adj* heedless; negligent.

caress (ka res'), *n.* an act or gesture of affection.

*__caret__ (kar' et), *n.* a mark indicating omission.

cargo (kär' gō), *n.* a ship's load of freight.

caribou (kar' i bōō), *n.* the North American reindeer.

caricature (kar' i ka tūr), *n.* a take-off; a drawing that exaggerates the characteristics of its subject.

*__caries__ (kā' ri ēz), *n.* decay of a bone or tooth.

*__carillon__ (kar' i lon), *n.* a set of bells, hung usually in a tower and operated either by hand or mechanically.

carillonneur (kar' i lo nûr), *n.* one who plays a carillon.

*__carminative__ (kär min' a tiv), *n.* a medicine for colic.

*__carmine__ (kär' min), *n.* a rich purplish red; the essential coloring principle of cochineal.

carnage (kär' nij), *n.* slaughter.
Syn. Massacre. *Carnage* usually refers to a heap of bloody, slaughtered bodies; *massacre* is wholesale slaughter including the slaying of non-resistants.

carnation (kär nā' shun), *n.* a variety of clove pink with spicy odor.

carnelian (kär nēl' yan), *n.* a red gem.

carnival (kär' ni val), *n.* a festival; riotous merry making.

*__carnivore__ (kär' ni vor), *n.* an animal that eats flesh.

carnivorous (kär niv' ō rus), *adj.* flesh-eating.

carol (kar' ul), *n.* a song or hymn of joy or praise, as Christmas *carols.*

*__carom__ (kar' um), *n.* a shot in which the billiard cue ball hits two other balls; in other games, a shot that strikes its mark after hitting something else imposed as an obstacle.

carom (kar' um), *v.i.* to rebound from one impact so as to make another which is desired; to rebound off an edge or obstacle.

*__carotid__ (ka rot' id), *n.* one of the two principal arteries on either side of the neck.

carouse (ka rouz'), *v.i.* to engage in noisy revelry.

carp (kärp), *n.* a freshwater foodfish with coarse scales.

carp (kärp), *v.i.* to find fault; complain.

carpal (kär' pal), *adj.* pertaining to the wrist.

carpenter (kär' pen tēr), *n.* one who works in wood.

carpet (kär' pet), *n.* a heavy fabric used to cover floors, usually made in strips.

carpetbag (kär' pet bag), *n.* a satchel made of carpeting.

carriage (kar' ij), *n.* the act of carrying or transporting; a vehicle in which persons are carried; manner of carrying oneself, bearing.

carrion (kar' i un), *n.* decayed or decaying flesh.

carron oil (kar' un oil), linseed oil and limewater, used for healing burns.

carrot (kar' ut), *n.* a plant with a reddish yellow root that is used as a vegetable; a reddish-yellow color.

*__carrousel__ (kar oo zel'), *n.* a merry-go-round.

carry (kar' i), *v.t. and v.i.* to transport, convey by hand, in a vehicle or by any means, as to *carry* the baby upstairs, a train *carries* mail, the wind *carries* dust or sound, telegraph wires *carry* messages, letters *carry* news, *carry* the words in your head; to win, as our troops *carried* the day, Roosevelt *carried* the election; to support, as two piers *carry* the bridge; keep for sale, as drugstores *carry* soap; to wear or have with one, as to *carry* arms; to conduct or hold, as to *carry* oneself with dignity; to bear or convey, as to fetch and *carry* for an hour; to reach to a distance, as your voice *carries.*

cart (kärt), *n.* a small, stout wagon, generally on two wheels; a light two-wheeled vehicle, hand-pushed, for carrying small loads.

cart (kärt), *v.t.* to transport in a cart.

*__cartel__ (kär' tel), *n.* a formal written arrangement between governments for exchange of prisoners; a union of producers to fix prices for their goods; a trust.

cartilage (kär' ti lij), *n.* The firm elastic tissue that makes up the skeleton of the embryos and the young of vertebrates, changing to bone in adults; gristle.

cartilaginous (kär ti laj' i nus), *adj.* of or like cartilage, gristly.

cartography (kär tog' ra fi), *n.* the making of maps.

carton (kär' ton), *n.* a cardboard container.

cartoon (kär tōōn'), *n.* a satirical or funny drawing of a public person or event, intended to mold public opinion.

cartridge (kär' trij), *n.* a case of metal or cardboard holding a bullet or charge of shot for a gun or revolver.

carve (kärv), *v.t.* to shape by cutting; to cut and serve meat at table.

carving (kärv' ing), *n.* a carved ornament.

cascade (kas kād'), *n.* a small waterfall; a series of electric condensers or amplifiers.

case (kās), *n.* something in which an object is enclosed; a state of things; the subject of a suit or trial at law; the relation of a noun or pronoun to other words, as the nominative, possessive, objective *cases.*

*casein (kā' se in), *n.* an acid substance produced in curdled milk.

*casement (kās' ment), *n.* a window sash hinged at the side.

cash (kash), *n.* money, coins, especially ready money.

cash (kash), *v.t.* to give cash for, as to *cash* a check.

cashier (kash ēr'), *n.* an officer of a firm or bank having charge of the handling of money.

cashmere (kash' mēr), *n.* a soft woolen fabric for shawls; a shawl made of it.

cask (kåsk), *n.* a wooden keg bound with metal hoops.

casket (kås' ket), *n.* a jewel chest; coffin.

casserole (kas' e rōl), *n.* a porcelain, glass or earthenware dish in which food is both cooked and served.

cassette (ka set '), *n.* part of a tape recorder which holds the magnetic tape.

*cassimere (kas' i mēr), *n.* a thin twilled woolen cloth used for men's garments.

cassock (kas' uk), *n.* a long, close-fitting garment worn by clergymen and choristers.

cassowary (kas' o wer i), *n.* a large Australian bird resembling the ostrich.

cast (kåst), *n.* the actors in a play; a throw, as of dice or a stone; an object shaped in a mold, as a plaster *cast* of a figure to be made in sculpture; the peculiar shape or design of a thing; a suggestion of color, as a greenish *cast.*

cast (kåst), *v.i. and v.t.* to make any kind of a cast, as to *cast* a stone, a glance, an aspersion, a vote or a play.

castanet (kas' ta net), *n.* a clapperlike musical instrument used especially in Spanish dances.

*caste (kåst), *n.* a class of society; social standing.

caster (kås' tēr), *n.* a small bottle for food seasonings, a cruet; a small swivelled wheel or roller used under heavy objects to facilitate moving.

castigate (kas' ti gāt), *v.t.* to punish; to chastise.

casting (kåst' ing), *n.* something shaped in a mold.

cast iron (kåst ī' ērn), *n.* iron melted and run into molds.

castle (kås' l), *n.* a fortified building, especially a nobleman's residence, fortress.

*casual (kazh' ū al), *adj.* happening by chance; careless.

casualty (kazh' ū al ti), *n.* an accident resulting in loss of life: *casualties,* losses of men in war by death or wounds.

casuistry (kazh' ū is tri), *n.* the science or doctrine of settling matters of conscience; clever but false reasoning on matters of morals.

cat (kat), *n.* a small carnivorous domestic animal, often a household pet; any of the feline species, as a lion or leopard.

*cataclysm (kat' a klizm), *n.* a catastrophe that changes the earth's surface, especially a devastating flood; any great upheaval in the social order.

*catacomb (kat' a kōm), *n.* an underground gallery with niches in the side used as tombs.

catalog or **catalogue** (kat' a log), *n.* an itemized list of names or articles arranged in alphabetic order or classified; a book containing such a list.

catamount (kat' a mount), *n.* any wild animal of the cat family, especially a cougar or lynx.

catapult (kat' a pult), *n.* an ancient war engine for hurling large stones.

cataract (kat' a rakt), *n.* a large waterfall; a disease of the eye in which the lens becomes opaque.

catarrh (ka tär'), *n.* inflammation of a mucous membrane, increasing the output of mucus.

catastrophe (ka tas' trō fē), *n.* a great disaster.

catbird (kat bûrd), *n.* a dark-gray American songbird that makes a cry like a cat's.

*catch (kach), *n.* anything caught, as a *catch* of fish; a device for fastening, as on a door or a garment.

catch (kach), *v.t. and v.i.* [*p.t.* and *p.p.* caught, *p. pr.* catching] to intercept in flight, as to *catch* a ball; to get to in time, as to *catch* a train; to surprise in the act, as to *catch* a liar; to attract, as red *catches* the eye; to pursue and overtake; to seize and hold, as briers *catch* at my dress; to take hold and stay fastened, as a lock *catches.*

catching (kach' ing), *adj.* contagious, as a disease; alluring, as a manner.

*catchup (kach' up), *n.* a sauce for food, as tomato *catchup;* also written *catsup, ketchup.*

catchy (kach' i), *adj.* attractive, taking the fancy, as a song; tricky, intended to trap, as a *catchy* problem.

catechism (kat' ē kizm), *n.* an elementary manual in the principles of a religion.

categorical (kat ē gor' i kal), *adj.* absolute, positive.

*category (kat' ē gō ri), *n.* a class, kind or division, as birds, beasts and fish are some of the *categories* into which the animal world is divided.

cater (kā' tēr), *v.i.* to furnish food, as for a banquet: *cater to,* to try to please.

caterpillar (kat' ēr pil ēr), *n.* the wormlike larva of a butterfly or moth.

catfish (kat' fish), *n.* a freshwater fish with feelers around the mouth, bullhead.

cathedral (ka thē' dral), *n.* the chief church of a diocese.

*****cathode** (kath' ōd), *n.* the negative pole of an electrolytic cell or vacuum tube: opposite of *anode.*

catholic (kath' ō lik), *adj.* universal, general, liberal.

Catholic (kath' ō lik), *adj.* pertaining to the Church of Rome or any other universal church.

catnip (kat nip), *n.* a strong-scented perennial herb of the mint family, which cats like.

cattle (kat' l), *n.* bulls, cows, calves, oxen, steers; sometimes any livestock, as sheep, goats, horses, hogs.

catwalk (kat' wôk), *n.* a plank path along a bridge or along the keel of a dirigible.

*****caucus** (kô' kus), *n.* a preliminary meeting of representatives of a political party to select candidates or fix upon a policy for a campaign.

caudal (kô' dal), *adj.* pertaining to a tail.

cauliflower (kô' li flou ẽr), *n.* a garden variety of cabbage with a solid head of white flower clusters.

cause (kôz), *n.* any person or thing that produces a result, as disease is often the *cause* of death; a reason, as *cause* for laughter; any principle or question supported by a person or party, as the *cause* of freedom, *cause* of social justice.

    Syn. Reason, motive. A *cause* is anything that produces a result; a *reason* explains a result; a *motive* is anything that prompts an action.

cause (kôz), *v.t.* to bring about; to make happen.

*****causeway** (kôz' wā), *n.* a raised roadway through a marshy region.

caustic (kôs' tik), *adj.* able to destroy by chemical action, as lye, burning, corrosive; sarcastic, sharp, as *caustic* remarks.

*****cauterize** (kô' tẽr iz), *v.* to burn or sear with a hot iron or with a caustic substance, as to *cauterize* a wound.

caution (kô' shun), *n.* a warning heedfulness; prudence in regard to danger.

caution (kô' shun), *v.t.* to warn, as against danger.

cautious (kô' shus), *adj.* exercising caution; heedful, wary.

cavalcade (kav al kād'), *n.* a procession of persons on horseback.

cavalry (kav' al ri), *n.* horsemen, especially mounted military troops.

cave (kāv), *n.* a hollow opening in the earth.

cave-in (kāv in), *n.* collapse; the act of caving in or collapsing, as of the walls of a mine.

cavern (kav' ẽrn), *n.* a very large cave.

cavernous (kav' ẽr nus), *adj.* hollow like a cavern.

*****caviar** (kav' i är), *n.* sturgeon roe, prepared as a relish.

*****cavil** (kav' il), *v.i.* to find flaws in; to raise captious or frivolous objections.

cavity (kav' i ti), *n.* a hollow space, as in a tooth.

*****cavort** (ka vôrt') *v.* to prance about, caper, as horses.

caw (kô), *n.* the cry of a crow.

caw (kô), *v.i.* to make a harsh sound like the caw of a crow.

C battery (bat' ẽri), an electric battery between the grid and the filament of an electron tube, to govern the amount of average plate current passing through.

cease (sēs), *v.i. and v.t.* to come to an end; to stop; to discontinue.

    Syn. Discontinue, stop. *Stop* refers to the ending of specific action, *cease* to the end of states of activity, as we *stop* playing the piano, but the music *ceases*; to *discontinue* is to interrupt the activity of something or to stop doing something habitual.

    Ant. Begin, commence, continue, start.

cedar (sē' dẽr), *n.* an evergreen tree with fragrant wood valued in building because of its great durability.

cede (sēd), *v.t.* to grant, as territory.

ceiling (sēl' ing), *n.* the overhead finish of a room; the top altitude an airplane can reach under specified conditions.

celebrate (sel' ē brāt), *v.i. and v.t.* to commemorate, observe joyfully, as an anniversary; to observe with formal rites, as Mass; to honor, praise.

    Syn. Commemorate. Any person or thing, past or present, is *celebrated* that is observed with outward ceremony, but nothing is *commemorated* but what is past and can be brought to memory.

    Ant. Despise, forget.

celebrity (sē leb' ri ti), *n.* fame, renown; one who is famous.

*****celerity** (sē ler' i ti), *n.* promptness, speed.

celery (sel' ẽr i), *n.* a plant with long leafstalks that are blanched for food.

*****celestial** (sē les' chal), *adj.* pertaining to the sky; heavenly, divine.

*****celibacy** (sel' i ba si), *n.* the state of being unmarried, especially single life followed from religious conviction or vows.

cell (sel), *n.* a small room for either voluntary or involuntary confinement, as in a monastery or a prison; the tiny unit of plant or animal tissues.

cellar (sel' ẽr), *n.* the underground floor of a house.

*****cello** (chel' ō), *n.* [*pl.* cellos] contraction of *violoncello.*

cellophane (sel' ō fān), *n.* a transparent waterproof tissue made from wood pulp.

cellular (sel' ū lẽr), *adj.* consisting of cells.

celluloid (sel' ū loid), *n.* an inflammable compound of camphor and pyroxylin, usually resembling ivory.

*****cement** (sē ment'), *n.* a mixture of lime, clay and water used while soft in building, for lining walls, making cellar floors; any substance which, applied while soft, hardens and causes two bodies to cohere, as glue or mortar.

cement (sē ment'), *v.t.* to fasten, line or cover with cement; to bind firmly.

*****cemetery** (sem' ē ter i), *n.* a burial place; graveyard.

cenotaph (sen' ō tåf), *n.* an empty tomb, or a monument in memory of one buried elsewhere.

censer (sen' sĕr), *n.* a vessel for burning incense, having a perforated cover.

*censor** (sen' sĕr), *n.* an ancient Roman magistrate who imposed taxes and regulated public morals; a modern official who examines books and plays to suppress the publication of objectionable works; one empowered to examine private correspondence and delete passages opposed to the public good; one who censures.

censorious (sen sō' ri us), *adj.* harshly critical.

*censure** (sen' shĕr), *n.* blame; harsh criticism.

censure (sen' shĕr), *v.t.* to condemn, criticize severely.

    Syn. Blame, condemn. To *censure* is in the main to criticize adversely; to *blame* is to find fault with or guilt in; to *condemn* implies thoughtful though adverse judgment.

census (sen' sus), *n.* an official count of population.

cent (sent), *n.* one one-hundredth of a dollar.

centaur (sen' tôr), *n.* a creature of ancient Greek mythology, half man and half horse.

centenarian (sen tē når' i an), *n.* a person a hundred years old.

*centenary** (sen' tē ner i), *n.* a hundred years; a celebration of a 100th anniversary.

centennial (sen ten' i al), *n.* a hundredth anniversary or its celebration.

center (sen' tĕr), *n.* the middle point of anything; that around which things form or toward which they move or tend; any place in the midst of activity, as a manufacturing *center*, a *center* of learning.

centigrade (sen' ti gråd), *adj.* separated into 100 degrees, as the scale of a *centigrade* thermometer.

centigram (sen' ti gram), *n.* a unit of weight equal to one one-hundredth of a gram.

*centimeter** (sen' ti mē tĕr), *n.* a unit of length equal to one one-hundredth of a meter.

centipede (sen' ti pĕd), *n.* a long-bodied worm-shaped animal with many joints and a pair of legs at each.

central (sen' tral), *adj.* pertaining to the center; at or near the middle; chief.

central (sen' tral), *n.* a telephone exchange; a telephone operator.

centralize (sen' tral iz), *v.i.* and *v.t.* to make central; to bring to a center; in government or business, to concentrate powers of direction.

*centrifugal** (sen trif' ū gal), *adj.* tending away from the center, as a *centrifugal* force.

*centripetal** (sen trip' ē tal), *adj.* tending toward the center, as a *centripetal* force.

century (sen' tū ri), *n.* a period of 100 years.

*cephalic** (sē fal' ik), *adj.* pertaining to the head.

cephalopoda (seph a lop' o da), *n.* mollusks having tentacles, including the nautilus and cuttlefish. See *illustration.*

*ceramics** (sē ram' iks), *n.* the art of making pottery.

cereal (sēr' ē al), *n.* any grass that yields an edible grain, as wheat, oats, rice, rye; any such grain prepared for food.

cereal (sēr' ē al), *adj.* pertaining to grains and the plants that produce them.

cerebellum (ser' ē bel' um), *n.* the lower back part of the brain, consisting of two lobes situated behind and above the medulla: called the *little brain.*

cerebral (ser' ē bral), *adj.* pertaining to the brain.

*cerebrum** (ser' ē brum), *n.* the major part of the brain, in front of and above the cerebellum, consisting of the two hemispheres that occupy the upper portion of the skull.

cerements (ser' ē ments), *n.* burial clothing.

ceremony (ser' ē mō ni), *n.* a rite or formality; formal procedure.

*cerise** (se rēz'), *n.* cherry color.

certain (sûr' tin), *adj.* fixed, specified, as a *certain* time, *certain* species; sure, reliable, as a *certain* cure; sure in mind, as to be *certain* of one's facts.

    Syn. *Certain* and *sure* are almost interchangeable. *Sure* implies, however, mere assurance; *certain* implies surety founded on definite proof.

    Ant. Doubtful, uncertain.

certainty (sûr' tin ti), *n.* the state of being sure; any sure and established fact.

*certificate** (sûr tif' i kit), *n.* written testimony to the truth of any fact, as a health *certificate.*

certify (sûr' ti fi), *v.t.* to attest; to guarantee; to testify in writing.

certitude (sûr' ti tūd), *n.* certainty; assurance.

*cerulean** (sē rōō' lē an), *adj.* sky-blue.

cervical (sûr' vi kal), *adj.* pertaining to the neck.

cervix (sûr' viks), *n.* the neck, especially the back part of the neck.

cessation (sә sā' shun), *n.* the act of ceasing or discontinuing; a stop.

cession (sesh' un), *n.* the giving up of territory; deeding of property; yielding a point in argument.

*cetacean** (sē tā' shun), *n.* a marine mammal, as the whale.

chafe (chāf), *v. i. and v. t.* to make or become sore by rubbing; to warm by rubbing, as cold feet; to fret and fume.

*chaff** (chåf), *n.* grain-husks; teasing, banter.

chaff (chåf), *v.t.* to tease, to make fun of good-naturedly.

chaffinch (chaf' inch), *n.* a songbird.

*chagrin** (shȧ grin'), *n.* distress caused by disappointment or humiliation; mortification.

chain (chān), *n.* a series of joined rings or links usually of metal; series of anything linked together, as a *chain* of mountains, telephone centrals or events; anything that binds or fetters.

chain (chān), *v. t.* to fasten or bind with a chain.

chair (châr), *n.* a movable seat with legs and a back; a position of honor or authority, as a professor's *chair: the chair*, a chairman.

chairman (châr' man), *n.* the head of a committee; one who presides at a meeting.

***chaise** (shāz), *n.* a two-wheeled carriage for two persons; any light carriage for pleasure driving.

***chalcedony** (kal sed' ō ni), *n.* a variety of pale-blue or gray quartz.

***chalice** (chal' is), *n.* a drinking cup, especially the cup used at the Lord's Supper.

chalk (chôk), *n.* a soft white kind of limestone; a stick of chalklike material used for drawing on a blackboard.

chalk (chôk), *v.t.* to write on or mark with chalk.

challenge (chal' enj), *n.* a defiance; a call to combat; a sentry's demand for the countersign.

challenge (chal' enj), *v.t.* to defy, call to combat; to demand the countersign; to dispute the accuracy of, as a statement.

***challis** (shal' i), *n.* a light woolen fabric.

chamber (chām' bēr), *n.* a room in a house, especially a bedroom; a councilroom; the council itself.

chamberlain (chām bēr lin), *n.* an officer who has charge of the private apartments of a sovereign or nobleman.

***chameleon** (ka mē' lē on), *n.* a lizard that can change its color according to its environment.

***champagne** (sham pān'), *n.* an effervescent wine.

champaign (sham pān'), *n.* flat, open country.

champion (cham' pi un), *n.* best of his or its class in a competition; one who defends the cause of another.

champion (cham' pi un), *v.t.* to advocate and work or fight for, as a cause; to contend for the rights of another.

chance (chàns), *n.* the unforeseeable way things happen; a happening; fortune, luck; lot; opportunity; a risk or gamble; a possibility; an imaginary power, fate.

chance (chàns), *v.i.* to happen unforeseeably or accidentally.

chance (chàns), *adj.* happening by accident, unintended; casual, as a *chance* meeting.

chancel (chàn' sel), *n.* the space in a church in which the altar stands; the space reserved for the clergy or choir.

chancellor (chan' sel ēr), *n.* a judge of a court of equity or chancery, the title of the head of some universities.

***chancery** (chàn' sēr i), *n.* a court judging cases on the simple principles of justice.

chandelier (shan de lēr'), *n.* a hanging support for a cluster of lights.

chandler (chàn' dlēr), *n.* one who makes and sells candles; a small merchant; retailer.

change (chānj), *n.* movement from one state of being to another; variation; small money; the balance returned to a customer when he offers more than is due.

change (chānj), *v.i. and v.t.* to progress from one state of being to another, as a grub *changes* to a beetle; to become

different, vary, as the colors of a sunset *change;* to pass from one phase to another, as the moon; to alter, make different, as to *change* the spelling of a word; to substitute one thing for another, as to *change* one's clothes; to give or receive the equal of something in smaller units, as to *change* $5.

channel (chan' el), *n.* the bed of a river; a deep passage through shallow waters; a grooved course; that through which anything flows, any passage; *v.t.* to guide.

chant (chànt), *n.* a solemn song; an intoned song.

chant (chànt), *v.i. and v.t.* to intone.

***chaos** (kā' os), *n.* a state of complete confusion; disorder.

chap (chap), *n.* a crack in the skin.

chap (chap), *v.i.* to crack, as the skin.

chapel (chap' el), *n.* a place of worship smaller than a church; a room set apart for worship in a cathedral, school or college.

***chaperon** (shap' ēr ōn), *n.* an older woman who accompanies young ladies to the theater, dances or houseparties for the sake of propriety.

chaplain (chap' lin), *n.* a clergyman serving as such in the army, navy or some institution.

chaps (chaps), *n. pl.* chaparejos; cowboys' leather breeches.

chapter (chap' tēr), *n.* a principal division of a book; a branch of a society.

char (chär), *v.t.* to scorch; to convert into charcoal.

character (kar' ak tēr), *n.* a sign or mark on an object to show ownership or origin, a brand or stamp; written or printed symbols, as letters or figures; a distinguishing quality, as the *character* of cats is to hunt birds; one's moral strength; a description of a person's qualities, as they gave him a good *character;* a person in literature, as Rowena is one of the *characters* in Ivanhoe.

characteristic (kar ak tēr is' tik), *adj.* representative, typical.

characterize (kar' ak tēr iz), *v.t.* to describe by peculiar qualities of; to typify or distinguish.

***charade** (sha rād'), *n.* a game in which several of the players dramatize the syllables of words for the others to guess.

charcoal (chär' kōl), *n.* wood partially burned.

charge (chärj), *n.* a price; an accusation; a sudden attack; a load, as of a gun; custody.

charge (chärj), *v.i. and v.t.* to advance in attack, to lay upon with authority, as I *charge* you with this trust; to make liable, as I *charge* you with a dollar's worth of goods; to accuse, as I *charge* him with burglary; to load, as a gun.

charger (chärj' ēr), *n.* a cavalry horse; a contrivance used in charging a storage battery.

chariot (char' i ut), *n.* an ancient two-wheeled vehicle for war or racing.

charisma (ka riz' ma), *n.* the special quality which enables a leader to attract others.

charity (char' i ti), *n.* kindness; benevolence; giving to the poor.

*****charlatan** (shär' la tan), *n.* a quack; pretender to knowledge not possessed.

charm (chärm), *n.* allurement; fascination; a magic spell; a small ornament, as a watch *charm.*

charm (chärm), *v. i. and v. t.* to cast a spell, use magic power, bewitch; to fascinate, attract, delight.

chart (chärt), *n.* a map; diagram; a graph.

chart (chärt), *v.t.* to show on a map or diagram, as to *chart* a ship's course.

charter (chär' tēr), *n.* a grant of rights.

charter (chär' tēr), *v.t.* to grant specified rights to; to empower to engage in business under certain conditions.

*****chary** (chär' i), *adj.* cautious; sparing.

chase (chās), *n.* pursuit; the hunting of game.

chase (chās), *v.t.* to pursue, put to flight; to hunt.

chasm (kazm), *n.* a yawning gap in the earth; a deep separation.

*****chassis** (shas' i), *n.* the frame and springs of a motor car; also, all other parts of the car, including the wheels.

chaste (chāst), *adj.* modest; pure.

*****chasten** (chās' n), *v.t.* to punish with the purpose to reform.

　Syn. Chastise, punish. To *chasten* is to afflict or distress for the sake of discipline or to develop the character, as whom the Lord loveth, He *chasteneth.* To *chastise* is to punish in anger to reform; to *punish* is to inflict a penalty upon for specific wrongdoing.

chastity (chas' ti ti), *n.* the state of being chaste; purity.

chat (chat), *v.i.* to talk lightly.

chattel (chat' l), *n.* any piece of personal property.

chatter (chat' ēr), *n.* meaningless prattle, idle talk.

*****chauffeur** (shō fûr'), *n.* one who earns his living by driving cars for others.

chauvinist (shō' ven ist), *n.* one who is excessive and often belligerent in the belief of personal superiority.

cheap (chēp), *adj.* low-priced; miserable; mean.

cheat (chēt), *n.* a fraud or sham; a deceiver, a swindler.

cheat (chēt), *v.i. and v. t.* to practice dishonesty, as to *cheat* in business; to defraud, swindle

　Syn. Defraud, trick. One *cheats* by direct and gross falsehood or artifice; one *defrauds* by a settled plan or contrivance; one *tricks* by taking advantage of the credulity of others.

check (chek), *n.* that which holds something back, impedes progress, puts a pause or stop to; a written order to a bank to pay out a depositor's money; a pattern in squares; an examination, comparison or verifying; that with which something is compared, a standard; a mark to show that something has been verified.

check (chek), *v.t.* to stop, repulse, hinder; to test or examine, as to *check* a list; to mark with a check; to deposit for convenience or safety, as *check* your hat at the door.

checkers (chek ērz), *n.* a game played by two persons with 24 disks on a board marked off in squares of black and white.

checkout (chek' out), *n.* the place to add up purchases as from a retail store or grocery store.

cheek (chēk), *n.* one side of the face; impudence.

cheer (chēr), *n.* a happy state of mind; a cry of applause.

cheer (chēr), *v.i. and v.t.* to applaud; to give comfort and reassurance to.

　Syn. Encourage, comfort. To *cheer* regards the spirits; to *encourage* the resolution. The sad need to be *cheered,* the timid to be *encouraged.* To *cheer* expresses more than to *comfort;* the former signifies calling forth hope or happiness, the lessening of pain.

　Ant. Dishearten, dismay.

cheerful (chēr' fool), *adj.* joyous; in good spirits.

cheese (chēz), *n.* a food made of solidified milk curds.

*****chef** (shef), *n.* a head cook; professional cook.

chemical (kem' i kal), *n.* a substance used in chemistry.

chemical (kem' i kal), *adj.* having to do with chemistry.

chemist (kem' ist), *n.* one skilled in chemistry.

chemistry (kem' is tri), *n.* the science of the composition of matter and its changes under certain influences.

*****chenille** (she nēl'), *n.* a tufted silk or worsted cord; a fabric made from it.

cherish (cher' ish), *v.t.* to hold dear; to treat tenderly; to protect; to cling to, as to *cherish* one's wrath.

　Syn. Foster, harbor. To *cherish* is both to hold dear and to treat as dear. To *foster* is to maintain and care for, to promote the growth of; to *harbor* is to entertain in the mind something like resentment or evil designs.

cherry (cher' i), *n.* a small round fruit with a smooth stone; the tree that bears it.

chess (ches), *n.* a game played by two persons with 16 pieces each on a board divided into 64 squares.

chest (chest), *n.* a large box with a lid, especially for holding valuables; the part of the body within the ribs and breastbone, the thorax.

chestnut (ches' nut), *n.* a nut within a bur, or the tree that produces it; the rich reddish brown color of the nut.

cheval glass (shē val' gläs), a full-length mirror in a swinging frame.

cheviot (chev' i ut), *n.* a cloth made from the wool of cheviot sheep.

chevron (shev' run), *n.* a V-shaped bar on uniform coat of a non-commissioned army officer or policeman, indicates rank or service.

chew (chōō), *v.t.* to masticate, grind with the teeth.

chicken pox (chik' en poks), a disease of

children, characterized by an itching rash.

*chicle (chĕk' l), n. a gum obtained from a tropical tree, used in making chewing gum.

chicory (chĭk' ō rĭ), n. a perennial plant with bright-blue flowers, and a root sometimes roasted as a substitute for coffee.

chide (chīd), v.t. to rebuke, scold.

chief (chēf), n. a commander or leader; the head of any organization.

Syn. Chieftain, commander, leader. A *chief* usually inherits his position as *chief* of a tribe or clan; as a government title, *chief* is used for civil rather than military offices, as a fire *chief*. *Chieftain* is limited to the leader of a robber band. *Commander* is a military or naval title. A political party 'has a *leader*, as does also a revolution, a cause, or any great social movement.

chief (chēf), adj. principal, most important; highest in rank.

*chiffon (shĭf' on), n. a gauzy silk fabric.

*chiffonier (shĭf' ō nēr), n. a high chest of drawers.

chilblain (chĭl' blān), n. a sore on the hands or feet caused by damp cold.

child (chīld), n. a young person between babyhood and youth; a son or daughter.

chill (chĭl), n. a small degree of coldness, as the *chill* of a cellar; a feeling of cold accompanied by shivering; a check upon enthusiasm or high spirits.

chime (chīm), n. the music of tuned bells; a set of bells musically tuned.

chime (chīm), v.i. and v.t. to ring in a musical way, as bells *chime;* to ring or play, as to *chime* bells; to indicate with chimes, as a clock *chimes* the hour.

*chimerical (kĭ mer' ĭ kal), adj. imaginary; fantastic.

chimney (chĭm' nĭ), n. [pl. chimneys] a structure, usually of brick, enclosing flues from a fireplace, stove or furnace.

*chimpanzee (chĭm' pan zē), n. an African ape.

chin (chĭn), n. the fore part of the lower jaw, under the mouth.

china (chī' na), n. a fine kind of porcelain.

*chinch bug (chinch bug), a small, black and white insect that destroys grain crops.

chinchilla (chin chĭl' a), n. a small South American rodent with soft, gray fur.

*chine (chīn), n. the backbone; a cut of meat from an animal or fish containing the backbone and surrounding flesh.

chink (chĭngk), n. a long narrow opening; a sharp metallic sound, the clink of metal objects shaken together.

chintz (chĭnts), n. a cotton cloth, usually glazed, printed in various colors.

chip (chĭp), n. a minute semiconductor material containing integrated circuits, making microcomputers possible.

chipmunk (chĭp' mungk), n. a small American squirrel with striped back.

*chirography (kĭ rog' ra fĭ), n. handwriting.

*chiropodist (kĭ rop' ō dĭst), n. one who treats foot troubles.

chirp (chûrp), n. a short, cheerful sound, as of a bird or cricket.

chirp (chûrp), v.i. to make a short, sharp sound, as a bird or cricket.

chisel (chĭz' l), n. a metal tool with a blade having a sharp-edged end, used for cutting wood, stone or metal.

chisel (chĭz' l), v.t. to cut with a chisel.

chivalrous (shĭv' al rus), adj. valorous; gallant; courteous.

*chivalry (shĭv' al rĭ), n. the spirit and manners of knighthood; courteous, gallant conduct.

chive (chīv), n. a perennial herb related to the leek and the onion.

*chloride (klō' rĭd), n. a compound of chlorine with another element.

*chlorine (klō' rēn), n. a greenish-yellow suffocating gas possessing great bleaching powers.

*chloroform (klō' rō fôrm), n. a liquid compound that yields a gas which dulls pain and causes unconsciousness.

*chocolate (chok' ō lĭt), n. a powder made by grinding roasted cacao nuts; a beverage made of it.

chocolate (chok' ō lĭt), adj. flavored with or the color of chocolate.

choice (chois), n. the act of choosing; preference; any person or thing chosen, as this is my *choice;* the best part or thing.

choice (chois), adj. worthy of being chosen; especially good.

choir (kwīr), n. a group of singers in a church; the space reserved for them.

choke (chōk), n. a device to check the flow of anything, as the valve in a carburetor that regulates the intake of air.

choke (chōk), v.i. and v.t. to suffocate; to be obstructed; to obstruct by clogging, as dead leaves *choke* a drain; to hinder the growth of, as weeds *choke* a flower bed.

cholera (kol' ēr a), n. a disease of the digestive tract, of which the symptoms are vomiting, diarrhea and cramps.

cholesterol (ko les ' te rōl), n. a fat soluble found especially in animal fats which can constrict blood vessels.

choose (chōōz), v.i. and v.t. to make a choice; to select one from two or more; to see fit, please, as I do not *choose* to go.

chop (chop), n. a small cut of meat off the loin or rib: *chops,* the jaws and the flesh around them; v.t. to cut with an ax.

choppy (chop' ĭ), adj. short, rough: said of waves.

choral (kō' ral), adj. pertaining to a chorus or choir.

chord (kôrd), n. combination of harmonious tones sounded together; straight line connecting ends of arc in a geometric figure.

chores (chōrs), n.pl. the daily routine work of a farm or household.

*chorister (kor' ĭs tēr), n. a member of a choir; a choir leader

*chorus (kō' rus), n. number of persons singing together, or expressing same opinion; refrain at the end of each song verse.

chow (chou), n. a breed of dogs originally from China.

chowchow (chou' chou), n. chopped mixed

pickles in a mustard sauce.

chowder (chou' dẽr), *n.* a savory stew of fish or clams with salt pork.

*__christen__ (kris' n), *v.t.* to baptize; to give a name to.

chromatic (krō mat' ik), *adj.* relating to color; written or sounded in half-tones of the diatonic scale.

chrome (krōm), *n.* chromium.

chromium (krō' mi um), *n.* a metallic element, steel-gray and rust-resisting.

chromo (krō' mō),` *n.* a colored lithographic print.

chronic (kron' ik), *adj.* continuing a long time or recurring : said of a disease.

chronicle (kron' i kl), *n.* a record of events in the order of their occurrence.

chronological (kron ō loj' i kal), *adj.* in order of time.

*__chronology__ (krō nol' ō ji), *n.* the recording of events in the order of their occurrence.

chronometer (krō nom' ē tẽr), *n.* any instrument for measuring off time; a ship's clock, safeguarded against irregularities due to change in temperature.

*__chrysalis__ (kris' a lis), *n.* the pupa of an insect in the shell or cocoon from which it emerges as a fully developed insect; the shell or cocoon of the pupa.

*__chrysanthemum__ (kris an' thē mum), *n.* a plant of the aster family with showy flowers that bloom in autumn.

chuck (chuk), *n.* the part of a beef carcass between the neck and the shoulder blade; a contrivance for holding a tool or a piece of material on which work is being done.

chuck (chuk), *v.t.* to toss, as a ball; to pat under the chin, as in playing with a child.

chuckle (chuk' l), *v.i.* to laugh in a quiet, suppressed way.

chum (chum), *n.* an intimate friend.

chunk (chungk), *n.* a short, thick piece.

chunky (chungk' i), *adj.* short and thick.

church (chûrch), *n.* a building devoted to worship; a religious system, including houses of worship, clergy and members; a christian denomination.

churl (chûrl), *n.* a peasant; a surly person.

churn (chûrn), *n.* a vessel in which milk and cream are agitated to make butter.

churn (chûrn), *v.i. and v.t.* to work a churn to get butter; to make, as butter, by agitating milk and cream; to agitate violently, as a thrashing fish *churns* the water.

chute (shōōt), *n.* a slide down which things are moved from any high place to a lower one; a flume.

*__cicada__ (si kā' da), *n.* a large, four-winged insect, the male produces prolonged chirping sound : often called a *locust*.

cider (sī' dẽr), *n.* apple juice, used as a drink and for making vinegar.

*__cigar__ (si gär'), *n.* a roll of tobacco leaves, for smoking.

cigarette (sig a ret'), *n.* tobacco rolled in paper, for smoking.

cilia (sil' i a), *n.pl.* the eyelashes; hairlike fuzz on plants and wings of insects.

cinch (sinch), *n.* a saddle girth secured by

loop and knots.

*__cinchona__ (sin kō' na), *n.* a Peruvian bark from which quinine is obtained.

cinder (sin' dẽr), *n.* a piece of burnt matter not reduced to ashes.

cinema (sin' ē ma), *n.* a motion picture or a motion picture theater.

cinnamon (sin' a mun), *n.* a spice made from the inner bark of an East Indian tree.

cipher (sī' fẽr), *n.* zero; something without value; a secret code.

cipher (sī' fẽr), *v.i.* to figure; to express in cipher.

circle (sûr' kl), *n.* a curved line of which every point is equally distant from a point within called the center.

circle (sûr' kl), *v.t.* to go all the way around anything, as if following a circular course, as to *circle* the city.

circuit (sûr' kit), *n.* a number of transistors which work together in a computer.

circuitous (sûr kū' i tus), *adj.* roundabout, indirect.

circular (sûr' kū lẽr), *n.* a piece of printed matter for general distribution.

circular (sûr' kū lẽr), *adj.* in a circle; like a circle.

circulate (sûr' kū lāt), *v.i. and v.t.* to make available to the reading public; to go around a specified course and return to the starting place, as the blood *circulates*.

circumference (sûr kum' fẽr ens), *n.* the perimeter or boundary line of a circle; the distance around a circle.

circumflex (sûr' kum fleks), *n.* an accent mark over a letter to indicate how it is to be sounded, with rising then falling tone.

circumlocution (sûr kum lō kū' shun), *n.* an indirect expression; a roundabout way of speaking.

circumscribe (sûr kum skrīb), *v.t.* to enclose within fixed bounds.

circumspect (sûr' kum spekt), *adj.* watchful on all sides; cautious; prudent.

circumstance (sûr' kum stans), *n.* any factor, as a condition or incident, accompanying a fact or event; an essential or a nonessential detail; an incident: *circumstances*, material environment, as brought up in good *circumstances;* all the factors of any situation, as he did well, under the *circumstances.*

circumvent (sûr kum vent'), *v.t.* to gain an advantage by stratagem or deception.

circus (sûr' kus), *n.* a show with many entertaining features, as acrobatics, trained animals, clowns, and the like; a level oblong space having tiers of seats on three sides where ancient Roman games and chariot races were held.

cistern (sis' tẽrn), *n.* a lined pit for holding water; a small reservoir.

citadel (sit' a del), *n.* the fortified part of a city.

citation (sī tā' shun), *n.* a quotation or the citing of a passage in a book; special mention, especially for heroism in military papers.

cite (sīt), *v.t.* to summon for an appearance in

court; to refer to as an authority.

Syn. Quote. To *cite* is to bring forth an author or his writings as authority for something; to *quote* is to repeat exactly in speech or writing someone else's words.

citizen (sit' i zen), *n.* one owing allegiance to a state.

*****citrate** (sit' rāt), *n.* a salt of citric acid.

citric acid (sit' rik as' id), an acid obtained from lemons, oranges, currants and other citrus fruits.

citron (sit' run), *n.* a lemonlike fruit, but larger and less acid than the lemon, having a thick rind used in cooking.

city (sit' i), *n.* a large town; an incorporated municipality.

civic (siv' ik), *adj.* having to do with a city or a citizen, as *civic* duties.

civics (siv' iks), *n.pl.* science of government.

*****civil** (siv'l), *adj.* relating to the ordinary life of citizens; not military; between citizens of the same country, as *civil* war; maintained for benefit of citizens, as *civil* service; polite; good-mannered.

Syn. Polite, courteous. *Civil* describes the minimum of good manners and implies a mere forbearing from actual rudeness; *polite* describes actions and speech prompted by consideration of others; *courteous* means not only considerate but dignified.

civilian (si vil' yan), *n.* one engaged in the pursuits of civil life, a person not in the army or navy.

civility (si vil' i ti), *n.* civil behavior; a polite act or speech.

civilization (siv i li zā' shun), *n.* the state or process of becoming civilized, as the *civilization* of a savage tribe; social progress and culture; a certain period or type of social culture, as Egyptian *civilization;* the whole enlightened or civilized world, as cannibalism is abhorrent to *civilization*.

civilized (siv' il izd), *adj.* of a country, having enlightened customs and government; of a person, versed in the arts and refinements of civilized life.

clack (klak), *n.* a sudden sharp sound; chatter.

claim (klām), *n.* a thing claimed; something demanded as a right; demand made on the grounds of right; land staked out by a miner.

claim (klām), *v.t.* to demand as one's right or due, as to *claim* the victory; to acknowledge or own, as to *claim* a child; to attract or win, as heroism *claims* our admiration.

clam (klam), *n.* an edible, bivalve shellfish.

clammy (klam' i), *adj.* cold, soft, wet, like a clam.

clamor (klam' ēr), *n.* continuous outcry.

clamor (klam' ēr), *v.i.* to shout, with confusion; make clamor.

clamp (klamp), *n.* a device used to hold things together.

clamp (klamp), *v.t.* to fasten together with a clamp.

clan (klan), *n.* a tribe; association of families.

*****clandestine** (klan des' tin), *adj.* secret; under cover.

clang (klang), *n.* a loud, sharp, ringing metallic sound.

*****clangor** (klang' gēr), *n.* constant clanging; continued outcry and uproar.

clank (klangk), *n.* a sharp metallic sound, not reverberant like a clang, as the *clank* of chains.

clannish (klan' ish), *adj.* holding together like the members of a clan.

clap (klap), *n.* a noise made by striking two things together, as the hands in applauding; a sharp sudden noise, as a *clap* of thunder.

clap (klap), *v.t.* to applaud by clapping the hands.

claret (klar' et), *n.* a dark red table wine.

clarify (klar' i fi), *v.t.* to make clear; free of impurities.

*****clarinet** (klar i net'), *n.* a wood-wind musical instrument, flaring at the end and having one reed.

*****clarion** (klar' i un), *n.* a small shrill trumpet.

clarion (klar' i un), *adj.* loud and clear.

clash (klash), *n.* the noise of contact between hard objects; a conflict of ideas or interests.

clash (klash), *v.i. and v.t.* to strike together hard; to conflict, as ideas or personalities.

clasp (klåsp), *n.* a fastening, as a catch or hook, by which things are fastened together, as the *clasp* of a bracelet; an embrace.

clasp (klåsp), *v.t.* to fasten with a clasp; to embrace; to grasp, as to *clasp* hands.

*****class** (klås), *n.* a number of things or persons with a common characteristic; a group of students to be promoted or graduated at the same time; a group of students studying the same subject, as a history *class;* social rank.

class (klås), *v.t.* to assign to a class, to classify.

classic (klas' ik), *n.* a work of literature or art of highest standard and lasting merit: *classics*, the literature of ancient Greece and Rome.

classical (klas' i kal), *adj.* pertaining to the classics, as a *classical* course in college.

classification (klas i fi kā' shun), *n.* division into classes.

classify (klas' i fi), *v.t.* to arrange in classes systematically.

clatter (klat' ēr), *n.* a continuing confusion of noises, as the *clatter* of dishwashing.

clatter (klat' ēr), *v.i.* to make a confusion of noises.

clause (klôz), *n.* a group of words forming part of a compound or complex sentence, having own subject and predicate; a section of document, as a constitution or law.

clavicle (klav' i kl), *n.* the collarbone.

claw (klô), *n.* a sharp hooked nail in the foot of a bird or animal.

claw (klô), *v.t.* to scratch, scrape, dig or tear with or as if with a claw.

clay (klā), *n.* thick, plastic earth; anything easily molded.

clean (klēn), *adj.* free of dirt; unsoiled; pure.

Syn. Clean, cleanly, pure. *Clean* expresses a freedom from dirt or soil; *cleanly* the disposition or habit of being clean. A person who keeps himself *clean* is *cleanly*. *Pure* is used in a moral sense; the heart should be *pure*.

clean (klēn), *v.t.* to make clean; to remove stains; to purify.

*cleanly (klen' li), *adj.* neat; tidy; of clean habits.

cleanse (klenz), *v.t.* to make clean; to purify morally.

clear (klēr), *n.* open space.

clear (klēr), *v.i. and v.t.* to make clear; to brighten; to render evident; to free of obstructions.

clear (klēr), *adj.* free from darkness; free from doubt or blame; free from obstructions or entanglement, as the ropes are *clear*, the road is *clear;* easily heard, distinct, as a *clear* voice; able to understand, as a *clear* mind; net, as *clear* profits.

Syn. Lucid. *Clear* means free from doubt or any kind of obstruction, plain and understandable. One has a *clear* conscience, sees one's way *clear*, gives a *clear* account of something. *Lucid* means sane or normal when it applies to a person or his mind; it means orderly and very easily understood when it applies to style of writing or speech.

clearing (klēr' ing), *n.* a piece of land cleared of timber.

clearly (klēr' li), *adv.* in a clear or distinct manner.

clearness (klēr' nes), *n.* the quality of being clear; distinctness.

cleat (klēt), *n.* a projecting piece of leather on the sole of a shoe to give a better grip; a strip of wood or metal on a floor to give a foothold; a wedge-shaped or two-armed device of wood or metal around which to make fast a rope.

cleat (klēt), *v.t.* to furnish with cleats.

cleave (klēv), *v.t.* to split apart.

cleave (klēv), *v.i.* to cling to.

cleaver (klēv' ēr), *n.* a butcher's square-bladed knife for cutting joints or chopping meat.

cleft (kleft), *n.* a fissure, a crevice.

cleft (kleft), *adj.* split; cleaved.

*clematis (klem' a tis), *n.* a perennial plant of the crowfoot family.

*clemency (klem' en si), *n.* mercy; mildness.

clement (klem' ent), *adj.* gentle; forbearing.

clergy (klûr' ji), *n.* a body of men trained for religious service, as priests and ministers.

clergyman (klûr' ji man), *n.* a minister of a church.

clerical (kler' i kal), *adj.* pertaining to the clergy; pertaining to clerks, as a *clerical* department.

clerk (klûrk), *n.* one who keeps accounts; a salesman in a store.

clever (klev' ēr), *adj.* quick and smart with the mind or hand; skillful; exhibiting skill, as a *clever* stunt.

Syn. Smart. *Clever* describes intellectual quickness, often implying a lack of intellectual value. *Smart* means witty or even pert.

clew (klōō), *n.* a fact that is or may be helpful in solving a mystery.

click (klik), *n.* a quick sharp sound as of two small bodies striking each other, like needles in knitting or two billiard balls.

click (klik), *v.i.* to come together with a clicking sound.

client (klī' ent), *n.* one for whom a lawyer acts; a person who employs another's services; a patron of a store.

*clientele (klī en tel'), *n.* a group of clients, as of a doctor or lawyer; a following.

cliff (klif), *n.* a high and steep rocky bank.

climate (klī' mit), *n.* the typical temperature and weather conditions of a region.

climax (klī' maks), *n.* the summit; peak; culminating point.

climb (klim), *v.t. and v.i.* to make one's way up or down with the hands and feet, as to *climb* a ladder, *climb* down a precipice; to ascend, as to *climb* a hill; to slope upward, as the road *climbs* for a mile; to rise in rank or honor, as to *climb* to be captain.

clime (klim), *n.* a climate or a region in respect to its climate.

clinch (klinch), *v.i. and v.t.* to come to grips; to fasten firmly, as with nails, or by doubling over a projecting part, as of a nail; to prove beyond doubt, as an argument.

cling (kling), *v.i.* to hold tightly, as by an embrace or twining; to stick, as wet clothes *cling* to the body.

clinic (klin' ik), *n.* free treatment of patients or performance of operations in the presence of students; a place for free or cheap medical service to the public.

clip (klip), *n.* an amount of wool sheared; a clasp to hold papers together; a pace or gait.

clip (klip), *v.t.* to shear wool or hair from; to fasten together with a clip.

*clique (klēk), *n.* a coterie; exclusive group.

cloak (klōk), *n.* a long, loose over garment.

cloak (klōk), *v.t.* to cover with a cloak; to conceal; to disguise.

clock (klok), *n.* a piece of machinery in a case for measuring off the passage of time.

clog (klog), *n.* a load or weight to hinder motion; a shoe with a wooden sole.

clog (klog), *v.t. and v.i.* to obstruct, choke up; to hinder; to become stopped up, as drains *clog*.

cloister (klois' tēr), *n.* a place of religious retirement.

clone (klōn), *n.* a group of organisms derived from a single individual by asexual means; an exact replica or duplicate of someone else.

close (klōz), *n.* the end.

close (klōz), *n.* an enclosed space.

close (klōz), *v.t. and v.i.* to shut, as to *close* a door; to end, as to *close* a debate or a business deal; to shut, as a door *closes;* to come near or together, grapple, as wrestlers *close*.

Syn. Conclude, end, finish. To *close* is the opposite of to *open*, hence the idea of open is presupposed whenever the word *close* is used. We *close* an open door, an open argument, or the wrestlers, as they grapple, close the open space between them.

To *end* implies absolute finality; a road *ends*, a war *ends*, we *end* a sentence with a period. To *conclude* is a formal word used for the ending of speeches or documents. To *finish* is to complete something already started, as to *finish* a day's work.

close (klōs), *adv.* near, as stand *close* together.

close (klōs), *adj.* near, as a *close* neighbor; tight, as a *close* fit; secretive; stingy; oppressive, unventilated, as *close* weather, a *close* room; following an original exactly, accurate, as a *close* translation, a *close* imitation; dear, intimate, as a *close* friend; nearly equal, as a *close* score; strict, as to keep a *close* watch.

closet (kloz' et), *n.* a little room off a larger one for storing clothes.

closure (klō' zhēr), *n.* that which encloses; a parliamentary rule by which debate may be ended to permit a vote being taken.

clot (klot), *n.* a lump formed by coagulation or thickening of a liquid, as the blood.

clot (klot), *v.i. and v.t.* to form or be formed into clots.

cloth (klôth), *n.* a woven fabric of some fibrous material; a piece of cloth for some special use, as a table*cloth.*

clothe (klō*th*), *v.t.* to put clothes on; to cover as if with clothing.

*****clothes** (klō*th*z), *n. pl.* garments.

clothier (klō*th*' yēr), *n.* one who makes or sells clothing.

clothing (klō*th*' ing), *n.* garments in general; any covering.

cloud (kloud), *n.* a mass of visible vapor in the sky; anything like a cloud, as a *cloud* of dust.

cloud (kloud), *v.i. and v.t.* to make dark or become dark as if with clouds.

clout (klout), *n.* a piece of cloth or leather, as a breech*clout;* the white center of a target in archery; a center shot; a blow of the hand, either open or clenched.

clove (klōv), *n.* the flower bud of a tropical tree, dried and used as a spice.

cloven (klō' ven), *n.* cleft; divided into sections, as a cow's hoof.

clover (klō' vēr), *n.* a low-growing forage plant, valuable for hay and pasture.

clown (kloun), *n.* a buffoon.

cloy (kloi), *v.t.* to fill to repletion; to surfeit.

club (klub), *n.* a heavy stick; a suit of cards marked with a trefoil; an association of persons for a common purpose, social, educational or commercial.

club (klub) *v.t.* to strike with a club; to combine, for a common cause.

clubfoot (klub' foot), *n.* a deformity of the foot.

cluck (kluk), *n.* a hen's call to her chicks.

clump (klump), *n.* a thick cluster of trees; a heavy tread.

clumsy (klum' si), *adj.* awkward; poorly done.

cluster (klus' tēr), *n.* a number of like objects grouped or growing together, as a flower *cluster.*

clutch (kluch). *n.* a tight, greedy grip; a set of eggs to be hatched; a device for throwing machinery into gear.

clutch (kluch), *v.t.* to grasp eagerly or greedily.

coach (kōch), *n.* a large, closed, four-wheeled carriage; a railroad passenger car; an automobile with two seats and only two doors; one who teaches a team in some form of sport.

coach (kōch), *v.t.* to tutor; to teach a team in athletics the fine points of a game or sport.

coagulate (ko ag' ū lāt), *v.i. and v.t.* to clot, congeal or curdle; to cause to clot.

coal (kōl), *n.* mineralized vegetable matter, used as fuel; an ember.

coal (kōl), *v.t.* to supply with coal, as to *coal* a ship.

coalition (kō a lish' un), *n.* an alliance of individuals, organizations or states for a common purpose.

coarse (kōrs), *adj.* composed of large particles, as *coarse* sand; large in texture; made of rough parts; rude, vulgar, unrefined.

coast (kōst), *n.* the strip of land along a large body of water; seashore.

coast (kōst), *n.* to travel along the coast; to run by momentum, as a vehicle, or a sled.

coastwise (kōst wiz), *adv.* along a coast.

coat (kōt), *n.* an outer garment covering the upper part of the body; a thin layer, as a *coat* of paint.

coat (kōt), *v.t.* to cover, as *coat* it with wax.

coax (kōks), *v.t.* to wheedle; to cajole.

cob (kob), *n.* a corncob; a strong, stocky horse.

*****cobalt** (kō' bōlt), *n.* a silver-white metallic element resembling nickel.

cobble (kob' l), *n.* a paving stone.

cobble (kob' l), *v.t.* to mend shoes.

cobbler (kob' lēr), *n.* one whose business it is to mend shoes.

COBOL (kō ´ bōl), *n.* an acronym meaning Common Business Oriented Language; a computer programming language used in data processing.

*****cobra** (kō' bra), *n.* a deadly poisonous snake of India, having hooded neck.

cobweb (kob' web), *n.* a spider's web; an accumulation of dust on a ceiling in fine threads like a spider's web.

coca (kō' ka), *n.* a powerful tonic made of the dried leaves of a South American shrub.

*****cocaine** (kō kān'), *n.* a drug made from the leaves of coca plant, used to deaden pain.

*****cochineal** (koch l nēl'), *n.* a scarlet dye made from the dried bodies of the females of a certain Mexican insect.

cock (kok), *n.* a male of birds, especially of the domestic breeds of fowl; a small conical heap of hay; the hammer of a gun; a faucet.

cockle (kok' l), *n.* a weed that grows in grainfields; an edible European shellfish; a kiln for drying hops.

*****cockney** (kok' ni), *n.* a native Londoner of the East End; the dialect peculiar to East End Londoners.

cockpit (kok' pit), *n.* a pit or ring in which

gamecocks fight; a space for care of the wounded on a warship; in small sailboats and yachts, a space slightly lower than the run of the deck; the space in which the pilot of an airplane sits.

cockroach (kok' rŏch), *n.* an insect pest.

cocoa (kŏ' kŏ), *n.* powdered seeds of the cacao tree; a beverage made from this powder.

coconut (kŏ' kŏ nut), *n.* the fruit of the coco palm.

cocoon (ko kōōn'), *n.* the silky oblong case enveloping the larvae of some insects, as caterpillars or silkworms in which they develop to the adult stage.

cod (kod), *n.* a large saltwater fish.

coddle (kod' l), *v.t.* to pet and pamper; to simmer in water but not boil, as eggs.

code (kŏd), *n.* a system of rules; system of signals, as a cipher *code.*

*codicil (kod' i sil), *n.* an appendix to a will.

coeducation (kŏ ed ū kā' shun), *n.* the education of boys and girls together in the same institution.

*coerce (ko ûrs'), *v.t.* to force or compel to act, enforce; to restrain by force.

*coffee (kof' i), *n.* the seeds from the fruit of a tropical tree, roasted and ground; the drink made from this substance.

coffer (kof' ēr), *n.* a casket or chest for valuable things; a kind of caisson or floating dock: *coffers,* treasure, funds.

coffin (kof' in), *n.* a case in which a dead person is placed for burial.

cog (kog), *n.* a tooth or projection on the circumference of a wheel, engaging with one on another wheel or shaft, to transmit motion in machinery.

cogent (kŏ' jent), *adj.* clear, forceful, convincing.

cogitate (kog' i tāt), *v.i. and v.t.* to think over, plan.

cognate (kog' nāt), *n.* a blood relation.

cognate (kog' nāt), *adj.* related by blood; of the same stock or origin, as languages or words.

cognizance (kog' ni zans), *n.* knowledge, perception; notice.

*cognomen (kog nŏ' men), *n.* a surname.

cohere (kŏ hēr'), *v.i.* to stick together, as paste; to be logically consistent.

coherence (kŏ hēr' ens), *n.* logical consistency.

cohesion (kŏ hē zhun), *n.* the state or act of sticking together.

*coiffure (kwa' fûr), *n.* arrangement of the hair; a headdress.

coil (koil), *n.* a series of rings or one ring in a series; anything wound in spirals, as a *coil* of rope.

coil (koil), *v.t.* to wind in a spiral, as rope.

coin (koin), *n.* a piece of minted money.

*coin (koin), *v.t.* to make metal into money; to invent, as a verbal expression.

coincide (kŏ in sīd'), *v.i.* to occupy the same space at the same time, as lines or angles *coincide;* to correspond exactly, as ideas.

coincidence (kŏ in' si dens), *n.* occurrence of events simultaneously, by chance.

coke (kōk), *n.* the residue of coal or petroleum after the gases have been expelled, used as fuel.

*colander (kul' an dēr), *n.* a pan or basin with perforated bottom.

cold (kōld), *n.* lack of heat; low temperature; an ailment of nose and throat.

cold (kōld), *adj.* lacking heat: opposite of *hot;* unemotional, unfeeling, as a *cold* heart; not warm enough for comfort, as the poor dog is *cold;* discouraging.

cold chisel (kōld chis' l), a chisel of highly tempered steel for cutting metals.

coleslaw (kōl' slô), *n.* cabbage salad.

colic (kol' ik), *n.* an acute pain in the abdomen or bowels.

*collaborate (ko lab' o rāt), *v.i.* to work together, especially in literature or art.

collapse (ko lops'), *n.* a breakdown; *v.i.* to break down, fall apart, cave in.

collar (kol' ēr), *n.* a band around the neck.

collar (kol' ēr), *v.t.* to take by the collar; to put a collar on.

collate (ko lāt'), *v.t.* to compare critically, as two manuscripts; to arrange in order.

collateral (ko lat' ēr al), *n.* property deposited as security for a loan.

collateral (ko lat' ēr al), *adj.* subordinate, auxiliary; parallel; coincident, as events; of the same ancestral stock, but not in the line of descent.

collation (ko lā' shun), *n.* a light meal.

*colleague (ko lēg'), *n.* an associate in office.

collect (kol' ekt), *n.* a short, opening prayer.

collect (ko lekt'), *v.t. and v.i.* to assemble; to bring things or people together; to obtain payment of bills or taxes; to gather specimens of, as to *collect* butterflies; to assemble or accumulate, as a crowd *collects.*

collection (ko lek' shun), *n.* the act of collecting; a group of articles of similar nature, as coins or stamps, books or pictures; voluntary contributions.

collective (ko lek' tiv), *adj.* formed by collecting, gathered into one unit, as the *collective* knowledge of medical science; relating to a group, as *collective* aims.

college (kol' ej), *n.* an institution of higher learning; a society of learned or powerful men, as the electoral *college.*

collide (ko līd'), *v.i.* to crash together.

collier (kol' yēr), *n.* a coal miner; a ship that carries cargoes of coal.

collision (ko lizh' un), *n.* a violent impact of two moving bodies, as vehicles.

colloquial (kŏ lō' kwi al), *adj.* used in common speech.

*colloquy (kol' ŏ kwi), *n.* a conversation.

collusion (ko lū' zhun), *n.* a secret agreement for a fraudulent or evil purpose.

colon (kō' lon), *n.* a mark of punctuation (:); the large intestine of the human body.

colonel (kûr' nel), *n.* a military officer ranking above a lieutenant colonel and below a brigadier general.

colonial (ko lō' ni al), *adj.* relating to a colony.

colonize (kol' ŏ nīz), *v.t. and v.i.* to form colonies in, as to *colonize* America; to establish in a colony, as to *colonize* surplus population; to go to and settle in a far country; to found a colony.

colonnade (kol on ād'), *n.* a series of columns in connection with a building.

color (kul' ẽr), *n.* the quality of things resulting from their property of reflecting some light rays and absorbing others; any of the hues of the rainbow; pigment.

colors (kul' ẽrz), *n.* a national flag; aboard ship or at a military post, the salute to the flag as it is hoisted or taken down.

*colossal (kŏ los' sal), *adj.* gigantic, huge.

colt (kōlt), *n.* the young of the horse, ass or zebra.

*column (kol' um), *n.* a round pillar to support or adorn a building; a vertical division of a page of print; a line of marching troops; a vertical arrangement of figures to be added; a permanent space in a daily newspper given over to a special feature.

*columnist (kol' um nist), *n.* the writer of a signed column in a newspaper.

coma (kŏ' ma), *n.* prolonged unconsciousness due to disease or injury.

*comatose (kom' a tōs), *adj.* lethargic.

comb (kōm), *n.* a toothed instrument to untangle and order or adorn the hair; the crest of a fowl or a wave; the wax celled casing in which bees enclose their honey.

comb (kōm), *v.t.* to run a comb through; to go through carefully in search for something; to break in a line of foam, as waves.

*combat (kom' bat), *n.* a battle, struggle, hand-to-hand contest.

*combat (kom' bat), *v.i. and v.t.* to struggle, contend, as to *combat* against a habit; to battle with, resist, as to *combat* disease.

combination (kom bi nā'shun), *n.* a joining of things; things combined; an association of persons for a common purpose.

combine (kom bīn'), *v.i. and v.t.* to join together; to unite.

*combine (kom' bīn), *n.* association of persons or corporations for common purpose, especially in restraint of trade; a threshing and harvesting machine that performs both operations.

combustible (kom bus' ti bl), *adj.* inflammable; capable of being ignited.

*combustion (kom bus' chun), *n.* the act of burning.

come (kum), *v.i.* [*p.t.* came, *p.p.* come, *pr.p.* coming] to move toward, draw near, as *come* here; to arrive, as the train *comes* at noon, May *comes* after April; to reach, as in space, as her hair *comes* to her shoulders; to reach, as an amount or condition, as the bill *comes* to $5, a liar *comes* to grief at last; to originate or develop, as to *come* of a royal line, a chicken *comes* from an egg; to be available, as diamonds *come* at a high price.

comedian (ko mē' dian), *n.* an actor in a comedy or a writer of comedies; a comical person.

comedy (kom' e di), *n.* an entertaining drama with a happy ending.

comely (kum' li), *adj.* of pleasing person and manner.

comet (kom' et), *n.* a luminous body moving through the heavens and following an orbit about the sun.

comfort (kum' fẽrt), *n.* ease of body and mind; consolation, solace; any person or thing that ministers to material ease or gives moral support.

comfort (kum' fẽrt), *v.t.* to console, give hope or moral strength to.

Syn. Console, solace. To *comfort* is to relieve pain or distress by substituting cheer, hope or strength; to *console* is to lessen grief or trouble without imparting actual cheer; to *solace* is to lessen loneliness or melancholy rather than something as sharp as grief or pain.

comic (kom' ik), *adj.* exciting mirth.

comity (kom' i ti), *n.* politeness, courtesy, friendliness, especially between governments.

comma (kom' a), *n.* a punctuation mark (,), used to separate words, phrases and clauses.

command (ko mánd'), *v.t.* to order with authority; to be chief officer of, as troops or a ship; to overlook, as a mountain peak *commands* the valleys.

Syn. Order, enjoin. *Command* is the formal and official word; a general *commands* his army, a captain *commands* his ship. To *order* is a more personal word and sometimes implies being peremptory in the use of authority, as to *order* someone off the grass. To *enjoin* means to command or order, but carries the idea of warning or admonition, as to *enjoin* obedience.

command (ko mánd'), *n.* an order; that which one commands, as a body of troops: authority; control.

commander (ko mán' dẽr), *n.* a naval officer next lower in rank than a captain.

commandment (ko mánd' ment), *n.* an order; one of the Ten Commandments.

commemorate (ko mem' ō rāt), *v.t.* to honor the memory of; to observe; to celebrate, as a national triumph.

commence (ko mens'), *v.i. and v.t.* to start; to begin; to set under way.

commencement (ko mens' ment), *n.* a beginning; the graduation of a class in school or college.

commend (ko mend'), *v.t.* to praise; to name as worthy.

*commensurate (ko men' shoo rit), *adj.* reducible to a common measure; equal in measure; in proportion.

comment (kom' ent), *n.* critical or explanatory statements; a remark.

comment (kom' ent), *v.i.* to say or write something about a person, thing, action or event.

*commentary (kom' en ter i), *n.* a body of explanatory notes, to accompany a text.

commerce (kom' ũrs), *n.* trade, especially interchange of goods between traders in different states or lands.

*commiserate (ko miz' er āt), *v.t.* to feel or express sympathy or pity for.

*commissary (kom' i ser i), *n.* an army officer in charge of provisions and supplies; a store selling food and other supplies, as in a mining camp.

commission (ko mish' un), *n.* a group of persons appointed to perform some public duty; the act of doing or committing, as *commission* of an errand, *commission* of a crime; the delegation of a responsible task to someone; a certificate of rank in the army or navy; the pay of an agent.

commission (ko mish' un), *v.t.* to give a commission to, as an officer; to put into service, as a ship; to empower to act, as an agent.

commit (ko mit'), *v.t.* to do (something specified), as to *commit* a crime; to give into custody or care, as to *commit* a man to prison, I *commit* the child to you; to entrust or consign, as to *commit* a poem to memory.

committee (ko mit' i), *n.* a group of persons appointed to attend to some particular activity of an organization.

commodious (ko mō' di us), *adj.* roomy and comfortable.

commodity (ko mod' i ti), *n.* an article of commerce, especially a profitable article of commerce; goods, merchandise.

common (kom' un), *n.* a tract of public land.

common (kom' un), *adj.* belonging to all of a group; ordinary; coarse and vulgar.

commonplace (kom' un plās), *adj.* ordinary, trite.

commonsense (kom' un sens), *adj.* sensible; characterized by ordinary, every day sense.

commonwealth (kom' un welth), *n.* the whole body of people under a government; a state.

commotion (ko mō' shun), *n.* excitement and confusion.

communicate (ko mū' ni kāt), *v.i. and v.t.* to exchange ideas through speech, writing or signal; to join, as rooms *communicate;* to impart, as to *communicate* the news of the day.

communion (ko mūn' yun), *n.* religious fellowship; the Lord's Supper, the Eucharist; the sharing or interchange of ideas.

communiqué (ko mū ni kā'), *n.* an official bulletin from scene of action.

communism (kom' ū nizm), *n.* a social system that puts property, capital and industry under the control of the community, and strives toward equal distribution of benefits.

communist (kom' ū nist), *n.* one who advocates or supports communism.

community (ko mū' ni ti), *n.* a body of people having common interests or living in one locality; possession of things or ideas in common.

commutation (kom ū tā' shun), *n.* a substitution of one kind of payment for another; the amount paid in substitutions; the reduction of a severe penalty to a lesser one.

commute (ko mūt'), *v.i. and v.t.* to travel back and forth regularly, as between one's home and the place where one works, on a commutation ticket; to reduce the severity of, as to *commute* a court's sentence.

compact (kom' pakt), *n.* an agreement or covenant; a small case in which women carry mirror, powder and rouge.

compact (kom pakt'), *adj.* closely packed, solid; terse; concise.

companion (kom pan' yun), *n.* a comrade; close associate; one who accompanies another.

company (kum' pa ni), *n.* an assemblage; visitors in a home; a group of persons associated in business with legal standing as a unit; a military unit commanded by a captain.

comparable (kom' pa ra bl), *adj.* capable or worthy of being compared.

comparative (kom par' a tiv), *adj.* estimated or studied by comparison; not positive, not exact, relative.

compare (kom pâr'), *v.i. and v.t.* to be like, as this *compares* favorably with that; to analyze one thing in terms of another to discover resemblances and differences; to inflect an adjective or adverb, giving the forms that express different degrees.

comparison (kom par' i sun), *n.* the act of comparing; an estimate of resemblances and differences; the change in form of an adjective or adverb to show difference in degree; a simile.

compartment (kom pärt' ment), *n.* a division made by a partition inside a closed space, as a *compartment* in a desk or in a railroad passenger car.

compass (kum' pás), *n.* an instrument indicating the directions, north, south, east, west, by means of a magnetic needle; an instrument for drawing circles.

compass (kum' pás), *v.i. and v.t.* to bring about a desired result; to encircle; to comprehend.

compassion (kom pash' un), *n.* sorrow for the sufferings of others; pity.

compatible (kom pat' i bl), *adj.* congruous, harmonious; able to get along together.

compel (kom pel'), *v.t.* to drive, take or restrain by force.

compendium (kom pen' di um), *n.* an abridgment of a text, a summary.

compensate (kom' pen sāt), *v.i. and v.t.* to recompense; to make amends for; to bring to a balance.

compensation (kom pen sā' shun), *n.* recompense; amends for damage of any kind; pay for services or work.

compete (kom pēt'), *v.i.* to strive or contend against the opposition of others.

competence (kom' pē tens), *n.* fitness, ability; a moderate fortune, enough to live on.

competent (kom' pē tent), *adj.* fit, able, capable.

competition (kom pē tish' un), *n.* rivalry; a match; effort to outdo a rival.

competitor (kom pet' i tẽr), *n.* one who competes; a rival.

compile (kom pīl'), *v.t.* to put existing materials together in fresh form, as a book; to assemble data.

complacence (kom plā' sens), *n.* contentment; self-satisfaction.

complacent (kom plā' sent), *adj.* contented, self-satisfied; exhibiting self-satisfaction.

complain (kom plān'), *v.i.* to express pain, sorrow or dissatisfaction; to find fault; to make a formal legal accusation.

complaint (kom plānt'), *n.* an expression of discontent; faultfinding; a formal charge; ailment.

***complement** (kom' plē ment), *n.* that which completes; the full number or amount to complete a set; the whole personnel of a vessel.

complete (kom plēt'), *v.t.* to bring to full number or accomplishment; to fill out; to supply a deficiency; to finish.

complete (kom plēt'), *adj.* lacking no part; finished; thorough.

complex (kom' pleks), *n.* in psychology, a group of associated ideas affecting the emotions and behavior.

***complex** (kom pleks'), *adj.* consisting of a number of parts or elements; intricate, not simple.

complexion (kom plek' shun), *n.* the coloring of the skin, especially of the face.

complexity (kom plek' si ti), *n.* intricacy; any complicated thing.

compliance (kom plī' ans), *n.* a yielding; consenting.

compliant (kom plī' ant), *adj.* yielding, disposed to oblige.

complicate (kom' pli kāt), *v.t.* to make intricate or difficult.

cómplicated (kom' pli kāt ed), *adj.* having many intricate parts; confusing, hard to solve, separate or analyze.

complication (kom pli kā' shun), *n.* the state of being complicated, entangled, intricate; that which complicates or causes confusion or difficulty; a confusing set of circumstances; a disease existing with and making more serious another disease.

complicity (kom plis' i ti), *n.* association in wrongdoing; a taking part in something, especially a crime.

***compliment** (kom' pli ment), *n.* an expression of praise or appreciation: *compliments,* formal greetings, as *compliments* of the author.

***complimentary** (kom pli men' ta ri), *adj.* conveying an expression of regard or appreciation; presented free, as a *complimentary* copy of a book.

comply (kom pli'), *v.i.* to yield or assent; to agree; to conform.

***component** (kom pō' nent), *n.* an elementary part, ingredient.

component (kom pō' nent), *adj.* forming a necessary part, helping to constitute.

***comport** (kom pōrt'), *v.t. and v.i.* to conduct, behave, as to *comport* oneself with dignity; to agree.

compose (kom pōs'), *v.t.* to form by combination of units or parts; to write, as poems or music; to calm, as to *compose* one's self; to constitute, make up, as the parts *compose* the whole; to reconcile, as differences of opinion; to set type. The parts *compose* the whole; the whole *comprises* the parts.

composed (kom pōzd'), *adj.* calm, cool, self-contained.

***composite** (kom poz' it), *n.* a compound or combination.

composite (kom poz' it), *adj.* compounded, made up of various parts.

composition (kom pō zish' un), *n.* the act or result of composing or compounding; a work of literature, painting, sculpture, music, in which various elements are brought together; setting of type for printing.

compositor (kom poz' i tér), *n.* one who composes, especially one who sets type.

***compost** (kom' pōst), *n.* a rotted mixture of leaf mold, manure and lime, used as a fertilizer.

composure (kom pō' zhér), *n.* calmness, coolness.

compound (kom' pound), *n.* the product of the mixture or union of parts.

***compound** (kom pound'), *v.t.* to unite into a whole, combine.

compound (kom' pound), *adj.* made of several different parts, composite.

comprehend (kom prē hend'), *v.t.* to include, contain or take in; to grasp with the mind, understand.

comprehension (kom prē hen' shun), *n.* mental grasp, understanding, ability to understand; inclusion.

comprehensive (kom prē hen' siv), *adj.* extensive, including much; able to understand.

compress (kom pres'), *v.t.* to press together; to condense.

compression (kom presh' un), *n.* condensation, pressing together.

comprise (kom prīz'), *n.* to take in, include, consist of.

compromise (kom' prō mīz), *v.i. and v.t.* to adjust by mutual concession; to expose to risk or suspicion; to reach an agreement by concession.

compulsion (kom pul' shun), *n.* force; constraint.

compulsory (kom pul' sō ri), *adj.* obligatory, enforced, required, as *compulsory* education.

compunction (kom pungk' shun), *n.* self-reproach, remorse; regret.

computation (kom pū tā' shun), *n.* the act or result of calculating; a calculation or reckoning.

compute (kom pūt'), *v.t.* to reckon, calculate.

computer (kom pū' ter), *n.* an electronic machine capable of accepting and processing data.

computerese (com pūt ´ er ēse), *n.* the language used by computer operators to communicate with each other.

concave (kon kāv'), *adj.* hollow and curved, like the inner surface of a sphere: opposite of *convex.*

conceal (kon sēl') *v.t.* to hide; to keep secret, to withhold, as information.

concede (kon sēd') *v.t.* to yield or allow; to admit or acknowledge; to grant, as a point in debate.

conceit (kon sēt'), *n.* exaggerated self-esteem, vanity; a quaint fancy.

conceivable (kon sēv' a bl), *adj.* capable of being thought of or understood; imaginable.

conceive (kon sēv'), *v.t. and v.i.* to think of, imagine or understand; to become pregnant; to think, have an idea.

***concentrate** (kon' sen trāt), *v.t.* to bring to

a center; to center attention on; to condense into a smaller but stronger quantity.

*concentric (kon sen' trik), *adj.* having the same center, as *concentric* circles.

concept (kon' sept), *n.* a thought or idea; a mental image.

conception (kon sep' shun), *n.* the act of forming an idea; understanding; beginning, especially the beginning of life in an ovum.

concern (kon sûrn'), *n.* something about which one cares or in which he is interested; interest in or regard for; a business company.

concern (kon sûrn'), *v.t.* to relate or belong to; affect, interest or engage; to implicate.

concerning (kon sûrn' ing), *prep.* relating to, regarding.

*concert (kon sûrt'), *v.t.* to contrive, devise or arrange in co-operation.

concert (kon' sûrt), *n.* a musical entertainment; harmony; co-operation.

concession (kon sesh' un), *n.* the act of yielding or that which is yielded; a privilege granted, as for mining or doing business in a certain place.

*conch (kongk), *n.* a large, spirally shaped seashell.

*conciliate (kon sil' i ăt), *v.t.* to reconcile; to win the favor or good opinion of.

concise (kon sīs'), *adj.* terse; condensed; short.

conclave (kon' klăv), *n.* a secret meeting; the meeting of cardinals to elect a pope.

conclude (kon klōōd'), *v.i. and v.t.* to come to an end; to bring to an end; to draw an inference.

conclusion (kon klōō' zhun), *n.* the end; an inference drawn; a final determination.

conclusive (kon klōō' siv), *adj.* decisive, final.

concoct (kon kokt'), *v.t.* to cook things together; to prepare by mixing; to devise, as a plan or scheme.

concomitant (kon kom' i tant), *n.* something attendant upon another thing; an attendant circumstance, as snow is not always a *concomitant* of cold weather.

concomitant (kon kom' i tant), *adj.* accompanying, attending.

*concord (kon' kôrd), *n.* harmony; agreement.

concordance (kon kôrd' ans), *n.* agreement; an index of words, with reference to the places where they occur in a text.

concourse (kon' kôrs), *n.* a coming together, as of many people; a place where many roads or paths meet.

*concrete (kon' krēt), *n.* a hard mass formed by mixing gravel or broken stone with sand, cement and water.

concrete (kon krēt'), *adj.* real; definite; made of concrete.

concur (kon kûr'), *v.i.* to acquiesce; to coincide or happen at the same time; to unite in expression of opinion or in action.

concurrent (kon kûr' ent), *adj.* existing or running together, as *concurrent* sentences for two or more crimes; acting jointly, as *concurrent* action by House and Senate.

concussion (kon kush' un), *n.* the shock of two objects in collision; a jarring, as of the brain, by a shock or blow.

*condemn (kon dem'), *v.t.* to pronounce guilty;

to declare forfeited from private to public use, as land; to declare unfit for use, as a building; to disapprove, as a policy of action or a person's conduct.

condensation (kon den să' shun), *n.* reduction in size or amount, as a synopsis is a *condensation* of a book or article; the process or product of changing from gaseous or vaporous form to liquid form.

condense (kon dens'), *v.t. and v.i.* to compress; to reduce in size or volume and pack into smaller space; to change from gaseous or vaporous to liquid form.

*condescend (kon dē send'), *v.i.* to stoop or descend to a less formal state; to be gracious to inferior persons; deign.

condiment (kon' di ment), *n.* a relish; seasoning.

condition (kon dish' un), *n.* a state of being, as healthy or sick, rich or poor, good or bad; a requirement for the doing of something, a stipulation; a qualification; external circumstances, as to work under bad *conditions.*

condole (kon dōl'), *v.i. and v.t.* to express sympathy, to grieve with another.

*condolence (kon dō' lens), *n.* sympathy; a message of sympathy.

condominium (kon' de min' ē um), *n.* a unit in an apartment house owned separately by individuals.

condone (kon dōn'), *v.t.* to find excuses for; to overlook, as a fault.

condor (kon'dēr), *n.* a South American vulture.

*conduce (kon dūs'), *v.i.* to tend; to help bring about.

conducive (kon dū' siv), *adj.* helping to bring about, as a result or condition, as health is *conducive* to happiness.

conduct (kon' dukt), *n.* personal behavior; management or direction, as of a business.

conduct (kon dukt'), *v.t.* to guide; to lead; to manage.

conductor (kon duk' tēr), *n.* one who or that which conducts, leads or guides; one who has charge of a public vehicle, as a train, bus or street car; a body or material through which an electric current can pass.

cone (kōn), *n.* a solid figure with a circular base, tapering upward to a sharp point; the cone-shaped fruit of certain evergreen trees; a hollow cone-shaped biscuit used to hold ice cream.

confection (kon fek' shun), *n.* anything conserved or compounded with sugar.

confectionery (kon fek' shun er i), *n.* candy; a candy shop.

confederacy (kon fed' ēr a si), *n.* an alliance or league for mutual support or action.

confederate (kon fed' ēr āt), *v.i. and v.t.* to unite or become united in a league of states or in a conspiracy.

confederate (kon fed' ēr it), *adj.* associated in a confederacy.

confer (kon fûr'), *v.t. and v.i.* to grant; to bestow upon, as a prize, a gift or a favor; to consult together, to engage in discussion.

conference (kon' fēr ens), *n.* a consultation;

a meeting for discussion of affairs.

confess (kon fes'), *v.i. and v.t.* to make confession; to admit or acknowledge, as a fault, sin or crime; to assert belief in, as a religious faith.

confessional (kon fesh' un al), *n.* the cabinet in which a priest sits while hearing confessions.

confessor (kon fes' ẽr), *n.* one who confesses; a priest who hears confessions.

confetti (kon fet' tē), *n. pl.* little pieces of colored paper used to toss into the air at a carnival or other festival.

*confidant (kon' fi dant), *n.* one to whom secrets are entrusted; a person in whom one confides or has faith.

confide (kon fīd'), *v.i. and v.t.* to have faith in, to trust; to entrust; to tell in confidence.

confidence (kon' fi dens), *n.* trust; assurance of one's own ability or fitness; a secret told in confidence.

confident (kon' fi dent), *adj.* self-assured; sure of.

confidential (kon fi den' shal), *adj.* revealed in confidence; to be kept secret.

configuration (kon fig ū rā' shun), *n.* outline, contour, shape.

confine (kon' fin), *n.* a boundary or limit.

confine (kon fin'), *v.t.* to restrict within limits; to imprison.

confirm (kon fûrm'), *v.t.* to strengthen, as faith; to ratify or verify, as news; to receive into the church.

*confiscate (kon' fis kāt), *v.t.* to adjudge forfeited and seize, because of violation of law; to appropriate for public use.

*conflagration (kon fla grā' shun), *n.* a great destructive fire.

conflict (kon' flikt), *n.* a fight or struggle for mastery; a clash of opinions or interests; an inner moral struggle.

conflict (kon flikt'), *v.i.* to clash; to fight for supremacy; to come into opposition.

confluence (kon' floo ens), *n.* the junction of two streams; the point at which they meet.

conform (kon fôrm'), *v.i. and v.t.* to be in or bring into agreement; to comply.

conformable (kon fôrm' a bl), *adj.* in agreement or harmony, as this is *conformable* to your designs; compliant.

conformation (kon fôr mā' shun), *n.* adaptation; formation, structure.

conformity (kon fôrm' i ti), *n.* agreement, correspondence, compliance.

confound (kon found'), *v.t.* to confuse, dismay; to astonish; to damn.

confront (kon frunt´), *v.t.* to stand face to face with hostility, as to *confront* an enemy; to put one face to face with, as to *confront* a critic with facts.

confuse (kon fūz'), *v.t.* to perplex, as to *confuse* a student; to bewilder, to mix, jumble together, as to *confuse* facts.

confusion (kon fū' zhun), *n.* disorder, turmoil, as *confusion* in the streets; mental agitation, bewilderment; embarrassment.

confute (kon fūt'), *v.t.* to prove false, as to *confute* previous arguments; to prove (a person) to be in error, as to *confute* the

judge.

congeal (kon jēl'), *v.i. and v.t.* to convert or be converted from a liquid to a solid state by freezing.

*congenial (kon jēn' yal), *adj.* having similar tastes, ideas and ideals; suitable to one's needs or desires, as a *congenial* environment.

congenital (kon jen' i tal), *adj.* existing since birth.

congested (kon jest' ed), *adj.* crowded, obstructed, as streets with traffic.

congestion (kon jes' chun), *n.* a crowded condition; an excessive accumulation of blood in some part of the body.

*conglomerate (kon glom' ẽr it), *adj.* gathered into a mixed mass.

congratulate (kon grat' ū lāt), *v.t.* to felicitate; to greet or address with pleasure because of some fortunate happening.

*congregate (kon' grē gāt), *v.i.* to assemble, as in a church.

congress (kon' gres), *n.* an assembly of representatives of state, especially of a republic.

*congruity (kong grōō i ti), *n.* agreement of things, harmony.

congruous (kon grōō' us), *adj.* fitly combining; in agreement, as facts one with another; consistent.

conjectural (kon jek' tūr al), *adj.* not certain, but surmised.

conjecture (kon jek' tūr), *n.* a guess; surmise; *v.i.* to guess; to surmise.

conjoin (kon join'), *v.i. and v.t.* to join together, combine.

conjoint (kon joint'), *adj.* associated.

*conjugal (kon' joo gal), *adj.* pertaining to marriage.

conjugate (kon' joo gāt), *v.t.* to inflect a verb or state its moods, tenses, voices, numbers, persons.

conjunct (kon jungt'), *adj.* joined together.

conjunction (kon jungk' shun), *n.* a part of speech connecting words, phrases and clauses; the apparent meeting of heavenly bodies.

*conjure (kon joor'), *v.i. and v.t.* to cast spells; to practice magic; to put a spell on.

connect (ko nekt'), *v.i. and v.t.* to associate or be associated; to join; to bring together; to form a line between.

connection (ko nek' shun), *n.* the act of connecting or state of being connected; relation, in thought or logic; a person associated with one in business or related by blood or marriage; boat and train transference in traveling; a hook-up of one telephone with another.

connivance (ko niv' ans), *n.* passive co-operation, especially in a crime or fault; collusion.

connive (ko niv'), *v.i.* to close the eyes to, pretend not to see, as to *connive* at a prisoner's escape; to be in secret- understanding with.

*connoisseur (kon i sûr'), *n.* an expert judge or critic, as of art.

connote (ko nōt'), *v.t.* to imply, suggest or point to a meaning in addition to the literal meaning.

connubial (ko nū' bi al), *adj.* matrimonial; pertaining to marriage or to a husband or wife.

*****conquer** (kong' kĕr), *v.t. and v.i.* to vanquish, subdue, overcome by force; to be victorious.

conqueror (kong' kĕr ēr), *n.* one who conquers, a victor.

*****conquest** (kong' kwest), *n.* the act of conquering, or that which is conquered; triumph.

conscience (kon' shens), *n.* the moral sense which distinguishes right from wrong.

*****conscientious** (kon shi en' shus), *adj.* guided by conscience, scrupulous.

conscious (kon' shus), *adj.* aware; self-conscious; mentally active; intentional.

consciousness (kon' shus nes), *n.* the full knowledge of what is in one's own mind; awareness.

conscript (kon' skript), *n.* one enrolled for compulsory military or naval service.

conscript (kon skript'), *v.t.* to draft into the army or navy.

conscription (kon skrip' shun), *n.* the system of drafting men for military service.

consecrate (kon' sĕ krāt), *v.t.* to set apart as sacred; to dedicate to God.

consecutive (kon sek' ū tiv), *adj.* following in order, successive; moving without interruption of thought, as a narrative.

consensus (kon-sen' sus), *n.* general agreement; representative trend, as of opinion.

consent (kon sent'), *n.* voluntary acceptance of a proposition or demand; approval; permission, as you have my *consent.*

consent (kon sent'), *v.i.* to comply, yield; to give permission or approval.

consequence (kon' sĕ kwens), *n.* that which follows, a result; importance.

consequent (kon' sĕ kwent), *adj.* following naturally or logically as a result.

consequential (kon sĕ kwen' shal), *adj.* self-important; following as a logical result.

conservation (kon sĕr vā' shun), *n.* the act of preserving resources from decay, loss or injury.

conservative (kon sûrv' a tiv), *adj.* cautious, prudent, moderate; opposed to great or sudden changes, supporting the existing regime, believing in established principles; not risky, as a *conservative* investment.

conservatory (kon sûrv' a tō ri), *n.* a greenhouse; a school of music, drama or oratory.

*****conserve** (kon sûrv'), *n.* a preparation of fruits in sugar.

conserve (kon sûrv'), *v.t.* to husband, as resources; to handle with care and safeguard against destruction.

consider (kon sid' ēr), *v.i. and v.t.* to deliberate; to ponder; to give attention to; to regard as.

considerable (kon sid' ēr a bl), *adj.* notable as in size or value.

*****considerate** (kon sid' ēr it), *adj.* ready to consider and act for the welfare of others.

consideration (kon sid ēr ā' shun), *n.* study; kindliness; a fact to be taken into account; a reward or inducement.

consign (kon sin'), *v.t.* to entrust; to set apart for special use or for use by some particular person; to ship goods to.

*****consignee** (kon sīn ē'), *n.* the person to whom goods are shipped.

consignment (kon sīn' ment), *n.* a shipment of goods; commitment of property to another than the owner for sale or safekeeping.

consist (kon sist'), *v.i.* to be made or composed of.

consistency (kon sis' ten si), *n.* the degree of density or thickness of a fluid; logical agreement, as between precept and practice or between two or more statements.

consistent (kon sis' tent), *adj.* free from self-contradiction; in harmony with.

console (kon sōl'), *v.t.* to comfort, in sorrow.

consolidate (kon sol' i dāt), *v.i. and v.t.* to make or become solid, united; to join two or more business concerns.

consommé (kon so mā'), *n.* a clear soup made by prolonged boiling of meats.

*****consonance** (kon' sō nans), *n.* agreement, harmony, especially of sounds.

consonant (kon' sō nant), *n.* a letter not a vowel.

consonant (kon' sō nant), *adj.* agreeing, consistent; having a sound like a consonant; having similar sounds, as *consonant* words.

consort (kon' sōrt), *n.* an associate; a husband or wife; a ship escorting another.

conspectus (kon spek' tus), *n.* a general view of a subject; survey.

conspicuous (kon spik' ū us), *adj.* showing prominently, very noticeable; outstanding.

*****conspiracy** (kon spir' a si), *n.* a plot; combination of persons for an evil purpose.

conspirator (kon spir' a tĕr), *n.* a plotter; one who engages in a conspiracy.

conspire (kon spīr'), *v.i.* to plot together; to combine secretly for an unlawful purpose.

*****constable** (kon' sta bl), *n.* an officer of the law comparable to a sheriff but of lower standing and working in a smaller field.

constancy (kon' stan si), *n.* steadfastness; stability.

Syn. Fidelity, faithfulness. *Constancy* is steadfastness, especially in love or friendship. *Fidelity* is unchanging adherence, sometimes to a person, but also to a trust or a cause. *Faithfulness* implies warm personal devotion.

constant (kon' stant), *adj.* steadfast, firm; not variable, as a *constant* light; continuous, as a *constant* drip of water.

constellation (kon ste lā' shun), *n.* a group of fixed stars to which a group name has been given.

consternation (kon stur nā' shun), *n.* dismay; confused fright.

constipation (kon sti pā' shun), *n.* inactivity of the bowels.

constituency (kon stit' ū en si), *n.* a body of followers; all the voters of a public officer's electoral territory.

constituent (kon stit' ū ent), *n.* a component part; one who follows and votes for an elected officer of the state.

constituent (kon stit' ū ent), *adj.* necessary

or serving as a part or element of a compound; empowered to elect.

constitute (kon sti tūt'), *v.t.* to compose or make up; to appoint, as to an office; to establish, as a law.

constitution (kon sti tū' shun), *n.* the composition or make-up of anything, as of the human body or the state; the system of fundamental laws of a nation or society.

constitutional (kon sti tū' shun al), *n.* a walk taken for the health.

constitutional (kon sti tū' shun al), *adj.* pertaining to a constitution, as *constitutional* law; in keeping with the constitution.

constrain (kon strān') *v.t.* to compel; to confine by force.

constraint (kon strānt'), *n.* compulsion or restraint; confinement; repression; embarrassment.

constrict (kon strikt'), *v.t.* to bind; to cramp.

construct (kon strukt'), *v.t.* to build; to put together.

construction (kon struk' shun), *n.* the act of building; a building; style of building; interpretation; the arrangement of words in a sentence or of sentences in a paragraph.

constructive (kon struk' tiv), *adj.* helping to build up, not destructive; helpful, as *constructive* suggestions.

*°construe (kon strōō'), *v.t.* to analyze the grammatical structure of a sentence; to interpret, as law.

*°consul (kon' sul), *n.* one of two chief magistrates of the ancient Roman republic; an officer commissioned by a government to reside in a foreign country to promote trade and safeguard the interests of his compatriots living or trading there.

consular (kon' sū lẽr), *adj.* pertaining to a consul or his duties and functions.

consulate (kon' sū lāt), *n.* the office and residence of a consul.

consult (kon sult'), *v.i. and v.t.* to confer with; to ask advice of, as to *consult* a physician; to have regard for, as to *consult* a friend's wishes; to refer to, as to *consult* a dictionary.

consultation (kon sul tā' shun), *n.* a conference for exchange of views, as of doctors in connection with a case of sickness.

consume (kon sūm'), *v.t.* to use up; to destroy, as by fire; to engross and waste, as passion *consumed* him.

consumer (kon sūm' ẽr), *n.* one who buys goods for his own use.

*°consummate (kon' su māt), *v.t.* to complete; to finish.

*°consummate (kon sum' it), *adj.* perfect; complete.

consummation (kon su mā' shun), *n.* completion; attainment of a desired end.

consumption (kon sump' shun), *n.* a disease that wastes the body; use of goods removing them from the market.

contact (kon' takt), *n.* a coming together of two objects so that they touch; close relations, as of a salesman with a possible customer; the junction of two electrical conductors.

contact (kon' takt), *v.t. and v.i.* to be or get in touch with; to touch.

contagion (kon tā' jun), *n.* transmission of disease by contact, which may be direct or indirect; the transmission of a mood, as the *contagion* of enthusiasm.

contagious (kon tā' jus), *adj.* catching, conveyed by contact, as a *contagious* disease, a *contagious* laugh.

contain (kon tān'), *v.t.* to hold within a certain space; to have capacity for; to include, as this book *contains* pictures; to control, as he could hardly *contain* his mirth.

contaminate (kon tam' i nāt), *v.t.* to pollute; to make impure; to defile.

Syn. Defile, pollute, taint, corrupt. Whatever is impure *contaminates;* what is gross and vile in the natural sense *defiles* and in the moral sense *pollutes;* what is contagious or infectious *corrupts*, and what is corrupted may *taint* other things.

Ant. Clean, clear, purify, whiten.

contemplate (kon' tem plāt), *v.t. and v.i.* to meditate on; to regard thoughtfully; to intend; to think over carefully.

Syn. Meditate, muse. Different species of reflection are marked by these terms. We *contemplate* what is present or before our eyes; we *meditate* on what is past or absent. The heavens are for us to *contemplate;* on the ways of Providence we may fitly *meditate*. One *muses* on events or circumstances which have been just passing.

*°contemplative (kon tem' pla tiv), *adj.* thoughtful.

contemporaneous (kon tem pō rā' nē us), *adj.* happening or existing at the same time; contemporary.

contemporary (kon tem' pō rer i), *n.* a person living at the same time as another; a person about the same age as another.

contemporary (kon tem' pō rer i), *adj.* happening or existing at the same time; having the same age.

contempt (kon tempt'), *n.* scorn; disdain; deliberate disregard for the orders or dignity of a court.

contemptible (kon tempt' i bl), *adj.* deserving scorn; despicable.

contemptuous (kon tempt' ū us), *adj.* manifesting contempt; disdainful.

contend (kon tend'), *v.i.* to strive in opposition; to assert; to present as an argument.

content (kon' tent), *n.* that which is contained, as the *contents* of a box; size or capacity for holding, as the *content* of this basket is a quart; meaning, subject matter, as the *content* of a text; contentment.

content (kon tent'), *adj.* satisfied with what one has; assenting, as to a vote.

contention (kon ten' shun), *n.* strife; conflict; that which one contends in argument or debate.

contentious (kon ten' shus), *adj.* quarrelsome; argumentative; causing contention.

contentment (kon tent' ment), *n.* the state of being satisfied with what one has.

contest (kon' test), *n.* a struggle to demonstrate superiority; rivalry for a prize.

Syn. Conflict, combat, fight. A *contest* is any rivalry, friendly rivalry, as an athletic *contest*, or hostile rivalry to win something. A *conflict* is a close fight. A *combat* is always an armed fight. A *fight* is usually a fist fight, but the word is also used of inner moral struggle.

contest (kon test'), *v.i. and v.t.* to take part in a struggle, as to *contest* against odds; to challenge the rightness or validity, as of a will; to struggle to hold or win, as a race or territory.

contestant (kon tes' tant), *n.* one who takes part in any kind of a contest.

context (kon' tekst), *n.* that part of a written discourse in which a certain word, phrase or passage appears, necessary to point the meaning, as it is hard to tell the exact meaning of a word out of *context*.

contiguity (kon ti gū' i ti), *n.* nearness; contact.

***contiguous** (kon tig' ū us), *adj.* touching; near.

continence (kon' ti nens), *n.* self-restraint, especially restraint in indulgence of the appetites.

continent (kon' ti nent), *n.* one of the six greatest divisions of the earth's land surface.

contingency (kon tin' jen si), *n.* something that may happen but of which there is no assurance; a chance.

contingent (kon tin' jent), *adj.* possible but not certain; accidental; depending, conditional, as success is *contingent* upon effort.

continual (kon tin' ū al), *adj.* uninterrupted; incessant.

Syn. Continuous, constant, perpetual. *Continual* describes almost unbroken recurrence in time, as *continual* questions, *continual* noise; *continuous* means unbroken and unceasing in both time and space, as a *continuous* line, *continuous* rain for three days; *constant* means persistent, as *constant* pain, *constant* hope; *perpetual* means unceasing, lasting, endless.

continuation (kon tin ū ā' shun), *n.* resumption after an interruption, as of a serial story.

continue (kon tin' ū), *v.i. and v.t.* to keep going; to persist; to resume after interruption; to prolong, as a line.

***continuity** (kon tin ū' i ti), *n.* uninterrupted advance or succession; dramatic sequence, the oneness of the plot and action; the filling in by a radio announcer of spaces between program items.

continuous (kon tin' ū us), *adj.* uninterrupted, unceasing.

contort (kon tôrt'), *v.t.* to twist; to wrench, make awry, as anger *contorted* his features.

contortion (kon tôr' shun), *n.* a twisting, writhing.

contour (kon' toor), *n.* an outline of some figure.

***contraband** (kon' tra band), *n.* goods forbidden by law to be exported or imported; smuggled merchandise.

contraband (kon' tra band), *adj.* illegal and subject to confiscation.

contract (kon' trakt), *n.* a formal agreement, as to supply goods or do work.

***contract** (kon trakt'), *v.i. and v.t.* to shrink into smaller space; to shorten; to make a contract; to incur, as an obligation.

contraction (kon trak' shun), *n.* a short form of something; a word shortened by omitting letters.

contradict (kon tra dikt'), *v.i. and v.t.* to reply with an opposite or contrary statement; to deny the truth of, gainsay.

Syn. Deny. To *contradict* is literally to say the opposite or contrary of something; to *deny* is to declare or reject as untrue.

contradictory (kon tra dik' tō ri), *adj.* not in agreement, inconsistent, as statements or views; presented in denial, as *contradictory* evidence; habitually contrary, as a *contradictory* pupil.

contradistinction (kon tra dis tingk' shun), *n.* differentiation by contrasting qualities.

***contrariety** (kon tra rī' e ti), *n.* variance.

***contrary** (kon' trer i), *n.* one of two opposite things, beliefs or conditions, as to assert the *contrary*.

contrary (kon' trer i), *adj.* opposite or different in meaning or effect; against, as *contrary* to orders; opposing, unfavorable.

contrast (kon' trast), *n.* a striking difference, dissimilitude; a person or thing strikingly different from another.

***contrast** (kon trast'), *v.i. and v.t.* to show difference, as black *contrasts* with white; to bring together so as to show difference.

contravene (kon tra vēn'), *v.t.* to infringe, violate, as a law; to oppose.

contribute (kon trib' ut), *v.i. and v.t.* to give something to a common cause or fund, as personal effort or money; to write for a periodical publication; to share in producing a result.

contribution (kon tri bū' shun), *n.* the act of contributing, or that which is contributed, as work, money, an article in a newspaper.

***contrite** (kon' trit), *adj.* penitent, thoroughly sorry.

contrition (kon trish' un), *n.* repentence; regret for fault or error.

contrivance (kon triv' ans), *n.* a device or invention; a scheme or plot.

contrive (kon triv'), *v.i. and v.t.* to plot, scheme; to devise, invent.

control (kon trōl'), *n.* the act or power of regulating, guiding or restraining; authority; rule or management; method of checking.

control (kon trōl'), *v.t.* to restrain, regulate, dominate; to check, as payments, costs, process in arithmetic.

***controversial** (kon trō vûr' shal), *adj.* subject to argument, disputable; contentious.

controversy (kon' trō vûr si), *n.* disputation; a clash of views or purposes, with debate and argument.

***controvert** (kon' trō vûrt), *v.t.* to oppose, as an argument or a claim, refute; to refuse, as a belief.

contumacious (kon tū mā' shus), *adj.* defiant

of authority; insubordinate, disobedient.

*contumacy (kon' tū ma si), n. insubordination, defiance.

Syn. Rebellion. *Contumacy* implies only occasional resistance; *rebellion* is systematic resistance. One engaged in acts of *contumacy* opposes the individual; one engaged in *rebellion* sets himself up against authority itself.

contumelious (kon tū mē' li us), *adj.* insolent, rude, contemptuous.

*contumely (kon' tū mē li), n. haughty and contemptuous language; insolence.

contusion (kon tū' zhun), n. a bruise, without breaking of the skin.

conundrum (kŏ nun' drum), n. a kind of riddle requiring a pun for an answer.

convalesce (kon va les'), v.i. to recover health after an illness; to improve in health.

convalescent (kon va les' ent), n. one who is recovering from illness.

convalescent (kon va les' ent), *adj.* recovering; regaining health and strength.

convalescence (kon va les' ens), n. a period of gradual recovery.

convene (kon vēn'), v.i. *and* v.t. to come together; to cause to assemble.

convenience (kon vēn' yens), n. suitability, fitness; freedom from discomfort, ease; that which gives ease and comfort or lightens labor, as domestic *conveniences*.

*convenient (kon vēn' yent), *adj.* suitable to one's circumstances or to an occasion; handy.

convent (kon' vent), n. a nunnery.

convention (kon ven' shun), n. a formal gathering of representatives of a group or profession; a meeting of political delegates; any fixed and generally accepted and followed custom.

conventional (kon ven' shun al), *adj.* in accord with general custom or a widely accepted rule.

converge (kon vûrj'), v.i. to tend toward one point.

*conversant (kon' vêr sant), *adj.* aware of; familiar with; proficient in.

conversation (kon vêr sā' shun), n. informal or familiar talk; oral discourse between persons.

Syn. Dialogue, conference, colloquy. A conversation is talk, the oral interchange of ideas or sentiments between two or more persons; a *dialogue* is confined to two persons. A *conference* is a formal exchange of opinions and advice between two or more persons. A *colloquy* is talk or conversation usually on a certain subject, as a *colloquy* on the law.

converse (kon vûrs'), v.i. to talk, take part in a conversation.

converse (kon' vûrs), *adj.* opposite, as a *converse* opinion; turned around, reversed in position or relation.

*conversely (kon vûrs' li), *adv.* on the other hand.

conversion (kon vûr' shun), n. change from one state to another, as *conversion* of coal to ashes; substitution of one thing for

another, as *conversion* of bonds into cash; a spiritual experience involving drastic change in belief.

*convert (kon' vûrt), n. one who is won over to a new belief or to a cause.

*convert (kon vûrt'), v.t. to change from one state or form to another; to persuade to allegiance to something.

convertible (kon vûr' ti bl), *adj.* capable of being converted, as heat is *convertible* into power.

convex (kon' veks), *adj.* curving outward like the outside of a globe: opposite of *concave*.

convey (kon vā'), v.t. to carry from one place to another, as a railroad train *conveys* freight and passengers; to impart, as an idea; to transfer, as a title to property.

conveyance (kon vā' ans), n. any vehicle in which persons or things are carried; a transfer of property ownership.

convict (kon' vikt), n. one who has been adjudged guilty of crime and sentenced.

convict (kon vikt'), v.t. to find guilty, as of a crime.

conviction (kon vik' shun), n. the act of convicting; state of being found guilty or of being convinced; strong belief.

convince (kon vins'), v.t. to cause to believe; to satisfy by evidence or persuade by argument.

convivial (kon viv' ial), *adj.* pertaining to a feast, festive; given to fellowship, gay.

convocation (kon vō kā' shun), n. the act of calling an assembly together; an assembly of clergymen.

convolution (kon vō lū' shun), n. the state of being wrapped or wound together; a fold in a surface, as of the brain.

convoy (kon voi '), v.t. to accompany, escort, usually for protection.

convulse (kon vuls'), v.t. to agitate violently, shake, as with spasms.

convulsion (kon vul' shun), n. agitation; an upheaval, as by a volcano; a muscular spasm.

coo (kŏŏ), n. the sound uttered by doves and pigeons, or a similar sound.

coo (kŏŏ), v.i. to make a sound like a dove or pigeon.

cook (kook), n. one who prepares food for eating.

cook (kook), v.i. *and* v.t. to prepare food with heat; to bake, boil, roast or stew, as to *cook* meat.

cookery (kook' ĕr i), n. art or practice of cooking.

cooky (kook' i), n. a small, flat, sweet cake.

cool (kōōl), *adj.* moderately cold.

cool (kōōl), n. coolness, as in the *cool* of the evening.

cool (kōōl), v.i. *and* v.t. to lose heat or ardor; to make moderately cold.

cooler (kōōl' ĕr), n. a refrigerator or a receptacle in which anything is kept cool.

coolie (kōōl' i), n. in the Far East, an unskilled laborer.

coon (kōōn), n. a raccoon.

coop (kōōp), n. a pen or enclosure, especially

for chickens; *v.t.* to put in coop or cage.

cooped up (kōōpt up), confined.

cooper (kōōp' ẽr), *n.* one who makes and repairs barrels and casks.

cooperage (kōōp' ẽr ij), *n.* a barrel factory.

***co-operate** (kō op' ẽr āt), *v.i.* to work or act together, as for a common purpose.

co-operation (kō op ẽr ā' shun), *n.* the act of working jointly; helpfulness.

***co-operative** (kō op' ẽr ā tiv), *n.* an organization of producers and sellers for mutual benefit in marketing.

co-operative (kō op' ẽr ā tiv), *adj.* working together; helpful.

co-ordinate (kō ôr' din āt), *v.t.* to place in the same class or order; to bring to harmonized action, as to *co-ordinate* eye and hand.

co-ordinate (kō ôr' din āt), *adj.* having the same rank or authority.

coot (kōōt), *n.* a certain short-tailed water bird of the rail family.

cope (kōp), *n.* a cape or cloak worn by priests.

cope (kōp), *v.i.* to strive or contend.

coping (kōp' ing), *n.* the layer of masonry capping or topping a wall.

copious (kō' pi us), *adj.* abundant, plentiful.

copper (kop' ẽr), *n.* a reddish, workable metal, used especially to conduct electricity.

copperhead (kop' ẽr hed), *n.* a venomous snake of the eastern U. S.

copra (kop' ra), *n.* the dried pulp of the coconut, from which coconut oil is obtained.

***copse** (kops), *n.* a thicket, as of trees and bushes, a coppice.

copy (kop' i), *n.* a reproduction, as of a text or a picture; one of many things made from one original, as a *copy* of a book.

copy (kop' i), *v.t.* to reproduce; to transcribe; to imitate.

copyright (kop' i rīt), *n.* the exclusive right, usually held by an author, artist or publisher, to reproduce, publish or sell for a number of years, a book or work of art.

***coquet** or **coquette** (kō ket'), *v.i.* to flirt or trifle, as with love.

coquetry (kō' ket ri), *n.* flirting or trifling.

coquette (kō ket'), *n.* a flirt, especially a woman who seeks to win a man's attention without intention of any return of affection.

***coral** (kor' al), *n.* the calcareous skeletons of certain marine animals, found in many shapes in tropical seas, including coral islands; the bright red color of some of these animals.

cord (kôrd), *n.* a string; something like string, as the spinal *cord;* a binding influence, as the *cords* of love; a stack of firewood, four feet by four by eight.

cordage (kôr' dij), *n.* cords collectively, especially the ropes used in rigging a ship.

cordate (kôr' dat), *adj.* heart-shaped.

cordial (kôr' jal), *n.* an aromatic, sweetened spirituous liquor.

cordial (kôr' jal), *adj.* hearty, sincere.

cordiality (kôr jal' i ti), *n.* heartiness; warm friendliness.

cordon (kôr' don), *n.* a cord or ribbon worn as the sign of membership in an order or

honorary society; an extended line of troops, forts or ships; a line or circle of persons, as a *cordon* of bandits.

corduroy (kôr' du roi), *n.* a thick, ribbed, durable cloth; a road made of logs laid crosswise.

core (kōr), *n.* the heart or innermost part of anything, as an apple or a mystery.

core (kōr), *v.t.* to remove the core from.

coreopsis (kō rē op' sis), *n.* a plant of the aster family with daisylike, brightly colored flowers.

corespondent (kō re spon' dent), *n.* a joint defendant, especially in a divorce suit.

cork (kôrk), *n.* the light and porous bark of the cork oak tree; a stopper for a bottle, commonly made of cork.

corn (kôrn), *n.* any cereal grain, especially maize; a hard and painful callus on the toe.

corn (kôrn), *v.t.* to preserve in brine, as beef.

corn borer (kôrn bôr' ẽr), a larva that eats the ear and stalks of growing corn.

corncob (kôrn' kob), *n.* the hard, woody center of an ear of corn; a smoking pipe.

cornflower (kôrn' flow ẽr), *n.* a plant, *Centaurea cyanus,* with white, pink, or blue flowers: also called *bachelor's-button.*

cornea (kôr' nē a), *n.* the transparent membrane of the eyeball.

corner (kôr' nẽr), *n.* the point at which two lines or surfaces meet, an angle; the intersection of two streets; a monopoly of a commodity, as wheat, formed by speculators to force the price up.

corner (kôr' nẽr), *v.t.* to put or drive into a corner, as to *corner* a rat; to force into a difficult position, as in an argument; to obtain control of stocks or commodities and compel buyers to pay the price demanded by the manipulators.

cornerstone (kôr' nẽr stōn), *n.* a stone at the corner of two walls; especially such a stone set in place with ceremony, and holding papers commemorating the occasion; any act or event of prime importance, as the signing of the Declaration of Independence is a *cornerstone* in American history.

cornet (kôr' net or kôr net'), *n.* a small brass-wind instrument resembling a trumpet.

cornice (kôr' nis), *n.* the highest or crowning course of a wall.

cornstarch (kôrn' stärch), *n.* starch made from Indian corn.

***corolla** (kō rol' a), *n.* the inner envelope of a flower around the sporophylls; all the petals of a flower, regarded collectively.

***corollary** (kor' o ler i), *n.* an additional deduction from a demonstrated proposition; a proposition following inevitably from one already proved.

corona (kō rō' na), *n.* a crownlike object; the flat projecting part of a cornice; a halo surrounding a heavenly body.

coronation (kor ō nā' shun), *n.* the ceremonial act of crowning a sovereign.

coroner (kor' ō nẽr), *n.* an officer who inquires into cases of sudden or accidental death by holding an inquest before a jury.

***coronet** (kor' ō net), *n.* a small crown worn

by nobles.

corporal (kôr′ pō ral), *n.* the lowest noncommissioned officer in a company, leading a squad of eight men.

corporal (kôr′ pō ral), *adj.* pertaining to the body, as *corporal* punishment.

corporate (kôr′ pō rit), *adj.* legally associated for transaction of business; incorporated.

corporation (kôr pō rā′ shun), *n.* a legally formed business company.

corporeal (kôr pō′ rē al), *adj.* possessing a physical body.

*****corps** (kôr), *n.* a body of men in a common service; two divisions of an army and auxiliary troops.

corpse (kôrps), *n.* a dead body: commonly with reference to a human body.

corpulence (kôr′ pū lens), *n.* excessive fatness or fleshiness.

*****corpuscle** (kôr′ pus l), *n.* a minute particle of matter; a cell of protoplasm in the blood or lymph.

*****corral** (ko ral′), *n.* a fenced enclosure for livestock.

correct (ko rekt′), *v.t.* to make right; to remove errors from, as to *correct* a manuscript; to reprove, as to *correct* a child; to amend, as to *correct* a bad habit.

correct (ko rekt′), *adj.* right, lacking fault or error; exact, accurate; proper, as *correct* behavior.

Syn. Accurate, exact. *Correct* means without fault according to a standard, as *correct* speech, a *correct* form of greeting. *Accurate* implies careful conformity to fact or truth, as an *accurate* account of what happened. *Exact* implies the very strictest conformity to fact or truth, as to quote the *exact* lines of a poem.

correction (ko rek′ shun), *n.* the act of setting right; an act of discipline.

corrective (ko rek′ tiv), *adj.* tending to set things right.

*****correlate** (kôr′ e lāt), *v.i. and v.t.* to have reciprocal relation; to bring into systematic relation, as to *correlate* physical and intellectual training.

*****correlative** (ko rel′ a tiv), *n.* one of two or more things in relationship; one of two words that are incomplete unless associated, as *if* and *then*, *whether* and *or*.

correspond (kor ē spond′), *v.i.* to be adequate or fit, as the donation *corresponds* to the need; to agree or match, as his appearance *corresponds* to your description of him; to communicate by exchange of letters.

Syn. Answer, suit. Things that *correspond* must be alike in size, shape, color and every minute particular; those that *answer* must be fitted for the same purpose; those that *suit* must have nothing disproportionate or discordant. In the moral application, actions are said not to *correspond* with professions; the success of an undertaking does not *answer* the expectation; particular measures do not *suit* the purpose of individuals.

correspondent (kor ē spon′ dent), *n.* one who writes letters, or sends news regularly to a

periodical.

*****corridor** (kor′ i dor), *n.* a passage or hallway in a building, with rooms opening off from it.

corroborate (ko rob′ ō rāt), *v.t.* to confirm, make certain.

corrode (ko rōd′), *v.i. and v.t.* to become worn or eaten away gradually; to wear away, eat away, as by chemical process.

corrosion (ko rō′ zhun), *n.* the process of being worn away, as metal by rust or morals by decay; the result of such a process, as rust is a *corrosion*, moral *corrosion*.

*****corrosive** (ko rō′ siv), *n.* that which causes corrosion.

*****corrosive** (ko rō′ siv), *adj.* eating away, wearing away, corroding.

*****corrugate** (kor′ ū gāt), *v.t.* to form in wrinkles or folds.

corrupt (ko rupt′), *v.i. and v.t.* to become rotten or putrid; to induce decay in something originally clean and sound; to deprave.

corruption (ko rup′ shun), *n.* decay; contamination; impurity.

*****corsage** (kôr säzh′), *n.* a bunch of flowers to be worn on a woman's dress, usually at the waist or shoulder.

corset (kôr′ set), *n.* a stiff, hooked or laced undergarment worn by women, covering the waist and hips.

cortex (kôr′ teks), *n.* bark; the outer layer of gray matter of the brain.

corundum (kō run′ dum), *n.* a mineral next to the diamond in hardness, designated by color, as ruby, sapphire, emerald, amethyst, topaz.

cosmetics (koz met′ iks), *n. pl.* creams, powders and the like, used for beautifying the skin or hair.

*****cosmic** (koz′ mik), *adj.* pertaining to the universe and the laws that govern it; vast and orderly, completely systematic.

cosmonaut (koz ′ mō nôt), *n.* a person trained to travel in outer space.

cosmopolitan (koz mō pol′ i tan), *n.* a citizen of the world; one who is at home anywhere.

cosmos (koz′ mos), *n.* the universe as a system: opposite of *chaos;* order, harmony.

cost (kost), *n.* the price paid for a thing, as money or work and suffering; loss, as at the *cost* of a limb.

Syn. Price, charge. The *cost* is what is actually paid for anything; the *price* is that which is asked in exchange for articles; the *charge* is that which is asked in exchange for services.

cost (kost), *v.i. and v.t.* to have a price; to be bought or sold for a certain price; to cause expenditure either in money or in other values.

costal (kos′ tal), *adj.* pertaining to the ribs.

costive (kos′ tiv), *adj.* constipated.

*****costume** (kos′ tūm), *n.* dress in general; clothing worn at one time; the special dress of a period, people or class; a masquerade outfit.

cot (kot), *n.* a cottage; a light, movable bed.

*cote (kōt), *n.* a shelter for sheep or doves.

*coterie (kō' te rĭ), *n.* a select clique or congenial social group.

cottage (kot' ĭj), *n.* a small dwelling; a small suburban or country house.

cotton (kot' n), *n.* a plant bearing seeds enclosed in a soft fibrous ball of hairy material from which a cloth is made; the cloth made from cotton bolls.

couch (kouch), *n.* a piece of furniture, a sofa or lounge, used for sleeping.

*cougar (kōō' gẽr), *n.* a large wild animal of the cat family native to the American continents: also called *catamount, puma, panther, mountain lion.*

cough (kof), *n.* a sudden expulsion of the breath with a characteristic vocal sound; this act and sound repeated incessantly as a symptom of disease.

could (kood), *auxiliary v.* [past tense of *can*] was able to, as he *could* sing when he was young; should be or would be able to, as he *could* sing if he were taught, how *could* you do such a thing to a friend.

coulee (kōō' lĭ), *n.* a deep dry gulch with steep sides.

council (koun' sĭl), *n.* a group of persons assembled for consultation; the administrative or legislative body of a town or city government or of an institution.

counsel (koun' sel), *n.* advice; a lawyer hired to give legal advice or argue a case for his client, or the lawyers collectively on one side of a case.

counsel (koun' sel), *v.i. and v.t.* to give advice or advise; to recommend, as a course of action.

count (kount), *n.* a reckoning; the number found by counting; an item in an indictment, as to be indicted on three *counts;* a European nobleman of a certain rank.

count (kount), *v.i. and v.t.* to reckon by units in order to find a total; to name the numerals in proper order; to matter, play a part, as your vote will *count.*

countenance (koun' tē nans), *n.* the face, especially the expression of the face; favor, approval, as to give *countenance* to an act.

countenance (koun' tē nans), *v.t.* to approve.

counter (koun' tẽr), *n.* one who counts; something used for counting; a table on which goods are shown in a shop.

counter (koun' tẽr), *adj.* adverse, contrary.

counterfeit (koun' tẽr fĭt), *v.t. and v.i.* to imitate in order to deceive, to forge, as to *counterfeit* money or a signature; to make fraudulent imitations, especially of money.

counterpane (koun' tẽr pān), *n.* a bed coverlet.

counterpart (koun' tẽr pärt), *n.* a closely corresponding or matching part or thing.

countersign (koun' tẽr sĭn), *n.* a watchword.

*countersign (koun´ tẽr sīn), *v.t.* to add a second person's signature to the first, as on a business paper to authenticate or confirm it.

countess (koun' tes), *n.* the wife of an earl or count.

countless (kount' les), *adj.* innumerable, too many to be counted.

country (kun' trĭ), *n.* the territory of a nation; a region, as farming *country;* the rural sections, in contrast to towns and cities.

county (koun' tĭ), *n.* a political subdivision of a state with a government of its own inferior to that of the state but with some powers over municipalities within it.

coup (kōō), *n.* a blow; a sudden brilliant move or act.

*coupé (kōō pā'), *n.* a four-wheeled two-seated closed carriage; a closed motor car smaller than a sedan or coach, with two doors and a single seat.

couple (kup' l), *n.* two of the same kind; a pair; a man and woman considered together, especially married, paired as in dancing or engaged.

couple (kup' l), *v.t.* to join two things together, as to *couple* railroad cars.

couplet (kup´ let), *n.* two consecutive rhyming lines of verse.

*coupon (kōō' pon), *n.* a part of a printed sheet of paper to be torn off, filled in and used in sending an order or for some similar purpose; a detachable certificate on a bond.

courage (kûr' ĭj), *n.* fearlessness; valor.

courageous (ku rā' jus), *adj.* brave, fearless

*courier (koor' ĭer), *n.* a special messenger.

course (kōrs), *n.* the line followed by an object in motion, as the *course* of a river or a comet; career; the part of a meal served at one time; a layer of brick or blocks in masonry; the ground traversed in a race or in certain games, as golf; a series, as of lectures or lessons, as a *course* in French, a series of acts or events, as the *course* of a life; a method, as a certain *course* of action.

court (kōrt), *n.* a hall of justice where accused persons are tried; the residence of a king or other noble; a level plot for games like tennis; a yard surrounded by walls homage, as to pay *court* to a sovereign.

court (kōrt), *v.t.* to woo; to seek to attract win, as to court favors, *court* disaster.

*courteous (kûr' tē us), *adj.* polite, formally well-mannered.

*courtesy (kûr' te sĭ), *n.* formal politeness favor instead of right, as in the bestowal of honors, as to hold a title by *courtesy.*

courtly (kōrt' lĭ), *adj.* refined, elegant.

court-martial (kōrt´ mär´ shal), *n.* court composed of army or navy officers to try cases of offense against the laws of the service.

courtship (kōrt' ship), *n.* the process or time of wooing.

*cousin (kuz' n), *n.* the son or daughter of one's uncle or aunt.

cove (kōv), *n.* a small sheltered inlet or bay.

covenant (kuv' e nant), *n.* an agreement formally made.

cover (kuv' ẽr), *n.* that which rests over anything or enwraps it; a lid; concealment, as under *cover* of darkness; underbrush in which game hides.

cover (kuv' ẽr), *v.i. and v.t.* to overspread; to enwrap; to put a lid or cover on; to hide;

to go over completely.

coverage (kuv' ẽr ĭj), *n.* in business, complete arrangements for a deal of protection as by insurance.

covert (kuv' ẽrt), *n.* a thicket, a hiding place for game.

covert (kuv' ẽrt), *adj.* hidden, concealed; furtive.

covet (kuv' et), *v.t.* to desire enviously that which belongs to another.

*covey** (kuv' ĭ), *n.* a small flock of birds, especially of partridges.

cow (kou), *n.* the mature female of any breed of cattle, or of certain other animals, as the elephant.

coward (kou' ẽrd), *n.* a timid, fearful person; one who lacks courage.

cower (kou' ẽr), *v.i.* to sink down, trembling with fear.

cowl (koul), *n.* a monk's hood; a cover for a chimney; the hood over the engine of an automobile.

coy (koi), *adj.* bashful, coquettishly shy.

cozy (kō' zĭ), *adj.* snug, warm and comfortable.

CPI, consumer price index.

CPU *n.* Central Processing Unit; in computer language this is one or more computer "brain" chips which process orders and information inside the computer.

crab (krab), *n.* a crustacean with flat body, ten legs, and the abdomen curled or folded under the body.

crack (krak), *n.* a chink or fissure; a sharp noise, as of something cracking; the report of a rifle.

crack (krak), *v.i. and v.t.* to break without being divided into separate parts; to split on the surface; to break or become harsh, as a voice *cracks;* to cause to make a sharp noise, as to *crack* a whip; to say cleverly, as to *crack* a joke; to *crack* up or crash.

cracker (krak' ẽr), *n.* a thin, brittle biscuit.

crackle (krak' l), *n.* a repeated rustling or snapping noise, as paper; a lacework of fine lines like little cracks in the glaze of certain pottery and chinaware, made intentionally as decoration.

crackle (krak' l), *v.i. and v.t.* to become covered with a network of fine fissures, as chinaware; to make repeated snapping, rustling sounds, as a fire or a paper; to cause something, as a sheet of paper, to make such sounds.

cradle (krā' dl), *n.* a baby's bed on rockers; a wooden or iron framework for holding a ship; a frame attached to a scythe to catch the grain as it is cut; a frame on rockers in which earth is washed for ore.

craft (kráft), *n.* cunning; guile; manual skill; a trade in which manual and mechanical skill are needed; a ship or airship.

cramp (kramp), *n.* an iron bar, bent at the ends, to brace blocks of stone or timbers; a tool with a tightening screw to hold things together; a painful tightening of a muscle.

cramp (kramp), *v.i. and v.t.* to contract painfully, as muscles; to fasten or hold with a clamping device; to restrain, hamper.

cranberry (kran' ber ĭ), *n.* the tart red berry of a plant that grows in bogs.

crane (krān), *n.* a long-legged, long-necked wading bird; a machine on wheels that moves a load vertically or horizontally; a traveling horizontal beam with a hoist; a metal arm on which cooking vessels are supported in a fireplace.

crane (krān), *v.i. and v.t.* to stretch out the neck, as a crane.

cranial (krān' ĭ al), *adj.* pertaining to the cranium or skull.

cranium (krā' nĭ um), *n.* the skull.

crank (krangk), *n.* a device for turning rotary motion into back-and-forth motion, or vice-versa; a bent handle, fixed or detachable, for turning things, as the *crank* of an automobile engine; a crotchety person; one who is almost fanatically absorbed in an idea.

cranky (krangk' ĭ), *n.* crotchety, cross; easily upset, as a boat.

cranny (kran'ĭ), *n.* a crack, as in a wall.

crape (krāp), *n.* a crinkly fabric of wool, silk or cotton; a piece of black crape used to symbolize mourning.

crash (krash), *n.* a smashing noise or the sound of large bodies in collision; a collision; complete failure of a business enterprise; a big break in the stock market; a coarse linen fabric.

crash (krash), *v.i. and v.t.* to collide; to sound with a great noise; to come down out of control and smash on the ground, as an airplane; to fail in business; to force noisily.

*crass** (kras), *adj.* dull, stupid; gross, coarse.

crate (krāt), *n.* a wickerwork hamper; a box made of slats with open spaces between.

crate (krāt), *v.t.* to pack, as for shipment, in a crate.

crater (krā' tẽr), *n.* the opening of a volcano.

*cravat** (kra vat'), *n.* a neckcloth, a necktie.

crave (krāv), *v.t.* to desire greatly, long for; to beg, as to *crave* a favor; to need.

craven (krā' ven), *n.* a coward.

craven (krā' ven), *adj.* cowardly, base.

craw (krô), *n.* a bird's crop.

crawl (krôl), *n.* a creeping motion; a swimming stroke.

crayfish (krā' fĭsh), *n.* a small freshwater shellfish resembling a lobster.

*crayon** (krā' on), *n.* a stick or pencil of charcoal or colored chalk, used in drawing; a drawing made with crayon.

craze (krāz), *n.* a flaw in the glaze of pottery; a fad, as the *craze* for antiques.

creak (krēk), *n.* a harsh sound like that of a rusty hinge.

creak (krēk), *v.i.* to make a squeaky sound like unoiled parts of a working machine.

cream (krēm), *n.* the rich, oily part of milk; the best of anything, as *cream* of the crop.

cream (krēm), *v.i. and v.t.* to turn into cream; to skim cream from or put cream in; to make creamy.

creamery (krēm' ẽr ĭ), *n.* a place where cream

and butter are kept or sold, or where butter and cheese are made.

creamy (krēm' i), *adj.* like cream, rich in cream.

crease (krēs), *n.* a mark made by wrinkling or folding.

crease (krēs), *v.i. and v.t.* to become marked by wrinkles or folds; to put a crease in.

create (krē āt'), *v.t.* to bring into existence.

creation (krē ā' shun), *n.* the act of creating or that which is created; the universe.

creator (krē ā' tēr), *n.* one who creates: *the Creator,* God.

*****creature** (krē' tūr), *n.* anything created, especially an animal.

*****credence** (krē' dens), *n.* belief, faith, trust.

credentials (krē den' shalz), *n. pl.* business references or recommendations; government papers attesting the authority of one appointed to a diplomatic position.

*****credible** (kred' i bl), *adj.* believable.

credit (kred' it), *n.* an item in an account in one's favor; time allowed for payment of a debt; deposits in a bank against which one may draw; the amount to which a person or firm can borrow; one who adds to the standing of some one or something, as Tom is a *credit* to his teacher and his college.

credit (kred' it), *v.t.* to believe, as to *credit* a story; to attribute to, as I *credit* you with intelligence; to give credit for.

credulity (krē dū' li ti), *n.* ready trust or belief.

*****credulous** (kred' ū lus), *adj.* inclined to trust or believe too easily; easily deceived.

creed (krēd), *n.* a brief authoritative statement of religious faith; any confession of religious belief.

*****creek** (krēk), *n.* a stream smaller than a river; an inlet from the sea.

creep (krēp), *v.i.* to crawl; to grow along a surface, as a vine.

*****cremate** (krē' māt), *v.t.* to burn to ashes, as a dead body.

*****crematory** (krē' ma tō ri), *n.* a place where the dead are cremated.

*****creosote** (krē' ō sōt), *n.* a heavy oily liquid distilled from wood tar, having a smoky smell and used as an antiseptic and to preserve wood.

crescent (kres' ent), *n.* the new moon, or something shaped like it.

crest (krest), *n.* the comb of a fowl; a tuft of feathers on a bird's head; the ridge of a mountain or wave; a coat of arms.

crestfallen (krest' fôl en), *adj.* dejected, dispirited.

*****cretaceous** (krē tā' shus), *adj.* like chalk or full of chalk.

*****cretonne** (krē ton'), *n.* a cotton fabric with printed colored patterns.

*****crevasse** (kre vas'), *n.* a deep fissure in a glacier.

crevice (krev' is), *n.* crack, a narrow opening caused by a split.

crew (krōō), *n.* a ship's company; a group of men working together on a job; rowing as a college sport, as to go out for *crew;* the oarsmen and coxswain of a racing shell.

crib (krib), *n.* a child's bed with high sides; rack or manger for horses and cattle; a slat-sided storage bin for corn; a frame of timber to prevent a cave-in; a translation, as of a foreign text, used to aid study.

crib (krib), *v.i. and v.t.* to plagiarize; to put into a crib, as to *crib* grain; to equip with cribbing, as a mine.

cribbage (krib' ij), *n.* a card game consisting of skill in securing number combinations, scored by pegs in a board.

cricket (krik' et), *n.* a small, leaping insect noted for the shrill chirping sound made by the males when they rub together parts of the forewings; a game.

crime (krīm), *n.* an act that violates the law

Syn. Vice, sin. A *crime* is a social offense; a *vice* is a personal offense; every action which does injury to others, either individually or collectively, is a *crime;* that which does injury to ourselves is a *vice.* *Crime* consists in a violation of human laws; *vice* is a violation of the moral law; *sin* is a violation of the divine law.

criminal (krim' i nal), *n.* one who commits crime; *adj.* having to do with crime.

crimp (krimp), *v.t.* to bend or twist into ridges and folds, as hair.

crimson (krim' zn), *n.* a deep red color; also any of various colors shading from red to purplish red.

cringe (krinj), *v.i.* to bend or crouch from fear or in servility; to flinch, as from pain.

cripple (krip' l), *n.* a lame or partially disabled person.

crisis (krī' sis), *n.* a turning point; a point in illness at which the patient becomes definitely better or worse; an emergency.

crisp (krisp), *n.* a state of crispness, as to bring to a *crisp; adj.* brittle; terse, curt.

crisp (krisp), *v.i. and v.t.* to come or bring to a crisp, as this bacon is nicely *crisped.*

crisscross (kris' krôs), *adj.* intersecting.

criterion (krī tēr' i un), *n.* a standard of criticism or judgment.

Syn. Standard. The *criterion* is employed only in matters of judgment; the *standard* is used in the ordinary concerns of life. The former serves for determining the characters and qualities of things; the latter for defining quantity and measure.

critic (krit' ik), *n.* one who analyzes things and forms a judgment on their value.

critical (krit' i kal), *adj.* having to do with critics or criticism; given to analysis; quick to find fault; of the nature of a crisis, as the *critical* moment.

criticism (krit' i sizm), *n.* the art of analyzing and estimating worth, as of literature or art; an unfavorable comment or faultfinding.

criticize (krit' i sīz), *v.t.* to examine sharply and form a judgment; to find fault.

croak (krōk), *n.* a deep, hoarse throaty sound like that made by a raven or frog.

*****crochet** (krō shā'), *v.i. and v.t.* to knit with one hooked needle.

crock (krok), *n.* an earthen jar; coloring matter that rubs off from dyed goods; soot on a kettle; a broken down horse.

crockery (krok' ẽr i), *n.* earthenware.

crocodile (krok' ō dīl), *n.* a large long-tailed amphibian reptile having a long head and pointed snout, native to Africa, Asia, Australia and the Americas.

crocus (krō' kus), *n.* a flowering bulbous plant of the iris family.

crone (krōn), *n.* an age-withered old woman.

crony (krō' ni), *n.* a pal, chum, close friend.

crook (krook), *n.* a shepherd's bent staff; a professional criminal; a bend, as the *crook* of the knee; *v.t.* to bend, as the elbow.

croon (krōōn), *v.i. and v.t.* to sing softly or plaintively.

crop (krop), *n.* a season's production of any growing thing, a harvest; a bird's craw; a riding whip with a leather loop.

crop (krop), *v.i. and v.t.* to reap or gather from the fields; to plant seeds for a later yield; to cut an animal's hair, ears or tail short; to graze; to appear unexpectedly.

croquet (krō kā'), *n.* a lawn game played with wooden balls and mallets.

croquette (krō ket'), *n.* a fried ball or cake of previously cooked minced food.

cross (krôs), *n.* an ancient instrument of punishment consisting of an upright stake with a crosspiece, to which a person was fastened and left to die : *the Cross,* the cross on which Christ was crucified; any representation of this; a crucifix; a badge or ornament in the shape of a cross; the intersection of two straight lines; a mixing of breeds or varieties, as of animals or plants.

cross (krôs), *v.i. and v.t.* to intersect, as two roads *cross;* to move or pass from one side to the other, as to *cross* over a brook; to interbreed; to make the sign of the cross upon, as to *cross* oneself; to lay athwart, as to *cross* one's fingers; to lie athwart, as railroads *cross* the continent; to travel over, as to *cross* the ocean, *cross* the continent; to intersect, as 5th Ave. *crosses* 42d St.; to cause to interbreed, as plants or animals.

cross (krôs), *adj.* crossing, as a *cross* street; contrary, as *cross* purposes; crotchety, peevish.

crosscut (krôs' kut), *adj.* used to cut across the grain, as a *crosscut* saw.

cross-examine (krôs eg zam' in), *v.t.* to question a witness with the purpose of revealing flaws in previous testimony.

cross-grained (krôs grānd'), *adj.* having an irregular grain or fiber, and hard to cut.

crosswise (krôs' wīz), *adv.* in the form of a cross; athwart.

crossword puzzle (krôs' wûrd puz' l), an arrangement of black and white squares in which letters are to be written making words that fill in the vertical and horizontal squares, crossing each other, definitions of the words to be guessed furnishing the clues to the letters to put in the squares.

crotch (kroch), *n.* a forking into two parts.

*****crotchety** (kroch' e ti), *adj.* whimsical; eccentric.

*****crouch** (krouch), *v.i.* to stoop low or cower, as in fear, or as an animal about to spring.

croup (krōōp), *n.* a disease of the throat, with painful coughing.

crow (krō), *n.* a large glossy black bird; the cry of the cock; a crowbar.

crow (krō), *v.i.* to make the loud, shrill cry of the cock; to brag, boast, exult noisily.

crowbar (krō' bär), *n.* an iron bar, wedge-shaped at one end, used as a pry or lever, to move heavy objects.

crowd (kroud), *n.* a number of persons or things collected in small space.

crowd (kroud), *v.i. and v.t.* to collect in large numbers; to shove or push; to squeeze something into small space.

crown (kroun), *n.* a royal headdress, symbol of sovereignty; top of the head; something like a crown, as the *crown* of a hill.

crown (kroun), *v.t.* to place a crown on the head of; to top off, furnish a finishing part.

crow's-foot (krōz' foot), *n.* a wrinkle around the eye; a decorative element shaped like a bird's footprint.

crow's-nest (krōz' nest), *n.* a lookout on the mast of a vessel.

CRT, cathode ray tube.

*****crucial** (krōō' shal), *adj.* cross-shaped; decisive, as a *crucial* moment.

crucible (krōō' si bl), *n.* a pot of earthenware in which metals and ores are melted.

crucifix (krōō' si fiks), *n.* a representation of Christ on the Cross.

crucifixion (krōō si fik' shun), *n.* the act of crucifying or being crucified : *Crucifixion,* the execution of Christ.

crucify (krōō' si fi), *v.t.* to put to death by hanging on a cross.

crude (krōōd), *adj.* in a natural state, as *crude* oil; bare, undisguised, as the *crude* facts; tactless, ungraceful, rude.

crudity (krōō' di ti), *n.* crudeness; rawness; a crude saying or action.

*****cruel** (krōō' el), *adj.* without mercy or pity; ready to give pain to others.

    Syn. Brutal, inhuman, savage. A person is *cruel* who is indifferent to the suffering of others or who takes pleasure in inflicting or beholding pain and suffering; he is *inhuman* if he withholds the common manifestations of tenderness and kindness; he is *brutal* or *savage* according to the manner in which he performs cruel acts.

cruelty (krōō' el ti), *n.* the state of being cruel, ruthlessness; a cruel act.

cruet (krōō' et), *n.* a small bottle for holding seasonings and relishes for table use; a caster.

cruise (krōōz), *n.* a voyage with no set destination.

cruise (krōōz), *v.i.* to sail about with no set destination, or touching at coastwise ports.

cruiser (krōōz' ẽr), *n.* a warship less heavily armed and faster than a battleship.

crumb (krum), *n.* a little piece, a mere fragment, as *crumbs* of bread, *crumbs* of hope.

crumble (krum' bl), *v.i. and v.t.* to break into small pieces or crumbs.

crumple (krum' pl), *v.i. and v.t.* to press into wrinkles, rumple.

crunch (krunch), *v.t.* to crush and chew with

the teeth; to press through with noise, as wheels *crunch* through snow.

crusade (krŏŏ sād′), *n.* one of the seven medieval expeditions to the Holy Land to take it from the Mohammedans; any enthusiastic undertaking, as for reform.

*****cruse** (krŏŏs), *n.* an earthen pot or dish; a vessel to hold water or oil.

crush (krush), *n.* a crowd causing pressure.

crush (krush), *v.t.* to press between two hard bodies; to squeeze out of shape.

crust (krust), *n.* the crisp outside of a loaf of bread; a dry piece of bread; the covering of a pie; the hard frozen surface of snow.

crust (krust), *v.i. and v.t.* to form into a crust; to encrust.

*****crustacean** (krus tā′ shun), *n.* a class of animals, usually aquatic, having a horny, crust-like shell, as barnacles, crabs, lobsters, shrimps and wood lice.

crusty (krus′ tl), *adj.* crisp, like a crust; having a crust.

crutch (kruch), *n.* a staff with a crosspiece at the top to fit under the arm, to help cripples in walking.

crux (kruks), *n.* a cross; anything difficult to explain; an important or critical point.

cry (krī), *n.* a loud call or utterance expressing fear, joy, surprise, pain or prayer; a prayer or appeal; an announcement or proclamation; public opinion expressed; the characteristic sound of a bird or animal; a weeping spell.

cry (krī), *v.i. and v.t.* to weep, shed tears; to make a loud call, as in prayer, pain, fear, anger or joy; to shout, proclaim.

crying (krī′ ing), *adj.* demanding notice, as a *crying* injustice.

crypt (kript), *n.* a subterranean cell or vault.

cryptic (krip′ tik), *adj.* hidden, secret, mysterious.

*****cryptogram** (krip′ tō gram), *n.* something written in cipher.

crystal (kris′ tal), *n.* transparent quartz; an inorganic body having plane surfaces that give it a certain geometrical form, as a snow *crystal*, a *crystal* of salt.

crystal (kris′ tal), *adj.* consisting of crystals; resembling a crystal; clear.

crystallize (kris′ tal īz), *v.i. and v.t.* to form in or into crystals.

cub (kub), *n.* a young fox, bear, wolf, lion.

cube (kūb), *n.* a solid body with six equal square faces or sides; the third power of a number.

cubic (kūb′ ik), *adj.* having the form of a cube; calculated or measured by cube-shaped units.

cubit (kūb′ it), *n.* an ancient linear measure of about 18 inches.

cuboid (kū′ boid), *adj.* approximately cubic in shape.

*****cuckoo** (kook′ ŏŏ), *n.* a European bird noted for its unpleasant habit of depositing its eggs in another bird's nest to be hatched; the American black-billed and yellow-billed cuckoo that raise their own young; the characteristic love call of the cuckoo.

cucumber (kū′ kum bĕr), *n.* the long juicy fruit of a creeping plant cultivated as a vegetable and used in making pickles.

cud (kud), *n.* food brought back from the first stomach to the mouth of certain animals, as all cattle, sheep, goats, deer, camels and giraffes, to be chewed and swallowed again.

cudgel (kuj′ el), *n.* a short thick club.

cudgel (kuj′ el), *v.t.* to beat with a club.

cue (kū), *n.* a catchword; a billiard stick.

cuff (kuf), *n.* the folded back part of a sleeve; a band worn over the wrist, as a part of the clothing; a blow with the open hand.

cuff (kuf), *v.t.* to strike with the open hand.

*****cuisine** (kwĕ zēn′), *n.* a place where cooking is done; a style of cookery.

*****culinary** (kū′ li ne ri), *adj.* pertaining to the kitchen or to cooking, as *culinary* utensils.

cull (kul), *n.* something worthless or inferior that is to be discarded.

cull (kul), *v.t.* to pick over and pick out the unfit of, as to *cull* apples.

culminate (kul′ mi nāt), *v.i.* to reach the highest point; to come to a climax.

culpable (kul′ pa bl), *adj.* deserving blame, faulty.

culprit (kul′ prit), *n.* a guilty person; one arraigned in court.

cult (kult), *n.* a particular ritual of worship of a god or goddess, as the *cult* of Venus; the devotees of a person or an idea or an intellectual fad; a sect.

cultivate (kul′ ti vāt), *v.t.* to work, as land in raising crops; to foster the growth of by labor and care; refine, as to *cultivate* one's mind; foster, cherish, as to *cultivate* good will.

*****culture** (kul′ tūr), *n.* tillage; the training or refining of the moral or intellectual faculties: the enlightenment and refinement acquired by such training; education; all the knowledge, crafts, art, literature, beliefs and customs of a people, as Greek *culture*, primitive *culture*.

culvert (kul′ vĕrt), *n.* an arched drain of masonry under a road or railroad.

cumber (kum′ bĕr), *v.t.* to hinder; to overload.

cumbrous (kum′ brus), *adj.* burdensome, large and troublesome, as a *cumbrous* package.

cumulative (kū′ mū lā tiv), *adj.* formed or growing by additions; to be added, if not paid when due, as interest or dividends, to the principal.

cunning (kun′ ing), *n.* guile; skill.

cunning (kun′ ing), *adj.* made with skill, clever; crafty, sly; cute.

cup (kup), *n.* a small drinking vessel; anything shaped like a cup, as the *cup* of a flower.

*****cupboard** (kub′ ĕrd), *n.* a small closet with shelves.

cupidity (kū pid′ iti), *n.* greedy desire for wealth.

*****cupola** (kū′ pō la), *n.* a rounded roof; a small structure, like a room with windows on all sides, on a roof.

cur (kûr), *n.* a mongrel dog.

*****curate** (kū′ rāt), *n.* any clergyman; one who

assists a vicar or rector.

*__curator__ (kū rā' tēr), *n.* the superintendent of a museum; a custodian, guardian.

__curb__ (kûrb), *n.* anything that restrains, a check; a strap or chain increasing the pressure of the bit; a stone street edging.

__curd__ (kûrd), *n.* the coagulated part of milk, containing casein and distinguished from whey, in cheesemaking.

__curdle__ (kûr' dl), *v.i. and v.t.* to thicken; to form curds, to coagulate, thicken, as to utter a blood-*curdling* warcry.

__cure__ (kūr), *n.* the act of healing; state of being healed; that which removes disease or evil; a remedy; spiritual care, as the *cure* of souls; the official position of a parish priest or curate, or the district over which he presides.

__cure__ (kūr), *v.t.* to heal; to restore to health.

Syn. Heal, remedy. To *cure* is employed for what is out of order; to *heal* for that which is broken; diseases are *cured*, wounds are *healed*. To *remedy*, in the sense of applying remedies, has a moral application; an omission, a deficiency or a mischief can be *remedied*.

__curfew__ (kûr' fū), *n.* an order in medieval times that fires be put out at a certain evening hour at the ringing of a bell; the ringing of a bell as a signal for children to go in from the streets.

__curiosity__ (kū ri os' i ti), *n.* inquisitiveness; anything curious or rare.

__curious__ (kū' ri us), *adj.* inquisitive; eager to learn; strange, odd or rare.

__curl__ (kûrl), *n.* a spiral lock of hair; anything that curls, as a *curl* of smoke; a plant disease that causes the leaves to curl up.

__curl__ (kûrl), *v.i. and v.t.* to become curled; to form in or into curls; to form into curves and coils.

__curlew__ (kûr lū), *n.* a bird of the snipe family.

__currant__ (kûr' ant), *n.* the acid berry of several shrubs used to make jelly and jam; a small seedless raisin.

__currency__ (kûr' en si), *n.* money in circulation; the state of being current; having common or general acceptance.

__current__ (kûr' ent), *n.* the flow of anything in a stream, as the *current* of a river, a *current* of air, an electric *current*.

__current__ (kûr' ent), *adj.* prevalent, as *current* styles; circulating, as *current* rumors; now passing or happening, as the *current* year.

__curriculum__ (ku rik' ū lum), *n.* a course of study; all the courses of study given in an educational institution.

__curry__ (kûr' i), *n.* a spiced condiment from India; a stew seasoned with curry.

__curry__ (kûr' i), *v.t.* to comb, as the hair of a horse; to dress leather; to seek by flattery, as to *curry* favor.

__curse__ (kûrs), *n.* a prayer for evil; an oath; a cause of great evil.

__curse__ (kûrs), *v.i. and v.t.* to swear profanely; to invoke evil upon.

__cursory__ (kûr' sō ri), *adj.* hasty; superficial.

__curt__ (kûrt), *adj.* abrupt.

__curtail__ (kûr tāl'), *v.t.* to cut short, abridge.

__curtain__ (kûr' tin), *n.* a hanging screen, especially one that can be drawn up and let down or fastened to one side.

*__curtsy__ (kûrt' si), *n.* a bow performed by girls and women as a gesture of respect.

__curvate__ (kûr' vāt), *adj.* curved.

*__curvature__ (kûr' va tūr), *n.* a curving, as *curvature* of the spine.

__curve__ (kûrv), *n.* a bending without an angle; a curved line; in baseball, a pitched ball that curves in toward or out from the batter.

__cushion__ (koosh' un), *n.* a soft pillow or pad; a case filled with air or soft material to ease the body in sitting, kneeling, reclining; a chamber, as of ar, to reduce shock.

__cusp__ (kusp), *n.* a pointed end, as a tooth; the horn of a crescent.

__custard__ (kus' tērd), *n.* a sweetened mixture of eggs and milk, baked.

__custodian__ (kus tō' di an), *n.* a keeper, guard.

__custody__ (kus' tō di), *n.* guardianship; imprisonment.

__custom__ (kus' tum), *n.* common usage or practice: *customs*, taxes on imports to a country.

Syn. Habit, practice. *Custom* is the fact of repetition; it carries the authority of long standing and public acceptance; it stands in the place of law, and regulates the conduct of men in the most important concerns of life. *Habit* is a settled tendency to repeat a certain thing because it has been done repeatedly before. Biting one's nails is a *habit*; sending Christmas cards is a *custom*. *Practice* is the repeated doing of something or the way of doing something.

__cut__ (kut), *n.* an opening made with an edged instrument, as a knife; an excavated channel; a piece cut off, as a *cut* of meat; a sharp blow, as a *cut* of the whip; a roadway or channel made by digging; a block or plate from which a picture is printed or a picture made from it, as the book has many *cuts*; an unexcused absence from class.

__cut__ (kut), *v.i. and v.t.* to operate as an edged tool, as this saw *cuts* clean; to be easily severed, as this wood *cuts* without much trouble; to cleave or sever with an edged instrument; to cause pain, as your words *cut* him to the quick; to reduce, as to *cut* prices; to hurt, as the ridicule *cut* him.

*__cutaneous__ (kū tā' nē us), *adj.* pertaining to the skin.

__cute__ (kūt), *n.* shrewd, clever; attractive because of a certain charm, as a *cute* puppy.

__cuticle__ (ku' ti kl), *n.* the epidermis; outer layer of the skin.

__cutlery__ (kut' lēr i), *n.* edged or cutting instruments, regarded collectively.

__cutlet__ (kut' let), *n.* a slice of meat to be broiled or fried.

__cutoff__ (kut' ôf), *n.* a road that provides a short cut; a mechanism to stop the flow of steam, water or gasoline.

__cuttle fish__ (kut' l fish), *n.* a cephalopod marine mollusk, having an internal shell, an inksac and ten tentacles.

*__cyanide__ (sī' a nīd), *n.* a compound of cyanogen with an element.

__cycle__ (sī' kl), *n.* a complete series of events,

coming back to a starting point as if having completed a circle, as the *cycle* of the seasons; an age, eon; the full round of values of an alternating electric current.

cyclecar (sī' kl kär), *n.* a light three or four-wheeled vehicle of narrow gauge propelled over the highway by a motor.

*****cyclic** (sī' klik), *adj.* pertaining to or moving in cycles.

cyclone (sī' klōn), *n.* a storm with high winds that blow spirally about a calm center; a hurricane.

*****cyclopedia** (sī clō pē' di a), *n.* an encyclopedia, a brief systematic treatment of all knowledge or of one special field.

*****cygnet** (sig' net), *n.* a young swan.

cylinder (sil' in dẽr), *n.* a body, either solid or hollow, with equal circular top and bottom, as a round tin can is a *cylinder;* the piston chamber of an engine.

cylindrical (si lin' dri kal), *adj.* having the form of a cylinder.

cymbal (sim' bal), *n.* one of a pair of brass disks which when struck together produce a ringing sound.

cynic (sin' ik), *n.* one of an ancient Greek school of philosophy that first sought virtue in self-control, later vehemently decried existing social evils; hence, a sarcastic, pessimistic person.

Syn. Misanthrope, pessimist. A *cynic* is one who sneeringly professes disbelief in sincerely good motives and altruistic conduct. A *misanthrope* has dislike for his fellow men and shuns their society. A *pessimist* distrusts all seeming good.

*****cynosure** (sī' nō shoor), *n.* an object of general attention.

cypress (sī' pres), *n.* a symmetrical cone-bearing evergreen tree, or its wood.

cyst (sist), *n.* a closed sac containing fluid or viscous diseased matter.

czar (zär), *n.* formerly, an emperor of Russia.

czarina (zär ē' na), *n.* an empress of Russia, or the wife of a czar.

D

dab (dab), *n.* a soft, gentle pat; a small, soft lump or portion, as a *dab* of cold cream.

dab (dab), *v.i. and v.t.* to strike softly; to put on in spots, as to *dab* a surface with paint.

dabber (dab' ẽr), *n.* one who dabs, or something used for dabbing, as a printers' pad for applying ink to certain surfaces.

dabble (dab' l), *v.t.* to dip repeatedly; paddle or splash gently in water, as the feet or hands; to do things without earnest effort.

dace (dās), *n.* a freshwater fish.

*****dachshund** (däks' hoont), *n.* a small German hound with elongated body and short legs.

daddy longlegs (dad' i lông' legz), a cranefly, a harvestman.

dado (dā' dō), *n.* the solid block forming the body of a pedestal; the lower part of the walls of a room when finished differently from the upper part; strip of wall between baseboard and chair rail.

daffodil (daf' ō dil), *n.* species of narcissus.

daft (dȧft), *adj.* simple, silly, soft-minded.

dagger (dag' ẽr), *n.* a short pointed weapon; in printing, a reference mark [†].

*****dahlia** (dȧl' ya), *n.* a tuberous rooted plant with brilliantly colored large flowers.

daily (dā' li), *n.* a newspaper published every day.

daily (dā' li), *adj.* happening every day.

Syn. Diurnal. *Daily* is used to distinguish daytime happenings from those that occur at night; *diurnal* is used for astronomical happenings. *Daily* is the simple word; *diurnal* the more poetic.

Ant. Nocturnal.

dainty (dān' ti), *n.* something choice or delicious; a delicacy.

dainty (dān' ti), *adj.* of delicate beauty or charm; fastidious.

Syn. Delicate, exquisite. A *dainty* thing or person is slight and elegant; *delicate* implies fineness and sometimes fragility; *exquisite* carries the sense of fineness in character or workmanship.

Ant. Coarse, gross, crude.

dairy (dâr' i), *n.* a place where milk is kept, to be made into butter and cheese; place where dairy products are sold.

dairy farm (dâr' i färm), a farm on which cattle are raised for production of milk.

dairying (dâr' i ing), *n.* the business of running a dairy.

dais (dā' is), *n.* a raised platform at the end of a room or hall.

daisy (dā' zi), *n.* a plant of the aster family, having long petals like rays surrounding a colored center.

dale (dāl), *n.* a glen, a vale or valley.

dalliance (dal' i ans), *n.* trifling; flirtatious play.

dally (dal' i), *v.i.* to trifle, play, linger, fool time away.

dam (dam), *n.* a barrier across a watercourse; female parent, especially of a quadruped.

dam (dam), *v.t.* to check the flow of, with a dam, as to *dam* a stream or lake.

damage (dam' ij), *n.* injury or harm to person or property.

damages (dam' ij ez), *n.* reparation in money for loss caused or damage done.

damage (dam' ij), *v.t.* to cause damage to, injure, harm.

*****damask** (dam' ȧsk), *n.* a rich silk fabric woven with elaborate patterns; a fine figured linen used for table cloths, etc.

dame (dām), *n.* a matron, an elderly woman; in Gt. Britain, a title, for women.

damn (dam), *v.t. and v.i.* to condemn as illegal or immoral; to doom to punishment; to swear at by saying *damn;* to curse.

damnable (dam' na bl), *adj.* deserving to be damned; outrageous.

damnation (dam nā' shun), *n.* the act of damning or the state of being damned.

damp (damp), *n.* moisture; gas formed in coal mines and other underground borings.

damp (damp), *v.t.* to choke, as a fire; stifle; check, restrain, as action; to make moist.

damp (damp), *adj.* moist, humid.

dampen (damp' en), *v.t.* to make moist; depress; stifle; deaden.

damsel (dam' zel), *n.* a maiden or girl.

*****damson** (dam' zun), *n.* a small dark-purple plum, originally from Damascus.

*****dance** (dàns), *n.* a rhythmic stepping in time to the beat of music; a social gathering for dancing; music written for dancing.

dance (dàns), *v.i. and v.t.* to move rhythmically, as in time to music; cause to dance; to cause by dancing: he *danced* me off my feet.

dandelion (dan' dē li un), *n.* a plant with bright yellow flowers.

dander (dan' dēr), *n.* anger.

dandle (dan' dl), *v.t.* to fondle.

dandruff (dan' druf), *n.* scurf on the scalp, falling in scales of dead skin.

dandy (dan' di), *n.* a fop, a dude.

danger (dān' jēr), *n.* hazard, peril, risk.

Syn. Jeopardy, hazard, peril, risk. *Danger* is harm or pain in the offing; *peril* is instant danger; *jeopardy* is exposure to danger; *hazard* is chance danger that can but may not occur; *risk* is the conscious taking of an adverse chance.

dangerous (dān' jēr us), *adj.* involving risk; causing peril; to be feared.

dangle - (dan' gl), *v.i. and v.t.* to hang or swing loosely; to hang about.

dank (dangk), *adj.* unpleasantly damp.

dapper (dap' ēr), *adj.* slight, spruce and trim.

dappled (dap' ld), *adj.* colored in spots or patches, as a horse.

dare (dâr), *n.* a challenge.

dare (dâr), *v.i. and v.t.* [*p.t.* dared, durst, *p.p.* dared, *pr.p.* daring] to have enough courage to do something; to venture to do; to challenge.

daring (dâr' ing), *n.* courage; venturesomeness.

dark (därk), *n.* absence of light; nightfall.

dark (därk), *adj.* having little or no light; approaching black, as a *dark* shade of blue; wicked, as *dark* doings; gloomy, as a *dark* view of life; obscure, as a *dark* saying; unenlightened, as the *Dark* Ages.

Syn. Dim, obscure, opaque. *Dark* means partly or wholly without light in all physical and mental senses. *Dim* means not bright, as a *dim* light, or not distinct, as a page looks *dim*. *Obscure* implies not enough light or the interposition of something that shuts off light, as fog makes the view *obscure,* or big words often make one's meaning *obscure*. *Opaque* means impervious to light.

darling (där' ling), *n.* one dearly beloved; a favorite.

darn (därn), *n.* a place that has been mended with interweaving stitches.

darn (därn), *v.t.* to mend a hole in torn fabric with interlacing stitches.

dart (därt), *n.* a sharp-pointed missile, as a javelin or arrow; a short seam bringing together the edges of a fabric where a V-shaped piece has been cut out of the goods; a quick darting motion.

dart (därt), *v.i.* to move suddenly and swiftly; to shoot out suddenly, as a flame *darts*.

dash (dash), *n.* a small quantity thrown into or over anything, as a *dash* of seasoning in food; a mark of punctuation used to indicate a break in the run of a sentence (—); a short running race, as the 100-yard *dash*; spirited action, as he works with a fine *dash*.

dash (dash), *v.i. and v.t.* to rush, as to *dash* out the door; to throw with violence, as to *dash* a plate on the floor; to wreck or shatter, as hopes; to perform quickly, as to *dash* off a letter.

dastard (das' tērd), *n.* a coward; poltroon.

*****data** (dā' ta), *n.* plural of *datum*.

data base (dā' ta bâs), *n.* a collection of organized facts and information needed to perform a task.

date (dāt), *n.* the fruit of an African and Asian palm tree; the day, month and year of a happening; an engagement to meet someone at a stated time and place.

date (dāt), *v.i. and v.t.* to belong to a certain period; to put a date upon; to make an engagement with.

datum (dā' tum), *n.* [*pl.* data (dā' ta)] something accepted as a base for inference; a fact on which reasoning is based.

*****daub** (dôb), *n.* a smear; material applied by smearing, as plaster.

daub (dôb), *v.t.* to apply by smearing; to paint unskillfully.

daughter (dô' tēr), *n.* the female offspring of human parents.

*****daunt** (dônt), *v.t.* to intimidate, frighten.

*****dauntless** (dônt' les), *adj.* fearless, undismayed.

dawdle (dô' dl), *v.i.* to move slowly; waste time.

dawn (dôn), *n.* daybreak; beginning, as the *dawn* of a new era, *dawn* of an idea.

dawn (dôn), *v.i.* to begin, as the day; rise, as the sun; come to mind, as an idea.

day (dā), *n.* the period, 24 hours, of the earth's revolution on its axis; the period from dawn to sunset; a time in history, as in Washington's *day*.

daybook (dā' book), *n.* the book in which a day's transactions in a business are recorded.

daybreak (dā' brāk), *n.* the dawn.

daydream (dā' drēm), *n.* a reverie; a happy illusion.

daystar (dā' stär), *n.* the morning star; also the sun.

daze (dāz), *n.* a confused mental state.

daze (dāz), *v.t.* to stupefy, with or as with a blow, as he was *dazed* with grief.

dazzle (daz' l), *v.t.* to blind momentarily with a blaze of light.

DBMS, data base management system.

deacon (dē' kun), *n.* a church lay officer who assists a minister; a cleric ranking next below; a priest.

dead (ded), *adj.* without life, motion or activity after being alive; dull; quiet; tasteless; lusterless; not valid.

deaden (ded' en), *v.t.* to reduce the force or effect of, as to *deaden* pain.

dead letter (ded let' ẽr), an undeliverable letter lacking proper address.

deadly (ded' li), *adj.* capable of causing death.

dead weight (ded wāt), any weight like that of a lifeless body; the weight of a vehicle apart from that of its load.

deaf (def), *adj.* lacking, or deficient in the sense of hearing.

deal (dēl), *n.* an act of buying and selling; the process, in card games, of handing cards to the players; a single round of a card game.

deal (dēl), *v.i. and v.t.* to have relations, do business; be concerned or engaged, as to *deal* in real estate; to conduct oneself, as he *dealt* kindly with the prisoner; to hand out one by one, as cards; to administer.

dean (dēn), *n.* the head of a chapter of church canons; a member of a college faculty with administrative duties; the oldest or senior member of a body of men.

dear (dẽr), *adj.* precious, beloved; valued; high-priced; *n.* a dear one.

dear (dẽr), *adv.* dearly; at a high price.

dearth (dûrth), *n.* scarcity; famine.

death (deth), *n.* the end of life.

deathwatch (deth' woch), *n.* a vigil beside a dying person; a certain small beetle whose ticking noise is thought to predict death.

debacle (de bä' kl), *n.* spring freshet; sudden collapse; stampede.

debar (dē bär'), *v.t.* to shut out; exclude.

debark (dē bärk'), *v.i. and v.t.* to disembark; land from a ship, dirigible or airplane.

debase (dē bās'), *v.t.* to bring to a lower level of value or conduct; degrade.

debatable (dē bāt' a bl), *adj.* open to debate.

debate (dē bāt'), *n.* a disputation or argument; discussion in arguments; a competitive presentation of arguments.

debate (dē bāt'), *v.i. and v.t.* to discuss controversially, argue; maintain a proposition by reasoning against arguments presented by an opponent; deliberate; consider a question from various approaches.

    Syn. Deliberate. To *debate* a question is to argue it out with another; to *deliberate* is to work it out in one's own mind.

debauch (dē bôch'), *v.i. and v.t.* to engage in acts of sensual pleasure; to corrupt in morals and principles.

debauchery (dē bôch' ẽr i), *n.* marked intemperance in the indulgence of any appetite; corruption of another's virtue.

*debenture** (dē ben' tũr), *n.* a certificate in acknowledgment of a debt.

debilitate (dē bil' i tāt), *v.t.* to weaken.

debilitated (dē bil' i tāted), *adj.* run down, weakened.

debility (dē bil' i ti), *n.* weakness from a run-down condition.

    Syn. Infirmity. *Debility* is a constitutional condition, affecting the whole body,

with its organic functions; *infirmity* is accidental, resulting from sickness or injury. *Debility*, as the word is commonly used, implies a general condition; *infirmity* is more commonly used to denote a localized condition, though it may quite properly apply to the body as a whole.

debit (deb' it), *n.* an entry in an account of an item owed.

debit (deb' it), *v.t.* to charge.

*debonair, debonaire** (deb ō når'), *adj.* courteous, gracious and gay.

debouch (dē bōōsh'), *v.i. and v.t.* to march from cover into open ground, as soldiers; emerge.

debris (de brē'), *n.* fragments, litter left after a smash; rubbish.

debt (det), *n.* that which is owed; the state of owing, as in *debt*.

debtor (det' ẽr), *n.* one who owes.

*debut** (dā bū'), *n.* a first appearance in formal society or on the stage.

decade (dek' ad), *n.* a group of ten; a period of ten consecutive years.

*decadence** (dē kā' dens), *n.* a state of decay or decline.

decagon (dek' a gon), *n.* a figure with ten sides.

Decalogue (dek' a lŏg), *n.* the Ten Commandments.

decamp (dē kamp'), *v.i.* to break camp and depart secretly; to run away.

decant (dē kant'), *v.t.* to pour gently so as not to stir up the dregs.

decanter (dē kant' ẽr), *n.* a vessel used to hold decanted liquors.

decapitate (dē kap' i tāt), *v.t.* to behead.

decathlon (dē kath' lon), *n.* an athletic competition in which each entrant performs in ten track or field events.

decay (dē kā'), *n.* the process of wasting away; corruption; rottenness.

decay (dē kā'), *v.i.* to waste away; rot.

    Syn. Deteriorate, decompose, putrefy, wither, waste. *Decay* indicates a change from a sound to an unsound state. To *decay* is natural to all things existing in time. To *decay* or to *decompose* is to disintegrate, without necessarily repulsive conditions. To *putrefy* implies foulness. To *rot* may or may not imply offensive conditions. Where *decay* suggests moving from one condition to another, to *rot* is to decay in stagnation.

decease (dē sēs'), *n.* death.

decease (dē sēs'), *v.i.* to die.

deceit (dē sēt'), *n.* effort or willingness to deceive; misrepresentation; falsehood.

    Syn. Deception, duplicity, guile, chicanery. *Deceit* is habitual intentional fraud or betrayal; a *deception* is the act of deceiving or the fraud practised. *Duplicity* is double-dealing. *Guile* implies subtlety and art in deceiving. *Chicanery* is trickery, especially in legal practice.

deceive (dē sēv'), *v.i. and v.t.* to practice fraud or deceit, mislead, cheat.

deceiver (dē sēv' ẽr), *n.* a cheat.

    Syn. Impostor. A *deceiver* is one who

practices any kind of deception; an *impostor* is one who studiously undertakes to pass himself off for what he is not.

decelerate (de sel' ēr ăt), *v.i. and v.t.* to slow up, move with decreasing speed.

decency (dē' sen si), *n.* [*pl.* decencies] the state or quality of being decent in words and conduct; that which is proper or seemly.

*decennial** (dē sen' i al), *adj.* happening once in ten years, or lasting ten years.

*decennium** (dē sen' i um), *n.* a ten-year period.

decent (dē' sent), *adj.* clean-spoken and right-acting; clean and neat; observing the proprieties; respectable; fairly good, as a *decent* share.

deception (dē sep' shun), *n.* the act of deceiving or state of being deceived; that which deceives or is done with intent to deceive; fraud; a trick or sham.

decide (dē sīd'), *v.i. and v.t.* to make up one's mind; bring to a conclusion; give a judgment; arbitrate.

decided (dē sīd' ed), *adj.* free from doubt or misgiving; determined.

Syn. Determined, resolute. A man who is *decided* has made up his mind; one who is *determined* is uninfluenced by the doubts, questions or arguments of others; one who is *resolute* is uninfluenced by fear.

decidedly (dē sīd' ed li), *adv.* positively, emphatically.

*deciduous** (dē sid' ū us), *adj.* having leaves that fall off in autumn, as certain trees; falling off at certain seasons or stages of growth, as the horns of deer.

decimal (des' i mal), *adj.* pertaining to or based upon the number 10; numbered by tens; *n.* a decimal fraction.

decimal system (des' i mal sis' tem), a system of measuring by 10 or powers of 10.

decimate (des' i māt), *v.t.* to destroy one tenth of; to destroy a considerable part of.

decipher (dē sī' fēr), *v.t.* to read secret writing or translate it into readable writing; to solve, unravel.

decision (dē sizh' un), *n.* the act of deciding; a conclusive judgment; the conclusion arrived at; determination, firmness, as this matter calls for *decision.*

Syn. Determination, resolution. *Decision* is the power of making up one's mind easily, usually as to action; *determination* is the quality of sticking to something obstinately; *resolution* is the quality of not being deterred by danger.

decisive (dē sī' siv), *adj.* final, conclusive; having the power of deciding; showing promptness.

deck (dek), *n.* the flooring of a ship; a pack of cards.

deck (dek), *v.t.* to array, adorn; to make a deck for, as to *deck* a ship.

declaim (dē klām'), *v.i. and v.t.* to speak in rhetorical style, recite a selection.

*declamation** (dek la ma' shun), *n.* the act or art of reciting; a reading or recitation of a literary selection before an audience.

declaration (dek la ra' shun), *n.* the act of declaring; an announcement, anything declared or proclaimed; also the document containing the proclamation.

*declarative** (de klar' a tiv), *adj.* affirmative, making a statement.

declare (dē klâr'), *v.t.* to make known openly, proclaim; to make an itemized statement of, as goods to pass through the customs.

Syn. Announce; proclaim. To *declare* means to make known plainly, publicly and formally; to *announce* is to make something known for the first time or to make known publicly beforehand something that is going to happen. To *proclaim* is to make known to the general public or to the world.

declension (dē klen' shun), *n.* the act of declining; a downward slope; the changes in the form of nouns and pronouns, showing their relation to the rest of a sentence, the case forms of nouns and pronouns.

declination (dek lin ā' shun), *n.* the act of deviating; a polite refusal.

decline (dē klīn'), *n.* a falling off, a wasting away, as of the mind or body; a downward slope; decay, as the *decline* of an empire.

decline (dē klīn'), *v.i. and v.t.* to turn aside, deviate; draw to an end, fail; refuse, reject; to inflect a noun or pronoun by stating its case forms.

declivity (dē kliv' i ti), *n.* a sloping, descending surface.

decoct (dē kokt'), *v.t.* to prepare by boiling, condense.

decoction (dē kok' shun), *n.* an extract made by boiling in water.

decode (dē kōd'), *v.t.* to translate a message from code into ordinary words.

decompose (dē kom pōs'), *v.i. and v.t.* to resolve into separate elements; to decay or rot.

decomposition (dē kom po zish' un), *n.* act of decomposing; state of rottenness or decay.

decorate (dek' ō rāt), *v.t.* to ornament, adorn; to give a badge of honor to.

decoration (dek ō rā' shun), *n.* the act of adorning; ornament; a mark of honor.

*decorous** (dek' ō rus), *adj.* marked by propriety; seemly, proper.

decorum (dē kō' rum), *n.* propriety, conformity to social standards; decency.

decoy (dē koi'), *n.* a fowl, real or artificial, used to lure wild birds within gunshot.

decoy (dē koi'), *v.t.* to lead or allure into a place of danger.

decrease (dē krēs'), *n.* the process of becoming less; amount by which anything is diminished.

decrease (dē krēs'), *v.i. and v.t.* to grow less; diminish in size or volume; abate.

decree (dē krē), *n.* an order with high authority, an edict.

decrepit (dē krep' it), *adj.* enfeebled by age or infirmity.

*decrepitude** (dē krep' i tūd), *n.* physical infirmity.

*decretal** (dē krē' tal), *n.* a decree, especially a papal decree.

decry (dē krī'), *v.t.* to blame publicly, cry

down; disparage, discredit.

decumbent (dē kum' bent), *adj.* lying on the ground, as the stems of certain plants.

dedicate (ded' i kāt), *v.t.* to consecrate with formal ceremonies; to set apart for a special use; to inscribe or address to someone as an honor, as to *dedicate* a book to John Smith.

Syn. Devote, consecrate, hallow. To *dedicate* is to set apart for any special use; to *devote* is to set apart wholly and exclusively, as to *devote* one's time to study. To *consecrate* is to set apart as being sacred; to *hallow* is to declare or make sacred.

dedication (ded i kā' shun), *n.* the act of dedicating; lines in the front of a book addressing it in honor to someone.

deduce (dē dūs'), *v.t.* to gather by reasoning, infer.

*deduct (dē dukt'), *v.t.* to take from.

deduction (dē duk' shun), *n.* the act or process of deducing or deducting; that which is arrived at by reasoning, a conclusion; that which is taken away.

deed (dēd), *n.* that which is done; exploit; a document conveying ownership of real estate.

deem (dēm), *v.i. and v.t.* to judge, consider as, suppose.

deep (dēp), *n.* deep water, the ocean; the middle; profundity.

deep (dēp), *adj.* extending far below the surface, extending far within, as a *deep* cut; coming from far within; profound, hard to understand; wise, also sly; absorbed, as *deep* in a book; rich and dark, as *deep* red; low-toned, as a *deep* voice.

deer (dēr), *n.* a family of wild, cud-chewing animals of which the male has antlers.

*deface (dē fās'), *v.t.* to mar, disfigure, remove important features of.

Syn. Disfigure, deform. To *deface* is to mar the face of something, as a poster or a wall; to *disfigure* is to inflict a deeper injury than to *deface;* to *deform* is to distort in structure.

*defalcate (dē fal' kāt), *v.i.* to embezzle.

*defamation (def a mā' shun), *n.* the act of injuring a person's reputation for honesty or virtue; calumny.

defame (dē fām'), *v.t.* to slander; injure the good name of.

default (dē fôlt'), *n.* a failure in duty or obligation, especially failure to pay a debt.

default (dē fôlt'), *v.i.* to fail to keep an agreement or meet an obligation, especially a financial obligation.

*defeasance (dē fē' zans), *n.* act of rendering null and void, as a deed.

defeat (dē fēt'), *n.* failure to win in strife; overthrow; frustration, vanquishment.

defeat (dē fēt'), *v.t.* to overcome, vanquish.

*defect (dē fekt'), *n.* an imperfection, fault.

defection (dē fek' shun), *n.* failure, voluntary failure in duty; desertion.

defective (dē fek' tiv), *adj.* faulty, imperfect; having flaws or shortcomings.

defend (dē fend'), *v.t.* to guard, protect, hold against danger or attack; maintain against

opposition, as a city or an argument.

Syn. Guard, protect. To *defend* is to intervene in any case of present danger or attack; to *protect* is to safeguard something against danger, present or future; to *guard* is to keep watch or to keep safe.

defense (dē fens', *n.* the act of resisting attack; that which wards off or protects from attack or danger; a guard; a defendant's answer or plea in a law case.

defer (dē fēr'), *v.t.* to put off, postpone.

*deference (def' ēr ens), *n.* the act of deferring; heed for the wishes of another.

defiance (dē fī' ans), *n.* the act of defying; a challenge.

deficiency (dē fish' en si), *n.* shortage, lack.

deficient (dē fish' ent), *adj.* lacking in some essential quality or element.

*deficit (def' i sit), *n.* a shortage in amount, especially of money.

defile (dē fīl'), *v.t.* to make unclean; to dishonor or tarnish, as a reputation.

defile (dē fīl'), *v.t. and v.i.* to march in a line.

*defile (dē fīl'), *n.* a narrow pass, as between cliffs or mountains.

definable (dē fīn' a bl), *adj.* capable of being defined.

define (dē fīn'), *v.t.* to fix the boundaries of; state the meaning of.

definite (def' i nit), *adj.* defined; having fixed limits; precise; exact.

definition (def i nish' un), *n.* the act of defining; a statement of meaning, as of a word.

*definitive (dē fin' i tiv), *adj.* conclusive, final; serving to define.

deflate (dē flāt'), *v.t. and v.i.* to reduce by letting out air or gas, as to *deflate* a balloon; to collapse, as a tire *deflates*.

deflect (dē flekt'), *v.t.* to turn from a straight line or course, as to *deflect* rays of light.

deflector (dē flek' tēr), *n.* an instrument for deflecting, averting, turning aside anything, as a ray of light.

deforest (dē for' est), *v.t.* to clear of growing trees.

deform (dē fôrm'), *v.t.* to spoil the shape of.

deformity (dē fôr' mi ti), *n.* a distortion, disfigurement; physical malformation.

defraud (dē frôd'), *v.t.* to deprive of a right or interest by trickery and deceit.

defray (dē frā'), *v.t.* to pay, as expenses.

deft (deft), *adj.* dextrous, skillful.

defunct (dē fungkt'), *adj.* dead; extinct.

defy (dē fī'), *v.t.* to challenge, dare.

degeneracy (dē jen' ēr a si), *n.* deterioration.

degenerate (dē jen' ēr āt), *v.i.* to become inferior or depraved.

degenerate (dē jen' ēr it), *adj.* degraded, deteriorated.

deglutition (dē glōō tish' un), *n.* the act of swallowing food.

degradation (deg ra dā' shun), *n.* a lowering in rank or position, disgrace, as the *degradation* of an officer; degeneration.

degrade (dē grād'), *v.t.* to reduce in grade or rank, deprive of office or dignity, disgrace; to corrupt.

degree (dē grē'), *n.* a step or grade in any

series; the 360th part of a circle; relative quantity or intensity, as of heat or cold; a division marked on a thermometer; a rank which college and university students attain on graduation; one of the three grades of an adjective or adverb, as the positive, comparative and superlative *degrees*.

deification (dē i fi kā' shun), *n.* the act of recognizing, worshiping or proclaiming as a god.

deify (dē' i fī), *v.t.* to worship as a god, as to *deify* the sun; to proclaim as a god.

*****deign** (dān), *v.i.* to condescend.

deity (dē' i ti), *n.* divine nature or rank; a god or goddess.

dejection (dē jek' shun), *n.* lowness of spirits; the state of being downcast.

Syn. Melancholy, sadness. *Sadness* is the all-inclusive term for lowness of spirits; *dejection* implies discouragement; *melancholy* is a chronic depression of the mind and spirit.

delay (dē lā'), *n.* postponement; detention.

delay (dē lā'), *v.t. and v.i.* to put off; postpone; hinder or detain temporarily; move slowly, linger.

delectable (dē lek' ta bl), *adj.* pleasing; delightful.

delegate (del' ē gāt), *n.* one empowered to act for another, a representative.

delegate (del' ē gāt), *v.t.* to commission to act for one, send as one's representative; to commit to the care of.

delegation (del ē gā' shun), *n.* a body of delegates sent to represent others.

delete (dē lēt), *v.t.* to cross off, remove.

*****deleterious** (del ē tēr' i us), *adj.* harmful.

deliberate (dē lib' ēr āt), *v.i. and v.t.* to ponder, reflect, weigh in the mind.

deliberate (dē lib' ēr it), *adj.* carefully considered; slow in making up one's mind.

deliberation (dē lib ēr ā' shun), *n.* calm and careful consideration.

delicacy (del' i ka si), *n.* a luxury or dainty, as food; fineness in form or texture, as the *delicacy* of lace; frailty, weakness; nicety, sensitiveness, as to have too much *delicacy* to be rude.

delicate (del' i kit), *adj.* nicely appreciative; mild, as a flavor; pleasing because of fineness; refined, considerate; finely made, marked by skill, as a *delicate* carving.

delicious (dē lish' us), *adj.* exquisitely pleasing to the taste.

delight (dē līt'), *n.* that which delights; great joy, extreme pleasure; capacity of giving pleasure.

delight (dē līt'), *v.t. and v.i.* to give pleasure, please, as music *delights* me; to be greatly pleased.

delightful (dē līt' fool), *adj.* pleasing, charming.

delineate (dē lin' ē āt), *v.t.* to show in outline, as by sketch or diagram; to describe accurately.

delinquency (dē ling' kwen si), *n.* a shortcoming, failure in duty; a wrongdoing, an offense.

delinquent (dē ling' kwent), *n.* one who offends or neglects duty or the law.

delinquent (dē ling' kwent), *adj.* offending, failing in duty.

*****deliquesce** (del i kwes'), *v.i.* to dissolve and become liquid by absorbing liquid from the air.

*****delirious** (dē lir' i us), *adj.* having delirium, out of one's head, raving.

delirium (dē lir' i um), *n.* temporary mental confusion or hallucination, often the result of high fever; extravagant enthusiasm.

deliver (dē liv' ēr), *v.t.* to rescue from danger, set free, release; to hand over to an addressee or purchaser, as a letter or package; to surrender, as to *deliver* oneself to the law; to utter, render in words, as to *deliver* an oration.

Syn. Release, discharge, free. To *deliver* means to set free from actual bondage or save from imminent or future danger; to *release* is to free from restraint; to *discharge* is to release or dismiss legally, as from custody; to *free* is to liberate in any sense, sometimes specifically to grant freedom, as Lincoln *freed* the slaves.

Ant. Bind, confine, imprison, restrain.

deliverance (dē liv' ēr ans), *n.* the act of delivering; state of being delivered.

dell (del), *n.* a small secluded valley.

delta (del' ta), *n.* the triangular mouth of a river, formed by deposits of alluvium.

deltoid (del'toid), *adj.* triangle-shaped; formed like the Greek letter delta (Δ).

*****delude** (dē lūd'), *v.t.* to deceive, mislead mentally.

*****deluge** (del' ūj), *n.* a flood; a great rush of anything, as a *deluge* of words.

delusion (dē lū' zhun), *n.* a misleading of the mind; a false belief.

delusive (dē lū' siv), *adj.* deceptive, misleading.

delve (delv), *v.i.* to dig, probe.

demagogue (dem' a gôg), *n.* a popular orator; a speaker who seeks personal success by appealing to common prejudice.

*****demand** (dē mànd'), *n.* the call for something; market for a commodity; the act of claiming something as due; an imperative call.

demand (dē mànd'), *v.t.* to claim as a right; request imperatively; require, as this situation *demands* study.

Syn. Require. We *demand* that which is owing and should be given or paid; we *require* that which we need. The creditor *demands* payment; we *require* food in order to live. To *demand* also means to call for with authority, as the police can *demand* entrance to a house; to *require* is to ask and expect as rightfully due.

*****demarcation** (dē mär kā' shun), *n.* the act of marking by limits or bounds; separation, especially by a boundary line.

demean (dē mēn'), *v.t.* to behave (oneself).

demean (dē mēn'), *v.t.* to lower or degrade, as he wouldn't *demean* himself by lying.

demeanor (dē mēn' ēr), *n.* behavior.

dementia (dē men' shi a), *n.* insanity.

demigod (dem' i god), *n.* a lesser deity.

demijohn (dem' i jon), *n.* a glass jug.

*demise (dē mīz'), *n.* transfer of property, as by lease; transfer of sovereignty, by death and inheritance; death.

demobilize (dē mō' bi līz), *v.t.* to disband.

democracy (dē mok' ra si), *n.* rule by the people; a community so governed; the quality of being democratic.

democrat (dem' ō krat), *n.* one who advocates or supports democratic government.

democratic (dem ō krat' ik), *adj.* pertaining to democracy.

demolish (dē mol' ish), *v.t.* to overthrow, destroy.

demolition (dem ō lish' un), *n.* destruction, ruin.

demon (dē' mun), *n.* an evil spirit, a devil.

*demoniac (dē mō' ni ak), *adj.* devilish, ruled by a demon.

*demonstrable (dē mon' stra bl), *adj.* capable of being demonstrated or proved.

*demonstrate (dem' un strāt), *v.t.* to prove true by reason or example.

demonstration (dem un strā' shun), *n.* proof; manifestation; a public parade or meeting of protest.

*demonstrative (dē mon' stra tiv), *adj.* exhibiting; quick to express feeling or display emotion.

demoralize (dē mor' al īz), *v.t.* to corrupt; disorganize; ruin courage or discipline of.

demountable (dē mount' a bl), *adj.* detachable, as an automobile wheel rim.

demur (dē mûr'), *v.i.* to object, take exception; to delay.

Syn. Hesitate, falter. To *hesitate* is the general term for all uncertain or undecided action; to *demur* is definitely to take exception or object to something; to *falter* is to weaken or waver.

demure (dē mūr'), *adj.* serious, grave; affectedly modest.

demurrer (dē mûr' ēr), *n.* an issue on a point of law.

den (den), *n.* the lair of a wild beast; an evil resort, as a *den* of thieves; any snug, private little room.

denaturalize (dē nat' ū ral īz), *v.t.* to deprive of citizenship.

*denatured (dē nā' tūrd), *adj.* changed in nature or character, as by chemical action, as *denatured* alcohol.

denial (dē nī' al), *n.* refusal to grant or acknowledge; rejection of a request; limitation in indulging the appetites.

denim (den' im), *n.* cotton drilling used for overalls, or a finer grade of coverings.

denizen (den' i zen), *n.* an inhabitant; a naturalized citizen.

denominate (dē nom i nāt), *v.t.* to designate, name.

denomination (dē nom in ā' shun), *n.* a class name; a group having a name; a sect; one of a series of units separately named, as the *denominations* of money.

denominator (dē nom i nā' tēr), *n.* the part of a simple fraction that shows into how many parts a thing is divided.

denote (dē nōt'), *v.t.* to indicate.

*denouement (dā nōō' män), *n.* the outcome of plot or any complicated situation.

denounce (dē nouns'), *v.t.* to threaten or accuse publicly; to give notice of intention to cancel a treaty.

dense (dens), *adj.* thick; crowded together; stupid.

density (den' si ti), *n.* compactness; the relation of weight to volume.

dent (dent), *n.* a small depression in a surface.

dent (dent), *v.t.* to put a dent in.

dental (den' tal), *adj.* pertaining to teeth.

*dentine (den' tēn), *n.* the hard tissue which forms the body of a tooth.

dentist (den' tist), *n.* one trained to treat and extract teeth and make artificial teeth.

dentistry (den' tis tri), *n.* the profession of treating and caring for teeth.

dentition (den tish' un), *n.* the process or period of cutting the teeth; the number, kind and arrangement of the teeth.

denture (den' tūr), *n.* a set of artificial teeth.

denude (dē nūd'), *v.t.* to make bare or naked.

*denunciation (dē nun si ā' shun), *n.* the act of denouncing; a public accusation.

deny (dē nī'), *v.t.* to declare untrue; refuse to believe or admit; reject, as a request; to disclaim, as to *deny* one's child.

Syn. Contradict, refute. To *deny* is merely to declare untrue or to reject as untrue; to *contradict* is to state the contrary; to *refute* is to prove untrue.

deodorant (de ō' dēr ant), *n.* anything that counteracts offensive odors.

deodorize (dē ō' dēr īz), *v.t.* to remove offensive odors.

depart (dē pärt'), *v.i.* to leave, go away.

department (dē pärt' ment), *n.* a subdivision, as of a business establishment or government; a special field of action or study.

departure (dē pär' tūr), *n.* the act of going away; deviation from a set course.

depend (dē pend'), *v.i.* to hang down; rely for support; to be based upon or decided by, as the answer *depends* on the question; to rely, trust.

dependence (dē pen' dens), *n.* the act of hanging, or state of being in suspension; support; reliance; that on which one relies.

dependency (dē pen' den si), *n.* a dependent territory.

dependent (dē pen' dent), *n.* one who looks to another for support.

depict (dē pikt'), *v.t.* to represent by a picture, portray.

deplete (dē plēt'), *v.t.* to empty, exhaust.

depletion (dē plē' shun), *n.* act of emptying; state of being emptied or exhausted, as the *depletion* of resources.

*deplorable (dē plôr' a bl), *adj.* regrettable.

deplore (dē plôr'), *v.t.* to lament; grieve for.

Syn. Lament. To *deplore* is to regret very deeply; to *lament* is to express regret or sorrow.

deploy (dē ploi'), *v.i. and v.t.* to go into more open formation, extend the front, as troops.

depone (dē pōn'), *v.i.* to testify under oath.

deponent (dē pō' nent), *n.* one who testifies under oath, often in writing.

depopulate (dē pop′ ū lāt), *v.t.* to deprive of inhabitants.

deport (dē pōrt′), *v.t.* to behave; to banish.

deportment (dē pōrt′ ment), *n.* conduct, behavior.

depose (dē pōs′), *v.t.* to deprive of office; to affirm under oath, as by affidavit.

deposit (dē poz′ it), *n.* anything that is laid down; money left in a bank subject to order; the natural occurrence of mineral in the earth, as a *deposit* of gold, oil or gas.

*****deposition** (dep ō zish′ un), *n.* the act of deposing; testimony under oath; sediment.

depositor (dē poz′ i tẽr), *n.* one who makes a deposit, as of money in a bank.

*****depository** (dē poz′ i tō ri), *n.* a place where things are deposited for safekeeping.

*****depot** (dē′ pō), *n.* a warehouse; a place where military supplies are stored; a railroad station.

deprave (dē prāv′), *v.t.* to make bad; corrupt.

depraved (dē prāvd′), *adj.* corrupt, debased.

*****depravity** (dē prav′ i ti), *n.* the state of being depraved; corruptness; a depraved act.

Syn. Corruption. *Corruption* is merely the loss of a former soundness or virtue; *depravity* is an unnatural falling away from normal soundness or purity.

deprecate (dep′ rē kāt), *v.t.* to pray against; to speak disapprovingly of.

depreciate (dē prē′ shi āt), *v.i. and v.t.* to lessen either in price or in value; to belittle.

depredate (dep′ rē dāt), *v.i. and v.t.* to plunder, pillage, lay waste.

depress (dē pres′), *v.t.* to lower, press down; to sadden.

depression (dē presh′ un), *n.* the act of depressing or state of being depressed; a sunken surface; lowness of spirits; a reduction of trade; a period of dull business.

*****deprivation** (dep ri vā′ shun), *n.* the act of taking away; loss.

deprive (dē prīv′), *v.t.* to take from; compel to do without, as to *deprive* one of a right.

depth (depth), *n.* that which is deep, especially sky or water; distance below the surface; profoundness; the middle, as the *depth* of night.

Syn. Profundity. *Depth* is indefinite in its signification, and *profundity* is a great degree of depth. *Depth* is used in both material and mental senses. The sea has *depth*, a well has *depth;* there are *depths* of wisdom, mind or philosophy; but *profundity* is confined to mental or moral matters.

deputation (dep ū tā′ shun), *n.* delegation; a delegation.

depute (dē pūt′), *v.t.* to appoint as an agent or deputy.

deputize (dep′ ū tīz), *v.t.* to depute.

*****deputy** (dep′ ū ti), *n.* one appointed to act for another.

derail (dē rāl′), *v.t.* to cause to leave the rails.

derange (dē rānj′), *v.t.* to throw into disorder and confusion.

derby (dûr′ bi), *n.* a stiff felt hat with a rounded crown.

*****derelict** (der′ e likt), *n.* anything voluntarily abandoned, especially a ship abandoned at sea; a social outcast.

derelict (der′ e likt), *adj.* abandoned.

dereliction (der e lik′ shun), *n.* default of duty; shortcoming; failure.

deride (dē rīd′), *v.t.* to mock.

*****derision** (dē rizh′ un), *n.* the act of deriding; contemptuous laughter; scorn.

derisive (dē rī′ siv), *adj.* expressing derision.

derivation (der i vā′ shun), *n.* that from which a thing is derived; the origin, as of a word.

derivative (dē riv′ a tiv), *n.* a thing taken or derived from another.

derive (dē rīv′), *v.i. and v.t.* to proceed, as from a source; to deduce; to receive, as from a source; to trace origin or descent of.

Syn. Deduce, trace. The act of *deriving* is immediate and direct; that of *tracing* is a gradual process; that of *deducing* is a process of reasoning. We discover sources and causes through *deriving;* we discover the history of things by *tracing;* we discover the grounds and reasons of things by *deducing.*

derma (dûr′ ma), *n.* the true, inner skin: also called *dermis.*

dermatology (dẽr ma tol′ ō ji), *n.* the science that treats of the skin.

dermis (dûr′ mis), *n.* the derma.

derogate (der′ ō gāt), *v.t.* to detract from; to disparage; to take something away from.

derogatory (dē rog′ a tō ri), *adj.* detracting, as from honor or reputation.

derrick (der′ ik), *n.* a hoisting apparatus consisting of a beam with tackle; the framework over a hole, as an oil well, supporting the tackle used in drilling or hoisting.

descend (dē send′), *v.i. and v.t.* to move from a higher to a lower position; to come down, as from a source, as to be *descended* from kings; to make a sudden attack, as to *descend* upon the enemy; to go down, as a mountain or ladder.

descendant (dē sen′ dant), *n.* one directly descended from an ancestor.

descendent (dē sen′ dent), *adj.* descending; moving downward.

descent (dē sent′), *n.* change from higher to lower position, rank, grade; origin, lineage; a downward step, as from honor or in value; a downward slope.

describe (dē skrib′), *v.t.* to represent or image in words; to draw the outline of, as a circle.

description (dē skrip′ shun), *n.* a word picture; class or kind, as furniture of any *description.*

*****descry** (dē skri′), *v.t.* to discover or spy with the eye, especially at a distance.

desecrate (des′ ē krāt), *v.t.* to violate the sanctity of; to divert from a sacred use.

*****desert** (dē zûrt′), *v.i. and v.t.* to abandon; to quit military service or leave a post of duty without permission.

*****desert** (dē zûrt′), *n.* merit; worthiness; what one deserves, a reward or punishment.

Syn. Merit, worth. *Desert* is the quality of deserving or earning either just reward or just punishment; *merit* is a quality that deserves reward; *worth* is the sum of all qualities that make a thing excellent.

desert (dez' ẽrt), *n.* a barren tract of land; sandy waste.

***deserve** (dē zûrv'), *v.t.* to earn; to be entitled to or worthy of.

***desiccate** (des' i kāt), *v.i. and v.t.* to dry up.

design (dē zīn'), *v.i. and v.t.* to make designs or plans; to draw a plan for, as to *design* a cathedral; to make as a pattern; to intend, set apart, as *designed* for a doctor.

design (dē zin'), *n.* a plan; pattern; purpose.
Syn. Aim, intention, purpose. A *design* is something skilfully and methodically planned; it requires time and study. A *purpose* is something previously decided upon. An *intention* is something one means to do, not necessarily what one is determined to do; an *aim* is a direct objective toward which one strives.

***designate** (dez' ig nāt), *v.t.* to indicate, show; to name; to set apart for a specified purpose.

designing (dē zin' ing), *adj.* scheming, artful.

desire (dē zīr'), *v.t.* to long for; to ask for.
Syn. Wish, want. To *desire* indicates strength or intensity of wanting; to *wish* is less intense, consisting often of a strong inclination; one often *wishes* for the impossible. To *want* implies need, as to *want* a drink, to *want* attention.

desirous (dē zīr' us), *adj.* full of or governed by desire; covetous; full of longing.

***desist** (dē zist'), *v.i.* to cease, stop.

desk (desk), *n.* a table for reading or writing, either open or with closable top.

desolate (des' ō lāt), *v.t.* to lay waste; to make wretched.

desolate (des' ō lit), *adj.* without inhabitants, deserted; gloomy; sad and lonely.

desolation (des ō lā' shun), *n.* the state of being laid waste; loneliness.

despair (dē spâr'), *n.* hopelessness; that which causes hopelessness.
Syn. Desperation, despondency. *Despair* is the complete collapse of all hope; *desperation* is despair expressed in violent action; *despondency* is a state of mind resulting from discouragement or a partial hopelessness.

***desperado** (des pẽr ā' dō), *n.* an utterly reckless criminal or outlaw.

desperate (des' pẽr it), *adj.* without hope; taking no heed of danger; reckless.

***despicable** (des' pik a bl), *adj.* contemptible.

despise (dē spīz'), *v.t.* to hold in contempt, to scorn.

despite (dē spīt'), *n.* spite; an act of spite or abuse; an injury.

despite (dē spīt'), *prep.* in spite of.

despoil (dē spoil'), *v.t.* to pillage, rob.

despond (dē spond'), *v.i.* to be downcast or disheartened.

despot (des' pot), *n.* absolute ruler; tyrant.

dessert (di zûrt'), *n.* a course of sweets, or pastry served at the end of a meal.

destination (des tin ā' shun), *n.* purpose for which something is designed; goal of jour-

ney, place to which anything to sent.

***destine** (des' tin), *v.t.* to appoint to a specific use, ordain, intend; to be bound, as a train *destined* for Chicago.

destiny (des' ti ni), *n.* fate, doom.
Syn. Fate, doom. *Destiny* is that which is irrevocable; death is the *destiny* of man; *fate* implies lot fixed without reason, but also irrevocable; *doom* is always final and usually calamitous.

destitute (des' ti tūt), *adj.* impoverished, lacking, in want, as *destitute* of food.

destitution (des ti tū' shun), *n.* great poverty.

destroy (dē stroi'), *v.t.* to tear down, ruin; to abolish; to kill.
Syn. Annihilate, demolish. *Destroy* is the inclusive word for any kind of ruin; to *demolish* is to tear down a structure, as to *demolish* a building, a city, a government or an argument; to *annihilate* is to put out of existence.

destruction (dē struk' shun), *n.* the act of destroying or state of being destroyed; ruin; death.

destructive (dē struk' tiv), *adj.* causing destruction; intended to ruin; deadly.

***desultory** (des' ul tō ri), *adj.* passing from one thing to another without logical connection; aimless.

detach (dē tach'), *v.t.* to disconnect.

detachment (dē tach' ment), *n.* something detached from a main body, as troops; aloofness: isolation; abstraction.

***detail** (dē tāl'), *n.* a minute portion; item; a man or body of men assigned to a particular task: *details*, all the parts, as the *details* of a plan; *in detail,* circumstantially, item by item.

***detail** (dē tāl'), *v.t.* to relate with minute particularity; to assign to a special task.

detain (dē tān'), *v.t.* to hold back, restrain; to delay.

detect (dē tekt'), *v.t.* to discover; to bring to light, especially something obscure.
Syn. Discover. To *detect* is to uncover something hidden; to *discover* is to learn or bring to light something hitherto unknown. We *detect* a person in a lie; we *discover* a new cure for a deadly disease, or a new road leading somewhere.

detection (dē tek' shun), *n.* the act of detecting; discovery.

detective (dē tek' tiv), *n.* one whose business is to detect crime, find criminals.

detention (dē ten' shun), *n.* the act of detaining or withholding; delay due to force.

deter (dē tûr'), *v.t.* to prevent by fear or discouragement, as one failure need not *deter* your efforts.

***deteriorate** (dē tēr' i ō rāt), *v.i. and v.t.* to grow worse; to make worse.

determinant (dē tûr' mi nant), *n.* that which determines.

determination (dē tûr mi nā' shun), *n.* the state of being determined; the act of bringing or coming to an end; resolution, persistence, mental decision and firmness.

determine (dē tûr' min), *v.i. and v.t.* to come to an end; to bring to an end; to resolve, decide; to give reason or impetus to, as circumstances *determine* the course of events.

*deterrent (dē ter' ent), *n.* anything that deters or prevents.

deterrent (dē ter' ent), *adj.* tending to hinder or prevent.

detest (dē test'), *v.t.* to abhor, loathe.

detestation (dē tes tā' shun), *n.* extreme dislike; abhorrence.

dethrone (dē thrōn'), *v.t.* to depose, as a sovereign.

*detonate (det' ō nāt), *v.i.* and *v.t.* to explode with a great noise.

detonation (det ō nā' shun), *n.* a loud explosion, sudden and shattering.

*detour (dē toor'), *n.* a deviation from a straight course; a diversion of traffic into side roads when a main road is closed off.

detract (dē trakt'), *v.i.* and *v.t.* to take away a part of, to defame; to subtract.

detraction (dē trak' shun), *n.* the taking away of reputation; a discrediting assertion, a disparagement.

detriment (det' ri ment), *n.* that which injures; damage.

detrimental (det ri men' tal), *adj.* harmful, injurious.

deuce (dūs), *n.* the two-spot of a suit of cards; a certain tie score in tennis, 40-all.

devastate (dev' as tāt), *v.t.* to lay waste, plunder.

develop (dē vel' up), *v.t.* and *v.i.* to advance to a more complete or complex form; to unfold gradually; to advance toward completion; to form by growth; to grow, evolve.

deviate (dē' vi āt), *v.i.* to turn aside from a course; to wander, as to *deviate* from the subject.

Syn. Wander, swerve, stray. To *deviate* is to leave a direct path; to *wander* is to move without a set course. To *swerve* is to turn aside suddenly, as a car *swerves* when a curve is too sharp or the driver loses control of the wheel. To *stray* is to move aimlessly, get lost. Men *swerve* from their duty to serve some selfish interest; the young *stray* from the paths of rectitude.

device (dē vīs'), *n.* anything made from a design, a contrivance; stratagem: *devices,* will or pleasure, as to be left to one's own *devices.*

devil (dev' l), *n.* an evil spirit, a demon.

devious (dē' vi us), *adj.* departing from the straight line; crooked or winding.

devisable (dē vīz' a bl), *adj.* capable of being bequeathed; capable of being devised.

devise (dē vīz'), *v.t.* to design; to contrive; to leave by will.

devoid (dē void'), *adj.* destitute, without, as *devoid* of honor.

devolve (dē volv'), *v.i.* and *v.t.* to pass or transfer from one to another.

devote (dē vōt'), *v.t.* to dedicate or consecrate; to give up entirely, as to *devote* oneself to reading.

devotion (dē vō' shun), *n.* religious piety; strong affection; loyalty; the act of devoting, as *devotion* of time to music.

devour (dē vour'), *v.t.* to eat up greedily; to destroy as if by eating; to take in eagerly, as to *devour* a book.

devout (dē vout'), *adj.* pious, religious; sincere, as this is my *devout* wish.

*dew (dū), *n.* moisture from the air condensed on the earth or any object that has cooled off, especially at night.

dewy (dū' i), *adj.* of or like dew; wet with dew.

dexterity (deks ter' i ti), *n.* adroitness, skill, especially with the hands.

dexterous (deks' tër us), *adj.* skillful, quick.

*diabetes (dī a bē' tēz), *n.* a disease characterized by too much sugar in the urine.

diabolic (dī a bol' ik), *adj.* devilish, fiendish.

diadem (dī a dem), *n.* a crown; tiara.

*diagnose (dī ag nōs'), *v.i.* and *v.t.* to recognize or ascertain by symptoms.

diagnosis (dī ag nō' sis), *n.* analysis of conditions, physical or mental, as a means of recognizing disease.

diagonal (dī ag' ō nal), *n.* a line running from corner to corner.

diagonal (dī ag' ō nal), *adj.* extending from corner to corner of a rectangle; oblique.

diagram (dī' a gram), *n.* a line drawing, a plan or chart, as a *diagram* of a park; an outline of a sentence showing the relation of the words to each other.

diagram (dī' a gram), *v.i.* and *v.t.* to make a plan, outline or graphic analysis.

dial (dī' al), *n.* the face of a watch or clock; a small plate inscribed with letters or numbers, used to make connections on telephones and radios: *sun dial,* a surface on which time is indicated by the shadow cast by the sun.

dial (dī' al), *v.t.* and *v.i.* to connect with, as by a telephone or radio dial; to work a dial.

dialect (dī' a lekt), *n.* a regional form of a language, differing from the standard.

*dialogue (dī' a lôg), *n.* a written or actual conversation between two persons.

diameter (dī am' ē tër), *n.* a line passing through the center of any object or figure, especially a circle; the length of this line.

diametric (dī a met' rik), *adj.* pertaining to, or having the nature of, a diameter; directly opposite, as a *diametric* argument.

*diamond (dī' a mund), *n.* a precious stone of crystallized carbon, noted for its hardness and for its brilliancy when cut in facets; any plane figure with straight sides and two acute and two obtuse angles; in baseball, the infield.

diaper (dī' a pēr), *n.* a white linen or cotton fabric having a certain weave; this fabric used as an infant's breechcloth.

*diaphanous (dī af' a nus), *adj.* so dainty as to be translucent or transparent.

*diaphragm (dī' a fram), *n.* a partition or dividing membrane, especially the muscular partition separating the chest from the abdomen; the vibrating disk of a telephone, as the receiving *diaphragm* and the transmitting *diaphragm* of the telephone.

diarrhea (dī a rē' a), *n.* persistent looseness of the bowels.

diary (dī′ a ri), *n.* a daily record; a blank-book for entering such a record.

diatonic (dī a ton′ ik), *adj.* of or designating a major or minor scale having eight tones to an octave.

diatribe (dī′ a trīb), *n.* a prolonged discussion; an abusive denunciation.

dibble (dib′ l), *n.* a pointed instrument for making holes in the ground for seeds or plants.

dice (dīs), *n.* small cubes marked with spots from one to six, used in gambling.

dichotomize (dī kot′ ō mīz), *v.i. and v.t.* to cut or separate into two parts.

dichromatism (dī krō′ ma tizm), *n.* the state of being able to perceive only two of the fundamental colors.

dicker (dik′ ẽr), *v.i.* to bargain; to barter.

***dicotyledon** (dī kot i lē′ dun), *n.* a plant having two cotyledons or seed leaves.

dictaphone (dik′ ta fōn), *n.* a phonographic instrument for recording and reproducing dictation; originally a trade name.

***dictate** (dik′ tāt), *v.t. and v.i.* to say, for another to write; to impose or require authoritatively, as to *dictate* the terms of surrender; to give orders.

dictation (dik tā′ shun), *n.* the act of dictating, or that which is dictated.

***dictator** (dik′ tā tẽr), *n.* one who dictates, especially one holding supreme authority; an absolute ruler of a state.

dictatorship (dik′ tā′ tẽr ship), *n.* rule by a dictator.

dictatorial (dik ta tō′ ri al), *adj.* overbearing; imperious.

diction (dik′ shun), *n.* choice and use of words; manner of speaking or writing.

dictionary (dik′ shun er i), *n.* a book giving the words and the meanings of the words in a language, often including etymology, pronunciation and notes on usage.

Syn. Lexicon, vocabulary, glossary, nomenclature. A *lexicon* is a dictionary of the dead languages; *dictionary* applies to the words of a modern, living language. A *vocabulary* is a special and partial kind of dictionary, giving the words used in a special branch of learning or science. A *glossary* commonly serves to define difficult terms; a *nomenclature* is a system of naming.

dictograph (dik′ tō grȧf), *n.* an instrument like a telephone with a mechanism for increasing the sound so that the usual mouthpiece is not needed and it can be used for getting evidence or for interoffice conversation; originally a trade name.

dictum (dik′ tum), *n.* an authoritative saying; judicial ruling on a certain point.

die (dī), *n.* [*pl.* dies] an engraved metal stamp used to make coins or medals or to emboss paper; a tool for cutting threads in screws; any of various other tools used to cut, shape and impress objects or substances.

die (dī), *n.* [*pl.* dice] a small cube, as of food, meat is often cut into *dice;* a small cube marked with 1 to 6 spots, used in gambling; chance: *the die is cast,* the course or event is irrevocably decided.

die (dī), *v.i.* to come to the end of life; to perish; to pass out of existence; to vanish or fade, as popularity *dies.*

Syn. Expire. To *die* is to become dead or cease to exist; living things *die,* old customs *die.* To *expire* is to come to an end, to breathe the last breath, or to terminate, as a lease.

diet (dī′ et), *n.* daily fare of food and drink; selection of food with reference to health; a plan of feeding to correct a disease.

diet (dī′ et), *v.i. and v.t.* to select foods for health; to eat according to a laid-out system of diet; to prescribe a diet.

dietetic (dī e tet′ ik), *adj.* pertaining to or regulating diet.

differ (dif′ ẽr), *v.i.* to be unlike; to disagree.

difference (dif′ ẽr ens), *n.* the state of being unlike; disagreement; a mark of distinction; what remains after subtracting one sum from another.

Syn. Distinction. *Difference* is unlikeness in material fact; *distinction* is unlikeness mentally perceived. We can see the *difference* between black and white; we make a *distinction* between good and evil.

Ant. Likeness, similarity.

different (dif′ ẽr ent), *adj.* unlike.

differential (dif′ ẽr en shal), *adj.* pertaining to or showing a difference according to outward circumstances, as a *differential* thermometer, a *differential* tariff; pertaining to the difference of two or more mechanical motions, as *differential* gear.

differentiate (dif ẽr en′ shi āt), *v.t. and v.i.* to distinguish between; to become different.

difficult (dif′ i kult), *adj.* hard to do, make, understand or deal with.

difficulty (dif′ i kul ti), *n.* a thing that can be done or understood only through much effort.

Syn. Hindrance, obstacle, obstruction. *Difficulty* is the general term for anything that takes exceptional skill to do or effort to understand or overcome. A *hindrance* is anything that checks movement or advance; an *obstacle* is some fixed thing that stands in the way; an *obstruction* is something that is put in the way to hinder or impede.

diffidence (dif′ i dens), *n.* bashfulness, timidity.

diffuse (di fūs′), *adj.* poured out, spread around; wordy.

diffuse (di fūz′), *v.t.* to spread in all directions, disseminate.

diffusion (di fū′ zhun), *n.* prolixity, as of speech.

dig (dig), *v.t. and v.i.* to use a spade or other implement or the hands to turn or take up earth; to bring up out of the earth, as to *dig* gold; to make by removing earth, as to *dig* a well; to delve.

digest (dī′ jest), *n.* information classified and condensed, as a *digest* of news.

***digest** (di jest′), *v.t. and v.i.* to convert food in the digestive tract into absorbable form; to classify, arrange and condense, as news; to think over; to become changed to absorbable form, as milk *digests* easily.

digestible (di jes′ ti bl), *adj.* capable of being digested.

digestion (di jes′ chun), *n.* the process of dissolving and changing food by chemical action of the digestive tract into substances that can be absorbed by the body.

digit (dij′ it), *n.* any of the Arabic numerals; a finger or toe.

digital (dij ′ i tūl), *adj.* a row of digits such as the digital clock showing time in a row of numbers.

dignify (dig′ ni fi), *v.t.* to confer dignity or honors upon.

dignitary (dig′ ni ter i), *n.* a person of exalted rank.

dignity (dig′ ni ti), *n.* nobleness of character, excellence; elevated rank, office or position; formality and reserve of manner.

*digress (di gres′), *v.i.* to turn aside, especially from the topic in speech or writing.

Syn. Deviate. Both *digress* and *deviate* mean turning out of a set course. To *digress* is essentially to depart from the straight line of a discourse; to *deviate* is to turn aside from a line of action.

dike (dik), *n.* a levee; bank of earth thrown up as a barrier against water.

dilapidated (di lap′ i dāt ed), *adj.* fallen into ruin.

*dilate (di lāt′), *v.i. and v.t.* to enlarge upon, as to *dilate* upon a subject; to expand in size, extend.

dilatory (dil′ a tō ri), *adj.* causing delay or intending to delay; slow.

dilemma (di lem′ a), *n.* an argument having two or more propositions, each equally adversely conclusive; a situation calling for decision between two equally bad alternatives; hence, any difficult choice.

*dilettante (dil e tan′ ti), *n.* one who pursues the arts superficially; a trifler.

diligence (dil′ i jens), *n.* close application, perseverance.

diligent (dil′ i jent), *adj.* hard-working, industrious.

Syn. Assiduous, busy, industrious. *Diligent* means earnest in application, as a *diligent* student; *assiduous* means unceasing and untiring, as to give *assiduous* care to a garden; *busy* means actively occupied, temporarily or habitually; *industrious* means devoted to working.

*dilute (di lūt′), *v.t.* to thin or make more liquid, as to *dilute* soup with water.

dilution (di lū′ shun), *n.* a liquid weakened or thinned by admixture with another.

dim (dim), *v.i. and v.t.* to become dim; to make dim.

dim (dim), *adj.* not bright, dull; faint, as sound; having poor vision, as *dim* eyes.

dime (dim), *n.* a silver coin equal to one-tenth of a dollar.

dimension (di men′ shun), *n.* measure in height, length and breadth.

diminish (di min′ ish), *v.i. and v.t.* to become smaller; make smaller.

diminutive (di min′ ū tiv), *adj.* very small, of less than average size.

dimity (dim′ i ti), *n.* [*pl.* dimities] a thin

corded cotton cloth, often having figures.

dimple (dim′ pl), *n.* a slight hollow on cheek or chin or elsewhere on surface of body.

din (din), *n.* an uproar, clamor, great noise.

dine (din), *v.i. and v.t.* to have dinner; to give a dinner to.

dingy (din′ ji), *adj.* grayish and grimy.

dinner (din′ ēr), *n.* the chief meal of the day, eaten either at midday or evening.

dint (dint), *n.* a mark left by a blow or pressure; force, power, as by *dint* of hard work.

*diocese (di′ ō sēs), *n.* the church district under authority of a bishop.

dioxide (di oks′ id), *n.* an oxide with two atoms of oxygen in each molecule.

dip (dip), *n.* the act of immersing and emerging rapidly, as a *dip* of a paddle, a quick downward movement of an airplane with an immediate turn to a higher elevation.

dip (dip), *v.i. and v.t.* to immerse and emerge quickly; to take up with a ladle, as to *dip* milk or gravy.

*diphtheria (dif thēr′ i a), *n.* a feverish infectious disease of the throat.

*diphthong (dif′ thong), *n.* a union of two vowels in one sound, as *oi* in oil is a diphthong.

*diploma (di plō′ ma), *n.* a certificate that a school or college course has been completed.

diplomacy (di plō′ ma si), *n.* the art of conducting negotiations between governments; tact.

diplomat (dip′ lō mat), *n.* one skilled or employed in intergovernmental negotiations.

dipper (dip′ ēr), *n.* a vessel used for dipping.

dire (dir), *adj.* dreadful, overwhelming, fatal.

direct (di rekt′), *v.t.* to put an address on, as a letter; to address, as to *direct* a speech to the laboring class; to cause to turn or follow, as to *direct* the eyes to a page, *direct* the attention to what is said; to manage, guide or lead, as to *direct* a business or an orchestra; to order with authority, as a judge *directs* a jury.

direct (di rekt′), *adj.* straight, not crooked, as a *direct* line between two points; straightforward, to the point, as a *direct* question; personal, as *direct* contact; immediate, not second-hand, as *direct* knowledge; lineal, as a *direct* descendant.

direction (di rek′ shun), *n.* guidance, management; an order or command; the course along which something moves or points, as to sail in a northerly *direction*.

director (di rek′ tēr), *n.* one who directs, superintends, manages or guides.

directorate (di rek′ tō rit), *n.* the office of a director; a body of directors.

directory (di rek′ tō ri), *n.* [*pl.* directories] a book of names and addresses.

dirge (dûrj), *n.* a funeral hymn; a poem or musical composition expressing grief.

*dirigible (dir′ ij i bl), *n.* a motor-driven airship having a cigar-shaped balloon.

dirigible (dir′ ij i bl), *adj.* capable of being steered.

dirk (dûrk), *n.* a dagger.

dirt (dûrt), *n.* loose earth, mud or dust; anything foul; uncleanness; litter; mess.

dirty (dir' ti), *adj.* defiled, soiled; base.

disability (dis a bil' i ti), *n.* incompetence, inability; lack of physical or mental ability.

lisable (dis ā' bl), *v.t.* to make unable, to cripple.

disabuse (dis a būz'), *v.t.* to undeceive.

disaffect (dis a fekt'), *v.t.* to alienate in feeling or loyalty; to fill with discontent.

disaffection (dis a fek' shun), *n.* disloyalty; discontent; ill will.

disagree (dis a grē'), *v.i.* to differ, be unlike; to differ in opinion, quarrel; to be unsuitable, as eggs *disagree* with the baby.

disagreeable (dis a grē' a bl), *adj.* not pleasing, offensive; ill-tempered.

disappear (dis a pēr'), *v.i.* to pass out of sight or existence; to vanish.

disappoint (dis a point'), *v.t.* to frustrate hope, fail to meet an expectation or hope.

disarm (dis ärm'), *v.i. and v.t.* to lay aside weapons; to take away weapons.

disarmament (dis är' ma ment), *n.* the act of disarming; formal reduction of military establishment.

disarray (dis a rā'), *v.t.* to throw into disorder; to undress.

disaster (di zås' tēr), *n.* a calamity, sudden misfortune.

disband (dis band'), *v.i. and v.t.* to break up, as an organization.

disbar (dis bär'), *v.t.* to deprive (a lawyer) of his professional standing.

disbelief (dis bē lēf'), *n.* lack of belief.

Syn. Unbelief. *Disbelief* is the actual rejection of something as untrue. *Unbelief* is a mere lack of belief.

disburden (dis bûr' den), *v.t.* to free from a burden; to unload; to relieve.

disburse (dis bûrs'), *v.t.* to expend, pay out.

discard (dis kard'), *v.t.* to cast aside as useless.

*•**discern** (di zûrn'), *v.t. and v.i.* to distinguish with the eye or mind, detect; to understand a distinction.

discernible (di zûrn' i bl), *adj.* perceptible.

discharge (dis chärj'), *n.* the act of discharging or of unloading; firing, as of guns; release, as from an obligation; release, acquittal; a flowing out, as a *discharge* of water; dismissal from employment.

discharge (dis charj'), *v.t. and v.i.* to relieve of a charge or burden; to permit or cause issuance of a liquid; to fire, as a gun; to unload, as a ship *discharges* cargo; to get rid of, as a debt or a duty; to release from service; to dismiss from employment; to go off, as a gun.

discipline (dis' i plin), *n.* training that strengthens; correction, punishment; control or order maintained; a system of rules for conduct.

disclaim (dis klām'), *v.t.* to disown; repudiate; deny knowledge of or responsibility for.

Syn. Disown. To *disclaim* is to throw off a claim; to *disown* is to refuse to admit as one's own.

disclose (dis klōz'), *v.t.* to uncover, reveal.

discolor (dis kul' ēr), *v.t.* to change from the natural color; to stain.

disco (dis ´ kō), *n.* informal word for discotheque; a kind of popular dance music with a strong beat.

discomposure (dis kum pō' zhēr), *n.* the state of being perturbed.

disconcert (dis kon sûrt'), *v.t.* to throw into disorder; to confuse.

disconsolate (dis kon' sō lit), *adj.* hopeless, sad, without cheer.

discontent (dis con tent'), *n.* lack of contentment, dissatisfaction.

discontinue (dis kon tin' ū), *v.t.* to break off, stop.

discord (dis' kôrd), *n.* disagreement, lack of harmony in opinion or sound; conflict.

Syn. Strife. *Discord* means general lack of harmony or agreement in opinion, specific lack of harmony in sound. *Strife* is active conflict.

Ant. Concord, harmony, unity.

discount (dis' kount), *n.* a deduction from a total sum or bill; a deduction made for interest on a bill or note; also the rate of interest charged.

discourage (dis kûr' ij), *v.t.* to lessen the courage of, dishearten.

discourse (dis' kôrs *or* dis kôrs'), *n.* conversation; formal written or spoken composition, as a *discourse* in physics.

discourse (dis kôrs'), *v.i.* to talk; to speak on a subject.

discover (dis kuv' ēr), *v.t.* to bring to light; to learn, find or see for the first time.

Syn. Invent. To *discover* is to find for the first time; to *invent* is to make for the first time. Gold was *discovered* in California but it had existed there for centuries unknown to men. Watt *invented* the steam engine, a device entirely new.

discovery (dis kuv' ēr i), *n.* the act of discovering, or that which is brought to light or knowledge.

discredit (dis kred' it), *n.* loss of credit or honor.

discreet (dis krēt'), *adj.* prudent, cautious, especially in speech.

discrepancy (dis krep' an si), *n.* inconsistency, variance.

discretion (dis kresh' un), *n.* free, individual judgment, as use your own *discretion;* prudence, reserve, especially in speech.

discriminate (dis krim' i nāt), *v.t. and v.i.* to distinguish; to make a distinction; to treat differently, as to *discriminate* between social classes.

discursive (dis kûr' siv), *adj.* digressive, rambling.

discuss (dis kus'), *v.t.* to debate, argue in detail.

Syn. Argue, debate. To *discuss* is to present and consider all the arguments for and against; to *argue* is to bring forth proofs and reasons in support of one's own issue; to *debate* is to argue formally and in public.

discussion (dis kush' un), *n.* a debate; argument pro and con.

disdain (dis dān'), *n.* contempt, scorn.

disdain (dĭs dān'), v.t. to view with scorn, consider unworthy.

*****disease** (dĭ zēz'), n. illness; any departure from health, either of mind or of body.

disfigure (dĭs fĭg' ūr), v.t. to mar or deform the figure of.

disfranchise (dĭs fran' chĭz), v.t. to deprive of the rights of citizenship, especially the vote.

disgrace (dĭs grās'), n. the state of being in dishonor, shame; anything that brings dishonor or shame, as littered streets are a *disgrace* to a town.

disguise (dĭs gĭz'), n. anything that conceals the identity or nature of a person or thing; especially garments intended to misrepresent.

disguise (dĭs gĭz'), v.t. to change the appearance of so as to conceal; to hide or mask.

disgust (dĭs gust'), n. a feeling of strong aversion or repugnance.

dish (dĭsh), n. a wide, concave or slightly concave vessel, bowl or platter for food; food served in a dish, as a *dish* of potatoes.

dish (dĭsh), v.t. to put into a dish; to make concave, as to *dish* a wheel.

dishearten (dĭs här' tn), v.t. to discourage.

dishonest (dĭs on' est), adj. devoid of honesty, untrustworthy.

dishonor (dĭs on' ẽr), v.t. to deprive of honor; to refuse to cash, as a check.

dishonorable (dĭs on' ẽr ȧbl), adj. lacking honor, disgraceful.

disillusion (dĭs ĭ lū' zhun), v.t. to free from a false belief, especially in the fineness of a person or thing.

disinfect (dĭs in fekt'), v.t. to free of infection by using some germ-killing substance.

disinherit (dĭs in her' ĭt), v.t. to deprive of an inheritance.

*****disintegrate** (dĭs in' tẽ grāt), v.i. and v.t. to break into parts, to crumble; to destroy the unity of.

disk (dĭsk), n. a flat circular plate, or anything resembling it; in computers a plate with magnetic coating.

diskette (dĭs ket'), n. (also known as 'floppy,') a flexible disk.

disk drive (dĭsk' drĭv), n. hardware used to read or write data.

dislike (dĭs lĭk'), n. repugnance, aversion.

dislike (dĭs lĭk'), v.t. to regard with repugnance or distaste.

*****dislocate** (dĭs' lō kāt), v.t. to put out of joint; disarrange.

dislodge (dĭs loj'), v.t. to drive from a place of rest or hiding.

disloyalty (dĭs loi' al tĭ), n. faithlessness; falseness to duty or allegiance.

dismal (dĭz' mal), adj. cheerless, depressing.

dismantle (dĭs man' tl), v.t. to strip of furniture and equipment, as a house or ship.

dismay (dĭs mā'), n. terrified surprise, consternation.

dismay (dĭs mā'), v.t. to strike with fear, terrify; discourage, as the amount of work *dismays* me.

Syn. Daunt, appall. To *dismay* is to crush the spirit with sudden fear; to *daunt* is to frighten or turn aside, as with something insurmounta-

ble; to *appall* is to overcome with awe, horror or fear.

dismember (dĭs mem' bẽr), v.t. to tear limb from limb; to cut into parts.

dismiss (dĭs mĭs'), v.t. to cause or permit to go, as to *dismiss* a class; to send away; to banish.

disorder (dĭs ôr' dẽr), n. lack of order; confusion; derangement of the physical system or the mind.

Syn. Disease. *Disorder* is a general term; one can have a *disorder* of some part of the body without *disease; disease* is an impairment of health, specifically a sickness caused by microorganisms.

Ant. Order.

disparage (dĭs par' ĭj), v.t. to speak slightingly of, depreciate, belittle.

disparity (dĭs par' ĭ tĭ), n. inequality; difference in age, rank, character or social or professional standing.

dispatch (dĭs pach'), n. a message sent; act of putting to death; speed, haste.

dispatch (dĭs pach'), v.t. to send, as a message or a messenger; to put to death; to dispose of, as business, with speed.

dispel (dĭs pel'), v.t. to drive away; to scatter.

Syn. Disperse. To *dispel* is to drive away without violence something intangible, as fears, hopes, grief; to *disperse* is to scatter in different directions, as to *disperse* a crowd.

dispense (dĭs pens'), v.t. and v.i. to deal out in portions; to distribute; to administer, as laws; to do without, as to *dispense* with the details of an explanation or narration.

Syn. Distribute. To *dispense* is an indiscriminate action; to *distribute* is to give to particular individuals. We *dispense* to all, collectively; we *distribute* to each, separately.

disperse (dĭs pûrs'), v.i. and v.t. to scatter in different directions.

dispirited (dĭs pĭr' ĭt ed), adj. disheartened, discouraged.

displace (dĭs plās'), v.t. to put out of place; to take the place of.

display (dĭs plā'), n. exhibition; ostentatious show.

display (dĭs plā'), v.t. to exhibit; show conspicuously.

display screen (dĭs plā' skrēn), n. a computer's device for visual representation of data.

displeasure (dĭs plezh' ẽr), n. annoyance, vexation; an offense.

Syn. Anger. *Displeasure* is a mild feeling compared to *anger* which is intense displeasure at an injury or injustice and is usually accompanied by the desire to punish.

disport (dĭs pôrt'), v.i. and v.t. to divert oneself; to make merry.

disposal (dĭs pōz' al), n. arrangement; bestowal.

Syn. Disposition. Disposal implies authority or power to deal with or settle a matter; *disposition* is the arrangement and ordering of things according to a plan.

disposition (dĭs pō zĭsh' un), n. the ordering or managing of things; power to control and arrange things; state of being arranged; inclination, mood, temper; the fixed qualities of one's nature or character.

Syn. Temperament. *Disposition* is a natural habit of mind; one has a happy or a gloomy *disposition; temperament* is more constitutional; one has a sanguine or a nervous *temperament.*

disprove (dis prōōv'), *v.t.* to demonstrate as false.

disputant (dis' pū tant), *n.* one who argues with another.

dispute (dis pūt'), *n.* a verbal controversy; a quarrel.

disquisition (dis kwi zish' un), *n.* an elaborate essay inquiring into a subject.

disregard (dis rē gärd'), *v.t.* to pay no heed to.

Syn. Neglect, slight. To *disregard* is merely to pay no attention to, as unimportant; to *neglect* is to fail in duty or care. We may *disregard* advice or discomfort, but to *neglect* to feed the dog is inexcusable. To *slight* is to disregard intentionally or scornfully.

disruption (dis rup' shun), *n.* forcible separation, a rending asunder.

*dissect** (di sekt'), *v.t.* to cut into separate parts for examination, as to *dissect* an animal or plant.

dissemble (di sem' bl), *v.t. and v.i.* to hide under a false appearance, pretend, feign; to conceal by pretense.

disseminate (di sem' i nāt), *v.t. and v.i.* to scatter, as seed; to spread, as knowledge.

dissension (di sen' shun), *n.* strong disagreement in opinion.

dissent (di sent'), *v.i.* to differ in opinion, disagree.

dissertation (dis ēr tā' shun), *n.* a long, written treatise on a certain subject; a thesis.

dissever (di sev' ēr), *v.i. and v.t.* to cut apart; to disunite.

dissimulate (di sim' ū lāt), *v.i. and v.t.* to dissemble; to pretend.

dissimulation (di sim ū lā' shun), *n.* pretense.

dissipate (dis' i pāt), *v.i. and v.t.* to live intemperately; to scatter, dispel, drive away, as sunlight *dissipates* darkness, faith *dissipates* fear; to squander, as money; to waste, as strength.

*dissociate** (di sō' shi āt), *v.i. and v.t.* to disjoin; to separate, disunite.

*dissoluble** (di sol' ū bl), *adj.* capable of being dissolved.

dissolute (dis' ō lūt), *adj.* loose in morals, profligate.

dissolution (dis ō lū' shun), *n.* the act of dissolving or of breaking up; disintegration; ruin.

*dissolve** (di zolv'), *v.i. and v.t.* to separate or be separated into particles and absorbed in a liquid; to break or cause to break into component parts, as a partnership.

dissonance (dis' ō nans), *n.* discord.

dissuade (di swād'), *v.t.* to advise against; divert from a purpose by argument or persuasion.

dissuasion (di swā' zhun), *n.* the act of turn-

ing from a purpose by persuasion.

*dissyllabic** (dis i lab' ik), *adj.* having two syllables.

distance (dis' tans), *n.* the space between two objects, or an interval of time; a far region, as to see hills in the *distance.*

distance (dis' tans), *v.t.* to outrun; to surpass.

distant (dis' tant), *adj.* remote, far off, away.

Syn. Far, remote. *Distant* is the opposite of *close* and means apart in space or time; *far* is the opposite of *near* and means a great way off; *remote* is very far removed from contact.

Ant. Close, near.

distasteful (dis tāst' fool), *adj.* unpleasant to the taste; displeasing to the feelings; offensive.

distemper (dis tem' pēr), *n.* an illness or malady, especially a serious, contagious disease of young dogs.

distend (dis tend'), *v.i. and v.t.* to stretch or cause to stretch out in all directions; to swell; to inflate; to bloat.

distention (dis ten' shun), *n.* swelling; inflation.

distil (dis til'), *v.i. and v.t.* to fall or cause to fall in drops; to vaporize and condense, as in making brandy from wine.

distinct (dis tingkt'), *adj.* plain, clear; unmistakably separated from anything else.

distinction (dis tingk' shun), *n.* the act of distinguishing; that by which things are distinguished one from another; the state of being distinguished from others, as socially or professionally; high standing or special quality.

distinguish (dis tin' guish), *v.t.* to separate from others by some mark or special quality.

distinguished (dis ting' gwisht), *adj.* eminent.

Syn. Conspicuous, noted, eminent, illustrious. A man is *distinguished* in proportion as he is distinct or separate from others; he is *conspicuous* in proportion as he is easily seen among his fellow men; *noted* in proportion to the extent of his renown; *eminent* as he stands out among rivals; *illustrious* as his name and fame may shine before the world.

distort (dis tôrt'), *v.t.* to twist out of natural shape, as things or facts.

distract (dis trakt'), *v.t.* to divert, as attention.

distraught (dis trôt'), *adj.* bewildered; confused; distracted.

distress (dis tres'), *n.* affliction; adversity.

Syn. Anxiety, anguish, agony. *Distress* is great physical or mental pain; *anxiety* involves uncertainty and has regard for the future. *Anguish* is almost torture of mind or body; *agony* is anguish so intense as to cause writhing.

distress (dis tres'), *v.t.* to afflict; to cause pain or suffering.

distribute (dis trib' ūt), *v.t.* to deal out; to apportion; to allot.

distribution (dis tri bū' shun), *n.* the act of distributing, apportionment, allotment; that which is distributed; manner of distributing.

*¤**district** (dĭs' trĭkt), n. a part of a municipality or state set apart as for administrative purposes.

distrust (dĭs trust'), n. lack of confidence or faith.

Syn. Suspicion, diffidence. We may look upon either ourselves or others with *distrust;* we can have *suspicion* only of others. *Distrust* of another makes one regard his words or acts with *suspicion. Distrust* of one's own powers may cause *diffidence.*

Ant. Assurance, confidence, conviction, certainty.

disturb (dĭs ṫûrb'), v.t. to trouble; to vex.

ditch (dĭch), n. a trench cut in the earth, as for drainage.

ditto (dĭt' ō), n. the same as before or above: expressed by two small marks (") and used in bills, accounts and lists to save repetition of items.

diurnal (dī ûr' nal), adj. daily, happening every day: opposite of *nocturnal.*

dive (dīv), n. a plunge into water or the downward swoop of a bird or an airplane.

dive (dīv), v.i. [p.t. either dived or dove, pr.p. diving] to plunge head first into water; to plunge forward and down, as an airplane.

divergence (dī vûr' jens), n. a moving of two things in different directions from a given point; deviation, as from a standard.

divers (dī' vērz), adj. several, various, as *divers* kinds of wares for sale.

diverse (dī vûrs'), adj. different, unlike; varied.

diversify (dī vûr' sĭ fī), v.t. to make different.

diversity (dī vûr' sĭ tĭ), n. difference, variety.

*¤**diversion** (dī vûr' shun), n. a turning aside; amusement.

divert (dī vûrt'), v.t. to turn aside from its course or away from a center, as to *divert* one's attention; to amuse.

*¤**divest** (dī vest'), v.t. to strip; to deprive of, as rights.

divide (dī vīd'), v.i. and v.t. to separate; to break apart; to apportion.

Syn. Separate, part. We *divide* something thought of as a whole; we *separate* or *part* parts that have been joined.

Ant. Join, unite.

divide (dī vīd'), n. a height of land forming a ridge between two drainage basins.

dividend (dĭv' ĭ dend), n. a number that is divided; a sum of money, earned profits, to be divided, as among shareholders.

divination (dĭv ĭ nā' shun), n. the art of foretelling events.

divine (dī vīn'), v.t. to foretell; to detect, through reasoning or intuition.

divine (dī vīn'), adj. pertaining to God; godlike.

divinity (dī vĭn' ĭ tĭ), n. the quality of divineness; a god; Divinity, God.

division (dī vĭzh' un), n. the act of dividing; state of being divided; one of the parts into which anything is divided; a U. S. army unit commanded by a major general and consisting of a headquarters, two infantry brigades, a light-artillery brigade and other

troops.

divisor (dĭ vī' zēr), n. the number by which another number is divided.

divorce (dĭ vōrs'), n. a legal dissolution of the marriage contract; separation of two things previously associated.

divorce (dĭ vōrs'), v.t. to separate from a husband or wife through legal action ending a marriage; to disunite.

*¤**divulge** (dĭ vulj'), v.t. to tell, reveal, as to *divulge* a plan.

do (dōō), v.i. and v.t. [p.t. did, p.p. done, pr.p. doing] to act; to perform; to accomplish; to finish; to achieve; to exert; to work at.

docile (dos' ĭl), adj. easy to teach, manageable.

docility (dō sĭl' ĭ tĭ), n. tractableness.

dock (dok), n. a landing place for boats, a wharf; a weed with a long taproot.

dock (dok), v.i. and v.t. to come to or be moored to a dock; to cut off or curtail, as wages or a horse's tail.

docket (dok' et), n. a list of cases due for trial; a bill tied to a shipment of goods; a label.

docking (dok´ ing), adv. the means by which two spacecraft are joined together.

doctor (dok' tēr), n. one learned or skilled in any particular branch of knowledge, especially a physician or surgeon; one who has a degree given for highest learning or attainment in some special field of knowledge or science.

doctor (dok' tēr), v.t. and v.i. to treat wounds or sickness of body or mind as a physician; to practice medicine.

doctrine (dok' trĭn), n. the principles or dogma of any branch of knowledge, especially of a sect or party; a belief held or taught.

Syn. Dogma, tenet. A *doctrine* is any body of teachings offered to others as true and practicable,

document (dok' ū ment), n. a formal or official paper.

documentation (doc ū men ta' shun), n. in connection with computers, the user's manual.

dodge (doj), v.i. and v.t. to evade, as a blow or a duty.

doe (dō), n. a female deer, antelope or hare.

doff (dof), v.t. to take off, as a hat: opposite of *don.*

dog (dôg), n. a domesticated animal, related in ancestry to the wolf, the companion and helpmate of man since prehistoric times; a male dog and the male of certain animals, as the fox; an andiron.

dog (dôg), v.t. to trail or follow closely; to worry.

dogma (dôg' ma), n. definite religious or theological doctrine; a tenet.

dogmatic (dôg mat' ĭk), adj. authoritative; stating or holding opinion for fact.

dogwood (dôg' wood), n. the wild cornel.

doily (doi' lĭ), n. a small ornamental table mat.

dole (dōl), n. charitable distribution of food or money; money from a public fund dealt out to the unemployed and needy.

dole (dōl), v.t. to deal out sparingly.

doleful (dōl' fool), adj. sorrowful, dismal.

doll (dol), n. a child's toy baby, a puppet.

dollar (dol' ẽr), n. a monetary unit of the United States and Canada, worth a hundred cents.

*__dolorous__ (dol' ẽr us), adj. sad, sorrowful.

dolphin (dol' fin), n. a sea mammal akin to the whale but much smaller: often called _porpoise_.

dolt (dōlt), n. a dull, stupid fellow.

domain (dō mān'), n. possession of land; land possessed and ruled over; lordship over a region; any sphere of action or thought, as within the _domain_ of science.

dome (dōm), n. a hemispherical roof or anything with a similar shape.

domestic (dō mes' tik), n. one who does housework for pay.

domestic (dō mes' tik), adj. pertaining to the house or home.

domesticate (dō mes' ti kāt), v.t. to make suitable for use or a place in the home; to tame.

domesticity (dō mes tis' i ti), n. the state of being suited to or devoted to home life.

*__domicile__ (dom' i sil), n. a dwelling or residence, a place of abode.

dominant (dom' i nant), adj. ruling, controlling; chief, predominating.

dominate (dom' i nāt), v.t. to govern, rule, control; to exercise chief power.

domineer (dom i nẽr'), v.i. and v.t. to exercise authority arrogantly or tyrannically.

dominion (dō min' yun), n. supreme authority; a territory subject to such authority as part of an empire but with much power of self-rule in local matters.

domino (dom' i nō), n. a costume of hood and a half mask used in a masquerade; an oblong piece of wood marked with dots with which the game _dominoes_ is played.

don (don), v.t. to put on: opposite of _doff_.

donate (dō' nāt), v.t. to give, contribute.

donkey (dong' ki), n. the ass; a stupid person.

*__donor__ (dō' nẽr), n. a giver.

doom (dōōm), n. fate; a sentence of punishment.

doom (dōōm), v.t. to pronounce judgment upon; to sentence.

doomsday (dōōmz' dā), n. the Judgment Day.

door (dōr), n. a hinged or sliding frame by which an opening into a building, room or piece of furniture is closed.

dormant (dôr´ mant), adj. sleeping; inactive.

dormer (dôr´ mẽr), n. a window set vertically in a sloping roof.

*__dormitory__ (dôr' mi tō ri), n. a sleeping room with a number of beds; a room or building in an institution in which the inmates sleep.

dormouse (dôr' mous), n. [pl. dormice] a small European squirrellike rodent.

dorsal (dôr´ sal), adj. pertaining to, or located on, the back, as a _dorsal fin_.

dory (dō´ ri), n. a flat-bottomed rowboat with a sharp prow and narrow stern.

dose (dōs), n. the quantity of medicine taken at one time.

dot (dot), n. a small point or speck.

*__dotage__ (dōt' ij), n. feebleness of mind, especially as due to old age.

double (dub' l), n. twice the quantity, size or amount; a duplicate; an understudy for an actor or singer.

double (dub' l), v.t. and v.i. to increase to twice the size, value or amount; to duplicate; to clench, as to _double_ the fists; to fold over, make of two thicknesses, as to _double_ cloth; to retrace a course, as a fox _doubles_ to confuse the scent; to substitute, as he _doubles_ for Tom in that role.

double (dub' l), adj. twofold; folded over; deceitful.

doubt (dout), n. mental indecision, uncertainty; misgiving.

Syn. Distrust, suspicion. _Doubt_ is lack of certainty about a fact or theory; _distrust_ is lack of trust or confidence in a person or thing; _suspicion_ is specific, active, sometimes unfriendly, and often unfounded, _distrust_.

Ant. Belief, faith.

doubt (dout), v.i. and v.t. to waver in opinion or belief; to question, distrust.

doubtful (dout' fool), adj. having doubts, uncertain.

douche (dōōsh), n. a jet of water or vapor; an instrument used to throw a jet of water or vapor.

dough (dō), n. a soft mass of flour paste, especially for bread.

doughy (dō' i), adj. doughlike, pasty.

dour (dōōr), adj. severe, stern, obstinate.

douse (dous), v.t. to plunge into a liquid.

dove (duv), n. any bird of the pigeon family, as the turtledove or mourning dove.

dovecot (duv' kot), n. a pigeonhouse.

dovetail (duv' tāl), v.t. to fasten with a joint resembling the spread out tail of a pigeon.

dowdy (dou' di), adj. untidy.

dowel (dou' el), n. a joint made by fitting a pin into a hole in another piece.

dower (dou' ẽr), n. a woman's life-share in her dead husband's estate.

down (doun), n. the soft feathers on young birds and beneath the stiff feathers on grown birds; anything resembling this, as the first hair on the human face or the fuzz on certain plant leaves.

down (doun), n. a sandy hill along a shore; an open upland region.

down (doun), v.t. to put down.

down (doun), adj. descending, as a _down_ slope.

down (doun), adv. toward a lower position, as he was going _down;_ to the utmost, as loaded _down;_ from the past, as handed _down_ from father to son.

down (doun), prep. along something in a descending line, as _down_ the hill.

downcast (doun' kåst), adj. dejected.

downers (doun´ erz), n. slang term for drugs such as barbiturates that depress the central nervous system.

downright (doun' rit), adj. thorough; blunt, informal.

*dowry (dou' rï), *n.* [*pl.* dowries] the property or money a woman brings to her husband when she marries.

doxology (doks ol' ŏ jî), *n.* one of several short hymns or chants of praise to God, as "Praise God from whom all blessings flow."

doze (dŏz), *v.i.* to sleep lightly or fitfully.

dozen (duz' n), *n.* a collection of twelve articles.

drab (drab), *n.* a kind of dull-brown or yellowish-brown woolen cloth.

draft or draught (dråft), *n.* an order for money to be paid from an account; the depth of water a boat or ship draws when loaded; a current of air; a preliminary sketch.

drag (drag), *n.* a dredge; slow, difficult motion; anything that drags.

drag (drag), *v.i. and v.t.* to trail; to lag; to haul over the ground; to search for with something that drags, as a hook.

dragon (drag' un), *n.* a fabulous huge serpent or lizard with wings.

dragoon (dra gŏŏn'), *n.* a mounted soldier.

drain (drån), *n.* that through which liquid is drained off, as a sewer or gutter.

drain (drån), *v.i. and v.t.* to flow off gradually; to be carried off, as water; to become empty because of the flowing off of water, as a sink *drains;* to empty of water, as a valley *drains* into a river; to draw off, as to *drain* water from a pond; to draw off water from, as to *drain* the pond.

drake (drāk), *n.* a male duck.

dram (dram), *n.* 1-18th of an ounce, troy measure; 1-16th of an ounce, avoirdupois measure.

*drama (drä' ma), *n.* a play in prose or verse depicting life or character.

dramatic (dra mat' ĭk), *adj.* pertaining to drama; theatrical; vivid, moving the emotions.

drape (dråp), *v.t.* to cover with curtains; to hang, as a curtain.

draper (dråp' ẽr), *n.* formerly, one who made cloths; now, a dealer in cloth.

drapery (drā' pẽr ĭ), *n.* textiles; hangings for a room or window, as curtains.

drastic (dras' tĭk), *adj.* acting fast and hard; severe, as *drastic* policies or punishment.

draw (drô), *v.t.* to drag or pull; represent in a picture or a lined figure.

Syn. Drag, haul, pull, pluck, tug. To *draw* is to put a body in motion toward oneself; to *drag* is to pull against resistance; to *haul* is to oppose still greater resistance; to *pull* may or may not be to move a thing, as horses may pull hard before they draw a load up a hill. To *pluck* is to pull with a sudden twitch; to *tug* is to pull with mighty effort.

drawback (drô' bak), *n.* resistance to a pull; in business, a rebate; a hindrance or loss of advantage.

drawer (drô' ẽr), *n.* one who or that which draws; (drôr) a sliding box in a desk or bureau: *drawers* (drôrz), undergarments for the lower part of the body and the legs.

drawing (drô' ing), *n.* the act of one who

draws; something drawn; a picture or diagram made with crayon, chalk, pen or pencil.

drawl (drôl), *n.* slow, lazy utterance.

drawl (drôl), *v.i. and v.t.* to speak or utter in a slow, lazy way.

dray (drā), *n.* a stout cart or truck.

dread (dred), *n.* great fear, especially of evil to come; reverence, awe.

dread (dred), *v.t.* to fear greatly, be afraid or.

dreadful (dred' fool), *adj.* causing fear or awe; shocking, horrible.

dreadnought (dred' nôt), *n.* a battleship having maximum armor and armament.

dream (drēm), *n.* thoughts and images experienced in sleep; any imaginary vision.

dream (drēm), *v.i.* to experience thoughts and images in sleep; to have daytime visions.

dreary (drēr'ĭ), *adj.* tiresome, monotonous; dismal, depressing.

dredge (drej), *n.* a machine for scraping the bed of a body of water or for digging a channel; a sifter, as for flour.

dredge (drej), *v.t.* to scrape, as the bed of a channel; to sprinkle with a sifted substance, as flour.

dregs (dregz), *n.* the sediment of liquors, grounds, lees; the worthless remains of anything.

drench (drench), *v.t.* to wet thoroughly.

dress (dres), *n.* costume or attire in general; a lady's gown.

dress (dres), *v.i. and v.t.* to attire, clothe, array; to arrange in line, as soldiers; to prepare for use, as to *dress* poultry; to prepare for display, as to *dress* a shop window; to treat and bandage, as a wound.

dresser (dres' ẽr), *n.* cupboard, bureau.

dressing (dres' ing), *n.* the act of putting on clothes; forcemeat; the stuffing of fowl for roasting; anything spread over land, as manure, broken rock or top-*dressing.*

dribble (drib' l), *v.i. and v.t.* to fall or cause to fall, drop by drop, or in a slow stream.

driblet (drib' let), *n.* a small bit of anything.

drift (drift), *n.* the slow movement of water or air, or of anything carried by them; the motion of a ship or plane apart from that which is controlled by engine or rudder; drifting matter.

drift (drift), *v.i.* to be carried along by a current of water or air.

drill (dril), *n.* an instrument for boring holes; any exercise, physical or mental, repeated with regularity; the training of soldiers in the manual of arms; a light furrow in which seed is sown; a heavy linen or cotton cloth.

drill (dril), *v.i. and v.t.* to go through a drill, as soldiers; to put through a drill, as to *drill* troops; to bore a hole; to make with a drill, as to *drill* a hole; to instruct or discipline, as to *drill* a student in algebra.

drink (dringk), *n.* any liquid to be swallowed; the amount drunk at one time.

drink (dringk), *v.i. and v.t.* to swallow a liquid; to swallow, as to *drink* milk; to receive through the senses, as to *drink* in beauty.

drip (drip), *n.* fall or escape of liquid in drops.

drip (drip), *v.i. and v.t.* to fall or let fall in drops.

drive (driv), *n.* the act of driving; a ride in a vehicle; a road for driving; a collection of logs floating down a stream; a mechanical device for giving motion to a machine; organized promotion of a project, as a *drive* to raise money or votes; a planned offensive advance of troops against an enemy.

drive (driv), *v.i. and v.t.* to rush with force; to impel, as a ball; to bore, as a tunnel; to direct, as a horse.

drizzle (driz' l), *n.* a light fall of rain.

droll (drōl), *adj.* amusing, odd, comical.

drollery (drōl' ēr i), *n.* buffoonery; humor, a jest.

*****dromedary** (drom' ē der i), *n.* the Arabian one-humped camel.

drone (drōn), *v.i. and v.t.* to make a monotonous sound; to read or speak in a low, dull tone.

droop (drōop), *v.i.* to hang down or bend, as with hunger or fatigue; to be depressed; to languish.

drop (drop), *n.* a globule of moisture; a fall, descent.

drop (drop), *v.i. and v.t.* to fall in drops or drip; to fall, as an apple *drops* to the ground; to let fall, as to *drop* a cup.

dropout (drop' out'), *n.* a student who leaves school before graduation; a person who abandons any project before its completion.

dross (drôs), *n.* the scum or slag of melted metal; waste matter; refuse.

*****drought** (drout), *n.* prolonged absence of rain; a long spell of dry weather; dearth.

drove (drōv), *n.* a group of cattle or sheep brought together for driving.

drown (droun), *v.i. and v.t.* to perish or to kill by suffocation in water; drowning is sometimes prevented by artificial respiration and use of restoratives.

drowsy (drou' si), *adj.* sleepy.

drudge (druj), *n.* one who does dull routine work; *v.i.* to work hard at dreary tasks.

drug (drug), *n.* a substance used as medicine, especially a narcotic preparation.

drug (drug), *v.t.* to dose with drugs; to stupefy with, or as if with a narcotic, as *drugged* with sleep.

drum (drum), *n.* a musical instrument consisting of a cylinder with a head of stretched skin, beaten with sticks.

drunk (drungk), *adj.* intoxicated with, or as if with, strong drink.

dry (drī), *v.i. and v.t.* to make or become dry.

dry (drī), *adj.* free from moisture, not wet or damp.

dual (dū' al), *adj.* composed of two, twofold, double.

duality (dū al' i ti), *n.* the state of being twofold.

dub (dub), *v.t.* to bestow knighthood or any title upon; to call, name.

dubious (dū' bi us), *adj.* doubtful; of uncertain result, as a *dubious* game; causing doubt.

duchess (duch' es), *n.* the wife or widow of a duke; a woman who rules a duchy.

duchy (duch' i), *n.* the territory controlled by a duke or duchess.

duck (duk), *n.* a flat-billed swimming bird with short legs and neck.

duct (dukt), *n.* a tube by which a fluid is conveyed, as a tear *duct.*

*****ductile** (duk' til), *adj.* capable of being drawn out into threads or hammered thin; tractable.

due (dū), *adj.* owed or owing, as *due* honors; owed as a debt; ascribable, caused by, as *due* to weather conditions.

duel (dū' el), *n.* a combat between two persons with deadly weapons.

duet (dū' et), *n.* a vocal or instrumental rendering of a musical selection by two performers; a composition for such rendering.

duke (dūk), *n.* one of the British or European nobility of highest rank next to a prince.

dulcet (dul' set), *adj.* sweet-sounding, melodious.

dull (dul), *v.t.* to make dull, as paper *dulls* scissors.

dull (dul), *adj.* stupid, sluggish, as a *dull* pupil, *dull* wits; slow-acting, listless; not sharp, as a *dull* knife; dim, as a *dull* star; not resounding, as a *dull* sound; cloudy, as *dull* weather; boring, as a *dull* book.

duly (dū' li), *adv.* in a fit and becoming manner, in due time.

dumb (dum), *adj.* incapable of speech, either permanently or momentarily; unusually stupid or unintelligent.

dump (dump), *n.* a place where rubbish is deposited.

dump (dump), *v.t.* to unload by tipping, as a truck; to empty a container by throwing its contents out in a mass, as to *dump* coal; to sell excess products abroad more cheaply than in the home market, to keep domestic prices up.

dun (dun), *n.* one who insistently demands payment; an urgent demand for payment.

dun (dun), *v.t.* to press for payment.

dun (dun), *adj.* dull brown in color.

dunce (duns), *n.* a stupid, ignorant person.

dune (dūn), *n.* a heap or hill of drifted sand.

dungeon (dun' jun), *n.* a dark cell, especially one underground.

duodecimal (dū ō des' i mal), *adj.* consisting of, or counted by, twelves.

duodecimo (dū ō des' i mō), *n.* a sheet of paper folded into twelve leaves; a book printed on paper so folded.

duodenum (dū ō dē' num), *n.* the upper part of the small intestine.

duotone (dū' ō tōn), *n.* a picture printed in two tones of one color.

duotype (dū' ō tip), *n.* a picture resulting from two halftone plates of the same negative differently etched.

dupe (dūp), *n.* one easily deceived; a victim of deception.

duplex (dū' plex), *adj.* double, twofold.

duplicate (dū' pli kāt), *n.* the exact match of anything; a reproduction or facsimile.

duplicate (dū' pli kāt), *v.t.* to make a duplicate of; to match; to repeat; to double.

duplicity (dū plis' i ti), *n.* deceit, double-dealing.

durable (dū' ra bl), *adj.* lasting, enduring.

Syn. Lasting, permanent. *Durable* means able to endure wear and tear; *lasting* means continuing long, sometimes forever; *permanent* is the opposite of *temporary*.

Ant. Fragile, fleeting, temporary.

durance (dūr' ans), *n.* imprisonment.

duration (dū rā' shun), *n.* continuance in time; the period of time a thing continues.

during (dūr' ing), *prep.* in the time of.

dusk (dusk), *n.* twilight or the darker part of dawn.

dust (dust), *n.* fine dry particles of earth suspended in the air or settled upon an object; any fine powder.

dutiable (dū' ti a bl), *adj.* subject to duty or tariff.

*****duty** (dū' ti), *n.* [*pl.* duties] obligatory service; moral obligation, as respect and obedience due to parents or superiors; that which is required by one's station or office; a tax on imports.

Syn. Obligation. *Duty* has to do with the conscience; an *obligation* arises from specific circumstances, and is a species of *duty*. He who guarantees payment of a sum of money assumes an *obligation;* he who marries contracts new *duties*.

dwarf (dwôrf), *n.* a human being, plant or animal of much less than average size.

dwarf (dwôrf), *v.t.* to prevent from growing to natural size; to diminish in proportions, either real or apparent.

dwarf computer (dwôrf com pū ´ ter), *n.* a computer which uses a small number of brain chips and memory chips, frequently found inside microwave ovens, electronic typewriters, etc.

dwell (dwel), *v.i.* to abide; to reside; to linger.

dwindle (dwin' dl), *v.i.* to become gradually less.

dye (dī), *n.* material used for coloring, a dyestuff.

dye (dī), *v.t.* to stain or color, especially by saturating with a dyestuff.

dynamic (dī nam' ik), *adj.* active, having energy and force.

dynamics (dī nam' iks), *n.* the division of mechanical science that treats of bodies in motion and forces that produce or change such motion.

dynamo (dī' na mō), *n.* a machine for converting mechanical energy into electric energy to be distributed in current form.

*****dynasty** (dī' nas ti), *n.* a line or succession of sovereigns from one family.

dysentery (dis ´ en ter i), *n.* a tropical disease akin to diarrhea.

dyspepsia (dis pep' sha), *n.* indigestion, disordered digestion.

E

each (ēch), *adj.* every one of two or more, as *each* child in the procession carried a flag.

each (ēch), *pron;* every one of a number of persons or things.

each (ēch), *adv.* apiece, as apples are two cents *each*.

eager (ē' gēr), *adj.* keenly desirous to do or obtain; ardent.

Syn. Ardent, burning, desirous.

Ant. Dull, indifferent.

eagle (ē'gl), *n.* a bird of prey noted for its size, strength, sharp sight and swift flight; a ten-dollar gold coin of the U. S.

ear (ēr), *n.* the organ of hearing; the external part of that organ.

earl (ûrl), *n.* an Irish or British nobleman ranking next below a marquis and above a viscount.

early (ûr' li), *adj.* coming relatively near the start of a period or series, as *early* American literature; happening before the usual or set time, as an *early* arrival; not late.

early (ûr' li), *adv.* in the first stages or period, as *early* in American history; ahead of set time, as to arrive *early*.

earmark (ēr' märk), *n.* a mark of identification on an animal's ear; any distinguishing mark.

earn (ûrn), *v.t.* to deserve as proper recompense for labor or service; to get by labor, as to *earn* $5.

earnest (ûr' nest), *n.* a pledge; an intent state of mind, as in *earnest*.

earnest (ûr' nest), *adj.* characterized by seriousness of purpose.

earnings (ûr' ningz), *n.* money received as compensation for work or services.

earring (ēr' ring), *n.* a ring passing through the lobe of the ear, worn as an ornament; any ornament worn on or hung from the ear.

earth (ûrth), *n.* the terrestrial globe on which mankind lives; soft ground, as distinguished from stone; land, as distinguished ·from air or water; the burrow of an animal, as the fox took to *earth*.

earthen (ûr' then), *adj.* made of earth, as an *earthen* pot.

earthquake (ûrth' kwāk), *n.* a localized trembling of the surface of the earth, due to disturbances underground.

earthwork (ûrth' wûrk), *n.* in military usage, a sheltering ditch with the dug dirt thrown up in front; any embankment of earth.

earthworm (ûrth' wûrm), *n.* the ordinary burrowing worm found in damp soil.

earthy (ûrth' i), *adj.* of the earth; like earth.

earwax (ēr' waks), *n.* waxlike secretion of the passages of the ear; cerumen.

ease (ēz), *n.* comfort; freedom from pain, distress or embarrassment.

Syn. Comfort. *Ease* is relaxation from toil or release from pain or distress; *comfort* is active enjoyment or content.

Ant. Discomfort, uneasiness.

easel (ē' zl), *n.* a frame to support a painter's canvas.

east (ēst), *n.* the direction toward the rising sun.

easterly (ēst' ēr li), *adj.* toward or from the east, as an *easterly* direction.

eastern (ēs' tērn), *adj.* of or toward the east.

easterner (ēs' tēr nēr), *n.* one who lives in the east especially the eastern part of the U. S.

eastward (ēst' wērd), *adj.* moving or looking toward the east, as an *eastward* window.

eastward (ēst' wērd), *adv.* toward the east, as to look *eastward*.

easy (ēz'i), *adj.* [*comp.* easier, *superl.* easiest] free from pain or worry; not hard to do.

Syn. Calm, manageable.

Ant. Uneasy, tense, difficult.

eat (ēt), *v.i. and v.t.* [*p.t.* ate, *p.p.* eaten, *pr.p.* eating] to take food; to chew and swallow; to destroy, wear away, as if by eating, as rust *eats* iron.

eaves (ēvz), *n. pl.* the overhanging edges of a roof.

eavesdrop (ēvz' drop), *v.i.* to listen secretly to others' talk.

ebb (eb), *n.* the flow of a tide back to the sea; a low state, as of health or fortune.

ebb (eb), *v.i.* to flow back, as a tide to the sea; to decline, as health or fortune.

*****ebony** (eb' un i), *n.* a hard, durable black wood.

*****ebullient** (ē bul' i ent), *adj.* boiling up.

ebullition (eb u lish' un), *n.* the act of boiling or bubbling up.

*****eccentric** (ek sen' trik), *n.* a circle not having the same center as another circle with which it partly coincides; an erratic person; a disk mounted on an axis which does not pass through the center and serves to change circular motion into a thrusting motion.

eccentric (ek sen' trik), *adj.* out of center; of persons, erratic, freakish.

eccentricity (ek sen tris' i ti), *n.* [*pl.* eccentricities] state of being eccentric; any oddity or deviation from what is usual.

*****ecclesiastic** (e klē zi as' tik), *n.* a clergyman.

ecclesiastic (e klē zi as' tik), *adj.* pertaining to the church.

echo (ek' ō), *n.* [*pl.* echoes] repetition of a sound, caused by reflection of the sound waves; any repetition of words or meaning, as this verse is an *echo* of Longfellow.

echo (ek' ō), *v.i. and v.t.* to give an echo, send back or repeat as a sound; to repeat or imitate, as he *echoes* his big brother.

*****éclat** (ā klä'), *n.* brilliant performance, showy actions; glory.

eclectic (ek lek' tik), *adj.* selecting; choosing from different sources, as *eclectic* teachings.

*****eclipse** (ē klips'), *n.* total or partial obscuration of a heavenly body by intervention of another; any overshadowing or disappearance, as the glory of the empire is in *eclipse*.

eclipse (ē klips'), *v.t.* to overshadow, obscure.

Syn. Obscure. The passing of one heavenly body between an observer and a second heavenly body *eclipses* the first heavenly body; anything that makes the appearance of a body less clear *obscures* it, as clouds *obscure* the sun.

Ant. Discover, reveal.

ecliptic (ē klip' tik), *n.* the apparent path of the sun through the heavens in a year.

eclogue (ek' lôg), *n.* a pastoral poem, an idyl.

ecology (i kol´ō jē), *n.* a division of biology which relates an organism to its environment.

*****economic** (ē kō nom' ik), *adj.* pertaining to the management of public affairs in connection with the accumulation, distribution and use of goods and money.

*****economical** (ē kō nom' i kal), *adj.* thrifty in handling wealth.

*****economics** (ē kō nom' iks), *n.* the science treating of the production and management of public wealth.

economize (ē kon' ō miz), *v.i.* to manage with care and frugality.

*****economy** (ē kon' ō mi), *n.* management of the affairs of a household or community; thrifty management, frugality.

*****ecru** (ek' rōō), *n.* a fabric having the color of raw silk or linen; the color beige.

ecru (ek' rōō), *adj.* beige-colored.

ecstasy (ek' sta si), *n.* [*pl.* ecstasies] a state of deep, especially joyous, emotion; rapture.

ecstatic (ek stat' ik), *adj.* causing or caused by ecstasy; rapturous.

ecumenical (ek ū men' i kal), *adj.* general, universal.

*****eczema** (ek' zē ma), *n.* an itching, scaly disease of the skin.

eddy (ed' i), *n.* a current of air or water moving contrary to the main stream; a body of air or water moving in a circle; a whirlpool.

eddy (ed' i), *v.i.* to move in a circle, as a current of air or water.

edge (ej), *n.* the thin, working side of a cutting instrument; the extreme border, as of a precipice or a body of water.

edge (ej), *v.i. and v.t.* to furnish with an edge; to move by degrees, as *edge* in.

edging (ej´ ing), *n.* material that forms a border.

edible (ed' i bl), *n.* anything fit to be eaten.

edible (ed' i bl), *adj.* fit to be eaten, eatable.

*****edict** (ē' dikt), *n.* a public proclamation or decree.

edification (ed i fi kā' shun), *n.* improvement, instruction, as for the *edification* of the public.

edifice (ed' i fis), *n.* a large, fine building or structure, such as capitols, parliament and reichstag houses, many court houses, city and town halls, churches, libraries, etc.

edify (ed' i fi), *v.t.* to build up mentally or morally; to teach, improve.

edit (ed' it), *v.t.* to revise and prepare for publication, as a manuscript; to direct the policies of, as a magazine or newspaper.

*****edition** (ē dish' un), *n.* the number of copies of a literary work put out at one time; a text as prepared by an editor, as Bentley's *edition* of Horace; any single printing of a newspaper, as the 10 o'clock *edition*.

educate (ed' ū kāt), *v.t.* to develop or train the mind of, teach; to prepare for a special profession or vocation.

education (ed ū kā' shun), *n.* moral and mental discipline gained by study and instruction; the process of acquiring this.
　Syn. Training, discipline. *Education* is the general term for all schooling; *training* is the practise of something to gain skill or ease. *Education* embraces many subjects; one takes *training* in a specific subject; *discipline* is systematic training to gain strength or effectiveness.

educator (ed' ū kā tēr), *n.* one who educates, a teacher.

educe (ē dūs'), *v.t.* to draw forth; to evolve.

eel (ēl), *n.* a long snakelike fish without scales or pelvic fins.

eerie or **eery** (ē' ri), *adj.* weird, uncanny.

*****efface** (e fās'), *v.t.* to erase, rub or strike out; to obliterate, destroy.

effect (e fekt'), *n.* the result of action; purport, as he spoke to the *effect* that—; a clear impression produced by an utterance or work of art.

effect (e fekt'), *v.t.* to cause, produce, bring about.
　Syn. Execute, accomplish. To *effect* is to bring about often in spite of resistance; to *execute* is to effect formally, as a law; to *accomplish* is to complete, as a task.

effective (e fek' tiv), *adj.* able to produce a particular result; efficient; in effect, as a law; impressive, as an *effective* remark.

*****effects** (e fekts'), *n.* personal property.

*****effectual** (e fek' tū al), *adj.* producing an effect.

effeminacy (e fem' i na si), *n.* the quality, in a man, of being womanish.

effeminate (e fem' i nit), *adj.* womanish.

*****efferent** (ef' ēr ent), *adj.* bearing out or away, as certain blood vessels are *efferent*.

effervesce (ef ēr ves'), *v.i.* to bubble and hiss, as a fermenting liquid; to be gay, merry, bubbling over with fun.

effervescent (ef ēr ves' ent), *adj.* bubbling.

effete (e fēt'), *adj.* no longer fertile or productive, as animals or plants; worn out, spent, as *effete* customs.

efficacious (ef i kā' shus), *adj.* producing a desired effect.

efficacy (ef' i ka si), *n.* the power of producing effects.

efficiency (e fish' en si), *n.* easy and quick production of desired results; skill and capability; the ratio of energy expended to power produced in a machine.

efficient (e fish' ent), *adj.* producing desired results easily; capable, skilful.

effigy (ef' i gy), [*pl.* effigies] a representation of a person.

effluvium (e floo' vi um), *n.* disagreeable exhalations from decaying matter.

effort (ef' ērt), *n.* exertion of power, physical or mental; an attempt; endeavor.

effrontery (e frun' tēr i), *n.* impudence, insolent boldness.

effulgence (e ful' jens), *n.* radiance of light.

effulgent (e ful' jent), *adj.* giving out light; shining.

effusion (e fū' zhun), *n.* the act of pouring out; gushing speech.

effusive (e fū' siv), *adj.* pouring forth; extravagant, gushing.

egg (eg), *n.* the oval or round body laid by birds from which their young are produced.

eggplant (eg' plånt), *n.* a plant with large ovoid fruit, used as a vegetable.

*****ego** (ē' gō), *n.* the conscious self.

*****egoism** (ē' gō izm), *n.* the doctrine that self-development is the end and motive of all action; hence, selfishness.

*****egotism** (ē' gō tizm), *n.* vanity, conceit.

*****egregious** (ē grē' jus), *adj.* remarkable, in a bad sense.

egress (ē' gres), *n.* departure; a way out, an exit, as *egress* from a building or a fix.

eider (ī' dēr), *n.* a large sea duck.

eight (āt), *adj.* one more than seven.

eighteen (ā tēn'), *adj.* one more than seventeen.

eighteenth (ā tēnth'), *adj.* next after 17th.

eighth (ātth), *adj.* next after seventh.

eightieth (ā' ti eth), *adj.* next after 79th.

eighty (ā' ti), *n.* one more than 79.

*****either** (ē' thēr), *adj.* one or the other of two, as wear *either* hat; one and the other of two, each, as the gate has a post at *either* side.

either (ē' thēr), *pron.* one of two, as choose *either* of the hats.

either (ē' thēr), *conj.* on one or the other supposition: correlative of *or*, as she is *either* laughing or crying.

either (ē' thēr), *adv.* any more than, also: used with *not*, as I am not hungry or thirsty *either*.

*****ejaculate** (ē jak' ū lāt), *v.t.* to utter suddenly.

ejaculation (ē jak ū lā' shun), *n.* an exclamation.

eject (ē jekt'), *v.t.* to throw out; to drive out, expel.

ejection (ē jek' shun), *n.* act of throwing out or of being driven out.

elaborate (ē lab' ō rāt), *v.t.* to work out in detail, perfect.

*****elaborate** (ē lab' ō rit), *adj.* carefully worked out, painstaking; complicated.

elapse (ē laps'), *v.i.* to slip away, as time.

elastic (ē las' tik), *n.* any fabric having India rubber woven into it; a rubber band.

elastic (ē las' tik), *adj.* capable of returning or springing back to shape after being stretched.

elasticity (ē las tis' i ti), *n.* the ability to return to shape after being stretched.

elate (ē lāt'), *v.t.* to raise the spirits of.

elation (ē lā' shun), *n.* exaltation.

elbow (el' bō), *n.* the joint of the arm; any bend resembling it.

elder (el' dēr), *n.* an older person; a certain church officer.

elderly (el' dēr li), *adj.* getting to be old.
　Syn. Aged, old. The *elderly* man has passed the meridian of life; the old man is fast approaching the end of life; the *aged* man has already reached or passed the average expectation of life.
　Ant. Young, youthful.

elect (ē lekt'), *n.* one who is chosen and set apart, as the *elect.*

elect (ē lekt'), *v.t.* to choose, set apart; to choose by vote, as for a public office.

election (ē lek' shun), *n.* the act of electing, as by votes; the taking of a public vote.

electioneer (ē lek' shun ēr), *v.i.* to work for, as one candidate or ticket, in an election.

*elective (ē lek' tiv), *n.* a college course chosen by a student, not required by the administration.

elective (ē lek' tiv), *adj.* subject to choice.

elector (ē lek' tēr), *n.* one who is qualified to vote.

*electorate (ē lek' tēr it), *n.* the whole body of persons entitled to vote.

electric (ē lek' trik), *adj.* pertaining to electricity; containing, caused by or run by, electricity.

electrician (ē lek trish' un), *n.* one skilled in the science of electricity; one who works with or on electrical apparatus.

*electricity (ē lek tris' i ti), *n.* an imponderable and invisible force of nature, used by man to produce light, heat and power.

electrify (ē lek' tri fi), *v.t.* to charge with electricity; to place, as a railroad line, under a system of electrical operation.

electrocute (ē lek' trō kūt), *v.t.* to put to death by an electric current.

electrode (ē lek' trōd), *n.* either terminal of an electric source, an anode or a cathode.

*electrolysis (ē lek trol' i sis), *n.* the decomposition of a chemical compound by electricity.

electron (ē lek' tron), *n.* a minute particle of matter charged with the smallest known quantity of negative electricity: opposite of *proton.*

electronics (ē lek´ tron´ iks), *n.* a science dealing with the action of electrons and transistors.

electroplate (ē lek' trō plāt), *v.t.* to plate, as with silver, through electrolytic process.

electrotype (ē lek' trō tip), *n.* a facsimile plate made by electroplating a wax impression.

*eleemosynary (el ē *a* mos' i ner i), *adj.* pertaining to alms, or the giving of alms.

elegance (el' ē gans), *n.* refinement, polish.

elegant (el' ē gant), *adj.* characterized by refinement and good taste, fastidious.

elegy (el' ē ji), *n.* a poem of lament, especially for the dead.

element (el' ē ment), *n.* a first or fundamental principle, as the *elements* of mathematics; one of four primary substances formerly believed to constitute the universe: earth, air, fire, water; any chemical substance that cannot be divided into other substances or ingredients, as gold, silver, oxygen; the natural or suitable environment of a person or thing, as to be in one's *element: elements,* the forces of nature as manifested in the weather.

elemental (el ē men' tal), *adj.* pertaining to one of the four primary elements of nature, as an *elemental* storm; fundamental, essential.

elementary (el ē men' ta ri), *adj.* primary, fundamental; rudimentary.

elephant (el' ē fant), *n.* a very large mammal, native to Asia and Africa, having a thick, nearly hairless hide, tusks and a trunk.

*elephantine (el ē fan' tin), *adj.* like an elephant, huge, unwieldy.

elevate (el' ē vāt), *v.t.* to raise, in physical position or in rank and standing.

elevation (el ē vā shun), *n.* the act of lifting or raising up; height, as of a hill or of rank.

elevator (el' ē vā' tēr), *n.* a hoisting machine for freight or passengers; an airplane airfoil used to make the craft rotate about its lateral axis.

eleven (ē lev' en), *adj.* one more than 10.

eleventh (ē lev' enth), *adj.* next after the 10th.

elf (elf), *n.* [*pl.* elves] a sprite, fairy.

elfin (el' fin), *adj.* pertaining to elves.

*elicit (ē lis' it), *v.t.* to draw out, educe.

elide (ē līd'), *v.t.* to omit, as the final letter or syllable of a spoken word.

eligibility (el i ji bil' i ti), *n.* the state of being fit to be chosen; suitability.

eligible (el' i ji bl), *adj.* fit to be chosen, suitable; meeting the requirements, as for office.

eliminate (ē lim' i nāt), *v.t.* to remove, get rid of, exclude; to ignore as unimportant.

elision (ē lizh' un), *n.* a cutting off or suppression; the dropping of a vowel before another vowel in a line of poetry to save a syllable, as *th' eternal.*

*elixir (ē lik' sēr), *n.* a tincture, essence or cordial.

elk (elk), *n.* the largest deer of Europe and Asia with broad antlers; the American wapiti.

ell (el), *n.* a measure formerly used for cloth, varying from 27 to 48 inches; an addition to a house at right angles, like an L, to the main structure.

*ellipse (e lips'), *n.* the figure made by a plane cutting through a cone on a slant.

ellipsis (e lip' sis), *n.* the omission of one or more words grammatically necessary but easily supplied by the reader; a printer's mark, as an asterisk, indicating omission of matter.

elliptic (e lip' tik), *adj.* having the nature of an ellipsis.

elm (elm), *n.* a shade tree noted for its symmetry.

elocution (el ō kū' shun), *n.* the art of declaiming.

elongate (ē lông' gāt), *v.t.* to make longer, stretch out.

elope (ē lōp'), *v.i.* to run away with a lover.

eloquence (el' ō kwens), *n.* fluency and persuasiveness in speaking.

else (els), *adj.* other, additional, as give me something *else;* different, as nothing *else* to say.

else (els), *adv.* otherwise, as study *else* you fail.

elsewhere (els' hwâr), *adv.* in another place.

*elucidate (ē lū' si dāt), *v.t. and v.t.* to explain, to make clear.

*elude (ē lūd'), *v.t.* to avoid or evade.

elusive (ē lū siv), *adj.* adroitly evading.

elusory (ē lū' sō ri), *adj.* evasive.

*emaciate (ē mā' shi āt), *v.t.* to make lean

through loss of flesh.

emanate (em' a nāt), v.i. to issue from, as a source.

emancipate (ē man' si pāt), v.t. to set free.

emancipator (ē man' si pā tēr), n. a liberator.

emasculate (ē mas' kū lāt), v.t. to deprive of masculine vigor, to weaken.

embankment (em bangk' ment), n. a bank of earth, as to hold water back.

embargo (em bär' go), n. a government ban on shipping through a port; a governmental act forbidding commerce with another nation.

embark (em bärk'), v.i. and v.t. to go aboard a ship for a voyage; to place aboard a ship; to launch upon a venture.

embarrass (em bar' as), v.t. to hinder or impede; to disconcert; to involve in money difficulties.

Syn. Abash, disconcert. To *embarrass* is to put a restraint on freedom and ease of any kind; one may be *embarrassed* by too much baggage or by a question one is unwilling to answer. To *abash* is to destroy self-possession; to *disconcert* is momentarily to disturb the poise.

Ant. Compose, relieve.

embassy (em' ba si), n. [pl. embassies] the position, business and responsibility of an ambassador; an ambassador and his official staff as a unit; the official residence of an ambassador.

embed (em bed'), v.t. to place in a bed or as in a bed.

embellish (em bel' ish), v.t. to adorn, decorate; to enrich, as a story with detail.

ember (em' bēr), n. a small, smoldering piece of coal or wood from a fire: *embers*, the smoldering bits of a dying fire.

embezzle (em' bez' l), v.t. to appropriate to one's own use that which has been entrusted to one for safekeeping.

embitter (em bit' ēr), v.t. to make bitter.

emblazon (em blā' zn), v.t. to mark with heraldic devices; to decorate in bright colors.

emblem (em' blem), n. a symbol; something that stands for an idea.

emblematic (em ble mat' ik), adj. symbolic.

embodiment (em bod' i ment), n. union into a whole; a visible example of something, as he is the *embodiment* of all the virtues.

embody (em bod' i), v.t. to typify, represent, as to *embody* the spirit of patriotism; to give expression to, as to *embody* ideas in a speech.

embolden (em bōl' den), v.t. to encourage.

embolism (em' bō lizm), n. the closing or obstruction of a blood vessel by a clot.

embosom (em booz' um), v.t. to hold in the bosom.

emboss (em bôs'), v.t. to ornament with bosses; to print in raised letters, as if by upward pressure from the under side of the sheet of paper.

embrace (em brās'), n. the act of putting one's arms around another; a hug.

embrace (em brās'), v.t. to clasp in the arms, hug; to adopt, include.

*embrasure (em brā' zher), n. an opening in a wall from which guns may be fired.

embrocation (em brō kā' shun), n. a lotion or liniment.

embroider (em broi' dēr), v.i. and v.t. to do fine needlework; to decorate with fine needlework.

embroil (em broil'), v.t. to throw into strife.

embryo (em' bri ō), n. the young of an animal in the first stages of life before being born or hatched; the young plant contained in a seed.

emend (ē mend'), v.t. to correct, especially to alter or correct, as faults in a written text; to improve.

*emendation (ē men dā' shun), n. alteration or correction, as of a text.

emerald (em' ēr ald), n. a precious stone of a deep shade of green; the color of an emerald.

emerge (ē mûrj'), v.i. to come out from anything, as a train *emerges* from a tunnel, a man from a house or from a state of unconsciousness.

emergency (ē mûr' jen si), n. [pl. emergencies] an unforeseen situation calling for immediate action; a crisis in affairs or relations.

emery (em' ēr i), n. an especially hard variety of carborundum, used for grinding and polishing.

emetic (ē met' ik), n. anything swallowed to cause vomiting.

*emigrant (em' i grarᵗ), n. one who quits his own country to settle in another.

emigrate (em' i grāt), v.i. to move from one country to another.

Syn. Immigrate. *Emigrate* and *immigrate* both come from *migrate*, which means to move from one country to another. To *emigrate* is to move out; to *immigrate* is to move in. Wandering tribes of men *migrate*, as do birds, in their seasonal flights.

eminence (em' i nens), n. a height, as of land; high standing, as in social or professional life.

eminent (em' i nent), adj. high; distinguished.

emissary (em' i ser i), n. a person sent on a mission in which he represents another, as a government; specifically, a secret agent.

emission (ē mish' un), n. the act of sending out; that which is sent out.

emit (ē mit'), v.t. to send out or give forth.

*emollient (ē mol' i ent), n. a soothing application that softens the skin.

emollient (ē mol' i ent), adj. softening, soothing.

emolument (ē mol' ū ment), n. profit or compensation from office or employment; remuneration for labor or services.

emotion (ē mō' shun), n. a strong feeling, as pleasure, joy, anger, pain, fear or sorrow.

emotional (ē mō' shun al), adj. easily moved, as an *emotional* child; arousing emotion, as *emotional* music.

*emperor (em' pēr ēr), n. the ruler of an empire.

*emphasis (em' fa sis), n. stress upon a spoken word; any stress or importance, as to lay the *emphasis* on speed in giving directions.

emphasize (em' fa siz), v.t. to stress, accentuate.

emphatic (em fat' ik), adj. emphasized, forceful; given to decisive speech or action, as an emphatic personality.

empire (em' pir), n. a group of states under the rule of a single monarch; control of wide regions.

Syn. Reign, dominion. Empire refers essentially to the lands and peoples ruled by an emperor; reign, to the act of ruling, hence essentially to the ruler, the one who reigns. Dominion has a wide field of meaning, and may be applied to man's rule over the beasts, to the power of the passions or to political overlordship.

*empirical (em pir' i kal), adj. based on experiment or experience, as empirical knowledge.

empiricism (em pir' i sizm), n. the philosophical theory that all knowledge springs from experience; quackery, unscientific practice, as of medicine or the healing arts.

employ (em ploi'), n. employment.

employ (em ploi'), v.t. to hire, as a man to do work; to use, as to employ drastic measures.

Syn. Hire. We employ whatever we take into our service or cause to subserve our convenience; we hire anyone to whom we pay wages.

employment (em ploi' ment), n. the state of being employed; that at which one is employed; an occupation.

emporium (em pō' ri um), n. a trade center; any big department store.

empower (em pou' ẽr), v.t. to confer power upon, authorize.

empress (em' pres), n. the wife of an emperor; a woman who rules over an empire.

empty (emp' ti), v.i. and v.t. to become empty; to make empty by removing the contents; to discharge, as a river.

empty (emp' ti), adj. without contents, void, vacant.

*empyrean (em pi rē' an), n. the highest heaven.

*emu (ē' mū), n. a large Australian bird, resembling the ostrich.

emulate (em' ū lāt), v.t. to strive to equal or excel.

emulsion (ē mul' shun), n. a fatty or oily medical preparation of the color and consistency of milk, for use as food or tonic; globules of one liquid suspended in another liquid.

enable (en ā' bl), v.t. to make able, empower; to make possible or easy.

enact (en akt'), v.t. to represent on the stage; to make into law.

enactment (en akt' ment), n. that which is enacted; a law.

enamel (en am' el), n. a smooth, tough, opaque substance used in coating surfaces of glass, porcelain, metal; a varnish with the qualities of enamel.

enamel (en am' el), v.t. [p.t. and p.p. enameled, pr.p. enameling] to apply enamel.

encamp (en kamp'), v.i. to make and go into a camp.

encampment (en kamp' ment), n. a camp.

enchain (en chān'), v.t. to bind with chains; to hold fast, as with a chain.

enchant (en chânt'), v.t. to captivate; to put a spell upon.

encircle (en sûr' kl), v.t. to enclose in, or as if in, a circle; to surround; to move all the way round, as to encircle the globe.

encomium (en kō' mi um), n. [pl. encomiums] high, formal praise.

Syn. Eulogy; panegyric. We bestow encomiums upon both persons and things. A eulogy is warmer and more personal praise than an encomium. A panegyric is often extravagant, and publicly addressed.

Ant. Abuse, defamation.

encompass (en kum' pås), v.t. to surround, enclose; to contain.

*encore (äng kōr'), n. the call from an audience for repetition of a part of a program.

encounter (en koun' tẽr), n. a hostile meeting, armed clash, combat, battle.

encounter (en koun' tẽr), v.t. to come upon suddenly; to meet face to face, especially as enemies.

encourage (en kûr' ij), v.t. to inspire with courage or hope.

encroach (en krōch'), v.i. to enter gradually or by stealth; to trespass; to invade, as the rights of another.

encumber (en kum' bẽr), v.t. to impede, retard; to load down, burden.

encyclical (en si' kli kal), n. a letter sent out by the Pope.

encyclical (en si' kli kal), adj. addressed to all members of a class or community; general.

*encyclopedia (en si klō pē' di a), n. a work made up of articles, often alphabetically arranged, covering all branches of knowledge or devoted to a certain branch of knowledge.

end (end), n. the final part or point, as the end of a road or a book; termination or conclusion; a purpose to be accomplished, an aim.

end (end), v.i. and v.t. to come to an end; to finish.

endanger (en dān' jer), v.t. to expose to danger, imperil.

endear (en dēr'), v.t. to make dear or loved.

endearment (en dēr' ment), n. a caress; words of affection.

endeavor (en dev' ẽr), n. effort; an attempt.

endeavor (en dev' ẽr), v.i. to strive or work.

Syn. Try. To try is the general term. To endeavor is to try or exert effort always with a specific end in view, as to endeavor to finish a lesson, endeavor to please.

endless (end' les), adj. lasting forever; eternal.

endorse (en dōrs'), v.t. to sign, as a check, on the back so that another may collect it; to approve, commend, sponsor.

endow (en dou'), v.t. to furnish with a permanent source of income.

endue (en dū'), v.t. to clothe, as to endue with a talent or grace.

endurable (en dūr' a bl), adj. bearable.

endurance (en dūr′ ans), *n.* ability to endure or strength to bear.

endure (en dūr′), *v.i. and v.t.* to continue unchanged; to bear, as pain or suffering.

enemy (en′ ē mi), *n.* [*pl.* enemies] one hostile to another, a foe; anything harmful, as dissipation is an *enemy* to health.

enemy (en′ e mi), *adj.* of or belonging to an enemy, as an *enemy* camp.

energetic (en ēr jet′ ik), *adj.* possessing energy, forceful; vigorous, active.

energy (en′ ēr ji), *n.* effective force; vigor; activity.

   Syn. Power, strength, vigor, force. *Power* is the general word. *Energy* is power as measured in work done or that can be done. *Strength* is the power that a living creature possesses of itself. *Vigor* is strength as indicated in the exercise of mind or body; *force* is power used against resistance.

*enervate (en′ ēr vāt), *v.t.* to weaken, physically or morally; to deprive of nervous force and vigor.

enfeeble (en fē′ bl), *v.t.* to make weak.

enforce (en fōrs′), *v.t.* to compel; to put into effect, as a law.

enfranchise (en fran′ chīz), *v.t.* to liberate, set free; to grant a franchise to; to admit to citizenship, with a right to vote.

engage (en gāj′), *v.t.* to put under pledge; to secure the services of; to employ; in mechanics, to come into gear with.

engagement (en gāj′ ment), *n.* betrothal; an appointment; a battle; in mechanics, the state of being in gear.

engender (en jen′ dēr), *v.t.* to beget; to bring forth; to produce.

engine (en′ jin), *n.* a machine by which power is applied to do work; a steam engine; an internal combustion engine.

engineer (en jin ēr′), *n.* one who runs an engine; one who is especially skilled in any branch of mechanical science, as a civil *engineer*, an electrical *engineer*.

engineer (en jin ēr′), *v.t.* to superintend, as the execution of a plan.

engineering (en ji nēr′ ing), *n.* the science and art of making and using machinery, building roads, bridges, canals, developing water power and mineral resources; skilful management, as in industry.

engrave (en grāv′), *v.t.* to cut deeply, as in stone or metal; to print from metal plates so cut.

engross (en grōs′), *v.t.* to write in a large round hand; to engage or occupy completely, as the attention.

enhance (en hans′), *v.t.* to augment; to intensify; to raise in esteem.

*enigma (ē nig′ ma), *n.* a riddle; a puzzling problem.

*enigmatic (ē nig mat′ ik), *adj.* puzzling.

enjoin (en join′) *v.t.* to command; to direct with authority; to prohibit, forbid.

enjoy (en joi′), *v.t.* to experience with pleasure; to derive pleasure from; to have the use or benefit of, as to *enjoy* good health.

enlarge (en lärj′), *v.i. and v.t.* to become larger; to make larger in size or capacity; to extend; to reproduce in a larger size, as a photograph; to amplify, as a written composition.

   Syn. Increase. To *increase* means to make more in value or number, greater in intensity, longer in time, as to *increase* wages or weight, *increase* one's fears. To *enlarge* is to increase the capacity or scope of, as to *enlarge* a room, *enlarge* the membership of a club.

   Ant. Decrease, lessen, diminish.

enlighten (en līt′ en), *v.t.* to inform, shed light upon in the way of truth or knowledge.

enlist (en list′), *v.i. and v.t.* to enroll, as in military service; to sign for service, as to *enlist* in the army; to win over, as to a cause.

enliven (en liv′ en), *v.t.* to make vigorous, active or more vivacious.

enmity (en′ mi ti), *n.* animosity, hostility.

   Syn. Animosity, hostility. *Enmity* lies in the heart; it is a feeling of hatred. *Hostility* is enmity expressed in action; *animosity* is ill will, often bitterly or resentfully expressed. *Enmity* often lies concealed in the heart and does not betray itself by any act of *hostility*.

   Ant. Friendship.

ennoble (e nō′ bl), *v.t.* to elevate to a place among the nobility; to raise to a loftier plane of character.

*ennui (än′ we), *n.* the state of being bored; listlessness.

enormity (ē nôr′ mi ti), *n.* the state of being huge; a horrible or atrocious offense.

enormous (ē nôr′ mus), *adj.* immense; far larger than the normal size or extent; atrocious.

   Syn. Immense, huge, vast. *Enormous* means abnormally large in size or abnormally great in degree; *immense* is larger than average; *huge* is great in bulk; *vast* is great in extent.

*enough (ē nuf′), *n.* a sufficiency, adequate quantity.

enough (ē nuf′), *adj.* sufficient.

   Syn. Adequate. *Enough* is sufficient to satisfy a wish or a need; *adequate* means in proportion to a specific requirement, as the sum is *adequate* for the trip.

   Ant. Inadequate, scanty.

enrage (en rāj′), *v.t.* to throw into a rage, make angry.

enrapt (en rapt′), *adj.* enraptured, fascinated.

enrapture (en rap′ tūr), *v.t.* to transport with delight.

enrich (en rich′), *v.t.* to make rich; to make fertile, as soil.

enroll (en rōl′), *v.t.* to put on record in a register; to enlist.

en route (än rōōt), on the way.

ensconce (en skons′), *v.t.* to fix securely; to hide, guard.

enshrine (en shrin′), *v.t.* to place in, or as in, a shrine; to consider as sacred.

enshroud (en shroud′), *v.t.* to cover with, or as if with, a shroud; to hide.

ensign (en′ sīn), *n.* a flag; the rank in the U. S. Navy between midshipman and junior grade lieutenant.

ensilage (en' si lij), *n.* fodder stored in a silo.

enslave (en slāv'), *v.t.* to make a slave of; to bring into a state of slavery.

ensnare (en snâr'), *v.t.* to catch in a snare or trap; to entrap; to inveigle.

ensue (en-sū'), *v.i. and v.t.* to follow as a consequence; to spring from, as a result.

entail (en tāl'), *n.* an estate settled upon a certain person and his descendants.

entail (en tāl'), *v.t.* to restrict an estate to a certain succession of heirs.

entangle (en tang' gl), *v.t.* to involve, tangle.

enter (en' tēr), *v.i. and v.t.* to go into; to inscribe, as to *enter* a name on a roll; to make a start in, as to *enter* college.

enterprise (en' tēr priz), *n.* an undertaking involving action or energy; business activity; active, progressive spirit.

entertain (en tēr tān'), *v.t.* to give pleasure to; to amuse; to receive as a guest; to consider or hold in the mind, as to *entertain* an idea.

enthrall (en thrōl'), *v.t.* to enslave; to fascinate.

enthrone (en thrōn'), *v.t.* to place upon a throne.

enthusiasm (en thū' zi azm), *n.* zeal; intense interest.

enthusiastic (en thū zi as' tik), *adj.* full of enthusiasm and intense interest.

entice (en tis'), *v.t.* to allure by waking hope or desire; to tempt.

entire (en tir'), *adj.* complete, whole, undivided.

entirety (en tir' ti), *n.* completeness, wholeness.

entitle (en ti' tl), *v.t.* to give a name or title to; to confer a legal right to; to give a right to, qualify, as age *entitles* him to respect.

entity (en' ti ti), *n.* a separate being; anything having reality in fact.

entomb (en tōōm'), *v.t.* to place in a tomb; to be a tomb for, as the fields of France *entomb* many Americans.

*entomology** (en tō mol' ō ji), *n.* the science that treats of insects.

entrails (en' trālz), *n. pl.* the intestines.

entrain (en trān'), *v.i. and v.t.* to go or put aboard a train.

entrance (en' trans), *n.* the act of entering; the way by which anything enters; admittance, as to *demand* entrance.

entrance (en trans'), *v.t.* to put or throw into a trance; to delight, as the tale *entranced* me.

entrap (en trap'), *v.t.* to take in a trap; to catch by trickery.

entreat (en trēt'), *v.t.* to beg, beseech, plead.

entreaty (en trēt' i), *n.* [*pl.* entreaties] an earnest petition, a supplication.

*entree** (än' trā), *n.* entrance, especially to a social group; a dish served at the beginning of a dinner, or between courses.

entry (en' tri), *n.* the act of entering; a place where one enters or goes in; the entering or recording of an item in a business account.

entwine (en twin'), *v.i. and v.t.* to twine around or twine together.

enumerate (ē nū' mēr āt), *v.t.* to count separately, name one by one.

*enunciate** (ē nun' shi āt), *v.i. and v.t.* to speak or pronounce distinctly.

enunciation (ē nun si ā' shun), *n.* articulation of speech; clear pronunciation.

envelop (en vel' up), *v.t.* to surround or cover; to enclose in.

*envelope** (en' ve lōp), *n.* a wrapper; a gummed paper folded to hold a letter.

envenom (en ven' um), *v.t.* to make poisonous; to fill with poison.

enviable (en' vi a bl), *adj.* exciting or deserving envy.

envious (en' vi us), *adj.* feeling or showing envy.

*environ** (en vi' run), *v.t.* to surround; to encircle; to enclose.

*environment** (en vi' run ment), *n.* surroundings; especially the conditions and influences under which one lives.

*environs** (en vi' runs), *n. pl.* the surrounding region of a town or city.

*envoy** (en' voi), *n.* a diplomatic representative ranking between an ambassador and a minister.

envy (en' vi), *n.* discontent because of the possessions or good fortune of another; covetousness.

envy (en' vi), *v.t.* to begrudge, covet.

enwrap (en rap'), *v.t.* to place in a wrapping.

*eon** (ē' on), *n.* an age in the earth's history, a geological age.

*epaulet** (ep' o let), *n.* an ornamental strap worn on the shoulder by officers of the army or navy.

*ephemeral** (e fem' ēr al), *adj.* existing for a day; quickly passing away, short-lived.

epic (ep' ik), *n.* a narrative poem commemorating heroic deeds written in an exalted style.

*epicure** (ep' i kūr), *n.* a person devoted to luxury.

*epicurean** (ep i kū rē' an), *adj.* luxurious; following a certain old Greek philosophy.

epidemic (ep i dem' ik), *n.* any disease that spreads unchecked through a community.

epidemic (ep i dem' ik), *adj.* attacking many at the same time, as an *epidemic* disease.

epidermis (ep i dûr' mis), *n.* the outer layer of skin; cuticle.

epiglottis (ep i glot' is), *n.* the leaf-shaped cartilage that covers the glottis at the upper part of the windpipe.

epigram (ep' i gram), *n.* a short witty or satirical verse; a witty thought tersely expressed.

epilepsy (ep' i lep si), *n.* a chronic nervous disease attended by fits and temporary unconsciousness.

epileptic (ep i lep' tik), *n.* a person afflicted with epilepsy.

epilogue (ep' i lŏg), *n.* a speech at the end of a play.

episcopacy (ē pis' kŏ pa si), *n.* church rule by bishops; the office of a bishop.

*episode** (ep' i sŏd), *n.* an incident in a story or play.

*epistle** (ē pis' l), *n.* a formal letter.

epistolary (ē pis' tō ler ĭ), *adj.* relating to letters; recorded in letters.

*epitaph (ep' ĭ tåf), *n.* a memorial inscription.

epithet (ep' ĭ thet), *n.* an adjective or phrase expressing a quality of a person or thing; as, Maine is known as the *pine tree* state.

*epitome (ē pĭt' ō mē), *n.* a concise summary.

epitomize (ē pĭt' ō mīz), *v.t.* to describe briefly; to condense, as a text.

*epoch (ep' ok), *n.* a point of time or a great event from which succeeding time is measured; a period of history marked by great events, as the *epoch* of invention.

*equability (ek wa bĭl' ĭ tĭ), *n.* evenness of temperament.

*equable (ek' wa bl), *adj.* even-tempered; uniform.

equal (ē' kwal), *n.* a person or thing of the same size, age, strength or rank; an equal number.

equal (ē' kwal), *adj.* the same in amount, degree, value or quality; equivalent; adequate, as *equal* to the undertaking.

Syn. Equivalent, identical. *Equal* means the same in degree, quantity, number, value, rank, age; *equivalent* means practically the same; *identical* means complete and absolute agreement; two copies of the same book are *identical*, no human faces are *identical*.

*equality (ē kwol' ĭ tĭ), *n.* the state of being equal.

equalize (ē' kwal ĭz), *v.t.* to make equal or uniform.

*equanimity (ē kwa nĭm' ĭ tĭ), *n.* evenness of temper or mind; composure.

*equation (ē kwā' zhun), *n.* a statement of equality between two mathematical expressions, as $2 + 2 = 4$ is an *equation*.

equator (ē kwā' tēr), *n.* the imaginary circle dividing the earth into two equal parts, the northern and southern hemispheres.

equatorial (ē kwa tō' rĭ al), *adj.* on or near the equator, characteristic of the regions near the equator, as *equatorial* plants.

equestrian (ē kwes' trĭ an), *n.* one who rides horseback.

equestrian (ē kwes' trĭ an), *adj.* pertaining to horses or to horsemanship; mounted.

equidistant (ē kwi dis' tant), *adj.* equally distant from two points.

equilateral (ē kwi lat' ēr al), *adj.* having all sides equal.

equilibrium (ē kwi lĭb' rĭ um), *n.* balance between two opposite weights or forces.

*equine (ē' kwīn), *adj.* pertaining to or like horses.

*equinoctial (ē kwi nok' shal), *adj.* pertaining to the time when day and night are equal; pertaining to the time when the sun crosses the equator.

equinox (ē' kwi noks), *n.* one of the two times in the year when the sun crosses the equator and day and night are equal: March 21 and September 23.

equip (ē kwip'), *v.t.* to furnish with things needed for a purpose, as arms for military service, education for a career.

equipment (ē kwip' ment), *n.* furnishings for any undertaking, service or career.

equipoise (ē' kwi poiz), *n.* equilibrium.

*equitable (ek' wĭ ta bl), *adj.* impartial, fair, just.

equity (ek' wi tĭ), *n.* [*pl.* equities] fairness; justice or right dealing.

*equivalent (ē kwiv' a lent), *n.* that which is practically the same as something else in value or effect.

equivalent (ē kwiv' a lent), *adj.* practically equal in value, size or effect.

equivocal (ē kwiv' ō kal), *adj.* ambiguous; doubtful.

Syn. Ambiguous, enigmatic. A statement that is *ambiguous* can be understood in more than one way; an *equivocal* statement also conveys more than one clear meaning, but is apt to be presented with intent to deceive, while an *ambiguous* statement may be only accidentally double in meaning. That which is *enigmatical* has to be guessed at.

Ant. Straightforward, frank, clear.

equivocate (ē kwiv' ō kāt), *v.i.* to use words of doubtful meaning in order to deceive.

*era (ē' ra), *n.* a period of history, especially as reckoned from a certain date.

eradicate (ē rad' ĭ kāt), *v.t.* to destroy; to exterminate, root up.

erase (ē rās'), *v.t.* to obliterate by rubbing.

eraser (ē rās' ēr), *n.* a piece of rubber used for rubbing out marks.

*erasure (ē rā' zhēr), *n.* the act of erasing; something erased.

erect (ē rekt'), *v.t.* to raise upright; to rear, as a structure; to set up for use.

erection (ē rek' shun), *n.* the act of building or rearing; that which is erected.

erg (ûrg), *n.* a unit of energy or work.

*ermine (ûr' min), *n.* a weasel common to both hemispheres whose coat turns white in the winter except for the black tail tip; the white winter fur of the ermine; state robes lined with ermine.

erode (ē rōd'), *v.t.* to wear away, as water *erodes* rock; to eat away, as rust *erodes* iron.

erosion (ē rō' zhun), *n.* wear by water or rust.

*err (ûr), *v.i.* to make a mistake; to go astray; to sin.

errand (er' and), *n.* a mission on which one is sent; a trip made to attend to some business.

errant (er' ant), *adj.* roving, wandering.

erratic (e rat' ĭk), *adj.* deviating from a course, eccentric; irregular, unreliable; queer.

*errata (e rā' ta), *n. pl.* errors made in printing.

erroneous (e rō' nē us), *adj.* wrong, marked by error.

error (er' ēr), *n.* false belief; a mistake.

Syn. Mistake, blunder. Every deviation from what is right may be called an *error;* a *mistake* is a misunderstanding or an oversight, not to be harshly judged; a *blunder* is an error arising from stupidity.

*erudite (er' oo dīt), *adj.* learned.

*erudition (er oo dish' un), *n.* learning derived

from the study of books.

eruption (ē rup' shun), *n.* a sudden bursting forth, as the *eruption* of a volcano or of war.

Syn. Explosion. *Eruption* is a sudden coming into view, a bursting forth; *explosion* is a bursting forth with loud noise. We speak of an *eruption* of flames, the *explosion* of gunpowder.

*****erysipelas** (er i sip' e las), *n.* a disease marked by inflammation of the skin and fever.

escalate (es´ ka lāt), *v.* to increase or to be increased as a war; to ascend or carry up as on an escalator.

escapade (es ka pād'), *n.* a prankish adventure; freakish stunt.

escape (es kāp'), *n.* the act of escaping; a means of escape, as a fire *escape.*

escape (es kāp'), *v.i. and v.t.* to avoid harm or evil; to break loose from captivity or restraint.

*****escheat** (es chēt'), *v.i.* to be forfeited through failure of heirs.

*****eschew** (es chōō), *v.t.* to shun, avoid.

escort (es' kôrt), *n.* one who accompanies another, for purposes of protection; an armed body of men acting as a guard; a ship sailing along with another to guard it.

esculent (es' kū lent), *adj.* eatable.

esophagus (ē sof' a gus), *n.* the tube between mouth and stomach through which food and drink are swallowed; the gullet.

especial (es pesh' al), *adj.* chief, particular.

especially (es pesh' al li), *adv.* chiefly, in particular.

*****espionage** (es' pi ô nij), *n.* the practice of spying; a system of spying.

espouse (es pouz'), *v.t.* to marry; to adopt or sponsor, as a cause.

espy (es pī'), *v.t.* [*p.t. and p.p.* espied, *pr.p.* espying] to see at a distance; to discover, as something hidden.

esquire (es kwīr'), *n.* formerly a knight's attendant; now used as a respectful form of address.

essay (es' ā), *n.* an attempt; a literary composition, generally confined to a single or personal phase of a subject.

*****essay** (e sā'), *v.t.* to try.

essence (es' ens), *n.* the fundamental characteristic of anything; substance; a concentrated extract, as *essence* of wintergreen.

essential (e sen' shal), *adj.* necessary, indispensable; absolute, perfect, as *essential* joy.

establish (es tab' lish), *v.t.* to set up, settle; to ordain, as laws; to found, as a colony; to gain recognition of, as to *establish* a reputation.

estate (es tāt'), *n.* one's condition in life; a person's property and possessions.

esteem (es tēm'), *n.* regard, respect, favorable opinion.

esteem (es tēm'), *v.t.* to set high value upon, respect, prize; to think, as I would *esteem* it a favor.

*****estimate** (es' ti māt), *n.* an appraisal; a calculation, as of probable cost; a judgment or opinion.

estimate (es' ti māt), *v.t.* to appraise; to form

an opinion of; to calculate approximately.

Syn. Appreciate, value. To *estimate* is to determine in one's mind an approximate figure; to *appreciate* is to perceive the exact worth of something; to *value* is to prize highly.

estrange (es trãng'), *v.t.* to alienate; to keep at a distance; to cause to change to indifference or dislike, as to *estrange* a friend.

estuary (es' tū er i), *n.* [*pl.* estuaries] the mouth of a tidal river; an inlet from the sea.

etch (ech), *v.t.* to engrave by biting out with an acid the design previously drawn with an etching needle.

etching (ech' ing), *n.* a picture or design etched on metal or glass.

eternal (ē tûr' nal), *adj.* everlasting; without beginning or end.

Syn. Endless, everlasting. *Eternal* applies to duration of time and means specifically without beginning or end; immortal, imperishable, as the *eternal* God; *everlasting* applies to future time and means enduring, without carrying the idea of no beginning; *endless* applies both to material length and duration of time.

Ant. Ephemeral, passing, temporary.

eternity (ē tûr' ni ti), *n.* [*pl.* eternities] infinite duration; immortality.

ether (ē' thēr), *n.* an extremely fine element lighter than air, supposed to pervade all space; a colorless liquid used to produce unconsciousness and insensibility to pain.

ethical (eth' i kal), *adj.* right, according to the principles of ethics.

ethics (eth' iks), *n.* the science of human behavior; the systematized principles of morally correct conduct.

ethnic (eth' nik), *adj.* racial, as *ethnic* differences; ethnological.

ethnology (eth nol' ō ji), *n.* the science which treats of the characteristics, origins and relations of different races of men.

*****ethyl** (eth' il), *n.* a compound of lead used in motor fuels.

etiquette (et' i ket), *n.* the conventional rules for correct behavior.

etymology (et i mol' ō ji), *n.* the branch of philology that treats of the origin of words.

euchre (ū' kēr), *n.* a card game.

eulogy (ū' lō ji), *n.* an oration in praise of a person or thing, especially a dead person; any high praise.

euphemism (ū' fem izm), *n.* a mild or inoffensive word or expression substituted for one deemed coarse, inelegant or improper.

euphonic (ū fon' ik), *adj.* pleasant-sounding.

*****euphony** (ū' fōn i), *n.* [*pl.* euphonies] sweet sound; the sound of words arranged so as to please the ear.

euphuism (ū' fū izm), *n.* an affected style of speaking and writing; artificially elegant diction.

eustachian tube (ū stā' ki an tūb), a passage leading from the middle ear to the pharynx.

euthenics (ū then' iks), *n.* the science that seeks improvement of mankind through improvement.

EVA *n.* an acronym for Extra-Vehicular Activity or space walking.

provement of living conditions.

evacuate (ē vak' ū āt), *v.t.* to make empty; to vacate; to withdraw from, as a fort or city.

*evade** (ē vād'), *v.t.* to elude; to dodge, as a question.

Syn. Elude. We *evade* a question by artfully turning the subject aside or skilfully distracting the attention of the inquirer; to *elude* is to avoid, slip away or baffle, but with less contrivance.

evanescent (ev *a* nes' ent), *adj.* disappearing, vanishing, fleeting.

*evangelical** (ē van jel' i kal), *adj.* pertaining to the Gospels.

evangelism (ē van' jel izm), *n.* preaching of the gospel.

evangelist (ē van' jel ist), *n.* one who brings the gospel; a traveling revivalist or minister without a fixed charge.

evaporate (ē vap' ō rāt), *v.i. and v.t.* to pass off in vapor or give off vapor; to change to vapor; to remove moisture from, as to *evaporate* fruits.

evaporation (ē vap ō rā' shun), *n.* conversion of liquid into vapor.

evasion (ē vā' zhun), *n.* the act of evading; the dodging of a question or a problem.

evasive (ē vā' siv), *adj.* seeking to evade, elusive, not frank.

eve (ēv), *n.* the evening before a holiday or anniversary, as Christmas *eve;* the period preceding some important event, as the *eve* of battle: short for *evening.*

even (ē' ven), *v.i. and v.t.* to be even; to make even; to make equal or level.

even (ē' ven), *adj.* equal; level; regular; smooth; steady.

even (ē' ven), *adv.* fully; quite: *even if,* although.

*evening** (ēv' ning), *n.* the last hours of the day and first of the night.

evenly (ē' ven li), *adv.* in an even, equal or regular manner; smoothly.

evenness (ē' ven nes), *n.* smoothness; uniformity; regularity.

event (ē vent'), *n.* an occurrence; anything that happens, especially a noteworthy occurrence.

Syn. Incident, occurrence. *Occurrence* is the general term for anything that happens; an *event* is an important occurrence; an *incident* is trivial or unimportant.

eventful (ē vent' fool), *adj.* crowded with events; momentous.

eventual (ē ven' tū al), *adj.* ultimate, final.

eventuality (ē ven tū al' i ti), *n.* [*pl.* eventualities] a possible occurrence, an outcome.

eventuate (ē ven' tū āt), *v.i.* to come about finally, result.

ever (ev' ẽr), *adv.* at any time; at all times.

everglade (ev' ẽr glād), *n.* a swampy tract of land.

evergreen (ev' ẽr grēn), *n.* a tree or plant which retains its foliage all year.

everlasting (ev ẽr làs' ting), *adj.* perpetual, eternal, endless.

evermore (ev ẽr mōr'), *adv.* forever.

every (ev' ẽr i or ev' ri), *adj.* all, taken one by one; each of a group.

evict (ē vikt'), *v.t.* to put out; to expel, by legal process.

*evidence** (ev' i dens), *n.* testimony; that which furnishes proof or gives ground for belief.

evident (ev' i dent), *adj.* plain, clear.

evidential (ev i den' shal), *adj.* based upon evidence.

evil (ē' vl), *n.* anything that causes harm or injury; misfortune; wickedness.

evil (ē' vl), *adj.* morally bad; wicked, as *evil* ways.

evince (ē vins'), *v.t.* to manifest, make evident.

evoke (ē vōk'), *v.t.* to call forth.

evolution (e vō lū' shun), *n.* development from one form of life to another; a gradual unfolding, as the *evolution* of a flower from the bud; that which is developed from a stated beginning, as baseball is an *evolution* from rounders.

evolve (ē volv'), *v.i. and v.t.* to develop from one state or stage of being to another.

ewe (ū), *n.* a female sheep.

ewer (ū' er), *n.* an ornamented vessel resembling a pitcher or jug.

*exact** (eg zakt'), *v.t.* to demand with authority; to require, call for.

Syn. Elicit. To *exact* is to draw forth by demand or force or authority, especially something considered rightfully due, as the teacher *exacts* obedience from a class; to *elicit* is to draw forth without force, as free discussion *elicits* truth.

exacting (eg zakt' ing), *adj.* making severe or unreasonable demands.

exaction (eg zak' shun), *n.* the act of exacting; that which is exacted; extortion.

exactness (eg zakt' nes), *n.* accuracy, precision.

*exaggerate** (eg zaj' ẽr āt), *v.i. and v.t.* to overstate; to see or represent as more than actually is the fact.

*exalt** (eg zôlt'), *v.t.* to elevate in rank, station or dignity.

examination (eg zam in ā' shun), *n.* investigation; critical or analytical study; careful inquiry; a test to measure knowledge of a subject or fitness for employment or service.

examine (eg zam' in), *v.t.* to investigate; to inquire into; to study, with analysis; to test for knowledge or fitness.

*example** (eg zàm' pl), *n.* a sample or specimen, one or a part used to show the quality of all; something to be followed or copied, a pattern or model; a problem in arithmetic; a warning.

Syn. Sample, specimen, instance. An *example* is a typical case of something, as a kind act is an *example* of courtesy; a *sample* is a piece or portion that shows the nature or quality of the whole, as a *sample* of lace; a *specimen* is one of a class, as a *specimen* of a butterfly; an *instance* is a fact or occurrence illustrating another, as this theft is an *instance* of his repeated stealing.

*exasperate** (eg zas' pẽr āt), *v.t.* to irritate; to make angry; to aggravate, embitter.

excavate (eks' ka vāt), *v.t.* to hollow out; to make by digging, as to *excavate* a cellar; to reveal by digging, as to *excavate* a buried city.

excavation (eks ka vā' shun), *n.* a hollow formed, as in the earth, by digging.

exceed (ek sēd'), *v.i. and v.t.* to be more than, or to surpass, something stated; excel, in size or quality.

exceedingly (ek sēd' ing li), *adv.* extraordinarily.

excel (ek sel'), *v.i. and v.t.* to surpass in good qualities; to outdo.

excellence (ek' sel ens), *n.* great merit.

excellent (ek' sel ent), *adj.* of great virtue or high quality, extremely good.

*****excelsior** (ek sel' si ōr), *adj.* higher; upward.

excelsior (ek sel' si ōr), *n.* fine wood shavings used in upholstering or for packing fragile articles.

except (ek sept'), *v.i. and v.t.* to enter an objection; to exclude one from a number of things presented together, omit.

except (ek sept'), *prep.* with exclusion of.

except (ek sept'), *conj.* unless.

exception (ek sep' shun), *n.* that which is excepted or excluded; an omission; an objection or complaint.

*****excerpt** (ek' sûrpt), *n.* an extract or passage copied from a text or book.

*****excess** (ek ses'), *n.* that which goes beyond usual or proper bounds or limits; intemperance; a remainder, the amount by which one number or quantity exceeds another.

Syn. Redundancy, superfluity. *Excess* is more than enough or too much of anything; the word may be used either in a favorable or in an unfavorable sense. A *superfluity* is more than is needed, implying a running into waste; a *redundancy* is an overabundance, implying more than necessary, but not implying waste.

Ant. Deficiency, lack, need, want.

excessive (ek ses' iv), *adj.* extreme; immoderate; unreasonable.

exchange (eks chānj'), *n.* the act of giving or taking anything in return for something else; the place where brokers gather to do business, as the stock *exchange.*

exchange (eks chānj'), *v.t.* to give or take one thing for another, trade; to substitute one thing for another.

exchequer (eks chek' ēr), *n.* a national treasury.

*****excise** (ek sīz'), *n.* a tax on the making, selling or consuming of goods within a country, as distinguished from import duties.

excise (ek sīz'), *v.t.* to cut out, remove.

excision (ek sizh' un), *n.* the act of cutting off, or state of being cut off.

excite (ek sīt'), *v.t.* to agitate; to arouse to action or feeling, stimulate.

Syn. Incite, provoke. To *excite* is to work upon the feelings or passions; to *incite* is to urge to external action; to *provoke* is to do either or both.

Ant. Calm, quiet, soothe.

excitement (ek sīt' ment), *n.* the state of being excited; agitation; commotion.

exclaim (eks klām'), *v.i.* to ejaculate; to cry out in surprise, wonder, anger, joy.

exclamation (eks kla mā' shun), *n.* an ejaculation; an abrupt cry of pain, delight or surprise.

exclude (eks klōōd'), *v.t.* to shut out or keep out, as to *exclude* a person from a place or a privilege.

exclusion (eks klōō' zhun), *n.* the act of shutting out or debarring; rejection.

exclusive (eks klōō' siv), *adj.* tending to exclude outsiders, limited to a chosen few, as an *exclusive* club; not sociable; not taking into account, as 10 oranges *exclusive* of the bad one.

excogitate (eks koj' i tāt), *v.t.* to discover or work out by thinking.

excommunicate (eks ko mū' ni kāt), *v.t.* to expel from membership in the church.

excoriate (eks kō' ri āt), *v.t.* to strip off the skin of, to flay.

excrescence (eks kres' ens), *n.* an unnatural outgrowth.

excretion (eks krē' shun), *n.* ejection of waste matter from the body.

*****excruciate** (eks krōō' shi āt), *v.t.* to torture.

*****exculpate** (eks' kul pāt), *v.t.* to free from blame, exonerate.

*****excursion** (eks kûr' zhun), *n.* an expedition; a pleasure trip.

Syn. Journey, tour, trip, jaunt. An *excursion* takes one out of his wonted courses, and usually involves more than one person; a *journey* involves extensive traveling and a specific destination; a *tour* is a more or less circuitous course, involving stops at various places; a *trip* is a short journey; a *jaunt* is a walk or ride taken gaily for pleasure.

excuse (eks kūs'), *n.* a reason presented for a default in duty, as an *excuse* for absence from school; a defense; an apology; a pretext.

excuse (eks kūz'), *v.t.* to offer or accept a reason or apology for default in duty or for real or seeming neglect of an obligation; to dismiss, as a student from attendance on classes.

Syn. Pardon. We *excuse* small faults and errors; we *pardon* serious offenses or crimes; we *forgive* a personal offense.

execrate (ek' sē krāt), *v.t.* to call down evil upon, curse.

execration (ek sē krā' shun), *n.* the act of execrating; the curse uttered; that which is execrated, a detested or accursed thing.

execute (ek' sē kūt), *v.i. and v.t.* to perform completely; to carry into effect; to write, sign and make effective, as a legal instrument; to put to death under a legal sentence.

Syn. Administer, enforce. To *execute* is to bring about or carry through to a stated end; to *administer* is to go through the process of carrying out; to *enforce* is to compel the execution of something, as a law.

execution (ek sē kū' shun), *n.* performance; capital punishment.

*****executive** (eg zek' ū tiv), *n.* an administrative officer.

executive (eg zek' ū tiv), *adj.* pertaining to the execution of plans, projects or business enterprise.

*executor** (eg zek' ū tēr), *n.* the administrator of a will.

exemplar (eg zem' plēr), *n.* a person or thing worthy of imitation; a model or ideal pattern.

*exemplary** (eg zem' pla ri), *adj.* worthy of imitation; serving as a type or example.

exemplify (eg zem' pli fi), *v.t.* to serve as an example of; to show by an example or sample.

*exempt** (eg zempt'), *v.t.* to free from an obligation, release from liability; to except, excuse.

exempt (eg zempt'), *adj.* free of responsibility or liability, as from some form of civic service.

exercise (ek' sēr siz), *n.* activity for training the mind or improving the physical condition; a drill in study: *exercises*, a program including songs and speeches to observe an event, as commencement.

exercise (ek' sēr siz), *v.i. and v.t.* to drill, practice, train; to use, as powers of mind and body.

exert (eg zûrt'), *v.t.* to put forth, as power or strength.

exertion (eg zûr' shun), *n.* effort; endeavor; use of strength.

*exhalation** (eks ha lā' shun), *n.* an exhaling or breathing out; that which is exhaled or breathed out.

*exhale** (eks hāl'), *v.i. and v.t.* to breathe out; to emit, as vapor.

exhaust (eg zôst'), *n.* the escape, as of used steam, from an engine; the steam or gas carried off after use; the device by which it escapes.

exhaust (eg zôst'), *v.t.* to use up completely, as to *exhaust* one's bank account or one's strength; to let out the contents of wholly, as to *exhaust* a boiler; to develop or discuss completely, as the speaker *exhausted* his subject.

exhaustion (eg zôs' chun), *n.* the act of using up completely; state of being completely used up; utter weariness, fatigue.

exhibit (eg zig' it), *v.t.* to show, display; to reveal by outward sign, as to *exhibit* anger.

exhibition (ek si bish' un), *n.* the act of showing or displaying; state of being displayed; that which is shown or displayed.

exhilarate (eg zil' a rāt), *v.t.* to make joyous, gladden, enliven.

exhort (eg zôrt'), *v.t.* to incite or urge; to warn earnestly.

*exhume** (eks hūm'), *v.t.* to take out of the ground; to disinter.

exigency (ek' si jen si), *n.* [*pl.* exigencies] something that demands immediate action or attention; a pressing necessity; emergency.

Syn. Emergency. *Exigency* stresses the idea of pressure and necessity; an *emergency* is a sudden and unexpected exigency.

*exile** (ek' sīl), *n.* the state of separation, either voluntary or enforced, from one's country; one thus separated from his native land.

*exile** (ek' sīl), *v.t.* to banish or expel from one's native land or the country of one's citizenship or allegiance.

exist (eg zist'), *v.i.* to be, have reality, to live.

existence (eg zis' tens), *n.* the state of being; life.

exit (ek' sit), *n.* the act of leaving or going out; the place at or through which one leaves.

exonerate (eg zon' ēr āt), *v.t.* to free from blame, clear, as of a charge or accusation.

Syn. Exculpate. To *exonerate* is to lift the burden of blame; to *exculpate* is merely to free from blame.

exorbitant (eg zôr' bi tant), *adj.* going beyond justified limits, excessive.

*exotic** (eks ot' ik), *adj.* not native, from a foreign land, as an *exotic* plant.

expand (eks pand'), *v.i. and v.t.* to reach out or grow in all directions; to become larger, swell; to spread out, distend or enlarge.

expanse (eks pans'), *n.* a wide area.

expansion (eks pan' shun), *n.* the state of expanding; that which is expanded or spread out.

expatiate (eks pā' shi āt), *v.i.* to expand upon a subject in speech or writing.

*expatriate** (eks pā' tri āt), *v.t. and v.i.* to banish, exile, drive out of one's own country; to withdraw from one's own country.

expect (eks pekt'), *v.t.* to look for, anticipate, await.

expectant (eks pek' tant), *adj.* waiting; anticipating; looking forward.

expectation (eks pek tā' shun), *n.* the act of expecting, anticipation; that which is looked for, as exceeding all *expectations*.

expectorate (eks pek' tō rāt), *v.i. and v.t.* to spit; spit out.

expediency (eks pē' di en si), *n.* that which serves one's purpose; the policy of working for one's own immediate advantage; suitability to an end or purpose.

*expedient** (eks pē' di ent), *n.* suitable means for achieving or attaining a purpose or end.

Syn. Resource. An *expedient* is any means that serves to accomplish a certain end; a *resource* is anything in which one depends for support or aid in doing something. A man of *resources* has great natural ability; a man resorts to *expedients* in lieu of better means.

expedient (eks pē' di ent), *adj.* of immediate advantage; convenient; suitable to a certain end, proper.

expedite (eks' pē dīt), *v.t.* to hasten, facilitate.

expedition (eks pē dish' un), *n.* haste, speed, promptness; a march or voyage by a number of persons, as an army, for a set purpose.

expel (eks pel'), *v.t.* to drive or force out; to deprive of membership or privileges, as to *expel* a child from school.

expend (eks pend'), *v.t.* to spend or use up, as money or strength.

expenditure (eks pen' di tūr), *n.* the laying out of money; expense.

expense (eks pens'), *n.* expenditure; the amount spent, outlay; a cause of spending, as a car is an *expense*.

expensive (eks pen' siv), *adj.* costly.

experience (eks pēr' i ens), *n.* the actual living through of events and emotions; skill or wisdom gained by actually doing things; knowledge gained by trial and practice.

experience (eks pēr' i ens), *v.t.* to undergo; to know or learn through one's own actions and reactions.

experiment (eks per' i ment), *n.* a trial, to test a theory or belief; a test.

expert (eks' pûrt), *n.* one who has special knowledge of a subject or special skill in a field of action.

*expert (eks pûrt'), *adj.* skilled.

expiate (eks' pi āt), *v.t.* to atone for.

*expiration (ek spi rā' shun), *n.* termination, end; death; anything breathed out, as air or a sound.

expire (ek spīr'), *v.i.* to breathe out, as air from the lungs; to come to an end; to die.

explain (eks plān), *v.t.* to expound; to make clear; to tell how and why.

explanation (eks pla nā' shun), *n.* the act of explaining or making clear; a statement that explains, an interpretation.

explanatory (eks plan' a tō ri), *adj.* serving to explain; offering an explanation.

*explicable (eks' pli ka bl), *adj.* capable of being explained.

explicit (eks plis' it), *adj.* clear and definite in language; outspoken, not disguised.

explode (eks plōd'), *v.i. and v.t.* to break forth with sudden noise and violence; to cause to burst with noise; to refute conclusively.

*exploit (eks' ploit), *n.* a feat or deed of skill or courage.

exploit (eks ploit'), *v.t.* to use, especially to one's own advantage.

exploitation (eks ploi tā' shun), *n.* the act of getting full value out of anything, as mineral deposits; selfish or unfair use of persons or resources, regardless of public interest.

exploration (eks plō rā' shun), *n.* the act of exploring, especially of unknown geographic regions; careful research; careful examination, as the *exploration* of a wound or an infected region.

explore (eks plōr'), *v.t.* to search into or examine thoroughly; to go through strange regions, taking observations and making maps.

*exponent (eks pō' nent), *n.* one who explains or interprets the principles of something; one who represents, as the *exponent* of a political party.

export (eks' pōrt), *n.* that which is exported or sent out of a country in international trade.

export (eks pōrt'), *v.t.* to carry or send abroad for trade.

expose (eks pōz'), *v.t.* to lay open, as to attack or criticism; to uncover; to subject to any influence, as to *expose* a film to light,

expose an invalid to a draft.

exposition (eks pō zish' un), *n.* an explanation; a written explanation or setting forth of a difficult subject; a public exhibition, as of paintings.

expositor (eks poz' i tēr), *n.* one who expounds or explains.

expostulate (eks pos' tū lāt), *v.i.* to remonstrate.

    Syn. Remonstrate. We *expostulate* in a tone of friendly authority; we *remonstrate* in a tone of protest or reproof. He who *expostulates* conveys earnest remonstrance; he who *remonstrates* presents reasons against something.

expound (eks pound'), *v.t.* to explain or interpret in detail.

express (eks pres'), *n.* a system of transportation of goods, luggage, money; a fast train or other passenger conveyance stopping only at important points.

express (eks pres'), *v.t.* to utter; to make known in words or by actions; to send by express.

expressive (eks pres' iv), *adj.* containing force or feeling, as an *expressive* voice; indicative, significant.

expulsion (eks pul' shun), *n.* a driving out, as the *expulsion* of the French by the English.

expulsive (eks pul' siv), *adj.* serving to drive out, as *expulsive* force.

expunge (eks punj'), *v.t.* to strike out, blot out, obliterate.

*expurgate (eks' pēr gāt), *v.t.* to clear a text of offensive, objectionable or incorrect material.

*exquisite (eks' kwi zit), *adj.* finely worked or made, as *exquisite* carving; keen and appreciative, as an *exquisite* ear for music; intense, as *exquisite* torture; pleasing because of beauty or daintiness.

extant (eks' tant), *adj.* still existing.

extemporaneous (eks tem pō rā' nē us), *adj.* unpremeditated, unstudied, extemporary.

extemporary (eks tem' pō rer i), *adj.* composed or delivered without preparation, impromptu, as an *extemporary* speech.

extemporize (eks tem' pō riz), *v.i. and v.t.* to make or speak impromptu; to improvise.

extend (eks tend'), *v.i. and v.t.* to stretch or reach, as our lands *extend* 10 miles; to stretch or draw out, lengthen, prolong; to enlarge, broaden.

extensive (eks ten' siv), *adj.* having great extent, broad, far-reaching.

extent (eks tent'), *n.* the space or amount to which a thing is extended; area, length, width, degree.

extenuate (eks ten' ū āt), *v.t.* to weaken, underestimate, excuse, as to *extenuate* an error.

exterior (eks tēr' i ēr), *n.* the outside surface or part of anything; outward conduct or appearance, as to be careful about *exteriors.*

exterior (eks tēr' i ēr), *adj.* external, outward.

exterminate (eks tûr' mi nāt), *v.t.* to destroy, kill off.

external (eks tûr' nal), *adj.* outward, outer; material, visible, as distinguished from mental, as *external* evidence; superficial, as *external* gratitude.

extinct (eks tingkt'), *adj.* extinguished; no longer in existence.

extinguish (eks ting' gwish), *v.t.* to put out, as a light; to destroy.

*****extirpate** (ek' stĕr pāt), *v.t.* to root up; to destroy.

*****extol** (eks tol'), *v.t.* [*p.t.* and *p.p.* extolled, *pr.p.* extolling] to praise highly.

extort (eks tôrt'), *v.t.* to obtain by threat or force.

extortion (eks tôr' shun), *n.* the offense of obtaining money or valuables not due by threat or force.

extra (eks' tra), *adj.* additional, beyond what is due or usual.

extract (eks' trakt), *n.* a selected passage from a text, a quotation; something taken from a substance by distilling or drawing out.

extraction (eks trak' shun), *n.* that which is extracted or drawn out; lineage.

extradite (eks' tra dīt), *v.t.* to surrender, as an accused person, to the government of another country, for trial. .

extraneous (eks trā' nē us), *adj.* not essential or to the point, as an *extraneous* argument; external; foreign.

Syn. Extrinsic. That which is *extraneous* is foreign and definitely external; *extrinsic* means not inherently belonging, unessential.

*****extraordinary** (eks trôr' di ner i), *adj.* out of the common or ordinary order or way, unusual, remarkable.

extravagant (eks trav' a gant), *adj.* wasteful; exceeding reasonable limits, excessive, as *extravagant* praise.

Syn. Excessive, exorbitant. *Excessive* is the general term describing whatever exceeds the usual amount or degree; *extravagant* means not only prodigal in spending, but exceeding the bounds of usual use or propriety; *exorbitant* applies to price and means unduly or unfairly excessive.

Ant. Moderate, temperate.

extreme (eks trēm'), *n.* the last limit of anything, the utmost: *extremes*, things utterly different and far removed from each other, as the *extremes* of joy and grief, or good and evil; first and last term in a proportion: opposite of *mean*.

extreme (eks trēm'), *adj.* last, final; radical, as *extreme* social ideas; farthest, as the *extreme* boundary; very great, as *extreme* joy.

extremity (eks trem' i ti), *n.* [*pl.* extremities] an end; the utmost degree; great need or danger.

extricate (eks' tri kāt), *v.t.* to free, as from difficulties; to release, as from entanglements.

extrinsic (eks trin' sik), *adj.* external, unessential.

extrorse (eks trôrs'), *adj.* facing outward.

*****extrude** (eks trōōd'), *v.t. and v.i.* to thrust or stick out, protrude.

extrusion (eks trōō' zhun), *n.* expulsion; protrusion.

exuberant (eg zū' ber ant), *adj.* copious, plenteous.

*****exude** (eks ūd'), *v.i. and v.t.* to discharge or be discharged from the body through the pores, as sweat.

exult (eg zult'), *v.i.* to rejoice triumphantly.

eye (I), *n.* the organ of sight; something resembling an eye, as the *eye* of a needle; vision, the ability to see, as an *eye* for a fine horse.

eye (I), *v.t.* to look at; to watch closely.

eyeball (ī' bôl), *n.* the globe of the eye.

eyebrow (ī' brou), *n.* the hairy arch over an eye.

eyelash (ī' lash), *n.* a hair growing from the edge of the eyelid.

eyelid (ī' lid), *n.* the shutter of skin that closes the eye.

eyesore (ī' sōr), *n.* anything that offends the sight.

eyetooth (ī' tōōth), *n.* [*pl.* eyeteeth] an upper canine tooth.

F

fable (fā' bl), *n.* a short fictitious narrative conveying a moral, especially one in which animals are personified.

fabric (fab' rik), *n.* a structure, as the *fabric* of a story; texture; manufactured cloth, woven or knit.

fabricate (fab' ri kāt), *v.t.* to construct; to weave, as textiles; to build in the imagination; to lie.

fabulous (fab' ū lus), *adj.* like a fable; fictitious; stretching belief.

*****facade** (fa säd'), *n.* the front of a building.

face (fās), *n.* the front part of the head, containing eyes, nose, mouth, cheeks, forehead, chin; the countenance; the expression of the countenance, as a cheerful *face;* the amount expressed on a banknote or bond; the front or principal side, as the *face* of a building; the side inscribed or printed for a certain use, as the *face* of a clock or of a playing card.

face (fās), *v.t.* to meet face to face; to confront; to stand with the face toward, as a house *faces* east; to oppose, resist, as to *face* the enemy; to contemplate with courage, as *face* the truth.

*****facet** (fas' et), *n.* a small face or surface, as of a cut stone.

facetious (fa sē' shus), *adj.* humorous, jocular.

Syn. Witty. A *facetious* remark is jocular, pleasant and laughable; *witty* means quick, cleverly *facetious.*

facial (fā' shal), *adj.* pertaining to the face.

facile (fas' l), *adj.* easily done; quick and sure, expert; easily persuaded, compliant.

facilitate (fa sil' l tāt), *v.t.* to make easy.

facility (fa sil' i ti), *n.* [*pl.* facilities] ease, dexterity resulting from skill or practice; anything that adds to ease of action, use or performance, as *facilities* for writing.

facing (fās' ing), *n.* a covering for the front of anything.

*facsimile (fak sim' i lē), *n.* an exact duplicate.

fact (fakt), *n.* anything actually done or existing.

faction (fak' shun), *n.* a group or clique within a party or state; also, party spirit or dissension.

factious (fak' shus), *adj.* given to faction or dissension.

factitious (fak tish' us), *adj.* artificial, sham; not natural.

factor (fak' tēr), *n.* an agent; steward of an estate; any element contributing to a result; any of the numbers or symbols which, multiplied together, form a product.

factory (fak' tō ri), *n.* a building or buildings equipped to manufacture.

factotum (fak tō' tum), *n.* a man of all work.

faculty (fak' ul ti), *n.* [*pl.* faculties] a physical or mental power, as the *faculty* of sight or memory; the teaching staff of a school.

fad (fad), *n.* a custom followed temporarily with exaggerated zeal; a hobby.

fade (fād), *v.i.* to lose color or distinctness.

fading (fād' ing), *n.* a variation in the intensity of received radio waves, while adjustments of sending and receiving devices remain unchanged.

fail (fāl), *v.i. and v.t.* to fall short of an end or purpose; to be unsuccessful; to waste away, decay; to be wanting or deficient in.

failing (fāl' ing), *n.* a fault or weakness.

failure (fāl' ūr), *n.* the act of failing; omission to perform or do; want of success; bankruptcy; a person who has failed.

faint (fānt), *n.* a swoon.

faint (fānt), *v.i.* to swoon; to lose courage.

faint (fānt), *adj.* feeble; weak, as in color; lacking distinctness.

fair (fâr), *n.* a meeting of buyers and sellers at a stated time and place; an exhibition of local arts and products, as a county *fair;* a showing of goods for sale, for charity, as a church *fair.*

fair (fâr), *adj.* pleasing to the eye; free from blemishes; light in hue, as a *fair* skin; neither very good nor very bad; honest and impartial, as a *fair* decision; of the weather, clear.

Syn. Impartial. *Fair* means not unjust; *impartial* means not swayed by preference or prejudice.

Ant. Unjust.

fairy (fâr' i), *n.* [*pl.* fairies] an imaginary being in human form, graceful and diminutive.

faith (fāth), *n.* religious belief; a doctrine believed; trust and confidence in another; fidelity, loyalty; honesty, as in good *faith.*

faithful (fāth' fool), *adj.* trusting; loyal; trustworthy; true, accurate, as a *faithful* story.

faithless (fāth' les), *adj.* lacking faith; given to breaking promises; untrustworthy.

Syn. Inconstant. *Faithless* means deceitful and treacherous, *inconstant* merely means changeable. An *inconstant* friend may turn to other interests or friends; a *faithless* friend may betray and deceive one.

Ant. Faithful, loyal.

fall (fôl), *n.* the act of falling or tumbling; overthrow, as of a besieged city; that which falls, as a *fall* of rain; autumn; decrease in prices; the rope on which one pulls in hoisting with a tackle; the distance anything drops, as a *fall* of ten feet.

fall (fôl), *v.i.* to drop in space or degree, as to *fall* out of bed, temperature *falls;* to be *sounded,* as music *falls* on our ears; to die, as men *fall* in battle; to pass into a certain condition or activity, as to *fall* into unconsciousness, *fall* to reminiscing; to happen, as Easter *falls* on Sunday, it *fell* upon a day in spring; to be arranged or divided, as Gaul *falls* into three parts.

fallacious (fa lā' shus), *adj.* based on a fallacy, misleading; delusive.

Syn. Misleading, deceitful, deceptive, fraudulent. *Fallacious* means deluding in appearance or because of false reasoning; what is *misleading* leads one to wrong judgments or conclusions; *deceptive* describes material things; *deceitful* applies usually to persons; *fraudulent* carries the idea of intentional deceit or trickery.

fallacy (fal' a si), *n.* [*pl.* fallacies] false appearance; false reasoning; a mistaken assumption.

fallible (fal' i bl), *n.* liable to error; not absolutely sure or reliable.

fallout (fôl ' out), *n.* when minute particles of radioactive material fall to earth after a nuclear explosion.

false (fôls), *adj.* untrue, wrong; faithless, disloyal; artificial, as *false* teeth.

falsetto (fôl set' ō), *n.* a tone of male voice pitched higher than the normal voice.

falsify (fôl' si fī), *v.i. and v.t.* to misrepresent; to make false statements; to change, as figures in a bill or report, fraudulently.

falsity (fôl' si ti), *n.* [*pl.* falsities] the quality of being false; a falsehood, a lie.

falter (fôl' tēr), *v.t. and v.i.* to speak or act with hesitation and timidity; to waver, give way, as troops *falter* before a sudden attack.

fame (fām), *n.* public reputation; wide renown.

Syn. Reputation. *Fame* is widespread; it usually refers to honor and glory, but also pertains to the much talked of; *reputation* is whatever the public thinks of one, good or bad.

familiar (fa mil' yēr), *adj.* intimate; informal; having detailed knowledge of, as to be *familiar* with Latin.

familiarity (fa mil i ar' i ti), *n.* [*pl.* familiarities] a state of intimate acquaintance, intimacy; anything done or said in an easy, informal manner, sometimes in excess of *family (fam' i li), n. a group composed of parents and children; a household group; a tribe or clan, lineage; a classification of animals or plants larger than a genus but less than an order.

famine (fam' in), n. general lack of food; a dearth of anything, as a paper *famine*.

famish (fam' ish), v.i. and v.t. to starve; to suffer or die of extreme hunger; to destroy or weaken with hunger.

famous (fā' mus), adj. renowned, celebrated.
Syn. Notorious. *Famous* and *notorious* both mean widely celebrated; *famous* is used in the honorable sense; *notorious* is used in the bad sense.

fan (fan), n. a light, flat, wide object used to move air against the face, for cooling; an instrument with constantly moving surfaces that agitate the air.

fan (fan), v.i. and v.t. to use a fan; to winnow grain with a fan; to make a fire blaze up by directing a current of air into it, as with a fan.

fanatic (fa nat' ik), n. one who is exaggeratedly zealous for a belief or cause.

fancied (fan' sēd), adj. imaginary, not real.

fanciful (fan' si fool), adj. guided by or based upon fancy rather than upon reason, whimsical; imaginary, not real.
Syn. Fantastic. *Fanciful* means indulging in, based on, or expressing whims or fancies rather than adhering to standards of taste or judgment; *fantastic* means extravagantly fanciful.

*fancy (fan' si), n. capricious imagination; whim; a liking based on caprice instead of reason, as to have a *fancy* for rainy days; an idea.

fancy (fan' si), v.i. and v.t. [p.t. and p.p. fancied, pr.p. fancying] to imagine; to have a liking for.

fancy (fan' si), adj. decorated, ornamented, not plain; beyond reason, as *fancy* prices.

fandango (fan dang' go), n. a Spanish dance.

*fanfare (fan' far), n. a flourish of trumpets; outward display.

fang (fang), n. an animal's long, sharp tooth; the long, hollow tooth of a poisonous snake.

fantail (fan' tāl), n. a variety of pigeon; a structural part resembling a spread fan.

*fantasia (fan ta zē' a), n. a fanciful musical composition unrestricted in form.

fantastic (fan tas' tik), adj. fanciful, whimsical; odd, grotesque.

far (fär), adj. remote in distance or time, as *far* places, the *far* future; more in degree, as *far* better.

far (fär), adv. to a great distance, as throw the ball *far*; very much, as you sing *far* better than I.

farad (far' ad), n. the unit of electrical capacity.

farce (färs), n. a comedy in which human traits and situations are satirized or made laughable; a ridiculous state of affairs.

farcical (fär' si kal), adj. unreal; ludicrous, laughable.

fare (fâr), n. provision, nourishment, sustenance; money paid for transportation.

fare (fâr), v.i. to experience, as good fortune or bad; to go or travel, as to *fare* forth.

farewell (fâr wel'), n. a parting salutation; wishes for another's welfare at parting.
Syn. Adieu, good-bye, valedictory. *Good-bye* is the homely and hearty word at parting; *farewell*, the formal one. A *valedictory* is a farewell address to a group, as a school or college graduating class.

farfetched (fär fecht'), adj. strained, forced.

*farina (fa rē' na), n. a meal or flour made from cereal grain or nuts.

*farinaceous (far i nā' shus), adj. consisting of or made of meal or flour.

farm (färm), n. a piece of land devoted to raising of crops or livestock, or devoted to any specific agricultural project.

farm (färm), v.i. and v.t. to cultivate land; to run a farm.

farmer (färm' ēr), n. one who owns, runs or works on a farm.

farming (färm' ing), n. agriculture.

faro (fâr' o), n. a gambling game played with cards.

farrier (far' i ēr), n. one who shoes horses, a blacksmith.

farrow (far' ō), v.i. and v.t. to give birth to pigs; n. a litter of pigs.

farsighted (fär sīt' ed), adj. seeing to a great distance; sagacious; always looking ahead.

farther (fär' thēr), adj. and adv. [compar. of far] to or at a greater distance, as *farther* lands, to go *farther*.

farthing (fär' thing), n. a British coin worth one-fourth of a penny.

fasces (fas' ēz), n. pl., a bundle of rods symbolizing the power of government.

fascinate (fas' i nāt), v.i. and v.t. to charm; to captivate, as by pleasing personality and manners.

fascination (fas i nā' shun), n. the act of fascinating or charming or state of being charmed; the quality of charm.

fashion (fash' un), n. a prevailing mode or style, as in clothes; conventional custom.

fashion (fash' un), v.t. to make; to shape or form.

fashionable (fash' un a bl), adj. modish, in style; conforming to the customs of the time.

fast (fàst), v.i. to abstain from food.

fast (fàst), adj. speedy, swift, as a *fast* horse; firmly fixed; ahead of the correct time, as my watch is *fast*; dissipated, dissolute.

fast (fàst), adv. with speed, rapidly, as the train went *fast*.

*fasten (fàs' n), v.t. to fix securely, as by locking; to join, as to *fasten* two pipe lengths together.

fastidious (fas tid' i us), adj. squeamish, fussy, hard to please.

fat (fat), n. oily or greasy animal tissue.

fat (fat), adj. corpulent, fleshy; greasy, oily.

fatal (fā' tal), adj. causing death, mortal, as a *fatal* wound.

fatalism (fā' tal izm), n. the doctrine that all things are preordained and determined by fate.

fatality (få tal' i tï), n. [pl. fatalities] determinism; anything decreed by fate; an accident resulting in death.

fate (fāt), n. destiny; one's predestined course of life.

fateful (fāt' fool), adj. charged with fate, momentous; inevitable.

father (fä' thẽr), n. a male parent.

father (fä' thẽr), v.t. to beget, be father to; to be the author of, or responsible for, as a writing or cause.

fathom (fath' um), v.t. to measure by sounding; to get to the bottom of; as to fathom a mystery.

fatigue (fa tēg'), n. weariness.
Syn. Weariness, lassitude. Fatigue is an exhaustion of either physical or mental powers; weariness, a wearing out of the strength or breaking of the spirits; lassitude, a general relaxation of the body.

fatten (fat' n), v.i. and v.t. to grow fat; to make fatter; to enrich.

fatty (fat' ĭ), adj. having fat or the quality of fat.

fatuity (fa tū' ĭ tĭ), n. stupidity.

***fatuous** (fat' ū us), adj. stupid, silly, inane.

***fauces** (fô' sēz), n. pl. the narrow passage from the mouth to the pharynx.

faucet (fô' set), n. a device on a pipe for drawing off liquids in regulated flow; a tap.

fault (fôlt), n. a slight offense; blemish; defect; an irregularity in the formation of subterranean strata, caused by a mass of rock slipping from its location.

faulty (fôl' tĭ), adj. imperfect.

fauna (fô' na), n. [pl. faunas or faunae] the animals characteristic of a given region or period.

favor (fā' vẽr), n. kindness; support; good will; an act of graciousness or kindness.

favor (fā' vẽr), v.t. to regard with favor; to show partiality toward.

favorable (fā' vẽr a bl), n. propitious; demonstrating approval.

favored (fā' vẽrd), adj. regarded with favor or partiality; gifted; having certain features or appearance, as an ill favored nag.

favorite (fā' vẽr ĭt), adj. preferred; specially esteemed.

favoritism (fā' vẽr ĭt izm), n. readiness to favor one more than another; partiality.

fawn (fôn), n. a young deer.

fawn (fôn), v.t. to seek favor by servile demeanor.

fawning (fôn' ing), n. gross or servile flattery.

fay (fā), n. an elf or fairy.

***fealty** (fē' al tĭ), n. loyalty; faithfulness to those having authority over one.

fear (fēr), n. alarm; apprehension of danger; awe or reverence for God.

fear (fēr), v.i. and v.t. to feel fear, be afraid; to be afraid of; have reverential regard for, as to fear God.

fearful (fēr' fool), adj. afraid; causing fear, as a fearful experience.
Syn. Dreadful, frightful, horrible, terrible are all more or less interchangeably used. To be fearful is to have fear about

something external, as fearful of the consequences; afraid means feeling fear.

fearless (fēr' les), adj. without fear; bold, daring.

feasible (fē' zĭ bl), adj. practicable, possible.

feast (fēst), n. a sumptuous repast; a festival, especially of the church.

feast (fēst), v.i. and v.t. to have or enjoy a feast; to give a feast to.

feat (fēt), n. a deed; a notable achievement involving skill or courage.

feather (feth' ẽr), n. a unit of the exterior covering of a bird: feathers, plumage.

feather (feth' ẽr), v.t. to put a feather on, as an arrow; in rowing, to turn (an oar) after a stroke so that the blade is horizontal with the water and will not catch wind.

feathery (feth' ẽr ĭ), adj. having or resembling feathers.

feature (fē' tūr), n. a prominent part of a make-up, as the features of the face, a feature in a newspaper, magazine or program of entertainment.

feature (fē' tūr), v.t. to play up prominently, as in a periodical publication or a program of entertainment.

febrifuge (feb' rĭ fuj), n. a remedy for fever.

***febrile** (fē' brĭl), adj. feverish.

***fecund** (fē' kund), adj. fruitful, fertile.

***fecundate** (fē' kun dāt), v.t. to make fruitful, fertilize.

***federal** (fed' ẽr al), adj. pertaining to a union of states.

federalism (fed' ẽr al izm), n. the doctrine or support of federal organization of government.

federalize (fed' ẽr al īz), v.t. to put under a central government, as a union of states.

fee (fē), n. a charge for professional services; a legally fixed charge for public services or privileges, as a license fee.

feeble (fē' bl), adj. weak in mind or body.

feed (fēd), n. that which is eaten, especially fodder for cattle or food for livestock.

feed (fēd), v.i. and v.t. to take food; to give food to.

feel (fēl), n. the sense of touch; feeling.

feel (fēl), v.t. and v.i. to sense by touching, as to feel an object; to be aware of, experience, as to feel joy; to be aware of being, as to feel cold.

feeler (fēl' ẽr), n. that which feels or touches, as the antennae of certain insects; a trial remark or action designed to draw comment.

feeling (fēl' ing), n. the experience of one who feels something, as an object or an emotion; a physical sensation; an emotional state.

feelings (fēl' ingz), n. pl. one's general state of emotional reaction or susceptibility, as you hurt my feelings.

***feign** (fān), v.i. and v.t. to make believe, pretend.
Syn. Assume, pretend. To feign is to invent and represent by sham, as one might feign sickness as an excuse for not keeping an engagement. To assume is to take upon oneself, as to assume an innocent air; to

pretend is to profess as true something false, as he *pretends* to be a doctor.

feint (fānt), *n.* a pretended blow taking an adversary off guard and opening the way for a real stroke, as in boxing, fencing or war; a pretended blow or attack upon a point where the attack is not to be made, exposing the point at which it actually is later to be directed.

*feldspar** (feld' spär), *n.* a group name for various crystalline minerals.

felicitate (fē lis' i tāt), *v.t.* to congratulate, wish well.

Syn. Congratulate. To *felicitate* is to make formal expression of good wishes; to *congratulate* is the common word for spontaneous and sincere well wishing.

felicitous (fē lis' i tus), *adj.* happily or aptly expressed.

felicity (fē lis' i ti), *n.* happiness; that which causes happiness.

*feline** (fē' lin), *n.* any animal of the cat family.

feline (fē' lin), *adj.* catlike, sly.

fell (fel), *n.* a moor; a down; a skin or hide.

fell (fel), *v.t.* to hew down, as a tree.

fell (fel), *adj.* sinister, cruel.

fellow (fel' ō), *n.* an individual; a companion, comrade; a college graduate receiving an allowance to support him in postgraduate study; a member of an incorporated literary or scientific society.

fellowship (fel' ō ship), *n.* companionship; an endowment to support a graduate student in college.

felon (fel' un), *n.* one who is guilty of felony; a painful abscess on a finger or toe near the nail.

felonious (fē lō' ni us), *adj.* of the nature of felony.

felony (fel' ō ni), *n.* a crime more serious than a misdemeanor.

felt (felt), *n.* an unwoven fabric of wool or fur compressed in manufacture, used for hats.

female (fē' māl), *n.* one of the female sex, a woman, girl or animal of this sex.

female (fē' māl), *adj.* of the sex that bears offspring; characteristic of the female sex: opposite of *male.*

Syn. Womanly, womanlike, womanish, effeminate. *Female* applies to the sex of persons, animals and plants; *feminine* is the opposite of *masculine* and applies to things characteristic of women, as *feminine* frills, *feminine* intuition; *womanly* applies to certain fine characteristics thought of as belonging especially to women, as *womanly* tenderness, devotion, pity; *womanlike* applies to certain undesirable characteristics typical of the weaknesses or faults of women, as a *womanlike* inconsistency; *womanish* is a scoffing word, as *womanish* fears; *effeminate* is an uncomplimentary word applied to men and means unmanly.

*feminine** (fem' i nin), *adj.* pertaining to or characteristic of the female sex: opposite of *masculine.*

*femoral** (fem' ō ral), *adj.* pertaining to the femur, or thigh.

*femur** (fē' mėr), *n.* the thighbone.

fen (fen), *n.* low marshland, a moor.

fence (fens), *n.* a barrier about a field to prevent the straying of animals.

fence (fens), *v.i. and v.t.* to practice fencing; to debate, exchanging thrusts and parries of argument, as if fencing; to enclose with a fence.

fencing (fens' ing), *n.* the art of thrusting and parrying with foil or sword; material used in making fences.

fend (fend), *v.t.* to ward off, as a blow.

fender (fen' dėr), *n.* that which wards off blows; a cushion on the side of a boat to prevent injury by collision with other boats or a dock; a wheelguard of an automobile.

fenestration (fen es trā' shun), *n.* the arrangement of windows on a building.

fennel (fen' el), *n.* an aromatic perennial herb of the carrot family.

feral (fē' ral), *adj.* untamed, wild; savage, like a wild animal.

*ferment** (fŭr' ment), *n.* any of certain living organisms, as yeasts or bacteria, or any enzyme that causes fermentation; tumult, agitation.

ferment (fŭr ment'), *v.i. and v.t.* to undergo fermentation, to work, as cider *ferments;* to cause fermentation, as yeast *ferments* dough; to agitate.

fern (fŭrn), *n.* a flowerless seedless plant with broad or feathery fronds or leaves.

fernery (fŭr' nėr i), *n.* [*pl.* ferneries] a place where ferns are cultivated.

ferocious (fē rō' shus), *adj.* fierce, savage.

ferocity (fē ros' i ti), *n.* fierceness, wildness.

ferret (fer' et), *n.* an animal of the weasel family.

ferret (fer' et), *v.i. and v.t.* to hunt like a ferret; to search relentlessly.

ferrotype (fer' ō tīp), *n.* a photograph taken on a sensitized iron plate.

ferrous (fer' us), *adj.* pertaining to or derived from iron.

ferruginous (fē rōō' ji nus), *adj.* brownish red, like iron rust.

*ferrule** (fer' il, fer' ōōl), *n.* a metal cap on the end of a walking stick, umbrella or tool handle to prevent splitting.

ferry (fer' i), *n.* [*pl.* ferries] a place where passengers, vehicles or freight are carried across a river or harbor; a ferryboat.

ferry (fer' i), *v.t.* to carry across a body of water, as a river, on a ferryboat.

fertile (fŭr' til), *adj.* productive, fruitful; rich, as *fertile* ground.

fertility (fėr til' i ti), *n.* the state of being fertile, the power to produce offspring.

fertilization (fŭr ti li zā' shun), *n.* enrichment, as of soil, to make it more productive.

fertilize (fŭr' ti līz), *v.t.* to enrich, as soil, so as to increase productiveness.

fertilizer (fŭr' ti līz ėr), *n.* that which fertilizes, as commercial products sold for the purpose.

*ferule** (fer' ōōl), *n.* a rod used for chastisement.

fervency (fŭr' ven si), *n.* ardor, warmth of

feeling.

fervent (fûr' vent), *adj.* ardent, warm, intense.

fervid (fûr' vid), *adj.* fiery; zealous.

fervor (fûr' vẽr), *n.* intensity of heat, feeling or expression.

Syn. Ardor. *Fervor* is the boiling over, the expression of intense feeling; *ardor* is itself the intense feeling.

Ant. Coolness, indifference.

festal (fes' tal), *adj.* pertaining to a feast, or holiday, festive.

fester (fes' tẽr), *n.* a small, suppurating sore.

fester (fes' tẽr), *v.i.* to produce pus; to cause soreness; to rankle.

festival (fes' ti val), *n.* a feast or joyous celebration; a periodical celebration.

festive (fes' tiv), *adj.* joyous, gay, as befits a time of feasting.

festivity (fes tiv' i ti), *n.* [*pl.* festivities] social gayety at an entertainment or feast.

festoon (fes tōōn'), *n.* a wreath or garland hanging in a curve.

festoon (fes tōōn'), *v.t.* to form in festoons; to decorate with festoons.

fetch (fech), *v.t.* to go and get and bring.

***fête** (fāt), *n.* a festival, especially an elaborate outdoor celebration.

fête (fāt), *v.t.* to honor with a festival.

***fetid** (fet' id), *adj.* giving forth an offensive smell.

***fetish** (fē' tish), *n.* an object supposed to possess powers of magic, such as curing the diseases of the owner.

fetlock (fet' lok), *n.* a tufted pad on the back of a horse's leg just above the hoof.

fetter (fet' ẽr), *n.* a chain or shackle for the feet; any restraint.

fettle (fet' l), *n.* good condition, readiness, as in fine *fettle*.

***feud** (fūd), *n.* a quarrel between families, carried from one generation to another; a fief.

fever (fē' vẽr), *n.* a diseased condition of the body attended by marked rise in temperature.

feverish (fē' vẽr ish), *adj.* having fever, having heat and thirst; excited and fitful, as *feverish* talk.

few (fū), *adj.* not many, as *few* children could answer the question.

few (fū), *n.* a small number, as a *few* knew the answer.

fez (fez), *n.* a brimless close-fitting felt hat, generally red with a black tassel, formerly worn by all Turkish men.

***fiancé** (fē än sā'), *n.* a betrothed man.

fiancée (fē än sā'), *n.* a betrothed woman.

***fiasco** (fē as' kō), *n.* a complete or ludicrous failure.

***fiat** (fī' at), *n.* a peremptory order or decree.

fiat money (fī' at mun' i), paper currency that has no backing in specie made legal by law.

fiber (fī' bẽr), *n.* a slender threadlike part of an organic tissue.

***fibrin** (fī' brin), *n.* a whitish fibrous protein substance that exists in the blood and causes coagulation.

fibrous (fī' brus), *adj.* having fibers or threadlike parts; composed of or resembling fibers.

fibula (fib' ū la), *n.* [*pl.* fibulae] the outer and smaller of the two bones of the lower leg below the knee.

fichu (fish'ōō), *n.* a light three-cornered cape or collar worn by women.

fickle (fik' l), *adj.* inconstant, capricious.

fiction (fik' shun), *n.* an invented story or narrative, especially a novel.

Syn. Figment, fabrication. *Fiction* is the creation of imagination, and does not necessarily imply an intent to deceive; *fiction* is the opposite of fact; a *fabrication* is definitely meant to deceive; a *figment* is something imaginary which the one who utters it may or may not believe to be true.

Ant. Fact, truth.

fictitious (fik tish 'us), *adj.* imaginary, invented; unreal.

fid (fid), *n.* a square bar of wood or iron supporting a topmast.

fiddle (fid' l), *n.* a violin.

fiddle (fid' l), *v.i. and v.t.* to play a violin; to play something on a violin; to trifle.

fiddlestick (fid' l stik), *n.* a bow for playing on the violin.

fidelity (fi del' i ti), *n.* faithfulness, loyalty; accuracy, as fidelity to a text.

fidget (fij' et), *v.i.* to move uneasily, restlessly.

fidgety (fij' e ti), *adj.* restless, uneasy.

***fiduciary** (fi dū shi er i), *n.* [*pl.* fiduciaries] a trustee.

fiduciary (fi du' shi er i), *adj.* of the nature of a trust.

fief (fēf), *n.* land held in fee, as to an overlord.

field (fēld), *n.* a piece of land for tillage or pasture, which may or may not be fenced in; a stretch of land with a single outstanding characteristic, as a coal *field*; the place where a battle is fought, a battle*field*; a certain department of study, as in the *field* of history; range or reach, as the *field* of vision.

field glass (fēld glås), a small telescope, often double.

fiend (fēnd), *n.* a diabolical person; a demon.

fiendish (fēnd' ish), *adj.* like a fiend, wicked and cruel.

***fierce** (fērs), *adj.* intense in anger; raging, as a *fierce* fire.

***fiery** (fī' ri), *n.* [*comp.* fierier, *superl.* fieriest] pertaining to, consisting of or resembling fire, hot, burning; spirited, passionate.

fife (fīf), *n.* a shrill-toned musical instrument of the flute class.

fifteen (fif tēn'), *n.* one more than fourteen.

***fifth** (fifth), *n.* one of five equal parts.

fifth (fifth), *adj.* next after the fourth.

fiftieth (fif' ti eth), *n.* one of 50 equal parts.

fiftieth (fif' ti eth), *adj.* next after the 49th.

fifty (fif' ti), *n.* one more than 49.

fig (fig), *n.* the edible pear-shaped fruit native to southwestern Asia.

fight (fīt), *n.* a physical struggle, a contest.

fight (fīt), *v.i. and v.t.* [*p.t.* and *p.p.* fought, *pr.p.* fighting] to contend with blows of the fist or with weapons; to oppose in order to defeat or destroy; to war against, as to

fight an enemy; to gain by fighting, as to *fight* one's way.

figment (fig' ment), *n.* an invention of the mind, a fiction.

figurative (fig' ŭr a tiv), *adj.* representing by a figure or symbol, symbolic; not literal, metaphorical.

figure (fig' ŭr), *n.* the shape or form of an object; the general conformation of one's body; a numerical symbol, as the *figure* 3; a drawing or diagram accompanying printed text.

figure (fig' ŭr), *v.i. and v.t.* to cipher; to calculate with numbers or symbols; to represent by a drawing or diagram.

figured (fig' ŭrd), *adj.* adorned with figures or patterns.

filament (fil' a ment), *n.* a fine thread; the thread of metal in an incandescent tube.

filbert (fil'bērt), *n.* the edible nut of the hazel, a hazelnut.

filch (filch), *v.t.* to pilfer, steal.

file (fil), *n.* a piece of steel with ridged surface for shaping metals by abrading; a systematic collection of papers, as business records; a row of soldiers, one behind another, or of objects so arranged.

file (fil), *v.i. and v.t.* to march or stand in a row, one behind another; to place in a cabinet or folder in a certain order, as papers; to abrade with a file.

*****filial** (fil' i al), *adj.* pertaining to, or proper to, a son or daughter.

filibuster (fil' i bus tēr), *n.* a freebooter, an irregular military adventure; an attempt to delay the action of a legislative assembly by speakers holding the floor against the opposing side.

filibuster (fil' i bus tēr), *v.i.* to act as a military freebooter; to delay action in a legislature by prolonging speeches or discussion.

filigree (fil' i grē), *n.* ornamental work of gold or silver wire.

filing (fil' ing), *n.* a fragment of metal rubbed off by a file.

fill (fil), *n.* a filled place, as in roadbuilding; a supply, as a *fill* for a pipe, to eat one's *fill*.

fill (fil), *v.i. and v.t.* to become full; to make full by putting or pouring, as to *fill* a hole with rocks; to occupy all of, as sugar *fills* a barrel; to raise the level of a low place, as in the land, by dumping something into the depression; to treat substances, such as cloth, wood, paper, with other substances in order to close the pores.

fillet (fil' et), *n.* a narrow band worn around the forehead to hold the hair in order; a piece of lean meat, sometimes rolled and tied for cooking.

filling (fil' ing), *n.* something used to fill an empty space or to replace lost matter.

filly (fil' i), *n.* [*pl.* fillies] a female colt.

film (film), *n.* a thin coating; a flexible thin sheet of cellulose nitrate treated for use in photography; a motion picture.

filmy (fil' mi), *adj.* having or resembling a film; delicately clouded, misty.

filter (fil' tēr), *n.* an apparatus or substance used for straining liquid to remove foreign substances.

filter (fil' tēr), *v.t.* to run through a filter, to strain.

filth (filth), *n.* foul matter; moral corruption.

filthy (fil' thi), *adj.* [*comp.* filthier, *superl.* filthiest] foul; nasty; unclean, physically or morally.

filtration (fil trā' shun), *n.* the process of straining.

fin (fin), *n.* a membranous attachment to the body of a fish resembling a wing or a paddle, which enables it to hold its balance and to move through the water; anything resembling a fin, as a *fin* keel on a boat or a small secondary plane on an airplane for balancing or for directing flight.

final (fi' nal), *adj.* coming at the end, last; conclusive.

Syn. Last, ultimate. *Final* means the last of a series, as the *final* event in a tournament, a *final* exam; that which is *last* comes at the end of others of like sort, as the *last* child in the row, the *last* page of a book; *ultimate* describes an end attained, as *ultimate* success.

*****finale** (fē nä' lā), *n.* the closing scene of a drama or opera; the last number on a program; the close or end.

finality (fi nal' i ti), *n.* completion; the act or state of coming to an end; conclusive decision.

*****finance** (fi nans'), *n.* the science of managing money; the actual management of monetary matters, as of a government or corporation.

financial (fi nan' shal), *adj.* pertaining to finance.

Syn. Fiscal, monetary, pecuniary. *Monetary* relates to actual money, coin, currency, as in the expression the *monetary* system. *Pecuniary* refers to that in which money is involved, as *pecuniary* interests. *Financial* applies especially to governmental revenues and expenditures, or to corporation management.

*****financier** (fin an sēr'), *n.* one skilled in the administration of money matters on a large scale.

finch (finch), *n.* any of various small singing birds, as sparrows, linnets, buntings.

find (find), *n.* something found.

find (find), *v.t.* [*p.t. and p.p.* found, *pr.p.* finding] to discover; to obtain by searching; to learn by study or experiment, as we *find* that insects have six legs.

finder (fin' dēr), *n.* an instrument for finding, as focus for a camera or range for a gun.

finding (fin' ding), *n.* the verdict of a jury, court or arbitrator: *findings,* equipment for an artisan, such as tools or materials.

fine (fin), *n.* money paid as a penalty.

fine (fin), *v.t.* to impose a fine or money penalty.

fine (fin), *adj.* delicate, as *fine* lace; sensitive, as a *fine* ear for music; not coarse, perfected, refined, as *fine* gold.

fine-drawn (fin drôn), *adj.* spun very fine; subtle.

finery (fin' er i), *n.* [*pl.* fineries] personal

adornment, as fine or showy clothes.

*finesse (fi nes'), n. artifice or stratagem; delicate skill; a certain play in card games.

finger (fing' gēr), n. one of the four digits of the hand, as distinguished from the thumb.

finger (fing' gēr), v.t. to handle with the fingers; to perform (on a musical instrument) with the fingers.

fingering (fing' gēr ing), n. manipulating with the fingers; the manner of using the fingers in playing a musical instrument.

fingerprint (fing' gēr print), n. an impression of a finger, or more commonly, a thumb, showing the characteristic lines of the skin, used as a means of identification.

finical (fin' i kal), adj. fastidious, fussy.

*finis (fī' nis), n. the end, as of a play or book.

finish (fin' ish), n. the end or conclusion; the final part of the process of making, that which completes or perfects, as to put a finish on a written article, the table has a shiny finish; social refinement.

finish (fin' ish), v.i. and v.t. to come to an end; to bring to an end, as to finish a song; to put the last touches on, as to finish a dress; to complete, as to finish one's schooling or work in the world.

finished (fin' isht), adj. concluded, complete; polished, in physical fact or in manner.

finite (fī' nīt), adj. having limits: opposite of infinite.

Syn. Limited. This world is finite; space is infinite. The power of a government is limited; the powers of mankind are finite. Ant. Infinite, unlimited.

*fiord (fyôrd), n. a long narrow inlet of the sea between high, rocky banks.

fir (fûr), n. a certain evergreen tree related to the pine; also its wood.

fire (fīr), n. combustion, with heat, flame and light; anything burning; something resembling fire, as the fire of your eye, the fire of a diamond.

fire (fīr), n. discharge of firearms, as the enemy's fire grew heavier.

fire (fīr), v.i. and v.t. to become ignited; to ignite; to keep a fire in, as to fire a furnace; to temper with heat, bake, as to fire pottery; to inflame, as to fire the passions; to discharge, as firearms.

firearms (fīr' ärmz), n. pl. guns; weapons discharged by means of explosive loads: usually small guns.

firebox (fīr' boks), n. the space in a furnace or stove that holds the fire.

firebrand (fīr' brand), n. a piece of burning wood; an incendiary; one who inflames the passions of others.

firebrick (fīr' brik), n. nonfusible brick, used for lining fireboxes.

firebug (fīr' bug), n. an incendiary.

fire clay (fīr klā), a clay that withstands extreme heat, used in making firebrick.

firedamp (fīr' damp), n. a combustible gas formed in coal mines.

firedog (fīr' dôg), n. an andiron.

fire-eater (fīr' ēt ēr), n. a juggler who pretends to eat fire; a defiant person.

firefly (fīr' flī), n. a small winged beetle which gives forth an intermittent luminous glow in the darkness.

fireman (fīr' man), n. one who serves in a fire-fighting department; one who fires furnaces.

fireproof (fīr' prōōf), adj. practically unburnable; proof against fire.

fireproof (fīr' prōōf), v.t. to make fireproof.

fire ship (fīr ship), a ship loaded with combustibles, ignited and sent to drift among the ships of an enemy.

fireside (fīr' sīd), n. the hearth; hence, domestic life and comfort.

fire test (fīr test), a test to discover the burning temperature of a lubricating oil; any other test by means of heat.

firetrap (fīr' trap), n. a non-fireproof building without proper provision for escape in case of fire.

firewarden (fīr' wôrd en), n. a public officer authorized to detect forest fires and direct fighting of same.

firing (fīr' ing), n. the methodical feeding of fuel into a furnace; exposure, as of pottery to extreme heat, to harden or glaze a surface; discharge of firearms, as the firing became heavier.

firkin (fûr' kin), n. a small wooden tub for holding butter or lard.

firm (fûrm), n. a business establishment or commercial house; a partnership.

firm (fûrm), v.t. to make compact, fix or set firmly.

firm (fûrm), adj. set solidly; compressed to hardness; unyielding; determined, as a firm voice.

Syn. Hard, solid. Firm means fixed, strong or steady in spite of pressure or shaking, as jelly is firm, a bridge is firm; hard means resisting pressure, impenetrable, as rocks; solid means compact and dense. Ant. Loose, unstable.

firmament (fûr' ma ment), n. the arch of the sky.

first (fûrst), n. the beginning, as the first of a book; anything that leads, as he is the first in his class.

first (fûrst), adj. preceding all others, as first choice, he was the first one here.

first (fûrst), adv. before all others in space, time or value, as you go first.

first-born (fûrst' bôrn'), n. the child born first in a family.

first-class (fûrst' klâs'), adj. of highest excellence.

firsthand (fûrst' hand'), adj. obtained directly from the producer or original owner.

firth (fûrth), n. a narrow arm of the sea: also called frith.

fiscal (fis' kal), adj. pertaining to the handling of public revenues, as in the fiscal year; financial, as fiscal affairs.

fish (fish), n. [pl. fish, fishes] a vertebrate animal living only in water, and having gills, fins and a long, slender, scale-covered body ending in a broad tail fin; a plate or strip of wood or metal strengthening the joint of two spars.

sh (fish), v.i. and v.t. to try to catch fish; to drag for submerged things; to try to get by indirect means, as to fish for compliments; to fasten, as spars, with a fish or fishplate.

isherman (fish' ĕr man), n. one who fishes for the market or sport.

ishery (fish' ĕr ĭ), n. [pl. fisheries] the business of catching fish for the market; the waters in which it is carried on.

ishy (fish' ĭ), adj. like fish, as this tastes fishy; incredible, as it sounds fishy.

issile (fis' il), adj. capable of being split.

ission (fish' un), n. the act of cleaving apart or splitting.

issure (fish' ĕr), n. a cleft or crack.

ist (fist), n. the hand closed with fingers curved tightly into the palm.

istula (fis' tū la), n. an ulcerous opening in the body.

it (fit), n. that which fits or is fitting, as the coat is a good fit.

it (fit), n. a paroxysm characteristic of certain bodily disorders, as an epileptic fit, a fit of coughing.

it (fit), v.i. and v.t. to conform in size and shape, as the suit fits well; to make fit or suitable.

it (fit), adj. appropriate, proper, as food fit for a king; ready, prepared, as fit for action.
Syn. Proper, suitable. Fit means adapted or qualified for a purpose, or able, as fit to work; suitable means in harmony or in accord with, as garments suitable for a bride; proper means correct or appropriate, as to have proper manners.

itful (fit' fool), adj. capricious, spasmodic, impulsive, unstable.

itting (fit' ing), n. making to conform in size and shape; trying on partly finished apparel; necessary part, as the fittings of a gymnasium.

itting (fit' ing), adj. suitable, appropriate.

ive (fiv), n. the number one more than 4.

ivefold (fiv fōld'), adj. and adv. in fives; five times as much or as great.

ix (fiks), n. a predicament, as I'm in a fix.

ix (fiks), v.i. and v.t. to become fixed or fastened; to make fast, secure or stable; to adjust, arrange; to repair.

ixation (fiks ā' shun), n. the act of making permanent or state of being made permanent, as the fixation of a chemical substance so that it will not undergo further change; concentration of gaze; arrested development; formation of a habit.

ixed (fikst), adj. firm, lasting, settled, permanent.

ixedly (fik' sed li), adv. steadily, firmly.

ixity (fiks' i ti), n. stability, permanence.

ixture (fiks' tūr), n. that which is firmly established; an article of furniture or equipment, taken as a permanent part of a house.

izz (fiz), n. a hissing noise, as of an effervescing liquid; a drink that fizzes.

izz (fiz), v.i. to effervesce, with a hissing sound.

flabby (flab' i), adj. without firmness; feeble; loose, lax.

*__flaccid__ (flak' sid), adj. limp, flabby; soft and weak.

flag (flag), n. a piece of bunting on which a device is shown, as the emblem of nationality; a plant of the iris family; a flat paving stone.

flag (flag), v.i. and v.t. to hang loose, droop; to lose vigor; to signal with a flag.

*__flagellate__ (flaj' e lāt), v.t. to whip, flog.

*__flageolet__ (flaj' ō let), n. a small musical wind instrument of the flute class.

flagging (flag' ing), n. a pavement of flagstones.

*__flagitious__ (fla jish' us), adj. atrocious, wicked.

*__flagon__ (flag' un), n. a large drinking vessel having a handle and sometimes a lid.

flagrant (flā' grant), adj. openly wicked, outrageous.

flagship (flag' ship), n. the ship carrying the commander of a fleet and flying his flag.

flagstone (flag' stōn), n. a flat stone used in paving, as for a sidewalk.

flail (flāl), n. an instrument for threshing grain.

flair (flâr), n. discernment by instinct, special aptitude; interest, bent.

flake (flāk), n. a loose, thin mass or scale of anything, as a flake of snow or soap.

flake (flāk), v.i. and v.t. to form into flakes or scales.

flaky (flāk' i), adj. formed in or like flakes, scales or tiny layers.

*__flamboyant__ (flam boi' ant), adj. ornate; marked by wavy, flamelike curves.

flame (flām), n. the blaze of combustion; a blaze; a flamelike glow, as of temper.

flame (flām), v.i. to burn with a flame or blaze, glow like a flame, burst into a blaze.

*__flamingo__ (fla ming' gō), n. a tropical aquatic bird.

*__flange__ (flanj), n. a raised or projecting rim to prevent a wheel from leaving a track.

flank (flangk), n. the side of an animal between ribs and hip; the side of anything; the right or left side of an armed force.

flank (flangk), v.t. to guard or strengthen the flank or side of, to attack or pass the side of; to be beside, border.

flannel (flan' el), n. a soft, loosely woven woolen cloth.

flap (flap), n. an overlapping surface; anything flat and limp that hangs loose; the motion of anything flat, wide or limp that hangs loose; the sound made by same.

flap (flap), v.i. and v.t. to beat or move loosely, as the bird's wings flap; to move with a beating motion, as a bird flaps its wings.

flare (flâr), n. a glaring light coming up suddenly and spreading; a blaze used for a signal; a sudden outburst.

flare (flâr), v.i. to burn with a flare; to give out a sudden, spreading blaze of light; to burst out, as her anger flared up; to spread outward, as a vase flares at the top.

flash (flash), n. a sudden, quickly passing emission of light; an outburst, as of wit.

flash (flash), v.i. and v.t. to break forth in a sudden or momentary flame; to act or speak with suddenness; to send out as if by flashes, as to *flash* the election returns.

flask (flásk), *n.* a small usually flattened bottle of glass, metal or leather, used to carry liquids or powder.

flat (flat), *n.* a level surface; the flat part of anything, as the *flat* of a sword blade, the *flat* of the hand; a suite of rooms on one floor of a building.

flat (flat), *adj.* level and horizontal, as *flat* lands; level and smooth, as a *flat* surface; spread out, prostrate; broad and thin, as a pancake; positive, unqualified, as a *flat* refusal; fixed, unvarying, as a *flat* rate; dull, monotonous, as a *flat* voice, a *flat* story; below the true pitch of a tone, minor.

flatten (flat' n), *v.t. and v.i.* to make flat or become flat in position, shape or quality.

flatter (flat' ĕr), *v.t.* to praise or gratify the vanity of, especially in self-interest; to over praise.

flatterer (flat' ĕr ĕr), *n.* one who flatters or blandishes or beguiles unduly.

flattery (flat' ĕr i), *n.* [*pl.* flatteries] insincere complimentary speech.

flatulence (flat' ü lens), *n.* distention of the abdomen by gases.

*flaunt (flônt), *v.i. and v.t.* to wave ostentatiously; to display defiantly.

flavor (flā' vẽr), *n.* distinctive taste, or odor; also, a distinguishing characteristic; as, his landscapes have the *flavor* of the West.

flavor (flā' vẽr), *v.t.* to impart a distinctive taste or odor to.

flaw (flô), *n.* a defect, blemish.

flax (flaks), *n.* a plant cultivated for its seeds and for its fiber, which is spun into linen.

flaxen (flaks' n), *adj.* made of flax, like flax; having the light straw color of flax.

flaxseed (flaks' sēd), *n.* the seed of flax, used in medicine and in making linseed oil.

flay (flā), *v.t.* [*p.t. and p.p.* flayed, *pr.p.* flaying] to strip off the skin of; to criticize scathingly.

flea (flē), *n.* a hard-bodied wingless blood-sucking insect.

fleck (flek), *n.* a spot; particle.

flection (flek' shun), *n.* a bend; a part that is bent.

fledge (flej), *v.i.* to acquire feathers necessary for flight.

fledgling (flej' ling), *n.* a young bird.

flee (flē), *v.i. and v.t.* [*p.t. and p.p.* fled, *pr.p.* fleeing] to run away.

fleece (flēs), *n.* the wool coat of a sheep.

fleece (flēs), *v.t.* to shear (sheep); to strip, plunder, as to *fleece* a man of money.

fleecy (flēs' i), *adj.* woolly.

fleer (flēr), *v.i. and v.t.* to laugh at, jibe, mock.

fleet (flēt), *n.* a group of warships under central command.

fleet (flēt), *adj.* swift, quickly passing away.

flesh (flesh), *n.* the muscular parts of an animal's body; the human body as distinguished from soul.

fleshly (flesh' li), *adj.* pertaining to the body, as distinguished from the spirit or soul.

fleshy (flesh' i), *adj.* [*comp.* fleshier, *superl.* fleshiest] corpulent, gross.

flexible (flek' si bl), *adj.* easily bent; compliant; yielding to persuasion.

Syn. Pliable, supple. *Flexible* is used in both the physical and moral sense; it means easily bent or adaptable to change of shape or opinion; *pliable* also means easily bent, but carries the added idea of being workable, as wax is *pliable; supple* implies ease of motion in any direction.

Ant. Rigid, stiff, unyielding.

*flexure (flek' shẽr), *n.* a bending or being bent; a bend or fold.

flick (flik), *n.* a light, quick stroke. *v.t.* to snap or jerk.

flicker (flik' ẽr), *n.* a brief, momentary wavering brightness, as the lamp gave a *flicker;* any brief stirring, as a *flicker* of the eyelid.

flicker (flik' ẽr), *n.* the North American golden-winged woodpecker.

flicker (flik' ẽr), *v.i.* to flutter, as wings; to waver, like a dying flame.

flight (flīt), *n.* the act of flying; a number of things passing through the air at once, as a *flight* of arrows; a series of steps in a staircase from one landing to the next.

flighty (flī' ti), *adj.* [*comp.* flightier, *superl.* flightiest] having or indicating flights of fancy, imagination or humor; capricious.

flimsy (flim' si), *adj.* unsubstantial, frail.

flinch (flinch), *v.i.* to shrink or draw back.

fling (fling), *n.* a throw; a lively dance; indulgence, as to have one's *fling. v.t.* [*p.t. and p.p.* flung, *pr.p.* flinging] to throw or hurl.

flint (flint), *n.* a hard kind of quartz that strikes a spark from steel.

flinty (flin' ti), *adj.* of or like flint, hard.

flip (flip), *n.* a flick, toss or jerk, as with a finger. *v.t.* to give a fillip to with the fingers, as to *flip* a coin.

flippancy (flip' an si), *n.* the quality of being light and pert.

flippant (flip' ant), *adj.* pert; regarding serious things lightly.

flipper (flip' ẽr), *n.* a broad limb used in swimming, as of the seal, walrus or whale.

flirt (flûrt), *n.* a quick throw; one who trifles with love.

flirt (flûrt), *v.i. and v.t.* to move jerkily or suddenly; to coquet; to make love insincerely, trifle with love; to move back and forth with swift action, as a fan.

flit (flit), *v.i.* to dart one way and another in short flights.

flitch (flitch), *n.* the side of a hog salted and cured, as a *flitch* of bacon.

float (flōt), *n.* something that floats; a vehicle without side boards, used for display in a parade; a tool for smearing and smoothing, like a plasterer's trowel.

float (flōt), *v.i. and v.t.* to lie on a liquid without sinking; to drift; to be or move suspended in air, as a balloon *floats;* to put on the market, as an issue of stocks; to cause to float.

*flocculent (flok' ü lent), *adj.* woolly; covered with a waxy fuzz resembling wool.

flock (flok), *n.* a group of birds or animals of the same kind moving about together; woolen or cotton refuse used as padding in

flock (flok), *v.i.* to move in flocks; to crowd together.

floe (flō), *n.* a large flat mass of floating ice.

flog (flog), *v.t.* to whip.

flood (flud), *n.* an abnormal flow of water, overrunning customary bounds; an inundation; deluge; any superabundance.

flood (flud), *v.t.* to overflow or inundate, as a river *floods* the land.

floodgate (flud' gāt), *n.* a movable barrier in a waterway to control the flow, a sluice.

floor (flōr), *n.* a surface in a structure on which one walks, as the *floor* of a room, the *floor* of a bridge; any bottom surface, as the ocean *floor;* the part of a legislative chamber in which the legislators sit; also the right to speak from one's seat in this space, as to have the *floor.*

floor (flōr), *v.t.* to furnish with a floor; to knock down, defeat in fight or argument, as to *floor* an opponent.

flop (flop), *n.* the act or sound of coming down with a jerk or slap.

flop (flop), *v.i. and v.t.* to turn over with a jerky motion and come down with a slap, as the fish *flopped* in the boat; to cause to flop.

floppy disk (flop' ē disk), *n.* a flexible disk.

flora (flō' ra), *n.* the plants of a region or period.

***floral** (flō' ral), *adj.* pertaining to or like flowers.

***floriculture** (flō' ri kul tūr), *n.* the cultivation of ornamental flowering plants.

***florid** (flor' id), *adj.* flowery, as *florid* speech; flushed, as a *florid* face.

***florist** (flōr' ist), *n.* one who grows and sells flowers.

floss (flôs), *n.* waste fibers of silk; an untwisted, soft silk thread, used in embroidery.

flossy (flôs' i), *adj.* like floss, downy, smooth and silky.

flotilla (flō til' a), *n.* a small fleet, or a fleet of small vessels.

flotsam (flot' sam), *n.* floating sea wreckage.

flounce (flouns), *n.* a narrow strip of goods sewed to the bottom of a skirt and along one edge only, so as to spread; a deep ruffle.

flounce (flouns), *v.i. and v.t.* to move the body impatiently, as she *flounced* out of the room; to put a flounce on, as the dress was *flounced.*

flounder (floun' dẽr), *n.* a flat-bodied sea fish.

flounder (floun' dẽr), *v.i.* to struggle awkwardly or with futile effort, as in trying to extricate oneself from any difficult situation.

flour (flour), *n.* finely ground grain meal, particularly of wheat.

flourish (flûr' ish), *n.* a fancy stroke, as with a pen; a waving motion, as with a wand; a threatening motion, as with a sword or stick; in music, a fanfare; any swaggering or challenging gesture.

flourish (flûr' ish), *v.i. and v.t.* to prosper; to embellish; to brandish.

flout (flout), *n.* a jeer, insult.

flout (flout), *v.t.* to mock, treat contemptuously.

flow (flō), *n.* the motion of water, as in a stream; the measure of liquid passing through a certain channel in a set time.

flow (flō), *v.i.* to run or spread, as water; to rise, as the tide *flows.*

flower (flou' ẽr), *n.* the bloom of a plant, the part that produces the seed; the best part of anything, as the *flower* of youth.

flower (flou' ẽr), *v.i. and v.t.* to produce flowers or blooms, to blossom; to adorn with flowers or with a floral design.

fluctuate (fluk' tū āt), *v.i.* to move, as a wave, go up and down or back and forth; to waver, vary, change.

Syn. Waver. To *fluctuate* is to move with irregular motion; to *waver* is to hesitate or falter. One's moods *fluctuate* from gay to sad; prices *fluctuate* between high and low; one *wavers* in purpose; courage *wavers.*

flue (flōō), *n.* a pipe or passage to carry off smoke.

fluency (flōō' en si), *n.* readiness of speech; smooth, easy flow.

fluent (flōō' ent), *adj.* flowing; easy; ready in use of words, smooth, as *fluent* writing.

fluff (fluf), *n.* a light down or the nap from cotton or fur.

fluffy (fluf' i), *adj.* fluff-covered; light and downy.

***fluid** (flōō' id), *n.* anything that flows, either a liquid or a gas.

flume (flōōm), *n.* a channel to direct the flow of water down an incline.

***fluorescence** (flōō ō res' ens), *n.* the quality, in some transparent substances, of colored luminosity, the special light thus produced.

***fluorine** (flōō' ō ren), *n.* a gaseous element related to chlorine found in the mineral fluorite.

***fluoroscope** (flōō' ō rō skōp), *n.* an instrument for observing and showing fluorescence.

flurry (flûr' i), *n.* a sudden stirring of the air; a sudden fall of rain or snow; any nervous flutter.

flurry (flûr' i), *v.t.* to agitate, excite, confuse.

flush (flush), *n.* a sudden rush, as of water; a rush of blood into the face, a blush; vigor, as in the *flush* of life.

flush (flush), *v.i. and v.t.* to flow and spread freely; to blush, glow; to wash with a sudden spreading flow of water.

flush (flush), *adj.* level with a surface or brim; brimful; vigorous, full of life.

fluster (flus' tẽr), *v.t.* to confuse, agitate.

flute (flōōt), *n.* a musical wind instrument; a decorative curved groove, as in architecture.

fluted (flōōt' ed), *adj.* ornamented with series of grooves; clear and flutelike.

fluting (flōōt' ing), *n.* in architecture, decoration with grooves.

flutter (flut' ẽr), *n.* a quick and irregular movement, as of wings; a state of mental and nervous agitation.

flutter (flut' ẽr), *v.i. and v.t.* to agitate the wings without flying; to make similar motions, as a flag in a light breeze; to be agitated and nervous; to flap rapidly, as to *flutter* the wings, *flutter* a handkerchief.

flux (fluks), *n.* a continuous flowing or passing; a mixture that helps produce fusion, as lime is a *flux* in metallurgy.

fly (flī), *n.* [*pl.* flies] a two-winged insect of many varieties; canvas stretched over the top of a tent; a flap on a garment covering a row of buttons; an artificial fly on a hook, used in fishing; the space over a stage from which scenery is handled.

fly (flī), *v.i. and v.t.* [*p.t.* flew, *p.p.* flown, *pr.p.* flying] to move through the air with wings, as a bird; to move through the air by means of any aircraft; to soar aloft, as a flag or kite; to wave or show, as to *fly* the colors; to flee from.

flying boat (flī'ing bōt), a seaplane.

flyleaf (flī' lēf), *n.* a blank leaf at the front of a book, preceding the title page.

flywheel (flī' hwēl), *n.* a heavy wheel in machinery to steady its motion.

foal (fōl), *n.* the young of any of the horse family, a colt or filly.

foam (fōm), *n.* the white froth formed on a liquid by agitation or fermentation.

foam (fōm), *v.i.* to form foam, effervesce frothily.

fob (fob), *n.* a small watch-pocket in men's trousers; a short ribbon or chain attached to a watch to hold a charm.

focal (fō' kal), *adj.* pertaining to a focus.

focalize (fō' kal īz), *v.t.* to bring to a focus.

focus (fō' kus), *n.* [*pl.* focuses or foci] the point where rays of light, sound or heat come to a point after being refracted; the adjustment necessary in eyes or lenses to obtain clear vision; any central point of activity or attention.

focus (fō' kus), *v.i. and v.t.* to center the vision upon; to bring to a focus; to set so as to form a perfectly clear image, as the lenses of eyeglasses, a telescope or a camera.

fodder (fod' ēr), *n.* coarse food for horses and cattle, as dried cornstalks.

foe (fō), *n.* an enemy, especially in war; an opponent, as a *foe* of democracy.

fog (fog), *n.* condensed water vapor in the air; a heavy mist; mental confusion.

fog (fog), *v.i. and v.t.* to become obscured as if with fog; to be or make misty.

fogbank (fog' bangk), *n.* a dense mass of fog at sea.

foggy (fog' i), *adj.* like fog; filled with fog; misty; mentally confused; indistinct.

fogy (fō' gi), *n.* a dull, old-fashioned, super-conservative person.

foible (foi' bl), *n.* a minor weakness of character.

foil (foil), *n.* a contrast, to set something off to advantage; metal hammered into thin leaves, a long thrusting weapon without point, used in fencing for sport.

foil (foil), *v.t.* to frustrate, baffle.

foist (foist), *v.t.* to pass off as genuine (that which is not genuine).

fold (fōld), *n.* a doubling over, as of cloth; an enclosed yard for sheep. *v.i. and v.t.* to form a fold, double over or form in folds;

to enclose sheep in a yard.

folder (fōl' dēr), *n.* one who or that which folds; a heavy sheet of paper folded so as to hold lighter sheets; a circular with several leaves that are not stitched or bound.

*****foliage** (fō' li ij), *n.* leafage; the whole leaf system of a plant or tree.

foliation (fō li ā' shun), *n.* the act of forming leaves or of forming a substance into leaves.

folio (fō' li ō), *n.* a sheet of paper folded over once; a book of the largest size, composed of sheets of paper folded only once, having 4 pages to a sheet; a leaf in a book or manuscript; a page number in a book.

folk (fōk), *n.* a group of kindred people, a tribe or nation; that great group of people within a nation that preserves its language and culture; the common people of any nation: *folks,* the plural, relations, family, people.

folklore (fōk' lōr), *n.* all the accumulated traditions, culture, beliefs, tales and learning of a people.

follow (fol' ō), *v.i. and v.t.* to go or come after in time or distance, as May *follows* April, the pup *follows* his master; to spring from, as sickness *follows* exposure; to accept and apply, as to *follow* advice.

Syn. Succeed, ensue. Either persons or things may *follow* or *succeed;* only things or ideas *ensue.* To *follow,* as said of persons, is to go in order, one after another; to *succeed* is to be in the same place as another after he has left it. To *ensue* is to follow as a result.

Ant. Lead, precede.

following (fol' ō ing), *n.* a body of followers or dependents.

folly (fol' i),*n.* [*pl.* follies] foolishness; light-mindedness; reckless action.

foment (fō ment'), *v.t.* to apply a warm lotion to, bathe with hot water; to stir up, incite, as to *foment* civic disorders.

fond (fond), *adj.* affectionate; foolishly doting.

fond (fon'), *n.* foundation, background, base, especially the main material of a cooked dish.

fondle (fon' dl), *v.t.* to caress.

*****font** (font), *n.* a stone receptacle holding the water used in baptizing; any fountain, spring or source; a type assortment.

food (fōōd), *n.* nutriment; solid edibles, as distinguished from liquids; anything that nourishes or strengthens.

fool (fōōl), *n.* a person who lacks judgment; a simpleton; a professional buffoon or jester.

fool (fōōl), *v.i. and v.t.* to act like a fool; to deceive.

foolhardy (fōōl' här di), *adj.* having courage without judgment; recklessly bold.

Syn. Adventurous, rash. The *foolhardy* man ventures because of his foolish recklessness; the *adventurous* man ventures for the love of daring and thrill; the *rash* man ventures without stopping to think.

Ant. Cautious, wary.

foolproof (fōōl' prōōf), *adj.* strong enough and simple enough to be handled or operated by a fool without damage or hindrance.

foot (foot), *n.* [*pl.* feet] the end part of the leg, on which an animal stands; that which covers the foot, as the *foot* of a sock; that on which anything stands, as the *foot* of a chair; the end opposite the top, as the *foot* of a mountain; a unit of measure equal to 12 inches; a certain group of syllables, the unit of meter, within a line of verse.

foot (foot), *v.i. and v.t.* to tread or dance to music; to go by foot, as to *foot* it; to dance through, as to *foot* a measure; to sum up, as the numbers in a column.

footage (foot' ij), *n.* length expressed in feet, as the *footage* of a fence.

football (foot' bôl), *n.* an inflated ball; a field game played by two teams of 11 men each.

footboard (foot' bôrd), *n.* a plank to stand on; a board at the foot of a bed.

footfall (foot' fôl), *n.* the sound of a footstep.

footgear (foot' gēr), *n.* shoes, stockings, boots, slippers, rubbers.

foothold (foot' hōld), *n.* a hold for the feet, a solid footing.

footing (foot' ing), *n.* ground or support for the feet, as an uncertain *footing*, a foothold; a relationship, as a friendly *footing*.

footman (foot' man), *n.* [*pl.* footmen] a liveried servant who attends a carriage.

footpad (foot' pad), *n.* a highwayman afoot.

foot-pound (foot' pound'), *n.* amount of power needed to raise a 1 lb. weight 1 foot.

foozle (foo' zl), *v.t. and v.i.* to bungle, mismanage.

fop (fop), *n.* a dandy.

for (fôr), *prep.* instead of, in place of, as Tom recited *for* John; on account of, in behalf of, as do it *for* me; to the extent of in space or time, as to walk *for* a mile, study *for* an hour; as being, as I took him *for* you; at the price of, as to sell *for* $5; suited to, as medicine *for* a cold; because of, as he could not talk *for* laughing; by the lack of, as to be embarrassed *for* funds; in support of, as cheer *for* our side; in spite of, as she can't sing, *for* all her efforts; considering, as tall *for* his age; intended or intending to reach or win, as to leave *for* Boston, try *for* a prize.

for (fôr), *conj.* because, since.

forage (for' ij), *n.* food for horses and cattle.

forage (for' ij), *v.i.* to hunt for provisions.

foray (for' ā), *n.* a sudden raid for spoils, as in war.

foray (for' ā), *v.i.* to ravage for spoils, pillage, make a raid in war.

forbear (fôr bâr'), *v.i. and v.t.* [*p.t.* forbore, *p.p.* forborne; *pr.p.* forbearing] to refrain, hold back; to do without.

forbearance (fôr bâr' ans), *n.* the act of forbearing; use of patience.

forbid (fôr bid'), *v.t.* [*p.t.* forbade, *p.p.* forbidden, *pr.p.* forbidding] to prohibit.

forbidding (fôr bid' ing), *adj.* repellent, disagreeable; repelling approach.

force (fôrs), *n.* strength, power; use of strength or power; violence; a body of men in readiness for action; the cause that changes bodies from state of rest to motion

or vice versa.

Syn. Violence. *Force* is a general term and means any physical power, as used in persons or things; *violence* is undue or unjust force, often accompanied by injury.

forceps (fôr' seps), *n.* [*pl.* forceps] a pair of pincers used in surgical operations and by dentists or watchmakers.

forcible (fôr' si bl), *adj.* brought about by using force; characterized by physical or mental power, as a *forcible* personality.

ford (fôrd), *n.* a shallow place in a stream where it may be crossed. *v.t.* to cross, as a stream at a shallow or passable place.

fore (fôr), *n.* the front, the front part.

fore-and-aft *adj.* lengthwise of a vessel, as *fore-and-aft* sails.

forearm (fôr' ärm), *n.* the part of the arm between wrist and elbow.

*****forebode** (fôr bōd'), *v.t.* to foretell, presage; to expect misfortune.

forecast (fôr' kåst), *n.* a prediction or prophecy; prevision, foresight.

*****forecast** (fôr kåst'), *v.t.* to predict, as to *forecast* the weather.

foreclose (fôr klōz'), *v.t.* to call for payment, as a mortgage when due, and cut off the further right of redemption.

foreclosure (fôr klō' zher), *n.* legal proceedings to end a mortgagor's right to redeem a mortgaged property.

forefather (fôr' fäth ēr), *n.* an ancestor.

*****forehead** (fôr' ed), *n.* the part of the face between the eyes and the hairline.

foreign (for' in), *adj.* situated or belonging outside of one's own country, as a *foreign* city; alien, not belonging to, as *foreign* to the argument.

forelock (fôr' lok), *n.* a lock of hair growing on the front part of the head.

foreman (fôr' man), *n.* the head man of a shop; spokesman of a jury.

foremost (fôr' most), *adj.* chief.

forensic (fô ren' sik), *adj.* having to do with courts of law or public debate; rhetorical.

foresight (fôr' sit), *n.* the act or power of foreseeing; care for the future.

forest (for' est), *n.* trees growing densely over a large area: figuratively, a *forest* of masts.

forestall (fôr stôl'), *v.t.* to obstruct, hinder or prevent by something done or said in advance; to outguess and outdo.

foretaste (fôr' tåst), *n.* anticipation.

foretell (fôr tel'), *v.t.* to predict, prophesy.

Syn. Prophesy, forecast, prognosticate. One may *foretell* coming events without being able to *prophesy* the future. One *foretells* by a simple calculation; to *prophesy* is to foretell by supernatural revelation; to *forecast* is really to guess ahead rather than to know what will happen; to *prognosticate* is to foretell from symptoms; it is an act of the understanding; a physician *prognosticates* the crisis of a disorder through scientific knowledge.

forethought (fôr' thôt), *n.* thinking beforehand, prudence.

forever (for ev' ēr), *adv.* eternally; incessantly.

foreword (fôr' wûrd), *n.* a word spoken ahead of time; a preface to a book.

***forfeit** (fôr' fit), *n.* a fine or penalty; that which is forfeited or lost through offense, neglect or failure.

forfeit (fôr' fit), *v.t.* to lose through offense, neglect or failure.

forge (fôrj), *n.* a furnace or a place with a furnace where metals are shaped by heating and hammering on an anvil; a smithy.

forge (fôrj), *v.t.* to shape by heating and hammering; to imitate falsely, especially to counterfeit, as a signature.

forgery (fôr' jer i), *n.* the crime of counterfeiting written papers or signatures.

forget (for get'), *v.i. and v.t.* [*p.t.* forgot, *p.p.* forgotten, *pr.p.* forgetting] to be unable to recall to mind; to fail to hold in memory.

forgetful (for get'ful), *adj.* of poor memory.

forgivable (for giv' a bl), *adj.* easily forgiven.

forgive (for giv'), *v.t.* [*p.t.* forgave, *p.p.* forgiven; *pr.p.* forgiving] to pardon, as to *forgive* an enemy; to cease to feel resentment for, as to *forgive* an offense.

    Syn. Pardon, condone. Individuals *forgive* each other personal offenses; we *pardon* offenses against law and morals. To *condone* is to forgive without comment.

forgo (for gō'), *v.t. and v.i.* to do without, give up; refrain, forbear.

fork (fôrk), *n.* an implement with prongs or tines, for use in eating, digging, pitching hay; a branch in a stream or road where it divides into two or more separate streams or roads; a crotch in a tree from which branches grow in different directions.

fork (fôrk), *v.i. and v.t.* to break into separate branches, as a road *forks;* to raise, throw or dig with a fork.

forked (fôrkt), *adj.* branching; fork-shaped.

forlorn (for lorn'), *adj.* deserted, forsaken, alone; wretched.

form (fôrm), *n.* the shape, figure or structure of a thing; a variety or kind, as seaweed is a *form* of algae; a conventional standard of conduct or ritual; a mold in which a substance is shaped.

form (fôrm), *v.i. and v.t.* to take form, arise; to give form to; to develop, as to *form* a friendship; to make up, compose, as oxygen and hydrogen *form* water.

    Syn. Fashion, mold, shape. A thing is *fashioned* when it is *formed* in some particular way. God *formed* man out of the dust; He *fashioned* him after His own image. A thing is *molded* when it is shaped to a pattern. It is *shaped* in a way that makes it visibly different from other things.

formal (fôr' mal), *adj.* according to fixed forms and rules; stiffly conventional.

***formaldehyde** (fôr mal' dē hīd), *n.* a gas obtained by the partial combustion of methanol, used as a disinfectant.

formality (fôr mal' i ti), *n.* strict observance of rule; precise conventionality.

formation (fôr mā' shun), *n.* the process of shaping; that which is shaped or formed.

formative (fôr' ma tiv), *adj.* giving form or shape to, plastic.

former (fôr' mẽr), *adj.* earlier; preceding; foregoing.

formerly (fôr' mẽr li), *adv.* in earlier times, previously.

***formidable** (fôr' mi da bl), *adj.* alarming; forbidding; awe inspiring; unapproachable.

formula (fôr' mū la), *n.* a definite set of words used in a ceremony; any set form, method or established rule; a general mathematical rule expressed in symbols.

formulate (fôr' mū lāt), *v.t.* to reduce to or express in a formula; to state definitely, as to *formulate* an idea.

forsaken (for sāk' n), *adj.* abandoned; deserted; forlorn.

fort (fôrt), *n.* an enclosed, strengthened place.

forte (fôrt), *n.* a special talent.

forth (fôrth), *adv.* onward in time, place or order of occurrence; out, as to send *forth* a messenger.

forthcoming (fôrth kum' ing), *adj.* about to appear.

***forthwith** (fôrth with'), *adv.* immediately.

fortieth (fôr' ti eth), *n.* one of 40 equal parts.

fortieth (fôr' ti eth), *adj.* next in order after the thirty-ninth.

fortification (fôr ti fi kā' shun), *n.* the act of building defensive works; a place strengthened for military defense, a fort.

fortitude (fôr' ti tūd), *n.* courageous endurance.

***fortnight** (fôrt' nīt), *n.* two weeks, 14 days.

FORTRAN (fôr ´ tran), *n.* acronym for *Formula* plus *Translation;* a computer programming language for problems expressed in algebraic terms.

fortress (fôr' tres), *n.* a place permanently fortified for defense.

fortuitous (fôr tū' i tus), *adj.* happening by chance.

***fortunate** (fôr' tū nit), *adj.* happening by good luck; favored by fortune, lucky.

***fortune** (fôr' tūn), *n.* the things, good or bad, that happen to one; chance, luck.

forty (fôr' ti), *n.* one more than 39.

forum (fō' rum), *n.* [*pl.* forums] a public meeting place; tribunal; a public meeting at which topics of interest are discussed by leaders and audience.

forward (fôr' wẽrd), *adj.* of or near the front; eager, also bold.

forward (fôr' wẽrd), *adv.* onward, as to go *forward.*

fossil (fos' il), *n.* any trace of a prehistoric animal or plant preserved in the earth or in rocks; an old fogy.

foster (fôs' tẽr), *v.t.* to nourish, cherish.

    Syn. Cherish, harbor. To *foster* is to keep with care and promote the welfare of; to *cherish* is to hold dear; to *harbor* is to give shelter to, especially in the mind, as he *harbors* resentment.

    Ant. Deaden, kill.

foul (foul), *n.* a blow or a play in a game that is not fair.

foul (foul), *v.t. and v.i.* to make dirty; to make an unfair play; to become entangled, as a rope.

foul (foul), *adj.* offensive; dirty; impure;

tangled, as a rope.

*foulard (foo lärd'), n. a light silk fabric with satin finish.

found (found), v.t. to establish, as to *found* a colony or a university; to cast, or melt and mold, metals.

foundation (foun dā' shun), n. that on which a structure rests, as the masonry supporting the walls of a house; a fund to support an institution; endowment; the premise on which a structure of argument rests.

Syn. Base, basis. *Foundation* means the solid groundwork supporting anything, as the *foundation* of a building, a system of government or an argument. *Base* is a material word; it is the bottom upon which anything stands, as the *base* of a column or a monument; *basis* is used figuratively to mean that on which anything is built up, as a rumor may have no *basis*, experiment is the *basis* of scientific knowledge.

founder (foun' dẽr), n. one who establishes something; one who founds or casts metals.

founder (foun' dẽr), v.i. to stumble and go lame, as a horse; to sink, as a ship.

foundling (found' ling), n. a child found after being deserted by its parents.

foundry (foun' dri), n. [pl. foundries] a mill where metals are cast.

fount (fount), n. a fountain; a spring; source.

fountain (foun' tin), n. an artificial, usually ornamental, jet or spray of water.

four (fôr), n. one more than three; symbol 4.

fourfold (fôr' fōld), adj. consisting of four parts; four times as much as a given quantity.

fourscore (fôr' skôr), adj. eighty, four times 20.

fourteen (fôr tēn´), n. one more than thirteen; symbol 14.

fourth (fôrth), n. one of four equal parts.

fourth (fôrth), adj. next after the third.

four-way (fôr' wā), adj. permitting passage of water or electric current any one of four different ways, as a *four-way* valve.

fowl (foul), n. [pl. fowl] a large edible bird, either game or domestic, as the ordinary chicken; the flesh of the domestic chicken used as food.

fox (foks), n. a wild animal of the dog family.

fox terrier (foks ter' i ẽr), a small, active dog bred for use in hunting foxes.

*foyer (fwä yā'), n. the lobby of a theatre.

*fracas (frä' kas), n. a noisy quarrel, a brawl.

fraction (frak' shun), n. a part broken off, a fragment; a part of a unit; one or more of a specified number of equal parts of a whole, as one-fifth, is a *fraction*.

fractious (frak' shus), adj. unruly, irritable.

fracture (frak' tūr), n. a break, as of a bone.

fracture (frak' tūr), v.t. to break, as a bone.

*fragile (fraj' il), adj. easily broken.

Syn. Frail, brittle. *Fragile* means so delicately made as to be easily broken, marred or destroyed, as a *fragile* piece of glassware, a fragile flower; *frail* means weak; *brittle* means easily snapped.

Ant. Hard, strong, tough.

*fragment (frag' ment), n. a part detached,

as by breaking, from the whole.

fragrance (frā' grans), n. sweetness of smell; a sweet odor.

fragrant (frā' grant), adj. sweet-smelling.

frail (frāl), adj. weak, physically or morally.

frame (frām), n. a structure composed of fitted parts; an open case in which something is hung, as a door *frame*, a picture *frame;* a state, condition or disposition, a mood, as a gay *frame* of mind.

frame (frām), v.t. to shape, fashion; compose, plan, as to *frame* a constitution; to express, as to *frame* a sentence; to provide with or enclose in a frame, as to *frame* pictures; to be a surrounding edge or frame for, as trees *frame* the view.

franc (frangk), n. a French silver coin.

*franchise (fran' chiz), n. a constitutional right, especially the right to vote; a particular right or privilege granted by a government to an individual or a corporation, as a street car *franchise*.

frank (frangk), n. the identifying mark on a telegram, or package that is to go free of postage or charge.

frank (frangk), v.t. to send at public expense, as the mail of a Congressman.

frank (frangk), adj. outspoken; candid; ingenuous.

*frankincense (frangk' in sens), n. a fragrant resin burned as incense.

frankness (frangk' nes), n. candor.

frantic (fran' tik), n. distracted, frenzied.

*fraternal (frá tûr' nal), adj. brotherly, as a *fraternal* greeting; designating a group of men bound together as brothers, as a *fraternal* society.

fraternity (frá tûr' ni ti), n. brotherhood, actual or in a formal association, as a college *fraternity*.

*fraternize (frat' ẽr niz), v.i. to associate together in brotherly or friendly fashion.

*fratricide (frat' ri sid), n. the crime of killing one's brother; one who kills his brother.

fraud (frôd), n. deliberate deceit; deception planned and executed with intent to deprive another of property or rights.

fraudulent (frôd' û lent), adj. characterized by cheating and deceit; obtained by dishonest means.

fraught (frôt), adj. laden, charged, freighted.

fray (frā), n. a fight, a turbulent commotion.

fray (frā), v.i. and v.t. to wear by rubbing; to ravel.

freak (frēk), ... a whim, caprice; an abnormal animal or plant.

freakish (frēk' ish), adj. whimsical, capricious; queer, abnormal.

freckle (frek' l), n. a brownish spot on the skin, caused by exposure to the sun.

freckle (frek' l), v.t. and v.i. to mark with freckles; to become freckled.

free (frē), v.t. to set at liberty; disengage of fastenings or entanglements.

free (frē), adj. [comp. freer, superl. freest] not subject to restraint; at liberty; independent; self-deciding; without obstruction; without charge.

free agent (frē ā´ jent), n. the athlete who is

contractually free to offer his services to any team.

freeborn (frē' bôrn), *adj.* not born in bondage or slavery.

freedman (frēd' man), *n.* [*pl.* freedmen] one who has been emancipated from slavery.

freedom (frē' dum), *n.* the state of being free; independence; liberty; lack of restraint; abuse of familiarity.

    Syn. Liberty. *Freedom* means absence of restraint; *liberty* is freedom from previous restraint; we value our *freedom* of speech in America; prisoners are set at *liberty*.

    Ant. Captivity, bondage, slavery.

free lance (frē lâns), a writer who finds his own market for his product; one who acts on his own responsibility.

freeman (frē' man), *n.* [*pl.* freemen] one who has political and civil liberty; a citizen.

Freemasonry (frē mā sn rǐ), *n.* the principles and fellowship of the secret societies called *Masons;* (*without cap.*) natural friendliness and mutual understanding.

freethinker (frē thĭngk' ẽr), *n.* one who refuses to accept dictated beliefs or formal creeds; an agnostic.

free will (frē wĭl'), the doctrine that man is free to exercise his will for good or evil.

freewill (frē wĭl'), *adj.* voluntary, as a *freewill* offering.

freeze (frēz), *v.i. and v.t.* [*p.t.* froze, *p.p.* frozen, *pr.p.* freezing] to be hardened or solidified into ice, congeal, as water *freezes;* to die with cold; to be stiff and formal; to form into ice or a congealed solid, as we *freeze* ice cream; to kill with cold, as a plant; to repel with formality.

freight (frāt), *n.* goods carried in bulk by ship, train or truck, cargo; the charge for such conveyance; a freight train.

freight (frāt), *v.i. and v.t.* to ship by freight; to load with goods for transportation.

frenzy (fren' zǐ), *n.* [*pl.* frenzies] violent agitation of the mind; delirious emotion; madness.

frequency (frē' kwen sǐ), *n.* [*pl.* frequencies] the repeated occurrence of anything at brief intervals; the number of repeated operations of a mechanical part in a unit of time, as in vibration or revolution; the number of cycles per second produced by the generator of an alternating electric current.

frequent (frē' kwent), *adj.* happening repeatedly at short intervals.

frequent (frē kwent'), *v.t.* to visit often or habitually.

    Syn. Haunt. To *frequent* is to visit or be in often and habitually, as a man may *frequent* a club or restaurant; to *haunt* is to visit continually and persistently, as a beggar *haunts* a rich man's door.

fresco (fres kō), *n.* [*pl.* frescos or frescoes.] a painting in water colors done on fresh plaster or on any plaster.

fresh (fresh), *adj.* new, recent; not previously used; unfaded, as *fresh* roses; in good condition, not stale, as *fresh* fish; clearly remembered, as a *fresh* impression; pure and

cool, as air; not salt; brisk, as a breeze.

freshen (fresh' en), *v.i. and v.t.* to become brighter or fresher in appearance; to become stronger, as the wind freshens; to refresh, revive.

freshet (fresh' et), *n.* any sudden flood, especially one caused by melting snow.

freshman (fresh' man), *n.* [*pl.* freshmen] a first-year student in high school or college.

fret (fret), *v.i. and v.t.* to be fussily irritated; to injure by rubbing, corrode; to tease, irritate.

fretwork (fret' wûrk), *n.* elaborate ornamental openwork.

friable (frī' a bl), *adj.* easily crumbled or reduced to a powder.

friar (frī' ẽr), *n.* a man belonging to a religious order, especially a mendicant order.

fricassee (frĭk a sē'), *n.* meat dish, as chicken, cut in small pieces, stewed in gravy.

friction (frĭk' shun), *n.* the act of rubbing; resistance of one surface to the motion of another surface rubbing over it; irritation caused by difference in views.

friend (frend), *n.* a person to whom one is attached by affection; an intimate acquaintance; one well inclined toward a cause, as a *friend* of democracy.

friendly (frend' lǐ), *adj.* like a friend; affable and amicable, as a *friendly* manner.

friendship (frend' ship), *n.* intimacy and mutual attachment; a friendly relationship, especially one of long standing.

frieze (frēz), *n.* the middle part of an entablature, between architrave and cornice, usually ornamented; coarse woolen cloth.

frigate (frig' it), *n.* a three-masted, square-rigged sailing vessel equipped for war.

fright (frit), *n.* a state of sudden fear; alarm; anything that causes sudden fear; an ugly or displeasing appearance.

frighten (frit' n), *v.t.* to terrify, alarm.

    Syn. Intimidate, scare. The danger that is sudden and unexpected *frightens;* to *intimidate* is to hinder by a show of violence; *scare* is a colloquial word for *frighten.*

frightful (frit' fool), *adj.* terrible, alarming, shocking.

frigid (frij' id), *adj.* excessively cold; lacking friendliness, stiffly formal.

frill (fril), *n.* a plaited or crimped edging to a garment; *frills,* showy but useless mannerisms or adornments.

frilling (fril' ing), *n.* gathered trimming or edging for garments.

fringe (frinj), *n.* an ornamental border of loose threads or cords; any border or edge resembling fringe, as a *fringe* of woods.

frippery (frip' ẽr ǐ), *n.* [*pl.* fripperies] cheap, tawdry ornament.

frisk (frisk), *v.i.* to gambol or dance in frolic.

frisky (frisk' ǐ), *adj.* lively, frolicsome.

frith (frith), *n.* a bay, a firth.

fritter (frit' ẽr), *n.* a small cake made of batter fried in deep fat. *v.t.* to waste, scatter.

frivolity (fri vol' ǐ tǐ), *n.* [*pl.* frivolities] levity; a trifling act or thought.

frivolous (friv' ō lus), *adj.* trifling, trivial; not serious, given to undue levity.

frizz (friz), *n.* something frizzed, as hair.

frizz (friz), *v.i. and v.t.* to curl or crisp, as hair; to form into tiny burs, as the nap of cloth.

frizzle (friz' l), *v.i. and v.t.* to cook with a sputtering sound; to curl tightly, as hair.

fro (frō), *adv.* away from, back, as *to and fro*.

frock (frok), *n.* the loose garment worn by monks; a dress or gown; a frock coat.

frog (frog), *n.* a small amphibious animal, web-footed and tailless; the tender pad in the middle of a horse's hoof; an oblong covered button fastening into a loop of cord; plate that guides wheels of railroad cars where tracks cross, as in a switch.

frolic (frol' ik), *n.* merrymaking; a prank.

frolic (frol' ik), *v.i.* [*p.t.* and *p.p.* frolicked, *pr.p.* frolicking] to play pranks; to make merry.

from (from), *prep.* forth, out of as a starting point, as to go *from* Chicago to Boston, come *from* the north, a mile *from* here; out of as an origin or source, as to come *from* a royal family, translated *from* the Latin; on account of, with, as dying *from* thirst.

*****frond** (frond), *n.* the leaf of a fern, palm or seaweed; a leaflike growth not separated into stem and leaf.

front (frunt), *n.* the fore part of anything, as of a building, of the field of operation in war, or of a shirt.

front (frunt), *v.i. and v.t.* to face; to face toward; to confront.

front (frunt), *adj.* pertaining to or situated at the fore part of anything, as a *front* door.

frontage (frunt' ij), *n.* extent of front, as of a plot of land along a street, road or river.

*****frontal** (frun' tal), *n.* a decorative covering for the front of an altar; an ornament on the forehead.

*****frontal** (frun' tal), *adj.* pertaining to the front especially to the forehead.

*****frontier** (frun tēr'), *n.* the border of a country toward another country or toward an unsettled region.

*****frontispiece** (frun' tis pēs), *n.* an illustration facing the title page of a book.

frost (frôst), *n.* frozen dew; minute frozen particles of moisture on a surface; a temperature that causes freezing.

frost (frôst), *v.t.* to form frost on; to give the appearance of frost; to injure or kill, as a plant, by frost.

frosted (frôst' ed), *adj.* covered with frost or with something that looks like frost.

frosting (frôst' ing), *n.* a preparation, as of fine sugar and beaten white of egg, spread over a cake; a certain finish of metal or glass without luster.

*****froth** (frôth), *n.* the foamy mass of bubbles formed on the surface of a liquid by agitation or fermentation.

frothy (frôth' i), *adj.* [*comp.* frothier, *superl.* frothiest] having froth, foamy; light, frivolous, unsubstantial.

frown (froun), *n.* a contraction of brow or wrinkling of forehead, as in doubt, deep thought or anger, a scowl. *v.i.* to contract brows sternly, scowl; to regard with disapproval.

frowzy (frouz' i), *adj.* untidy.

frozen (frō' zn), *adj.* excessively cold; transformed into ice, congealed.

*****frugal** (frōō' gal), *adj.* thrifty, economical.

frugality (frōō gal' i ti), *n.* thrift, economy.

Syn. Economy, miserliness, parsimony. *Frugality* is the opposite of wastefulness; *economy* is a wise and careful management of one's resources; *parsimony* is excessive economy; *miserliness* is the denial of ordinary comforts for the sake of hoarding.

fruit (frōōt), *n.* any product of a plant useful to man, as cotton or vegetables; a seed or seeds and the surrounding envelope, as a walnut or a bean pod, especially the edible pulp around a seed or seeds, as of an apple; any result, as the *fruits* of toil.

fruitful (frōōt' fool), *adj.* prolific; producing results.

fruition (frōō ish' un), *n.* the bearing of fruit; realization, as of a plan or enterprise.

frustrate (frus' trāt), *v.t.* to baffle; to defeat in a purpose; to prevent from accomplishing.

frustum (frus' tum), *n.* [*pl.* frustums or frusta] the part of a cone or pyramid left when the top is truncated or cut off.

fry (frī), *v.t.* [*p.t.* and *p.p.* fried, *pr.p.* frying] to cook in hot fat in a pan.

fuchsia (fū' sha), *n.* a garden plant of the evening-primrose family.

fuel (fū' el), *n.* combustible material to feed a fire, as coal, wood or oil; anything that starts or sustains the fires of passion.

fugitive (fū' ji tiv), *n.* one who flees from danger or the law. *adj.* fleeing, as from danger; not fixed, temporary, evanescent.

fugue (fūg), *n.* a musical form combining several themes.

*****fulcrum** (ful' krum), *n.* [*pl.* fulcrums or fulcra] the point on which a lever turns.

fulfill (fool fil'), *v.t.* to carry to completion, as a plan; to keep, as a promise; to realize, as a purpose.

fulfillment (fool fil' ment), *n.* accomplishment; completion.

full (fool), *n.* the highest measure, as the *full* of the moon, I enjoyed it to the *full*.

full (fool), *v.t.* to thicken, as cloth, by damping, heating and pressing; to scour and thicken in a mill.

full (fool), *adj.* filled; having no empty space; complete, as a *full* load, a *full* moon; deep and strong, as a *full* tone.

full (fool), *adv.* entirely; completely, as *full*-fledged; very, as *full* often.

fuller (fool' ēr), *n.* one who fulls cloth in a mill.

fulminate (ful' mi nāt), *n.* a detonating salt of fulminic acid.

fulminate (ful' mi nāt), *v.i. and v.t.* to detonate; to thunder; to issue forth, as decrees or orders, with threats.

*****fulsome** (fool' sum), *adj.* extravagant; elaborate; insincere; as, *fulsome* compliments.

fumble (fum' bl), *v.i. and v.t.* to grope about awkwardly; to handle awkwardly.

*****fume** (fūm), *n.* vapor or smoke, as the *fumes* of incense; a stifling smoke or gaseous substance, as the *fumes* of acids. *v.i.* to fuss and fret; to give forth smoke or vapor.

fumigate (fū′ mi gāt), *v.t.* to disinfect by the action of smoke or vapor.

fun (fun), *n.* sport, mirth, amusement, play.

function (fungk′ shun), *n.* normal and characteristic action, as the *function* of the liver; special purpose or duty, as the *functions* of a judge. *v.i.* to fulfill a normal activity; to perform duty of an office.

functionary (fungk′ shun er i), *n. pl.* functionaries one charged with certain official duties.

fund (fund), *n.* money set apart for some special purpose; an accumulation or store, a supply; *funds*, money available for use.

fundamental (fun da men′ tal), *adj.* pertaining to a foundation or basis; essential; elementary.

fundamentalism (fun da men′ tal izm), *n.* a religious movement emphasizing certain historical beliefs as fundamental and opposing modernism.

*****funeral** (fū′ něr al), *n.* the ceremony of burying the dead, with a procession of mourners.

funereal (fū něr′ e al), *adj.* pertaining to or suitable for a funeral; sad; mournful.

fungous (fung′ gus), *adj.* like a fungus.

*****fungus** (fung′ gus), *n.* [*pl.* funguses or fungi] a plant growth that reproduces by spores, as molds, mildews, rusts, mushrooms.

funnel (fun′ el), *n.* a wide-mouthed conical vessel terminating in a spout for pouring liquids; the chimney of a steamship.

funny (fun′ i), *adj.* [*comp.* funnier, *superl.* funniest] laughable, amusing, comical.

fur (fûr), *n.* the soft thick hair of certain animals; a furry hide used for clothing.

furbelow (fûr′ bē lō), *n.* a flounce on a woman's dress; any fancy or fussy adornment.

furbish (fûr′ bish), *v.t.* to brighten by rubbing; to polish, burnish; to renovate.

furious (fū′ ri us), *adj.* raging with anger, frantic; tempestuous, rushing, violent.

furl (fûrl), *v.t.* to roll up and make fast, as a flag or sail.

*****furlong** (fûr′ lông), *n.* a measure of length equal to one-eighth of a mile.

*****furlough** (fûr′ lō), *n.* leave of absence.

furnace (fûr′ nis), *n.* an enclosed structure in which fuel is burned to make heat.

furnish (fûr′ nish), *v.t.* to supply with needed things; to fit out; to equip.

furnishings (fûr′ nish ingz), *n.* furniture, fixtures.

*****furniture** (fûr′ ni tūr), *n.* the necessary equipment for a house.

*****furor** (fū′ rôr), *n.* a great outburst of excitement; a rage, craze or fad.

furrier (fûr′ i ēr), *n.* one who sells furs.

furrow (fûr′ ō), *n.* the trench made in the

ground by a plow; a groove; wrinkle.

furrow (fûr′ ō), *v.t. and v.i.* to plow; to make grooves in.

furry (fûr′ i), *adj.* covered with fur; like fur.

further (fûr′ thēr), *v.t.* to promote, as plans or enterprises.

further (fûr′ thēr), *adj.* [*no positive; superl.* furthest] more remote; additional, as *further* places, *further* facts.

further (fûr′ thēr), *adv.* at or to a greater distance or degree, as to go *further.*

furtherance (fûr thēr ans), *n.* advancement.

furthermore (fûr′ thēr môr), *adv.* moreover, besides.

furthermost (fûr′ thēr mōst), *adj.* most remote.

furtive (fûr′ tiv), *adj.* secret, sly, stealthy.

fury (fū′ ri), *n.* [*pl.* furies] violent rage; great anger.

furze (fûrz), *n.* a hardy, spiny, evergreen shrub of Europe with yellow flowers, gorse.

*****fuse** (fūz), *n.* a tube or cord filled or saturated with combustible substances and used for setting off explosives; a fusible plug in an electric system that melts when the current exceeds the limit of safety.

fuse (fūz), *v.t. and v.i.* to liquefy by means of heat, melt; to melt and run together or blend, as metals.

fuselage (fū′ ze lij), *n.* the body of an airplane, with a seat for the pilot and containing the engine and controls.

fusel oil (fū′ zel oil), an oily, colorless, poisonous liquid found in raw or insufficiently distilled liquors, as corn whiskey; amyl alcohol.

fusible (fū′ zi bl), *adj.* capable of being fused or melted.

*****fusillade** (fū zi lād′), *n.* a simultaneous discharge of firearms.

*****fusion** (fū′ zhun), *n.* the act or process of melting metals by heat; union by melting; a uniting of political parties or factions for a campaign.

fuss (fus), *n.* unnecessary activity, confusion.

fuss (fus), *v.i.* to worry, be bothered about trifles.

fussy (fus′ i), *adj.* given to fussing, too particular; requiring much care, as a *fussy* job.

fustian (fus′ chan), *n.* a kind of coarse twilled cotton cloth; corduroy; velveteen.

fustian (fus′ chan), *adj.* made of fustian; pompous in manner but lacking ability; cheap.

*****futile** (fū′ til), *adj.* ineffectual, useless; trifling.

futility (fū til′ i ti), *n.* uselessness.

*****future** (fū′ tūr), *n.* time yet to come.

future (fū′ tūr), *adj.* still to happen.

fuzz (fuz), *n.* fine light particles of down, fluff.

G

*gabardine (gab ẽr dẽn'), a woolen or cotton fabric resembling serge but having a ribbed appearance on only one side.

gabble (gab' l), n. meaningless chatter; the noise made by geese.

gabble (gab' l), v.i. to talk fast; to jabber; to utter inarticulate sounds fast, as a goose.

gable (gā' bl), n. the triangular part of a wall of a building between the edges of a sloping roof; the end wall of a building, as distinguished from the front or side.

*gad (gad), n. a pointed metal bar used in breaking up or loosening ore; a goad for oxen.

gad (gad), v.i. to go about aimlessly.

gadfly (gad' fli), n. [pl. gadflies] a fly that bites and torments cattle; a horsefly.

gaff (gaf), n. a pole with a sharp hook on one end for landing big fish; a steel spur on the leg of a gamecock; a spar supporting the upper edge of a fore-and-aft sail.

gaff (gaf), v.t. to land or strike with a gaff, as a fish.

gag (gag), n. something thrust into the mouth to prevent speech or sound; any rule or subterfuge that prevents debate; a tool for straightening rails.

gag (gag), v.t. and v.i. [p.t. and p.p gagged, pr.p. gagging] to restrain from speech by force or authority, as the dictator gags the press; to retch, strain, as in violent nausea.

gage (gāj), n. something given as security for the fulfillment of an obligation or pledge; a cap or glove thrown upon the ground as a challenge.

gage, see gauge.

gaiety (gā' e ti), n. [pl. gaieties] the state or quality of being merry, liveliness, vivacity, jollity.

gaily (gā' li), adv. merrily, blithely, gleefully; with fine display, as the city was gaily decked with flags.

gain (gān), n. advantage, profit, advancement, increase.

gain (gān), v.i. and v.t. to increase, as to gain in health; to obtain; to advance, as he gained on his pursuer; to win, as he gained his point.

*gainsay (gān sā'), v.t. [p.t. and p.p. gainsaid, pr.p. gainsaying] to contradict, dispute, oppose, deny.

gait (gāt), n. the manner of walking or running, as an easy gait.

gaiter (gā' tẽr), n. a legging; spat.

*gala (gā' la), adj. festive.

*galaxy (gal' ak si), n. an assemblage of brilliant persons; Galaxy, the Milky Way.

gale (gāl), n. a strong wind, slightly less violent than a hurricane; an outburst, as a gale of laughter.

*gall (gôl), n. the bile; the gall bladder; anything bitter to experience; rancor.

gall (gôl), n. a sore on the skin, caused by chafing, especially on a horse's back.

gall (gôl), n. a protective growth on the leaves or bark of trees and plants, especially oak trees, surrounding insect larvae developing from eggs deposited in a wound made by the parent insect.

gall (gôl), v.i. and v.t. to become sore as the result of chafing; to make sore by chafing; to irritate, harass.

*gallant (gal ant'), n. a beau; a man of fashion who makes a point of paying small attentions to women.

*gallant (gal' ant), adj. brave; dashing, chivalrous; stately, as a gallant ship.

gallantry (gal' an tri), n. bravery; elaborate politeness to women.

*galleon (gal' ē un), n. a broad-beamed, high-sterned ship of the 15th and later centuries having three or four decks.

*gallery (gal' ẽr i), n. [pl. galleries] a corridor; a section of seats built out from the wall of a theater or church; a room used for the showing of works of art.

galley (gal' i), n. a single-decked vessel of medieval times, propelled by both sails and oars; a large rowboat; the kitchen quarters of a ship; a long tray in which type is placed when set; a proof of a galley of type on a long strip of paper called galley proof.

galling (gôl' ing), adj. chafing, irritating.

gallon (gal' un), n. a liquid measure equal to four quarts.

gallop (gal' up), n. the springing gait of a horse at full speed; the act of riding at this gait. v.i. and v.t. to run or ride at full speed; to put to this pace, as to gallop a horse.

*gallows (gal' ōz), n. a wooden structure used for hanging condemned criminals.

gallstone (gôl' stōn), n. a hard lump of matter formed in the bladder or the bile duct.

galore (ga lōr'), adv. in great abundance.

galosh (ga losh'), n. a rubber overshoe, especially one with a high top.

galvanic (gal van' ik), adj. relating to a direct electrical current, especially one from a battery; stimulating, arousing.

*galvanism (gal' va nism), n. the branch of electrical science that treats of currents arising from the chemical action of certain bodies placed in contact or of acid on metal.

galvanize (gal' va niz), v.t. to cause to undergo the action of electric currents; to plate or coat with metal through application of an electric current; to stimulate or arouse, as if by an electric current.

gambier (gam' bẽr), n. a vegetable extract used medicinally and in tanning and dyeing.

gambit (gam' bit), n. a chess opening in which the first player gives his opponent a piece or pawn to gain an advantage in position.

gamble (gam' bl), n. any act accompanied by

risk of loss. *v.i. and v.t.* to play a game for money; to risk money on uncertain gain.

gambler (gam' blẽr), *n.* one who plays games of chance, especially as a profession.

*gamboge (gam bōj'), *n.* a reddish-yellow color; the orange-red tree gum from which this color is made.

gambol (gam' bul), *n.* a frolic; act of dancing or frisking about.

gambol (gam' bul), *v.i.* [*p.t. and p.p.* gamboled, *pr.p.* gamboling] to skip about sportively, frolic.

gambrel (gam' brel), *n.* the hock of a horse; a gambrel roof.

game (gām), *n.* a contest of strength, skill or chance, for sport or for a stake; a scheme or plan; animals hunted for sport.

game (gām), *adj.* plucky.

gamin (gam' in), *n.* a child of the streets; a street Arab.

*gamut (gam' ut), *n.* the entire range or extent, as of a musical scale.

gander (gan' dẽr), *n.* a male goose; a simpleton.

gang (gang), *n.* a number of persons banded together in a common pursuit, as of crime; a group of workers under one boss; a set of tools or implements arranged to work together, as the shares of a *gang* plow.

*ganglion (gang' gli un), *n.* [*pl.* ganglia or ganglions] a collection of nerve cells forming a nerve center.

gangplank (gang' plangk), *n.* a movable bridge of cleated planks by which to board or leave a ship at its dock.

*gangrene (gang' grēn), *n.* mortification of tissue in a living body.

gangster (gang' stẽr), *n.* a member of an organization of criminals.

gangway (gang' wā), *n.* space in which to pass.

gantlet (gônt' let), *n.* formerly a military punishment in which the partially naked offender ran between two lines of soldiers who struck at him with clubs; a series of difficult tests.

*gaol (jāl), *n.* a jail.

gap (gap), *n.* an opening; cleft; a pass, as a *gap* in the mountains.

*gape (gāp), *n.* the act of opening the mouth and staring in amazement or surprise; a yawn. *v.i.* [*p.t. and p.p.* gaped, *pr.p.* gaping] to open the mouth wide, as in astonishment; to yawn; to stare stupidly.

Syn. Stare, gaze. *Gape* connotes stupid wonder; to *stare* implies impertinence or absent-mindedness; to *gaze* is to look with astonishment, pleasure or admiration.

*garage (ga räzh'), *n.* building where automobile is kept; auto repair shop.

garb (gärb), *n.* dress, particularly of a special kind, as nurses' *garb*.

garbage (gär' bij), *n.* kitchen or market refuse.

garble (gär' bl), *v.t.* to select only such parts as will serve a purpose; to mutilate, misrepresent, as to *garble* a story.

garden (gär' dn), *n.* ground given up to cultivation of flowers, fruits, vegetables.

gardenia (gär dēn' ia), *n.* a plant cultivated for its fragrant, showy flowers.

gargle (gär' gl), *n.* an antiseptic liquid used for washing the throat or mouth.

gargle (gär' gl), *v.i. and v.t.* to use a gargle; to take a liquid in the mouth and agitate it by expelling air slowly from the lungs.

gargoyle (gär' goil), *n.* a grotesquely carved stone waterspout usually projecting from the upper part of a building.

garish (gâr' ish), *adj.* gaudy, dazzling, flashy.

garland (gär' land), *n.* a chaplet or wreath of flowers.

garlic (gär' lik), *n.* a plant with onionlike root, having pungent taste and odor, used in cooking.

garment (gär' ment), *n.* any article of clothing.

garner (gär' nẽr), *n.* a storehouse for grain.

garner (gär' nẽr), *v.t.* to gather up and store.

garnet (gär' net), *n.* a precious and semiprecious mineral used as a gem; the deep red color of the precious stone.

garnish (gär' nish), *n.* an ornament, decoration; something laid around a steak or fish on a platter, as a *garnish* of parsley.

garnish (gär' nish), *v.t.* to decorate, adorn.

garnishee (gär nish ē'), *n.* one who holds the property of another pending its final disposal by a court with regard to claims of a third person. *v.t.* to attach property pending court decision as to its disposal.

*garniture (gär' ni tūr), *n.* embellishment.

garret (gar' et), *n.* the top floor of a house, generally unfinished, an attic.

garrison (gâr' i sun), *n.* a body of troops stationed in a fort; a fortified place where such troops are stationed.

garrison (gâr' i sun), *v.t.* to furnish troops for a fortification.

garrulity (ga rōō' li ti), *n.* incessant talk, loquacity.

garrulous (gar' ū lus), *adj.* talkative, loquacious.

garter (gär' tẽr), *n.* an elastic band or strap to hold up a stocking.

garter snake (gär' tẽr snǎk), a small, harmless American snake.

gas (gas), *n.* [*pl.* gases] an airlike liquid without definite shape or volume, tending to expand indefinitely when unconfined; any combustible gaseous vapors used for light and heat; any vapor used to induce anesthesia; a vaporous substance used to make breathing painful or to cause death, as in warfare; gasoline.

gas (gas), *v.t.* [*p.t. and p.p.* gassed, *pr.p.* gassing] to attack with a deadly vapor.

gas bomb (gas bom), a shell used in trench fighting, charged with poison gas.

gas engine (gas en' jin), an engine run by the burning of a mixture of gas and air.

*gaseous (gas' ē us), *adj.* having the nature of gas.

gash (gash), *n.* a deep cut with gaping edges.

gash (gash), *v.t.* to make a deep cut in.

gasify (gas' i fī), *v.i. and v.t.* [*p.t. and p.p.* gasified, *pr.p.* gasifying] to become gas; to convert a substance into gas.

gas mask (gas măsk), a covering for the face used as protection against poison gas.

*gasoline (gas' ō lēn), *n.* a liquid distilled from petroleum, used as a fuel, for cleaning and in internal combustion engines.

*gasometer (gas om' ē tēr), *n.* a device for holding and measuring gas.

gasp (găsp), *n.* a convulsed, painful effort to catch the breath.

gasp (găsp), *v.i.* to breathe with pain and difficulty, with the mouth open.

gastric (gas' trik), *adj.* pertaining to the stomach.

gastric juice (gas' trik jōōs), a fluid secreted in the stomach that acts as chief agent in digestion.

*gastritis (gas trī' tis), *n.* inflammation of the stomach.

gastronomic (gas trō nom' ik), *adj.* pertaining to the art of good eating.

gastronomy (gas tron' ō mi), *n.* the art of good eating, epicurism.

gate (gāt) *n.* a frame of wood or metal on hinges to open and close a passageway, as through a fence.

gather (gath' ēr), *v.i. and v.t.* to congregate, as a crowd *gathered;* to generate pus, as a boil; to increase, as storm clouds *gathered;* to bring together, collect, as grain; to draw together in folds, as cloth; to summon, as courage; to accumulate, as to *gather* wealth; to infer, as to *gather* an idea.

Syn. Collect. To *gather* is to bring things together in one place; to *collect* implies selection resulting in a more orderly whole. Pebbles are *gathered* in a heap; people *collect* stamps.

Ant. Disperse, scatter.

gathering (gath' ēr ing), *n.* the act of assembling; an assemblage; an abscess.

gaudy (gôd' i), *adj.* [*comp.* gaudier, *superl.* gaudiest] showy; gay or fine in a vulgar way.

gauge or **gage** (gāj), *n.* a standard of measurement; the distance between the rails of a railroad; a measuring instrument.

gauge or **gage** (gāj), *v.t.* to measure; to calculate the contents of, as a barrel; to bring into conformity with a standard.

*gaunt (gônt), *adj.* pinched and lean; forbidding, desolate, as a *gaunt* landscape.

*gauntlet (gônt' let), *n.* a mailed glove; a glove with a long wristpiece.

*gauze (gôz), *n.* a very thin, light, transparent fabric of silk, cotton or linen; a fabric resembling such material, as wire.

gauzy (gôz' i), *adj.* thin and light, semitransparent, like gauze.

gawk (gôk), *n.* an awkward dull person.

gawky (gôk' i), *adj.* awkward, clumsy.

gay (gā), *adj.* lively and merry.

gaze (gāz), *n.* a steady, intent look.

gazelle (ga zel'), *n.* a small, graceful and swift antelope with large, lustrous eyes.

gazette (ga zet'), *n.* a newspaper; an official journal giving news of honors, bankruptcies and public notices.

gazette (ga zet'), *v.t.* to publish in an official journal.

*gazetteer (gaz e tēr'), *n.* a dictionary of geographical names; one who writes or is appointed to publish news.

gear (gēr), *n.* apparatus, equipment, clothing, tackle, tools; a part of machinery that performs a special function, as the steering gear of an automobile; the engagement of revolving parts with each other, as in *gear;* a toothed wheel or cogwheel. *v.t.* to put in gear, equip with gears.

gearing (gēr' ing), *n.* the parts of a machine that transmit motion from one section to another.

gee (jē), *interj.* a call directing a team of oxen to turn to the off side or to the right, away from the driver: opposite of *haw.*

*gelatin or gelatine (jel' a tin), *n.* a translucent substance derived from animal tissues such as cartilage and hoofs.

gem (jem), *n.* a precious or semiprecious stone; any perfect specimen of its kind, as this essay is a *gem;* a light muffin.

gender (jen' dēr), *n.* one of three classifications into which English nouns and pronouns naturally fall (masculine, feminine and neuter), as the noun *boy* is in the masculine *gender, box* is neuter *gender, she* is feminine *gender, it* is neuter *gender.*

*genealogy (jen ē al' ō ji), *n.* [*p*'. genealogies] a chronological record tracing the descent of a person or family from an ancestor; lineage, pedigree.

general (jen' ēr al), *n.* a general principle as distinguished from a particular; the highest rank of a commissioned officer in the army.

general (jen' ēr al), *adj.* pertaining to a whole; pertaining to all, as a *general* order; not specific, vague, as a *general* statement; pertaining to the typical, as it is the *general* thing to have two eyes; prevailing, as it is the *general* custom to dine at seven; not specialized, as a *general* store; signifying superiority in rank, as attorney *general.*

Syn. Universal. What is *general* applies to all or nearly all; what is *universal* applies to all, without exception.

Ant. Local, limited.

*generally (jen' ēr al i), *adv.* commonly, in most instances, as a rule, in a broad sense.

generalship (jen' ēr al ship), *n.* the office or term of office of a general; skill in command, tactical and strategical ability.

generate (jen' ēr āt), *v.t.* to beget, as children; to produce, as heat, power, ideas.

generation (jen ēr ā' shun), *n.* the act or process of producing; all the individuals of any one genealogical period; one stage in a line of descent, as father and son are of different *generations;* the period of time between parent and child, about 33 years.

generator (jen' ēr ā tēr), *n.* anyone or anything that causes or originates; a machine producing steam, gas or electric power.

*generic (je ner' ik), *adj.* pertaining to a genus; general: opposite of *specific.*

generosity (jen ēr os' i ti), *n.* [*pl.* generosities] the quality of being liberal; benevolence.

*generous (jen' ēr us), *adj.* liberal in action or ideas; openhanded, magnanimous.

*genesis (jen' ē sis), *n.* the beginning, origin.

genial (jēn' yal), *adj.* kindly, sympathetic, cordial; pleasingly warm and friendly.

genius (jēn' yus), *n.* extraordinary aptitude for creative artistic work; a person of marked ability in any field; as a person who exerts great influence over another, as an evil *genius*.

genteel (jen tēl'), *adj.* polite, well bred: now used only humorously or sarcastically.

gentian (jen' shan), *n.* a plant valued for its deep blue flowers; the roots of the yellow gentian, used as a tonic.

gentility (jen til' i ti), *n.* [*pl.* gentilities] noble birth; good breeding; courtesy, dignity, good manners.

gentle (jen' tl), *adj.* wellborn; mild, kindly, docile, soft, soothing, as a *gentle* voice; moderate, as a *gentle* breeze.

Syn. Tame. Any unbroken horse might be *gentle* by nature, but not *tame;* a horse that is broken in will be *tame,* but may not be *gentle. Gentle* connotes natural disposition; *tame,* having been brought under subjection.

Ant. Tempestuous, severe, violent.

*gentleman (jen' tl man), *n.* [*pl.* gentlemen] a well-bred and honorable man.

gentlewoman (jen' tl woom an), *n.* [*pl.* gentlewomen] a woman of good birth and breeding.

gentry (jen' tri), *n.* people of good birth and education; those next in standing to the nobility in England, as the landed *gentry.*

*genuflection (jen ū flek' shun), *n.* a bending of the knee in worship or homage.

*genuine (jen' ū in), *adj.* real, unadulterated.

genus (jē' nus), *n.* [*pl.* genera] a classification between family and species and including a number of species, as the *genus Felis* includes the lion, tiger and cat; class, kind.

geography (jē og' ra fi), *n.* [*pl.* geographies] the science that deals with the surface of the earth, its natural divisions, mountain ranges, rivers, climatic conditions, plant and animal life, agriculture and commerce; the natural features of a specific area.

geology (jē ol' ō gi), *n.* the science that deals with the structure of the earth and its physical changes, especially as recorded in the rocks.

geometry (jē om' ē tri), *n.* the branch of mathematics treating of the measurement and relationships of lines, angles, planes and solids.

*georgic (jôr' jik), *n.* a poem on agriculture.

geranium (jē rā' ni um), *n.* a plant cultivated for its brilliant red flowers.

germ (jûrm), *n.* the rudimentary form of an organism; a bud, seed; that from which anything springs, as the *germ* of an idea.

germane (jûr mān'), *adj.* related or relevant, appropriate.

germicide (jûr' mi sīd), *n.* any substance used to destroy disease germs.

germinal (jûr' mi nal), *adj.* pertaining to a germ or seed bud; incipient, leading to, as the *germinal* idea.

germinate (jûr' mi nāt), *v.i. and v.t.* to de-velop, sprout, bud; to cause to develop or sprout.

germination (jûr mi nā' shun), *n.* the beginning of development in a seed, bud or germ.

gerund (jer' und), *n.* the present participial form of a verb used as a noun, as *being* is a *gerund* in the sentence, your being here is a joy to me.

gesticulate (jes tik' ū lāt), *v.i.* to make motions to attract attention or gestures to emphasize a meaning.

*gesture (jes' tūr), *n.* a movement, as of the limbs, body or face to express emotion or to emphasize an assertion; something said or done for effect, as his offer of help was just a *gesture.*

get (get), *v.i. and v.t.* [*p.t.* got, *p.p.* got or gotten, *pr.p.* getting] to arrive at or bring oneself into a certain state or condition, as to *get* free; to become, as to *get* tired; to acquire, as property; to procure, obtain, as to *get* help; to learn, as a lesson; to understand, perceive, as an idea; to prepare, as a meal; to contract, as a cold.

*gewgaw (gū' gô), *n.* a showy trifle.

G-Forces (gē' fôr' sēs), *n.* the forces astronauts experience when the spacecraft changes speed, either to accelerate or slow down.

*ghastly (gȧst' li), *adj.* horrible; gruesome; haggard, pale, ghostlike in appearance.

*gherkin (gûr' kin), *n.* a small cucumber used for pickling.

ghetto (get' ō), *n.* a financially depressed city area populated usually by minority groups.

ghost (gōst), *n.* the spirit of a dead person; apparition; specter or phantom; a faint approximation, as the *ghost* of an idea.

ghostly (gōst' li), *adj.* pertaining to or like a ghost; supernatural.

ghost writer (gōst rit' ēr), one who writes a literary work for which another receives credit.

*ghoul (gōōl), *n.* an evil spirit that robbed the dead and fed on corpses; a grave robber; one whose pursuits or interests are repulsive.

giant (jī' ant), *n.* an imaginary person of great size and power; a person, plant or animal of unusual size; a person of extraordinary ability, as an intellectual *giant.*

giant (jī' ant), *adj.* like a giant; huge; of great height or bulk, as a *giant* rock.

*gibber (jib' ēr), *v.i.* to speak incoherently.

*gibberish (jib' ēr ish), *n.* fast, incoherent talk; senseless chatter.

*gibbet (jib' et), *n.* a gallows. *v.t.* to hang on a gibbet; to expose to public ridicule.

*gibe (jīb), *n.* a taunt; sneering or sarcastic comment; a quick sharp note of derision.

gibe (jīb), *v.i. and v.t.* to scoff, taunt.

giblet (jib' let), *n.* any of the edible internal parts of poultry, as heart or gizzard.

giddy (gid' i), *adj.* [*comp.* giddier, *superl.* giddiest] dizzy; having a whirling sensation; light-headed; producing dizziness, as a *giddy* height.

gift (gift), *n.* something given; a present; a natural talent, as a *gift* for writing.

Syn. Donation, aptness, bent. A *gift* implies ability expressed without difficulty; *aptness* implies natural or potential ability; *bent* expresses a tendency of mind or disposition; *donation* suggests a contribution, especially to a public institution.

gigantic (jī gan' tĭk), *adj.* huge, immense.

giggle (gĭg' l), *n.* a silly, nervous laugh.

giggle (gĭg' l), *v.i.* to laugh in a foolish, nervous manner; to titter.

*****gigolo** (jĭg' ō lō), *n.* a man who serves as escort or dancing partner to women for pay.

gild (gĭld), *v.t.* to cover with a thin coating of gold; to color with gold.

gilding (gĭld' ĭng), *n.* an overlay of gold or something that looks like gold.

gill (gĭl), *n.* the breathing organ of fish and animals that live in water.

*****gill** (jĭl), *n.* one-fourth of a pint.

gilt (gĭlt), *n.* gilding; a covering of gold or of something resembling gold.

gilt (gĭlt), *adj.* gilded.

*****gimbals** (jĭm' balz), *n.* a device for suspending something, as a ship's compass, so that it will remain level.

gimcrack (jĭm' krak), *n.* a thing that is showy but of no use; gewgaw.

gimlet (gĭm' let), *n.* a small tool for boring holes.

gimp (gĭmp), *n.* a narrow twisted trimming used on furniture or clothing.

gin (jĭn), *n.* a distilled liquor flavored with juniper berries. *n.* machine for separating seeds from cotton fiber; a trap. *vt.* [*p.t.* and *p.p.* ginned, *pr.p.* ginning] to clear of seeds by a gin, as cotton.

ginger (jĭn' jẽr), *n.* a tropical herb; a plant cultivated for its spicy rootstalk; the ground root used as a spice or medicine.

gingerbread (jĭn' jẽr bred), *n.* a dark-colored cake sweetened with molasses and flavored with ginger; a cheap, vulgar ornamentation.

gingerly (jĭn' jẽr lĭ), *adv.* in a cautious, fearful manner.

gingham (gĭng' am), *n.* a cotton cloth usually having stripes or checks.

ginseng (jĭn' seng), *n.* an Oriental plant with scarlet berries.

*****giraffe** (jĭ răf'), *n.* an African ruminant animal, the tallest of the quadrupeds, with an extraordinarily long neck; the camelopard.

*****gird** (gûrd), *v.t.* [*p.t.* and *p.p.* girded, girt, *pr.p.* girding] to bind with a girdle or flexible band; to encircle; to equip; to prepare.

girder (gûrd' ẽr), *n.* a spanning beam supporting the joists of a floor.

girdle (gûr' dl), *v.t.* to encircle; to bind with, or as if with, a belt; to cut the bark of a tree entirely around.

girl (gûrl), *n.* a female child; a young woman.

girth (gûrth), *n.* the circumference; the band by which a saddle is held on a horse.

*****gist** (jĭst), *n.* the essence of a matter, as the *gist* of an argument.

give (gĭv), *v.t.* and *v.i.* [*p.t.* gave, *p.p.* given, *pr.p.* giving] to bestow, as to *give* support; to deliver, as to *give* a message; to administer, as an oath of office; to pronounce, as an opinion; to supply, as the furnace *gives* heat; to furnish, as entertainment, as to

give a party; to proffer, as the hand; to present for consideration, as to *give* a reason; to cause to have, as a disease; to contribute, as he *gave* generously; to yield under pressure, as the door *gave* under the force of his blow.

given (gĭv' n), *adj.* addicted to, disposed, as *given* to boasting; fixed, stated, as a *given* time.

gizzard (gĭz' ẽrd), *n.* the second stomach of a bird.

*****glacial** (glā' shal), *n.* pertaining to a glacier; pertaining to ice or its action; frozen, icy.

*****glacier** (glā' shẽr), *n.* a vast accumulation of ice and snow, formed in cold regions, that moves slowly down a slope or covers Arctic regions with an ice sheet.

glad (glad), *adj.* joyous, cheerful, gay, pleased; causing joy, as *glad* news.

gladden (glad' n), *v.t.* to make glad or joyful.

glade (glād), *n.* an open space in a forest.

*****gladiator** (glad' ĭ ā tẽr), *n.* one who fought with a sword in public in ancient Rome.

*****gladiolus** (glad ĭ ō' lus), *n.* a bulbous plant of the iris family.

gladsome (glad' sum), *adj.* joyous; pleasing.

glair (glâr), *n.* the white of egg or a size made from it, as in bookbinding; viscous matter.

glairy (glâr' ĭ), *adj.* smooth, slick, viscous, slimy.

*****glamour** (glam' ẽr), *n.* enchantment, delusive charm, fascination, a romantic spell.

*****glance** (glàns), *n.* a quick look or view; an oblique movement; ore with a metallic luster. *v.i.* to look quickly; to strike on a slant and fly off, as a bullet *glanced*.

gland (gland), *n.* an organ secreting a fluid to be used in, or eliminated from, the body.

glandular (glan' dū lẽr), *adj.* pertaining to glands, or having to do in any way with glands.

glare (glâr), *n.* a dazzling light; a fierce, piercing look; a slippery surface. *v.i.* to shine dazzlingly; to look piercingly.

glaring (glâr' ĭng), *adj.* giving a dazzling light; conspicuous, flagrant, as a *glaring* fault; fierce, furious, as a *glaring* eye.

   Syn. Barefaced. *Glaring* characterizes the thing; *barefaced*, the one who does it. A *glaring* lie is one that flashes forth as a falsehood; a *barefaced* lie marks the effrontery of him who utters it.

*****glass** (glàs), *n.* a hard, brittle substance, usually transparent; anything made of glass; the quantity that fills a drinking glass, as a *glass* of milk.

glasses (glàs' ez), *n.* eyeglasses, spectacles.

glassful (glàs' fool), *n.* the amount a glass holds.

glassware (glàs' wâr), *n.* glass articles.

glaucoma (glô kō' ma), *n.* an eye disease.

glaze (glāz), *n.* a vitreous coating, as on pottery; a smooth, glossy surface or finish; a film over eye. *v.t.* to fit, or equip with glass, to give a glossy finish to, as to *glaze* pottery.

*****glazier** (glā' zhẽr), *n.* one who fits panes of glass into window or door frames.

glazing (glāz' ĭng), *n.* the act of setting glass;

a coating of glass or a glasslike substance; the act of applying glaze.

gleam (glēm), *n.* a faint, brief flash of light; anything resembling it, as a *gleam* of hope.

gleam (glēm), *v.i.* to send forth rays of light; to become suddenly visible, flash, as lights *gleamed* in the darkness.

glean (glēn), *v.t. and v.i.* to gather after the reapers, as grain; to assemble, collect, bit by bit, as facts.

glee (glē), *n.* exuberant joy; a musical composition for unaccompanied voices in harmony.

glen (glen), *n.* a narrow, secluded valley; a shady nook in the woods.

glib (glib), *adj.* smooth-spoken, plausible.

glide (glīd), *v.i.* to slide smoothly; to drop down obliquely without a motor, as an airplane or motorless aircraft.

glider (glīd'ẽr), *n.* a form of aircraft resembling an airplane but having no motor.

glimmer (glim'ẽr), *n.* a faint light; a faint perception, as a *glimmer* of hope.

glimmer (glim'ẽr), *v.i.* to shine in a faint, unsteady manner.

glimpse (glimps), *n.* a quick, passing view; a vague idea, inkling.

glimpse (glimps), *v.t.* to see quickly; to catch a fleeting view of.

Syn. Glance. A *glimpse* connotes a swift, passing appearance; a *glance* implies the action of the eye seeking the object. One catches a *glimpse* of an object and casts a *glance* at it.

glint (glint), *n.* a gleam of light; reflected light. *v.i. and v.t.* to flash, gleam, glitter.

*****glisten** (glis'n), *v.i.* to sparkle with light; to shine with a soft luster, gleam.

glister (glis'tẽr), *n.* glitter.

glitch (glich), *n.* a malfunction or mishap; an error.

glitter (glit'ẽr), *n.* brilliancy, dazzling brightness. *v.i.* to sparkle with light.

gloaming (glōm'ing), *n.* twilight.

gloat (glōt), *v.i.* to gaze fixedly; to feast the eyes or mind; to rejoice over with cruel satisfaction.

globe (glōb), *n.* a sphere; a ball-shaped object; a representation of the shape of the earth, covered with maps; the earth itself.

*****globular** (glob'ū lẽr), *adj.* shaped spherically, like a globe; consisting of globelike particles.

globule (glob'ūl), *n.* a small spherical body; a round drop.

gloom (glōōm), *n.* partial darkness, obscurity; a melancholy state.

gloomy (glōōm'i,, *adj.* [*comp.* gloomier, *superl.* gloomiest] dismal, melancholy.

glorify (glō'ri fī), *v.t.* to honor, reverence, adore, as to *glorify* God, to give radiance, as her smile *glorified* her face, to make glorious, elevate by praise, as to *glorify* the commonplace.

glorious (glō'ri us), *adj.* honored, illustrious; resplendent, as a *glorious* occasion.

*****glory** (glō'ri), *n.* great honor, popular praise, renown; splendor, as the *glory* of the hills; that in which one glories. *v.i.* [*p.t.* and *p.p.*

gloried, *pr.p.* glorying] to rejoice in, exult.

*****gloss** (glôs), *n.* a smooth, glistening finish; deceptive appearance.

gloss (glôs), *v.t.* to make smooth and shiny; to furnish with comments, as a book; to *gloss* over, to conceal defects.

glossary (glôs'a ri), *n.* [*pl.* glossaries] a special list of words, with definitions; a vocabulary explaining special uses of words.

glossy (glos'i), *adj.* [*comp.* glossier, *superl.* glossiest] polished, shining; lustrous.

glove (gluv), *n.* a hand covering with a separate compartment for each finger; a padded leather protector for the hand.

glow (glō), *n.* shining heat; warmth of color, as the *glow* of health; warmth of body, as in a *glow;* ardor.

glow (glō), *v.i.* to throw out heat and light without flame; to be moved by eagerness or zeal; to be warm and flushed, as to *glow* from healthy exercise.

*****glower** (glou'ẽr), *v.i.* to stare with a threatening expression.

*****glucose** (glōō'kōs), *n.* a form of sugar occurring in fruits and honey; a sirup containing natural glucose and other ingredients.

*****glue** (glōō), *n.* a hard gelatin derived from the boiled and jellied skins, hoofs and bones of animals, used for fastening things together, as pieces of wood, broken articles.

glue (glōō), *v.t.* [*p.t.* and *p.p.* glued, *pr.p.* gluing] to unite or fasten with glue.

glum (glum), *adj.* gloomy, moody, sullen.

glut (glut), *n.* an oversupply, superabundance.

glut (glut), *v.t.* to overload, as a market; to oversupply; to fill to repletion, satiate.

gluten (glōō'ten), *n.* a nutritious substance in certain grains, especially wheat.

glutinous (glōō'ti nus), *adj.* sticky, viscous.

glutton (glut'n), *n.* a greedy eater.

*****glycerin or glycerine** (glis'ẽr in), *n.* a clear, almost colorless liquid used in medicine and in making explosives.

*****gnarl** (närl), *n.* a knot in wood; a large knot on the bark of a tree.

gnarled (närld), *adj.* full of knots, twisted.

gnash (nash), *v.t.* to strike or grind together, as the teeth.

gnat (nat), *n.* a tiny, stinging winged insect.

gnaw (nô), *v.t.* [*p.t.* and *p.p.* gnawed, *pr.p.* gnawing] to bite at, slowly, repeatedly, persistently; to wear away with the teeth.

*****gnome** (nōm), *n.* a dwarf supposed to be the guardian of treasures buried in the earth, the guardian spirit of miners.

*****gnu** (nōō), *n.* an African antelope with an oxlike head, a mane, flowing tail and downward-curving horns.

go (gō), *v.i.* [*p.t.* went, *p.p.* gone, *pr.p.* going] to depart, as they *went* away yesterday; to proceed, move, advance, as to *go* home from school, a letter *goes* by air mail; to be relinquished or abolished, as graft must *go;* to operate, work, as the clock *goes;* to pass, as a week *goes* quickly; to extend, reach or lead, as this path *goes* through the woods; to be in a certain condition, as to *go* in rags; to become, as to *go* deaf; to have a certain tune or phrasing, as the song *goes* like this; to put oneself, as to *go* to trouble; to belong, as the bread *goes* in the breadbox; to harmonize, suit, as yellow *goes* well with brown; to have recourse to, as to *go* to law; to make a special sound, as cows *go* moo.

goad (gōd), *n.* a pointed stick used to make oxen go faster; a prod.

goad (gōd), *v.i. and v.t.* to use a goad; to drive with a goad; to urge to greater activity.

goal (gōl), *n.* the final aim in a contest; a marking on each side of an athletic field, in some games, toward which the players attempt to propel the ball in order to score; ultimate object of endeavor.

goat (gōt), *n.* a ruminant, hollow-horned quadruped.

goatee (gōt ē'), *n.* a tuft of hair on the chin, trimmed to a point.

gobble (gob' l), *n.* the cry of the male turkey.

gobble (gob' l), *v.i. and v.t.* to make a noise like a turkey; to eat fast.

goblet (gob' let), *n.* a drinking glass with a base and stem.

goblin (gob' lin), *n.* a mischievous sprite.

god (god), *n.* a being with divine powers; an idol.

God (god), *n.* the Supreme Being; the Creator.

godchild (god' chīld), *n.* one for whom another is sponsor at baptism.

goddess (god' es), *n.* a female deity.

godlike (god' līk), *adj.* superb; magnificent; fit for or like a god; superlatively good.

godly (god' li), *adj.* devout, pious.

godsend (god' send), *n.* unexpected good fortune.

goggle (gog' l), *n.* a rolling of the eyes.

goggle (gog' l), *v.i.* to roll the eyes; to stare.

goggles (gog' lz), *n. pl.* glasses to protect the eyes from dust.

goiter (goi' tēr), *n.* an enlargement of the thyroid gland, causing neck swelling.

gold (gōld), *n.* a metallic element, dense, soft, ductile and malleable, used in making jewelry and in coinage.

golden (gōl' den), *adj.* made of gold; like gold; having the color of gold, valuable, precious, as *golden* moments.

goldenrod (gōl' den rod), *n.* a tall plant with yellow flowers.

goldfinch (gōld' finch), *n.* a songbird with yellow body and black wings, tail and crown.

goldfish (gōld' fish), *n.* an orange-hued freshwater fish prized for aquariums.

goldsmith (gōld' smith), *n.* a worker in gold.

gold standard (gōld stan' dērd), use of gold alone as the basis of values for a system of coinage.

golf (golf), *n.* a game played with a small resilient ball and long-handled clubs over a course called *links*.

*****gondola** (gon' dō la), *n.* a long, narrow Venetian pleasure boat, propelled with one oar; a flat, open-sided freight car; in aviation, a long narrow car hung under a dirigible balloon.

gondolier (gon dō lēr'), *n.* the oarsman of a gondola.

gong (gông), *n.* a piece of metal like a shallow dish, struck with a mallet to give a bell-like signal.

good (good), *adj.* [*comp.* **better**, *superl.* **best**] suitable for a purpose, as *good* to eat; considerable, as a *good* deal; having excellent qualities, as a *good* mother; agreeable, pleasant, as *good* company; beneficial, as *good* counsel; proper, becoming, as a *good* rule to follow; reliable, as *good* material; admirable, as a *good* book; of unquestioned standing, as a *good* Republican; commercially sound, as a *good* risk.

goods (goodz), *n. pl.* possessions; merchandise.

good will (good wil), benevolence, kindly feeling, friendly disposition; the value of a business establishment over and above its cash assets and material property.

goody (good' i), *n.* a sweetmeat; anything good to eat.

goose (gōōs), *n.* [*pl.* geese] a web-footed, flat-billed bird, like a large duck or a short-necked swan; a silly, gooselike person.

*****gooseberry** (gōōz' ber i), *n.* [*pl.* gooseberries] a plant with a prickly, hairy, acid berry; the shrub that bears this berry.

*****gopher** (gō' fēr), *n.* a North American burrowing rodent.

gore (gōr), *n.* clotted blood.

gore (gōr), *n.* a triangular piece sewn into a dress or sail; a wedge-shaped piece used in making the dome of an umbrella.

gorge (gôrj), *n.* a narrow ravine between hills; an obstruction in a channel such as is caused by a jammed float of logs; the throat. *v.i.* to swallow greedily; to stuff oneself with food.

*****gorgeous** (gôr' jus), *adj.* glittering, splendid, magnificent.

gorilla (gō ril' a), *n.* an African manlike ape.

*****gosling** (goz' ling), *n.* a young goose.

gospel (gos' pel), *n.* good tidings; something accepted as true: *the Gospels*, the story of Christ's life as told in the books of Matthew, Mark, Luke and John.

gossamer (gos' a mēr), *n.* a film of cobwebs; a thin, soft, filmy gauze; a thin waterproof cloak.

gossip (gos' ip), *n.* idle talk about other people's affairs; one who discusses private affairs of others. *v.i.* to go about telling idle tales about others.

*****gouge** (gouj), *n.* a chisel with a concave blade used for cutting grooves in wood. *v.t.* to scoop out with, or as with, a gouge.

*****goulash** (gōō' läsh), *n.* a highly seasoned stew of beef or veal.

*****gourd** (gōrd), *n.* a plant bearing a fruit resembling a pumpkin or melon; the dried rind often used as a dipper.

gourmand (goor' mand), *n.* a gluttonous eater; one who enjoys luxurious food, an epicure.

gourmet (gōōr' mā), *n.* a connoisseur of food and drink.

gout (gout), *n.* a painful inflammatory disease

of the joints or extremities.

govern (guv' ẽrn), *v.i.* *and* *v.t.* to exercise authority; to rule; to direct and control; to determine; to require to be in, as a transitive verb *governs* the objective case.

    Syn. Rule, conduct, supervise. To *govern* is to rule with judgment and knowledge. To *rule* is to use a more unqualified degree of power. A king *governs* his people by wise laws and an upright administration; a despot *rules* by arbitrary decision. *Conduct* has the idea of management; *supervise* that of overseeing.

governess (guv' ẽr nes), *n.* a woman who trains and teaches children in their own home.

government (guv' ẽrn ment), *n.* the act of governing; administration of public affairs.

    Syn. Administration. *Government* implies *administration*, and *administration* involves a degree of *government*. But *government* includes every exercise of authority, while *administration* covers only that exercise of authority which consists in applying certain rules and laws.

gown (goun), *n.* a woman's dress, especially one for formal wear; a loose robe worn as part of an academic costume.

grab (grab), *v.i.* *and* *v.t.* to make a sudden motion of grasping; to seize suddenly and with force.

grab (grab), *n.* a sudden and forceful seizure.

grace (grās), *n.* ease, charm, attractiveness in form or manner; sense of propriety, as to have the *grace*, to do what is proper; a term of relief from an obligation, as thirty days' *grace;* a blessing asked at meals.

    Syn. Mercy. *Grace* implies spontaneous favor; *mercy*, compassionate treatment of the suffering.

graceful (grās' fool), *adj.* easy and beautiful in form or motion.

gracious (grā' shus), *adj.* showing kindness or mercy; polite, charming.

gradation (grā dā' shun), *n.* the act of arranging in rank according to some set requirement, as size; a regular arrangement; progress step by step; gradual change, as *gradations* in color.

grade (grād), *n.* a step or degree in rank, dignity, quality, order; the proportion of rise in a road or railroad to a certain horizontal distance; a division of a school course covering a year's work; the pupils in such a division; a rating in school work, as a good *grade*. *v.t.* to arrange in an orderly series, class, sort; to level, as a lawn; mark, as to *grade* compositions.

*****gradual** (grad' ū al), *adj.* proceeding by degrees; slow but steady in progress, as *gradual* improvement.

graduate (grad' ū ăt), *n.* one who has completed a course in school or college and received a diploma. *v.i* *and* *v.t.* to pass the final tests of a school or college course; to mark with degrees, as on a scale. *adj.* for graduates, as a *graduate* school.

graduation (grad ū ā' shun), *n.* the act of receiving a diploma testifying that the student has completed a certain course; the ceremony attending the giving of diplomas; division into degrees, as of a thermometer; a line or mark that divides a scale.

graft (gråft), *n.* a small cutting from one plant or tree inserted into a slit in the stem or trunk of another plant or tree, of which it becomes a growing part; a piece of living skin transplanted from one part of the body to another. *n.* the acquisition of money by questionable means, as the use of official position for personal gain. *v.t.* to insert a cutting from one plant in the stem of another; to transplant living skin, bone or tissue from one part of body to another or from one body to another.

grain (grān), *n.* a small, hard particle of matter; collectively, the seed of cereal plants such as wheat; a small unit of weight in avoirdupois and troy measures; the texture of things, as wood or stone; the natural disposition or instincts of a person, as that goes against the *grain*.

gram (gram), *n.* the unit of weight in the metric system.

grammar (gram' ẽr), *n.* the science that deals with classes of words and their relation to each other; the use of words with reference to custom and rules; a book on this subject.

grammarian (gra mâr' i an), *n.* one who specializes in the study of the form and use of words.

grammatical (gra mat' i kal), *adj.* pertaining to grammar; in accordance with the rules of grammar.

gramophone (gram' ō fōn), *n.* an instrument for recording and reproducing sound: originally a trade name.

grampus (gram' pus), *n.* a sea mammal allied to the blackfish; the killer whale.

granary (grăn' a ri), *n.* [*pl.* granaries] a storehouse for grain.

grand (grand), *adj.* superior in rank or dignity, foremost; large, main, as the *grand* ballroom; magnificent, sumptuous, as entertaining on a *grand* scale; impressive, as scenery; distinguished, as a *grand* old man.

grandchild (grand' child), *n.* the child of one's son or daughter.

grandfather (grand' fåth ẽr), *n.* a father's or mother's father.

grandparent (grand' pâr' ent), *n.* a parent's father or mother, as paternal *grandparents*.

*****grandeur** (gran' dūr), *n.* greatness in size or dignity, eminence, magnificence, majesty.

grandiloquent (gran dil' ō kwent), *adj.* speaking pompously, bombastic.

grandiose (gran' di ōs), *adj.* impressive, magnificent; assuming a false splendor.

grange (grānj), *n.* a farm with its buildings; a local branch of the national organization of farmers.

granite (gran' it), *n.* a hard rock composed of quartz and orthoclase or microline.

granivorous (gra niv' ō rus), *adj.* grain-eating; living on seeds.

grant (grant), *n.* something conferred, as land or rights or money.

grant (grånt), *v.t.* to give or confer, as land or rights; to concede, as a point in argument.

granular (gran' ū lẽr), *adj.* composed of grains; like grains.

granulate (gran' ū lāt), *v.i.* and *v.t.* to form grains; to make into or cover with grains or crystals.

granule (gran' ūl), *n.* a small grain, or grain-like particle.

grape (grāp), *n.* the fruit of the grapevine, a smooth-skinned, juicy berry growing in clusters and used as table fruit or in making wine; a cluster of small iron balls used as ammunition for cannons, grapeshot.

graph (gråf), *n.* a diagram having lines, dots or other conventional symbols to show relative size or importance or the change over a period of time.

graphic (graf' ik), *adj.* pertaining to the art of writing; describing vividly; of or pertaining to those arts, as painting, drawing, engraving, that express ideas by means of marks or lines on a flat surface.

graphite (graf' it), *n.* a soft, black carbon used in pencils.

grapnel (grap' nel), *n.* a small anchor with several claws, used for small boats and for balloons; a grappling iron.

grapple (grap' l), *n.* a close hold, as in wrestling; a device for gripping. *v.i.* and *v.t.* to use a grappling iron; to struggle at close quarters; to lay fast hold of, as in a fight or wrestling match.

****grasp** (gråsp), *n.* the act of seizing with the hand; power of understanding.

grasp (gråsp), *v.i.* and *v.t.* to try to seize, as to *grasp* at anything; to seize, grip, clasp and hold; to lay hold of mentally, as to *grasp* an idea.

grass (gràs), *n.* herbage having hollow stalks, jointed, long, narrow and spear-shaped blades and seeds like grain.

grate (gråt), *n.* a framework of iron bars to hold a coal fire. *v.i.* and *v.t.* to scrape and make a harsh noise; to grind, with harsh sounds, as metals scraping together; to have an irritating effect, as to *grate* on one's nerves; to pulverize by rubbing against a rough surface, as to *grate* cheese.

grateful (gråt' fool), *adj.* thankful; giving pleasure, welcome.

grater (gråt' ẽr), *n.* a kitchen utensil having a rough surface for rubbing off small portions of anything, as a nutmeg *grater.*

gratification (grat i fi kā' shun), *n.* the act of pleasing or state of being pleased; that which gratifies.

gratify (grat' i fi), *v.t.* to give pleasure or satisfaction to, indulge, as to *gratify* a whim.

Syn. Indulge, humor. To *gratify* is to give pleasure to, to *indulge* implies a yielding of the will, sometimes through weakness; to *humor* is, commonly, to make concessions to the whims of others.

grating (gråt' ing), *n.* an open framework or lattice of bars. *adj.* harsh, irritating.

****gratis** (grā' tis), *adv.* without charge, as a favor.

gratitude (grat' i tūd), *n.* gratefulness, thankful appreciation.

gratuitous (gra tū' i tus), *adj.* freely bestowed, without recompense; voluntary.

gratuity (gra tū' i ti), *n.* [*pl.* gratuities] a free gift; a reward for minor services, as a tip.

****gravamen** (gra vā' men), *n.* [*pl.* gravimina] the material part of a legal grievance or charge.

grave (grāv), *n.* an excavation for burial of a dead person.

grave (grāv), *v.t.* to cut or carve as with a chisel, engrave; to impress or fix indelibly.

grave (grāv), *adj.* serious, important, momentous, as a *grave* decision; solemn, sedate, as a *grave* manner.

Syn. Serious, solemn, earnest. *Grave* implies austerity as if from consideration of weighty matters; *serious,* deep thought or reflection; *solemn,* extreme gravity; *earnest,* restrained eagerness and always connotes sincerity.

gravel (grav' el), *n.* fragments of rock, coarser than sand; pieces of hard matter in the bladder or kidneys.

gravel (grav' el), *v.t.* to cover with gravel.

gravitate (grav' i tāt), *v.i.* to be acted upon by the force of gravity; to be attracted toward, as boy gravitates toward girl.

gravitation (grav i tā' shun), *n.* the force that attracts bodies toward each other.

gravity (grav' i ti), *n.* the force that tends to draw all bodies toward the center of the earth; seriousness.

gravy (grā' vi), *n.* [*pl.* gravies] a sauce for food, as chicken *gravy;* the juice that drips from meat while it is cooking, often serving as a base for such sauce.

gray (grā), *n.* a color resulting from blending black and white; an animal of this color, as the horse was a *gray.*

gray (grā), *adj.* having the color of white mixed with black, as *gray* cloth; turning white, as *gray* hair; dismal, as a *gray* day.

graze (grāz), *v.i.* and *v.t.* to feed on growing grass; to put cattle out in pasture to feed on growing herbage; to scrape in passing, as the bullet barely *grazed* its mark.

****grease** (grēs), *n.* soft animal fat; oily matter used for lubrication. *v.t.* to apply grease to; to lubricate with oily matter.

****greasy** (grēs' i), *adj.* [*comp.* greasier, *superl.* greasiest] like grease; smeared or spotted with grease.

great (grāt), *adj.* large in size, number or quantity, as a *great* sum of money; eminent, able and honored, as a *great* man; of extraordinary magnitude or intensity, as a *great* flood; long continued, as for a *great* many years; more remote by one generation, as *great*-grandchild.

Syn. Large, big. *Great* expresses degree; *large* connotes breadth, scope, generosity; *big* expresses size, bulk or extent.

greed (grēd), *n.* avarice, cupidity, inordinate desire, as *greed* for power.

greedy (grēd' i), *adj.* [*comp.* greedier, *superl.* greediest] inordinately desirous, as of wealth, avaricious; ravenous.

green (grēn), *n.* a color uniting blue and yellow; a grass plot, as the square of turf about a hole in a golf course.

green (grēn), *adj.* having the color made by blending blue and yellow; fresh and flourishing, as *green* memories; unripe, as *green* fruit; inexperienced, as a *green* worker; not seasoned, as *green* lumber; having an unhealthy color.

greenback (grēn' bak), *n.* a piece of paper money printed on the back with green ink.

greenhorn (grēn' hôrn), *n.* an inexperienced person, a novice.

greenhouse (grēn' hous), *n.* a glass-roofed building in which plants are grown.

greens (grēnz), *n.* evergreen branches used for decoration, especially at Christmas; vegetable leaves, as of spinach or turnips, used as food.

greet (grēt), *v.t.* to welcome; to salute in friendly, hospitable manner; to appear before, as a strange sight *greeted* our eyes.

greeting (grēt' ing), *n.* a salutation, welcome; a written salutation sent to, or received from, someone absent.

***gregarious** (grē gãr' i us), *adj.* associating in herds or companies.

***grenade** (grē nād'), *n.* an explosive shell, with a time fuse, thrown by hand or fired from a rifle; a flask filled with chemicals, thrown upon a fire to extinguish it.

grenadier (gren a dēr'), *n.* an infantryman who throws grenades; a member of a special corps or company in the army.

greyhound (grā' hound), *n.* a slender, long-bodied, fast-running dog with keen sight, used extensively for hunting and racing.

grid (grid), *n.* a gridiron or grated iron implement used for broiling; a lead plate used in a storage battery; an electrode controlling the current between plate and filament of an electron tube.

griddle (grid' l), *n.* a metal plate for cooking pancakes.

gridiron (grid' ī ẽrn), *n.* a grated iron utensil for broiling meat or fish; anything marked with parallel lines resembling a gridiron, as a football field.

grief (grēf), *n.* great sorrow, affliction; that which causes sorrow; misfortune, as to come to *grief*.

Syn. Sadness, woe, anguish. *Grief* is acute mental pain resulting from a definite cause; *sorrow* is sadness over loss or disappointment; *woe* is inconsolable misery; *anguish* is excruciating distress of mind or body.

Ant. Joy, happiness, delight.

grievance (grēv' ans), *n.* a sense of wrong; a cause of annoyance and resentment.

grieve (grēv), *v.i.* and *v.t.* to feel sorrow or grief; to cause sorrow and grief.

grievous (grēv' us), *adj.* causing pain or sorrow; serious, as a *grievous* wrong.

griffin (grif' in), *n.* a fabulous animal with the body and legs of a lion, the wings and beak of an eagle.

grill (gril), *n.* a gridiron; an apparatus for broiling; a dish of broiled meat, as a mixed

grill. *v.t.* to cook on a grill, broil; to subject to cross-examination.

grille (gril), *n.* a wrought iron or bronze grating in a window or gateway.

grim (grim), *adj.* [*comp.* grimmer, *superl.* grimmest] of forbidding aspect, unyielding, relentless; repellent, as a *grim* duty; ghastly, as a *grim* tale.

***grimace** (gri mās'), *n.* a facial distortion, wry face; a twisting of the face, as in pain.

grimace (gri mās'), *v.i.* to make a face.

grime (grim), *n.* dirt, soot.

grimy (grim' i), *adj.* covered with dirt.

grin (grin), *n.* a broad smile.

grin (grin), *v.i.* to smile broadly.

grind (grind), *n.* the act of grinding; tiresome work, dreary routine, as it was a hard *grind*.

grind (grind), *v.t.* and *v.i.* to rub together, as to *grind* the teeth; to reduce grain to meal by rubbing between hard surfaces, as to *grind* corn; to operate by turning a crank; to polish or whet, as to *grind* scissors.

grindstone (grīnd' stŏn), *n.* a circular stone turning on an axle, on which tools are ground and sharpened.

grip (grip), *n.* a firm grasp with the hand; a mechanical device for taking hold of something firmly; force of hold, either physical or mental, as the *grip* of disease, a good *grip* on the problem; strength of the hand, as he has a mighty *grip*.

grip (grip), *v.t.* to seize strongly with the hand; to hold firmly; to give a handclasp to; to hold fixed in rapt attention, as the speaker's words *gripped* the audience.

gripe (grip), *n.* a pain in the intestines; distress, hardship, as the *gripe* of poverty.

grippe (grip), *n.* a heavy cold accompanied by fever and pain in the joints, influenza.

gripping (grip' ing), *adj.* intensely interesting, so as to catch and hold attention to the end, as a gripping story or dramatic situation.

grisly (griz' li), *adj.* [*comp.* grislier, *superl.* grisliest] ghastly, hideous, gruesome.

grist (grist), *n.* grain for grinding; ground corn.

gristle (gris' l), *n.* a tough, rubberlike, translucent substance in animal tissue, cartilage.

gristmill (grist' mil), *n.* a mill where grain or corn is ground.

grit (grit), *n.* rough, hard particles, as of sand; courage.

grits (grits), *n. pl.* grain coarsely ground, as corn.

gritty (grit' i), *adj.* of or like small, hard particles of sand; brave, plucky.

grizzly (griz' li), *n.* [*pl.* grizzlies] the grizzly bear, a large, fierce bear of the western North American mountain regions. *adj.* streaked with gray, as hair.

groan (grŏn), *n.* a sound uttered in pain and sorrow and sometimes intentionally to manifest ridicule.

Syn. Moan. A *groan* is a deep, often spasmodic sound indicating acute distress; a *moan* is a plaintive, sustained sound.

groan (grŏn), *v.i.* to utter a moaning sound, as in great pain, sorrow, or to express ridicule.

grocer (grō' sẽr), *n.* one whose business it is to sell foodstuffs, as tea, coffee, sugar, fruits.

grocery (grō' sẽr ĭ), *n.* [*pl.* groceries] a shop selling food commodities.

grog (grog), *n.* a mixture of spirits and water without sweetening; any intoxicating drink.

groggery (gŏg' ẽr ĭ), *n.* a grogshop, barroom.

groggy (grog' ĭ), *adj.* tipsy; dazed, as if by drink.

grogshop (grog' shŏp), *n.* a liquor saloon.

groin (groin), *n.* the part of the body between the thigh and the abdomen; the curve made by the intersection of two arches.

grommet (grom' et), *n.* a metal ring for receiving a cord or rope, as on sails or mailbags.

groom (grōōm), *n.* one who has charge of horses. *n.* a man about to be married or recently married. *v.t.* to curry and feed a horse and keep it in good condition: *well groomed,* glossy, sleek, as a horse; neat in appearance, well dressed, as a person.

groove (grōōv), *n.* a channel or furrow, especially when cut in something by a tool; habit, routine.

groove (grōōv), *v.t.* to make grooves in.

grope (grōp), *v.i.* to feel one's way in the dark with the hands; to feel about for something, physically or mentally, as to *grope* for an idea.

grosbeak (grōs' bēk), *n.* a big-beaked songbird related to the finches.

grosgrain (grō' grain), *n.* a stout, double-corded silk.

gross (grōs), *n.* twelve dozen; the entire amount. *adj.* large and coarse, unrefined; total, as of earnings; flagrant, as *gross* neglect.

grotesque (grō tesk'), *adj.* fantastic, bizarre, incongruous.

grotto (grot' ō), *n.* a natural cavern in the earth; an artificial place of retreat resembling a cave.

grouch (grouch), *n.* one who is habitually cross and sulky.

grouch (grouch), *v.i.* to grumble, complain, as he always has something to *grouch* about.

ground (ground), *n.* the earth underfoot; land; foundation for belief, good reason; extent to be covered; the bottom, as of a body of water; contact of an electric conductor with the earth, as in *ground* wire; *grounds,* sediment, dregs; foundation, cause, reason.

ground (ground), *adj.* having been reduced to particles through a process of grinding; relating to the ground, as *ground* water; near the earth, as the *ground* floor.

groundhog (ground' hog), a thickset, North American burrowing rodent; woodchuck.

groundless (ground' les), *adj.* without reason, not founded in fact.

groundwork (ground' wûrk), *n.* the foundation for an enterprise, preparation.

group (grōōp), *n.* a small assemblage of things having some relation; cluster, as of buildings.

group (grōōp), *v.i. and v.t.* to form in a group; to organize a group.

grouse (grous), *n.* a game bird, with a plump body and reddish-brown plumage.

grout (grout), *n.* coarse meal; mortar or cement mixed with gravel; plaster for ceilings.

grove (grōv), *n.* a group of trees; a small wood; a group of cultivated trees, as an orange *grove.*

grovel (grov'l), *v.i.* to lie face downward; to creep on the ground; to crawl and cringe, as in submission or appeal.

grow (grō), *v.i. and v.t.* [*p.t.* grew, *p.p.* grown, *pr.p.* growing] to increase in size through natural processes; to flourish; to change by degrees, increase in any way, as to *grow* older and wiser; to cultivate, as to *grow* corn.

growl (groul), *n.* a deep angry, throaty noise, as of a dog.

growl (groul), *v.i.* to utter a growl; to grumble.

growth (grōth), *n.* the gradual development of a plant or animal; increase in size or amount; something that grows, as the hill was covered with green *growth;* a tumor or cancer.

grub (grub), *n.* the thick, wormlike larva of some insects, as beetles.

grub (grub), *v.i. and v.t.* to dig with effort; to uproot, as tree stumps; to drudge; to clear by digging.

grudge (gruj), *n.* secret ill will in resentment of a real or fancied wrong.

grudge (gruj), *v.t.* to grant with visible reluctance; to give with regret.

gruel (grōō' el), *n.* thin porridge.

gruesome (grōō' sum), *adj.* ghastly, inspiring horror.

gruff (gruf), *adj.* blunt, rough, surly, hoarse and rough, as a *gruff* voice.

grumble (grum' bl), *n.* a subdued murmur, complaint.

grumble (grum' bl), *v.i.* to find fault, complain.

grumpy (grump' ĭ), *adj.* surly, cross, ill-tempered.

grunt (grunt), *n.* the guttural noise a pig makes; an inarticulate sound expressing indifference or contempt.

grunt (grunt), *v.i.* to make a guttural sound, as a pig.

guano (gwä' nō), *n.* the droppings of sea birds found in large deposits especially off the coast of Peru and used as fertilizer.

guarantee (gar an tē'), *n.* anything that assures a certain thing will happen or be done; a solemn statement that a thing is as it is represented to be, a guaranty.

guarantee (gar an tē'), *v.t.* to give assurance that a thing is as represented, especially when reparation for defects is provided; to be legally responsible for.

guarantor (gar' an tôr), *n.* one who guarantees; one who assumes legal responsibility for the debt or default of another.

guaranty (gar' an tĭ), *n.* assumption of responsibility for meeting of obligations by another; property pledged as security for

fulfilment of an obligation.

guard (gärd), *n.* one who watches over and protects; a protecting part, as a mud*guard*, a watch*guard;* act of guarding: *on guard*, on the watch, as in military service.

guard (gärd), *v.t. and v.i.* to watch over; to check, restrain, keep under control, as to *guard* one's speech; to be cautious, prudent, as to *guard* against want.

  Syn. Safeguard, shelter, curb. To *guard* is to stand watch over and maintain in safety; to *safeguard* is to provide means of protection from danger; to *curb* is to restrain.

*****guardian** (gär' di an), *n.* one who has the care of another's property or person or both, especially a custodian appointed by law.

*****guava** (gwä' va), *n.* a tree of tropical America, yielding a pear-shaped fruit, used in making jelly; the fruit of this tree or the jelly made. from it.

*****gubernatorial** (gū bĕr na tō' ri al), *adj.* pertaining to a governor or the governorship, as a *gubernatorial* campaign.

gudgeon (guj' un), *n.* an iron pin or shaft on which a wheel revolves; a socket in which a turning pin rests, as in a hinge or the rudder setting of a small boat.

guernsey (gûrn' zi), *n.* a close-fitting knitted woolen shirt.

*****guerrilla** (ge ril' a), *n.* one of an irregular band of raiders, not a regular part of an army.

guerrilla (ge ril' a), *adj.* pertaining to irregular warfare.

guess (ges), *n.* a conjecture, surmise, opinion not founded on evidence.

guess (ges), *v.i. and v.t.* to form an opinion without evidence to give it support; to work out by conjecture, as to *guess* the answer to a riddle.

  Syn. Conjecture, surmise, divine, fancy. To *guess* is to attempt to hit upon the correct answer at random or without sufficient evidence; to *conjecture* is to form an opinion on what is acknowledged as insufficient data; to *surmise* is to infer on still slighter grounds; to *divine* is to perceive through sympathy or intuition; to *fancy* is to believe without being sure.

guest (gest), *n.* one who is entertained at the house or table of another; a lodger or boarder at a hotel or inn.

guffaw (gu fô'), *n.* a rude, boisterous laugh.

guidance (gīd' ans), *n.* the act of directing; supervision; assistance, as with advice.

guide (gīd), *n.* one who leads or directs; a small book containing information for travelers, a guidebook; the end man on a line of soldiers.

guild or gild (gild), *n.* an association of persons engaged in a common trade or calling, for mutual advantage and protection.

guile (gīl), *n.* deceit, duplicity, treachery.

*****guillotine** (gil' ō tēn), *n.* an apparatus for beheading condemned persons by means of a heavy knife sliding between uprights.

guilt (gilt), *n.* the state of having committed an offense or crime; the fact of having violated a law.

guiltless (gilt' les), *adj.* innocent.

guilty (gilt' i), *adj.* [*comp.* **guiltier, superl.** guiltiest] justly chargeable with an offense or crime; not innocent, as a *guilty* mind.

guinea fowl (gin' i foul), a barnyard fowl having grayish blue feathers with white dots, originally imported from Guinea.

guinea pig (gin' i pig), a small rodent having short ears and nearly tailless.

*****guise** (gīz), *n.* external appearance, dress; cloak, mask, pretense.

*****guitar** (gi tär'), *n.* a six-stringed musical instrument played with the fingers.

gulch (gulch), *n.* a gully, ravine.

gulf (gulf), *n.* an arm of the sea extending into the land and larger than a bay; an abyss.

gull (gul), *n.* a web-footed sea bird with long wings; a person easily deceived or cheated.

gull (gul), *v.t.* to deceive, cheat.

gullet (gul' et), *n.* the tube that leads from the mouth to the stomach, the throat.

gullible (gul' i bl), *adj.* easily deceived or imposed upon.

gully (gul' i), *n.* [*pl.* gullies] a dry channel or groove in the earth, worn by water.

gulp (gulp), *n.* the act of swallowing hastily; a large amount swallowed at once.

gulp (gulp), *v.i. and v.t.* to catch the breath, as if by swallowing; to swallow eagerly or greedily.

gum (gum), *n.* a sticky substance that exudes from certain trees; a preparation of elastic substances flavored and used for chewing; tissue of the jaws in which teeth are set.

gum (gum), *v.i. and v.t.* [*p.t.* and *p.p.* gummed, *pr.p.* gumming] to turn into gum, make into gum; to fasten with gum.

gumbo (gum' bō), *n.* the okra plant or its pods; a soup thickened with okra pods.

gummy (gum' i), *adj.* consisting of, containing or producing a sticky substance; covered with a sticky substance.

gun (gun), *n.* a weapon which discharges an explosive carrying a charge of shot or a bullet.

guncotton (gun' kot n), *n.* cotton or other vegetable fiber treated with acids and used as an explosive.

gun metal (gun' met' l), an alloy of copper and tin, formerly used in making cannon; a dark-gray color having a bluish-red tinge.

gunner (gun' ĕr), *n.* one who works a gun; a warrant officer in charge of ordnance on a ship; one who hunts game with a gun.

gunpowder (gun' pou dĕr), *n.* an explosive substance composed of saltpeter, sulphur and charcoal.

*****gunwale** (gun' el), *n.* the upper part of a boat where topsides and deck meet.

gurgle (gûr' gl), *n.* a bubbling sound or the sound of water flowing from a narrow-necked bottle or jug.

gurgle (gûr' gl), *v.i.* to flow in a broken, rushing stream; to make a bubbling sound.

*****gush** (gush), *n.* a sudden strong flow of liquid from an enclosed space; an outburst, as of words.

gush (gush), v.i. to flow forth suddenly, strongly and in volume.

gusher (gush' ĕr), n. an oil well with voluminous. natural flow.

gusset (gus' et), n. a triangular piece of cloth inserted in a garment to enlarge or reinforce it.

gust (gust), n. a sudden blast or puff of wind; an outburst, as of anger.

*****gustatory** (gus ta tŏ' ri), adj. pertaining to the taste.

gusto (gus' tō), n. zest, relish.

gut (gut), n. an intestine; a narrow channel.

gut (gut), v.t. to remove the intestines from; to destroy the inside of, as fire gutted the building.

gutta-percha (gut' a pûr' cha), a white-to-brown, rubberlike substance obtained from evergreen trees of the Malay Archipelago, used in commerce and industry.

gutter (gut' ĕr), n. a channel for carrying away water, as from the streets or from the eaves of a house.

*****guttural** (gut' ĕr al), adj. pertaining to the throat; sounded in the throat, as a guttural tone.

guy (gī), n. a rope or chain for steadying anything, as a pole or mast; a queer-looking or oddly dressed person.

guzzle (guz' zl), v.i. and v.t. to drink greedily and immoderately.

*****gymnasium** (jim nā' zi um), n. [pl. gymnasiums] a building or room for athletic exercises; a European high school, especially in Germany.

gymnast (jim' nast), n. one who excels in gymnastics.

gymnastics (jim nas' tiks), n. pl. physical exercises with weights or on bars, fixed or swinging, and various apparatus requiring strength and skill in their use.

*****gynecology** (jin ē kol' ŏ ji), n. the branch of medical science that treats of the physical functions and diseases of women.

*****gypsum** (jip' sum), n. calcium sulphate, used in making plaster of Paris.

gypsy (jip' si), n. a member of a dark-skinned, wandering race of Oriental origin.

gyral (jī' ral), adj. rotatory, whirling.

gyrate (jī' rāt), v.i. to revolve around a central point, rotate, as a cyclone gyrates.

gyration (jī rā' shun), n. the act of turning or whirling around a center.

*****gyrocompass** (jī' rŏ kum pas), n. a type of continuously driven gyroscope, so constructed that the axis always points to the true north.

*****gyroplane** (jī rŏ plān), n. an aircraft whose balance and support depend upon swiftly rotating horizontal or slightly inclined planes.

*****gyroscope** (jī' rŏ skōp), n. an instrument used for stabilizing airplanes, monorail cars, ships, compasses.

H

haberdasher (hab' ĕr dash ĕr), n. a dealer in small goods, ribbons, needles, thread; in the U. S., a dealer in men's furnishings.

habiliments (ha bil' i ments), n. pl. dress, costume, garb.

habilitate (ha bil' i tāt), v.t. to clothe; to fit out for work, equip, as a mine.

habit (hab' it), n. dress, clothing for special use or occasion, as a riding habit; a characteristic produced by constant repetition of an action.

habitable (hab' i ta bl), adj. fit to live in.

*****habitat** (hab' i tat), n. the region in which an animal or plant naturally lives.

*****habitation** (hab i tā' shun), n. a dwelling place.

    Syn Home, residence, domicile. A habitation is merely a place of abode; a residence is a permanent dwelling place; a home is a dwelling endeared as the scene of domestic ties and family life.

*****habitual** (ha bit' ū al), adj. done by habit, customary.

*****habituate** (ha bit' ū āt), v.t. to accustom oneself to certain conditions or actions through constant use or repetition.

habitué (ha bit ū ā'), n. one who frequents a certain place, as he is a habitué of this restaurant.

hack (hak), n. a carriage let out for hire; a literary drudge, doing odd jobs of writing; a short, dry cough; a tool for breaking up surfaces of land; a gash inflicted by a sharp instrument; a notch cut in a tree trunk.

hack (hak), v.t. and v.i. to cut unevenly, gash, as to hack a tree; to give a short, dry cough, as he hacks continually.

hackle (hak' l), n. the neck feathering of a fowl; a certain feathered fly for angling.

hackle (hak' l), v.t. to clean flax or hemp by combing.

hackney (hak' ni), n. [pl. hackneys] a breed of horses for riding and driving; a hack, a carriage for hire.

hackneyed (hak' nĕd), adj. worn, commonplace, as a hackneyed expression.

hack saw (hak' sô), a narrow, close-toothed saw, set in a frame, used for cutting metal.

haddock (had' uk), n. an edible sea fish similar to the cod but smaller.

*****haft** (hâft), n. the handle of a tool or knife, a hilt.

hag (hag), n. a witch; an ugly old woman.

haggard (hag' ĕrd), adj. worn, gaunt, lean and hollow-eyed.

hail (hāl), n. frozen rain; anything scattered in abundance, as a hail of bullets; a salutation. v.i. and v.t. to pour down small, icy particles; to shower dówn with force; to greet with a cry of salutation, as I hailed my friend; to call after.

hair (hâr), *n.* a threadlike growth from the skin of an animal; the entire growth of hair on an animal or on a human head; a very small distance, as to miss by a *hair.*

hairbreadth (hâr' bredth), *n.* a minute distance.

hairsplitting (hâr' split ing), *n.* the act of drawing very fine distinctions.

hairspring (hâr' spring), *n.* an extremely delicate spring regulating the movement of a balance wheel, as that of a watch.

hairy (hâr' i), *adj.* covered with hair; like hair.

***halcyon** (hal' si un), *adj.* peaceful, happy, calm.

hale (hāl), *adj.* physically sound, healthy.

hale (hāl), *v.t.* to move a person by force, as to *hale* him to court.

***half** (häf), *n.* [*pl.* halves] one of two equal parts. *adj.* consisting of half.

half (häf), *adv.* to the extent of one-half, as *half* past four; partly, as I was *half* drowned.

half blood (häf blud), *n.* one whose parents are of different races, a half-breed.

half-breed (häf' brēd), *n.* a person of mixed blood; especially in the U. S., the offspring of an American Indian and white person.

***halibut** (hal' i but), *n.* a large, flat sea fish, prized as a food fish.

halitosis (hal i tō' sis), *n.* disagreeable breath.

hall (hôl), *n.* a large room; a corridor or passage; a vestibule; a college building; a public building.

hallow (hal' ō), *v.t.* to consecrate, devote to sacred purposes.

hallucination (ha lū si nā' shun), *n.* belief in something purely imaginary and nonexistent as though it were real, a delusion.

halo (hā' lō), *n.* a ring of light appearing to encircle a luminous body; the bright ring shown in works of art around the heads of holy persons; the glory that surrounds a person or thing idealized.

halt (hôlt), *n.* a stop in marching; a break in any progress; lameness.

halt (hôlt), *v.i. and v.t.* to stop in marching; to bring to a stop; to check any progress, as to *halt* proceedings.

halt (hôlt), *adj.* lame, crippled.

halter (hôl' tēr), *n.* a rope on a headstall for leading or holding an animal, as a horse; a hangman's rope; an article of clothing worn by girls and women, tied around the neck and waist, leaving the shoulders bare.

halting (hôl' ting), *adj.* lame, limping, hesitant, as *halting* speech.

halve (häv), *v.t.* to divide into two equal parts.

***halyard** (hal' yērd), *n.* a rope or tackle for hoisting a flag or sail.

ham (ham), *n.* the back part of the thigh of an animal, especially of a pig; a hog's thigh, salted and smoked.

hame (hām), *n.* one of the two curved bars on a draft horse's harness to which the traces are attached.

hamlet (ham' let), *n.* a small village.

hammer (ham' ēr), *n.* a tool with a handle and an iron head for driving nails; any-

thing of similar construction, as the *hammer* of a gun, the *hammer* or padded mallet striking the wires in a piano, the weight on a handle used in throwing the *hammer.*

hammer (ham' ēr), *v.i. and v.t.* to strike heavy blows; to pound or drive with a hammer.

hammock (ham' uk), *n.* a swinging couch, usually of network or canvas; a hummock or ridge.

hamper (ham' pēr), *n.* a wicker basket usually having a cover, as a clothes *hamper.*

hamper (ham' pēr), *v.t.* to impede, obstruct.

hamstring (ham' string), *v.t.* [*p.t.* and *p.p.* hamstrung, *pr.p.* hamstringing] to lame by cutting the tendons at the back of the leg.

hand (hand), *n.* the part of the body with which one grasps; the broad flat member at the lower end of the arm, connected with it by the wrist and divided into thumb, fingers and palm; anything resembling a hand in appearance, structure or use, a pointer, as the *hands* of a clock; a measure of 4 inches; style of penmanship, as to write a good *hand;* cards dealt to one player in one round of the game; a manual worker, as a farm-*hand;* assistance, as to lend a *hand;* ability, as try your *hand* at this; direction, side, as on the right *hand;* source, as first*hand* knowledge; any part in an action, as I had a *hand* in that.

hand (hand), *v.t.* to give or pass with the hand, as *hand* me that book.

hand (hand), *adj.* associated with or done by the hand, as *hand*work.

handcuff (hand' kuf), *n.* a manacle, a metal ring that can be locked around the wrist, used to fetter criminals.

handicap (han' di kap), *n.* a hindrance, disadvantage; a disadvantage (or advantage) to a contestant to make the match more even, as in a race.

handicraft (han' di kráft), *n.* an occupation requiring manual skill; expertness in working with the hands.

handiwork (han' di wûrk), *n.* work done by hand; the product of personal effort, as that bookcase is my own *handiwork.*

***handkerchief** (hang' kēr chif), *n.* a square of cloth for wiping the eyes, face or nose; a similar square worn about the neck, a neckerchief.

handle (hand' l), *n.* the part of anything made and meant for grasping with the hand.

handle (hand' l), *v.t.* to touch or feel with the hand; to manage, manipulate, control, as I will *handle* that business.

handmaid (hand' mād), *n.* a female personal attendant.

***handsome** (han' sum), *adj.* good-looking, as a *handsome* person; considerable, generous.

handspike (hand' spīk), *n.* a wooden lever for moving heavy weights; a capstan bar.

handy (hand' i), *adj.* [*comp.* handier, *superl.* handiest] skilled in using the hands; convenient, nearby.

hang (hang), *v.t. and v.i.* [*p.t.* and *p.p.* hung or hanged, *pr.p.* hanging] to suspend, to fasten to something above, as to *hang* curtains; to hold or carry in a lowered position, as to *hang* the head; to suspend by the neck until dead, as to *hang* a murderer; to dangle, be suspended, as the fruit *hung* just out of reach; to threaten, hover, as misfortune *hangs* over him.

*hangar (hang' ĕr), *n*. a shed for aircraft.

hanger (hang' ĕr), *n*. that by which something is suspended, a form upon which an article of clothing is hung; one who suspends, as a paper hanger.

hangings (hang' ingz), *n. pl.* draperies, curtains and wall decorations.

hangman (hang' man), *n.* [*pl.* hangmen] a public executioner.

hangnail (hang' nāl), *n.* a small piece of skin hanging from the root of a fingernail.

hank (hangk), *n.* two or more skeins of silk or yarn fastened together.

hanker (hang' kĕr), *v.i.* to desire keenly, as to *hanker* for ice cream.

haphazard (hap haz' ĕrd), *adv.* by chance, at random.

hapless (hap' les), *adj.* unfortunate, unlucky.

happen (hap' en), *v.i.* to occur, come about, befall.

Syn. Chance. To *happen* is to take place or occur; to *chance* is to occur by accident.

happily (hap' i li), *adv.* fortunately; joyously.

happiness (hap' i nes), *n.* the state of being happy, joyousness.

happy (hap' i), *adj.* [*comp.* happier, *superl.* happiest] enjoying life, contented; causing joy or happiness, as a *happy* chance; expressing joy, as a *happy* smile; apt, as a *happy* reply.

harangue (ha rang'), *n.* a ranting public speech.

*harass (har' as), *v.t.* to annoy, vex, weary; to pillage, raid, lay waste.

*harbinger (här' bin jĕr), *n.* a forerunner, messenger, as birds are *harbingers* of spring.

harbor (här' bĕr), *n.* a port or haven for ships, a sheltered arm of a large body of water, with docks and piers.

harbor (här' bĕr), *v.t.* to shelter or protect; to cherish; to entertain, indulge, as to *harbor* ill will.

hard (härd), *adj.* compact and solid; difficult to pierce or break; difficult to do; stern, unyielding.

Syn. Difficult, arduous. That is *hard* which will not yield to a compressing force; a *difficult* task is one that requires skill; *arduous* suggests wearisome exertion.

hard coal (härd kōl) anthracite.

hard disk (härd' disk), *n.* a disk that is not flexible.

harden (här' dn), *v.i. and v.t.* to become hard or harder, as mortar *hardens*; to make hard or harder, as to *harden* the heart.

hardheaded (härd hed' ed), *adj.* obstinate.

hardhearted (härd här' ted), *adj.* cruel, unsympathetic.

hardly (härd' li), *adv.* laboriously; scarcely.

Syn. Scarcely. *Hardly* means with difficulty; *scarcely* means with scant margin.

hardship (härd' ship), *n.* privation; anything hard to bear.

hardware (härd' wâr), *n.* metal manufactured

articles, as tools, utensils, nails.

hardy (här' di), *adj.* vigorous, sturdy, strong; bold, brave.

hare (hâr), *n.* a rabbit-like rodent, timid, herbivorous.

harebrained (hâr' brānd), *adj.* heedless, flighty.

harelip (hâr' lip), *n.* a malformation of the upper lip, dividing it in the middle, like a hare's lip.

*harem (hā' rem), *n.* the apartments in a Mohammedan home for women and children; the women of a Mohammedan family.

hark (härk) *v.i.* to listen. *interj.* listen!

*harlequin (här' lē kwin), *n.* the buffoon in a pantomime.

harm (härm), *n.* injury, damage.

harm (härm), *v.t.* to hurt, injure, damage.

harmonic (här mon' ik), *adj.* having concord of sounds; pertaining to harmony as distinguished from melody and rhythm.

harmonica (här mon' i ka), *n.* a mouth organ.

harmonics (här mon' iks), *n. pl.* the science of musical sounds.

harmonious (här mō' ni us), *adj.* concordant, adapted one to another; peaceful.

harmonize (här' mō niz), *v.i. and v.t.* to produce harmony; to bring into harmony.

harmony (här' mō ni), *n.* [*pl.* harmonies] concordance of sounds; the science treating of musical composition in chords; agreement and co-operation.

harness (här' nes), *n.* the working gear of a horse; equipment.

harness (här' nes), *v.t.* to put harness on.

harp (härp), *n.* a large musical instrument of triangular shape, wired, and played with the fingers; any object or contrivance resembling a harp.

harp (härp), *v.i.* to dwell upon a subject with tedious repetition: used with on or *upon*, as she *harps* on his faults.

harpoon (här pōōn'), *n.* a long, barb-headed spear having a line attached to the shaft, used in hunting whales.

harpsichord (härp' si kôrd), *n.* a stringed instrument with a keyboard, an early form of the piano.

harpy (här' pi), *n.* a greedy, covetous, grasping person; one resembling the Harpies of classical mythology.

harrow (har' ō), *n.* an agricultural implement, drawn over plowed land to break up clods of earth and smooth the soil. *v.t.* to run a harrow over, as plowed land; to torment and torture, as it *harrows* my very soul.

harrowing (har' ō ing), *adj.* agonizing, as a *harrowing* experience.

harry (har' i), *v.t.* [*p.t. and p.p.* harried, *pr.p.* harrying] to annoy greatly, harass.

harsh (härsh), *adj.* discordant, hard-toned; rough; austere.

hart (härt), *n.* the male of the red deer, a stag.

hartebeest (härt' bēst), *n.* a large African antelope, having erect curved horns, no mane.

harvest (här' vest), *n.* the reaping season; the gathering in of crops; that which is reaped and gathered.

harvest (här' vest), *v.i. and v.t.* to reap and gather, as a crop; to win, as a reward or gain from service or investment.

hash (hash), *n.* a dish of chopped meat and vegetables; a jumble or botch.

hash (hash), *v.t.* to cut up and mix; to botch, as a job: *hash* over, to go over and over the same ground in discussion.

hasp (hásp), *n.* a small bar secured by a padlock.

haste (hāst), *n.* quick action, speed, impatient hurrying.

Syn. Precipitancy, hurry, bustle. *Haste* denotes rapidity and urgency; *hurry* implies confusion and flurry; *bustle* denotes commotion; *precipitancy* is headlong, excessive or rash haste.

haste (hāst), *v.i. and v.t.* to hurry, cause to go faster, hasten.

hasten (hās' n), *v.i. and v.t.* to cause to make haste; to expedite; to hurry, as he *hastened* into the building.

hasty (hās' ti), *adj.* [*comp.* hastier, *superl.* hastiest] hurried, fast, impetuous, impulsive, rash.

hat (hat), *n.* an article of clothing worn on the head.

hatch (hach), *n.* an opening in a floor, deck or roof, as at the top of a ladderway, with flat, removable covering or lid; lower half of a divided door. *n.* brood of young birds leaving the eggs at one time.

hatch (hach), *n.* one of the fine, crossed lines used in a drawing or etching to shade the picture. *v.t. and v.i.* to produce, as from eggs, as to *hatch* chickens; to produce young, as the eggs *hatched* today. *v.i.* to mark with fine cross lines, as a drawing.

hatchery (hach' ĕr i), *n.* a place where eggs are hatched artificially, as by incubators.

hatchet (hach' et), *n.* a small ax.

hatchway (hach' wā), *n.* a rectangular opening in a ship's deck for passage by men or goods.

hate (hāt), *n.* intense dislike, detestation.

hate (hāt), *v.t.* to dislike intensely, detest.

Syn. Detest, abhor, abominate, loathe. To *hate* is a general term signifying intense aversion, especially accompanied by ill will; to *abhor* implies deep-rooted antagonism or repugnance; to *abominate* is to detest in the highest degree; to *loathe* is to regard with utter disgust.

Ant. Love.

hateful (hāt' fool), *adj.* malignant, obnoxious, extremely offensive.

Syn. Odious, obnoxious, offensive. *Hateful* implies something that excites actual aversion; *odious* something exceedingly disagreeable; *obnoxious* implies something objectionable; *offensive* applies to that which is displeasing or insulting, as an *offensive* odor; an *offensive* attitude.

hatred (hā' tred), *n.* bitter aversion, malevolence, sustained hostility of feeling.

haughtiness (hô' ti nes), *n.* the quality of being haughty.

Syn. Disdain, arrogance. *Haughtiness* is

founded on a high opinion of oneself; *disdain*, on a low opinion of others. *Arrogance* combines the two feelings. *Haughtiness* and *disdain* are essentially mental states; *arrogance*, a mode of action springing from a state of mind.

Ant. Humility, meekness, modesty.

*****haughty** (hô' ti), *adj.* [*comp.* haughtier, *superl.* haughtiest] proud, overbearing, disdainful.

haul (hôl), *n.* a strong pull, as I gave it a *haul;* distance traversed by something pulled, as a long *haul;* things obtained by means of a pulling action, as a *haul* of fish in a net. *v.t.* to pull; to move by pulling, as to *haul* a train.

*****haunch** (hônch), *n.* the leg and loin of an animal taken together; this part used as meat.

haunt (hônt), *n.* a place to which one frequently resorts.

*****haunt** (hônt), *v.t.* to frequent, as a place; to appear and reappear, as a ghost; to fill the mind constantly, as the idea *haunts* me.

*****hauteur** (hō tûr), *n.* a disdainful manner or bearing, air of conscious superiority.

have (hav), [*p.t.* and *p.p.* had, *pr.p.* having] to hold, as I *have* a pen in my hand; to own, possess, as he *has* a farm, to *have* fears, I *have* an idea; to experience, as to *have* fun; to enjoy, as every dog *has* his day; to give birth to, as to *have* a baby; to be under obligation or compulsion, as we *have* to leave soon; to cause to be or do, bring about, as we *had* the garden weeded; *have* nothing to do with dishonest practices. As an auxiliary verb *have* is used to form the present perfect, past perfect and future perfect tenses of other verbs, as I *have* walked, I *had* walked, I shall *have* walked.

haven (hā' ven), *n.* a harbor; a port or shelter for ships; any place of refuge.

havoc (hav' uk), *n.* destruction, devastation, ruin, waste.

haw (hô), *interj.* a driver's call to a draft animal or team directing it toward the driver or to the left: opposite of *gee.*

hawk (hôk), *n.* a fast-flying, strong bird of prey.

hawk (hôk), *v.t.* to peddle, as wares by crying them in the street.

*****hawser** (hô' zēr), *n.* a thick rope or cable used in towing, mooring or anchoring a ship.

hawthorn (hô' thorn), *n.* a prickly shrub or tree of the rose family.

hay (hā), *n.* grass, clover, alfalfa, cut and dried for use as fodder.

haycock (hā' kok), *n.* a conical pile of hay in a field.

hazard (haz' ĕrd), *n.* a risk; something risked as in a gamble.

hazard (haz' ĕrd), *v.t.* to risk; to stake on a chance, as money.

Syn. Risk, venture. One *hazards* an opinion; he *hazards* money in a card game; *hazards* his life in a battle. One *risks* his life in trying to save another. He *ventures* (money) in business, taking the chance of losing in order to be in line for profits.

hazardous (haz' ẽrd us), *adj.* risky, perilous, chancy.

haze (hāz), *n.* a slight fog or mist; dimness of sight; mental confusion or vagueness.

hazel (hāz' el), *n.* a shrub or tree bearing an edible nut.

hazel (hāz' el), *adj.* made of hazel wood; having a soft reddish-brown color.

hazy (hā' zi), *adj.* misty; obscure.

he (hē), *pron.* [*pl.* they] the man mentioned; anyone, as *he* who runs may read: the masculine pronoun of the third person, singular.

head (hed), *n.* the highest part of the human body, holding the brain and the face, with eyes, nose and mouth in front, the ears on the sides; the principal part of anything, as the *head* of a hill; a leader, commander or chief executive; the top part or upper end of anything, as the *head* of a cane, a bed, a line of persons, a *head* of cabbage, the *head* of an article in a newspaper; the *head* of a boil; intellect, as a good *head* for figures; the source, as the *head* of a stream; an individual, as 20 *head* of cattle, $5 a *head*.

head (hed), *v.t.* and *v.i.* to lead; to stand at the head of, as to *head* a line; to supply with a heading, as to *head* a newspaper article; to form a head, as cabbage *heads* heavily.

head (hed), *adj.* principal or chief, as the *head* man; coming from in front, as a *head* wind; leading, as the *head* horse.

heading (hed' ing), *n.* a headline or set of headlines over an article.

headland (hed' land) *n.* a promontory; unplowed land strip at sides of a field.

headline (hed' lin), *n.* a line of type at the top or head of a page or column in a book, newspaper, magazine, giving a title.

headlong (hed' lông), *adv.* headfirst.

headphone (hed' fōn), *n.* a receiver for telephone or radio held over the ear by a band worn around the head.

headquarters (hed' kwôr tẽrz), *n.* a central establishment, as the *headquarters* of a business enterprise, *headquarters* of a brigade; the quarters of a high commanding officer.

headstrong (hed' strông), *adj.* ungovernable, self-willed.

headway (hed' wā), *n.* the momentum or a vehicle; distance run after power is shut off; progress; the interval, especially of time, between two trains or the like running in the same direction; any kind of progress, as we are making good *headway;* clearance, as under a bridge.

heady (hed' i), *adj.* precipitate; intoxicating.

heal (hēl), *v.i.* and *v.t.* to become well or sound, as the wound *heals* slowly; to make well or sound, as the doctor *healed* me quickly.

health (helth), *n.* mental, physical or moral soundness; freedom from disease.

healthful (helth' fool), *adj.* promoting health, salubrious.

healthy (helth' i), *adj.* [*comp.* healthier, *superl.* healthiest] sound and well, free

from disease.

    Syn. Wholesome, salubrious, salutary, healthful. The outdoor life keeps one *healthy*. Good food is *wholesome*. Fresh air is *salubrious*. That which serves to remove a disorder is *salutary*. Exercise is *healthful*.

    Ant. Delicate, diseased, frail, sick.

heap (hēp), *n.* a number of things or quantity of one thing thrown together in a mass.

heap (hēp), *v.t.* to form into a heap; to pile up.

hear (hẽr), *v.t.* and *v.i.* [*p.t.* and *p.p.* heard, *pr.p.* hearing] to listen to, perceive through the ear; to heed; to have the sense of hearing.

hearing (hẽr' ing), *n.* the sense by which sounds are perceived; a judicial investigation in which principals and their witnesses are heard.

hearsay (hẽr' sā), *n.* common report.

hearsay (hẽr' sā), *adj.* heard at second hand, as *hearsay* evidence.

hearse (hûrs), *n.* a vehicle for carrying the dead to the grave.

heart (härt), *n.* the organ, in animals, by which the blood is pumped through the system; the core or center of anything, as the *heart* of the city, the *heart* of a melon; tenderness, sympathy, sweetness of character, one of a suit of cards marked with red hearts.

heartburn (härt' bûrn), *n.* a burning sensation in the stomach caused by indigestion.

*****hearth** (härth), *n.* an open fireplace; the family circle.

hearty (här' ti), *adj.* [*comp.* heartier, *superl.* heartiest] cordial, sincere, warm, kindly; vigorous, strong, as a *hearty* laugh.

    Syn. Warm, sincere, cordial. A man should be *hearty;* his heart should be *warm;* his talk should be *sincere;* his reception of others *cordial*.

    Ant. Cold, distant, formal.

heat (hēt), *n.* the sensation produced by near approach to or contact with a hot body; high temperature; ardor.

heat (hēt), *v.t.* to make hot, increase the temperature of.

heated (hēt' ed), *adj.* excited, animated, as a *heated* discussion.

heath (hēth), *n.* a tract of land covered with a growth of heather.

*****heathen** (hē *then*), *n.* a pagan, idolator.

heathenish (hē' *then* ish), *adj.* irreligious, ignorant, unenlightened.

*****heather** (heth' ẽr), *n.* a low evergreen shrub.

heat shield (hēt shēld), *n.* the outside covering on the spacecraft which protects the craft from the heat of re-entry.

*****heave** (hēv), *n.* an effort in moving or throwing a heavy object.

heave (hēv), *v.t.* and *v.i.* to hoist or lift up; to throw a heavy object with great effort, as to *heave* a boulder; to bring up from inside, as to *heave* a sigh; to rise and fall alternately, as his shoulders *heaved*.

heaven (hev' en), *n.* the abode of God and the blessed; the sky; a state of bliss.

heavenly (hev' en li), *adj.* blissful.

heavy (hev' i), *adj.* [*comp.* heavier, ~~swperl.~~ heaviest] having much weight, as a *heavy* load; dejected, as a *heavy* heart; dull, as a *heavy* discourse; of more than the usual amount, as a *heavy* fall of snow.

*hebdomadal (heb dom' a dal), *adj.* weekly, every seven days.

heckle (hek' l), *v.t.* to bait; to harass, bother, as by questions or taunts.

hectic (hek' tik), *adj.* pertaining to the wasting away of animal tissues, as in consumption, as a *hectic* flush.

hector (hek' tẽr), *v.t.* to bully, domineer.

hedge (hej), *n.* a fence of bushes or shrubs, closely grown.

hedgehog (hej' hog), *n.* a small, insectivorous animal having quills on its back; a porcupine.

heed (hẽd), *n.* close attention.

heed (hẽd), *v.i.* and *v.t.* to give attention; to take notice of; to listen to and accept, as to *heed* a warning.

heedful (hẽd' fool), *adj.* attentive, mindful.

heel (hẽl), *n.* the hinder part of a foot or of an article of footgear, as a shoe or stocking.

heel (hẽl), *v.i.* and *v.t.* to supply with a heel, as to *heel* a shoe; to follow at one's heels, as a dog; to tilt or incline, as a sailboat.

heft (heft), *n.* weight. *v.t.* to raise; to try the weight of; to try to lift.

hefty (hef' ti), *adj.* heavy, as a *hefty* load.

*heifer (hef' ẽr), *n.* a young cow.

*height (hit), *n.* the measure of anything from bottom to top; stature; elevation; an elevated piece of land; the topmost reach, as the *height* of folly.

heighten (hit' n), *v.t.* and *v.i.* to give more height to; to intensify; to rise in height, increase.

*heinous (hã' nus), *adj.* hateful, atrocious, flagrant.

Syn. Flagrant, flagitious, atrocious. A crime is *heinous* that seriously offends against the laws of man; a sin is *heinous* that seriously offends against God's will; an error is *flagrant* that is glaring and inexcusable; *flagitious* is that which is villainous, scandalous or corrupt; a crime is *atrocious* when it is accompanied by inhumane conduct.

heir (âr), *n.* one who succeeds to a title or inherits property.

heiress (âr' es), *n.* a female heir.

heirloom (âr' lōōm), *n.* a piece of personal property handed down from one generation to another.

helical (hel' i kal), *adj.* spiral in shape, like the thread of a screw or a coiled spring.

helicopter (hel' i kop tẽr), *n.* a flying machine that can rise horizontally.

*heliograph (hẽ' li ō gráf), *n.* an apparatus to give signals by flashing sunlight from a mirror.

helioscope (hẽ' li ō skōp), *n.* a telescope so made as to protect the eyes when observing the sun.

*heliotrope (hẽ' li ō trōp), *n.* a plant with dainty flowers that turn toward the sun; the purplish color of its flowers.

*helium (hẽ' li um), *n.* a very light and non-inflammable gas used for inflating the gasbag of a dirigible.

hell (hel), *n.* the place of punishment for the wicked after death.

hello (he lō'), an exclamation used in informal greeting, calling the attention, answering a telephone.

helm (helm), *n.* the rudder of a boat or ship with the tiller or wheel by which the helmsman controls it; a post of command.

helmet (hel' met), *n.* a piece of leather or metal armor for the head; any protective covering for the head, in sport or war.

help (help), *n.* aid, assistance, support, succor; relief; a portion of food; servants or assistants collectively.

help (help), *v.t.* and *v.i.* to aid, as to *help* a friend; to render aid; to give assistance to; to serve food, as at the table.

Syn. Assist, aid, succor, relieve. To *help* is to do good to; to *assist* is to place oneself beside another to give him strength; to *aid* is to promote another's effort toward an end; to *succor* is to go to the help of anyone; to *relieve* is to alleviate. We *succor* one who is in danger; *relieve* one who is in distress.

Ant. Hinder, hamper, weaken.

hem (hem), *n.* the edge of a garment doubled and sewn, to prevent fraying.

hemisphere (hem' is fẽr), *n.* half a globe; half the earth, as the eastern and western *hemispheres.*

hemlock (hem' lōk), *n.* a large evergreen tree of the pine family; a wild poisonous plant of the carrot family.

hemorrhage (hem' o rij), *n.* a strong flow of blood.

hemorrhoids (hem' o roidz), *n. pl.* bleeding piles.

hemp (hemp), *n.* a tough-fibered plant from which rope and certain coarse fabrics are made.

hemstitch (hem' stich), *n.* a particular kind of ornamental stitching.

hen (hen), *n.* the female of the domestic fowl and other birds.

hence (hens), *adv.* from here; for this reason.

henceforth (hens fôrth'), *adv.* from this time on.

henchman (hench' man), *n.* [*pl.* henchmen] a follower, as in politics.

hepatic (hẽ pat' ik), *adj.* pertaining to the liver.

hepatica (hẽ pat' i ka), *n.* a plant of the crowfoot family.

*heptagon (hep' ta gon), *n.* a figure having seven sides and seven angles.

her (hûr), *pron.* objective and possessive case, singular, of *she.*

herald (her' ald), *n.* an official who proclaims messages from a sovereign; a messenger, forerunner, one who brings tidings. *v.t.* to proclaim, announce, usher in.

*heraldic (he ral' dik), *adj.* pertaining to the science of armorial bearings.

heraldry (her' ald ri), *n.* the art or science of

armorial bearings and coats of arms.

herb (ûrb), n. a plant with a soft stem that produces seed and then withers; a plant with commercial uses, especially medicine.

*__herbage__ (ûr′ bĭj), n. grasses; foliage and young stems of plants.

*__herbarium__ (hûr bâr′ ĭum), n. [pl. herbariums or herbaria] a place where dried plants are classified and kept for study.

herbiferous (hûr bĭf′ ẽr us), adj. producing herbs and grasses.

herbivorous (hûr bĭv′ ŏ rus), adj. feeding on herbs and grasses.

herd (hûrd), n. a group of cattle; a crowd, mob.

herd (hûrd), v.i. and v.t. to go together; to form into a herd.

here (hēr), adv. in this place; at this point.

hereafter (hēr ăf′ tẽr), n. the future; the life after this one.

hereafter (hēr ăf′ tẽr), adv. after this moment or time; henceforth.

hereby (hēr bī′), adv. by virtue of this or by means of this.

hereditary (hē red′ ĭ ter ĭ), adj. inheritable; inherited, acquired by inheritance.

heredity (hē red′ ĭ tĭ), n. the transmission of physical or mental qualities from one generation to another; the tendency of any living thing to reproduce the characteristics of its ancestors.

herein (hēr ĭn′), adv. in or into this.

heresy (her′ e sĭ), n. [pl. heresies] a belief contrary to that which is commonly accepted or maintained by authority.

heretic (her′ e tĭk), n. one who rejects the commonly accepted beliefs.

heretofore (hēr too fōr′), adv. up to the present; until now.

herewith (hēr wĭth′), adv. with this.

*__heritage__ (her′ ĭ tĭj), n. an estate acquired through birthright, an inheritance.

hermit (hûr′ mĭt), n. one who lives apart from human companionship.

hermitage (hûr′ mĭ tĭj), n. a secluded residence; the home of one who has retired from the world.

hernia (hûr′ nĭa), n. a rupture.

*__hero__ (hē′ rō), n. [pl. heroes] a man of extraordinary courage; one who performs great deeds; the principal figure in a story or play.

heroic (hē rō′ ĭk), adj. like a hero; marked by great courage; larger than lifesize.

*__heroine__ (her′ ō ĭn), n. a female hero.

*__heroism__ (her′ ō ĭzm), n. the assembled qualities of a hero; splendid courage.

heron (her′ un), n. a wading bird with long neck and legs.

heronry (her′ un rĭ), n. a place where herons breed.

herpes (hûr′ pēz), n. a virus disease which causes eruptions of small blisters on the skin.

*__herring__ (her′ ĭng), n. an edible sea fish that moves in great schools.

herringbone (her′ ĭng bōn), n. a pattern made up of rows of parallel lines sloping at opposite angles like a herring's backbone.

hers (hûrz), pron. the possessive form of she,

used alone, as the book is hers.

herself (hûr self′), pron. a form of the pronoun for the feminine third person singular used for emphasis, as she herself told me; reflexive form of her, as she hurt only herself; her normal or true self, as wait until she is herself again.

hesitancy (hez′ ĭ tan sĭ), n. hesitation; indecision.

*__hesitate__ (hez′ ĭ tāt), v.i. to pause in doubt, speak with a stammer.

Syn. Falter, demur. To hesitate is to be undecided; to falter suggests unsteadiness, wavering, flinching, as his courage faltered; to demur is to delay because of some objection.

*__heterodox__ (het′ ẽr ŏ doks), adj. differing from accepted standards of belief; opposed to orthodox.

heterodoxy (het′ ẽr ŏ dok sĭ), n. [pl. heterodoxies] an unorthodox belief.

*__heterogeneous__ (het ẽr o jē′ nē us), adj. dissimilar, composed of unlike parts.

hew (hū), v.i. and v.t. [p.t. hewed, p.p. hewn or hewed, pr.p. hewing] to use an ax; to cut or shape, with or as with, an ax.

hexagon (hek′ sa gon), n. a plane figure having six sides and six angles.

hexameter (heks am′ ē ter), n. a verse with six feet or metrical divisions, especially the Greek and Latin heroic verse, dactylic hexameter.

*__hiatus__ (hī ā′ tus), n. a break, interruption of continuity, a gap.

*__hibernal__ (hī bûr′ nal), adj. wintry.

hibernate (hī′ bẽr nāt), v.i. to den up and sleep for the winter as a bear; to pass the winter season, without vegetating, as the spores and winter buds of various plants.

*__hiccough__ (hik′ up), n. a sound like a sharp gasp, with sudden drawing in of breath, caused by convulsive contraction of the diaphragm and throat.

hickory (hik′ ŏ rĭ), n. [pl. hickories] an American nut-bearing tree with very hard wood; the wood of this tree.

hide (hīd), n. the skin of an animal.

hide (hīd), v.i. and v.t. [p.t. hid, p.p. hidden, pr.p. hiding] to conceal oneself; to conceal some object; to make a secret of, as to hide the facts.

hidebound (hīd′ bound), adj. having a tight skin, as an animal, or bark, as a tree; narrow-minded, prejudiced, obstinate.

*__hideous__ (hĭd′ ē us), adj. ugly, horrible, repulsive.

hie (hī), v.i. [p.t. and p.p. hied, pr.p. hieing] to hurry.

*__hierarchy__ (hī′ ẽr är kĭ), n. the clergy of a church, according to rank.

*__hieroglyphic__ (hī′ ẽr ŏ glĭf′ ĭk), n. a symbol or picture used as writing by the ancient Egyptians.

high (hī), adj. elevated, as high land; strong, as high winds.

highroad (hī′ rōd), n. a main road.

highhanded (hī han′ ded), adj. arbitrary, overbearing.

highway (hī′ wā), n. a public road.

highwayman (hī' wā man), *n.* one who robs those who travel on a public road.

*****hilarious** (hi lâr' i us), *adj.* noisily merry.

*****hilarity** (hi lar' i ti), *n.* [*pl.* hilarities] noisy merriment.

hill (hil), *n.* a natural elevation of land not as great as a mountain; a small stack of dirt, as an ant*hill*, or a *hill* of potatoes.

hill (hil), *v.t.* to form into a hill; to draw earth around, as to *hill* potatoes.

hillbilly (hil' bil i), *n.* a Southern mountaineer or backwoodsman.

hillock (hil' uk), *n.* a small hill.

hilly (hil' i), *adj.* [*comp.* hillier, *superl.* hilliest] abounding in hills; steep.

hilt (hilt), *n.* a handle of a sword or dagger.

him (him), *pron.* the objective case of *he,* as I asked *him.*

himself (him self'), *pron.* a form of the pronoun for the masculine third person singular, used for emphasis; as a simple objective, as he bought it for *himself;* in apposition, as John *himself* did it; reflexively, as he cut *himself.*

hinder (hin' dẽr), *adj.* belonging to or constituting the back or rear.

*****hinder** (hin' dẽr), *v.t.* to prevent; to obstruct, thwart, impede.

hindmost (hind' mōst), *adj.* furthest from the front; in the extreme rear.

hindrance (hin' drans), *n.* an obstruction, impediment, obstacle to progress.

hinge (hinj), *n.* the joint on which a door, gate or lid turns or swings; a natural joint, as of an oyster shell.

hinge (hinj), *v.i. and v.t.* to turn upon, as the argument *hinges* on this fact; to furnish with hinges.

hint (hint), *n.* an indirect allusion or suggestion. *v.i. and v.t.* to suggest indirectly.

hip (hip), *n.* the upper fleshy part of the thigh; the joint of two sloping parts of a roof.

hippie (hip´ ē), *n.* one of a group of young people who wears informal and eccentric clothing, has a preoccupation with drugs, and an interest in communal living.

hippodrome (hip' ō drōm), *n.* a course for chariot races, surrounded with tiers of seats; any arena.

*****hippopotamus** (hip ō pot' a mus), *n.* [*pl.* hippopotamuses or hippopotami] a huge thick-skinned amphibious animal that lives in and along African rivers.

hire (hīr), *n.* the act of hiring; wages paid for personal work; that which is paid for use of anything belonging to another. *v.t.* to employ for wages; to engage for temporary use, as to *hire* an automobile; to place at another's service, temporarily, for pay.

hireling (hīr' ling), *n.* one who serves for hire; one who will sell his honor for personal gain.

*****hirsute** (hûr' sūt), *adj.* hairy.

his (hiz), *pron.* the possessive form of *he,* adjective or pronoun, as it is *his* book; this book is *his.*

hiss (his), *n.* a whistling noise made by forcing breath between tongue and upper teeth.

v.i. and v.t. to express disapproval by means of a hiss; to utter with a hiss; to condemn by hissing, as they *hissed* him off the stage.

histology (his tol' ō ji), *n.* the scientific study of plant and animal tissues.

historian (his tō' ri an), *n.* a writer or student of history.

historic (his tor' ik), *adj.* having a history, as a *historic* place.

*****historical** (his tor' i kal), *adj.* pertaining to history, as *historical* studies.

*****history** (his' tō ri), *n.* [*pl.* histories] a full account of the past, as of a nation or country, with interpretive and explanatory comment that distinguishes it from mere annals or chronicles; a history text; any narrative or story; a historical drama.

histrionic (his tri on' ik), *adj.* pertaining to acting, to actors or to the stage in a general way; theatrical.

hit (hit), *n.* a stroke or blow; a success, as the play was a *hit. v.i. and v.t.* [*p.t.* and *p.p.* hit, *pr.p.* hitting] to collide; to strike; to deliver a blow.

hitch (hich), *n.* a sudden jerk; a limp, as to walk with a *hitch;* an obstacle, impediment, as a *hitch* in the plans; a temporary noose, loose knot or other means of connecting two things. *v.i. and v.t.* to become entang: d; to move jerkily, as he *hitched* forward; to fasten or tie, as *hitch* your horse to the tree; to pull with a jerk, as *hitch* up your socks.

hither (hith' ẽr), *adj.* on the side toward the speaker, as the *hither* side. *adv.* to this place, as come *hither.*

hitherto (hith ẽr tōō'), *adv.* up to this time; until now.

hive (hīv), *n.* a house for bees; the bees that live in it; any place crowded with busy workers.

hive (hīv), *v.i. and v.t.* to gather in a hive; to place in a hive, as bees; to store up, as honey.

hives (hīvz), *n. pl.* a skin disease with itching blotches, caused by inability to digest certain foods, as shellfish and strawberries.

hoar (hōr), *n.* white frost. *adj.* gray or white with age, ancient.

hoard (hōrd), *n.* a secret store or treasure.

hoard (hōrd), *v.t. and v.i.* to accumulate secretly, and store, as to *hoard* gold; to amass money, as to *hoard* for the future.

hoarding (hōrd' ing), *n.* a temporary board fence in front of a building under construction; a billboard.

hoarfrost (hōr' frôst), *n.* white particles of frozen dew.

hoarse (hōrs), *adj.* rough and harsh in sound, as the voice when one has a bad cold.

hoax (hōks), *n.* a mischievous deception, especially of the public, by means of an imaginary story presented as true.

hoax (hōks), *v.t.* to deceive with a trick.

hob (hob), *n.* the flat part of a grate on which things are set to be kept warm; the peg at which quoits are thrown.

hobble (hob' l), *v.i. and v.t.* to walk with a limp; to cause to limp, lame, as to *hobble* a horse; to fetter.

hobby (hob' i), n. [pl. hobbies] a favorite pursuit or object.

hobnail (hob' nāl), n. a short thick nail with a heavy head for studding shoe soles.

hobnob (hob' nob), v.i. to associate in an intimate, free-and-easy way.

hock (hok), n. the hind ankle of a horse; a cut of pork just above the foot.

hockey (hok' i), n. a game played on ice or turf, with sticks and a puck.

hocus-pocus (hō' kus pō' kus), n. a juggler's word; a juggling trick; tomfoolery.

hod (hod), n. a wooden trough on a long handle, held over the shoulder, for carrying mortar and bricks.

hodgepodge (hoj' poj), n. a mixture of different things, a disorderly collection.

hoe (hō), n. an implement with a flat blade and a long handle, for use in gardening.

hoe (hō), v.i. and v.t. [p.t. and p.p. hoed, pr.p. hoeing] to work with a hoe; to cultivate by hoeing.

***hog** (hog), n. a swine; a greedy, gluttonous person. v.i. to become buckled or curved like a hog's back, as a ship's bottom when strained.

hogshead (hogz' hed), n. a liquid measure; a large cask.

***hoist** (hoist), n. an apparatus for lifting things; a tackle; an elevator.

hoist (hoist), v.t. to lift, as with tackle.

hold (hōld), n. the cargo space in the interior of a ship. n. a firm grip; a place where prisoners are held, as a jail; a fortified place, stronghold. v.t. and v.i. to have possession of; to retain; to contain; to harbor, as to hold a grudge; to carry on or join in, as to hold a meeting; to maintain in a specified state, as to hold oneself prepared; to remain steadfast or faithful, cleave, as to hold to an ideal; to persist, as the law still holds.

holding (hōl' ding), n. anything held or owned, as stocks and bonds or a farm.

hole (hōl), n. an opening through something, as a coat or a wall; a pit; cavity; a metal cup sunk in the ground, into which a golf ball must be struck.

holiday (hol' i dā), n. a day of celebration of some great event in the past; a day off from work.

holiness (hō' li nes), n. the quality of being consecrated to the worship of God; freedom from sin: His Holiness, the Pope.

Syn. Sanctity, righteousness. Holiness suggests an inherent quality; sanctity, an acquired state, often implying sacredness and inviolability as well; righteousness denotes unswerving obedience to the divine law rather than complete spiritual purity and freedom from sin.

holland (hol' and), n. a fine unbleached linen or cotton.

hollow (hol' ō), n. a cavity; an unfilled space; a lower space between bordering hills.

hollow (hol' ō), v.t. and v.i. to make hollow, excavate, scoop out; to become hollow.

hollow (hol' ō), adj. having a void space within, as a hollow tree; insincere; super-

ficial; muffled, deep sounds, as if coming from a hollow body.

holly (hol' i), n. a stubby tree with prickly, shiny leaves and red berries.

hollyhock (hol' i hok), n. a tall plant of the mallow family.

holster (hōl' stēr), n. a leather case for a pistol.

holy (hō' li), adj. [comp. holier, superl. holiest] morally and spiritually perfect; sinless; consecrated.

***homage** (hom' ij), n. respect manifested in external action, deference, reverence.

home (hōm), n. one's place of residence; the dwelling place of a family; a benevolent institution providing a dwelling place for persons without homes of their own. adj. pertaining to one's dwelling place, as home ties or to one's country, as home industries; domestic. adv. to or at home, as to go home.

homely (hōm' li), adj. [comp. homelier, superl. homeliest] simple, plain, comfortable; plain of feature, not handsome.

homesick (hōm' sik), adj. having an intense longing for home.

homestead (hōm' sted), n. dwelling and land of a family, especially of early settlers in the West.

***homicide** (hom' i sīd), n. the killing of one human being by another, whether by intention or not; manslaughter, murder or justifiable homicide, as in self-defense.

homiletics (hom i let' iks), n. the branch of theology that treats of sermons and their composition.

homily (hom' i li), n. [pl. homilies] a formal public sermon; a formal private discourse on religious topics.

hominy (hom' i ni), n. hulled corn, coarsely ground.

***homogeneity** (hō mō jē nē' i ti), n. the quality of being similar, uniformity.

***homogeneous** (hō mō jē' nē us), adj. composed of similar parts, uniform throughout.

***homonym** (hom' ō nim), n. one of two or more words with identical pronunciation but different spelling and meaning, as rain, rein, reign.

***hone** (hōn), n. a fine whetstone for sharpening razors. v.t. to sharpen on whetstone, as to hone a razor; to long or yearn, as he honed for his friends.

***honest** (on' est), adj. trustworthy, true, as honest measure; frank, sincere and open, as an honest manner.

honesty (on' es ti), n. the quality of being truthful.

honey (hun' i), n. a thick, sweet substance that bees make from nectar.

honeydew (hun' i dū), n. a sweet deposit left on leaves by plant lice and on which ants, bees and other insects feed; a kind of cantaloupe.

honeymoon (hun' i mōōn), n. the first month after marriage; a journey by a newly married couple.

honeysuckle (hun' i suk l), n. a climbing plant with sweet flowers.

***honor** (on' ēr), n. a fine sense of what is just

and right with readiness to apply it to one's own conduct in relation to others; great respect; wide and good reputation; any token of recognition for distinguished services or high merit. *v.t.* to treat with respect, revere; to bestow honors upon; to recognize, as a business obligation and meet it, as to *honor* a claim; to recognize as correct and pay, as to *honor* a draft.

Syn. Respect, esteem. To *honor* is an outward act; to *esteem* is to hold in high regard, appreciate, prize.

honorable (on' ĕr a bl), *adj.* guided by the sense of honor; worthy of being honored; upright, straightforward and honest; used also as a title of distinction, as the *Honorable* John Smith.

*****honorarium** (on ŏ rär' i um), *n.* a fee paid to a professional man for services, where professional ideals forbid the setting of a price.

honorary (on' ĕr er i), *adj.* done, or conferred, as an honor, as an *honorary* degree.

hood (hood), *n.* a soft, loose covering for the head; an ornamental fold on the back of an academic gown.

hoof (hōōf), *n.* [*pl.* hoofs or hooves] the foot of certain animals, as the horse, cow, deer, hard and horny.

hoofbound (hōōf' bound), *adj.* suffering from a disease in which the hoof dries and contracts painfully.

hook (hook), *n.* a curved piece with which to catch hold of things; a cape of which the end points inland or toward a mainland, as Sandy Hook. *v.i. and v.t.* to have shape of a hook, as the cape *hooks* inward; to catch with a hook, as to *hook* a fish; to fasten with a hook, as she *hooks* her cape together.

hoop (hōōp), *n.* a circular band holding something together, as a barrel; a ring for the finger; a circular piece of wood or metal rolled along the ground by children for sport.

hoot (hōōt), *n.* the cry of an owl, or a sound resembling it; a jeer. *v.i. and v.t.* to make a sound like the owl's cry; to jeer.

hop (hop), *n.* a vine whose pistillate cones are used in making medicine and to give a bitter taste to malt liquors. *n.* a jump taking off and landing with the same foot; the leap of a frog, in which all the feet leave the ground and come down at once; a flight by airplane. *v.t. and v.i.* to jump or leap about or over, as to *hop* a wall; to jump, as the bird *hopped*.

hope (hōp), *n.* the desire and expectation of good, anticipation; the act of hoping; that for which one hopes, as my *hope* is that you may succeed.

hope (hōp), *v.i.* to desire, with expectation of fulfilment, as to *hope* for the best.

hope chest (hōp chest), a collection of clothes and linens accumulated by a young woman in anticipation of her marriage.

hopeful (hōp' fool), *adj.* full of hope; inspiring hope and promising success, as a *hopeful* outlook, a *hopeful* sign.

horde (hôrd), *n.* a multitude.

horehound (hôr' hound), *n.* a bitter mint plant with whitish fuzzy leaves used for coughs and colds or as flavoring in candy.

*****horizon** (hō rī' zn), *n.* the circular line where the sky seems to meet the earth or sea; the limit of vision, physical or mental.

horizontal (hor i zon' tal), *adj.* related to the horizon, level, not vertical.

hormone (hôr' mōn), *n.* a chemical substance or secretion which when it is carried by the blood from the organ in which it originates to another, stimulates the second organ.

horn (hôrn), *n.* a pointed process or growth on the head of a hoofed animal, as the bull or deer; something resembling such a growth or something made of horn; the substance of which horns are composed; a wind instrument, originally made of hollow horns.

hornblende (hôrn' blend), *n.* a common hard mineral, dark green or black.

hornet (hôrn' net), *n.* a stinging wasp.

hornpipe (hôrn' pip), *n.* a lively dance.

horoscope (hor' ŏ skōp), *n.* a representation of the heavens at any given time, by which astrologers profess to foretell the future of persons born at that time.

horrible (hor' i bl), *adj.* terrible, dreadful.

*****horrid** (hor' id), *adj.* hideous; dreadful.

horrify (hor' i fi), *v.t.* [*p.t.* and *p.p.* horrified, *pr.p.* horrifying] to fill with horror, strike with horror.

horror (hor' ĕr), *n.* the greatest fear or dread.

hors de combat (ôr de kon bä'), disabled, as from fighting.

hors d'oeuvres (ôr dŭ' vr), a small portion of food, especially something tart, served as an appetizer before meals.

horse (hôrs), *n.* a four-footed, solid-hoofed animal, used for riding or for pulling loads; a framework to support things, as a sawhorse.

horsefly (hôrs' fli), *n.* a large fly that sucks blood from animals.

horsepower (hôrs' pou ĕr), *n.* a unit of mechanical power equal to the power needed to raise 33,000 pounds at the rate of one foot per minute, as a *horsepower* of 120.

horse-radish (hôrs rad' ish), *n.* a plant with a long root having a pungent flavor, ground and used as a relish.

horticulture (hôr' ti kul tūr), *n.* the art or science of growing trees or plants.

hose (hōs), *n.* coverings for the legs, stockings.

hose (hōs), *n.* a flexible tube for carrying water or other fluids.

hosiery (hō' zher i), *n.* stockings.

*****hospitable** (hos' pi ta bl), *adj.* generous and warm hearted in receiving and entertaining visitors.

hospital (hos' pit al), *n.* a medical institution for the care of the sick.

hospitality (hos pit al' i ti), *n.* the practice of entertaining visitors with kindness.

host (hōst), *n.* one who entertains another; the proprietor of an inn; an organism giving nourishment to a parasite.

host (hōst), *n.* the consecrated bread of the Eucharist.

hostage (hos' tĭj), *n.* one held by an enemy as a pledge for fulfilment of certain stated conditions.

hostile (hos' tĭl), *adj.* pertaining to an enemy; showing ill will, unfriendly.

hostility (hos tĭl' ĭ tĭ), *n.* [*pl.* hostilities] the state of being an enemy; an act of enmity.

hostler (hos' lẽr), *n.* one who takes care of horses.

hot (hot), *adj.* [*comp.* hotter, *superl.* hottest] having great heat; burning, fiery, passionate, furious; having a sharp taste, as highly spiced food.

Syn. Fiery, burning, ardent. A temper is said to be *hot* or *fiery*; the mind is *ardent* in pursuit of an object. Zeal may be *hot, fiery, burning* and *ardent*.

Ant. Cold, indifferent.

hotel (hō tel'), *n.* an establishment that provides lodging and meals for pay.

hothouse (hot' hous), *n.* glass-roofed, heated building for cultivation of plants out of season.

hound (hound), *n.* a hunting dog. *v.t.* to pursue, with dogs or as if with dogs; to track down; to pursue relentlessly.

hour (our), *n.* one twenty-fourth of a day, 60 minutes; an appointed time.

hourglass (our' glås), *n.* a device for measuring time, by running sand from one bulb to another; a sandglass that marks off one hour.

house (hous), *n.* a building for residence, one of the divisions of a legislative body; a business establishment.

house (houz), *v.t.* to furnish with a house; to shelter.

household (hous' hōld), *n.* a group of persons who live together; a family in one home.

***hovel** (huv' el), *n.* a shed; a mean home, shack.

***hover** (huv' ẽr), *v.i.* to flutter over or about; to settle over, as a hen her chicks.

how (hou), *adv.* in what manner, as *how* do you do that? to what degree or extent, as *how* far are you going?

however (hou ev' ẽr), *adv.* in whatever manner or degree; nevertheless; notwithstanding.

howitzer (hou' ĭt sẽr), *n.* a short cannon.

howl (houl), *n.* a prolonged cry, like that of a wolf; the whistle of the wind.

howl (houl), *v.i.* to utter a mournful cry; to make a cry of pain or distress.

hoyden (hoi' dn), *n.* a boisterous girl, tomboy.

hub (hub), *n.* the turning point of a wheel; a central part; the peg used in pitching quoits.

hubbub (hub' ub), *n.* uproar.

huckleberry (huk' l ber' ĭ), *n.* [*pl.* huckleberries] a low-growing shrub with a seedy, berrylike fruit; the fruit of this shrub.

huckster (huk' stẽr), *n.* a peddler, one who sells a variety of small goods, as from a cart.

huddle (hud' l), *n.* a crowd; a group of persons in close contact.

huddle (hud' l), *v.i.* to crowd together.

***hue** (hū), *n.* a shade of color.

huff (huf), *n.* a fit of petulance.

huff (huf), *v.i. and v.t.* to puff; to bully; to remove a piece that has failed to jump in a game of checkers.

hug (hug), *n.* a close embrace. *v.t.* to embrace; stay close to, as the boat *hugged* shore.

huge (hūj), *adj.* very large.

hulk (hulk), *n.* the body of a ship, especially when old and disabled.

hulking (hulk' ĭng), *adj.* unwieldy, clumsy, as a *hulking* fellow.

hull (hul), *n.* the outer covering or husk of a seed; the body of a ship.

hullabaloo (hul' a ba lōō), *n.* an uproar.

hum (hum), *n.* the noise made by bees and other insects in flying; the sound of distant machinery or a plane aloft.

hum (hum), *v.i.* to make a noise like that of a bee in heavy flight; to make a noise like the sustained sound of *m,* or sing with the lips closed, as to *hum* a tune; to bring about great activity, as to make things *hum*.

***human** (hū' man), *adj.* pertaining to mankind.

humane (hū mān'), *adj.* kind, merciful.

Syn. Charitable, compassionate, sympathetic, tender hearted. Whereas *human* indicates the ordinary attributes of humanity, *humane* denotes what may rightly be expected of mankind at its best. The *compassionate* man sympathizes with and desires to relieve suffering.

Ant. Cruel, harsh, ruthless, merciless.

humanitarian (hū man ĭ târ' ĭ an), *n.* a philanthropist. *adj.* philanthropic.

humanity (hū man' ĭ tĭ), *n.* [*pl.* humanities] mankind; the qualities of kindness and sympathy.

***humble** (hum' bl), *adj.* modest, unassuming.

Syn. Lowly. A man is *humble* from a sense of his imperfections; he is *modest* inasmuch as he sets little value on his qualifications and acquirements.

Ant. Proud, arrogant, haughty.

humbug (hum' bug), *n.* a fraud; an impostor.

humdrum (hum' drum), *adj.* dull, monotonous, commonplace.

humerus (hū' mẽr us), *n.* [*pl.* humeri] the bone of the upper arm, from the shoulder to the elbow.

humid (hū' mid), *adj.* damp, moist.

humidity (hū mid' ĭ tĭ), *n.* dampness, especially with reference to the condition of the air.

humiliate (hū mil' ĭ āt), *v.t.* to bring low, humble, put to shame, as he *humiliated* me publicly.

humility (hū mil' ĭ tĭ), *n.* modesty, mildness, freedom from pride; unpretentiousness.

hummingbird (hum' ĭng bûrd), *n.* a small, long-beaked bird.

hummock (hum' uk), *n.* a small mound; a ridge or pile of ice on an ice floe.

***humor** (hū' mẽr), *n.* the quality in anything that appeals to a sense of the comic and provokes mirth; the faculty that makes it possible to discover, appreciate and express things that are funny; a mood, as in a good *humor;* any fluid of the human body or

other organism. *v.t.*, to indulge, gratify, as to *humor* one's whims.

hump (hump), *n.* a rounded protuberance, especially that formed by a deformed spine.

humus (hū' mus), *n.* a black or brown substance found in soil, formed by decaying animal or vegetable matter.

hunch (hunch), *n.* a hump.

hunch (hunch), *v.t.* to round, as he *hunched* his shoulders.

hundred (hun' dred), *n.* one more than 99.

hundredth (hun' dredth), *n.* one of a hundred equal parts.

hundredth (hun' dredth), *adj.* following the 99th.

hunger (hung' gĕr), *n.* keenness of appetite; desire for food.

hunger (hung' gĕr), *v.i.* to long for; to be hungry.

hungry (hung' gri), *adj.* [*comp.* hungrier, *superl.* hungriest] wanting food.

hunt (hunt), *n.* the act of pursuing, a chase.

hunt (hunt), *v.i. and v.t.* to seek, as I *hunted* everywhere; to pursue, as game or wild animals; to search for.

hurdle (hûr' dl), *n.* a barrier to be jumped in a race.

hurl (hûrl), *v.t.* to throw with violence; to overthrow; to utter with violence, as to *hurl* accusations.

hurly-burly (hûr li' bur li), *n.* great confusion.

hurricane (hûr' i kān), *n.* a cyclone, usually accompanied by rain, thunder and lightning.

hurry (hûr' i), *n.* [*pl.* hurries] haste, as to go in a *hurry.* *v.i. and v.t.* to hasten.

hurt (hûrt), *n.* an injury; pain of body or mind. *v.i. and v.t.* to feel pain; to cause pain or damage; to cause physical pain to, as the blow *hurt* him; to wound the feelings of, as his words *hurt* her.

hurtful (hûrt' fool), *adj.* injurious, harmful.

hurtle (hûrt' l), *v.t. and v.i.* to fling, with force; to clash; to clatter; to move rapidly or rush suddenly.

husband (huz' band), *n.* a man who has a wife.

husband (huz' band), *v.t.* to manage economically, as to *husband* one's resources; to *husband* one's strength.

husbandman (huz' band man), *n.* [*pl.* husbandmen] a farmer.

hush (hush), *n.* a silence. *v.t.* to conceal, as a fact, by keeping silent. *interj.* be still!

husk (husk), *n.* the dry outer covering, as of an ear of corn.

husky (husk' i), *adj.* [*comp.* huskier, *superl.* huskiest] like husks; rough, as a voice; burly, strong.

hussar (hoo zär'), *n.* a member of the cavalry of a European army.

*hussy** (huz' i), *n.* [*pl.* hussies] a worthless woman; saucy girl.

*hustle** (hus' l), *v.t. and v.i.* to push roughly; to jostle.

hut (hut), *n.* a cabin, shanty.

hutch (huch), *n.* a bin, box or chest for storing things, as grain; a coop or pen for animals, as a rabbit *hutch.*

hyacinth (hī' a sinth), *n.* a handsome bulbous flowering plant of the lily family.

hyaline (hī' a lin), *adj.* transparent, like glass.

hybrid (hī' brid), *n.* an animal or plant produced by crossing two separate varieties.

hydrant (hī' drant), *n.* a vertical pipe through which water is drawn from a main, as for use in flooding streets or fighting fire.

hydrate (hī' drāt), *n.* a chemical compound containing water. *v.t. and v.i.* to combine with water.

hydraulic (hī drô'lik), *adj.* pertaining to water or other fluids in motion; operated by water.

*hydraulics** (hī drô' liks), *n.* *pl.* the science of fluids in motion.

*hydride** (hī' drid), *n.* a compound of hydrogen with another element.

hydrocarbon (hī drō kär' bon), *n.* a compound of hydrogen and carbon.

hydrogen (hī' drō jen), *n.* a colorless, gaseous, inflammable substance, the lightest element known.

hydrometer (hī drom' ē tĕr), *n.* a metal or glass tube that floats in a vertical position, used to determine specific gravities.

hydroplane (hī drō plān), *n.* motor driven racing boat of peculiar design adapted to operation only at high speed.

hydrophobia (hī drō fō' bi a), *n.* abnormal fear of water; a disease caused by the bite of a mad dog; rabies.

hydrophone (hī' drō fōn), *n.* an instrument for listening to sound transmitted through water, used in detecting submarines.

hydrostatics (hī drō stat' iks), *n.* the branch of physics that treats of fluids at rest, their pressure and equilibrium.

hydrotherapy (hī drō ther' a pi), *n.* treatment of disease with water.

hydrous (hī' drus), *adj.* containing water; watery.

hyena (hī ē' na), *n.* a wolf-like carnivorous animal of Asia and Africa.

*hygiene** (hī' jēn), *n.* the science of health; sanitary living.

hymn (him), *n.* a sacred song expressing adoration.

hymnal (him' nal), *n.* a church songbook.

*hyperbole** (hī pûr' bō lē), *n.* a figure of speech, obviously exaggerating.

hypertension (hī ' per ten ' shun), *n.* abnormally high blood pressure.

hyphen (hī' fen), *n.* a mark (-) joining two words compounded, or separating syllables, as at the end of a line of print.

*hypnotism** (hip' nō tizm), *n.* a method of inducing a trancelike sleep.

*hypocrisy** (hī pok' ris i), *n.* the act of pretending to be what one is not.

hypocrite (hip' ō krit), *n.* an insincere person; one who pretends to be what he is not.

*hypodermic** (hī pō dûr' mik), *adj.* inserted under the skin.

*hypotenuse** (hī pot' ē nūs), *n.* the side of a right-angled triangle opposite the right angle: formerly spelled *hypothenuse.*

*hypothesis (hǐ poth' ē sis), n. [pl. hypotheses] something assumed for the purpose of argument.

hypothetical (hǐ pō thet' ĭ kal), adj. assumed for the purpose of argument.

hysteresis (his tēr ē' sis), n. the property of a magnetic substance whereby it tends to continue in any state of magnetization.

*hysteria (his tēr' ĭ a), n. a nervous affection characterized by emotional excitement and lack of control, especially in fits of alternate laughing and crying.

I

I (I), pron. [pl. we] nominative singular of the first personal pronoun; the person speaking.

*ibex (i' beks), n. a wild goat, especially of the Swiss and Italian mountains.

*ibis (i' bis), n. a wading bird of the heron family with a long curved beak.

ice (is), n. frozen water; a frozen dessert not containing cream, as sherbet, orange ice; a substance resembling ice, as camphor ice.

ice (is), v.t. to cool with ice; to cover with frosting, as a cake.

ice age (is āj), the era in which the earth's surface was covered with ice or glaciers.

iceberg (is' bûrg), n. a floating mass of ice at sea, broken off from a glacier.

iceboat (is' bōt), n. a frame mounted on runners like skate blades and propelled over the ice by sails; a strong, heavy steamboat used to break a way through ice in rivers and harbors: also called icebreaker.

icebox (is' boks), n. a refrigerator.

ice floe (is flō), a floating field of ice at sea.

ice pack (is pak), a field of broken and drifting ice; a rubber bag filled with cracked ice, used to bring down a swelling or fever.

ichthyology (ik thi ol' ō ji), n. the branch of zoology that treats of fishes.

*icicle (i' sik l), n. a hanging cone of ice formed by water freezing as it drips.

icily (i si li), adv. in a cold, repelling manner.

icing (is' ing), n. a coating of fine sugar, white of egg and sometimes a flavoring, spread over a cake.

*icon (i' kon), n. [pl. icons] a sacred image.

*iconoclast (i kon' ō klast), n. a breaker of images; one who opposes cherished beliefs.

icy (i' si), adj. [comp. icier, superl. iciest] pertaining to or like ice; covered with ice; cold; frosty, as an icy window pane; cold in manner.

idea (i dē' a), n. a mental picture or pattern, as my idea of a whale; a plan, an intention, as my idea is to start on Tuesday; notion, an indefinite fancy.

*ideal (i dē' al), n. a mental picture of perfection as a model toward which to strive; a supreme standard; a person thought of as perfect enough to be imitated.

Syn. Pattern. An ideal is a standard of perfection, either real or mentally conceived; a pattern is something by which something else is made or something thought of as worthy of imitation.

ideal (i dē' al), adj. existing in the mind or in imagination only: opposite of real; conforming to a standard of perfection, as an ideal day to go fishing.

idealism (i dē' al izm), n. pursuit of perfection in life or art; the quality of seeing things as we wish they were instead of as they are: opposite of realism; the philosophical doctrine that mind and spirit are the only realities.

idealist (i dē' al ist), n. one who believes that reality is mental; one who in art or literature shows things as they should be instead of as they are; one who strives for perfection; a dreamer, an impractical person.

idealize (i dē' al iz), v.i. and v.t. to form ideals; to adopt as a standard of perfection; to attribute perfection to, as she idealizes her sister.

identical (i den' ti kal), adj. same, as this identical book; precisely alike, as fingerprints are never identical.

identify (i den' ti fi), v.t. [p.t. and p.p. identified, pr.p. identifying] to prove that something is the thing meant or involved, as in a case at law; to prove that something is one's own, as a piece of stolen property.

identity (i den' ti ti), n. sameness; a state of exact likeness; distinctive individuality, as to conceal one's identity.

*ideology (id ē ol' ō ji), n. the science of ideas; the philosophy that holds that ideas are derived only from experience; the system of beliefs characteristic of a person or of a school of thought.

idiocy (id' i ō si), n. a permanent condition of lack of intelligence due to an undeveloped brain or an abnormal brain condition.

idiom (id' ium), n. a turn of expression peculiar to a language or to an individual writer or speaker.

idiomatic (id i ō mat' ik), adj. expressed in idioms; characteristic of a language, as an idiomatic expression.

*idiosyncrasy (id i o sing' kra si), n. [pl. idiosyncrasies] a marked peculiarity of a person's nature or temperament.

idiot (id' i ut), n. a person born without the capacity to develop intelligence.

idle (i dl), adj. unemployed; lazy; futile; groundless, as an idle rumor.

Syn. Lazy, indolent. An idle person is one who is not busy, not actively occupied. lazy is a disparaging term and means not inclined or willing to work or to make an effort; indolent means fond of ease and not fond of exertion.

Ant. Active, busy, industrious.

idle (i' dl), v.i. to waste time by doing noth-

ing; to saunter; to run slowly in neutral, as an automobile engine.

*idol (I' dul), *n.* an image of a god; an object of worship or devotion.

idolater (I dol' *a* tẽr), *n.* an idol-worshiper.

idolatry (I dol' *a* tri), *n.* the worship of idols or images; any excessive devotion.

idolize (I' dul īz), *v.t.* to make an idol of; to adore with exaggerated reverence, as to *idolize* a hero.

*idyl or **idyll** (I' dil), *n.* a short description of rural scenes in poetry or prose.

idyllic (I dil' ik), *adj.* like an idyl; picturesquely rural or rustic; charming in simplicity.

if (if), *conj.* providing, on condition that, as I'll go *if* John goes; supposing that, as you will like the book *if* you read it; although, as the speech was witty *if* short; whether, as see *if* you can lift that rock.

igloo (ig' loo), *n.* an Eskimo house, usually made of snow or ice blocks.

igneous (ig' nē us), *adj.* pertaining to fire; caused by the action of fire and heat within the earth, fused, as *igneous* rocks.

ignite (ig nīt'), *v.i. and v.t.* to take fire; to set fire to, kindle.

ignition (ig nish' un), *n.* the act of kindling or state of being kindled; device for exploding gasoline charge in an engine.

ignoble (ig nō' bl), *adj.* of low birth or station; of mean character.

*ignominious (ig nō min' i us), *adj.* disgraceful; dishonorable, humiliating.

*ignominy (ig' nō min i), *n.* [*pl.* ignominies] public disgrace or dishonor.

*ignoramus (ig nō rā' mus), *n.* a hopelessly ignorant person.

ignorance (ig' nō rans), *n.* the state of being without knowledge.

ignorant (ig' nō rant), *adj.* destitute of knowledge; knowing little or nothing, uninformed; unaware, as I was *ignorant* of your arrival.
    Syn. Illiterate. An *ignorant* person is one lacking in education or knowledge; *illiterate* means definitely deficient in primary schooling, unable to read and write. A learned man may be *ignorant*, without knowledge, of many things outside his special field; the *illiterate* person may have much knowledge of practical things yet not be able to read or write.
    Ant. Learned, wise.

ignore (ig nōr'), *v.t.* to disregard; to treat as though unknown.

iguana (' gwä' na), *n.* a large herbivorous lizard of South and Central America.

iliac (il' i ak), *adj.* relating to the upper portion of the hipbone.

ilium (il' i um), *n.* the upper bone of the hip.

ill (il), *n.* an evil, a misfortune; an injurious fact, condition or influence; disease.

ill (il), *adj.* sick; unpropitious, as an *ill* wind; faulty, not proper as *ill* manners; bad, disagreeable, as an *ill* temper.

ill (il), *adv.* badly, poorly, as an *ill* done task, *ill* furnished.

illegal (il lē' gal), *adj.* contrary to law.

illegible (il lej' i bl), *adj.* undecipherable;

hard to read, as *illegible* writing.

illegitimate (il lē jit' i mit), *adj.* unlawful; born out of wedlock; illogical, as an *illegitimate* excuse.

illiberal (il lib' ẽr al), *adj.* not broadminded, bigoted; ungenerous.

*illicit (il lis' it), *adj.* forbidden, contrary to law or rule; improper, as *illicit* pleasures.

illimitable (il lim' it *a* bl), *adj.* without limits, immeasurable.

illiteracy (il lit' ẽr *a* si), *n.* lack of learning, especially inability to read and write.

illiterate (il lit' ẽr it), *adj.* unable to read and write, uneducated.

illness (il' nes), *n.* the condition of being ill, sickness, disease.

illogical (il loj' i kal), *adj.* not logical, not correctly reasoned.

illuminate (i lūm' i nāt), *v.t.* to light up, give light, enlighten; to throw light on, as to *illuminate* an obscure problem.
    Syn. Illumine, enlighten. We *illuminate* by means of artificial lights; the sun *illuminates* the world with its own light. Preaching and instruction *enlighten* the minds of men. *Illumine* is a poetic variation of *illuminate*.
    Ant. Darken, obscure.

illumination (i lū mi nā' shun), *n.* a lighting up; decoration with lights; intellectual or spiritual enlightenment.

illusion (i lū' zhun), *n.* a deceptive or unreal appearance; hallucination; a belief based on faulty reasoning.

*illusory (i lū' sō ri), *adj.* misleading, deceiving.

*illustrate (il' us trāt), *v.t.* to make clear, explain by examples; to adorn, as a book, with pictures.

*illustrative (i lus' tra tiv), *adj.* tending to elucidate or explain; serving as an example or picture.

illustrious (i lus' tri us), *adj.* distinguished, famous, eminent.

*image (im' ij), *n.* an imitation of a person or object, as a picture or statue; an exact likeness, as she is the *image* of her mother; a figure of speech.

*imagery (im' ij ri), *n.* [*pl.* imageries] representation by images; use of figures of speech in writing or talking; mental pictures, the result of memory or imagination.

imaginable (i maj' i na bl), *adj.* capable of being imagined or pictured in the mind.

imaginary (i maj' i nẽr i), *adj.* existing only in the mind, unreal, fancied.

imagination (i maj i nā' shun), *n.* the power of the mind to form pictures; a mental image or conception; creative mental power.

imagine (i maj' in), *v.i. and v.t.* to make mental images; to form a mental picture of; to fancy; to surmise.

*imbecile (im' bē sil), *n.* a person of feeble, simple mind, but not an idiot or moron.

*imbecile (im' bē sil), *adj.* mentally feeble.

imbibe (im bīb'), *v.t.* to drink in; to take in as if by drinking, as to *imbibe* knowledge.

imbrication (im bri kā' shun), *n.* overlapping of edges, as of shingles on a roof.

imbue (im bū'), *v.t.* to saturate with; to dye; to cause to be permeated, as the mind with ideas.

imitate (im' i tāt), *v.t.* to produce a likeness of, as to *imitate* another person's mannerisms; to take as a model, copy, mimic; to resemble.

imitation (im i tā' shun), *n.* act of copying or mimicking; a copy. *adj.* not genuine, artificial as *imitation* silk.

immaculate (i mak' ū lit), *adj.* spotless, pure; excessively clean, as *immaculate* linens.

immanent (im' a nent), *adj.* indwelling, inherent, subjective.

immaterial (im ma tēr' i al), *adj.* not composed of matter, spiritual; irrelevant, unimportant.

immature (im a tūr'), *adj.* not full-grown; unripe; crude, childish.

immeasurable (i mezh' ēr a bl), *adj.* beyond possibility of being measured, limitless.

immediate (i mē' di it), *adj.* next, not separated in time or space; close, with nothing intervening; direct, as *immediate* causes; belonging to the present moment, present, as *immediate* needs; nearest in relation, as one's *immediate* family.

*__immemorial__ (im mē mō' ri al), *adj.* extending back beyond the range of memory or record; very ancient.

immense ·(i mens'), *adj.* very large, vast, huge.

immensity (i men' si ti), *n.* [*pl.* immensities] vastness; huge bulk or wide extent.

immerse (i mūrs'), *v.t.* to plunge into and under water; to baptize by submerging the entire body; to engross, as to be *immersed* in one's work.

immigrant (im' i grant), *n.* a native of one country who enters another to settle permanently.

immigrate (im' i grāt), *v.i.* to enter a country of which one is not a native with the intention of establishing permanent residence.

imminent (im' i nent), *adj.* promising or threatening to happen at once, as *imminent* misfortune.

Syn. Impending. *Imminent* means about to happen immediately. *Impending* excludes the idea of the instant; it means hanging over indefinitely or accumulating. One may be in *imminent* danger of death; financial ruin may be *impending* for months.

immobility (im ō bil' i ti), *n.* the state of being fixed, stable, not in motion.

immoderate (im mod' ēr it), *adj.* excessive, intemperate, extravagant, extreme.

immodest (im mod' est), *adj.* bold, forward.

immolate (im' ō lāt), *v.t.* to offer as a sacrifice, kill in a sacrificial ceremony.

immoral (im mor' al), *adj.* not guided by the commonly accepted ideas of rightness in conduct, unprincipled.

immortal (i mōr' tal), *n.* one of imperishable fame.

immortal (i mōr' tal), *adj.* deathless, imperishable.

immune (i mūn'), *adj.* exempt, free, as *immune* from taxation; protected from a dis-

ease, as by vaccination or inoculation.

immune (i mūn'), *n.* one who is not subject to a certain disease.

immunity (i mū' ni ti), *n.* [*pl.* immunities] exemption from ordinary duties and burdens; the state of not being subject to a disease.

immure (i mūr'), *v.t.* to enclose within walls, imprison; to shut up as if within walls.

*__immutable__ (i mū' ta bl), *adj.* unchanging, unalterable.

imp (imp), *n.* a little devil, a goblin; a mischievous child.

impact (im' pakt), *n.* a collision; a forcible striking together that sets the struck body in motion.

impair (im pâr'), *v.t.* to weaken, damage; to lessen in quality.

Syn. Injure. To *impair* is to employ a progressive mode of injuring. To *injure* is to damage either through slow, sustained action or through an instantaneous act. Straining of the eyes *impairs* the sight; a blow *injures* rather than *impairs* the eye.

impale (im pāl'), *v.t.* to transfix, as with a stake.

impalpable (im pal' pa bl), *adj.* imperceptible to the touch; unsubstantial.

impanel (im pan' el), *v.t.* [*p.t.* and *p.p.* impaneled, *pr.p.* impaneling] to list or enroll for jury service; to select a jury from a list.

impart (im pärt'), *v.t.* to give a share of, bestow; to make known, disclose, as to *impart* knowledge or news.

*__impartial__ (im pär' shal), *adj.* fair to all concerned, showing no favoritism, just.

impasse (im pàs'), *n.* an unpassable road; anything that blocks advance; an unescapable predicament.

impassioned (im pash' und), *adj.* moved by, or showing strong or deep feeling, ardent.

impassive (im pas' iv), *adj.* lacking emotion, apathetic, indifferent, serene.

*__impatient__ (im pā' shi ent), *adj.* restless under stress, as of pain or opposition; eager, restless, hasty.

impeachment (im pēch' ment), *n.* the arraignment of a public officer for misconduct in office; a challenge to the credibility or validity, as of testimony.

impeccable (im pek' a bl), *adj.* faultless.

impecunious (im pē kū' ni us), *adj.* having no money; habitually poor.

impede (im pēd'), *v.t.* to obstruct, hinder, prevent the progress of.

impediment (im ped' i ment), *n.* anything that hinders or obstructs; an organic defect that hinders a function, as an *impediment* of speech.

impel (im pel'), *v.t.* [*p.t.* and *p.p.* impelled, *pr.p.* impelling] to drive forward; to force, constrain, as duty *impels* me.

impend (im pend'), *v.i.* to hang over and be or seem ready to fall; to be at hand or about to happen.

impenetrable (im pen' ē tra bl), *adj.* not to be entered, as a dense forest, pierced, as a wall, or solved, as a mystery; closed to argument, as a mind, or to sympathy, as a heart.

impenitence (im pen' i tens), *n.* absence of regret for faults or misdeeds.

imperative (im per' a tiv), *n.* the mood of a verb expressing command.

imperative (im per' a tiv), *adj.* expressing command, authoritative; obligatory, compulsory.

*__imperceptible__ (im pēr sep' ti bl), *adj.* beyond perception by the senses or the mind.

imperfect (im pûr' fekt), *adj.* incomplete, defective; denoting action continuing in the past but not completed, as in the sentence he was doing his chores, *was doing* is in the *imperfect* tense.

imperial (im pēr' i al), *adj.* pertaining to an empire or an emperor; supreme, as *imperial* power; designating the system of weights and measures used in the United Kingdom, as an *imperial* gallon.

imperil (im per' il), *v.t.* to place in danger, jeopardize.

imperious (im pēr' i us), *adj.* domineering, overbearing; urgent, as *imperious* necessity.

Syn. Imperative, peremptory. *Imperious* always means arrogant and overbearing; *imperative* means commanding, especially commanding with authority; *peremptory* means admitting of no denial or refusal.

imperishable (im per' ish a bl), *adj.* indestructible; not subject to decay; permanently enduring.

impermeable (im pûr' mē a bl), *adj.* not permitting passage through, especially not permitting liquids to pass through.

impersonal (im pûr' sun al), *adj.* without personality; not referring to any particular person; not expressing the action of a person or thing, having *it* for a subject, as an *impersonal* verb.

impersonate (im pûr' sun āt), *v.t.* to give personality to, personify; to imitate and mimic the appearance and mannerisms of another person.

impertinence (im pûr' ti nens), *n.* unfitness, as of words to an occasion or a subject; incivility; sauciness.

imperturbable (im pēr tûr' ba bl), *adj.* not easily disturbed or agitated, calm.

impervious (im pûr' vi us), *adj.* impenetrable.

*__impetuous__ (im pet' ū us), *adj.* hasty or rash in action, as a person, impulsive; rushing violently, as a stream.

*__impetus__ (im' pē tus), *n.* [*pl.* impetuses] a driving force; impulse to motion; incentive for action.

impiety (im pī' e ti), *n.* [*pl.* impieties] ungodliness, irreverence.

impinge (im pinj'), *v.i.* to strike, dash or collide; to come into close contact.

*__impious__ (im' pi us), *adj.* not pious, profane, irreverent.

*__implacable__ (im plā' ka bl), *adj.* not to be appeased, relentless.

implant (im plânt'), *v.t.* to cause to take root, as a plant in the ground, a principle in the mind.

implement (im' plē ment), *n.* an instrument

or tool for doing something.

implicate (im' pli kāt), *v.t.* to involve, bring into connection.

Syn. Involve. To *implicate* is literally to fold something into something else; to *implicate* therefore means to entangle and often to incriminate; to *involve* means to draw into, as one becomes *involved* in a quarrel, *implicated* in an accusation.

Ant. Extricate, remove.

implication (im pli kā' shun), *n.* an entanglement; something implied, from which an inference can be made.

implicit (im plis' it), *adj.* implied; understood but not expressed, as an answer is often *implicit* in a question; complete, utter, as *implicit* faith.

implore (im plōr'), *v.t.* to entreat, supplicate, pray.

imply (im plī'), *v.t.* [*p.t.* and *p.p.* implied, *pr.p.* implying] to suggest in a manner justifying an inference, without direct statement, to hint, to involve, as learning *implies* study.

impolite (im pō līt'), *adj.* ill-mannered, rude.

impolitic (im pol' i tik), *adj.* contrary to good policy, unwise.

*__import__ (im' pōrt), *n.* meaning; significance: *imports*, merchandise brought into a country from abroad.

import (im pōrt'), *v.t.* to bring in from abroad, as goods to be sold; to imply; to suggest.

important (im pōr' tant), *adj.* of much import or significance, momentous.

*__importune__ (im pōr tūn'), *v.t.* to address with repeated appeals, to request or urge persistently.

impose (im pōz'), *v.i. and v.t.* to take advantage, presume, as to *impose* on someone's hospitality; to place, inflict, lay, as to *impose* a burden on a friend, a tax on the public; to lay out, as pages of type, in order and lock up in the frame for printing.

imposing (im pōz' ing), *adj.* impressive in size or power.

impossible (im pos' i bl), *adj.* not capable of happening, being or being done; objectionable, as an *impossible* person.

impost (im' pōst), *n.* that which is imposed or levied, as a tax or duty, especially a customs duty.

*__impostor__ (im pos' tēr), *n.* one who deceives others by presenting himself in an assumed character or pretending to knowledge he does not possess; a swindler.

*__impotence__ (im' pō tens), *n.* feebleness of mind or body, weakness.

impound (im pound'), *v.t.* to shut up in a pen, as stray dogs; to seize and hold by law, confiscate; to collect (water) for irrigation.

impoverish (im pov' ēr ish), *v.t.* to make poor, reduce to poverty; to exhaust, as land.

impracticable (im prak' ti ka bl), *adj.* unworkable, unusable; not feasible.

imprecation (im prē kā' shun), *n.* the invoking of evil, a curse.

impregnable (im preg' na bl), *adj.* not to be captured, unconquerable, as a fortress;

unassailable, as an argument.

impregnate (im preg' nāt), *v.t.* to make pregnant, get with young; to saturate, imbue, as the mind with principles.

impress (im pres'), *v.t.* to mark, as with a die; to affect deeply, as your letter *impressed* me.

impression (im presh' un), *n.* the mark made by a die or stamping machine; an image in the mind, an effect of sensation or influence; a vague notion or memory.

impressionable (im presh' un *a* bl), *adj.* easily impressed or influenced.

imprint (im' print), *n.* a mark caused by pressure; the publisher's name and address on the title page of a book.

imprison (im priz' n), *v.t.* to put in prison; to confine in any way.

improbable (im prob' *a* bl), *adj.* unlikely to be or to occur; not easy to believe or expect.

impromptu (im promp' tū), *adj.* without preparation, extemporaneous, as an *impromptu* speech. *adv.* without preparation, on the spur of the moment, as he spoke *impromptu.*

improper (im prop' ẽr), *adj.* unsuitable, as garments *improper* for a wedding; not in accord with conventional conduct or good taste; indecent; incorrect, as the *improper* use of a word: *improper fraction,* a fraction having a numerator larger than the denominator, as 7/4.

impropriety (im prō prī' e ti), *n.* [*pl.* improprieties] the quality of being improper; an improper act; a mistake in grammar or usage.

improve (im proov'), *v.i. and v.t.* to grow better; to make better; to increase value of, as piece of land, by erecting buildings on it.

improvement (im proov' ment), *n.* anything that contributes to betterment; the state of becoming better, as in health or value: *improvements,* buildings enhancing the value of land, or permanent fixtures added to a house.

improvidence (im prov' i dens), *n.* lack of foresight or forethought, lack of thrift.

improvise (im' prō vīz), *v.i. and v.t.* to compose extemporaneously; to make or do on the spur of the moment, as to *improvise* a shelter.

imprudent (im proo' dent), *adj.* indiscreet, unwise, not cautious.

impudent (im' pū dent), *adj.* boldly forward, pert, insolent, saucy.

impugn (im pūn'), *v.t.* to assail with arguments; to attack or challenge as false.

impulse (im' puls), *n.* the act of driving onward; sudden force causing motion forward; any incitement to unconsidered action, as the *impulse* to laugh; a motive or instinctive tendency; as a man of inexplicable *impulses.*

impulsive (im pul' siv), *adj.* acting on impulse or feeling; caused by feeling, as an impulsive word; having power to impel or move forward.

impunity (im pū' ni ti), *n.* [*pl.* impunities] freedom from punishment or painful consequences.

impure (im pūr'), *adj.* mixed with extraneous matter or with some inferior substance, adulterated; dirty, unwholesome, as *impure* water.

impurity (im pū' ri ti), *n.* [*pl.* impurities] the state of not being clean or of being mixed with inferior substances; a defect in physical composition or moral character.

imputation (im pū tā' shun), *n.* the making of insinuations; an insinuation.

impute (im pūt'), *v.t.* to ascribe or charge, as to *impute* a mistake to ignorance.

in (in), *prep.* not beyond the limits of in space or time, within, as London is *in* England, a bird *in* a cage, *in* 1895 A.D.; during, as it happened *in* the spring, *in* parting, let me say; after, at the end of, as come back *in* an hour; within an enclosing substance, as dressed *in* velvet, wrapped *in* paper, soaked *in* milk; within as a condition or activity, as *in* fear, rule *in* splendor, live *in* ease, be *in* publishing; within the scope of, as not *in* the memory of man; within the ability of, as it is *in* her to succeed; uttered or written according to, as a letter *in* cipher, a book *in* English; by way of, as *in* apology.

in (in), *adv.* to or toward the inside, as come *in,* the ship is headed *in.*

in (in), *adj.* incoming, as the *in* traffic.

inaccurate (in ak' ū rit), *adj.* not strictly correct, inexact, having error.

inactive (in ak' tiv), *adj.* inert; sluggish, indolent; idle.

inadequate (in ad' ē kwit), *adj.* not enough; not equal to a need.

inadvertent (in ad vûr' tent), *adj.* done without attention, inattentive, unintentional.

inalienable (in āl' yen *a* bl), *adj.* not to be removed or transferred, as *inalienable* rights.

inane (in ān'), *adj.* empty, pointless, meaningless.

inanimate (in an' i māt), *adj.* without life, as a chair is an *inanimate* object; dull, not animated, as an *inanimate* expression.

inanity (in an' i ti), *n.* [*pl.* inanities] senselessness; emptiness, as of speech; an empty pointless saying.

inarticulate (in är tik' ū lāt), *adj.* not uttered clearly or so as to be understood; unable to speak, dumb, as *inarticulate* animals; lacking joints, as certain animals.

inasmuch (in az much'), *adv.* in like degree; insofar: *inasmuch as,* because, since.

inaudible (in ô' dibl), *adj.* too low or distant to be heard.

inaugural (in ô' gū ral), *adj.* pertaining to an inauguration, as an *inaugural* address.

inauspicious (in ôs pish' us), *adj.* ill-omened, unfavorable, unpromising.

inborn (in' bôrn), *adj.* natural, innate.

inbred (in' bred), *adj.* natural, innate; born of related parents.

incalculable (in kal' kū la bl), *adj.* too great or too numerous to be reckoned.

incandescent (in kan des' ent), *adj.* glowing with heat, so as to give light.

incantation (in kan tā' shun), *n.* a magical formula spoken or sung.

incapacitate (in ka pas' i tāt), *v.t.* to deprive

of ability to act or function.

incapacity (in ka pas' i ti), *n.* [*pl.* incapacities] lack of power; legal disqualification.

incarcerate (in kär' sẽr āt), *v.t.* to imprison.

incarnation (in kär nā' shun), *n.* assumption of flesh; embodiment in human form.

incautious (in kô' shus), *adj.* unwary, reckless.

*** incendiary** (in sen' di er i), *n.* [*pl.* incendiaries] a person guilty of arson; one who inflames public passions.

incendiary (in sen' di er i), *adj.* pertaining to deliberate setting afire of property; tending to inflame the passions of the people.

*** incense** (in' sens), *n.* any aromatic substance burned for fragrance, as during religious ceremonials.

incense (in sens'), *v.t.* to make angry.

incentive (in sen' tiv), *n.* a motive for action.

inception (in sep' shun), *n.* the beginning, as of an idea, institution or custom.

incessant (in ses' ant), *adj.* unceasing, continual.

inch (inch), *n.* the twelfth part of a foot in linear measure.

*** inchoate** (in kô' it), *adj.* just begun, incomplete, rudimentary.

incidence (in' si dens), *n.* the act of falling upon or affecting, as a ray of light upon a surface.

incident (in' si dent), *n.* an occurrence. *adj.* appertaining to, as duties *incident* to office; impinging upon, as an *incident* ray.

incidental (in si den' tal), *adj.* constituting a minor element of some action or occurrence, casual.

incinerate (in sin' ẽr āt), *v.t.* to burn to ashes.

incipient (in sip' i ent), *adj.* beginning to be or appear.

*** incise** (in sīz'), *v.t.* to cut lines or characters into the surface of; to engrave.

incision (in sizh' un), *n.* a cut, as in surgery.

*** incisive** (in sī' siv), *adj.* cutting, sharp; trenchant, as words.

incite (in sīt'), *v.t.* to rouse to action; to stir up, as to *incite* to rebellion.

incivility (in si vil' i ti), *n.* [*pl.* incivilities] the quality of impoliteness; a rude act.

inclement (in klem' ent), *adj.* harsh; merciless; stormy, as the weather.

inclination (in kli nā' shun), *n.* a slant; a leaning or tendency of the mind; propensity.

   Syn. Tendency, propensity, proneness. All these terms are used to designate the state of the will toward an object. *Inclination* denotes the first movement in that direction; a *tendency* is a continuing *inclination*. *Propensity* and *proneness* both designate, etymologically, a downward direction, and therefore refer commonly to that which is bad or low; one has a *propensity* or *proneness* to lying.

   Ant. Disinclination, repulsion.

*** incline** (in' klīn), *n.* a slope; a slanting flat surface.

incline (in klīn'), *v.i.* and *v.t.* to lean or slope; to cause to lean or slope; to have a mental tendency, as to *incline* toward business.

inclose (in klōz'), *v.t.* to shut in, as with a fence; to insert with something else, as a card is *inclosed* with a letter; to enclose.

include (in klōōd'), *v.t.* to contain as a part; to class with; to inclose.

*** inclusive** (in klōō' siv), *adj.* inclosing; including all, as the 15th to the 21st *inclusive*.

incoherence (in kō hēr' ens), *n.* lack of cohesion; the state of not holding together; lack of logic, in speech or writing; inconsistency.

incombustible (in kom bus' ti bl), *adj.* not to be consumed by fire.

incommensurate (in ko men' shoo rit), *adj.* out of proportion to; inadequate.

*** incommunicable** (in ko mū' ni ka bl), *adj.* not able or fit to be told.

*** incomparable** (in kom' pa ra bl), *adj.* beyond compare; without an equal.

incompatible (in kom pat' i bl), *adj.* incapable of harmonious relations; incongruous.

incompetent (in kom' pē tent), *adj.* deficient in ability or fitness; not legally qualified; inadmissible, as evidence.

incomplete (in kom plēt'), *adj.* not finished, lacking some part, imperfect.

incomprehensible (in kom prē hen' si bl), *adj.* not to be grasped by the mind; beyond belief.

inconceivable (in kon sēv' a bl), *adj.* incapable of being conceived or pictured by the mind, unthinkable.

*** inconclusive** (in kon klōō' siv), *adj.* leading to no final settlement; unconvincing.

*** incongruity** (in kong grōō' iti), *n.* [*pl.* incongruities] lack of mutual fitness; something that is unsuitable to a situation.

*** incongruous** (in kong' groo us), *adj.* reciprocally disagreeing; not associating harmoniously.

inconsequent (in kon' sē kwent), *adj.* not springing logically from preceding acts or statements; lacking logical connection with the subject.

inconsiderable (in kon sid' ẽr a bl), *adj.* not worth considering, unimportant.

inconsiderate (in kon sid' ẽr it), *adj.* lacking proper regard for the comfort, welfare or feelings of others.

inconsistent (in kon sis' tent), *adj.* illogical; self-contradictory.

inconsolable (in kon sōl' a bl), *adj.* not to be comforted.

inconspicuous (in kon spik' ū us), *adj.* too small or unimportant to attract notice or attention; not standing out in the surroundings.

inconstant (in kon' stant), *adj.* unstable, subject to change, fickle, variable.

incontestable (in kon tes' ta bl), *adj.* beyond dispute; incontrovertible.

incontrovertible (in kon trō vûr' ti bl), *adj.* not admitting of controversy, argument or debate.

*** inconvenience** (in kon vēn' yens), *n.* the state of not being convenient; that which causes discomfort or annoyance. *v.t.* to go against another's comfort and ease; to cause discomfort or annoyance, to trouble.

Syn. Annoy, molest. We *inconvenience* others by causing them trouble and bother. We *annoy* or *molest* by doing that which is positively irritating, painful or harmful. We may be *inconvenienced* by another's absence, or *annoyed* by his presence. To *molest* is to cause injury or seriously to disturb.

inconvertible (in kon vûr' ti bl), *adj.* not to be changed into something else or exchanged for something else.

inconvenience **incorporate** (in kôr' pŏ rāt), *v.i. and v.t.* to unite with another body, forming a new unit, as in business; to unite, as individuals, groups, organizations or firms, into a new legally recognized unit.

incorporation (in kôr pŏ rā' shun), *n.* the act of incorporating; the result of such action, or the new entity so formed: also called *corporation*.

incorporeal (in kôr pŏ' re al), *adj.* having no material or bodily existence.

incorrect (in ko rekt'), *adj.* having error; inaccurate; improper, as *incorrect* behavior.

incorrigible **incorrigible** (in kor' i ji bl), *adj.* too hopelessly bad to be corrected.

incorruptible (in ko rup' ti bl), *adj.* incapable of physical decay; not subject to moral contamination; not to be influenced by offers of bribes.

increase (in' krēs), *n.* growth in size or number; the amount by which anything is enlarged.

increase (in krēs'), *v.i. and v.t.* to grow in size or number; to augment.

Syn. Grow. To *increase* is to become larger either by instantaneous act or by gradual process; to *grow* is to enlarge only through the latter method.

Ant. Decrease, fade, decline.

incredible (in kred' i bl), *adj.* beyond belief.

incredulity (in krē dū' li ti), *n.* the act of withholding belief, unbelief.

incredulous (in kred' ū lus), *adj.* indicating disbelief or unbelief; not credulous, doubting, skeptical.

increment (in' krē ment), *n.* an increase; an added amount, as the *increment* of money at interest.

incriminate (in krim' i nāt), *v.t.* to charge with a crime, indicate guilt, accuse.

incrust (in krust'), *v.t.* to cover with a crust.

incrustation (in krus tā' shun), *n.* a crusty covering.

incubator (in' kū bā tēr), *n.* an apparatus for hatching eggs artificially or for maintaining the life of a premature or delicate baby.

incubus (in' kū bus), *n.* [*pl.* incubuses or incubi] a nightmare; an oppressive weight or burden.

inculcate **inculcate** (in kul' kāt), *v.t.* to plant in the mind, as principles, by constant admonition.

inculpate (in kul' pāt), *v.t.* to blame; to incriminate; to accuse, expose to blame.

incumbent (in kum' bent), *n.* the present holder of an office. *adj.* imposed as a duty, as it is *incumbent* on me to go.

incur (in kûr'), *v.t.* [*p.t.* and *p.p.* incurred,

pr.p. incurring] to become subject to, as to *incur* displeasure; to contract, as a debt.

incurable (in kūr' a bl), *n.* a person diseased beyond hope of recovery. *adj.* beyond possibility of cure.

incursion (in kûr' zhun), *n.* an inroad, raid, invasion.

indebted (in det' ed), *adj.* resting under obligation.

Syn. Obliged. We are *indebted* to one who renders an essential service, *obliged* to one who confers any service. A man is *indebted* to one who saves his life; *obliged* to another for an ordinary act of civility.

indecent (in dē' sent), *adj.* not decent; unfit to be seen or heard; offensive to the common standards of propriety.

indecision **indecision** (in dē sizh' un), *n.* a wavering, faltering state of mind, irresolution.

indecisive **indecisive** (in dē sī' siv), *n.* not leading to a decision, inconclusive.

indecorous **indecorous** (in dē ko' rus), *adj.* contrary to the dictates of good manners.

indecorum (in dek' ŏ rum), *n.* a violation of propriety or good manners.

indeed (in dēd'), *adv.* in fact, just so, truly.

indefatigable (in dē fat' i ga bl), *adj.* not to be wearied, tireless.

indefeasible (in dē fēz' ibl), *adj.* not to be annulled or made void, as an *indefeasible* title.

indefensible (in dē fen' si bl), *adj.* not capable of being convincingly defended or excused.

indefinable (in dē fīn' a bl), *adj.* incapable of being accurately described or explained.

indefinite (in def' i nit), *adj.* inexact; not precise; having no defined limit; vague.

indelible (in del' i bl), *adj.* not to be erased, as from paper or the mind.

indelicacy (in del' i ka si), *n.* [*pl.* indelicacies] lack of refinement; an act or a word of a coarse nature.

indemnify (in dem' ni fi), *v.t.* to compensate for damage done or loss caused.

indemnity (in dem' ni ti), *n.* [*pl.* indemnities] compensation for damage done or loss caused an individual, corporation or nation.

indent (in dent'), *v.t.* to make a notch or notches in the edge of; to set a line of writing or printing in from the margin.

indentation (in den tā shun), *n.* a small depression of a surface caused by a dent.

indention (in den' shun), *n.* the act of setting a line of writing or printing in from the margin; space left by this act, as at beginning of paragraph; distance in from outside measure, as the edge of the type page.

indenture (in den' tūr), *n.* a covenant or deed; in former times, a contract binding an apprentice or servant to an employer or master. *v.t.* to bind by written agreement.

independence (in dē pen' dens), *n.* freedom from assistance by others or from rule by others.

independent (in dē pen' dent), *n.* one who will not adhere to an organization, as a party or established church. *adj.* free, uncontrolled by another, as an *independent* store, contrasted with a chain, an *independent* mind, an *independent* income; self-reliant, as too *independent* to take relief; opposite of *dependent*.

indestructible (in dē struk' ti bl), *adj.* incapable of being destroyed.

indeterminate (in dē tûr' mi nāt), *adj.* not definitely fixed, not precise or distinct, vague.

index (in' deks), *n.* [*pl.* indexes or indices] something that points out, as the *index* finger; an alphabetical list of references to the contents of a book.

India rubber (in' di a rub' ĕr), Caoutchouc, made from juice of a tropical plant.

indicate (in' di kāt), *v.t.* to point out; to suggest.

*****indicative** (in dik' a tiv), *n.* the mood of the verb that declares or affirms or asks a direct question.

indicator (in' di kā tĕr), *n.* a device that points, especially a device to show relation between pressure and volume of steam in cylinder of a steam engine.

*****indict** (in dīt'), *v.t.* to charge formally with an offense or a crime.

*****indictment** (in dīt' ment), *n.* a formal, official charge against an accused person.

indifferent (in dif' ĕr ent), *adj.* unconcerned, not caring how things go, apathetic; neutral.
    Syn. Unconcerned. One who is *indifferent* has no interest, choice or feeling about a matter. One who is *unconcerned* feels no anxiety.
    Ant. Interested, anxious.

indigence (in' di jens), *n.* poverty.

*****indigenous** (in dij' ē nus), *adj.* native; innate, inborn.

*****indigent** (in' di jent), *adj.* destitute, needy, poor.

indigestion (in di jes' chun), *n.* inability to digest food; dyspepsia.

indignant (in dig' nant), *adj.* justly angry.

indignation (in dig nā'shun), *n.* angry scorn for acts of an unworthy, dishonorable or unjust nature.

indignity (in dig' ni ti), *n.* [*pl.* indignities] an offense against the personal dignity of another.

indigo (in' di gō), *n.* a blue dyestuff; the plant from which it is obtained; a deep violet blue color.

*****indirect** (in di rekt'), *adj.* oblique, circuitous; not straightforward, misleading; remotely not immediately connected, as an *indirect* result.

indiscreet (in dis krēt'), *adj.* imprudent, injudicious.

indiscretion (in dis kresh' un), *n.* imprudence; an imprudent act.

indiscriminate (in dis krim' i nit), *adj.* without discrimination or distinction; promiscuous; miscellaneous.

indispensable (in dis pen' sa bl), *adj.* absolutely necessary.

indisposition (in dis pō zish' un), *n.* a slight ailment.

*****indisputable** (in dis' pū ta bl), *adj.* beyond argument, unquestionable.

*****indissoluble** (in di sol' ū bl), *adj.* not capable of being dissolved or annulled.

indistinct (in dis tingkt'), *adj.* not clear; vague; faint, to hearing or sight.

indistinguishable (in dis ting' gwish a bl), *adj.* not clearly enough outlined to be identified.

indite (in dīt'), *v.t.* to compose, write.

individual (in di vid' ū al), *n.* a single person or thing considered separately from the class or group.

individual (in di vid' ū al), *adj.* pertaining to or characteristic of a single person or thing; for use by one person, as *individual* cups.

individuality (in di vid ū al' i ti), *n.* [*pl.* individualities] existence as an individual; distinctive character.

indivisible (in di viz' i bl), *adj.* not capable of being separated into parts.

indolence (in' dō lens), *n.* love of ease; laziness.

indomitable (in dom' i ta bl), *adj.* untamable, invincible.

indorse (in dôrs'), *v.t.* to sign on the back, as a check; to support with approval.

*****indubitable** (in dū' bi ta bl), *adj.* not to be doubted or questioned, too plain or true to be doubted.
    Syn. Unquestionable, indisputable, incontrovertible. When a fact is supported by such evidence as admits of no doubt, it is *indubitable*. The character of a man whose integrity cannot be impeached establishes his assertions as of *unquestionable* authority. A fact of universal acceptance must be regarded as *indisputable*, and arguments that have never been controverted are fairly to be termed *incontrovertible*.
    Ant. Doubtful, debatable.

induce (in dūs'), *v.t.* to influence to action, prevail upon, bring on, cause.

inducement (in dūs' ment), *n.* that which induces, a motive; that which provides a missing incentive.

induct (in dukt'), *v.t.* to install in office.

induction (in duk' shun), *n.* the formal establishment of a person in an office; the process of reasoning from particular instances to general conclusions; a conclusion reached by that method; electric or magnetic influence without contact.

inductive (in duk' tiv), *adj.* proceeding from or reached by the logical method of generalizing from instances; in electricity, produced by induction.

indue (in dū'), *v.t.* to clothe or invest, furnish; to assume, put on.

indulge (in dulj'), *v.i. and v.t.* to gratify tastes and desires; to gratify, as desires; to humor, favor, as to *indulge* a child.

indulgence (in dul' jens), *n.* gratification, especially self-gratification; the act of gratifying or humoring; a favor.

indurate (in' dū rāt), *v.i. and v.t.* to grow hard; to make hard.

industrial (in dus' tri al), *adj.* pertaining to production of goods for trade.

industrious (in dus' tri us), *adj.* hard-working.

*****industry** (in' dus tri), *n.* [*pl.* industries] steadiness in toil; the whole establishment of productive enterprise in a country; the part of it devoted to production of one kind of goods, as the automobile *industry*.

inebriate (in ē' bri āt), *n.* a habitual drunkard.

ineffable (in ef' a bl), *adj.* inexpressible; too sacred for utterance.

ineffective (in e fek' tiv), *adj.* not producing the desired action or result; incompetent.

ineffectual (in e fek' tū al), *adj.* unavailing, useless, futile.

inefficient (in e fish' ent), *adj.* not producing the desired effect; not capable or proficient.

inelegant (in el' ē gant), *adj.* offensive to good taste, unrefined.

ineligible (in el' i ji bl), *adj.* not qualified, as to vote or be voted for.

inept (in ept'), *adj.* not fitting, unsuitable, awkward, as a remark.

inequality (in ē kwol' i ti), *n.* [*pl.* inequalities] a difference in favor of one over another; disparity; unevenness of surface.

*•**inequitable** (in ek' wi ta bl), *adj.* not according to equity or fairness.

inequity (in ek' wi ti), *n.* [*pl.* inequities] injustice or an instance of injustice.

inert (in ûrt'), *adj.* without power to move, act or resist.

*•**inertia** (in ûr' sha), *n.* lack of energy or activity; the property by which matter, either at rest or in motion, tends to continue in the same state unless acted upon by an outside force.

inestimable (in es' ti ma bl), *adj.* not computable; beyond specific mensuration or valuation.

inevitable (in ev' i ta bl), *adj.* unavoidable.

inexact (in eg zakt'), *adj.* not precise, not accurate.

inexcusable (in eks kūz' a bl), *adj.* not to be excused, unpardonable.

*•**inexhaustible** (in ek zôs' ti bl), *adj.* too great to be used up; tireless, never giving out.

*•**inexorable** (in ek' sō ra bl), *adj.* not to be moved by entreaty, unyielding.

*•**inexpedient** (in eks pē' di ent), *adj.* not prudent, practicable or advisable.

inexpiable (in eks' pi a bl), *adj.* not to be atoned for.

*•**inexplicable** (in eks' pli ka bl), *adj.* not capable of being explained or accounted for.

inexpressible (in eks pres' i bl), *adj.* beyond the power of words to express.

inextinguishable (in eks ting' gwish a bl), *adj.* not to be quenched, as a fire.

*•**inextricable** (in eks' tri ka bl), *adj.* too snarled to be disentangled.

infallible (in fal' i bl), *adj.* unerring, certain.

*•**infamous** (in' fa mus), *adj.* having a bad reputation, notoriously bad, scandalous.

infamy (in' fa mi), *n.* [*pl.* infamies] public disgrace, loss of reputation, ignominy; an infamous or evil act.

infancy (in' fan si), *n.* the first years of life; the early, formative period of anything, as a custom or institution.

infant (in' fant), *n.* a baby, a very young child; a person not yet old enough to vote.

*•**infantile** (in' fan til), *adj.* pertaining to infants or the period of infancy; very childish.

*•**infatuate** (in fat' ū āt), *v.t.* to inspire with foolish passion.

infect (in fekt'), *v.t.* to poison, as a wound, with disease germs or bacteria; to contaminate, taint.

infectious (in fek' shus), *adj.* communicated by, or bearing, germs; tending to spread; catching, as an *infectious* laugh.

infelicitous (in fē lis' i tus), *adj.* not appropriate, as an *infelicitous* remark.

infelicity (in fē lis' i ti), *n.* [*pl.* infelicities] an ill-timed, inappropriate remark or act; the state of being unhappy.

infer (in fûr'), *v.i. and v.t.* to derive by reasoning from facts; to conclude.

inference (in' fér ens), *n.* the act of judging one thing by another; a logical conclusion from first facts.

inferential (in fér en' shal), *adj.* derived by reasoning from data.

inferior (in fēr' i ēr), *adj.* lower in grade or quality, mediocre; set below the type line in printing.

inferiority (in fēr i or' i ti), *n.* the state of being lower in grade, quality or office.

infernal (in fûr' nal), *adj.* related to or resembling hell; devilish.

infest (in fest'), *v.t.* to overrun; to plague persistently.

infidel (in' fi del), *n.* one who rejects a faith, as Christianity.

infidelity (in fi del' i ti), *n.* [*pl.* infidelities] faithlessness; disloyalty, as to one's mate.

infiltrate (in fil' trāt), *v.i. and v.t.* to percolate; to pass through the pores of; to filter into or through.

infinite (in' fi nit), *adj.* extending immeasurably or inconceivably.

infinitesimal (in fi ni tes' i mal), *adj.* infinitely small; less than any assigned quantity, as the *infinitesimal* calculus.

infinitive (in fin' i tiv), *n.* the verb form expressing the general sense without limitation in person or number; used with *to*, as *to read.*

infinity (in fin' i ti), *n.* [*pl.* infinities] unlimited time or space, boundlessness; eternity.

infirm (in fûrm'), *adj.* feeble, weak; not stable.

infirmary (in fûr' ma ri), *n.* [*pl.* infirmaries] institution for care of sick or injured, especially school or college hospital.

infirmity (in fûr' mi ti), *n.* [*pl.* infirmities] a weak or sick condition; any particular form of weakness or sickness.

inflame (in flām'), *v.t.* to set afire; to kindle, as to *inflame* anger; to excite.

inflammable (in flam' a bl), *adj.* easily ignited; easily excited.

inflammation (in fla mā' shun), *n.* a diseased condition of any part of the body accompanied by pain, redness, heat and swelling.

inflammatory (in flam' a tō ri), *adj.* causing inflammation; tending to arouse passions or cause tumultuous uprisings.

inflate (in flāt), *v.i. and v.t.* to puff up; to fill with air or gas.

inflation (in flā' shun), *n.* an artificial stimulus to circulation of money.

inflect (in flekt'), *v.t. and v.i.* to modulate, as

the voice; to change the form of for different grammatical relations, as to *inflect* a verb or noun; to be modified in form, as this verb *inflects* thus.

inflection (in flek' shun), *n.* rising and falling of the voice; change in the form of nouns and verbs to indicate number, person, mood and tense.

inflexible (in flek' si bl), *adj.* incapable of being bent, rigid; firmly fixed, as in purpose.

inflict (in flikt'), *v.t.* to cause to be suffered or endured, as pain; to impose, as a punishment.

*influence (in' floo ens), *n.* that which tends to produce results by invisible means; power springing from rank, station or office; ability to secure favors from those in power.

influence (in' floo ens), *v.t.* to affect by any invisible power; to affect, as the conduct or condition of persons or things, as the weather *influences* the crops.

influential (in floo en' shal), *adj.* having or exerting power; effective toward an end.

influenza (in floo en' za), *n.* an epidemic disease resembling a severe cold.

influx (in' fluks), *n.* an inflow, a pouring in.

inform (in fôrm'), *v.t.* to give form to; to give information, knowledge, news; to tell.

informal (in fôr' mal), *adj.* unceremonious.

informality (in fôr mal' i ti), *n.* [*pl.* informalities] departure from regular custom or from the strict rules of etiquette; any particular instance of such departure.

information (in fôr mā' shun), *n.* communicated knowledge or news.

infraction (in frak' shun), *n.* a violation or breach, as of the law or a treaty.

infrequent (in frē' kwent), *adj.* happening not often but at long and irregular intervals; rare, uncommon.

infringe (in frinj'), *v.i. and v.t.* to encroach, as to *infringe* upon the rights or property of another; to break, as a law.

infuriate (in fū' ri āt), *v.t.* to enrage.

infuse (in fūz'), *v.t.* to pour in, as a liquid; to instill, as principles; to steep without boiling.

infusion (in fū' zhun), *n.* that which is poured in or instilled, a mixture; the process of steeping a substance in water to draw out its essential qualities; the liquid thus obtained.

*ingenious (in jēn' yus), *adj.* endowed with great skill, inventive; cleverly contrived.

ingenuity (in jē nū' i ti), *n.* cleverness in designing or contriving.

Syn. Wit. *Ingenuity* comprehends invention; *wit* is of the imagination, which forms new and sudden conceptions of things. One is *ingenious* in matters either of art or of mechanics; one is *witty* only in matters of intellect.

*ingenuous (in jen' ū us), *adj.* frank, open, sincere, artless, candid.

inglorious (in glō' ri us), *adj.* obscure, humble; disgraceful, shameful.

ingot (ing' got), *n.* a cast mass of metal.

ingrained (in grānd'), *adj.* worked into the fabric, as dye in woolen yarns; deeply rooted, as *ingrained* honesty.

ingratiate (in grā' shi āt), *v.t.* to insinuate (oneself) into the favor of another.

ingratitude (in grat' i tūd), *n.* absence of gratefulness; failure to appreciate kindness.

ingredient (in grē' di ent), *n.* a component part; an element in a mixture.

*ingress (in' gres), *n.* entrance, the way in.

inhabit (in hab' it), *v.t.* to live in, as a house or country.

inhale (in hāl'), *v.i. and v.t.* to draw air or smoke into the lungs; to breathe in.

*inherent (in hēr' ent), *adj.* existing as part of the nature of anything, inborn.

inherit (in her' it), *v.i. and v.t.* to acquire through heirship; to come into possession of through the death of the owner or holder, as an estate or a title; to acquire the characteristics of, as an ancestor.

inhibit (in hib' it), *v.t.* to restrain; to forbid; to repress.

*inhospitable (in hos' pi ta bl), *adj.* not cordial to strangers or guests; affording no shelter.

inhuman (in hū' man), *adj.* lacking the good qualities of mankind; cruel.

*inimical (in im' i kal), *adj.* hostile, adverse.

inimitable (in im' i ta bl), *adj.* defying imitation; matchless.

iniquitous (in ik' wi tus), *adj.* wicked.

iniquity (in ik' wi ti), *n.* [*pl.* iniquities] state of wickedness; a wicked act; great injustice.

initiate (i nish' i āt), *v.t.* to instruct in the elements of anything; to set something going, as to *initiate* a custom; to introduce into a secret society with rites, as a new member.

inject (in jekt'), *v.t.* to throw or force in.

injector (in jek' tẽr), *n.* apparatus for injecting water into a steam boiler.

injudicious (in jōō dish' us), *adj.* imprudent, unwise.

injunction (in jungk' shun), *n.* an order, especially from a court.

injure (in' jẽr), *v.t.* to hurt or damage.

injurious (in joor' i us), *adj.* hurtful; detrimental.

injury (in' jẽr i), *n.* [*pl.* injuries] that which causes harm or damage; the damage or hurt done.

injustice (in jus' tis), *n.* the quality of being unfair; a wrong.

Syn. Wrong. *Injustice* is the opposite of whatever is fair and just; a *wrong* is a deeper thing; a *wrong* is an actual violation of personal rights.

ink (ingk), *n.* a fluid used for writing; a paste used in printing.

ink (ingk), *v.t.* to put ink upon, mark with ink.

inkling (ingk' ling), *n.* an intimation or hint.

inland (in' land), *adj.* back from the coast.

*inlay (in lā'), *v.t.* [*p.t.* and *p.p.* inlaid, *pr.p.* inlaying], to ornament the surface of an object by setting in pieces of ivory, hard wood, metal.

inlet (in' let), *n.* a small bay or creek; an opening by which water is admitted, as to a tank.

inn (in), *n.* a tavern.

*****innate** (in' năt), *adj.* inborn, not acquired.

inner (in' ẽr), *adj.* internal; pertaining to the mind or spirit, as an *inner* experience.

innocent (in' ō sent), *adj.* without guilt, sinless; inexperienced in worldly ways.

innocuous (i nok' ū us), *adj.* harmless.

innovation (in ō vā' shun), *n.* a change from established custom; a new thing or method.

*****innoxious** (i nok' shus), *adj.* not injurious.

innuendo (in ū en' dō), *n.* [*pl.* innuendos or innuendoes] an indirect expression of derogation, an insinuation.

*****innumerable** (i nū' mẽr a bl), *adj.* without number; too great a number to be counted.

inoculate (in ok' ū lāt), *v.t.* to inject the virus of a disease into as an immunizing measure.

inoperative (in op' ẽr ă tiv), *adj.* not working; without effect.

inordinate (in ôr' di nit), *adj.* immoderate, excessive.

inorganic (in ôr gan' ik), *adj.* not belonging to the animal or vegetable kingdoms, inanimate, as rocks.

inquest (in' kwest), *n.* a judicial inquiry, especially by a coroner into the cause of a death.

inquire (in kwīr'), *v.i. and v.t.* to ask a question; to investigate, examine; to ask about.

*****inquiry** (in kwī' ri), *n.* [*pl.* inquiries] a question; investigation.

inquisitive (in kwiz' i tiv), *adj.* given to asking questions, curious.

inroad (in' rōd), *n.* an invasion; encroachment.

*****insane** (in sān'), *adj.* mentally deranged.

insanity (in san' i ti), *n.* derangement of mind; utter folly.

*****insatiable** (in sā' shi a bl), *adj.* not capable of being satisfied or appeased.

inscribe (in skrīb'), *v.t.* to write upon or engrave; as to *inscribe* a book or memorial tablet; to address to a person or group, as a poem; to draw one figure within another with certain specified contacts, as in geometry.

inscription (in skrip' shun), *n.* that which is written; a dedication.

inscrutable (in skrōō' ta bl), *adj.* beyond understanding; incomprehensible to the human mind, as an *inscrutable* Providence.

insect (in' sekt), *n.* one of a class of invertebrate animals, often having wings but always having bodies composed of head, thorax and abdomen, with three pairs of jointed legs.

insensate (in sen' sāt), *adj.* lacking sensation, inanimate, as *insensate* rocks; lacking sense, foolish; without feeling, brutal.

insensibility (in sen si bil' i ti), *n.* want of physical feeling or of emotion.

insensible (in sen' si bl), *adj.* by nature destitute of feeling or sensation or having possessed and lost those powers; unconscious; apathetic.

inseparable (in sep' a ra bl), *adj.* incapable of being separated; always together.

insert (in' sûrt), *n.* something inserted or put in, as extra paper or an additional paragraph in a text.

*****insert** (in sûrt'), *v.t.* to thrust or place in; to introduce.

insertion (in sûr' shun), *n.* the act of inserting or being put in, as the advertisement is to have two *insertions;* that which is put in, especially trimming put in between pieces of plain material in making a dress.

inshore (in' shôr), *adj.* located near the shore or moving toward the shore.

inside (in' sīd'), *n.* the inner part, as the *inside* of a box. *adj.* interior, as *inside* lining; confidential and supposedly authoritative, as *inside* information. *adv.* within, as go *inside. prep.* within, as *inside* the house.

*****insidious** (in sid' i us), *adj.* sly, crafty, working in secret, treacherous.

insight (in' sīt), *n.* perception of the inner nature of things; keen understanding; mental vision, intuition.

*****insignia** (in sig' ni a), *n. pl.* distinguishing marks; symbols of office or of rank or membership in an organization, as the army.

insignificant (in sig nif' i kant), *adj.* having little importance or meaning.

insincere (in sin sẽr') *adj.* not absolutely honest; not frank and open, hypocritical.

insinuate (in sin' ū āt), *v.t.* to work in or penetrate by slow or artful means; to suggest indirectly or in derogation; to hint.

Syn. Ingratiate. A person who *insinuates* himself into favor does so with persistence and smooth, sly easiness; he who *ingratiates* himself works his way to favor by special, not always dignified, attentions.

insipid (in sip' id), *adj.* flavorless, dull, as *insipid* talk, an *insipid* beverage.

insist (in sist'), *v.i.* to demand, urge persistently.

Syn. Persist. To *insist* is to take a stand and stick to it; to *persist* is to move actively for fulfilment of one's aims. We *insist* on something by constantly maintaining it; we *persist* in a thing by continuing to do it.

Ant. Desist, leave, abandon.

insistent (in sist' ent), *adj.* urgent, compelling notice.

insolent (in' sō lent), *adj.* haughtily contemptuous, extremely disrespectful.

insoluble (in sol' ū bl), *adj.* not to be solved, as a problem; impossible to dissolve, as a substance.

insolvency (in sol' ven si), *n.* bankruptcy.

Syn. Failure, bankruptcy. *Insolvency* is a state; *failure* an act flowing from that state; *bankruptcy*, the result of that act. *Insolvency* is inability to meet one's financial obligations; *failure* is a cessation of business for want of means with which to carry it on; *bankruptcy* is a legal surrender of one's remaining assets into the hands of one's creditors.

Ant. Solvency, success, prosperity.

insomnia (in som' ni a), *n.* sleeplessness.

*****insouciance** (in sōō' si ans), *n.* indifference, unconcern, lack of interest.

inspect (in spekt'), *v.t.* to examine critically, as for defects; to test officially.

inspiration (in spi rā' shun), *n.* inbreathing;

that which stirs the creative impulse in art; that which is created by this impulse.

inspire (in spir'), *v.i. and v.t.* to breathe in, inhale; to imbue with ideas and ambitions; to arouse the creative impulse in art.

instability (in sta bil' i ti), *n.* lacking firmness and steadiness; the state of being easily moved or upset; changeability of character or mood.

install (in stôl'), *v.t.* to induct into office, as with ceremonial exercises; to put in place, as machinery.

instalment (in stôl' ment), *n.* one of a series of scheduled payments; one of the parts in which a serial story is published.

instance (in' stans), *n.* an example or typical case: *for instance,* by way of example.

instant (in' stant), *n.* a moment or even smaller time unit. *adj.* now present, urgent, as the *instant* need.

instantaneous (in stan tā' nē us), *adj.* acting or occurring in a moment or at a given moment.

instate (in stāt´), *v.t.* to put in office or in place, as to *instate* oneself in another's favor.

instead (in sted'), *adv.* in its place, as I want this *instead;* in the place of, as I will go *instead* of him, that is, as his substitute.

instep (in' step), *n.* the arched upper surface of the forward part of the human foot.

instigate (in' sti gāt), *v.t.* to urge on, incite.

instill (in stil'), *v.t.* [*p.t.* and *p.p.* instilled, *pr.p.* instilling] to pour in by drops; to introduce, as good principles, gradually: sometimes *instil.*

*****instinct** (in' stingkt), *n.* any natural impulse that takes the place of thinking and reasoning; a sense of things apart from any process of reasoning, as the *instinct* of self-protection.

institute (in' sti tūt), *v.t.* to establish; to originate, as a custom.

*****institution** (in sti tū' shun), *n.* the act of establishing or that which is established; a fixed custom; a society devoted to special works.

instruct (in strukt'), *v.t.* to teach; to direct.

instrument (in' stroo ment), *n.* that by means of which something is done, a means; a device for making musical sounds; a tool or implement.

instrumentality (in stroo men tal' i ti), *n.* [*pl.* instrumentalities] an agency or means.

insubordinate (in su bôr' di nit), *adj.* refusing to recognize authority, mutinous.

insubstantial (in sub stan' shal), *adj.* not material; frail and flimsy.

insufferable (in suf' ẽr a bl), *adj.* unendurable.

insufficient (in su fish' ent), *adj.* not enough, deficient.

*****insular** (in' sū lẽr), *adj.* pertaining to an island; dwelling on an island; isolated; narrowminded, limited.

insulate (in' sū lāt), *v.t.* to prevent passage of electricity or heat from one body to another by covering the conductors with nonconducting material.

insulin (in' sū lin), *n.* a substance obtained

from the pancreas of cattle or sheep, used in cases of diabetes: originally a trade name.

insult (in' sult), *n.* an affront; a remark or act offensive to the feelings or dignity of its object.

insult (in sult'), *v.t.* to treat with insolence or rudeness.

insuperable (in sū' pẽr a bl), *adj.* not to be overcome, insurmountable, as a difficulty.

*****insure** (in shoor'), *v.i. and v.t.* to make certain, assure; to provide for indemnity against loss, as by death, fire, flood.

insurgent (in sûr' jent), *n.* a rebel; a member of a political party who joins with other members in opposing policies adopted by the party. *adj.* rebellious against constituted authority.

insurrection (in su rek' shun), *n.* an uprising in resistance to constituted authority; rebellion.

inswept (in' swept), *adj.* having the front end narrower than the rear, as some automobile bodies.

intact (in takt'), *adj.* unbroken, undamaged, whole after a blow or shock.

*****intaglio** (in tal' yō), *n.* [*pl.* intaglios or intagli] a gem stone with a design cut into the surface: opposite of *cameo.*

intake (in' tāk), *n.* the place at which a pipe or channel takes in a fluid.

intangible (in tan' ji bl), *adj.* not perceptible through touch; vague, difficult to define.

*****integer** (in' tē jẽr), *n.* a whole number.

*****integral** (in' tē gral), *adj.* complete or necessary to completion.

integrate (in' tē grāt), *v.t.* to bring parts together to make a whole.

integrity (in teg' ri ti), *n.* uprightness, soundness of character, moral wholeness.

integument (in teg' ū ment), *n.* an external covering or skin.

intellect (in' te lekt), *n.* the mind, the power to reason as distinguished from the power to feel.

    Syn. Intelligence, mind. *Mind* is the general term that embraces both *intelligence* and *intellect. Intelligence* is a quickness to understand; *intellect* is great mental power.

intelligence (in tel' i jens), *n.* ability to apply the mind effectively to any situation, study or problem; clear thinking plus good judgment; news or knowledge.

intelligible (in tel' i ji bl), *adj.* easily understood; clearly stated.

intemperance (in tem' pẽr ans), *n.* lack of self-restraint, overindulgence.

intend (in tend'), *v.t. and v.i.* to have in mind as a purpose, to plan or purpose; to have an aim or intention; to mean to do.

intense (in tens'), *adj.* developed to high degree, as *intense* anxiety, *intense* light; ardent; strained.

intensify (in ten' si fī), *v.t.* [*p.t.* and *p.p.* intensified, *pr.p.* intensifying] to render more intense, heighten, aggravate.

intensive (in ten' siv), *adj.* giving more force to; thorough, deep, concentrated, as *intensive* study; increasing production per unit of land, as *intensive* farming.

intent (in tent'), *n.* a purpose or aim. *adj.* giving concentrated attention.

intention (in ten' shun), *n.* purpose; meaning.

inter (in tùr'), *v.t.* to bury.

intercede (in tẽr sēd'), *v.i.* to mediate, plead in behalf of another.

intercept (in tẽr sept'), *v.t.* to stop and seize on the way, cut off, block.

intercession (in tẽr sesh' un), *n.* the act of interceding, mediation.

interchangeable (in tẽr chān' ja bl), *adj.* capable of being substituted one for the other.

intercourse (in' tẽr kōrs), *n.* communication; relations between individuals or groups.

*****interest** (in' ter est), *n.* concern in a thing; command of attention, as this story holds my *interest*; money paid for the use of money; money earned by capital loaned or invested.

interface (in' tẽr fās), *n.* computers communicating from one system to another.

interfere (in tẽr fēr'), *v.i.* to interpose or meddle in the affairs of others; to strike one foot against the opposite foot or ankle in walking or running, said of horses.

interference (in tẽr fēr' ens), *n.* a confusion of received radio signals, or that which causes such confusion.

interim (in' tẽr im), *n.* an intervening period of time, an interval, the meantime.

interior (in tẽr' lẽr), *n.* the inside part of anything; the inland part of a country.

interior (in tẽr' lẽr), *adj.* inner, internal.

interjection (in tẽr jek' shun), *n.* an exclamation.

interlinear (in tẽr lin' ē ẽr), *adj.* written or printed between lines on a page; having matter written or printed between the lines, as an *interlinear* translation.

*****interloper** (in' tẽr lōp ẽr), *n.* an intruder.

interlude (in' tẽr lūd), *n.* a short entertainment between acts of a play in the early days of the theater; a short passage played between major sections of a musical rendition; any interval of time between events.

intermediary (in tẽr mē' di er i), *n.* one who stands or acts between, a mediary.

interment (in tùr' ment), *n.* burial.

interminable (in tùr' mi na bl), *adj.* endless.

intermittent (in tùr mit' ent), *adj.* coming and going, alternating; ceasing for brief periods and then recurring, as an *intermittent* fever; unsustained, as *intermittent* effort.

intern (in tùrn'), *v.t.* to force to stay in one place, as men or ships of a belligerent, discovered in neutral territory.

intern (in tùrn'), *n.* a doctor serving a period of residence and practice in a hospital.

internal (in tùr' nal), *adj.* pertaining to, from or on the inside.

international (in tẽr nash' un al), *adj.* relating to or affecting two or more nations at once.

interpolate (in tùr' pō lāt), *v.t.* to insert, as new matter in a text; to alter or corrupt thus.

interpose (in tẽr pōz'), *v.i. and v.t.* to be between others; to place between others.

interpret (in tùr' pret), *v.t.* to translate, explain, construe.

interregnum (in tẽr reg' num), *n.* the period between two reigns or governments.

interrogation (in ter ō gā' shun), *n.* a question; the act of questioning.

*****interrupt** (in te rupt'), *v.t. and v.i.* to break into, as a sentence; to stop a speaker by breaking in with a remark of one's own.

intersect (in tẽr sekt'), *v.i. and v.t.* to cross, as two lines; to cut across, as one line *intersects* another.

intersperse (in tẽr spûrs'), *v.t.* to set here and there among other things, as to *intersperse* shrubs among trees; to adorn or moderate with (something) scattered here and there, as to *intersperse* a lecture with jokes.

*****interstice** (in tûr' stis), *n.* a narrow space between two things, a crevice, a chink.

interval (in' tẽr val), *n.* time between events or space between objects.

intervene (in tẽr vēn'), *v.i.* to come, be or happen in between; to pass, as time; to come between in order to hinder, as to *intervene* in a fight.

intervention (in tẽr ven' shun), *n.* a coming between, mediation; any interference.

interview (in' tẽr vū), *n.* a formal conference or meeting; a meeting with a news reporter or the published account of the conversation.

intestate (in tes' tāt), *adj.* dying without a will; not disposed of by will, as property.

intestinal (in tes' ti nal), *adj.* pertaining to the bowels.

intestine (in tes' tin), *adj.* internal; within a country, domestic, as an *intestine* war.

intimacy (in' ti ma si), *n.* [*pl.* intimacies] close friendship, familiarity.

intimate (in' ti māt), *n.* a close friend or associate. *v.t.* to make known in an indirect manner, hint, indicate.

intimate (in' ti mit), *adj.* in close association, familiar, as he is my *intimate* friend; confidential, personal, as an *intimate* communication; detailed, gained by close study, as *intimate* knowledge.

intimation (in ti mā' shun), *n.* an indirect suggestion, a hint, as he gave no *intimation* of his plans.

intimidate (in tim' i dāt), *v.t.* to make afraid, frighten.

into (in' tōō), *prep.* from without to within in space, occupation or condition, as go *into* the house, go *into* politics, change sorrow *into* rejoicing.

intolerable (in tol' ẽr a bl), *adj.* unendurable.

intolerance (in tol' ẽr ans), *n.* lack of forbearance, narrowmindedness with regard to the opinions and beliefs of others; inability to endure, as *intolerance* of noise or violence.

intolerant (in tol' ẽr ant), *adj.* bigoted; unable to endure: used with *of.*

intonation (in tō nā' shun), *n.* the act or manner of intoning or sounding musical notes, chanting; the rise and fall in the tones of the human speaking voice.

intone (in tōn'), *v.t. and v.i.* to utter in prolonged tones, chant, as in some religious observances; to recite in a monotone.

intoxicant (in tok' si kant), *n.* that which

makes drunk. *adj.* intoxicating.

intoxicate (in tok' si kāt), *v.t.* to make drunk, as alcoholic liquor; to overstimulate; to excite the sensations or passions.

intractable (in trak' ta bl), *adj.* unmanageable, hard to control.

intractile (in trak' til), *adj.* incapable of being drawn out in the form of a wire.

intransitive (in tran' si tiv), *adj.* unable to have an object, as the verbs *to live, to glow.*

intrench (in trench'), *v.i. and v.t.* to go into the trenches, as troops in war; to make trenches or furrows in; to fortify with trenches or ditches; to encroach: used with *upon.*

intrepid (in trep' id), *adj.* daring, bold, fearless.

*intricacy** (in' tri ka si), *n.* [*pl.* intricacies] entanglement, complication.

intricate (in' tri kit), *adj.* complicated, complex, entangled, elaborately interwoven, as an *intricate* plot.

*intrigue** (in trēg'), *n.* secret scheming, a plot.

*intrigue** (in trēg'), *v.i. and v.t.* to plot or scheme in secret; to interest greatly, puzzle, arouse the curiosity of by a baffling quality.

intrinsic (in trin' sik), *adj.* inherent; part of the nature of a person or thing, as *intrinsic* merit: opposite of *extrinsic.*

introduce (in trō dūs'), *v.t.* to bring in; to bring into acquaintance; to present in formal manner, as a resolution.

introspection (in trō spek' shun), *n.* the act of looking within one's own mind, self-analysis.

intrude (in trōōd'), *v.i. and v.t.* to enter without invitation or without being wanted; to force upon.

    Syn. Obtrude. To *intrude* is to force one's way without right, unasked or unwanted; to *obtrude* is to impose oneself or one's opinions unnecessarily, as don't *obtrude* personal matters into a general conversation.

intrusion (in trōō' zhun), *n.* the act of trespassing, invasion.

intuition (in tū ish' un), *n.* instinctive knowledge, perception of facts or conditions without reasoning; instantaneous comprehension.

intuitive (in tū' i tiv), *adj.* having instinctive comprehension, perceived without process of reasoning.

*inundate** (in' un dāt), *v.t.* to cover with water or as with water, to flood, overflow.

inure (in ūr'), *v.t.* to make accustomed to, harden, as Eskimos are *inured* to low temperatures.

invade (in vād'), *v.t.* to enter with hostile intentions, as a foreign land; to infringe upon, as the rights of another.

invalid (in' va lid), *n.* a sick or disabled person. *adj.* sickly; adapted for the sickly, as *invalid* diet.

invalid (in val' id), *adj.* null and void.

invalidate (in val' i dāt), *v.t.* to make null and void; to deprive of force and effect.

invaluable (in val' ū a bl), *adj.* beyond valuation, priceless.

invariable (in vâr' i a bl), *adj.* unchanging, constant, uniform.

invasion (in vā' zhun), *n.* the act of entering a foreign land with hostile intention; infringement.

invective (in vek' tiv), *n.* bitter denunciation, wordy abuse.

*inveigh** (in vā'), *v.i.* to speak bitterly; to reproach: used with *against.*

*inveigle** (in vē' gl), *v.t.* to coax, persuade with flattery.

invent (in vent'), *v.t.* to devise, discover or contrive, as to *invent* a good excuse, *invent* a machine.

invention (in ven' shun), *n.* the act of inventing or the thing invented; creative imagination; a fabrication or falsehood.

inventor (in vent' ẽr), *n.* one who invents, as Edison was a great *inventor.*

inventory (in' ven tō ri), *n.* [*pl.* inventories] stocktaking, an itemized list of goods and their value.

*inverse** (in vûrs'), *adj.* contrary in direction or effect.

*inversion** (in vûr' shun), *n.* reversal of position, order or relation.

invert (in vûrt'), *v.t.* to turn inside out, upside down, or so as to face the other way; to reverse in order or relation, as to *invert* a sentence or phrase.

invertebrate (in vûr' tē brāt), *n.* an animal that has no backbone. *adj.* having no backbone; lacking character.

invest (in vest'), *v.t.* to clothe, as with office, power or dignity; to surround, as a fort; to besiege; to put money into in expectation of profit, as an enterprise.

    Syn. Endue, endow. One is *invested* with that which is external; *endued* with that which is internal. We *invest* a person with an office or a dignity; he is *endued* with good qualities. To *endow* is but a variation of to *endue.* We may say a person is either *endued* or *endowed* with a good understanding, but of the imagination we say that it *endues* things with properties.

investigate (in ves' ti gāt), *v.t.* to examine in a systematic manner; to ascertain by careful inquiry.

investiture (in ves' ti tūr), *n.* vestment; the act of installing in office.

investment (in vest' ment), *n.* the act of laying out money in expectation of profit; the sum so placed.

inveterate (in vet' ẽr it), *adj.* deep-rooted, as hatred; habitual, fixed in a habit.

*invidious** (in vid' i us), *adj.* likely to lead to ill will, offensive; discriminating unfairly.

invigorate (in vig' ẽr āt), *v.t.* to impart new vigor to, strengthen, enliven.

invincible (in vin' si bl), *adj.* unconquerable.

inviolable (in vi' ō la bl), *adj.* not to be profaned, as church premises; not to be broken, as a promise.

invisible (in viz' ibl), *adj.* incapable of being seen; out of sight.

invitation (in vi tā' shun), *n.* a request to attend, do or belong; the spoken or written words in which one is invited; an enticement.

invite (in vīt'), v.t. to request the attendance of at a certain place and time; to tempt or attract, as his manner *invites* rebuke.

inviting (in vīt' ing), adj. attractive, alluring.

invoice (in' vois), n. a notice that goods have been shipped with itemized statement of their nature, quality and prices.

invoke (in vōk'), v.t. to call upon in supplication or prayer; to call upon for aid; to call up, as evil spirits, conjure.

involuntary (in vol' un ter i), adj. not done willingly or by choice.

involution (in vō lū' shun), n. the act of folding in or around; the state of being complicated or entangled.

involve (in volv'), v.t. to infold, complicate, entangle; to contain or include by implication or necessity, as success *involves* work.

invulnerable (in vul' nēr a bl), adj. incapable of being wounded, having no weak point; unassailable.

inward (in' wērd), adj. on the inside, situated within, internal; mental or spiritual, as *inward* joy; toward the inside, ingoing, as *inward* traffic.

inward (in' wērd), adv. toward the inside; within the mind, as look *inward*.

*iodine** (I' ō dīn), n. a nonmetallic element found in mineral springs and seaweed.

*iodoform** (I ō' dō fôrm), n. a crystalline compound of iodine.

*ion** (I' on), n. an electrically charged particle that enables electricity to pass through air and solutions.

iota (I ō' ta), n. the Greek letter corresponding to English *i*; an insignificant amount.

*ipecac** (ip' ē kak), n. a South American creeping plant; a tincture from its roots used in medicine.

*irascible** (I ras' i bl), adj. easily angered.

*irate** (I' rāt), adj. wrathful, angry.

ire (Ir), n. anger, wrath.

iridescence (ir i des' ens), n. a shimmering play of rainbow colors, as in a sunlit bubble.

iris (I' ris), n. [pl. irises] a perennial plant with large, many-colored flowers and sword-shaped leaves: also called *flag* or *fleur-de-lis;* the colored part of the eye about the pupil.

irk (ûrk), v.t. to trouble, annoy, vex; to weary, bore.

iron (I' ērn), n. the most common and useful of the metals; an instrument made of iron, especially one for smoothing or pressing cloth: *irons*, fetters. v.t. and v.i. to smooth or press cloth or clothes with a flatiron. adj. made of iron, as an *iron* bar; strong, unbending, as an *iron* will.

ironclad (I' ērn klad), adj. protected by a covering of iron plates.

ironical (I ron' i kal), adj. meaning the opposite of what is said; having the nature of light ridicule, humor or mockery.

*irony** (I' rō ni), n. subtle sarcasm or humor implying the opposite of what is expressed.

irradiate (i rā' di āt), v.t. to throw rays of light upon, to brighten; to shed or diffuse, as to *irradiate* light or joy; to treat with radiant heat or ultraviolet rays, as to *irradiate* foods.

irrational (ir rash' un al), adj. without the power to reason, as an animal; lacking reason, unreasonable, as an *irrational* request.

Syn. Unreasonable. *Irrational* means contrary to reason and therefore foolish, as to have *irrational* hopes; *unreasonable* means contrary to reason and therefore impracticable and carries the idea of excessiveness, as *unreasonable* expenses.

irreclaimable (in rē klām' a bl), adj. incapable of being recovered or restored.

*irrefutable** (ir ref' ū ta bl), adj. incapable of being refuted or proved incorrect.

irregular (ir reg' ū lar), adj. not straight or even, not uniform in shape or order; not conforming to established law, method or usage; not following the normal rules of grammatical inflection or conjugation, as an *irregular* verb.

*irreparable** (i rep' a ra bl), adj. damaged beyond possibility of repair.

irresistible (ir rē zis' ti bl), adj. not to be successfully withstood.

irresolute (i rez' ō lūt), adj. lacking determination, wavering.

irrespective (ir rē spek' tiv), adj. regardless, independent, as *irrespective* of rank or station.

irresponsible (ir rē spon' si bl), adj. not to be trusted; not answerable for consequences; insolvent.

irrevocable (i rev' ō ka bl), adj. not capable of being recalled or undone, as *irrevocable* words, an *irrevocable* mistake.

irrigate (ir' i gāt), v.t. to supply with water or liquid by artificial means, as land or a wound.

irritable (ir' i ta bl), adj. easily provoked or exasperated, impatient.

irritate (ir' i tāt), v.t. to provoke, annoy, cause impatience or anger.

irritation (ir i tā' shun), n. the state of being annoyed or impatient, exasperation; an oversensitive condition of an organ or part of the body.

irruption (i rup' shun), n. a bursting in, as of a flood of water or throng of persons.

isinglass (I zing glȧs), n. a semitransparent form of gelatin prepared from the air bladder of the sturgeon, cod; mica in thin sheets.

island (I' land), n. a body of land surrounded by water; anything detached from a main body or resembling an island in its isolation.

isle (Il), n. a small island: used in poetry.

*isolate** (I' sō lāt), v.t. to place alone, to set apart from others.

isolation (I sō lā' shun), n. the state of being set apart from others; seclusion.

*isosceles** (I sos' e lēz), adj. having two equal sides, as an *isosceles* triangle.

issue (ish' ū), n. that which flows or passes out; offspring; an edition of a publication; a point of contention.

*issue** (ish ū), v.i. and v.t. to come or flow forth; to send forth; to put into circulation, as a newspaper or money.

*isthmian** (is' mi an), adj. relating to an isthmus.

*isthmus (is' mus), *n.* a narrow neck of land connecting two larger bodies of land.

itch (ich), *n.* a feeling of irritation in the skin; a constant desire, as an *itch* for adventure.

itch (ich), *v.i.* to be afflicted with an irritated condition of the skin; to have a constant desire for something, as he simply *itches* for excitement.

item (i' tem), *n.* a separate unit in a list; a particular article in a newspaper, as a short note; a sum entered in an account.

iteration (it ẽr ā' shun), *n.* repetition.

itinerant (i tin' ẽr ant), *adj.* wandering.

itinerary (i tin' ẽr er i), *n.* the route of a journey.

ivory (i' vō ri), *n.* the hard, white substance of elephant or walrus tusks. *adj.* made of, resembling or color of ivory.

ivy (i' vi), *n.* a climbing or creeping woody vine with shiny, ornamental leaves.

J

jab (jab), *v.i.* and *v.t.* [*p.t.* and *p.p.* jabbed, *pr.p.* jabbing] to make a sudden thrust with something sharp; to poke; to stab an object with a thrusting motion or with something sharp.

jabber (jab' ẽr), *n.* talk that is incoherent or unintelligible. *v.i.* to talk fast and indistinctly, chatter.

jack (jak), *n.* the male of some animals, as the rabbit or the ass; the knave of any suit in a pack of playing cards; any of various kinds of levers, lifts or similar mechanical devices; a man of the common people; often written *Jack. v.t.* to raise with a jack, as *jack* up a rear wheel.

*jackal (jak' ôl), *n.* a wild carnivorous animal of the dog family that hunts at night and in packs.

jackass (jak' ås), *n.* the male ass; a blockhead.

jackdaw (jak' dô), *n.* a European bird of the crow family.

jacket (jak' et), *n.* a short, tailless coat.

jade (jād), *n.* an old, worn-out horse; a saucy young woman; a hard semiprecious stone used for ornament and in jewelry.

jagged (jag' ed), *adj.* having irregular, notched or sharp edges.

*jaguar (jag' wär),), *n.* a large wildcat found in southwestern U. S. and South America.

jail (jāl), *n.* a prison, especially one for those guilty of lesser offenses and sentenced to comparatively short terms.

jam (jam), *n.* a dense crowding of persons or things; a conserve of fruit boiled with sugar. *v.i.* and *v.t.* to become squeezed or crushed together; to stick or become unworkable by wedging; to crowd together or stick in tightly, as to *jam* clothing in a trunk; to block, as to *jam* traffic.

jamb (jam), *n.* an upright piece forming the side of an opening, as of a door.

jangle (jang' gl), *n.* a sound like that of untuned bells ringing together; a noisy quarrel. *v.i.* and *v.t.* to make discordant sounds; to cause something to make such sounds; to wrangle.

janitor (jan' i tẽr), *n.* one who serves as caretaker of a building.

japan (ja pan'), *n.* a hard glossy varnish, Japanese lacquer; articles finished with this kind of varnish. *v.t.* [*p.t.* and *p.p.* japanned, *pr.p.* japanning] to cover with hard, brilliant varnish or lacquer.

jar (jär), *n.* an approximately barrel-shaped, broad-mouthed vessel of earthenware or glass; as much as a jar will hold, as to cook a *jar* of cherries. *n.* a sudden shaking or jolt; a mental shock; a clash of opinions; a discordant sound. *v.i.* and *v.t.* to shake with vibration; to clash, produce a harsh sound, as it *jars* on my ears; to cause to shake, to jolt, as the shock *jarred* the house.

*jardiniere (jär di nẽr'), *n.* an ornamental stand or pot for flowers or plants; a large, fancy flower pot.

jargon (jär' gon), *n.* confused, unintelligible talk; the special speech or vocabulary of a class, as of technicians, artists, thieves.

*jasmine (jas' min), *n.* a shrub of the olive family with fragrant flowers; perfume made from jasmine flowers.

jasper (jas' pẽr), *n.* a variety of quartz stained red, brown, green or yellow, polished and used for ornament.

*jaundice (jôn' dis), *n.* a disease marked by yellow coloring of the eyeballs and skin, caused by the blood taking up bile.

jaunt (jônt), *n.* a short walk or ride for pleasure. *v.i.* to go for a walk, ride or short excursion.

*jaunty (jôn' ti), *adj.* gay; sprightly and nonchalant; dashingly gallant.

javelin (jav' lin), *n.* a light spear to be thrown by hand.

jaw (jô), *n.* the upper or lower part of the bony framework of mouth in which the teeth are set; anything that resembles a jaw, as a mechanical contrivance for gripping.

jay (jā), *n.* a bird related to the crow, especially the blue *jay.*

jaywalker (jā' wôk ẽr), *n.* one who crosses streets carelessly or at the wrong places.

jazz (jaz), *n.* a type of American music of Negro origin, developed from ragtime and used especially for dance music.

jealous (jel' us), *adj.* characterized by anxiety, envy, distrust; fearing faithlessness in love; suspicious.

jealousy (jel' us i), *n.* envy; suspicion; the demand for exclusive affection or attention.

*jean (jēn), *n.* a twilled cotton cloth: *jeans,* clothes made of this cloth.

jeer (jẽr) *n.* a sneer, taunting mockery. *v.i.*

and v.t. to sneer, scoff, ridicule.

jelly (jel' i), *n.* [*pl.* jellies] a semitransparent, semisolid substance obtained by the prolonged boiling of fruit juices or meats; a food preparation of such nature, *v.i. and v.t.* to become jelly; to make into jelly.

jenny (jen' i), *n.* a machine used in spinning; the female of certain animals, as the ass; an airplane used for training fliers.

*****jeopardize** (jep' ër dīz), *v.t.* to expose to hazard or risk.

jeopardy (jep' ër di), *n.* a state of risk or hazard, peril.

jerk (jûrk), *n.* a sudden pull or twist, spasmodic movement, *v.i. and v.t.* to move as in a spasm; to push, pull or twist suddenly and sharply.

jersey (jûr' zi), *n.* a knitted fabric, as of wool; a shirtlike garment made of it.

jest (jest), *n.* a joke, a quip, *v.i.* to make jokes; to make fun of, make light of.

jester (jest' ër), *n.* a buffoon or clown in a royal or noble household of medieval time to create mirth or amusement; a king's fool.

jet (jet), *n.* a sudden gush of liquid or gas through a narrow opening; a spout for emission of a stream of liquid or gas, as a gas *jet. n.* a velvety-black form of anthracite coal, polished and used in making ornaments, as buttons. *v.i. and v.t.* to shoot forth in a sudden stream, as a liquid or gas; to cause to spurt or shoot out, as to *jet* steam. *adj.* made of, or having color and appearance of jet.

jet lag (jet ' lag), *n.* when the body is disrupted with changes of sleep and hunger due to changes in time zones usually caused by jet travel.

jetsam (jet' sam), *n.* pieces of cargo thrown overboard to lighten a vessel in distress; such goods washed ashore.

jettison (jet' i sun), *v.t.* to throw overboard or abandon goods in time of peril.

jetty (jet' i), *n.* [*pl.* jetties] a wall run out from shore into the water to furnish protection against the wash of the waves.

*****jewel** (jōō' el), *n.* a valuable ornament, a cut and mounted precious stone; a valuable piece of hard substance used to make a bearing in a watch.

jeweler (jōō' el ër), *n.* one who makes or sells jewels.

*****jewelry** (jōō' el ri), *n.* jewels collectively; personal ornaments, especially those set with jewels, as bracelets, necklaces, pins.

jib (jib), *n.* a triangular sail rigged from the head of the foremast to the jib boom; the arm of a crane from which the load is suspended. *v.i.* to move sideways or backward, shift or swing around.

jibe (jīb), *v.i. and v.t.* to shift from one side of a vessel to the other, as a sail *jibes;* to change a vessel's course so that such a shift occurs; to tack.

jiffy (jif' i), *n.* a moment.

jig (jig), *n.* a quick, lively dance or music for it; mechanical device for jolting up and down. *v.i. and v.t.* to dance a jig; to use a jig.

jilt (jilt), *n.* a person who discards a suitor

previously accepted.

jilt (jilt), *v.t.* to discard a lover.

jingle (jin'gl), *n.* a sharp tinkling metallic sound as the *jingle* of sleighbells; a short verse with a simple, repeated rhyme.

jingle (jing' gl), *v.i. and v.t.* to make or cause to make a sharp, tinkling, metallic sound, as the bells *jingled,* he *jingled* the coins in his pocket.

jingo (jing' gō), *n.* one who talks war, boasts of his country's prowess in war or advocates warlike policies.

job (job), *n.* a piece of work; regular employment, as to have a good *job;* any scheme for private gain. *v.t.* to buy and sell odd lots of goods. *adj.* done by the piece, as *job* work; bought, sold or considered as a total, as a *job* lot.

jobbery (job' ër i), *n.* the act of scheming or trading for one's own gain at public expense, graft.

jockey (jok' i), *n.* one who makes a profession of riding horses in races. *v.i. and v.t.* to cheat; to deceive; to play for position in a contest or for advantage in a business deal.

jocose (jō kōs'), *adj.* given to joking, jolly, humorous.

jocular (jok' ū lër), *adj.* making jokes or done as a joke.

jocularity (jok ū lar' i ti), *n.* merriment.

*****jocund** (jok' und), *adj.* jolly, gay, playful.

*****jodhpurs** (jōd' poorz), *n.* riding breeches that fit tightly from knee to ankle.

jog (jog), *n.* a slight shake or push; a slow trot; a slight turning aside, as a *jog* in a road. *v.t. and v.i.* to push or shake slightly; to trot slowly to make a slight turn, as the road jogs left.

join (join), *v.i. and v.t.* to come together; to bring together, to unite; to become a member, as to *join* a club; to engage in, as *join* battle.

joint (joint), *n.* a uniting place, a junction; the hinge where two bones of an animal body meet, as knee, hip or elbow; one of the large pieces into which a carcass is cut, as a *joint* of beef. *adj.* united; shared; held in common, as *joint* stock.

jointure (join' tūr), *n.* a settlement by which a wife agrees to accept a specified inheritance on her husband's death instead of a life interest or dower right in his entire estate.

*****joist** (joist), *n.* a floor timber or beam, running parallel from wall to wall.

joke (jōk), *n.* something said or done to excite laughter, a jest, witticism. *v.i.* to jest, make merry.

jollification (jol i fi kā' shun), *n.* merrymaking.

jollity (jol' i ti), *n.* the state of being merry or jolly, gaiety.

jolly (jol' i), *adj.* lively, merry, gay.

jolt (jōlt), *n.* a sudden jerk or shock; a knock or blow. *v.i. and v.t.* to bump, as the wagon *jolted* along; to push or jar, as the blow *jolted* him.

*****jonquil** (jong' kwil), *n.* a bulb-rooted plant

with fragrant white or yellow flowers.

joss (jos), *n.* a Chinese household idol.

*****jostle** (jos' l), *v.t.* to push against; to push with the elbow.

jot (jot), *n.* a small particle, as not a *jot* or tittle. *v.t.* to note in writing, make a memorandum of, as to *jot* it down on paper.

jounce (jouns), *v.t. and v.i.* to jolt, shake up and down, especially by rough riding.

journal (jûr' nal), *n.* a daily record of events, as a newspaper, diary, or legislative minutes; commercial entry book for daily business transactions. *n.* the part of a mechanical rotating shaft or spindle that turns on a bearing.

journalist (jûr' nal ist), *n.* one who writes for or edits a newspaper.

journey (jûr' ni), *n.* travel from one place to another, a trip. *v.i.* to travel.

*****joust** (just) *n.* a combat between two mounted knights with lances in medieval times.

*****jovial** (jō' vi al), *adj.* convivial, merry.

joy (joi), *n.* gladness, happiness, rejoicing, bliss.

Syn. Pleasure, delight, gladness. *Pleasure* is the general term for any emotion aroused by gratification; *delight* is keen pleasure; *gladness* is happiness, especially as apparent in facial expression or bearing; *joy* is a deep and spiritual experience.

Ant. Sorrow, grief, pain, displeasure.

joyful (joi' fool), *adj.* full of happiness, causing happiness, as *joyful* tidings.

joyous (joi' us), *adj.* causing happiness; blithe, gay, lighthearted, as a *joyous* child.

jubilation (jōō bi lā' shun), *n.* a shouting for joy; declaration of triumph.

jubilee (jōō' bi lē) *n.* the 50th (or 25th) anniversary of any event; any occasion of joyousness.

judge (juj), *n.* presiding officer of a court; a person presiding over a competition such as a debate and deciding which side wins; one competent to draw critical conclusions on merit of an artistic próduction, as a *judge* of music; an arbitrator. *v.i. and v.t.* to consider a case and pass sentence; to form an opinion about, as to *judge* a point at issue; to make critical estimate of, as to *judge* a work of art.

judgment (juj' ment), *n.* the pronouncing of a formal opinion or decision; the decision made; ability to make right decisions, as he has good *judgment.*

Syn. Discretion, prudence. *Judgment* is conclusive; it decides by positive inference, it enables a person to discover the truth. *Discretion* is intuitive; it discerns or perceives what is in all probability right. *Prudence* guards against the chance of evil.

Ant. Heedlessness, recklessness.

judicial (jōō dish' al), *adj.* pertaining to judges, courts or decisions or to the administration of justice.

*****judiciary** (jōō dish' i eri), *n.* judges collectively.

judicious (jōō dish' us), *adj.* prudent, based on good judgment, wise.

jug (jug), *n.* an earthenware vessel with narrow neck and a handle.

juggle (jug' l), *v.i. and v.t.* to do sleight-of-hand tricks; to perform tricks with, as to *juggle* Indian clubs.

*****jugular** (jug' ū lēr), *n.* any of certain veins on side of neck, especially one of the two large veins that return blood from the head, *adj.* relating to throat or neck, as the *jugular* vein.

juice (jōōs), *n.* the fluid part of plant or animal tissues, as apple *juice,* meat *juices.*

juicy (jōōs' i), *adj.* full of juice, succulent.

jumble (jum' bl), *n.* disorder; a disordered collection of things; a kind of cookie.

jumble (jum' bl), *v.t.* to assemble or mix in a disordered collection.

jump (jump), *n.* a leap; the space or thing leaped over, as a *jump* of 10 feet. *v.i. and v.t.* to leap; to spring up suddenly; to leap over, as to *jump* a fence; to cause to leap, as to *jump* a horse.

junction (jungk' shun), *n.* the act of joining; the state of being joined; the meeting place of two lines of any kind, as a railroad *junction,* the *junction* of two rivers.

juncture (jungk' tūr), *n.* the point or line formed by two bodies being joined together; an occasion formed by a grouping of circumstances, as at this *juncture.*

jungle (jung' gl), *n.* a dense tropical forest.

junior (jōōn' yēr), *adj.* younger in age or service or of lower standing, as a *junior* partner; a student in high school or college in the third year of the course, one year below the senior class.

juniper (jōō' ni pēr), *n.* a tree or shrub of pine family with aromatic blue fruits resembling berries having a pungent flavor.

junk (jungk), *n.* discarded articles of all kinds, waste. *n.* a Chinese sailing vessel. *v.t.* to discard, scrap.

junket (jung' ket), *n.* a dish made of sweetened milk jellied by the action of rennet; a feast or outing, especially at public expense.

junta (jun' ta or Spanish hōōn' tä), *n.* a legislative assembly or council in Latin countries.

junto (jun' tō), *n.* [*pl.* juntos] a secret council of state, faction, cabal.

juridical (joo rid' i kal), *adj.* pertaining to law and the administration of justice.

jurisdiction (joor is dik' shun), *n.* legal power or authority; extent of authority and power.

*****jurisprudence** (joor is proo' dens), *n.* the science of law; the system of laws of a country.

jurist (joor' ist), *n.* one who is skilled in the science of law.

*****juror** (joor' ēr), *n.* one who serves on a jury.

*****jury** (joor' i), *n.* a group of persons, usually 12, sworn to listen to the evidence at a trial and pronounce a true verdict; a group of persons selected to award prizes, as in an art competition.

just (just), *adj.* conformable to law, human and Divine; impartial, fair, honest in dealing with others. *adv.* exactly, as placed *just* to the left; only, as *just* lately; very recently, as I have *just* heard the news;

barely, as it *just* missed the mark.

justice (jus' tis). *n.* the quality of being just; the principle or practice of dealing justly with others, fairness; administration of law, as a court of *justice*; a judge or magistrate.

justice (jus' tis). *n.* the quality of being just; demonstrably right, defensible.

*justifiable (jus' ti fi a bl). *adj.* excusable; demonstrably right, defensible.

justification (jus ti fi kā' shun). *n.* the act of justifying; that which justifies, vindication.

justify (jus ti fi), *v.t.* to prove just or right;

to prove or pronounce blameless; to space type so that lines end evenly.

jut (jut) *v.i.* to project beyond a main body, as the cape *juts* to the east.

jute (joot). *n.* the fiber of an East Indian plant used in making ropes, twine or burlap.

*juvenile (jōō' ve nil). *adj.* young; suitable for children, as *juvenile* books.

juxtaposition (juks ta pŏ zish' un), *n.* the act of placing side by side or state of being so placed.

K

k (kā), the symbol for the quantity 1,024. Used to designate memory capacity, as 48K RAM. K is generally taken to mean 1,000.

kale (kāl), *n.* a kind of cabbage with open, curled leaves: also spelled *kail*.

*kaleidoscope (ka li' dō skōp), *n.* a cylinder containing loose pieces of colored glass, and mirrors that show the pieces in ever-changing patterns as the cylinder is turned.

kangaroo (kang ga rōō'), *n.* an Australian leaping animal with short forelegs, long, powerful hind legs, a muscular tail and (in the female) a pouch for carrying the young.

*kaolin (kā' ō lin), *n.* a pure white clay used in making porcelain.

karakul (kar' a kul), *n.* a sheep of Asia; the curly black coat of the new lambs of this breed, used as fur.

karat (kar' at), *n.* a unit of weight for precious stones; one twenty-fourth, used in measuring the fineness of gold: also spelled *carat*.

*kayak (kī' ak), *n.* an Eskimo canoe.

*keel (kēl), *n.* the lengthwise foundational timber or metal structure of a ship, extending from stem to stern at the bottom of the hull; the corresponding part of an airplane body serving to maintain balance.

keel (kēl), *v.i. and v.t.* to turn bottom up, as to *keel* over; to furnish with a keel; to turn up the bottom of, as to *keel* up a boat.

keen (kēn), *n.* a wailing lamentation for the dead. *v.i. and v.t.* to lament for the dead with wailing. *adj.* sharp, cutting, acute, as a *keen* edge on a knife, a *keen* or cutting wind, *keen* criticism.

keep (kēp), *v.i. and v.t.* to continue, as to *keep* happy, *keep* going, the fruit *keeps* well; to maintain, as to *keep* a horse; to preside over, as to *keep* house, *keep* a store; to observe or honor, as to *keep* the Sabbath, *keep* a promise; to detain, as to *keep* a pupil after school.
    Syn. Preserve, save. The idea of having in one's possession is common to all these terms. The elementary meaning of *keep* is to retain in one's possession. To *preserve* is to *keep* with care, and free of all injury. To *save* something is to *keep* it laid up in a safe place.
    Ant. Relinquish.

keepsake (kēp' sāk), *n.* something kept as a souvenir of the giver.

keg (keg), *n.* a small, heavy barrel of 10 gallons or less.

kelp (kelp), *n.* a large coarse brown seaweed; ashes of seaweed from which iodine is obtained.

ken (ken), *n.* knowledge, comprehension, as beyond my *ken*.

kennel (ken' el), *n.* a house for a dog: *kennels*, a place where dogs are raised or kept.

kennel (ken' el), *v.i. and v.t.* to live in a kennel; to keep in a kennel.

kerchief (kûr' chif), *n.* a piece of cloth, usually square, worn as a head covering, around the neck or for ornament; a handkerchief.

kernel (kûr' nel), *n.* a grain or seed; the inner part of a nut or fruit pit; a whole grain of wheat or corn; the essence or core, as of a plan or an argument.

kerosene (ker' ō sēn), *n.* refined petroleum, also distilled from bituminous shale and called *coal oil*.

ketchup (kech' up), *n.* a table sauce made of tomatoes and other ingredients; catsup or catchup.

kettle (ket' l), *n.* a metal vessel in which liquids are boiled, especially a tea*kettle*.

key (kē), *n.* a metal instrument used to operate a lock; a lever producing the desired action in an instrument, as a piano *key*, a typewriter *key*; the clue to the solution of a problem or riddle, or the deciphering of a code; a device for opening and closing an electric circuit, as a telegraph *key*; a pitch or tone of voice; a system of musical tones based upon a certain note, the *keynote*. *n.* a low island or reef. *v.i. and v.t.* to lock with a key; to regulate the pitch and tone of, as in music.

keynote (kē' nōt), *n.* the first or tonic note of a scale; a fundamental idea, as the *keynote* of a speech.

keystone (kē' stōn), *n.* the topmost stone in an arch, wedge-shaped and holding the entire structure solidly in place.

*khaki (kä' ki), *n.* olive drab or brown cloth used in making uniforms.

*khan (kän), *n.* a prince, lord or governor in Persia, Afghanistan and other Asiatic countries.

khan (kän), *n.* a roadside inn of the Far East.

*khedive (ke dēv'), *n.* title of the Turkish

viceroy of Egypt from 1867 to 1914.

kick (kik), *n.* a blow with the foot; recoil, as of a gun. *v.i. and v.t.* to strike out with the foot; to strike something with the foot; to recoil, as a gun.

kid (kid), *n.* the young of the goat; the flesh, fur, or skin of a kid.

kidnap (kid' nap), *v.t.* to carry away, as a person, against his will and hold for ransom; to abduct.

kidney (kid' nĕ), *n.* [pl. kidneys] one of two oblong, flattened organs that separate waste from the blood, passing it off as urine; anything shaped like a kidney, as a *kidney bean;* temperament or constitution, sort or kind, as one of that *kidney.*

kill (kil), *v.t.* to deprive of life; to weaken or destroy, as to *kill* the flavor of; in printing and editing, to order withheld from publication.

*kiln (kil), *n.* an oven in which things are dried or hardened, as a brick *kiln.*

kilocycle (kil' ō si kl), *n.* a unit, 1,000 cycles per second, used in measuring the frequency of an alternating current.

kilogram (kil' ō gram), *n.* a unit of weight and mass in the metric system equal to 1,000 grams or 2.2046 pounds avoirdupois.

kilometer (kil' ō mē tēr), *n.* a unit of distance in the metric system equal to 1,000 meters or 3,280.8 feet, about 5/8 of a mile.

kilowatt (kil' ō wot), *n.* a unit of electrical power equal to 1,000 watts.

kilt (kilt), *n.* a knee-length, plaited skirt of tartan cloth worn by men in the Scottish Highlands.

*kimono (ki mō' nō), *n.* a dressing gown made like loose outer robe worn by Japanese.

kin (kin), *n.* a group of persons of the same stock or family; relatives collectively.

kind (kind), *n.* a natural group, class or division; sort, as this *kind* of candy; nature, character, quality.

kind (kind), *adj.* benevolent, indulgent, sympathetic and considerate.

kindle (kin' dl), *v.i. and v.t.* to catch fire; to set fire to; to inflame.

kindling (kin' dling), *n.* any easily lighted material used to start a fire.

kindly (kīnd' li), *adj.* humane, benevolent, kind. *adv.* in a kind manner, graciously.

kindness (kīnd' nes), *n.* the quality of being benevolent and well-disposed; a kind act.

kindred (kin' dred), *n.* relationship, kinship; persons related by birth or marriage, relations. *adj.* related; alike in nature or character.

*kinematics (kin ē mat' iks), *n.* the science of pure motion.

*kinetic (ki net' ik), *adj.* pertaining to motion; imparting motion.

kinetics (ki net' iks), *n.* the science that treats of the action of forces in producing changes of motion.

king (king), *n.* a male sovereign; a card in each suit of a pack of playing cards carrying a picture of a king; a piece in checkers that can be moved in any direction; the principal piece in chess.

kingdom (king' dum), *n.* a land ruled by a king; one of the three great divisions of existence, as the animal, vegetable and mineral *kingdoms.*

kingly (king' li), *adj.* befitting or like a king, royal, noble, regal.

kink (kingk), *n.* a twist, curl or loop in a rope or string; an odd, fanciful whim.

kink (kingk), *v.i. and v.t.* to form twists or loops, as this thread *kinks;* to form into twists or curls, as to *kink* the hair.

kinsfolk (kinz' fōk), *n.* relatives.

kipper (kip' ēr), *n.* a salmon or herring, cleaned, salted and smoked.

kiss (kis), *n.* a caress with the lips.

kiss (kis), *v.i. and v.t.* to caress with the lips.

kit (kit), *n.* an outfit of equipment, as a tool *kit.*

*kitchen (kich' en), *n.* a room set apart for cooking.

kite (kit), *n.* a bird of prey of the hawk family; a light frame of wood covered with paper or cloth, to be flown in the air.

kith (kith), *n.* friends and acquaintances.

kitten (kit' n), *n.* a young cat.

kleptomania (klep tō mā' ni a), *n.* a form of neurotic weakness marked by irresistible desire to steal.

kleptomaniac (klep tō mā' ni ak), *n.* a person afflicted with kleptomania.

knack (nak), *n.* adroitness, dexterity, a special gift for doing something, as he has the *knack* of making people feel at ease.

knapsack (nap' sak), *n.* a case to hold personal articles and carried on the back, as by soldiers.

knave (nāv), *n.* a dishonest person, a rascal; a card in each suit of a pack of playing cards with the picture of a servant on it, a jack.

knavery (nāv' ēr i), *n.* [pl. knaveries] dishonesty; action befitting a knave.

knead (nēd), *v.t.* to mix by working with the hands, as dough; to massage; to mold into shape with the hands, as clay.

knee (nē), *n.* the joint uniting the leg and thigh bones; anything resembling a knee, as a bent piece of timber used in boatbuilding.

kneecap (nē' kap), *n.* the flat, oval, movable bone at the front of the knee, the patella; a protective covering worn over the knee.

kneel (nēl), *v.i.* [p.t. and p.p. knelt or kneeled, pr.p. kneeling] to bend the leg and stoop forward so as to rest the weight of the body on a knee or the knees.

kneepan (nē' pan), *n.* the patella.

knell (nel), *n.* the sound of a bell, especially when tolled for a funeral; anything that indicates death or failure.

knickknack (nik' nak), *n.* an ornamental trifle.

knife (nif), *n.* [pl. knives] a sharp-edged steel blade set in a handle; a cutting instrument with several blades that hinge into a case used as a handle. *v.t.* to stab or cut with a knife.

knight (nit), *n.* one who holds non-hereditary rank next below a baronet in Great Britain; a member of any of certain orders or societies, as the *Knights* of Columbus; a certain chess piece, placed between castle and bishop.

knit (nǐt), *v.i.* and *v.t.* to weave yarn into a fabric with needles; to make something by knitting; to draw together and unite closely.

knob (nob), *n.* a rounded handle, as of a door or a cane; a round protuberance; a hill or mountain.

knock (nok), *n.* a stroke with something hard and heavy; a rap with the knuckles, as on a door; a sound in machinery caused by a defect. *v.i.* and *v.t.* to strike a blow with something hard; to rap on a door; to give a blow to; to make a pounding noise, as an engine.

knockout (nok' out), *n.* a mechanical device used to throw out finished work; a blow that produces unconsciousness.

knoll (nōl), *n.* a rounded small hill.

knot (not), *n.* an arrangement of cords or ropes in such a way that they will hold together, or hold something without slipping or loosening; an entanglement or difficulty; a tough spot in a board caused by hard fibers that grew around the joining of a branch with the trunk; a unit of measure of a ship's speed, equal to a nautical mile (6080.20 ft.), as to make 8 *knots* per hour.

knot (not), *v.i.* and *v.t.* to make a knot or knots; to tie in a knot; to fasten with knots.

knotty (not' ĭ), *adj.* [*comp.* knottier, *superl.* knottiest] full of knots; tangled; difficult, as a *knotty* problem.

know (nō), *v.i.* and *v.t.* [*p.t.* knew, *p.p.* known, *pr.p.* knowing] to have knowledge; to be certain of; to recognize; to have acquaintance or experience with, as to *know* a thing is so, to *know* Latin, to *know* how to do something, to *know* the way home, to *know* someone, to *know* sorrow.

knowledge (nol' ej), *n.* clear perception of a truth, fact or subject; that which is known; information gained and preserved; learning.

Syn. Wisdom, science, information. *Wisdom* is the understanding and insight that come from experience; *science* is precise and classified knowledge; *information* is knowledge gained from books or instruction.

Ant. Ignorance.

knuckle (nuk' l), *n.* the projecting joint at the base of a finger; the knee joint of a calf or pig.

knurl (nûrl), *n.* a hard twisted knot or protuberance, as on a tree; one of the ridges on the edge of a coin, a nut or a screwhead.

knurl (nûrl), *v.t.* to bead, ridge or mill, as the edges of a coin.

knurly (nûr' lĭ), *adj.* [*comp.* knurlier, *superl.* knurliest] knarly.

koala (kō ä'/la), *n.* an arboreal tailless marsupial of Australia, resembles a bear.

kudu (kōō' dōō), *n.* a large handsome African antelope.

kumquat (kum' kwot), *n.* a small citrus fruit of China, used in making preserves.

L

label (lā' bel), *n.* a small piece of paper, cloth or metal attached to anything to show ownership, contents, destination and the like; a catch phrase or descriptive word. *v.t.* [*p.t.* and *p.p.* labeled or labelled, *pr.p.* labeling or labelling] to attach a label to; to classify, as if with a label.

labial (lā' bĭ al), *n.* a sound formed by the lips; a letter representing such a sound, as the consonants *p, b, m, f, v.*

labial (lā' bĭ al), *adj.* pertaining to the lips; formed by the lips, as a *labial* sound.

labor (lā' bēr), *n.* work, toil; exertion or effort, either physical or mental; those who work for wages, especially in industrial establishments, or engineering works or in the trades; childbirth. *v.i.* and *v.t.* to toil; to struggle; to have heavy going of it, advance with difficulty, as a wagon *labors* over a muddy road or a ship *labors* in heavy seas.

laboratory (lab' ō ra tō rĭ), *n.* [*pl.* laboratories] a building or room in which scientific experiments are conducted, or where drugs, chemicals, explosives are tested and compounded.

laborious (la bō' rĭ us), *adj.* difficult, toilsome, involving much effort.

labyrinth (lab' ĭ rinth), *n.* an intricate arrangement, as of paths in a garden or halls and rooms in a building; a maze.

labyrinthine (lab ĭ rin' thin), *adj.* intricate;

puzzling.

lace (lās), *n.* an ornamental fabric of fine thread, woven in patterns; braid used on uniforms, as gold *lace;* a cord run through eyelets to hold things together, as a shoelace.

lace (lās), *v.t.* to adorn with lace; to fasten with a lace; to lash or whip.

lacerate (las' ēr āt), *v.t.* to mangle, tear, wound with jagged cuts; to harrow the feelings.

laceration (las ēr ā' shun), *n.* the act of mangling; a jagged cut; deep injury to the feelings.

lachrymal (lak' rĭ mal), *adj.* pertaining to tears.

lachrymose (lak' rĭ mōs), *adj.* tearful; inclined to weep.

lack (lak), *n.* deficiency, need; the thing needed or wanting. *v.i.* and *v.t.* to be deficient in or in want of; to be destitute of.

lackadaisical (lak a dā' zĭ kal), *adj.* affectedly pensive or sentimental; languishing; listless.

lackey (lak' ĭ), *n.* a menial attendant; footman.

laconic (la kon' ĭk), *adj.* using few words, concise, terse, pithy.

lacquer (lak' ēr), *n.* a transparent varnish; Chinese or Japanese woodwork finished with a hard, heavy varnish.

lacquer (lak' ẽr), v.t. to finish with lacquer.

*__lacrosse__ (la krôs'), n. a game played by teams of 12 players.

lacteal (lak' tē al), adj. milky; of or like milk.

lad (lad), n. a boy or youth.

ladder (lad' ẽr), n. a framework having two long parallel side-pieces with parallel cross-pieces called rounds, regularly spaced, used in climbing; any similar device for climbing or scaling; as shrouds and ratlines on a ship or a fish ladder.

lade (lād), v.t. [p.t. laded, p.p. laded or laden, pr.p. lading] to load; to scoop up and throw out, as to lade water out of a tub.

lading (lād' ing), n. the act of loading; the act of bailing; a load or cargo.

ladle (lād'l), n. a deep long-handled spoon, a scoop. v.t. to dip or serve liquid with a ladle or dipper.

lady (lād' i), n. [pl. ladies] a well-bred woman; a titled woman.

ladybird (lā' di bûrd), n. a red and black speckled beetle, ladybug.

lag (lag), n. a retardation of movement, as in machinery; a stave of a cask.

lag (lag), v.i. to move slowly, fall behind.

laggard (lag' ẽrd), n. a slow or sluggish person, loiterer. adj. slow-moving.

lagoon (la gōōn'), n. a shallow lake formed at the mouth of a river.

*__lair__ (lâr), n. the den of a wild animal.

*__laity__ (lā' i ti), n. the people as distinguished from the clergy; all people outside a stated profession.

lake (lāk), n. a large inland body of water.

lake (lāk), n. a coloring matter made of insoluble metallic compounds; a deep red color.

lama (lā' ma), n. a Buddhist priest of Tibet.

lamb (lam), n. a young sheep.

lambent (lam' bent), adj. playing over a surface, as flame; flickering softly, as light.

lambskin (lam' skin), n. the skin of a lamb dressed with the fleece on; leather made from it.

lame (lām), adj. crippled or disabled in the limbs; not sound or convincing, as a lame excuse. v.t. to cripple.

lament (la ment'), n. an expression of sorrow; an elegy.

*__lament__ (la ment'), v.i. and v.t. to feel sorrow, mourn; to express sorrow for.

*__lamentable__ (lam' en ta bl), adj. deplorable; sorrowful.

lamp (lamp), n. a vessel in which oil is burned through a wick to give light; any electrical or gas device for producing artificial light or heat, as an arc lamp, a sun lamp.

lampoon (lam pōōn'), n. a satire designed to bring a person into contempt or ridicule. v.t. to ridicule a person in a satire.

lamprey (lam' pri), n. an aquatic animal resembling an eel; has gill pockets or branchial openings on sides.

*__lance__ (làns), n. a weapon consisting of a shaft with a sharp metal head, wielded by thrusting. v.t. to pierce with a lance; to cut with a lancet.

lancet (làn' set), n. a pointed, two-edged sur-

gical instrument.

land (land), n. the portion of the earth's surface not covered by water; ground, earth; a national territory; the country as set apart from the city, as back to the land; tracts of ground, as public land, to inherit land.

Syn. Country, ground. The term land in its elementary sense does not include the idea of habitation; the term country is not centered upon the land as land but conveys the idea of a region under one government. We speak of the land as rich or poor according to what it yields; of a country as rich or poor according to what its people possess. Ground means earth or soil as distinguished from water. v.i. and v.t. to come ashore from a ship or to earth from an airship, to alight; to set ashore, as a ship's or airship's passengers; to bring to land, as a fish; to take or win, as to land a prize.

landing (land' ing), n. the coming or putting ashore of passengers or goods from a vessel; the alighting on earth, as of an airplane; also a place where passengers or cargo are discharged; a small level platform at the top or at a turn in a staircase.

landlocked (land' lokt), adj. entirely or nearly surrounded by land, as a harbor.

landlubber (land' lub ẽr), n. a sailor's term for one who is not a sailor.

landmark (land' märk), n. any object on land easily seen from sea, that guides a pilot; any object that serves as a guide.

lane (lān), n. a narrow road; a little-traveled path; a regular route, as air lanes, ocean lanes, traffic lanes.

*__language__ (lang' gwij), n. human speech; the speech of one people as distinguished from that of others; specialized words and phrases of a certain trade, profession or subject, as scientific language, the language of baseball, of the turf, of the movies.

languid (lang' gwid), adj. deficient in energy, spiritless, apathetic, as a languid manner.

languish (lang' gwish), v.i. to become weak or spiritless, droop, pine.

*__languor__ (lang' gẽr), n. lack of physical or mental energy; listlessness.

lank (langk), adj. lean, slender.

lanky (langk' i), adj. tall, thin and loose-jointed.

lansdowne (lanz' doun), n. a fine fabric of silk and wool.

lantern (lan' tẽrn), n. a transparent case to protect a lamp from the weather, sometimes portable or sometimes stationary, as the glassed room enclosing a lighthouse beacon.

lap (lap), n. the part of the body from waist to knees of a seated person; the margin by which one surface extends beyond another, as the lap of shingles; one length of a course which has to be passed over more than once in a race. n. the act of lapping; as much liquid as can be taken with one lick of the tongue, as a lap of milk. v.t. and v.i. to gain a lap in a race on a circular track, to take up liquid with the tongue, as a cat laps milk; to lay together so that one projects over the other, as to *lap* shingles; to project over another, as the shingles *lap*.

lap dog (lap dŏg), *n.* a small pet dog.

lapel (la pel'), *n.* the turned over part of a coat, from the collar to the front of the body part

lappet (lap' et), *n.* a hanging fold of a garment; a flap of flesh, as a bird's wattle.

lapse (laps), *n.* steady passage, as of time; a slip or fault, as a *lapse* of memory, a *lapse* from virtue.

lapwing (lap' wing), *n.* a crested plover of the Old World.

larceny (lär' se ni), *n.* theft.

larch (lärch), *n.* a coniferous, deciduous tree of the pine family; its tough wood.

lard (lärd), *n.* hog's fat, melted and cooled.

lard (lärd), *v.t.* to smear with lard; to enrich by inserting strips of pork or bacon before roasting, as meat.

larder (lär' dēr), *n.* a pantry; a supply of household provisions.

large (lärj), *adj.* of great size; extensive, as a *large* forest; of more than average power or scope; *at large*, unconfined, as the murderer is still *at large;* representing a whole state or section, not a single district, as a representative *at large*.

Syn. Great, bulky, big, ample. A *large* house is the opposite of a small house; a *great* house is so large or magnificent as to cause wonder or be famous; a *bulky* package is not only large but unwieldy. *Big* refers to physical size or volume, as a *big* dog, a *big* voice, or to mental or spiritual largeness, as a *big* heart. An *ample* meal is large enough to be plentiful or sufficient; an *ample* dress is overlarge.

Ant. Little, mean, narrow, small.

lariat (lar' i at), *n.* a rope or leather thong with a running noose to lasso horses or cattle, or to picket grazing animals.

lark (lärk), *n.* a European songbird; a frolic.

larkspur (lärk' spûr), *n.* a plant with showy blue, pink or white flowers having spurs like the claws of a lark.

larva (lär' va), *n.* [*pl.* larvae or larvas] an insect in the early, wingless, wormlike stage of its development after it leaves the egg and before it becomes a chrysalis; the early stage in the changes of other animals that pass through several phases of development.

*•laryngeal** (la rin' jē al), *adj.* pertaining to the larynx.

*•laryngitis** (lar in ji' tis), *n.* inflammation of the larynx.

*•larynx** (lar' ingks), *n.* [*pl.* larynges] a formation of cartilage and muscles in the throat, containing the vocal cords.

laser (lā´ zer), *n.* a device in which energy is released in a narrow beam of light from an atomic or molecular system.

lash (lash), *n.* thong of a whip; a hair that grows out from eyelid. *v.t.* to strike with a whip; to scourge with satire.

lass (las), *n.* a girl or young woman.

lassitude (las' i tūd), *n.* weariness, languor.

*•lasso** (las' ō), *n.* a rope or rawhide cord with a noose used in catching horses or cattle.

last (lȧst), *n.* a wooden or metal block on which shoes are shaped. *n.* the end; the final stage, as this is the *last* of it. *v.i.* to remain in existence or operation, endure. *adj.* coming after all others in time, place or order; final, conclusive. *adv.* after all others, as you come *last*.

lasting (lȧst' ing), *adj.* durable, continuing.

latch (lach), *n.* the catch of a door that holds it closed. *v.t.* to secure or fasten with a latch.

late (lāt), *adj.* [*comp.* later, *superl.* latest] after the usual or set time; tardy; recently deceased. *adv.* after a set time, as you came *late;* recently.

*•latent** (lā' tent), *adj.* present but not apparent, as *latent* energy.

lateral (lat' ēr al), *adj.* having to do with the side, as equi*lateral;* situated on the side, as *lateral* wings.

latex (lā' teks), *n.* a milky juice of certain plants, as the rubber tree.

*•lath** (lȧth), *n.* any of the thin, narrow strips of wood nailed to the timbers of a house to afford a hold for wall plaster; metal sheets used for the same purpose; laths collectively.

*•lathe** (lā*th*), *n.* a machine in which pieces of wood or metal are shaped by turning against a cutting tool as it revolves.

lather (la*th*' ēr), *n.* a thick foam made by moistening soap; foam caused by profuse sweating, as on a horse's hide.

latitude (lat' i tūd), *n.* distance, in degrees, north or south of the equator; freedom from close restrictions; liberality of thought.

latter (lat' ēr), *adj.* the second of two things mentioned; recent, as in *latter* times; toward the end, as the *latter* part of the year.

*•lattice** (lat' is), *n.* a crisscross openwork of wood or metal strips.

laud (lôd), *v.t.* to praise highly.

laudable (lôd' a bl), *adj.* praiseworthy.

*•laudanum** (lô' da num), *n.* a preparation of opium.

laudatory (lôd' a tō ri), *adj.* expressing praise.

laugh (lȧf), *n.* the sound caused by and expressing merriment.

*•laugh** (lȧf), *v.i. and v.t.* to express merriment by convulsive sounds accompanied by opening of the mouth and wrinkling of the face; to produce an effect by means of laughter, as we *laughed* him out of it.

laughable (lȧf' a bl), *adj.* ludicrous, comical.

laughingstock (lȧf' ing stok), *n.* a person who is the object of ridicule.

laughter (lȧf' tēr), *n.* the act or sound of laughing.

*•launch** (lônch), *n.* an open pleasure boat, usually propelled by steam, gas or electricity; the largest boat carried by a warship.

*•launch** (lônch), *v.t.* to cause to slide into the water, as a newly built ship; to hurl, as a spear; to initiate, as an enterprise.

*•laundress** (lôn' dres), *n.* a woman who washes and irons clothes.

*•laundry** (lôn' dri), *n.* [*pl.* laundries] a place where clothes are washed and ironed; clothes to be washed.

laureate (lô' rē ăt), *adj.* crowned with laurel as a symbol of honor or praise.

*laurel (lô' rel), *n.* an evergreen shrub; a symbol of fame.

laurels (lô' relz), *n. pl.* honors, distinctions.

*lava (lä' va), *n.* melted rock thrown from a volcano; this fluid in solid form.

lavatory (lav' a tō rĭ), *n.* [*pl.* lavatories] a washroom or washbasin.

lave, *v.i. and v.t.* to bathe or wash.

lavender (lav' en dēr), *n.* a fragrant plant of the mint family; the perfume made from it; the pale purplish color of its flowers.

lavish lav' ish), *adj.* profuse, extravagant. *v.t.* to bestow with profusion; to squander.

law (lô), *n.* a rule of action sustained by authority; a statute; a rule or axiom of science or art.

lawful (lô' fool), *adj.* comformable to law; sanctioned by law.

lawless (lô' les), *adj.* heedless of the law, in violation of law.

lawn (lôn), *n.* a carefully kept plot of grass, closely mown; fine cotton or linen fabric.

lawyer (lô' yer), *n.* one learned or skilled in the law; one who practices professionally in the law courts.

lax (laks), *adj.* loose, vague, weak; slack.

laxative (lak' sa tiv), *n.* a mildly purgative or cathartic medicine.

lay (lā), *n.* a lyric; a short narrative poem.

lay (lā), *v.t.* [*p.t. and p.p.* laid, *pr.p.* laying] to cause to lie; to put down or place in a certain position or order, as a hen *lays* an egg, we *lay* a carpet, a floor, a cable or a line of rails; to effect a change in the condition of something, as an invader *lays* a country waste; to suppress or calm, as rain *lays* dust; to fell, as a blow *laid* him low; to impose, as a government *lays* taxes; to place or impute, as we *lay* the blame on someone; to set in a certain place or period, as a scene; to spread, as cement.

Syn. Put, place, calm, appease, impose.

layman (lā' man), *n.* [*pl.* laymen] one of the people as distinguished from the clergy; one not of a stated profession.

lazy (lā' zǐ), *adj.* [*comp.* lazier, *superl.* laziest], disinclined to work, indolent.

*lea (lē), *n.* grassland; a meadow.

leach (lēch), *v.t.* to wash with water in order to separate some soluble element from, as to *leach* wood ash to obtain lye; to obtain by this process, as to *leach* lye from wood ashes.

lead (led), *n.* a soft, heavy, easily melted, malleable metal used in making water pipes and in many alloys and compounds; the metal strip used to separate lines in printing. *adj.* made of lead. *v.t.* to furnish with lead for some particular use, as to *lead* type by separating lines with thin bars of type metal.

lead (lēd), *v.t. and v.i.* to guide or conduct by going first, as he *led* the party home; to go or be first, as Tom *led* up the hill, Tom *leads* in spelling; to guide by influence, as to *lead* someone astray; to direct, as he *leads* the orchestra; to act as guide or director, as she *leads* at choir practice; to be the best among, as Tom *leads* his class; to conduct oneself in the course of, as to *lead* a merry life; to take a certain course, as the road *leads* to Boston; to begin a card game or hand with, as *lead* trumps; to play first, as in a game of cards.

Ant. Rebuff, repel.

leaden (led' n), *adj.* of or like lead; sluggish.

leaf (lēf), *n.* [*pl.* leaves] a unit of the foliage of a plant; anything flat and thin, as a page or the movable part of a table top; a very thin sheet of metal, as gold *leaf.*

league (lēg), *n.* an alliance to promote mutual interests; a confederation. *v.i. and v.t.* to form an alliance; to join together. *n.* a measure of distance, about three miles.

leak (lēk), *n.* an opening that lets something as a gas or a liquid, in or out accidentally, as in a boat or a pipe. *v.i. and v.t.* to let a liquid or other substance in or out accidentally through a crack or hole, as a tank or boat *leaks;* to lose by leaking, as this barrel *leaks* oil; to escape accidentally through an opening, as sugar *leaks* out of a bag; to become gradually or secretly spread about, as news *leaks* out.

leakage (lēk' ĭj), *n.* that which leaks in or out; the quantity that leaks in or out.

lean (lēn), *adj.* not fat, as meat; thin, gaunt; poor, unproductive, as to fall on *lean* days.

lean (lēn), *v.i. and v.t.* [*p.t. and p.p.* leaned, *pr.p.* leaning] to deviate or cause to deviate from an upright position; to rest one's weight, as to *lean* on a gate; to cause to rest, as to *lean* a broom against a wall; to look to for support, as to *lean* on a friend for help; to be in sympathy with, to incline to, as to *lean* towards Communism.

leaning (lēn' ing), *n.* a tendency or inclination of the mind, as a *leaning* toward mathematics.

leap (lēp), *n.* a jump; the distance covered in a jump, as a *leap* of 20 feet.

leap (lēp), *v.i. and v.t.* [*p.t. and p.p.* leaped, *pr.p.* leaping] to jump or spring; to pass over by leaping, as to *leap* a ditch or fence.

*learn (lûrn), *v.t. and v.i.* [*p.t. and p.p.* learned, *pr.p.* learning] to gain knowledge of, or skill in, as to *learn* history or knitting; to assimilate facts or information, as to *learn* quickly.

learning (lûrn' ing), *n.* knowledge acquired through study and instructions; scholarship.

lease (lēs), *n.* a written contract for the letting of property for a stated term of time and at a fixed price. *v.t.* to let property to or rent it from another.

leash (lēsh), *n.* a thong or cord by which an animal is held. *v.t.* to hold or control with a thong or cord.

least (lēst), *adj.* [*superl.* of little] smallest in degree, size, value, importance.

least (lēst), *adv.* in the lowest or smallest degree, as the *least* desirable house.

leather (leth' ēr), *n.* the tanned and curried skin or hide of an animal.

leathern (leth' ērn), *adj.* made of leather.

leave (lēv), *n.* permission, as you have my *leave* to go; departure, as to take one's *leave;* a furlough, as *leave* of absence.

leave (lēv), *v.i. and v.t.* [*p.t.* and *p.p.* left, *pr.p.* leaving] to go away, depart, as to *leave* home; to bequeath, as he *left* a fortune; to cause to remain behind, as *leave* a tip, *leave* the dog home.

Syn. Quit, forsake. To *leave* merely means to go away; to *quit* means to leave with no intention of returning. *Forsake* carries the idea of *leaving* in the lurch.

Ant. Remain, stay.

leaven (lev' en), *n.* a substance that causes fermentation, especially in dough or liquids, as yeast; any influence working silently and unseen that brings about fundamental changes. *v.t.* to produce fermentation in, literally or figuratively.

lecture (lek' tūr), *n.* a formal discourse on a set subject; a wordy reprimand.

lecture (lek' tūr), *v.i. and v.t.* to deliver a discourse; to address a discourse to, as an audience; to reprove with many words.

ledge (lej), *n.* a shelflike projection from a wall or the side of a building, as a window *ledge,* a horizontal projection from a wall of rock or a hillside.

ledger (lej' ēr), *n.* the principal account book of a business establishment, containing the credits and debits.

lee (lē), *n.* shelter from the wind, given by some intervening object, as in the *lee* of a high wall; the side away from the wind.

lee (lē), *adj.* away from the wind, as the *lee* side of a ship; in the same direction as the wind blows, as a *lee* tide.

leech (lēch), *n.* a flat bloodsucking worm that lives in water and was formerly used by doctors to bleed patients.

leek (lēk), *n.* a bulbous plant resembling the onion.

leer (lēr), *n.* a sly sidelong look expressing malice or evil. *v.i.* to look sideways with expression of sly malice or evil thought.

*•***leeward** (lē' wērd), *adj. and adv.* away from the wind, as the *leeward* side, steer to *leeward.*

leeway (lē' wā), *n.* the sideways drift of a ship from the course on which it is headed; an extra allowance of space or time, as give me a little *leeway* on this lesson.

left (left), *adj.* the side which, as one faces north, is to the west: opposite of *right.*

left-handed (left han' ded), *adj.* using the left hand better than the right; insincere or indirect, as a *left-handed* compliment.

leg (leg), *n.* one of the limbs by means of which animals stand and walk; anything resembling a leg in form or function, as the *leg* of a chair; the length of one tack covered by a vessel in sailing; either side of a triangle, distinguished from the base.

legacy (leg' a si), *n.* [*pl.* legacies] money or property left to one by a will; something inherited, as a *legacy* of character.

legal (lē' gal), *adj.* pertaining to law; in accordance with or permitted by law.

legality (le gal' i ti), *n.* [*pl.* legalities] lawfulness; technical interpretation of law.

legalize (lē gal īz), *v.t.* to make lawful.

*•***legate** (leg' it), *n.* a person who represents his country in a foreign land.

legation (lē gā' shun), *n.* an envoy and his associates; the official establishment of a diplomatic representative, especially an ambassador.

*•***legend** (lej' end), *n.* any story coming out of the past, based on history but not verifiable; the inscription on a monument, descriptive lines under an illustration in a book.

*•***legerdemain** (lej ēr dē mān'), *n.* sleight of hand.

leggings (leg' ingz), *n. pl.* long gaiters; extra covering for the legs.

*•***leghorn** (leg' hôrn), *n.* a dark, unbleached straw made in Leghorn (Livorno), Italy; a hat made from this straw.

legible (lej' i bl), *adj.* easy to read; readable.

*•***legion** (lē' jun), *n.* a division of the ancient Roman army; a military force; a multitude.

legionnaire (lē jun âr'), *n.* a legionary.

legionary (lē' jun er i), *n.* [*pl.* legionaries] a member of a legion.

legionary (lē' jun er i), *adj.* pertaining to legions; multitudinous.

legislate (lej' is lāt), *v.i. and v.t.* to enact a law; to effect by means of laws, as to *legislate* industrial improvement.

legislation (lej is lā' shun), *n.* the act of making laws; the laws made by a representative body.

*•***legislator** (lej' is lā tēr), *n.* a lawmaker; a member of a lawmaking assembly.

*•***legislature** (lej' is lā tūr), *n.* the lawmaking body of a state of the U. S.

*•***legitimate** (lē jit' i mit), *adj.* according to the law or accepted standards; born in wedlock; reasonable, as a *legitimate* argument.

*•***legume** (leg' ūm), *n.* a two-valved seed vessel having a row of seeds attached along the seam where the parts join, as in a pod of peas.

*•***leisure** (lē' zhēr), *n.* spare or free time. *adj.* free from the pressure of work and responsibilities, as *leisure* hours.

lemon (lem' un), *n.* the small acid fruit of a tropical citrus tree; its light yellow color. *adj.* having flavor or color of a lemon. disease.

lemonade (lem un ād'), *n.* a drink made of water, sugar and lemon juice.

lemur (lē' mur), *n.* a primate mammal of eastern hemisphere tropics, related to monkeys; varieties are numerous.

lend (lend), *v.i. and v.t.* [*p.t.* and *p.p.* lent, *pr.p.* lending] to make a loan; to turn over to another for temporary use; to provide, as to *lend* assistance.

*•***length** (length), *n.* measure from end to end; duration of time: as *length* of a string, a road, a meeting, life, time; a *length* of rope: *at length,* at last, after a long time.

lengthen (leng' then), *v.i. and v.t.* to become or make longer, as the days *lengthen,* to *lengthen* a dress.

lengthy (leng' thi), *adj.* [*comp.* lengthier, *superl.* lengthiest] long; long and tiresome, as a *lengthy* discourse.

*lenient (lē' ni ent), *adj.* mild; merciful; not severe.

*lenity (len' i ti), *n.* gentleness; mildness.

lens (lenz), *n.* [*pl.* lenses] a piece of glass having one or more curved surfaces used to change the course of rays of light so as to focus the view; the crystalline structure of the eye, which focuses light on the retina.

lentil (len' til), *n.* a plant of the pea family, with edible seeds.

*leonine (lē' ō nīn), *adj.* lionlike.

leopard (lep' ērd), *n.* a large flesh-eating cat of Asia and Africa, with yellow coat spotted with black.

leper (lep' ēr), *n.* a person afflicted with leprosy.

leprosy (lep' rō si), *n.* [*pl.* leprosies] a skin disease.

lesion (lē' zhun), *n.* injury; a change in any organ or bodily tissue due to injury or disease.

less (les), *n.* a smaller amount, as you have little, but I have *less*. *adj.* [comp. of little] not so large, many or much; fewer. *prep.* minus, as five *less* two equals three.

lessee (les ē'), *n.* a tenant holding a lease.

lessen (les' n), *v.i. and v.t.* to grow or make smaller in quantity or degree; to diminish.

lesser (les' ēr), *adj.* smaller, inferior.

lesson (les' n), *n.* an assignment for study; that which is taught and learned at one time; anything learned, through instruction or experience, as that sickness gave me a *lesson*.

*lessor (les' ôr), *n.* an owner who leases property to a tenant.

lest (lest), *conj.* so that not; for fear that, as judge not, *lest* ye be also judged.

let (let), *v.t. and v.i.* [*p.t.* and *p.p.* let, *pr.p.* letting] to permit, as *let* him go; to lease to a tenant, or from an owner, as we *let* a house to or from some one; to be leased, as the house *lets* for $1.00 a month.

*lethal (lē' thal), *adj.* deadly; fatal.

*lethargic (lē thär' jik), *adj.* morbidly drowsy; sluggish, dull.

lethargy (leth' ēr ji), *n.* morbid drowsiness, deep sleep; sluggishness; apathy, indifference.

letter (let' ēr), *n.* a symbol for a certain sound; a character in the alphabet; a communication in writing; exact meaning, as the *letter* of the law.

letter (let' ēr), *v.t.* to inscribe with letters.

letterpress (let ēr pres), *n.* typed text as distinguished from illustrations.

letters (let' ērz), *n. pl.* learning; literature.

*lettuce (let' is), *n.* a garden plant with crisp leaves, used as a salad.

*levee (lev' ē), *n.* formerly, an assembly held in the morning by a monarch; a morning reception; an official reception. *n.* an artificial embankment to hold a river in its channel in time of flood. *v.t.* to line a river course with embankments to check spread of flood waters.

level (lev' el), *n.* a horizontal plane or line; even altitude, as the top of this table is on a *level* with that; a carpenter's instrument having one bubble of air in a glass tube nearly full of alcohol or ether, used to determine whether a surface is horizontal or inclined by centering the bubble. *v.t.* to make even or equal in elevation. *adj.* smooth and flat; horizontal.

level off (lev' el ôf), to fly horizontally over the ground before landing, as an airplane.

*lever (lē' vēr), *n.* a bar turning on a fixed point called the fulcrum, used to transmit power.

*leverage (lē vēr ij), *n.* the power gained by using a lever; power of influence.

leviathan (lē-vī' a than), *n.* a large unidentified ocean mammal, mentioned in the Bible; anything huge.

levity (lev' i ti), *n.* buoyancy; lightness in conduct; frivolity, lack of seriousness.

levy (lev' i), *n.* [*pl.* levies] the act of raising money or men for service by drafting; the amount or number so raised. *v.t.* [*p.t.* and *p.p.* levied; *pr.p.* levying] to draft men or money; to impose a tax.

*lewd (lūd), *adj.* vulgar, impure, lustful.

lexicographer (lek si kog' ra fēr), *n.* one who engages in the writing or editing of a dictionary.

lexicon (lek' si kon), *n.* a dictionary, especially of an ancient language.

liability (lī a bil' i ti), *n.* [*pl.* liabilities] susceptibility, as to sickness; responsibility, as for debts: *pl.*, debts of a business house as opposed to *assets*.

liable (lī' a bl), *adj.* susceptible, as to a disease; responsible, as for payment of debt; distinguished from *likely*.

*liaison (lē ā zōn), *n.* a linking together of the operations of different forces, as separate divisions of an army; co-operation, intercommunication.

liar (lī ēr), *n.* one who tells lies.

libation (lī bā' shun), *n.* the act of pouring out wine or oil in honor of a god; the liquid that is poured.

libel (lī bel), *n.* defamation, especially in writing or print; publication of matter unjustly injurious to someone's reputation.

libel (lī'bel), *v.t.* [*p.t.* and *p.p.* libeled or libelled, *pr.p.* libeling or libelling] to state, write or publish matter unjustly injurious to another's reputation.

liberal (lib' ēr al), *n.* one who is progressive in thinking or principles. *adj.* openhanded, generous; broadminded, especially as to religious or political ideas.

liberality (lib ēr al' i ti), *n.* [*pl.* liberalities] generosity; broadmindedness.

liberate (lib' ēr āt), *v.t.* to set free.

liberty (lib' ēr ti), *n.* [*pl.* liberties] freedom.

librarian (lī brâr' i an), *n.* a person in charge of a library.

*library (lī' brer i), *n.* [*pl.* libraries] a collection of books; a room or building in which a collection of books is kept.

license (lī' sens), *n.* a legal permit to engage in a certain activity or carry on a certain business; abuse of freedom. *v.t.* to authorize by legal permit.

*licentiate (lī sen' shǐ ăt), n. one who is licensed by the proper authorities to preach or to practice a profession.

licentious (lī sen' shus), adj. disregardful of law or the principles of morality; dissolute.

*lichen (lī' ken), n. a flowerless plant without leaves that grows on tree bark, fences and rocks.

lick (lĭk), n. a small quantity; a saline deposit to which animals go to get salt.

lick (lĭk), v.t. to stroke with the tongue; to lap up; to make a sudden flickering movement, as a tongue of flame licks wood.

licorice (lĭk' ō rĭs), n. the root or thickened juice of a certain tropical plant.

lid (lĭd), n. a movable cover for the opening of a box or other container; the eyelid.

lie (lī), v.t. [p.t. lay, p.p. lain, pr.p. lying] to rest in or take a reclining position, as to lie down; to be or remain in a flat or prostrate position on some surface, as the book lies on the table; to be situated, as Boston lies north of New York; to extend, as all life lies before you; to be, as health lies in right living. v.i. [p.t. and p.p. lied, pr.p. lying] to utter a falsehood. n. a falsehood, an untruth.

lief (lēf), adv. gladly, willingly, as I should as lief have that one.

*liege (lēj), n. a vassal; a lord or sovereign.

liege (lēj), adj. entitled to loyalty and devotion, as a lord; bound to give service as to a lord; loyal.

*lien (lē' en), n. a legal claim upon property to cover an unpaid debt made with the property as security, as for work done.

*lieu (lū), n. place; stead, as in lieu of.

life (līf), n. animate existence; the time between birth and death; animation, spirit, zest; living beings in general, as plant life, insect life, human life; a biography, as a life of Lincoln; period of usefulness, as the life of a machine.

lift (lĭft), n. the act of raising, also the load raised; a ride given to a pedestrian, hence, help; an elevator; a hoisting apparatus.

lift (lĭft), v.i. and v.t. to rise, as the fog lifted slowly; to raise with steady pulling or a heave; to hold up, as lift your head.

Syn. Raise, hoist, elevate. To raise means to lift something into an upright position or to its original position. To lift is to pick something up from its original position. We lift a chair from the floor. We raise a flagpole or a fallen people. Hoist implies an exceptionally heavy weight or the use of tackle in lifting it. To elevate is to raise above the usual position in place or dignity.

Ant. Lower, drop.

ligament (lĭg' a ment), n. a strong tissue connecting the ends of bones in the body or supporting some internal organ.

ligature (lĭg' a tūr), n. something narrow that binds, as a bandage, or a thread for tying blood vessels together; two letters cast on one type body; a curving mark placed over two letters to show they are to be printed as a single character.

light (lĭt), n. the quality of environment that makes vision possible, the opposite of darkness; rays issuing from some illuminating body, as the sun, fire or a lamp; anything used for illumination, as a lamp or candle, as bring a light; daylight; a window pane; the condition of being seen or known, public knowledge, as graft brought to light; that which gives mental illumination or understanding, as this throws light on the problem, in the light of history. v.i. and v.t. [p.t. and p.p. lit or lighted; pr.p. lighting] to shine, be bright, as the sky lights up; to make bright, as a lamp lights a room; to kindle, as a fire; to guide with or as with a light, as the moon lighted us home. adj. illuminated; bright; clear and shining; not heavy; gay and carefree.

lighten (lĭt' n), v.t. to illuminate.

lighten (lĭt' n), v.t. to make less heavy.

lighter (lĭt' ẽr), n. a barge used in loading and unloading vessels lying offshore.

lightning (lĭt' ning), n. a sudden flash of electricity as it passes from cloud to cloud or from the clouds to the earth.

lightship, n. a moored vessel with lights to protect shipping.

ligneous (lĭg' nē us), adj. like wood, woody.

like (lĭk), n. that which resembles another, as its like does not exist.

like (lĭk), v.t. to have a taste for, be fond of, enjoy. adj. resembling in appearance or quality; equal or nearly so, as a like quantity; characteristic of, as it is like you to laugh; having the indications of, as it looks like a storm. prep. similar to, as you look like him; in the manner of, as sing like her; befitting, as speak up like a man.

liken (lĭk' n), v.t. to compare.

likeness (lĭk' nes), n. similarity; a portrait, copy; semblance, guise.

Syn. Resemblance, similarity, semblance. Likeness is used to indicate a very close sameness. Similarity indicates that things are somewhat alike. Resemblance is used of external similarity. Semblance indicates only a seeming likeness.

Ant. Difference, dissimilarity, unlikeness.

likewise (lĭk' wīz), adv. in like manner; also.

lilac (lī' lak), n. a shrub with pale purple or white flowers in heavy clusters; a pale purple color.

lilt (lĭlt), n. a lively, merry tune; cadence.

lily (lĭl' ĭ), n. a plant with bulbous root and showy flowers.

*limb (lĭm), n. a jointed part of the body; a leg or arm; a branch of a tree.

limber (lĭm' bẽr), n. the detachable front part of a gun carriage. v.i. and v.t. to become or to make flexible. adj. flexible, supple.

*lime (lĭm), n. a white, powdery substance obtained by the action of heat upon limestone, used to sweeten land and in making cement. n. a small sour fruit resembling the lemon and orange. n. the linden tree.

limelight (lĭm' lĭt), n. a strong light thrown upon the stage in a theater; publicity.

limestone (lĭm' stōn), n. a rock having carbonate of lime as the basis of its composition.

limit (lĭm′ ĭt), *n.* a boundary; the furthest extent. *v.t.* to restrict; to hold within fixed bounds.

limitation (lĭm ĭ tā′ shun), *n.* restriction; that which qualifies something.

*limn (lĭm), *v.t.* to paint or draw a picture of; to depict.

*limousine (lĭm oo zēn′), *n.* a motor car with a large closed body and a separate open but roofed seat for the driver.

limp (lĭmp), *n.* a halt in one's gait. *v.i.* to walk with a halting gait, walk lamely. *adj.* lacking stiffness; lacking character.

limpet (lĭm′ pet), *n.* a clinging shellfish.

limpid (lĭm′ pĭd), *adj.* clear, transparent, as the water in a pool.

linage (līn′ ĭj), *n.* amount of advertising measured in agate lines, that is one-twelfth of an inch in depth and one column in width, as this paper has more *linage* than that.

linchpin (lĭnch′ pĭn), *n.* a piece of iron passed through the end of an axle to keep the wheel in place.

linden (lĭn′ den), *n.* a tree with heart-shaped leaves and small clusters of cream-colored flowers.

line (līn), *n.* a distinct mark made by pen, pencil, chalk or the like, having length but little breadth; a drawn mark representing a true mathematical line; an extended rope, wire, piping, rail or row of objects, as telegraph *lines,* a railroad *line,* a water *line,* a *line* of boys; a measure of length, the twelfth part of an inch; a unit of print or poetry; a wrinkle, as the *lines* of a face; a series of ancestors, as to come from a long *line* of poets; a boundary, as crossing the *line* into Mexico; the equator; a limit, as we draw the *line* at murder; *lines,* a role in a play, as he knows his *lines.*

line (līn), *v.i. and v.t.* to form in line; to make lines in or on; to put a lining in, as a coat.

*lineage (lĭn′ ē ĭj), *n.* an ancestral line of descent, as he has an aristocratic *lineage.*

lineal (lĭn′ ē al), *adj.* in direct descent from an ancestor.

*lineament (lĭn′ ē a ment), *n.* a feature, as of the face; outline.

linear (lĭn′ ē ēr), *adj.* pertaining to lines or composed of lines; pertaining to length, as *linear* measure.

linen (lĭn′ en), *n.* a thread or cloth made from flax; articles made of linen, as household *linen. adj.* made of linen.

liner (līn′ ēr), *n.* a passenger carrying ship operated by a steamship line engaged in regular service.

linger (lĭng′ gēr), *v.i.* to delay, tarry; to hesitate.

Syn. Loiter. To *linger* is to remain in a place or at an occupation or to be slow in quitting or departing. We may *linger* from reluctance. To *loiter* is to delay from idleness, or aimlessness, especially in a place.

Ant. Hasten, hurry, speed.

*lingerie (lan zhe rē′), *n.* women's underwear; any linen goods.

lingo (lĭng′ gō), *n.* a special language, dialect or vocabulary as used by some particular class of persons; jargon, as sailors' *lingo.*

lingual (lĭng′ gwal), *adj.* pertaining to or formed by the tongue, as the letters *t, d* or *s.*

linguist (lĭng′ gwist), *n.* a student of languages, one who knows several languages.

liniment (lĭn′ ĭ ment), *n.* a thin medicated liquid to be rubbed into the skin.

lining (lī′ nĭng), *n.* an inside covering, as the *lining* of a coat, the *lining* of a furnace.

link (lĭngk), *n.* a single division of a chain; in surveying, a measure of 7.92 inches; a connection. *v.i. and v.t.* to be connected; to connect with or as with links or a chain.

links (lĭngks), *n.* a golf course.

linoleum (lĭ nō′ lē um), *n.* a floor-covering made of ground cork and oxidized linseed oil applied to a burlap or canvas back.

linotype (lĭn′ ō tĭp), *n.* a machine that sets and casts type in line units.

linseed (lĭn′ sēd), *n.* the seed of flax.

lint (lĭnt), *n.* scrapings of linen used in dressing wounds; cotton fiber; raw cotton.

lintel (lĭn′ tel), *n.* the horizontal top piece over a door or window.

linter (lĭn′ tēr), *n.* short fibers that stick to the cotton seed; a machine to remove these short fibers.

lion (lī′ un), *n.* a large, powerful carnivorous animal native to Africa and southern Asia; a famous person sought after in social circles.

lionize (lī′ un īz), *v.t.* to treat as a celebrity at social gatherings.

lip (lĭp), *n.* one of the two borders of the mouth; an edge that resembles a lip, as the *lip* of a pitcher.

lipstick (lĭp′ stĭk), *n.* rouge for the lips put up in stick form.

liquefaction (lĭk wē fak′ shun), *n.* the process of transforming or being transformed from a solid to a liquid state.

liquefy (lĭk′ wē fī), *v.i. and v.t.* to become liquid; to convert a solid into a liquid.

liquid (lĭk′ wid), *n.* a substance that is neither solid nor gas. *adj.* readily flowing, like water; neither solid nor gaseous; smooth and flowing like sounds or *l* and *r.*

liquidate (lĭk′ wi dāt), *v.i. and v.t.* to pay debts; to pay off, as a debt; to settle the affairs of a business establishment, as in bankruptcy.

*liquor (lĭk′ ēr), *n.* any liquid substance, especially any alcoholic beverage.

lisle (lĭl), *n.* a fine cotton thread or a fabric made of it.

lisp (lĭsp), *n.* imperfect pronunciation of *s* and *z. v.i. and v.t.* to pronounce *s* and *z* as *th;* to say or recite something in a lisping manner.

list (lĭst), *n.* a catalog, roll or register or the series of names or items therein, as a passenger *list;* the edge or selvage of cloth; a ridge thrown up alongside a furrow in plowing. *n.* a sidewise leaning, as of a ship. *v.t.* to place in a list, as a catalog, inventory, roll or register; to cover with strips of cloth; to plow in such a way as to turn up ridges between the furrows. *v.i.* to tilt to one side, as a ship.

•**listen** (lis' n), *v.i.* to attend closely so as to hear.

listless (list' les), *adj.* languid, apathetic; without energy.

litany (lit' a nl), *n.* a solemn responsive form of prayer, especially in a church service.

•**liter** (lē' tēr), *n.* a measure of capacity in the metric system equal to 61.026 cubic inches, .9081 dry quarts or 1.0567 liquid quarts.

literal (lit' ēr al), *adj.* consisting of letters; pertaining to letters; according to the exact words, precise, not exaggerated.

•**literary** (lit' ēr er i), *adj.* pertaining to literature; versed literature or engaged in its production.

literate (lit' ēr it), *adj.* knowing letters, able to read and write.

•**literature** (lit' ēr a tūr), *n.* the best writings; the best books of a country or a period; the collective writings upon a given subject or in a particular field, as the *literature* of sport; any kind of printed matter, as the advertising *literature* of a wholesale house.

•**lithe** (lith), *adj.* supple, pliant.

lithograph (lith' ō gráf), *n.* a print reproduced from a drawing on stone or, by same process, from a drawing on zinc or aluminum. *v.t.* to draw on stone and transfer to paper.

litigate (lit' i gāt), *v.i. and v.t.* to engage in a lawsuit; to contest in a court of law.

litmus (lit' mus), *n.* a purple dye obtained from certain lichens, which turns red in the presence of acids and turns blue in the presence of alkalis.

litter (lit' ēr), *n.* a stretcher on which a sick or wounded person is carried; a confusion of things, scattered odds and ends; a bedding, as of straw, for animals; the young of certain animals produced at one birth. *v.i. and v.t.* to bring forth young: said of animals; to scatter things about, as in a room; to put down bedding for horses or cattle.

little (lit'l), *n.* a small quantity, as a *little* of this or that. *adj.* [*comp.* less, *superl.* least] small; unimportant; petty: as a *little* man, a *little* space of time, a *little* mistake.

Syn. Small, diminutive, tiny. *Small* and *little* are often used interchangeably. *Little* is definitely the opposite of *big, small* often indicates less than what is usual or expected in reference to amount, quantity or number. *Little* often carries an implication of tenderness or charm, as a sweet *little* song. *Diminutive* is smaller than *little*. *Tiny* is exceedingly *little*.

Ant. Great, large, broad, noble.

little (lit' l), *adv.* in a small degree, as he *little* knows.

liturgy (li tûr' ji), *n.* [*pl.* liturgies] the prescribed forms or rites for public worship, especially in certain Christian churches.

live (liv), *v.i. and v.t.* to be alive, exist; to reside, as I *live* here; to pass or experience, as to *live* a good life; to put into practice, as he *lived* what he taught.

live (liv), *adj.* having life; burning, charged with electricity, as a *live* coal, a *live* wire; brilliant, as a *live* color; spirited, as a *live* argument.

livelihood (liv' li hood), *n.* means of living.

livelong (liv' long), *adj.* entire, long, as the *livelong* day.

lively (liv' li), *adj.* [*comp.* livelier, *superl.* liveliest] full of life; brisk, animated; alert, as *lively* interest.

liver (liv' ēr), *n.* a glandular organ that secretes bile.

livery (liv' ēr i), *n.* [*pl.* liveries] uniforms worn by servants; the keeping of horses for pay or the business of hiring out horses and vehicles.

livid (liv' id), *adj.* discolored by a bruise; pale as ashes.

living (liv' ing), *n.* the state of being alive; the means of keeping alive, maintenance, as to earn a *living*.

lizard (liz' ērd), *n.* a small, long-tailed scaly-bodied reptile usually having four short legs, each with five toes and claws.

llama (lä' ma), *n.* a mammal of South America, related to the camel but has no hump.

llanos (lä' nōz), *n.pl.* the grassy plains of South America.

lo (lō), *interj.* behold!

load (lōd), *n.* a burden; as much as can be carried at one time, as a wagon *load;* the charge of a gun; a mental burden.

load (lōd), *v.t.* to put a load on or into, as to *load* a ship or freight car; to place a charge in, as a gun; to burden, weigh down.

loadstone or **lodestone** (lōd' stōn), *n.* a magnetic ore of iron; anything that strongly attracts.

loaf (lōf), *n.* a formed mass of bread, cake or sugar. *v.i.* to idle time away.

loam (lōm), *n.* rich vegetable mold mixed with earth; earth consisting of clay, vegetable matter and enough sand to loosen it.

loan (lōn), *n.* anything borrowed or lent, especially a sum of money put out at interest. *v.i. and v.t.* to lend.

loath (lōth), *adj.* reluctant.

loathe (lōth), *v.t.* to hold in detestation, dislike intensely.

lobby (lob' i), *n.* [*pl.* lobbies] a small hall or waiting room; the part of a legislative hall to which the public has access; a group of persons trying to influence legislation.

lobby (lob' i), *v.i.* [*p.t. and p.p.* lobbied, *pr.p.* lobbying] to put pressure on legislators in order to secure passage of a bill.

lobbyist (lob' i ist), *n.* one who makes a practice of lobbying.

lobe (lōb), *n.* any rounded projection or subdivision of an organ, as a *lobe* of the brain or ear.

lobster (lob' stēr), *n.* a large edible crustacean that lives in the sea and has five pairs of legs, the front pair having powerful pinching claws; the meat of the lobster used as food.

local (lō' kal), *n.* a branch of a labor union whose members live in or near the city where its headquarters are; a railroad train

locality making all stops; a newspaper item of strictly neighborhood interest. *adj.* pertaining to place or a particular place.

locality (lō kal' ĭ tĭ), *n.* [*pl.* localities] a region, section or neighborhood.

localize (lō' kal ĭz), *v.t.* to fix in a stated place; to confine to a particular place.

*****locate** (lō' kāt) *v.i. and v.t.* to settle or take up residence in a place; to place something; to find the position of, as to *locate* buried treasure.

location (lō kā' shun), *n.* place or situation; a place, not in a studio, where a moving picture (or part of it) is being filmed.

lock (lok), *n.* a mechanical device with spring and bolt used to fasten a door, box lid or safe, operated by a key or a secret combination; an arrangement of gates by which boats are raised or lowered from one level to another in a dock or canal.

lock (lok), *v.i. and v.t.* to fasten a lock; to fasten with a lock, as *lock* the box; to shut in or out; to make immovable by the interlinking of parts, as to *lock* wheels.

lockjaw (lok' jô), *n.* a kind of tetanus in which the lower jaw is drawn shut and becomes rigidly fixed.

locksmith (lok' smith), *n.* one who makes or mends locks.

locomotion (lō kō mō' shun), *n.* the act or power of moving from place to place.

locomotive (lō kō mō' tiv), *n.* a steam or electric engine to haul railroad cars.

locust (lō' kust), *n.* a migratory and destructive winged grasshopper; a tree of North America.

locution (lō kū' shun), *n.* a special style of speech; a particular phrase.

lode (lōd), *n.* a deposit of mineral ore running in a vein or rock fissure.

lodestar (lōd' stär), *n.* any star used to steer by, especially the North Star.

lodestone, see **loadstone**.

lodge (loj), *n.* a small house in the woods for hunters; a gatekeeper's or gamekeeper's dwelling on an estate; the meeting place of a secret society; the society itself.

lodge (loj), *v.i. and v.t.* to live in rented rooms; to fall and come to rest; to furnish with a temporary place of residence.

loft (lôft), *n.* a room directly under a roof; an upper floor in a storehouse; a floor or gallery above the main floor, as a hay*loft*, or organ *loft*.

lofty (lôf' ti), *adj.* [*comp.* loftier, *superl.* loftiest] very high, exalted.

log (log), *n.* an undressed piece of timber; device for measuring speed of ship; book in which ship's daily record is kept.

loganberry (lō' gan ber ĭ), *n.* a plant obtained by crossing the red raspberry with the blackberry; the fruit of this plant; also a variety of dewberry.

.arithm (lôg' a rith m), *n.* the exponent, or in le < of the power to which a fixed number, the base, must be raised in order to produce a given number.

loggerhead (lôg' ĕr hed), *n.* an iron tool used hot to melt pitch; a large sea turtle: *at log-* *gerheads,* quarreling.

*****loggia** (lo' ji a), *n.* a covered outside gallery or portico.

logic (loj' ik), *n.* the science of reasoning.

logic circuit (loj ' ik ser ' kit), *n.* that within a computer which processes information, does arithmetic, and makes decisions.

logical (loj' ik al), *adj.* according to the rules of logic, correctly reasoned.

logician (lō jish' an), *n.* one who is skilled in logic.

logrolling (lôg' rōl ing), *n.* exchange of support by two political groups in order to obtain what each wants.

loin (loin), *n.* the lower part of the back of a quadruped or man.

loiter (loi' tẽr), *v.i.* to linger along a way, hang about, waste time.

loll (lol), *v.i.* to lounge at ease.

lone (lōn), *adj.* solitary, without company.

lonely (lōn' li), *adj.* [*comp.* lonelier, *superl.* loneliest] deserted, unfrequented; depressed because lacking companionship.

lonesome (lōn' sum), *adj.* without companionship; depressed because of solitude.

long (lông), *adj.* extended to great length in time or space: the opposite of *short*; taking more time to pronounce than a shorter sound, as the *a* in *fate* is long in comparison with the short *a* in *fat. adv.* to a great extent in time or space, as all day *long*, make the dress *long. v.i.* to desire intensely: used with *for*, as I *long for* a vacation.

*****longevity** (lon jev' ĭ tĭ), *n.* great length of life.

longitude (lon' ji tūd), *n.* distance measured in degrees east or west from zero meridian.

look (look), *n.* the act of looking; appearance; facial expression. *v.i. and v.t.* to direct the eyes so as to see, as to *look* at a book; to appear, as you *look* well; to observe, examine, as *look* this over.

loom (lōōm), *n.* a frame or machine used in weaving cloth.

loon (lōōn), *n.* a large diving bird of the northern hemisphere.

loop (lōōp), *n.* a doubling or fold of a string or rope; a ring or circular figure resembling such a doubling, as in a railroad; an airplane maneuver. *v.i. and v.t.* to make a loop; to form into loops or fasten with loops.

loose (lōōs), *adj.* not held fast or fitting tightly, as a *loose* knot, *loose* clothes, a *loose* tooth; vague, as *loose* thinking; lax, as *loose* morals; not compact, as *loose* as ashes. *v.t.* to let fly, as *loose* an arrow; to set free, undo, disengage, untie; to relax.

loot (lōōt), *n.* plunder. *v.t.* to pillage and plunder, as a captured city.

lop (lop), *v.i. and v.t.* to hang limply; to cut off.

loquacious (lō kwā' shus), *adj.* talkative.

lord (lôrd), *n.* a ruler or governor; a British nobleman. *v.i.* to rule; to domineer; often used with *it* as to *lord* it over others.

lore (lōr), *n.* learning; a body of tradition or knowledge of some particular subject or field, or possessed by a certain group, as f lk*lore,* animal *lore.*

lose (lōōz), *v.i. and v.t.* [*p.t.* and *p.p.* lost, *pr.p.* losing] to be deprived of, fail to keep, as we may *lose* money, health or *lose* our way; to waste, as to *lose* time or a chance; to fail to follow mentally, as to *lose* the point of an argument, *lose* track of something; to fail to win, as a battle or a game; to forget the identity of, as to *lose* oneself in a book.

Syn. Miss, forfeit, mislay. What one *loses* may be gone forever; what one *misses* may be temporarily out of sight or merely unobserved; what one *forfeits* is lost through fault or error. To *mislay* is to lose something by forgetting where it was put. *Ant.* Gain, find.

loss (lôs), *n.* the fact of losing or state of having been lost; that which is lost, waste; failure to obtain or to keep; defeat.

lot (lot), *n.* fortune or fate, as one's lot in life; a piece of land, as a building *lot;* any object or counter used to make a choice or decision by chance, as to draw *lots;* a number of articles handled as one, as this *lot* of goods.

lotion (lō' shun), *n.* a medicated fluid for the skin.

lottery (lot' ẽr i), *n.* [*pl.* lotteries] a distribution of prizes by drawing lots.

lotus (lō' tus), *n.* a plant of the waterlily family, held sacred by the early Egyptians.

loud (loud), *adj.* high or full sounding; noisy; conspicuous, as *loud* clothing.

lounge (lounj), *n.* an upholstered couch or sofa; a comfortably furnished waiting room in a hotel or clubhouse; a lazy gait in walking. *v.i.* to walk or behave in leisurely manner; to loll; to waste time.

louse (lous), *n.* [*pl.* lice] a parasitic wingless insect living on plant or animal bodies; 3 varieties live on human beings.

lout (lout), *n.* a clumsy, awkward fellow.

lovable (luv' a bl), *adj.* worthy of or inspiring love.

love (luv), *n.* a strong and deep feeling of attachment, great affection; passionate attraction and ardent affection, especially for one of the opposite sex; fondness, as *love* of books.

Syn. Affection, attachment, charity. *Affection* is usually applied only to a feeling for living or responsive beings, but one may have an *attachment* for an old hat. *Attachment* also implies unchanging devotion to a person, whereas *affection* may be a mere fondness. *Love* is the strongest word; it connotes passionate, ardent devotion. *Charity* is benevolent love for mankind in general or a merciful attitude towards an individual.

lovely (luv' li), *adj.* [*comp.* lovelier, *superl.* loveliest] beautiful.

low (lō), *adj.* having little elevation; below standard level; vulgar; cheap; of sounds, not loud: opposite of *high.*

lower (lou' ẽr), *v.i.* to have a threatening look, as a *lowering* sky; to scowl.

lower (lō' ẽr), *v.t.* to lessen or bring down; to weaken; to reduce.

lowermost (lō' ẽr mōst), *adj.* lowest.

lowing (lō' ing), *n.* the bellowing of cattle.

lowland (lō' land), *adj.* pertaining to a low or level region.

lowlands (lō' landz), *n.pl.* a low, flat country.

lowly (lō' li), *adj.* [*comp.* lowlier, *superl.* lowliest] humble; of low rank.

low-pressure (lō presh' ẽr), *adj.* using or needing only a small amount of steam pressure.

loyal (loi' al), *adj.* faithful, as to one's country, duty or friend.

*****lozenge** (loz' enj), *n.* an equilateral figure with two acute and two obtuse angles, a rhomb; a candy made in rhomb shape.

LSD *n.* a drug producing states of hallucination.

lubber (lub' ẽr), *n.* one who is clumsy or lazy; an incompetent sailor.

*****lubricant** (lū' bri kant), *n.* a substance, as an oil, used to reduce friction in the moving parts of a machine.

*****lubricate** (lū' bri kāt), *v.t.* to act as a lubricant, as oil *lubricates* machinery; to supply with a lubricant to reduce friction, as to *lubricate* an engine.

lucid (lū' sid), *adj.* shining; transparent; clear; easy to understand.

lucifer (lū' si fẽr), *n.* a match ignited by means of friction.

luck (luk), *n.* whatever happens by chance, fortune, as good *luck,* bad *luck.*

lucky (luk' i), *adj.* [*comp.* luckier, *superl.* luckiest] having good luck; fortunate.

*****lucrative** (lū' kra tiv), *adj.* profitable.

*****lucubration** (lū kū brā' shun), *n.* close, hard study.

*****ludicrous** (lū' di krus), *adj.* ridiculous.

lug (lug), *v.t.* to carry or drag with effort or inconvenience.

luggage (lug'ij), *n.* baggage.

lukewarm (lūk' wôrm), *adj.* moderately warm; indifferent.

lull (lul), *n.* a calm interval in a storm, or a momentary cessation of noise or activity.

lull (lul), *v.i. and v.t.* to become quiet, calm down; to soothe and make quiet.

lullaby (lul' a bī), *n.* [*pl.* lullabies] a cradle song.

lumbago (lum bā' gō), *n.* rheumatism of the loin muscles.

lumbar (lum' bẽr), *adj.* pertaining to the region of the loins.

lumber (lum' bẽr), *n.* timber sawed and dressed for use in building; rubbish.

*****luminary** (lū' mi nẽr i), *n.* [*pl.* luminaries] a body emitting light, especially a heavenly body.

luminous (lū' mi nus), *adj.* emitting or radiating light, shining; enlightening, intelligent.

lump (lump), *n.* a small shapeless mass; a swelling. *v.i. and v.t.* to form in lumps; to place together in a mass or a new unit, as to *lump* the charges.

lumpy (lump' i), *adj.* [*comp.* lumpier, *superl.* lumpiest] full of lumps; covered with choppy waves, as a *lumpy* sea.

lunacy (lū' na si), *n.* [*pl.* lunacies] mental unsoundness; foolish behavior.

lunar (lū′ nĕr), *adj.* pertaining to the moon; measured by the moon, as a *lunar* month.

lunatic (lū′ na tĭk), *n.* an insane person.

lunatic (lū′ na tĭk), *adj.* crazy, as *lunatic* actions; for the insane, as a *lunatic* asylum.

lunch (lunch), *n.* a light meal usually the meal between breakfast and dinner; luncheon.

*****luncheon** (lun′ chun), *n.* a light meal, a lunch.

lung (lung), *n.* one of the two organs for breathing in air-breathing animals.

lunge (lunj), *n.* a sudden thrust, as with a sword; a plunge or leap forward. *v.i.* to make a sudden thrust; to plunge forward.

lurch (lûrch), *n.* a sudden roll to one side, as of a ship; a stumbling, staggering motion.

lurch (lûrch), *v.i.* to roll suddenly sidewise, as a ship; to stagger.

*****lure** (lūr), *n.* anything used to attract; a decoy; artificial bait for fish. *v.t.* to entice.

*****lurid** (lūr′ ĭd), *adj.* pale, wan; having the look of flame seen through a cloud of smoke; vivid, shocking, as *lurid* headlines.

lurk (lûrk), *v.i.* to lie in secret hiding; to linger around stealthily; to sneak about.

*****luscious** (lush′ us), *adj.* extremely sweet; delicious.

lush (lush), *adj.* juicy; rich in vegetation, as *lush* land.

lust (lust), *n.* strong desire to possess or enjoy, as the *lust* for money; sensuous desire.

luster (lust′ ĕr), *n.* brightness; splendor.

lusty (lus′ tĭ), *adj.* [*comp.* lustier, *superl.* lustiest] robust; vigorous.

*****lute** (lūt), *n.* a stringed musical instrument.

*****luxuriant** (luks ū′ rĭ ant), *adj.* growing vigorously; profuse or florid, as *luxuriant* writing.

*****luxuriate** (luks ū′ rĭ āt), *v.i.* to live in luxury; to indulge unrestrainedly, as to *luxuriate* in music.

*****luxurious** (luks ū′ rĭ us), *adj.* indulging in or contributing to luxury.

*****luxury** (luk′ shoo rĭ), *n.* [*pl.* luxuries] indulgence in costly or easy living; any rare or costly object that contributes to fine living.

lyceum (lī sē′ um), *n.* a course of instruction by means of lectures, concerts or performances; a building used for such a course of instruction.

lyddite (lĭd′ īt), *n.* a high explosive used as a bursting charge for shells.

lye (lī), *n.* an alkaline solution made from wood ashes, used in washing and making soap.

*****lymph** (lĭmf), *n.* a colorless, sticky fluid in animal bodies.

lynch (lĭnch), *v.t.* to kill, in mob excitement, a person supposed to be guilty of a crime without permitting him to have a legal trial.

lynx (lĭnks), *n.* [*pl.* lynxes] a fierce wildcat with short tail and tufted ears.

*****lyre** (līr), *n.* a stringed, harplike musical instrument of ancient times.

lyre bird (līr bûrd), *n.* Australian ground dwelling bird, male's tail plumage is displayed in form of a lyre.

*****lyric** (lĭr′ ĭk), *n.* originally a song meant to be sung to the lyre; now, any short, emotional, personal poem. *adj.* pertaining to song or to short, musical poem.

M

macadamize (mak ad′ am ĭz), *v.t.* to fill in and pack a roadbed with crushed stone and roll so as to form a smooth hard surface, the so-called macadam or *macadamized* road.

*****macaroni** (mak a rō′ nĭ), *n.* a food made by forming a fine wheat paste into long thin tubes; a buffoon.

macaroon (mak a rōon′), *n.* a small cake made with ground almonds or coconut.

*****mace** (mās), *n.* a heavy-headed staff carried before an official to symbolize authority; a mace-bearer. *n.* a spice made of the hulls of the nutmeg.

macerate (mas′ ĕr āt), *v.t.* to soften by soaking; to cause to waste away.

*****machination** (mak ĭ nā′ shun), *n.* plotting; a plot, especially an evil plot.

*****machine** (ma shēn′), *n.* a contrivance to apply mechanical energy to the doing of work; the working organization of a political party.

machinery (ma shēn′ ĕr ĭ), *n.* engines and machine tools in general; the working system of any organization, as the *machinery* of government.

machine gun (ma shēn′ gun), a small, continuous and rapid-firing gun.

machine tool (ma shēn′ tōōl), a tool operated by means of mechanical power, as a lathe.

machinist (ma shēn′ ist), *n.* one who is skilled in the principles and use of machinery.

macho (ma′ chō), *n.* a man who takes special pride in his virility.

*****mackerel** (mak′ ĕr el), *n.* an ocean food fish.

mackintosh (mak′ in tosh), *n.* a waterproof overcoat made of thin rubber-coated cloth.

macramé (mak′ re mā), *n.* trimming or fringe made of knotted string or cord.

macrobiotics (mak′ rō bī ot′ iks), *n.* a diet plan for prolonging life which uses whole grained cereals instead of red meat.

*****macron** (mā′ kron), *n.* the short, straight horizontal line (‾) placed over a vowel to indicate that it is pronounced with a long sound.

mad (mad), *adj.* mentally disordered, insane; having rables, rabid, as a *mad* dog; crazy, as a *mad* enterprise; disorderly, as a *mad* rush; enraged, angry, as to be *mad* at injustice.

madam (mad′ am), *n.* a complimentary title or form of courteous address to a lady.

madden (mad′ n), *v.t.* to make mad, as if crazy with fury, infuriate, enrage.

*mademoiselle (măd mwà zel'), *n.* a title of courtesy given in France to a young woman; miss.

madness (mad' nes), *n.* insanity; folly.

Syn. Frenzy, rage, fury. *Madness* is a confirmed derangement in the organ of thought; *frenzy* is a temporary derangement, coming from the violence of a disease or passion. *Rage* refers more immediately to the anger or agitation that exists within the mind; *fury*, to that which shows itself outwardly. A person contains or stifles his *rage*, but his *fury* breaks into some form of open violence, in word or act.

Madonna (ma don' a), *n.* [*pl.* Madonnas] a representation of the Virgin Mary, usually with the infant Christ; (*not cap.*) madame, my lady.

maelstrom (măl' strom), *n.* a whirlpool, a turmoil; any destructive far-reaching influence.

Mafia (ma´ fè a), *n.* a secret society in Sicily which breaks the law; a similar crime organization which exists in other countries.

*magazine (mag a zēn'), *n.* a warehouse; place for storing military supplies, especially ammunition; a chamber in a gun; a periodical publication.

*magenta (ma jen' ta), *n.* a red dye obtained from coal tar; the purplish red color of this dye.

maggot (mag' ut), *n.* the grublike larva of certain insects, as the housefly, especially one that hatches in decaying matter, as meat.

magic (maj' ik), *n.* the art of producing results through the help of superhuman beings or the occult forces of nature, sorcery, witchcraft.

magic (maj' ik), or magical (maj' i kal), *adj.* relating to or produced by supernatural means; exercising magic; charming, bewitching.

magician (ma jish' an), *n.* one skilled in magic, a sorcerer; one who does sleight-of-hand tricks in a public performance.

magisterial (maj is tēr' i al), *adj.* pertaining to a master or a magistrate.

magistrate (maj' is trāt), *n.* a civil officer invested with certain judicial and executive powers; a justice of the peace.

magma (mag' ma), *n.* the molten or fused mass from which igneous rocks were formed.

magnanimity (mag na nim' i ti), *n.* a combination of fine qualities of mind and soul; freedom from petty ways of thinking and acting.

magnanimous (mag nan' i mus), *adj.* great-minded; liberal, generous.

*magnate (mag' nāt), *n.* a person prominent and influential in a major industry, as a steel *magnate.*

*magnesia (mag nē' sha), *n.* a white tasteless earthy substance, oxide of magnesium, used to correct acid conditions in the body and in making asbestos.

magnesium (mag nē' shi um), *n.* a silvery white metallic element, used in signaling and photography because of the powerful light with which it flares.

*magnet (mag' net), *n.* the loadstone, a kind of iron ore that has the power to attract iron; a piece of steel or iron artificially endowed with this property.

magnetize (mag' ne tiz), *v.t.* to endow with the power to attract iron; to make a magnet of.

magneto (mag nē' tō), *n.* a dynamo generating current for the ignition in an internal combustion engine.

magnification (mag ni fi kā' shun), *n.* the apparent enlargement obtained by viewing through a magnifying lens; the state of being magnified or exalted.

magnificence (mag nif' i sens), *n.* grandeur, splendor of appearance or surroundings.

Syn. Splendor, pomp. *Magnificence* lies not only in the number and extent of the objects presented, but in the degree of richness as to their coloring and quality. *Splendor* is but a characteristic of magnificence.

magnificent (mag nif' i sent), *adj.* grand in appearance, splendid; exalted, noble.

magnify (mag' ni fi), *v.t.* to increase the apparent size of, as by viewing through a lens; actually to enlarge; to exaggerate.

magnitude (mag' ni tūd), *n.* size, greatness of bulk or extent; importance.

*magnolia (mag nō' li a), *n.* a tree with handsome foliage and large pink or white flowers.

magpie (mag' pi), *n.* a black and white chattering bird of the crow family.

mahogany (ma hog' a ni), *n.* a tree of tropical America with very hard dark reddish brown wood; the wood of this tree.

maid (mād), *n.* a young unmarried woman; a female servant.

maiden (mād' n), *n.* an unmarried girl or woman. *adj.* pertaining to or like a maiden; unused; first, as a ship's *maiden* voyage.

maidenhair (mād' n hâr), *n.* a handsome and delicately leafed fern.

maidenly (mād' n li), *adj.* like, or suitable to, a maiden, modest.

mail (māl), *n.* defensive body armor of steel, either in plates or in network. *n.* a government system of conveying letters and packages; the matter thus carried. *v.t.* to post or send by mail.

maim (mām), *v.t.* to cripple or mutilate.

main (mān), *n.* the ocean; the essential point; strength or power, as with might and *main;* the principal pipe in a water system.

main (mān), *adj.* principal, as a *main* line; sheer, as by *main* strength.

mainframe (mān' frām), *n.* the computer device which contains the central control.

mainstay (mān' stā), *n.* the stay or big rope from the maintop to the foot of the foremast; any main support, as her son is the *mainstay* of her old age.

mainstream (mān' strēm), *n.* the dominant course or trend.

maintop (mān' top), *n.* the square platform at the head of the lower mainmast of a ship.

maintain (mān tān'), *v.t.* to support, sustain.

*maintenance (mān' tē nans), *n.* sustenance, support; defense; means of sustenance; upkeep.

maize (māz), *n.* Indian corn.

majestic (ma jes' tik), *adj.* having great dignity of person or mien; stately, grand.

majesty (maj' es ti), *n.* [*pl.* majesties] sovereignty; a king or queen, emperor or empress; grandeur, nobility: *Majesty,* the title of address of a sovereign, as Your *Majesty,* His *Majesty.*

major (mā' jēr), *n.* an army officer next in rank above a captain; a course of study in which a high school or college student specializes. *adj.* greater in number, amount, extent, rank or importance.

major general (mā' jer jen' ēr al), an army officer next in rank below a lieutenant general and next above a brigadier general.

majority (ma jor' i ti), *n.* a number greater than half of a given number; the difference between this number and the remainder of the total, as a *majority* of 189; the status of legal age, 21 years; the rank and office of a military major.

*make (māk), *n.* shape or style of construction; brand or manufacturing source, as this *make* of shoe; character, disposition. *v.i. and v.t.* to move or tend, as peace *makes* for prosperity; to create, fashion or compose, as to *make* dresses or poems; to gain, as to *make* friends; to establish in position, as his courage will *make* or break him; to come to, arrive at, as to *make* harbor; to constitute, amount to, as 60 minutes *make* an hour.

maladjustment (mal a just' ment), *n.* lack of fitness or harmony; unsuitability to environment or situation.

*maladroit (mal a droit'), *adj.* unskilful, clumsy, awkward.

malady (mal' a di), *n.* [*pl.* maladies] any illness of mind or body.

*malapropos (mal ap rō pō'), *adj.* inappropriate. *adv.* inappropriately.

*malaria (ma lâr' i a), *n.* a disease produced by the bite of a certain mosquito and accompanied by great exhaustion, sweats and intermittent chills and fever.

malcontent (mal' kon tent), *n.* one who is always discontented with things as they are.

male (māl), *n.* a person, plant or animal of male sex. *adj.* belonging to the sex that begets young: opposite of *female;* made up of men, as a *male* quartet.

*malediction (mal ē dik' shun), *n.* the act of calling evil upon anyone, a curse: opposite of *benediction.*

malefaction (mal ē fak' shun), *n.* the doing of evil; an evil deed.

malefactor (mal' ē fak tēr), *n.* a doer of evil, criminal.

*malevolence (ma lev' ō lens), *n.* ill will; desire to injure others.

malevolent (ma lev' ō lent), *adj.* malicious; wishing evil to others.

Syn. Malicious. To be *malevolent* is to have evil so deeply rooted in the character as to color one's intentions and influence; *malicious* means full of hate and spite. *Malicious* acts and sayings are petty and may express only a temporary spite; but a *malevolent* man wishes evil and radiates

evil.

*malfeasance (mal fē' zans), *n.* a wrong doing, especially an illegal act performed by one in public office.

malice (mal' is), *n.* spite, ill will.

malicious (ma lish' us), *adj.* spiteful; done or said from spiteful or mischievous motives.

malign (ma līn'), *v.t.* to speak evil of, slander, defame.

malignant (ma lig' nant), *adj.* maliciously disposed; tending to cause death, virulent, as a *malignant* tumor.

malignity (ma lig' ni ti), *n.* the state of being malignant, virulence.

*mall (môl), *n.* a mallet used in the game of pall-mall, played in an alley; a shady public walk.

malleable (mal' ē a bl), *adj.* capable of being extended, shaped or worked by hammering or rolling.

mallet (mal' et), *n.* a short-handled wooden-headed hammer, used for driving a chisel; a long-handled stick with a hammerlike head, used to play croquet.

malnutrition (mal nū trish' un), *n.* undernourishment, due either to lack of food, want of certain necessary elements in the diet or poor assimilation.

malodorous (mal ō dēr us), *adj.* having a bad smell.

malpractice (mal prak' tis), *n.* wrong treatment of a case by a physician or surgeon, or neglect in caring for a patient; illegal action by one engaged in a profession.

*malt (môlt), *n.* barley or other grain prepared for use in brewing and distilling.

maltreat (mal trēt'), *v.t.* to handle roughly, abuse.

mammal (mam' al), *n.* a member of the highest class of vertebrate animals, including man, that nourish their young with milk.

mammography (ma mog' rŭ fē), *n.* X-ray examination of the breast to determine tumors before they can be seen or felt.

mammon (mam' un), *n.* worldly gain.

mammoth (mam' uth), *n.* an extinct species of huge hairy elephant; anything unusually large.

man (man), *n.* [*pl.* men] a human being, especially a mature male human being; the human race, mankind. *v.t.* to furnish with men, as to *man* a ship.

manacle (man' a kl), *n.* a handcuff.

manacle (man' a kl), *v.t.* to put handcuffs on.

manage (man' ij), *v.i. and v.t.* to get along, as I can manage; to administer, conduct, as to *manage* a business.

manageable (man' ij a bl), *adj.* easily controlled.

management (man' ij ment), *n.* the act of managing or directing; the directing staff of any enterprise or institution.

manager (man' ij ēr), *n.* one who directs or conducts anything, as a business.

manatee (man a tē'-, *n.* a herbivorous mammal inhabiting coastal waters of tropical America and western Africa, nearly hairless, about 11 feet long; known as seacow: there are several species.

mandate (man' dāt), *n.* an order or command issued upon high authority; an order by a court; the placing or entrusting of a small conquered country's affairs in the hands of a major Power by the League of Nations; tacit instructions to a political party implied in its being voted into power, as Roosevelt's re-election seemed a *mandate* for social legislation.

*****mandatory** (man' da tōr i), *adj.* required by authority; obligatory.

mandrill (man' dril), *n.* a large short tailed baboon of west Africa.

mane (mān), *n.* the long hair on the back of a horse's neck, or about the neck of a lion.

*****maneuver** (ma nōō' vēr), *n.* an adroit, swift movement of troops or ships in war; any artful course of action; a stratagem. *v.i. and v.t.* to contrive and execute swift movements of troops or ships in war; to manage with skill, as to maneuver a battle; to handle or cause to make certain movements, as to *maneuver* troops.

manful (man' fool), *adj.* sturdy, brave.

*****manganese** (mang' ga nēz), *n.* a hard, brittle, gray-colored metallic element.

*****mange** (mānj), *n.* a skin disease of dogs and other animals with hairy coats.

manger (mān' jēr), *n.* a feeding trough for horses and cattle.

mangle (mang' gl), *n.* a machine with rollers to iron clothes. *v.t.* to lacerate, cut or bruise; to mutilate, to make a botch of. *v.t.* to smooth in a mangle.

mango (mang' gō), *n.* the yellowish-red fruit of a tropical tree.

mangosteen (mang' gō stēn), *n.* a fruit grown in East India and the Philippines.

*****mangrove** (mang' grōv), *n* a tropical tree whose branches send down roots which rapidly grow into a dense thicket.

mangy (mān' ji), *adj.* afflicted with mange.

manhood (man' hood), *n.* the state of being a man; the qualities that befit a man, as strength and courage.

*****mania** (mā' ni a), *n.* violent insanity; a craze, as a *mania* for writing.

maniac (mā' ni ak), *n.* a madman.

*****maniacal** (ma nī' a kl), *adj.* affected with mania, insane, mad.

manicure (man' i kūr), *n.* one who makes a business of taking care of hands and fingernails; the care of the hands; a treatment to care for the hands. *v.t.* to treat and care for the hands and fingernails.

manifesto (man i fes' tō), *n.* a proclamation by a government or a body of persons concerning political measures or intentions.

manifold (man' i fōld), *n.* a copy of a paper made by a duplicating machine; a pipe with several outlets for connecting with other pipes. *v.t.* to make numerous copies of at one time; to multiply. *adj.* having many sides or phases; multiplied.

manila (ma nil' a), *n.* a Philippine cigar or cheroot; a hemplike fiber obtained from a Philippine tree, used in making ropes, textiles and paper.

manipulate (ma nip' ū lāt), *v.t.* to operate by means of the hands; manage in a clever way so as to bring about a desired effect.

manipulation (ma nip ū lā' shun), *n.* the act of doing things with the hands; clever management of affairs to attain one's ends.

mankind (man kīnd'), *n.* the human race; men in general as distinguished from women in general.

manly (man' li), *adj.* [*comp.* manlier, *superl.* manliest] having the qualities proper to a man, courageous, resolute.

Syn. Masculine, male. *Masculine* is the opposite of *feminine* and is applied to what is characteristic of men, as *masculine* clothes, *masculine* reasoning; *manly* is applied to a man's fine qualities and means strong, brave, worthy of a fine man; *male* is the opposite of *female* and refers to sex.

manna (man' a), *n.* the food miraculously supplied to the Israelites in the wilderness; the sap and juice of the flowering ash, used in medicine.

manner (man' ēr), *n.* method, mode of action; kind, as what *manner* of man is this; style in literature or art, as in the *manner* of Rubens: *manners,* deportment, social conduct.

mannequin (man' e kin), *n.* an artist's, tailor's or dressmaker's dummy or lay figure; a woman employed as a model to display clothes.

mannerism (man' ēr izm), *n.* a peculiarity of style, action or bearing, especially if it is affected.

man-of-war (man ov wär), *n.* a large fighting ship; a naval ship of the line, heavily armed.

*****manor** (man' ēr), *n.* the district over which a lord held authority in medieval England; a tract of land held by tenants in fee to a landlord.

manse (mans), *n.* the residence of a Presbyterian minister in Scotland; any parsonage.

mansion (man' shun), *n.* a large and stately dwelling house.

manslaughter (man' slô tēr), *n.* the killing of a human being, done without malice or premeditation.

mantel (man' tl), *n.* a narrow ornamental slab above a fireplace.

mantis (man' tis), *n.* a large orthopterous insect, also called praying-mantis.

mantle (man' tl), *n.* a long cloak; a conical network that becomes incandescent when heated.

mantle (man' tl), *v.i. and v.t.* to blush; to take on a covering, as of scum; to overspread, as a blush *mantled* her brow; to cover with a cloak; to disguise, conceal.

manual (man' ū al), *n.* a handbook. *adj.* relating to hands; done by hands.

manufactory (man ū fak' tō ri), *n.* [*pl.* manufactories] a place where goods are made by machines and labor; a factory.

manufacture (man ū fak' tūr), *n.* the conversion of raw materials into goods ready for use; anything manufactured. *v.t.* to convert, especially by use of machinery, raw materials into goods ready for use.

manure (ma nūr'), *n.* fertilizer, especially

waste matter from stables.

manuscript (man' ū skript), *n.* a text written by hand, whether with pen, pencil or typewriter; writing as distinguished from print. *adj.* written by hand.

many (men' ĭ), *n.* a large number; a multitude of people. *adj.* [*comp.* more, *superl.* most] numerous, consisting of a great number.

manzanilla (man za nil' a), *n.* a kind of small olive usually stuffed with pimentos when pickled; a certain kind of sherry wine.

map (map), *n.* a representation on a flat surface, as paper, of all or part of the surface of the earth, showing land outlines, continents, seas, mountain ranges and rivers, countries, states and cities; a chart of the heavens. *v.t.* to delineate in a map; to plan, as to *map* out a tour.

maple (mā' pl), *n.* a tree valued for its shade, its wood and in some varieties for its sap, from which maple sugar is made; the wood of this tree used in making furniture.

mar (mär), *v.t.* to disfigure, damage.

*****marabou** (mar' a bōō), *n.* a large African stork with soft feathers used on women's clothing; the long soft feathers of this bird, collectively.

*****maraschino** (mar a skē' nō), *n.* a cordial made from the fermented juice of the marasca, a small bitter cherry.

marasmus (ma raz' mus), *n.* emaciation.

marathon (mar' a thon), *n.* a footrace of 26 miles, 385 yards; any of various endurance competitions, as in dancing.

maraud (ma rôd'), *v.i.* and *v.t.* to wander in search of plunder, raid; to make a raid upon.

marble (mär' bl), *n.* a hard limestone, white or colored, and taking a fine polish; a sculpture in marble; a small clay, stone or glass ball used by boys in a game. *v.t.* to stain in imitation of marble. *adj.* made of or resembling marble; cold and hard like marble.

marbles (mär'blz), *n. pl.* a boys' game played with small balls of clay or glass.

marcel wave (mär sel' wäv), a style of waving the hair in tiers.

march (märch), *n.* a movement of persons arranged in rank and file and walking in step, as soldiers; the distance traversed in marching from one stopping place to another; a steady onward movement, as the *march* of time; a musical composition timed for marching. *n.* a border or frontier; a country or territory. *v.i. and v.t.* to move with regular steps and all in step, as soldiers; to make march, as he *marched* his men down the road.

*****marchioness** (mär' shun es), *n.* the wife or widow of a marquis; a woman holding the rank of a marquis.

mare (mâr), *n.* the female of the horse, donkey or zebra.

margin (mär' jin), *n.* an edge, a border; the unused edge of a printed page; the difference between the amount of net sales and the cost of goods sold, as a *margin* of profit; an extra amount of time or money allowed,

as a *margin* of ten minutes to catch a train.

marginal (mär' ji nal), *adj.* relating to a margin or edge; placed in the margin, as *marginal* notes.

marigold (mar' i gōld), *n.* a garden plant with showy flowers, usually golden yellow.

marimba (ma rim' ba), *n.* a musical instrument resembling the xylophone.

marine (ma rēn'), *n.* a soldier assigned to duty on a warship; a member of the U. S. Marine Corps, under the Navy Department, serving in foreign lands and moving from port to port on warships; the collective shipping of any country; a picture of a scene at sea. *adj.* relating to the sea.

mariner (ma' rin ēr), *n.* a sailor.

marionette (mar i ō net'), *n.* a puppet, a doll made to move and act by strings.

marital (mar' i tal), *adj.* pertaining to marriage.

*****maritime** (mar' i tĭm), *adj.* pertaining to the sea; situated near the sea; relating to navigation or to trade at sea; nautical, as a *maritime* phrase.

marjoram (mär' jō ram), *n.* a genus of aromatic plants of the mint family.

mark (märk), *n.* a visible sign by which anything is known, as a brand or trade-mark; a distinguishing feature, as a *mark* of genius; a fixed standard; a line or an object that indicates position; a target; any aim or goal; a line or written symbol, as to make *marks* on a page; an ancient gold or silver coin; the German monetary unit; a border, a march, a territory.

mark (märk), *v.i.* and *v.t.* to make a mark; to notice; to make marks on, as to *mark* a wall; to correct and grade by symbols, as the teacher *marks* the papers; to characterize, show up, as chatter *marks* the fool.

market (mär' ket), *n.* a public place for the buying and selling of goods; a possible field for the selling of any particular line or kind of goods, as Russia is a *market* for American machinery. *v.i.* and *v.t.* to buy or sell in a public place; to put up for sale or to sell in a market.

marksman (märks' man), *n.* [*pl.* marksmen] one who shoots well, one skilled in hitting the mark.

*****marline** (mär' lin), *n.* a small two-stranded cord used for binding cable ends in splicing.

marlinespike (mär' lin spĭk), *n.* a pointed piece of iron used to separate the strands of a rope in splicing.

marmalade (mär' ma lād), *n.* a jamlike preserve made from the juice, pulp and rind of fruits, as oranges, pineapple, grapefruit.

maroon (ma rōōn'), *v.t.* to leave on a desert island; to leave alone and helpless.

maroon (ma rōōn'), *n.* a rich deep red color.

*****marquis** (mär' kwis), *n.* a nobleman ranking next below a duke and above an earl.

marquise (mär kēz'), *n.* the wife of a marquis; a marchioness.

marquisette (mär kwis et'), *n.* a sheer cloth of cotton or silk.

marriage (mar' ij), *n.* the state of being legally wedded; the wedding ceremony; any close union.

marrow (mar' ō), *n.* the soft substance that fills the hollow of a bone; the essence of anything.

marry (mar' i), *v.i. and v.t.* [*p.t. and p.p.* married, *pr.p.* marrying] to wed; to perform the ceremony of uniting a man and woman in wedlock; to espouse, take as husband or wife.

marsh (märsh), *n.* a swampy stretch of land.

marshal (mär' shal), *v.t.* to arrange in order, as a parade; to set in order for use in argument or debate, as data; to lead.

marsupial (mär sū' pi al), *n.* an order of mammals, including the kangaroos, bandicoots and opossums, of which the females have a pouch or pocket in the abdomen in which to carry the young.

mart (märt), *n.* a market.

marten (mär' ten), *n.* a small fur-bearing animal that lives in trees.

martial (mär' shal), *adj.* warlike.

Syn. Warlike, military. *Martial* describes the pomp, verve and ceremonies of war, as *martial* music, to walk with a *martial* air, *martial* law; *warlike* means literally like war, fond of war, easily provoked to war, or it characterizes the tools and activities of war; *military* describes soldiers and all that pertains to them or to the conduct of war on land.

martin (mär' tin), *n.* any of various insect-eating birds of the swallow family.

martyr (mär' tēr), *n.* one who dies rather than give up his faith; one who sacrifices life or possessions for any cause. *v.t.* to put to death or to cause to suffer for adherence to a belief.

martyrdom (mär' tēr dum), *n.* the death or sufferings of a martyr.

marvel (mär' vel), *n.* something extraordinary and astonishing; a prodigy. *v.i.* to feel surprise, wonder or astonishment.

marvelous (mär' vel us), *adj.* occasioning surprise and wonder; almost incredible, astonishing.

mascot (mas' kot), *n.* any person or thing supposed to bring good luck.

masculine (mas' kū lin), *adj.* characteristic of, suitable for or used by men; virile.

mash (mash), *n.* a soft pulpy mass; a mixture of bran and water. *v.t.* to crush into a soft, pulpy state.

mask (mask), *n.* a complete or partial cover for the face to disguise or protect the wearer, as a gas *mask;* a cast of the face after death, a death *mask;* a masquerade festival; a masquerader; any pretense or subterfuge. *v.i. and v.t.* to masquerade; to cover or conceal, as one's face or true feelings and intentions.

mason (mā' sn), *n.* one who works in stone or brick.

masquerade (mas kēr ād'), *n.* a festive gathering at which everybody wears a mask; concealment of one's true feelings or intentions; pretence of being what one is not. *v.i.* to attend a party where everyone wears a mask; to make a false appearance.

Mass (mas), *n.* celebration of the Eucharist.

mass (mas), *n.* a quantity of matter concentrated as a single body; a number of things taken together as a unit; bulk. *v.i. and v.t.* to come together in a solid unit; to make into a lump or unit.

masses (mas' ez), *n.* the people.

*****massacre** (mas' a kēr), *n.* cruel and indiscriminate slaughter of many human beings; butchery. *v.t.* [*p.t. and p.p.* massacred, *pr.p.* massacring] to kill human beings in great numbers with great cruelty.

*****massage** (ma säzh'), *n.* a rubbing and kneading of the body to tone muscles, improve circulation and promote physical well-being, frequently with remedial purpose and effect. *v.t.* to rub and knead body for remedial or hygienic effect.

*****masseur** (ma sûr'), *n.* [*fem.* masseuse (ma sûz')] one who applies massage.

massive (mas' iv), *adj.* bulky, weighty; impressive in size.

mast (mast), *n.* a long round tapering timber of wood or steel rising from the keel of a ship through the decks, to support the rigging and sails, a spar.

master (mas' tēr), *n.* one who commands others; a director, as of a school; one who has upper hand in a contest; an artist of supreme eminence, as the old *masters;* in university rating, one between a bachelor and a doctor, as *Master* of Arts. *v.t.* to subdue, overcome, as to *master* a lion or a habit; to learn thoroughly, as to *master* a lesson. *adj.* showing the power or skill of a master, as a *master* builder, *master* mechanic, a *master*piece.

masterful (mas' tēr fool), *adj.* having the qualities, as skill or power, of a master; inclined to use power, domineering.

mastery (mas' tēr i), *n.* command of a situation; art or skill; conquest.

mastic (mas' tik), *n.* a tree that produces a valuable resin; the resin of the mastic tree, used in varnishes and drugs.

*****masticate** (mas' ti kāt), *v.t.* to chew.

*****mastiff** (mas' tif), *n.* a large smooth-coated dog, esteemed as a watchdog.

mastodon (mas' tō don), *n.* a prehistoric extinct animal resembling an elephant, with long tusks and molar teeth cular for their projections; anything huge and monstrous.

mat (mat), *n.* a flat piece of heavy woven fabric; such a piece of fabric laid in a doorway on which to wipe the feet; a small piece of knitted or woven material, used for ornament or for hot dishes; anything closely woven as a tangle of weeds; a matrix for producing stereotypes. *v.i. and v.t.* to twist, weave or form into a mat; to cover or furnish with mats.

matador (mat' a dōr), *n.* the man picked to kill the bull in a bullfight.

match (mach), *n.* anything that is exactly like another; an equal, as he has never met his *match;* a contest; marriage. *n.* a small piece of wood or heavy paper tipped with a substance easily ignited by friction. *v.i. and v.t.* to be exactly alike, as these ribbons *match* in color; to equal, as his income *matches* mine; to find or supply something like, as *match* this material; to arrange a contest for, as they *matched* him against the champion.

matchless (mach' les), *adj.* unequalled, without a rival, peerless.

mate (māt), *n.* a companion or associate; a husband or wife; an officer ranking next below the captain on merchant vessels; a petty naval officer, as a gunner's *mate;* one of a pair, as the *mate* to a stocking. *n.* in chess, a checkmate, winning the game, or stalemate, making it a draw. *v.t.* to marry; to pair, as animals, for breeding. *v.t.*, in chess, to place the opponent's king in a position under attack and from which he cannot escape.

material (ma tēr' ial), *n.* the substance of which anything consists; data, subject matter, as *material* for a book; fabric, as *material* for a dress. *adj.* consisting of matter, not spiritual; essential, as it is a *material* point in my argument; pertaining to physical existence, as *material* needs.

maternal (ma tûr' nal), *adj.* motherly.

maternity (ma tûr' ni ti), *n.* the state of being a mother; character or relationship of a mother.

mathematical (math ē mat' i kal), *adj.* relating to mathematics; done by means of mathematics; exact, precise.

mathematics (math ē mat' iks), *n. pl.* the science of quantities and magnitudes, the relations between them, and the methods by which unknown quantities can be found from those known or supposed, expressed or calculated in numbers or other symbols.

matin (mat' in), *adj.* pertaining to the morning.

matins (mat' inz), *n. pl.* morning prayers; prayers for the morning, said at midnight.

*matinee** (mat i nā'), *n.* a reception, concert or dramatic performance in the afternoon.

*matriarch** (mā tri ärk), *n.* a woman who is head of a tribe, clan or family.

*matricide** (mā' tri sīd), *n.* the murder of one's mother; one who murders his mother.

matriculate (ma trik' ū lāt), *v.i.* and *v.t.* to register as a successful applicant for admittance to college; to record on the college rolls as admitted.

matrimonial (mat ri mō' ni al), *adj.* pertaining to marriage.

matrimony (mat' ri mō ni), *n.* marriage.

*matrix** (mā' triks), *n.* [*pl.* matrices] a cavity in which anything is formed or cast; a mold in which type is cast for a typesetting machine; a mold or mat, usually of papier mâché, for making a stereotype.

*matron** (mā' trun), *n.* a married woman, especially one who has had children; a woman who does the housekeeping in an institution, such as a hospital.

matted (mat' ed), *adj.* covered with mats or matting; tangled, as *matted* hair.

matter (mat' ēr), *n.* that which occupies space and is perceptible by the senses; substance: the opposite of mind or spirit; anything

sent through the mail; affair, as it's a small *matter;* difficulty, as what's the *matter;* an instance or occasion, as no laughing *matter, matter* for thought; pus. *v.i.* to signify; to be of importance.

matting (mat' ing), *n.* mats collectively; material of which mats are made.

mattock (mat' uk), *n.* a pickax with one end flat for use in grubbing.

*mattress** (mat' res), *n.* a case made of heavy cloth and stuffed with soft materials and used to sleep upon or to make a bed comfortable; a frame covered with heavy material and filled with springs, for the same purpose.

*mature** (ma tūr'), *adj.* full-grown; ripe; perfected, as a *mature* plan; pertaining to full development, as a *mature* person.

maturity (ma tu' ri ti), *n.* [*pl.* maturities] the state of being full-grown or ripe; the period of full growth and development; ripeness; time for payment of principal, as on insurance policies or an issue of bonds.

*matutinal** (ma tū' ti nal), *adj.* pertaining to the morning; happening early in the day.

maudlin (mŏd' lin), *adj.* easily moved to tears; weakly sentimental.

maul (môl), *n.* a large hammer or mallet used in driving spikes.

*mausoleum** (mô sō lē' um), *n.* a stately tomb.

*mauve** (mōv), *n.* a soft lilac, violet or purple color.

maw (mô), *n.* the stomach of an animal: sometimes used to denote the jaws, gullet and stomach together.

mawkish (môk' ish), *adj.* affectedly or sickishly sentimental.

maxim (mak' sim), *n.* an established principle or general truth; a wise or proverbial saying.

maximum (mak' si mum), *n.* the greatest possible or attainable number or quantity: opposite of *minimum.*

may (mā), *v. aux.* [*p.t.* might] to be possible, as it *may* happen; to be permitted, as you *may* have it; would that, as *may* it happen soon.

maybe (mā' bē), *adv.* perhaps.

mayonnaise (mā o nāz´), *n.* a sauce of oil and egg yolk used on salads and sandwiches.

*mayor** (mā' ēr), *n.* the chief administrative officer of a municipality.

maze (māz), *n.* a labyrinth; a bewildering tangle of lines or ideas.

mead (mēd), *n.* a meadow.

meager (mē' gēr), *adj.* lean, thin, poor, barren.

meal (mēl), *n.* coarsely ground grain; a repast; the food eaten at one time, as at breakfast, lunch or dinner.

mean (mēn), *n.* the middle point or situation; an approximate or adjusted average. *v.i. and v.t.* to be disposed, as to *mean* well; to intend, as he *means* trouble; to design, as he *meant* it as a compliment; to imply, as money *means* power; to signify, as the German *ja means* yes. *adj.* lacking in position, power, dignity, character or generosity, as a *mean* station in life, a *mean* manner, *mean* with his money

meaning (mēn' ing), *n.* significance, as the words *yes* and *yea* have the same meaning.

means (mēnz), *n. pl.* methods; ways of doing, as there are many *means* for acquiring wealth; middle terms in a proportion, as in 2:4=6:8 the product of the *means* equals the product of the *extremes*; resources, substance, as his *means* were limited.

meander (mē an' dēr), *v.i.* to flow in a winding course; to wander aimlessly.

meantime (mēn' tīm), *n.* an intervening space of time, as in the *meantime. adv.* in the intervening time, as *meantime* I shall be considering the matter.

measles (mē' zlz), *n. pl.* an infectious disease, with fever, and small red spots on the skin.

*****measure** (mezh' ēr), *n.* the standard by which the size, extent or volume of anything is found and expressed; the extent or dimensions of anything; any device used to find size, extent or capacity, as a foot rule or a quart *measure;* a system of measuring, as linear *measure;* a limit, as the *measure* of life is 70 years; a legislative enactment, as a reform *measure;* rhythm in poetry or music.

measure (mezh' ēr), *v.i. and v.t.* to ascertain the dimensions or volume, as it's better to *measure* than to guess; to compute the extent or quantity of, as to *measure* a board.

meat (mēt), *n.* the flesh of animals used as food; gist, as the *meat* of an argument.

meaty (mēt' i), *adj.* [*comp.* meatier, *superl.* meatiest] containing meat, like meat, nourishing; substantial, pithy, as a *meaty* essay.

*****mechanic** (mē kan' ik), *n.* a skilled workman in machinery; an artisan.

mechanical (mē kan' i kal), *adj.* operated by machinery; done in a machinelike way or acting in a machinelike way; interested in machinery, as he has a *mechanical* turn of mind.

medal (med' l), *n.* a coin-shaped piece of metal impressed with a device or an inscription commemorating some distinguished event or person.

medallion (mē dal' yun), *n.* a large medal, or a tablet with a design in relief.

meddle (med' l), *v.i.* to interfere without right or necessity; to interpose officiously or impertinently; to take a hand in affairs of others.

meddlesome (med' l sum), *adj.* inclined to meddle, officious.

median (mē' di an), *n.* a median number, point or line. *adj.* being intermediate; indicating a relation between higher and lower items; having the nature of an average but not as exact.

mediate (mē' di āt), *v.i. and v.t.* to be judge or peacemaker between other parties as equally interested in each; to bring about by acting as peace maker in a quarrel or war, as to *mediate* an agreement.

mediation (mē di ā' shun), *n.* intercession, peacemaking.

medical (med' i kal), *adj.* pertaining to medicine or its use.

*****medicinal** (mē dis' i nal), *adj.* having the properties of medicine, curative or healing.

medicine (med' i sin), *n.* any preparation used to cure disease; the science of curing disease.

*****medieval** (mē di ē' val), *adj.* pertaining to the Middle Ages.

*****mediocre** (mē' di ō kēr), *adj.* of medium excellence, ordinary.

meditate (med' i tāt), *v.i. and v.t.* to reflect, ponder, as to *meditate* on repentance; to think upon, plan, consider, as to *meditate* a change.

medium (mē' di um), *n.* that which rests between extremes; an intervening substance through which force acts; agency; a person claiming to receive communications from the dead. *adj.* occupying a position between extremes; average; ordinary, as a *medium* grade of goods.

medley (med' li), *n.* a confused mixture of unlike ingredients; parts of tunes put together to make a new tune.

meek (mēk), *adj.* modest, mild, submissive.

*****meerschaum** (mēr' shum), *n.* a light claylike mineral substance found in Spain and Asia Minor; a pipe with a bowl made of it.

meet (mēt), *n.* a gathering, meeting, as a hunt *meet,* a track *meet. v.i. and v.t.* to come upon, in approaching from opposite directions; to come face to face with; to be introduced to; to confront in battle; to pay, as a bill; to conform to, as to *meet* the rules.

*****megalomania** (meg a lō mā' nia), *n.* a craze of personal greatness, delusions of grandeur; strong tendency to exaggeration.

megaphone (meg' a fōn), *n.* a large funnel used to speak through in order to magnify sound, as the cheer leaders use *megaphones.*

melancholy (mel' an kol i), *n.* despondency; a state of meditative sadness. *adj.* depressed; feeling or causing or arising from a feeling of sadness, as a *melancholy* person.

melee (mā lā'), *n.* a confused fight between many hand to hand combatants.

*****meliorate** (mēl' yō rāt), *v.i. and v.t.* to grow better; to cause to improve; to make more tolerable.

mellifluous (me lif' lū us), *adj.* honey-sweet; smooth-flowing, as speech.

mellow (mel' ō), *v.i. and v.t.* to become soft and tender, to ripen; to become sweetened with age. *adj.* soft and tender because ripe; mature, sweet because mature.

melodious (mē lō' di us), *adj.* having or making melody, musical.

melody (mel' ō di), *n.* [*pl.* melodies] a song or tune; the principal part in a harmonized composition.

melon (mel' un), *n.* a trailing plant with juicy fruit, as the musk*melon* and water*melon.*

melt (melt), *v.i. and v.t.* to change, or cause to change, from a solid to a liquid state; to soften, as the story *melted* his heart.

melt down (melt doun), *n.* the accidental melting of uranium pellets and/or the rods that contain them.

member (mem' bēr), *n.* a limb or organ of the body; a single part; one who belongs to an association.

membrane (mem' brān), *n.* a thin fold or layer

of animal tissue forming a covering for some part or organ.

memento (mē men' tō), *n.* [*pl.* mementos] a souvenir, a token.

memoir (mem' wär), *n.* a history written from personal experience, knowledge and memory.

memorable (mem' ō ra bl), *adj.* worthy of being remembered.

memorial (mē mō' ri al), *n.* something intended to preserve a person or event in the people's memory; a written statement addressed to a government, or by one government to another, often containing a petition. *adj.* of or pertaining to memory; said or done in remembrance, commemorative.

memorize (mem' ō riz), *v.t.* to commit to memory, learn by heart.

memory (mem' ō ri), *n.* [*pl.* memories] the power of remembering or recalling to the mind things that are past; something remembered, as a happy *memory.*

  Syn. Remembrance, recollection, reminiscence. *Memory* is the general term for any mental recalling of experience; *remembrance* is the state of recalling or keeping in mind;

memory capacity (mem' o rē ka pas' i te), *n.* the maximum number of storage positions in a computer's memory.

memory circuit (mem ' ōr ē ser ' kit), *n.* that within a computer which stores programs and information.

menagerie (mē naj' ēr i), *n.* a place where animals are kept for exhibition; a collection of wild or strange animals.

mend (mend), *n.* improvement, as on the *mend;* a repair, as he made a good *mend.*

mend (mend), *v.i. and v.t.* to repair as to *mend* a shoe; to improve, reform, as *mend* your ways.

mendacious (men dā' shus), *adj.* false; given to falsehood.

mendicant (men' di kant), *n.* a beggar. *adj.* begging.

menial (mē' ni al), *n.* a servant. *adj.* pertaining to servants; servile.

meningitis (men in ji' tis), *n.* inflammation of the membranes enclosing the brain and spinal cord.

mensuration (men shoo rā' shun), *n.* the act of measuring; a system of measurement; the branch of mathematics that deals with length, area and volume.

mental (men' tal), *adj.* pertaining to the mind.

mentality (men tal' i ti), *n.* mental capacity; mind as a part of one's individuality.

menthol (men' thōl), *n.* a crystalline substance derived from oil of peppermint, used in medicines and toilet preparations.

mention (men' shun), *n.* passing notice; incidental reference. *v.t.* to speak of very briefly; to name.

menu (men' ū), *n.* bill of fare; a list of alternative actions displayed on the computer screen for selection by the user.

mercantile (mûr' kan til), *adj.* commercial; pertaining to trade or to merchants.

  Syn. Commercial. *Mercantile* activities have to do with the actual buying and sell-

ing of goods; *commercial* relates to the theory and practice of commerce. We speak of a *mercantile* house, a *mercantile* situation, but of a *commercial* education, a *commercial* people.

mercenary (mûr' sē ner i), *n.* [*pl.* mercenaries] a soldier hired into the service of a foreign country; one who serves only for pay. *adj.* acting always and only for gain; springing from greed for gain, as a *mercenary* crime.

merchandise (mûr' chan diz), *n.* goods bought and sold; articles of trade.

merchant (mûr' chant), *n.* a trader; one who carries stocks of goods for sale.

merciful (mûr' si fool), *adj.* showing mercy, lenient, compassionate.

merciless (mûr' si les), *adj.* without mercy, unfeeling, cruel.

mercurial (mûr kū' ri al), *adj.* having the properties of mercury or quicksilver; fickle, changeable.

mercury (mûr' kū ri), *n.* quicksilver, a heavy silver-white metallic element, liquid at ordinary temperatures.

mercy (mûr' si), *n.* [*pl.* mercies] the disposition to forgive, spare or pity; compassion; an act of clemency; compassionate treatment.

  Syn. Clemency, leniency, lenity. *Mercy* is expressed in compassionate and forgiving treatment of offenders and pity and help for those undergoing suffering; *clemency* is a weaker word than *mercy;* it means *mildness* especially in meting out penalties; *lenity* is very mild; *leniency* is an easygoing avoidance of severity.

  Ant. Cruelty, harshness.

mere (mēr), *adj.* [*superl.* merest] such and no more, simple, nothing but, as a *mere* child.

merge (merj), *v.i. and v.t.* to unite; to unite with; to blend; to join together.

merger (mer' jēr), *n.* combination of several business concerns under central control.

meridian (me rid' i an), *n.* an imaginary circle about the earth, passing through the poles; a line on a map representing such a circle. *adj.* pertaining to midday.

meringue (mē rang'), *n.* a frosting made of sugar and the beaten white of egg.

merino (me rē' nō), *n.* [*pl.* merinos] a breed of sheep with a fine wool.

merit (mer' it), *n.* excellence; worthiness of commendation or reward.

meritorious (mer i tō' ri us), *adj.* having merit; worthy of commendation or reward.

mermaid (mēr' mād), *n.* a fabled marine creature having the upper part like a woman and the lower part like a fish.

merriment (mēr' i ment), *n.* fun, gaiety.

merry (mer' i), *adj.* [*comp.* merrier, *superl.* merriest] full of mirth and good humor; jolly.

mesh (mesh), *n.* an opening between threads of a net; the engagement of the teeth of gears. *v.i. and v.t.* to engage, as gear teeth; to entangle, as if in a net.

mesmerize (mes' mēr iz), *v.t.* to induce an abnormal state of the nervous system in which the thoughts and acts of the patient are controlled by the will of the operator, to hypnotize.

mess (mes), *n.* a number of persons who eat together, especially in the military and naval services; the meal for which they assemble; a state of disorder and confusion; a disagreeable mixture of things.

message (mes' ij), *n.* a communication, written or oral; a formal communication from a chief executive to a legislative body, as the President's *message* to Congress.

*metabolism (me tab' ŏ lizm), *n.* the process by which the cells or tissues of a living body transform food materials into their own vital substance.

metacarpus (met *a* kar' pus), *n.* the part of the hand between the wrists and the fingers.

metal (met' l), *n.* a substance, usually an element and usually heavy and solid, having any of certain characteristics, such as luster, ductility, malleability, fusibility by heat, conduction of electricity, as gold, silver, iron, tin, brass are *metals;* platinum is a precious *metal. adj.* made of metal.

*metallurgy (met' l ûr ji), *n.* the art or process of separating metals from their ores and of using metals and alloys in manufacture; metalworking.

*metamorphosis (met *a* môr' fŏ sis), *n.* change of form or structure; transformation, as of a caterpillar into a butterfly.

metaphysics (met *a* fiz' iks), *n. pl.* mental philosophy, dealing with the nature and causes of being and knowing.

*metempsychosis (mē temp si kō' sis), *n.* the passage of a soul from one body into another at time of death; transmigration of souls.

*meteor (mē' tē ēr), *n.* a celestial body entering the earth's atmosphere with great speed and becoming hot and glowing with the friction of its passage through the air, as a shooting star.

meteoric (mē tē or' ik), *adj.* pertaining to, caused by or like a shooting star; momentarily dazzling and wonderful.

*meteorite (mē' tē ēr it), *n.* a stony or metallic mass which has fallen upon the earth out of space.

*meteorology (mē tē ēr ol' ŏ ji), *n.* the science that treats of atmospheric conditions and phenomena, the science of the weather.

meter (mē' tēr), *n.* an instrument that registers the measurement of currents that pass through it, as a water *meter,* electric *meter,* gas *meter. n.* rhythm, the measured arrangement of syllables in a line of verse, with certain stresses or lengths of sound; rhythm and time.

meter or **metre** (mē' tēr), *n.* the unit of length in the metric system, equal to 39.37 inches.

methane (meth' ān), *n.* an odorless, gaseous hydrocarbon, rising from decomposing matter in marshes and mines.

methinks (mē thingks'), *impersonal v.* [*p.t.* methought] it seems to me.

method (meth' ud), *n.* a systematic arrangement of things or ideas; a way of doing.

methodical (mē thod' l kal), *adj.* systematic.

methyl (meth' il), *n.* the hydrocarbon radical of which methane is the hydride.

metric (met' rik), *adj.* involving measurement; pertaining to the decimal system of weights and measures, which uses the meter as a measure of length and the gram as a measure of weight.

metrical (met' ri kal), *adj.* pertaining to rhythm; pertaining to measure, metric.

metrograph (met' rō gráf), *n.* an apparatus to register the mileage run by a locomotive and the number and time of its stops.

*metronome (met' rō nōm), *n.* an instrument that beats time for music.

metropolis (mē trop' ŏ lis), *n.* a chief city, in size and activity.

metropolitan (met rō pol' i tan), *adj.* pertaining to a metropolis.

mettle (met' l), *n.* the general quality of a man's character, ardor, spirit.

mettlesome (met' l sum), *adj.* high-spirited.

mews (mūz), *n. pl.* stables opening upon a court.

*mezzanine (mez' *a* nēn), *n.* a mid-floor between two ordinary floors, as the gallery between the main floor and second floor is the *mezzanine.*

*mezzotint (med' zō tint), *n.* a variety of copper engraving, producing soft tones in the print.

*mica (mī' ka), *n.* a mineral silicate that forms into thin, transparent leaves.

microcomputer (mī crō kom pū' ter), *n.* a small computer; a personal computer.

*microcosm (mī' krō kozm), *n.* a miniature world, especially mankind as representing the universe.

micrometer (mī krom' ē tēr), *n.* an instrument to measure accurately minute distances.

microorganism (mī krŏ ôr' gan izm), *n.* a minute organism that can be seen only through the microscope, such as bacteria and protozoa.

microphone (mī' krō fōn), *n.* a device used in radio broadcasting stations to receive and transmit sounds.

*microscope (mī' krō skōp), *n.* an optical instrument that magnifies minute objects so that they can be studied.

microwave (mī ´ krō wāv), *n.* an electromagnetic wave with a wave length longer than red light and shorter than radio waves; a modern oven which uses that wave.

mid (mid), *adj.* [*superl.* midmost] middle: usually in combination, as *mid*day, *mid*night, *mid*-ocean.

middle (mid' l), *n.* a portion equally distant from the extremes, as in the *middle* of his speech. *adj.* equally distant from the extremes; being between two others, as the *middle* one of three houses.

middling (mid' ling), *adj.* of medium size or quality.

midget (mij' et), *n.* a very small person. a dwarf.

midriff (mid' rif), *n.* the diaphragm.

midnight (mid' nīt), n. twelve o'clock at night.

midshipman (mid' ship man), n. one ranking next below an ensign in the U. S. Navy; a U. S. Naval Academy student.

midst (midst), n. the middle; the very central part thought of as being surrounded, as in the *midst* of danger, in the *midst* of the battle or the feast.

*****mien** (mēn), n. general appearance, air, manner, bearing.

might (mīt), n. great strength, power, force.

might (mīt), v.i. past tense of *may.*

*****mignonette** (min yun et'), n. a garden plant with fragrant greenish-white flowers.

migrate (mī' grāt), v.i. to move from one place to another, or from one country to another, to establish new residence; to move or pass from one region or climate to another, as certain birds and animals do.

mikado (mi kä' dō), n. the title given to the Emperor of Japan by foreigners.

milch (milch), adj. yielding milk, as a *milch* cow.

mild (mīld), adj. of gentle disposition; moderate, as *mild* weather.

mildew (mil' dū), n. any of certain minute fungi that grow on plants or decaying matter; plant disease produced by these fungi; mold growing on cloth, leather and other substances when damp, due to these fungi. v.t. and v.i. to cause mildew or become mildewed.

mile (mīl), n. a measure of length equal to 5,280 feet, also called the *statute mile;* the *sea mile* or *nautical mile,* 6080.2 feet.

mileage (mīl' ij), n. distance traversed, measured in miles; an allowance of so much per mile to legislators, salesmen for traveling expenses.

militant (mil' i tant), adj. warlike or engaged in war, fighting; aggressive.

militarism (mil' i ta rizm), n. the maintenance of a strong army and navy as a national policy; the idealizing of warlike spirit and martial virtues; government by the military class.

military (mil' i ter i), adj. pertaining to soldiers, armies or warfare.

militia (mi lish' a), n. a body of civilians enrolled as a military force, drilled and trained for defense, but called into active service only in times of emergency.

milk (milk), n. the white fluid produced by female mammals to feed their young; any white fluid resembling milk, as the juice of the *milk*weed, the *milk* of the coconut, *milk* of magnesia.

mill (mil), n. a machine that grinds; a building equipped with grinding machinery; a manufacturing plant in other industries, as a steel *mill* or cotton *mill.*

mill (mil), v.i. and v.t. to move aimlessly in circles, as cattle; to subject to such operations as are commonly done in a mill, like sawing timber, crushing ore, rolling steel.

millennium (mil len' i um), n. a thousand years: *the millennium,* the 1000 years referred to in Rev. 20: 1-7 as the time when Christ will rule on earth; a period of perfection.

miller (mil' ẽr), n. one who operates a mill, especially a flour mill; a moth with wings dusted as if with flour.

milliner (mil' i nẽr), n. one who makes and sells women's hats.

*****millinery** (mil' i ne ri), n. women's headgear; the business of making and selling women's hats.

million (mil' yun), n. a thousand thousand.

*****millionaire** (mil yun âr'), n. a man of great fortune, having a million or more dollars.

millrace (mil' rās), n. a swift current of water driving the machinery of a mill.

mimic (mim' ik), n. one who imitates. v.t. [p.t. and p.p. mimicked, pr.p. mimicking] to imitate, ape; ridicule by imitating.

mimicry (mim' ik ri), n. the act of one who mimics; in zoology, the protection afforded some edible or defenseless creatures by the likeness borne to a fierce or inedible creature, or to a leaf, a flower or other object.

minaret (min a ret'), n. a tall, slender turret, from which a muezzin or crier calls Mohammedans to prayer.

mince (mins), v.t. and v.i. to cut or chop fine; to utter with voluntary moderation, tone down, as to *mince* words; to walk or talk affectedly and primly.

mind (mīnd), n. the intellectual reasoning, thinking, remembering and conscious faculty. v.i. and v.t. to obey; to be troubled; to be careful, as *mind* your step; to heed; to object to; to obey; to watch or tend, as to *mind* a baby.

mindful (mīnd' fool), adj. bearing in mind, attentive.

mine (mīn), n. an excavation in the earth from which minerals are taken; a tunnel dug under a fort or position of enemy troops containing explosives; the explosives planted in a mine; explosives moored at sea, slightly submerged, to destroy enemy ships. v.i. and v.t. to make a mine; to dig up metals or ores; to set explosives under land or water to damage an enemy; to dig into for ores, as to *mine* a region; to get by digging, as to *mine* coal. *possessive form of the personal pronoun I*: belonging to me, as that hat is *mine.*

mineral (min' ẽr al), n. any inorganic chemical substance existing naturally; ore; anything not animal or vegetable in nature, though sometimes (coal, for instance) organic in origin. adj. pertaining to, consisting of or impregnated with minerals, as *mineral* water.

mineralogy (min ẽr al' ō ji), n. the science that treats of minerals.

Minerva (min ẽr' va), n. ancient mythical goddess of war, wisdom, arts and sciences.

mingle (ming' gl), v.i. and v.t. to intermix.

*****miniature** (min' i a tūr), n. a very small painting, especially a portrait on ivory. adj. diminutive, represented or existing on a very small scale.

minim (min' im), n. the smallest liquid measure, a sixtieth of a fluid dram, about equal to a drop.

minimize (min' im iz), *v.t.* to reduce to a minimum; to underestimate; to understate.

minimum (min' i mum), *n.* [*pl.* minima] the least possible quantity: opposite of *maximum*.

mining (min' ing), *n.* the act of making mines or working them.

minion (min' yun), *n.* a servile attendant or flattering dependent, a favorite; a size of type (7 point).

minister (min' is tēr), *n.* a clergyman; a diplomatic agent, of lower rank than an ambassador; the head of a governmental department. *v.i.* to serve; to serve as pastor of a church; to *minister* to, to give aid.

ministerial (min is tēr' i al), *adj.* pertaining to ministry of any kind.

ministry (min' is tri), *n.* the position of a minister; the clergy collectively. *n.* [*pl.* ministries] a government department presided over by a minister; all the heads of government departments, particularly those forming the cabinet.

mink (mingk), *n.* a carnivorous animal allied to the weasel, yielding a valuable fur.

minnow (min' ō), *n.* a small freshwater fish.

minor (min' ēr), *n.* a person less than 21 years old. *adj.* less; smaller; inferior.

***minority** (mi nor' i ti), *n.* [*pl.* minorities] the smaller of two groups within a total; the party casting less than half the votes in a two-party election. *n.* the state of being a minor; the period of life before attaining legal age.

minstrel (min' strel), *n.* a wandering medieval entertainer who sang songs and accompanied them with harp or lute; a member of a blackface troupe, entertaining audiences with songs and jokes.

mint (mint), *n.* a place where money is coined by government authority. *n.* an odoriferous plant yielding a pungent essential oil, as the pepper*mint*. *v.t.* to coin, as money, in a mint.

***minuet** (min ū et'), *n.* a slow stately dance; the music for it.

minus (mi' nus), *n.* the sign (—) of subtraction. *adj.* less, decreased by, as 5 *minus* 4 is 1.

minute (min' it), *n.* the 60th part of an hour equal to 60 seconds; the 60th part of the degree of an arc: *minutes*, memoranda; the detailed record of the proceedings of a formal meeting, as of a business organization, society or legislative body.

***minute** (mi nūt'), *adj.* small; insignificant; noting what is small, as a *minute* account of the game.

minutiae (min ū' shi ē), *n. pl.* [*sing.* minutia] small or trivial details.

minx (mingks), *n.* a pert girl.

miracle (mir' a kl), *n.* any occurrence that cannot be explained by the laws of nature; a marvel.

miraculous (mi rak' ū lus), *adj.* supernatural, wonderful.

***mirage** (mi räzh'), *n.* an optical atmospheric illusion by which the image of a distant object is seen as if inverted; any deceptive appearance or illusion.

mire (mīr), *n.* deep mud. *v.i.* and *v.t.* to sink in mud; to cause to sink in mud; to dirty with or as if with mud.

mirror (mir' ēr), *n.* a looking glass; any smooth, reflecting surface. *v.t.* to reflect, as if in a mirror.

mirth (mirth), *n.* merriment, jollity, especially with laughter.

misadventure (mis ad ven' tūr), *n.* a misfortune, mishap, mischance.

misalliance (mis a lli' ans), *n.* an undesirable or unhappy marriage.

***misanthrope** (mis' an thrōp), *n.* a hater of mankind; one who distrusts and dislikes others.

misapprehend (mis ap rē hend'), *v.t.* to misunderstand.

miscarry (mis kar' i), *v.i.* to turn out badly; to be unsuccessful.

miscellaneous (mis e lā' nē us), *adj.* made up of many different things, kinds or parts; mixed.

***miscellany** (mis' e lā ni), *n.* [*pl.* miscellanies] a mixture of various kinds of things, especially literary material.

mischance (mis chȧns'), *n.* a mishap, bad luck.

mischief (mis' chif), *n.* harm; damage; action intended to vex or annoy.

***mischievous** (mis' chiv us), *adj.* causing injury or damage; playing pranks intended to annoy.

misconceive (mis kon sēv'), *v.t.* to misunderstand, misjudge, interpret wrongly.

misconception (mis kon sep' shun), *n.* a false opinion; a wrong understanding.

***misconstrue** (mis kon strōō'), *v.* to interpret wrongly.

miscreant (mis' krē ant), *n.* a villain, wretch.

miscreant (mis' krē ant), *adj.* villainous, unscrupulous.

misdemeanor (mis dē mēn' ēr), *n.* a crime of less degree than a felony.

miser (mi' zēr), *n.* one who hoards money for its own sake and not for use.

miserable (miz' ēr a bl), *adj.* unhappy; worthless.

misery (miz' ēr i), *n.* pain; distress; great unhappiness.

misfit (mis fit'), *n.* anything too large or too small, as this shoe is a misfit; a person out of place in his environment.

misfortune (mis fôr' tūn), *n.* adversity, bad luck; a calamity.

misgiving (mis giv' ing), *n.* doubt about the future; a premonition of evil.

mishap (mis' hap), *n.* an unfortunate accident.

mislay (mis lā'), *v.t.* to put in the wrong place; to lose for a time.

misnomer (mis nō' mēr), *n.* a wrong name, especially misnaming some one in a legal document.

***misogynist** (mis oj' i nist), *n.* a woman-hater.

misplace (mis plās'), *v.t.* to put in the wrong place.

misrepresent (mis rep rē zent'), *v.t.* to report incorrectly.

miss (mis), *n.* a failure to hit, reach or attain.

miss (mis), *n.* an unmarried girl or woman.

miss (mis), *v.i.* and *v.t.* to fail of a mark;

to fail to hit; to feel the loss or absence of.

missal (mis' al), *n.* the book containing everything said or sung in the Roman Catholic Mass for every day of the year.

missile (mis' il), *n.* anything to be thrown or hurled as a spear, arrow, bomb, bullet.

mission (mish' un), *n.* the act of sending or state of being sent with certain powers, especially to propagate religion; a body of persons sent to represent an organization or a government for a special purpose.

missionary (mish' un er i), *n.* a person who is sent to propagate religion.

missive (mis' iv), *n.* a letter or message.

mist (mist), *n.* a visible watery vapor in the atmosphere; fog.

mistake (mis tāk'), *n.* an error.

mistake (mis tāk'), *v.i. and v.t.* [*p.t.* mistook, *p.p.* mistaken, *pr.p.* mistaking] to err in judgment or opinion; to identify wrongly, as I *mistook* you for John.

*ast**mistletoe** (mis' l tō), *n.* an evergreen plant, parasitic on the oak tree.

mistress (mis' tres), *n.* a woman who exercises authority, as the female head of a family or school.

misunderstand (mis un dėr stand'), *v.t.* to take in a wrong sense; to mistake the meaning of.

misuse (mis ūs'), *n.* wrong use, abuse.

misuse (mis ūz'), *v.t.* to use in a wrong way, mistreat.

mite (mit), *n.* a minute animal of the spider family often infesting cheese and other stored foods; a very small quantity; a tiny object or person.

miter (mi' tėr), *n.* a headdress made in two sections, worn by church officers. the joining of two surfaces at a 45-degree angle.

mix (miks), *v.i. and v.t.* to mingle with; to unite or blend into one mass.

Syn. Mingle, blend, confound. To *mix* is here a general and indefinite term, signifying simply to put together; we may *mix* two or several things. We *mingle* several objects. Things *mixed* lose all distinction; but they may be *mingled* and yet retain their individuality. To *blend* is only partially to *mix*, as colors *blend* which fall into each other. To *confound* is to confuse.

mixture (miks' tūr), *n.* the product of mixing; a compound or mass formed by mixing; a blend.

*ast**mnemonics** (nē mon' iks), *n.* the art or science of developing the power of memory.

moa (mō' a), *n.* large wingless bird, about 12 feet tall, of New Zealand, now extinct, related to the cassowary and ostrich.

moan (mōn), *n.* a low, prolonged sound of the voice expressing sorrow or pain; a sound resembling this, as the *moan* of the wind.

moan (mōn), *v.i.* to utter a low, prolonged sound expressing pain or grief.

moat (mōt), *n.* a deep, wide, water-filled ditch around the rampart of a castle or fortress, forming a protection against invaders.

mob (mob), *n.* a rough and disorderly crowd; people in general, as he writes for the *mob*.

mob (mob), *v.t.* to attack, in a disorderly

rabble, as they *mobbed* the jail.

*ast**mobile** (mō' bil), *adj.* easily moved; changing expression, as a *mobile* face.

*ast**mobilize** (mō' bi liz), *v.t.* to assemble and make ready for active service, as to *mobilize* troops.

moccasin (mok' a sin), *n.* a soft deerskin footcovering worn by the North American Indians and now used by hunters and campers; a poisonous American snake.

*ast**mocha** (mō' ka), *n.* a fine coffee that came originally from Mocha in Arabia.

mock (mok), *v.t.* to ridicule; to mimic; to jeer at.

mockery (mok' er i), *n.* the act of ridiculing; a sham, as it's a hollow *mockery*.

*ast**mode** (mōd), *n.* method, form, custom; in grammar, the mood of a verb in expressing the manner of being or doing.

*ast**model** (mod' l), *n.* a pattern of something to be made or reproduced; an example worthy of imitation. *v.t. and v.i.* to make a figure of, as to *model* a head; to form objects out of clay; to serve as a subject for an artist or sculptor, to try on clothes and exhibit them to prospective customers.

modem (mō' dem), *n.* a telephone hookup device.

moderate (mod' ėr it), *n.* one of conservative views and action. *adj.* reasonable, mild, calm, not extreme or violent.

moderate (mod' ėr āt), *v.i. and v.t.* to become less intense, as cold, or more mild, as the weather; to lessen, as to *moderate* a pressure.

modern (mod' ėrn), *adj.* pertaining to recent or present time.

modernism (mod' ėr nizm), *n.* a religious movement stressing ethical and critical values rather than theological creeds and dogmas.

modest (mod' est), *adj.* not boastful, unassuming, retiring, unpretentious; virtuous.

modification (mod i fi kā' shun), *n.* a slight reduction, as in statement; alteration.

modify (mod' i fi), *v.t.* [*p.t.* and *p.p.* modified, *pr.p.* modifying] to change the form of, slightly, qualify, as to *modify* rules; limit, reduce; to restrict the meaning of, as an adjective *modifies* a noun.

*ast**modiste** (mō dēst'), *n.* a fashionable dressmaker.

*ast**modulate** (mod' ū lāt), *v.i. and v.t.* to pass from one musical key to another by using tones related to both keys; to vary the tone of, as the voice; to regulate amplitude and frequency of, as an electric current.

module (moj ' ōōl), *n.* a standard or unit of measurement; any of a set of units to be fitted together; a detachable unit with a specific function as in a spacecraft.

*ast**moiety** (moi' et i), *n.* a small portion or share.

*ast**moist** (moist), *adj.* containing liquid, as *moist* earth; damp, humid.

moisture (mois' tūr), *n.* a moderate degree of dampness; that which makes damp.

Syn. Humidity, dampness. *Moisture* is any small degree of infusion of a liquid into a substance or body. *Humidity* is the same thing expressed with more scientific limitation, referring especially to the air. *Dampness* is that species of *moisture* which arises from gradual accumulation of water in bodies capable of containing it; we find *dampness* in cellars.

molar (mō' lẽr), *n.* a double, grinding tooth. *adj.* pertaining to grinding; adapted to grinding. *adj.* relating to matter considered in a mass, not in its molecular nature.

molasses (mō las' ez), *n.* the thick sirup left after refining cane sugar; treacle.

mold (mōld), *n.* a fuzzy, exterior fungous growth on damp or decaying animal or vegetable matter; a hollow form in which anything is poured for shaping, as a pudding *mold;* distinctive character, as a man of that *mold. v.t.* to form in or as in a mold; to knead into a required consistency or shape.

molder (mōl' dẽr), *v.i.* to crumble away in decay.

molding (mōl' ding), *n.* a strip of material used as ornamental edging in building.

mole (mōl), *n.* a dark-colored spot or growth on the skin; a small, soft-furred burrowing animal with minute eyes; a breakwater at the mouth of a harbor.

molecule (mol' ē kūl), *n.* the smallest quantity of an element or compound which can exist separately.

molehill (mōl' hil), *n.* a small mound of earth left by the burrowing mole; a trifling annoyance or obstacle, as to make mountains out of *molehills.*

molest (mō lest'), *v.t.* to annoy or interfere with, harass, pester.

mollify (mol' i fī), *v.t.* to soothe, calm, as to *mollify* a person.

mollusk (mol' usk), *n.* one of various soft-bodied animals, most of which have protective shells, as slugs, snails, clams, oysters.

molt (mōlt), *v.i.* to shed the feathers, horns, hair or skin.

molten (mōl' ten), *adj.* melted; made by melting and casting.

moment (mō' ment), *n.* an instant of time; import or importance, as news of great *moment.*

momentary (mō' men ter i), *adj.* lasting only for an instant; done in an instant; quickly passing, not lasting.

momentous (mō men' tus), *adj.* very important.

momentum (mō men' tum), *n.* the measure of motion in a body found by multiplying mass by velocity, impetus.

monad (mon' ad), *n.* an atom; a minute, simple organism or organic unit.

monarch (mon' ẽrk), *n.* a supreme ruler, sovereign.

monarchy (mon' ẽr ki), *n.* [*pl.* monarchies] a form of government with a king or emperor as supreme head; a country so governed.

monastery (mon' as ter i), *n.* [*pl.* monasteries] a secluded residence for persons under religious vows, especially monks.

monastic (mō nas' tik), *adj.* pertaining to monasteries or monks.

monetary (mon' ē ter i), *adj.* pertaining to money.

monetize (mon' ē tīz), *v.t.* to give a standard value to, as a metal for use in coin.

money (mun' i), *n.* gold, silver or other metal coined and issued by a government as a medium of exchange; standardized medium of exchange and measure of value; anything that represents cash, as any form of bank credit.

moneyed (mun' id), *adj.* wealthy.

mongoose (mong' gōōs), *n.* a small, ferretlike animal of India and Egypt that attacks and kills poisonous snakes.

mongrel (mung' grel), *n.* anything of mixed breed or kind; especially a dog of mixed breed.

monism (mon' izm), *n.* the doctrine that there is only one kind of substance or final reality, as mind or matter.

monition (mō nish' un), *n.* warning, notice, caution.

monitor (mon' i tẽr), *n.* one who warns or advises; a pupil appointed to oversee younger ones, as on a playground; the earliest type of armor-clad warship, with a revolving turret on an open deck.

monk (mungk), *n.* a man who devotes himself exclusively to a religious life and lives in a monastery, under church discipline.

monkey (mung' ki), *n.* [*pl.* monkeys] one of the primates, especially one of the long-tailed forms smaller than the ape.

monkish (mungk' ish), *adj.* like a monk; monastic.

monocle (mon' ō kl), *n.* an eyeglass for one eye.

monocular (mō nok' ū lẽr), *adj.* having only one eye; adapted for use by one eye, as a *monocular* telescope.

monogamy (mō nog' a mi), *n.* marriage of one wife only.

monogram (mon' ō gram), *n.* a character formed by uniting two or more letters, as one's initials.

monograph (mon' ō gráf), *n.* a treatise closely limited to one subject or phase.

monolith (mon' ō lith), *n.* a pillar or column formed of a single block of stone.

monologue (mon' ō lôg), *n.* a long speech by one person.

monomania (mon ō mā' ni a), *n.* mental derangement in regard to one subject only.

monoplane (mon' ō plān), *n.* an airplane with only one main supporting surface.

monopolist (mō nop' ō list), *n.* one who has a monopoly or complete control, especially of an industrial or commercial field.

monopolize (mō nop' ō līz), *v.t.* to acquire control of, as the entire product or service in some special field, so as to regulate the market; to keep all or practically all to oneself, as to *monopolize* a conversation.

monopoly (mō nop' ō li), *n.* complete control of a market by a single manufacturer or distributor.

monosyllable (mon' ō sil a bl), *n.* a word of

one syllable.

monotheism (mon' ō thē izm), n. the doctrine or belief that there is only one god.

monotone (mon' ō tōn), n. speech in unchanging tone; utterance all on one note.

monotony (mō not' ō ni), n. unbroken uniformity, dull repetition; continuance of tone.

*monsoon (mon sōōn'), n. a periodic wind in the Indian Ocean and southern Asia.

monster (mon' stēr), n. an animal, plant or thing that departs from the customary course of nature in its kind; an ugly or cruel person.

monstrosity (mon stros' i ti), n. [pl. monstrosities] anything hideously abnormal or deformed.

monstrous (mon' strus), adj. deformed, hideous; huge; horrible.

month (munth), n. one of the twelve major divisions of the year: lunar month, the period from one new moon to another, not quite 30 days.

monument (mon' ū ment), n. a memorial structure; any conspicuous and enduring example, as a monument of genius.

moo (mōō), n. [pl. moos] the lowing sound made by a cow.

*mood (mōōd), n. style; state of mind; the change in form of a verb to indicate manner of being or doing.

moody (mōōd' i), adj. [comp. moodier, superl. moodiest] given to changes in the state of mind.

*moon (mōōn), n. the satellite that revolves about the earth in monthly cycles. v.i. to wander and look about in abstracted manner.

moonshine (mōōn' shīn), n. moonlight; idle talk, empty show; liquor made illegally.

moonstone (mōōn' stōn), n. a translucent, semiprecious stone of yellowish color.

moon-struck (mōōn' struk), adj. lunatic.

*moor (moor), n. a tract of waste land, especially one covered with heather. v.i. and v.t. to secure in a certain place, as a ship; to fasten to, as a dock, with a cable.

mooring (moor' ing), n. the act of securing a vessel in a particular place; the place where a ship is moored.

*moose (mōōs), n. a large, North American deer resembling the European elk.

moot (mōōt), adj. debatable, as a moot question.

mop (mop), n. an implement for washing floors, having a bundle of cloth or yarn at the end of a long handle; an abundant head of hair, as a mop of hair. v.t. to wash or dry, as to mop a floor; to swab or wipe up, as to mop the water on the floor.

mope (mōp), v.i. to go about with a drooping air; to be silent, dull, dispirited.

moraine (mō rān'), n. a ridge of rocks and gravel deposited by a glacier.

*moral (mor' al), adj. conforming to generally accepted ideas of what is right and just in human conduct.

*morale (mō ral'), n. the mental state that makes it possible to sustain courage, determination and endurance in times of test and trouble.

morality (mō ral' i ti), n. [pl. moralities] right living, virtue; conformity to generally accepted standards of conduct.

moralize (mor' al īz), v.i. to present a lecture on right conduct; to render right and just.

morals (mor' alz), n. pl. right conduct in an inclusive sense; the principles of good behavior.

morass (mō ras'), n. a swamp, bog.

morbid (mōr' bid), adj. diseased, unhealthy; mentally unwholesome; gloomy, as she has a morbid nature.

mordant (mōr' dant), n. a substance that eats into a surface, a corrosive. adj. biting, as an acid; sarcastic, keen, as a mordant wit.

more (mōr), n. a greater quantity or number, as I wanted more. adj. [comp. of many and much] being greater in number, volume or extent. adv. in or to a greater degree or extent; again.

moreover (mōr ō' vēr), adv. besides, furthermore.

morgue (mōrg), n. a public establishment where the bodies of unknown dead are held for identification.

*moribund (mor' i bund), adj. dying.

morning (mōr' ning), n. the early part of the day; forenoon. adj. relating in any way to the early part of the day, the forenoon.

morning-glory (mōr' ning glō' ri), n. a twining plant with white, purple or pink blossoms.

morocco (mō rok' ō), ' . a fine-grained leather of goatskin.

*moron (mō' ron), n. a person who is deficient in mental ability.

morose (mō rōs'), adj. sullen, gloomy.

morphia (mōr' fi a), n. the narcotic principle of opium.

*morphine (mōr' fēn), n. an alkaloid of opium, used in medicine.

morphinism (mōr' fin izm), n. a morbid state induced by excessive use of opium.

morphology (mōr fol' ō ji), n. the science of forms in the organisms of plants and animals.

morris (mor' is), n. an English country dance of Moorish origin.

morrow (mor' ō), n. the day following any day specified, tomorrow.

*morsel (mōr' sel), n. a small piece; a mere bite, as a morsel of food.

*mortal (mōr' tal), n. a being subject to death, a human being. adj. subject to death; causing death, fatal, as a mortal wound; deadly, as a mortal enemy.

mortality (mōr tal' i ti), n. [pl. mortalities] the condition of being subject to death; number of deaths in proportion to population.

mortar (mōr' tēr), n. a vessel in which substances are pounded with a pestle; a cement of lime, sand and water, used in building; a short, stubby cannon used to fire shells at a high angle, dropping them on a mark.

*mortgage (mōr' gij), n. a legal paper pledging property to cover a debt, as he holds a mortgage on my house. v.t. to pledge as security, as to *mortgage* a house.

mortification (môr ti fi kā' shun), *n.* self-denial, discipline; humiliation, chagrin; gangrene.

mortify (môr' ti fi), *v.t. and v.i.* to deaden; to discipline by self-denial, as to *mortify* the flesh; to humiliate, embarrass, as her child's behavior *mortified* her; to lose vitality and organic structure; to gangrene, as the flesh *mortified.*

mortise (môr' tis), *n.* a hole or hollowed-out space in a timber, in which to insert a tenon. *v.t.* to join with mortise and tenon, as timbers.

mortmain (môrt' mān), *n.* tenure of land by a corporation.

mortuary (môr' tū er i), *n.* [*pl.* mortuaries] a building for the dead pending burial, a morgue.

mosaic (mō zā' ik), *n.* a design made by inlaying pieces of material of different colors.

mosque (mosk), *n.* a Mohammedan place of worship.

mosquito (mus kē' tō), *n.* [mosquitoes] a two-winged insect, the females of which puncture the human skin with a proboscis, causing irritation and in some species carrying the germs of malaria or yellow fever.

moss (môs), *n.* a small, leafy plant that grows like a thick mat in crevices, on trees, rocks and damp ground.

most (mōst), *n.* the greatest number, quantity or value. *adj.* [superl. of more] greatest in number, quantity or degree.

mote (mōt), *n.* a very small particle.

*****moth** (môth), *n.* a night-flying insect with four wings, related to the butterfly; any of several small, yellowish or buff-colored insects whose larvae eat woolen fabrics and furs, as the clothes *moth.*

mother (muth' ẽr), *n.* a female parent.

motif (mō tēf'), *n.* the central idea or theme of a work, as in music, art or literature; a melody that may be repeated many times with variations throughout a musical composition.

motion (mō' shun), *n.* the act of moving; passage from one place to another; a gesture; a formal proposal in a deliberative assembly.

motive (mō' tiv), *n.* that which leads to action; an incentive; the animating idea, as in a work of music, art or literature; a motif.

motley (mot' li), *n.* [*pl.* motleys] a mixture, as of colors. *adj.* consisting of or clothed in different colors; composed of varying elements, as a *motley* gathering.

motor (mō' tẽr), *n.* an engine that produces motion, as a gas or electric *motor. adj.* producing motion; driven by a motor, as a *motorboat. v.i. and v.t.* to travel by motor car; to transport by automobile or motor truck.

mottle (mot' l), *v.t.* to color in blotches.

mottled (mot' ld), *adj.* dappled, spotted.

motto (mot' ō), *n.* [*pl.* mottoes] a word, phrase or expression inscribed on anything to set forth its guiding principle, character or use; adage, maxim.

mound (mound), *n.* a hillock; an artificial hill.

mount (mount), *n.* a hill or mountain. *n.* a riding horse; a structure on which anything is permanently set, as a *mount* for a cannon or a picture. *v.i. and v.t.* to rise, as prices; to climb, as we *mounted* the hill with effort; to seat oneself on, as to *mount* a horse.

*****mountain** (moun' tin), *n.* a great height of land that projects above its surroundings.

mountaineer (moun ti nēr'), *n.* one who lives in a mountain region; one who climbs mountains.

mountebank (moun' tē bangk), *n.* one who sells quack medicines; a charlatan.

*****mourn** (môrn), *v.i. and v.t.* to grieve, as she *mourned* for years; to grieve for, as the dog *mourned* his master.

mournful (môrn' fool), *adj.* expressing sorrow, overborne by grief, sad.

mourning (môrn' ing), *n.* expression of grief; the dress of one who has lost a friend or relative; tokens of public loss by death, as black draperies in public buildings or flags at half mast.

mouse (mous), *n.* [*pl.* mice] a small rodent of the fields or one that infests houses, granaries.

mousse (mōos), *n.* a frozen dessert or salad of flavored whipped cream.

*****mouth** (mouth), *n.* the opening of the head in animals through which they take food and utter sounds.

*****mouth** (mouth), *v.t. and v.i.* to utter in a pompous fashion; to rant; to speak affectedly or with grimaces.

mouthful (mouth' fool), *n.* [*pl.* mouthfuls] the amount required to fill the mouth.

mouthpiece (mouth' pēs), *n.* the part of a wind instrument to which the lips are applied; a spokesman.

movable (mōov' a bl), *adj.* capable of being moved.

move (mōov), *v.i. and v.t.* to change place or position, as I tried to take a picture but she *moved;* to cause to change place or position, as *move* the chair over here; to offer a motion or resolution in a deliberative assembly.

moving (mōov' ing), *adj.* changing place or posture; affecting the feelings.

Syn. Affecting, pathetic. That which is *moving* excites the emotions, as a *moving* appeal; *affecting* is a more general term applying to anything that stirs the feelings; that which is *pathetic* arouses sympathy, pity and sorrow.

moving picture (mōov' ing pik' tūr), a series of pictures taken so actions photographed as static are projected with such rapidity that the characters seem to move as if alive.

*****mow** (mou), *n.* the space in a barn where hay or grain is stored.

mow (mō), *v.t.* to cut down, as grass or wheat.

much (much), *n.* a great quantity, as I don't want *much. adj.* [*comp.* more, *superl.* most] great in quantity, as *much* money. *adv.* to a great degree or extent, as I don't want it *much.*

*mucilage (mū' sil ij), *n.* a gummy substance used in medicine and as an adhesive.

muck (muk), *n.* heavy, moist earth, especially mixed with manure.

mucous (mū' kus), *adj.* pertaining to the thick fluid secreted by the mucous membranes; resembling mucus; secreting mucus, slimy.

mucus (mū' kus), *n.* the thick fluid secreted by the mucous membranes.

mud (mud), *n.* soft wet earth, mire.

muddle (mud' l), *n.* a confused state.

muddle (mud' l), *v.i. and v.t.* to be confused or aimless; to confuse or stupefy; to handle in a bungling way.

muff (muf), *n.* a warm soft cover, as of fur, to keep hands warm; a bungling attempt. *v.t.* to bungle; to fail, especially to drop a ball one is trying to catch.

muffin (muf' in), *n.* a quick bread or biscuit baked in a cup-shaped tin.

muffle (muf' l), *v.t.* to wrap up warmly; to deaden the sound of by covering, as to *muffle* a bell.

mug (mug), *n.* an earthenware or metallic drinking cup with a handle.

muggy (mug' i), *adj.* [*comp.* muggier, *superl.* muggiest] warm, damp, close, as a *muggy* day.

mugwump (mug' wump), *n.* a voter belonging to a party but not always following its lead or voting for its candidates; an independent.

*mulatto (mū lat' ō), *n.* [*pl.* mulattoes] a person one of whose parents is white and the other a Negro.

mulberry (mul' ber i), *n.* [*pl.* mulberries] the sweet dark purple fruit of a tree of the genus *Morus;* a tree of this genus with whitish berries on which the silkworm feeds.

mulch (mulch), *n.* a collection of straw, used to protect the roots of plants in winter.

mulch (mulch), *v.t.* to protect with mulch.

*mulct (mulkt), *n.* a fine. *v.t.* to punish with a fine; to deprive of by fraud, as they *mulcted* him of five dollars.

mule (mūl), *n.* the offspring of a male ass and a mare.

mull (mul), *n.* a thin, soft muslin. *v.t.* to warm, spice and sweeten, as ale.

multigraph (mul' ti graf), *n.* a small cylinder printing press for form letters.

multiplane (mul' ti plān), *n.* an airplane with more than two main planes superimposed.

multiple (mul' ti pl), *n.* a number or quantity which contains another an exact number of times, without a remainder.

multiplex (mul' ti pleks), *adj.* combining many in one, as this dictionary combines definitions, pronunciations, spellings, synonyms and antonyms.

*multiplication (mul ti pli kā' shun), *n.* the act or process of multiplying.

multiplicity (mul ti plis' i ti), *n.* the quality of being multiplex, manifold or various; a great number, as a *multiplicity* of reasons.

multiply (mul' ti pli), *v.i. and v.t.* to increase in number or extent, as the number of cases *multiplies* rapidly; to find the number

equal to a given number taken a specified number of times, as to *multiply* 2 by 5.

multitude (mul' ti tūd), *n.* a great number, crowd, assembly; people in general.

multitudinous (mul ti tū' din us), *adj.* consisting of a great number.

mum (mum), *adj.* silent.

mumble (mum' bl), *v.i. and v.t.* to speak indistinctly, as to *mumble* to oneself; to utter indistinctly, as to *mumble* one's words.

mummery (mum' ēr i), *n.* [*pl.* mummeries] masquerading with buffoonery.

mummy (mum' i), *n.* [*pl.* mummies] a dead body embalmed after the manner of the ancient Egyptians.

mumps (mumps), *n.* a contagious disease with fever and a swelling of neck glands.

munch (munch), *v.i. and v.t.* to chew slowly or noisily, as he was *munching;* the children *munched* the candy.

*municipal (mū nis' i pal), *adj.* pertaining to a city or town as an incorporated, self-governing political unit.

municipality (mū nis i pal' i ti), *n.* [*pl.* municipalities] a corporate town, borough or city.

*munificence (mū nif' i sens), *n.* great generosity, lavishness in giving.

munitions (mū nish' unz), *n. pl.* military stores of materials.

mural (mū' ral), *n.* a painting on a wall. *adj.* relating in any way to a wall.

murder (mûr' dēr), *n.* homicide with malice aforethought. *v.t.* to kill a person unlawfully with malice aforethought.

*murk (mûrk), *n.* darkness, as lost in the *murk.*

murky (mûrk' i), *adj.* [*comp.* murkier, *superl.* murkiest] dark, gloomy, obscure.

murmur (mûr' mer), *n.* a low, indistinct sound, like that of a running stream or of voices at a little distance. *v.i. and v.t.* to make a sound like that of a running stream or the hum of bees at a distance; to utter in a murmuring tone.

*muscle (mus' l), *n.* a highly contractile organ of fibrous tissue by which movement is effected in an animal body; bodily strength.

muscular (mus' kū lēr), *adj.* relating to muscles; equipped with muscles; strong-bodied.

muse (mūz), *n.* any of the nine goddesses who presided over the arts and sciences.

muse (mūz), *v.i.* to ponder, meditate.

museum (mū zē' um), *n.* a collection of natural, scientific or literary curiosities or works of art; the building in which such a collection is kept, as a *museum* of fine arts.

mush (mush), *n.* boiled corn meal; anything soft and thick like mush.

mushroom (mush' rōōm), *n.* an edible fungus.

music (mū' zik), *n.* the art or science of harmonic sounds; harmony or melody; printed representation of notes to be sung or played.

musician (mū zish' an), *n.* one who knows the science or art of music; one who sings or plays a musical instrument.

musk (musk), *n.* a strong-scented substance obtained from a certain deer; an artificial product resembling musk in odor.

musket (mus' ket), *n*. the firearm formerly used by infantry, a gun like a rifle, but having a smooth bore.

musk ox (musk oks), *n*. a ruminant gregarious mammal of arctic North America, related to both sheep and cattle, has curved horns and musky odor, eats grass and mosses.

muskrat (musk' rat), *n*. an aquatic rodent having a long, scaly tail, webbed hind feet and dark, glossy brown fur, sometimes called Hudson seal.

*muslin** (muz' lin), *n*. a fine, thin cotton fabric.

muss (mus), *n*. confusion and disorder.

muss (mus), *v.t.* to disorder, as clothing.

mussel (mus' l), *n*. a bivalve found either in the sea or in fresh water.

must (must), *v.i.* to be obliged or compelled, as he *must* do it; to be required; to be logically necessary, as this *must* be what you want.

*mustache, moustache** (mus täsh'), *n*. the growth of hair on the upper lip.

mustang (mus' tang), *n*. the small, tough, half-wild horse of the western prairies.

mustard (mus' tĕrd), *n*. a plant with seeds that are ground and used as seasoning; a hot condiment made of these ground seeds, for use on meats.

muster (mus' tĕr), *n*. an assembly of troops, for review or for active service; a register, as of troops. *v.t.* to assemble, as troops; to gather together, as to *muster* all one's resources.

musty (mus' ti), *adj*. [*comp.* mustier, *superl.* mustiest] moldy, spoiled by age, as *musty* cheese; stale, as a *musty* proverb.

mutability (mū ta bil' i ti), *n*. the quality of being subject to change, instability.

mutable (mū' ta bl), *adj*. capable of or susceptible to change; inconstant.

mute (mūt), *n*. a person who lacks the power of speech; a letter that is not pronounced; a consonant pronounced with breath stopping—*p, b, t, d, k, g*; a device to soften the tone of a musical instrument. *v.t.* to muffle the tone of, as a musical instrument. *adj*. lacking the power of speech; dumb; silent.

mutilate (mū' ti lāt), *v.t.* to disfigure or maim, as by cutting off a limb or essential part; to mangle and cut, as a text.

mutilation (mū ti lā' shun), *n*. the act of mutilating; a serious disfigurement or injury through cutting off some essential part.

mutineer (mū ti nēr'), *n*. one who is guilty of mutiny.

mutinous (mū' ti nus), *adj*. partaking of the nature of mutiny; inclined to mutiny; engaging in mutiny.

mutiny (mū' ti ni), *n*. insurrection against or forcible resistance to constituted authority, especially among troops or aboard ship.

mutter (mut' ĕr), *n*. a low, indistinct utterance, generally ill-natured; a growl.

mutter (mut' ĕr), *v.i. and v.t.* to utter in a low, indistinct tone and generally in a surly manner; to grumble.

mutton (mut' n), *n*. the flesh of sheep.

*mutual** (mū' tū al), *adj*. reciprocal, shared in common.

muzzle (muz' l), *n*. snout; the end of a firearm from which the missile emerges; a device to keep a dog from biting, by covering its muzzle. *v.t.* to put a muzzle on.

my (mī), *pron*. possessive form of me, as that is *my* hat.

myriad (mir' i ad), *n*. ten thousand; any very large number, as he has a *myriad* of friends.

myriad (mir' i ad), *adj*. consisting of a very great number, innumerable.

*myrrh** (mûr), *n*. the aromatic, gummy resin of an Oriental plant.

myself (mī self'), *pron*. [*pl*. ourselves] an emphasized form of the pronoun for the first person singular, as I *myself* heard it; as a reflexive, as I cut *myself*.

mysterious (mis tēr' i us), *adj*. partaking of the nature of mystery; not clear to the understanding, baffling.

Syn. Abstruse, cabalistic, dark, enigmatical, hidden, unfathomable, inexplicable, inscrutable, mystic, mystical, obscure, occult, recondite, secret. That is *mysterious* which excites and at the same time baffles; That is *mystic* or *mystical* which has some *hidden* or *abstruse* meaning. That is *inscrutable* which is *unfathomable* and incapable of interpretation.

*mystery** (mis' tĕr i), *n*. [*pl*. mysteries] something secret, obscure or unexplainable; that which is beyond human comprehension.

mystic (mis' tik), *adj*. mysterious, related to divine revelation, baffling, puzzling, incomprehensible.

mystification (mis ti fi kā' shun), *n*. the act of baffling; the state of being baffled or puzzled.

mystify (mis' ti fī), *v.t.* [*p.t.* and *p.p.* mystified, *pr.p.* mystifying] to involve in mystery, baffle, puzzle.

myth (mith), *n*. a story rooted in the most ancient religious beliefs and institutions of a people, usually dealing with gods, goddesses or natural phenomena; an imaginary thing.

*mythology** (mi thol' ō ji), *n*. [*pl*. mythologies] the scientific study of myths; a collection of myths.

N

nabob (nā' bob), *n*. a native governor of a province in India, under the Mogul empire; a very wealthy man.

*nadir** (nā' dĕr), *n*. the part of the heavens directly under the place where one stands; opposed to *zenith*.

nag (nag), *n.* a small horse, pony; any horse.

nag (nag), *v.i. and v.t.* to scold constantly, as she *nags* continually; to find fault with, as she *nags* her husband.

nail (nāl), *n.* the horny protective plate at the end of a finger or toe, as finger*nail*, toe*nail;* the claw of a bird or other animal. *n.* a pointed piece of metal, usually with a broad head, that can be driven into wood to fasten pieces together. *v.t.* to fasten with a *nail*; to clinch, as to *nail* a bargain; to expose, as to *nail* a lie.

*naive (nä ēv'), adj. artless, ingenuous, unaffectedly simple, unsophisticated.

*naiveté (nä ēv tā'), n. artlessness; unaffected naturalness.

*naked (nā' ked), adj. unclothed, bare, unassisted, as the *naked* eye; plain, as the *naked* truth.

name (nām), *n.* that by which a person or thing is called; fame, as he has a great *name* in radio; something thought of as having lost its real existence, as chivalry has become a *name*.

Syn. Designation, denomination, appellation, title. *Name* is a general term; *appellation* suggests a descriptive name, as one *appellation* of Maine is the Pine Tree State; a *designation* is a specific name; *denomination* denotes a class or division; a *title* indicates rank, office or distinction. *v.t.* to give a name to; to call by name, mention by name; to set, as *name* a price.

nankeen (nan kēn'), *n.* a buff-colored cotton cloth, originally made in Nanking, China.

nap (nap), *n.* a short slumber, a brief doze. *n.* the fuzzy surface of some fabrics. *v.i.* to sleep lightly and for a short time.

nape (nāp), *n.* the back of the neck.

napery (nāp' ẽr i), *n.* table linen.

napkin (nap' kin), *n.* a small piece of cloth, especially one on which to wipe the hands and lips.

narc (närk), *n.* slang for a police undercover agent usually from the Federal Bureau of Narcotics.

narcosis (när kō' sis), *n.* stupefaction from the effects of a drug.

narcotic (när kot' ik), *n.* a drug that alleviates pain and induces sleep. *adj.* producing coma or torpor.

*narrate (na rāt'), v.t. to tell, as a story.

narration (na rā' shun), *n.* a story; the telling of a story, a recital of events.

narrative (nar' a tiv), *n.* a story or a recital of events. *adj.* pertaining to story-telling, as a good *narrative* sense.

narrow (nar' ō), *adj.* having little width, of small dimension from side to side; lacking breadth of view; with little to spare, as a *narrow* escape; limited, as in a *narrow* sense. *v.i. and v.t.* to become less broad; to lessen the width of.

narrows (nar' ōz), *n. pl.* a narrow passage connecting two large bodies of water.

narwhal (när' hwal), *n.* an animal of the Arctic ocean, about 15 feet long, related to the dolphin, resembles a small whale; the male has a spirally grooved tusk about 7 feet long projecting forward.

NASA (nas' a), *n.* National Aeronautics and Space Administration.

*nasal (nā' zal), adj. pertaining to the nose; pronounced, as the letters *m* and *n*, through the nose.

*nascent (nas' ent), adj. beginning to be, just coming into existence, as a *nascent* idea.

nasturtium (na stûr' shum), *n.* a garden plant with spicy stem and seeds and showy red and yellow flowers.

nasty (nås' ti), *adj.* [*comp.* nastier, *superl.* nastiest] disgustingly dirty; mean; indecent; serious, as a *nasty* cut.

*natal (nā' tal), adj. pertaining to birth, as one's *natal* day.

natation (nā tā' shun), *n.* the art of swimming.

natatorial (nā ta tō' ri al), *adj.* pertaining to swimming.

natatorium (nā ta tō' ri um), *n.* a swimming pool, especially indoors.

nation (nā' shun), *n.* a race, the people of one country under one government.

*national (nash' un al), n. a citizen of a country, member of a nation. adj. pertaining to a nation.

nationalism (nash' un al izm), *n.* devotion to one's own country; support of national independence; a policy that advocates state ownership and control of industries.

*nationality (nash un al' i ti), n. the state of belonging to or being a member of a nation; the state of being a nation.

native (nā' tiv), *n.* one born in a stated country or place. *adj.* born in a stated country or place; growing naturally in a stated region; not acquired, as a *native* gift for languages.

Syn. Indigenous, natural, original. *Native* means inborn and increases the contrast between what is natural and artificial; *natural* is that which belongs to something by nature; *indigenous* is that which grows or lives naturally in a certain country or climate, as cotton is *indigenous* to America; *original* signifies that which precedes all others in its category, as the *original* inhabitants of a continent.

nativity (nā tiv' i ti), *n.* [*pl.* nativities] time, place and manner of birth.

*natural (nat' û ral), adj. pertaining to nature; inborn, not artificial or acquired; conforming to the customary sequence or character of things and events.

naturalist (nat' û ral ist), *n.* one who makes a special study of animals and plants.

naturalism (nat' û ral izm), *n.* the doctrine that scientific laws account for all phenomena, materialism; realism in art and literature.

*naturalize (nat' û ral īz), v.t. to confer the rights, privileges and duties of a native citizen upon, as to *naturalize* an immigrant.

*nature (nā' tûr), n. the universe; the forces or powers that animate and regulate it; the sum of an individual's personality and character; any marked characteristic, as he has a scholarly *nature*.

naughty (nô ti), *adj.* [*comp.* naughtier, *superl.*

naughtiest] mischievous, disobedient.

*nausea (nô' shē a), n. sickness of the stomach, especially seasickness, accompanied by desire to vomit; great disgust.

*nauseous (nô' shus), adj. disturbing to the stomach; disgusting.

nautical (nô' ti kal), adj. having to do with ships and navigation.

nautilus (nô' ti lus), n. [pl. nautiluses or nautili] a mollusk with a spiral shell.

naval (nā' val), adj. pertaining to a navy.

nave (nāv), n. the cross-shaped central part of a church between the aisles. n. the central block of a wheel, the hub.

navel (nā' vel), n. the depression in the middle of the lower part of the abdomen; the umbilicus.

navigable (nav' i ga bl), adj. capable of being passed over by boats or ships; steerable, as a navigable balloon.

navigate (nav' i gāt), v.i. and v.t. to sail a ship; to travel by water; to direct the course of.

navy (nā' vi), n. a nation's entire equipment for war at sea, including ships, yards, stations, trained officers and men and supplies; especially the ships.

nay (nā), n. a negative vote; a negative voter. adv. no; not this merely, but also, as I believe, nay I know.

neap (nēp), adj. lowest, as neap tide.

neap tide (nēp tīd), the smallest high tide of the lunar month, when the moon is at first or third quarter.

near (nēr), v.i. and v.t. to approach, as the time nears, the ship nears port. adj. not distant in time or space, close; intimate, as a near friend; missing by little, as a near escape; of draft animals, the one on the driver's side, as the near horse; stingy, closefisted. adv. almost; closely.

near-by (nēr' bī'), adv. and adj., at hand, close.

neat (nēt), n. cattle, cows, bulls, oxen, as distinct from horses and sheep. adj. bovine, as neat cattle. adj. tidy, trim, as a neat person; adroit, as a neat reply.

neb (neb), n. a bird's beak.

nebula (neb' ū la), n. [pl. nebulas or nebulae] a faint misty patch of light in the heavens, produced by clustered stars or by masses of diffused gaseous matter.

nebulous (neb' ū lus), adj. pertaining to a nebula; faint and vague, indistinct, as the plan is still nebulous.

necessary (nes' e ser i), n. [pl. necessaries] something essential or indispensable: necessaries, requisite things, as the necessaries of life. adj. indispensable; inevitable, as a necessary result.

necessitate (nē ses' i tāt), v.t. to make necessary; to require; to compel, as the situation necessitates immediate action.

necessity (nē ses' i ti), n. [pl. necessities] something that is indispensable, as food is a necessity; that which is unavoidable; great need, as call me in case of necessity; poverty.

neck (nek), n. the part of the body between the head and trunk; a long narrow part of an object, as the neck of a vase; a narrow strip, as a neck of land; the part of a garment that covers or fits about the neck, as the neck of a dress.

neckerchief (nek' ēr chif), n. a piece of cloth or decorative handkerchief worn about the neck.

necklace (nek' lis), n. a string of beads or ornaments, worn around the neck, as pearls.

necktie (nek' ti), n. a scarf or narrow band passed around the collar and tied in front.

*necrology (ne krol' ō ji), n. a list or register of deaths within a certain period, as the necrology of 1937.

*necromancy (nek' rō man si), n. the pretended power to foretell the future by communicating with the dead, magic.

necropolis (ne krop' o lis), n. cemetery, especially an ancient old world city of the dead.

nectar (nek' tēr), n. the wine of the gods; any especially delicious drink; the sweet fluid of flowers from which bees make their honey.

*nectarine (nek' tēr ēn), n. a variety of peach having a smooth skin.

nee (nā), adj. born: used in giving the maiden name of a married woman, as Mrs. Chester, nee Barton.

need (nēd), n. necessity, lack of anything requisite or useful; poverty.

need (nēd), v.i. and v.t. to be obliged, as you need not take it; to be in want; to stand in want of, require, as the car needs gas.

needle (nēd' l), n. a small sharp-pointed piece of steel with an eye through which a thread is passed, used in sewing; anything resembling a needle, in appearance or use, as a pine needle, the needle of a compass.

needless (nēd' les), adj. unnecessary.

needs (nēdz), adv. necessarily, as they needs must fight.

needy (nēd' i), adj. poverty-stricken; in dire want.

*ne'er (når), adv. a contraction of never.

ne'er-do-well (når' dōō wel), n. one who fritters away his time; a good-for-nothing.

nefarious (nē får' i us), adj. extremely wicked, infamous.

negation (nē gā' shun), n. denial, as he shook his head in negation.

negative (neg' a tiv), n. a denial, as his answer was a negative; the side of a debate that tries to refute what the opposite side tries to prove, as we had the negative; a photographic film or plate for printing positive pictures. v.t. to prove the contrary of; to deny or refuse; to vote down. adj. expressing negation, as a negative reply; deficient in positive qualities, as she is a negative person; expressing opposition, as a negative vote; opposite of positive, as negative electricity.

*neglect (neg lekt'), n. failure to attend to business or meet obligations; lack of care, as the house was in a state of neglect. v.t. to omit performance of, as a duty; to fail to care for, as he neglects his home; to disre-

gard, as he *neglected* my principal argument.
Syn. Disregard, slight. To *neglect* is to
fail to give proper attention to some duty
or obligation; to *disregard* is to neglect intentionally; to *slight* is to treat with indifference and often contempt.

*negligee (neg li zhā'), *n.* a loosely fitting
gown; informal dress, as she was in *negligee.*

negligence (neg' li jens), *n.* carelessness, indifference.

negligent (neg' li jent), *adj.* careless, neglectful.

negligible (neg' li ji bl), *adj.* of little moment;
unworthy of attention, as it was a *negligible*
loss.

*negotiable (nē gō' shi a bl), *adj.* capable of
being negotiated, transferred or exchanged.

negotiate (nē gō' shi āt), *v.i. and v.t.* to treat
with others in business or in public or
private affairs, as they *negotiated* for many
weeks; to bring about by conferring, as to
negotiate a treaty; to sell, convert into
cash, as to *negotiate* bonds.

*negotiation (nē gō shi ā' shun), *n.* the discussion preliminary to the signing of a
contract or a treaty.

*neigh (nā), *n.* the cry of a horse, whinny.

neigh (nā), *v.i.* to utter the cry of a horse,
whinny.

*neighbor (nā' bēr), *n.* a person living nearby,
as a next-door *neighbor. adj.* near-by.

neighborly (nā' bēr li), *adj.* friendly, kind.

*neither (nē' thēr), *pron.* not the one or the
other, as *neither* is a trustworthy person.

*neither (nē' thēr), *adj.* not either, as *neither*
hat will do.

*neologism (nē ol' ŏ jizm), *n.* a new word or
phrase introduced into a language, a coined
word; an old word used in a new and different sense.

*neophyte (nē' ŏ fīt), *n.* a novice, a beginner;
a new member, convert.

*nephew (nef' û), *n.* the son of one's brother
or sister.

*nephritis (ne frī' tis), *n.* inflammation of the
kidneys.

*nepotism (nep' ŏ tizm), *n.* favoritism to relatives.

nerve (nûrv), *n.* one of the cordlike fibers
that convey sensation from all parts of the
body to the brain; coolness in action.

nerve (nûrv), *v.t.* to give vigor and courage to.

*nervine (nûr' vēn), *n.* any tonic for the
nerves.

nervous (nûr' vus), *adj.* pertaining to the
nerves in any way; having weak nerves;
restless, uneasy, irritable and excitable.

nervy (nûr' vi), *adj.* [*comp.* nervier, *superl.*
nerviest] showing coolness and courage;
bold, self-assured.

nest (nest), *n.* the dwelling place of a bird,
where it lays its eggs and rears its young;
a structure made by an insect as a hatching
place, as a wasp's *nest;* a set of bowls,
tables or boxes that fit one inside another.
v.i. to build a nest, to live in a nest.

*nestle (nes' l), *v.i. and v.t.* to lie close and
snug; to cherish, cuddle, as she *nestled* the

puppy in her arms.

nestling (nest' ling), *n.* a young bird that has
not left the nest.

net (net), *n.* a meshed fabric used in catching fish, birds, butterflies; any meshed
fabric, as a hair *net;* a snare; a ball hit into
a tennis net.

net (net), *v.t.* to take with a net; to capture
by trick; to hit a ball into a tennis net. *v.t.*
to take as clear profit, as to *net* $1,000 on a
transaction. *adj.* clear, remaining after all
expenses and costs are deducted, as a *net*
income or profit.

*nether (neth' ēr), *adj.* lying beneath, as the
nether garments; lower, as the *nether* regions.

Ant. Upper.

netting (net' ing), *n.* nets in general; material of which nets are made; any network,
as mosquito *netting.*

nettle (net' l), *n.* a coarse herb having stinging hairs. *v.t.* to sting, irritate.

neural (nū' .al), *adj.* belonging to a nerve.

*neuralgia (nū ral' ja), *n.* acute pain in a
nerve.

*neurasthenia (nū ras thē' ni a), *n.* exhaustion of the nervous system.

neuritis (nū rī' tis), *n.* inflammation of a
nerve or nerves.

*neurosis (nū rŏ' sis), *n.* a disturbance of the
bodily system springing from disordered
nerves.

neurotic (nū rot' ik), *adj.* pertaining to the
nervous system; having a disorder of the
nerves; hysterical, as a *neurotic* person.

*neuter (nū' tēr), *adj.* neither masculine nor
feminine, as a *neuter* noun.

*neutral (nū' tral), *adj.* supporting or favoring neither party in a dispute; without bias;
lacking strong character, as a *neutral* color.

neutralize (nū' tral iz), *v.t.* to counteract; to
make of no effect; to destroy the peculiar
properties of, as a chemical.

never (nev' ēr), *adv.* at no time; in no degree, as *never* mind.

nevermore (nev ēr mōr'), *adv.* at no future
time, never again.

nevertheless (nev ēr thē les'), *adv.* notwithstanding; in spite of that.

*new (nū), *adj.* of recent origin; young, as
the *new* year; fresh, as a *new* start.

Syn. Novel, modern, fresh, recent. *New*
expresses the idea of having existed or been
known only a short time; *novel* implies
something different from the usual; the
modern is the thing of today; *fresh* denotes
something just made, done or received;
recent suggests something lately formed,
created or developed.

Ant. Old, familiar, usual, common.

new (nū), *adv.* lately; newly.

newel (nū' el), *n.* the upright pillar or post
in a winding staircase about which the
steps turn in their course; the post at the
foot or landing of a stairway.

*news (nūz), *n.* a report of recent events, tidings; something unknown to the listener or
reader, as that's *news* to me.

Syn. Tidings, intelligence. *News* is a

general term; *tidings* is now rarely used except in poetic or elevated speech; *intelligence* implies news more or less formally communicated.

newsprint (nūz′ print), *n.* a wood-pulp paper used for newspapers.

newt (nūt), *n.* a small salamander, eft.

next (nekst), *adj.* immediately following or preceding, as *next* in line; nearest in time, as the *next* hour; nearest in place, as the *next* house; nearest in rank or degree.

nib (nib), *n.* a point, as of a pen; a handgrip on the shaft of a scythe. *v.t.* to furnish with a nib; to sharpen a point.

nibble (nib′ l), *n.* a small bite. *v.i.* and *v.t.* to bite off in little bits; to make successive small bites, as a fish *nibbles* at the bait.

niblick (nib′ lik), *n.* a heavy, iron-headed golf club with slanting face, used to loft the ball.

nibs (nibz), *n. pl.* crushed beans of cocoa or or coffee.

*nice (nis), *adj.* fastidious, precise; pleasing, well-mannered, as a *nice* child; discriminating, as a *nice* ear for music.

*nicety (nī′ se ti), *n.* [*pl.* niceties] a minute distinction, as the *niceties* of argument; exactness of perception; accuracy, as the proportions were calculated to a *nicety*.

*niche (nich), *n.* a recess in a wall, especially one to hold a statue.

nick (nik), *n.* a notch or broken place in any surface, as the vase has a *nick;* an exact point of time, moment of crisis, as you arrived in the *nick* of time. *v.t.* to make nicks in, chip, as to *nick* a plate.

nickel (nik′ el), *n.* a silver-white ductile metal, tough and noncorrosive; a five-cent coin made of a nickel and copper alloy.

nickel-plate (nik′ el plāt), *n.* a thin layer of nickel spread over a metal surface by means of electrolysis, to improve its appearance or to prevent rusting.

nickel silver (nik′ el sil′ vēr), German silver, an alloy of copper, zinc and nickel, usually in proportion 3, 1 and 1.

nickel steel (nik′ el stēl), steel with a percentage of nickel, harder and stronger than carbon steel, used in building automobiles.

*nicotine (nik′ ō tēn), *n.* a colorless, poisonous oil contained in tobacco, used as an insecticide.

nidus (nī′ dus), *n.* the nest of spiders and insects.

*niece (nēs), *n.* the daughter of one's brother or sister.

niggard (nig′ ērd), *n.* a stingy person.

niggard (nig′ ērd), *adj.* stingy, covetous.

niggardly (nig′ ērd li), *adj.* miserlike; meanly small, as a *niggardly* allowance. *adv.* in the manner of a niggard; stingily, meanly.

nigh (nī), *adj.* near; on the side toward the driver, as the *nigh* horse. *adv.* almost; near in time, place, relationship, likeness or course of events. *prep.* near to.

night (nīt), *n.* the time between sunset and sunrise; the close of the day.

nightingale (nīt′ in gāl), *n.* a bird of the thrush family about six inches long, noted for the male's song at night.

nightjar (nīt′ jär), *n.* a night-flying insectivorous bird.

nightmare (nīt′ mâr), *n.* a dreadful dream accompanied by physical uneasiness.

nightshade (nīt′ shād), *n.* any of several plants including the potato plant, eggplant and bittersweet, especially the poisonous or medicinal varieties.

*nihilism (nī′ i lizm), *n.* the doctrine that the present social organization is so bad that it should be destroyed even if it cannot be improved; terrorism; anarchism.

*nihilist (nī′ i list), *n.* one who advocates or supports the theory that destruction of the present order is desirable; an anarchist.

nimble (nim′ bl), *adj.* active, as a *nimble* mind; quick, lively, as *nimble* fingers.

nimbus (nim′ bus), *n.* the halo of light surrounding the heads of divinities and saints.

nine (nīn), *n.* one more than 8.

nineteen (nīn tēn′), *n.* one more than 18.

ninety (nīn′ ti), *n.* one more than 89.

ninny (nin′ i), *n.* a simpleton.

ninth (nīnth), *n.* one of 9 equal parts.

ninth (nīnth), *adj.* next after the 8th.

nip (nip), *n.* a pinch between the fingers; sudden, sharp cold, as·the *nip* of the wind; a tang, as in strong cheese.

nip (nip), *v.t.* to pinch between the fingers, as to *nip* off a flower; to bite lightly, as your dog *nipped* me; to blight, as frost *nipped* the peach buds.

nipper (nip′ ēr), *n.* one who or that which pinches; a horse's front tooth; the claw of a crab.

nippers (nip′ ērz), *n.* pincers.

nipple (nip′ l), *n.* the protuberance of the female breast through which a baby or young animal draws milk; the rubber mouthpiece of a nursing bottle.

*nirvana (nir vä′ na), *n.* complete renunciation; freedom from desire, hate and false belief; sinless calm.

nit (nit), *n.* the egg of a parasitic insect such as a flea or louse; the young insect.

niter (nī′ tēr), *n.* a white salt, potassium nitrate or saltpeter, used in making gunpowder.

nitrate (nī′ trāt), *n.* a salt of nitric acid; especially of potassium or sodium used as fertilizer.

*nitrogen (nī′ trō jen), *n.* a colorless, tasteless and odorless gaseous element that forms a large part of the atmosphere.

nitrogenous (nī troj′ ē nus), *adj.* pertaining to the colorless and odorless gaseous element that forms a large part of the atmosphere; containing this element.

*nitroglycerin or **nitroglycerine** (nī trō glis′-ēr in), *n.* a highly explosive, oily liquid prepared by subjecting glycerin to the action of nitric and sulphuric acids.

nitrous (nī′ trus), *adj.* resembling a white, crystalline salt, potassium nitrate; obtained from this salt or impregnated with it.

no (nō), *n.* [*pl.* noes] a denial, as my no was emphatic; a negative vote: *noes*, the voters in the negative, as the *noes* have it. *adj.* not any; as he has *no* sense; not one, as there is

no chance. *adv.* not so: opposite of *yes.*

nobility (nō bil' i ti), *n.* the quality of being noble, fine character; the peerage or aristocracy.

noble (nō' bl), *n.* a member of the titled aristocracy. *adj.* [*comp.* nobler, *superl.* noblest] of high character; of great excellence or worth; grand, imposing; of the aristocracy.

nobleman (nō' bl man), *n.* a member of the titled aristocracy; a peer.

nobody (nō' bod i), *n.* [*pl.* nobodies] a person of no importance. *pron.* not anybody.

nocturnal (nok tûr' nal), *adj.* pertaining to night.

nod (nod), *n.* a quick and slight inclination of the head. *v.i. and v.t.* to incline the head; to express by a quick, slight inclination of the head, as to *nod* assent; to bend or incline the upper part forward, as the flowers *nodded* in the wind; to make a mistake, as even Homer sometimes *nods.*

*node (nōd), *n.* a knot, knob, swelling; the knotty formation on a plant stem from which a leaf springs.

*nodule (nod' ūl), *n.* a small knot or lump.

nog (nog), *n.* a block of wood set in masonry as a place for nailing; one of the square logs used in a pile to support the roof of a mine; a mixed drink, as eggnog.

noise (noiz), *n.* loud sound; confusion of sounds; clamor.

*noisome (noi' sum), *adj.* noxious; injurious to health; foul.

noisy (noiz' i), *adj.* [*comp.* noisier, *superl.* noisiest] full of confused sounds; boisterous.

*nomad (nō' mad), *n.* one who wanders from place to place.

nomad or **nomadic** (nō' mad, nō mad' ik), *adj.* wandering, unsettled.

*nom de plume (nom' dē plŏōm), a pen name; an assumed name under which an author writes.

*nomenclature (nō' men klā tūr), *n.* the names or technical terms used in any art or science.

nominal (nom' i nal), *adj.* pertaining to a name or to names; in name only, negligible, trifling, as a *nominal* sum.

nominate (nom' i nāt), *v.t.* to propose for office, name as a candidate, appoint.

    Syn. Name. To *nominate* and to *name* are both to mention by name, but to *nominate* is to mention for a specific purpose, to *name* may be for any purpose or no purpose beyond simple identification.

*nonage (non' āj), *n.* minority; the first 21 years of living.

*nonagenarian (non a jē nâr' i an), *n.* a person between the ages of 90 and 100 years.

*nonce (nons), *n.* the time being, as say no more for the *nonce.*

*nonchalance (non' sha lans), *n.* indifference; lack of interest or enthusiasm: airy unconcern.

nonchalant (non' sha lant), *adj.*, unconcerned, indifferent.

*noncombatant (non kom' ba tant), *n.* one whose military duties do not include taking an active part in fighting, as a member of an ambulance corps.

noncommittal (non ko mit' al), *adj.* concealing one's purposes and opinions; not committing oneself to any action.

nondescript (non' dē skript), *n.* a person or thing not easily described. *adj.* unclassified or unclassifiable; having no distinctive features, as a *nondescript* hat.

none (nun), *pron.* not any, as I have *none.*

none (nun), *adv.* in no way; not at all, as *none* the worse for wear.

nonentity (non en' ti ti), *n.* [*pl.* nonentities] the state of not existing, or existing only in the imagination; a person or thing absolutely unimportant.

*nonfeasance (non fē' zans), *n.* neglect or omission of an official or legal duty.

*nonpareil (non pa rel'), *n.* a person or thing without an equal, peerless; a size of type. *adj.* having no equal, peerless.

non partisan (na·n' par' ta san), *n.* not adhering to a faction.

nonplus (non' plus), *v.t.* to puzzle; to perplex completely, as my reply *nonplused* him.

nonsense (non' sens), *n.* that which is without meaning; words or language without meaning; anything absurd; trifles.

nonstop (non' stop), *adj.* without a break, especially in aviation, as a *nonstop* flight.

nonsuit (non' sūt), *n.* a decision against the plaintiff in a law suit because he has not prosecuted his case or established sufficient cause of action; a dismissal of complaint.

noodle (nōō' dl), *n.* a narrow strip of dried dough, often used in soup.

*nook (nook), *n.* a secluded recess or corner.

noon (nōōn), *n.* the middle point of the day, midday.

noose (nōōs), *n.* a running knot that holds more tightly as it is subjected to weight or pull. *v.t.* to catch or snare in a noose.

nor (nôr), *conj.* likewise not, and not; or not: a negative connecting word after *neither* or *not* used to complete the meaning, as neither the man *nor* the child saw the approaching automobile, not by word *nor* look did she betray herself.

norm (nôrm), *n.* an established standard, rule, pattern.

normal (nôr' mal), *adj.* according to standard or rule, regular, natural, customary, as *normal* procedure.

north (nôrth), *n.* one of the four points of the compass, the point directly opposite to the south and to the left of a person facing due east; the northern part of any country, as the *north* of Europe. *adj.* situated in the north, as the *North Pole*; facing or proceeding north, as the *north* passage of a ship; coming from the north, as a *north* wind. *adv.* to, in or toward the north, as the ship will proceed *north* from Chile.

northeast (nôrth ēst'), *n.* the point of the compass halfway between due north and due east.

northern (nôr' thẽrn), *adj.* having to do with the north, as the *northern* part of the state.

northerner (nôr' thẽr nẽr), *n.* a person living

in the northern section of the United States, as distinguished from a southerner.

northern lights (nôr′ thẽrn līts), the aurora borealis.

northwest (nôrth west′), *n.* the point of the compass halfway between due north and due west.

nose (nōz), *n.* the organ of smell; snout; anything resembling a nose, as the *nose* of a torpedo. *v.i. and v.t.* to sniff, as the dogs *nosed* about; to rub with the nose, as the horses *nosed* each other; to find, detect, as to *nose* out a secret.

***nosology** (nō sol′ ō ji), *n.* the classification of diseases.

***nostalgia** (nos tal′ ji a), *n.* homesickness.

nostril (nos′ tril), *n.* one of the two open passages of the nose.

nostrum (nos′ trum), *n.* a quack medicine, cure-all.

***notable** (nō′ ta bl), *adj.* worthy of notice, memorable.

notary (nō′ ta ri), *n.* [*pl.* notaries] one permitted by law to attest legal documents.

notation (nō tā′ shun), *n.* the practice of recording by marks or symbols; a method of using symbols instead of words; the act of noting or making a note.

notch (noch), *n.* a nick or cut in the edge of something; a narrow way between two mountains. *v.t.* to mark with notches; to cut notches in.

note (nōt), *n.* a memorandum; a brief explanatory comment, as the *notes* to a text; a paper promising to pay money owed in a certain time; renown, as a man of *note;* a musical sound, or a sign representing one; a tone, as a *note* of joy in the voice; a short letter, as a *note* of acceptance.

note (nōt), *v.t.* to mark down, make a memorandum of; to mention, as to *note* in passing; to pay attention, as *note* what I say.

noted (nōt′ ed), *adj.* celebrated.

nothing (nuth′ ing), *n.* no thing, not anything, a nonentity. *adv.* not at all, as *nothing* loath; by no means, as *nothing* less.

notice (nō′ tis), *n.* observation by mind or eye, attention; an announcement, as *notice* of a meeting; an order, as *notice* to vacate; critical comment, as a *notice* of a play. *v.i. and v.t.* to take note of, as I did not *notice;* to observe, perceive, give attention to, as she failed to *notice* my presence; to mention, as he *noticed* the book in his column.

Syn. Remark, observe. To *notice* is a more cursory action than to *remark*. We may *notice* a thing by a single glance, but to *remark* is to react with the mind. We *observe* things in order to judge of them or draw conclusions from them.

noticeable (nō′ tis a bl), *adj.* capable of being seen, conspicuous, as a *noticeable* limp; worthy of observation.

notification (nō ti fi kā′ shun), *n.* the act of making known or of giving notice; a notice given; a document by which a legal information is conveyed.

notify (nō′ ti fi), *v.t.* [*p.t. and p.p.* notified,

pr.p. notifying] to give notice to; to inform of.

notion (nō′ shun), *n.* an idea or conception of something; a belief; inclination, as I have a *notion* to go.

notoriety (nō tō ri′ e ti), *n.* the state of being publicly known in an unfavorable way.

notorious (nō tō′ ri us), *adj.* noted, famous; widely discussed in an unfavorable or scandalous way; as he is a *notorious* gambler.'

notwithstanding (not *with* stan′ ding), *adv.* nevertheless, however, yet. *prep.* in spite of, as *notwithstanding* your opposition. *conj.* although.

nougat (nōō′ gat), *n.* a sweet candy made of almonds, pistachio and other nuts.

nought (nôt), *n.* nothing; a worthless thing or person; zero, the mathematical symbol 0, a cipher.

noun (noun), *n.* the name of a person, place or thing.

nourish (nûr′ ish), *v.t.* to feed, support; to maintain; to promote the growth of, as sunshine *nourishes* plants.

***novel** (nov′ el), *n.* a long fictitious prose narrative with a plot. *adj.* recently introduced or discovered, new, strange or unusual.

novelist (nov′ el ist), *n.* one who writes books of fiction.

novelty (nov′ l ti), *n.* [*pl.* novelties] newness and strangeness; something that is new and strange.

***novice** (nov′ is), *n.* a beginner; a monk or nun on probation.

novitiate (nō vish′ i āt), *n.* the state of being a beginner; a period of testing and training before final admission to a religious order.

now (nou), *adv.* at this time; at that time; immediately, as I must go *now;* under the present circumstances, as *now* what shall we do? *conj.* since; seeing that, as *now* that you have brought up the matter I may as well confess.

nowadays (nou′ a dāz), *adv.* in these times.

nowise (nō′ wīz), *adv.* in no way, manner or degree.

***noxious** (nok′ shus), *adj.* harmful, deadly, pernicious.

nozzle (noz′ l), *n.* a spout, as of a hose, teapot, teakettle.

***nuance** (nū ans′), *n.* a slight variation; a small gradation, as a delicate *nuance* of color or tone.

nuclear (nū′ klē r), *adj.* of, like, or forming a nucleus; of or using energy of an atomic nuclei.

***nucleus** (nū′ klē us), *n.* the central mass around which matter accumulates or grows; anything that serves as a center of development, as the *nucleus* of the army was this regiment.

nude (nūd), *adj.* naked, bare.

nudge (nuj), *v.t.* to push gently, as I *nudged* him with my elbow.

nugget (nug′ et), *n.* a lump, as of native gold; any small thing of much value; as *nuggets* of wisdom.

***nuisance** (nū′ sans), *n.* anything that causes vexation or annoyance.

null (nul), *adj.* having no legal force or effect, invalid, void, not binding.

nullification (nul i fi kā′ shun), *n.* the act of nullifying.

nullify (nul′ i fi), *v.t.* [*p.t.* and *p.p.* nullified, *pr.p.* nullifying] to annul or render void, make ineffective.

nullity (nul′ i ti), *n.* the quality or condition of being without force or effect.

*****numb** (num), *v.t.* to deprive of feeling.

numb (num), *adj.* without power of feeling.

number (num′ bér), *n.* the total count of aggregated units, the symbol that stands for this amount; a certain numeral that serves to identify a person or thing from others, as I noted down the *number* of the bus; a considerable company, as a *number* of people; a single one of a series, as the June *number* of a magazine. *v.t.* to count; to put a number on, as a house.

numberless (num′ bér les), countless, innumerable.

numeral (nū′ mér al), *n.* a symbol or word that expresses a number. *adj.* pertaining to numbers; denoting a number.

numeration (nū mér ā′ shun), *n.* the act of numbering; the art of reading numbers.

numerator (nū′ mér ā tér), *n.* the number above the line in fractions, indicating the number of fractional units taken, as two is the *numerator* in the fraction two-thirds.

numerical (nū mer′ i kal), *adj.* pertaining to or expressed in numbers.

numerous (nū′ mér us), *adj.* consisting of a great number of persons or things; many.

*****numismatics** (nū miz mat′ iks), *n. pl.* the study of coins and medals.

numskull (num′ skul), *n.* a blockhead.

nun (nun), *n.* a woman devoted to a religious life and usually living in a convent under vows.

*****nuncio** (nun′ shi o), *n.* a papal ambassador.

nunnery (nun′ ér i), *n.* [*pl.* nunneries] a convent.

*****nuptial** (nup′ shal), *adj.* pertaining to marriage.

nuptials (nup′ shalz), *n.* a marriage ceremony.

nurse (nûrs), *n.* a woman who cares for infants; one who tends the sick. *v.i. and v.t.* to do nursing; to suck milk from a mother; to nourish and suckle, as a baby; to tend the sick; to treat, as to *nurse* a fever; to foster, as to *nurse* a grievance.

nursery (nûr′ sé ri), *n.* a room in a house set aside for the care and play of young children; a place where trees, shrubs and vines are grown for transplanting.

nurseryman (nûr′ sé ri man), *n.* a man who grows plants for sale.

nurture (nûr′ tūr), *n.* nourishment; education, training. *v.t.* to rear, care for and educate, foster.

nut (nut), *n.* the fruit of certain trees, consisting of a kernel in a shell; a threaded head for a bolt.

nutcracker (nut′ krak ér), *n.* an instrument for cracking nuts.

nutmeg (nut′ meg), *n.* the aromatic kernel of the fruit of an East Indian tree, grated and used as spice.

*****nutrient** (nū′ tri ent), *adj.* promoting growth, nourishing

nutriment (nū′ tri ment), *n.* nourishment, food; that which promotes development.

nutrition (nū trish′ un), *n.* that which nourishes, food; the process by which plants and animals absorb and utilize nourishment.

nutritious (nū trish′ us), *adj.* affording nourishment.

nutritive (nū′ tri tiv), *adj.* pertaining to or having the quality of nutrition.

nuzzle (nuz′ l), *v.t. and v.i.* to rub or snuff with the nose, as the horse *nuzzled* its master's hand; to nestle, lie close.

*****nymph** (nimf), *n.* a goddess of nature inhabiting the mountains, woods or streams; an insect in the pupa stage of development.

O

oaf (ōf), *n.* a dull-witted person, simpleton, dolt.

oak (ōk), *n.* a tree that bears a one-celled fruit, called an acorn, set in a scaly cup; its hard wood.

oaken (ōk′ en), *adj.* made of or like oak.

oakum (ō′ kum), *n.* loose hemp obtained by untwisting old ropes and used aboard ship with pitch, to calk seams.

*****oar** (ōr), *n.* a wooden shaft with a broad blade at one end, for use in rowing a boat.

oar (ōr), *v.t.* to row.

*****oasis** (ō ā′ sis), *n.* [*pl.* oases] a fertile spot in the midst of a desert.

oast (ōst), *n.* a kiln for drying malt or hops.

oaten (ōt′ n), *adj.* made of oats or oatmeal.

oats (ōtz), *n.* a grain used as feed for livestock and its meal ground and used as a breakfast cereal.

oath (ōth), *n.* [*pl.* *oaths, pronounced ōths*] a solemn declaration of intention to tell the truth; a holy name used profanely, as in anger.

*****obduracy** (ob′ dū ra si), *n.* stubbornness.

*****obdurate** (ob′ dū rāt), *adj.* not to be moved by argument or appeal; intractable. inflexible, unyielding.

*****obedience** (ō bē′ di ens), *n.* submission to authority; the act of obeying commands.

obedient (ō bē′ di ent), *adj.* submissive to authority, yielding, compliant.

Syn. Yielding, compliant, dutiful, obsequious. *Obedient* implies willing submission to control; *compliant* and *yielding* suggest ready and sometimes weak, conformance with another's wishes; *dutiful* implies obedience from a sense of obligation, as to a parent; *obsequious* carries the suggestion of servility and fawning.

*obeisance (ō bā' sans), *n.* a bow or a bend of the knee indicating submission or homage.

*obelisk (ob' e lisk), *n.* a high, four-sided pillar of stone tapering as it rises, and having a pyramidal top; a printing mark (†) in a text referring the reader to a footnote similarly marked.

obese (ō bēs'), *adj.* corpulent.

*obesity (ō bēs' i ti), *n.* excessive fatness.

obey (ō bā'), *v.i. and v.t.* to do as bidden, as the child *obeyed* instantly; to yield to the authority of, as to *obey* one's parents.

*obfuscate (ob fus' kāt), *v.t.* to darken, obscure; to confuse, bewilder; to dim, as his vision was *obfuscated.*

*obituary (ō bit' ū er i), *n.* [*pl.* obituaries] a printed notice of a death; an article about one who has very recently died.

object (ob' jekt), *n.* anything that can be perceived by the senses; a person or thing toward whom or which an act or feeling is directed, as the *object* of a campaign, an *object* of pity; a word or clause naming that which receives the action indicated by a verb, as in the sentence, he climbed the steps, steps is the *object* of climbed.

object (ob jekt'), *v.i. and v.t.* to regard with disfavor, as I *object;* to offer in opposition, as I *object* that the house is too old.

Syn. Oppose. To *object* to a thing is to propose or start something against it; to *oppose* it is to set oneself steadily and actively against it.

Ant. Favor, further.

objectionable (ob jek' shun a bl), *adj.* not fit for acceptance; reprehensible, offensive.

objective (ob jek' tiv), *n.* the end toward which action is directed, as success is his *objective;* the accusative case. *adj.* serving as a goal; existing outside the mind; detached, impersonal, as an *objective* point of view: opposite of *subjective;* accusative, as the verb governs a pronoun in the *objective* case.

*objurgate (ob' jēr gāt), *v.t.* to chide, reprove.

*oblate (ob' lāt), *adj.* flattened at the poles, as the earth is an *oblate* spheroid.

*oblate (ob' late), *n.* one devoted to the monastic life or to some special mission.

*oblation (ob lā' shun), *n.* a religious offering or sacrifice; any offering to a church or charity.

obligate (ob' li gāt), *v.t.* to put under legal or moral indebtedness, as he obligates me by his continued kindness.

obligation (ob li gā' shun), *n.* the binding power of a promise or contract; the state of being indebted for a favor.

*obligatory (ob lig' a tō ri), *adj.* binding, imposing a duty.

oblige (ō blīj'), *v.t.* to put under obligation, constrain; to do a favor for, as the singer *obliged* the audience with an encore.

obliging (ō blīj' ing), *adj.* ready to do favors.

*oblique (ob lēk'), *adj.* between the horizontal and the vertical, slanting, as a line; deviating from the perpendicular; indirect, as

oblique methods.

obliquity (ob lik' wi ti), *n.* [*pl.* obliquities] the state of being neither horizontal nor vertical, lack of perpendicularity; deviation from correct principles.

obliterate (ob lit' ēr āt), *v.t.* to blot out, efface.

oblivion (ob liv' i un), *n.* the state of forgetting completely or of being completely forgotten.

oblivious (ob liv' i us), *adj.* forgetful; not noticing, as *oblivious* of his surroundings.

*oblong (ob' lông), *n.* a right-angled figure with more length than breadth.

oblong (ob' lông), *adj.* having right angles and being more long than broad.

*obloquy (ob' lō kwi), *n.* [*pl.* obloquies] reproachful language; the condition of being censured or held in contempt.

obnoxious (ob nok' shus), *adj.* offensive, odious.

*oboe (ō' bō), *n.* [*pl.* oboes] a slender, woodwind musical instrument having a double reed and producing a thin, plaintive tone; organ stop producing tone of an oboe.

*obscene (ob sēn'), *adj.* indecent, offensive to modesty, lewd.

*obscenity (ob sen' i ti), *n.* [*pl.* obscenities] an act or expression of indecent nature.

obscure (ob skūr'), *adj.* dim, indistinct, clouded; hard to understand, vague, as an *obscure* paragraph; humble, lowly, as he rose from an *obscure* position.

obscurity (ob skū' ri ti), *n.* [*pl.* obscurities] indistinctness; state of being without fame.

obsecrate (ob' sē krāt), *v.t.* to entreat.

obsecration (ob sē krā' shun), *n.* an earnest entreaty; a petition in the Roman church litany beginning with the word *by.*

*obsequies (ob' sē kwiz), *n. pl.* funeral rites.

*obsequious (ob sē' kwi us), *adj.* servile, fawning.

observance (ob zûr' vans), *n.* the act of conforming to or heeding, as laws and customs.

observant (ob zûr' vant), *adj.* watchful; taking notice.

observation (ob zûr vā' shun), *n.* the act of taking notice; something noticed; a remark.

Syn. Observance. *Observation* now commonly applies to that which is carefully considered, as a patient is under *observation* so that his physician may study his symptoms; *observance* implies conformance with laws and customs, as he is strict in his *observance* of traffic regulations.

observatory (ob zûr' va tō ri), *n.* [*pl.* observatories] a place fitted up with telescopes for studying the sky and stars; a high place that affords an extensive view.

observe (ob zûrv'), *v.t. and v.i.* to keep in view; to take notice of; to comply with, as to *observe* rules; to celebrate, as to *observe* a holiday; to take notice; to comment.

observing (ob zûr' ving), *adj.* quick to notice, as an *observing* person.

obsess (ob ses'), *v.t.* to beset, haunt or harass, as the threat of war *obsesses* him.

obsession (ob sesh' un), *n.* the state of being ruled by one idea or desire; a ruling idea, a mania.

obsolescent (ob sō les' ent), *adj.* going out of use.

obsolete (ob' sō lēt), *adj.* out of use, discarded, as an *obsolete* word or custom.

obstacle (ob' sta kl), *n.* an obstruction, impediment, that which stands in the way, as an obstacle to progress.

obstetrics (ob stet' riks), *n.* the branch of medicine that pertains to childbirth.

obstinacy (ob' sti na si), *n.* [*pl.* obstinacies] the state or quality of being stubborn; unreasonable adherence to a purpose or opinion; a stubborn attitude or act.

obstinate (ob' sti nit), *adj.* pertinaciously adhering to one's opinions or purposes; stubborn; not yielding to treatment, as a *stubborn* disease.

Syn. Obdurate, inflexible, headstrong, willful, dogged, stubborn, pertinacious, intractable; refractory. *Obstinate* implies not yielding to argument, persuasion or pleading; *dogged* denotes a tenacious and sometimes sullen pursuit of a certain course or idea; *stubborn* usually indicates native perseverance; *pertinacious* connotes an irritating persistence, as a *pertinacious* salesperson; *intractable* and *refractory* imply resistance to control, although an *intractable* child usually resists less actively than a *refractory* one.

Ant. Yielding, pliant, docile, tractable.

obstreperous (ob strep' ĕr us), *adj.* clamorous, turbulent, unruly.

obstruct (ob strukt'), *v.t.* to block up, impede as the passage of something; to retard; to cut off, as to *obstruct* the view.

*obtain (ob tān'), *v.i.* and *v.t.* to be established in custom or use, as the custom *obtains* in that country, to get possession of, gain, acquire, win, procure, as to *obtain* permission.

*obtrude (ob trōōd'), *v.i.* and *v.t.* to force oneself upon others; to thrust in or upon.

*obtrusive (ob trū' siv), *adj.* inclined to push forward.

*obtuse (ob tūs'), *adj.* not acute, as an *obtuse* angle; not having keen sensibilities, dull, stupid, as an *obtuse* person.

*obverse (ob' vŭrs), *n.* a front surface, especially the head or date side of a coin: opposite of *reverse. adj.* facing observer; having the base narrower than top, as an *obverse* leaf.

obviate (ob' vi ăt), *v.t.* to meet and dispose of; to clear away, remove, as that will *obviate* the necessity of writing.

obvious (ob' vi us), *adj.* evident, plain.

*occasion (o kā' zhun), *n.* occurrence; cause, as that was the *occasion* of the trouble; a favorable opportunity, as when the *occasion* arises; opportunity; a special event or ceremony.

Syn. Occasion, cause. *Occasion* implies something that directly or indirectly provides an opportunity to act, as I seized the *occasion* to tell him; the *cause* is that

which actually makes something happen, as he was the *cause* of the misunderstanding.

occasional (o kă' zhun al), *adj.* occurring at intervals, as an *occasional* week end in the country; referring to some special event, as an *occasional* poem; incidental, as *occasional* comments, *occasional* meetings.

*occident (ok' si dent), *n.* the west: opposite of *orient.*

occipital bone (ok sip' i tal bōn), the bone at the lower part of the back of the skull.

occiput (ok' si put), *n.* [*pl.* occipita] the back of the skull or head.

*occlude (o klōōd'), *v.i.* and *v.t.* to shut up, to close or obstruct; to shut in or out as by closing a passage, as to *occlude* light.

*occult (o kult'), *adj.* pertaining to magic, astrology and other arts using divination or incantation; mysterious.

occupancy (ok' ū pan si), *n.* the act of living in, as a house; act of holding in possession; the term during which one occupies premises.

occupant (ok' ū pant), *n.* one living in a house, a tenant.

occupation (ok ū pā' shun), *n.* the act of occupying; one's business or calling.

occupy (ok' ū pi), *v.t.* to dwell in; to devote to or apply oneself to, as to *occupy* one's time or oneself with work; to take up, fill, as the estate *occupies* many acres of ground.

occur (o kûr'), *v.i.* to happen, as it must not *occur* again; to come to mind, as it suddenly *occurred* to me.

occurrence (o kûr' ens), *n.* something that happens, an event, incident.

ocean (ō' shun), *n.* the vast expanse of salt water covering nearly three fourths of the globe; one of the major divisions of this expanse, as the Pacific *Ocean.*

ocher (ō' kĕr), *n.* an earthy, yellow or red ore, used as a pigment in paints.

*octagon (ok' ta gon), *n.* a plane figure having eight sides and eight angles.

*octave (ok' tāv), *n.* the harmonic combination of two musical tones eight diatonic degrees apart; the whole series of tones that they comprise.

*octavo (ok tā' vō), *n.* [*pl.* octavos] a book made by folding a sheet into eight leaves or 16 pages.

*octopus (ok' tō pus), *n.* [*pl.* octopuses, octopodes or octopi] a sea mollusk having eight arms projecting from a saclike body and ending in suckers with which it grasps and holds its prey.

ocular (ok' ū lĕr), *adj.* pertaining to the eyes or to sight.

oculist (ok' ū list), *n.* one who treats diseases of the eye.

odd (od), *adj.* not paired or matched with another; extra; peculiar, queer.

oddity (od' i ti), *n.* [*pl.* oddities] strangeness, eccentricity, a queer or peculiar person or thing.

odds (odz), *n.pl.* inequality, advantage, as the *odds* are in his favor; an advantage in an amount wagered to compensate for smaller chances of winning, as 4 to 1 *odds*.

*ode (ōd), *n.* a formal poem in exalted style, generally written in commemoration of some great event or in honor of some distinguished person.

*odious (ō′ di us), *adj.* hated or abhorred, offensive.

odium (ō′ di um), *n.* hatred, dislike.

odor (ō′ dẽr), *n.* smell, scent, that which affects the sense of smell, as the *odor* of newly baked bread, the *odor* of burning rubber.

odoriferous (ō dẽr if′ ẽr us), *adj.* giving out an odor.

odorous (ō′ dẽr us), *adj.* having a scent.

of (ov), *prep.* from, indicating separation; source, as *of* noble birth; from as cause, as he died *of* pneumonia; by, as the novels *of* Galsworthy; with, as means or material, as it is made *of* glass; about, relating to, as to talk *of* the past; distinguished by, as a time *of* fear; from, amongst, out of, as to give *of* one's time, some *of* the crowd; belonging to, connected with, as the right *of* the owner; during, as *of* recent years.

off (ôf), *adj.* being absent or away, as he is *off* to the country; removed, as his coat is *off;* inaccurate, as he is *off* in his figures; below standard, as an *off* season; more removed or distant, as on the *off* side.

off (ôf), *adv.* so as to move away, out from a place or position, as to push *off;* from, so as not to be on, as take *off* your coat; so as to end or be rid of, as the pain passed *off;* so as to decrease, as inquiries fell *off;* away from work, as a day *off;* at a distance, as he stood a block *off.*

off (ôf), *prep.* not on; away from, as take it *off* the table; distant from, as a mile *off* shore; temporarily freed from, as *off* duty; below the standard, as *off* one's game.

off (ôf), *interj.* begone! away with you!

*offal (ôf′ al), *n.* the waste parts of a butchered animal, carrion, refuse.

offend (o fend′), *v.t. and v.i.* to cause to feel hurt, make angry, as he *offended* his best friend; to transgress a moral or divine law, sin; to displease.

offender (o fend′ ẽr), *n.* one who breaks a law or causes displeasure.

offense (o fens′), *n.* an affront; a transgression, as an *offense* against the law; the feeling of injury, as to take *offense;* the attacking side; the act, plan or system of attack.

offensive (o fen′ siv), *n.* the attacking side; system of attack. *adj.* displeasing, disagreeable.

offer (ôf′ ẽr), *n.* the act of proposing a deal, as to make an *offer;* naming of price, as fifty dollars is my *offer.*

offer (ôf′ ẽr), *v.i. and v.t.* to occur or present itself for acceptance or rejection, as opportunity *offers;* to place before one for acceptance or rejection, as to *offer* money; to propose, as to *offer* a solution; name, as a price; to do, make or give, as to *offer* resistance; to proffer, as to *offer* advice.

offering (ôf ẽr ing), *n.* the act of making a proposal; that which is offered; a gift.

offertory (ôf′ ẽr tō ri), *n.* the offering to God of bread and wine in the sacrament; a hymn or prayer at this time; the collection of money at a religious service.

offhand (ôf hand′) *adv.* without preparation; casually.

office (ôf′ is), *n.* a position of trust and authority; a place of public or private business; a duty or service, as he tendered his good *offices;* any prescribed religious service, as the *office* of the dead.

*official (o fish′ al), *n.* one who holds office.

official (o fish′ al), *adj.* pertaining to an office, as *official* duties; having proper authority.

*officiate (o fish′ i āt), *v.i.* to perform the duties of an office, as the minister *officiated.*

*officious (o fish′ us), *adj.* meddling, intrusive.

offing (ôf′ ing), *n.* the deep sea, far offshore; distance, as in the *offing.*

*offset (ôf set′), *v.t.* to make up for, balance, as the beauty of the place *offset* the gray weather.

offset (ôf′ set) *n.* something that counterbalances or sets off; an offshoot; a smudged impression from a printed sheet to another sheet; a method of lithography.

offshoot (ôf′ shōot), *n.* a shoot or branch from a main stem.

offshore (ôf′ shore), *adj.* coming, moving or directed away from the shore, as an *offshore* breeze; situated away from the shore.

offspring (ôf′ spring), *n.* one's child or children; descendants; the young of animals; a result.

Syn. Progeny, issue. *Offspring* is applicable to one or many children in a family. *Progeny* is employed only in referring collectively to a number. *Issue* is used in an indefinite manner without regard to number.

*often (ôf′ en), *adv.* many times, frequently.

*ogle (ō′ gl), *n.* an amorous glance. *v.t.* to look at fondly with amorous glances.

ohm (ōm), *n.* the unit of electrical resistance.

oil (oil), *n.* an inflammable and greasy liquid obtained from various animal, vegetable and mineral substances and used for lighting, lubrication, medicine.

*oil (oil), *v.t.* to lubricate with oil.

oilcloth (oil′ klôth), *n.* canvas coated with linseed oil and used for covering floors, tables, shelves.

oilskin (oil′ skin), *n.* cloth treated with oil and used for waterproof garments.

oily (oil′ i), *adj.* containing or like oil, greasy.

ointment (oint′ ment), *n.* an oily preparation applied to wounds; a salve used to make the skin smooth and soft.

*okra (ō′ kra), *n.* a West Indian plant with seedpods valued for use in soups, stews and pickles; also, a dish made from its pods.

old (ōld), *adj.* advanced in years, no longer young; long in use, as an *old* hat; belonging to the distant past, as an *old* spinning wheel.

olden (ōld′ n), *adj.* ancient; bygone, as *olden* times.

oleaginous (ō lē aj' ĭ nus), *adj.* oily, greasy, unctuous.

***oleander** (ō lē an' dẽr), *n.* a poisonous evergreen shrub with handsome, fragrant flowers.

***oleomargarine** (ō lē ō mär' ga rēn), *n.* imitation butter.

***olfactory** (ol fak' tō rĭ), *adj.* pertaining to or used in smelling.

***oligarchy** (ol' ĭ gär kĭ), *n.* [*pl.* oligarchies] rule by a few; a government in which all power is in the hands of a few persons.

olive (ol' ĭv), *n.* an Old-World evergreen tree; the oily fruit of this tree; the dull green color of this fruit before it ripens.

olive (ol' ĭv), *adj.* having a greenish-yellow or yellowish-brown color, as an *olive* skin.

***omega** (ō mē' ga), *n.* the last letter of the Greek alphabet; the last thing, the end.

***omelet** (om' e let), *n.* a dish made of eggs and milk (or water), beaten and cooked in a pan.

omen (ō' men), *n.* a sign of some future event, portent.
   Syn. Prognostic, presage. The *omen* and the *prognostic* are both drawn from external objects; the *presage* is drawn from one's own feelings.

omen (ō' men), *v.t. and v.i.* to foretell by signs, prognosticate; to forebode.

ominous (om' ĭ nus), *adj.* foreboding evil, inauspicious, threatening.

omission (ō mĭsh' un), *n.* the act of leaving out of account or neglecting to do; a thing omitted.

omit (ō mĭt'), *v.t.* to leave out, neglect to do, fail to mention.

omnibus (om' nĭ bus), *n.* a public vehicle carrying passengers over a fixed route.

omnipotence (om nĭp' ō tens), *n.* unlimited power: *Omnipotence*, the Deity.

omnipotent (om nĭp' ō tent), *adj.* having unlimited power, all-powerful.

omnipresence (om nĭ prez' ens), *n.* universal presence; the state of being everywhere at once.

***omniscient** (om nĭsh' ent), *adj.* knowing all things; infinitely wise, as the *omniscient* God.

omnivorous (om nĭv' ō rus), *adj.* eating all kinds of food, animal and vegetable alike.

on, *prep.* over and in contact with, as the hat lies *on* the shelf; in connection or activity with, as he is *on* the staff; with, as a basis or ground of action or opinion, as I have it *on* good authority; at, in the region that is toward, as the ocean lies *on* the east; during, as *on* Monday; upon the occasion of, as cash *on* delivery; in a state of, as *on* sale; towards, to the account of, as fortune smiled *on* him; in relation to, as to agree *on* a plan. *adv.* not off; onward, forward. *adj.* in progress, as the race is *on;* open, as the switch is *on.*

***once** (wuns), *adv.* at one time, formerly; one time, as I went only *once.*

one (wun), *n.* the number 1 or its symbol; a person. *adj.* single in number.

***onerous** (on' ẽr us), *adj.* burdensome,

weighty, oppressive.

***onion** (un' yun), *n.* a plant with a bulbous root that is used as food.

onlooker (on' look ẽr), *n.* a spectator.

only (ōn' lĭ), *adj.* sole. single, as this is the *only* one I have. *adv.* exclusively, singly, as I have *only* this one.

***onomatopœia** (on ō mat ō pē' ya), *n.* the formation or putting together of words to resemble the sounds made by the thing signified, as *buzz.*

onrush (on' rush), *n.* a rushing onward, as the child was frightened by the *onrush* of the crowd.

onset (on' set), *n.* an assault, attack; the first stage, as the *onset* of a disease.

onslaught (on' slôt), *n.* a furious attack.

ontology (on tol' ō jĭ), *n.* the branch of metaphysics that deals with the essential nature, properties and relations of things; the science of reality.

onus (ō' nus), *n.* a duty, a responsibility, burden of proof (Latin *onus probandi*), as the *onus* falls on you.

onward (on' wẽrd), *adv.* forward.

***onyx** (on' ĭks), *n.* a variety of quartz in layers of various colors.

***oolong** (ōō' long), *n.* a Chinese tea.

ooze (ōōz), *n.* soft mud or slime; an almost imperceptible flow. *v.i. and v.t.* to flow almost imperceptibly; to exude as through pores.

opacity (ō pas' ĭ tĭ), *n.* the quality of being impervious to light.

***opal** (ō' pal), *n.* a precious stone of milky hue, exhibiting in the light a play of various colors.

opalescent (ō pal es' ent), *adj.* resembling opal in its play of colors under changing light.

***opaque** (ō pāk'), *adj.* not transparent, impervious to light.

***open** (ō' pen), *n.* wide space, clear of obstructions to the view, as out in the *open.*

***open** (ō' pen), *v.i. and v.t.* to unclose; to unfold, as a flower; to make a first move; to unclose, as a door; to clear, as to *open* a road blocked by snow; to inaugurate, as to *open* the season, *open* a show. *adj.* not closed, as an *open* door; clear of obstruction, as *open* country; uncovered, as an *open* boat; frank, unconcealed, as *open* criticism; undecided, as an *open* question; free to all, as an *open* meeting.

***opening** (ō' pen ing), *n.* an aperture; cavity; beginning, as of a play.

openly (ō' pen lĭ), *adv.* without concealment, as *openly* jealous.

opera (op' ẽr a), *n.* a musical drama.

opera house (op' ẽr a hous), *n.* a building designed and constructed for the production of operas and seating of audiences.

operate (op' ẽr āt), *v.i. and v.t.* to produce a certain effect; to run, conduct, as to *operate* a machine, to *operate* a business.

operatic (op ẽr at' ĭk), *adj.* having to do with opera; resembling opera.

operation (op ẽr ā' shun), *n.* the act, method or result of operating; regular action, as the factory is in *operation;* a surgery on the living body.

operative (op' ẽr a tiv), *adj.* working, effective.

operetta (op ẽr et' a), *n.* a light musical play with slight plot and spoken dialogue.

*ophthalmia** (of thal' mi a), *n.* inflammation of the eyeball.

*ophthalmic** (of thal' mik), *adj.* pertaining to the eye.

*opiate** (ō' pi ăt), *n.* a medicine compounded with opium to induce sleep or dull the sense of pain.

*opinion** (ō pin' yun), *n.* belief or judgment, estimation, as my *opinion* of him is good.

opinionated (ō pin' yun ăt ed), *adj.* firm or obstinate in one's opinions.

opium (ō' pi um), *n.* a drug made from the dried juice of the poppy.

*opossum** (ō pos' um), *n.* a gray-furred American animal that feigns death in moments of danger; a similar Australian animal.

*opponent** (o pō' nent), *n.* an adversary, antagonist. *adj.* in opposition.

*opportune** (op' or tūn), *adj.* well timed, seasonable, suitable.

opportunist (op or tū' nist), *n.* one who takes advantage of circumstances.

opportunity (op or tū' ni ti), *n.* [*pl.* opportunities] a favorable opening for moves to one's own advantage; a convenient time or occasion.

*oppose** (o pōz'), *v.t.* to act against, as to *oppose* a measure; to contend against; to set up in opposition or contrast.

opposite (op' ō zit), *adj.* placed over against, fronting, as the *opposite* side; contrary, adverse, antagonistic, as an *opposite* opinion.

opposition (op ō zish' un), *n.* the act of placing one thing in contrast to or against another; that which is so placed; resistance, as the plan met with *opposition.*

oppress (o pres'), *v.t.* to burden, crush by hardship or severity, as the monarch *oppressed* his subjects; to lie heavily upon, as discouragement *oppressed* him.

oppressive (o pres' iv), *adj.* unjustly severe; burdensome, as *oppressive* heat.

*opprobrium** (o prō' bri um), *n.* disgrace that follows wrongdoing, infamy.

*oppugn** (o pūn'), *v.t.* to assail with argument.

optic (op' tik), *adj.* pertaining to vision.

optician (op tish' an), *n.* one who makes or sells eyeglasses and other instruments for the eyes.

optics (op' tiks), *n.* the science of the properties of light and vision.

optimism (op' ti mizm), *n.* the doctrine that all is for the best; the habit of looking at the brighter side of life.

optimist (op' ti mist), *n.* one who believes that things are all right and takes a cheerful and hopeful view of life; opposite of *pessimist.*

option (op' shun), *n.* power or right of choosing, a choice; privilege of buying or selling at a certain figure within a set time, as I have an *option* on the house.

optional (op' shun al), *adj.* subject to choice, as an *optional* or elective course in college.

optometrist (op tom' ē trist), *n.* one who examines the eyes for the purpose of prescribing glasses.

opulence (op' ū lens), *n.* great wealth.

opulent (op' ū lent), *adj.* rich, wealthy, as an *opulent* person; profuse; luxuriant.

*opus** (ō' pus), *n.* a work, especially a musical composition.

or (ôr), *conj.* else, otherwise.

oracle (or' a kl), *n.* the response of a deity to some inquiry; one who speaks with inspiration or authority; the answer or judgment given by an oracle.

oracular (ō rak' ū lẽr), *adj.* like an oracle; dogmatically magisterial.

*oral** (ō' ral), *adj.* spoken, not written, as an *oral* examination.

*orange** (or' enj), *n.* a tree with a golden-colored, round juicy fruit; the fruit; the color of the fruit, yellow with a slight tinge of red.

*orangutan** (ō' rang ōō tan), *n.* a large man-like (anthropoid) ape found in Borneo and Sumatra.

oration (ō rā' shun), *n.* a formal speech, especially one prepared for an important occasion.

orator (or' a tẽr), *n.* one who speaks eloquently in public.

*oratorio** (or a tō' ri ō), *n.* a musical composition with a sacred theme.

*oratory** (or' a tō ri), *n.* the art of public speaking, eloquence; part of a chapel; a society of priests.

orb (ôrb), *n.* a sphere; heavenly body, especially a major one, as the sun or moon; the eye.

orbicular (ôr bik' ū lẽr), *adj.* orb-shaped.

orbit (ôr' bit), *n.* the path of a planet in space; the bony cavity in which the eye is set.

orchard (ôr' chẽrd), *n.* a large piece of land on which fruit trees, nut-bearing trees or sugar maples are cultivated; the trees on such a piece of land.

*orchestra** (ôr' kes tra), *n.* a group of musicians playing together on instruments; the space in which they perform; the main floor of a theatre.

orchid (ôr' kid), *n.* a plant having showy blossoms with three petals, one of which varies greatly from the others in shape and is often spurred; a blue-red color.

ordain (ôr dān'), *v.t.* to admit to the ministry or priesthood; to establish by decree or law; to destine, as fate *ordained* his career.

*ordeal** (ôr dē' al), *n.* a severe trial or test of fortitude; an ancient method of determining guilt or innocence.

order (ôr' dẽr), *n.* regular arrangement, as the house is in good *order;* state of being arranged systematically, as in numerical *order;* a group of persons, as a fraternal *order;* a zoological classification larger than a family and smaller than a class, as an *order* of plants or animals; command or authority, as by *order* of the President; public peace, as law and *order;* working conditions, as out of *order;* a direction to buy, sell or supply goods, as to place an *order. v.t.* to command, as to *order* a person to appear in court; to manage, as the President *orders* the affairs of the nation; to give an order for, as to *order* supplies.

ordinal (ôr' di nal), *n.* a number noting order of position in a series, as first, second, third. *adj.* noting order, as an *ordinal* number.

*ordinance (ôr' di nans), *n.* that which is ordained; a rule or law.

*ordinary (ôr' di ner i), *adj.* usual, customary, according to general rule or common experience; commonplace.

ordination (ôr di nā' shun), *n.* the act of conferring holy orders or state of being ordained, the ceremony of admission to the ministry.

*ordnance (ôrd' nans), *n.* artillery.

*ore (ōr), *n.* metal in its raw state as extracted from the earth.

organ (ôr' gan), *n.* that part of a living body by which some special function is discharged; a newspaper speaking semi-officially for a government or a party; a means of accomplishing something; a musical wind instrument whose tones are produced by flue and reed pipes controlled by a keyboard.

organdy (ôr' gan di), *n.* a fine, thin muslin having a stiff finish.

organic (ôr gan' ik), *adj.* pertaining to bodily organs, as an *organic* disease; pertaining to or derived from living bodies, as plants or animals.

organism (ôr' gan izm), *n.* a living body.

organist (ôr' gan ist), *n.* one who plays an organ.

organize (ôr' gan iz), *v.i. and v.t.* to get together for action, as the workers *organized;* to bring together for action, as we *organized* a glee club; to arrange related parts into a unified whole, as to *organize* a business.

*orgy (ôr' ji), *n.* [*pl.* orgies] a drunken revel.

*oriel (ō' riel), *n.* a bay window, especially on an upper floor.

orient (ō' ri ent), *n.* the east, especially the countries of Asia or in the eastern part of the Mediterranean. *v.t.* to set facing the east; to place in correct position or relation to, as to *orient* oneself to unfamiliar surroundings.

orientation (ō ri en tā' shun), *n.* adjustment; getting one's bearings; being set in correct relation to some standard.

orifice (or' i fis), *n.* a mouth or aperture.

origin (or' i jin), *n.* the beginning of anything; place and time of beginning; cause.

original (ō rij' i nal), *n.* that from which anything is copied; the language in which a book is first written, as he read it in the *original. adj.* first in a series, as an *original* inhabitant; not a copy, as an *original* painting; not translated; new, as an *original* idea; inventive, creative, as an *original* writer.•

originality (ō rij i nal' i ti), *n.* the ability to invent or create something unusual.

originate (ō rij' i nāt), *v.i. and v.t.* to begin to exist, as the river *originates* in the mountains; to bring into being, as he *originated* the idea.

*oriole (ō' ri ōl), *n.* a bird, yellow or orange and black, that builds a hanging nest.

ormolu (ôr' mo lōō), *n.* brass ornament for furniture, imitating gold.

*ornament (ôr' na ment), *n.* anything that adorns. *v.t.* to furnish with ornaments or ornamentation; to adorn, as to *ornament* a Christmas tree.

*ornate (ôr nāt'), *adj.* elaborately adorned, or embellished.

ornithology (ôr ni thol' ō ji), *n.* the scientific study of birds and bird life.

*orotund (ō' rō tund), *adj.* of clear, smooth sound, as if spoken with rounded lips; as an *orotund* voice; pompous.

orphan (ôr' fan), *n.* a child either or both of whose parents is dead.

orthodox (ôr' thō doks), *adj.* holding, or in accordance with, established belief, especially in connection with religion; approved, accepted, as she does all the *orthodox* things.

*orthoëpy (ôr' thō e pi), *n.* correct pronunciation.

orthography (ôr thog' ra fi), *n.* correct spelling.

orthopedics (ôr thō pē' diks), *n.* the correction or treatment of deformities in young children.

oryx (ō' riks), *n.* an antelope of Arabia and Africa, having long upstanding nearly straight horns; there are four species including white oryx, sandy oryx, beisa and gemsbok.

oscillate (os' i lāt), *v.i.* to swing back and forth like a pendulum; to waver, as between two opinions.

oscillation (os i lā' shun), *n.* the act of swinging back and fourth, wavering, indecision.

osculate (os' kū lāt), *v.i. and v.t.* to kiss.

*osier (ō' zhér), *n.* a kind of willow tree of which the twigs are used in making baskets and furniture; the twig or rod used for basket making.

ossification (os i fi kā' shun), *n.* the process that converts animal tissues into bone.

ossify (os' i fi), *v.t. and v.i.* to turn into bone; to become callous, hard.

ostensible (os ten' si bl), *adj.* apparent, professed, specious, as *ostensible* friendship often conceals a bitter hostility.

ostentation (os ten tā' shun), *n.* outward show, vulgar display.

ostentatious (os ten tā' shus), *adj.* fond of display, gaudy.

osteology (os tē ol' ō ji), *n.* the science of the structure and diseases of bones.

osteopath (os' tē ō path), *n.* one who treats bodily ailments by manipulating bones, joints and nerve centers.

ostracize (os' tra siz), *v.t.* to banish by vote; to bar from favor.

*ostrich (os' trich), *n.* a flightless bird of

Africa, with long legs and having wing and tail feathers that are valuable in commerce.

other (uth' ẽr), *pron.* the opposite one of two, as one or the *other* of you.

other (uth' ẽr), *adj.* being the remaining, as her *other* sons; additional, as without *other* source of income; not the same, different, as I have *other* things to do; second, alternate, as every *other* one was drafted.

otherwise (uth' ẽr wiz), *adv.* in a different way. *conj.* else, as I am afraid it would spoil your enjoyment, *otherwise* I would tell you the story.

ought (ôt), *auxiliary v.* to be obliged by duty or conscience, as I *ought* to write two letters; to be forced by necessity or expediency, as we *ought* to dress warmly in winter; to follow naturally as a result, as this *ought* to be the mate to this shoe; to need, as this hole *ought* to be darned.

ounce (ouns), *n.* a measure of weight, 1/16th of a pound avoirdupois, 1/12 of a pound troy.

our (our), *pron.* belonging to us, as that is *our* dog.

oust (oust), *v.t.* to eject, put out, as they *ousted* him from power.

out (out), *adv.* away from the inside, as to stay *out;* not within the limits, as *out* of town; abroad, away from home, as to send a suit *out* to be pressed; not in a state or condition, as *out* of form; forth, as the sun came *out;* in bloom, as my roses are *out;* into the open, as the news is *out;* in error, as your figures are *out;* clear of obstruction, as to clean *out* a desk; loudly, as to cry *out.*

outboard (out' bõrd), *adj.* attached to the outside of a boat, as an *outboard* motor.

outbreak (out' brāk), *n.* an eruption, as an *outbreak* of disease, an *outbreak* of disorder.

outburst (out' bûrst), *n.* a violent outbreak, as of anger.

outcast (out' kåst), *n.* one who is cast out, an exile; one excluded from fellowship.

outcast (out' kåst), *adj.* driven forth, rejected.

outclass (out klås'), *v.t.* to excel or surpass in quality or skill, as the new boat outclassed all its rivals.

outcome (out' kum), *n.* result, consequence.

outcrop (out' krop), *n.* the projection of layers of rock above ground. *v.i.* to come to the surface.

outcry (out' krī), *n.* clamor, tumult.

outdo (out' dōō), *v.t.* to excel.

outlaw (out' lô), *n.* one who has lost his legal rights; a dangerous criminal at large; a fugitive. *v.t.* to deprive of legal standing; as to *outlaw* a rule.

outlay (out' lā), *n.* expenditure.

outlet (out' let), *n.* a vent, a means of escape; a stream emptying a lake; a means of distribution, as of goods.

outline (out' līn), *n.* a line that bounds or defines a figure; a first draft of a literary composition. *v.t.* to sketch in contour; to give the plan of.

outlive (out liv'), *v.t.* to live longer than, survive.

outlook (out' look), *n.* a view from a point of vantage; prospect for the future.

outrage (out' rãj), *n.* wanton wrong done to others, a gross violation of what is commonly regarded as right and decent.

outrageous (out rā' jus), *adj.* atrocious, grossly violating standards of decency.

outright (out rīt'), *adv.* completely and without reservation; at once, as he was killed *outright.*

outside (out sīd'), *n.* the external surface of anything, apart from the interior. *adj.* external. *adv.* beyond an enclosure, as to go *outside;* on the exterior, as decorated *outside.*

outstanding (out stan' ding), *adj.* prominent, as an *outstanding* achievement; due and unpaid, as debts.

outward (out' wẽrd), *adj.* external; visible.

outwit (out wit'), *v.t.* to surpass in wisdom; to defeat by superior skill or cunning, as to *outwit* an adversary.

outwork (out' wûrk), *n.* a defense constructed beyond the main body of a fort.

outwork (out wûrk'), *v.t.* to do more work than.

outworn (out' wõrn), *adj.* out-of-date.

oval (ō' val), *n.* anything shaped like an egg.

oval (ō' val), *adj.* shaped like an egg.

ovation (ō vā' shun), *n.* a hearty demonstration of favor by a crowd or audience.

oven (uv' en), *n.* a chamber in a stove used for baking; a similar space used for heating substances in course of manufacture.

over (ō' vẽr), *adv.* beyond or away from the perpendicular, as to fall *over;* so as to face oppositely, as to turn *over;* across the brim, as running *over;* in excess of a certain quantity, as children of nine years or *over;* again, as to do the work *over.*

over (ō' vẽr), *prep.* above; in authority, power, dignity, value; more than or better than in quality or degree; upon the surface of, as to wander *over* the earth; along the course of, as to drive *over* a new road; across, as to jump *over* a puddle; during, as to keep *over* night.

overawe (ō vẽr ô'), *v.t.* to restrain by awe.

overbearing (ō vẽr bâr' ing), *adj.* arrogant.

overboard (ō' vẽr bõrd), *adv.* over the side of a ship.

overflow (ō' vẽr flō), *n.* water or other liquid that runs over after filling a receptacle.

overflow (ō vẽr flō'), *v.i. and v.t.* to run over, as a liquid after filling a receptacle; to flood, as a region.

overhear (ō vẽr hẽr'), *v.i. and v.t.* to hear by accident.

overpower (ō vẽr pou' ẽr), *v.t.* to crush by superior force.

overproduction (ō vẽr prō duk' shun), *n.* production in excess of demand.

overseer (ō' vẽr sē ẽr), *n.* a superintendent.

overt (ō' vẽrt), *adj.* open, public.

overtake (ō vẽr tāk'), *v.t.* to catch by pursuit; to come upon as punishment.

overthrow (ō vẽr thrō'), *v.t.* to push or throw over, defeat.

overturn (ō vẽr tûrn'), *v.t.* to upset.

overwhelm (ō vẽr hwelm'), *v.t.* to crush or destroy; to overcome with emotion.

overweening (ō vẽr wēn' ing), *adj.* unduly confident, arrogant.

*oviparous (ō vip' a rus), *adj.* producing young by laying and hatching eggs.

ovoid (ō' void), *adj.* shaped like an egg.

owe (ō), *v.t.* to be indebted to; to be under obligation to pay or make, as to *owe* an apology.

owl (oul), *n.* a bird of prey that flies by night.

own (ōn), *v.i. and v.t.* to admit; to possess rightfully. *adj.* belonging to.

ox (oks), *n.* [*pl.* oxen] a domesticated bovine beast of burden.

*oxide (ok' sīd), *n.* a compound of oxygen and a base.

oxidize (ok' si dīz), *v.i. and v.t.* to take up oxygen or combine with it; to convert into an oxide.

*oxygen (ok' si jen), *n.* a gas without color or smell, essential to all life, animal and vegetable.

*oyer (ō' yẽr), *n.* a hearing or trial of legal causes.

*oyez (ō' yes), *interj.* hear ye, attention; a word three times called in a courtroom to secure silence and attention.

*oyster (ois' tẽr), *n.* a sea mollusk with a two-leaved, hinged shell, used as food.

*ozone (ō' zōn), *n.* a gas resembling oxygen, occurring in the air.

P

pace (pās), *n.* one step in walking; rate of speed, gait; a certain gait of a horse.

pace (pās), *v.i. and v.t.* to walk with long, even steps; to move with the feet on the same side simultaneously, as a horse; to measure off by steps; to set the speed for, as a runner in a race.

pachyderm (pak' i dûrm), *n.* an animal having very thick skin, as the elephant or rhinoceros.

pacific (pa sif' ik), *adj.* conciliatory, peaceful, mild.

*pacification (pa sif i kā' shun), *n.* the act of making peace between combatants.

*pacifist (pas' i fist), *n.* one who opposes war and advocates the settling of disputes by arbitration.

pacify (pas' i fi), *v.t.* to calm, quiet, reconcile; to bring out of a state of anger.

pack (pak), *n.* a bundle tied up to be carried; a set, as a *pack* of cards; a number of animals hunting together. *v.i. and v.t.* to press together into a mass, as snow *packs;* to form into a bundle; to put together, as clothes in a trunk; to press into a mass, as *pack* the dirt well; to crowd, as into a space, as to *pack* passengers into a subway train.

package (pak' ij), *n.* a bundle of goods, parcel.

packaged software (pak' ijd sôft' wâr), *n.* an off-the-shelf software program marketed for widespread use.

pact (pakt), *n.* an agreement.

pad (pad), *n.* a soft cushion; the cushionlike part of the feet of some animals; a block of sheets of paper. *v.t.* to add extra material, as to *pad* the shoulders of a coat, *pad* an essay.

padding (pad' ing), *n.* material used for stuffing; unnecessary material used to expand writing.

paddle (pad' l), *n.* a short broad-bladed oar used without leverage to propel and steer a canoe; an instrument of similar shape used in stirring and mixing. *v.i. and v.t.* to wade in shallow water; to propel with a paddle, as a canoe.

paddock (pad' uk), *n.* a space where horses are exercised; a small field used for pasture.

padlock (pad' lok), *n.* a lock with a link to be passed through the staple of a hasp, or the links of a chain. *v.t.* to fasten with a padlock.

pagan (pā' gan), *n.* a heathen, one having no religious beliefs. *adj.* heathen, irreligious.

page (pāj), *n.* one side of a leaf of a book or manuscript. *n.* a boy servant; a male attendant on a legislative body; in the days of chivalry, a young fellow serving a knight as the first stage of training for his own knighthood. *v.t.* to number the pages of, as a book or manuscript. *v.t.* to call by means of a page, as in the lobby of a hotel.

*pageant (paj' ent), *n.* a display or procession of persons in costume representing a past period, frequently with re-enactment of historic scenes; mere show and pompous display.

*pagoda (pa gō' da), *n.* a sacred temple or tower of the Far East.

*pail (pāl), *n.* a metal or wooden open vessel, with a handle over the top, used to carry liquids.

pain (pān), *n.* physical or mental suffering; a penalty, as on *pain* of death: *pains*, labor, careful and diligent effort, as she took great *pains* with the work.

pain (pān), *v.i. and v.t.* to suffer, give pain; to cause suffering to, to hurt or distress.

paint (pānt), *n.* pigment mixed with oil or water and applied to a surface with a brush. *v.i. and v.t.* to apply paint; to spread paint on; to make a picture with paint; to depict.

Syn. Depict. To *paint* is to represent figures on canvas, or, figuratively, to describe in words. To *depict* is to use words alone to make the mental picture.

painter (pān' tẽr), *n.* one whose occupation

is to paint; an artist skilled in depicting subjects in colors.

pair (pâr), n. two things of a kind, similar in form, suited to each other and associated.

pajamas (pa jä′ maz), n. a sleeping costume consisting of coat and loose trousers.

*****palace** (pal′ is), n. the residence of a sovereign or of a bishop; any magnificent house or building.

palatable (pal′ it a bl), adj. agreeable to the taste; savory.

palatal (pal′ a tal), n. a sound formed with the blade of the tongue almost touching the hard palate, as the sound of ch in chin is a palatal. adj. pertaining in any way to the palate.

palate (pal′ it), n. the roof of the mouth, including the hard, bony front part or the hard palate, and the soft back part, called the soft palate or the velum.

*****palatial** (pa lä′ shal), adj. suitable to a palace; like a palace.

*****palaver** (pa lav′ ẽr), n. chatter, talk; conference.

pale (pāl), n. a fence picket; a district or territory shut in as if by a fence. adj. lacking color, faint; wan, white, ashen. v.i. to turn white, lose color.

paleobotany (pā lē ŏ bot′ a ni), n. the science of fossil plants.

*****paleolithic** (pā lē ŏ lith′ ik), adj. characterizing the period of human development when chipped stone tools were used; belonging to the earlier part of the Stone Age.

*****paleontology** (pā lē on tol′ ŏ ji), n. the science of fossil remains.

*****palette** (pal′ et), n. a thin oval plate of wood or porcelain (usually with a thumb hole) on which an artist mixes colors; a set or range of colors.

palfrey (pôl′ fri), n. a horse.

*****palimpsest** (pal′ imp sest), n. a sheet on which the original writing has been erased to make room for new writing.

palindrome (pal′ in drōm), n. anything that reads the same backward and forward—like Madam, I'm Adam.

palisade (pal i sād′), n. a fence or fortification formed of stakes driven into the ground and pointed at the top: palisades, a line of high barrierlike cliffs.

*****pall** (pôl), n. a cloak or mantle; a covering for a coffin; anything likened to it, as a pall of smoke. v.i. to become insipid and tiresome.

palladium (pa lä′ di um), n. a rare grayish metallic element belonging to the platinum group.

pallet (pal′ et), n. a small rough bed.

*****palliate** (pal′ i āt), v.t. to lessen, reduce, as to palliate a sickness; to excuse, as an offense against the law.

palliative (pal′ i ā tiv), n. that which tends or is intended to cloak guilt or lessen pain.

palliative (pal′ i ā tiv), adj. tending or intended to cloak guilt or lessen pain.

pallid (pal′ id), adj. pale, wan, lacking color.

pallor (pal′ ẽr), n. paleness.

*****palm** (päm), n. the inner part of the hand; the part of a glove that covers it; anything with a broad flat shape, as an oar or an antler.

palm (päm), n. a tropical tree with a straight high slender unbranching trunk with long leaves clustered at the top; a leaf of the palm tree as a symbol of victory.

palmetto (pal met′ ŏ), n. a species of palm tree of the West Indies and southern United States; the leaves of this tree used for weaving.

*****palmistry** (päm′ is tri), n. the art of foretelling the future or analyzing character by reading the lines in the palm of the hand.

palpable (pal′ pa bl), adj. perceptible by or as if by touch, tangible, visible, audible; plain, obvious, as a palpable error.

palpitate (pal′ pi tāt), v.i. to beat or throb fast, flutter.

palpitation (pal pi tā′ shun), n. a rapid, irregular beat, as palpitation of the heart.

*****palsy** (pôl′ zi), n. paralysis, especially with a trembling of the limbs. v.t. [p.t. and p.p. palsied, pr.p. palsying] to paralyze.

paltry (pôl′ tri), adj. worthless; contemptible.

pamper (pam′ pẽr), v.t. to treat with excessive indulgence.

pamphlet (pam′ flet), n. a small unbound book, usually on some current topic or containing propaganda.

pan (pan), n. a broad shallow vessel used in cooking, mining or manufacture; anything of similar shape. v.i. and v.t. to appear in a miner's pan, as gold; to cook in a pan, as fish; to wash in a pan, as gravel for gold.

*****panacea** (pan a sē′ a), n. a cure-all.

*****pancreas** (pan′ krē as), n. a large fleshy gland situated under and behind the stomach, secreting a digestive fluid; it is called the sweetbread when it is used as food.

pancreatin (pan′ krē a tin), n. an albuminoid principle in the fluid of the pancreas.

pandemonium (pan dē mō′ ni um), n. a place of wild disorder; confused uproar.

pander (pan′ dẽr), v.i. to cater to the desires of others.

pane (pān), n. the sheet of glass in a section of a window or door.

*****panegyric** (pan ē jir′ ik), n. a eulogy; a formal literary or oratorical expression of high praise.

panel (pan′ el), n. a rectangular section of cloth or wood in a structure; a division of a wall or ceiling; a light section set in a heavier frame, as in a door; a movable part bolted to the main structure of a wing of an airplane; the list from which a jury is drawn; a painting on a thin board.

panel (pan′ el), v.t. [p.t. and p.p. paneled or panelled, pr.p. paneling or panelling] to form in panels; to furnish with panels.

pang (pang), n. a sudden sharp thrust of pain; mental agony.

panic (pan′ ik), n. a sudden and general fright; a sudden loss of business confidence by the public.

*****pannier** (pan′ yẽr), n. a basket carried on

the back of a pack animal, usually slung in pairs; a frame to spread a skirt at the hips.

panoply (pan' ŏ pli), *n.* a complete suit of armor; any complete protective covering.

***panorama** (pan ō rä' ma), *n.* a view in all directions; a scene that moves before one's eyes; a great painting of scenes made to move past the onlooker.

pansy (pan' zi), *n.* [*pl.* pansies] a garden plant with velvety-petaled flowers of brilliant mixed colors.

pant (pant), *v.i. and v.t.* to breathe fast and hard, as after exertion: to long, desire, as we *pant* for life; to pronounce breathlessly, as the runner *panted* a single word.

pantaloon (pan ta lōōn'), *n.* a buffoon in pantomime: *pantaloons*, trousers.

pantheism (pan' thē izm), *n.* belief that God is in all things; worship of all gods indiscriminately.

***pantheon** (pan thē' on), *n.* a temple to all the gods.

panther (pan' thër), *n.* a leopard; a large American wildcat, also called *cougar* or *puma.*

***pantomime** (pan' tō mĭm), *n.* a representation in a dumb show; a play without words.

pantry (pan' tri), *n.* [*pl.* pantries] a small room where kitchen supplies are kept and from which food is served.

pap (pap), *n.* any soft food for infants; juicy pulp of certain fruits.

***papacy** (pā' pa si), *n.* the office and authority of the Pope; the popes collectively.

***papal** (pā' pal), *adj.* pertaining to the Pope.

paper (pā' për), *n.* a material made in thin sheets from rags, wood pulp and other materials, used for writing and printing, covering walls and wrapping packages; a newspaper; a literary composition, as he read a *paper* on woman suffrage. *v.t.* to cover with paper. *adj.* made of paper; on paper only and not existing in reality, as *paper* profits.

papoose (pa pōōs'), *n.* a North American Indian baby or small child.

***papyrus** (pa pi' rus), *n.* [*pl.* papyri] a species of Egyptian reed from which the ancients made paper; a manuscript on papyrus.

par (pär), *n.* a fixed standard from which values are measured, as the *par* of stocks; equality, as to be on a *par* with others; in golf, the number of strokes figured as a perfect score for a hole or over an entire course.

parable (par' a bl), *n.* a short story carrying a clear moral.

parabola (pa rab' ō la), *n.* in geometry, the figure formed by the intersection of a cone with a plane parallel to its side.

parachute (par' a shōōt), *n.* an umbrella-shaped apparatus in which aviators drop from a plane to the ground in emergency.

parade (pa räd'), *n.* a formal march or procession; any ostentatious display, as a *parade* of learning. *v.i. and v.t.* to march in a parade; to form and lead in display, as he

paraded his regiment; to march through, as to *parade* the avenue; to make ostentatious display of, as to *parade* one's talents.

***paradise** (par' a dĭs), *n.* the Garden of Eden; heaven.

paradox (par' a doks), *n.* something apparently absurd or incredible, yet possibly true.

paradoxical (par a dok' sik al), *adj.* of the nature of a paradox; apparently self-contradictory, yet possibly true.

***paraffin** (par' a fin), *n.* a waxy substance without taste, color or odor, obtained by distillation from wood, coal, or from crude petroleum and used in candlemaking, as waterproofing material, in sealing preserve jars.

paragon (par' a gon), *n.* a model or pattern of perfection.

paragraph (par' a gräf), *n.* a subdivision of a written text, containing sentences dealing with one topic.

parallel (par' a lel), *n.* one of two or more equidistant lines or planes; something closely resembling another; a statement of similarity, as to draw a *parallel* between mathematics and music; an imaginary circle about the earth equidistant at all points from the equator. *v.t.* to state a likeness as to *parallel* mathematics and music; to be literally equidistant from at all points, as to *parallel* the equator; to resemble, as to *parallel* another's line of reasoning. *adj.* equally distant, as one line or plane to another, at all points; having the same course; having close resemblance.

paralysis (pa ral' i sis), *n.* loss of the powers of sensation and of movement.

paralyze (par' a līz), *v.t.* to deprive of sensation or the power of movement; to unnerve; to render inactive.

parameter (pâ ram´ ĭ ter), *n.* the value which determines the form of expression, function, etc.; a number expressing some aspect of the behavior of a physical system; a fixed limit or guideline.

***paramount** (par' a mount), *adj.* superior to all others; eminent or chief, as the *paramount* issue in a political campaign.

parapet (par' a pet), *n.* a low wall along the edge of a roof, a bridge, balcony; a protective wall or rampart in a fortification; breastwork, as a bank of earth or sandbags along the forward edge of a trench.

paraphernalia (par a fër nä' lia), *n. pl.* ornaments of dress generally; articles of equipment; trappings.

paraphrase (par' a fräz), *n.* a free translation; statement of the same thing in other words. *v.t.* to translate freely, not word for word but giving the sense; to say the same thing in other words.

parasite (par' a sīt), *n.* an animal or plant nourished by another to which it attaches itself; a person who does no work but lives at the expense of others.

***parasol** (par' a sŏl), *n.* a sunshade.

parboil (pär' boil), *v.t.* to boil partially.

***parcel** (pär' sel), *n.* a small package; a plot, as a *parcel* of land.

parcel (pär' sel), *v.t.* to divide, distribute.

parch (pärch), *v.i. and v.t.* to dry with heat, as the skin *parches* during fever, the sun *parches* the grass; to scorch.

parchment (pärch' ment), *n.* the skin of a sheep or goat dressed and prepared for writing; a document, as a diploma, on parchment.

pardon (pär' dn), *n.* forgiveness; the act of an executive in freeing a convicted person from the legal penalty; the remission of penalty. *v.t.* to forgive; to release from a legal penalty.

pardonable (pär' dn a bl), *adj.* forgivable, excusable.

****pare** (pâr), *v.t.* to cut away little by little, as to *pare* a horse's hoofs; to reduce, as to *pare* profits in order to make a sale; to cut off a skin or rind, as to *pare* potatoes.

paregoric (par ē gor' ik), *n.* a tincture of opium used to ease pain.

paregoric (parē gor' ik), *adj.* relieving pain.

****parent** (pâr' ent), *n.* a father or mother; the source of a living thing, as the *parent* of a plant.

****parentage** (pâr' en tij), *n.* the relationship of parent to child; descent, as of good *parentage*.

parental (pa ren' tal), *adj.* pertaining to parents or parenthood; resembling a parent, as *parental* care of a foundling.

parenthesis (pa ren' thē sis), *n.* [*pl.* parentheses] an explanatory word or clause inserted in a sentence; the marks that set it off, ( ).

****paresis** (pa rē' sis), *n.* incomplete paralysis.

parietal (pa rī' e tal), *n.* one of two bones of the skull, wall bones.

parietal (pa rī' e tal), *adj.* pertaining to a wall or side; forming the wall or side, as the *parietal* bones of the head.

parish (par' ish), *n.* district under the particular charge of a clergyman; a unit of local government, the equivalent of a county in Louisiana.

parity (par' i ti), *n.* equality; likeness; equivalence in currency.

park (pärk), *n.* an area of ground set aside for public use; a city square with walks, lawn and seats.

park (pärk), *v.i. and v.t.* to leave standing idle, as an automobile; to arrange artillery when not in use.

parlance (pär' lans), *n.* conversation; discourse or debate; a special way of speaking, diction.

parley (pär' li), *n.* a conference, especially with an enemy, with a view to making peace. *v.i.* to confer, especially with an enemy.

****parliament** (pär' li ment), *n.* a representative legislative assembly; the paramount legislature of the United Kingdom of Great Britain and Northern Ireland.

parliamentary (pär li men' ta ri), *adj.* according to the rules and customs of deliberative assemblies, as *parliamentary* law.

parlor (pär' lẽr), *n.* a reception room; a drawing room; any shop fitted out for the comfort and ease of patrons and with some show of elegance, as a beauty *parlor*.

parochial (pa rō' ki al), *adj.* pertaining to a parish, as a *parochial* school; narrow-minded, as if with no concern for things outside one's own parish.

parody (par' ŏ di), *n.* [*pl.* parodies] a burlesque imitation of a serious composition.

parody (par' ŏ di), *v.t.* [*p.t.* and *p.p.* parodied, *pr.p.* parodying] to use as subject for burlesque imitation.

****parole** (pa rōl'), *n.* a word of honor, as given by a prisoner of war conditionally released; the system of releasing prisoners from jail under condition of good behavior and periodical reports to the authorities.

parole (pa rōl'), *v.t.* to release conditionally, as prisoners of war or persons convicted of breaking laws.

paroxysm (par' ok sizm), *n.* a sudden spasm or fit of acute pain.

****parquet** (pär kā'), *n.* a flooring made of wooden inlay; the floor space of a theater between the orchestra rail and the parquet circle.

parquetry (pär' ket ri), *n.* wooden inlay for floors; mosaic flooring.

parricide (par' i sīd), *n.* the murder of one's father, mother or other close relative; one who commits such a murder.

parrot (par' ut), *n.* a tropical bird with a hooked bill, brilliant plumage, and ability to imitate human speech.

parry (par' i), *n.* [*pl.* parries] a turning aside of a thrust or blow, as in fencing or boxing; a defensive argument repelling attack in a debate. *v.i. and v.t.* to make a parry; to ward off, as a thrust, blow or argument.

parse (pärs), *v.i. and v.t.* to be in agreement with the rules of grammar, as this sentence *parses* correctly; to analyze according to the rules of grammar, telling the parts of speech and the syntax, as *parse* this sentence.

parsimonious (pär si mō' ni us), *adj.* frugal to a fault; miserly.

parsimony (pär' si mō ni), *n.* [*pl.* parsimonies] stinginess, excessive thrift; an act of stinginess.

parsley (pärs' li), *n.* a garden plant with leaves used as a garnish and as flavoring.

parsnip (pärs' nip), *n.* a garden plant with an edible root, like that of the carrot, but white instead of yellow.

parson (pär' sn), *n.* the incumbent of a parish; a clergyman, a preacher.

parsonage (pär' sn ij), *n.* the residence of a clergyman in charge of a parish; the home provided for a parson by his parish.

part (pärt), *n.* something less than the whole, as take only *part* of it; a piece or portion; the representation of a character in a play, as to play the *part* of Macbeth; a share, as in a business or enterprise, as I'll have no *part* in it.

Syn. Piece, portion, fragment. A *part* is an essential piece or section of a whole; a *portion* is a piece or section separated from a whole to be allotted or assigned to a person or a purpose, as a *portion* of pie, one's *portion* of the day's work; a *piece* is a part detached from some larger source and regarded as a thing in itself, as a *piece* of string; a *fragment* is a piece broken off.

part (pärt), *v.i. and v.t.* to separate; to take leave; to divide into portions, as *part* the apple between you two, *part* your hair on the side.

partake (pär tāk'), *v.i.* [*p.t.* partook, *p.p.* partaken, *pr.p.* partaking] to take or receive a share in common with others, as to *partake* of food or shelter.

partial (pär' shal), *adj.* pertaining to a part, incomplete, not entire; showing favoritism, biased.

*__partiality__ (pär shi al' i ti), *n* [*pl.* partialities] favoritism, bias.

participant (pär tis' i pant), *n.* one who takes part, one who shares.

participate (pär tis' i pāt), *v.i.* to take part, share with others, as to *participate* in a game.

*__participle__ (pär' ti si pl), *n.* a part of a verb that partakes of the nature both of verb and of adjective.

particle (pär' ti kl), *n.* the smallest possible separable amount of anything; a word without inflection, as an article, a preposition or conjunction, or a word used alone, as an interjection.

*__particular__ (pẽr tik' ū lẽr), *n.* an individual thing or point or quality, as in this *particular*.

*__particular__ (pẽr tik' ū lẽr), *adj.* distinct from others; peculiar or unusual; exact; fussy.
    Syn. Individual, special. *Particular* means specifically one and only one out of many others like it, as I want this *particular* puppy; *individual* means belonging to one only or very characteristic of one person or thing, as one's *individual* beliefs, an individual manner of speech; *special* means unusual, as this is a *special* favor.

particularize (pẽr tik' ū lẽr īz), *v.i. and v.t.* to be attentive to single things or details; to give the particulars of.

parting (pär' ting), *n.* separation; the place of separation, as the *parting* of the ways; leavetaking, as *parting* is such sweet sorrow.

*__partisan__ (pär' ti zan), *n.* one who takes sides; an adherent of a political party or of one side in a dispute. *adj.* pertaining to a party, as in politics; favoring one side or party, as in politics or a dispute.

partition (pär tish' un), *n.* the act of dividing; state of being divided; a dividing wall apart from those in the original construction of a building. *v.t.* to divide into parts or shares; to subdivide by adding walls.

partner (pärt' nẽr), *n.* one who is associated with another or with several others in an enterprise; one who teams with another against an opposing team of partners in certain games.

partridge (pär' trij), *n.* a game bird related to the quail and pheasant.

party (pär' ti), *n.* a number of persons organized for a special purpose, as in politics; a social gathering; a participator, as the *parties* in a case at law, or the *party* of the first part in a contract, as for the purchase of property.

*__pasha__ (pa shä'), *n.* a Turkish title formerly given to high officials: sometimes spelled *bashaw.*

*__pass__ (pås), *n.* a narrow way, as between mountains; a permit for free transportation or admission, as a *pass* to the ball park; a state of affairs, as things have come to a bad *pass;* a movement of the hand as by one person mesmerizing another or a *pass* made by a juggler to cover his real action.

pass (pås), *v.i. and v.t.* to meet and go by, as the cars *passed* here; to be promoted from one class to another or go through an examination successfully, as I *passed;* to elapse or go by, as time *passes* slowly; to move from one to another, hand, as please *pass* the salt; to *pass* bad money; to approve, as the Senate *passed* the bill; to be approved by, as the bill *passed* the Senate.

*__passage__ (pas' ij), *n.* the act of moving from one place to another or of changing from one condition to another; progress, as of time; a voyage; a way by which one passes, as my room is down the *passage;* enactment, as *passage* of laws; a portion, as of an essay or speech, as he quoted this *passage.*

passing (pås' ing), *n.* the act of going or of going by; death. *adj.* temporary, casual.

passion (pash' un), *n.* violent agitation of mind in anger; intense desire; suffering.

passionate (pash' un it), *adj.* emotional, ardent, intense, as a *passionate* desire.

passive (pas' iv), *adj.* submissive; suffering without resistance; the form of a verb indicating that the subject does not act but is acted upon; the condition of an aircraft not under its own power or without power of its own.

passport (pås' pōrt), *n.* a license to travel in a foreign country.

past (påst), *n.* time gone by; a person's life history to date. *adj.* having been, as *past* times; gone by, as this *past* hour; former, as a *past* president; expert, as a *past* master. *adv.* near or by, as the train just went *past. prep.* by or beyond, as the train went *past* the station, it is *past* noon.

paste (påst), *n.* a wet and sticky mixture for fastening things together, such as cloth or paper; any sticky, moist substance.

paste (påst), *v.t.* to fasten with paste; to stick things together.

pastel (pas tel'), *n.* a colored crayon; a picture made with this kind of crayon in delicate colors. *adj.* soft-toned, pale and highly brilliant, as pastel shades or colors.

*__pasteurize__ (pas' tẽr īz), *v.t.* to sterilize by heating to 131°–158° F. for 30 minutes, as milk.

pastille (pas tēl'), *n.* a small cone of aromatic paste, burned slowly to fumigate a room; a medicated lozenge.

pastime (pas' tĭm), *n.* diversion, sport, pleasant occupation, recreation.

*__pastor__ (pás' tẽr), *n.* a minister having charge of a church and its congregation.

pastoral (pás' tō ral), *n.* a poem or play showing the lives of shepherds and shepherdesses; a literary composition or a painting depicting country life. *adj.* pertaining to shepherds or to simple country life.

pastry (pās' trĭ), *n.* [*pl.* pastries] pies, tarts and other baked products, made of rich crust with various fillings.

pasture (pás' tŭr), *n.* grassland on which cattle graze; grass or other fodder eaten by grazing cattle. *v.i. and v.t.* to graze; to put in grassland to graze.

__pasty__ (pas' tĭ), *n.* a pie, usually of meat, with a crust all around it.

pasty (pās' tĭ), *adj.* like paste in consistency or color, as a *pasty* mess, a *pasty* skin.

pat (pat), *n.* a quick light caressing touch with the hand; a small lump, as a *pat* of butter. *v.t.* to touch lightly with the hand, as in a caress, as to *pat* a dog. *adj.* apt, exact, as a *pat* answer. *adv.* aptly, as he spoke *pat* and to the point.

patch (pach), *n.* a piece of material applied over a hole; a plot of ground; a small area differing from its surroundings, as a *patch* of trees, a *patch* of white on a black cat.

patch (pach), *v.i. and v.t.* to repair with a patch; to put a patch on; to mend clumsily.

pate (pāt), *n.* the crown of the head.

patella (pa tel' a), *n.* the kneecap.

paten (pat' en), *n.* a thin round metal plate; the plate used for the bread in the Eucharist.

*__patent__ (pat' ent), *n.* a right or privilege granted to an inventor by the government to make or use a particular invention for a term of years without competition by other users of the same thing; a grant of land by a government; the certificate evidencing such a grant. *v.i. and v.t.* to issue or receive a grant of special rights to the use of an invention or a tract of land. *adj.* covered by a patent; high grade, as *patent* flour.

patent (pā' tent), *adj.* apparent, obvious, as a *patent* excuse.

paternal (pa tûr' nal), *adj.* relating in any way to a father or to the state of being a father.

paternity (pa tûr' ni tĭ), *n.* [*pl.* paternities] fatherhood; male parentage; authorship.

path (páth), *n.* a footway; a course of conduct, as the right *path*.

pathetic (pa thet' ĭk), *adj.* evoking sorrow and sympathy, touching.

pathological (path ō loj' i kal), *adj.* pertaining to the science of diseases, as a *pathological* lecture; diseased, as a *pathological* organ.

*__pathos__ (pā' thos), *n.* the quality in an experience or in a literary description of an experience that arouses sympathy.

*__patience__ (pā' shens), *n.* calm endurance without complaint; forbearance.

patient (pā' shent), *n.* a sick person under the care of a doctor or nurse.

patient (pā' shent), *adj.* enduring calmly, uncomplaining; forbearing; persevering.

patriarch (pā' tri ärk), *n.* the founder or head of a family; a venerable old man; a bishop or archbishop in the Oriental Church.

patrician (pa trish' an), *n.* a member of the ancient Roman aristocracy; any aristocratic person. *adj.* of aristocratic birth: opposite of *plebeian*.

patrimony (pat' ri mō ni), *n.* [*pl.* patrimonies] an estate that has descended through a family line.

*__patriot__ (pā' tri ut), *n.* one who is devoted to his country.

*__patriotic__ (pā tri ot' ik), *adj.* devoted to one's own country and ready to serve it.

*__patriotism__ (pā' tri ut izm), *n.* devotion to one's country; national loyalty.

*__patrol__ (pa trōl'), *n.* a guard that goes the rounds; the act of moving about a district to guard it; a group of men on guard duty.

patrol (pa trōl'), *v.i. and v.t.* to be on guard duty; to walk back and forth or around to guard and protect, as a policeman *patrols* a neighborhood.

patrolman (pa trōl' man), *n.* a policeman on a beat.

*__patron__ (pā' trun), *n.* a guardian or protector; a regular customer, as patron of a shop; a man who gives his support to a social or charitable undertaking. *adj.* aiding or guarding, as a *patron* saint.

*__patronage__ (pā' trun ij), *n.* aid, support; condescension; the power to control political nominations.

*__patronize__ (pā' trun īz), *v.t.* to act as a guardian toward; to be a customer of, frequent, as a restaurant or a shop; to treat with condescension.

*__patronymic__ (pat rō nim' ik), *n.* a name derived from an ancestor. *adj.* derived from the name of an ancestor; denoting ancestry.

patter (pat' ẽr), *n.* a quick, steady succession of light sounds, as the *patter* of raindrops, the *patter* of children's feet. *n.* rapid empty talk. *v.i.* to move with quick, light steps; to strike with a swift steady succession of light blows, as the child *pattered* down the stairs, the rain *patters* on the roof.

pattern (pat' ẽrn), *n.* a model to be copied; a design from which to work, as a *pattern* for a dress; the design of a fabric, as lace or a rug. *v.i. and v.t.* to follow after, copy; to form in a pattern; to design.

patty (pat' ĭ), *n.* [*pl.* patties] a pastry shell filled with food, as an oyster *patty*.

*__paucity__ (pô' si ti), *n.* smallness of number or quantity; fewness; scantiness, insufficiency.

*__paunch__ (pônch), *n.* the belly, abdomen.

pauper (pô' pẽr), *n.* one deep in poverty, especially so poor as to require support at public expense.

pauperize (pô' pẽr īz), *v.t.* to make a pauper of, to impoverish completely.

pause (pôz), *n.* a momentary or brief stop or suspension of activity; an interruption of progress. *v.i.* to stop for a moment; to hesitate.

pave (pāv), *v.t.* to cover with stones, brick

or wood, as to *pave* streets; to make smooth and easy, as to *pave* the way to success.

pavement (pāv' ment), *n.* a paved roadway or sidewalk.

paving (pāv' ing), *n.* materials for making a pavement.

pavilion (pa vil' yun), *n.* a large open-sided tent or shelter.

*****paw** (pô), *n.* the foot of a quadruped with claws, as distinguished from a hoof.

paw (pô). *v.i. and v.t.* to scrape with the forefoot; to handle awkwardly.

*****pawn** (pôn), *n.* the chess piece of least value, representing a foot soldier. *n.* something deposited as security on a loan; the state of being pledged, as my ring is in *pawn. v.t.* to place in pawn; to deposit as security.

pawnshop (pôn' shop), *n.* a place where money is lent on articles deposited as security for repayment.

*****pay** (pā), *n.* money received for work done, services rendered or goods sold.

pay (pā), *v.i. and v.t.* to make recompense in money, as we *pay* on Friday; to give money for work, services or goods; to be profitable, as it *pays* to do right; to *pay* out, let run, as a rope.

payload (pā' lōd), *n.* the cargo of a spacecraft.

pea (pē), *n. [pl.* peas or pease] a pod-bearing vine and its edible seed.

peace (pēs), *n.* a state of tranquillity; absence of war; a pact to end a war; freedom from disorderly disturbances; freedom from fears or worries.

Syn. Quiet, calm, tranquillity. *Peace* brings exemption from private quarrels or from war. *Quiet* goes with freedom from noise or interruption. *Calm* is a species of *quiet;* it predicates the absence of violent motion as well as of noise. *Tranquillity* marks either a situation of the present moment or the permanent condition of immovable objects.

Ant. Agitation, excitement, contention, war.

peaceable (pēs' a bl), *adj.* not disposed to war or quarreling, calm.

peaceful (pēs' fool), *adj.* at peace; free from war or disturbance; tranquil, calm.

peach (pēch), *n.* a tree with downy-skinned juicy fruit; the fruit of this tree.

peacock (pē' kok), *n.* a bird with handsome tail feathers marked with iridescent spots.

peak (pēk), *n.* a sharp summit; a mountain jutting up among others or standing alone; the edged or pointed end of anything, as the *peak* of a mast or a roof; the highest development or point of anything, as the *peak* of a man's career, the *peak* of production; the highest value of an alternating electric current.

peaked (pēk' ed), *adj.* sharp-featured, thin, sickly; pale and drawn-looking.

*****peal** (pēl), *n.* a loud and prolonged sound, as a *peal* of thunder; a set of tuned bells.

peal (pēl), *v.i. and v.t.* to give forth loud or solemn sounds, as the organ *pealed* forth; to cause to sound forth, as to *peal* a bell.

peanut (pē' nut), *n.* a plant of tropical origin with underground nuts in shell-like pods; the groundnut.

pear (pâr), *n.* an orchard tree with juicy thin-skinned fruit; the fruit of this tree.

*****pearl** (pûrl), *n.* a hard, smooth, grayish-white iridescent gem formed in the shell of the oyster; anything very choice or valuable, as a pearl of girlish beauty.

pearly (pûr' li), *adj.* [*comp.* pearlier, *superl.* pearliest] containing, made with or resembling pearls; clear.

*****peasant** (pez' ant), *n.* a rustic laborer, farmer or countryman.

*****peat** (pēt), *n.* decayed vegetable matter, resembling turf, cut from bogs for fuel.

pebble (peb' l), *n.* a small rounded stone, worn smooth by the action of the elements.

*****pecan** (pē kan'), *n.* a species of North American hickory; the nuts produced by this tree.

peccability (pek a bil' i ti), *n.* the state of being subject to sin.

peccadillo (pek a dil' ō), *n.* a trifling fault.

peccary (pek' a ri), *n.* an American wild hog.

peck (pek), *n.* a unit of dry measure, a quarter of a bushel. *n.* a quick sharp stroke with or as with the beak of a bird. *v.i. and v.t.* to pick up food with the beak; to strike with the beak, as birds do; to strike with a pointed instrument, such as an icepick.

*****pectin** (pek' tin), *n.* a substance occurring in various fruits, which aids in the formation of jelly, used in making preserves.

pectoral (pek' tō ral), *n.* a remedy for diseases of the chest; an ornament worn on the breast; a priest's or an abbot's cross or breastplate.

peculate (pek' ū lāt), *v.i.* to appropriate public money to one's own use; to embezzle.

*****peculiar** (pē kūl' yẽr), *adj.* one's own; distinctive; odd.

*****peculiarity** (pē kū li ar' i ti), *n. [pl.* peculiarities] something distinctively characteristic.

*****pecuniary** (pē kū' ni er i), *adj.* pertaining to money; monetary.

*****pedagogue** (ped' a gog), *n.* one who teaches children; a schoolmaster.

*****pedal** (ped' al), *n.* a treadle or foot lever, as on a bicycle or organ. *v.i. and v.t.* to use a treadle or foot lever; to operate by means of a treadle or foot lever, as to *pedal* a bicycle. *adj.* pertaining to the foot.

*****pedant** (ped' ant), *n.* one who makes an ostentatious display of his learning; one who pursues knowledge for its own sake rather than for its uses.

peddle (ped' l), *v.i. and v.t.* to travel about selling small wares; to sell in small quantities, especially from door to door.

pedestal (ped' es tal), *n.* the base of a column or statue.

pedestrian (pē des' tri an), *n.* one who goes afoot. *adj.* going afoot; slow-moving; dull.

pedigree (ped' i grē), *n.* lineage, family tree, line of descent; a certificate showing the ancestors by name, as the pedigree of a dog or horse.

*****pedometer** (pē dom' ē tẽr), *n.* a watch-shaped instrument to record distances in walking.

peek (pēk), v.i. to look with the eye half closed; to peep or pry.

peel (pēl), n. the skin or rind of certain fruits and vegetables, as orange *peel*. v.t. to remove the skin or rind from, as to *peel* an orange, *peel* the bark off a birch tree.

peep (pēp), v.i. to chirp, as young birds; to look through a crevice or out from a hiding place.

peer (pēr), n. one of the same rank, an equal; a nobleman.

peeress (pēr′ es), n. the wife of a peer; a noblewoman.

peerless (pēr′ les), adj. without an equal, matchless.

peevish (pē′ vish), adj. fretful, irritable.

peewit (pē′ wit), n. the lapwing or crested plover of the Old World, so called because of its cry.

peg (peg), n. a small pointed wooden pin; a piece of wood projecting from a wall on which to hang things.

pelf (pelf), n. wealth, especially stolen goods; lucre, gain.

pelican (pel′ i kan), n. a large aquatic bird with a huge pouched bill in which it catches fish.

*pellagra (pe lā′ gra), n. a disease due to faulty diet.

pellet (pel′ et), n. a little ball, as of food or medicine.

pell-mell (pel mel′), adv. in wild confusion, headlong, as they rushed out *pell-mell*.

*pellucid (pe lū′ sid), adj. perfectly clear; easily understood.

Syn. Transparent. Anything *pellucid* is pervious to light, and the eye can penetrate into it. *Transparent* things are bright throughout their substance. A stream is *pellucid;* it admits light, but it is not *transparent* for the eye.

pelt (pelt), n. the undressed skin of an animal with a furry coat. v.i. and v.t. to beat down, as hail; to strike repeatedly with missiles.

pelvis (pel′ vis), n. the bone-enclosed cavity in the lower part of the abdomen.

pemmican (pem′ i kan), n. lean meat, dried, pounded and pressed into cakes.

pen (pen), n. a small inclosure for animals or fowl; the animals or birds so confined, as a *pen* of Plymouth Rocks. n. a split-pointed piece of metal used in a holder for writing with ink. v.t. to confine in a pen or coop; to write with a pen, as to *pen* a letter.

*penal (pē′ nal), adj. relating to punishment for crime; punitive.

penalty (pen′ al ti), n. punishment for any crime or offense; a fine; anything paid or forfeited for breaking a rule, as in a game.

*penance (pen′ ans), n. suffering or self-sacrifice as an expression of sorrow for having sinned.

pence (pens) n. the plural of penny in quoting a price in British pennies.

*penchant (pän chän′), n. a taste, a liking, as

he has a *penchant* for art.

pencil (pen′ sil), n. graphite or colored chalk inside a stick of wood, used in writing and drawing. v.t. to write or draw with a pencil.

pend (pend), v.i. to await settlement, to be undecided, as the case is *pending*.

pendant (pen′ dant), n. a hanging ornament.

pendant (pen′ dant), n. a hanging ornament often worn about the neck.

pending (pen′ ding), adj. hanging; imminent, as *pending* evil; unsettled, as a *pending* lawsuit. prep. during, through, as *pending* the suit; until, while one is waiting for, as *pending* the final settlement of the estate.

*pendulum (pen′ dū lum), n. a body suspended from a fixed point so that it may swing freely back and forth, as in a clock case.

penetrable (pen′ ē tra bl), adj. capable of being entered or pierced.

penetrate (pen′ ē trāt), v.i. and v.t. to pass in; to pierce something; to enter into, pierce.

penetration (pen ē trā′ shun), n. the act of entering or piercing; mental acuteness, insight.

*penguin (pen′ gwin), n. a large sea bird of the Southern Hemisphere with rudimentary wings used in swimming.

penicillin (pen′ a sil′ in), n. an antibiotic obtained from certain molds or produced synthetically.

peninsula (pen in′ sū la), n. a projecting piece of land almost cut off from the mainland by water.

penitence (pen′ i tens), n. repentance, sorrow for sins or faults.

penitentiary (pen i ten′ sha ri), n. [pl. penitentiaries] a prison, house of correction.

penknife (pen′ nīf), n. a small pocketknife.

penmanship (pen′ man ship), n. the art of writing with a pen; skill in writing with a pen; a special or a personal style of writing.

pennant (pen′ ant), n. a long narrow flag or streamer flown on a vessel; a triangular flag; any flag used as a symbol of victory in an athletic contest, especially the *pennant* of professional baseball.

penny (pen′ i) [pl. pennies] the U.S. and Canadian cent.

pennyweight (pen′ i wāt), n. a weight equal to 24 grains troy measure or 1/20 of an ounce.

penology (pē ncl′ ō ji), n. the scientific study of punishment for crime, of the management of penal institutions and the reformation of criminals.

*pension (pen′ shun), n. an allowance paid for past services after retirement, by a government or a private employer.

pension (pän syôn′), n. a boarding house; a boarding school.

pension (pen′ shun), v.t. to grant a pension to.

pensive (pen′ siv), adj. quietly thoughtful.

pentagon (pen′ ta gon), n. a plane figure with five sides and five angles.

pentameter (pen tam′ ē tēr), n. a verse having five metrical feet.

*pentathlon (pen tath' lon), *n.* an athletic contest in the modern Olympics in which each entrant takes part in five events and total scores are counted.

*penult (pē' nult), *n.* the next to last syllable of a word.

penultimate (pē nul' ti mit), *adj.* last but one, as the *penultimate* word in a sentence.

penumbra (pē num' bra), *n.* a partial shadow around the rim of the total shadow of the moon or earth in an eclipse; the half-shadow along the edge of any shadow.

penurious (pē nū' ri us), *adj.* miserly, grudging, stingy.

Syn. Parsimonious, stingy. *Parsimonious* means exceedingly sparing; *penurious* means grudgingly and meanly sparing; *stingy* is the general term that means grudging of any expense whatsoever.

Ant. Generous, liberal, openhanded.

penury (pen' ū ri), *n.* want of the necessaries of life; poverty.

*peony (pē' ō ni), *n.* a perennial plant with handsome flowers.

people (pē' pl), *n.* [*pl.* peoples] a race or a nation, inhabitants, as the French *people;* human beings, men, women and children; relatives, ancestry, as to come of fine *people;* all the voters of a nation, as to take the issue to the *people.*

pepper (pep' ēr), *n.* a hot pungent spice made of the ground berries of an East Indian plant and called *black pepper;* the ground seeds of the same plant, called *white pepper;* capsicum, red pepper.

peppermint (pep' ēr mint), *n.* an aromatic herb; a cordial prepared from it; a candy flavored with it.

*pepsin (pep' sin), *n.* a nitrogenous ferment contained in the gastric juices; a preparation made from the stomach of a pig, sheep or calf to aid the human digestive system.

per (pûr), *prep.* through, by, as know *per* this document; for each, as 60 miles *per* hour, a dollar *per* dozen.

perambulation (pēr am bū lā' shun), *n.* the act of walking about, especially to inspect a tract or property.

perceive (pēr sēv'), *v.t.* to obtain knowledge of through the senses; to understand; to discern.

per cent (pēr sent), *literally,* per centum, by the hundred; so many to each hundred, as 80 *per cent* is 80 to each hundred.

perceptible (pēr sep' ti bl), *adj.* capable of being perceived.

perception (pēr sep' shun), *n.* awareness, consciousness; knowledge obtained through the senses.

perceptive (pēr sep' tiv), *adj.* having the faculty of perceiving; quick to understand.

perch (pûrch), *n.* a freshwater fish. *n.* a measure of length equal to 5½ yards, a rod; a measure of surface equal to 30¼ square yards, a square rod; a cubic measure used in masonry, usually 24¾ cubic feet, as 10 *perches* of brick. *n.* a pole or bar for birds to roost on; any high seat. *v.i. and v.t.* to alight

and rest on something, as a bird on a perch; to place or set on a perch.

perchance (pēr chàns'), *adv.* perhaps.

*percolate (pûr' kō lāt), *v.i. and v.t.* to seep through small spaces; to pass boiling water through coffee; to prepare coffee by filtering boiling water through it.

percussion (pēr kush' un), *n.* violent collision; the impact of a gun hammer on the cap that holds the powder; tapping, as the chest, to discover internal conditions; producing tone by a stroke or blow, as the piano and drum are instruments that produce tone by *percussion.*

perdition (pēr dish' un), *n.* total destruction; ruin; loss of the hope of happiness in a future life.

peregrination (per ē gri nā' shun), *n.* the act of going about; journeying; a journey.

*peremptory (pēr emp' tō ri), *adj.* positive, final; arrogant, as a *peremptory* command.

perennial (pēr en' i al), *n.* a plant that lives from year to year. *adj.* lasting all year; living from year to year, as *perennial* plants.

*perfect (pûr' fekt or pûr fekt'), *v.t.* to make perfect; to complete or finish.

perfect (pûr' fekt), *adj.* complete; without defect or blemish.

perfectible (pēr fek' ti bl), *adj.* capable of being perfected.

perfection (pēr fek' shun), *n.* the state of being without defect, flaw or blemish.

*perfidious (pēr fid' i us), *adj.* not true to a trust, treacherous, faithless.

perfidy (pûr' fi di), *n.* [*pl.* perfidies] betrayal of a trust; treachery.

perforate (pûr' fō rāt), *v.t.* to pierce through; to make holes through.

perforation (pûr fō rā' shun), *n.* the act of perforating; a hole made by boring or piercing.

perforce (pēr fôrs'), *adv.* by necessity.

perform (pēr fôrm'), *v.i. and v.t.* to act a part; to effect, execute, do; to carry out, as a vow.

performance (pēr fôrm' ans), *n.* the carrying out of something, as a vow; a deed; a presentation of a play, rendition of a musical composition or presentation in public of an act of entertainment, as of gymnastics or sleight of hand.

*perfume (pûr' fūm), *n.* fragrance, as of a flower; a substance, usually a liquid, used to give fragrance to things.

*perfume (pēr fūm'), *v.t.* to impart fragrance to; to fill with a fragrant odor.

perfumery (pēr fūm' er i), *n.* [*pl.* perfumeries] perfumes in general; a place where perfumes are made.

perfunctory (pēr fungk' tō ri), *adj.* done carelessly, done merely to discharge a duty without interest in the process or result; careless, as a *perfunctory* day's work.

*perhaps (pēr haps'), *adv.* possibly, maybe.

*pericardium (per i kär' di um), *n.* [*pl.* pericardia] the membrane that surrounds the heart.

*perihelion (per i hē' li on), *n.* [*pl.* perihelia]

the point in the orbit of a heavenly body nearest the sun.

peril (per' il), *n.* danger, jeopardy; risk of damage, injury or loss.

perilous (per' i lus), *adj.* full of danger, hazardous.

perimeter (pe rim´ ē tēr), *n.* the outer boundary of any plane figure; the distance around a circle or total lengths of all the sides of an angular figure.

period (pēr' i ud), *n.* a cycle; interval of time; a dot used in punctuation (.).

periodic or **periodical** (pēr i od' ik, -ik al), *adj.* occurring at regular intervals of time.

periodicity (pēr i ō dis' i ti), *n.* [*pl.* periodicities] quality of happening at regular time intervals; having periodic quality.

peripatetic (per i pa tet' ik), *adj.* walking about.

peripheral (per if´ feral), *n.* any device of a computer that is external to the CPU and main memory (for example, printer, modem, terminal) but attached to it by the appropriate electrical connections.

*****periphery** (pe rif´ ēr i), *n.* [*pl.* peripheries] the circumference of any curved figure, plane or solid.

periptery (pe rip' tēr i), *n.* [*pl.* peripteries] the region about an aircraft in which there are circular or whirling air movements.

perish (per' ish), *v.i.* to die; to be destroyed.

perishable (per' ish a bl), *adj.* liable to decay or death; easily spoiled, as fruits or vegetables.

*****peritonitis** (per i tō nī' tis), *n.* acute inflammation of the peritoneum.

periwig (per' i wig), *n.* a wig, a peruke.

periwinkle (per' i wing kl), *n.* a creeping plant; a small sea snail.

perjure (pûr' jēr), *v.t.* to cause (oneself) to swear falsely by lying while under oath to tell the truth.

perjury (pûr' jēr i), *n.* [*pl.* perjuries] deliberate falsehood under oath.

permanence (pûr' ma nens), *n.* the state or quality of being enduring or fixed.

permanent (pûr' ma nent), *adj.* lasting indefinitely; continuing in the same state.

    Syn. Abiding, constant, durable, fixed, immutable, invariable, lasting, perpetual, stable, steadfast. *Durable* applies to material substances that resist wear. *Lasting* may apply to either physical or spiritual things. A thing that is *permanent* is not subject to change. *Immutable* applies to that which resists both time and change.

    Ant. Perishable, evanescent, changeful.

permeable (pûr' mi a bl), *adj.* capable of being passed through or penetrated.

permeate (pûr' mē āt), *v.t.* to penetrate and pass through the pores of; to saturate, pervade.

permissible (pēr mis' a bl), *adj.* fit to be permitted, allowable.

permission (pēr mish' un), *n.* the act of allowing; consent.

*****permit** (pēr mit'), *v.t.* to allow; to give leave; to tolerate.

permute (per mūt'), *v.t.* to interchange things

in a series, so as to obtain all the possible combinations.

pernicious (pēr nish' us), *adj.* harmful in the extreme, destructive, deadly.

peroration (per ō rā' shun), *n.* the concluding part of a speech; the summing up of an argument.

peroxide (pēr ok' sīd), *n.* that oxide of a base which contains the largest proportion of oxygen; hydrogen peroxide, used for bleaching, as the hair.

perpendicular (pûr pen dik' ū lēr), *n.* a line at right angles to another line or surface. *adj.* at right angles to a horizontal line or plane; upright, vertical.

perpetrate (pûr' pē trāt), *v.t.* to do; to perform; to commit, as to *perpetrate* a crime.

*****perpetual** (pēr pet' ū al), *adj.* never ceasing, not temporary, endless.

perpetuate (pēr pet' ū āt), *v.t.* to make perpetual, give lasting existence to, preserve.

perpetuity (pûr pet ū' i ti), *n.* [*pl.* perpetuities] lasting existence, duration or worth; endless time; anything that lasts forever.

perplex (pēr pleks'), *v.t.* to puzzle, embarrass, confuse.

perplexity (pēr plek' si ti), *n.* [*pl.* perplexities] the state of being perplexed, as I am in great *perplexity;* that which puzzles and embarrasses, as the situation has many *perplexities.*

perquisite (pûr' kwi zit), *n.* a gain in addition to regular pay arising from one's position, as *perquisites* of office.

persecute (pûr' sē kūt), *v.t.* to harass and oppress, particularly because of differences in religion.

perseverance (pûr sē vēr' ans), *n.* steadiness in seeking a goal; persistent effort.

persevere (pûr sē vēr'), *v.i.* to persist in any undertaking.

*****persiflage** (pûr' si fläzh), *n.* banter, raillery, light talk.

persimmon (pēr sim' un), *n.* the pulpy plum-like fruit of an American tree, puckery until completely ripe or frosted.

*****persist** (pēr sist'), *v.i.* to continue steadily in any course of action; to apply oneself with unrelaxing effort and attention.

persistence (pēr sis' tens), *n.* uninterrupted effort in an undertaking or purpose.

persistent (pēr sis' tent), *adj.* persevering, as a *persistent* student; tenacious, enduring, as *persistent* superstitions; constantly recurring, uninterrupted, as *persistent* questions.

person (pûr' sn), *n.* an individual human being; bodily presence, as he will be here in person.

personal (pûr' sun al), *adj.* pertaining to a particular person, private, as *personal* beliefs, *personal* affairs; direct, not delegated, as a *personal* welcome; pertaining to the individual appearance or character, as to have *personal* charm; relating to an individual's appearance or affairs, especially familiar, as a *personal* question.

*****personality** (pûr su nal' i ti), *n.* [*pl.* personalities] existence as a person; the assemblage of qualities, physical, mental and moral, that set one apart from others; distinctive individuality, as he is a man of strong *personality;* a too intimate, or offensive remark about a person, as don't indulge in *personalities.*

personate (pûr' sun āt), *v.t.* to pretend to be, especially in order to defraud.

personification (pẽr son i fi kā' shun), *n.* representation or endowment of an abstract quality with an individual character, as Cupid is the *personification* of love; embodiment, as he is the *personification* of honor.

personify (pẽr son' i fī), *v.t.* to be a marked example of, as he *personifies* honor; to attribute personality to, as to *personify* nature.

personnel (pûr so nel'), *n.* the persons employed in a business establishment, government service or other group.

*****perspective** (pẽr spek' tiv), *n.* the art of depicting objects on a plane so as to show three dimensions and indicate distance away from the observer.

perspicacity (pẽr spi kas' i ti), *n.* acuteness of mental vision, quick, clear understanding.

perspicuity (pẽr spi kū' i ti), *n.* clearness of thought and expression.

*****perspiration** (pûr spi rā' shun), *n.* sweat.

*****perspire** (pẽr spīr'), *v.i.* to excrete waste matters, in liquid form, through the pores of the skin, to sweat.

persuade (pẽr swād'), *v.t.* to influence to believe or do, prevail upon by means of argument, advice, entreaty; to convince; to win over; to urge.

persuasion (pẽr swā' zhun), *n.* the act of urging, or state of being won over; belief, especially religious belief, as I am of the Christian *persuasion.*

  Syn. Belief, conviction. A *persuasion* is an opinion or belief to which one has been won over and of which one is assured; a *belief* is that to which one assents; a *conviction* is an unshakable belief.

  Ant. Skepticism.

*****persuasive** (pẽr swā' siv), *adj.* having power to persuade, convince, influence.

pert (pûrt), *adj.* saucy, bold.

pertain (pẽr tān'), *v.i.* to relate, belong, be a part.

*****pertinacious** (pûr ti nā' shus), *adj.* obstinately persistent.

pertinent (pûr' ti nent), *adj.* fitting or appropriate; to the point.

perturb (pẽr tûrb'), *v.t.* to agitate, disturb, disquiet, especially in the mind.

*****peruse** (pẽ rōōz'), *v.t.* to read with careful attention.

pervade (pẽr vād'), *v.t.* to be in or pass through every part of, permeate.

pervasive (pẽr vā' siv), *adj.* passing through, permeating.

perverse (pẽr vûrs'), *adj.* obstinate, persistent in wrong, deviating from the normal, right or true.

  Syn. Contrary, factious, fractious, froward, intractable, obstinate, petulant, stub-

born, wayward. *Perverse* signifies willfully wrong. The *stubborn* or *obstinate* person will not do what another desires or requires. The *petulant* person frets. The *perverse* individual is willfully *intractable.* The *wayward* person has a *perverse* disregard for morality and duty.

  Ant. Conscientious, dutiful, yielding.

*****perversion** (pẽr vûr' zhun), *n.* a turning from truth or from the proper use or meaning; misrepresentation, corruption, as a *perversion* of the story.

perversity (pẽr vûr' si ti), *n.* [*pl.* perversities] an act of perversion; the quality of being perverse.

pervert (pûr' vẽrt), *n.* one who has turned from the right to the wrong, especially to abnormal vice.

pervert (pẽr vûrt') *v.t.* to turn from the true end or proper purpose; to misapply.

pervious (pûr' vi us), *adj.* penetrable; receptive, accessible, as to new ideas.

pesky (pes' ki), *adj.* annoying.

pessimism (pes' i mizm), *n.* the tendency to exaggerate in thought the evils of life: opposite of *optimism.*

pessimist (pes' i mist), *n.* one who looks on the worst side of everything.

pest (pest), *n.* a plague; anything that annoys, as locusts or a teasing child.

pester (pes' tẽr), *v.t.* to annoy.

pestiferous (pes tif' ẽr us), *adj.* conveying pestilence; noxious; annoying.

pestilence (pes' ti lens), *n.* plague; an infectious or contagious disease.

pestilent (pes' ti lent), *adj.* obnoxious, physically or mentally.

pestilential (pes ti len' shal), *adj.* pertaining to or producing a pestilence; pernicious.

*****pestle** (pes' l), *n.* an instrument with which to pound or grind things in a mortar.

pet (pet), *n.* a tame animal that is fondled; a favorite person.

pet (pet), *n.* a spell of peevishness.

pet (pet), *v.t.* to fondle; to be indulgent to.

*****petal** (pet' l), *n.* one of the separate parts of the corolla of a flower.

*****petard** (pē tärd'), *n.* a case filled with explosives and attached to a wall or gate to blow it open; a kind of firecracker.

*****petition** (pē tish' un), *n.* an earnest supplication; a document addressed to someone in authority or to a governing agency containing a request for action and signed by many persons.

petition (pē tish' un), *v.t.* to supplicate; to present a petition.

petit jury (pet' i joo' ri), a trial jury as distinguished from a grand jury.

*****petrel** (pet' rel), *n.* a web-footed, strong-winged sea bird.

petrifaction (pet ri fak' shun), *n.* the process by which animal and vegetable matter becomes stone.

petrify (pet' ri fī), *v.i. and v.t.* to become stone; to change, as organic matter, into stone; to paralyze, make rigid, as with fear or amazement.

petroleum (pē trō' lē um), *n.* crude oil, refined by distillation to yield gasoline, naphtha, benzine, kerosene and lubricating oils.

pettish (pet' ish), *adj.* peevish, fretful.

***petty** (pet' i), *adj.* small; trifling; minor, as a *petty* offense; small-minded.

petulant (pet' ū lant), *adj.* cross, irritable, querulous.

***petunia** (pē tū' ni a), *n.* a garden plant of the nightshade family with handsome funnel-shaped flowers.

pew (pū), *n.* a long seat in a church; formerly an inclosed space with seats for a group of persons, as a family.

pewter (pū' tẽr), *n.* an alloy of tin and lead or tin and copper; articles made of this alloy.

phantasm (fan' tazm), *n.* a vision or specter, a figment of the imagination, a fantasy.

phantom (fan' tum), *n.* an apparition, ghost.

phantom (fan' tum), *adj.* having appearance without substance, as a *phantom* horse.

pharisaical (far i sā' i kal), *adj.* hypocritical, self-righteous.

***pharmaceutics** (fär ma sū' tiks), *n.pl.* the science of preparing and using drugs.

pharmacist (fär' ma sist), *n.* a person skilled in pharmacy, a druggist.

pharmacy (fär' ma si), *n.* [*pl.* pharmacies] the art of preparing, compounding and dispensing medicines; a drugstore.

***pharynx** (far' ingks), *n.* [*pl.* pharynges] the cavity or passage at the upper end of the esophagus.

***phase** (fāz), *n.* an aspect that changes; a stage in development.

***pheasant** (fez' ant), *n.* a game bird with showy feathering.

phenix (fē' niks), *n.* a fabulous bird of the Arabian desert, supposed to live 500 years and after death by fire to rise to new life; a symbol of immortality; also phoenix.

phenomenal (fē nom' ē nal), *adj.* having the nature of a phenomenon; very extraordinary, unusual.

phenomenon (fē nom' ē non), *n.* [*pl.* phenomena] a very extraordinary occurrence; anything that is known through the physical senses.

phial (fi' al), *n.* a small glass bottle.

***philanthropic, philanthropical** (fil an throp'ik, -i kal), *adj.* well disposed toward all mankind, benevolent.

philanthropist (fi lan' thrŏ pist), *n.* one who loves and seeks to benefit mankind.

***philanthropy** (fi lan' thrŏ pi), *n.* [*pl.* philanthropies] love of mankind; benevolence.

***philatelist** (fi lat' e list), *n.* one who collects and studies postage stamps.

philippic (fi lip' ik), *n.* a speech of vehement invective.

***philology** (fi lol' ŏ ji), *n.* scientific study of languages, including structure, development, history and relationships; linguistics.

***philoprogenitiveness** (fil ŏ prŏ jen' i tiv nes), *n.* the instinctive love of offspring.

philosopher (fi los' ŏ fẽr), *n.* a student of philosophy; one noted for calm judgment and practical wisdom.

philosophic (fil ŏ sof' ik), *adj.* pertaining to

philosophy; calm, wise and thoughtful.

philosophize (fi los' ŏ fīz), *v.i.* to reason like a philosopher.

***philosophy** (fi los' ŏ fi), *n.* [*pl.* philosophies] study of the causes and relations of things and ideas; the serene wisdom that comes from calm contemplation of life and the universe.

***phlegm** (flem), *n.* mucus secreted especially in the air passages of the throat.

***phlegmatic** (fleg mat' ik), *adj.* sluggish, dull, apathetic, calm.

phobia (fō' bi a), *n.* a morbid fear that has no reasonable basis and cannot be controlled.

phonetic (fō net' ik), *adj.* relating to the voice or to sounds in speech; representing sounds of speech, as *phonetic* spelling.

phonetics (fō net' iks), *n. pl.* the science of sounds in speech.

***phonogram** (fō' nŏ gram), *n.* a symbol used to represent a word, syllable or sound; a phonograph record.

phonograph (fō' nŏ gráf), *n.* an instrument to record and reproduce sounds.

phosphate (fos' fāt), *n.* a salt of phosphoric acid; a carbonated drink.

phosphorescence (fos fō res' ens), *n.* emission of light without heat.

phosphorescent (fos fō res' ent), *adj.* luminous, without heat.

phosphoric (fos for' ik), *adj.* pertaining to, resembling or obtained from phosphorus.

***phosphorous** (fos' fō rus), *adj.* containing phosphorus.

phosphorus (fos' fō rus), *n.* a yellowish, waxlike, non-metallic poisonous element, luminous in the dark.

photograph (fō' tō gráf), *n.* a picture made by exposing sensitive film to the action of light. *v.t.* to take a photograph of.

***photography** (fō tog' ra fi), *n.* the art of making pictures by exposing sensitized film to the action of light.

photostat (fō' tō stat), *n.* a reproducing device for documents, drawings, etc.

phrase (frāz), *n.* a group of two or more words without subject or predicate, usually introduced by a preposition, and having the force of a single part of speech, as an *adverbial* phrase; a brief expression packed with meaning; diction, phraseology. *v.t.* to put into words, as to *phrase* an idea.

phraseology (frā zē ol' ŏ ji), *n.* style of expression; peculiarity of expression or selection of words.

***phrenology** (frē nol' ŏ ji), *n.* the reading of character through the conformation of the skull.

phylactery (fi lak' tẽr i), *n.* [*pl.* phylacteries] a charm or talisman, an amulet; a small leather box containing slips inscribed with Scriptural passages.

phylum (fi' lum), *n.* one of the large, primary divisions into which plants and animals are divided, ranking below a kingdom and above an order.

***physic** (fiz' ik), *n.* a cathartic.

physic (fiz' ik), *v.t.* to administer cathartics.

physical (fiz' i kal), *adj.* relating to the body: opposite of *mental;* pertaining to nature, material, natural; pertaining to the science of physics or the laws and forces of physics, as *physical* computations.

    Syn. Bodily, corporal, corporeal. *Bodily* means definitely of or belonging to the body, as *bodily* ills; it is the opposite of *mental; physical* also means bodily, but embraces everything in the material world; it is the opposite of *spiritual* or *physical; corporal* means bodily, but is used to describe infliction, as *corporal* punishment; *corporeal* means having a body; it is the opposite of *immaterial.*

    Ant. Mental, spiritual, immaterial.

*__physician__ (fi zish' an), *n.* a doctor of medicine.

*__physicist__ (fiz' i sist), *n.* a student of physics or the natural sciences.

physics (fiz' iks), *n. pl.* the science of matter, motion and energy.

*__physiognomy__ (fiz i og' nō mi), *n.* [*pl.* physiognomies] the face; facial expression of character; the art of identifying qualities of mind through interpretation of facial characteristics.

physiology (fiz i ol' ō ji), *n.* [*pl.* physiologies] the science that treats of the vital functions performed by the organs of animals and plants; a book on this science.

*__physique__ (fi zēk'), *n.* the whole physical constitution of a person.

*__pianist__ (pi an' ist), *n.* one who plays the piano.

*__piano__ (pi an' ō), *n.* [*pl.* pianos] a musical instrument played by striking keys which in turn cause hammers to strike wires of various lengths and tensions.

*__pianoforte__ (pi an ō for' tē), *n.* a piano.

*__piazza__ (pi az' a), *n.* a plaza; an open space surrounded by buildings; a veranda.

*__pica__ (pī' ka), *n.* a size of type, 12 point; a unit of type measure 1/6 inch, to measure column width or the length of a line of type.

*__picayune__ (pik a yōōn'), *n.* a certain small silver coin of old times; anything of trifling value. *adj.* of little value, paltry.

piccolo (pik' ō lō), *n.* [*pl.* piccolos] a small flute sounding an octave higher than the ordinary flute.

pick (pik), *n.* a tool for loosening earth or breaking stone, consisting of a curved iron bar with two sharp ends set on a stout wooden handle. *n.* choice, as take your *pick. v.t.* to strike with a pick or as if with a pick; to open with a pointed tool, as to *pick* a lock; to pluck, as to *pick* apples; lift, as *pick* it up; to choose or select, as *pick* the one that will do the most good; to rob, as *pick* pockets.

pickax (pik' ax), *n.* a pick, with one end of the iron bar bladed for chopping, the other pointed for picking.

pickerel (pik' ēr el), *n.* a freshwater foodfish of the pike family, smaller than a pike.

picket (pik' et), *n.* a fence paling; a stake to which a horse is tethered; a patrol of union workers before a shop where nonunion labor is employed or where the practices are unfair to the workers, as during a strike; a military guard stationed outside the lines to give warning of the approach of an enemy. *v.i. and v.t.* to act as a picket; to tether, as a horse; to place a picket guard; to place pickets outside a shop in time of strike; to patrol in front of such a shop.

pickle (pik' l), *n.* brine for preserving food; anything preserved in brine or vinegar, especially a small cucumber.

picnic (pik' nik), *n.* a short pleasure trip by a party carrying its own food to be eaten outdoors. *v.i.* [*p.t. and p.p.* picnicked, *pr.p.* picnicking] to go on or hold a picnic; to eat as informally as when on a picnic.

pictorial (pik tō' ri al), *adj.* having pictures; told in pictures, as a story.

picture (pik' tūr), *n.* a painting, drawing or photograph depicting something, as persons, objects, landscapes; a mental image or representation; an embodiment, as he is the *picture* of health; a scene suitable for reproduction in a painting or drawing, as isn't that child a *picture. v.t.* to depict; to represent in a painting or drawing, or in descriptive words, as who could *picture* that scene.

picturesque (pik tūr esk'), *adj.* like a picture, vivid, striking, colorful.

pie (pī), *n.* a food dish consisting of filling made of meat, fruit, custard or the like, baked between two pastry crusts or in one bottom crust.

*__piece__ (pēs), *n.* a separated part; fragment; division, as a *piece* of land; a quantity used as a unit in manufacture, as a *piece* of goods; one of a set, as each *piece* in this set of dishes, a *piece* in a chess set; a unit of work, as we hire them to work by the *piece;* a coin, as a 50-cent *piece;* a literary or musical composition, as that was a pretty *piece* you played.

piece (pēs), *v.t.* to patch; to put together, piece by piece.

piecemeal (pēs' mēl), *adv.* piece by piece, gradually.

*__pied__ (pīd), *adj.* variegated, spotted, piebald.

*__pier__ (pēr), *n.* a mass of masonry supporting an arch, as of a bridge; a projecting wharf or dock.

*__pierce__ (pērs), *v.t.* to penetrate, especially with a pointed instrument, to perforate; to thrust into or through, to stab; to break through, as an enemy's lines in war.

piety (pī' eti), *n.* [*pl.* pieties] the quality of being pious; reverence for God and a sense of duty toward Him; a pious act.

pig (pig), *n.* the young of swine; a swine; a mass of molten metal poured into a mold to cool and harden.

*__pigeon__ (pij' un), *n.* a bird of the dove family, often domesticated.

pigeonhole (pij' un hōl), *n.* a compartment in a desk for papers.

pigment (pig' ment), *n.* coloring matter; the coloring matter in animals and plants.

pike (pīk), *n.* a voracious freshwater fish.

pilaster (pi las' tēr), *n.* a rectangular column or pillar, partly built into a wall.

pile (pīl), *n.* a large beam or pointed stake driven into the ground to make a foundation, ferry slip, wharf wall or similar structure. *n.* a mass or heap, a large building or group of buildings. *n.* close-set, high-standing threads or fibers of a thick fabric like velvet or a heavy carpet; standing hairs of fur. *v.t.* to heap up.

pilfer (pil' fēr), *v.t.* to steal in small quantities.

pilgrim (pil' grim), *n.* one who travels; especially one who goes to a distant place to pay homage or worship at a shrine.

pill (pil), *n.* a small ball of medicinal substance.

pillage (pil' ij), *n.* the act of plundering; spoil, booty. *v.t.* to despoil; to rob, plunder and lay waste.

pillar (pil' ēr), *n.* a supporting column; a monumental shaft.

Syn. Column. The word *pillar* is the general term and carries the idea of strength and support; *column,* on the other hand, is used only in connection with fine architecture and usually refers to a type or order, as a Doric *column.*

pillion (pil' yun), *n.* a cushion fastened behind a horse's saddle for a woman or child to ride on.

pillow (pil' ō), *n.* a case filled with feathers or some soft stuffing material, used as a head rest. *v.t.* to rest on a pillow or as on a pillow, as to *pillow* one's head; to furnish with a soft cushion.

pilot (pī' lut), *n.* one who steers a ship or aircraft; the cowcatcher of a locomotive; a mechanical device regulating action or motion. *v.t.* to guide, steer, direct on a course.

*****pimento** (pi men' tō), *n.* [*pl.* pimentos] allspice; pimiento.

*****pimiento** (pē myen' tō), *n.* [*pl.* pimientos] a variety of sweet pepper used in salads and as a flavoring for cheese.

pimpernel (pim' pēr nel), *n.* a plant of the primrose family with blooms that close when bad weather is coming.

pimple (pim' pl), *n.* a small pustule.

pin (pin), *n.* a short, sharp-pointed piece of wire, with a head, used to fasten pieces of cloth or paper together; any kind of peg to hold parts together, as in machine. *v.t.* to fasten together with any kind of pin.

pinafore (pin' a fōr), *n.* a loose apron.

*****pincers** (pin' sērz), *n. pl.* an instrument with which to grip and hold, having two handles and two grips working on a hinged fulcrum.

pinch (pinch), *n.* a squeeze or nip, as he gave me a *pinch,* a *pinch* of salt; an emergency, as in a *pinch. v.t.* squeeze or nip; economize.

pine (pīn), *n.* a cone-bearing evergreen tree with needlelike leaves; the wood of this tree. *v.i.* to waste away, as from grief or anxiety.

pineapple (pīn' apl), *n.* a tropical plant; its cone-shaped, edible fruit.

pine needle (pīn nē' dl), the leaf of the pine.

pinion (pin' yun), *n.* the last joint of a bird's wing; a wing; a feather. *n.* the smaller of two geared wheels. *v.t.* to bind or secure, as by binding the wings or arms; to confine.

pink (pingk), *n.* a color made by mixing red and white; a pale red. *n.* a garden flower with spicy fragrance. *v.t.* to punch small round holes into; to scallop the edge of, as cloth, in dressmaking.

pinnacle (pin' a kl), *n.* a small turret on the top of a building, generally with a spire; the peak or summit of anything, as the *pinnacle* of fame.

pint (pint), *n.* one-eighth of a gallon, liquid measure.

pioneer (pī ō nēr'), *n.* an early settler in a frontier land; one who builds roads in advance of an army on the march; one who is first in experiments or exploration, as Marconi was a radio pioneer. *v.i. and v.t.* to settle early in a frontier region; to lead the way in any advance or development; to open up, as new unbroken country.

*****pious** (pī' us), *adj.* dutiful to God, reverent, religious.

pip (pip), *n.* a small seed, as of an apple; a disease of poultry; a spot on a playing card or a domino.

pipe (pīp), *n.* a long hollow tube; a tube with a bowl at one end for smoking tobacco, opium or the like; a musical instrument having a tube or tubes of wood, reed or metal.

pipe (pīp), *v.i. and v.t.* to make a shrill sound; to whistle a tune; to equip with pipes, as to *pipe* a house; to carry through tubes, as to *pipe* gas into a city; to call with a pipe, as to *pipe* all hands on deck.

pippin (pip' in), *n.* a variety of apple.

*****piquancy** (pē' kan si), *n.* [*pl.* piquancies] the quality of being agreeably stimulating to the palate or provoking to the mind.

*****piquant** (pē' kant), *adj.* pleasantly sharp to the taste; stimulating or provocative, as *piquant* comment; keen and clever, as *piquant* wit.

*****pique** (pēk), *n.* resentment, offense, wounded pride. *v.t.* to wound the pride of, sting the feelings of.

piracy (pī' ra si), *n.* [*pl.* piracies] robbery of vessels on the high seas; infringement of a copyright on a literary work or of a patent.

pirate (pī' rit), *n.* one who plunders ships on high seas; one who infringes copyright or patent. *v.i. and v.t.* to practice robbery; to publish a literary work in infringement of a copyright; to take without permission or compensation.

*****pirouette** (pir oo et'), *n.* a dancer's whirl on the toes; a comparable whirl by a horse.

pirouette (pir oo et'), *v.i.* to whirl on the toes.

*****piscatorial** (pis ka tō' ri al), *adj.* relating to fish or to fishing.

*****pismire** (pis' mir), *n.* an ant.

pistil (pis' til), *n.* the seed-bearing organ in the center of a flower.

pistillate (pis' ti lāt), *adj.* having pistils.

pistol (pis' tl), *n.* a small short-barreled hand gun.

piston (pis' tun), *n.* a small disk or cylinder fitting exactly and moving up and down in the barrel of a pump or the cylinder of an engine; a sliding valve in a musical wind instrument.

pit (pit), *n.* a deep hole in the earth; a hollowed part of the body, as the arm*pit;* a depression in the skin, like the *pits* left by smallpox; a depressed space in which a contest of animals is held, as a cock*pit;* the shaft of a mine; the lowest part of a theater; part of a commodity exchange for special trading, as the grain *pit.*

pit (pit), *v.t.* to mark with hollows or holes; to match in a contest, as to *pit* my wits against yours; to place in a pit; to remove the pits of fruit.

pitch (pich), *n.* the solid black resinous stuff that remains after coal tar is distilled; a slope or plunge forward or down, as the *pitch* of a roof; a degree, as a high *pitch* of feeling; the height or depth of a tone, determined by the speed of vibration.

pitch (pich), *v.i. and v.t.* to slope; to plunge; to hurl or throw; to set up, as to *pitch* a tent; to set the key for, as to *pitch* the voice high or low.

pitcher (pich' ẽr), *n.* an earthen or metal vessel having a handle and a spout, used to pour liquids.

pitchy (pich' ĭ), *adj.* [*comp.* pitchier, *superl.* pitchiest] full of pitch, like pitch or smeared with pitch.

piteous (pit' ē us), *adj.* exciting pity; showing pity.

Syn. Doleful, woeful, rueful. *Piteous* is applicable to one's external expression of body or to one's state of mental pain. A child makes *piteous* lamentations when it suffers from hunger or has lost its way. *Doleful* applies to those sounds which convey the idea of pain; there is something *doleful* in the tolling of a funeral bell or in the sound of a muffled drum. *Woeful* applies to the circumstances and situations of men; a scene is *woeful* in which we witness a family of young children suffering from sickness and want. *Rueful* applies to the outward manifestations of inward sorrow depicted in the looks or countenance.

Ant. Happy, cheerful, joyous.

pitfall (pit' fŏl), *n.* a pit lightly covered over so that wild beasts may fall into it; any unrecognized source of danger, as the *pitfalls* of life in a great city.

pith (pith), *n.* the soft spongy substance inside a plant stem; marrow; quintessence, substance, force.

pithy (pith' ĭ), *adj.* [*comp.* pithier, *superl.* pithiest] having the nature of, or being filled with, pith; forcible, terse and pointed, as a *pithy* remark.

pitiable (pit' ĭ a bl), *adj.* commanding or worthy of pity; insignificant.

pitiful (pit' ĭ fool), *adj.* moving to compassion; full of pity; worthy of contempt, pitiable.

pitiless (pit' ĭ les), *adj.* without pity or compassion, merciless.

pittance (pit' ans), *n.* a small allowance, portion or wage.

pity (pit' ĭ), *n.* [*pl.* pities] sympathy for those in distress; compassion; a cause for distress, something to be regretted, as it's a *pity.*

Syn. Compassion, sympathy. *Pity* is excited principally by the distress, weakness or degraded condition of another; *compassion* is deep sympathy for the sufferings of another; *sympathy* is the fellow feeling for the pain or distress of another.

pivot (piv' ut), *n.* a point on which something turns or revolves.

pivot (piv' ut), *v.i. and v.t.* to turn on a pivot; to supply with a pivot.

pizza (pēt ´ sa), *n.* a doughy crust overlaid with tomato sauce, spices, and cheese.

*****placability** (plă ka bil' ĭ tĭ), *n.* the quality of being easily pacified or appeased.

*****placable** (plā' ka bl), *adj.* easy to appease or satisfy.

*****placard** (plak' ärd), *n.* a card shown in public, giving notice of some forthcoming event or advertising something.

*****placard** (pla kärd'), *v.t.* to announce or advertise with placards.

*****placate** (plā' kāt), *v.t.* to appease or pacify.

place (plās), *n.* a special spot, location or locality; a city square; situation; site; station in life, as he knows his *place.*

place (plās), *v.t.* to put in any situation; to recognize, as I don't *place* you; to arrange, as to *place* a loan; to repose, as to *place* faith or trust in an associate.

*****placer** (plas' ẽr), *n.* a surface mineral deposit, distinguished from a vein of ore.

placid (plas' id), *adj.* calm, peaceful.

*****plagiarism** (plā' jĭ a rizm), *n.* literary theft, passing off as one's own the words or ideas of another.

plagiarist (plā' jĭ a rist), *n.* one who steals the ideas, words or phrases of another and passes them off as his own.

*****plague** (plāg), *n.* a malignant epidemic; anything exceedingly troublesome or annoying.

*****plaid** (plad), *n.* a checkered woolen cloth; the distinctive checkered pattern of Scottish tartans.

plain (plān), *n.* a stretch of level ground.

*****plain** (plān), *adj.* level, flat; smooth; simple; clear, evident.

plaint (plānt), *n.* lamentation; complaint.

plaintiff (plān' tĭf), *n.* the complainant in a suit at law.

plaintive (plān' tĭv), *adj.* mournful; expressing grief or sorrow.

*****plait** (plēt), *n.* a flat fold of cloth doubled over upon itself; a pleat. *v.t.* to double over in folds, as cloth. *v.t.* to braid, as hair.

plait (plat), *n.* braid of hair.

plan (plan), *n.* a drawing on paper showing the outline and construction of anything, as a house; a scheme or project.

plan (plan), *v.t.* to design; to form a plan for.

plane (plān), *n.* a flat surface; a flat supporting surface of an airplane. *n.* a broad-leaved tree, one variety of which is the sycamore. *n.* a carpenter's tool for smoothing a wooden surface, making it flat and even. *v.t.*

to smooth with a plane.

*planet (plan' et), *n.* a heavenly body revolving around the sun.

planetary (plan' e ter i), *adj.* having to do in any way with the being or nature of a planet.

plank (plangk), *n.* a long, heavy board; an item in a political party platform.

plant (plånt), *n.* any vegetable organism; the machinery or fixtures, with buildings, of a business, enterprise or institution.

plant (plånt), *v.t.* to place in the ground to grow; to establish, as an idea or an institution; to stock, as to *plant* a river with trout.

*plantain (plan' tin), *n.* a tropical tree yielding an edible fruit similar to the banana; a common weed that grows almost everywhere.

planter (plån' tẽr), *n.* one who plants; the owner of a plantation.

*plaque (plak), *n.* a thin, flat plate of metal or other substance, carved or ornamented.

plash (plash), *n.* a small pool of water; the sound of water splashing. *v.i. and v.t.* to splash; to dash with water; to interweave the twigs of, as to *plash* a hedge.

*plasma (plaz' ma), *n.* the colorless fluid of the blood in which the red corpuscles float; the fluid in muscle; protoplasm.

plaster (plås' tẽr), *n.* a composition of lime, sand and water to coat a wall; a substance with healing qualities spread on cloth and applied to an affected part of the body to ease the pain and cure the disease. *v.i. and v.t.* to spread plaster; to spread like a plaster; to spread with a plaster.

plastic (plas' tik), *adj.* capable of being formed or molded in desired shapes, as wax is *plastic*; easily impressed, as a *plastic* nature; formative, creative. *n.* sculpture, the art of modeling; a product of synthetic chemistry, like celluloid or bakelite.

plat (plat), *n.* a braid; a plot of ground.

plate (plåt), *n.* a thin flat piece of hard substance, as metal, porcelain, wood or glass; a shallow round dish from which to eat; a plateful, as a *plate* of food; dishes and utensils, especially those made of precious metals; a metal surface engraved for reproduction. *v.t.* to coat, as a metal, with another metal, especially by electrolysis; to make a duplicate printing plate from an original.

*plateau (pla tō'), *n.* [*pl.* plateaux] a tableland; a stretch of high, flat land.

platen (plat' n), *n.* flat part or bed of printing press where paper is pressed down on type; typewriter roller around which paper passes.

platform (plat' fôrm), *n.* a flat floor of wood or stone raised above the ground; a political party's declaration of policy.

platinum (plat' i num), *n.* a grayish-white metal, very hard and ductile, resisting rust, hard to melt and highly valued in the making of chemical utensils and settings for jewelry.

platitude (plat' i tūd), *n.* insipidity; dullness; a stale, trite remark.

platitudinous (plat i tū' di nus), *adj.* commonplace, trite.

platoon (pla tōon'), *n.* a body of soldiers, consisting of four squads of 8 men each; a similar squad in the organization of a police system.

platter (plat' ẽr), *n.* a large flat dish from which food is served.

plaudit (plô' dit), *n.* applause, clapping, approval.

*plausible (plô' zi bl), *adj.* specious; seeming true, but not proved true; easily believed but possibly not meriting belief.

play (plå), *n.* sport; light, quick, irregular motion, as the *play* of light over a surface; freedom for action, as the *play* of a steering wheel; action or use, as to bring all one's powers into *play*. *v.i. and v.t.* to have fun, as in a game; to run and frolic, as the children are *playing;* to move lightly, flicker, as light *plays* over a surface; to imitate for fun, as to *play* soldiers; to act the character of, as to *play* Macbeth; to take part in, as a game, as to *play* ball; to make music on, as to *play* the piano.

playful (plå' fool), *adj.* sportive; gay, lively.

*plaza (plå' za), *n.* an open square or marketplace.

plea (plē), *n.* [*pl.* pleas] an excuse or apology; urgent entreaty; legal pleading, as court of common *pleas*.

plead (plēd), *v.i. and v.t.* to argue before a court of law; to supplicate; to discuss or defend by arguments; to offer as an excuse, as I can only *plead* illness.

pleasant (plez' ant), *adj.* grateful to the senses or the mind; delightful; cheerful.

Syn. Agreeable, pleasing. *Pleasant* are those qualities in a person or thing that gives pleasure; *pleasing* describes the effect the pleasant person or thing has upon us; *agreeable* means harmonious to the taste or wish.

Ant. Disagreeable, unpleasant.

pleasantry (plez' ant ri), *n.* [*pl.* pleasantries] a merry trick or joke; a good-natured quip.

please (plēz), *v.i. and v.t.* to have the wish, as if you *please;* to give pleasure to; to gratify.

pleasure (plezh' ẽr), *n.* gratification; agreeable emotions or sensations; delight; enjoyment; diversion, recreation.

*plebeian (plē bē' yan), *adj.* pertaining to the common people.

*plebiscite (pleb' i sīt), *n.* the vote of the common people, especially the direct vote of all the people of a region on a question of public policy.

pledge (plej), *n.* a promise; anything placed as security. *v.i. and v.t.* to make a promise or pledge; to place as security.

*plenary (plē' na ri), *adj.* full; complete; absolute, as *plenary* powers.

*plenipotentiary (plen i pō ten' shi er i), *n.* [*pl.* plenipotentiaries] an agent sent abroad with full power to represent his government. *adj.* having full power.

*plenitude (plen' i tūd), *n.* fulness, abundance.

*plenteous (plen' tē us), *adj.* abundant; amply sufficient.

plentiful (plen' ti fool), *adj.* existing in great

quantity; yielding abundantly.

plenty (plen' ti), *n.* [*pl.* plenties] abundance; a sufficiency, as that is *plenty*.

pleonasm (plē' ō nazm), *n.* use of extra, unnecessary words in speaking or writing.

***plethora** (pleth' ō ra), *n.* overabundance.

pleura (ploor' a), *n.* [*pl.* pleurae] a delicate serous membrane covering the interior of the thorax and the surface of each lung.

***pleurisy** (ploor' i si), *n.* inflammation of the pleura.

plexus (plek' sus), *n.* [*pl.* plexus or plexuses] a network, as of blood vessels or nerves.

pliability (pli a bil' i ti), *n.* the quality of being pliable or bending easily, flexibility.

pliable (pli' a bl), *adj.* easily bent; easily influenced.

pliant (pli' ant), *adj.* easily bent or bending, flexible; yielding readily to moral suasion.

pliers (pli' ērz), *n.* *pl.* small pincers used for seizing and bending wires and like articles.

***plight** (plit), *n.* an unfavorable situation or distressed condition, as a sorry *plight*.

plight (plit), *v.t.* to pledge, as to plight troth, one's hand, one's honor.

plinth (plinth), *n.* the lowest square part of the base of a column or pedestal.

plod (plod), *v.i.* to travel laboriously; to drudge, toil slowly and patiently, as he *plods* through his lessons.

plot (plot), *n.* a small, marked-off piece of ground; a scheme or secret plan; the plan of a story or play, with complications to be worked out at the end.

plot (plot), *v.i. and v.t.* to scheme or plan; to conspire; to make a plan or map of; to contrive complications for a story or play.

***plover** (pluv' ēr), *n.* a shore bird resembling the sandpiper but having a shorter bill and plumper, more compact body.

***plow, plough** (plou), *n.* a farm implement for turning the soil over before planting; a similar implement for turning packed substances aside, as a snow*plow*.

plow (plou), *v.t.* to turn or move with a plow, as to *plow* a field, *plow* a path through the snow.

plowshare (plou' shâr), *n.* the blade of a plow, the part that cuts the soil.

pluck (pluk), *n.* courage; the heart, liver and lungs of an animal or fowl.

pluck (pluk), *v.t.* to pick or gather, as fruit or flowers; to twitch, twang, as the strings of an instrument, as to *pluck* a guitar; to take the feathers from, as *pluck* this chicken.

plucky (pluk' i), *adj.* [*comp.* pluckier, *superl.* pluckiest] having plenty of courage.

plug (plug), *n.* a piece of wood or other substance to stop a hole. *v.t.* to stop, as a hole, with a plug.

plum (plum), *n.* a fruit tree; its fruit, smooth-skinned, juicy, and having a stone or pit; a prize; something worth struggling for.

plumage (ploom' ij), *n.* the feathering of a bird.

***plumb** (plum), *n.* a heavy body, usually a lump of lead, suspended at the extremity of a line to test the perpendicularity of something, as a post or wall; a similar weight on a line to measure the depth of water; perpendicular position, as out of *plumb*.

plumb (plum), *v.t.* to test with a plumb line; to measure the depth of with a plumb line; to penetrate, as depths; to solve, as a mystery. (plum), *adv.* vertically, perpendicularly, exactly.

plumber (plum' ēr), *n.* one who engages in the business of installing or repairing water and gas pipes, cisterns and other fixtures.

plumcot (plum' kot), *n.* a fruit resulting from crossing the plum and the apricot.

plume (plūm), *n.* a feather; crest. *v.t.* to adjust the feathers of, as a bird *plumes* itself; to preen; to take pride in, as he *plumes* himself on his ability.

plummet (plum' et), *n.* a lead weight attached to a line and used for sounding water depths or determining a true vertical.

plump (plump), *adj.* round and sleek.

plump (plump), *adv.* suddenly, heavily, directly, as he fell *plump* into the lake.

plump (plump), *v.i. and v.t.* to drop or fall heavily; to drop, cast or plunge all at once or suddenly and heavily, as to *plump* oneself or another down on a bench.

plumy (ploom' i), *adj.* [*comp.* plumier, *superl.* plumiest] feathered; adorned with feathers.

plunder (plun'dēr), *n.* pillage, loot. *v.t.* to loot, take by force, as in war.

plunge (plunj), *n.* a sudden dive; a headlong fall; a forward rush.

plunge (plunj), *v.i. and v.t.* to dive or leap forward; to throw or push into a liquid.

pluperfect (ploo' pûr fekt), *adj.* denoting an action completed prior to some other past action, as I was there early, but the car *had gone*; also called *past perfect*.

***plural** (ploor' al), *n.* the form of a word denoting more than one, as men is the *plural* of man. *adj.* consisting of more than one, as *plural* marriage.

plurality (ploo ral' i ti), *n.* [*pl.* pluralities] the state of consisting of more than one; in a two-party contest, the majority; in a three-party election, the greatest number of votes for one ticket; the margin of one vote over another, as A had a *plurality* of 937 over B.

***plus** (plus), *n.* the sign (+) indicating that addition is to be performed: opposite of *minus*. *adj.* indicating addition, as the *plus* sign; positive, not negative.

***plush** (plush), *n.* a heavy cloth with a pile longer and softer than velvet.

***plutocracy** (ploo tok' ra si), *n.* [*pl.* plutocracies] rule by the rich.

plutocrat (ploo' tō krat), *n.* one who has influence or power through his great wealth.

ply (pli), *n.* [*pl.* plies] a fold or twist, as in fabrics: frequently used in combination to show the number of folds, as three-*ply*. *v.i.* [*p.t.* and *p.p.* plied, *pr.p.* plying] to run on schedule between two ports. *v.t.* [*p.t.* and *p.p.* plied, *pr.p.* plying] to work at, as to *ply* a trade; to wield, as to *ply* an ax

***pneumatic** (nū mat' ik), *adj.* pertaining to air; inflated with air, as a rubber tire:

operated by air pressure, as a machine.

pneumatics (nū mat′ iks), *n.* the science that treats of the physical properties and phenomena of air or gas.

*pneumonia (nū mō′ ni a), *n.* acute inflammation of the lungs.

*poach (pōch), *v.i.* to trespass; to hunt on another's posted property. *v.t.* to cook in boiling water or other liquid, especially an egg.

pock (pok), *n.* a pustule on the skin containing eruptive matter.

pocket (pok′ et), *n.* a bag worked permanently into an article of clothing, as coat, trousers or skirt, to hold small articles; any cavity to hold things; a deposit of ore apart from the main vein; a space where the density of the air differs from that in the surrounding region. *v.t.* to put into a pocket; to conceal, suppress, as to pocket one's pride.

pod (pod), *n.* covering of certain seeds, as of pea and bean, holding the seeds in a row. *v.i. and v.t.* to form into pods; to remove from the pod.

podiatry (pō di′ a tri), *n.* the science and care of diseases of the feet.

*poem (pō′ em), *n.* a verse composition, with meter and with or without rhyme, expressing fine thoughts in a beautiful manner.

poet (pō′ et), *n.* one who writes verse.

poetic (pō et′ ik), *adj.* having the form or spirit of poetry; suitable for expression in a poem.

poetry (pō′ et ri), *n.* the art of writing poems; expression of fine thought in metrical forms.

*poignancy (poin′ yan si), *n.* the quality of being keen, piercing.

*poignant (poin′ yant), *adj.* keen, stinging, as *poignant* wit; painfully affecting, as *poignant* grief.

*poinsettia (poin set′ i a), *n.* a Central American plant with showy flowers.

point (point), *n.* a sharp end. as the *point* of a needle; a projection of land into water; an outstanding feature, as he has good *points;* a special application, as the *point* of a story; a mark of punctuation; an exact spot, as the *point* where roads meet; an exact condition, as indicated by a degree on a scale, as the freezing *point;* the position of a dog when marking down game, as the dog came to a *point;* a unit in scoring in certain games.

point (point), *v.i. and v.t.* to indicate by directing a finger toward; to indicate in words, as to *point* out a fact; to aim, as to *point* a gun; to sharpen, as to *point* a pencil; to indicate the presence of game, as a dog does by assuming a certain pose.

point-blank (point blangk), *adj.* going straight to the mark, as a shot; direct, unqualified, as a *point-blank* refusal. *adv.* directly; without mincing words, as he asked the question *point-blank*, the gun was fired *point-blank*.

pointer (poin′ tēr), *n.* something that indicates position; a large hunting dog trained to stop and show the place where game is hidden.

*poise (poiz), *n.* equilibrium, balance, as mental *poise. v.i. and v.t.* to be in a state of equilibrium; to balance.

Syn. Balance. To *poise* is properly to keep the weight from pressing on either side; to *balance* is to keep the balance even. The idea of bringing to an equilibrium is common to both these terms, but a thing is *poised* as respects itself, *balanced* as respects other things.

poison (poi′ zn), *n.* anything noxious or destructive by chemical action to the life or health of a living body into which it is introduced.

Syn. Venom. *Poison* usually connotes something taken or administered in food or drink; *venom* is the *poison* secreted by certain serpents, spiders and scorpions that makes their bite injurious and sometimes fatal. *v.t.* to administer an injurious or deadly substance to, as to *poison* a dog; to infuse with poison, as to *poison* food; to corrupt, as to *poison* one's morals.

poke (pōk), *n.* a thrusting or pushing motion, as he gave me a *poke* with his cane; a projecting rim on front of woman's bonnet; wooden collar with stick hanging down from it, to prevent cattle from leaping fences. *v.i. and v.t.* to dawdle along; to prod, as with a stick; to thrust or push.

poker (pōk′ ēr), *n.* a metal bar for stirring up a fire. *n.* a card game with a pool of bets on their cards made by the players.

poky (pōk′ i), *adj.* [*comp.* pokier, *superl.* pokiest] cramped, shabby; dull, slow.

polar (pō′ lēr), *adj.* pertaining in any way to either pole of the earth.

polarity (pō lar′ i ti), *n.* the property possessed by certain bodies, by which they exert forces in opposite directions, with a positive pole having power to attract and a negative pole having power to repel.

pole (pōl), *n.* a long staff or rod, as a bean *pole;* a unit in land measure.

pole (pōl), *n.* either extremity of the axis of the earth; the region in a magnetized body where the greatest force of attraction or repulsion is exerted.

polecat (pōl′ kat), *n.* a skunk, a ferret.

polemic, polemical (pō lem′ ik, -i cal), *adj.* controversial.

polemics (pō lem′ iks), *n.* the art of disputation, especially in matters of theology.

polestar (pōl′ stär), *n.* the North Star; a directing principle.

*police (pō lēs′), *n.* an organized force of civil officers to preserve order in a municipality.

policy (pol′ i si), *n.* [*pl.* policies] management of affairs in the interest of the civic body; a particular course of action planned by a governing body in public relations or administration of government; course of conduct, as it is good *policy* to keep one's own counsel. *n.* [*pl.* policies] a contract of insurance.

polish (pol′ ish), *n.* the act of making smooth or glossy by rubbing; the fine finish obtained by rubbing; a substance used in polishing; fine manners. *v.t.* to make smooth or glossy by friction.

polite (pō līt'), *adj.* well-bred, refined, courteous.

Syn. Gentle, genteel. *Polite* implies culture and refinement; *gentle* denotes good or aristocratic birth; *genteel* has come to mean vulgar affectation of the qualities associated with good breeding.

Ant. Crude, coarse, boorish.

*politic** (pol' i tik), *adj.* shrewd, expedient, wise in policy.

political (pō lit' i kal), *adj.* pertaining to government.

politics (pol' i tiks), *n.* the art or science of government; matters connected with the selection of officers of government and their administration of office after being elected.

polity (pol' i ti), *n.* [*pl.* polities] the form or constitution of the civil government of a state; constitution of any organization similarly administered; political constitution.

polka (pōl' ka), *n.* a gay round dance Bohemian in origin.

*poll** (pōl), *n.* the head, especially the top and back parts, covered by hair; a register of qualified voters; a voting place; an election. *v.t.* to lop, clip or shear; to cast, as a ballot; to count the individual votes of, as to *poll* a jury; to receive votes, as he *polled* a large majority.

pollard (pol' ērd), *n.* a tree lopped back to the trunk to stimulate growth of foliage; a stag or ox without horns.

pollen (pol' en), *n.* the fertilizing powder in the cell of a flower anther.

polliwog (pol' i wog), *n.* a tadpole.

pollute (po lūt'), *v.t.* to defile, render unclean, taint, corrupt.

pollution (po lū' shun), *n.* the act of defiling or state of being defiled; that which taints or causes impurity.

polo (pō' lō), *n.* a game resembling hockey but played on horseback, with long-handled mallets.

poltroon (pol trōōn'), *n.* a skulking coward.

polyandry (pol' i an dri), *n.* the practice of having more than one husband at the same time.

polychrome (pol' i krōm), *adj.* in many colors, as polychrome statues.

*polygamy** (pō lig' a mi), *n.* the practice of having more than one wife at the same time.

polyglot (pol' i glot), *adj.* written in several languages; knowing many languages.

polygon (pol' i gon), *n.* a plane closed figure having many angles.

*polysyllabic** (pol i si lab' ik), *adj.* having more than two syllables.

polytechnic (pol i tek' nik), *adj.* giving instruction in a number of arts and sciences with special regard for their use in making a living, as a *polytechnic* school or institute.

polytheism (pol' i thē izm), *n.* the belief that there are many gods.

*pomade** (pō mād'), *n.* a perfumed ointment to dress the hair.

*pomato** (pō mā' tō), *n.* a plant produced by grafting tomato buds or shoots on potato

plants. The fruit is tomatolike, and is usually eaten raw in salads.

*pomegranate** (pom' gran it), *n.* a tree yielding a reddish berry about the size of an orange, with many seeds in a crimson pulp, and a pleasant, acid flavor.

pomelo (pom' e lō), *n.* the grapefruit or shaddock.

*pommel** (pum' el), *n.* the knob on a sword hilt; the high part of a saddle-bow.

pommel (pum' el), *v.t.* to beat and bruise.

pomology (pō mol' ō ji), *n.* the science of cultivating fruit trees.

pomp (pomp), *n.* ceremonious display, magnificence.

pompadour (pom' pa dōr), *n.* a manner of dressing the hair by brushing it straight back from the forehead without a part.

pompon (pom' pon), *n.* an ornamental ball of silk or feathers worn on a woman's costume or a soldier's uniform; a small buttonlike chrysanthemum.

pompous (pomp' us), *adj.* self-important, ostentatious.

poncho (pon' chō), *n.* a loose, Spanish-American cloak consisting of a blanket with a hole in the middle for the head; a similar cloak of rubber or other waterproof material.

pond (pond), *n.* a small lake.

ponder (pon' dēr), *v.t.* to deliberate; to weigh mentally, as to *ponder* a question.

ponderable (pon' dēr a bl), *adj.* capable of being weighed.

ponderous (pon' dēr us), *adj.* very heavy, dull.

pone (pōn), *n.* bread made of corn meal: also called corn *pone.*

pongee (pon jē'), *n.* a soft, light silken fabric.

*poniard** (pon' yērd), *n.* a small dagger.

pontiff (pon' tif), *n.* a bishop; the Pope.

*pontifical** (pon tif' i kal), *adj.* pertaining to a bishop, especially the Pope.

*pontoon** (pon tōōn'), *n.* a small, flat-bottomed boat; a buoyant, flat-bottomed structure supporting a floating military bridge; a buoyant structure on a hydroplane, used in coming down on water.

pony (pō' ni), *n.* [*pl.* ponies] a small horse.

*pool** (pōōl), *n.* a small body of still water, a pond. *n.* a game resembling billiards. *n.* a sum of money consisting of stakes put up by a number of persons betting together; a combination of natural competitors to control a market. *v.t.* to form a common fund; to put into a common fund, as to *pool* resources.

poop (pōōp), *n.* the raised deck in the stern of a ship.

*poor** (poor), *adj.* needy, having small means; deficient in quality, unsatisfactory, as a *poor* substitute; scanty, inadequate, as a *poor* harvest.

pop (pop), *n.* a short, snapping sound, as the *pop* of a firecracker; a soft drink.

pop (pop), *v.i.* to make a snapping sound; to burst open, like popcorn; to burst into sight, as he *popped* in on us.

pope (pōp), *n.* a priest of the Greek church: *the Pope,* the head of the Roman Catholic

Church.

poplar (pop' lẽr), *n.* a fast-growing tree with light wood.

poplin (pop' lin), *n.* a fabric of silk and worsted.

popover (pop' ō vẽr), *n.* a hotbread made of batter, milk and eggs that becomes a hollow shell when baked.

poppy (pop' ĭ), *n.* a plant with showy flowers, one species of which yields opium.

populace (pop' ū lĭs), *n.* the common people.

*popular (pop' ū lẽr), *adj.* pertaining to the common people; in general favor.

popularity (pop ū lar' ĭ tĭ), *n.* the state of being liked by many people.

popularize (pop' ū lẽr ĭz), *v.t.* to render popular, establish in general favor.

populate (pop' ū lāt), *v.t.* to furnish with inhabitants; to inhabit.

population (pop ū lā' shun), *n.* total number of inhabitants; the inhabitants collectively.

*populous (pop' ū lus), *adj.* thickly peopled.

*porcelain (pôr' se lĭn), *n.* a fine, white glazed earthenware; articles made of it.

*porch (pôrch), *n.* an open but roofed vestibule; a veranda.

porcupine (pôr' kū pĭn), *n.* a rodent having spines or quills in its hairy coat that it uses as weapons of defense in time of danger.

*pore (pôr), *n.* a minute hole in the skin through which perspiration passes. *v.i.* to read studiously: used with *over*.

*pork (pôrk), *n.* the flesh of swine used as meat.

porosity (pō ros' ĭ tĭ), *n.* the quality of having pores; the state of being permeable by liquids.

porous (pō' rus), *adj.* having pores; permeable by liquids.

porphyry (pôr' fĭ rĭ), *n.* [*pl.* porphyries] a hard fine-grained stone embedded with small crystal grains.

*porpoise (pôr' pus), *n.* the sea hog, an animal of the whale family from 5 to 8 feet long; the bottle-nosed dolphin.

porridge (por' ĭj), *n.* oatmeal boiled slowly in water until it thickens.

porringer (por' in jẽr), *n.* a small dish for porridge, broth or similar foods.

port (pôrt), *n.* a place where ships come in, unload, reload and depart; a harbor; a place of refuge, as any *port* in a storm. *n.* a round window in the side of a ship. *n.* the left side of a ship as one faces the bow. *n.* a wine originally made in Portugal; a wine resembling it. *v.t.* to place so that the upper end is to the left, as a rifle, as *port* arms; to turn to the left, as a ship, as *port* your helm.

portable (pôr' ta bl), *adj.* able to be carried; easy to carry.

portage (pôr' tĭj), *n.* the carrying of boats and supplies overland from one navigable body of water to another.

portal (pôr' tal), *n.* a gate or entrance, especially an archway.

*portent (pôr' tent), *n.* an omen, especially of impending evil.

portentous (pôr ten' tus), *adj.* ominous, threatening.

porter (pôr' tẽr), *n.* the keeper of a door or gate; one whose occupation is to carry baggage for passengers or do errands for pay, as for guests at a hotel; one who serves passengers on sleeping cars.

*portfolio (pôrt fō' lĭ ō), *n.* [*pl.* portfolios] a portable case for loose papers; the office or duties of the head of a governmental department.

porthole (pôrt' hōl), *n.* a round opening in the side of a ship, as for a window.

*portico (pôr' tĭ kō), *n.* [*pl.* porticos] a structure like a porch, with a roof supported by columns.

portiere (pôr tyâr'), *n.* a curtain or piece of drapery hung across a doorway.

*portion (pôr' shun), *n.* a piece or part, a share; a helping of food.

portly (pôrt' lĭ), *adj.* dignified in bearing; corpulent.

*portrait (pôr' trāt), *n.* a painting of a person; a fine photograph of a person's face or whole figure; a word picture of a person.

*portraiture (pôr' trāt tūr), *n.* the art of making portraits; the art of describing persons in words that produce clear pictures.

portray (pôr trā'), *v.t.* to paint or draw the likeness of, depict, delineate.

*pose (pōz), *n.* attitude or position of the body; an assumed mental attitude, affectation, as his interest in the common people is only a *pose. v.i. and v.t.* to assume a particular attitude or position, as to *pose* for a photograph; to fix in place, as to *pose* a subject for a painting; to present as a proposition or puzzling question.

*position (pō zish' un), *n.* the state of being set or placed; the place where a person or thing is set, in relation to others; an attitude of mind or body, as his *position* in the debate was untenable; employment; the placement of troops; the ground to be held against attack.

Syn. Posture, attitude, pose. The *position* is that in which a body is placed in respect to other bodies, as standing with one's back toward another is a *position*. A *posture* is that *position* which a body assumes with respect to itself, as a sitting or reclining *posture; attitude* is posture consciously or unconsciously expressive of a mood or feeling; *pose* is an attitude deliberately assumed.

positive (poz' ĭ tĭv), *adj.* clearly expressed; strongly affirmative; having a clear, strong character of its own; not subject to change, as *positive* instructions; having as the elementary unit the proton, having on its surface more protons than electrons. *n.* that which is affirmative, active, effective in any sense; a photographic plate, film or slide reproducing the light and shade of the original: more than zero, as a positive number: opposite of *negative*.

positron (poz' ĭ tron), *n.* a particle produced in the breaking up of atoms, like an electron with positive instead of negative charge.

*posse (pos' ē), *n.* a force of men brought together by a sheriff for special duty, as to hunt down a criminal.

*possess (po zes'), *v.t.* to own, to have and keep; to enter into and control, as the passion for wealth *possessed* him.

possession (po zesh' un), *n.* ownership; occupancy; anything possessed: frequently in the plural, as his *possessions* are great.

*possessive (po zes' iv), *adj.* denoting ownership or a desire to own, as a *possessive* nature or manner, the *possessive* case.

possessor (po zes' ẽr), *n.* owner, one who possesses.

posset (pos' et), *n.* a drink of hot milk curdled with wine or ale and spiced.

possibility (pos i bil' i ti), *n.* [*pl.* possibilities] the state of being possible; something that is possible; potentiality, as the plan has great *possibilities*.

possible (pos' i bl), *adj.* capable of happening or being done.

post (pōst), *n.* an upright piece, as of timber, supporting a structure. *n.* the system of carrying mail. *n.* a place where one is stationed in the line of duty; a place of trust; a military station. *v.t.* to publish, as if by nailing a placard to a post; to place on a list; to mail; to transfer from journal to ledge, as an entry in bookkeeping; to station at a post of duty, as a soldier.

postage (pōs' tij), *n.* the charge for carrying in the mail; the sum paid for such carriage.

postal (pōs' tal), *adj.* of or pertaining to the post office or mail service, as *postal* rates.

poster (pōs' tẽr), *n.* a large advertising placard.

*posterior (pōs tēr' i ẽr), *adj.* subsequent in time or place; hinder.

posterity (pos ter' i ti), *n.* [*pl.* posterities] succeeding generations; descendants.

postgraduate (pōst grad' ū āt), *adj.* of or pertaining to studies pursued after graduation from a school or college. *n.* one who is studying after receiving an academic degree.

posthaste (pōst hāst'), *adv.* with great speed.

*posthumous (pōs' tū mus), *adj.* born after the death of the father; published after the death of the author; occurring after one's death, as *posthumous* fame.

*postilion (pōs til' yun), *n.* the rider on the near-side leader of a four-horse team.

postmaster (pōst' mås tẽr), *n.* the superintendent of a post office.

postmeridian (pōst mē rid' i an), *adj.* after noon.

post-mortem (pōst môr tem), *adj.* occurring, made or done after death, as a *post-mortem* examination.

*postpone (pōst pōn'), *v.t.* to put off, delay, defer.

postponement (pōst pōn' ment), *n.* the act of deferring to a future time.

*postscript (pōst' skript), *n.* matter added to a letter or document after the writer has signed it.

postulate (pos' tū lāt), *n.* a self-evident proposition, accepted without requirement of proof. *v.t.* to assume without requirement of proof.

posture (pos' tẽr), *n.* attitude; the placing or position of parts of the body; physical carriage, bearing; a mental attitude.

postwar (pōst wôr ´), *adj.* after a war.

posy (pō' zi), *n.* [*pl.* posies] a flower or a bunch of flowers, bouquet.

pot (pot), *n.* a metal vessel for holding liquids or boiling them; an earthenware vessel, as a bean *pot*, tea*pot*, flower*pot*.

pot (pot), *v.t.* to put in a pot, as to *pot* a plant; to preserve in a pot, as to *pot* ham.

pot (pät), *n.* slang for marijuana.

potash (pot' ash), *n.* a powerful alkali obtained from wood ashes.

potassium (pō tas' ium), *n.* a silvery-white metallic element found in soils and mineral deposits and in various compounds, and used in photography, electroplating and tanning.

potation (pō tā' shun), *n.* a draft or drink; the act of drinking, especially liquor.

potato (pō tā' tō), *n.* [*pl.* potatoes] the edible tuber of a widely cultivated plant, one of mankind's staple foods.

potent (pō' tent), *adj.* powerful; having great authority.

potentate (pō' ten tāt), *n.* one who possesses great power; a mighty ruler.

*potential (pō ten' shal), *adj.* possible; not actually existing, but imaginable or expectable; latent.

*potion (pō' shun), *n.* a draft or drink.

potluck (pot luk), *n.* whatever may be provided for a meal; informal hospitality.

potpie (pot' pī), *n.* a meat pie cooked in a pot, especially with dumplings.

*potpourri (pō pōō rē'), *n.* a dish composed of various kinds of meats and vegetables; a medley.

pot shot (pot shot), an unsportsmanlike shot to secure food.

pottage (pot' ij), *n.* a stew or rich soup of meat and vegetables.

pottery (pot' ẽr i), *n.* [*pl.* potteries] earthenware of all kinds; a place where it is made.

*pouch (pouch), *n.* a small bag or pocket.

poultice (pōl' tis), *n.* a soft mixture applied to a sore or inflamed part of the body.

*poultry (pōl' tri), *n.* domestic fowl.

pounce (pouns), *v.i.* to swoop upon and seize, as a cat *pounces* upon a mouse.

pound (pound), *n.* a measure of weight, 16 ounces avoirdupois, 12 ounces troy; a British unit of money, equal to 20 shillings; an inclosure to hold stray cattle, dogs, or other animals.

pound (pound), *v.t. and v.i.* to beat, as with a hammer; to tamp, as earth; to move or come down heavily, as with the feet, as he *pounded* up the stairs; to beat heavily, as the waves *pounded* against the rocks.

*pour (pōr), *v.i. and v.t.* to rush out, as water from a broken tank; to cause to flow from, as to *pour* water from a pitcher; to discharge in a continuous stream.

pout (pout), *n.* any of several fresh-water catfish; an eel*pout*. *n.* a pushing out of the lips, as when sulky. *v.i.* to push the lips out, as in a sulky fit.

poverty (pov' ĕr ti), *n.* the state of being poor, indigence, great need; lack, as a *poverty* of ideas.

powder (pou' dĕr), *n.* a dry substance reduced to fine particles. *v.i. and v.t.* to use powder, as for cosmetic purposes, as she *powders* too much; to reduce to powder, as by pounding; to dust with powder, as she *powders* her face.

power (pou' ĕr), *n.* the faculty of doing or performing; energy, force, strength; authority; one who possesses power, as he is a *power* in the community; with capital initial letter, a great nation, as the U.S. is a world *Power*.

powerful (pou' ĕr fool), *adj.* having power, mighty, strong; efficacious.

Syn. Potent, puissant. *Powerful* applies to whatever is capable of producing great effect, as a *powerful* engine, a *powerful* athlete, a *powerful* corporation; *potent* suggests some inherent quality that works out its effect with certainty, as a *potent* drug, a *potent* medicine; *puissant* refers chiefly to persons, especially princes and potentates, and connotes the outward aspects of power, as a *puissant* monarch.

Ant. Powerless, feeble, weak, impotent.

powerless (pou' ĕr les), *adj.* weak, lacking in force or energy; unable to bring about a desired effect.

pox (poks), *n.* an eruptive disease, causing pustules or pocks on the skin, as small*pox* or syphilis.

practicability (prak ti ka bil' i ti), *n.* the state of being practicable or feasible.

practicable (prak' ti ka bl), *adj.* capable of being done, feasible.

practical (prak' ti kal), *adj.* capable of being put to use; useful not theoretical.

practically (prak' ti kal i), *adv.* really, virtually, as *practically* useless.

practice (prak' tis), *n.* frequent or customary action; pursuit of a profession, as the *practice* of law or medicine; drill as a means of acquiring skill.

practitioner (prak tish' un ĕr), *n.* one engaged in the practice of a profession.

pragmatism (prag' ma tizm), *n.* the philosophy that makes results the test of truth.

*prairie (prâr' i), *n.* an extensive tract of level or slightly undulating land without trees and covered with tall, coarse grass.

praise (prāz), *n.* commendation, approbation.

praise (prāz), *v.t.* to commend; to approve and give credit for merit.

*prance (prāns), *v.i.* to spring or bound; to step high and gaily.

prank (prangk), *n.* a playful trick.

*prate (prāt), *v.i.* to talk idly, chatter

prattle (prat' l), *n.* childish talk.

pray (prā), *v.i. and v.t.* to ask earnestly; to say prayers, especially to God; to entreat, implore; to beg for, as he *prayed* forgiveness.

*prayer (prâr), *n.* a solemn address to the Supreme Being; act of praying; an earnest entreaty.

*preach (prēch), *v.i. and v.t.* to proclaim, to deliver a sermon; to recommend earnestly, as to *preach* economy.

preamble (prē' ambl), *n.* an introductory passage affixed to a document of state, a legal enactment or a petition; any introduction to a speech or writing.

precarious (prē kâr' i us), *adj.* depending on the will of another or on chance; uncertain, risky, hazardous, as a *precarious* perch.

precaution (prē kô' shun), *n.* a measure employed to prevent disaster or misfortune.

precede (prē sēd'), *v.t.* to go before in time, place, rank or importance.

*precedence (prē sēd' ens), *n.* priority.

precedent (pres' ē dent), *n.* a parallel case in the past, especially as a guide for present action or ground for decision, as she did not intend to establish a *precedent* by giving her permission.

precedent (pre sē' dent), *adj.* going before.

precept (prē' sept), *n.* a rule of action or moral conduct, a maxim.

*precinct (prē' singkt), *n.* an inclosed district, as a police *precinct*, a voting *precinct: precincts*, neighborhood, environment.

*precious (presh' us), *adj.* of great value, prized.

*preciosity (presh i os' i ti), *n.* overcareful use of words; overrefinement.

*precipice (pres' i pis), *n.* a steep descent, an almost vertical cliff.

precipitant (prē sip' i tant), *n.* a chemical agent that causes the indissoluble elements in a liquid to separate and settle to the bottom of the container. *adj.* falling or rushing headlong, hasty.

*precipitate (prē sip' i tāt), *n.* a chemical substance that separates in solid form when the other elements dissolve. *v.t.* to throw headlong; to hasten a crisis. *adj.* impulsive, hasty, rash.

precipitous (prē sip' i tus), *adj.* like a precipice, steep; rash; hasty.

*precise (prē sīs'), *adj.* exact, strict, accurate, definite.

*preclude (prē klōod'), *v.t.* to shut out from access or consideration; to prevent.

*precocious (prē kō' shus), *adj.* prematurely developed, especially mentally, as a *precocious* child.

precocity (prē kos' i ti), *n.* the state of being developed before the normal time; especially premature mental development in a child.

preconceive (prē kon sēv'), *v.t.* to form, as an opinion, in advance, as I *preconceived* the idea that I would not like her.

preconception (prē kon sep' shun), *n.* a prejudice; an opinion formed without knowledge.

precursor (prē kûr' sĕr), *n.* forerunner, omen.

predatory (pred' a tō ri), *adj.* rapacious, plundering; living by preying upon others, as a *predatory* animal.

*predecessor (pred ē ses' ĕr), *n.* one who has preceded another in the same office or position.

predestination (prē des ti nā' shun), *n.* the doctrine that whatever comes to pass was ordained long in advance.

*predicable (pred' i ka bl), *adj.* capable of being affirmed.

*predicament (prē dik' a ment), *n.* an unpleasant, unfortunate or puzzling situation.

*predicate (pred' i kāt), *n.* that part of a sentence which makes a statement about the subject. *v.t.* to affirm or assert.

predict (prē dikt'), *v.t.* to foretell, prophesy.

*predilection (prē di lek' shun), *n.* preference beforehand, partiality.

predispose (prē dis pōz'), *v.i. and v.t.* to incline oneself beforehand; to influence others in advance of an event or situation, as a courteous manner in people *predisposes* us in their favor.

predominant (prē dom' i nant), *adj.* having superior strength or influence, controlling.

predominate (prē dom' i nāt), *v.i.* to be superior in strength, authority or influence; to prevail, as tragedy usually *predominates* in opera.

pre-eminent (prē em' i nent), *adj.* superior to all others, especially in excellence.

pre-empt (prē empt'), *v.t.* to establish a right or claim to before others make a claim.

preen (prēn), *v.t.* to clean and smooth, as with a beak, as a bird *preens* his feathers.

*preface (pref' is), *n.* preliminary matter explaining the nature and purpose, as of a book; an introduction. *v.t.* to introduce, explain what is coming.

prefatory (pref' a tō ri), *adj.* introducing and explaining.

*prefect (prē' fekt), *n.* a civil magistrate in ancient Rome; the governor of a department in modern France; a student with some of a teacher's authority, a monitor.

prefecture (prē' fek tūr), *n.* the office, jurisdiction or official quarters of a prefect.

prefer (prē fûr'), *v.t.* to regard or esteem more than something else.

*preferable (pref' ēr a bl), *adj.* more to be desired, as I think the black hat is *preferable.*

preferably (pref' ēr a bli), *adv.* rather than something else, by choice, as come to see me soon, *preferably* this week.

preference (pref' ēr ens), *n.* the act of preferring or the thing preferred; choice of one rather than another.

preferential (pref ēr en' shal), *adj.* giving or receiving preference.

preferment (prē fûr' ment), *n.* promotion to a higher position; a high post of honor, dignity or advantage, especially in the church.

prefix (prē' fiks), *n.* a letter, word or syllable at the beginning of a word that gives a new shade of meaning.

pregnant (preg' nant), *adj.* about to have offspring; fertile; teeming, as with ideas.

prehensile (prē hen' sil), *adj.* adapted for holding or grasping.

prehistoric (prē his tor' ik), *adj.* pertaining to or existing before historical records.

prejudice (prej' oo dis), *n.* premature judgment, bias.

Syn. Bias, partiality. **prepossession** pre-

sumption. A *prejudice* or *prepossession* is grounded often on feeling, fancy, associations. A *prejudice* against foreigners is very common in retired communities. A *prepossession* is always favorable, a *prejudice* always unfavorable, unless the contrary is expressly stated.

prejudicial (prej oo dish' al), *adj.* damaging, as to a case or cause.

*prelate (prel' it), *n.* a dignitary of the church, as a bishop or archbishop.

preliminary (prē lim' i ner i), *n.* [*pl.* preliminaries] an introductory act or exercise.

preliminary (prē lim' i ner i), *adj.* preceding, introductory, as *preliminary* remarks.

*prelude (prel' ūd), *n.* a short piece of music played as an introduction to a longer composition.

*premature (prē ma tūr'), *adj.* arriving, occurring or done before the set or proper time.

premeditate (prē med' i tāt), *v.t.* to design or plan beforehand.

*premier (prē' mi ēr), *n.* a prime minister. *adj.* first, chief; earliest in time.

*premise (prem' is), *n.* a proposition assumed in advance of argument.

premise (prē mīz'), *v.t.* to explain in advance of discussion.

premises (prem' is ez), *n.* real estate; a house and lot on which it stands.

premium (prē' mi um), *n.* a reward, bonus, something given free to a purchaser of goods to encourage buying; the amount by which the value of a stock market security exceeds par value; the periodic payment on an insurance policy.

premonition (prē mō nish' un), *n.* a sense of impending events, a foreboding.

premonitory (prē mon' i tō ri), *adj.* giving warning in advance of the event.

preoccupied (prē ok' ū pīd), *adj.* having the attention fixed upon other matters.

preordain (prē ōr dān'), *v.t.* to decree or order beforehand.

*preparation (prep a rā' shun), *n.* the act of making ready for use, a mixture prepared for a particular use, as a medical *preparation;* the state of being prepared, as *preparation* for war.

preparatory (prē par' a tō ri), *adj.* serving to make ready or fit.

prepare (prē pâr'), *v.t. and v.i.* to fit for a special purpose, make ready, as to *prepare* a room for occupancy; to make mentally ready, as to *prepare* a person for bad news; to make things or oneself ready, as to *prepare* for winter, to *prepare* for an ordeal.

prepense (prē pens'), *adj.* premeditated, as malice *prepense.*

prepay (prē pā'), *v.t.* to pay charges upon in advance, as to *prepay* a package.

preponderant (prē pon' dēr ant), *adj.* outweighing.

preponderate (prē pon' dēr āt), *v.i.* to outweigh; to exceed in power and influence; with *over.*

preposition (prep ō zish' un), *n.* a word placed before a noun or pronoun to indicate its relation to some other word in the sentence.

prepossessing (prē po zes' ing), *adj.* charming, attractive.

preposterous (prē pos' tēr us), *adj.* contrary to nature or reason, beyond belief, incredible.

prerogative (prē rog' a tiv), *n.* an exclusive or special privilege.

presage (pres' ij), *n.* a foreboding, presentiment.

*****presage** (prē sāj'), *v.t.* to forebode, predict.

presbyter (prez' bi tēr), *n.* an elder, minister or priest.

*****presbytery** (prez' bi ter i), *n.* [*pl.* presbyteries] a court composed of the pastors and ruling elders of a group of Presbyterian churches in a given district; the group of churches ruled by such a body and forming with other presbyteries a synod; the part of a cathedral between the choir and altar.

*****prescient** (prē' shi ent), *adj.* knowing in advance.

prescribe (prē skrīb'), *v.i.* and *v.t.* to write medical directions, as to *prescribe* for a person; to order authoritatively; to order the use of, as a medicine.

prescription (prē skrip' shun), *n.* the act of prescribing; that which is prescribed; a doctor's written directions for the preparation of a medicine.

presence (prez' ens), *n.* the state of being present; immediate neighborhood, as in the presence of the enemy; the appearance and person of a man, as he has a good *presence*: *presence of mind,* quickness in understanding and dealing with a situation.

present (prez' ent), *n.* a gift; the immediate moment, as there's no time like the *present.*

present (prez' ent), *adj.* at hand, as the *present* moment, I was *present* at the meeting.

present (prē zent'), *v.t.* to offer, introduce; to exhibit, as to *present* a play; to aim or point.

presentable (prē zent' a bl), *adj.* suitable to be offered, given or introduced; fit to be seen.

*****presentation** (prez en tā' shun), *n.* the act of introducing formally; the act of exhibiting to the public, as a theatrical *presentation;* the act of bestowing, as the *presentation* of awards.

*****presentiment** (prē zen' ti ment), *n.* a foreboding of things to happen.

presently (prez' ent li), *adv.* shortly, before long, as I will see him *presently.*

preservation (prez ēr vā' shun), *n.* the act of keeping or state of being kept from injury or decay.

preservative (prē zûr' va tiv), *n.* that which prevents injury and keeps intact. *adj.* having the power of keeping from injury or decay.

preserve (prē zûrv'), *n.* fruit cooked with sugar and put up in various ways to keep it for future use: commonly used in the plural.

preserve (prē zûrv'), *v.t.* to keep from injury; to protect; to maintain, as to *preserve* silence; to put up for future use, as food.

*****preside** (prē zīd'), *v.i.* to direct, as a meeting.

president (prez' i dent), *n.* one who presides, as over an organization or a republic.

press (pres), *n.* a machine for printing; a ma-

chine to form things by means of pressure; periodical print, as the power of the *press;* crowding, with pressure one against another; a closet for storage, as a clothes *press;* urgent demands, as the *press* of work.

press (pres), *v.i.* and *v.t.* to bear down heavily; to push forward; to squeeze or crush; to urge as to *press* a person for an answer; to make smooth by pressure, commonly with heat, as to *press* clothes.

pressing (pres' ing), *adj.* urgent, as a *pressing* need.

pressman (pres' man), *n.* one who operates or works about a printing press.

pressure (presh' ēr), *n.* a weight or burden, as of distress; weight of influence or authority, as *pressure* was brought to bear; urgent demand, as financial *pressure;* force exerted on a body, tending to change its shape or volume.

*****prestidigitation** (pres ti dij i tā' shun), *n.* sleight of hand, legerdemain.

*****prestige** (pres tēzh'), *n.* high standing due to past actions, renown, reputation.

presto (pres' tō), *adv.* quickly, suddenly.

presume (prē zūm'), *v.i.* and *v.t.* to venture without actual authorization; to take for granted; to imply, as promotion *presumes* merit.

presumption (prē zump' shun), *n.* something taken for granted; that which encourages belief, without proof, as the *presumption* is that he will accept; unwarranted assurance; unjustified assumption, as I dislike his constant *presumption.*

presumptive (prē zump' tiv), *adj.* based on supposition, apparent but not proved, as the *presumptive* heir to a throne.

*****presumptuous** (prē zump' tū us), *adj.* arrogant; bold, overconfident.

Syn. Arrogant, insolent. One is *presumptuous* who encroaches beyond the bounds of good taste and takes undue liberties; one is *arrogant* who makes exorbitant claims to importance; *insolent* suggests offensive disregard for the feelings of others.

presuppose (prē su pōz'), *v.t.* to take for granted; to require as antecedent, as action *presupposes* an agent.

*****pretend** (prē tend'), *v.i.* and *v.t.* to make believe; to present a claim, as to a title; to simulate, as he *pretended* good will.

pretender (prē ten' dēr), *n.* one who claims what is not rightfully his; one who makes a claim, especially a false claim, to anything.

*****pretense** (prē tens'), *n.* a false or hypocritical profession, as under *pretense* of friendliness; sham, pretext, claim, as without pretense of accuracy.

Syn. Sham, affectation, subterfuge. A *pretense* applies to that which is deceitfully held out as true, as a *pretense* of honesty; a *sham* usually applies to a substitution, imitation or counterfeit purporting to be the real thing; *affectation* denotes something consciously assumed and insincere; *subterfuge* suggests a deliberate deception for the sake of escape from punishment or an awkward situation.

pretension (prē ten' shun), *n.* a claim that is doubtful or false; unwarranted appearance of power, influence.

pretentious (prē ten' shus), *adj.* assuming an air of superiority.

*__pretext__ (prē' tekst), *n.* an ostensible motive put forward to conceal the real one.

*__pretty__ (prit' i), *adj.* [*comp.* prettier, *superl.* prettiest] pleasing to the eye, without being beautiful; pleasing to the mind, as a *pretty* sense of humor; moderately large, as a *pretty* inheritance; fine, as a *pretty* thing to do. *adv.* fairly, moderately, as *pretty* good.

*__pretzel__ (pret' sel), *n.* a brittle biscuit, twisted like a knot, glazed and crusted with salt.

*__prevail__ (prē vāl'), *v.i.* to succeed, gain mastery, rule, as truth shall *prevail;* to urge successfully, as we *prevailed* upon him to accept.

*__prevalence__ (prev' a lens), *n.* preponderance; the state of being widely distributed or generally accepted, as the *prevalence* of patriotic spirit.

prevalent (prev' a lent), *adj.* widespread, predominant.

prevaricate (prē var' i kāt), *v.i.* to evade the truth, equivocate.

*__prevent__ (prē vent'), *v.t.* to stop from being done or coming to pass; to hinder, obstruct.
Syn. Preclude, avert. *Prevent* is a general term for hindering, stopping or obstructing; to *preclude* is to prevent by anticipative action; to *avert* is to forestall some threatened evil.

prevention (prē ven' shun), *n.* the act of hindering or obstructing; a hindrance or obstruction.

preventive (prē ven' tiv), *n.* that which tends to stop undesired things from happening; something that keeps disease away, as *preventive* medicine. *adj.* tending to prevent.

*__previous__ (prē' vi us), *adj.* going before, preceding.
Syn. Earlier, foregoing, former. *Previous* indicates anything that has gone before, especially in time; *foregoing* applies almost exclusively to preceding statements; *former* applies to that which precedes in time, place or order.

prevision (prē vizh' un), *n.* foresight; foreknowledge.

*__prey__ (prā), *n.* any creature which another creature seizes to kill or eat; act of seizing to eat; a person who is the victim of any hostile or injurious person or thing.

prey (prā), *v.i.* to plunder; to seize and devour or destroy; to wear down, as grief *preys* upon one's mind.

price (prīs), *n.* cost, value, amount of money asked for something to be sold.

priceless (prīs' les), *adj.* without price; invaluable.

prick (prik), *n.* a sharp-pointed instrument; the stinging sensation caused by a jab with such an instrument or something likened to it, as a pin*prick* or the *prick* of conscience.

prick (prik), *v.t.* to pierce or puncture with a sharp-pointed instrument; to annoy, as his conscience *pricked* him.

prickle (prik' l), *n.* a small, sharp point; a spine or thorn on a plant. *v.i. and v.t.* to tingle; to cause a stinging sensation in the skin.

prickly (prik' li), *adj.* [*comp.* pricklier, *superl.* prickliest] full of prickles; causing a stinging, tingling sensation.

pride (prīd), *n.* inordinate self-regard; a proper feeling of esteem for one's own qualities or achievements; that which one prizes, as my record is my *pride.*
Syn. Arrogance, egotism, superciliousness, haughtiness, disdain, vainglory, vanity, conceit. *Pride* is an absorbing sense of one's own greatness. *Haughtiness* thinks highly of itself and poorly of others. *Arrogance* claims much for itself and concedes little to others. *Disdain* sees contemptuously the inferiority of others to itself. *Vanity* is eager for admiration and praise, is elated if they are rendered, and pained if they are withheld. *Conceit* is offensive and overweening self-confidence; *Vainglory* is more pompous and boastful than *vanity.*
Ant. Humility, meekness, diffidence, modesty.

*__prig__ (prig), *n.* one who poses or is overprecise in manners, speech, morals.

*__prim__ (prim), *adj.* precise, neat, sedate and fastidious.

primacy (prī' ma si), *n.* [*pl.* primacies] the state of being first in rank; the office and dignity of an archbishop.

primal (prī' mal), *adj.* primary; principal; original, early.

*__primary__ (prī' mer i), *n.* [*pl.* primaries] a meeting of voters to name candidates for office. *adj.* original, first in time or importance; elementary.

primary colors (prī' mer i kul' ērz), the principal colors of the spectrum, red, green and blue.

*__primate__ (prī' mit), *n.* the highest dignitary in a national church; a creature belonging to the highest order of mammals (plural, *primates,* pronounced prī mā' tēs).

prime (prīm), *n.* the first stage of full development, as *prime* of life. *v.t.* to prepare for firing, as a gun, by placing a firing charge; to prepare for operation by some preliminary act, as to *prime* a pump by pouring water into it; to prepare, as to *prime* one who is to testify in court. *adj.* first in order of time, primitive; first in rank or importance; first in quality; primary as opposed to derivative, as a *prime* cause.

*__primer__ (prīm' ēr), *n.* that which primes, as the fulminating powder used to set off a gun or explosive charge.

*__primer__ (prim' ēr), *n.* a manual of elementary instruction; a size of type, 10-point or 18-point.

*__primeval__ (prī mē' val), *adj.* relating in any way to the earliest time; very ancient.

priming (prīm' ing), *n.* the first coat of paint; powder used to set off a main charge of explosive, as the *priming* of a gun.

primitive (prim' i tiv), *n.* a word not derived from another; a line, figure or number from which another is derived; anything with the characteristics of early times or an original state. *adj.* pertaining to the beginning or early times; extremely old-fashioned; simple, crude, as *primitive* living conditions.

primogeniture (prī mō jen' i tūr), *n.* seniority of birth; in older times, in English law, the eldest son's exclusive right of inheritance.

primordial (prī môr' di al), *adj.* existing from the beginning, original.

primp (primp), *v.i. and v.t.* to deck oneself in a prim or affected manner; to fuss over one's appearance.

primrose (prim' rōz), *n.* an early spring flower, generally reddish-yellow.

prince (prins), *n.* a ruler; a son of a sovereign; a leader, as a merchant *prince*.

*****princess** (prin' ses), *n.* the daughter of a sovereign; wife of a prince.

principal (prin' si pal), *n.* a person in first authority; the head of a school; a person of first concern in a business transaction; one of the makers of a contract; a capital sum put out at interest. *adj.* chief; essential.

principality (prin si pal' i ti), *n.* [*pl.* principalities] the domain of a prince.

principally (prin' si pal i), *adv.* chiefly.

principle (prin' si pl), *n.* a rule or law of action or conduct; the essential characteristic, as the *principle* of the thing; uprightness, as he stands by his *principles*.

  Syn. Rule. *Principle* emphasizes the idea of that which exercises governing or guiding influence; *rule* implies more limited and specific regulation.

prink (pringk), *v.i.* to dress up in fussy, showy fashion; to primp.

print (print), *n.* a mark made by impression, as a foot*print;* reading matter produced from type passed through a press, as I saw it in *print;* a picture made by impression of a plate, especially of a wood block.

print (print), *v.i. and v.t.* to write in letters resembling type; to make impressions from type or plates; to stamp, as with a pattern.

printer (prin' tēr), *n.* one whose trade is the setting of type or putting it through the press.

printing (print' ing), *n.* the art of producing from type matter to be read, including setting type and putting it through the press.

prior (prī' ēr), *n.* the head of a religious house or group of monks; the coadjutor of an abbot. *adj.* earlier, previous.

prioress (prī' ēr es), *n.* a woman heading a religious house of nuns; one ranking next below the abbess.

priority (prī or' i ti), *n.* precedence; the state of being first in rank or time of service.

priory (prī' ō ri), *n.* [*pl.* priories] a religious establishment of monks or nuns next in dignity to an abbey.

*****prism** (prizm), *n.* a solid whose bases are similar, equal and parallel to each other, and whose sides are parallelograms; a refracting optical instrument.

prison (priz' n), *n.* a place or state of restraint; a public building in which criminals are confined.

*****pristine** (pris' tēn), *adj.* pertaining to a very early period, original.

*****privacy** (prī' va si), *n.* [*pl.* privacies] a state of retirement, seclusion, freedom from interruption by others.

  Syn. Retirement, seclusion, solitude. *Privacy* implies freedom from the observation and association of others; *retirement* implies a withdrawing from public life, although the person who retires may still enjoy friendly intercourse; he who goes into *seclusion* shuts himself away from the world, usually seeing only the members of his household and intimate friends; *solitude* usually implies the presence of no other person, as a hermit lives in *solitude*.

  Ant. Company, society, association, companionship, fellowship.

private (prī' vit), *n.* an enlisted man in an army. *adj.* peculiar to oneself, personal, not public.

privateer (prī va tēr'), *n.* a privately owned ship licensed by a government to attack the ships of an enemy.

*****privation** (prī vā' shun), *n.* the state of lacking something; poverty, hardship.

*****privative** (priv' a tiv), *n.* a syllable that changes the sense of a word from positive to negative, as in *unwilling;* a quality that is due only to lack of possession of another quality, as whiteness is due to absence of color.

privet (priv'et), *n.* an evergreen shrub for hedges.

privilege (priv' i lij), *n.* a favor or right granted to one with exclusion of others; a right granted by a constitutional government to its citizens, as the *privilege* of assembly, prerogative.

prize (prīz), *n.* a reward gained in competition with others. *n.* a lever, leverage, means of prying up, as a weight. *v.t.* to place high value on, esteem greatly. *v.t.* to move with a lever, pry.

pro (prō), *adv.* on the affirmative side, as they argued *pro* and con.

probability (prob a bil' i ti), *n.* [*pl.* probabilities] that which is likely to happen; the state of being likely to happen, as it is a *probability*, in all *probability*.

*****probate** (prō' bāt), *n.* the official proof of wills; the official copy of a will, with certificate of its legal proof. *v.t.* to prove legally, as a will.

probation (prō bā' shun), *n.* test or trial of character and responsibility; the period over which such a test extends, as I am employed on *probation*.

*****probe** (prōb), *n.* a surgical instrument to examine a wound; a close inquiry.

probe (prōb), *v.t.* to explore or examine with a probe; to conduct a searching inquiry into affairs or conditions.

probe (prōb), *n.* a spacecraft designated to explore and transmit data about the upper atmosphere to the earth.

*****probity** (prob' i ti), *n.* integrity, honesty.

problem (prob' lem), *n.* a question for solution; a difficult matter requiring settlement; an exercise for students to work out.

problematic, problematical (prob lem at' ik, -i kal), *adj.* having the nature of a problem; hard to work out, puzzling, uncertain.

*__proboscis__ (prō bos' is), *n.* [*pl.* proboscises or proboscides] the elongated snout of certain animals, as the elephant; the projecting mouth parts of some insects.

*__procedure__ (prō sē' dūr), *n.* a manner of taking action; way of conducting, as a case at law, as the correct *procedure*.

*__proceed__ (prō sēd'), *v.i.* to advance; to go ahead; to get on with, as *proceed* as you are, *proceed* according to rule.

*__proceeds__ (prō' sēdz), *n. pl.* the profits from a transaction or public performance, as the *proceeds* will go to charity.

*__process__ (pros' es), *n.* a progressive course; a series of acts aimed at a single end; an outgrowth from a body, as a horn is a *process* on the head of an animal.

procession (prō sesh' un), *n.* orderly progress; a number of persons organized for a formal march.

*__proclaim__ (prō klām'), *v.t.* to announce or declare officially.

proclamation (prok la mā' shun), *n.* an official announcement to the public, an edict.

proclivity (prō kliv' i ti), *n.* [*pl.* proclivities] an inclination, tendency.

procrastinate (prō kras' ti nāt), *v.i.* to put off action from time to time, delay.

procreation (prō krē ā' shun) *n.* the production of young.

proctor (prok' tēr), *n.* one employed to enforce discipline or keep a watch on classes taking examinations in college.

procurable (prō kūr' a bl), *adj.* obtainable.

procurator (prok' ū rā tēr), *n.* one who manages affairs for another, especially legal interests.

*__procure__ (prō kūr'), *v.t.* to get, obtain.

prod (prod), *n.* a goad; a punch with a goad, as he gave me a *prod* with his cane. *v.t.* to poke with a pointed stick; to urge on; to stimulate, as to *prod* one's memory.

prodigal (prod' i gal), *n.* a spendthrift, a wasteful person. *adj.* reckless with money, wasteful, lavish.

prodigality (prod i gal' i ti), *n.* [*pl.* prodigalities] wastefulness; extravagance.

*__prodigious__ (prō dij' us), *adj.* enormous; amazing.

*__prodigy__ (prod' i ji), *n.* [*pl.* prodigies] an extraordinary person, as an infant *prodigy;* a wonder; a freak of nature.

produce (prod' ūs), *n.* that which is yielded or brought forth, as farm *produce*.

*__produce__ (prō dūs'), *v.i. and v.t.* to yield or bring forth; to bring to view; to place before the public, as a play.

*__product__ (prod' ukt), *n.* that which is produced, as the *product* of the fields, *product* of one's labors.

production (prō duk' shun), *n.* the act of bringing forth; that which is brought out by nature or through man's wit and toil; a

play on the stage.

Syn. Performance, work. The term *production* cannot be employed without reference to the source from which the thing in question is produced, as the *production* of art, a *production* of the mind. A *performance* cannot be spoken of without some reference to the agent, as we speak of this or that person's *performance*. We speak either of the *work* of one's hands or of a *work* of the imagination.

productive (prō duk' tiv), *adj.* having the power of yielding or bringing forth; fruitful, fertile.

*__profanation__ (prof a nā' shun), *n.* the act of treating sacred things with disrespect.

*__profane__ (prō fān'), *v.t.* to desecrate. *adj.* not sacred, secular; irreverent, blasphemous.

profess (prō fes'), *v.i. and v.t.* to make an avowal; to make open declaration of.

profession (prō fesh' un), *n.* the act of avowing, as *profession* of faith; that which is declared; a vocation that requires learning rather than work with the hands.

professional (prō fesh' un al), *n.* one who engages in a learned vocation; one who engages in sport for pay. *adj.* pertaining in any way to any kind of learned vocation.

professor (prō fes' ēr), *n.* one who makes an avowal, as of faith; a college teacher of the highest grade.

proffer (prof' ēr), *v.t.* to offer something that may be accepted or declined; to tender, as to *proffer* aid.

proficiency (prō fish' en si), *n.* skill in any branch of knowledge, science, business or art.

proficient (prō fish' ent), *adj.* skilled, expert.

*__profile__ (prō' fil), *n.* the outline of anything seen from the side, as a face, a hill.

profit (prof' it), *n.* pecuniary gain; benefit from an act done, business transacted or investment made.

profitable (prof' it a bl), *adj.* yielding gain or advantage; bringing returns, as an investment; bringing in more than goes out, as a business.

profiteer (prof i tēr'), *n.* a person who makes excessive profits, especially in time of war.

profiteer (prof i tēr'), *v.i.* to make excessive profits, especially in time of war.

profligacy (prof' li ga si), *n.* dissolute living.

profligate (prof' li gāt), *adj.* dissolute; living in vice.

Syn. Abandoned, reprobate. A *profligate* man has given himself up to vice. An *abandoned* person has yielded completely to passion. The *reprobate* is one who has become insensible to reproof and is beyond reform.
Ant. Virtuous, controlled.

profound (prō found'), *adj.* deep, as *profound* depths of the ocean; penetrating, as *profound* thought; reaching the depths of one's nature, as *profound* grief.

profundity (prō fun' di ti), *n.* [*pl.* profundities] great depth, as *profundity* of feeling.

*__profuse__ (prō fūs'), *adj.* very liberal; too liberal; lavish, abundant, as *profuse* flowering.

profusion (prō fū' zhun), *n.* a lavish outpouring, abundance.

progenitor (prŏ jen' ĭ tẽr), *n.* an ancestor, forefather.

progeny (proj' e nĭ), *n.* offspring; descendants.

prognosticate (prog nos' tĭ kāt), *v.i. and v.t.* to predict, foretell, especially the weather.

program (prō' gram), *n.* a schedule of events; plan of action; a list of items in an entertainment, with names of the speakers, singers, actors; the complete sequence of instructions and routines needed to solve a problem or to execute directions in a computer.

programmer (prō´ gram er), *n.* a computer specialist who writes programs.

*****progress** (prŏ gres'), *v.i.* to move onward, advance, develop.

progression (prŏ gresh' un), *n.* advancement; mathematical series.

progressive (prŏ gres' ĭv), *n.* a person or a party favoring changes and reforms in policy or administration. *adj.* moving forward; interested in improvement or advance.

*****prohibit** (prŏ hib' ĭt), *v.t.* to forbid; to interdict by authority.

prohibitionist (prŏ ĭ bish' un ĭst), *n.* one who favors forbidding manufacture or traffic in alcoholic liquors.

prohibitive (prŏ hib' ĭ tĭv), *adj.* tending to put a stop to; having the nature of a ban.

*****project** (prŏj' ekt), *n.* a plan or design; school work planned by student and teacher together to test the student's ability to make practical use of his knowledge.

*****projectile** (prŏ jek' tĭl), *n.* an object thrown through the air by hand or a gun, as a spear or a bullet.

projection (prŏ jek' shun), *n.* that which juts out; representation on a plane surface of a three-dimensional object, as a flat map of the earth is a *projection* of the globe.

projector (prŏ jek' tẽr), *n.* an appliance made to throw a picture on a screen by reflecting light.

prolapse (prŏ laps'), *n.* a falling forward out of place.

*****proletariat** (prŏ lē tãr ĭ at), *n.* the lowest class of society; those who work for daily wages and have no capital.

proliferous (prŏ lif' ẽr us), *adj.* producing new plants by budding; developing buds from flowers or fruit.

prolific (prŏ lif' ĭk), *adj.* productive, fertile, fruitful.

*****prologue** (prō' lŏg), *n.* an introduction, especially to a play.

prolong (prŏ lŏng'), *v.t.* to lengthen, extend.

prolongation (prŏ lŏng gā' shun), · *n.* an extension in time or in space.

*****promenade** (prom ē näd'), *n.* a public place for walking; a walk for pleasure; a school or college dance. *v.i.* to walk merely for pleasure and in a leisurely way.

prominence (prom' ĭ nens), *n.* the state of being outstanding; a projection.

prominent (prom' ĭ nent), *adj.* outstanding, projecting, conspicuous; distinguished.

Syn. Conspicuous, salient, signal. What is *prominent* stands out in such a way as to

attract attention; what is *conspicuous* is plainly visible to the eye or mind; what is *salient* immediately arrests the attention, as the *salient* point in an argument; what is *signal* is out of the ordinary, as a *signal* honor.

Ant. Obscure, inconspicuous.

promiscuous (prŏ mis' kũ us), *adj.* mingled, indiscriminate.

promise (prom' ĭs), *n.* an engagement to do or not to do something; ground for expectation of good things in the future, as he is a young man of great *promise.*

Syn. Engagement, pledge, word. *Promise* is a general term; *engagement* implies a binding agreement, carrying certain definite obligations, a *pledge* denotes a solemn *promise* or guarantee of performance.

promise (prom' ĭs), *v.t. and v.i.* to engage to do, make or obtain, as I *promised* the work by Friday; to make a promise of, as to *promise* a book; to give one's promise to, as I *promised* her my support; to make a promise; to afford hopes, give grounds for expecting much, as the weather *promises* well.

promissory (prom' ĭ sŏ rĭ), *adj.* containing a pledge to pay, as a *promissory* note

promontory (prom' un tŏ rĭ), *n.* [*pl.* promontories] a high cape, a point of land jutting out into the sea.

promote (prŏ mōt'), *v.t.* to advance, push forward; to contribute to the development of; to pass a student to the next higher class.

promoter (prŏ mōt' ẽr), *n.* one who organizes and starts new companies, especially by raising funds; one who encourages or fosters.

promotion (prŏ mō' shun), *n.* advancement to a higher standing or stage of development; the act of bringing about such advancement; the act of organizing and advancing, as an industry or commercial project.

prompt (prompt), *v.t.* to urge to action; to cause an action, inspire; to supply the next words to a speaker or actor who has forgotten them. *adj.* ready and quick to act as occasion demands; done without delay.

prompter (promp' tẽr), *n.* one whose business it is to help actors who forget their lines.

promptitude (promp' tĭ tūd), *n.* quickness of decision and action, readiness.

*****promulgate** (prŏ mul' gāt), *v.t.* to make known to the public, announce.

prone (prōn), *adj.* lying with the face downward; mentally inclined, as *prone* to error.

proneness (prōn' nes), *n.* the state of being mentally inclined; propensity; tendency.

prong (prŏng), *n.* a sharp-pointed piece of metal, as the *prong* of a pitchfork; a point of a deer's antler.

pronominal (prŏ nom' ĭ nal), *adj.* pertaining to or used as a pronoun.

pronoun (prō' noun), *n.* a word referring to or used in place of a noun.

*****pronounce** (prŏ nouns'), *v.t.* to articulate the sounds of, as words; to utter formally, as to *pronounce* the benediction, to *pronounce* sentence upon a convicted criminal.

pronounced (prŏ nounst'), *adj.* strongly

marked; decided, as *pronounced* features, in a *pronounced* manner.

*pronunciation (prŏ nun si ā' shun), *n.* the act of uttering words; manner of uttering, as in giving letters the correct sound, placing the accent correctly.

proof (prŏof), *n.* testimony or convincing evidence; a demonstration of correctness; a trial printing on which errors are marked for correction before the final impression is made.

proofreader (prŏof' rĕd ēr), *n.* one whose business it is to read trial impressions of printed matter and mark errors for correction.

prop (prop), *n.* a support or stay to hold up something. *v.t.* to sustain or support, as we shall have to *prop* the shed roof.

*propaganda (prop a gan' da), *n.* methods and measures for spreading doctrines, principles, printed matter or speeches, for the purpose of promoting a cause, political, religious or military.

propagate (prop' a gāt), *v.i. and v.t.* to have offspring; to cause to increase in number, as plants; to disseminate, as news; to extend through space, as light.

*propel (prŏ pel'), *v.t.* [*p.t.* and *p.p.* propelled, *pr.p.* propelling] to drive forward, as an automobile or boat.

propeller (prŏ pel' ēr), *n.* a screw, with broad blades, driving a ship or airplane with power coming from the engines.

propensity (prŏ pen' si ti), *n.* [*pl.* propensities] a natural tendency, inclination.

proper (prop' ēr), *adj.* denoting a particular person or thing, as a *proper* noun; fitting or appropriate to, as the *proper* thing to do.

property (prop' ēr ti), *n.* [*pl.* properties] that which is owned by exclusive right; a special quality, as the *properties* of iron; things used in a play except scenery and costumes.

*prophecy (prof' ē si), *n.* [*pl.* prophecies] a prediction of something that is to happen; the power or act of predicting the future.

*prophesy (prof' ē sī), *v.i. and v.t.* [*p.t.* and *p.p.* prophesied, *pr.p.* prophesying] to predict.

prophet (prof' et), *n.* one who foretells future events; one under divine inspiration as a teacher of God's will to the people, as a Biblical *prophet*.

*prophylactic (prŏ fi lak' tik), *n.* a medicine to prevent disease or protect against it.

propinquity (prŏ ping' kwi ti), *n.* nearness in time or place or relationship; kinship.

*propitiate (prŏ pish' i āt), *v.t.* to conciliate; to make favorable.

propitious (prŏ pish' us), *adj.* favorable; favorably inclined.

proportion (prŏ pōr' shun), *n.* comparative relation in size or degree; ratio; a fair share or return, as you will be paid in *proportion* to service rendered.

proportionate (prŏ pōr' shun it), *adj.* adjusted to something else according to a certain rate of common valuation.

proposal (prŏ pōz' al), *n.* that which is offered for consideration or acceptance; an

offer of marriage.

propose (prŏ pōz'), *v.t.* to bring forward for consideration; to make an offer of marriage.

proposition (prop ŏ zish' un), *n.* the presentation of a topic for debate; statement of a problem for solution; that which is offered for consideration.

propound (prŏ pound'), *v.t.* to offer for consideration.

proprietary (prŏ prī' e ter i), *n.* [*pl.* proprietaries] one who possesses in his own right; a body of proprietors. *adj.* under exclusive ownership; made under exclusive ownership, as a *proprietary* medicine may be made and sold only by the patent owner.

proprietor (prŏ prī e tēr), *n.* a legal owner.

propriety (prŏ prī' e ti), *n.* [*pl.* proprieties] the state of being fit and appropriate; conformity to established custom.

propulsive (prŏ pul' siv), *adj.* having power to drive forward.

*pro rata (prŏ rā'ta), in proportion.

*prosaic (prŏ zā' ik), *adj.* commonplace, dull.

*proscenium (prŏ sē' ni um), *n.* [*pl.* prosceniums or proscenia] the part of a stage between the curtain and the orchestra.

proscribe (prŏ skrīb'), *v.t.* to punish by outlawing; to condemn, prohibit.

prose (prōz), *n.* ordinary spoken or written language, composition without metrical form.

prosecute (pros' ē kūt), *v.i. and v.t.* to go to law; to accuse of a crime before a legal tribunal; to pursue or carry on, as to *prosecute* an enterprise; to bring legal proceedings against, as to *prosecute* a swindler.

prosecution (pros ē kū' shun), *n.* pursuit; the institution and carrying on of a suit at law; the side in a criminal case representing the public against an accused person.

prosecutor (pros' ē kū tēr), *n.* one who brings suit against another; the officer of the state who represents the public in criminal cases.

*proselyte (pros' ē līt), *n.* a convert to some religion or belief; one who has been won over from one belief or party to another.

*prosody (pros' ŏ di), *n.* the part of grammar that treats of quantity, accent and the laws of versification.

prospect (pros' pekt), *n.* a view of the country; expectation; a possible customer or client. *v.i. and v.t.* to explore for minerals, as to *prospect* for gold; to examine the possibilities of.

prospective (prŏ spek' tiv), *adj.* looking forward; acting with foresight; expectable.

prospector (pros' pek tēr), *n.* one who searches for valuable ores and minerals.

prospectus (pros pek' tus), *n.* [*pl.* prospectuses] an outline of plans for a project or institution whose establishment is desired.

prosper (pros' pēr), *v.i. and v.t.* to succeed, as the business *prospered*; to flourish, as fruit *prospers* in that climate; to render successful, as God *prospered* His servant.

prosperity (pros per' i ti), *n.* success; good fortune; state of thriving.

prosperous (pros' pēr us), *adj.* successful, thriving.

*prostrate (pros'trāt), *adj.* lying stretched out; lying flat; overthrown. *v.t.* to bow low, as in supplication, as to *prostrate* oneself before an altar; to break down, as sickness *prostrated* him.

*prosy (prōz'ĭ), *adj.* [comp. prosier, superl. prosiest] dull, tiresome.

*protean (prō'tē an), *adj.* readily assuming different shapes.

protect (prō tekt'), *v.t.* to guard against danger; to shield from harm; to defend through high tariff, as domestic products.

protection (prō tek'shun), *n.* the act of safeguarding; that which shields from harm; defense of domestic products through high tariffs against competition by cheap imports.

protector (prō tek'tẽr), *n.* one who or that which guards and defends; one ruling in place of a king not yet come of age.

protectorate (prō tek'tẽr ĭt), *n.* an arrangement by which a great and powerful nation assumes responsibility for the safety of a small one; government by a regent, as the *protectorate* of Cromwell.

*protégé (prō'te zhā), *n.* one who is under the care or patronage of another.

*protein (prō'tē in), *n.* one of a class of nitrogenous compounds, as albumin, fibrin, casein, which form animal tissue; the gelatinous, semitransparent substance obtained from albumin, fibrin or casein, the essential principle of food.

protest (prō'test), *n.* an earnest declaration of opinion against some act or condition, statement of disapproval; notice that a note or check has been presented and payment refused.

*protest (prō test'), *v.i. and v.t.* to object; to express disapproval and dissent; to declare dishonored, as a check or note; to assert solemnly, as he *protested* his sincerity.

*protestation (prot es tā'shun), *n.* a declaration of dissent; an earnest affirmation.

protocol (prō'tō kol), *n.* a preliminary official memorandum serving as the basis for a final treaty or convention.

proton (prō'ton), *n.* the smallest unit of positive electricity.

protoplasm (prō'tō plazm), *n.* a semifluid, albuminous substance, regarded as the ultimate basis of physical life, from which all living organisms are developed.

prototype (prō'tō tīp), *n.* the original from which others are copied, or in likeness to which they are formed.

protract (prō trakt'), *v.t.* to prolong in time or space.

protractor (prō trak'tẽr), *n.* a mathematical instrument for making and measuring angles on a sheet of paper.

protrude (prō trōōd'), *v.i. and v.t.* to project; to thrust forward.

protrusion (prō trōō'zhun), *n.* the act of thrusting forward or state of being thrust forward, a projection.

protuberant (prō tū'bẽr ant), *adj.* swelling, bulging.

proud (proud), *adj.* haughty; properly self-respecting; giving cause for pride.

prove (prōōv), *v.t.* to test; to demonstrate, with argument; to supply evidence; to make a trial impression of, as in printing.

proven (prōōv'en), *adj.* demonstrated, established, as not proven—a verdict in Scots law, the only correct use of *proven;* in all other uses *proved* is correct.

provender (prov'en dẽr), *n.* dry feed for horses and cattle, such as hay.

proverb (prov'ûrb), *n.* a short, pithy saying, adage.

proverbial (pro vûr'bĭ al), *adj.* pertaining to adages; well-known.

provide (prō vīd'), *v.i. and v.t.* to take care of, as the Lord will *provide;* to furnish supplies, as we *provided* food.

provided (prō vīd'ed), *conj.* on condition that.

providence (prov'ĭ dens), *n.* preparation for meeting future needs; foresight; prudence; economy.

Providence (prov'ĭ dens), *n.* God's care for mankind.

provident (prov'ĭ dent), *adj.* thoughtful in arranging to meet future needs; economical.

providential (prov ĭ den'shal), *adj.* springing from divine care for mankind; fortunate, as a *providential* meeting.

province (prov'ins), *n.* a division of an empire or state; a dependent country; a sphere of influence or field of responsibility; country or small city, contrasted with a metropolis.

provincial (prō vin'shal), *n.* one who belongs to a province; one who lives far from big cities; a countryman. *adj.* pertaining to or characteristic of life in the dependencies; not possessing the metropolitan qualities; narrow in outlook, limited.

provision (prō vizh'un), *n.* the act of preparing in advance; accumulation of stores and supplies.

provisional (prō vizh'un al), *adj.* conditional; temporary.

provisions (prō vizh'unz), *n.* food.

*proviso (prō vī'zō), *n.* [pl. provisos] a conditional stipulation; a clause, as in a statute or deed, introducing a condition.

*provocation (prov ō kā'shun), *n.* that which causes anger; the act of angering or state of being angered; that which stirs emotion, thought or action, a challenge.

provocative (prō vok'a tiv), *adj.* producing a state of anger or vexation; producing a responsive emotion, thought or action, as a *provocative* glance, a *provocative* remark.

*provoke (prō vōk'), *v.t.* to make angry, irritate; to excite, arouse.

*provost (prov'ust), *n.* a superintendent; an official head; the chief magistrate of a Scottish city.

*prow (prou), *n.* the bow of a ship; the nose of an airplane fuselage or of a dirigible.

prowess (prou'es), *n.* bravery, valor; skill.

*prowl (proul), *v.i.* to creep about stealthily.

proximate (prok'si mit), *adj.* nearest, either preceding or following.

proximity (proks im'ĭ ti), *n.* nearness in time or place.

proxy (prok'si), *n.* [pl. proxies] one who is

authorized to vote or act for another; the certificate of such authorization.

*prude (prōōd), *n.* an exaggeratedly proper person.

*prudence (prōō' dens), *n.* wisdom in practical affairs; care and caution.

prudent (prōō' dent), *adj.* wise in practical affairs; careful, cautious.

prudential (prōō den' shal), *adj.* characterized by care and caution; springing from practical wisdom.

prune (prōōn), *n.* a dried plum.

prune (prōōn), *v.t.* to trim trees, bushes or vines by cutting off twigs and branches; to cut down or reduce, as to *prune* expenses.

prunella (prōō nel' a), *n.* a woolen fabric used in making gaiters.

*prussic acid (prus' ik as' id), hydrocyanic acid, a deadly poison.

pry (prī), *v.i. and v.t.* to examine inquisitively, *pry* into; to prize or move with a lever, *pry* up or *pry* loose.

*psalm (säm), *n.* a sacred song.

*pseudonym (sū' dō nim), *n.* a fictitious name.

psychedelic (sī kē del ´ ik), *adj.* having to do with abnormal alterations of perception as in psychedelic drugs.

psychic (sī' kik), *n.* a spiritualistic medium.

psychical (sī' kik al), *adj.* pertaining to the soul or spirit; pertaining to the mind.

*psychological (sī kō loj' i kal), *adj.* pertaining to the mind or the science of the mind.

*psychology (sī kol' ō ji), *n.* [*pl.* psychologies] the science of the mind; mental philosophy; a book on the science of the mind.

*psychopathic (sī kō path' ik) *adj.* afflicted with mental disorder.

*psychophysics (sī kō fiz' iks), *n.* the science that treats of the relations between mind and matter.

*ptomaine (tō' mān), *n.* an alkaloid of a highly poisonous nature, originating in decaying matter such as food.

public (pub' lik), *n.* the people; a special following among the people, as an author needs a large *public*. *adj.* belonging to the people, as a *public* library; known to almost everybody; affecting the people in general, as a *public* disgrace.

publication (pub li kā' shun), *n.* the business of printing and selling; something printed for sale, as a book or newspaper; the act or process of making anything public.

publicist (pub' li sist), *n.* one who writes upon affairs, as international relations, political science and current events of national concern.

publicity (pub lis' i ti), *n.* the state of being a subject of common knowledge; circulation of printed matter advertising a business, institution or cause; notoriety.

publish (pub' lish), *v.t.* to make known by announcing or proclaiming; to print and put on sale, as books, newspapers and magazines.

publisher (pub' lish ẽr), *n.* a person or firm engaged in the business of printing books, magazines or newspapers and offering them for sale.

puck (puk), *n.* a hard, rubber disk used in the game of ice hockey.

pucker (puk' ẽr), *n.* a small fold or wrinkle.

pucker (puk' ẽr), *v.t. and v.i.* to gather into small folds; to wrinkle; to become drawn up into small folds, as the cloth *puckered.*

puckery (puk' ẽr i), *adj.* having a tendency to wrinkle easily, as *puckery* material; contracting to the tissues inside the mouth as a *puckery* fruit.

*pudding (pood' ing), *n.* a soft food, made of flour, milk, eggs and various flavorings, usually a sweetened dish used as dessert.

puddle (pud' l), *n.* a little pool of muddy water on a sidewalk or in a road; clay and sand kneaded when wet to make a mixture impervious to water; a heavy tamp used in packing ballast on a railroad track.

puddle (pud' l), *v.t.* to work clay into a waterproof mixture; to line with kneaded clay; to make iron in a reverberatory furnace.

puddle iron (pud' l ī' ẽrn), iron made by subjecting pig iron and oxidizing elements to intense heat in a reverberatory furnace.

puddling (pud' ling), *n.* the method of turning melted pig iron into wrought iron in a reverbatory furnace with oxidizing elements to remove impurities.

pudgy (puj' i), *adj.* short and fat, as a *pudgy* figure.

*pueblo (pweb' lō), *n.* [*pl.* pueblos] a community dwelling place of the Pueblo Indians in the Southwest of the U. S., built of adobe and arranged in terraces.

*puerile (pū' ẽr il), *adj.* childish.

puerility (pū ẽr il' i ti), *n.* [*pl.* puerilities] childishness; a childish act.

puff (puf), *n.* a single sudden emission of breath or gust of wind; a whiff, as a *puff* of smoke; a fungous ball filled with dust, also called *puff*ball; any of various small round objects formed as if inflated, such as a powder *puff;* a light sort of cake formed in a hollow sphere and filled with some creamlike mixture, as a cream*puff;* empty praise, especially that in a newspaper, as the drama critic gave the new actress quite a *puff*. *v.i. and v.t.* to emit air, smoke, breath, in single gusts; to breathe fast and hard, as after exertion; to inflate with air or with importance, as to *puff* up with pride; to blow out in whiffs, as to *puff* smoke.

puff adder (puf ad ´ ẽr), *n.* a poisonous South African snake of the viper family, that inflates itself with air which it puffs out as a warning sound.

puffy (puf' i), *adj.* [*comp.* puffier, *superl.* puffiest] distended or inflated; coming in gusts, as a *puffy* breeze; having an inflated style, as a *puffy* sort of essay.

pug dog (pug' dŏg), *n.* a small dog with face and nose like a bulldog's, and a tightly curled tail.

pugging (pug' ing), *n.* the operation of working up clay for pottery or bricks.

*pugilism (pū' ji lizm), *n.* the art of boxing; prize fighting.

*pugnacious (pug nā' shus), *adj.* always ready to fight, quarrelsome.

pugnacity (pug nas' i ti), n. readiness to fight, quarrelsomeness.

*****puissant** (pū' i sant), adj. powerful, strong; mighty, as a puissant ruler.

puling (pūl' ing), adj. whining; infantile.

pull (pool), n. a haul, as it was a long pull up that hill; something operated by tugging, as a bellpull; the state of having influence with those in power, as in politics.

pull (pool), v.i. and v.t. to cause motion toward a compelling force; to drag, haul, tug.

pullet (pool' et), n. a young hen.

pulley (pool' i), n. [pl. pulleys] a turning wheel over which a rope, belt or chain runs in doing work, as in lifting weights, transmitting power to machinery.

*****pulmonary** (pul' mō ner i), adj. pertaining to or affecting the lungs.

*****pulmotor** (pul' mō tẽr), n. a machine for producing artificial respiration in cases of asphyxiation.

pulp (pulp), n. a soft, wet mass, as the pulp of an orange, or the pulp of ground cloth or wood, from which paper is made.

pulpit (pool' pit), n. an inclosed elevated reading desk in a church, from which the sermon is spoken.

pulpwood (pulp' wood), n. wood that is made into a soft mass for manufacturing purposes, especially making paper.

pulpy (pul' pi), adj. [comp. pulpier, superl. pulpiest] consisting of a soft, wet mass.

pulsate (pul' sāt), v.i. to throb or beat.

pulsation (pul sā' shun), n. a throb or beat.

*****pulse** (puls), n. the rhythmic throb of an artery as the blood passes through, matching the beat of the heart.

pulverize (pul' vẽr iz), v.t. to reduce to powder.

*****pumice** (pum' is), n. a hard, light spongy volcanic stone, used for cleaning and polishing, as a pumice stone.

pump (pump), n. a machine to raise water or other liquids or to move gases, as an air pump. v.t. to raise or move fluids by means of a machine; to seek information through persistent questioning, as I pumped the news out of him.

*****pumpkin** (pump' kin), n. a plant of the gourd family with large, round, yellow or orange-colored fruit.

pun (pun), n. a play upon words, exploiting similarity in sound with difference of meaning.

punch (punch), n. a tool for stamping or perforating; a blow with the closed hand; a drink made from fruit juices.

punch (punch), v.t. to make a hole or impression with a stamping or perforating tool; to strike with the fist.

punctilio (pungk til' i ō), n. [pl. punctilios] a fine point in behavior or ceremony; fastidious preciseness.

*****punctilious** (pungk til' i us), adj. attentive to the fine points of etiquette or conduct.

*****punctual** (pungk' tū al), adj. in exact agreement with appointed time; on time.

punctuality (pungk tū al' i ti), n. the characteristic of being on time.

punctuate (pungk' tū āt), v.i. and v.t. to mark with points indicating breaks in the run of a sentence, as the comma or period; to interrupt, as his speech was punctuated with applause.

punctuation (pungk tū ā' shun), n. the act or art of pointing sentences with commas, semicolons and other marks.

puncture (pungk' tūr), n. a small hole made by a sharp instrument, as a puncture in a pneumatic tire. v.t. to make a hole in.

*****pungent** (pun' jent), adj. sharp and stinging to taste or to smell; sarcastic; keen, as a pungent wit.

*****punish** (pun' ish), v.t. to cause loss or pain to, as a penalty for fault or crime; to chastise, correct.

punishable (pun' ish a bl), adj. liable to penalty.

punishment (pun' ish ment), n. the act of chastising; a penalty for a crime or a fault.

punitive (pū' ni tiv), adj. done as a measure of chastisement; having the nature of chastisement.

punk (pungk), n. decayed wood that is useful for tinder.

puny (pū' ni), adj. [comp. punier, superl. puniest] inferior in strength or size; weak, as a puny man makes puny efforts.

pup (pup), n. a young dog, puppy.

pupa (pū' pa), n. the intermediate stage in the life of an insect, after the larval stage, chrysalis.

*****pupil** (pū' pil), n. a young student; the dark center of the eye, the apple of the eye.

puppet (pup' et), n. a small doll or image, especially one used in a mock drama, and moved by hands, wires or strings; a person controlled by another and having no initiative.

puppy (pup' i), n. [pl. puppies] a young dog.

purblind (pûr' blind), adj. seeing obscurely, nearly blind.

purchase (pûr' chis), n. something bought; a good hold or grip on an object to lift or move it, leverage. v.t. and v.i. to buy, as to purchase a hat; to obtain, as for a price, as to purchase one's freedom; to apply a mechanical device for raising or moving to; to make a purchase, as that is the suit I purchased last week.

*****pure** (pūr), adj. free from physical or moral defilement; without admixture; sheer, as pure folly; genuine, as pure kindness.

purgation (pûr gā' shun), n. the act of cleansing, as of physical impurities, or clearing, as of guilt.

purgatory (pûr' ga tō ri), n. in the Roman Catholic Church, the state of purification through suffering after death from venial sins done in this life; any state of misery.

purge (pûrj), n. that which cleanses; removal of elements of population not desired by the governing class. v.i. and vt. to become or make free of impurities; to rid of unfriendly elements, as Hitler purged the Nazi party.

purify (pū' ri fi), v.t. [p.t. and p.p. purified, pr.p. purifying] to free from corruptions or barbarisms.

purist (pūr' ĭst), *n.* one who is scrupulously exact in choice of words and style of expression.

puritan (pū' rĭ tan), *n.* a person who is extremely strict in his religious life and morals; one who urges a reform of the Church.

purity (pū' rĭ tĭ), *n.* the quality of being free of blemishes and without admixture.

*****purl** (pûrl), *n.* an embroidered border; a reversed knitting stitch, producing a ribbed appearance. *n.* a small swirl of water; the sound of a murmuring stream. *v.i.* and *v.t.* to invert the stitches in knitting. *v.i.* to make a sound like the murmur of a flowing stream.

*****purlieus** (pûr' lūz), *n. pl.* environs, the outskirts of a city.

purloin (pûr' loin), *v.t.* to steal.

purple (pûr' pl), *n.* the color obtained by blending blue and red.

*****purport** (pûr' pōrt), *n.* meaning, signification.

purport (pûr pōrt'), *v.t.* to mean or seem to mean; to be intended for understanding in a certain way; to profess.

purpose (pûr' pus), *n.* design, intention, a desired end. *v.t.* to intend; to propose to oneself as an end.

purposely (pûr' pus lĭ), *adv.* intentionally, deliberately, as he *purposely* ignored her comment.

purr (pûr), *n.* the murmuring sound made by a cat that is comfortable and content.

purse (pûrs), *n.* a small holder for money, to be carried in the pocket or hand; a sum of money offered as a prize. *v.t.* to pucker or wrinkle, as the lips.

purser (pûr' sēr), *n.* a clerk on a passenger steamer having charge of tickets, accounts, freight.

pursuant (pēr sū' ant), *adj.* acting or done in consequence of or according to.

*****pursue** (pēr sū'), *v.t.* to chase; to follow, as an occupation; to seek, as to *pursue* pleasure.

*****pursuit** (pēr sūt'), *n.* the act of chasing; an occupation.

purulent (pū' roo lent), *adj.* consisting of or containing pus.

purvey (pûr vā'), *v.i.* and *v.t.* to procure or provide, as food.

purveyance (pûr vā' ans), *n.* the procuring of food; the food provided.

*****pus** (pus), *n.* matter secreted in sores.

push (poosh), *n.* a shove; pressure or the exertion of pressure; a major forward movement, as of military forces. *v.i.* and *v.t.* to press against with continuing force; to shove; to promote, with steady endeavor; to dun, as to *push* a debtor.

pusher (poosh´ er), *n.* an active or energetic person; in slang, an illegal seller of narcotics or drugs.

*****pusillanimity** (pū sĭ la nĭm' ĭ tĭ), *n.* [*pl.* pusillanimities] cowardice; a cowardly act.

*****pusillanimous** (pū sĭ lan' ĭ mus), *adj.* cowardly; mean-spirited.

*****pustule** (pus' tūl), *n.* a small swelling in the skin, containing pus.

put (poot), *v.t.* and *v.i.* to place, as to *put* the papers in the desk; to cause to be in a certain condition, as to *put* the house in order; to set, as to *put* a price on something; to express, as to *put* thoughts into words; to hurl with an overhand motion of the arm, as to *put* the shot; to betake oneself, as to *put* to sea.

*****putative** (pū' ta tĭv), *adj.* supposed, reputed, as the putative father of the baby.

putrefaction (pū trē fak' shun), *n.* the process of decomposition; rottenness.

putrefy (pū' trē fī), *v.i.* and *v.t.* to decay; to cause to rot.

putrescent (pū tres' ent), *adj.* decaying, rotting.

putridity (pū trid' ĭ tĭ), *n.* rottenness.

putsch (pootsh), *n.* an unsuccessful uprising against the government, especially in Germany.

putt (put), *n.* a short, careful stroke in golf to place the ball in or near the hole.

putter (put' ēr), *n.* a golf club used for playing a short, careful stroke.

putty (put' ĭ), *n.* a compound of whiting and linseed oil used to fasten glass in sashes and frames and to fill holes in wood or plaster.

puzzle (puz' l), *n.* something that tries the ingenuity or perplexes; a riddle.

puzzle (puz' l), *v.i.* and *v.t.* to think hard, as to *puzzle* over a problem; to confuse and perplex, as the situation *puzzles* me.

pygmy (pig' mĭ), *n.* a very small person or thing, a dwarf: Pygmy, one of a dwarf people in Central Africa.

pylon (pī' lon), *n.* a tower or monumental gateway at the entrance to an ancient temple; a flag pole or metallic tower marking an airport; a metallic scaffold or tower supporting a long span of electric wires.

*****pylorus** (pī lō' rus), *n.* [*pl.* pylori] the opening of the stomach into the intestines.

*****pyramid** (pir' a mid), *n.* a solid body having triangular sides rising to an apex: the *Pyramids,* huge stone structures built as tombs for ancient Egyptian kings and Peruvian emperors.

*****pyramidal** (pī ram' ĭ dal), *adj.* having triangular sides rising to an apex.

pyre (pīr), *n.* a funeral pile for burning the corpse.

*****pyrites** (pī rī' tēz), *n.* a native compound of sulphur with iron or copper.

*****pyrography** (pī rog' ra fĭ), *n.* the art of decorating materials, such as wood and leather, by burning designs into their surface with a hot iron.

pyromania (pī rō mā' nĭ a), *n.* an insane longing to set fire.

*****pyrometer** (pī rom' ě tēr), *n.* an instrument to measure extremely high degrees of heat, as in furnaces, and for measuring the expansion of substances under great heat.

*****pyrotechnics** (pī rō tek' niks), *n.* the art of making and handling fireworks; fireworks.

*****python** (pī' thon), *n.* a large nonvenomous serpent, the boa or anaconda.

*****pyx** (piks), *n.* the box in which the consecrated wafer is kept; the box in which coins are tested in the British mint before being placed in circulation.

Q

quack (kwak), *n.* the cry of the duck; a pretender to medical skill or to skill of any kind. *v.i.* to make a noise like the cry of a duck.

quackery (kwak' ĕr ĭ), *n.* claim to medical skill not actually possessed; imposture.

*****quad** (kwod), *n.* a quadrangle or court of a college; a block of metal used to space between type letters.

quadrangle (kwod' rang gl), *n.* a plane figure with four angles and four sides; an open square surrounded by buildings.

quadrangular (kwod rang' gŭ lẽr), *adj.* having four sides and four angles.

*****quadrant** (kwod' rant), *n.* the fourth part of a circle, contained within an angle of 90°: an arc of 90°; an instrument with which the altitude of heavenly bodies is measured, used in navigating ships.

quadrate (kwod' rāt), *adj.* having four equal sides and four right angles.

quadratic (kwod rat' ĭk), *adj.* involving the square but no higher power of an unknown quantity, as a *quadratic* equation.

quadratics (kwod rat' ĭks), *n.* the part of algebra that deals with equations involving the square but no higher power of an unknown quantity.

quadrennial (kwod ren' ĭ al), *adj.* occurring once in four years; consisting of four years, as a *quadrennial* term of office.

quadrilateral (kwod rĭ lat' ẽr al), *n.* a four-sided plane figure.

*****quadrille** (kwo drĭl'), *n.* a dance by four couples; the music for it.

quadroon (kwod rōōn'), *n.* the offspring of a white person and a mulatto; a person of quarter negro blood.

quadruped (kwod' roo ped), *n.* a four-footed animal. *adj.* four-footed.

*****quadruple** (kwod' roo pl), *adj.* fourfold.

*****quadruple** (kwod roo' pl), *v.i. and v.t.* to increase fourfold; to multiply by 4.

*****quadruplet** (kwod' roo plet), *n.* a group of four of one kind; four offspring of one mother born within a few minutes of each other.

*****quaff** (kwȧf), *v.t. and v.i.* to drink copiously of, as he *quaffed* the water in great swallows; to drink deeply, as he *quaffed* thirstily.

*****quagmire** (kwag' mĭr), *n.* a bog; a stretch of soft, wet ground.

quail (kwāl), *n.* a bird related to the partridge; the bob white. *v.i.* to shrink from danger, cower.

quaint (kwānt), *adj.* pleasingly old-fashioned; attractively unusual in looks or ways.

quake (kwāk), *n.* a shaking or trembling, especially an earthquake.

quake (kwāk), *v.i.* to tremble or shake; to quiver with agitation.

qualification (kwol ĭ fĭ kā' shun), *n.* the act of

proving oneself fit or worthy; that which demonstrates fitness; a limitation, as to meaning of a word; fitness, as for office.

*****qualify** (kwol' ĭ fī), *v.i. and v.t.* to be fit or to prove one's fitness for any particular service, office or employment; to make limiting statement or restricting condition about; to describe, limit or modify, as an adjective *qualifies* a noun, an adverb a verb.

qualitative (kwol' ĭ tā tĭv), *adj.* pertaining to peculiar properties; determining the nature of component parts.

quality (kwol' ĭ tĭ), *n.* [*pl.* qualities] any peculiar power or property; essential nature, attribute, characteristic; degree of excellence, as a material of fine *quality.*

*****qualm** (kwäm), *n.* a sudden fit of sickness, nausea; compunction; sudden fear.

*****quandary** (kwon' da rĭ), *n.* [*pl.* quandaries] a state of difficulty or perplexity.

quantitative (kwon' tĭ tā tĭv), *adj.* pertaining to bulk, amount or number.

*****quantity** (kwon' tĭ tĭ), *n.* [*pl.* quantities] any indeterminate or measurable bulk, weight or number; a large portion, sum or mass; the length or duration of a sound, as in music or in distinguishing between short and long vowels.

quantum (kwon' tum), *n.* the smallest amount of energy radiated or absorbed by matter, varying as the frequency of the vibration associated with the ether wave.

*****quarantine** (kwor' an tēn), *n.* the time during which a vessel suspected of carrying germs of disease is prohibited from intercourse with the shore; the place at which such vessels are held; an enforced restriction placed on a person or place because of contagious disease, as the house is in *quarantine.*

*****quarrel** (kwor' el), *n.* an angry dispute.

quarrelsome (kwor' el sum), *adj.* inclined to wrangle; contentious.

quarry (kwor' ĭ), *n.* [*pl.* quarries] a place where building stone is dug out of the earth.

quarry (kwor' ĭ), *n.* [*pl.* quarries] game; anything hunted. *v.t.* [*p.t.* and *p.p.* quarried, *pr.p.* quarrying] to take stone from; to excavate, as to *quarry* land.

*****quart** (kwôrt), *n.* a unit of liquid measure, two pints or one-fourth of a gallon; a unit of dry measure equal to one-eighth of a peck.

quarter (kwôr' tẽr), *n.* one of four equal parts of anything; a silver coin worth one-fourth of a dollar, 25 cents; one of the four major points of the compass, as which *quarter* does the wind blow from; one of the four limbs of an animal, with the surrounding parts, for use as meat; mercy to a wounded enemy, as the victors gave no *quarter;* a section or district, as the Latin *quarter* of Paris.

quarter-deck (kwôr' tẽr dek), *n.* the part of a

ship's upper deck aft of the mainmast.

quarterly (kwôr' tẽr li), *n.* [*pl.* quarterlies] a publication issued every three months.

quarterly (kwôr' tẽr li), *adj.* happening every three months. *n.* [*pl.* quarterlies] a quarter of the year.

quartermaster (kwôr' tẽr mȧs tẽr), *n.* an officer whose function is to find food and supplies for a regiment; a petty officer of the navy who assists the navigator.

quarters (kwôr' tẽrz), *n.* lodgings, especially for troops.

quartet (kwôr tet'), *n.* any group of four; a musical composition in four parts; the four singers or players who perform it.

quarto (kwôr' tō), *n.* [*pl.* quartos] the size of a book or its page made by folding each sheet into four leaves with a page about 9½ by 12½ inches. *adj.* having four leaves to a sheet.

quartz (kwôrts), *n.* a crystalline form of silica, the commonest solid mineral, occurring in granite and many other kinds of stone.

quasar (kwä´ zär), *n.* a distant starlike object which emits light or powerful radio waves.

*****quash** (kwosh), *v.t.* to put down, as a rebellion; to set aside, make void, as to *quash* an indictment.

*****quassia** (kwosh' i a), *n.* a South American tree yielding excessively bitter bark and wood, from which a tonic is made.

*****quaternion** (kwa tûr' ni un), *n.* a set of four parts, things or persons.

quatrain (kwot' rān), *n.* a stanza having four lines, which usually rhyme alternately.

quaver (kwā' vẽr), *n.* a vibration, as of the voice. *v.i.* to shake or tremble; to vibrate.

*****quay** (kē), *n.* a wharf at which ships load and unload cargo.

queen (kwēn), *n.* a female ruler; consort of a king.

queenly (kwēn' li), *adj.* [*comp.* queenlier, *superl.* queenliest] of, like, or suitable to a king's consort.

queen post (kwēn pōst), one of two vertical timbers in a roof truss at equal distances from the tie beam.

*****queer** (kwēr), *adj.* odd, singular, droll, strange. *v.t.* to interfere with, as to *queer* one's chances.

quell (kwel), *v.t.* to crush, put down, as a riot or rebellion; to calm, allay, as rage or a fever.

quench (kwench), *v.t.* to extinguish, as a fire; to allay, as thirst.

quern (kwern), *n.* a primitive hand mill to grind grain.

querist (kwēr' ist), *n.* one who asks a question.

*****querulous** (kwer' ū lus), *adj.* fretful, complaining.

*****query** (kwēr' i), *n.* [*pl.* queries] a question.

query (kwēr' i), *v.t.* to question; to challenge the correctness of.

quest (kwest), *n.* a search.

*****question** (kwes' chun), *n.* an inquiry, interrogation; subject discussed.

question (kwes' chun), *v.t. and v.i.* to inquire of, query, as to *question* a witness; to dis-

pute, challenge, as to *question* a decision; to inquire.

Syn. Ask, inquire, interrogate. To *question* or *interrogate* means to ask repeated questions in order to ascertain certain facts; to *ask* is the general term for putting a question; to *inquire* is to request information, as we *inquired* the way.

questionable (kwes' chun a bl), *adj.* open to inquiry; subject to suspicion.

queue (kū), *n.* the tail of a wig; a braid of hair hanging down the back; a waiting line, as of people or vehicles.

*****quibble** (kwib' l), *n.* a petty argument advanced to evade the truth; a diversion from the point under discussion.

quibble (kwib' l), *v.i.* to evade the truth by intruding petty arguments; to cavil, as to *quibble* over the meaning of a word.

quick (kwik), *adj.* lively, animated, active, brisk, ready, hasty.

quicken (kwik' en), *v.i. and v.t.* to act or move with more speed, as the story *quickens;* to cause to act or move more rapidly, as you should *quicken* the action in your story; to refresh, as the cool breeze *quickened* me.

quicklime (kwik' līm), *n.* lime burned and unslaked.

quicksand (kwik' sand), *n.* a bed of wet sand so loose and mobile that any heavy body sinks into it.

quicksilver (kwik' sil vẽr), *n.* mercury; an amalgam of tin and mercury.

quick-witted (kwik wit' ed), *adj.* mentally alert, as a *quick-witted* answer.

quiddity (kwid' i ti), *n.* [*pl.* quiddities] the essence of anything; a trifling nicety.

quidnunc (kwid' nungk), *n.* one who is curious about what goes on around him, a gossip.

quiescent (kwī es' ent), *adj.* inactive, still.

*****quiet** (kwī' et), *n.* absence of noise, stillness, silence, peace.

quiet (kwī' et), *adj.* noiseless; tranquil; not conspicuous, as *quiet* colors.

quiet (kwī' et), *v.i. and v.t.* to become silent; to calm or pacify; to still, hush, tranquillize.

quietude (kwī' e tūd), *n.* a state of stillness, repose, tranquillity.

*****quietus** (kwī ē' tus), *n.* that which causes suspension or cessation of action; death· final settlement of an account.

quill (kwil), *n.* a large feather of a bird's wing or tail; the hollow stem of a feather; one of the long sharp spines of the porcupine; a feather with the end of the shaft sharpened to use as a pen; a plectrum or pick for a stringed instrument, made from the shaft of a feather.

quilt (kwilt), *n.* a bed covering with a layer of soft material between two pieces of cloth.

quilt (kwilt), *v.i. and v.t.* to work at the making of a quilt; to interline, in the same way that a quilt is made.

quilting (kwilt' ing), *n.* the making of quilts; the material from which quilts are made.

*****quince** (kwins), *n.* a small, tough tree with hard yellow-skinned fruit, sometimes used in making jelly.

*quinine (kwī' nĭn), n. an alkaline substance obtained from the bark of the cinchona tree used as a tonic and as a remedy for malaria.

quinquennial (kwĭn kwen' ĭ al), adj. occurring every five years; lasting five years.

quinsy (kwĭn' zĭ), n. a severe soreness of the throat and tonsils with inflammation, swelling and pus.

quint (kwĭnt), n. a set or sequence of five.

quintessence (kwĭnt es' sens), n. concentrated essence; typical example.

*quintessence (kwĭnt es' ens), n. the concentrated essence of anything; a typical embodiment, as he is the quintessence of patriotism.

quintillion (kwĭn tĭl' yun), n. a thousand quadrillions, 1 followed by 18 ciphers, in France and the U.S.; a million quadrillions, 1 followed by 30 ciphers, in Great Britain.

quintet (kwĭn tet'), n. a musical composition for five voices or instruments; the five performers; any set of five.

quintuple (kwĭn' tū pl), adj. fivefold, multiplied by five.

quintuplets (kwĭn' tū plets), n. five offspring of the same mother born within a few minutes of each other.

quip (kwĭp), n. a sarcastic remark, clever retort.

quire (kwīr), n. a unit of measure of paper, one-twentieth of a ream or 24 sheets; formerly, four sheets folded to make eight leaves.

quirk (kwûrk), n. a quick twist or flourish of the pen; a quick play of fancy; a quip, quibble, clever evasion.

*quit (kwĭt), v.i. and v.t. to cease; to desist from; to resign; to discharge a debt.

quite (kwīt), adv. wholly, completely, entirely.

quits (kwĭts), adj. on even terms, all square.

quittance (kwĭt' ans), n. discharge of a debt.

quitter (kwĭt' ẽr), n. one who gives up a task before it is finished, a shirk.

quiver (kwĭv' ẽr), n. a case to hold arrows; a tremor.

quiver (kwĭv' ẽr), v.i. to tremble, shake.

*quixotic (kwĭks ot' ĭk), adj. chivalrous to the point of being ridiculous; queer, eccentric.

quiz (kwĭz), n. a test, as of a class, by questions; an enigma or obscure question designed to puzzle. v.t. to puzzle with odd questions; to make fun of; to test, as a class in school, with questions.

quizzical (kwĭz' ĭ kal), adj. having fun while pretending to be serious, bantering, teasing, as a quizzical look.

*quoin (koĭn), n. an exterior angle of a building, or one of the shaped stones used to make it; a wedge-shaped printing device used to lock type in a frame.

*quoit (kwoĭt), n. a flat, iron ring pitched at a peg in the game called quoits.

*quorum (kwō' rum), n. the number of members whose presence is required before a meeting can legally take action.

quota (kwō' ta), n. the part or share assigned to each, either in work to be done, money to be collected or advantages reaped.

quotation (kwō tā' shun), n. the act of repeating the words of another; that which is repeated; current price in a market.

quote (kwōt), v.i. and v.t. to repeat or copy a passage from another's speech or writing; to state the current price of in a market.

*quoth (kwōth), v.i. said: an archaic form, usually followed by the subject noun or pronoun, as quoth he.

*quotient (kwō' shent), n. the number resulting from division of one number by another.

R

rabbet (rab' et), n. a cut in one piece of wood to permit joining with another piece; a joint made in this way. v.t. to join two pieces of wood by making cuts in one or both.

*rabbi (rab' ĭ), n. [pl. rabbis] a Jewish interpreter and teacher of the law.

rabbit (rab' ĭt), n. a small burrowing rodent related to the hare, with long ears and a short fluffy tail; Welsh rabbit, a dish of melted or toasted cheese on toast or crackers, sometimes called rarebit.

rabble (rab' l), n. an iron bar to stir hot metal in puddling. n. a mob, a noisy crowd: the rabble, the riffraff element in the common people.

rabid (rab' ĭd), adj. furious, raging; fanatic; having rabies or pertaining to rabies, as a rabid sympton, a rabid dog.

*rabies (rā bĭ ēz), n. a fatal disease of the nervous system, especially of dogs and other carnivorous animals, transmitted only by the bite of an infected animal; hydrophobia.

raccoon (ra kōōn'), n. a small, arboreal, carnivorous animal of North America with a bushy ringed tail; the fur of this animal.

*race (rās), n. a swiftly coursing channel of water, as a millrace; a contest of speed; groove holding balls in a ball bearing.

race (rās), n. a division of mankind having traits that set it apart as a distinct human type, as the white race; a tribe, people or group of peoples or a nation descended from the same common stock or having the same root language or culture, as the Latin race; family, lineage, as to come of a royal race.

race (rās), v.i. and v.t. to run swiftly; to take part in a contest of speed, as time races, the stream races, life races away; horses race, thoughts race through one's mind.

racial (rā' shal), adj. pertaining to stock or lineage.

rack (rak), n. a mass of high, broken clouds.

rack (rak), n. a framework on which to hang clothes; a barred grating on a manger to hold fodder; a framework on a hay wagon; a bar with teeth that mesh with those of a geared wheel. *n.* an old-time apparatus to inflict torture by stretching the body; anguish, physical or mental. *v.t.* to strain, stretch or exert; to torture.

racket (rak' et), *n.* noise of a confused kind; a confusion of noises.

racket (rak' et), *n.* an organized criminal operation systematically exacting tribute from legitimate business and thus from the public in general. *n.* a frame filled with network of catgut used to strike the ball in tennis and other games, as lacrosse.

radar (rā´ där), *n.* a device which detects, locates, and indicates the speed of aircraft, ships, and objects by means of reflected microwaves.

radial (rā' di al), *adj.* spreading, like rays of light; pertaining to the radius, the bone of the forearm.

radiance (rā' di ans), *n.* brilliant brightness.

*•***radiant** (rā' di ant), *adj.* emitting rays of light or heat; shining, brilliant, as *radiant* beauty; beaming with joy, love or hope, as a *radiant* face.

*•***radiate** (rā' di āt), *v.i. and v.t.* to emit rays of light or heat; to give forth, diffuse, as to *radiate* courage.

radiation (rā di ā' shun), *n.* the emission of rays of light or heat.

radiator (rā' di ā tēr), *n.* a coil or drum throwing out heat; any appliance used to cool by spreading water or air, as the *radiator* of an automobile.

radical (radi' kal), *adj.* fundamental; going to the roots of anything; revolutionary.

radicate (rad' i kāt), *v.i. and v.t.* to take root; to plant, establish.

radio (rā' di ō), *n.* [*pl.* radios] a system of sending and receiving signals, messages, speeches, music and other sounds, by electric waves without the use of connecting wires; radiotelegraphy and radiotelephony; a radio receiving set.

radioactive (rā' di ō ak' tiv), *adj.* emitting rays of energy or rays of electrified particles; exhibiting the properties possessed by radium.

radio-frequency (rā di ō frē' kwen si), *n.* a succession of vibrations too fast to be perceived by the ear. more than 15,000 per second.

radiogram (rā' di ō gram), *n.* a message sent by radiophone or by wireless telegraphy.

radiograph (rā' di ō gráf), *n.* a picture made on a photographic plate by means of radiation other than light; an X-ray photograph.

radiography (rā' di og' rā fi), *n.* the process of making radiographs.

radiometer (rā di om' ē tēr), *n.* an instrument to measure radiant energy.

radiophone (rā' di ō fōn), *n.* a wireless telephone.

radiotherapy (rā di ō ther'a pi), *n.* the use of radioactivity to treat disease.

radish (rad' ish), *n.* a garden plant with a pungent fleshy root which is eaten without cooking.

radium (rā' di um), *n.* a rare metallic element, found in pitchblende and possessing strong radioactivity with no apparent loss of energy or weight from giving out actinic rays.

*•***radius** (rā' di us), *n.* [*pl.* radii] a straight line from the central point of a circle or sphere to its circumference or surface; one of two bones of the human forearm or of the front leg of higher vertebrates.

radix (rā' diks), *n.* a root; the root or first form of a word; the base of a system of logarithms.

radon (rā' don), *n.* a heavy gaseous element resembling argon, but radioactive.

raff (raf), *n.* a jumbled heap; the rabble, as in *riffraff*.

raffle (raf' l), *n.* a drawing for a prize to be won by one of the individuals who collectively provide it. *n.* rubbish, waste. *v.t.* to put up as a prize on which *c*hances are sold.

*•***raft** (ráft), *n.* a floating platform, made of logs, planks or metal supported by buoyant cylinders, to carry a load by water or for use as a life*raft* at a bathing beach.

raft (ráft), *v.i.* to work on a float of logs; to transport by float.

rafter (ráf' tēr), *n.* one of the sloping beams in a roof.

rag (rag), *n.* an old piece of cloth: *rags*, old, worn and tattered clothes, he was in *rags* and tatters.

ragamuffin (rag' a muf in), *n.* a ragged, mischievous loafer.

rage (rāj), *n.* anger, fury.

ragged (rag' ed), *adj.* worn out; tattered; dressed in tatters.

*•***ragout** (ra gōō'), *n.* a highly seasoned stew.

ragtime (rag' tim), *n.* rhythm marked by syncopation of the melody; music having a syncopated melody standing out against a regular rhythmic accompaniment.

*•***raid** (rād), *n.* a hostile or predatory incursion; an attack by airplanes, or a night attack on the enemy's trenches; a forced entrance by police upon premises where gambling or other offenses are going on.

*•***raid** (rād), *v.t.* to attack suddenly and return quickly; to enter and make arrests in enforcing the law.

rail (rāl), *n.* a horizontal bar in a fence; a horizontal bar along the side of a deck, stairway or balcony, to protect those passing; one of a series of long flanged steel bars forming a track for trains. *n.* a wading bird related to the cranes; a marsh-hen or crake. *v.t.* to equip with rails, to fence. *v.i.* to scold or scoff, address with bitter, scornful language.

railhead (rāl' hed), *n.* the furthest point to which a track has been laid in construction of a railroad.

railing (rāl' ing), *n.* material for rails; a fence made of posts and rails.

*•***raillery** (rāl' ēr i), *n.* [*pl.* railleries] satire touched with pleasantry, kindly ridicule, banter.

railroad (rāl' rōd), *n.* a line of track consisting of two parallel lines of heavy steel rails laid on ties over a ballasted roadbed, on which cars are drawn by steam or electric engines; a system of such trackage, with equipment, as rolling stock, stations, roundhouses, shops, signals.

railway (rāl' wā), *n.* a railroad carrying lighter traffic, as a trolley *railway.*

raiment (rā' ment), *n.* clothing, garments.

rain (rān), *n.* water in drops discharged from the clouds; anything likened to rain with its countless drops, as a *rain* of bullets.

rain (rān), *v.i. and v.t.* to fall in drops from the clouds; to fall like rain; to cause to occur as if in showers, as to *rain* compliments upon one.

rainbow (rān' bō), *n.* the bow or arc formed in the sky opposite the sun by sunlight shining through raindrops or mist and showing the colors of the spectrum.

rainfall (rān' fôl), *n.* the amount of rain that falls upon a given area in a given time.

raise (rāz), *v.t.* to cause to rise; to lift up; to cause to grow, as to *raise* a crop; to collect, as to *raise* a fund; to build, erect, as to *raise* a building; to bring up from below, as to *raise* a sunken ship; to put on a higher level, as to *raise* prices.

raisin (rā' zn), *n.* a dried grape of a special variety.

rake (rāk), *n.* a farmer's or gardener's toothed implement with a long handle, sometimes mounted on wheels, and used to smooth the soil or collect loose hay, leaves or litter from the ground. *n.* a dissolute man. *n.* inclination from the perpendicular, as the slant of a mast or funnel. *v.i. and v.t.* to use a rake; to gather or smooth with a rake, as to *rake* a lawn; to gather with a rake, as to *rake* leaves. *v.i.* to slant, as a ship's mast. *v.t.* to direct gunfire lengthwise, as our guns *raked* the deck of the ship.*v.t.* to cut a wing tip of an airplane back at an angle so that the after part is wider than the forward part.

rally (ral' i), *n.* [*pl.* rallies] a recovery from disorder or depression, as the team made a *rally* on the goal line, there was a strong *rally* in stocks; a mass meeting, as there will be a football *rally* tonight.

rally (ral' i), *v.i. and v.t.* to recover after disorder or depression; to reassemble, as troops in retreat; to revive, as you must *rally* your drooping spirits.

RAM (ram) *n.* random access memory; a computer memory that can be read and written into.

ram (ram), *n.* a male sheep; an apparatus for battering; the plunger of a force pump; the pounding weight used in a pile driver.

ram (ram), *v.t.* to force down by heavy impacts; to drive against, hard.

ramble (ram' bl), *n.* aimless wandering from place to place; an idle stroll. *v.i.* to roam about; to go from place to place idly; to wander in thought; to talk or write without progress toward a definite conclusion.

ramification (ram i fi kā' shun), *n.* a division or separation into branches, a subdivision, as the subject has many *ramifications.*

ramify (ram' i fi), *v.i. and v.t.* to spread out into branches; to separate into divisions.

*ramose** (rā' mōs), *adj.* branched, branching, having branches.

ramp (ramp), *n.* a slope connecting two levels for vehicles or pedestrians.

rampage (ram' pāj), *n.* a state of great excitement, as he is on the *rampage.*

rampage (ram pāj'), *v.i.* to storm and rage; to be furious.

rampant (ram' pant), *adj.* overleaping restraint or natural bounds; rearing on the hind legs with one foreleg raised above the other, as a lion *rampant* in a coat of arms.

rampart (ram' pärt), *n.* a mound or wall surrounding a fortified place; anything interposing between a threatened person and the source of the threat, as wealth is a *rampart* against need.

ramrod (ram' rod), *n.* a rod used to push down the charge of a muzzle-loading gun.

ramshackle (ram' shak l), *adj.* dilapidated, rickety.

*ranch** (ranch), *n.* a large cattle, horse or sheep farm; a large plantation of one crop, as a fruit *ranch.*

rancid (ran' sid), *adj.* having the rank smell or taste of spoiled fat, as this butter is *rancid.*

*rancor** (rang' kẽr), *n.* deep and spiteful dislike; implacable enmity.

rancorous (rang' kẽr us), *adj.* malignant, spiteful.

random (ran' dum), *n.* a haphazard course; lack of definite purpose, as at *random. adj.* without definite aim, haphazard.

range (rānj), *n.* a line or row, a series, as a mountain *range;* an area over which livestock may roam or feed; compass, reach, scope, as the *range* of prices, the *range* of a voice, the gun has a long *range;* line or direction, as to keep in *range* with a buoy; the whole region in which a plant or animal is naturally found; a place for target shooting, as a rifle *range;* a kitchen stove.

*range** (rānj), *v.i. and v.t.* to wander widely and freely; to differ within limits, as the prices *range* from $5 to $10; to set in rows; to place in a certain order.

ranger (rān' gẽr), *n.* a rover; the keeper of a royal English park or forest; one of a body of mounted men who patrol an extensive area; a forest guard.

rangy (rān' ji), *adj.* [*comp.* rangier, *superl.* rangiest] long-limbed and lank.

*rank** (rangk), *n.* a row of objects or men; station or position in life or in an organization; a grade of official position, as the *rank* of major. *v.i. and v.t.* to hold a certain position, as he *ranks* high in the organization; to rate, as I *rank* him high among those in his profession. *adj.* coarse and abundant in growth, as *rank* vegetation; strong and offensive, as a *rank* odor.

rankle (rang' kl), *v.i.* to fester; to irritate, as the remark *rankled.*

*ransack** (ran' sak), *v.t.* to search minutely; to plunder.

ransom (ran' sum), *n.* money asked or paid for release of a captive. *v.t.* to free from captivity by payment of money.

rant (rant), *n.* noisy, empty declamation.

rant (rant), *v.i.* to bluster; to be noisily wordy; to shout and gesture.

rap (rap), *n.* a quick, sharp, light blow.

rap (rap), *v.t.* to strike with a quick blow.

rap (rap), *v.* to have a frank discussion or talk either in a group or on a one-to-one basis.

*rapacious (ra pā' shus), *adj.* given to plundering; seeking prey; grasping.

rapids (rap' idz), *n.* a part of a river where the water rushes in a swift descent generally over a rocky stretch.

rape (rāp), *n.* a taking by force, robbery.

rape (rāp), *v.t.* to seize and take by force.

rapid (rap' id), *adj.* fast-moving, very swift.

rapier (rā' pi ẽr), *n.* a long slender-bladed sword for thrusting.

*rapine (rap' in), *n.* pillage and destruction.

*rapprochement (ra prōsh' män), *n.* a state of agreement; an understanding, as between two governments.

rapscallion (rap skal' yun), *n.* a rascal.

rapt (rapt), *adj.* transported with delight.

rapture (rap' tūr), *n.* ecstasy, great joy.

rare (rār), *adj.* [*comp.* rarer, *superl.* rarest] uncommon; precious because scarce; not cooked thoroughly, as meat.

rarebit (rār' bit), *n.* a Welsh rabbit, a dish of toasted or melted cheese on toast or crackers.

rare earth (rār ûrth), **rare earth metal** (met' l), one of a group of metals with properties common to all the group, occurring in various minerals; as cerium, terbium and yttrium are *rare earth metals.*

*rarefaction (rār ē fak' shun), *n.* the act of rendering less dense.

*rarefy (rār' ē fī), *v.i.* and *v.t.* to make or become thin or less dense.

rarely (rār' li), *adv.* seldom.

*rarity (rar' i ti), *n.* [*pl.* rarities] thinness; scarceness; excellence.

*rascal (ras' kal), *n.* a mean fellow; a tricky person.

rascality (ras' kal' i ti), *n.* [*pl.* rascalities] the state of being mean and tricky; an act such as is to be expected from such a person.

rash (rash), *n.* an eruption of red spots on the skin. *adj.* hasty; reckless, lacking caution and prudence.

rasher (rash' ẽr), *n.* a thin slice as of bacon or ham.

*rasp (rásp), *n.* a coarse file.

*raspberry (raz' ber i), *n.* [*pl.* raspberries] a bramble or prickly shrub of the rose family with juicy fruit, usually red or black.

rat (rat), *n.* an animal like the mouse but larger and more voracious.

ratable (rāt' *a* bl), *adj.* subject to taxation; capable of being rated or estimated.

ratchet (rach' et), *n.* a hinged piece that goes over the teeth of a geared wheel as it moves but drops in behind each tooth as it passes and prevents reverse revolution.

rate (rāt), *n.* ratio or proportion; price, according to a scale or standard, as *rates* at a hotel, postage *rates;* the amount or degree of one thing measured in terms of another, as a *rate* of miles per hour. *v.i. and v.t.* to belong in a certain class, have a certain standing or rank; to appraise, value, fix the value or degree of, as I *rate* studiousness highly.

*rather (ráth' ẽr), *adv.* more willingly, preferably, as I would *rather* stay home; instead, as take me *rather* than another; somewhat, as come *rather* early.

ratification (rat i fi kā' shun), *n.* the act of confirming, as the *ratification* of the 18th Amendment came in wartime.

ratify (rat' i fī), *v.t.* to express formal approval and acceptance of; to confirm, as to *ratify* a treaty.

*ratio (rā' shō), *n.* [*pl.* ratios] the relation or proportion of one quantity to another.

*ratiocination (răsh i os i nā' shun), *n.* the process of thinking a thing to a conclusion, reasoning.

*ration (rā' shun), *n.* an allowance, especially a daily allowance of food in the army or navy. *v.t.* to furnish with an allowance of food or other supplies, distribute, as *ration* it out among the men.

*rational (rash' un al), *adj.* according to reason.

*rationale (rash un ā' lē), *n.* a reasoned exposition; the underlying principles or reason.

rationalism (rash' un al izm), *n.* a doctrine which makes the basis for interpreting the universe human reason rather than sense perceptions or divine revelation.

rationality (rash un al' i ti), *n.* the power or practice of reasoning.

rationalize (rash' un al iz), *v.t.* to explain in terms of human reasoning, justify according to reason; to divest of all unreasonable or unexplainable elements, as to *rationalize* a miracle; to standardize by scientific management.

ratline (rat' lin), *n.* a rope forming one of the rounds of a ladder in a ship's rigging, strung between shrouds.

*rattan (ra tan'), *n.* a climbing palm with long, smooth, reedlike stems; a stem from such a palm; a walking stick made from this stem; wickerwork made of these flexible stems.

rattle (rat' l), *n.* a swift, continuous succession of short, sharp sounds, as the *rattle* of hail on a roof; a child's toy that makes a clattering sound.

rattle (rat' l), *v.i. and v.t.* to make a continuous clattering sound; to cause to make such a sound, as to *rattle* a stick on a picket fence; to move with such a sound, as the cart *rattled* over the rough road.

rattler (rat' lẽr), *n.* one who or that which makes a rattling noise; a rattlesnake.

rattlesnake (rat' l snāk), *n.* a venomous snake with hard bony rings on its tail that produce a rattling sound.

raucous (rô' kus), *adj.* rough sounding, harsh, hoarse.

ravage (rav' ij), *v.i. and v.t.* to cause ruin; to lay waste, pillage and burn.

ravage (rav' ij), *n.* pillage and destruction;

havoc; waste, as the *ravages* of disease.

rave (rāv), *v.i.* to talk like a madman; to wander mentally; to be delirious.

ravel (rav' l), *v.i. and v.t.* to become unwoven or unwound; to fray.

raven (rā' ven), *n.* a glossy black bird of the crow family.

raven (rav' en), *v.i. and v.t.* to seek and devour prey; to devour greedily.

*__ravenous__ (rav' en us), *adj.* rapacious and voracious; greedy for food.

ravine (ra vēn'), *n.* a deep gully worn by the action of a stream or torrent.

*__ravish__ (rav' ish), *v.t.* to seize and carry away by force; to transport with delight or joy.

*__raw__ (rô), *adj.* uncooked; unprepared, in the natural state, as *raw* materials.

rawboned (rô bōnd'), *adj.* with the bones sticking out; very lean, gaunt.

rawhide (rô' hīd), *n.* untanned skin; a cowhide whip.

ray (rā), *n.* a line of light proceeding from a radiant point; a beam of energy from a central source, as a heat *ray;* a line of radiation; a glimmer, as a *ray* of understanding.

rayon (rā' on), *n.* a fiber resembling silk made from cellulose by forcing it through small holes and drying the threads thus formed; the cloth made from these fibers.

raze (rāz), *v.t.* to level to the ground, tear down, as a building.

razor (rāz' ẽr), *n.* a sharp blade in a handle for cutting hair smooth to the skin.

reach (rēch), *n.* the distance within which one can touch anything; the act of stretching out to touch or grasp, as it took a long *reach* to get the apple, within *reach;* a straight-ahead stretch, as a long *reach* of the river; the bar that connects the rear axle of a wagon with the front; the distance a ship sails on one tack. *v.i. and v.t.* to stretch out in order to touch, as he *reached* for it; to arrive at, as we *reached* our destination.

react (rē akt'), *v.i.* to act in return, have a return influence, rebound; to respond to a stimulus.

reaction (rē ak' shun), *n.* return action, an opposite tendency, as conservatism is the *reaction* to radicalism; response, as honesty is the *reaction* to trust, one's *reaction* to good news.

read (rēd), *v.i. and v.t.* [*p.t.* and *p.p.* read (red), *pr.p.* reading] to take the meaning of written or printed words through the eye and the mind; to peruse.

readable (rēd' a bl), *adj.* fit to be read; easy to peruse; entertaining to a reader.

reader (rēd' ẽr), *n.* one who reads; a book used in teaching young pupils how to read.

readiness (red' i nes), *n.* the state of being prepared; promptness; willingness.

reading (rēd' ing), *n.* perusal of books; printed matter; a rendition of a prose, poetical or dramatic composition; what is registered by a gauge or meter, as the *reading* of the speedometer was 65 miles.

ready (red' i), *adj.* [*comp.* **readier,** *superl.*

readiest] prepared; in condition for immediate action or use; prompt, quick, as a *ready* answer; willing, as *ready* to work; available, as *ready* cash.

*__real__ (rē' al), *adj.* actually existing, not fictitious or imaginary, genuine, true; fixed, immovable, as *real* property is distinct from personal.

real estate (rē' al es tāt'), lands and all appertaining to them, as buildings.

*__realism__ (rē' al izm), *n.* the representation in art and literature of things as they actually are: opposite of *idealism* and *romanticism.*

realistic (rē al is' tik), *adj.* true to nature and fact, as *realistic* literature.

reality (rē al' i ti), *n.* [*pl.* realities] that which has actual existence; fact, truth; an actual person or thing.

*__realization__ (rē al i zā' shun), *n.* perception of the true nature of anything; accomplishment of a plan; turning of hope or expectation into actual happening.

realize (rē' al iz), *v.t.* to bring into actual existence, as to *realize* a hope; to perceive, understand, as to *realize* the truth; to sell and turn into cash, as to *realize* on real estate.

*__really__ (rē' al i), *adv.* actually, in truth.

realm (relm), *n.* a kingdom or empire; a domain, as the *realm* of poetry.

realty (rē' al ti), *n.* real estate.

ream (rēm), *n.* a measure of quantity in paper: 20 quires, or 480 sheets; a printer's ream, 516 sheets.

reap (rēp), *v.i. and v.t.* to gather grain; to receive a reward; to gather, as grain.

rear (rēr), *n.* the back part or last part, as the *rear* of a car, the *rear* of a procession; space behind, as the henhouse is at the *rear* of the stables. *v.i. and v.t.* to rise, as the horse *rears* on its hind legs; to raise or build, as they *reared* a house.

*__reason__ (rē' zn), *n.* the mental faculty which enables man to deduce principles from facts and to distinguish between right and wrong; a motive for action, as the *reason* for my doing it was simple; sanity, sense; a sane view, as that sounds like reason.

reason (rē' zn), *v.i.* to exercise the mental powers of induction and deduction; to argue; to consider both sides, debate, as let us *reason* it out.

reasonable (rē' zn a bl), *adj.* able to proceed, step by step, in thought, to a proper conclusion; governed by sound sense; moderate; acceptable.

reasoning (rē' zn ing), *n.* the process of arriving at sound conclusions through inferences and deductions; a course of argument.

*__rebate__ (rē' bāt), *n.* a discount or refund. *v.t.* to allow a discount on; to return part of.

*__rebel__ (reb' el), *n.* one who revolts against authority.

*__rebel__ (rē bel'), *v.i.* to revolt against authority; to take arms against one's government or sovereign.

rebellion (rē bel' yun), *n.* the act of resisting the government; open defiance of constituted authority; insubordination.

rebellious (rĕ bel′ yus), *adj.* defying lawfully constituted authority; resisting control.

*****rebound** (rĕ bound′), *n.* the act of springing back to place after a shock or blow. *v.i.* to spring back after a shock or blow.

rebuff (rĕ buf′), *n.* an abrupt refusal; a snub; any sharp check or repulse. *v.t.* to repel sharply; to snub; to beat back.

rebuke (rĕ būk′), *n.* a reprimand, reproof. *v.t.* to reprove sharply, reprimand, chide.

rebus (rē′ bus), *n.* [*pl.* rebuses] an enigmatic representation of a word, words or phrase by pictures or symbols.

rebuttal (rĕ but′ al), *n.* the act of answering directly an opponent's arguments in debate; giving evidence to offset evidence offered by the opposite side in a lawsuit.

*****recalcitrant** (rĕ kal′ si trant), *adj.* refractory; stubbornly refusing to comply, obstinate.

recall (rĕ kôl′), *n.* the act of summoning back; a signal ordering troops back from an advance; the power of an electorate to remove from office one whom it has previously elected. *v.t.* to summon back, as to *recall* a messenger; to bring back to mind, as to *recall* something that happened last year; to take back, as to *recall* an offensive remark.

recant (rĕ kant′), *v.i. and v.t.* to renounce opinions formerly asserted; to withdraw; to abjure.

recantation (rĕ kan tā′ shun), *n.* a declaration recalling and canceling a former one.

recapitulate (rē ka pit′ ū lāt), *v.i. and v.t.* to go over the main points of what has already been said; to summarize.

recede (rĕ sēd′), *v.i.* to move back; to retreat.

recede (rĕ sēd′), *v.t.* to deed back to a former owner: may be written *re-cede.*

*****receipt** (rĕ sēt′), *n.* the act of receiving or the state of being received, as on *receipt* of your letter; a written acknowledgment of payment or of a shipment's having been properly delivered; that which is taken in, as today's *receipts;* a recipe.

receipt (rĕ sēt′), *v.t.* to sign in acknowledgment of something paid or delivered.

receive (rĕ sēv′), *v.t.* to take or accept, as a gift, payment, or goods in a business transaction; to welcome and entertain, as guests.

receiver (rĕ sēv′ ēr), *n.* a recipient; a person appointed by a court to manage a property in controversy, especially in bankruptcy.

recension (rĕ sen′ shun), *n.* expert revision, as of a text; a revised text.

recent (rē′ sent), *adj.* of late origin or occurrence; new.

*****receptacle** (rĕ sep′ ta kl), *n.* something to hold other things, a container, as a pocketbook is a *receptacle* for money.

receptive (rĕ sep′ tiv), *adj.* ready to take in and hold; quick to take in impressions, and strong in holding perceptions, as a *receptive* mind.

*****recess** (rĕ ses′), *n.* an alcove; a secluded nook; a short intermission in work.

recession (rĕ sesh′ un),*n.* withdrawal. *n.* the act of deeding a property back.

recessional (rĕ sesh′ un al), *n.* the hymn sung at the close of a church service while the clergy and the choir are withdrawing.

*****recipe** (res′ i pē), *n.* a formula for mixing a medicine, directions for preparing a dish for the table.

recipient (rĕ sip′ i ent), *n.* one who receives, as the *recipient* of favors.

*****reciprocal** (rĕ sip′ rō kal), *adj.* mutual; interchangeable.

reciprocate (rĕ sip′ rō kāt), *v.i. and v.t.* to repay in kind, as to *reciprocate* a favor; to give in return for.

*****reciprocity** (res i pros′ i ti), *n.* [*pl.* reciprocities] an arrangement between two parties for mutual advantage, as nations in permitting each other's goods to pass the border without paying tariff.

*****recital** (rĕ sīt′ al), *n.* narration; a statement of particulars; a musical performance by one person or from the works of one composer.

recite (rĕ sīt′), *v.i. and v.t.* to answer questions in class at school; to repeat from memory, as she *recited* the whole poem; to tell in detail, as to *recite* their many grievances.

reckless (rek′ les), *adj.* heedless, careless, venturesome.

reckon (rek′ un), *v.i. and v.t.* to rely or count on; to make a computation; to compute, calculate, as to *reckon* the cost of a journey; to consider, as to *reckon* another among one's friends.

reckoning (rek′ un ing), *n.* calculation; an accounting; itemized bill; the calculation of a ship's position at sea or a plane's position, as to fly by dead *reckoning.*

reclaim (rĕ klām′), *v.t.* to demand return of, as to *reclaim* a payment made in error; to reform, as to *reclaim* a criminal; to bring to usefulness, as to *reclaim* waste land.

recline (rĕ klīn′), *v.i. and v.t.* to lie down to rest; to cause to lean back.

*****recluse** (rĕ kloōs′), *n.* one who lives in retirement, a hermit.

recognition (rek og nish′ un), *n.* the act of knowing again or state of being known again; acknowledgment, as of a brave act.

*****recognize** (rek′ og nīz), *v.t.* to know again someone or something previously seen or known; to give full credit, as to *recognize* merit in an action; to give the floor to, entitle to a hearing, as to *recognize* one who wishes to speak.

recoil (rĕ koil′), *v.i.* to retreat, as troops *recoil* before an attack; to spring back, as a spring; to react, as a lie *recoils* on the liar.

*****recollect** (rek o lekt′), *v.t.* to recall to memory.

recollect (rē ko lekt′), *v.t.* to gather together again.

recollection (rek o lek′ shun), *n.* the act of calling back to the mind; something remembered; memory, as I have no *recollection* of it.

*****recommend** (rek o mend′), *v.t.* to commend to another; to introduce favorably; to advise.

recommendation (rek o men dā′ shun), *n.* the

act of commending to another; a favorable introduction.

recommit (rē ko mit'), v.t. to submit anew, as to *recommit* a bill to a committee.

***recompense** (rek' om pens), n. an equivalent given in return; compensation; reward. v.t. to give an equivalent to; to requite.

***reconcilable** (rek' on sīl a bl), adj. capable of being restored to a state of harmony.

reconcile (rek' on sīl), v.t. to restore to a state of harmony after a break in relations; to adjust harmoniously, make consistent, as to *reconcile* science and religion.

reconciliation (rek on sīl i ā' shun), n. renewal of friendship after a break; the act of harmonizing or making consistent, as *reconciliation* of the contradictory stories.

***recondite** (rek' un dīt), adj. deep, abstruse, learned; hidden from view, concealed.

***reconnaissance** (rē kon' i sans), n. the act of reconnoitering, a survey.

***reconnoiter** (rē ko noi' tēr), v.i. and v.t. [p.t. and p.p. reconnoitered, pr.p. reconnoitering] to examine, as the surrounding country, especially before making a military movement.

reconstruct (rē kon strukt'), v.t. to build again, especially something that has been destroyed or fallen into decay, as to *reconstruct* an ancient temple.

***record** (rek' ērd), n. the facts in the history of anything; a written or printed presentation of those facts; the official report of a governmental or other body of its acts preserved for future reference; the cylinder, disk or roll from which sounds are reproduced in a phonograph or similar instrument; the best performance in any sporting event. adj. best or greatest of its kind to date, as a *record* jump, a *record* volume of business.

record (rē kôrd'), v.t. to make a record of; to set down for future reference; to preserve for mechanical reproduction, as to *record* an opera on the phonograph.

recount (rē' kount), n. a second counting, as of votes in a disputed election.

re-count (rē' kount), v.t. to enumerate a second time.

recount (rē kount'), v.t. to recite, tell in detail, as to *recount* one's adventures.

recoup (rē kōōp'), v.t. to make good, as a loss; to indemnify for a loss.

***recourse** (rē kôrs'), n. a source of aid or protection; an appeal for assistance, as *recourse* to a court.

recover (rē kuv' ēr), v.t. and v.i. to regain, get back after losing; to get well after sickness, or regain consciousness.

re-cover (rē kuv' ēr), v.t. to cover again; to put a new cover on.

recovery (rē kuv' ēr i), n. [pl. recoveries] the act of getting something back; restoration to any lost state, as health.

***recreant** (rek' rē ant), n. a coward; deserter. adj. cowardly; unfaithful to a cause.

***recreation** (rek rē ā' shun), n. refreshment of strength or spirit after toil; relaxation; amusement, as workers need *recreation.*

recrimination (rē krim i nā' shun), n. the act of meeting an accusation with an accusation; a counter accusation.

***recrudescence** (rē krōō des' ens), n. a fresh outbreak of a disease; a second attack of illness; any renewal or reopening.

***recruit** (rē krōōt'), n. one who has just been enlisted in any cause; one who has newly joined army or navy. v.t. to enlist new members, as for army or navy or any organization; to recover, renew, refresh, as to *recruit* one's health.

rectangle (rek' tang gl), n. a four-sided figure with four right angles.

rectification (rek ti fi kā' shun), n. the act of setting right.

rectify (rek' ti fī), v.t. to set right; to correct; to remove errors from; to refine by distillation; to change from alternating to direct electric current.

rectifier (rek' ti fī ēr), n. a device for changing an alternating into a direct electric current.

***rectitude** (rek' ti tūd), n. uprightness; correctness of principles and practice; honesty.

rector (rek' tēr), n. clergyman in charge of a parish; the head of a school or college.

rectory (rek' tō ri), n. [pl. rectories] the house of a parish head.

recumbent (rē kum' bent), adj. reclining; lying down.

recuperate (rē kū' pēr āt), v.t. and v.i. to regain, as health; to recover strength, health or losses; to convalesce.

recur (rē kûr'), v.i. to go back to; to come back to the mind; to return, as an attack of sickness.

***recusant** (rek' ū zant), n. one who refuses to conform, especially to established church; a nonconformist. adj. refusing to conform, especially to practices of established church service.

red (red), n. one of the primary colors.

red (red), adj. having the color of red.

redbreast (red' brest), n. the robin.

redden (red' n), v.t. and v.i. to make or become red; to blush or flush.

reddish (red' ish), adj. somewhat red.

redeem (rē dēm'), v. to ransom from bondage; to make atonement for, as to *redeem* a fault; to free from incumbrance, as by paying a mortgage or other debt; to pay, as a note; to fulfill, as a promise.

redeemer (rē dēm' ēr), n. one who frees by paying a price: *the Redeemer*, Christ.

***redemption** (rē demp' shun), n. the act of freeing or state of being freed by payment of a ransom or price.

***redolent** (red' ō lent), adj. fragrant; odorous; suggestive, as *redolent* of youth.

redoubt (rē dout'), n. a field work for strengthening a military position without flanks.

redoubtable (rē dout' a bl), adj. formidable; valiant.

redound (rē dound'), v.i. to come as a result, result, turn out, as your gift *redounds* to your credit.

***redress** (rē dres'), n. reparation; amends.

redress (rē dres'), v.t. to set right, as to *re-*

dress a wrong; to make amends to.

re-dress (rē dres'), *v.i. and v.t.* to dress again.

redsear (red' sēr), *v.i.* to break or crack under the hammer, as iron when hot.

reduce (rē dūs'), *v.i. and v.t.* to become less, as the swelling is *reducing;* to lower in rank, degrade, as to *reduce* an officer to the ranks; to lessen or lower in amount, size, value or degree; to change from one state to another, as to *reduce* wood to paper or fuel to ashes; to change to a simpler form, as to *reduce* a fraction or a chemical compound.

reducible (rē dus' i bl), *adj.* capable of being lessened, diminished or lowered in degree.

reduction (rē duk' shun), *n.* diminution; conquest or subjugation; the changing of quantities from one denomination to another, as *reduce* 20 quarts to gallons.

redundance (rē dun' dans), *n.* excess, superfluity; use of unnecessary words.

reduplicate (rē dū' pli kāt), *v.t.* to redouble, repeat.

redwood (red' wood), *n.* evergreen coniferous tree, native of California and Oregon; attains great age and size.

reed (rēd), *n.* a tall grass with slender stems growing in wet land; a musical pipe made of a hollow stem; a part in a weaver's loom.

reef (rēf), *n.* the part of a sail that can be taken up by means of small ropes so as to lessen the area exposed to the wind.

reef (rēf), *n.* a ridge of rock or sand, at or close to the surface of the water; a lode, vein or ledge, as a quartz-reef.

reef (rēf), *v.i. and v.t.* to shorten sail by lessening area of canvas exposed to wind.

reefer (rēf' ēr), *n.* a sailor's jacket.

reek (rēk), *n.* smoke, steam, vapor.

reek (rēk), *v.i. and v.t.* to emit smoke or fumes; to expose to smoke.

reel (rēl), *n.* a revolving frame on which cord may be wound, as a fisherman's *reel,* a hose *reel;* a bobbin; a spool of motion picture film. *n.* a lively country dance or the music for it. *v.i. and v.t.* to wind on a reel or bobbin, as he *reeled* too much line. *v.i.* to stagger; to whirl; to dance a reel.

re-entry (rē en' trē), *n.* the moment when a spacecraft reenters the atmosphere at the conclusion of a space mission.

refection (rē fek' shun), *n.* a light meal.

*refectory** (rē fek' tō ri), *n.* [*pl.* refectories] a dining hall.

*refer** (rē fūr'), *v.i. and v.t.* to allude, as I am *referring* to ancient Rome; to consult, as he *referred* to the dictionary; to submit for criticism, information or decision, as we must *refer* this matter to a higher authority.

*referable** (ref' ēr a bl), *adj.* capable of being submitted; ascribable.

referee (ref ēr ē'), *n.* one to whom a dispute or contest is left for decision; an official who sees to it that the rules of a game are observed; one to whom legal cases of a certain kind are turned over.

reference (ref' ēr ens), *n.* the act of submitting a question to authority or applying to a source for information; a source of infor-

mation or authority, as this book is a *reference;* relation, as in *reference* to that matter; an allusion, as he made *reference* to the story; a written statement of a person's character and qualifications, as she gave her cook a good *reference.*

referendum (ref ēr en' dum), *n.* [*pl.* referendums or referenda] submission of a legislative act to people for a decisive vote.

refine (rē fin'), *v.i. and v.t.* to become pure; to free of worthless matter and remove impurities, as to *refine* oil.

refined (rē find'), *adj.* purified; cultivated, polished, as manners; subtle, as *refined* humor, *refined* cruelty.

refinement (rē fin' ment), *n.* the act of purifying; elegance of manner; freedom from coarseness in act, thought and speech.

refinery (rē fin' ēr i), *n.* [*pl.* refineries] a place where anything, as oil, ore, sugar, is purified.

reflect (rē flekt'), *v.t. and v.i.* to throw back, especially rays, as of light or heat; to show an image, as a mirror; to ponder, think over.

reflection (rē flek' shun), *n.* that which is reflected, as one's *reflection* in a mirror; the backthrow of rays, as *reflection* of light from a polished surface; reproach, blame, discredit, as a *reflection* on his honesty; thought, especially of a meditative, backward-turning nature.

*reflex** (rē' fleks), *n.* reflection; a reflection or image; involuntary action in response to a nerve impulse, as of a muscle.

reflex (rē' fleks), *adj.* turning backward, as *reflex* thought; acting in a backward or returning direction, as a *reflex* influence.

reflexible (rē flek' si bl), *adj.* capable of being reflected.

reflexive (rē flek' siv), *adj.* indicating action upon the subject itself, as a *reflexive* verb, *himself* is a *reflexive* pronoun.

reflux (rē' fluks), *n.* a flowing back.

*reform** (rē fôrm'), *n.* amendment of what is evil or undesirable; correction of social wrongs.

reform (rē fôrm'), *v.i. and v.t.* to change for the better; to improve one's ways; to make better by removing faults or flaws.

reformatory (rē fôr' ma tō ri), *n.* [*pl.* reformatories] an institution for detention of offenders in which their correction is sought rather than punishment.

refract (rē frakt'), *v.t.* to deflect from a straight line, as a ray of light.

refraction (rē frak' shun), *n.* deflection, as of rays of light, from a straight line.

refractory (rē frak' tō ri), *adj.* disobedient; hard to work, as a metal; obstinately resisting cure, as a disease or wound. *n.* material that resists action of heat or corrosion, used as a furnace lining or in crucibles.

refrain (rē frān), *n.* the phrase or verse repeated at the end of each stanza of a poem or song.

refrain (rē frān'), *v.i.* to forbear; to restrain oneself, hold oneself back, as to *refrain* from action.

refrangible (rē fran' ji bl), *adj.* capable of being refracted.

refresh (rē fresh'), *v.* to revive, reinvigorate; to quicken, as the mind.

refreshment (re fresh' ment), *n.* the act of reinvigorating or state of being reinvigorated; that which reinvigorates: *refreshments,* food and drink.

refrigerate (rē frij' ēr āt), *v.t.* to cool and keep cool.

refrigerator (rē frij' ēr ā tēr), *n.* a box or room in which perishable foods are cooled and kept cool; a device for artificially producing coldness.

*refuge (ref' ūj), *n.* a place of safety and shelter.

*refugee (ref ū jē'), *n.* one who flees, especially from an attacked city or from political oppression.

refulgent (rē ful' jent), *adj.* emitting brilliant light.

*refund (rē fund'), *v.t.* to pay back; to arrange in a new form, as a public debt.

refusal (rē fūz' al), *n.* rejection of a proposal; denial of a request; the right to make a final decision, as on purchase of property, before a deal is closed with others.

refuse (rē fūz'), *v.i. and v.t.* to decline to accept an offer or proposal; to be unwilling to grant, as to *refuse* permission; to decline, as to *refuse* an invitation.

refute (rē fūt'), *v.t.* to prove false or erroneous; to disprove.

regain (rē gān'), *v.t.* to recover possession of.

regal (rē' gal), *adj.* royal.

regale (rē gāl'), *v.t.* to entertain royally, as with feasting.

regalia (rē gā' lia), *n. pl.* insignia of royalty; decorations worn on the person as symbols of rank or office.

regard (rē gärd'), *n.* close attention, consideration, respect: *regards,* good wishes.

regard (rē gärd'), *v.t.* to follow with close attention; to esteem; to relate to.

regarding (rē gärd' ing), *prep.* about, concerning, in reference to.

regardless (rē gärd' les), *adj.* without regard for, as he is quite *regardless* of personal danger.

regatta (rē gat' a), *n.* a series of boat races in one program.

regency (rē' jen si), *n.* [*pl.* regencies] the office or jurisdiction of a substitute ruler; term of service in that office.

regenerate (rē jen' ēr āt), *v.t.* to endow with new life and vigor; to renew spiritually.

regent (rē' jent), *n.* one who rules in place of another, as during the minority of a king.

*regicide (rej' i sid), *n.* the murder of a king; one who murders a king.

*regime (rā zhēm'), *n.* a prevailing system of management or government, as under the present *regime* at Washington.

regimen (rej' i men), *n.* systematic regulation, as of diet.

region (rē' jun), *n.* an indefinitely large area of land; a surrounding area; a part or division of the body, as the *region* of the stomach; a field of thought or study.

register (rej' is tēr), *n.* a record or roll or the book in which it is kept; a grated opening in a floor or wall through which heat is piped from a furnace below; correct placing of the parts of a picture or map in colors; the range of a voice or instrument.

register (rej' is tēr), *v.i. and v.t.* to write one's name in a book of record, as at a hotel; to enter in a book of record; to protect by recording in an official list, as to *register* a letter; to enroll or record; to indicate by pose and expression, as to *register* delight; to read or mark, as the thermometer *registers* 72°.

registrar (rej' is trär), *n.* an official who keeps a list or record of names.

registration (rej is trā' shun), *n.* the act of entering in a book of record, as the *registration* of voters.

registry (rej' is tri), *n.* [*pl.* registries] the place where a record of names is kept.

*regnant (reg' nant), *adj.* reigning, ruling; prevailing.

regret (rē gret'), *n.* concern, as for a loss or bad conduct: *regrets,* a note politely declining an invitation. *v.t.* to remember with wish it had been otherwise; to deplore, as an action, and wish it could be done over and done differently.

*regular (reg' ū lēr), *n.* a person who follows the rules and accepts all the principles of an organization, as a *regular* in politics; a soldier in the *regular* army. *adj.* according to rule or custom; happening at set intervals; methodical.

regulate (reg' ū lāt), *v.t.* to place under fixed rules; to govern by custom; to adjust to a state of constancy, as to *regulate* a watch.

regulation (reg ū lā' shun), *n.* act of adjusting or state of being adjusted; a rule, as the rules and *regulations* require it.

regurgitate (rē gûr' ji tāt), *v.t. and v.i.* to throw back; to raise after swallowing; to be thrown back.

rehabilitate (rē ha bil' i tāt), *v.t.* to restore to a former capacity, reinstate; to vindicate.

rehash (rē hash'), *v.t.* to present over again in another form, as to *rehash* old arguments.

rehearse (rē hûrs'), *v.t.* to repeat; to practice by repeating, as a part in a play.

rehearsal (rē hûr' sal), *n.* the act of practicing in private; a private performance before something is presented to the public, as a theatrical *rehearsal.*

*reign (rān), *n.* supreme rule; the period of a sovereign's rule. *v.i.* to rule, as a sovereign; to prevail, as custom *reigns* here.

reimburse (rē im bûrs'), *v.t.* to pay back; to compensate, as for a loss.

*rein (rān), *n.* one of the long straps fastened to a horse's bit by which to drive.

reincarnation (rē in kär nā' shun), *n.* the belief that the souls of the dead return to earth in new forms or bodies.

reindeer (rān' dēr), *n.* a large deer of the Arctic regions.

reinforce (rē in fōrs'), *v.t.* to strengthen with new force or forces, as to *reinforce* a foundation, to *reinforce* an army.

reins (rānz), *n.* kidneys or loins, especially as the seat of feelings and passion.

reinstate (rē in stāt′), *v.t.* to restore to a former condition or office.

reiterate (rē it′ ēr āt), *v.t.* to repeat again and again.

reject (rē jekt′), *v.t.* to refuse to accept; to throw away, discard.

rejoice (rē jois′), *v.i. and v.t.* to feel joy; to express gladness, exult; to make glad or happy, as your news *rejoices* me.

rejoin (rē join′), *v.t. and v.i.* to join again after separation, reunite with; to answer to a reply, as for a defendant to meet the plaintiff's answer to the first defense.

rejoinder (re join′ dēr), *n.* an answer to an answer; a retort.

rejuvenate (rē joo′ vĕ nāt), *v.t.* to make young again, as the brisk mountain air *rejuvenated* her.

relapse (rē laps′), *n.* a return, after apparent recovery or reform, to an earlier state of illness or vice. *v.i.* to fall back into a state of illness or bad living after apparent recovery or reform.

relate (rē lāt′), *v.i. and v.t.* to refer, as my story *relates* to the war; to tell, narrate, as he *related* a strange tale.

relation (rē lā′ shun), *n.* the act of telling; a narrative or recital of facts; mutual connection, as the *relation* of heat to fire; the character of personal contact, as my *relation* with him is pleasant; a kinsman or relative.

relative (rel′ a tiv), *n.* a person connected by kinship; something considered in connection with something else, as a *relative* of a proposition. *adj.* relating or related to, as a point *relative* to the subject in hand; not absolute, having force or meaning only in connection with something else.

relax (rē laks′), *v.i. and v.t.* to become less firm or severe, as discipline *relaxes* when officers are indifferent to their duties; to slacken, as he *relaxed* his grip; to mitigate, abate, free from strain, as *relax* your mind.

*relaxation (rē laks ā′ shun), *n.* diminution of tension; diversion or recreation.

relay (rē lā′), *n.* a new supply, as of horses for use on a long journey; the place at which new horses are ready; a race in which several runners, forming a team, take up the competition successively, each running a certain part of the distance; an arrangement by which one electrical circuit, when it is opened or closed, opens or closes another. *v.t.* to send by series of carriers.

re-lay (rē lā′), *v.t.* to lay a second time, as to *re-lay* a pavement.

relays (rē′ lās), *n.* mechanical arms which control and route the flow of electrical power in early computers.

release (rē lēs′), *n.* liberation from restraint; deliverance from pain or distress; the giving out of a news item or first presentation of a moving picture film; the escape of used steam or the fumes of fuel from an exhaust.

release (rē lēs′), *v.t.* to set free; to let go; to permit publication of, as a news item that has been held back; to permit the showing of, as a film.

relegate (rel′ ē gāt), *v.t.* to send away, as out of a country into exile; to remove, as to *relegate* furniture to the attic; to consign to a place in the background of attention; to assign, as to a class or sphere, as to *relegate* a new species to a certain family.

relent (rē lent′), *v.i.* to become less severe in judgment or action, have pity.

relevant (rel′ ē vant), *adj.* applicable, related, pertinent.

reliable (rē lī′ a bl), *adj.* trustworthy.

reliance (rē lī′ ans), *n.* confidence, trust; that on which one depends, as you are my chief *reliance* in this situation.

reliant (rē lī′ ant), *adj.* trusting, relying on.

relic (rel′ ik), *n.* that which remains of something dead, ruined or destroyed; an object of reverence or worship once belonging to Christ, the Virgin or one of the Saints, especially a part of the body; a keepsake or souvenir.

relict (rel′ ikt), *n.* a widow.

*relief (rē lēf′), *n.* that which lessens pain or distress; the state of being released from distress or pain; assistance given to the needy or unemployed from public funds; the person who takes one's place on a post of duty; sharpness of outline due to contrast, as a church spire stands out in *relief* against the sky.

relieve (rē lēv′), *v.t.* to free from distress or pain; to take the place of, as to *relieve* a sentry; to set off by contrast; to lessen, as monotony.

*religion (rē lij′ un), *n.* a system of faith or worship; conscientious devotion to a principle or ideal, as honest dealing is his *religion.*

relinquish (rē ling′ kwish), *v.t.* to give up claim to, leave, surrender, desist from.

reliquary (rel′ i kwer i), *n.* [*pl.* reliquaries] a small box or casket for keeping or exhibiting a relic.

relish (rel′ ish), *n.* zest, enjoyment; pleasing flavor; a condiment. *v.t.* to like taste of; to enjoy.

reluctant (rē luk′ tant), *adj.* unwilling, disinclined, done or made without desire, as a *reluctant* concession.

rely (rē lī′), *v.i.* to depend upon, have confidence in, as I *rely* upon your advice.

*remain (rē mān′), *v.i.* to stay, be left; to continue in a certain state, as to *remain* indifferent under persuasion.

remainder (rē mān′ dēr), *n.* that which is left after anything is taken away; the quantity left after subtraction.

remains (rē mānz′), *n.* things left, the body after death.

remand (rē mand′), *v.t.* to recommit or send back, as the state *remanded* him to prison.

remark (rē märk′), *n.* a brief observation or statement, comment; notice. *v.t. and v.i.* to take note of, observe, as we *remarked* his sad expression; to comment.

remarkable (rē märk′ a bl). *adj.* noteworthy, extraordinary.

remedial (rē mē′ dl al), *adj.* having power to cure or correct.

*remedy** (rem′ ē dĭ), *n.* [*pl.* remedies] a medicine, application or treatment meant to cure, as a *remedy* for a mind diseased. *v.t.* to relieve or cure, as sickness; to correct or relieve, as a bad social, or business condition.

remember (rē mem′ bēr), *v.t.* to recall to mind; to keep in mind.

remembrance (rē mem′ brans), *n.* the act of recalling, as to hold in *remembrance;* recollection, as I have no *remembrance* of the affair; the extent of recollection, as the great blizzard is not within my *remembrance;* a memento, as a *remembrance* of those happy days.

remind (rē mīnd′), *v.t.* to cause to recollect, as *remind* me when the time comes, your story *reminds* me of old times.

reminiscence (rem ĭ nĭs′ ens), *n.* the recalling of the past; a story of the past in which one had a part.

remiss (rē mĭs′), *adj.* careless or negligent in the performance of duty or meeting of obligations.

remission (rē mĭsh′ un), *n.* the act of remitting, or that which is remitted; cancellation, discharge or annulment of a liability or debt, as the *remission* of sins is a central idea in Paul's theology.

remit (rē mĭt′), *v.i. and v.t.* to moderate, as the fever remits; to send money in payment; to pardon; to give up, as to *remit* a fine.

remittance (rē mĭt′ ans), *n.* the sending of money; the money sent.

remittent (rē mĭt′ ent), *adj.* moderating, abating, lessening, as a *remittent* fever.

remnant (rem′ nant), *n.* a leftover part; remainder, especially a short length of fabric at the end of a bolt after the rest has been sold, usually offered at a reduced price.

remodel (rē mod′ l), *v.t.* to make over, as to *remodel* a house.

remonstrance (rē mon′ strans), *n.* the act of making objection or protest, expostulation, reproof.

*remonstrate** (rē mon′ strāt), *v.i.* to object, expostulate, plead, as I *remonstrated* with him.

remorse (rē môrs′), *n.* anguish caused by a sense of wrongdoing; great repentance.

remote (rē mōt′), *adj.* distant in time or space; inconsiderable, as a *remote* likelihood.

removable (rē mōōv′ a bl), *adj.* capable of being placed elsewhere.

removal (rē mōōv′ al), *n.* the act of taking away; the state of being taken away; dismissal.

remove (rē mōōv′), *v.i. and v.t.* to depart, go away, as they *removed* to the country; to change the location of, transfer; to dismiss from a position of responsibility.

remunerate (rē mū′ nēr āt), *v.t.* to repay, compensate, give in money an equivalent for service.

*renaissance** (ren e säns′), *n.* a new birth or revival of interest, especially along artistic and literary lines: *Renaissance,* the transitional movement in Europe between the 14th and 16th centuries, marked by a revival of classic influence.

*renascent** (rē nas′ ent), *adj.* returning to existence, reviving.

rend (rend), *v.t.* to tear apart, split, rip; to wrest.

render (ren′ dēr), *v.t.* to give in, requite, as to *render* thanks; to present, as to *render* a bill; to deliver, as to *render* a decision; to furnish, as to *render* aid; to translate, as to *render* a Latin text into English, to express, interpret, perform, as to *render* a piece of music; to purify by melting, as lard.

*rendezvous** (rän′ de vōō), *n.* a place of meeting agreed upon in advance; a meeting by appointment, as I have a *rendezvous* with death. *v.i. and v.t.* to meet, or to bring together, at an appointed time or place, as troops or warships.

rendition (ren dĭsh′ un), *n.* a version or translation, as a good *rendition* of a Latin text; style of presenting, as a fine *rendition* of the part of Macbeth.

renegade (ren′ ē gād), *n.* one who renounces his faith, an apostate, traitor.

renegade (ren′ ē gād), *adj.* traitorous.

*renew** (rē nū′), *v.t.* to restore, renovate, refresh; to resume, as to *renew* activity; to continue, as a subscription; to grant or obtain an extension of, as to *renew* a note.

renounce (rē nouns′), *v.t.* to disown, reject, repudiate; to withdraw from, as to *renounce* a pact or treaty.

renovate (ren′ ō vāt), *v.t.* to make as if new again; to restore to freshness.

renown (rē noun′), *n.* fame, distinguished standing, acclaim.

rent (rent), *n.* a rip or tear; a split, as in opinion or belief. *n.* periodic payment for the use of property. *v.t. and v.i.* to lease or hire from an owner; to lease or hire; to be leased or for hire, as the boat *rents* for ten dollars a day.

rental (ren′ tal), *n.* amount paid for use of property; income from property leased to tenants.

*renunciation** (rē nun sǐ ā′ shun), *n.* the act of giving up; the act of casting off.

repair (rē pâr′), *n.* the act of restoring to good condition that which has been broken or worn by use; the state of being sound and in good order, as the car is in good *repair. v.t.* to restore to good condition after having been broken or worn by use; to set right, as to *repair* a mistake. *v.i.* to go back, as to *repair* to one's old home.

*reparation** (rep a rā′ shun), *n.* amends or compensation for loss or damage.

*repartee** (rep ēr tē′), *n.* a quick, clever reply; a conversation containing many such replies.

*repast** (rē pást′), *n.* a meal.

repay (rē pā′), *v.t.* to give back an equivalent; to make a return, as to *repay* a kindness.

*repeal** (rē pēl′), *n.* the recall of a law.

repeal (rē pēl′), *v.t.* to withdraw or cancel, call back and annul, as a law.

repeat (rē pēt′), *v.i. and v.t.* to say over again,

do again; to do or say a second time, as to *repeat* an order; to say over from memory, recite; to pass on, as to *repeat* gossip.

repeater (rē pēt' ēr), *n.* one who or that which does or says something again; a voter who casts more than one vote; a rapid-firing revolver with a reservoir of cartridges; a watch that strikes the hour when a spring is pressed; a decimal fraction with the same figure recurring, as 0.33 is a *repeater* or repetend.

repel (rē pel'), *v.t.* to drive back, as to *repel* an enemy; to resist successfully, as to *repel* an invasion; to refuse to consider, reject, as a suitor; to disgust, as the idea *repels* me.

repellent (rē pel' ent), *adj.* resisting; repulsive, disgusting.

repent (rē pent'), *v.i.* to regret deeply anything said or done; to change one's ways because of contrition.

repentance (rē pen' tans), *n.* contrition, penitence.

repercussion (rē pēr kush' un), *n.* a forcing or driving back or the state of being forced or driven back; reverberation, as of sound; a result or effect, especially indirect.

*****repertoire** (rep' ēr twär), *n.* the list of dramas, operas and parts that an individual or a company is prepared to perform.

repetition (rep ē tish' un), *n.* the act of doing or saying again; that which is done or said again.

repetitious (rep ē tish' us), *adj.* characterized by repeating; given to going over the same ground more than once.

repine (rē pīn'), *v.i.* to languish; to complain, grumble, fret.

replenish (rē plen' ish), *v.t.* to renew, as a stock of goods; to fill again.

replace (rē plās'), *v.t.* to restore to a former place or position, as to *replace* a book on the shelf; to take the place of, as my new pen *replaces* the one I lost; to provide an equivalent for, as to *replace* something broken.

replete (rē plēt'), *adj.* completely filled, abounding in or with.

*****replevin** (rē plev' in), *n.* recovery of goods alleged to have been illegally seized, on presentation of security for restoration if the seizure is sustained by a court.

*****replica** (rep' li ka), *n.* an exact reproduction.

replication (rep li kā' shun), *n.* the plaintiff's answer to the defendant's plea.

reply (rē plī'), *n.* [*pl.* replies] an answer.

reply (rē plī'), *v.i.* to answer.

report (rē pōrt'), *n.* an official presentation of facts; an account of an event, especially for publication; rumor, fame, reputation; a record of proceedings; a loud and sudden noise, as the *report* of a gun.

report (rē pōrt'), *v.i. and v.t.* to present oneself for duty; to give an account of; to state as fact; to make a charge against.

reporter (rē pōr' tēr), *n.* one who gives an account; one who gathers news for a newspaper; one who attends court trials and legislative debates and records proceedings.

repose (rē pōz'), *n.* the act of resting or state of being at rest, as I need *repose*, the caged lion was in *repose.*

repose (rē pōz'), *v.i. and v.t.* to lie down, rest; to lay, place, as the king *reposes* all his confidence in the prime minister.

repository (rē poz' i tō ri), *n.* [*pl.* repositories] a place for deposit and safekeeping, as a *repository* of useful information.

reprehend (rep rē hend'), *v.t.* to censure.

reprehensible (rep rē hen' si bl), *adj.* deserving censure, culpable.

represent (rep rē zent'), *v.t.* to give an account or picture of; to act or speak for, as he *represents* a large constituency; to impersonate; to stand for, as each letter *represents* a sound.

representation (rep rē zen tā' shun), *n.* portrayal, a likeness; the state of being acted for by others, as our *representation* in Congress; those who thus act for others.

representative (rep rē zen' ta tiv), *n.* one who acts for others, as the *Representatives* in the lower house of Congress.

repress (rē pres'), *v.t.* to check or restrain; to hold down.

reprieve (rē prēv'), *n.* temporary suspension of a sentence; temporary relief from pain or escape from danger.

reprieve (rē prēv'), *v.t.* to grant a delay of punishment to; to free temporarily from pain or danger.

*****reprimand** (rep' ri mánd), *n.* a severe reproof or rebuke. *v.t.* to rebuke; to censure officially and formally.

reprisal (rē prīz' al), *n.* an act of retaliation.

reproach (rē prōch'), *n.* censure, rebuke; a cause of dishonor or the state of being in dishonor, as his conduct is a *reproach* to the family name.

reproachful (rē prōch fool), *adj.* expressing rebuke, as a *reproachful* look.

reprobate (rep' rō bāt), *n.* a depraved person, a profligate. *v.t.* to condemn strongly. *adj.* hopelessly sinful, vicious, corrupt.

reprobation (rep rō bā' shun), *n.* condemnation.

reproduce (rē prō dūs'), *v.t.* to bring into existence again; to produce offspring; to duplicate; to make a copy of; to present or exhibit again, as a play.

reproof (rē prōōf'), *n.* censure; rebuke without bitterness.

reprove (rē prōōv'), *v.t.* to rebuke without bitterness.

*****reptile** (rep' til), *n.* a cold-blooded, air-breathing, scaly vertebrate that crawls on its belly or by means of short legs, as a snake or lizard.

republic (rē pub' lik), *n.* a state in which the sovereign power is vested in representatives chosen by the people and responsible to them.

republican (rē pub' li kan), *adj.* pertaining to or characteristic of government of the people through representatives of their own choosing.

repudiate (rē pū' di āt), *v.t.* to refuse to recognize; to refuse to honor a debt; to disavow.

*****repugnance** (rē pug' nans), *n.* aversion, dislike.

repugnant (rē pug' nant), *adj.* extremely distasteful, offensive.

repulse (rē puls'), *n.* the act of putting off or driving back; or state of being put off or driven back; a firm refusal, rejection.

repulse (rē puls'), *v.t.* to beat back, as to *repulse* an attack; to drive away, rebuff.

repulsion (rē pul' shun), *n.* aversion, deep dislike.

repulsive (rē pul' siv), *adj.* repellent, disgusting.

reputable (rep' u ta bl), *adj.* of good standing, worthy of esteem.

reputation (rep ū tā' shun), *n.* good standing; the opinion or regard in which one is generally held, as he has a *reputation* for honor.

repute (rē pūt'), *n.* good or bad standing; the regard in which one is held, as he is a man of good *repute*.

request (rē kwest'), *n.* the act of asking for something, as to make a *request;* that which is sought, as this is my *request;* the condition of being much sought after, as this book is in great *request. v.t.* to ask for, as to *request* a favor; to express an appeal to, as she *requested* him to hurry.

requiem (rē' kwi em), *n.* a mass for repose of the soul of a dead person; a solemn hymn in honor of the dead.

require (rē kwīr'), *v.t.* to claim as a right; to demand as with authority; to need, call for.

requirement (rē kwīr' ment), *n.* that which is needed or demanded.

requisite (rek' wi zit), *n.* that which is indispensable. *adj.* necessary, indispensable.

requisition (rek wi zish' un), *n.* a formal official demand; a formal request for things needed in work; an official order for supply of such things. *v.t.* to order, as to *requisition* supplies.

requital (rē kwit' al), *n.* repayment of good or bad acts in the same kind, compensation, retaliation.

requite (rē kwit'), *v.t.* to meet good or bad acts with acts of the same nature; to avenge or reward, rightly or wrongly, as to *requite* a favor with ungratefulness.

rescind (rē sind'), *v.t.* to annul, revoke, repeal.

rescue (res' kū), *n.* the act of delivery from danger. *v.t.* to save from danger or deliver from imprisonment.

research (rē sûrch'), *n.* deep study or investigation; the quest for new information through examination of source material.

resemblance (rē zem' blans), *n.* likeness, similarity.

resemble (rē zem' bl), *v.t.* to look like or to have similar character.

resent (rē zent'), *v.t.* to feel keen displeasure over; to show anger because of.

resentment (rē zent' ment), *n.* strong displeasure, deep sense of injury.

reservation (rez ẽr vā' shun), *n.* something held back or kept from sight or knowledge; retention for oneself, as *reservation* of all advantages from a deal; limitation or qualification, as I offer this view with some *reservations;* accommodations, as a hotel *reservation;* a tract of land set apart for some special use.

reserve (rē zûrv'), *n.* something kept back; qualification; extra supplies; restraint in manner; funds held from circulation to back credit; funds laid aside by a business concern as a safeguard against future needs; troops held in readiness to assist field forces when hard pressed. *v.t.* to set aside or hold back for future needs.

reservoir (rez' ẽr vwôr), *n.* a place where water is collected and stored; a store of anything, as the banks are *reservoirs* of wealth.

reside (rē zīd'), *v.i.* to live, especially for a long term, as to *reside* in one house ten years; to be inherent or vested in, as all power *resides* in the government.

residence (rez' i dens), *n.* a domicile; the time during which one lives at a certain place, as during my ten years' *residence* here.

residuary (rē zid' ū er i), *adj.* pertaining to a remainder, as a *residuary* bequest, disposing of whatever property may be left after the specific part of a will is carried out.

residue (rez' i dū), *n.* remainder.

residuum (rē zid' ū um), *n.* [*pl.* residua or residuums] that which is left after any process or operation that subtracts from an original mass or body.

resign (rē zīn'), *v.t.* and *v.i.* to surrender formally, as a position or office in government, business or a civil organization; to relinquish, as to *resign* a claim; to give up one's office or position, as the secretary *resigned.*

resignation (rez ig nā' shun), *n.* the act of giving up an office voluntarily; a document stating intent to give up an office; calm acceptance of misfortune.

resilient (rē zil' ient), *adj.* springing back, elastic, buoyant.

resin (rez' in), *n.* a solid substance obtained from certain trees that exude it as gum.

resist (rē zist'), *v.t.* to meet any force with a contrary one, oppose; to withstand; to strive against.

resistance (rē zis' tans), *n.* the act of opposing; that which checks progress, as a healthy child has good *resistance* to disease; that which checks motion, as an airplane has to overcome the *resistance* of the air; the opposition that substances, even conductors, offer to the passage of an electric current.

resistless (rē zist' les), *adj.* not to be opposed successfully.

resolute (rez' ō lūt), *adj.* firm in purpose, determined.

resolution (rez ō lū' shun), *n.* constancy of purpose; a resolve; a formal expression of opinion by a deliberative body, as there is a *resolution* before the house.

resolve (rē zolv'), *v.t.* and *v.i.* to separate the constituent parts of, analyze; to make up one's mind.

resonant (rez' ō nant), *adj.* resounding, rich and vibrant in sound.

*resort (rē zôrt'), *n.* a resource, as this is my last *resort;* a much visited place, as a seaside *resort.* *v.i.* to go frequently or in great numbers; to turn to for help; to have recourse to, as to *resort* to force.

*resound (rē zound'), *v.i.* to be filled with sound; to reverberate, as his name *resounds* throughout the land.

*resource (rē sôrs'), *n.* a source of help or supply: *pl. resources,* wealth; the various means within a nation's possession for meeting the needs of its people, as America leads the world in natural *resources.*

respect (rē spekt'), *n.* regard, esteem; an aspect, as in some *respects;* reference, as in *respect* to. *v.t.* to hold in high esteem, have regard for, as to *respect* the rights of others; to concern, as this policy *respects* national prosperity.

respectable (rē spek' ta bl), *adj.* worthy of high esteem, well regarded.

respectful (rē spekt' fool), *adj.* showing regard for; acting with proper deference.

respecting (rē spek' ting), *prep.* in view of; with regard to.

respective (rē spek' tiv), *adj.* relating to each of several, as our *respective* interests; relative.

respiration (res pi rā' shun), *n.* the act of breathing; one breath, including inhalation and exhalation.

*respiratory (rē spir' a tō ri), *adj.* pertaining to breathing, or connected with it in any way, as the *respiratory* organs.

respite (res' pit), *n.* a period of relief, as a *respite* from pain; a temporary delay in the execution of a sentence.

resplendent (rē splen' dent), *adj.* shining with brilliant luster, dazzling.

respond (rē spond'), *v.i.* to answer or reply; to react, as the horse *responded* to the spur.

response (rē spons'), *n.* an answer or reply; reaction, as in *response* to my urging, he yielded.

responsible (rē spon' si bl), *adj.* answerable, as you are *responsible* to the law; fit to be trusted with the carrying out of a charge or duty; able and ready to meet obligations.

responsive (rē spon' siv), *adj.* answering or reacting; done through responses, as *responsive* reading; easily swayed, as a *responsive* audience.

rest (rest), *n.* a state of ease; absence of motion, as I need *rest,* the machine is at *rest;* a pause from labor or exertion; repose; a support, as a book*rest.* *n.* that which remains after removal of a part. *v.i. and v.t.* to desist from toil; to enjoy repose; to lay, place, as *rest* your head on my shoulder, I *rest* my faith in you.

*restaurant (res' tō rant), *n.* a public dining place.

restitution (res ti tū' shun), *n.* the act of restoring to the original owner, making good a loss, indemnification.

restive (res' tiv), *adj.* impatient, uneasy.

restless (rest' les), *adj.* uneasy, always in motion, bringing no repose, as *restless* sleep.

*restoration (res tō rā' shun), *n.* the act of re-

turning to an original state or condition; the act of giving anything back to an owner; anything that has been thus returned.

restore (rē stôr'), *v.t.* to return to a former owner; to bring back to a former state or condition.

*restrain (rē strān'), *v.t.* to check, control, restrict.

restraint (rē strānt'), *n.* the act of hindering or state of being hindered; loss of freedom in action.

restrict (rē strikt'), *v.t.* to confine or limit.

restrictive (rē strik' tiv), *adj.* limiting, holding within fixed bounds.

*result (rē zult'), *n.* that to which any course leads, consequence, effect of action. *v.i.* to follow as an effect of action.

*resume (rē zūm'), *v.t.* to begin again; to take up again after interruption, as to *resume* work; to take back, take again, reoccupy, as he *resumed* his place.

résumé (rez´ ōo mā´), *n.* a summary of one's employment record or education made up when applying for a job.

*resumption (rē zump' shun), *n.* the act of beginning again.

resurrect (rez u rekt'), *v.t.* to restore to life; to bring into use or view again, as to *resurrect* an old hat.

resuscitate (rē sus' i tāt), *v.t.* to revive; to restore to consciousness.

*retail (rē' tāl), *n.* the selling of goods in small quantities: *at retail,* in small quantities: opposite of *at wholesale.*

retail (rē' tāl), *v.i. and v.t.* to sell in small quantities; to pass along, tell in detail, as to *retail* the news of a neighborhood.

retain (rē tān'), *v.t.* to keep possession of.

retainer (rē tān' ēr), *n.* one who serves a person of rank; a fee paid to counsel to engage his services later.

retaliate (rē tal' i āt), *v.i. and v.t.* to give like for like; to repay (as a wrong), with a like thing.

retard (rē tärd'), *v.t.* to hold back, obstruct; to hinder, delay.

*retch (rech), *v.i. and v.t.* to strain as in vomiting; to vomit.

retention (rē ten' shun), *n.* the act of keeping in possession; holding in mind or memory.

retentive (rē ten' tiv), *adj.* able to keep in possession, as a *retentive* memory.

*reticent (ret' i sent), *adj.* not much inclined to talk; reserved.

*reticular (rē tik' ū lēr), *adj.* like a network; complicated.

*reticule (ret' i kūl), *n.* a lady's handbag or workbag, originally one made of network.

*retina (ret' i na), *n.* the inner coating of the eyeball where the optic nerve ends; the part of the eye on which images of objects are reflected.

*retinue (ret' i nū), *n.* the attendants of a person of high station; a body of followers.

retire (rē tir'), *v.i. and v.t.* to go to some place where one may be private; to go to bed; to give up active work and live on one's income; to take out of action, as to *retire* a worker because of age; to dismiss honorably from service, as to *retire* an army officer at a certain age; to withdraw from circulation, as to *retire* an issue of government bonds.

retirement (rē tīr′ ment), *n.* the act of withdrawing from business or public life; a state of being secluded, as he lives in *retirement*.

retort (rē tôrt′), *n.* a sharp answer to a remark; a quick, witty reply. *v.i. and v.t.* to reply sharply and cleverly or angrily.

retract (rē trakt′), *v.i. and v.t.* to take back something that has been said; to recall an utterance; to withdraw from a position taken in argument; to draw back or draw in, as the cat *retracts* her claws.

retractile (rē trak′ til), *adj.* capable of being drawn back or drawn in, as the turtle's head is *retractile*.

retreat (rē trēt′), *n.* retirement of troops before an enemy; the act of going back or withdrawing from a position; a place of privacy and safety; a home for nervous and insane persons; a period of withdrawing from worldly affairs and spending time in prayer and meditation. *v.i.* to retire from attack; to withdraw from a position, as I pressed him with arguments and he *retreated;* to go into seclusion and retirement, as to *retreat* from the world.

retrench (rē trench′), *v.i. and v.t.* to reduce expenses; to economize; to lessen, as to *retrench* the people's rights; to strengthen a line of defense with a second, inner line.

****retribution** (ret ri bū′ shun), *n.* a proper return for actions, particularly bad; especially just punishment, as it was a case of righteous *retribution*.

retrieve (rē trēv′), *v.i. and v.t.* to bring in game that has been shot by a hunter, as the dog soon learned to *retrieve;* to fetch, as the dog *retrieved* the bird; to recover, as I *retrieved* a large part of my loss.

retriever (rē trēv′ ēr), *n.* a dog trained to find and bring to the hunter game which has been shot, as the water spaniel is a good *retriever*.

****retroactive** (ret ro ak′ tiv), *adj.* operating in previous time, as the law passed in 1896 was *retroactive;* suits were brought under it for offenses committed in 1893.

****retrocede** (ret rō sēd′), *v.t. and v.i.* to grant back to the original owner; to move back; to withdraw, as he *retroceded* from his first stand in the debate.

****retrograde** (ret′ rō grād), *adj.* going or moving backward; going from a better to a worse condition of body, mind or morals.

****retrogression** (ret rō gresh′ un), *n.* the act of moving back; the act of losing ground or retreating; change to a worse condition.

retro-rocket (ret ′ rō rōk ′ it), *n.* a rocket which goes against the direction of travel to act as a brake.

****retrospect** (ret′ rō spekt), *n.* a backward view or review of the past.

****retrospection** (ret rō spek′ shun), *n.* thought about things that are past; a review in the mind of things that have happened; the habit of thinking of the past.

return (rē tûrn′), *n.* the act of coming back to anything from which one has been away, as a *return* to one's native place, a *return* to happiness after trouble; recovery of something lost, as the *return* of my pocketbook will be much appreciated; profit, as the *returns* from an investment; report of results, as election *returns*.

return (rē tûrn′), *v.i. and v.t.* to go back to, as I shall *return* to my home; to come again, as robins *return* in the spring; to give back, as I am *returning* your pencil; to pay or repay, as study will *return* a profit.

reunion (rē ūn′ yun), *n.* a meeting of persons who have not been together for some time, as a class *reunion*, a family *reunion;* the act of meeting again, as I look forward to a *reunion* with you.

reunite (rē ū nīt′), *v.i. and v.t.* to come together again; to bring together again.

reveal (rē vēl′), *v.t.* to make known; to bring to light something that has been hidden; to disclose, as to *reveal* a secret.

****reveille** (rev e lē′), *n.* the signal on drum or bugle sounded about sunrise for soldiers or sailors to get up in the morning.

revel (rev′ el), *n.* noisy merrymaking, a convivial celebration, a carouse. *v.i.* to engage in riotous merrymaking; to take great delight in, as I *revel* in sports.

revelation (rev e lā′ shun), *n.* the act of making known something that has been a secret; the thing that is made known, as this book is a *revelation* to me, any amazing disclosure.

revenge (rē venj′), *n.* the doing of an injury in return for another; the desire to return evil for evil; a chance to get even, as you shall have your *revenge*. *v.t.* to inflict pain or punishment because of, as to *revenge* a defeat: to avenge for a wrong done, as to *revenge* oneself.

revenue (rev′ e nū), *n.* the returns from investment of money; the income from property; the income of a government from public taxes, customs, duties and rents.

reverberate (rē vûr′ bēr āt), *v.i. and v.t.* to sound and sound again, echo and re-echo, resound; to cause to give back a sound in echo; to reflect rays of heat and light.

revere (rē vēr′), *v.t.* to regard with the greatest respect; to regard with a mixture of affection and awe.

****reverence** (rev′ ēr ens), *n.* deep respect with awe and affection; a title of respect to a priest, as your *Reverence*.

reverend (rev′ ēr end), *adj.* worthy of deep respect: a title of respect to a clergyman, as the *Reverend* John Smith.

reverent (rev′ ēr ent), *adj.* showing deep respect; expressing a mixture of love and awe.

****reverie** (rev′ ēr i), *n.* the state of being lost in thought, day-dreaming; deep musing.

reverse (rē vûrs′), *n.* the opposite, as it is just the *reverse* of what you think; a mechanical gear causing the opposite motion, as the engine is in *reverse;* misfortune, check, as he met with *reverses. adj.* opposite, as in the *re-*

verse direction. *v.i. and v.t.* to move the other way, as I *reversed;* to cause to go or work the opposite way, as I *reversed* the engine; to turn something the other way, either backward or upside down, as he *reversed* the bucket; to change, as let us *reverse* our positions.

reversible (rē vûr' sĭ bl), *adj.* capable of being turned the other way; finished on both sides, as *reversible* silk.

*reversion** (rē vûr' shun), *n.* tendency of any growing thing, as a plant or animal, to turn back or return to an earlier form; the return of property to its former owner.

revert (rē vûrt'), *v.i.* to return; to go back, as to a former position or condition, as let us not *revert* to that subject; to return to a former owner, the estate *reverts* to his uncle.

review (rē vū'), *n.* a second view of anything; the act of repeating lessons already learned and recited, as a *review* of a month's work in history; a criticism, as a *review* of a new book; a magazine devoted to considering the news again and to noticing new books or works of art; the march of troops or movement of ships of the navy before a high officer for general inspection of their fitness for service. *v.i. and v.t.* to look over again; to study again; to write a notice of a book; to inspect, as troops or ships.

revile (rē vīl'), *v.i. and v.t.* to use bad language; to address with abusive words.

revise (rē vīs'), *n.* a printer's proof, once corrected, showing the type as changed and presented for a second critical reading.

revise (rē vīs'), *v.t.* to review and correct, as a printer's proof; to examine and make corrections in, as to *revise* an essay or *revise* one's opinions.

revision (rē vizh' un), *n.* the act of reading again and correcting; the composition after being corrected.

revive (rē vīv'), *v.i. and v.t.* to recover consciousness and strength, as a person after sickness or injury, a plant after drooping; to bring back to normal condition; to produce again, as an old opera.

revivify (rē vĭv' ĭ fī), *v.t.* [*p.t. and p.p.* revivified, *pr.p.* revivifying] to bring back to life and vigor.

*revocable** (rĕv' ō ka bl), *adj.* capable of being canceled or called back.

*revocation** (rev ō kă' shun), *n.* the act of calling back, as an order or decree; canceling; repeal; reversal, as of a decision.

revoke (rē vōk´), *v.t.* to call back or repeal; to cancel; in cardplaying, to fail to follow suit when one should and is able to.

revolt (rē vōlt´), *n.* an uprising against those in power, rebellion.

revolt (rē vōlt'), *v.i. and v.t.* to rebel; to be disgusted; to cause disgust, as such conduct *revolts* me.

revolution (rev ō lū' shun), *n.* motion around a center; the act of a body in moving all the way around a center; a great change in the way of doing things; a radical change in thought, government or custom; an effort to overthrow a government and set up a new one by violent means.

revolutionist (rev ō lū' shun ĭst), *n.* one who believes in and works for radical changes.

revolutionize (rev ō lū' shun īz), *v.t.* to cause a great or complete change in, as to *revolutionize* methods of manufacture.

revolve (rē volv'), *v.i. and v.t.* to move in a circular course about a center, as the earth *revolves* about the sun; to cause to move about a center or turn on an axis.

revulsion (rē vul' shun), *n.* a sudden and deep change of feeling; the act of drawing back from something with keen dislike.

reward (rē wôrd'), *n.* that which is given for anything received, either good or bad, but especially something given in recognition and appreciation of merit, as a *reward* for his efforts. *v.t.* to give something in recognition of service or merit, as to *reward* the finder for returning money to the owner.

rhapsody (rap' sō dĭ), *n.* [*pl.* rhapsodies] an oration or any emotional utterance or piece of writing full of exaggerated expression of feeling; an emotional musical composition irregular in form.

rheostat (rē' ō stat), *n.* an instrument regulating the strength of an electric current by controlling the amount of resistance.

*rhetoric** (ret' ō rĭk), *n.* the art of speaking or writing with correctness, clearness and strength; a textbook on this subject; fine writing, especially in prose; pretentious, artificial elegance in writing or speech.

rhetorician (ret ō rish' un), *n.* one skilled in the art of correct speech or one who teaches it.

*rheum** (rōōm), *n.* a watery or mucous discharge, especially from the eyes or nose, as in catarrh.

*rheumatism** (rōō' ma tĭzm), *n.* a painful, inflamed condition of muscles or joints, accompanied by swelling and stiffness.

*rhinoceros** (rī nos' ēr os), *n.* a huge thickhided animal of Asia and Africa, with one or two horns projecting from its snout.

*rhododendron** (rō dō den' dron), *n.* one of a genus of ornamental shrubs or trees (mostly evergreen) of the heath family.

rhomboid (rom' boid), *n.* a four-sided figure having its opposite sides equal and parallel, but the adjacent sides unequal and the angles all oblique angles.

rhombus (rom' bus), *n.* a four-sided figure with all sides equal in length, with opposite sides parallel and with two obtuse angles and two acute right angles.

rhubarb (rōō' bärb), *n.* a hardy garden plant with large leaves and a fleshy pink stalk; the stalks of this plant used for food, having, when cooked, a tart flavor; an extract from the root of a similar oriental plant, used in medicine.

rhyme or **rime** (rīm), *n,* a likeness of sound between two words, especially at the ends of lines in verse; a word that resembles another in sound, as star is a *rhyme* for far. *v.i. and v.t.* to accord in sound, end in the same sound in one or more syllables, as motion *rhymes* with ocean; to put words that match in sound at the ends of lines in verse.

*rhythm (rith' m), n. regular, repeated movement, as the *rhythm* of waves beating on a beach; cadence in written or spoken language, especially in poetry, caused by the metrical arrangement of accents and pauses; the regular flow of movement and beat in music; any certain pattern of time and accent in music, as waltz *rhythm*, two-four *rhythm*.

rib (rib), n. one of the curved bones attached to the spinal column and together forming a framework in which the lungs are enclosed; anything resembling or likened to one of these bones, as a *rib* of a ship's hull, the *ribs* of an umbrella; the main stem in a leaf; a fore-and-aft part of the wing structure of an airplane.

rib (rib), v.t. to enclose in or equip with anything resembling the bones of the chest or the ridges these bones make on the skin of the chest, as to *rib* knitting.

*ribald (rib' ald), adj. coarse and indecent, as language or conduct.

ribaldry (rib' ald dri), n. [pl. ribaldries] indecency of speech, or coarse conduct.

ribbon (rib' un), n. a strip of silk or other fine fabric used for ornament; a narrow inked strip of cloth, as the *ribbon* in a typewriter; any long thin strip resembling a ribbon, as a *ribbon* of moonlight.

'rice (ris), n. a valuable cereal grass usually grown on flooded fields in tropical countries; the seed of this grass used for food.

*rich (rich), adj. having more than ordinary amounts of money or possessions; expensive and fine, as *rich* clothing; abundant, as a *rich* harvest; fertile and productive, as this is *rich* soil; having plenty of, as *rich* in memories; brilliant and strong, as *rich* colors or tones.

riches (rich' ez), n. pl. valuable possessions, wealth; plenty.

Richter scale (rik' ter skăl), n. the measure of the energy released by earthquakes from the minimum 1 to the maximum 10.

rick (rik), n. a pile or heap, especially, a heap of hay or straw carefully built up, rounded at the top and covered over.

rickets (rik' ets), n. a disease of children in which the bones are softened.

*ricochet (rik ō shā'), v.i. and v.t. [p.t. and p.p. ricocheted, pr.p. ricocheting] to rebound or skip on a flat surface; to strike and glance off, as the shot *ricocheted* from the wall of the fort; to cause to skip or glance from a surface, as see if I can *ricochet* this flat stone across the pond.

rid (rid), v.t. to free, as a burden or affliction, as to *rid* a place of vermin, *rid* a friend of his distress. adj. freed, as at last I am rid of that cold.

riddance (rid' ans), n. the act of freeing from something undesirable; the state of being delivered from annoyance, as his departure is a good *riddance*.

riddle (rid' l), n. an enigma, a conundrum, especially a trick question with a puzzling answer. n. a coarse sieve, used to sift sand or ashes. v.t. to pierce with many holes, making the object like a sieve, as to *riddle* a car with shots; to refute, as to *riddle* another's statement with opposite arguments; to sift in a coarse sieve, as to *riddle* gravel.

ride (rid), n. a journey on horseback or in any kind of conveyance; a path for saddlehorses.

ride (rid), v.i. and v.t. to be carried along on the back of a horse, on a bicycle, or in a wagon, car, ship, airplane or other conveyance; to move, as the car *rides* easily; to be carried through or over, as the ship *rode* the waves; to survive, as the ship *rode* the storm; to sit on, control and proceed, as to *ride* a horse or a bicycle.

rider (rid' er), n. one who is carried, as a horseback *rider*, the car accommodates six *riders*; a section or clause added to a statute or enactment, generally to bring about something not included in the original purpose.

ridge (rij), n. any raised line on a surface, as a *ridge* of land; the line where two slopes unite, as the *ridge* of a roof.

ridge (rij), v.i. and v.t. to be marked with raised lines; to put raised lines in.

ridicule (rid' i kūl), n. banter, mockery, derision; the act of making fun of. v.t. to make fun of, laugh at in derision.

ridiculous (ri dik' ü lus), adj. deserving to be laughed at, comical, absurd, as what a *ridiculous* argument, he cut a *ridiculous* figure.

rife (rif), adj. prevalent; common; widespread; general, as suspicion was *rife* among those present, sickness is *rife* in town.

rifle (ri' fl), n. a firearm with a long barrel, grooved spirally on the inside to give spin to the bullet, increasing the accuracy of fire. v.t. to groove spirally, as a gun barrel v.t. to rob, pillage, plunder.

rift (rift), n. an opening in anything caused by splitting; a fissure; a separation into parts, as a *rift* in the clouds.

rift (rift), v.t. and v.i. to burst open; to split open; to separate into parts, as the clouds *rifted*.

rig (rig), n. a way of arranging the masts, sails and ropes of a ship; an outfit of clothing or equipment, as he wore a strange *rig*.

rig (rig), v.t. to fit with sails, spars and ropes, as to *rig* a ship; to fit out, equip; to dress oddly, as you should have seen the way he was *rigged*.

rigging (rig' ing), n. the entire system of sails and ropes on a sailing vessel; gear and tackle in general.

*right (rit), n. that which is correct and in accordance with accepted standards of justice and truth; opposite of *wrong*, as we will fight for the *right*; that to which one has a just and proper claim, as we will fight for our *rights*; the right-hand side, as it is on your *right*; *the Right*, the conservative party in politics.

right (rit), v.t. to put in order, as to *right* a messy lot of papers; to correct, as to *right* a wrong; to recover correct position, as the ship *righted* easily after the great wave struck her. *adj.* in accordance with justice and honor, as he is a man of *right* conduct; straight, as a *right* line; made by one line perpendicular to another, as a *right* angle; suitable, as the *right* answer; pertaining to the side of the body which most people use the most: opposite of *left.*

right (rīt), *adv.* correctly, as you answered *right;* directly, as the shot went *right* to the mark; in the proper way, as do it *right.*

right angle (rīt ang' gl), an angle of 90°, formed by one straight line perpendicular to another straight line.

***righteous** (rī' chus), *adj.* just, equitable; ruled by what is right; blameless; upright, as a *righteous* man, a *righteous* cause, *righteous* wrath.

rightful (rīt' fool), *adj.* having a just and proper claim, as the *rightful* owner; in accord with justice, as a *rightful* demand.

***rigid** (rij' id), *adj.* not pliant, stiff, inflexible, unyielding; strict, severely just.

rigmarole (rig' ma rōl), *n.* a jumble of words; disconnected talk with little sense.

rigor (rig' ẽr), *n.* stiffness; severity; an act or condition of severity, as the *rigors* of a northern climate.

rigorous (rig' ẽr us), *adj.* stern, inflexible, unyielding, severe.

rill (ril), *n.* a small stream or rivulet.

rim (rim), *n.* a border, margin or edge; a raised border; brim.

rim (rim), *v.t.* to furnish with a border, especially a raised border; to serve as an edge around something, as the bowl is *rimmed* with silver.

***rime** (rīm), *n.* hoarfrost, white frost.

rime (rīm), *n.* rhyme.

rimy (rīm' i), *adj.* [*comp.* rimier, *superl.* rimiest], frosted.

***rind** (rīnd), *n.* the thick outer skin as of an orange or squash; the outer coating, as bark of a tree.

***rinderpest** (rin' dẽr pest), *n.* a serious and contagious disease of cattle, cattle plague.

ring (ring), *n.* a circle; something circular in form, as a finger *ring;* persons standing in a circle about a center of interest; a combination of men for a common purpose, usually a selfish or criminal one, as a political *ring,* a drug *ring;* an enclosed space for a contest or exhibit, as a boxing *ring.*

ring (ring), *n.* the sound of a bell; the sound given out by metal free to vibrate when struck; a certain quality of sound or meaning, as his statement has the *ring* of truth.

***ring** (ring), *v.t.* to encircle; to furnish or decorate with anything of circular form.

***ring** (ring), *v.i. and v.t.* to sound musically, resound, as a bell when struck; to sound a bell as a summons, as to *ring* for service, *ring* up on the phone; to resound, as his fame will *ring* throughout the land; to have a sensation as of bells sounding or a buzz, as my ears *ring;* to make resound, as to *ring* a bell· to repeat over and over, as to *ring*

rink (ringk), *n.* an inclosed space with a surface of ice on which to skate or play such games as hockey; a smooth floor for roller-skating.

rinse (rins), *v.t.* to wash lightly, especially without soap; to wash off with clean water to remove soap and suds, as to *rinse* dishes.

riot (rī' ut), *n.* uproar; tumult; a disorderly outbreak; vivid confusion, as a *riot* of color or sound. *v.i.* to raise an uproar; to take part in a public disturbance; to revel noisily; to act without restraint.

riotous (rī' ut us), *adj.* turbulent, disorderly, seditious.

rip (rip), *n.* an opening made in fabric by the giving way of a seam; a saw that cuts with the grain of the wood, called a *ripsaw;* a rough area on the surface of water caused by reversing tides or currents.

***riparian** (ri pâr' i an), *adj.* having to do in any way with the banks of a river or lake; pertaining to a shore, as those who own property along a stream have *riparian* rights.

ripe (rīp), *adj.* in a state of maturity or perfection, as *ripe* fruit, grain *ripe* for the harvest; mellow, matured, highly developed, as a *ripe* scholar; ready, as *ripe* for trouble.

ripen (rīp' en), *v.i. and v.t.* to become matured or ready for use; to hasten the development of.

ripple (rip' l), *n.* a small curling wave, as a *ripple* on the water, a *ripple* of hair; the sound made by wavelets, or a sound resembling it, as the *ripple* of the breeze.

ripple (rip' l), *v.i.* to become ruffled on the surface, have little curling waves, as the lake *ripples* in the breeze, her hair *ripples.*

riprap (rip' rap), *n.* a loose foundation of stones especially on a soft bottom in deep water.

***rise** (rīz), *n.* the act of going up; an ascent; the extent to which anything goes up, as a *rise* of 10 percent in prices; a small hill, as a *rise* of land; the coming up, as of the sun, sun*rise;* advance in office, station or importance, as his *rise* in the world was swift.

rise (rīz), *v.i.* [*p.t.* rose, *p.p.* risen, *pr.p.* rising] to go higher; to ascend; to extend upward, as the mountain *rises* to an elevation of 1,500 feet; to get up after kneeling or lying down; to come over the horizon, as the sun *rises* late in winter; to swell up, as the dough is *rising;* to become greater or go up, as prices *rose* last week; to go up in the world, as he rose fast.

riser (rīz' ẽr), *n.* one who rises; the upright front of a step or seat.

risibility (riz i bil' i ti), *n.* [*pl.* risibilities] readiness to laugh; laughter; the sense of what is funny.

rising (rīz' ing), *n.* the act of getting up or going up, as the *rising* of the moon; a revolt, as a *rising* of the people.

risk (risk), *n.* possibility of loss or danger; peril, as at the *risk* of his life he rescued them. *v.t.* to take the chance; to imperial; to stake, hazard, as I would *risk* my life on his skill.

rite (rīt), *n.* a solemn religious act; a formal

ceremony, as funeral *rites.*

ritual (rit′ ū al), *n.* the manner of performing a religious service; a book of forms for a religious service; any set form or ceremony.

rival (rī′ val), *n.* a competitor; antagonist; one who strives for the same object as another.

rival (rī′ val), *v.t.* to compete; to strive to equal or excel; to emulate. *adj.* competing; having similar claims, emulous.

rivalry (rī′ val rī), *n.* [*pl.* rivalries] competition; effort to equal or excel.

rive (rīv), *v.i. and v.t.* to split; to tear apart.

river (riv′ ēr), *n.* a large running stream of water flowing into a bay, gulf, sea or another river.

rivet (riv′ et), *n.* a short metal bolt with a head on one end and hammered to a head on the other end while it is hot and after it has been passed through two plates of metal to hold them together.

rivet (riv′ et), *v.t.* to secure with a metal bolt by hammering; to put a head on a bolt by pounding; to fasten as if with bolts, as to *rivet* a friendship.

rivulet (riv′ ū let), *n.* a little stream.

roach (rōch), *n.* a freshwater fish related to the carp, found in European waters.

roach (rōch), *n.* a cockroach, an insect pest in ships and houses.

road (rōd), *n.* a public way for vehicles; a path or route to be followed, as his *road* through life was hard; an open offshore stretch of water where ships may ride at anchor.

roam (rōm), *v.i. and v.t.* to wander about without any definite object or destination; to wander over or through, as to *roam* the woods.

roan (rōn), *n.* a horse with a coat of bay, sorrel or chestnut sprinkled heavily with white hairs; the color of such a horse.

roan (rōn), *n.* a soft grained sheepskin used in bookbinding to imitate morocco.

roar (rōr), *n.* the deep full cry of one of the larger animals, as the lion; a loud, prolonged sound, as a *roar* from the crowd, the *roar* of heavy traffic. *v.i.* to make a long deep sound like the cry of a lion, to bellow.

roast (rōst), *n.* a joint of meat to be cooked before a fire or in an oven.

roast (rōst), *v.i. and v.t.* to be cooked before an open fire or in an oven; to feel the heat severely, as I am *roasting* in this sun; to cook before an open fire, in an oven or in embers, as to *roast* a joint of beef, to *roast* corn or potatoes.

rob (rob), *v.i. and v.t.* to steal; to deprive of something rightfully owned.

robber (rob′ ēr), *n.* a thief.

robbery (rob′ ēr ī), *n.* [*pl.* robberies] theft; the criminal act of taking money or goods belonging to another; an act of theft.

robe (rōb), *n.* a loose outer garment; the dressed hide of an animal used to cover the lap when driving, as a buffalo *robe*: *robes,* garments of state.

robe (rōb), *v.i. and v.t.* to put on a formal garment; to array in garments of state.

robot (rō′ bot), *n.* an efficient, automatic type of worker; an automaton; a word created by Karel Capek to designate artificially created mechanical workmen that appeared in his play "R.U.R."

robust (rō bust′), *adj.* hardy, strong, muscular, vigorous.

rock (rok), *n.* a large mass of stone or of stony matter; that which may wreck a person or a business, as we are on the *rocks.*

rock (rok), *v.i. and v.t.* to move to and fro or back and forth, as a cradle *rocks;* to cause to move back and forth, as to *rock* a cradle; to shake, as an earthquake *rocks* a village.

rocker (rok′ ēr), *n.* one of the curved pieces on which a cradle or chair sways.

rocket (rok it), *n.* a reaction propelled device that carries its own supply of fuel and oxygen to support combustion in airless-space.

rod (rod), *n.* a straight, slim stick of wood or metal, as a fishing *rod;* a switch used to enforce discipline among unruly children; discipline. *n.* a unit of linear measure equal to 5½ yards.

rodent (rō′ dent), *n.* any of various small gnawing animals, such as mice, rats, rabbits, squirrels.

rodeo (rō′ dē ō or rō dā′ ō), *n.* a market where cattle are collected; an exhibition featuring cowboy horsemanship and cattle roping.

roe (rō), *n.* a small deer native to Europe and Asia; the female of the red deer.

roe (rō), *n.* a mass of fish eggs.

rogue (rōg), *n.* a dishonest person, knave; a sly, mischievous person, a rascal.

roguery (rōg′ ēr ī), *n.* [*pl.* rogueries] knavish or dishonest practices; cheating; mischievous or waggish conduct.

roguish (rōg′ ish), *adj.* mischievous; dishonest in a sly way.

roil (roil), *v.t.* to stir up and make muddy, as he *roiled* the spring; to vex and harass.

*role (rōl), *n.* a part or character in a play or an opera, as he plays the *role* of a martyr; a function or pose.

roll (rōl), *n.* the act of turning over and over or from side to side; anything turned round and round upon itself or that revolves, as a *roll* of cloth, a phonograph *roll;* a kind of biscuit doubled over; a long deep sound as a *roll* of thunder, the *roll* of drums; a wavelike surface, as a *roll* of land. *n.* a list of names, as a class *roll. v.i. and v.t.* to turn over and over or from side to side, as a horse *rolls,* a ship *rolls;* to produce a long, deep sound, as thunder *rolls;* to cause to move by turning over and over, as to *roll* a log; to cause to move on wheels by pushing, as to *roll* a wheeled chair; to press down with something that turns over and over, as to *roll* turf.

roller (rōl′ ēr), *n.* one who or that which rolls; a cylinder in a machine; a tumbling pigeon; a canary bred and trained to have a special roll or trill in its song.

rollick (rol′ ik), *v.i.* to move in a swaggering, carefree manner; to frolic.

rolling (rōl′ ing), *adj.* rotating; moving on or as if on wheels; having undulations, as *rolling* country; rumbling, as thunder.

ROM (rom), *n.* read only memory; a permanent computer memory containing fixed data or instructions; the memory cannot be changed.

*romance (rō mans'), *n.* a work of fiction stressing adventure and incident; delight in what is fanciful, adventurous and picturesque. *v.i.* to make up stories, tell fanciful tales, fib.

romantic (rō man' tik), *adj.* picturesque and strange; marked by the spirit of adventure and variety; fanciful, unreal.

romp (romp), *v.i.* to play in a rough or frolicking manner.

rood (rŏŏd), *n.* a cross, a crucifix: *holy rood,* the cross of Christ.

rood (rŏŏd), *n.* a square measure equal to one-fourth of an acre or 40 square rods.

*roof (rŏŏf), *n.* the top covering of a house or building. *v.t.* to place a top cover on a house or other building; to supply with shelter, as if taking under a roof.

*rook (rook), *n.* a bird of the crow family; a swindler.

rookery (rook' ēr i), *n.* [*pl.* rookeries] a breeding place of a colony of rooks; a breeding place of a colony of gulls or seals; a ramshackle tenement house.

*room (rŏŏm), *n.* a walled-in part of a house; a chamber; space not occupied.

room (rŏŏm), *v.i.* to lodge, as he *rooms* here.

roomy (rŏŏm' i), *adj.* [*comp.* roomier, *superl.* roomiest] spacious.

roost (rŏŏst), *n.* the pole or perch upon which birds rest at night.

roost (rŏŏst), *v.i.* to sit or sleep on a perch.

rooster (rŏŏs' tēr), *n.* a male fowl, especially the domestic cock.

*root (rŏŏt), *n.* the part of a plant that is underground, holding the plant in place and taking moisture and nourishment from the earth; the origin or source, as the *root* of a word, the *root* of the difficulty; a number or quantity that multiplied by itself gives as a product a given number, as 3 or —3 is the second or square *root* of 9, and 3 is the third root of 27.

root (rŏŏt), *v.i. and v.t.* to take hold in the ground; to implant deeply and firmly; to dig or burrow with the snout, as pigs *root*: *root up,* to take out of the ground.

rope (rōp), *n.* a thick cord or small cable; objects braided, twisted or strung together, as a *rope* of pearls, a *rope* of daisies; a thick thread of matter that forms in a liquid. *v.t.* to fasten with cords; to lasso, as to *rope* cattle.

ropy (rōp' i), *adj.* [*comp.* ropier, *superl.* ropiest] like cord; viscous.

*rosaceous (rō zā' shus), *adj.* pertaining to roses; having several petals arranged in a circular form.

*rosary (rō' za ri), *n.* [*pl.* rosaries] a place where roses grow; a garland of roses; a string of beads by which prayers are counted.

rose (rōz), *n.* a thorny plant or in some varieties a climbing vine, with thorny stems and fragrant flowers, red, white or other colors; the flower of this plant.

*roseate (rō' zē ăt), *adj.* like a rose; rose-colored.

*rosemary (rōz' mâr i), *n.* [*pl.* rosemaries] a sweet-smelling evergreen shrub from which an aromatic water is distilled.

*rosette (rō zet'), *n.* a cluster of ribbons arranged in the form of a rose; any ornament made in the shape of a rose.

rosewood (rōz' wood), *n.* a hard, dark-red Brazilian wood used in cabinet work and to make fine furniture.

*rosin (roz' in), *n.* resin, the product left after distilling crude turpentine, used in varnishes and soaps and on violin bows.

rosin (roz' in), *v.t.* to rub with rosin, as I must *rosin* this violin bow.

*roster (ros' tēr), *n.* a list of officers and men enrolled for duty in the military and naval services; any list of names, as of members in a club.

rostral (ros' tral), *adj.* having a beak; relating to a beak; resembling a beak.

rostrum (ros' trum), *n.* [*pl.* rostrums or rostra] a platform or pulpit from which an oration may be delivered; a beak, as of a bird or a ship.

rosy (rōz' i), *adj.* [*comp.* rosier, *superl.* rosiest] red; blushing; favorable, as *rosy* prospects.

rot (rot), *n.* decay; the process of decaying; a disease of sheep; a disease attacking plants; nonsense.

rot (rot), *v.i. and v.t.* to decay; to cause to decay, as wet weather *rots* plants.

*rotary (rō' ta ri), *adj.* turning on an axis, as a wheel; made with parts that turn on an axis, as a *rotary* printing press.

*rotate (rō' tāt), *v.i. and v.t.* to turn on an axis, as the wheel *rotates* more easily when greased; to cause to turn on an axis, as *rotate* that wheel in the opposite direction.

rotation (rō tā' shun), *n.* the act of turning on an axis or hub; alternation or regular succession; the act of alternating, first one and then another, as *rotation* of crops.

rote (rōt), *n.* mechanical routine; repetition without understanding, as you know the lesson by *rote,* but do not seem to know what it really means.

rotten (rot' n), *adj.* decayed; decomposed; dirty and corrupt, as *rotten* government.

rotund (rō tund'), *adj.* plump and rounded out, as a *rotund* figure; full-toned, as he speaks in *rotund* tones; using high-sounding words, as a *rotund* style.

rotunda (rō tun' da), *n.* a circular, domed building; a large circular room with domed ceiling, as the *rotunda* of the Capitol.

*roué (rŏŏ ā'), *n.* a dissolute man, a rake.

*rouge (rŏŏzh), *n.* a cosmetic used to redden the cheeks or lips; a red powder used for polishing gems, glass and metals.

rouge (rŏŏzh), *v.i. and v.t.* to use a cosmetic to redden the cheeks or lips; to tint with red, as to *rouge* the cheeks.

*rough (ruf), *n.* an unfinished state, as in the *rough;* a rowdy.

rough (ruf), *v.t.* to make uneven; to do hastily

and incompletely, as to *rough* out a plan; to handle without gentleness, as do not *rough* the child.

rough (ruf), *adj.* having an uneven surface; rugged; not smooth, as a *rough* road; not gentle, as *rough* play; harsh in manner; crude; hastily or only approximately made or done, as a *rough* guess, a *rough* sketch.

roughage (ruf′ ij), *n.* coarse food that cannot be completely digested and that stimulates action of the intestines.

roulette (rōō let′), *n.* a game of chance played with a revolving disk and a ball.

round (round), *n.* a circle or globe; a fixed course, as a policeman must make his *round* in so many minutes; a series, as a *round* of parties; a volley of sounds, as a *round* of applause; one of a series, as the *rounds* of a boxing match; a ladder rung; a certain cut of beef, as a steak off the *round*. *v.i.* and *v.t.* to become curved out with fullness, as the balloon will *round* out; to give a curved form to, as *round* out this line; to pass, as the ship *rounded* the cape. *adj.* circular; curved; complete, as a *round* hundred; going out and back, as a *round* trip; full and clear, as *round* tones. *adv.* in all directions, as the leaves blow *round;* in rotation, as clock hands go *round;* so as to reach all present, as pass the candy *round;* in circumference, as 10 feet *round;* here and there, as the dog follows him *round.*

round (round), *prep.* about, so as to encircle, as pass the rope *round* the post, sit *round* the table; from behind, as peek *round* a fan; from all sides toward, as the crowd gathered *round* the bulletin board; in all directions from, as look *round* the camp.

roundelay (roun′ de lā), *n.* a song or dance of old times with one strain or a simple melody frequently repeated.

round robin (round rob′ in), a petition with signatures written in a circle so that no one can tell who signed first.

roundsman (roundz′ man), *n.* a police officer who goes through a district to see how the patrolmen are covering their beats.

rouse (rouz), *v.i.* and *v.t.* to stir suddenly from sleep; to awaken or be awakened suddenly; to stir to thought or action.

rout (rout), *n.* total defeat and disorderly flight; a disorderly crowd; disorder.

rout (rout), *v.t.* to defeat and put to flight; to drag forth, as to *rout* out the late sleepers. *v.i.* and *v.t.* to dig with the snout, as a pig; to root up; to dig out, gouge.

*route (rōōt), *n.* the way or road traveled; the course of a journey; a certain course to be covered, as a newsboy's *route*. *v.t.* to send over a certain road or combination of roads, as to *route* a shipment of goods.

*routine (rōō tēn′), *n.* a course of business, official or domestic duties regularly pursued; fixed methods of action; uniform habits or practice.

rove (rōv), *v.i.* and *v.t.* to wander or ramble; to roam, as we *roved* in the woods, we *roved* the woods.

row (rō), *n.* a line, file or rank of persons or things. *n.* a ride in a boat propelled by oars, as we had a good *row*. *v.i.* and *v.t.* to wield an oar or a pair of oars; to propel a boat with oars.

row (rou), *n.* a noisy disturbance, quarrel, brawl.

row (rou), *v.i.* to make or take part in a disturbance or quarrel.

rowdy (rou′ di), *n.* [*pl.* rowdies] a rough, riotous fellow. *adj.* [*comp.* rowdier, *superl.* rowdiest] rough and noisy.

*rowel (rou′ el), *n.* a tiny wheel with sharp teeth on the rim, as on a spur.

rowlock (rō′ lok), *n.* a device to keep an oar from slipping on the side of a rowboat, a pair of wooden or metal pins, a notch cut in or a metal crotch: also called *oarlock.*

royal (roi′ al), *adj.* pertaining to a king; befitting or like a king; regal; pertaining to the government of a kingdom, as *royal* decrees; holding a charter from a king or queen, as a *royal* colony.

royalist (roi′ al ist), *n.* an adherent of a king or advocate of rule by a sovereign.

royalty (roi′ al ti), *n.* the character, status or family of a sovereign; royal personages.

royalty (roi′ al ti), *n.* [*pl.* royalties] a percentage paid to an author, composer or inventor for use of a patent or copyright, as the author of this book receives a *royalty* of 20 cents on every copy sold by the publishers.

rub (rub), *n.* the act of passing over with friction, as give this glass a *rub;* a difficulty or hindrance, as there's the *rub.*

rub (rub), *v.i.* and *v.t.* to pass over or be passed over with friction, as this collar *rubs;* to clean or scour, as *rub* the glass with a wet rag; to polish.

rubber (rub′ ẽr), *n.* an elastic substance obtained from the sap of various plants that grow in tropical lands; a piece of this substance used for erasing; anything made of India rubber, as an overshoe; the decisive game in a series after a tie score.

rubbish (rub′ ish), *n.* trash; waste fragments; anything of no value.

rubble (rub′ l), *n.* rough undressed stone; builders' rubbish.

rubescent (rōō bes′ ent), *adj.* becoming red, reddening.

rubicund (rōō′ bi kund), *adj.* red or inclined to redness; ruddy, as a *rubicund* complexion.

rubric (rōō′ brik), *n.* the ritual forms printed in a prayerbook; the heading of a statute; so called because formerly written in red.

rubricate (rōō′ bri kāt), *v.t.* to mark or distinguish with red.

*ruby (rōō′ bi), *n.* [*pl.* rubies] a precious stone, varying in color from carmine to crimson; a rich red color like that of this gem.

ruche (rōōsh), *n.* frilled or plaited lace, net or silk used as an edging for a dress or as a collar.

ruche (rōōsh), *v.t.* to adorn with a ruche.

ruching (rōōsh′ ing), *n.* material used in making frilled edges for a dress; ruches collectively.

ruck (ruk), *n.* the ordinary crowd, especially a group of horses running far behind the winner: *in the ruck,* unimportant, undistinguished. *v.i. and v.t.* to wrinkle or crease.

rudder (rud' ẽr), *n.* a broad flat frame of wood or metal by which a boat, ship, airplane or dirigible is steered.

ruddy (rud' i), *adj.* [*comp.* ruddier, *superl.* ruddiest] approaching redness; tinged with red; florid, as a *ruddy* countenance.

*rude (rōōd), *adj.* rough; uncultivated; uncivil; impolite; harsh.

*rudiment (rōō' di ment), *n.* a first principle; elementary stage; that which is incompletely developed.

rudimentary (rōō di men' ta ri), *adj.* elementary; undeveloped.

rue (rōō), *n.* an herb of bitter taste and strong odor. *v.t.* to regret, be sorry for, repent of, as you shall *rue* this action.

rueful (rōō' fool), *adj.* mournful, melancholy, regretful.

ruff (ruf), *n.* a large frilled collar; a thick covering of feathers or fur about the neck of a bird or animal.

*ruffian (ruf' i an), *n.* a rough, lawless, boisterous fellow.

ruffle (ruf' l), *v.t.* to wrinkle, pucker or disarrange; to annoy or vex, as your conduct *ruffles* me. *v.t.* to equip or adorn with folds or gathers. *v.t.* to raise or make stand out, as a bird *ruffles* its feathers; to make ripples upon, as a light breeze *ruffled* the water; to rumple, as to *ruffle* one's hair.

rug (rug), *n.* a floor covering of heavy fabric usually made in one piece and not tacked down; a lap robe; a fur mat.

*rugged (rug' ed), *adj.* rough, shaggy, as a *rugged* beard; strongly marked, as a *rugged* range of mountains; sturdy, as a *rugged* body, a *rugged* nature.

ruin (rōō' in), *n.* destruction; overthrow; downfall; complete loss, as of wealth or happiness: *ruins,* remains, as the *ruins* of an ancient city. *v.t.* tear down, destroy, wreck, as you have *ruined* my happiness, the house is *ruined,* our business will be *ruined.*

ruinous (rōō' i nus), *adj.* fallen into a state of destruction; decayed; consisting of surviving fragments or parts; causing destruction.

*rule (rōōl), *n.* a standard or guide; a maxim or precept; a fixed course of action; controlling power or the use of it, as the king had a long *rule,* the *rules* of a game; an instrument for measuring.

rule (rōōl), *v.i. and v.t.* to be in command; to prevail; to govern; to decide a disputed matter, as the referee *ruled* in our favor; to mark with lines, as if with the aid of a ruler, as he *ruled* the sheet for a ledger account.

ruler (rōōl' ẽr), *n.* one who governs or commands; a smooth-edged strip of wood or metal with which to draw straight lines of given lengths or to measure distances.

ruling (rōōl' ing), *n.* a decision by a court or referee.

*rum (rum), *n.* an alcoholic liquor distilled from molasses or the juice of the sugar cane.

rumble (rum' bl), *n.* a low, heavy, continued, rolling sound; a seat or space for baggage at the back of an automobile. *v.i.* to make a long heavy rolling sound.

*ruminant (rōō' mi nant), *n.* a herbivorous animal, such as the cow, sheep, goat, deer, camel, giraffe, that swallows its food unchewed and regurgitates it in the form of a cud for chewing. *adj.* chewing the cud; quiet and thoughtful.

ruminate (rōō' mi nāt), *v.i. and v.t.* to chew a cud; to think over again, meditate, ponder.

rumination (rōō mi nā' shun), *n.* the act of chewing the cud; meditation.

rummage (rum' ij), *v.i. and v.t.* to ransack, search through a collection of things.

rumor (rōō' mẽr), *n.* a report passing from one person to another without evidence of truth; public gossip, hearsay. *v.t.* to circulate a report without investigating the truth or falseness of it.

rump (rump), *n.* the hind end of an animal.

rumple (rum' pl), *n.* an irregular fold, a wrinkle, a crease. *v.t.* to make uneven, crumple, muss, as do not *rumple* my hair.

rumpus (rum' pus), *n.* a disturbance; a great to-do.

run (run), *n.* a pace faster than a walk; the act of running, as the dog had a good *run;* a distance covered, as by a car or train, as a 100-mile *run;* a small stream; a series of performances, as the play had a long *run;* free use, as you have the *run* of the house; the customary sort, as the general *run* of mankind; a panic, as a *run* on the bank; a long ravel in a knitted fabric.

run (run), *v.i.* [*p.t.* ran, *p.p.* run, *pr.p.* running] to go at a faster pace than a walk; to be a candidate, compete, as to *run* for mayor; to make regular trips, ply, as the steamer *runs* between New York and Savannah; to flow, as a river *runs,* the water *ran* out; to act, operate, as a watch *runs;* to dissolve and spread, as the color in that blouse *runs;* to have a certain direction, as the road *runs* north; to discharge a fluid, as my eyes *run,* his nose *runs.*

run (run), *v.t.* [*p.t.* ran, *p.p.* run, *pr.p.* running] to cause to go faster than a walk, as do not *run* that horse too hard; to do by going faster than a walk, perform, as to *run* a race; to manage or conduct, as to *run* a home or a business; to operate, as to *run* a sewing machine; to incur, as danger; to thrust, as to *run* a sword through a rival; to mark out, as to *run* a boundary line.

rune (rōōn), *n.* a character in the ancient Teutonic alphabet of northern Europe used from the 3d century by the Anglo-Saxons and Scandinavians; a magic mark or verse: *runes,* old Finnish or old Norse poetry.

rung (rung), *n.* a round of a ladder; a crosspiece of a chair, bracing the structure; a floor timber in a ship; one of the grips on a ship's steering wheel.

runt (runt), *n.* an undersized animal; the

weakest one in a brood or litter; a person of less than normal size.

*rupture (rup' tūr), *n.* the act of breaking apart or state of being broken apart; a break in friendly relations; a hernia or torn muscle. *v.i. and v.t.* to break, as some some tissues *rupture* more easily than others; to burst, as he *ruptured* a blood vessel; to interrupt or break off, as friendly relations.

*rural (roor' al), *adj.* having to do with the country or with country life, as *rural* scenes.

rural free delivery (roor' al frē dē liv' ē i), a system of free delivery of mail to persons living in country districts maintained by the Federal Government.

*ruse (rōoz), *n.* a trick; stratagem; action intended to mislead another.

*rush (rush), *n.* violent motion with haste; pressure, as a *rush* of business; the hurrying of many people to a new place, as the California gold *rush*. *n.* a grasslike herb growing in wet land and having round, limber hollow stems, growing to a height of 4 feet or more. *v.i. and v.t.* to move forward hastily, hurry; to cause to hurry, as you are *rushing* me too fast; to attack fast and hard, as to *rush* an enemy outpost.

rusk (rusk), *n.* a light, sweetened biscuit; a sweetened bread baked dry.

russet (rus' et), *n.* a brown color varying from a red-yellow to a more reddish red-yellow; cloth or clothes of that color; a coarse homespun cloth or garments made of it; a winter apple with a rough russet-colored skin.

rust (rust), *n.* the reddish matter that forms on iron or steel through the action of air and moisture; a destructive disease of plants due to a fungus, which causes reddish spots on stems and leaves. *v.i. and v.t.* to become coated with reddish matter, red oxide of iron, through action of air and moisture on the metal, as iron *rusts* easily; to cause such a condition, as the damp air has *rusted* these hinges; to become worn from lack of occupation, as until I can get a job I shall simply *rust*.

rustic (rus' tik), *n.* a countryman; a peasant.

rustic (rus' tik), *adj.* pertaining to the country or characteristic of it and its people; unpolished, unadorned.

rusticate (rus' ti kāt), *v.i. and v.t.,* to reside for a time in the country; to send into the country, especially as a punishment, as he was *rusticated* from college for three months.

rusticity (rus tis' i ti), *n.* [*pl.* rusticities] rural manners; the simplicity characteristic of countryfolk; awkwardness.

rustle (rus' l), *n.* a light sound, as of dead leaves moved on the ground by one walking.

rustle (rus' l), *v.i. and v.t.* to make a sound like that of dead leaves being moved about, as your dress *rustles* when you walk; to steal cattle on the range.

rustler (rus' lēr), *n.* an energetic, successful man; one who steals cattle on the range.

rusty (rus' ti), *adj.* [*comp.* rustier, *superl.* rustiest] covered with the red matter forming on iron and steel when exposed to air and moisture; suffering from lack of use or work, as my mind is *rusty* after a long vacation; having the reddish color of rust.

rut (rut), *n.* a deep track worn by the wheels of passing vehicles; a settled way of thinking or doing things, as do not let your mind get into a *rut*.

*ruthless (rōoth' les), *adj.* having no pity or compassion; cruel and unsparing.

rye (rī), *n.* a grain related to wheat, used to make flour and whisky and as fodder for livestock.

S

Sabbath (sab' ath), *n.* the seventh day of the week, from sundown on Friday to sundown on Saturday, kept as a day of rest and worship by the Jews.

sabbatical (sa bat' i kal), *adj.* pertaining to the Sabbath.

saber (sā' bēr), *n.* a heavy cavalry sword with curving blade.

sable (sā' bl), *n.* a small flesh-eating animal related to the marten, native to northern Europe and Siberia, and valued for its fine fur; the fur of this animal or a garment made of it; its color, black; a mourning garment.

*sabot (sà bō'), *n.* a wooden shoe worn by the peasants of various countries of Europe.

sabotage (sab ō täzh), *n.* deliberate damage done to an employer's property, whether goods, machinery or plant; refusal to work, and interference with other workers.

sac (sak), *n.* a baglike organ in a plant or animal body, generally containing a special fluid.

saccate (sak' āt), *adj.* having the form of a sac or pouch.

saccharin (sak' a rin), *n.* a white crystalline product of coal tar, several hundred times as sweet as cane sugar, used as a substitute for sugar in special diets.

*saccharine (sak' a rin), *adj.* having the qualities of sugar; yielding sugar; extremely sweet or too sweet.

*sacerdotal (sas ēr dō' tal), *adj.* pertaining to priests or to the priesthood.

sachem (sā' chem), *n.* a high chief of the North American Indians, in some tribes an office passing from father to son; any leader or ruler.

*sachet (sa shā'), *n.* a small bag or cushion filled with perfumed powder.

sack (sak), *n.* a bag, especially a large one, as of burlap, to hold something heavy like grain or potatoes; a loose coat for women or children; also written *sacque*; the plundering of a captured city, as the *sack* of Troy.

sack (sak), *v.t.* to put into a coarse bag; to plunder, pillage, ravage a town or land.

sackcloth (sak' klŏth), *n.* a coarse material of which heavy bags are made; coarse cloth worn as a token of mourning or penitence.

sacking (sak' ing), *n.* coarse material, like burlap, used in making sacks.

*****sacrament** (sak' ra ment), *n.* a solemn religious rite, as baptism or the Eucharist, the Lord's Supper.

*****sacred** (sā' kred), *adj.* set apart for religious use; pertaining to God or religion; consecrated; to be held in reverence.

*****sacrifice** (sak' ri fis), *n.* the act of offering something to God in atonement as an act of worship; what is thus offered; the act of giving up something one has or wants for the good of others: also, *self-sacrifice;* the selling of goods at cost or under cost, involving loss; any grievous loss, as to win a war at the *sacrifice* of men.

*****sacrifice** (sak' ri fis), *v.i. and v.t.* to make an offering to God; to give up, lose, renounce or destroy for a cause, as to *sacrifice* one's life for one's country; to sell at a loss, as the property was *sacrificed* for $5,000.

*****sacrilege** (sak' ri lej), *n.* the act of violating sacred things; a word or act that profanes anything sacred.

*****sacrilegious** (sak ri lēj' us), *adj.* violating sacred things; impious.

sacristan (sak' ris tan), *n.* one who has the care of church vessels, vestments and the like; a sexton.

*****sacristy** (sak' ris ti), *n.* [*pl.* sacristies] the room in a church where the sacred vessels and vestments are kept; a vestry.

sacrosanct (sak' rō sangkt), *adj.* very sacred, very holy, not to be profaned.

*****sacrum** (sā' krum), *n.* [*pl.* sacra or sacrums] the five united vertebrae at the lower end of the spinal column, connected with the pelvis.

sad (sad), *adj.* having grief or sorrow; expressing grief or sorrow; mournful; causing sorrow; somber; dark-colored.

sadden (sad' n), *v.i. and v.t.* to become or make sorrowful; to cause sorrow to; to cause to mourn or grieve.

saddle (sad' l), *n.* a seat, usually of leather, for one riding horseback; the hindquarters or loins of a meat carcass, as a *saddle* of mutton; the lower part of the back of a fowl resembling a saddle in shape.

saddlebow (sad' l bō), *n.* the front, arched part of a saddle, the pommel.

saddler (sad' lēr), *n.* one who makes and sells fittings for riding and driving.

saddlery (sad' lēr i), *n.* [*pl.* saddleries] saddles and fittings for horseback riding or driving; the business or shop of a saddler.

sadiron (sad' i ērn), *n.* a flatiron, a heavy implement used for smoothing and pressing dampened cloth or clothes.

safe (sāf), *adj.* free from threat of harm, loss or danger; unharmed, having escaped injury; secure; involving no risk, as a *safe* investment; trustworthy, as a *safe* bridge.

safe (sāf), *n.* a strong structure in which to store money, papers or valuables, generally with a secret lock and providing security against fire, and burglars.

safeguard (sāf' gärd), *n.* one who or that which protects; defense; protection given by a government to one from another country. *v.t.* to protect, defend, keep from harm, as to *safeguard* health.

safety (sāf' ti), *n.* freedom from danger, injury or damage; the state of being protected against harm.

safety pin (sāf' ti pin), a pin so made that its point is held within a metal cap when it is fastened.

safety valve (sāf' ti valv), an automatic release on a boiler that permits escape of steam when the pressure reaches the danger point; any relief or vent for dangerous emotion.

*****saffron** (saf' run), *n.* a plant resembling the crocus having a bulbous root and flowers whose pistils yield a deep-yellow dye; the color of this dye. *adj.* having a deep-yellow color.

sag (sag), *n.* a downward bend or depression, as a *sag* in a roof; a drop in prices.

sag (sag), *v.i.* to depart from a normal and proper line, as a towrope *sags* of its own weight, a roof *sags* because the timbers yield; to be depressed, as one's spirit *sags* under a weight of trouble.

*****saga** (sä' ga), *n.* a legend or story of an Icelandic hero or family line of medieval times; any prose or verse narrative celebrating a line of events or the history of a family.

*****sagacious** (sa gā' shus), *adj.* mentally quick and discerning, shrewd, wise.

sagacity (sa gas' i ti), *n.* quick, keen judgment; ability to see promptly what should be done in a difficult situation; the quality of quick, sure decision.

sagamore (sag' a mōr), *n.* a tribal chief of certain North American Indians, ordinarily not quite so high a title as sachem.

*****sage** (sāj), *n.* an old man of great wisdom; a profound philosopher. *n.* a plant of the mint family, genus *Salvia,* used in cookery. *adj.* wise, discerning, profound, as *sage* advice.

sago (sā' gō), *n.* a kind of granulated food starch prepared from the pith of certain East Indian palm trees called *Sago* palms.

*****sail** (sāl), *n.* a sheet of canvas spread to catch the wind, by means of which a vessel is driven forward in the water; a ride in a sailboat, as we had a delightful *sail.*

sail (sāl), *v.i. and v.t.* to move across water propelled by wind and sail; to travel by water on any vessel; to glide through the air, as a buzzard *sails;* to travel over in a ship, as to *sail* the seven seas; to manage and steer, as to *sail* a boat.

sailor (sāl' ēr), *n.* a seaman; mariner; a member of the crew of any ship but especially a sailing ship.

saint (sānt), *n.* a holy or sanctified person, especially one canonized by the Church; one who is eminent for piety and virtue.

sake (sāk), *n.* cause or objective, as do this for the *sake* of law and order; welfare or benefit, as do it for my *sake*.

*__salaam__ (sa läm'), *n.* a salutation used in oriental lands, combining a deep bow with placing of the right palm on the forehead.

salable (sāl' a bl), *adj.* marketable; sure to find a buyer.

salacious (sa lā' shus), *adj.* indecent, impure.

salad (sal' ad), *n.* a dish of cold green vegetables dressed with vinegar or oil; any cold dish of fruit, meat, fish or vegetables served with mayonnaise or other dressing; a green herb grown for these dishes, as lettuce or endive.

salamander (sal' a man dẽr), *n.* any of various small amphibians, shaped like lizards but having a soft, scaleless skin; a mythical lizard-shaped animal fabled by the ancients to live unharmed in fire; a small stove to keep new building construction from freezing.

*__salary__ (sal' a ri), *n.* [*pl.* salaries] regular yearly, monthly or weekly recompense paid for services rendered in business or the professions.

sale (sāl), *n.* exchange of goods for a price in money; offering of goods at lowered prices, as a special *sale* of kitchenware; existence of a market or demand, as there is no *sale* for these goods.

salience (sā' li ens), *n.* the quality of standing out prominently, prominence.

*__salient__ (sā' li ent), *n.* a forward-bulging section of a military line, as of trenches; a projecting angle in a fortification.

salient (sā' li ent), *adj.* standing out prominently, noticeable; projecting outwardly, greater than two right angles, as the arc that measures a *salient* angle takes in more than half the circumference of a circle.

saline (sā' lin), *adj.* salty; consisting of, containing or like salt.

saliva (sa li' va), *n.* the watery fluid secreted in the mouth; spittle.

*__salivary__ (sal' i ver i), *adj.* pertaining to the spittle or to the glands that produce it.

salivate (sal' i vāt), *v.t. and v.i.* to produce an excess of spittle in; to secrete saliva.

sallow (sal' ō), *n.* a small broad-leaved willow tree that grows in Europe and Asia; a twig of willow.

sallow (sal' ō), *adj.* having a pale, sickly yellow color, as he has a *sallow* complexion.

sally (sal' i), *n.* [*pl.* sallies] a rush of men from a fort or defended place to attack the forces besieging it; a swift outburst of wit or fancy, as his *sallies* of wit kept us amused. *v.i.* to rush out suddenly; to set out boldly, as to *sally* forth in quest of adventure.

*__salmon__ (sam' un), *n.* a sea fish that swims into fresh-water rivers and streams to spawn, having silvery, black-spotted sides, and highly valued as food.

salmonella (sal ' mō nel ' a), *n.* the genus of bacteria which cause food poisoning and diseases such as typhoid fever.

*__salon__ (sa lŏn'), *n.* a fine reception room; a fashionable assemblage; a gathering, at set times, of noted persons: *the Salon*, in Paris, an annual exhibition of the work of artists of the day.

*__saloon__ (sa lŏon'), *n.* a drawing room; the main cabin of a passenger steamship; in the U. S., a barroom.

salsify (sal' si fi), *n.* the oyster plant, grown for its edible root.

*__salt__ (sôlt), *n.* sodium chloride, used for seasoning and preserving foods; a compound of any alkali with any acid; something that gives character or flavor, as the *salt* of wit. *v.t.* to sprinkle, season, treat with salt, as to *salt* meat to preserve it; to supply with salt, as to *salt* livestock.

salt (sôlt), *adj.* seasoned or preserved with sodium chloride.

*__saltation__ (sal ta' shun), *n.* a leaping or dancing.

saltcellar (sôlt sel' ẽr), a small dish to hold salt for the table.

saltpeter (sôlt pē' tẽr), *n.* a white crystalline substance used in making gunpowder and to preserve food.

salubrious (sa lū' bri us), *adj.* healthful, as a *salubrious* climate.

*__salutary__ (sal' ū ter i), *adj.* good for the health; tending to improve; wholesome.

salutation (sal ū tā' shun), *n.* a greeting; the act of greeting.

*__salute__ (sa lūt'), *n.* a mark of military respect shown by raising the hand to the cap or by holding a rifle or sword in a prescribed position; a salvo of cannon or dipping of the flag aboard ship in honor of guests of high rank or ships of another navy.

salvable (sal' va bl), *adj.* capable of being saved.

salvage (sal' vij), *n.* the saving of a ship or its cargo from loss at sea; money paid to those who prevent such loss; any act of saving goods or property from being lost or destroyed, as *salvage* from a business that fails; the property that is saved.

salvage (sal' vij), *v.t.* to save a ship or its cargo from being lost at sea; to save something when loss of all is threatened.

salvation (sal vā' shun), *n.* the act of saving; state of being saved; the deliverance of the soul from sin and death.

*__salve__ (säv), *n.* a healing ointment; anything that heals or soothes, as your words are a *salve* to my hurt feelings. *v.t.* to apply a healing substance to a wound; to soothe, as injured feelings.

*__salver__ (sal' vẽr), *n.* a tray on which anything is presented, as he brought the letters on a silver *salver*.

salvo (sal' vō), *n.* [*pl.* salvos] a discharge of a number of pieces of artillery as a salute; a volley of applause.

same (sām), *adj.* being one, identical, as the *same* man that was here yesterday; corresponding exactly or indistinguishably, as my hat is the *same* size as yours; equal, as to walk the *same* distance every day.

sameness (sām' nes), *n.* likeness, similarity.

*__samovar__ (sam' ō vär), *n.* a Russian urn of brass or copper containing a charcoal burner to keep water hot for tea.

sampan (sam' pan), *n.* a flat-bottomed boat propelled by scull and sail, used in the rivers and harbors of China and Japan.

*sample (sam' pl), *n.* a specimen; a part taken to show the nature of the whole.

sample (sam' pl), *v.t.* to test by taking a part as representative of the whole; to show one of a series or line as an example of the others; as to *sample* a shipment of fruit.

sampler (sam' plēr), *n.* one who tests by taking representative parts of anything; a sort of needlework, so called because originally done as a test of a beginner's skill.

*sanatorium (san a tō' ri um), *n.* [*pl.* sanatoriums or sanatoria] a health retreat; an institution where resident patients are treated for particular diseases, as a *sanatorium* for nervous cases.

sanatory (san' a tō ri), *adj.* conducive to health; contributing to a cure.

sanctify (sangk' ti fi), *v.t.* [*p.t. and p.p.* sanctified, *pr.p.* sanctifying] to set apart as holy; to consecrate.

sanctimonious (sangk ti mō' ni us), *adj.* hypocritical; pretending to be more holy than one actually is.

sanction (sangk' shun), *n.* the act of giving authority to do something or approving that which has been done: *sanctions*, provisions to assure execution of law or performance of pledge. *v.t.* to approve; to confirm; to ratify, as the Department of State *sanctions* the ambassador's course of action.

sanctity (sangk' ti ti), *n.* [*pl.* sanctities] holiness, sacredness; saintliness of character.

sanctuary (sangk' tū er i), *n.* [*pl.* sanctuaries] the most secluded and sacred part of a temple; a place of certain shelter, a refuge.

sanctum (sangk' tum), *n.* a sacred place; a place of utmost privacy.

sand (sand), *n.* fine particles of rock that has been crushed or worn by the elements through long periods of time, heavier than dust but much finer than gravel: *sands*, a region of loose, grainy soil, a beach; loose particles of sand in an hourglass and hence moments, as the *sands* of time. *v.t.* to add sand to; to sprinkle with sand.

sandal (san' dal), *n.* a kind of outer footwear consisting of a sole held by straps; a loose slipper.

sandalwood (san' dal wood), *n.* a yellowish fragrant wood of an Indo-Malayan tree, used in cabinetmaking.

sandpaper (sand pā' pēr), *n.* heavy paper coated with sand to smooth and polish.

sandpiper (sand' pi pēr), *n.* a wading bird resembling the plovers and living on the shores of inland rivers and ponds.

*sandwich (sand' wich), *n.* two slices of bread with meat, cheese or the like between them.

sandy (san' di), *adj.* [*comp.* sandier, *superl.* sandiest] composed of, covered with or resembling sand.

sane (sān), *adj.* mentally sound and healthy; coming from or befitting a sound mind, as *sane* advice.

*sanguinary (sang' gwi ner i), *adj.* attended

with much bloodshed, bloody, as a *sanguinary* battle; bloodthirsty, murderous.

*sanguine (sang' gwin), *adj.* having a warm, cheerful and hopeful nature, confident; of the color of blood, red.

sanitarian (san i tār' i an), *n.* one who advocates or promotes measures of health.

sanitarian (san i tār' i an), *adj.* pertaining to health or the laws of health.

*sanitarium (san i tār' i um), *n.* [*pl.* sanitariums or sanitaria] an institution for the treatment and care of invalids; a sanatorium or health retreat.

sanitary (san' i ter i), *adj.* pertaining to, connected with or tending to promote health; hygienic.

sanitation (san i tā' shun), *n.* use of scientific knowledge in providing means to preserve health; use of things that contribute to hygiene and health; as good plumbing, drainage and the like.

sanity (san' i ti), *n.* soundness of mind, mental health.

sans (sanz), *prep.* without, as *sans* everything.

sap (sap), *n.* the juice of plants that circulates through them and supports them in growth; vital fluid; vitality.

*sapience (sā' pi ens), *n.* wisdom; knowledge along with keen discernment.

sapient (sā' pi ent), *adj.* wise, sagacious.

sapling (sap' ling), *n.* a young tree; a youth.

*saponaceous (sap ō nā' shus), *adj.* relating to or like soap; soapy, slippery.

saponify (sa pon' i fi), *v.i. and v.t.* [*p.t. and p.p.* saponified, *pr.p.* saponifying] to become soap; to make into soap.

*sapphire (saf' Ir), *n.* a transparent precious stone of deep-blue corundum; a pure transparent variety of corundum whitish or yellowish in color; a greenish-blue color.

sappy (sap' i), *adj.* [*comp.* sappier, *superl.* sappiest] full of sap; juicy.

saraband (sar' a band), *n.* a Spanish dance; the music for it.

sarcasm (sär' kazm), *n.* language that bites or taunts; a bitter, cutting style of expression.

sarcastic (sär kas' tik), *adj.* bitterly scornful; ironic in an unkind way; taunting.

sarcophagus (sär kof' a gus), *n.* [*pl.* sarcophagi or sarcophaguses] a stone coffin; a large coffin open to view within a tomb.

*sardine (sär dēn'), *n.* a small food fish resembling the herring, found in European waters and preserved in oil for export.

*sardonic (sär don' ik), *adj.* scornful and bitter; derisive, as a *sardonic* smile.

*sargasso (sär gas' ō), *n.* a tropical seaweed from which the Sargasso Sea takes its name.

*sarsaparilla (sär sa pa ril' a), *n.* a twining shrub native to Mexico, from the dried roots of which medicine and a soft drink are made; a preparation made from these dried roots.

sartorial (sär tō' ri al), *adj.* pertaining to tailors or to tailoring.

sash (sash), *n.* an ornamental band worn around the waist or over the shoulder; a frame to hold a pane of glass: windows collectively, as the house needs new *sash*.

sassafras (sas' *a* fras). *n.* a tree related to the laurel, with soft yellow wood and yellow flowers, with roots having an aromatic bark from which a medicinal preparation is made and which is sometimes used as a flavoring.

*Satan (sā' tan), *n.* the Devil.

satanic (sā tan' ĭk), *adj.* resembling Satan; diabolical, devilish.

satchel (sach' el), *n.* a small bag in which to carry belongings; a handbag; a small valise.

*sate (sāt), *v.t.* to satisfy, as the appetite; to weary by overabundance.

sateen (sa tēn'), *n.* a cotton cloth with a glossy finish resembling satin.

*satellite (sat' e lĭt), *n.* a heavenly body that revolves around a larger one, as the moon is the earth's *satellite;* a follower or attendant, always subordinate; any devoted follower.

*satiate (sā' shi āt), *v.t.* to fill full or ·gratify completely; to satisfy every need or desire of, glut. *adj.* filled full, satisfied, sated.

*satiety (sa tī' e tĭ), *n.* the state of being filled or satisfied so completely that there is no need or desire for more.

satin (sat' ĭn), *n.* a closely woven silk fabric with glossy surface but dull back.

satin (sat' ĭn), *adj.* like satin, smooth, glossy; made of satin, as a *satin* dress.

*satire (sat' ĭr), *n.* sarcasm, wit and irony; a composition holding vices or follies up to ridicule, as Gulliver's Travels is a *satire* on the life of its author's times.

satiric (sa tir' ĭk), *adj.* of the nature of satire, sarcastic, ironical and ridiculing; severely scornful and censorious of men and manners.

satirist (sat' ĭr ĭst), *n.* one who writes satire, holding people and customs up to ridicule.

satirize (sat' ĭr ĭz), *v.t.* to use as the subject for satire, hold up to ridicule, attack with ridicule.

satisfaction (sat ĭs fak' shun), *n.* the act of satisfying or fulfilling; the state of being satisfied, gratified, fulfilled; contentment; gratification; settlement or payment, as this bill calls for *satisfaction;* reparation or apology, as he gave me *satisfaction* for the injury done.

satisfactory (sat ĭs fak' tō rĭ), *adj.* acceptable; meeting requirements.

satisfy (sat' ĭs fī), *v.i. and v.t.* [*p.t. and p.p.* satisfied, *pr.p.* satisfying] to give pleasure; to gratify; to make content; to settle, as an account; to discharge, as to *satisfy* a claim; to convince, as I *satisfied* him of your ability to do the job.

saturate (sat' ū rāt), *v.t.* to soak; to cause to become completely charged with something, as to *saturate* the mind with learning; to fill till it can hold or absorb no more, as to *saturate* a sponge with water; to charge with magnetism to the full extent of capacity, as a mass of iron or steel, such as the field or armature core of a dynamo.

*saturnine (sat' ẽr nĭn), *adj.* dull; gloomy; morose; sullen.

*satyr (sat' ẽr), *n.* a Greek forest deity with a man's body but the horns and legs of a goat.

*sauce (sôs), *n.* a condiment or seasoning for food; pulp of fruit stewed and sweetened, as apple*sauce*.

saucer (sô' sẽr), *n.* a small dish on which a cup is set or used for serving side dishes.

sauciness (sô' sĭ nes), *n.* impertinence, impudence.

*saucy (sô' sĭ), *adj.* [*comp.* saucier, *superl.* sauciest] pert, impudent.

sauna (sou´ nū), *n.* a steam bath where water is run over hot stones to produce steam or the room or enclosure for that bath.

*saunter (sôn' tẽr), *n.* a stroll, an idle walk, a leisurely, unconcerned way of walking.

saunter (sôn' tẽr), *v.i.* to wander about idly, stroll, loiter.

sausage (sô' sĭj), *n.* seasoned minced meat, sometimes smoked or cooked, stuffed into a casing or molded into cakes ready for cooking.

sauté (sō tā'), *adj.* fried quickly, with little grease in the pan.

*savage (sav' ĭj), *n.* a wild, uncivilized person; one who is brutal in his ways. *adj.* uncivilized, wild, fierce, cruel.

savanna (sa van' a), *n.* an extensive open plain or meadow without trees.

*savant (sa vän'), *n.* a man of great learning in some special field, a scholar.

save (sāv), *v.i. and v.t.* to be economical; to lay aside, as money, for future use; to remove from danger; to preserve from evil; to rescue. *prep.* except, not including, as all is lost *save* honor.

savings (sāv' ĭngz), *n. pl.* money laid away for future use.

savior (sāv' yẽr), *n.* one who saves or delivers.

savor (sā' vẽr), *n.* flavor, taste; relish; a distinguishing quality, as the *savor* of great learning is in this book; scent, as the kitchen was full of the pleasant *savor* of roasting beef. *v.i. and v.t.* to possess a distinguishing quality, as this *savors* of rebellion; to flavor, season, as to *savor* a stew; to taste or smell with pleasure, as to *savor* one's food.

savory (sā' vẽr ĭ), *n.* a hardy aromatic herb of the mint family, used in cooking.

savory (sā' vẽr ĭ), *adj.* pleasing to taste or smell, as a *savory* meal.

*savoy (sa voi'), *n.* a winter cabbage with crisp, curled leaves.

saw (sô), *n.* a saying, a proverb, a maxim.

saw (sô), *n.* a cutting instrument with a thin, flat blade having a toothed edge.

saw (sô), *v.i. and v.t.* [*p.t.* sawed, *p.p.* sawed or sawn, *pr.p.* sawing] to use a saw; to be cut with a saw, as this wood *saws* hard; to cut with a saw, as to *saw* wood.

sawyer (sô' yẽr), *n.* one who saws logs or timber, especially either one of two workmen (top *sawyer* and bottom *sawyer*) who saw timbers over a saw pit.

saxophone (sak' sō fōn), *n.* a brass wind instrument having a conical tube with finger keys and a clarinet reed mouthpiece.

say (sā), *n*. what one has uttered or desires to utter, as I must have my *say*.

say (sā), *v.i. and v.t. [p.t. and p.p.* said, *pr.p.* saying] to speak, tell, utter in words.

scab (skab), *n*. a crust formed over a wound or sore; a disease of plants in which scales form on stem or leaf; a contagious disease of sheep, resembling mange; a worker who takes the place of one who is on strike.

scabbard (skab′ ẽrd), *n*. the sheath of a sword.

scaffold (skaf′ ōld), *n*. a temporary structure for workmen to stand or walk on while putting up a building; a platform on which a condemned criminal stands to be hanged.

scaffolding (skaf′ ōld ing), *n*. the structure about a building under erection for workmen to walk on; materials for making such a structure.

scalawag (skal′ *a* wag), *n*. a scamp, a rascal.

*scald (skōld), *n*. a burn or injury to the skin caused by a hot liquid or steam.

scald (skōld), *v.t.* to burn with hot liquid or steam; to heat, as a liquid, without boiling; to cleanse with boiling water.

scale (skāl), *n*. a balance on which to weigh things: *scales*, any form of weighing machine, large or small, movable or fixed. *n*. one of small bony or horny plates covering bodies of most fishes and reptiles; a similar but much lighter growth on wings of some insects; any thin flaky crust on skin of animals or bark of trees caused by certain diseases; a metallic flake caused by oxidation, as of rust. *n*. a series, going up step by step, as a *scale* in music, the *scale* marked on a thermometer; proportion, as the map is on the *scale* of one inch to the mile and it is carefully drawn to *scale;* size, extent, as we do business on a large *scale*. *v.i. and v.t.* to come off in thin layers; to form into flakes, as rust in a boiler; to remove the hard skin plates from, as to *scale* a fish; to throw in such a way that the missile skips on the water, as to *scale* a stone across a pond; to throw a flat object in a similar way through the air. *v.t.* to climb up the side of, as

scale (skāl), *v.t.* to climb up the side of, as to *scale* a cliff; to make according to a common standard of measurement, as to *scale* one drawing to another; to reduce by a certain ratio, as to *scale* wages up or down.

*scalene (skā lēn′), *adj*. having the sides and angles unequal, as a *scalene* triangle.

*scallop (skol′ up), *n*. edible salt-water mollusk or shellfish with two ribbed or fluted shells; one of curved sections in an edge with even round notches all along it.

scallop (skol′ up), *v.t.* to bake after thickening with crumbs and a sauce, as to *scallop* oysters; to ornament an edge by cutting a uniform series of semicircular notches all along it, as to *scallop* a cookie.

scalp (skalp), *n*. the skin on the top and back of the head on which the hair grows; the skin and hair of the head together; a part of it cut off by the American Indians in warfare as a token of victory.

scalp (skalp), *v.t.* to cut off a section of skin and hair from the head, as the Indians *scalped* many captives.

*scalpel (skal′ pel), *n*. a surgeon's knife, small and very sharp.

scaly (skāl′ i), *adj. [comp.* scalier, *superl.* scaliest] covered with small hard plates; flaky.

scamp (skamp), *n*. a rascal, a fellow who does not amount to much. *v.i. and v.t.* to do poor work, as you are *scamping* on the job; to do inadequately, hurriedly and carelessly, as to *scamp* a job.

scamper (skam′ pẽr), *n*. a hasty flight. *v.i.* to run fast and lightly; to run about in play; to run away as if in fright.

scan (skan), *v.i. and v.t.* to scrutinize; to examine carefully; to separate into units of meter, as to *scan* a line of verse.

scandal (skan′ dal), *n*. something said that is false and injurious to another; malicious gossip, slander; a cause of reproach, anything that offends or disgraces, as his conduct was a neighborhood *scandal*.

scandalous (skan′ dal us), *adj.* offending the sense of what is right and decent; causing offense or shame, as your conduct is *scandalous*, a *scandalous* situation or affair.

scant (skant), *v.t.* to stint, limit closely. *adj.* not full or abundant, as *scant* measure; scarcely sufficient, as *scant* rations.

scantling (skant′ ling), *n*. a long thin narrow timber used for rough, covered work in building; set of specifications for plates or flooring of ship under construction.

scanty (skan′ ti), *adj. [comp.* scantier, *superl.* scantiest] barely enough, meager; stingy.

scape (skāp), *n*. the shaft of a column; the shaft of a feather; a long flower stem rising from a clump of leaves or from a covered part in the ground, as the *scape* of a daffodil.

scapegoat (skāp′ gōt), *n*. one who bears the blame for the sins or faults of others.

scapegrace (skāp′ grās), *n*. an irresponsible or unprincipled fellow.

*scapula (skap′ ū la), *n*. the shoulderblade.

*scar (skär), *n*. a mark left on the skin after a wound heals; a marring mark on the surface of anything, as a table; the memory of an injury, as his action left *scars* on my mind. *v.i. and v.t.* to heal over and leave a mark on the skin; to mar or mark.

*scarab (skar′ ab), *n*. a certain beetle that was worshiped by the ancient Egyptians as a symbol of immortality; a gem made in the form of this beetle and inscribed with ancient Egyptian symbols.

*scarce (skårs), *adj.* not common; not plentiful; not equal to the demand.

scarcely (skårs′ li), *adv.* barely, hardly, almost not, as I *scarcely* saw him, I *scarcely* made the train; certainly not, as we can *scarcely* suppose that this is true.

scarcity (skår′ si ti), *n*. dearth, insufficiency.

*scare (skår), *n*. a sudden fright or panic.

scare (skår), *v.i. and v.t.* to take fright, as he *scares* easily; to cause fright; to alarm, as you *scared* me.

scarf (skärf), *n.* [*pl.* scarfs or scarves] a neckerchief; a long wide band worn about the neck; a strip of cloth or lace to cover a bureau, sideboard or the like. *n.* [*pl.* scarfs or scarves] a groove cut into wood; a piece of timber cut or notched so as to make a joint with another notched timber. *v.t.* to join two timbers by notching or two metal pieces by bolting.

scarify (skar' i fī), *v.t.* [*p.t.* and *p.p.* scarified, *pr.p.* scarifying] to scratch or cut lightly; to furrow, as the ground for planting; to hurt, as another's feelings, as if by cutting.

*****scarlatina** (skär la tē' na), *n.* scarlet fever.

scarlet (skär' let), *n.* a brilliant red with a tinge of yellow; cloth of such a color.

scarlet fever (skär' let fē' vēr), a contagious disease marked by sore throat, fever and a bright red rash, scarlatina.

scarp (skärp), *n.* the sharp, almost perpendicular inner slope of a ditch about a fortification; any steep descent.

scarp (skärp), *v.t.* to cut down almost perpendicularly, as to *scarp* the face of a rock.

scathe (skā*th*), *v.t.* to injure by fire, scorch; to denounce witheringly.

scathing (skā*th*' ing), *adj.* damaging, withering, severe or bitter, as a *scathing* rebuke.

scatter (skat' ēr), *v.i. and v.t.* to disperse, as the crowd *scattered;* to strew or throw about; to cause to disperse, as the police *scattered* the crowd.

scavenge (skav' enj), *v.t.* to cleanse, as streets, of mud and filth.

scavenger (skav' en jēr), *n.* a street cleaner; an animal or bird that feeds on carrion or waste matter.

*****scenario** (sē när' i ō), *n.* [*pl.* scenarios] a synopsis of the plot of a play or an opera, indicating scenes and the actions of the players; the outline of a play for a motion picture.

scene (sēn), *n.* the time and place in which the action of a story or play is laid, the setting; anything viewed as a whole, as the political *scene;* a view, as of a landscape; a part of a play or story presenting one episode, the parts of an act; a painting on canvas hung at the back of a stage to make the setting realistic, scenery; any extraordinary exhibition of excitement, as do not make a *scene* here.

scenery (sēn' ēr i), *n.* views in nature; the painted wings, backdrop and views used to give proper setting for a stage performance.

*****scenic** (sēn' ik), *adj.* pertaining to views in nature or settings on the stage.

scent (sent), *n.* the sense of smell; an odor; the odor left by a person or animal, as a hound follows the *scent* of a fleeing animal; hence any trail or track, as the clever fugitive threw his pursuers off the *scent.*

scepter, sceptre (sep' tēr), *n.* a staff borne by a sovereign as an emblem of royal authority.

*****schedule** (sked' ūl), *n.* a formal list or inventory; a list of things to be done in a certain order or time; a written or printed plan or statement of regularly timed events or operations, a timetable, as railroad trains run on *schedule.*

schedule (sked' ūl), *v.t.* to place in a list of things to be done; to arrange a timetable for, as to *schedule* trains, boats, airplanes.

scheme (skēm), *n.* a plan, purpose or plot; arrangement of ideas or things in systematic order; a sketch showing arrangement of parts.

scheme (skēm), *v.* to plot; to plan; to devise: often with the suggestion of trickery.

*****schism** (sizm), *n.* division or separation, especially of an organization into factions; the offense of causing a split in a church organization; a faction that breaks away from an organization.

*****schismatic** (siz mat' ik), *adj.* tending to cause factional division.

*****schist** (shist), *n.* any rock that splits readily into slabs or sheets.

scholar (skol' ēr), *n.* a student; a person of advanced learning in a special field.

scholarship (skol' ēr ship), *n.* great and thorough learning, erudition; aptitude for advanced learning; a fund to assist worthy students at college.

scholastic (skol as' tik), *adj.* relating to schools or advanced learning, academic; pedantic.

school (skōōl), *n.* a place where instruction is given; a schoolhouse; a body of students divided into classes; the followers of a great leader of thought or a body of persons holding to one doctrine or belief; any field or means of learning, as the *school* of hard knocks. *n.* a large number of fish swimming together. *v.t.* to teach or train; to discipline or educate, as to *school* oneself to obey, to *school* children in English. *v.i.* to swim together in large numbers, as fish.

schooling (skōōl' ing), *n.* formal education; book learning; education from any source, as he had his *schooling* in business.

*****schooner** (skōōn' ēr), *n.* a sailing vessel with two or more masts fore-and-aft rigged.

*****schottische** (shot' ish), *n.* a round dance similar to the polka.

sciatic (sī at' ik), *adj.* relating to the hip.

sciatica (sī at' ik a), *n.* neuralgia of the sciatic nerve in the hip and thigh.

science (sī' ens), *n.* systematized knowledge of any one department of the study of mind or matter, as the *science* of physics.

scientific (sī en tif' ik), *adj.* pertaining to a science, as *scientific* books; following the laws and exact principles of science, as *scientific* farming; systematic, as *scientific* management.

scientist (sī' en tist), *n.* one who seeks exact knowledge through study and experiment.

*****scimitar** (sim' i tēr), *n.* an oriental saber with a curved blade.

*****scintilla** (sin til' a), *n.* a spark, an almost imperceptible trace, as not a *scintilla* of evidence.

scintillate (sin' til āt), *v.i.* to emit sparks or fire with flash and glitter; to sparkle, as wit *scintillates.*

*****scion** (sī' un), *n.* a sprout or shoot of a plant, such as is used in grafting; a descendant, as he is the *scion* of an ancient family: also spelled *cion*.

scissors (siz' ērz), *n.* a cutting instrument with two pivoted blades; small shears.

sclerosis (sklē rō' sis), *n.* the hardening of body tissues.

scoff (skof), *n.* a jeer, an expression of contempt, mockery or derision. *v.i. and v.t.* to mock, jeer, treat with scorn, deride.

scold (skōld), *v.i. and v.t.* to chide sharply or rudely; to find fault with; to berate.

scold (skōld), *n.* one who finds fault habitually and violently.

*sconce (skons), *n.* a wall bracket to hold a lamp or candle; a covered lantern; a small fort.

*scoop (skōōp), *n.* a large ladle; a deep shovel. *v.i. and v.t.* to take out or up, as with a ladle.

scope (skōp), *n.* room or opportunity for free outlook or action; the extent of ability; range or field taken in, as the *scope* of knowledge, *scope* of a book.

*scorbutic (skôr bū' tik), *adj.* relating to scurvy.

*scorch (skôrch), *n.* a mark caused by heat, as the iron left a *scorch* on the skirt.

scorch (skôrch), *v.t. and v.i.* to burn the surface of, as the laundry *scorched* this handkerchief; to become parched, shriveled or withered by heat, as the grass *scorches* in the sun.

*score (skōr), *n.* a notch cut into something; an account or bill, as my *score* at the general store; a grudge, as I have a *score* to settle with him; a record of points made in a game; the notes of a musical composition; twenty. *v.i. and v.t.* to keep tally, keep count of points made in a game; to make points in a game; to mark with notches or grooves; to criticize harshly.

*scorn (skôrn), *n.* great contempt, haughty disdain; an object of contempt. *v.t.* to hold in contempt; to regard with disdain

scornful (skôrn' fool), *adj.* contemptuous, disdainful.

scorpion (skôr' pi un), *n.* a tropical insect-eating animal resembling a spider, with pinching claws and a poisonous sting.

scotch (skoch), *n.* a cut on the surface; a score; a line on the ground in the game of hopscotch. *n.* a wedge or block to prevent slipping or rolling. *v.t.* to cut or wound slightly; to scratch; to disable, as to *scotch* a snake. *v.t.* to block a wheel or log with a wedge-shaped object.

scoundrel (skoun' drel), *n.* a man without honor or virtue.

*scour (skour), *n.* the act of rubbing to remove dirt, as this pot needs a good *scour;* the action of a stream that clears the bed of loose stones. *v.t.* to clean by washing, rubbing; to form by erosion, as a stream *scours* a channel. *v.t.* to pass over swiftly as in search, to search thoroughly, as to *scour* the fields for rabbits.

*scourge (skûrj), *n.* a whip with handle and lash; a cause of great or widespread affliction and destruction, as the *scourge* •of

drought. *v.t.* to whip severely; to cause great and widespread affliction.

*scout (skout), *n.* a person sent out to make observations and bring back information, especially of the movements of an enemy; a member of the Boy Scouts or Girl Scouts.

scout (skout), *v.i.* to look or search about for observation and information, especially to learn the whereabouts, strength or movements of an enemy; to reconnoiter.

scout (skout), *v.t.* to mock or jeer at, to scoff at, as he *scouted* my suggestion.

scoutmaster (skout' mas' tēr), *n.* the leader of a troop of Boy Scouts.

scow (skou), *n.* a large flat-bottomed boat with square ends.

scowl (skoul), *v.i.* to lower the brows and wrinkle the forehead in anger, sullenness or deep thought.

scrag (skrag), *n.* anything lean and tough; a bony person or animal; a bony end of meat, as the neck.

scraggy (skrag' i), *adj.* [*comp.* scraggier, *superl.* scraggiest] lean, bony; rough, rugged; jagged.

scramble (skram' bl), *n.* a confused effort of a number of persons to get something that is loose, as a *scramble* for the ball.

scramble (skram' bl), *v.i. and v.t.* to climb with hands and feet, as to *scramble* up a cliff; to struggle in confused manner, as five players *scrambled* for the ball; to mix up; to stir eggs while cooking in a pan.

*scrap (skrap), *n.* a small detached piece; fragment: *scraps,* leftover food or odds and ends of metal. *v.t.* to break up to obtain its metal, as to *scrap* a ship; to discard, as to *scrap* old methods.

*scrape (skrāp), *n.* a scratchy sound; a difficulty, especially of one's own making; a narrow escape, as that was a close *scrape.*

scrape (skrāp), *v.i. and v.t.* to rub with something sharp-edged so as to make a grating sound; to rub with a sharp tool so as to remove, as to *scrape* paint; to draw a road grader over, as to *scrape* a road; to assemble little by little, as I can *scrape* up $10; to manage with difficulty, as he *scrapes* along.

*scratch (skrach), *n.* a mark or tear on a surface, as the skin or a table, made by drawing something sharp-pointed over it; the grating sound of a pen on paper; the starting line in a race, as he started from *scratch,* the others had head starts. *v.i. and v.t.* to make a grating sound, as a pen on paper; to mark by drawing something with a sharp edge or point over the surface of; to draw over a rough surface, as to *scratch* a match; to draw the fingernails over, as to *scratch* a mosquito bite.

*scrawl (skrôl), *n.* a piece of careless or illegible writing.

scrawl (skrôl), *v.i. and v.t.* to write hastily and badly; to scribble, as to *scrawl* a note.

scrawny (skrô' ni), *adj.* [*comp.* scrawnier, *superl.* scrawniest] bony; lean and lank.

*scream (skrēm), *n.* a shrill cry, as of pain or fear; any long shrill penetrating sound.

as the *scream* of a fire siren. *v.i. and v.t.* to utter a shrill cry, as of pain or fear; to utter in loud, shrill tones.

screech (skrēch), *n.* a harsh, shrill cry, as the brakes went on with a *screech*.

*screed (skrēd), *n.* a tirade, spoken or written; a long speech or an article, of a ranting nature; a long strip, as a *screed* of wood or a *screed* of plaster, put on at intervals to gauge the line of the whole surface.

*screen (skrēn), *n.* a light structure to conceal things, shut something out or protect, as a window *screen*, a fire *screen*, a smoke *screen;* a coarse sieve; the curtain on which motion pictures are projected. *v.t.* to conceal, shelter or protect by means of something that intervenes, as to *screen* windows, *screen* off a corner of a room; to pass through a coarse sieve, as to *screen* gravel; to show on a curtain, as motion pictures.

*screw (skrōō), *n.* a fastening device of metal with a spiral thread; anything that works by turning in such a medium as air or water, as the propeller of a ship or airplane.

screw (skrōō), *v.i. and v.t.* to advance by turning round and round, as this peg *screws* in; to twist, as do not *screw* up your face; to fasten with threaded metal pieces, as to *screw* a lid on a box.

scribble (skrib′ l), *n.* scrawled writing, careless penmanship. *v.i. and v.t.* to write carelessly.

*scribe (skrīb), *n.* a writer; a teacher or copyist of the Jewish law.

*scrim (skrim), *n.* a thin fabric of cotton or linen used in upholstery, linings and window curtains.

scrimmage (skrim′ ij), *n.* a confused struggle; in football, a single play from the snapping of the ball to the moment it is downed, especially the struggle between the two lines as the play starts.

scrimp (skrimp), *v.i. and v.t.* to economize pinchingly; to hold to a small allowance.

scrip (skrip), *n.* a certificate given in place of money; a bit of paper with writing on it; a wallet or small satchel.

script (skript), *n.* handwriting; type designed to look like handwriting; manuscript; the written material of a play for the stage, radio or screen.

*scripture (skrip′ tūr), *n.* any sacred writings: *the Scriptures,* the Old and New Testaments, the Bible, often called the *Holy Scriptures.*

*scrofula (skrof′ ū la), *n.* a disease with swelling of the glands of the neck and inflammation of the bones and joints.

scroll (skrōl), *n.* a roll of paper or parchment with writing on it; ornamentation with spiral lines.

scrub (skrub), *n.* a vigorous rubbing; a stunted tree; a growth of dwarfed vegetation; a person who is undersized.

scrub (skrub), *v.i. and v.t.* to rub vigorously, as a floor or clothes in the wash.

scrub (skrub), *adj.* stunted; worthless, inferior; second-rate, as a *scrub* team that plays practice games with the regular team.

scruple (skrōō′ pl), *n.* 20 grains, apothecaries′ measure; a minute quantity; hesitation from conscientious motives or from the desire to distinguish what is right from what is merely expedient.

scrupulous (skrōō′ pū lus), *adj.* conscientious; exact; punctilious.

scrutinize (skrōō′ ti nīz), *v.t.* to inspect or examine closely.

scrutiny (skrōō′ ti ni), *n.* [*pl.* scrutinies] close inspection, detailed critical examination, minute inquiry.

scud (skud), *n.* light clouds driven by the wind; clouds of spray or masses of foam driven by the sea winds.

scud (skud), *v.i.* to move or run fast; to be driven before the wind or run before a gale with little or no sail set.

scuff (skuf), *n.* a dragging of the feet; a rough, worn spot, as on a shoe.

scuff (skuf), *v.i. and v.t.* to drag or scrape the feet on the ground; to wear off the surface; to rub off the polish of.

scuffle (skuf′ l), *n.* a disorderly struggle; a confused contest or fight. *v.i.* to engage in a confused, disorderly struggle.

scull (skul), *n.* an oar used in a notch at the stern of a boat with a side-to-side, twisting motion instead of a pull; one of a pair of light, broad-bladed oars less than 10 feet long. *v.t.* to propel, as a boat, with a single oar over the stern worked with a back-and-forth motion.

scullery (skul′ ĕr i), *n.* [*pl.* sculleries] a room where cooking utensils are cleaned and kept.

scullion (skul′ yun), *n.* a servant in a scullery who cleans pots and pans and does kitchen chores.

sculptor (skulp′ tĕr), *n.* one who makes figures and statues by carving them from stone or wood or modeling them in soft substances such as clay and wax.

*sculpture (skulp′ tūr), *n.* the art of carving figures from stone or modeling them in such substances as clay and wax. *v.i. and v.t.* to decorate with carved or molded figures; to make such figures.

scum (skum), *n.* heavy foam on a liquid, especially on a boiling or fermenting liquid, containing the impurities of the mass; masses of tiny vegetable growths floating on stagnant water; debased persons collectively, as the *scum* of society.

scupper (skup′ ĕr), *n.* a hole in a ship′s side to let deck water run off or a gutter along the edge of a deck for the same purpose.

scurf (skûrf), *n.* flakes of dead skin; dandruff; any flaky scales adhering to a surface.

scurrile (skûr′ il), *adj.* befitting a buffoon or vulgar jester.

scurrility (skur il′ i ti), *n.* [*pl.* scurrilities] vulgar or vile joking; an abusive or obscene flow of words.

scurrilous (skûr′ i lus), *adj.* indecent, vulgar and vile; abusive, as *scurrilous* language.

scurry (skûr′i), *n.* [*pl.* scurries] hurried movement, scampering. *v.i.* [*p.t. and p.p.* scurried, *pr.p.* scurrying] to hasten, move rapidly, as the clouds *scurry* on a windy day.

scurvy (skûr′ vĭ), *n.* a disease caused by lack of green food (vitamin C) and marked by bleeding gums and great weakness.

scurvy (skûr′ vĭ), *adj.* [*comp.* scurvier, *superl.* scurviest] mean, contemptible, low.

scutch (skuch), *n.* an implement of wood used in beating flax and hemp; a bricklayer's hammer and chopper.

scutcheon (skuch′ un), *n.* a shield with a coat of arms, an escutcheon.

scuttle (skut′ l), *n.* a hatchway with a cover on the roof of a house or a ship's deck; a coal hod.

scuttle (skut′ l), *v.t.* to sink a ship by making holes in the hull.

*scythe (sīth), *n.* an implement for mowing hay and grain having a curved long blade on a long double-curved handle.

sea (sē), *n.* the ocean; a great body of salt water smaller than an ocean; a very large inland body of water, especially salt water; a heavy swell or wave on the ocean; something covering a large area or so closely filled that it might be likened to the surface of a great body of water, as a *sea* of faces.

sea cucumber (sē kū′ kum bĕr), *n.* the holothurian or sea slug, a wormlike marine animal.

sea dog (sē′ dôg), *n.* a dogfish; any of certain seals, especially the harbor seal; an old experienced sailor.

seafaring (sē′ fâr ing), *adj.* engaged in sea voyages; following a mariner's life.

*seal (sēl), *n.* any of various fish-eating sea mammals of the north and south cold regions, valued for their hides and oil, and in some species for their fur.

sea lion (sē lī′ un), *n.* a large seal of the Pacific Ocean, having ears and sometimes reaching a length of 12 feet.

*seam (sēm), *n.* the line made by joining two pieces, as of cloth, plank or metal; a layer of mineral matter in the earth, as a *seam* of coal *v.i. and v.t.* to show a line of joining or of separating into parts, as the rock *seams* right down the middle; to mark with lines, as time *seams* our faces with wrinkles; to join together in such a way as to make a line.

sea mew (sē mū), *n.* a kind of sea gull.

*seamstress (sēm′ stres), *n.* a needlewoman; one who makes her living by sewing for others.

seamy (sēm′ ĭ), *adj.* [*comp.* seamier, *superl.* seamiest] showing lines; showing the rougher part of stitching; the worst, as the *seamy* side of life.

*séance (sā äns′), *n.* a sitting; a session; a meeting of persons in quest of messages from the spirit world; a demonstration by a spiritualist medium, talking with the dead.

seaplane (sē′ plăn), *n.* an airplane so devised that it can rise from or alight on the water.

seaport (sē′ pōrt), *n.* a harbor, town or city situated on a seacoast, accessible to seagoing vessels and engaged in overseas commerce.

sear (sēr), *v.t.* to burn, cauterize, as to *sear* a wound; to brown the surfaces of meat by exposing them briefly to a very hot fire, in a dry pan or broiler, so that the juices are retained during the slower cooking that follows; to harden, make callous, as wicked ways *sear* the conscience.

search (sûrch), *n.* a quest, a seeking; thorough investigation, as I have made a *search* of the records. *v.i. and v.t.* to seek, make a quest or inquiry; to look for.

searching (sûrch′ ing), *adj.* penetrating, thorough, as a *searching* question.

searchlight (sûrch′ līt), *n.* a powerful light with a reflector and mounted on a swivel so that it can be turned at will upon any object; a flashlight.

*season (sē′ zn), *n.* a particular time distinguished from other periods, as one of the four *seasons* of the year; a special period, as the football *season: in season,* at a good time, as you came just *in season;* able to be caught or killed legally, as rabbits are *in season. v.i. and v.t.* to become dry, as lumber; to become mature; to make dry and hard, as lumber; to add relish to, as to *season* food with salt and pepper; to make less dull, dry or severe, as to *season* a discourse with wit or a censure with sympathetic kindness.

seasonable (sē′ zn a bl), *adj.* occurring in good time, fit for a certain time, timely.

seasonal (sē′ zn al), *adj.* pertaining to, happening at or influenced by certain times of the year, as *seasonal* storms.

seasoning (sē′ zn ing), *n.* that which is added to food to give it greater relish, a condiment.

sea spiders (sē spī′ dĕrs), *n.* marine anthropods or *Pantopoda* of several species; some found in deep water, others under stones at edge of water.

seat (sēt), *n.* that on which a person sits or anything rests; the spot where anything is established, as a *seat* of learning.

seat (sēt), *v.t.* to supply a place to sit; to cause to sit; to place; to supply, as a chair, with a surface on which to sit.

seaweed (sē′ wēd), *n.* any plant that grows in the sea, especially certain algae, as kelp or dulse.

seaworthy (sē′ wûr thǐ), *adj.* fit to go to sea, sound enough to weather sea storms.

secant (sē′ kant), *adj.* cutting, as a *secant* line.

secede (sē sēd′), *v.i.* to withdraw from any fellowship, association or union, especially of political or religious nature.

secession (sē sesh′ un), *n.* the act of separating; withdrawal.

*seclude (sē klōōd′), *v.t.* to keep apart, isolate.

seclusion (sē klōō′ zhun), *n.* retirement, solitude, privacy.

seclusive (sē klōō′ sĭv), *adj.* keeping apart from others; seeking privacy.

second (sek′ und), *n.* a time unit, the 60th part of a minute; the 60th part of a degree of angular measure.

second (sek′ und), *n.* the one after the first; one who attends another, as a boxer's *second;* an article or piece of goods of inferior grade, as these gloves are *seconds*. *v.t.* to act as an attendant or assistant, as to *second* a boxer; to give formal support to, as a motion made by another. *adj.* following or appearing immediately after the first, as the *second* house on the right. *adv.* in next rank or degree after the first, as you come *second*.

*secondary (sek' un der i), *adj.* not of the first order of importance; following the primary, as a *secondary* school; subordinate, as speed is *secondary* to accuracy in this test.

secondhand (sek' und hand), *adj.* used before, not new, as *secondhand* clothes; derived from a source, not direct, as *secondhand* news.

secondly (sek' und li), *adv.* in the next or second place.

secrecy (sē' kre si), *n.* [*pl.* secrecies] an act of concealing; concealment; the habit of being reticent.

*secret (sē' kret), *n.* something kept in concealment; anything unrevealed or kept from the knowledge of others; a hidden cause; a mystery. *adj.* hidden, concealed, withheld from the knowledge of others; private, secluded.

*secretary (sek' rē ter i), *n.* [*pl.* secretaries] a person employed to assist in correspondence; one who keeps records for an organization; the head of a department of the U. S. Government, as the *Secretary* of State; a writing desk with pigeonholes and drawers and sometimes bookshelves.

secretary bird (sek' rē ter i bûrd), *n.* a large African bird of prey, about four feet high, has long scaly legs and long quills at back of head, its diet includes snakes, lizards and insects.

secrete (sē krēt'), *v.t.* to hide or conceal; to keep, as information, to oneself; to separate from the blood of an animal body or from the sap of a plant and change into a new substance, as the liver *secretes* bile.

secretion (sē krē' shun), *n.* the act of creating new substances out of substances separated from the blood of an animal or sap of a plant body; any substance thus produced.

secretive (sē krē' tiv), *adj.* tending to keep secrets, especially one's affairs to oneself, reticent.

sect (sekt), *n.* a number of persons united in some particular faith or doctrine.

*sectarian (sek târ' i an), *n.* a member of an organization devoted to one belief or doctrine; a narrow, bigoted person. *adj.* pertaining to a separated group believing a certain doctrine; prejudiced.

*section (sek' shun), *n.* the act of cutting; separation by cutting; a separate part or subdivision of anything, as a *mining* section, a residential *section*, a *section* of seats in the grandstand.

sectionalism (sek' shun al izm), *n.* regard for one part of the country rather than for the whole nation; local pride at the expense of true patriotism.

sector (sek' tẽr), *n.* the part of a circle included within two radii and the arc which they inclose.

secular (sek' ū lẽr), *adj.* pertaining to this world and this life, earthly, not religious or spiritual; not ecclesiastical, civil; extending over ages of time.

secure (sē kūr'), *v.t.* to make safe, protect, as to *secure* a treasure; to make fast, as to *secure* a boat to a dock; to gain possession of, as to *secure* a health certificate.

secure (sē kūr'), *adj.* free from danger, safe, protected; confident.

security (sē kū' ri ti), *n.* [*pl.* securities] the state of being safe or sure; protection; a pledge for the payment of a debt: *securities*, stocks and bonds.

*sedan (sē dan'), *n.* a closed motor car with no separate compartment for the driver and with seats for five to seven passengers; a covered chair slung on poles and carried by two men.

*sedate (sē dāt'), *adj.* calm, composed; quiet and dignified.

*sedative (sed' a tiv), *n.* a medicine that quickly allays pain and quiets the patient.

sedative (sed' a tiv), *adj.* soothing the nerves, assuaging pain, producing calm.

*sedentary (sed' en ter i), *adj.* spending much of the time sitting; requiring a great deal of sitting, as a person of *sedentary* habit, a *sedentary* calling.

sedge (sej), *n.* a solid-stemmed grasslike herb that grows in wet land.

sediment (sed' i ment), *n.* the matter that sinks to the bottom of a container full of liquid; dregs, lees.

sedimentary (sed i men' ta ri), *adj.* consisting of or formed by matter settling to the bottom of a body of liquid.

sedition (sē dish' un), *n.* an offense against the state in word or act, less grave than insurrection or treason; the stirring up of rebellious feelings among the people.

seditious (sē dish' us), *adj.* tending to cause discontent among the people; fostering the spirit of rebellion.

*seduce (sē dūs'), *v.t.* to lead into error or wrongdoing; to tempt; to cause to stray from duty or virtue.

seduction (sē duk' shun), *n.* the act of leading astray; that which tempts to wrongdoing.

sedulous (sed' ū lus), *adj.* persevering, hardworking, steadily industrious.

see (sē), *n.* the office and authority of a bishop, or an archbishop: *Holy See*, the Pope's court in Rome.

see (sē), *v.i. and v.t.* to have the power of sight or vision; to understand; to perceive with the eye, as I *see* the dog; to perceive meanings with the mind, understand, as I *see* the reason now; to visit, as to go to *see* him; to receive, as he will not *see* you.

Syn. Look.

seed (sēd), *n.* the fertilized ovule of a plant or tree from which reproductive process may develop, generally in form of grain or nut or contained within fruit; that from which anything develops; origin, as *seeds* of rebellion. *v.t.* to sow, as we must *seed* the lawn again; to remove pits or seeds from.

seedling (sēd' ling), *n.* a plant grown from

seed; any young tree.

seedy (sēd' ĭ), *adj.* [*comp.* seedier, *superl.* seediest] full of seeds, as blackberries are *seedy;* having run to seed; shabby.

seeing (sē' ĭng), *n.* the power of vision, sight.

seeing (sē' ĭng), *conj.* inasmuch as, considering, since it is so, as *seeing* it is going to rain, we had better hurry.

seek (sēk), *v.t.* [*p.t. and p.p.* sought, *pr.p.* seeking] to look for, go in search of; to try to find or obtain, as to *seek* health.

seem (sēm), *v.i.* to appear to be, as there *seem* to be two ships in the distance; to give the effect of being, as the time *seems* long; to appear to oneself, as I *seemed* to be in trouble.

seeming (sēm' ĭng), *n.* appearance; surface show as differing from inner reality.

seeming (sēm' ĭng), *adj.* apparent; apparent but not real, as a *seeming* interest.

seemly (sēm' lĭ), *adj.* [*comp.* seemlier, *superl.* seemliest] fit, suitable or becoming; decent, proper.

seep (sēp), *v.i.* to leak through small outlets slowly, ooze.

***seer** (sēr), *n.* a prophet, one who foresees.

seethe (sēth), *v.i. and v.t.* to boil as the oil *seethes* in the caldron; to be in a violently agitated state, as the maelstrom *seethes,* emotions *seethe.*

segment (seg' ment), *n.* a separated part, an individual piece, as the *segments* of an orange; the part of a circle inclosed between a line drawn from one point on the circumference to another and the arc between the ends of this line.

segregate (seg' rē gāt), *v.i. and v.t.* to become separated; to cause to be separated or placed apart from others.

***seine** (sān), *n.* a fishing net with floats at the top and sinkers at the bottom, set out in a circle and drawn in to a central point so that the fish may be taken out.

***seismic** (sĭz' mĭk), *adj.* relating to earthquakes; like an earthquake or produced by an earthquake.

***seismograph** (sĭz' mō grăf), *n.* an instrument to record disturbances caused by earthquakes.

***seismology** (sĭz mol' ō jĭ), *n.* the scientific study of earthquakes.

seizable (sēz' a bl), *adj.* capable of being grasped.

seize (sēz), *v.t.* to grasp or clutch; to take by force; to arrest, as to *seize* a criminal; to confiscate, annex, as to *seize* territory.

seizure (sē' zhēr), *n.* the act of taking possession of by force; the sudden attack of a disease.

seldom (sel' dum), *adv.* rarely, infrequently.

***select** (sē lekt'), *v.t.* to pick out, choose; to take instead of others, as to *select* a book.

select (sē lekt'), *adj.* chosen; picked; taken in preference to others; superior.

selection (sē lek' shun), *n.* the act of choosing; the thing chosen; possibility of choice, as we have a good *selection.*

selectivity (sē lek tĭv' ĭ tĭ), *n.* the ability of a radio set to respond to impulses of the frequency to which it is adjusted or tuned, and to give no response to other frequencies.

***selenium** (sē lē' nĭ um), *n.* a nonmetallic element resembling sulphur and tellurium.

self (self), *n.* [*pl.* selves] the identity of any person or thing; one's own person; personality; personal interest; selfishness.

self-conscious (self' kon' shus), *adj.* aware of being a living entity; aware of one's failings to the point of losing poise, embarrassed.

self-government (self' guv' ērn ment), *n.* self-control; government by the whole population of a civil unit, democratic government.

selfish (sel' fish), *adj.* caring only for one's own needs or desires; not generous.

self-respect (self' rē spekt'), *n.* proper pride and esteem for oneself.

self-righteous (self rī' chus), *adj.* overconfident of one's own integrity.

selfsame (self' sām), *adj.* identical, the very same, as we came and went the *selfsame* day.

sell (sel), *v.i. and v.t.* to be sold, find a buyer; to make sales; to transfer to another for payment; to betray for a reward.

selvage (sel' vij), *n.* the edge of cloth finished off in such a way as to prevent raveling.

semaphore (sem' a fōr), *n.* a signaling apparatus that works projecting bars, flags or lights according to a code; a system of signaling by placing one's arms in different positions relative to the body.

semaphore (sem' a fōr), *v.i. and v.t.* to signal by means of movements of mechanically moved objects or by changing the position of the arms; to express in this manner, as I shall *semaphore* your message.

semblance (sem' blans), *n.* likeness; pretense, as a *semblance* of honesty is all he has; a picture.

semiannual (sem ĭ an' ū al), *adj.* issued or happening twice a year or every six months, as a *semiannual* publication, a *semiannual* convention.

semicircle (sem' ĭ sûr kl), *n.* half a circle; anything shaped or formed like half a circle, as a *semicircle* of spectators.

semicolon (sem' ĭ kō lon), *n.* a mark of punctuation (;) indicating a break next greater that that which is marked by a comma.

seminary (sem' ĭ ner ĭ), *n.* [*pl.* seminaries] an academy or school, especially a school or college of theology; the place where anything is trained or schooled, as a *seminary* of crime.

senate (sen' ĭt), *n.* the upper house of a legislature; the upper house of the U. S. Congress; a council of state; a council of students in school or college having charge of some points of school management.

senator (sen' a tēr), *n.* a member of the upper house of a state legislature or the Congress.

send (send), *v.t.* [*p.t. and p.p.* sent, *pr.p.* sending] to cause to go, dispatch, as *send* a messenger, *send* it by mail.

***senile** (sē' nĭl), *adj.* pertaining to, characteristic of or caused by old age.

senility (sē nil' ĭ tĭ), *n.* [*pl.* senilities] feebleness of body or mind caused by old age; an act befitting an old and feeble person.

senior (sēn' yẽr), *n*. an older person; one of longer service or higher rank than another; an old person; a member of the graduating class in a school or college.

senna (sen' a), *n*. a tropical plant of the cassia family whose leaves are dried for use in medicine.

sensation (sen sā' shun), *n*. perception by sight, taste, touch, hearing or smell; a feeling caused by such perception; any bodily feeling, an emotion.

sensational (sen sā' shun al), *adj*. involving the physical or mental feelings; exciting interest or emotion.

sense (sens), *n*. one of the five physical faculties, sight, taste, touch, hearing and smell, by which impressions of the world outside oneself are received; discernment; understanding; mental perception; good judgment; meaning, as the *sense* of a sentence.

senseless (sens' les), *adj*. incapable of feeling; unconscious; devoid of meaning.

sensibility (sen si bil' i ti), *n*. [*pl*. sensibilities] the state of being able to perceive or the quality of being easily affected; delicacy of feeling.

sensible (sen' si bl), *adj*. manifesting correct judgment; perceived or able to be perceived through the physical faculties.

sensitive (sen' si tiv), *adj*. easily affected, excited or offended; having any of the physical faculties of perception well developed, as *sensitive* to sound; affected by light, as *sensitive* photographic film used in photography.

sensory (sen' so ri), *adj*. pertaining to sensation or to any one of the five senses, as *sensory* experience; carrying nerve impulses from the sense organs to the brain or other nerve center.

sensual (sen' shoo al), *adj*. relating to the physical nature; given to overindulgence of physical desires, voluptuous.

sensuous (sen' shoo us), *adj*. relating to any of the physical faculties of perception; influenced by sense impressions, sensitive to beauty.

sentence (sen' tens), *n*. a series of words so arranged as to present a unit of statement or thought; a final judgment made effective by imposing a penalty upon a guilty person.

sentence (sen' tens), *v.t*. to condemn by judgment of a court and impose a penalty, as to *sentence* the murderer to life imprisonment.

sententious (sen ten' shus), *adj*. expressing ideas in the form of proverbs, pithy; given to speaking or writing in an axiomatic, moralizing style.

sentient (sen' shent), *adj*. having ability to feel and perceive.

sentiment (sen' ti ment), *n*. a thought prompted by feeling, as a Christmas *sentiment;* emotional feeling or utterance; an opinion, as these are my *sentiments*.

sentimental (sen ti men' tal), *adj*. full of, caused by or expressing emotion; mawkishly emotional.

sentinel (sen' ti nel), *n*. one who watches or guards against the approach of enemies; a sentry.

sentry (sen' tri), *n*. [*pl*. sentries] a soldier placed on guard to challenge any who approach his post of duty and to halt those not entitled to pass.

sepal (sē' pal), *n*. one of the ring of leaflike growths that form the calyx of a flower, the cuplike structure surrounding the petals.

separable (sep' a ra bl), *adj*. capable of being divided; capable of being taken from the whole to which it belongs.

separate sep' a rāt), *v.i. and v.t*. to become detached from the whole; to draw apart; to go different ways; to divide; to break away from the whole; to keep apart, as a stream *separates* the two towns.

separate (sep' a rit), *adj*. divided from the rest; disconnected; distinct.

sepia (sē' pi a), *n*. a dark-brown pigment made from a secretion of the cuttlefish; the cuttlefish. *adj*. made of or colored with dark-brown pigment; having that color, however produced.

sepoy (sē' poi), *n*. a native soldier in the British army in India.

sepsis (sep' sis), *n*. blood poisoning.

septennial (sep ten' i al), *adj*. occurring once in 7 years or lasting 7 years, as a *septennial* event, a *septennial* period.

septet (sep tet'), *n*. a musical composition for seven voices or instruments.

septic (sep' tik), *adj*. relating to or produced by putrefaction and poisonous dec y.

septuagenarian (sep tū a jē nâr' i an), *n*. a person aged 70 to 79, inclusive.

sepulcher, sepulchre (sep' ul kẽr), *n*. a tomb, a burial vault.

sepulchral (sē pul' kral), *adj*. suggestive of the tomb, funereal, dismal in appearance; deep, solemn and hollow-toned, as a voice.

sepulture (sep' ul tūr), *n*. burial.

sequel (sē' kwel), *n*. a following part, as of a story; a result.

sequence (sē' kwens), *n*. order of succession; things or thoughts following one after another.

sequester (sē kwes' tẽr), *v.t*. to remove property from the owner's control while a claim is being adjusted or a point of law decided; to seclude.

seraglio (sē ral' yō), *n*. [*pl*. seraglios] the women's quarters of a Mohammedan residence, a harem.

seraph (ser' af), *n*. [*pl*. seraphs or seraphim] an angel of the highest order.

seraphic (sē raf' ik), *adj*. angelic.

sere (sēr), *adj*. dry, withered.

serenade (ser e nād'), *n*. evening music in the open air; music played or sung by a lover to his lady, especially under her window at night.

serenade (ser e nād'), *v.t*. to entertain with evening song; to honor with special open-air music at night, as we *serenaded* the newcomers.

serene (sē rēn'), *adj*. calm, undisturbed, placid.

serenity (sē ren' i ti), *n*. calm, peace. undisturbed quiet.

serf (sûrf), *n.* a worker regarded in the Middle Ages as part of an estate, passing with it to any new owner; a slave.

serge (sûrj), *n.* a twilled woolen fabric.

*****sergeant** (sär′ jent), *n.* a noncommissioned army officer ranking next above a corporal; a police officer ranking below a lieutenant.

sergeant major (sär′ jent mā′ jẽr), the chief noncommissioned officer of a regiment; the master sergeant at headquarters assisting the adjutant.

serial (sēr′ i al), *n.* a story issued in successive parts; any composition presented in installments in print, movies, or radio broadcasts.

serial (sēr′ i al), *adj.* pertaining to a sequence; occurring as part of a sequence; published in successive instalments, as a *serial* story.

sericulture (ser′ i kul tūr), *n.* the business of raising silkworms for the raw silk.

*****series** (sēr′ ēz), *n.* an arrangement of things or events in orderly succession; a sequence or a related group.

seriocomic (sēr i ō kom′ ik), *adj.* having a mixture of earnestness and fun.

serious (sēr′ i us), *adj.* thoughtful, grave in manner or disposition; not jesting, in earnest, as I am *serious* about this; gravely important, as we have suffered *serious* losses.

*****sermon** (sûr′ mun), *n.* a public discourse delivered by a clergyman and based on a text from the Bible; any serious discourse, especially one with pious exhortation.

serous (sēr′ us), *adj.* pertaining to the secretions of certain membranes of the body, as the peritoneum; thin and watery, like these secretions.

*****serpent** (sûr′ pent), *n.* a large snake.

*****serpentine** (sûr′ pen tēn), *n.* a kind of rock resembling marble, often dull green and mottled like a snake's skin and taking a high polish; sinuous, crooked.

*****serried** (ser′ id), *adj.* crowded together; compact; standing in rows, like soldiers.

serum (sēr′ um), *n.* [*pl.* serums] the thin watery fluid left after any body fluid clots, as blood *serum;* the thin watery secretion of certain glands; fluid from the blood of an animal used by injection as an antitoxin to make people and other animals immune to infectious diseases like smallpox.

servant (sûr′ vant), *n.* one who is employed to do work for another, as a house *servant;* one who is devoted to something and works for it, as George Washington was a *servant* of his country.

serve (sûrv), *v.i. and v.t.* to work for another; to be in the army or navy; to be convenient and satisfactory, as this will *serve* for the present; to work for; to provide and place before, as to *serve* a meal or a summons.

*****service** (sûr′ vis), *n.* the performance of work done for another for hire; assistance; an organization whose members work for the public, as the civil *service* or the army and navy; the performance of duty in the army or navy; religious rites, as church *services;* provision at table, as the *service* is very good in this restaurant.

service (sûr′ vis), *v.t.* to keep in good repair, as to *service* a car.

serviceable (sûr′ vis a bl), *adj.* useful; fit for long, hard use.

*****servile** (sûr′ vil), *adj.* pertaining to slaves; having a slavish spirit; submissive, cringing.

servility (sẽr vil′ i ti), *n.* [*pl.* servilities] the spirit of a slave; cringing submission; an act befitting a slave.

*****servitude** (sûr′ vi tūd), *n.* the condition of a slave; subjection.

*****sesame** (ses′ a mē), *n.* a plant of India yielding flat seeds from which a valuable oil is made.

session (sesh′ un), *n.* a meeting of an assembly, such as a legislative house, a class at school or college; the term during which an assembly is in action, as a *session* of court or Congress; governing body of Presbyterian church, composed of pastor and elders.

sestet (ses tet′), *n.* a verse composition of six lines; the last six lines of a sonnet.

set (set), *n.* a number of things of the same kind intended to be used together, as a *set* of dishes; a clique or social group, as the smart *set;* a young plant placed in the ground to grow; drift or course, as the *set* of the tide; the artificial scenery for an episode in a motion picture or a play.

set (set), *v.i. and v.t.* to sink below the horizon, as the sun *sets* in the west; to pass from a soft or fluid state to one of hardness, as concrete *sets* slowly; to take a certain course, as the tide *sets* in, then out; to put in a certain place or position, as *set* this chair on the porch; to put a hen on eggs to hatch them; to name or fix, as you *set* the date; to place in order, as to *set* type ready to print; to bring to a certain state or condition, as *set* your thoughts upon this lesson; to adjust or prepare, as we *set* sail, *set* the clock, *set* the table for dinner.

settee (se tē′), *n.* a long seat with a back and with or without arms.

setter (set′ ẽr), *n.* a hunting dog of a breed trained formerly to crouch, now to point at game.

setting (set′ ing), *n.* the arrangement or surroundings in which anything is placed, as the house has a lovely *setting* in a grove of trees, a stage *setting;* a collection of eggs to be hatched by a hen.

settle (set′ l), *n.* a long wooden seat with a high back. *v.i. and v.t.* to become fixed or permanent; to sink to the bottom of a liquid as sediment *settles;* to free from uncertainty; to pay, as to *settle* a bill or account; to colonize, as the Dutch *settled* New York.

settlement (set′ l ment), *n.* adjustment of affairs, as we must come to a *settlement;* colonization; a region or place newly peopled by those who intend to remain there, as the early *settlements* in the Mohawk Valley; an institution for the benefit of the people in a poor city neighborhood, giving instruction and entertainment.

settler (set′ lẽr), *n.* a colonist; a pioneer who makes a home in new territory.

seven (sev′ en), *n.* the sum of one and six;

the symbol representing that number.

sevenfold (sev' en fōld), *adv.* seven times as much; having seven similar parts.

seventeen (sev en tēn'), *n.* one more than 16; the symbol representing it, 17.

seventeenth (sev en-tēnth'), *adj.* the next after the 16th.

seventh (sev' enth), *n.* the next after the sixth; one of seven equal parts.

seventh (sev' enth), *adj.* following the sixth.

seventieth (sev' en ti eth), *n.* the next after the 69th; one of 70 equal parts.

seventy (sev' en ti), *n.* [*pl.* seventies] one more than 69.

sever (sev' ẽr), *v.i. and v.t.* to part from one another, as we must *sever;* to separate, keep apart; to break or divide, as it is time for us to *sever* relations with those people.

several (sev' ẽr al), *adj.* consisting of more than two but not many, as we went *several* miles farther; taken individually, as our *several* interests in this enterprise.

severance (sev' ẽr ans), *n.* the act of separation or state of being separated.

severe (sē vẽr'), *adj.* strictly adhering to rule; harsh, hard, merciless, austere, as a *severe* manner of speaking, a *severe* person, a *severe* rebuke, a *severe* master, a *severe* headache.

severity (sē ver' i ti), *n.* [*pl.* severities] harshness; extreme strictness.

sew (sō), *v.i. and v.t.* [*p.t.* sewed, *p.p.* sewed or sewn, *pr.p.* sewing] to work as a seamstress, as to *sew* for a living; to join together with needle and thread.

*sewage (sū' ij), *n.* waste matter carried off in underground pipes.

sewer (sū' ẽr), *n.* a line of underground pipes to carry off waste matter.

sewerage (sū' ẽr ij), *n.* a system of lines of underground pipe to carry off waste matter; the matter carried off.

sex (seks), *n.* the distinction between male and female; males or females collectively.

*sexagenarian (sek sa jē nâr' i an), *n.* a person aged 60 to 69, inclusive.

sextant (seks' tant), *n.* the sixth part of a circle; an instrument for measuring angular distance between objects, used in finding latitude at sea through altitude of sun.

sextet (seks tet'), *n.* a musical composition for six voices or instruments; the six persons who render it; anything consisting of six parts.

sexton (seks' tun), *n.* a lesser official of a church who takes care of the building or has charge of funerals, vestments and sacred vessels.

shabby (shab' i), *adj.* [*comp.* shabbier, *superl.* shabbiest] threadbare or worn; mean, despicable, as *shabby* conduct.

shack (shak), *n.* a hut or cabin; a rickety old house.

shackle (shak' l), *n.* a fetter; handcuff; clasp to hold the arms or legs of a prisoner and prevent his escape. *v.t.* to fasten fetters on; to impede; to embarrass or hinder.

shad (shad), *n.* a food fish of the sea that swims into rivers in the spring to spawn.

shade (shād), *n.* relative darkness caused by something that intercepts the rays of light, as in the *shade* of a tree; obscurity, as he is smart, but his brother puts him in the *shade;* a relative degree, as of color, tone or meaning; something that dims the light from outside, as a window *shade: shades,* the spirits of those who have died, as *shades* of my esteemed ancestors.

shadow (shad' ō), *n.* an outlined figure of an object made when it intercepts the light; shade within limits set by the shape of that which interrupts the passing of light rays; something without substance, as dreams are the *shadows* of our waking life.

shady (shād' i), *adj.* [*comp.* shadier, *superl.* shadiest] sheltered from the glare of the sun; questionable, avoiding the light, as a man of *shady* ways.

*shaft (shȧft), *n.* a weapon with a stem, as a spear or an arrow; anything that darts and wounds like an arrow, as *shafts* of sarcasm; the long, narrow entrance to a mine; a round bar that carries power from a motor to the machinery of a mill or factory; one of the wooden pieces between which a horse is hitched to a wagon; the body of a column.

shafting (shȧf' ting), *n.* a set of turning bars that carry power from a motor to machinery.

shag (shag), *n.* a rough-cut, coarse tobacco; rough, woolly hair; a rough nap on cloth.

shaggy (shag' i), *adj.* [*comp.* shaggier, *superl.* shaggiest] having thick, rough hair or wool.

shah (shä), *n.* the title of the former ruler of Persia, now known as Iran.

shake (shāk), *n.* a combination of push and pull, as he gave me a *shake;* a movement up and down or back and forth, as a hands*hake;* a trembling or tremor, as a *shake* of the earth.

shake (shāk), *v.i. and v.t.* [*p.t.* shook, *p.p.* shaken, *pr.p.* shaking] to move as if shivering, tremble, as he *shook* with fear; to move vibratingly, as the house *shakes* in the wind; to quake, as the earth is *shaking;* to disturb greatly, as this news *shakes* me.

shakespearian (shāk spēr' i an), *adj.* relating to William Shakespeare or his works.

shaky (shāk' i), *adj.* [*comp.* shakier, *superl.* shakiest] trembling, infirm, unsteady.

shale (shāl), *n.* a soft rock that splits easily into leaves or layers.

shall (shal), *auxiliary v.* [*p.t.* should] am to, am going to, as I *shall* do it; must, imperatively or due to obligation, as you *shall* do as you are told.

shallow (shal' ō), *n.* a shoal; a stretch of water without much depth.

shallow (shal' ō), *adj.* having little depth, as *shallow* water, *shallow* words.

sham (sham), *n.* a fraud, a tricky thing, as this scheme is a *sham;* make-believe; a pretender, as this man is a *sham.*

sham (sham), *adj.* pretended, false, unreal, as a *sham* battle, *sham* words.

shaman (shä' man), *n.* a priest believed to be in communication with gods and demons; also a medicine man of certain North American Indian tribes.

shamble (sham' bl), *n.* a shuffling way of walking. *v.i.* to walk in a shuffling awkward way.

shambles (sham' blz), *n.pl.* a slaughterhouse; any place or scene of bloodshed.

shame (shām), *n.* a painful sense of guilt or dishonor; deep regret; modesty; something that causes reproach or disgrace, as it is a *shame* to do it. *v.t.* to cause disgrace to, bring reproach upon, as your conduct *shames* me.

shamefaced (shām' fāst), *adj.* bashful, shrinking, shy.

shameful (shām' fool), *adj.* disgraceful, indecent, offensive.

shameless (shām' les), *adj.* without shame or modesty, bold.

*shampoo (sham poo'), *n.* a washing of the head and hair; a preparation used to make lather with which to wash the head and hair. *v.t.* to wash the head and hair, first with a lather, then with clear water to rinse.

shamrock (sham' rok), *n.* a three-leafed plant resembling the white clover, used as the national emblem of the Irish people.

shanghai (shang' hī), *v.t.* to drug and kidnap a sailor to get hands to man a ship.

shank (shangk), *n.* the leg from knee to ankle; the part connecting the grip and the cutting or working part, as the *shank* of a tool.

shanty (shan' ti), *n.* [*pl.* shanties] a rude hut.

shape (shāp), *n.* the form or figure of an object or animal; a planned form, as I have my ideas in *shape* for the debate. *v.i.* and *v.t.* to take form, as my ideas are *shaping* in preparation for the debate; to give form to.

shapely (shāp' li), *adj.* [*comp.* shapelier, *superl.* shapeliest] well-formed; symmetrical; gracefully formed.

share (shâr), *n.* an individual's portion or part of something divided or distributed among a number of persons; a unit of stock in a business enterprise; a fair part, as I had my *share*, I did my *share*.

share (shâr), *n.* the blade of a plow or cultivator. *v.t.* to possess in common or to divide equally, as we *share* the room, we *share* the profits; to distribute in fair or equal parts, as it was *shared* between you.

shark (shärk), *n.* a large, voracious and destructive sea fish with many sharp teeth.

sharp (shärp), *n.* a sign in music indicating that a note is to be raised half a tone. *v.i.* and *v.t.* to raise the pitch; to sing or play above pitch. *adj.* having a very thin cutting edge or penetrating point; coming to an acute angle, as a *sharp* peak; keen-minded, as a *sharp* child; close and exact, as *sharp* questioning; piercing, bitter, pungent, as a *sharp* wind, a *sharp* tongue, a *sharp* taste like that of vinegar.

sharpen (shär' pen), *v.t.* to impart a cutting edge to; to make more keen.

sharpshooter (shärp' shoot ẽr), *n.* a skilled marksman; in military rating, the next grade below expert rifleman.

shatter (shat' ẽr), *v.i.* and *v.t.* to break into many pieces, smash; to overthrow.

shave (shāv), *n.* the act of cutting hair close to the skin; a blade within two grips for smoothing wood; a narrow escape, as that was a close *shave*. *v.i.* and *v.t.* to cut hair close to skin; to make smooth or bare by drawing a sharp edge over; to slice thin; to reduce, as to *shave* prices in a sale.

shaving (shāv' ing), *n.* the act of using a razor on the face; a thin paring, as of wood.

shawl (shôl), *n.* a square or oblong piece of cloth thrown over the shoulders for warmth.

she (shē), *feminine pron.* one particular woman or girl, as *she* said it; any female person or animal.

sheaf (shēf), *n.* [*pl.* sheaves] a bundle held together by a cord or band, as a *sheaf* of grain, a *sheaf* of papers.

*shear (shēr), *v.t.* to cut or clip the hair or wool of, as to *shear* sheep; to cut or clip off, as to *shear* wool; to deprive of, strip, as they *sheared* him of all he owned.

shears (shērz), *n.pl.* a cutting instrument of two pivoted crossing blades, as a large pair of scissors; anything that works in similar fashion, like hoisting *shears*.

*sheath (shēth), *n.* a case or scabbard for a sword; a case in which part of a plant stem is inclosed.

*sheathe (shēth), *v.t.* to put into a case, as to *sheathe* a sword.

sheave (shēv), *v.t.* to gather and tie into bundles.

shed (shed), *n.* a small, low building, frequently with open front or sides; a hangar for airplanes. *v.t.* to cause to flow, as to *shed* tears; to discard, as a snake *sheds* its skin; to give forth, diffuse, as a lamp *sheds* light.

sheen (shēn), *n.* brightness; splendor; luster, as *sheen* of silky fabrics.

sheep (shēp), *n.* [*pl.* sheep] a cud-chewing animal prized for its meat and wool; a timid person with no courage, lacking initiative.

sheepcote (shēp' cōt), *n.* a pen for sheep, a sheepfold.

sheepish (shēp' ish), *adj.* like a sheep in timidity, awkwardly bashful or silly.

sheepshead (shēps' hed), *n.* a food fish of the North Atlantic coast.

sheepskin (shēp' skin), *n.* the skin of a sheep or anything made of it, as a coat or parchment; a college diploma.

sheer (shēr), *n.* a change in the course of a ship; upward slope of a ship's build toward bow. *v.i.* to turn from the course, as a road *sheers* to the left, to *sheer* off, as in order to avoid collision. *adj.* complete, absolute, as *sheer* foolishness; very thin, as *sheer* fabrics. *adv.* steeply; almost perpendicularly, as the cliff fell *sheer* below us.

sheet (shēt), *n.* a large thin piece of anything, as a *sheet* of paper, glass or metal; a rectangular piece of linen used in making up a bed; a rope attached to a sail by which to change its position. *v.t.* to cover, as ice *sheets* a sidewalk.

*sheik (shēk), *n.* the head of a Bedouin family, tribe or clan; a man irresistibly fascinating to women.

*shekel (shek' el), *n.* an ancient Jewish coin.

shelf (shelf), *n.* [*pl.* shelves] a board set horizontally against a wall or into a bookcase or cabinet to hold things; any flat horizontal ledge as a *shelf* of rock.

shell (shel), *n.* a hard covering enclosing a nut, egg or animal body, as the *shell* of a hickory nut, a hen's egg or a turtle; the material of which such a casing is composed; a hollow case filled with explosives to be discharged from a firearm; the case in which the charge of a breech-loading gun is packed; an empty form without reality, as he is a mere *shell* of a man; a racing boat propelled by oars. *v.t.* to remove from a natural case, as to *shell* peanuts; to remove from cob, as to *shell* corn; to attack with explosive charges, as to *shell* a fort.

*****shellac** (she lak'), *n.* a resinous substance found on trees in India, used in making varnish; a solution of this substance in alcohol, used as a hard varnish.

shelter (shel' tẽr), *n.* a place of safety; cover from a storm; a refuge; protection. *v.t.* to protect or shield, as from harm.

shelve (shelv), *v.i. and v.t.* to slope, as the bay bottom *shelves* off gradually; to equip with horizontal boards on which to set things; to lay aside or postpone, as the resolution was promptly *shelved* until the following meeting.

shelving (shelv' ing), *n.* material for making ledges on which to set things; shelves collectively.

*****shepherd** (shep' ẽrd), *n.* one who tends sheep; a pastor.

*****sherbet** (shûr' bet), *n.* a cooling beverage of water, sugar and fruit juices; a water ice with fruit flavor.

sheriff (sher' if), *n.* the chief law-enforcing officer of a county or shire.

sherry (sher' i), *n.* [*pl.* sherries] a white wine, originally made in Jerez, Spain.

shield (shẽld), *n.* a piece of armor carried on the left arm; anything that protects by warding off harm; an escutcheon or emblem, as the Shield of David formed by two crossed triangles. *v.t.* to protect, ward off danger from.

shift (shift), *n.* a change from one position to another; an effort, ways and means, as to make shift to go; an artifice; a force of workingmen or the time during which it is working, as the day *shift;* the moving of football players into a different line-up before the ball is put in play; a woman's chemise or nightgown.

shiftless (shift' les), *adj.* not resourceful, lazy, improvident.

shifty (shif' ti), *adj.* [*comp.* shiftier, *superl.* shiftiest] tricky; artful.

shillelagh (shil lā' la), *n.* a club or cudgel.

shilling (shil ' ling), *n.* a British silver coin, replaced by the 5 pence piece.

shimmer (shim' ẽr), *n.* a gleam of wavering light; the sheen of such fabrics as satin, as this material has a wonderful sheen and *shimmer.*

shin (shin), *n.* the fore part of the leg between ankle and knee.

shine (shīn), *n.* the quality of brightness in surfaces, as the *shine* of polished metal; illumination, as the *shine* of a lamp, sun*shine;*

sheen luster. *v.i. and v.t.* to emit light steadily; to have brightness; to cause to glisten, as the sun *shines,* he has a *shining* wit; to polish, as I must *shine* my shoes.

shingle (shing' gl), *n.* a thin, flat piece of wood or other material used to cover roofs; the pebbles on a sea beach; a small signboard, as a doctor's *shingle. v.t.* to cover a roof with small, thin slabs of wood or other material in overlapping rows; to cut short, as to *shingle* hair.

shiny (shīn' i), *adj.* [*comp.* shinier, *superl.* shiniest] diffusing light, bright; glossy, having sheen or polish.

ship (ship), *n.* any large seagoing vessel that carries freight and passengers; specifically, a full square-rigged sailing vessel with three, four and sometimes five masts.

ship (ship), *v.i. and v.t.* to go aboard a ship; to join a ship as a member of the crew; to send by ship or any conveyance carrying freight, as to *ship* goods.

shipmaster (ship' màs tẽr), *n.* the captain or master of any merchant vessel.

shipmate (ship' māt), *n.* a fellow member of a crew.

shipment (ship' ment), *n.* the act of sending goods by any kind of conveyance, as rail *shipment,* water *shipment;* the goods that are sent.

shipping (ship' ing), *n.* vessels collectively, as the *shipping* of New York Harbor.

shipshape (ship' shāp), *adj.* well arranged, all in order.

shipwreck (ship' rek), *n.* total or partial loss of a vessel at sea; ruin, failure, as the *shipwreck* of a business.

shipyard (ship' yärd), *n.* a waterside establishment where ships are built or repaired.

shire (shīr), *n.* an English district or county.

shirk (shûrk), *v.t.* to shun, neglect or evade, as to *shirk* one's duty.

shirt (shûrt), *n.* a loose garment with sleeves worn by men and boys under the coat and vest; a close-fitting undergarment for the upper body.

shiver (shiv' ẽr), *n.* a trembling, as with cold or fear, as the *shivers* ran up and down me. *n.* a small piece or splinter broken off, as the mirror was smashed to *shivers. v.i. and v.t.* to tremble or quiver, as with cold or terror; to break into tiny fragments, as the rock *shivered* the window panes.

shoal (shōl), *n.* a great number thronging together, as a *shoal* of fish. *v.i.* to school, as fish. *n.* a shallow place in a body of water; a sandbank or bar less than 6 fathoms under water. *adj.* shallow, as *shoal* water ahead.

shoat (shōt), *n.* a pig, a young hog.

shock (shok), *n.* a heavy blow; concussion; a violent disturbance of the feelings, as this news is a *shock* to me; the disturbance of the body caused by electric current passing through it.

shock (shok), *v.t.* to shake with a heavy blow; to pass an electric current through; to move with surprise or horror, as the news *shocked* me.

shocking (shok' ing), *adj.* extremely disturbing; disgusting, horrifying.

shoddy (shod' l), *n.* [*pl.* shoddies] cloth made of old cloth shredded; wool fibers from old cloth; cheap display. *adj.* [*comp.* shoddier, *superl.* shoddiest] made of old cloth torn into shreds; not genuine; sham; cheap, vulgar.

shoe (shoo), *n.* an outer covering for the foot, reaching little if any above the ankle; something resembling a shoe, either in the way it is used or in its position, as a brake *shoe.*

shoe (shoo), *v.t.* [*p.t. and p.p.* shod, *pr.p.* shoeing] to furnish with footgear; to put a bar or plate on a horse's hoofs for protection on hard or rough roads.

shoot (shoot), *n.* a young branch or growth on a plant; a match at marksmanship.

shoot (shoot), *v.i. and v.t.* to fire a gun; to move swiftly, as an arrow *shoots* through the air; to dart, as a pain *shoots* up his arm; to grow out, as the leaves will soon *shoot.*

shop (shop), *n.* a place where goods are sold at retail, a store; a place where mechanical operations are performed, as a print *shop;* one's own business, as to talk *shop.*

shop (shop), *v.i.* to go to stores to buy; to go from one store to another, looking for the most satisfactory goods or prices.

shore (shor), *n.* the land adjacent to a large body of water, such as a sea, bay or lake. *n.* a heavy beam used as a prop or support. *v.t.* to support with props, as this wall will have to be *shored* up.

short (short), *adj.* not long, in space or time; abrupt; not complete; crisp.

shortage (shor' tij), *n.* less than the required amount, deficit.

shorten (shor' tn), *v.i. and v.t.* to lose length, become shorter, as the days *shorten* as winter comes on; to take length from, as I must *shorten* this dress; to make light and friable as piecrust.

shortening (shor' tn ing), *n.* any fat used to make pastry or cake light and easily broken.

shorthand (short' hand), *n.* any system of writing using characters and strokes to make for rapidity of writing, stenography.

shortly (short' li), *adv.* soon, after a little while; briefly, concisely; curtly.

shot (shot), *n.* the discharge of a firearm or delivery of a hand-thrown missile; the small pellets of lead with which a scattering fire is delivered from a shotgun; a marksman, as he is a good *shot;* a metal ball thrown in a contest of strength and skill; the pictures composing a single scene in motion pictures.

should (shood), *auxiliary v.* [*p.t.* of *shall*] ought to, as you *should* go; providing that, as *should* we miss the train we shall be in trouble: used in quoting a phrase originally containing *shall*, as I said I *should* go for the original statement *I shall go.*

shoulder (shol' der), *n.* the part of the human body where the arm joins the trunk; in a quadruped, the upper end of the foreleg where it joins the body; a part of anything that juts like the top of the arm, as a *shoulder* of a mountain; that which bears burdens, as the responsibility is on his *shoulders. v.i. and v.t.* to push or jostle

with the upper body, as I *shouldered* him aside; to carry across the upper part of the back or on one shoulder, as he *shouldered* the load.

shout (shout), *n.* a loud and sudden cry; an outburst of cheers from an assemblage.

shove (shuv), *n.* a strong push, as give the boat a *shove. v.i. and v.t.* to push, as stop *shoving, shove* that rock over.

shovel (shuv' l), *n.* an implement consisting of a scoop with a handle, for digging or moving such things as dirt, coal. *v.t.* to dig or move with a scoop on a long handle.

show (sho), *n.* a public exhibition, as a dog *show;* demonstration or proof, as a *show* of strength; presentation of a program of entertainment; pretense or false semblance; ostentation, pomp.

show (sho), *v.i. and v.t.* to be seen or visible, as the spot on your dress *shows;* to present to the eye or attention, exhibit, as he *showed* me his toys; to explain, teach, as *show* me how to do this; to *prove,* as *show* that you are right; to manifest or bestow, as he had *shown* me great kindness.

shower (shou' er), *n.* a fall of rain, hail or snow that does not last long; good things coming in abundance, as a *shower* of blessings; a party at which gifts are made to an engaged girl, as a linen *shower. v.i. and v.t.* to sprinkle; to pour out; to give generously, as to *shower* with presents or kindness.

showy (sho' i), *adj.* [*comp.* showier, *superl.* showiest] ostentatious, attracting attention, gaudy.

shred (shred), *n.* a torn-off strip; fragment; particle, as he hasn't a *shred* of kindness in his make-up. *v.t.* to tear into pieces.

*****shrew** (shroo), *n.* scolding woman. *n.* a small animal, resembling mouse and related to the mole, that feeds on insects and worms.

shrewd (shrood), *adj.* sharp-witted, clever in practical affairs, not easily fooled.

*****shriek** (shrek), *n.* a shrill outcry, as of pain or fear. *v.i. and v.t.* to cry out in a shrill and piercing tone, as she *shrieked* with pain or fear.

shrift (shrift), *n.* confession by and absolution for a dying person: *short shrift,* small allowance of time for confession before death; prompt execution of a sentence.

shrill (shril), *adj.* sharp in sound, piercing, as a *shrill* tone.

shrimp (shrimp), *n.* a small edible shellfish related to the lobster.

shrine (shrin), *n.* a case in which sacred relics are kept; a place, such as a small chapel, consecrated to a saint or some sacred relic.

shrine (shrin), *v.t.* to keep in a hallowed place, enshrine.

shrink (shringk), *v.i. and v.t.* to diminish by contracting, as cloth *shrinks* when it is wet; to cause to diminish by wetting and drying; to draw back, as in fear or distaste, as I *shrink* from this ordeal.

shrivel (shriv' l), *v.i. and v.t.* [*p.t. and p.p.* shriveled, *pr.p.* shriveling] to shrink and wrinkle, wither; to dry and curl up.

shroud (shroud), *n.* a dress or covering for the

dead; a winding sheet. *n.* one of the ropes rigged in sets numbering three to five to support a mast, and having crossropes called *ratlines,* forming a ladder leading to the masthead; any guy rope. *v.i. and v.t.* to clothe for burial; to cover with a winding sheet; to veil, conceal, as the clouds *shroud* the tops of lofty mountains.

shrub (shrub), *n.* a woody plant or bush smaller than a tree, having many separate stems growing from one root in the ground.

shrubbery (shrub' ẽr ĭ), *n.* [*pl.* shrubberies] a collection of bushes.

shrug (shrug), *n.* a raising of the shoulders to indicate indifference or doubt. *v.i. and v.t.* to raise the shoulders as an expression of doubt or indifference.

shuck (shuk), *n.* a shell or husk, as a corn *shuck,* peanut *shucks,* oyster *shucks.*

shuck (shuk), *v.t.* to remove the shells or husks from, as to *shuck* corn, peanuts or oysters.

shudder (shud' ẽr), *n.* a trembling or shivering caused by fear or horror. *v.i.* to shiver with fear or horror.

shuffle (shuf' l), *n.* a scraping of the feet, as to walk with a *shuffle;* a dance in which the feet are pushed along the floor; a change in the relative positions, as a *shuffle* of playing cards; evasion, trickiness, deceit, *v.i. and v.t.* to scrape the feet along the ground in walking or dancing; to rearrange, as to *shuffle* cards; to evade, deceive.

shun (shun), *v.t.* to avoid, keep away from; to refrain from, as to *shun* evil ways.

shunt (shunt), *n.* a turning aside, as of a freight train from the open line to a siding; a device to divert part of an electric current. *v.i. and v.t.* to turn off a main line to a side line; as railroad cars onto a siding; to divert, as part of an electric current.

shut (shut), *v.i. and v.t.* to close so as to prevent entrance or exit, as a door shuts; to close, as to *shut* a book.

shut (shut), *adj.* closed, not open.

shutter (shut' ẽr), *n.* an outside window cover set on hinges; a device to regulate the fall of light on the plate or film of a camera.

shuttle (shut' l), *n.* a device to carry the weft back and forth through the threads of the warp to make cloth; a device in a sewing machine that locks the stitches; a train going back and forth on a short connecting line between two main points; the track for such a train between two main points. *v.i. and v.t.,* to move alternately back and forth.

shy (shī), *n.* [*pl.* shies] a fling, toss, trial, as let me take a *shy* at it. *n.* [*pl.* shies] a sudden leap forward or to the side, as by a frightened horse, *v.t.* [*p.t. and p.p.* shied, *pr. p.* shying] to fling, as to *shy* a stone. *v.i.* [*p.t. and p.p.* shied, *pr. p.* shying] to leap forward or aside in fear, as a horse. *adj.* [*comp.* shyer, *superl.* shyest] timid, bashful; wary.

*****sibilant** (sib' ĭ lant), *n.* a hissing sound; a letter representing such as sound, as *s. adj.* having hissing sound.

*****sibyl** (sib' ĭl), *n.* a woman possessing powers of prophecy.

sick (sik), *adj.* ill; indisposed; having nausea; disgusted, as I am *sick* of this job.

sicken (sik' en), *v.i. and v.t.* to become ill or disgusted; to make ill or disgusted.

sickle (sik' l), *n.* a cutting tool having a small curved blade on a handle, used for cutting grass; with a hammer the symbol of the Soviets.

sickly (sik' li), *adj.* [*comp.* sicklier, *superl.* sickliest] ailing; mawkish.

side (sīd), *n.* a straight line forming a unit in the boundary of a plane figure, as a *side* of a square; a surface forming part of the inclosure of a solid, as a *side* of a cube; one of two contrasting surfaces, as the inner and outer *sides;* one of the surfaces of a fixed cubic structure that is neither front nor back, as the *sides* of a house; the part of an animal's body that is neither front nor back, as the right or left *side;* one of two opposing forces, as which *side* am I or. in the debate; a line of descent, as on my mother's *side. v.i.* to take one part or position against another, as I *side* with you in this debate, the U. S. *sided* with the Allies. *adj.* lateral; not at the front or back, as a *side* door; along the edge, as a *sidewalk* along a street; minor, indirect as a *side* remark.

sideboard (sīd' bŏrd), *n.* a piece of dining-room furniture to hold dishes or silverware, a buffet.

sidecar (sīd kär), a small car attached to the side of a motorcycle.

*****sidereal** (sĭ dēr' ēal), *adj.* relating to the stars; measured by the stars, as *sidereal* time or ages.

sidetrack (sīd' trak), *n.* a siding on a railroad. *v.t.* to switch onto a siding, as to *sidetrack* a freight car; to switch or turn aside, as he was *sidetracked* from his purpose.

siding (sīd' ing), *n.* a short additional stretch of railroad track running off from the main line to which cars are switched or shunted to load and unload freight or to permit other trains to pass; a sidetrack.

sidle (sī' dl), *v.i.* to move obliquely and unobtrusively, as the dog *sidled* up to me.

siege (sēj), *n.* the surrounding of a fortified place to compel its garrison to surrender because of lack of supplies; a continued effort to win something.

sienna (si en' a), *n.* red or orange-yellow clay used as a pigment.

sieve (siv), *n.* a utensil for separating the finer from the coarser parts of a substance, as sand or gravel, by passing it through a network of fine or coarse meshes.

sift (sift), *v.t.* to put through a screen; to scrutinize with a view to rejecting some and retaining the rest, as to *sift* evidence.

*****sigh** (sī), *n.* a long deep audible breath, expressing relief, weariness or sadness. *v.i.* to take a long deep breath with sound of voice expressing weariness, regret, relief; to long for, as to *sigh* for the past.

*****sight** (sīt), *n.* the power or act of perceiving through the eyes; that which is thus perceived; range of vision; point of view; a

device to assist in aiming, as a gun *sight;* something shocking to behold, as when they pulled him out of the river, he was a *sight;* a view of interesting things, as to see the *sights* of the big city. *v.i. and v.t.* to perceive with the eye; to aim, as to *sight* a gun.

sign (sīn), *n.* that by which anything is known or represented; a symbol, a token; a gesture used instead of speech.

signal (sig′ nal), *n.* a motion with a meaning; a sound, an object or a motion used to convey an order or information; an event that moves to action, as that assassination was the *signal* for war. *v.i. and v.t.* to make signs, as she *signaled* for me to come; to make signs to, as to *signal* a ship; to communicate by means of signs, motions, flags, lights, as the ship *signals* distress. *adj.* memorable, remarkable, distinguished, as a *signal* event in the history of the state.

signature (sig′ na tūr), *n.* the name of a person written by himself; the writing of one's name to show authorship, as the *signature* on a letter.

signet (sig′ net), *n.* a seal; imprint made, as in wax, by a seal.

significant (sig nif′ i kant), *adj.* having meaning; important, as a *significant* look, a *significant* event.

signification (sig nif i kā′ shun), *n.* meaning.

signify (sig′ ni fī), *v.i. and v.t.* [*p.t. and p.p.* signified, *pr.p.* signifying] to have importance, as it does not *signify;* to indicate, as a meaning; to betoken, as this *signifies* war.

silage (sī′ lij), *n.* fodder cut and preserved for winter use by fermentation in a silo: often called *ensilage.*

silence (sī′ lens), *n.* the absence of sound, stillness. *v.t.* to cause to be quiet or still, as I *silenced* him; to hush, as to *silence* rumors.

silent (sī′ lent), *adj.* soundless, making no noise; speechless, taciturn; inactive, as a *silent* partner in a business.

ᶜsilhouette (sil ōō et′), *n.* an outline drawing filled in with solid color.

silhouette (sil ōō et′), *v.i. and v.t.* to appear in outline and solid color, as his figure was *silhouetted* on the window shade.

⋆silica (sil′ i ka), *n.* a colorless mineral substance, occurring in many forms, as quartz, crystal, opal, sand, and used in making glass and pottery.

⋆silicon (sil′ i kon), *n.* a nonmetallic element found in rocks and sand.

silicon (sil ′ ē kon′), *n.* that which conducts the flow of electricity from one pathway to another.

silk (silk), *n.* a fine soft fiber spun by the silkworm in making its cocoon; thread or cloth made of this fiber; anything resembling this fiber, as corn *silk.*

silkworm (silk′ wûrm), *n.* the larva of a certain moth that spins a strong fiber to wind its cocoon.

silky (sil′ ki), *adj.* [*comp.* silkier, *superl.* silkiest] pertaining to or made of the threads of the silkworm; soft, fine and glossy, as *silky* hair.

sill (sil), *n.* a timber laid horizontally to form the base or foundation of a structure, such as a door or window.

silly (sil′ i), *adj.* [*comp.* sillier, *superl.* silliest] weak-minded; foolish, unwise, as a *silly* thing to do.

silo (sī′ lō), *n.* a storing pit or closed airtight structure for fermenting fodder into silage.

silt (silt), *n.* mud or sand deposited by a stream. *v.i. and v.t.* to fill with sediment.

silver (sil′ vêr), *n.* a soft metallic element, lustrous, malleable and ductile, one of the precious metals used in making coins, jewelry and fine ornamental wares; coins made of this metal, as I will have to pay you in *silver;* the luster of this metal. *v.i. and v.t.* to take on a shining grayish color, as his hair is *silvering;* to cover or plate with silver. *adj.* having the color and luster of silver, as *silver* threads among the gold.

silvery (sil′ vêr i), *adj.* having the color and luster of silver; clear, as *silvery* tones.

simian (sim′ i an), *n.* an ape or monkey. *adj.* like or pertaining in any way to apes or monkeys; apelike.

similar (sim′ i lêr), *adj.* having a general likeness or correspondence; like in any quality or property.

similarity (sim i lar′ i ti), *n.* [*pl.* similarities] resemblance, likeness; a point of likeness.

⋆simile (sim′ i lē), *n.* [*pl.* similes] a figure of speech in which one thing is directly likened to another, as we flew *like the wind.*

simmer (sim′ êr), *v.i. and v.t.* to boil gently.

simon-pure (sī′ mon pūr), *adj.* genuine, real, original.

⋆simony (sim′ ō ni), *n.* the act of buying or selling places of honor in the church.

⋆simoom (si mōōm′), *n.* a hot dry sand-laden wind blowing suddenly in the desert.

simper (sim′ pêr), *n.* an affected or silly smile. *v.i.* to smile in affected or silly manner.

simple (sim′ pl), *adj.* single, not complex; plain, unaffected, unadorned; natural, not artful.

simpleton (sim′ pl tun), *n.* a foolish or weak-minded person.

simplicity (sim plis′ i ti), *n.* [*pl.* simplicities] the state or quality of having no complex or intricate nature or construction; artlessness, lack of guile; plainness in manner of living; silliness.

simplify (sim′ pli fī), *v.t.* [*p.t. and p.p.* simplified, *pr.p.* simplifying] to make more clear and understandable, do away with complexities; to make easier.

simulate (sim′ ū lāt), *v.t.* to pretend, imitate.

simulation (sim ū lā′ shun), *n.* pretense, imitation, make-believe.

⋆simultaneous (sī mul tā′ nē us), *adj.* happening, done or existing at the same time.

sin (sin), *n.* offense against the laws of God; wickedness. *v.i.* to break the laws of God; to transgress, do wrong.

since (sins), *adv.* from that time, as I have never been there *since. prep.* from the time of, as I have been here ever *since* the war. *conj.* after the time that, as *since* the war ended, the map of Europe has changed completely; because, seeing that, considering, as *since* you do not like it, I shall change it.

sincere (sin sēr'), *adj.* true, honest, without affectation or pretense, real.

sincerity (sin ser' i ti), *n.* the state or quality of being pure, genuine, simple and unaffected, frank and honest.

***sinecure** (si' nē kūr), *n.* a position or office in which one is well paid and has few duties or responsibilities.

sinew (sin' ū), *n.* a tendon; anything supplying strength or providing resources, as the *sinews* of war.

sinful (sin' fool), *adj.* wicked, impious, unholy.

sing (sing), *v.i. and v.t.* to make musical sounds with the voice; to celebrate with verse or song, as arms and the man I *sing*.

***singe** (sinj), *n.* a slight burn on the surface. *v.t.* to burn slightly; to scorch surface of; to remove hair from by passing over flame.

single (sing' gl), *adj.* consisting of or performed by one only; alone; separate; unmarried; honest, sincere. *v.t.* to select, as one person or thing from many, as I *singled* him out from the crowd.

singly (sing' gli), *adv.* by ones; one at a time.

singsong (sing' sông), *adj.* having a monotonous tone or rhythm.

***singular** (sing' gū lēr), *n.* the form of a word that denotes only one of a kind, as tree is the *singular* of trees; the form of a word used to denote that it is used of or with or for one person or thing, as I, he, she, it are all *singular* pronouns; has is a *singular* form of to have.

singular (sing' gū lēr), *adj.* not plural; not dual; having to do with only one; extraordinary, strange, as you are making a *singular* request.

singularity (sing gū lar' i ti), *n.* [*pl.* singularities] the state of oneness; the state of being extraordinary; a special characteristic

***sinister** (sin' is tēr), *adj.* inauspicious, unlucky; ill-omened, boding evil; dishonest, ill-intentioned.

sink (singk), *n.* a basin with a drain to carry off waste liquids. *v.i. and v.t.* to go or fall downward as iron *sinks* in water; to decline gradually; to subside; to cause to go down, as to *sink* a ship.

sinuous (sin' ū us), *adj.* bending, having in and out curves, winding, as the *sinuous* course of a river; erring, crooked, as *sinuous* conduct or policies.

***sinus** (si' nus, *n.* [*pl.* sinuses] a cavity in a bone or an air cavity in the head connecting with the nose.

sip (sip), *n.* a mere taste of a liquid.

sip (sip), *v.i. and v.t.* to take a liquid a taste at a time; to drink slowly in small amounts.

***siphon** (si' fon), *n.* a bent pipe or tube with one short leg and one longer one, for drawing off liquids from a higher to a lower level or from one container to another, through air pressure. *v.t.* to draw off by means of a pipe, as to *siphon* a liquid from a tub into bottles.

sir (sir), *n.* a term of respectful address to a man.

sire (sir), *n.* a title of respect to a ruler; a father, a head of a family. *v.t.* to be the father of, beget.

siren (si' ren), *n.* a mythological alluring sweet-voiced creature, half woman and half bird that lured mariners to their death; a device to give warning, as of fire or the passage of a police vehicle, with a screaming whistle.

***sirloin** (sûr' loin), *n.* a cut of beef from the upper part of the loin.

***sirocco** (si rok' ō), *n.* [*pl.* siroccos] a hot dust-laden wind that blows from the Libyan deserts toward Italy and Sicily.

***sirup** (sir' up), *n.* a thick, sweet liquid made from the juice of fruits boiled with sugar or from the sap of the sugar maple; also syrup.

***sisal** (si' sal), *n.* an agave plant that grows in Central America and the West Indies; the fiber of this plant used in making rope.

sister (sis' tēr), *n.* the daughter of one's parents; a female member of a religious order, a nun.

sisterhood (sis' tēr hood), *n.* a number of women or girls, belonging to one society.

sit (sit), *v.i.* to rest upon the lower part of the trunk of the body; to be in session, as the court *sits* today; to cover eggs to be hatched, as the hen *sits*.

site (sit), *n.* a location; a plot of land set aside for special use.

sitting (sit' ing), *n.* a session, as a *sitting* of court.

situate (sit' ū āt), *v.t.* to fix a location for; to locate; assign to a certain place or position.

situation (sit ū ā' shun), *n.* a position, location; circumstance, as in this *situation*; employment, a job.

six (siks), *n.* one more than five; the symbol 6, representing this number.

sixteen (siks tēn'), *n.* one more than 15; the symbol 16, representing this number.

sixteenth (siks tēnth'), *n.* one of 16 equal parts. *adj.* next following 15th.

sixth (siksth), *n.* one of six equal parts; the one after the fifth.

sixth (siksth), *adj.* next following the fifth.

sixtieth (siks' ti eth), *n.* one of 60 equal parts; the one after the 59th. *adj.* next after 59th.

sixty (siks' ti), *n.* one more than 59.

sizable (siz' a bl), *adj.* of considerable magnitude, quite large.

size (siz), *n.* magnitude, bulk or dimensions, as a house of great *size*. *n.* a thin, weak glue used to glaze a surface, as of paper. *v.t.* to gloss with a paste; to classify according to bulk or measure.

sizzle (siz' l), *n.* a hissing sound. *v.i.* to give out hissing sound or sound of frying.

skate (skāt), *n.* a runner or blade of steel, usually fitted to a shoe, on which one glides over ice; a similar device having wheels ir place of runners or blades, called a roller *skate*. *n.* a flatfish of the ray family. *v.i.* to move over ice on runners or blades attached to the shoes; to move on small wheels attached to a plate affixed to the shoes.

skein (skān), *n.* a coil of thread or yarn.

skeleton (skel' ē tun), *n.* the framework of bones of men and animals; any framework, as the *skeleton* of a building.

*****skeptic** (skep' tik), *n.* one who doubts things commonly accepted as basic; a doubter; especially one who doubts religious theories; also spelled *sceptic.*

skeptical (skep' ti kal), *adj.* doubting, unable or unwilling to believe, especially the theories of religion.

skepticism (skep' ti sizm), *n.* a state of doubt or unbelief; the doctrine that all human knowledge is uncertain.

sketch (skech), *n.* an outline; a rough draft; a simple drawing rapidly made. *v.i. and v.t.* to make quick, simple drawings; to draw in outline, make outline of.

skew (skū), *n.* a slanting motion or position; a twist or slant. *v.t.* to make or set on the skew or to one side. *adj.* placed obliquely or on a slant; not symmetrical.

skewer (skū' ēr), *n.* a pin of wood or metal to hold a roast of meat folded together. *v.t.* to fasten with a wood or metal pin.

*****ski** (skē), *n.* [*pl.* skis] one of a pair of long narrow runners of wood attached to the shoe for gliding over snow: the Continental pronunciation is *shē.* *v.i.* to slide over snow on long runners attached to the shoes.

skid (skid), *n.* a log used as a track to slide heavy objects; a slip to the side, as of automobile or airplane; one of the two sledlike runners on some kinds of aircraft to simplify landing. *v.i. and v.t.* to slip sidewise, as an automobile; to haul over timbers laid as a track.

*****skiff** (skif), *n.* a small light rowboat.

skillet (skil ' et), *n.* a small frying pan or stewpan.

skillful (skil ' fool), *adj.* expert, clever, as a *skillful* artist; showing expertness, as *skillful* carving.

skill (skil), *n.* expertness; knowledge and the ability to apply it in practical ways and in art.

skim (skim), *v.i. and v.t.* [*p.t. and p.p.* skimmed, *pr.p.* skimming] to glide over a surface; to remove matter from the surface of, as to *skim* milk; to read rapidly.

skimp (skimp), *v.i. and v.t.* to be stingy; to supply meanly; to do work in a slighting, negligent way.

skin (skin), *n.* the outer covering of an animal body; an outer covering of a vegetable body, as the *skin* of an apple. *v.t.* to take the skin from, as to *skin* a deer.

skinflint (skin' flint), *n.* stingy, avaricious person.

skinny (skin' i), *adj.* [*comp.* skinnier, *superl.* skinniest] thin, lean, bony.

skip (skip), *n.* a light leap or jump; an omission. *v.i. and v.t.* to caper, jump lightly; to omit, leave out.

skipper (skip' ēr), *n.* the master of a ship, a sea captain.

skirmish (skûr' mish), *n.* a battle between small forces; a minor clash or part of a battle. *v.i.* to take part in a minor engagement in war.

*****skirt** (skûrt), *n.* a woman's garment that hangs from the waist; a petticoat; the loose lower part of a man's coat; a hanging flap, as the *skirt* of a saddle. *v.t.* to border; to pass along the edge of.

skit (skit), *n.* a short piece of writing, satirical or humorous.

skittish (skit' ish), *adj.* shy, easily frightened, timid and nervous.

skulk (skulk), *v.i.* to keep hidden or move about slyly, furtively.

skull (skul), *n.* the bony frame of the head.

skunk (skungk), *n.* a small animal, with dark fur and a white stripe on each side of the back, emitting an offensive odor when disturbed; the fur of this animal.

sky (skī), *n.* [*pl.* skies] the arch of the heavens overhead.

skylark (skī' lärk), *n.* a bird that sings as it flies upward.

skylarking (skī lärk ing), *n.* merrymaking, frolicking.

sky line (skī līn), the horizon; the outline of trees, hills, buildings against the sky.

skyscraper (skī' skrāp ēr), *n.* a very high building.

slab (slab), *n.* a thick flat piece of stone or a thick slice of stone; a thick slice of anything, as bacon or cheese.

slack (slak), *n.* the part of anything that hangs loose, as the *slack* of a rope. *v.i. and v.t.* to become or make less tight, loosen; to be negligent in work or the performance of a duty; to neglect, as work or duty. *adj.* hanging loose; careless; sluggish.

slacken (slak' en), *v.i. and v.t.* to become loose, sag; to become slower, as the pace *slackens;* to make slower, as to *slacken* speed.

slacker (slak' ēr), *n.* one who shirks a duty, especially in wartime.

slacks (slaks), *n. pl.* loose, wide trousers.

slag (slag), *n.* the dross of a metal; metallic waste separated from ores when melted; cinders from a blast furnace.

slake (slāk), *v.t.* to quench, extinguish, make less, as to *slake* one's thirst.

slam (slam), *n.* a banging noise, as a *slam* of a door.

slander (slan' dēr), *n.* a false report circulated to damage the reputation of a person.

slander (slan' dēr), *v.t.* to circulate false reports calculated to injure someone.

slang (slang), *n.* the use of words not approved for careful or formal written language, but which make speech colorful and vivid; inelegant, trashy word fads; the speech of a certain group, as thieves' *slang.*

slant (slant), *n.* a slope, an inclined plane; obliqueness, as the road goes off at a slant.

slant (slânt), *v.i. and v.t.* to go off at an angle from a straight line; to slope.

slap (slap), *n.* a blow with the open hand; a blow given with anything flat. *v.t.* to strike with open hand or with any flat object.

slash (slash), *n.* a cut made with a sweeping stroke. *v.i. and v.t.* to strike out violently and wildly with a knife or a whip; to cut with a sweeping stroke, gash.

slat (slat), *n.* a thin narrow strip of wood or metal, as a bed *slat.*

slate (slāt), *n.* a kind of rock that splits easily into thin plates; a plate of such rock for roofing or to write on. *n.* a list of candidates to represent a party in an election. *v.t.* to offer as a candidate for election, as one of a party list of candidates.

slattern (slat' ẽrn), *n.* a careless, untidy, slovenly woman.

*****slaughter** (slô' tẽr), *n.* the killing and butchering of animals for food; great destruction of life; massacre.

slaughterhouse (slô' tẽr hous), *n.* a place where animals are butchered.

slave (slāv), *n.* a human being held in bondage; a victim of a habit; one who drudges with small reward. *v.i.* to live a life of drudgery, to drudge or toil.

slavery (slāv' ẽr ĭ), *n.* the state of being subject to the will of another; the practice of holding human beings in bondage or the state of being held in bondage.

slaw (slô), *n.* sliced or chopped cabbage.

slay (slā), *v.t.* to kill, especially in a violent and sudden manner.

*****sleazy** (slā' zĭ), *adj.* [*comp.* sleazier, *superl.* sleaziest] flimsy; poorly woven.

sled (sled), *n.* a conveyance on runners to travel over snow and ice.

sledge (slej), *n.* a heavy sled to carry loads over snow and ice. *n.* a heavy hammer such as blacksmiths use, or such as is used to break up stone, a sledgehammer.

sleek (slēk), *v.t.* to make smooth and glossy by rubbing or brushing, as to *sleek* the hair.

sleek (slēk), *adj.* smooth, glossy.

sleep (slēp), *n.* a natural temporary period of almost complete unconsciousness, normally at night, in which the body rests, slumber; torpor. *v.i.* to rest, in a temporary unconscious state, as at night; to repose with the mind inactive and the eyes closed.

sleeper (slēp' ẽr), *n.* one who sleeps; a strong piece of timber, stone or metal used to support and hold in place a heavy structure, a railroad tie; a railroad sleeping car.

sleepy (slēp' ĭ), *adj.* drowsy; sluggish, dull; conducive to slumber.

sleet (slēt), *n.* rain freezing as it falls.

sleeve (slēv), *n.* the part of a garment that covers the arm.

*****sleigh** (slā), *n.* a conveyance on runners for traveling on snow or ice; a sled with seats.

sleight (slīt), *n.* dexterity; a trick done so smoothly and fast that the eye cannot see how it is done.

slender (slen' dẽr), *n.* small or narrow in proportion to the length or height; slim, slight.

sleuth (slōōth), *n.* a bloodhound; a detective.

slew (slōō), *v.i. and v.t.* to slide around, to twist, to veer; to slue.

slice (slīs), *n.* a piece cut off across the broad surface of a larger body; a knife with a broad blade; a spatula to spread paint or thick ink. *v.t.* to cut layers off, as to *slice* bread.

slick (slĭk), *adj.* smooth; slippery.

slicker (slĭk' ẽr), *n.* an oilskin coat.

slide (slīd), *n.* a smooth slippery surface, as a toboggan *slide;* a slanting surface down which things may run; a fall of ice and snow down a mountainside.

*****slight** (slīt), *n.* an act of neglect toward another person; a show of indifference toward another; intentional withholding of due courtesy. *v.t.* to treat with discourtesy; to neglect; to do carelessly, as you *slighted* this lesson.

slim (slĭm), *adj.* slender, scant, meager; mean, sly, tricky.

slime (slīm), *n.* soft sticky mud; any moist mucuslike matter, as the *slime* on a snail.

slimy (slīm' ĭ), *adj.* [*comp.* slimier, *superl.* slimiest] moist, sticky and resembling mucus; vile, contemptible.

sling (sling), *n.* a pouchlike piece as of leather with a cord or thong at each end, used to hurl a stone; an arrangement of ropes or chains with hooks to grip a heavy object and lift or hoist it; a loop of cloth hung from neck to support an injured arm. *v.t.* to throw or hurl; to hoist with tackle.

slink (slingk), *v.i.* [*p.t. and p.p.* slunk, *pr.p.* slinking] to go as if ashamed, furtively; to sneak.

slip (slĭp), *n.* a slide; a missing of one's footing; an error or fault in speech or conduct; a landing place for vessels; a space between lines of piling or piers where a ship or ferryboat docks; a cutting from a plant, to be planted; a one-piece garment worn under a dress; a loose case that goes on and off easily, as a pillow *slip;* a leash to hold a dog, as the hound was on a *slip. v.i. and v.t.* to miss one's foothold; to make an unintentional misstatement, as my tongue *slipped;* to do something wrong without bad intention, as I *slipped* that time; to take a cutting from a plant; to put on easily, as he *slipped* the ring over her finger.

slipper (slĭp' ẽr), *n.* a low and light shoe, easily put on or taken off.

slippery (slĭp' ẽr ĭ), *adj.* smooth enough to slide on; affording no foothold; elusive, as he is a *slippery* person to deal with.

slipshod (slĭp' shod), *adj.* wearing old, worn loose shoes; slovenly, careless, as a *slipshod* way of speech.

slit (slĭt), *n.* a long cut; a narrow opening.

slit (slĭt), *v.t.* to make a long cut in; to cut lengthwise in strips.

*****sliver** (slĭv' ẽr), *n.* a splinter, as a *sliver* of wood. *v.t.* to break or cut into long thin pieces.

slogan (slō' gan), *n.* the war cry of a Highland clan; any rallying cry; any watchword; an expression used to draw attention and to identify, as the firm has a *slogan.*

sloop (slōōp), *n.* a fore-and-aft rigged vessel with only one mast.

slop (slop), *n.* spilled liquid; puddles of dirty liquid spilled on a clean floor; wet swill, as *slop* for pigs: *slops,* wet waste.

slop (slop), *v.i. and v.t.* to splash dirty water; to spill mussily; to soil by splashing dirty liquid on, as don't *slop* the floor.

slope (slōp), *n.* an incline; a slanting surface; slant, as this roof should have more *slope*. *v.i. and v.t.* to slant; to cause to slant.

slot (slot), *n.* a short and narrow opening, as a mail *slot* in a door. *v.t.* to cut a short and narrow opening in.

*****sloth** (slōth), *n.* laziness, idleness, unwillingness to work or engage in any activity, slowness. *n.* a South American animal that lives in trees and hangs upside down on the branches.

slouch (slouch), *n.* an ungainly gait; an awkward person. *v.i.* to walk or move in an awkward, ungainly manner, with drooping shoulders and shuffling feet.

*****slough** (slou), *n.* a miry spot, a bog, a swamp; depression, gloom. *n.* a low spot in a prairie, either dry or miry.

slough (sluf), *v.t. and v.i.* to shed, as a snake

slough (sluf), *n.* a skin shed by a snake; dead tissue cast off by the skin. *v.t. and v.i.* to shed, as a snake *sloughs* its skin; to cast off dead skin tissues.

*****sloven** (sluv′ en), *n.* a habitually untidy person.

slovenly (sluv′ en li), *adj.* untidy; careless of personal appearance.

slow (slō), *adj.* lacking speed; behind time, as the clock is *slow*; requiring much time, as this is *slow* work; sluggish-minded.

slue (slōō), *n.* a swamp, a slough.

slue (slōō), *v.i. and v.t.* to slide around, turn from side to side, as a car *slues* through the mud; to turn or swing about a fixed point, as to *slue* a boom around a mast.

slug (slug), *n.* a mollusk without a shell; a land creature like a snail but having no shell, as this garden is full of *slugs*. *n.* a chunk of metal; a bar of type metal used between lines of type for spacing; a heavy bullet. *v.i. and v.t.* to strike heavily.

sluggard (slug′ ẽrd), *n.* a person who is habitually lazy and idle.

sluggish (slug′ ish), *adj.* heavy, dull, lazy.

*****sluice** (slōōs), *n.* a gate to regulate flow of water; an artificial channel for a stream of water. *v.t.* to wash ore in an artificial channel of water; to float logs down such a waterway.

slum (slum), *n.* a poor, densely populated run-down section of a city.

slumber (slum′ bẽr), *n.* sleep. *v.i.* to sleep.

slump (slump), *n.* a fall, as in prices; a business depression; a slouching attitude.

slump (slump), *v.i.* to be depressed, as business *slumps*; to fall, as prices; to let oneself go heavily, as he *slumped* into a chair.

slur (slûr), *n.* a disparaging remark or act; an insult; implied reproach. *v.t.* to disparage; to pronounce indistinctly by running together, as to *slur* a syllable.

slush (slush), *n.* the slop of melting snow; a greasy mixture for lubricating machines; sentimental or silly talk or writing.

sly (slī), *adj.* [*comp.* slyer or slier, *superl.* slyest or sliest] crafty; artfully cunning; deceitful; roguish.

smack (smak), *n.* a quick sharp blow or slap; a quick sharp sound of the lips; a taste, as give me a *smack* of the jelly; a smattering, as a *smack* of science. *n.* a small one-masted vessel, used by fishermen. *v.i. and v.t.* to strike a sharp and sudden blow, to have the taste, flavor or character of, as this *smacks* of treason; to slap or strike.

small (smôl), *n.* the lesser part, as the *small* of the back. *adj.* little in quantity or degree; of relatively inferior dimensions; mean; little-minded.

*****smallpox** (smôl′ poks), *n.* a severe contagious disease with fever and pus-filled spots in the skin.

smart (smärt), *n.* a stinging sensation, as the *smart* of a wound; a pang of grief. *v.i. and v.t.* to have or to cause a sharp stinging pain. *adj.* quick-witted, sharp; brilliant, clever; stylish in dress.

smash (smash), *n.* a crash causing destruction, as that car must have been in a terrible *smash;* ruin, as the *smash* of a business concern. *v.i. and v.t.* to shatter into many pieces; to go to pieces, fail, as a business; to dash violently into something; to break into pieces, as to *smash* a cup or a window.

smattering (smat′ ẽr ing), *n.* superficial knowledge, as he has but a *smattering* of Latin.

smear (smēr), *n.* a blot or stain of some greasy substance, ink, paint or the like.

smell (smel), *n.* the sense by which we perceive odors; an odor. *v.i. and v.t.* to have an odor; to perceive an odor.

smelt (smelt), *v.t.* to melt, as an ore, in order to separate the metal; to refine.

smilax (smī′ laks), *n.* a delicate trailing plant with greenish blossoms.

smile (smīl), *n.* a facial expression indicating pleasure or amusement, or irony or derision, with lips curled. *v.i.* to express amusement, pleasure, approval or derision through curling of lips.

smirch (smûrch), *n.* a smear or stain, as a *smirch* or paper or a *smirch* on one's reputation. *v.t.* to soil, smear; to disgrace.

smirk (smûrk), *n.* an affected smile. *v.i.* to smile in self-conscious or affected manner.

smite (smīt), *v.t.* [*p.t.* smote, *p.p.* smitten, *pr.p.* smiting] to strike hard; to devastate.

smith (smith), *n.* a worker in metals, as a gold*smith*, silver*smith*, black*smith*.

smithy (smith′ i), *n.* [*pl.* smithies] a place where metals are shaped by hammering; a blacksmith's shop.

smock (smok), *n.* a long, loose garment or coat, usually washable, to protect one's clothes while working; any other loose garment.

smog (smog), *n.* a combination of smoke and fog, as Pittsburgh is famous for *smog*.

smoke (smōk), *n.* the visible fine particles that pass into the air from a burning substance; the act of using tobacco in a pipe, cigar or cigarette, as this is a good *smoke*.

smoke (smōk), *v.i. and v.t.* to give out fumes and clouds of fine particles when burning; to make fumes, as the lamp *smokes;* to burn tobacco in a pipe, cigar or cigarette, taking the vapors into the mouth and blowing them out again; to cure with smoke, as to *smoke* a ham or a fish; to drive from a retreat or hiding place, as to *smoke* out the criminals.

smokehouse (smōk' hous), *n.* building in which meats are cured by means of smoke.

smokestack (smōk' stak), *n.* a chimney or pipe through which fumes pass from a factory, locomotive or the like.

smolder (smōl´dēr), *v.i.* to burn slowly and in a smothered manner making smoke without flames; also smoulder.

***smooth** (smooth), *adj.* even-surfaced; without roughness; bland; flattering; clever and persuasive, as he is a *smooth* talker.

***smother** (smuth' ēr), *v.i.* and *v.t.* to suffocate; to stifle; to cover over, as a fire, so that little air reaches it; to kill by depriving of air.

smudge (smuj), *n.* a smear or stain; a dirty mark, as a *smudge* of grease on an apron; a heavy smoke made to keep off mosquitoes and gnats or to protect fruit on the trees from frost. *v.t.* to smear, soil, stain.

smug (smug), *adj.* affectedly precise or prim; self-satisfied.

smuggle (smug' gl), *v.i.* and *v.t.* to send or carry goods across a national boundary or through a port without paying customs duties; to bring foreign labor into a country against the law.

smut (smut), *n.* a spot or stain made by dirty matter; a plant disease; sooty spots or stains; obscene talk.

smutty (smut' i), *adj.* [*comp.* smuttier, *superl.* smuttiest] spotted or stained by dirty matter, such as soot; improper, indecent, as a *smutty* joke.

snaffle (snaf' l), *n.* a horse's bit with a joint in the middle and rings at the ends; a bit without a curb.

snag (snag), *n.* a short rough branch of a tree; a tree trunk fixed in the bed of a river; impediment, as we struck a *snag*.

snail (snāl), *n.* a small creeping animal, some species living on land and some in water, carrying a spiral-shaped shell into which it can withdraw and having tentacles on its head; a sluggard.

snake (snāk), *n.* a long, slender, crawling reptile having a scaly body, no legs or feet, living upon insects and small animals and, in some species, having poisonous fangs; a treacherous person.

snap (snap), *n.* a sharp, quick sound, as the *snap* of a dead twig that breaks; a sudden breaking; a device that fastens by closing with a sharp sound; a quick bite or attempt to bite, as the dog made a *snap* at my hand.

snap (snap), *v.i.* and *v.t.* to make a quick, sharp sound, as frosty snow *snaps* underfoot; to fasten with a sharp clicking sound, as the lock *snapped* shut; to break with a sudden sharp sound, as I *snapped* that dead twig off; to seize suddenly, as he *snapped* up my offer; to close with a sharp sound, as *snap* the lock.

snapdragon (snap' drag un), *n.* a plant bear-

ing showy flowers thought to resemble a dragon's face; a game in which raisins are picked from a dish of burning brandy.

snapper (snap' ēr), *n.* a food fish of tropical seas; a snapping turtle.

snapping turtle (snap' ing tûr' tl), a freshwater turtle with strong jaws, valued as food.

snare (snâr), *n.* a noose set to catch animals; anything that entangles or entraps; a cord across a drumhead to regulate the quality of the sound. *v.t.* to catch in a noose; to entangle, entrap.

snarl (snärl), *n.* a sharp harsh sound, not as deep as a growl, made by an angry animal. *n.* a tangle as of hair or yarn, as this string is all in a *snarl;* any entanglement or complication, as this business is in a *snarl*. *v.i.* to make a sharp harsh sound of anger, not so deep as a growl. *v.i.* and *v.t.* to tangle or knot or to cause to tangle or knot; to complicate.

snatch (snach), *n.* something taken hastily, as a *snatch* of lunch. *v.i.* and *v.t.* to grasp at or seize something suddenly, as to *snatch* at a coin or an opportunity.

sneak (snēk), *n.* one who does things in a mean, sly and underhand way. *v.i.* to go stealthily; to act with sly deceit.

sneer (snēr), *n.* a facial expression of contempt or derision; an utterance of contempt or scorn. *v.i.* to show contempt or scorn by an expression of the face; to scoff, speak contemptuously.

sneeze (snēz), *n.* a sudden and violent involuntary expulsion of air usually through the nose or mouth with a sound like "a-tchoo!" *v.i.* to expel air involuntarily and noisily through the nose or mouth.

snicker (snik' ēr), *n.* a half-suppressed laugh, a giggle. *v.i.* to laugh foolishly and in a half-suppressed way; to giggle.

sniff (snif), *n.* the act of smelling with a quick drawing in of breath through the nose; a whiff of an odor. *v.i.* and *v.t.* to draw the breath in through nose in order to catch and identify an odor; to express contempt by quick passage of air through nostrils, as he *sniffed* at the plan.

snip (snip), *n.* a quick cut with scissors; a bit cut off; as a *snip* of cloth; an insignificant person or thing, as he is only a *snip* of a boy. *v.i.* and *v.t.* to make swift, light cuts with shears or scissors; to cut off with scissors.

***snipe** (snip), *n.* a shore bird with a long beak.

snipe (snip), *v.i.* and *v.t.* to take a long-range shot, as at an enemy, from concealment.

snivel (sniv' el), *n.* the act of snuffling or drawing up mucus or moisture in the nose; a hypocritical whining.

snivel (sniv' el), *v.i.* to run at the nose; to cry in a whining way with snuffling.

snob (snob), *n.* a vulgar person who makes a pretense of fine manners; one who cringes to superiors and condescends to inferiors.

***snood** (snood), *n.* a band worn about the hair; a fillet.

snoop (snoop), *v.i.* to pry into things, meddle.

snooze (snōōz), *n.* a nap, a short, light sleep.

snooze (snōōz), *v.i.* to take a nap, sleep for a short time lightly.

*snore (snōr), *n.* the sound of heavy breathing, as made when sleeping deeply.

snore (snōr), *v.i.* to breathe noisily in sleep.

snort (snôrt), *v.i.* to blow air noisily through the nostrils, as the horse *snorts*.

*snout (snout), *n.* the projecting nose of an animal.

snow (snō), *n.* crystals of frozen water vapor falling from the clouds; these crystals lying in a mass on the ground or on objects. *v.i. and v.t.* to fall from clouds in flakes or frozen crystals; to cover with snow or as if with snow; to overwhelm, as his opponent was *snowed* under in the election.

snowplow (snō' plou), *n.* a machine used to clear snow from roads and railroad tracks.

snowshoe (snō' shōō), *n.* a wooden oval-shaped frame strung with a leather network and fastened to the foot by thongs, used for walking on the surface of soft snow.

snub (snub), *n.* an intended slight. *v.t.* to check the motion of and make fast; to stop quickly by turning a rope around a post, as to *snub* a boat; to check contemptuously; to rebuff or slight intentionally. *adj.* short and stubby, as a *snub* nose.

snuff (snuf), *n.* fine-ground tobacco used for sniffing into the nostrils or dipping with a small brush into the mouth.

snuff (snuf), *v.i. and v.t.* to sniff; to draw in through the nose, as pulverized tobacco.

snuffle (snuf' l), *n.* the sound of breathing heavily through the nose. *v.i.* to breathe heavily and noisily through the nose.

snug (snug), *adj.* fitting close, as a *snug* shirt; comfortable, cozy, as a *snug* cottage.

snuggle (snug' gl), *v.i. and v.t.* to draw close, nestle; to hold close.

so (sō), *adv.* in like manner, as Tom can jump the fence, *so* can Bob; to such extent or degree, as *so* fat she can't run.

so (sō), *conj.* therefore, as you will not agree, and *so* I am withdrawing from the deal.

so (sō), *interj.* as you were; that's enough.

soak (sōk), *n.* the act or state of saturating or being saturated, as I gave the clothes a good *soak. v.i. and v.t.* to absorb moisture, lie in water till saturated, as the clothes *soaked* all morning; to wet thoroughly, as I *soaked* the clothes.

soap (sōp), *n.* a compound of a fatty acid with an alkali, used for washing and cleansing.

soapstone (sōp' stōn), *n.* a soft greasy sort of stone, steatite.

*soar (sōr), *v.i.* to fly aloft; to engage in exalted thought, aspire; to fly an airplane without motor power under impetus of the wind; to rise above any level, as prices *soared.*

sob (sob), *n.* a convulsive sigh or cry with tears and catching of the breath.

sob (sob), *v.i.* to weep with audible convulsive catching of the breath.

sober (sō' bẽr), *adj.* temperate, calm, sedate; not drunk. *v.i. and v.t.* to become calm; to make calm.

sobriety (sō brī' e tı), *n.* habitual temperance; the state of being calm and serious.

*sobriquet (sō' brı kā), *n.* a nickname.

soccer (sok' ẽr), *n.* association football.

*sociable (sō' sha bl), *n.* a social gathering of an informal nature.

sociable (sō' sha bl), *adj.* companionable, pleasant in company.

*social (sō' shal), *adj.* pertaining to human life; pertaining to life in a governed community; disposed to maintain orderly relations with others; flocking or living together in a community, as ants are *social* insects.

*socialism (sō' shal ızm), *n.* a theory that land, industries and goods produced should be owned, managed and distributed by a government representing the people; any system aimed to put these ideas into practical application.

socialist (sō' shal ıst), *n.* an advocate of public ownership of land and management of industries; a member of a party supporting these measures.

*society (sō sī' e tı), *n. [pl.* societies] human beings in general taken in relation to one another; an organized community; a body of persons united for some common purpose; the more cultivated or more fashionable part of the community.

*sociology (sō sı ol' ō jı), *n.* the science of human relations, especially those between the community and the individual.

sock (sok), *n.* a short-legged stocking.

socket (sok' et), *n.* a hollow or opening into which something is fitted, as a *socket* for an electric-light bulb.

*sod (sod), *n.* turf, sward; a single piece of cut turf. *v.t.* to cover with cut pieces of turf fitted closely and packed down to make an even surface.

soda (sō' da), *n.* sodium carbonate, a white powdery salt used in making soap, paper and glass; sodium bicarbonate, used in cooking; any of many compounds of soda.

soda water (sō' da wō' tẽr), a bubbling solution of bicarbonate of soda with an acid that produces effervescence; water charged with carbonic acid and flavored with fruit sirups, taken as a beverage.

sodden (sod' n), *adj.* dull and heavy with dissipation, as a *sodden* face; soaked, wet and heavy, saturated; half-cooked and soggy.

sodium (sō' dı um), *n.* a white alkaline metallic element, very abundant in common salt.

*sofa (sō' fa), *n.* a long, upholstered seat with back and arms.

soft (sôft), *adj.* soothing and agreeable to any of the five senses; yielding easily to pressure, not hard; not loud or harsh, as a *soft* voice; easily moved, as a *soft* heart; relaxed, untrained, as *soft* muscles; free from calcium and magnesium salts, as *soft* water; not alcoholic, as ginger ale is a *soft* drink; bituminous, not anthracite, as *soft* coal.

*soften (sôf' en), *v.i. and v.t.* to become soft; to make soft or softer.

software (sôft' wâr), *n.* the programs that make the computer perform a function.

*soil (soil), *n.* land, earth, that part of the

surface of the earth that can be dug, plowed and planted; any substance in which something grows, as *poverty* is the soil of discontent. *n.* a stain or spot; anything that makes dirty. *v.i. and v.t.* to become dirty, as this fabric *soils* easily; to smudge, smear make dirty, as to *soil* one's clothes.

*****sojourn** (sō' jûrn), *n.* any temporary stay elsewhere than at home.

*****sojourn** (sō jûrn'), *v.i.* to live temporarily, as to *sojourn* in a foreign land.

*****solace** (sol' is), *n.* consolation; comfort in sorrow; the source of relief or consolation. *v.t.* to comfort in sorrow, console.

solar (sō' lẽr), *adj.* relating to or from the sun, as *solar* light; measured in terms of the earth's relation to the sun, as the *solar* year.

solar cell (sō ´ lẽr sẽl ´), *n.* a battery which converts energy in sunlight into electricity.

solar system (sō' lẽr sis' tem), the sun and the heavenly bodies that revolve around it.

*****solder** (sod' ẽr), *n.* a metallic alloy, commonly of tin and lead, used, when melted to join metals or mend breaks in metal objects.

*****soldier** (sōl' jẽr), *n.* a person engaged in military service; an enlisted man, a private as distinguished from an officer.

soldier (sōl' jẽr), *v.i.* to engage in military service; to make a mere pretense of working; in the latter sense often pronounced sō' jẽr.

*****sole** (sōl), *n.* the bottom of the foot; the bottom of a shoe or boot. *n.* an edible flatfish of Europe; any of the edible flatfishes of the Pacific Coast of the U. S. *v.t.* to furnish with a flat bottom, as to *sole* shoes. *adj.* alone, only, as I am the *sole* occupant of this house; one and one only, as the *sole* survivor.

*****solecism** (sol' ē sizm), *n.* a breach of the rules of grammar or violation of the established idiom of a language.

*****solemn** (sol' em), *adj.* inspiring awe; impressive; earnest.

solemnity (sō lem' ni ti), *n.* [*pl.* solemnities] impressiveness; deep seriousness; a religious rite or ceremony.

solicit (sō lis' it), *v.i. and v.t.* to canvass; to ask for with earnestness.

solicitation (sō lis i tā' shun), *n.* persistent asking; importunity.

solicitor (sō lis' i tẽr), *n.* one who entreats; an attorney; a canvasser, especially for charity funds.

solicitous (sō lis' i tus), *adj.* eager, anxious, concerned.

*****solicitude** (sō lis' i tūd), *n.* concern, anxiety.

solid (sol' id), *n.* a body with fixed shape; a substance not gaseous or fluid; an object with three dimensions.

solid (sol' id), *adj.* having fixed shape; compact; not hollow; heavy; substantial.

solidarity (sol i dar' i ti), *n.* community of interests and responsibilities.

solidify (sō lid' i fī), *v.i. and v.t.* [*p.t. and p.p.* solidified, *pr.p.* solidifying] to become or to make dense, firm and fixed in shape.

solidity (sō lid' i ti), *n.* the state of being fixed in shape; firmness of character; substantial soundness, validity, as *solidity* of argument.

soliloquize (sō lil' ō kwiz), *v.i.* to talk to oneself; to deliver a monologue.

soliloquy (sō lil' ō kwi), *n.* [*pl.* soliloquies] a monologue; a speech with only oneself as audience.

*****solitaire** (sol i târ), *n.* a game played by only one person; a gem set or mounted alone.

solitary (sol' i ter i), *adj.* alone; separate from all others; without companions.

solitude (sol' i tūd), *n.* loneliness; seclusion; a deserted place.

solo (sō' lō), *n.* [*pl.* solos or soli] a musical composition for a single voice or instrument; rendition by a single singer or player; anything performed by one person without help, as a dance or an airplane flight.

*****solstice** (sol' stis), *n.* either of the two points at which the sun is farthest from the earth's equator; the time at which the sun passes either of these points, about June 21 and December 21.

soluble (sol' ū bl), *adj.* able to be dissolved; capable of being solved.

*****solution** (sō lū' shun), *n.* the act of dissolving in a liquid; a preparation made by dissolving any substance in another; the act of solving; the answer to a problem.

solvable (sol' va bl), *adj.* capable of being solved.

solve (solv), *v.t.* to explain; to make clear; to find a desired answer by calculating.

solvent (sol' vent), *n.* any liquid in which a substance can be dissolved. *adj.* able to dissolve substances; able to pay all debts.

somber (som' bẽr), *adj.* melancholy; dark and gloomy.

*****sombrero** (som brā' rō), *n.* [*pl.* sombreros] a broad-brimmed hat, such as is worn by men in South and Central America and on the plains of the southwestern United States.

some (sum), *pron.* an indefinite quantity or number as distinguished from the rest, as *some* will come. *adj.* of indeterminate quantity or number, as have *some* cake. *adv.* approximately, as *some* 20 houses lined the street.

somebody (sum' bod i), *n.* a person not named, as *somebody* will like it; a person of standing and importance, as he is *somebody* in this town.

somehow (sum' hou), *adv.* in one way or another.

somersault (sum' ẽr sôlt), *n.* an acrobatic feat in which a person turns heels-over-head in the air and comes down on his feet.

something (sum' thing), *n.* an object, unknown or not specified.

sometime (sum' tim), *adv.* at an unfixed date or hour.

sometimes (sum' tims), *adv.* occasionally, now and then.

*****somewhat** (sum' hwot), *n.* an uncertain quantity.

somewhat (sum' hwot), *adv.* in an uncertain degree.

*****somnambulism** (som nam' bū lizm), *n.* sleep walking, the act of walking in one's sleep.

*somnolent (som' nŏ lent), adj. sleepy, drowsy; tending to make one sleepy.

son (sun), n. a male offspring; one identified by relation to a calling, as a farmer is a son of the soil.

*sonata (sō nä' ta), n. a musical composition with several related movements and usually for a single instrument, as the piano, and never for more than two instruments.

song (song), n. vocal music; a musical composition to be rendered vocally; a lyric poem; a trifle, as the house was sold for a song.

son-in-law (sun' in lô), n. [pl. sons-in-law] the husband of one's daughter.

sonnet (son' et), n. a poem of 14 lines, usually arranged in two groups, one of eight lines and one of six.

*sonorous (sō nō' rus), adj. giving forth sound when struck; full-sounding and deep-toned.

*soon (sōōn), adv. in a short time; quickly, without delay.

*soot (soot), n. a soft greasy black substance forming in chimneys from the smoke and vapors of burning fuel and consisting largely of fine particles of carbon.

*sooth (sōōth), n. truth; reality.

*soothe (sōōth), v.t. to calm, quiet and reassure; to ease, as to soothe pain; to comfort.

*soothsayer (sōōth' sā ẽr), n. one who foretells the future.

sop (sop), n. anything softened in a liquid; something given as a bribe or a conciliatory offering. v.t. to dip in a liquid, as to sop toast in coffee.

*sophism (sof' izm), n. clever, formal argument containing a fallacy or intended to deceive.

*sophist (sof' ist), n. one who argues smartly but evades the truth, a fallacious reasoner; an ancient Greek teacher of rhetoric.

sophisticated (sō fis' ti kāt ed), adj. wise in the ways of the world.

sophistry (sof' is tri), n. subtle or deceptive reasoning.

sophomore (sof' ō mōr), n. a student in the second year of high school or college.

*soporific (sō pō rif' ik), n. a preparation that tends to cause sleep; a narcotic.

*soprano (sō prä' nō), n. [pl. sopranos or soprani] the highest-ranging singing voice, the treble; the musical part for voices in that range; one who sings in that range.

sorcerer (sôr' sẽr ẽr), n. a magician, wizard or enchanter.

sorceress (sôr' sẽr es), n a woman who practices sorcery or magic, a witch.

sorcery (sôr' sẽr i), n. [pl. sorceries] magic; doing of tricks with pretended help from evil spirits, witchcraft.

sordid (sôr' did), adj. mean, vile, base, low; dirty, muddy in color.

sore (sōr), n. a painfully diseased spot in or on a living body; a bruised or inflamed spot; a wound; a sorrow; a hurt feeling. adj. tender and sensitive; painful; severe, as sore trouble. adv. grievously; severely, as he was sore hurt, the knight was sore stricken.

sorghum (sôr' gum), n. a canelike grass resembling broomcorn; sirup prepared from a species of this grass.

sorority (sō ror ´ i ti), n. a girls' or women's organization.

*sorrel (sor' el), n. a docklike plant; a reddish-brown or yellow-brown color; a horse of this color.

sorrow (sor' ō), n. mental pain or affliction; grief.

*sorry (sor' i), adj. [comp. sorrier, superl. sorriest] regretful; penitent; serving its purpose poorly, as a sorry excuse.

*sort (sôrt), n. a kind or species; class, group; quality, character.

sort (sôrt), v.t. to arrange in classified groups.

sot (sot), n. a habitual drunkard.

*sough (suf), n. a sighing sound such as the wind makes in pine trees. v.i. to blow with sound like that of sighing.

*soul (sōl), n. the spiritual, nonmaterial part of man's being; the immortal part, that which survives after death of the body; the essence of anything; a human being.

sound (sound), n. the sensation perceived through the hearing organs; any noise; distance to which one can hear, as to be within sound; speech, music and all noises reproduced by radio or sound pictures. n. a long and comparatively narrow body of water connecting large open bodies of water. v.i. and v.t. to give or be made to give vibrations perceptible by the organs of hearing. v.i. and v.t. to measure water depths; to ascertain the depth of. adj. complete, whole; unbroken; free of decay; firm; safe; strong; wholesome.

sounding (sound' ing), n. a measurement of the depth of water taken by line or plummet; the depth measured: soundings, any water shallow enough to be measured with a hand line.

soup (sōōp), n. a liquid food generally based on meat stock with vegetables and seasoning added, served either thick or strained.

sour (sour), adj. having an acid, sharp taste; acid from fermentation, as milk; disagreeable; ill-natured; bitter.

source (sōrs), n. that from which anything originates, as the source of a river, a source of knowledge, sources of power.

souse (sous), n. anything steeped or preserved in pickle; pickled meats; a dip or plunge into water. v.t. to steep in pickle; to dip or plunge, as I soused the dog in the tub.

south (south), n. the point of the compass directly opposite north or to the right of one facing toward the sunrise; a region lying in this direction: the South, that part of the U. S. below the Mason and Dixon line.

southeast (south ēst'), n. the point of the compass between east and south.

*southerly (suth' ẽr li), adj. pertaining to, toward or coming from the south, as to steer a southerly course, a southerly wind.

southern (suth' ẽrn), adj. pertaining to, situated in or proceeding from the regions directly opposite the north.

southwest (south west'), n. the point of the compass between the west and the south.

*souvenir (sōō vĕ nĕr'), *n.* a memento or keepsake.

*sovereign (sov´ ĕr in), *n.* a supreme ruler; a king or queen, the emperor or the empress; a former British gold coin worth one pound sterling; *adj.* royal, supreme in power; effectual and potent, as a *sovereign* remedy.

sovereignty (sov' ĕr in tī), *n.* [*pl.* sovereignties] supreme power or dominion.

soviet (sō' vi et), *n.* a council : *Soviet,* one of the primary organs of government in Russia.

*sow (sou), *n.* a female hog.

*sow (sō), *v.i. and v.t.* to scatter seed; to plant seed; to disseminate; to impart, as to *sow* knowledge.

spa (spä), *n.* a mineral spring; a resort or a sanitarium with mineral springs.

space (spās), *n.* continuous extension; the whole extent of the universe within which all matter and all bodies exist, as the stars are in *space;* room in which to move; room in which to do things or keep things, I want office *space* for myself and the members of my staff.

space (spās), *v.t.* to arrange at desired intervals, separate, as you have not *spaced* the lines in your essay neatly.

space shuttle (spās shut ´l), *n.* a spacecraft used to transport persons and equipment from Earth to the space station.

space station (spās stä´shan), *n.* the structure or platform used to launch the space shuttle.

spacious (spā' shus), *adj.* extending far and wide; roomy.

spade (spād), *n.* a tool for digging, like a shovel but with a flat blade; a black figure, heart-shaped but with a handle, on one suit in a pack of playing cards; any card of that suit; the suit bearing this figure. *v.i. and v.t.* to dig with a flat-bladed shovel.

span (span), *n.* the clear stretch of an arch or bridge between supports; a matched team of horses; the wingspread of an airplane, from the tip of one wing to the tip of the other; a measure of length, approximately 9 inches.

span (span), *v.t.* to arch across, as the bridge *spans* the river.

spangle (spang' gl), *n.* a small plate or boss of shining metal; any glittering ornament. *v.t.* to adorn with glittering ornaments; to sprinkle with bright objects.

spank (spangk), *v.t.* to slap on the buttocks with the open hand.

spar (spär), *n.* any mast, yard, boom or gaff in a vessel's sailing equipment; any round timber used in rigging mechanical apparatus, as the boom in a steam scoop. *n.* a shining crystalline mineral. *v.i.* to box; to deliver and ward off blows in a boxing match.

spare (spâr), *n.* an extra wheel and tire for an automobile for emergency use; any emergency equipment. *v.t.* to be forgiving, show mercy to; to withhold punishment; to refrain from, as to *spare* no expense; to use frugally or rarely, as to *spare* the sugar in war time; to dispense with, as I can *spare* a dollar. *adj.* thin, gaunt; scarce, scanty.

spark (spärk), *n.* a bit of burning matter thrown off by a fire; a glowing bit of metal thrown off by a metallic body under the heat of great friction; the flash of a discharge of electric current; any tiny bit of matter that glows momentarily; anything that illuminates flashingly, as a *spark* of wit.

sparkle (spär kl), *v.i.* to throw off sparks; to flash and twinkle.

sparrow (spar' ō), *n.* a small brown bird of the finch family.

sparse (spärs), *adj.* thinly scattered or distributed, as population.

spasm (spazm), *n.* a sudden, violent and involuntary contraction of the muscles; a violent emotion quickly passing, as a *spasm* of anger.

spasmodic (spaz mŏd' ik), *adj.* convulsive; violent but of short duration, as *spasmodic* anger, *spasmodic* effort, a *spasmodic* cough.

spatial (spā' shal), *adj.* of or pertaining to space.

spatter (spat' ĕr), *n.* a sprinkle, as a *spatter* of shot. *v.i. and v.t.* to sprinkle or scatter in drops or particles.

spatula (spat' ū la), *n.* a broad, thin, flexible blade used for spreading and for lifting things such as slices of pie or portions of fish at table.

spavin (spav' in), *n.* a disease that causes stiffening of the hock joint in horses.

spawn (spŏn), *n.* the eggs of fishes, oysters and the like, deposited in massy formations.

spawn (spŏn), *v.i.* to deposit eggs : said of fishes and shellfish.

speak (spēk), *v.t. and v.i.* to use a certain language, as to *speak* French; to deliver an address, as he *spoke* at the meeting; to be expressive, as this scene *speaks* to humanity; to recognize, as I do not *speak* to him; to talk, utter words.

speaker (spēk' ĕr), *n.* one who makes utterance; the presiding officer of a legislature, as the *Speaker* of the House.

speaking (spēk' ing), *adj.* articulate, as man is a *speaking* animal; used for transmitting speech, as a *speaking* tube; lifelike, as the *speaking* image of a person.

spear (spēr), *n.* a weapon with a sharp head on a long shaft; a leaf or stalk, as of grass.

spear (spēr), *v.t.* to pierce with a pointed thrusting weapon; to impale upon such a weapon, as to *spear* a fish.

*special (spesh' al), *n.* a person or thing set aside for a particular use or service, as a train. *adj.* designed or set apart for a particular purpose; distinctive; uncommon, out of the ordinary.

specialist (spesh' al ist), *n.* one who devotes himself to a particular branch of science or service, as a *specialist* in nervous diseases.

specialize (spesh' al iz), *v.i.* to apply oneself to a particular form of service or a particular science, as he *specializes* in diseases of the nerves.

specie (spē' shi), *n.* coin; metal that has been made into coin.

*species (spē' shiz), *n. sing. and pl.* a group of animals or plants smaller than a genus, belonging to that genus, but differing in some details; a kind, sort or form.

specific (spĕ sif' ĭk), *adj.* particular; relating definitely to one as distinguished from others of its kind; detailed and exact, as a *specific* program.

specification (spes ĭ fĭ kā' shun), *n.* exact statement; an item in a list of things to be done or supplied; *specifications,* itemized requirements, as the *specifications* for a building or the details of a contract.

specify (spes' ĭ fī), *v.t.* [*p.t. and p.p.* specified, *pr.p.* specifying] to mention in detail; to name particularly and individually or item by item.

specimen (spes' ĭ men), *n.* a sample; a representative individual.

*specious (spē' shus), *adj.* plausible; ostensible; appearing to be true, but not true.

speck (spek), *n.* a tiny spot; a tiny bit of anything. *v.t.* to mark with tiny spots.

speckle (spek' l), *v.t.* to mark with spots of a different color.

speckled (spek' ld), *adj.* marked with spots of a different color from that of the main body, as a *speckled* hen.

spectacle (spek' ta kl), *n.* an unusual sight or view; pageant; show; a painful sight, as he was a *spectacle* when he came home.

spectacles (spek ta klz), *n.* eyeglasses held in place by hinged bows that rest above or hold behind the ears.

spectacular (spek tak' û lẽr), *adj.* showy, sensational.

spectator (spek' tã tẽr), *n.* an onlooker; one who beholds.

specter, spectre (spek' tẽr), *n.* an apparition, a ghost, a phantom.

spectral (spek' tral), *adj.* like a ghost; pertaining to the spectrum or scheme of primary colors.

spectrum (spek' trum), *n.* [*pl.* spectrums or spectra] the colors of the rainbow as shown through a prism that breaks rays of light into elementary colors.

speculate (spek' û lãt), *v.i.* to meditate; to ponder; to guess; to take chances; to invest for quick profit; to gamble on a rising or falling market.

speech (spĕch), *n.* the utterance of ideas in words; the act of uttering; a language; a particular way of uttering, as his *speech* was slow and mumbling.

speed (spĕd), *n.* velocity; rate of progress or advance. *v.i. and v.t.* to make haste; to expedite; to cause to go faster.

speedometer (spĕd om' ē tẽr), *n.* an indicator of the rate at which a vehicle is going.

speedy (spĕd' ĭ), *adj.* [*comp.* speedier, *superl.* speediest] going fast, swift.

spell (spel), *n.* a form of magic words; a charm, incantation; fascination, sway, as the *spell* of his personality. *n.* a turn of work in relief of another, as I took my *spell* at midnight; any period of time with one characteristic, as a rainy *spell*. *v.i. and v.t.* to make charms; to cast a charm upon; to represent, as a word in speech or writing letter by letter; to mean or imply, as

this *spells* ruin.

spellbound (spel' bound), *adj.* fascinated.

spelling (spel' ing), *n.* the proper arrangement of letters to form a word; the act of representing words letter by letter.

spend (spend), *v.i. and v.t.* to pay out money; to pay out, as to *spend* money; to employ or use, as to *spend* time or effort; to wear out, use up, as to *spend* one's strength.

spendthrift (spend' thrift), *n.* one who is prodigal or lavish with money. *adj.* prodigal, lavish, extravagant.

*spermaceti (spûr ma sē' ti), *n.* a white waxy substance obtained from the head of the sperm whale.

sperm whale (spûrm hwāl), a whale that lives in tropical seas and has a square head with teeth in the lower jaw only, valued for sperm oil and spermaceti found in the head.

spew (spū), *v.i. and v.t.* to spit out, vomit, eject.

*sphere (sfēr), *n.* a globe or globular body; a solid every point of whose surface is equally distant from a central point; a field of action or influence, as that is not within my *sphere*.

*spherical (sfer' ĭ kal), *adj.* globular; having the shape of a globe; having a rounded surface of which every point is equally distant from the point within called the *center*.

sphinx (sfingks), *n.* [*pl.* sphinxes] a mythological monster with a lion's body and a human head, ram's head or hawk's head; a hawk moth; a person whose ideas cannot be guessed or whose personality is wrapped in mystery.

spice (spīs), *n.* any aromatic and pungent vegetable substance used for flavoring food; something that adds a flavor, as the *spice* of wit. *v.t.* to season or flavor with aromatic, pungent vegetable substances.

spick-and-span (spik and span), *adj.* brand new; fresh; unsoiled by wear or use.

spicy (spīs' ĭ), *adj.* [*comp.* spicier, *superl.* spiciest] flavored with spice; aromatic and pungent; sharp; witty, racy, as a *spicy* story.

spider (spī' dẽr), *n.* a small invertebrate animal having eight legs and two or more pairs of spinnerets with which it spins a silky thread to make cocoons for eggs, nests to live in or webs to catch prey, such as flies and other insects. *n.* a long-handled frying pan.

spigot (spig' ut), *n.* a faucet in the venthole of a cask; any faucet.

spike (spīk), *n.* a very large nail with a heavy head; a projecting piece of metal on the sole of a shoe to prevent slipping. *v.t.* to equip or fasten with sharp points or large nails; to pierce with something sharp; to stop the vent of a cannon with a metal bar; to finish, end, make ineffective.

spikenard (spīk' nẽrd), *n.* an aromatic plant from which a costly ointment was prepared by the ancients; the ointment made from this plant.

spill (spil), *n.* a slender strip of wood or a long fold of paper used in lighting lamps, or in place of matches. *n.* the act of overflowing; the overflow of a dam. *v.i. and v.t.* to run over, as the water *spills* over the dam; to lose by pouring or overflowing, as to *spill* the milk from a pitcher.

spin (spin), *n.* a rapid whirling. *v.t. and v.i.* to draw out into threads; to cause to whirl fast, as a top; to whirl; to let an airplane descend while turning on its own axis.

spinach (spin' ich), *n.* an edible plant with pulpy leaves that are used as pot herbs.

spinal (spi' nal), *adj.* relating to the backbone.

spinal column (spi' nal kol' um), the backbone.

spindle (spin' dl), *n.* a rod in a spinning wheel for twisting the thread.

spine (spin), *n.* the backbone; any ridge that stands out like the vertebrae.

***spinet** (spin' et), *n.* a small keyboard musical instrument, one of the early forms of the piano.

spinster (spin' ster), *n.* an unmarried woman, an old maid.

spiny (spin' i), *adj.* having thorns or prickles.

spiral (spi' ral), *n.* a curve winding away from a center, as if going upward around the surface of a cone. *adj.* winding upward from a center like the thread of a screw.

spire (spir), *n.* a single turn of a spiral.

spire (spir), *n.* a high steeple; a spear of grass; a summit or peak.

***spirit** (spir' it), *n.* the soul; personality; vivacity; the essence of anything; courage and enthusiasm; the ruling feeling, as the *spirit* of '76. *v.t.* to carry off suddenly and secretly, as to *spirit* the evidence away.

spirited (spir' i ted), *adj.* full of life, animated.

spirits (spir' its), *n. pl.* liquor; mood, as in high *spirits*.

***spiritual** (spir' it ū al), *n.* a religious song of the American Negro. *adj.* not material; having to do with the soul.

spiritualism (spir' it ū al izm), *n.* the belief that the dead communicate with the living.

spirituous (spir' it ū us), *adj.* containing alcohol, as *spirituous* liquors.

spit (spit), *n.* saliva. *n.* a rod on which meat is impaled and roasted before a fire. *n.* an image, as he is the living *spit* of his father. *v.i.* to eject saliva from the mouth. *v.t.* to impale, as meat, on a sharp-pointed rod; to run through as with a sword.

spite (spit), *n.* ill will, hatred; petty malice.

spite (spit), *v.t.* to treat with malice; to injure or annoy in a spirit of meanness.

spitfire (spit' fir), *n.* a quick-tempered person.

spittle (spit' l), *n.* saliva.

splash (splash), *n.* the act of striking a liquid; the liquid thrown up by a blow or the fall of a body into it; the sound of a body falling into a liquid; an irregular spot, as a *splash* of color. *v.i. and v.t.* to dash water about; to spatter with liquid.

splat (splat), *n.* a vertical slat or bar in a chair back.

splay (splā), *adj.* spread out, broad, awkward, ill-formed, as *splay* feet. *n.* an opening with a slanted or beveled edge. *v.t.* to dislocate, as a shoulder-bone; to slope or slant, as the sides of a door or window.

splayfooted (splā foot' ed), *adj.* having feet spread out abnormally broad and flat.

***spleen** (splēn), *n.* an organ near the stomach the secretion of which affects the blood; ill temper, spite.

splendid (splen' did), *adj.* magnificent, imposing, inspiring, glorious.

splendor (splen' dēr), *n.* magnificence, pomp, richness, conspicuous greatness.

splice (splis), *n.* a union, as of the ends of two ropes. *v.t.* to join as two rope ends by intertwining the strands.

splint (splint), *n.* a thin piece of wood to keep a broken bone in position; a strip of wood used in making baskets and chair seats.

splinter (splin' tēr), *n.* a sharp piece of wood broken from a board or any timber. *v.i. and v.t.* to break into small pieces.

split (split), *n.* a lengthwise break; a breaking apart, as between two factions in an organization. *v.i. and v.t.* to divide lengthwise; to break into factions. *adj.* divided lengthwise, as *split* logs, *split* fish.

splotch (sploch), *n.* a stain; daub, as a *splotch* of ink.

***spoil** (spoil), *n.* plunder, booty, loot: *spoils*, the gains of war or political success in patronage and power, as to the victor belong the *spoils*.

spoke (spōk), *n.* one of the bars of a wheel radiating from the hub to the rim.

spoliation (spō li ā' shun), *n.* the act of plundering.

***sponge** (spunj), *n.* the porous, elastic, fibrous framework left when certain sea creatures perish; this fibrous matter dried for use in cleaning or bathing; a person who absorbs his living from others instead of working for it. *v.i. and v.t.* to live dependent upon another; to gather sponges; to clean with a sponge.

sponsor (spon' sēr), *n.* a godfather; one who vouches for something or stands back of it, as the *sponsor* of a radio program or of a new political organization.

spontaneous (spon tā' nē us), *adj.* unforced; voluntary; done of one's own will; self-generated, as *spontaneous* combustion.

spool (spōol), *n.* a cylinder on which thread is wound; a drum on which wire or cable is wound.

spoon (spōon), *n.* a kitchen or table utensil consisting of a bowl attached to a handle; a golf club with slanted face and short shaft.

sporadic (spō rad' ik), *adj.* occurring irregularly, scattered, isolated.

spore (spōr), *n.* a minute particle in certain plants that acts as a seed and produces new plants.

sport (spōrt), *n.* diversion, amusement, entertainment; a pastime; a competition in athletic games.

sportive (spōr' tiv), *adj.* frolicsome, merry, playful.

spot (spot), *n.* a particular place; a stain or blot. *v.t.* to mark with stains; to disgrace or blemish, as to *spot* one's record or reputation.

spouse (spouz), *n.* a husband or wife.

spout (spout), *n.* a tube or pipe through which a liquid runs off, as a rain*spout*, the *spout* of a kettle. *v.i. and v.t.* to pour forth in a stream; to speak or recite in a fluent and affected fashion, as to *spout* poetry.

sprain (språn), *n.* a wrench of a ligament.

sprain (språn), *v.t.* to wrench, as the ligaments of the ankle or any joint.

sprat (sprat), *n.* a small fish resembling the herring; a young herring.

sprawl (sprôl), *n.* a relaxed, ungraceful position. *v.i.* to lie with the arms and legs stretched out.

spray (språ), *n.* a small branch bearing flowers; a slender, graceful branch of flowers. *n.* drops of water carried by the wind or blown by an atomizer or squeezed bulb. *v.i. and v.t.* to blow in drops; to blow upon in fine drops, as to *spray* the throat.

spread (spred), *n.* extension; expanse of a surface, as the *spread* of a sail; something that is extended over a surface, as a *spread* for a bed; a feast, as this is a noble *spread;* something laid over a surface, as a *spread* for a slice of bread; difference, as the wide *spread* between cost and price. *v.i. and v.t.* to be extended over a surface; to distribute evenly over a surface; to circulate, as *spread* news.

sprig (sprig), *n.* a shoot of a tree, bush or plant; an ornament resembling a spray of leaves or flowers; a nail without a head, a brad; a lad.

sprightly (sprit'li), *adj.* [*comp.* sprightlier, *superl.* sprightliest] vivacious, brisk, animated, full of life and spirit.

spring (spring), *n.* a contrivance devised so as to resume its first shape on being released from distortion, used to ease shock on the axles of a vehicle and its occupants; a coil of metal to make a bed or chair resilient and more comfortable; elastic quality, recoil; a leap or a bound; a flow of water from the earth; any source of supply, as a *spring* of knowledge or joy; the season following winter when plants begin to grow, usually March, April and May in the North Temperate Zone.

springy (spring'i), *adj.* [*comp.* springier, *superl.* springiest] giving and recovering under weight or pressure, elastic, resilient; having many springs, wet, as *springy* land; light and full of vigor, as a *springy* step.

sprinkle (spring'kl), *n.* a light scattering of liquid in drops, as a *sprinkle* of rain.

sprinkle (spring'kl), *v.i. and v.t.* to fall lightly, as rain; to scatter in drops; to scatter on, as to *sprinkle* a cake with sugar.

sprint (sprint), *n.* a short distance run at top speed. *v.i.* to run a short distance at top speed.

sprocket (sprok'et), *n.* a wheel with teeth on the outer rim to engage the links of a chain; one of the teeth or cogs on such a wheel.

sprout (sprout), *n.* a new shoot or bud on a plant or a root. *v.i.* to put forth new shoots; to germinate, as these seeds are *sprouting*.

sprouts (sprouts), *n. pl.* the edible buds of a kind of cabbage, called *Brussels sprouts.*

spruce (sprōōs), *n.* an evergreen tree with needles and cones; wood of this tree. *adj.* smart and trim in appearance.

spry (spri), *adj.* [*comp.* spryer or sprier, *superl.* spryest or spriest] nimble, agile, quick and active.

spunk (spungk), *n.* courage, pluck, mettle.

spur (spûr), *n.* a sharp point worn on the heel of a horseman's boot to urge or discipline a saddle horse; anything that incites to action. *v.i. and v.t.* to urge or discipline a horse with the heel; to incite to action, urge on.

spurious (spū'ri us), *adj.* false, counterfeit, not genuine.

spurn (spûrn), *v.t.* to drive away with the foot, kick; to reject with scorn or contempt; to turn aside from with disdain.

spurt (spûrt), *n.* a sudden or forcible ejection of a liquid, a gush; a strong, brief effort.

spurt (spûrt), *v.i. and v.t.* to come forth or be forced out in a sudden stream; to jet; to make a sudden earnest effort at something.

Sputnik (spoot ′ nik), *n.* the name of a satellite in Russia.

sputter (sput'er), *n.* excited and incoherent talk, fuss; moist matter ejected in small particles; the sound of spluttering.

sputter (sput'er), *v.i.* to speak rapidly ejecting saliva in small particles from the mouth.

sputum (spū'tum), *n.* saliva, spittle.

spy (spi), *n.* [*pl.* spies] one who secretly watches others; one who secretly observes an enemy force and reports its movements.

spy (spi), *v.i. and v.t.* [*p.t. and p.p.* spied, *pr.p.* spying] to observe in secret and by stealth; to catch sight of.

spyglass (spi glàs), *n.* a small telescope.

squab (skwob), *n.* a young pigeon.

squabble (skwob'l), *n.* a noisy quarrel. *v.i.* to wrangle, quarrel noisily.

squad (skwod), *n.* a small group of persons; a unit of police or of a military organization; seven infantry soldiers commanded by a corporal; any small group engaged in common effort or activity, as a football *squad,* a clean-up *squad.*

squadron (skwod'run), *n.* a military unit consisting of the headquarters and two or more cavalry troops; a subdivision of a fleet of naval vessels; a division of a military air fleet consisting of three flights of three to six airplanes each.

squalid (skwol'id), *adj.* very dirty; poverty-stricken.

squall (skwôl), *n.* a sudden, hard gust of wind; a screaming outcry.

squalor (skwol'er), *n.* wretched poverty.

squander (skwon'der), *v.t.* to spend lavishly, waste.

square (skwâr), *n.* a plane figure with four equal sides and four right angles; a device for measuring right angles, used by draughtsmen and builders; anything with four equal sides, as a city *square;* the product of a number multiplied by itself, as the *square* of 2 is 4. *adj.* having four equal sides and four right angles; forming a right angle; honest, fair; satisfying, sufficient, as a *square* meal. *v.i. and v.t.* to form in a right angle, as this board *squares*; to make even, as to *square* an account; to multiply a number by itself.

square root (skwâr rōōt), the number obtained when a number that is multiplied by itself is reduced to its original factors, as the *square root* of 4 is 2.

*squash (skwosh), *n.* the fleshy edible fruit of a field or garden plant of the gourd family.

squat (skwot), *v.i.* to settle down as if sitting; to settle land either under a government lease so as ultimately to take title to it or without right or title. *adj.* short and stocky, crouching.

squatter (skwot' ĕr), *n.* one who occupies land either without right or under government lease in expectation of acquiring ownership.

squaw (skwô), *n.* an American Indian woman.

*squeak (skwēk), *n.* a thin, sharp, penetrating sound, as the *squeak* of an ungreased wheel.

squeak (skwēk), *v.i.* to make a shrill penetrating cry or sound like that of a mouse or an unoiled hinge.

*squeal (skwēl), *n.* a sharp, shrill cry, prolonged like that of a pig. *v.i.* to utter a shrill cry like that of a pig.

squeamish (skwēm' ish), *adj.* easily shocked; easily affected with nausea; very particular.

squeegee (skwē' jē), *n.* an implement with a straight-edged strip of rubber used to remove water from windows.

squeeze (skwēz), *n.* a tight jam; a crowding together.

squeeze (skwēz), *v.i. and v.t.* to make one's way by pressing or crowding, as I *squeezed* in; to get by pressure, force, as to *squeeze* juice from an orange; to press or compress as to *squeeze* an orange; to press or jam, as to *squeeze* passengers into a car.

squelch (skwelch), *v.t.* to silence; to suppress; to discourage, disconcert.

squib (skwib), *n.* a kind of firework that burns with a sizzling sound or explodes with a crack; a short satirical composition.

squid (skwid), *n.* a kind of cuttlefish having a tapering body with 10 arms and two fins near the tail; bait shaped like a squid or made from squid.

squint (skwint), *n.* a sidelong look; a condition of the eyes in which they look obliquely.

squint (skwint), *v.i.* to look obliquely or with the eyes half closed.

squint-eyed (skwint' id'), *adj.* cross-eyed.

squire (skwir), *n.* a knight's attendant; a justice of the peace; the proprietor or landholder of a rural English district.

squire (skwir), *v.t.* to escort.

squirm (skwûrm), *v.i.* to wriggle, writhe.

*squirrel (skwûr' el), *n.* a small, agile rodent with a bushy tail.

squirt (skwûrt), *n.* a spurt of liquid; a syringe to throw a small stream of water.

squirt (skwûrt), *v.i. and v.t.* to spurt out; to eject in a small quick jet.

stab (stab), *n.* a thrust with a short, pointed weapon, as a dagger; a wound made by such a thrust; a thrust of pain or grief.

stab (stab), *v.i. and v.t.* to thrust with a dagger; to wound as with a dagger.

stability (sta bil' i ti), *n.* firmness in position; ability to resist a force tending to overthrow; firmness of character, constancy.

*stabilize (stā' bi līz), *v.t.* to make steadfast, firm, dependable; to secure and keep the balance of, as to *stabilize* a boat, an airplane or a government.

*stabilizer (stā' bil iz ēr), *n.* a device to steady the motion and maintain the balance of an airplane or a ship.

stable (stā' bl), *n.* a building in which horses or cattle are kept. *v.t.* to put in a barn; to supply stalls for, as horses. *adj.* firmly set; resisting anything tending to overthrow; constant and reliable.

stack (stak), *n.* a large orderly pile of hay or wood; any systematically arranged pile; a pipe or chimney to carry off smoke as from a factory, steamship or locomotive.

stack (stak), *v.t.* to arrange in an orderly pile.

*stadium (stā' di um), *n.* [*pl.* stadiums or stadia] a structure in the shape of an oval or round bowl with seats for spectators of athletic contests held on the inclosed space; an old Greek linear measure, about 606¾ feet.

staff (stàf), *n.* [*pl.* staves or staffs] a stick carried for use in walking or for personal defense; support.

stag (stag), *n.* the male of the red deer; a man attending a social function without escorting a lady; a party or entertainment for men only.

stage (stāj), *n.* the raised platform on which a theatrical performance is presented; a swinging scaffold for workmen; a float on which workers stand to paint the hull of a ship; a field of action; a section of a journey, as we proceeded by easy *stages;* a period or phase in the development of anything, as the enterprise did very well in its early *stage;* a large coach for the conveyance of passengers. *v.i. and v.t.* to be exhibited, as this play will *stage* well; to present in public, as he has *staged* two plays this season.

stagger (stag' ēr), *n.* a reeling or tottering: *staggers,* a disease of horses that causes them to totter and fall, sometimes called *blind staggers. v.i. and v.t.* to reel; to shock and upset, as your news *staggers* me; to arrange alternately so as to avoid crowding or congestion, as in planting trees or in traveling to or from business at different hours.

staging (stāj' ing), *n.* a scaffold; manner of presentation of a play to an audience.

stagnant (stag' nant), *adj.* not flowing but standing, foul from standing, as *stagnant* water; dull, as *stagnant* business.

stagnate (stag' nāt), *v.i.* to stand without flowing, as water *stagnates* in a hollow; to become inactive and inert, as he is simply *stagnating* in that job.

stagy (stāj' i), *adj.* artificial, theatrical.

staid (stād), *adj.* sober, sedate, steady.

stain (stān), *n.* discoloration, a spot or blot; taint or blemish on one's character.

stain (stān), v.i. and v.t. to discolor, as this cloth *stains* easily, I have *stained* the table-cloth; to color, as with dye or varnish.

stair (stâr), n. one of a series of steps leading from a lower to a higher level, as from one floor of a house to the next: *stairs*, a flight of steps, as front or back *stairs*.

staircase (stâr' kās), n. a flight of steps with railings in a house.

stairway (stâr' wā), n. a flight of steps.

stake (stāk), n. a stick of wood sharpened at one end to be driven into the ground; a post to which a person was bound to be burned alive, as he died at the *stake*. n. something wagered; something to be gained or won at a risk, as our future is the *stake* in this deal. v.t. to risk, wager, contend for, as I *staked* everything on his honesty; to mark the boundaries of, as he *staked* his claim.

stalactite (sta lak' tīt), n. an iciclelike mass hanging from the roof of a cavern, formed by the drip of water with lime in it.

stalagmite (sta lag' mīt), n. a cone of carbonate of lime built up on the floor of a cavern by water dripping from above.

stale (stāl), v.i. and v.t. to become old and flavorless; to deprive of interest. adj. having lost freshness, as *stale* bread; vapid, tasteless; trite, as *stale* ideas.

stalemate (stāl' māt), n. a position in which a chess player cannot move without putting his king in check, a draw; a standstill, as the negotiations are now in a *stalemate*.

stalk (stôk), n. the stem of a plant or flower, as a *stalk* of corn; the stem of an object, as a goblet. n. a haughty way of stepping.

stalk (stôk), v.t. and v.i. to creep up on stealthily, as to *stalk* a deer; to walk in haughty manner, as to *stalk* out of the room.

stall (stôl), n. an inclosed space in a stable in which a horse or cow is kept; a small booth from which goods are sold; a close cover as for a hurt finger; a seat, often carved and canopied, in the choir section of a church.

stall (stôl), v.i. and v.t. to keep in a closed space within a stable; to lose the action of, as I have *stalled* my engine; to cause to stop by becoming stuck, as the soft sand *stalled* the car; to become stuck in mud, as the wagon *stalled* at the foot of the hill.

stalwart (stôl' wẽrt), n. a strong person; a loyal member of a party. adj. strong, sturdy, tall and well-built.

stamen (stā' men), n. the organ of a flower that holds the pollen.

stamina (stam' i na), n. staying power, vitality, vigor, endurance.

stammer (stam' ẽr), n. a halting manner of speech; hesitation in uttering words.

stammer (stam' ẽr), v.i. and v.t. to speak in a halting way; to utter with hesitation and in a nervous manner.

stamp (stamp), n. a mark made by impression; an implement or machine for making such impressions on paper, cloth or in metal; a printed, gummed piece of paper sold by a government to be affixed to mail matter as evidence that postage has been paid; evidence of a distinctive quality, as the *stamp*

of culture. v.i. and v.t. to strike upon the ground, as the foot; to make a mark on by means of pressure; to place postage upon; to crush, as to *stamp* ore.

stampede (stam pēd'), n. a sudden wild rush of cattle; panicky flight or action by many persons together. v.i. and v.t. to rush off in a herd, as cattle in fright; to make a sudden rush in alarm, as the crowd *stampeded* when the gun was fired; to cause to rush away in panic; to throw a crowd of persons into a panic.

stanch (stänch) or **staunch** (stônch), v.t. to stop the flow of, as blood from a wound. adj. firm, faithful, loyal, dependable.

stand (stand), n. a structure upon which things may be set; a small platform on which a witness is placed when giving testimony in a courtroom, the witness *stand;* a small structure at which goods are sold, as a fruit *stand;* a position firmly held, as I take my *stand* upon this plank of the party platform; a growth of crops in the field, as a fine *stand* of corn. v.i. and v.t. [p.t. and p.p. stood, pr.p. standing] to be in upright position on the feet; to be a substitute for, as these letters *stand* for the company's name; to conform, as it *stands* to reason; to take sides, as I *stand* for justice; to be in a certain state, as I *stand* ready to help; to set upright, as *stand* the vase on the table.

standard (stan' dẽrd), n. an established measure or model; an upright timber used as a support in building; a flag or emblem.

standardize (stan' dẽr dīz), v.t. to cause to conform to certain uniform specifications, as to *standardize* equipment.

standing (stand' ing), n. good reputation; continuance, as a policy of long *standing*.

standing (stand' ing), adj. not flowing, stagnant, as water; remaining in effect indefinitely, as a *standing* invitation.

standpoint (stand' point), n. a position or standard that forms the basis of an opinion or judgment, as that is unwise from the *standpoint* of health.

standstill (stand' stil), n. a cessation of motion; a definite stop.

stannary (stan' a ri), n. [pl. stannaries] a tin mine or works.

stannous (stan' us), adj. pertaining to tin.

stanza (stan' za), n. a subdivision of a poem, with several lines or verses taken as a unit.

staple (stā' pl), n. a major article of commerce, universally dealt in; raw material for manufacture; a chief element; fiber of wool, cotton or flax, as cotton of long *staple*. n. a U-shaped piece of metal with pointed ends to fasten something to wood, as use plenty of *staples* when you put up that chicken wire; a piece of wire with which sheets of paper are fastened together. v.t. to fasten with U-shaped pieces of wire driven into wood, as *staple* that wire fence generously; to secure. adj. regularly produced and traded in; established in commerce; standard and essential, as *staple* foods.

star (stär), n. a far-distant heavenly body that

shines at night; anything compared to such a body; a five- or six-pointed figure; an asterisk (*) used to draw the attention of a reader, as to footnotes; a brilliant, outstanding person as this reporter is our *star*, a stage, screen or radio *star*. *v.i. and v.t.* to shine in one's calling; to be prominent or pre-eminent; to mark with an asterisk, as *star* this footnote; to play up strongly, as we shall *star* you in our next play.

starboard (stär' bĕrd), *n.* the right-hand side of a ship as one faces the bow. *adj.* pertaining to the right-hand side of a ship, as the *starboard* light.

*starch** (stärch), *n.* a white substance without taste or odor found in plants; a commercial product used in laundering; formality; backbone. *v.t.* to stiffen with starch, as clothes in laundering.

*stare** (stãr), *n.* a fixed look with eyes wide open. *v.i. and v.t.* to look fixedly with wide-open eyes, gaze at; to face, confront; to embarrass, as she *stared* him out of countenance.

starfish (stär' fish), *n.* a carnivorous marine animal of many species all having radiating arms; a pest to oyster growers.

stark (stärk), *adj.* rigid; barren, unrelieved; complete, as *stark* madness.

stark (stärk), *adv.* utterly, as *stark* mad.

starling (stär' ling), *n.* a common black-feathered bird about 9 inches long.

start (stärt), *n.* a beginning; the beginning place; an advantage in a contest of speed, as to get a good *start* over one's opponents; a quick motion or twitch, as of one suddenly alarmed, as a *start* of surprise.

start (stärt), *v.i. and v.t.* to rise or move suddenly, as he *started* from his chair; to give a sudden, involuntary jerk, as from surprise; to move in a fixed direction, as he *started* off in pursuit; to set in motion, as to *start* a car, to *start* a rumor.

startle (stär' tl), *v.i. and v.t.* to move suddenly, in surprise or alarm; to disturb with sudden speech or act, as you came in so quietly you *startled* me.

startling (stär' tling), *adj.* amazing, alarming.

starvation (stär vã' shun), *n.* long-continued unsatisfied hunger; the condition of suffering or dying from lack of food.

starve (stärv), *v.i. and v.t.* to suffer extreme hunger; to die for want of food; to withhold food from.

state (stãt), *n.* the condition in which a person or thing is; style of living, as he lives in high *state*; a nation: *State*, one of the 48 major divisions of the United States of America.

stated (stãt' ed), *adj.* set, fixed, regular, as *stated* intervals.

stately (stãt' li), *adj.* [*comp.* statelier, *superl.* stateliest] grand, majestic, dignified.

statement (stãt' ment), *n.* the act of declaring or affirming; that which is declared or affirmed.

stateroom (stãt' rōōm), *n.* a ship cabin; a private compartment in a Pullman or parlor car.

statesman (stãts' man), *n.* [*pl.* statesmen] one who is skilled or experienced in the management of governmental affairs.

*static** (stat' ik), *n.* sharp, crackling noises in a radio receiving set, caused by electrical disturbances in the air.

*static** (stat' ik), *adj.* pertaining to bodies at rest or in equilibrium or to electric charges at rest as distinguished from electric currents.

statics (stat' iks), *n.* the branch of mechanics that treats of bodies at rest.

station (stã' shun), *n.* the place where a person or thing stands; position; a stopping place or terminal, as on a railroad; the headquarters of a force of men or its central working place; a radio broadcasting center, as *Station* KDKA; social standing, as he married beneath his *station*. *v.t.* to assign to a certain location or position.

*stationary** (stã' shun er i), *adj.* fixed, settled in one place, not advancing in any way.

stationer (stã' shun ĕr), *n.* one who sells paper, pencils and other writing materials.

*stationery** (stã' shun er i), *n.* writing materials of all kinds, especially paper for correspondence.

statistical (sta tis' ti kal), *adj.* pertaining to figures and numbers as they are used in classifying and explaining facts.

*statistician** (stat is tish' un), *n.* one who makes a business of collecting and classifying numerical facts.

*statistics** (sta tis' tiks), *n.* the science of numerical facts; the collection and arrangement of such facts.

statuary (stat' ū er i), *n.* the art of making figures in stone or metal; one who engages in this art; such figures regarded collectively.

*statue** (stat' ū), *n.* the representation of a living or symbolic figure carved in wood or stone or modeled in clay or wax and cast in metal, cement or plaster.

*statuesque** (stat ū esk'), *adj.* having the impressiveness, modeling or pose of a carved or molded figure.

statuette (stat ū et'), *n.* a small carved, modeled or cast figure.

stature (stat' ūr), *n.* the actual natural height of an animal body; a man's size with respect to character, ability and reputation, as he is a statesman of giant *stature*.

*status** (stã' tus), *n.* standing, condition, rank.

statute (stat' ūt), *n.* a written law; a permanent rule adopted officially by a university.

statutory (stat' ū tō ri), *adj.* legally enacted; deriving authority from law.

stave (stãv), *n.* a strip of wood forming a unit in the side of a cask or barrel.

stave (stãv), *v.t.* [*p.t. and p.p.* staved or stove, *pr.p.* staving] to break or break in, the side of a cask or barrel; to make a hole in by the force of a collision; to break down, as *stave* the door in; to push aside, as to *stave* off disaster.

stay (stã), *n.* a prop or support, either rigid or a rope. *n.* a visit; duration of a visit or sojourn; a postponement, as by court action.

stay (stā), *v.i. and v.t.* to tarry, wait, halt, reside temporarily; to postpone, as the court *stayed* the case; to stop the movement of, as moved by sudden pity, he *stayed* his hand.

*****stead** (sted), *n.* the place another might or should have, as I went in his *stead;* service, as it stood me in good *stead.*

steadfast (sted' fåst), *adj.* firmly fixed; resolute, unwavering.

steady (sted' ĭ), *v.i. and v.t.* to become or make fixed and firm.

steady (sted' ĭ), *adj.* [*comp.* steadier, *superl.* steadiest] stable, firmly fixed; resolute, unwavering; regular in action or movement.

steak (stāk), *n.* a thick slice across a larger cut of meat, especially beef, as a *steak* from the round.

steal (stēl), *v.i. and v.t.* [*p.t.* stole, *p.p.* stolen, *pr.p.* stealing] to commit theft; to go in secret or furtive manner, as to *steal* away; to take without right and by furtive methods.

stealth (stelth) *n. sly,* secret, underhand procedure or action; secrecy.

stealthy (stel' thĭ), *adj.* furtive, secret, as *stealthy* movements.

steam (stēm), *n.* vapor into which water is changed by boiling, invisible until it condenses in cooler air. *v.i. and v.t.* to turn into vapor in boiling; to move by power of water vapor in cylinders of engines; to cook or saturate by means of vapor of boiling water.

steamer (stēm' ẽr), *n.* a ship that is propelled by steam; a utensil for exposing articles to steam.

steamship (stēm' ship), *n.* a seagoing ship propelled by steam power, as a transatlantic liner, a steamer.

steed (stēd), *n.* a horse, especially a spirited horse.

steel (stēl), *n.* iron refined and combined with carbon. *v.t.* to cover or plate with carbonized iron; to make hard and unyielding or composed, as *steel* yourself for a shock.

*****steelyard** (stēl' yärd), *n.* a balance for weighing that consists of a beam, a weight sliding on a graduated scale and hooks to hold the thing being weighed.

steep (stēp), *n.* a hillside almost perpendicular; a precipice. *v.i. and v.t.* to soak in a liquid, as tea; to imbue, as he is *steeped* in crime. *adj.* precipitous, having a sharp incline.

steeple (stēp' l), *n.* a tower tapering to a point; a spire, as a church *steeple.*

steeplechase (stēp' l châs), *n.* a race on horseback over open country with obstacles, such as fences and ditches or especially prepared barriers.

steer (stēr), *n.* a male of the ox kind, raised for beef. *v.i. and v.t.* to direct one's course or conduct; to hold to a set course, as to *steer* a ship, *steer* clear of the rocks.

steerage (stēr' ĭj), *n.* the least desirable quarters on a ship, available at the lowest rate for passage.

stein (stĭn), a large, earthenware drinking cup or mug, with a handle, used especially

for beer; the quantity of beer in such a container.

stellar (stel' ẽr), *adj.* relating to stars, either the heavenly bodies or persons prominent in their callings, as *stellar* space, a *stellar* performance.

stem (stem), *n.* the trunk of a tree; the corresponding part of a shrub or smaller plant; the slender stalk that connects a fruit, flower or leaf to the branch; any slender part resembling a stalk, as the *stem* of a goblet, the *stem* of a smoker's pipe; the farthest forward part of a ship, where its sides slope in to the prow; the part of a word that remains unchanged when the word is inflected; the part of a watch by which it is wound; a highway or railroad line, as this is the main *stem. v.t.* to remove stems from, as to *stem* cherries; to put stems on, as to *stem* artificial flowers. *v.t.* to hold back, as you cannot *stem* the ocean tides; to make way against, as we had to *stem* a strong current.

stench (stench), *n.* a strong, offensive odor.

stencil (sten' sil), *n.* a thin plate of metal, parchment or paper, with a design or letters cut out to use for marking decorations or printing addresses by applying wet color with a brush. *v.t.* to mark by means of a plate that has a cut-out design or lettering.

stenographer (ste nog' ra fẽr), *n.* one who writes shorthand and transcribes the notes.

stenographic (sten ō graf' ik), *adj.* pertaining to or written in shorthand, as *stenographic* notes.

stenography (ste nog' ra fĭ), *n.* the art of writing shorthand and transcribing it.

step (step), *n.* a stride; the distance covered in one stride; a surface on which the foot is set in moving up or down a flight of stairs; a single act toward a desired state or situation, as a *step* toward success; a way of walking, as he has a springy *step;* a series of related foot-and-body movements in dancing, as that is an intricate *step.*

step (step), *v.i. and v.t.* to move the feet, as in walking, as *step* this way; to come into a certain position or condition without effort, as to *step* from one job into another; to push down with the foot, as to *step* on the accelerator; to set or place, as the foot, to measure the distance of, as we *stepped* off the length of the living room; to insert a pole or mast in a socket to hold it up.

steppes (steps), *n.* the vast, barren plains of Siberia.

step rocket (step' rŏk' et), *n.* a particular type of rocket used in space launchings.

stereo (ster' ē ō), *n.* a stereophonic record player, record, or tape.

*****stereopticon** (ster ē op' ti kon), *n.* a magic lantern for showing photographic slides.

*****stereoscope** (ster' ē ō skōp), *n.* an instrument held before the eyes by which two slightly different pictures of the same object are made to appear as one, and give the illusion of having three dimensions.

*****stereotype** (ster' ē ō tīp), *n.* a printing plate made from a papier-mâché or plaster cast or mold of a form of a printing surface; anything mechanically monotonous, especially a phrase or figure of speech.

stereotyped (ster' ē ō tīpt), *adj.* usual, dull, monotonous.

*sterile (ster' ĭl), *adj.* barren, unproductive; free from disease germs; destitute of ideas, as this is a *sterile* essay.

sterility (ste ril' ĭ tĭ), *n.* barrenness, lack of fertility.

sterilize (ster' ĭ līz), *v.t.* to deprive of fertility; to free of disease germs.

sterling (stûr' lĭng), *adj.* genuine; of high merit; guaranteed as to fineness on a scale set by the British Government, as *sterling* silver.

stern (stûrn), *n.* afterpart of a ship. *adj.* austere, severe, strict, harsh, forbidding.

sternum (stûr' num), *n.* [*pl.* sternums or sterna] the breastbone.

*stethoscope (steth' ō skōp), *n.* an instrument used by doctors to listen to sounds in the heart and lungs, to detect any pathological condition.

stevedore (stē' ve dōr), *n.* a person who loads and unloads ship cargoes.

stew (stū), *n.* a dish of meat and vegetables boiled slowly. *v.i. and v.t.* to boil slowly, as meat and vegetables together.

*steward (stū' ērd), *n.* one who manages an estate for another; an employee in charge of food service in a club, hospital or ship.

stewardess (stū' ērd es), *n.* a woman who attends female passengers aboard ship.

stick (stĭk), *n.* a small branch or shoot cut off a tree; a walking stick; a slender piece, as a *stick* of candy; a metal holder in which type is set by hand. *v.i. and v.t.* [*p.t. and p.p.* stuck, *pr.p.* sticking] to project, as to *stick* out, *stick* through; to pierce, stab, jab, as this pin *stuck* me. *v.i. and v.t.* [*p.t. and p.p.* stuck, *pr.p.* sticking] to adhere; to cause to adhere, as *stick* a stamp on the envelope; to thrust, as he *stuck* his head in the door.

stickle (stĭk' l), *v.i.* to argue about things of little importance.

stickler (stĭk' lēr), *n.* one who insists on matters of little importance.

sticky (stĭk' ĭ), *adj.* [*comp.* stickier, *superl.* stickiest] adhesive, glutinous, viscous.

stiff (stĭf), *adj.* rigid, not flexible; not fluid, as this paint is *stiff*; strong, as a *stiff* breeze; cool and formal in manner, overdignified.

stifle (stī' fl), *n.* a joint in the hind leg of a horse. *v.i. and v.t.* to suffocate; to extinguish, as *stifle* that flame; to kill by withholding air; to put out, as a fire.

stigma (stig' ma), *n.* [*pl.* stigmas or stigmata] a mark of disgrace or dishonor; a blemish, a birthmark; the upper part of a flower pistil on which the pollen is deposited.

stigmatize (stig' ma tĭz), *v.t.* to brand as disgraceful or dishonored.

stile (stīl), *n.* a set of steps leading over a fence or wall.

stiletto (sti let' ō), *n.* [*pl.* stilettos] a small dagger with a slender blade.

still (stĭl), *n.* an apparatus for distilling

liquids. *n.* a picture that does not show movement, especially an individual photograph taken from a motion-picture scene and used in advertising. *v.t.* to hush, silence, put to rest, pacify. *v.t.* to make by distilling. *adj.* not moving or moving without excitement or disturbance, as *still* water in a pond, *still* waters run deep; silent, quiet, not noisy, as a *still* small voice, the winds were *still*. *adv.* neveretheless, notwithstanding, as *still*, I intend to go; to this time, as I am *still* here; continuously, as before, as he was *still* worried; in a greater degree, *still* more.

stilt (stĭlt), *n.* one of a pair of slender poles with a footrest on which to walk high above the ground.

stilted (stĭl' ted), *adj.* artificial, formal, as *stilted* speech.

stimulant (stim' û lant), *adj.* serving to accelerate, as action of heart. *n.* anything that spurs to faster, more effective or more intense action, as good reading is a *stimulant* to the mind; a medicine that increases the activity of an organ, as the heart.

stimulate (stim' û lāt), *v.i. and v.t.* to rouse to greater activity, spur.

stimulus (stim' û lus), *n.* a spur; anything that leads to greater activity or arouses, as your talk was a *stimulus* to study.

sting (sting), *n.* the sharp, poisonous weapon with which some insects are armed, as the *sting* of a bee; anything sharp that causes a wound to body or feelings, as your words are a *sting* to my conscience; the thrust of a poisonous, sharp weapon. *v.i. and v.t.* [*p.t. and p.p.* stung, *pr.p.* stinging] to pierce or wound, as your words *sting*; to cause a sharp sensation to, as red pepper *stings* the tongue.

stingy (stin' jĭ), *adj.* [*comp.* stingier, *superl.* stingiest] mean, not ready to give; meager.

stink (stingk), *n.* a strong, offensive odor. *v.i.* [*p.t.* stank, *p.p.* stunk, *pr.p.* stinking] to emit a strong, offensive odor.

*stint (stint), *n.* the amount of work to be done in a specified time, as my daily *stint* of study. *n.* a restriction or limitation, as give without *stint*. *v.i. and v.t.* to provide scantily, begrudge; to limit or restrict, as to *stint* a boy's allowance.

*stipend (stī' pend), *n.* a salary; an allowance paid periodically.

stipple (stip' l), *v.t.* to engrave or draw with dots; to apply light dots of paint to, as to *stipple* a wall.

stipulate (stip' û lāt), *v.t.* to mention specifically, to specify as part of terms of an agreement.

stir (stûr), *n.* activity, excitement, agitation, tumult.

stir (stûr), *v.i. and v.t.* to be in motion, especially to be busy and energetic; to put into motion, as the breeze *stirred* the leaves; arouse, as to *stir* a person to action; to instigate, as to *stir* up trouble.

*stirrup (stir' up), *n.* a footrest hung from the side of a saddle.

stitch (stich), *n.* a single pass of a threaded

needle through material, or of knitting needles or a crochet needle; a style of sewing, knitting or crocheting; a sharp, sudden pain, especially in the side; a small part of one's dress, as she had to change every *stitch* she had on. *v.i. and v.t.* to sew.

stoa (stō' a), *n.* a portico, porch or colonnade, especially in ancient Greek architecture.

stock (stok), *n.* the trunk or stem of a tree or plant; a line of family descent, ancestry; shares in the capital of a company; cattle, live*stock;* an old-fashioned formal necktie; meat juice or extract used as the base for soup; the supply of goods for sale in a store; grip of a gun, a gun*stock;* a common flowering plant. *v.i. and v.t.* to lay in supplies, as to *stock* up; to provide with supplies of goods to be sold, as to *stock* a store. *adj.* kept on hand, as goods in a store, as a *stock* china pattern; frequently used, as that is one of your *stock* arguments.

stockade (stok ād'), *n.* a line of posts or timbers set closely to form a barrier and afford protection. *v.t.* to defend by means of a line of close-set posts.

stocking (stok' ing), *n.* a close-fitting covering for the foot and leg.

stocks (stoks), *n. pl.* an arrangement of boards with openings cut to receive hands or feet in which persons were formerly fastened and exposed to public gaze as a punishment.

stock-still (stok' stil), *adj.* motionless, fixed like a set post.

stocky (stok' i), *adj.* having a short, thick, heavy-set body.

stodgy (stoj' i), *adj.* heavy, indigestible, as *stodgy* food; dull, commonplace, prosaic, as a *stodgy* person.

stogy (stō' gi), *n.* a coarse rough cigar.

stoke (stōk), *v.i. and v.t.* to tend a fire; to furnish with fuel, as to *stoke* a furnace.

stoker (stōk' ẽr), *n.* a fire tender; one who feeds a furnace with fuel; a device to feed a furnace.

stole (stōl), *n.* a long narrow scarf with fringed ends, worn by clergymen.

*stolid (stol' id), *adj.* impassive, expressionless, dull, stupid.

stomach (stum' ak), *n.* the principal organ of digestion. *v.t.* to put up with, endure, as I cannot *stomach* his talk.

stone (stōn), *n.* hard mineral matter, rock; a piece broken off from a rock; the pit or hard seed shell of certain fruits, as a cherry *stone;* a British measure of weight equal to 14 pounds; a gem. *v.t.* to throw pieces of rock at; to remove pits from, as to *stone* peaches; to line with rock, as a well.

stone age (stōn āj), *n.* the period of time preceding the bronze age, characterized by the use of flint and stone implements.

stoned (stōnd), *adj.* slang for drunk from alcohol or under the influence of a drug or narcotic.

stoneware (stōn' wâr), *n.* a coarse kind of glazed pottery.

stony (stōn' i), *adj.* [*comp.* stonier, *superl.* stoniest] rocky, hard; pitiless, as a *stony* silence, a *stony* look.

stool (stōōl), *n.* a seat without a back and often with three legs but sometimes four.

stoop (stōōp), *n.* a forward bend of the upper body, as he walks with a *stoop;* a platform in front of a house door; a drinking vessel.

stoop (stōōp), *v.i.* to bend forward; to lean forward and downward, as to pick something off the ground; to condescend, as I would not *stoop* to do that.

stop (stop), *n.* a halt, pause; a station on a railroad line; an organ pipe; a punctuation mark indicating a pause to be made in reading; end, finish, as at last the lecture came to a *stop. v.i. and v.t.* to cease moving; to cause to cease moving; to prevent passage; to keep from doing, as if you try it, I shall *stop* you.

stopgap (stop' gap), *n.* a temporary expedient.

stopover (stop' ō vẽr), *n.* a pause or stop at an intermediate point in a journey, as a *stopover* in Chicago on the way to the Pacific coast.

*stoppage (stop' ij), *n.* an obstruction.

stopper (stop' ẽr), *n.* a plug or cork preventing flow from a bottle, jug or basin.

stopple (stop' l), *n.* a plug, cork or bung. *v.t.* to close with a plug, cork or bung.

*storage (stōr' ij), *n.* the keeping of goods in safety when not in use; the placing of such goods in a warehouse; the charge for space for such keeping.

*store (stōr), *n.* a collection of goods or articles put away for future use; a shop. *v.t.* to put away for future use; to accumulate, hoard, as to *store* up treasures.

stores (stōrz), *n.* provisions and supplies in large quantities, as aboard a ship, at an army post or camp.

stork (stōrk), *n.* a large wading bird with long legs and a long, pointed bill.

storm (stōrm), *n.* a violent disturbance of the air, with wind, snow, hail or rain; a commotion of any sort; an outburst, as a *storm* of anger, a *storm* of laughter; a violent attack. *v.i. and v.t.* to blow and rain, hail or snow; to rage; to attack with violence, as to *storm* a fortified position.

story (stō' ri), *n.* [*pl.* stories] a tale; a narrative, short or long; a fib; an account of experiences or explanation of something done, as I have heard his *story*, now what is yours? a stage of a building, the distance and space from one floor to another, as the building has three *stories*, each 9 feet high.

stout (stout), *adj.* resolute, as a *stout* heart; strong, as a *stout* string; corpulent, large-bodied; as a *stout* person.

stove (stōv), *n.* a structure (often metal) in which fuel is burned to give heat for cooking or for warming a room, as an electric *stove*, a gas *stove;* a kiln or dryer.

stow (stō), *v.t.* to put away in small space, pack tightly.

stowage (stō' ij), *n.* space for keeping packed things; charge for packing and putting in a safe place.

stowaway (stō' a wā), *n.* one who hides himself aboard a vessel to avoid paying fare.

straddle (strad′ l), *n.* a position with the legs wide apart as if in a saddle; an attempt to favor both sides of a question at once.

straddle (strad′ l), *v.i. and v.t.* to stand or walk with the legs wide apart; to sit astride of; to take both sides of a question.

straggle (strag′ l), *v.i.* to wander apart from a group of which one is supposed to be a part, stray; to spread out, as this vine *straggles.*

*straight** (strāt), *adj.* without a bend or turn, not crooked, direct, as *straight* thinking.

straight (strāt), *adv.* in a direct manner, as go *straight* home.

straighten (strāt′ n), *v.t.* to take the bends and turns out of.

straightforward (strāt fôr′ wêrd), *adj.* undeviating, honest, direct.

straightway (strāt′ wā), *adv.* at once, immediately.

*strain** (strān), *n.* stock, race, breed; a violent effort; a wrench, as a muscle. *n.* a tune or melody, as the *strains* of the national hymn. *v.i. and v.t.* to make violent effort; to wrench, harm by overexertion, as to *strain* a muscle; to filter, as to *strain* a fruit juice.

strainer (strān′ êr), *n.* a sieve through which a liquid may be poured to separate it from solid matter, as a coffee *strainer.*

strait (strāt), *n.* a narrow passage of water connecting two seas: *straits*, poverty, as in dire *straits*. *adj.* narrow, confined, difficult.

straiten (strāt′ n), *v.t.* to make narrow; to confine within close limits; to subject to need.

straitjacket (strāt jak′ et), a canvas coat so made as to hold down the arms of a violently insane, delirious or unruly person.

straitlaced (strāt lāst), *adj.* very strict in manners and morals.

strand (strand), *n.* the shore of a large body of water; one of the twists of a rope; a single lock of hair, a string, as a *strand* of pearls. *v.t. and v.i.* to run aground; to be reduced to a state of financial embarrassment.

strange (strānj), *adj.* not known or met before, unaccountable, surprising.

stranger (strān′ jêr), *n.* a person with whom one is not acquainted.

strangle (strang′ gl), *v.i. and v.t.* to choke; to choke to death, as the murderer *strangled* his victims; to force back, as to *strangle* a cry of despair.

strangulation (strang gū lā′ shun), *n.* the act of choking to death.

strap (strap), *n.* a long narrow piece of leather, especially one with holes and a buckle to hold things together.

strap (strap), *v.t.* to fasten or bind with a long piece of leather or canvas fitted with holes and a buckle; to beat with a long strip of leather; to sharpen, as to *strap* a razor.

strapping (strap′ ing), *adj.* tall and well built, husky.

*stratagem** (strat′ *a* jem), *n.* a trick to deceive an enemy or opponent; a shrewd maneuver.

strategy (strat′ ē ji), *n.* [*pl.* strategies] the science of military movements; use of artifice and sometimes of deceit.

*strategic** (stra tē′ jik), *adj.* showing skilful planning, as a *strategic* move.

stratify (strat′ i fi), *v.i. and v.t.* [*p.t. and p.p.* stratified, *pr.p.* stratifying] to form or be formed into layers.

stratosphere (strā′ tō sfēr), *n.* the highest portion of the atmosphere, almost 7 miles above the earth, where the temperature changes only slightly with altitude.

*stratum** (strā′ tum), *n.* [*pl.* strata] a bed of earth or rock constituting a layer.

straw (strô), *n.* a dried stalk of grain; such stalks collectively.

strawberry (strô′ ber i), *n.* [*pl.* strawberries] a vine with a juicy, red, fruit for which it is widely cultivated.

straw vote (strô vōt′), an informal vote to determine the relative strength of a candidate or the public sentiment on a political issue.

stray (strā), *n.* a lost and wandering person or animal; a homeless waif. *v.i.* to wander from a proper or natural place or way; to deviate from the path of duty. *adj.* wandering, lost; incidental, as a *stray* remark.

*streak** (strēk), *n.* a line of color different from that of its background; a vein, as a *streak* of vanity; a layer, as a *streak* of fat in meat. *v.t.* to mark with stripelike lines.

stream (strēm), *n.* a current of water; anything moving along continuously, as a *stream* of talk, traffic, light, air.

stream (strēm), *v.i.* to flow, move steadily, as talk, traffic, light, air; to wave with the winds, as a banner.

streamer (strēm′ êr), *n.* a long, narrow flag or pennon; a ribbon fastened at one end; a headline running all the way across a newspaper page.

streamline (strēm′ lin), *n.* shape that offers little resistance to the air; path of a fluid. *adj.* planned with curved contours and no sharp angles to offer resistance to air or water, as a *streamline* train.

street (strēt), *n.* a public road in a city or town.

streetcar (strēt′ kär), *n.* a passenger car on a railway in a city.

street railway (strēt rāl′ wā), a system of tracks for trolley cars in a city.

strength (strength), *n.* power, force; intensity, as the *strength* of an acid.

strengthen (streng′ then), *v.i. and v.t.* to increase in power or intensity; to reinforce.

strenuous (stren′ ū us), *adj.* urgent, ardent, zealous; requiring great exertion.

stress (stres), *n.* compulsion, pressure; emphasis; forces exerted against each other by two surfaces in contact, as *stress* and strain in a bridge structure. *v.t.* to emphasize, give importance to, as accuracy cannot be too strongly *stressed* in this work.

stretch (strech), *n.* the act of drawing anything out; anything drawn out, as a long *stretch* of road. *v.i. and v.t.* to reach out; to be elastic, as this material *stretches;* to loosen the muscles, as I must *stretch* my legs; to draw out or extend; to exaggerate, as to *stretch* a story.

stretcher (strech' ẽr), *n.* a litter to carry injured persons or dead bodies upon; a device for extending something in a desired shape, as a sweater *stretcher*.

*****strew** (strōō), *v.t.* to spread by scattering, as seeds.

stricken (strĭk' en), *adj.* afflicted, as with illness; incapacitated, wounded.

strict (strĭkt), *adj.* severe, exacting, as a *strict* law, a *strict* teacher; exact, as a *strict* translation.

stricture (strĭk' tūr), *n.* censure; contraction of a tube or channel in the body, as an intestine.

stride (strīd), *n.* a long step; the length of such a step. *v.i. and v.t.* [*p.t. and p.p.* strode, *pr.p.* striding] to take long steps.

strident (strī' dent) *adj.* harsh, shrill, grating, as a *strident* voice.

strife (strīf), *n.* struggle, conflict, discord.

strike (strīk), *n.* the act of hitting; stoppage of work by employees; discovery of a deposit of ore; unexpected good fortune or success. *v.i. and v.t.* [*p.t. and p.p.* struck, *pr.p.* striking] to hit; to cease working in order to bring an employer to terms; to discover, as a vein of ore; to lower, as a flag in token of surrender; to indicate by sound, as a clock *strikes* the hour; to cause to ignite, as to *strike* a match; to assume, as to *strike* a pose; to arrive at, as to *strike* a bargain

strikebreaker (strīk' brāk ẽr), *n.* a person employed to substitute for a striking workman.

striking (strīk' ing), *adj.* impressive, remarkable.

string (string), *n.* a small cord or thick thread; a series of connected things, as a *string* of troubles; a group of things held by a cord, as a *string* of beads; the thread of a pod, as the string of *string* beans; a tightly stretched cord of catgut or a wire used for certain musical instruments, as the guitar, mandolin. *v.t. and v.i.* [*p.t. and p.p.* strung, *pr.p.* stringing] to put on a cord or thread, as to *string* beads; to remove the long tough fiber from a pod, as to *string* beans; to fit with cords, as to *string* a tennis racket; to form a loose line, as the cars *string* out over a mile.

stringed (stringd), *adj.* equipped with strings, as a *stringed* instrument.

stringent (strin' jent), *adj.* strict, severe, rigidly enforced, binding.

stringy (string' i), *adj.* [*comp.* stringier, *superl.* stringiest] fibrous; having many hard fibers, as *stringy* meat; lifeless and noncurling, as my hair is *stringy*; viscid.

strip (strip), *n.* a long, narrow piece, as a *strip* of cloth, wood or metal, a *strip* of road or river. *v.i. and v.t.* to come off in long pieces; to undress; to take the covering from, as a hide from a carcass; to deprive of, take away, as the depression *stripped* him of every dollar; to milk dry, as to *strip* a cow.

stripe (strīp), *n.* a long, narrow band of color on a background of different color; a long

narrow streak; a welt on the skin caused by a stroke with a whiplash; a color, kind or sort, as persons of that *stripe*. *v.t.* to mark with lines or bands of different colors.

stripling (strip' ling), *n.* a youth, a boy.

strive (strīv), *v.i.* to try hard; to struggle, as to *strive* for success, *strive* to win a race.

stroke (strōk), *n.* a blow; one of a series of movements, as the *stroke* of oars; an effort, action, as a bold *stroke* for freedom; anything happening suddenly and unexpectedly, as a *stroke* of luck, a paralytic *stroke;* the sounding of the hour by a clock, as on the *stroke* of midnight; the oarsman farthest aft in a racing shell.

stroll (strōl), *n.* a leisurely ramble for pleasure. *v.i.* to wander afoot in leisurely manner and for pleasure.

*****strong** (strông), *adj.* having physical power, muscular, full of vigor, as a *strong* fighter; forceful, as *strong* words; alcoholic, as *strong* drink; firm, as a *strong* foundation for a building or a belief; intense in degree or quality, as a *strong* mixture.

stronghold (strông' hōld), *n.* a fortress, a well-defended place of safety.

strop (strop), *n.* a strip of leather upon which to sharpen a razor. *v.t.* to sharpen on a leather strip; to strap, as a razor.

*****strophe** (strō' fē), *n.* the part of a choral dance in ancient Greek stage art in which the dancers move in a body to one side; the music played and sung during this movement; a stanza, verse.

*****structure** (struk' tūr), *n.* a building; a union of parts, as in a machine; the manner in which a machine or a body is put together.

struggle (strug' l), *n.* a violent effort; a contest. *v.i.* to try hard, strive; to contend.

strum (strum), *v.i. and v.t.* to play on a stringed instrument noisily and without expression.

strut (strut), *n.* an affected step or walk.

strut (strut), *v.i.* to walk in a manner indicating conceit or affectation.

*****strychnine** (strĭk' nin), *n.* a poisonous alkaloid extracted from nux vomica, used in medicine to stimulate the heart and nerves.

stub (stub), *n.* a tree stump; any short piece left after main part has been removed, as the *stubs* in a checkbook; a pen point that is short and blunt. *v.t.* to strike, as the toes, against some projecting object underfoot.

stubble (stub' l), *n.* the short pieces of stalk left in a field after grain or heavy grass has been cut; a short, rough growth of beard.

stubborn (stub' ẽrn), *adj.* obstinate, unyielding; hard to treat, as a *stubborn* case.

stucco (stuk' ō), *n.* [*pl.* stuccos or stuccoes] fine plaster in walls inside a building; coarser plaster as an outside covering for the walls of a house. *v.t.* [*p.t. and p.p.* stuccoed, *pr.p.* stuccoing] to use a certain kind of plaster for decorating walls or as an outer coat for a house.

stud (stud), *n.* a large-headed ornamental nail; an upright timber in a building, to which laths are nailed; a removable ornamental button, as a shirt *stud*. *n.* a group of horses kept for breeding. *v.t.* to adorn with close-set knobs or ornamental points, as stars *stud* the sky.

studding (stud' ing). *n.* joists for use in the walls of houses.

*student (stū' dent), *n.* a pupil in school; a member of a college body; one seeking knowledge, a scholar.

studied (stud' id), *adj.* carefully thought out, as a *studied* compliment.

studio (stū' di ō), *n.* a room in which an artist works; a place where motion pictures are filmed; a room having the mechanical equipment for radio broadcasting.

*studious (stū' di us), *adj.* devoted to the acquisition of knowledge.

*study (stud' i), *n.* [*pl.* studies] the act of using the mind to acquire knowledge; a branch of learning; close examination into a particular subject, as a *study* of school management; a room set apart and furnished for reading, writing and thinking; a sketch for a picture to be painted; a piece of music designed to give practice in some special field or phase; a memorizer of a theatrical part, as this actor is a very quick *study*. *v.i. and v.t.* to apply the mind in quest of knowledge; to investigate closely, as to *study* labor conditions; to think upon closely, as to *study* a situation.

stuff (stuf), *n.* materials out of which things are made; the fundamental quality, as you have the *stuff* of a martyr; rubbish.

stuffing (stuf' ing), *n.* the material used to fill anything; a highly seasoned filling for a roast or other dish.

stuffy (stuf' i), *adj.* [*comp.* stuffier, *superl.* stuffiest] close, poorly ventilated; choked up, having the nasal passage closed, as from a head cold.

stultify (stul' ti fī), *v.t.* [*p.t. and p.p.* stultified, *pr.p.* stultifying] to cause to appear foolish or absurd.

stumble (stum' bl), *n.* a tripping as one walks or runs; a blunder. *v.i.* to trip on something when walking or running; to blunder; to find unexpectedly, as to *stumble* upon the answer.

stump (stump), *n.* the part of a tree or shrub left after the trunk is cut down; anything resembling it or compared to it, as the *stump* of a pencil, of an amputated limb or a tail; a political platform. *v.i. and v.t.* to clump the feet in walking; to travel about making speeches, as in a political campaign; to lop off, to hinder and perplex, as this problem *stumps* me.

stun (stun), *v.t.* to render senseless by a blow; to make numb with shock, as the news *stuns* us.

stunt (stunt), *n.* a notable feat of strength, skill or daring. *v.i.* to perform spectacular feats of strength, skill or great daring. *v.t.* to check the growth of, prevent development, dwarf.

stupefaction (stū pē fak' shun), *n.* insensibility, the state of being stunned.

stupefy (stū' pē fī), *v.t.* [*p.t. and p.p.* stupe-

fied, *pr.p.* stupefying] to deprive of sensibility; to knock, shock or drug into a state of unconsciousness or complete stupidity.

*stupendous (stū pen' dus), *adj.* so vast as to benumb the senses of one who beholds; of extraordinary size or degree, completely amazing.

*stupid (stū' pid), *adj.* deficient in perception and understanding; dull-witted; tiresome, as a *stupid* lecture.

stupidity (stū pid' i ti), [*n. pl.* stupidities] extreme dullness of perception or understanding, slowness of mind.

stupor (stū' pẽr), *n.* mental numbness; lethargy; inactivity of the senses.

sturdy (stûr' di), [*adj. comp.* sturdier, *superl.* sturdiest] hardy, robust, strong, vigorous; resolute.

*sturgeon (stûr' jun), *n.* a large food fish of northern waters having air bladders from which isinglass is made and producing a roe from which caviar is prepared.

stutter (stut' ẽr), *n.* hesitation in speech, with repetition of a part of a word. *v.i.* to speak with hesitation, repeating a single part of a word.

sty (stī), *n.* [*pl.* sties] a pigpen. small swelling on edge of an eyelid with inflammation.

style (stīl), *n.* manner of doing; manner of expressing thought; fashion; the marker of a sundial; the stemlike part of a flower bearing the stigma; a title, descriptive form of address. *v.t.* to make fashionable; to address or name with a descriptive title of courtesy.

stylish (stīl' ish), *adj.* fashionable.

stylist (stīl' ist), *n.* one who is a master of method in art; one who advises on matters of dress.

stylus (stī' lus), *n.* a sharp-pointed writing instrument used for making carbon copies, for recording sounds or for reproducing sounds.

stymie (stī' mi), *n.* a situation in golf when the ball nearer the hole on the putting green lies in the direct line of play of the other ball which is about to be played.

styptic (stip' tik), *n.* a substance which when applied to a cut stops its bleeding.

suasion (swā' zhun), *n.* persuasion; the act of convincing, as moral *suasion*.

*suave (swäv), *adj.* smooth in manner, pleasingly polite.

*suavity (swäv' i ti), *n.* [*pl.* suavities] smoothness of manner, politeness.

subacid (sub as' id), *adj.* slightly tart.

*subaltern (sub ôl tẽrn), *n.* a commissioned officer in the army below a captain in rank; a subordinate.

subconscious (sub kon' shus), *adj.* pertaining to the mental activity that goes on beneath the surface of conscious thought.

*subdue (sub dū'), *v.t.* to overcome or conquer; to tone down; to tame.

*subject (sub' jekt), *n.* one under the rule of another; a person or thing studied or treated in some particular way, as the *subject* of an essay, a picture or study; the part of a sentence about which a statement is made.

adj. under the rule of another; liable, as he is *subject* to delusions; dependent upon, as our decision is *subject* to your wishes.

*subject (sub jekt'), v.t. to bring under control, tame, subdue, expose to action.

subjection (sub jek' shun), *n.* the act of subduing; state of being a subject.

subjective (sub jek' tiv), *adj.* relating to the person who is thinking, saying or doing something rather than to the object considered.

subjugate (sub' joo gāt), *v.t.* to subdue completely, bring under dominion, enslave.

subjunctive (sub jungk' tiv), *n.* a verb in the mood expressing doubt or possibility. *adj.* expressing doubt, possibility or the state of being conditional.

sublimate (sub' li māt), *n.* a solid deposit produced by condensing a vapor formed by heating a solid. *v.t.* to convert a solid into vapor by heating and then condense the vapor into another solid; to refine; to divert the energy of, as a natural impulse, to a more worth-while channel.

sublime (sub līm'), *n.* that which is exalted, majestic or solemn. *adj.* exalted, majestic, solemnly grand.

sublimity (sub lim' i ti), *n.* [*pl.* sublimities] grandeur, solemnity, exalted state or style.

submarine (sub' ma rēn), *n.* a boat that can be propelled under water.

submarine (sub ma rēn'), *adj.* existing or operating below the surface of the sea.

submerge (sub mûrj), *v.i. and v.t.* to go below the surface, as a submarine; to place completely under water.

submission (sub mish' un), *n.* the act of yielding; obedience to the will of another.

submit (sub mit'), *v.i. and v.t.* to surrender; to yield to the authority or will of another; to present for judgment or decision by another.

subordinate (su bôr' di nit), *n.* one of lesser rank. *adj.* having lower rank or importance; subject to another's will or authority.

subordinate (su bôr' di nāt), *v.t.* to assign to a lesser rank or lower position; to make second to something else in importance.

suborn (sub ôrn'), *v.t.* to induce to commit perjury, to hire or persuade to swear falsely.

subornation (sub ôr nā' shun), *n.* the act of inducing a person to swear falsely in court.

*subpoena (su pē' na), n. a court order for appearance at a named time and place with a penalty for disobedience.

*subpoena (su pē' na), v.t. to serve or summon with an order to appear in court with a penalty for disobedience.

subscribe (sub skrīb'), *v.t. and v.i.* to sign one's name to; to agree to take a magazine or newspaper regularly; to pledge a contribution, to contribute; to approve formally.

subscription (sub skrip' shun), *n.* the affixing of a signature; a contribution or the pledge of a contribution; an order for regular delivery of a magazine or newspaper.

subsequent (sub' sē kwent), *adj.* later, following, coming after, either in time or order.

subserve (sub sûrv'), *v.t.* to advance an inter-

est, contribute to a result, help in carrying out a purpose.

subservient (sub sûr vi ent), *adj.* acting in the interest of another; servile.

*subside (sub sīd'), v.i. to sink to a lower level; to quiet down, as the storm *subsided.*

*subsidence (sub sīd' ens), n. the act of sinking or quieting down.

*subsidiary (sub sid' i er i), n. [pl. subsidiaries] an auxiliary, an organization maintained by another, as the *subsidiaries* of a large corporation. *adj.* auxiliary, assisting, under higher authority.

subsidize (sub' si dīz), *v.t.* to support or assist with a fixed schedule of financial aid, as governments *subsidize* private ships for mail carriage.

subsidy (sub' si di), *n.* [*pl.* subsidies] a grant of public money to assist private operators in serving the public; any financial help given by one individual to another.

*subsist (sub sist'), v.i. to be maintained, to live, to continue.

subsistence (sub sis' tens), *n.* means of supporting life, maintenance.

substance (sub' stans), *n.* matter or material; the essential part, as the *substance* of an argument.

*substantial (sub stan' shal), adj. consisting of matter, essential; actual; solid; responsible, as a *substantial* citizen; considerable, as a *substantial* gift.

*substantiate (sub stan' shi āt), v.t. to establish the truth of, with evidence; to confirm, verify.

substantive (sub' stan tiv), *n.* a noun or a phrase or clause used as a noun. *adj.* essential, real, lasting.

substitute (sub' sti tūt), *n.* a person or thing taking the place of another; a person serving for another; a thing used instead of another. *v.i. and v.t.* to take the place of another; to use instead of something else.

substitute (sub' sti tūt), *adj.* taking the place of another person or thing.

substratum (sub strā' tum), *n.* a layer beneath the surface, as of soil or rock, a foundation.

subterfuge (sub' tēr fūj), *n.* an evasion or artifice, pretense to conceal a real motive.

subterranean (sub te rā' ne an), *adj.* below the surface of the earth.

*subtile (sub' til or sut' l), adj. subtle in the different senses of that word.

subtitle (sub tī' tl), *n.* a subhead or secondary title; the name of a book repeated on a page after the title page; a short explanation of a coming scene on a motion-picture screen.

*subtle (sut' l), adj. artful, crafty, wily, sly, as a *subtle* opponent; delicate, elusive, as a *subtle* perfume; ingenious, as a *subtle* argument.

subtlety (sut' l ti), *n.* mental keenness; craftiness; elusive delicacy.

subtract (sub trakt'), *v.i. and v.t.* to perform the operation of lessening by a set amount; to take away from, deduct.

subtrahend (sub' tra hend), *n.* the quantity to be taken from another quantity in the process of subtraction.

*suburb (sub' ûrb), *n.* a town or district adjacent to a city of which it may or may not be a part.

suburban (sub ûr' ban), *adj.* living in or pertaining to the outlying residential districts of a city.

subvention (sub ven' shun), *n.* a government grant or subsidy.

subversion (sub vûr' shun), *n.* overthrow, ruin.

subvert (sub vûrt'), *v.t.* to turn upside down, overthrow, destroy.

subway (sub' wā), *n.* an underground passage; a tunnel beneath the surface of a city street with an electric railway running through it; the railway in such a tunnel.

succeed (suk sēd'), *v.i. and v.t.* to follow, be next in order; to get what one wants and strives for; to prosper in business; to follow after, as he *succeeded* his father; to follow immediately after in time, as Tuesday *succeeds* Monday.

success (suk ses'), *n.* accomplishment of a purpose; one who has prospered or won high standing, as he is a *success* in life.

successful (suk ses' fool), *adj.* prosperous; achieving what was desired.

succession (suk sesh' un), *n.* the act of following in order; a number of things in a series, as a *succession* of severe winters; the act of coming into an inheritance.

successive (suk ses' iv), *adj.* occurring in order, consecutive.

*successor (suk ses' ẽr), *n.* one who follows in the place of another.

*succinct (suk singkt'), *adj.* tersely expressed, concise.

succor (suk' ẽr), *n.* help, relief, assistance. *v.t.* to go to the relief or assistance of.

succotash (suk' ō tash), *n.* green corn and beans boiled together.

succulent (suk' ū lent), *adj.* juicy, having watery tissues, as a plant; not dry or dull, as a *succulent* discourse.

succumb (su kum'), *v.i.* to yield to a greater force; to die.

such (such), *pron.* that kind of a person or thing; those who, as *such* as wish to may come. *adj.* of that kind, as *such* questions should be more widely discussed; of the same class, as *such* composers as Mozart and Chopin.

suck (suk), *n.* the act of drawing into the mouth, as give me a *suck* of that lollypop; act of drawing in, as that pump has a strong *suck.* *v.i. and v.t.* to draw milk from the mother's breast; to absorb, as this paper *sucks* ink; to draw into the mouth, as to *suck* a stick of candy.

suckle (suk' l), *v.i. and v.t.* to nurse at the breast; to bring up, rear, foster.

suckling (suk' ling), *n.* an unweaned child or animal.

suction (suk' shun), *n.* the act or power of drawing up liquid.

sudden (sud' n), *adj.* happening unexpectedly, hasty, abrupt, as a *sudden* decision.

suds (sudz), *n. pl.* soapy water, with bubbles on it or in a lathery state.

sue (sū), *v.t. and v.t.* to go to law; to plead, start legal proceedings against, as to *sue* a person for libel.

suède (swãd), *n.* a soft kidskin used with the napped flesh side out, for gloves, shoes, purses and similar articles; a cloth with a similar soft surface.

suet (sū' et), *n.* the hard fat that accumulates around the kidneys and loins of sheep, beef cattle and hogs and from which tallow or leaf lard is rendered.

suffer (suf' ẽr), *v.i. and v.t.* to have pain or distress, as he *suffered* greatly; to undergo, as to *suffer* a change; to permit, as *suffer* little children to come unto me.

sufferance (suf' ẽr ans), *n.* toleration, acceptance without having given direct permission, as we are here by *sufferance* of the authorities.

*suffice (su fis'), *v.i. and v.t.* to be enough; to satisfy the need.

sufficiency (su fish' en si), *n.* adequacy, competency, as means; plenty, as I have a *sufficiency* for the present.

sufficient (su fish' ent), *adj.* enough, adequate, satisfying present needs.

suffix (suf' iks), *n.* a letter or syllable added at the end of a word to indicate a shade of meaning. *v.t.* to add at the end to form a new word.

suffocate (suf' ō kāt), *v.i. and v.t.* to be choked; to perish for want of air; to stifle, smother.

suffrage (suf' rij), *n.* the right to vote, electoral franchise.

suffragette (suf ra jet'), *n.* a woman who advocated and agitated for women's right to vote before that right was granted.

*suffuse (su fūz'), *v.t.* to overspread with color, as glorious tints of sunset *suffused* the evening sky, or with mist or liquid, as eyes *suffused* with tears.

sugar (shoog' ẽr), *n.* a sweet crystalline substance chiefly obtained from sugar cane, sugar beets and maple sap. *v.t. and v.i.* to form sweet crystals, as the juice is *sugaring* fast.

*suggest (su jest'), *v.t.* to intimate; to bring up, as an idea, through mention of something connected or related to it; to propose, as to *suggest* a plan.

*suggestion (su jes' chun), *n.* a hint; that which brings one thing to mind by referring to another somehow connected with it; that which is offered for consideration.

suicidal (sū i sī' dal), *adj.* pertaining to the taking of one's life; fatal to one's own interests or welfare.

*suicide (sū' i sīd), *n.* self-destruction; one who kills himself.

*suit (sūt), *n.* a group or series of things of the same kind or used together, as a *suit* of clothes, a *suit* of playing cards; a legal action for remedy of a wrong; a courtship.

suitable (sūt' a bl), *adj.* fitting, appropriate.

suitcase (sūt' kās), *n.* a flat handbag to carry clothing.

suite (swēt), *n.* a retinue of attendants, as the monarch and his *suite;* a group of rooms, as in a hotel; a set of furniture.

suitor (sū' tẽr), *n.* one who entreats, especially

one who woos a woman.

sulk (sulk), *v.i.* to be sullen, moody and silent.

sulky (sul' ki), *n.* [*pl.* sulkies] a light vehicle with two wheels and a seat for only one person and drawn by one horse, used in trotting races. *adj.* [*comp.* sulkier, *superl.* sulkiest] silently sullen.

sullen (sul' en), *adj.* morose, ill-tempered in a quiet, gloomy way; somber, as *sullen* skies.

sully (sul' i), *v.t.* [*p.t. and p.p.* sullied, *pr.p.* sullying] to tarnish or soil; to stain.

sulphur (sul' fẽr), *n.* a nonmetallic element, brittle, yellow in color and burning with suffocating fumes: also spelled *sulfur*.

sulphurate (sul fū' rāt), *v.t.* to combine with sulphur or subject to its action.

sulphureted (sul' fū ret ed), *adj.* having sulphur in its composition, as *sulphureted* hydrogen.

sulphuric (sul fū' rik), *adj.* obtained from sulphur or containing it.

sulphurous (sul fū' rus), *adj.* containing or resembling sulphur; fiery, blasphemous, as *sulphurous* speech.

*****sultan** (sul ' tan), *n.* a Mohammedan ruler, especially the ruler of Turkey before World War I.

sultry (sul' tri), *adj.* [*comp.* sultrier, *superl.* sultriest] hot, close and oppressive; heavy with moist heat, as a *sultry* day.

sum (sum), *n.* the whole, a total; an indefinite amount, as of money; the number obtained by adding.

*****sumac** (shoo' mak), *n.* a shrub having heavy, solid clusters of small flowers that turn into berries, and of which some varieties are used in tanning and dyeing.

summarize (sum' a riz), *v.t.* to state concisely, sum up.

summary (sum' a ri), *n.* [*pl.* summaries] a briefer form of a document or composition presenting its principal features in small space. *adj.* concise; immediate, taking effect without delay, as a *summary* discharge from a position.

summation (sum ā' shun), *n.* the act of forming a total; review of the arguments in a case in court.

summer (sum' ẽr), *n.* the part of the year between spring and autumn; the hottest months, as from mid-June to the middle of September.

summit (sum' it), *n.* the peak or highest point, as the *summit* of a mountain or a career.

summon (sum' un), *v.t.* to order or invite to appear, send for; to call into action.

summons (sum' unz), *n.* [*pl.* summonses] an order to appear in court.

*****sumptuary** (sump' tū er i), *adj.* pertaining to expense; regulating expenses, as *sumptuary* laws were passed to suppress luxurious living.

*****sumptuous** (sump' tū us), *adj.* expensive, luxurious, magnificent.

sun (sun), *n.* the light-giving body around which the earth and other planets revolve; sunshine. *v.t.* to bask in the open light of day; to expose to the rays of the sun.

suncup (sun' kup), *n.* a variety of evening primrose bearing yellow flowers, found in California.

sunder (sun' dẽr), *v.t.* to part, sever, rend.

sundial (sun' dī al), *n.* a device that indicates the time of day by means of a shadow cast upon a dial by a pointer or style.

sundown (sun' doun), *n.* the time of day when the sun appears to descend below the horizon.

sundries (sun' driz), *n. pl.* items not specified individually in a statement.

sundry (sun' dri), *adj.* various, several.

sunken (sungk' en), *adj.* deeply depressed, as *sunken* eyes; on the bottom or under the water; on a lower level of ground, as *sunken* gardens.

sunny (sun' i), *adj.* [*comp.* sunnier, *superl.* sunniest] bright, warm, cheerful.

sunshine (sun' shīn), *n.* daylight.

sunstroke (sun' strōk), *n.* prostration caused by direct exposure to the rays of the sun.

sunup (sun' up), *n.* sunrise, the time the sun comes up.

sup (sup), *v.i. and v.t.* to have a light evening meal; to sip, take a fluid into the mouth a small amount at a time.

superannuated (su pẽr an' ū āt ed), *adj.* too old to work.

superb (sū pũrb'), *adj.* grand, stately, magnificent.

supercomputer (sōo ' per com pūt ' er), *n.* a large computer made of hundreds of tiny computer chips all wired together.

superficial (sū pẽr fish' al), *adj.* on the surface, not deep, not profound.

*****superfluous** (sū pũr' flū us), *adj.* more than enough, being more than is needed.

superhuman (sū pẽr hū' man), *adj.* beyond ordinary human power or capacity, as a *superhuman* task.

superintend (sū pẽr in tend'), *v.t.* to oversee, direct, have charge of.

superintendent (sū pẽr in ten' dent), *n.* an overseer; one directing and in charge.

superior (sū pẽr' i er), *n.* one of higher rank or greater excellence. *adj.* higher in station or rank; more excellent.

superlative (sū pũr' la tiv), *n.* something of the highest degree of excellence; a word indicating such a quality; the highest degree of comparison in adjectives and adverbs.

supernal (sū pũr' nal), *adj.* celestial, heavenly.

supernatural (sū pẽr nat' ū ral), *adj.* beyond the laws of nature; not governed or explained by mere physical laws; miraculous.

supernumerary (sū pẽr nū' mẽr er i), *n.* [*pl.* supernumeraries] a person or thing beyond the required or customary number; an actor without a speaking part in a play.

superscription (sū pẽr skrip' shun), *n.* the address on a letter; writing or engraving on the outside or top of anything.

supersede (sū pẽr sēd'), *v.t.* to take the place of.

*****superstition** (sū pẽr stish' un), *n.* belief in supernatural things; reverence founded on fear; belief in omens and signs.

superstructure (sū' pẽr struk tūr), *n.* anything built or founded on something else; the part of a building above the foundation; part of a ship above the main deck.

supervene (sū pĕr vēn'), *v.i.* to come as something extra; to follow closely after.

supervise (sū' pĕr vīz), *v.t.* to oversee and direct.

supervisor (sū' pĕr vī zĕr), *n.* an overseer or superintendent.

supervisory (sū pĕr vī' zō rī), *adj.* serving in the capacity of an overseer or superintendent.

supine (sū' pīn), *adj.* lying on the back; indifferent, careless.

supper (sup' ĕr), *n.* the evening meal.

supplant (su plănt'), *v.t.* to displace, supersede.

supple (sup' l), *adj.* flexible, pliant, lithe; yielding; compliant.

supplement (sup' lē ment), *n.* something added; an additional or extra section, as a newspaper *supplement*. *v.t.* to add to; to make more complete by an additional part.

suppliant (sup' lī ant), *n.* one who supplicates, one who seeks humbly. *adj.* humbly beseeching, entreating.

supplicate (sup' lī kāt), *v.i. and v.t.* to ask humbly and earnestly; to beg for.

supplication (sup lī kā' shun), *n.* humble and earnest entreaty or prayer.

supply (su plī'), *n.* [*pl.* supplies] the amount on hand of anything that is or may be needed. *v.t.* [*p.t. and p.p.* supplied, *pr.p.* supplying] to furnish with needed things; to provide.

support (su pōrt'), *n.* that which sustains.

support (su pōrt'), *v.t.* to sustain, bear up; to endure; to uphold; to provide for.

*****suppose** (su pōz'), *v.i. and v.t.* to imagine; to believe without proof; to accept as true for purposes of reasoning.

*****supposition** (sup ō zish' un), *n.* an assumption; a hypothesis.

*****supposititious** (su poz ī tish' us), *adj.* assumed, conjectural; false; pretended.

suppress (su pres'), *v.t.* to subdue, quell, keep down; to withhold from publication; to keep from giving expression to, as to *suppress* a smile.

suppurate (sup' ū rāt), *v.i.* to form pus.

suppurative (sup' ū rā tiv), *adj.* tending to form pus, as a *suppurative* wound.

supremacy (sū prem' a sī), *n.* the state of being over all, in quality or authority; the highest excellence.

supreme (sū prēm'), *adj.* highest in authority or power; most excellent; highest in degree, as *supreme* daring.

surcharge (sur' charj), *n.* an overcharge; collection of more than is right; an additional printing on the face of a stamp, changing the price or value; a stamp thus overprinted.

surcingle (sûr' sing gl), *n.* a girth in a horse's harness.

*****sure** (shoor), *adj.* fit to be depended upon, certain, reliable, unfailing; confident, having no doubt. *adv.* undoubtedly.

surety (shoor' tī), *n.* [*pl.* sureties] one who guarantees payment of another's obligation;

something put up as a pledge to cover a future payment; assurance, certainty.

surf (sûrf), *n.* the waves of the sea breaking along the shore with roar and foam.

surface (sûr' fīs), *n.* the outer face of a solid body; the level of a body of water. *adj.* pertaining to outer face of anything; superficial, false, as *surface* feelings.

surfeit (sûr' fīt), *n.* excess, especially in eating or drinking.

surfeit (sûr' fīt), *v.i. and v.t.* to overeat, overindulge; to overfeed, satiate, cloy.

surge (sûrj), *n.* a billow; a great roll of anything resembling a billow, as a *surge* of emotion, a *surge* of popular resentment.

surge (sûrj), *v.i.* to rise high; to advance in volume, as the crowd *surged* forward.

surgeon (sûr' jun), *n.* a doctor who performs operations.

surgery (sûr' jēr ī), *n.* [*pl.* surgeries] the act and art of treating wounds or internal diseases by means of operations.

surly (sûr' lī), *adj.* [*comp.* surlier, *superl.* surliest] ill-humored, rudely cross, morose.

surmise (sûr mīz'), *n.* a conjecture, suspicion; an opinion with little evidence supporting it. *v.t.* to guess, conjecture; to assume on small evidence.

surmount (sûr mount'), *v.t.* to rise above, overcome, conquer.

*****surname** (sûr' nām), *n.* a family name, last name.

surpass (sēr pås'), *v.t.* to exceed; to excel.

surplice (sûr' plis), *n.* a loose, linen vestment worn by the clergy and choir singers.

surplus (sûr' plus), *n.* [*pl.* surpluses] an excess over requirement. *adj.* exceeding requirements, extra.

*****surprise** (sēr priz'), *n.* something that happens unexpectedly; the state of being taken unaware.

surprise (sûr priz'), *v.t.* to take unaware; to astonish with something unexpected.

surrender (su ren' dĕr), *n.* the act of yielding; act of giving something up, under pressure; submission to superior force.

surrender (su ren' dĕr), *v.i. and v.t.* to yield, give up under pressure or superior force; to relinquish possession of.

surreptitious (sûr ep tish' us), *adj.* done by secret means, stealthy.

surrogate (sûr' ō gāt), *n.* a substitute; a bishop's deputy; a county officer having charge of the proving of wills; a probate judge.

surround (su round'), *v.t.* to inclose on all sides, encompass.

surroundings (su round' ingz), *n.* the influences, circumstances and conditions that go to make up environment.

surtax (sûr' taks), *n.* a tax in addition to a normal tax.

*****surtout** (sûr tōot'), *n.* a wide-skirted coat reaching below the knees.

*****surveillance** (sûr vāl' ans), *n.* the act of watching; state of being watched.

*****survey** (sûr' vā), *n.* a determination of area and boundaries; a study and report, as a health *survey*.

*survey (sẽr vā'), *v.t.* to ascertain the exact area and boundaries of; to study some particular aspect of.

surveyor (sẽr vā' ẽr), *n.* one whose business it is to calculate areas and locate boundary lines.

survival (sẽr vīv' al), *n.* continuance, the act of outliving another; act of outlasting; anything that comes down from earlier times.

survive (sẽr vīv'), *v.i. and v.t.* to continue living after others die; to live through, as to *survive* a battle.

survivor (sẽr vīv' ẽr), *n.* one who outlives another; one who escapes with his life.

*susceptible (su sep' ti bl), *adj.* easily acted upon; impressible; sensitive or subject to, as *susceptible* to colds, *susceptible* to flattery; capable of, as *susceptible* of proof.

sushi (sū' shē), *n.* a Japanese dish made of raw fish.

suspect (sus' pekt), *n.* a person thought to be guilty.

suspect (sus pekt'), *v.t.* to believe guilty; to imagine to exist; to distrust.

suspend (sus pend'), *v.t.* to hang, as to *suspend* something from a beam; interrupt or postpone, as to *suspend* operations, *suspend* a business, *suspend* judgment.

suspense (sus pens'), *n.* a state of uncertainty as to what is going to happen; eager expectancy.

suspension (sus pen' shun), *n.* a withholding of judgment or decision; temporary dismissal, as *suspension* from school; a temporary cessation of operation.

suspicion (sus pish' un), *n.* a belief with little or no supporting evidence; a very small amount of something; an inkling; mistrust, doubt.

suspicious (sus pish' us), *adj.* subject to question; having doubt.

sustain (sus tān'), *v.t.* to hold up or support; to endure; to prove, as to *sustain* an accusation; to maintain, as to *sustain* a conversation; to suffer, as to *sustain* an injury.

sustenance (sus' tē nans), *n.* that which supports life, food.

*suture (sū' tūr), *n.* the drawing together of the edges of a wound by sewing; the union or articulation of the bones in the skull.

*swab (swob), *n.* a mop for cleaning floors or decks; a small piece of cotton or cloth used in applying medicine to the mouth or throat and in washing wounds and sores.

swab (swob), *v.t.* to clean with a heavy mop; to wash or apply medicine to.

swagger (swag' ẽr), *n.* a strutting, arrogant way of walking; noisy boasting. *v.i.* to strut with an insolent air; to brag and boast.

swain (swān), *n.* a country boy; a lover.

swallow (swol' ō), *n.* the act of taking one mouthful of food or drink into the stomach; the mouthful thus acted upon. *n.* a small migratory bird with short bill, long wings and forked tail. *v.t.* to take food down the throat into the stomach; to make invisible, as the darkness *swallowed* him; to accept readily, as to *swallow* a story; to accept an

insult without action.

*swamp (swomp), *n.* an area of wet or boggy land. *v.t. and v.i.* to sink by filling with water, as a huge wave *swamped* the boat; to overwhelm, ruin; to become submerged.

*swan (swon), *n.* a web-footed bird with a very long, curved neck.

swan's-down (swonz' doun), *n.* the soft feathers of the swan, used in trimming and for powder puffs.

*swap (swop), *n.* a trade, a bargain. *v.i. and v.t.* to trade, give one thing for another, barter.

*sward (swôrd), *n.* a stretch of thick turf.

*swarm (swôrm), *n.* a crowd or multitude in motion; colony of bees. *v.i. and v.t.* to gather in great numbers; to move about in throngs; to contain a throng of people moving about, as the city *swarms* with sightseers; to fly from one hive to another, as the bees *swarmed* today; to throng, as people *swarmed* upon the beaches.

*swarthy (swôr' thi), *adj.* [*comp.* swarthier, *superl.* swarthiest] dark-hued, dark-skinned.

swash (swosh), *n.* a splashing of water against something; a narrow channel of water between a sandbank and the shore; a bar over which the waves dash and splash. *v.i. and v.t.* to dash and splash, as waves over a bar.

swashbuckler (swosh' buk lẽr), *n.* a swaggering, boasting soldier.

*swastika (swas' ti ka), *n.* an ancient religious symbol resembling a plus sign with each point marking a right angle made by an added short, straight line used as the emblem of the Nazi party in Germany.

swat (swot), *v.t.* to hit violently, crush, as to *swat* a fly.

swatch (swoch), *n.* a sample of cloth or leather.

*swath (swôth), *n.* the space cut by a mowing machine or scythe in one course; the path of mown grass or grain left by the mower.

*swathe (swāth), *v.t.* to bind with a long strip of cloth; to wrap, as she *swathed* herself in furs.

sway (swā), *n.* a swinging motion, as the *sway* of a tree in wind; governing power; rule, dominance. *v.i. and v.t.* to swing from side to side; to cause to incline; to influence in judgment, as the speaker *swayed* his audience; to dominate.

swaybacked (swā' bakt), *adj.* having a back that sags, as a horse.

*swear (swâr), *v.i. and v.t.* [*p.t.* swore, *p.p.* sworn, *pr.p.* swearing] to take an oath; to make a solemn promise; to declare on oath; to speak profanely.

sweat (swet), *n.* the moisture that exudes from the pores of the skin, perspiration; any gathering of moisture in tiny drops on a surface. *v.i. and v.t.* to exude moisture in small drops, perspire; to cause to perspire, as it would be good to *sweat* that horse a little; to overwork, as in a sweat-shop.

sweater (swet' ẽr), *n.* a knitted or crocheted jacket.

sweep (swēp), *n.* the act of using a broom; a long swinging motion, as a *sweep* of the hand, the *sweep* of an oar; a long, heavy oar; one who cleans chimneys, as a chimney *sweep;* the act of getting rid of something or a state of complete accomplishment, as our party made a clean *sweep* of the election; a wide stretch, as a great *sweep* of grassland. *v.i. and v.t.* to use a broom; to move fast, as the cars *swept* down the road; to move in a dignified manner, as she *swept* out of the room; to have wide extent, as this meadow *sweeps* to the river; to clean with a broom, as to *sweep* a floor; to range over, as searchlights *sweep* the river at night.

sweeping (swēp′ ing), *adj.* extensive, all-embracing, as a *sweeping* victory; covering much ground, as a *sweeping* statement.

sweepstakes (swēp′ stāks), *n.* a race in which all the money risked may be won by a few; a race in which all the prize money goes to one contestant; a lottery of prizes based on the winner of such a race.

*****sweet** (swēt), *n.* a darling or beloved person; *sweets,* candies, cakes and the like, as you mustn't eat too many *sweets. adj.* tasting like sugar; not sour, as *sweet* milk; pleasing to the senses, as a *sweet* sound or smell; fresh, not salted, as *sweet* butter; pleasant, agreeable, equable, as a *sweet* disposition.

sweetbread (swēt′ bred), *n.* the pancreas or the thymus gland of a calf or lamb used as food.

sweetbrier (swēt′ brī ēr), *n.* a thorny shrub having fragrant pink blossoms.

sweeten (swēt′ n), *v.i. and v.t.* to become more sugarlike in taste; to cause to taste like sugar; to make more pleasing or attractive.

sweetening (swēt′ n ing), *n.* that which makes things taste more like sugar, as the pie needs more *sweetening.*

sweetheart (swēt′ härt), *n.* a lover; a loved one.

sweetmeat (swēt′ mēt), *n.* a confection made with sugar.

sweet potato (swēt pō tā′ tō), the edible root of a creeping vine.

swell (swel), *n.* a long rolling wave; the roll of the sea far from land; a rolling ridge of land; an increase in volume of sound, as the *swell* of the organ. *v.i. and v.t.* to expand or enlarge, as by inflation; to cause to rise or increase; to puff up, as to *swell* the chest.

swelter (swel′ tēr), *n.* a hot, moist, heavy state of the atmosphere. *v.i.* to be oppressed by the heat.

swerve (swûrv), *n.* a swing aside from the path of progress, as the car gave a sudden *swerve. v.i. and v.t.* to make or cause to make a turn out of a course, deviate; to deflect, as you can't *swerve* me from my aim.

swift (swift), *n.* a bird related to the swallow, famous for its speedy flight. *adj.* moving far in little time; doing much in a short time, as he is a *swift* worker; fast, rapid.

swill (swil), *n.* kitchen refuse fed to pigs. *v.i.*
and *v.t.* to drink greedily or grossly.

swim (swim), *n.* the act of propelling oneself in the water, as I had a good *swim;* a whirl, as my head is in a *swim;* a gliding motion; the full tide of life, business or society, as he is in the *swim. v.i. and v.t.* [*p.t.* swam, *p.p.* swum, *pr.p.* swimming] to propel oneself forward in water by natural means, as by using the legs and arms, fins or the like; to float on a liquid; to be submerged in, as her eyes *swam* with tears; to become dizzy, giddy, as the blow made the fighter's head *swim;* to whirl, as the lights swam before my eyes; to cross by swimming, as he *swims* the cove regularly.

swindle (swin′ dl), *n.* a gross fraud.

swindle (swin′ dl), *v.i. and v.t.* to defraud, obtain money under false pretenses, cheat.

swine (swīn), *n.* [*pl.* swine] a hog; hogs or pigs collectively.

swing (swing), *n.* a free back-and-forth motion; the distance through which anything suspended moves back and forth, as the pendulum has a *swing* of 4 inches; a contrivance of ropes and a seat on which to move back and forth through the air; strongly emphasized rhythm, as a marching song with a good *swing,* the *swing* of band music.

swing (swing), *v.i. and v.t.* [*p.t. and p.p.* swung, *pr.p.* swinging] to hang, suspend, as by a cord, rope or chain; to sway back and forth; to turn, as on a hinge, as the gate *swung* open; to march with a long, free stride, as the soldiers *swung* down the street; to move or cause to move to and fro, as he *swung* the child for an hour; to brandish, as to *swing* a weapon; to conclude successfully, as to *swing* a big deal.

swipe (swīp), *n.* a bar or lever, as for starting an engine or working a pump. *v.t.* to strike with a side swing, as of the arm.

swirl (swûrl), *n.* a whirling or eddying motion, as a *swirl* of water. *v.i. and v.t.* to move in eddies; to cause to eddy.

swish (swish), *n.* a whistling sound like that of a lash cutting through the air; a rustling sound, as of stiff silk when moved. *v.i. and v.t.* to move or cause to move with a whistling noise, as to *swish* a whip.

switch (swich), *n.* a slender, flexible stick; a tress of hair used to make a woman's hair look more abundant; a device to break an electric current or transfer it to another conductor; a device for moving the rails so that cars or trains can pass from one line of track to another; a shift, as a *switch* of public opinion. *v.t. and v.i.* to whip with a slender stick; to move from one track to another, as a streetcar or railroad train; to change from one opinion or policy to another; to change from one circuit to another or into or out of a circuit, as to *switch* a light on; to twitch suddenly, as a cow *switches* its tail; to alter a course suddenly.

swivel (swiv′ l), *n.* a device for coupling things together that permits either part to turn; a pivot arrangement that permits turning in all directions, as this dog leash is good because it hooks on with a *swivel.*

swivel (swiv' l), *v.i. and v.t.* to fasten or be fastened with a coupling device that permits turning in all directions; to pivot.

swoon (swōōn), *n.* fainting fit. *v.i.* to faint.

swoop (swōōp), *n.* a sudden downward sweep like that of a hawk darting at its prey. *v.i. and v.t.* to dart downward; to fall upon and seize, as to *swoop* a ball.

sword (sōrd), *n.* a keen-edged, long-bladed weapon for cutting and thrusting.

sycamore (sĭk' a mōr), *n.* the buttonwood or plane tree, distinguished by the shedding of its bark, making the trunk and branches look white or gray in patches.

*sycophant (sĭk' ō fant), *n.* a flatterer; one who, to gain favors, pretends to agree with everything someone else says.

syllabication (sĭ lab ĭ kā' shun), *n.* division of a word into parts: sometimes *syllabification*.

syllable (sĭl' a bl), *n.* the letters that represent a separately pronounced part of a word, as *syl* is the first syllable of the word *syllable;* a unit of pronunciation within a word, consisting of a vowel ordinarily combined with one or more consonants.

syllabus (sĭl' a bus), *n.* an outline, as of a lecture; a brief statement of the main points of a discourse.

*syllogism (sĭl' ō jĭzm), *n.* an argument presented in logical form, with two statements called the premises leading to a conclusion, which may be either correct or false according to the correctness of the premises, as an animal lives, a tree lives, therefore a tree is an animal (false: two senses of *live*)..

sylph (sĭlf), *n.* an imaginary being living in the air, a kind of fairy; a slim, graceful young girl.

sylvan (sĭl' van), *adj.* pertaining in any way to forests, woods or groves.

symbol (sĭm' bul), *n.* an emblem or sign, as the dove is a *symbol* of peace, figures are *symbols* of number.

symbolism (sĭm' bul ĭzm), *n.* the giving of fanciful meanings to well-known objects, especially in literature and the fine arts.

symbolize (sĭm' bul īz), *v.t.* to serve as a sign or emblem of; to represent, as the lion *symbolizes* courage.

symmetry (sĭm' ē trĭ), *n.* [*pl.* symmetries] proper proportion in the arrangement of parts; correct balance between the two halves of an outline; graceful proportioning; the beauty of harmonious arrangement of parts.

sympathy (sĭm' a thĭ), *n.* [*pl.* sympathies] the sharing of feelings, as of pleasure or pain; compassion, pity; likeness of disposition, as we are in *sympathy* with each other.

*symphony (sĭm' fō nĭ), *n.* [*pl.* symphonies] harmony of sound; a musical composition fully orchestrated in sonata form; a har-

mony of colors, as her costume was a *symphony* of blues.

*symposium (sĭm pō' zĭ um), *n.* [*pl.* symposiums or symposia] a collection of utterances by different persons on one subject.

symptom (sĭmp' tum), *n.* a special condition of any part of the body indicating the presence of disease; any condition indicating a cause, as *symptoms* of popular discontent.

synagogue or synagog (sĭn' a gog), *n.* a Jewish house of worship; the group or congregation of believers worshiping in such a place.

*synchronism (sĭng' krō nĭzm), *n.* coincidence of time; the state of happening at the same time as something else.

synchronize (sĭng' krō nĭz), *v.t.* to cause to agree in time, as to *synchronize* two clocks.

*synchronous (sĭng' krō nus), *adj.* happening at the same time, as *synchronous* events.

syncopate (sĭng' kō pāt), *v.t.* to contract a word by omitting letters from the middle of it; to write or play music in measures that start on an unaccented beat and end on an accented one.

*syncope (sĭng' kō pē), *n.* the omission of letters from the middle of a word; fainting, sudden cessation of breathing, sensation and consciousness.

syndicate (sĭn' dĭ kāt), *n.* a combination or association of persons or companies to provide larger funds for carrying on an enterprise; a company that buys manuscripts, comic strips and other special articles and sells them to a number of newspapers to be published in each on a set date.

*synod (sĭn' ud), *n.* a church council.

*synonym (sĭn' ō nĭm), *n.* a word of the same or almost the same meaning as another word.

synopsis (sĭn op' sĭs), *n.* [*pl.* synopses] an outline of a literary or dramatic composition.

syntax (sĭn' taks), *n.* the part of grammar that treats of the construction of sentences and the relationship of words to one another in a sentence.

synthetic (sĭn thet' ĭk), *adj.* made of parts or elements combined in a new form; composed artificially; produced artificially.

*syringa (sĭ rĭng' ga), *n.* a shrub with flowers resembling orange blossoms: also called *mock orange.*

*syringe (sĭr' ĭnj), *n.* a device with which to inject fluid, consisting of a rubber bulb to produce suction and a hose and nozzle through which the liquid passes.

system (sĭs' tem), *n.* a combination of parts into a whole, as the bodily *system,* the digestive *system,* a railroad *system,* the solar *system;* orderly arrangement, as you need more *system* in your work.

T

tab (tab), *n.* a flap or tag, as on a garment.

tabby (tab' ĭ), *n.* [*pl.* tabbies] a brindled cat; any domestic cat.

tabby (tab' ĭ), *adj.* [*comp.* tabbier, *superl.* tabbiest] brindled, as a *tabby* cat; marked in waves, as watered silk.

*tabernacle (tab' ẽr nak' l), *n.* a tent, a lightly constructed dwelling; the movable, tentlike structure in which the Israelites worshiped as they wandered in the wilderness; a small receptacle for the consecrated Host in Roman Catholic churches; any place of worship.

tabes (tā' bēz), *n.* a gradual wasting away of the body.

*table (tā' bl), *n.* an article of furniture with a flat, horizontal top that is set on legs; a collection of items in orderly arrangement, as a *table* of contents in a book, a railroad time*table. v.t.* to place on a table, as the card had already been *tabled;* to lay aside, as to *table* a resolution in a deliberative assembly.

*tableau (tab' lō), *n.* [*pl.* tableaux or tableaus] a scene represented by persons posed, motionless and silent.

tableland (tā' bl land), *n.* a high, level area of land; a plateau of considerable area.

tablet (tab' let), *n.* a flat surface to write on; a pad of writing paper; a flat panel fastened in a wall and carrying an inscription; medicine or candy in a small, flat disk.

tabloid (tab' loid), *n.* a compressed tablet or pill, originally a trade name; anything that is especially brief, compact and concentrated; a newspaper with small pages and numerous photographs. *adj.* condensed and brief, as *tabloid* news of the day.

taboo or **tabu** (ta bŏō'), *n.* a religious (prohibition) of the Polynesians by which persons and things were rendered sacred and inviolable; a ban on anything.

taboo (ta bŏō'), *v.t.* to forbid approach to or use of. *adj.* under a ban, prohibited.

tabor (tā' bẽr), *n.* a small drum shaped like a tambourine and beaten with one stick : also *tabour.*

*taboret (tab' ō ret), *n.* a small stool or stand, often handsomely carved or inlaid : also *tabouret.*

tabular (tab' ū lẽr), *adj.* in the form of a table or schedule, arranged in columns.

tabulate (tab' ū lāt), *v.t.* to arrange in an orderly list.

tachometer (ta kom' ē tẽr), *n.* an instrument that measures and makes a record of speed.

*tacit (tas' it), *adj.* implied but not expressed, granted by silence, where a spoken negative might have been expected, as *tacit* consent; silent.

*taciturn (tas' i tûrn), *adj.* habitually silent, uncommunicative.

tack (tak), *n.* a small, sharp nail with a broad head, flat or curved; one leg of a sailing

ship's course when she goes against the wind; a veering of a ship's course to take advantage of a side wind; a change in policy; new line of action. *v.i. and v.t.* to change a ship's course to suit the wind; to fasten with short, broad-headed nails; to fasten lightly, as with stitches.

*tackle (tak' l), *n.* apparatus of blocks and ropes for lifting and lowering; implements or gear in general, as fishing *tackle. v.t.* to grapple with; to lay hold of; to deal with or attack vigorously, as I must *tackle* this algebra lesson.

*tact (takt), *n.* fine understanding and nice discernment with delicate skill in saying or doing the right thing; consideration for others.

tactician (tak tish' an), *n.* one who is skilled in the science of military movements; one skilled in adroit maneuvers for the accomplishment of any purpose.

tactics (tak' tiks), *n.* the science of military and naval operations, apart from strategy; any adroit maneuver for the accomplishment of a purpose.

*tactile (tak' til), *adj.* perceptible by touch.

tactual (tak' tū al), *adj.* pertaining to the sense or organs of touch.

tadpole (tad' pōl), *n.* a young frog or toad with gills and a long tail.

taffeta (taf' ē ta), *n.* a fine, thin, glossy silken fabric, slightly stiff.

taffrail (taf' rāl), *n.* the railing around the stern of a ship; the upper afterdeck.

taffy (taf' ĭ), *n.* candy made of molasses or brown sugar boiled down.

tag (tag), *n.* an identifying card or label attached to something, as baggage; a loose end; a children's game. *v.t. and v.i.* to attach a label to; to overtake and touch; to follow closely, as I'll just *tag* along.

tag day (tag dā), a special day for contributions to a cause, each contributor receiving a badge or token.

tail (tāl), *n.* the appendage at the hind end of an animal's body, a prolongation of the backbone; anything hanging loose, as the *tail* of a kite; the rear end of anything, as the *tail* of the procession.

tailboard (tāl' bōrd), *n.* the removable piece at the back of a truck or wagon.

tailings (tāl' ings), *n. pl.,* refuse, waste material, as in flour manufacture, petroleum refining or ore dressing, chaff in threshing.

tail light (tāl lit), a red lamp at the rear of an automobile.

tailor (tā' lẽr), *n.* one who makes suits and outer garments.

*taint (tānt), *n.* a spot indicating corruption or decay; presence of undesirable foreign matter. *v.i. and v.t.* to become spoiled, as meat; to infect, poison; to defile, corrupt.

take (tāk), *n.* the act of acquiring; amount

acquired, as a *take* of fish with nets; a single portion of copy to be set in type.

take (tāk), *v.t. and v.i.* [*p.t.* took, *p.p.* taken, *pr.p.* taking] to gain possession of; to grasp; to seize; to interest, attract; to select, as to *take* material from a book; to consume, as it *takes* time; to occupy, as the grand piano *takes* too much space; to endure, as to *take* punishment; to photograph; to be successful; to have the desired effect.

taking (tāk' ing), *adj.* pleasing, as you have a *taking* personality.

*talc (talc), *n.* a soft, greasy mineral substance: also called *soapstone.*

tale (tāl), *n.* a narrative or story; a count of things, as the *tale* of a day's receipts in a store; detrimental talk, gossip.

*talent (tal' ent), *n.* ability, special fitness for any particular occupation; an ancient unit of weight or money.

*talesman (tālz' man), *n.* one summoned to make up a deficiency in a jury.

*talisman (tal' iz man), *n.* a charm; a figure in metal or stone supposed to have magic qualities.

talk (tôk), *n.* speech, vocal utterance, conversation; rumor, as idle *talk.*

talk (tôk), *v.i. and v.t.* to utter words; to speak, converse; to exert influence upon, as we *talked* him into accepting; to express oneself orally in, as to *talk* French.

talkative (tôk' a tiv), *adj.* loquacious, fond of conversing.

tall (tôl), *adj.* high in stature; lofty; exaggerated, as *tall* talk.

tallow (tal' ō), *n.* the melted fat or suet of cattle and sheep, used in making candles, soap, oleomargarine.

tally (tal' i), *n.* [*pl.* tallies] a count kept by marking down each unit; originally done by notching sticks which were then split and one half held by each interested party.

tally (tal' i), *v.i. and v.t.* [*p.t. and p.p.* tallied, *pr.p.* tallying] to agree in count; to keep count of by marking items down one at a time.

*tallyho (tal i hō'), *n.* a four-in-hand coach. *interj.* huntsman's cry urging on hounds.

talon (tal' un), *n.* the claw of a bird of prey.

*tamale (ta mä' lē), *n.* a Mexican dish of minced meat and cornmeal, seasoned with red pepper, wrapped in corn husks, dipped in oil and steamed.

tamarack (tam' a rak), *n.* the American black larch.

tamarind (tam' a rind), *n.* a tropical tree that has yellow flowers and fruit with acid pulp.

tambour (tam' boor), *n.* a small drum; an embroidery hoop.

tambourine (tam boo rēn'), *n.* a small hand drum with jingling disks attached to the hoop.

tame (tām), *v.t.* to subdue; to domesticate.

tame (tām), *adj.* domesticated; spiritless, dull.

tamp (tamp), *n.* a heavy flat-surfaced block with a handle at the upper end, used to pound down loose earth or sod.

tamp (tamp), *v.t.* to plug a blast hole with packed clay; to pack and harden with re-

peated blows, as to *tamp* turf.

tamper (tam' pēr), *v.i.* to meddle, to change objectionably, as don't *tamper* with that machine; to bribe, corrupt.

tampion (tam' pi un), *n.* a plug stopping the muzzle of a cannon when not in use.

tan (tan), *n.* the bark of certain trees, as the oak, used in dressing hides; a yellowish-brown color with a reddish tinge; the dark coloring of the skin after long exposure to the sun. *v.i. and v.t.* to take on a dark color from exposure to the sun, as my skin *tans* easily; to dress hides in making leather by using vegetable, mineral or chemical compounds.

tang (tang), *n.* the part of a knife or fork that fits up inside the handle; a strong, piquant flavor; a characteristic quality, as his speech has the *tang* of the mountain country.

tangent (tan' jent), *n.* a straight line that touches a curve but does not cut it; a course leading away from its proper point, as he went off at a *tangent. adj.* touching; in contact at only one point.

tangerine (tan je rēn'), *n.* a small, sweet and juicy orange having a distinctly reddish skin, called a mandarin orange.

tangible (tan' ji bl), *adj.* perceptible to the touch; evident, discernible, real.

tangle (tang' gl), *n.* a confused mass of intertwined threads or strings, as my hair is in a *tangle;* a confusion of words or things.

tangle (tang' gl), *v.i. and v.t.* to form in a confused, intertwining collection, as these ropes *tangle;* to knot, entangle, as I *tangled* the yarn; to confuse, as with arguments.

tango (tang' gō), a dance originating in Spanish America; music suited for that dance.

tank (tangk), *n.* a large receptacle for liquids, as a water *tank* on a roof, a swimming *tank;* an armored motor car with caterpillar treads for cross-country operations in war. *v.t.* to place or store in a large receptacle, as we had better *tank* a lot of water.

tankard (tangk' ērd), *n.* a large drinking vessel with a lid.

tanker (tangk' ēr), *n.* a ship equipped with large containers for transporting oil, molasses and other liquids in bulk.

tannery (tan' ēr i), *n.* [*pl.* tanneries] a works where hides are dressed in making leather.

tannic (tan' ik), *adj.* pertaining to or made from bark.

tannic acid (tan' ik as' id), a substance obtained from bark and nutgalls used in dressing hides.

tansy (tan' zi), *n.* [*pl.* tansies] a bitter, aromatic plant with small, yellow flowers.

tantalize (tan' ta liz), *v.t.* to tease; to torment by raising hopes or fears that will not be realized.

tantamount (tan' ta mount), *adj.* equivalent to in meaning or value, as your words are *tantamount* to a promise.

tantrum (tan' trum), *n.* a sudden outburst of temper.

tap (tap), *n.* a spigot, faucet; a branch conductor leading away from a main electric circuit; a playful touch; a light knock, as a *tap* on a door. *v.i. and v.t.* to rap lightly, as he *tapped* on the door; to draw liquid by opening a spigot, as to *tap* beer.

tape (tāp), *n.* a long narrow band of linen, silk or cotton; a narrow strip of paper used in a stock ticker; a long strip of stout fabric marked with a scale for measuring; a rope across a track to mark the finish line of a race.

taper (tā′ pẽr), *n.* a thin wax candle; a gradual decrease in size toward the end, as that mast has a graceful *taper. v.i. and v.t.* to grow or cause to grow more slender at one end. *adj.* growing smaller toward one end.

***tapestry** (tap′ es tri), *n.* [*pl.* tapestries] a heavy fabric of wool or silk woven with a design and used for hangings or upholstery.

tapeworm (tāp′ wûrm), *n.* a flat, ribbonlike parasite that infests the intestines of man and other animals, causing malnutrition.

***tapioca** (tap i ŏ′ ka), *n.* a starchy food substance obtained from the roots of the cassava.

***tapir** (tā′ pẽr), *n.* a large animal of South and Central America and Malaysia that has short legs and a flexible snout.

***tapis** (tap′ ē), *n.* carpet, tapestry; floor, as on the *tapis*, meaning under discussion.

taproot (tap′ rŏŏt), *n.* the main underground stem of a plant that strikes straight down into the earth.

taps (taps), *n.* the closing signal of the day in the army or navy, sounded by the drum, bugle or trumpet as an order to extinguish lights; this signal sounded as an honorary ceremony at the burial of a soldier.

tar (tär), *n.* a thick, dark-colored, oily substance obtained by distilling coal or wood rich in resin. *n.* a sailor. *v.t.* to cover with tar.

***tarantula** (ta ran′ tū la), *n.* a large spider of tropical or near-tropical regions, with hairy body and a painful sting.

tardiness (tär′ di nes), *n.* the state of being late or moving with slow, reluctant pace.

tardy (tär′ di), *adj.* [*comp.* tardier, *superl.* tardiest] late, behindtime; moving with slow, reluctant pace.

tare (târ), *n.* a weed that grows in grain fields; the darnel. *n.* an allowance for the weight of the container, subtracted from the price charged a purchaser.

target (tär′ get), *n.* a mark shot at in practice with bow and arrow, rifle, or artillery; anything aimed at, as I am a *target* for his wit; a small shield.

tariff (tar′ if), *n.* a schedule of charges to be levied against various kinds of imported goods; the customs duty on any particular imported article, as the *tariff* on watches; any schedule of charges and rates, as for a railroad or a hotel.

tarn (tärn), *n.* a small mountain lake.

tarnish (tär′ nish), *v.i. and v.t.* to lose luster, become dull; to become discolored from the action of air and moisture; to take the brightness from, stain, as your remarks *tarnish* his reputation.

***tarpaulin** (tär′ pô lin), *n.* stout, waterproof canvas or a cover or garment made of it.

tarry (tar′ i), *v.i.* [*p.t. and p.p.* tarried, *pr.p.* tarrying] to stay behind, linger, delay.

tarsier (tär′ si ẽr), *n.* an East Indian tree-dwelling mammal with large staring eyes, long ankle bones and specialized toes ending in disks.

tarsus (tär′ sus), *n.* the ankle; the thin cartilage that stiffens the eyelid.

tart (tärt), *n.* a small shell of pastry, filled with fruit, jam, or jelly. *adj.* sharp and sour of taste, acid; severe, as *tart* speech.

tartan (tär′ tan), *n.* a plaid woolen fabric, worn especially in the Scottish Highlands; the distinctive pattern of such plaids, as the *tartan* of this clan is blue and green.

***tartar** (tär′ tẽr), *n.* an acid substance formed in fermenting grape juice; the crusty deposit that forms at the base of a tooth.

***tartaric acid** (tär tar′ ik as′ id), a substance found in the juice of grapes and berries.

***task** (täsk), *n.* a definite piece of work to be done. *v.t.* to assign work to; to burden with work; to test one's strength or ability, as this problem *tasks* my mind: *to take to task*, to reprimand.

***tassel** (tas′ l), *n.* an ornament consisting of a tuft of loose threads at the end of a cord and left hanging, as from a curtain; anything thought of as resembling such an ornament, as a corn *tassel*.

taste (tāst), *n.* the sensation produced on the tongue and palate by anything taken into the mouth; that one of the five physical senses by which such a sensation is perceived; a characteristic flavor, as the *taste* of bananas; a small quantity taken into the mouth, as a *taste* of that pickle; special liking or aptitude for any art or study, as he has a *taste* for mathematics; good judgment in selecting, matching or harmonizing things, as she dresses with good *taste*.

tasteful (tāst′ fool), *adj.* showing refinement and good judgment.

tasty (tāst′ i), *adj.* [*comp.* tastier, *superl.* tastiest] savory, flavorful.

tat (tat), *v.t. and v.i.* to make by knotting thread wound on a shuttle, as to *tat* lace; to be occupied with such work, as she *tats* by the hour. *n.* a blow, as tit for *tat*.

tatter (tat′ ẽr), *n.* a ragged, hanging piece on clothing: *tatters*, ragged clothes, hanging in shreds.

tatterdemalion (tat ẽr dē mäl′ yun), *n.* a ragamuffin; a person in rags and tatters.

tatting (tat′ ing), *n.* a kind of knotted work like lace, made by hand with a shuttle.

tattle (tat′ l), *v.i. and v.t.* to talk idly, prate; to gossip, tell tales.

tattoo (ta tŏŏ′), *n.* a signal by drum or bugle shortly before taps for soldiers or sailors to go to their quarters at night; any continuous rattling noise, as he beat a *tattoo* on the door. *v.t.* to mark the body with a design by puncturing the skin with a needle and inserting a lasting stain or dye into the wounds or by scarring with cuts.

***taunt** (tônt), *n.* a bitter or sarcastic remark,

a jeer or jibe. *v.t.* to address with insulting language, jeer, jibe.

taupe (tōp), *n.* a dull yellowish-gray color like that of a mole, mole-gray.

taut (tôt), *adj.* stretched tight, as a rope.

tavern (tav' ẽrn), *n.* an inn, a roadhouse.

taw (tô), *n.* a marble used as a shooter; a game of marbles; the line from which one shoots in this game.

***tawdry** (tô' dri), *adj.* [*comp.* tawdrier, *superl.* tawdriest] showy, without good taste, gaudy.

tawny (tô' ni), *adj.* [*comp.* tawnier, *superl.* tawniest] of a yellowish-brown color.

tax (taks), *n.* a charge, at a certain percentage of valuation, on income, real estate or other property, levied by a government for its own support; an imposition, as your request is a *tax* on my good nature. *v.t.* to place a compulsory levy upon, as income or property, to raise funds to support governmental needs, pay for public works and the like; to subject to a strain, as his request may *tax* your good nature; to accuse.

taxable (taks' a bl), *adj.* subject to a levy by government.

taxation (taks ā' shun), *n.* the act of collecting a percentage on the valuation of private property to raise public funds; the amount thus collected.

taxi (taks' i), *n.* [*pl.* taxis] a taxicab. *v.i.* to run over water or land in taking off or coming down, as airplane or seaplane; to ride in a hired motor vehicle, as I *taxied* downtown.

taxicab (tak' si kab), *n.* a public motor car, especially one with a mechanical device registering the distance traveled and indicating the amount of fare due; often abbreviated to *taxi.*

taxidermist (tak' si dûr mist), *n.* one who stuffs and mounts the skins of dead animals.

***taxidermy** (tak' si dûr mi), *n.* the art of stuffing and mounting the skins of dead animals so as to give them a lifelike appearance.

***taximeter** (tak' si mē tẽr), *n.* a mechanism to show a passenger in a taxicab what the fare is at any moment and for printing a card with the charge at the end of a ride.

tea (tē), *n.* the dried leaves of an oriental shrub; the beverage made by steeping such leaves in boiling water; any infusion or extract used as a medicine or beverage, as beef *tea;* an afternoon or evening meal; a social gathering at which tea and other refreshments are served to the assembled guests.

teach (tēch), *v.i. and v.t.* [*p.t. and p.p.* taught, *pr.p.* teaching] to give instruction; to impart knowledge to; to cause to learn; to direct the development of.

Syn. Discipline, drill, educate, enlighten, inculcate, indoctrinate, inform, initiate, instill, instruct, nurture, school, train, tutor. To *teach* is simply to communicate knowledge. To *instruct* is to impart knowledge with special method and completeness. To *educate* is to draw out and develop harmoniously and in the fullest sense the mental and moral powers. To *train* is to direct

to a certain result talents already existing. To *discipline* is to train under strict control and restraint. To *nurture* is to foster and *educate* in a less formal manner.

teal (tēl), *n.* a small, wild fresh-water duck.

team (tēm), *n.* two or more horses or other draft animals harnessed to the same vehicle or to a plow; a number of players on a side in an athletic contest, as a baseball *team;* any group with similar interests and aims. *v.t. and v.i.* to join a group, as to *team* up with one's friends; to move or transport with horses, as to *team* the baggage to the city.

tear (tēr), *n.* a small drop of fluid secreted by the eye.

***tear** (târ), *n.* a rent, as in a fabric or garment. *v.i. and v.t.* [*p.t.* tore, *p.p.* torn, *pr.p.* tearing] to part on being pulled; to be rent; to pull apart, rend, lacerate; to move with violence, as to *tear* a door off its hinges.

tear gas (tēr gas), an irritating vapor that causes weeping and is used in war and by the police.

***tease** (tēz), *n.* the act of plaguing someone, a person who likes to torment others.

***tease** (tēz), *v.t.* to irritate and annoy; to ask persistently; to tear apart, to comb, to unravel, as to *tease* wool or cotton fibers.

teasel (tē' zl), *n.* a plant somewhat like the thistle, with prickly flower heads, used to make a nap on woolen cloth; any instrument resembling the burs of this plant and used to raise a nap.

teaspoon (tē' spōōn), *n.* a small spoon for general use at table, holding about one-third as much as a tablespoon.

technical (tek' ni kal), *adj.* relating to some particular art, science or trade; having to do with the mechanical part of an art or science, as a *technical* school or college.

technicality (tek ni kal' i ti), *n.* [*pl.* technicalities] an exact point in connection with some particular art, science or trade; a very strict and close interpretation of a rule.

***technique** (tek nēk'), *n.* the manner of handling details in the execution or performance of an undertaking, especially in the arts, as the pianist has a fine *technique.*

technology (tek nol' ō ji), *n.* the science underlying industrial arts; education in the branches of learning useful in manufacture and industry.

***tedious** (tē' di us), *adj.* wearisome, tiresome; going on drearily.

***tedium** (tē' di um), *n.* tiresomeness, monotony.

tee (tē), *n.* the mark aimed at in quoits and curling; a small cone of sand or earth from which a ball is driven for the first stroke on each hole of a golf course; the square of turf in which this cone stands: *to a tee,* to an exact or precise point, as that is the situation *to a tee. v.t.* to place golf ball on cone of sand or earth before driving it.

teem (tēm), *v.i.* to be prolific; to be full or abundantly stocked, as the river *teems* with fish.

teens (tēnz), *n.* the years of one's age from 13

to 19 inclusive.

teeter (tē′ tẽr), v.i. and v.t. to seesaw; to waver precariously; to cause to waver precariously, jiggle, as to *teeter* a board.

*teethe (tēth), v.i. to cut teeth.

teething (tēth′ ing), n. the process of cutting the first set of teeth.

teetotaler (tē tō′ tl ẽr), n. one who uses no alcoholic beverage, a total abstainer.

tegmen (teg′ men), n. [pl. tegmina] a covering; the inner layer of a seed coat.

tegument (teg′ ū ment), n. a natural outer covering, as the skin.

telegram (tel′ ē gram), n. a message electrically flashed by wire in a code of dots and dashes.

telegraph (tel′ ē gráf), v.i. and v.t. to send a message over a wire by opening and closing an electric circuit; to send a message by radio or wireless telegraphy; to send a message to, as to *telegraph* a friend.

*telegrapher (tē leg′ ra fẽr), n. one who operates the key opening and closing the electric circuit in sending code messages of dots and dashes over a wire.

*teleology (tel ē ol′ ō ji), n. the belief that natural phenomena are designed for a specific end: opposed to *mechanism.*

*telepathy (tē lep′ a thi), n. communication without words; the transmission of thought from one mind to another without use of anything acting on or through the physical senses; thought transference.

telephone (tel′ ē fōn), n. an instrument that reproduces sounds, especially speech, at a distant point by means of electricity.

telephotography (tel ē fō tog′ ra fi), n. the art of photographing distant objects through a special lens; the transmission of pictures by reproducing them at a distance by telegraph.

telescope (tel′ ē skōp), n. an instrument that makes it possible to see objects at great distances, as the farther stars.

*telescope (tel′ ē skōp), v.i. to slip into each other like the separate parts of a telescope; to come together with such force that one body enters another, as cars of a train in a collision, as two cars *telescoped.*

*teletypewriter (tel′ e tīp rit ẽr), n. a telegraphic device by which work done on one typewriting machine is simultaneously produced by another.

*television (tel′ ē vizh un), n. the transmission and reproduction of a distant scene by means of electricity and light rays; the device by which this is done.

tell (tel), v.t. and v.i. [p t. and p.p. told, pr.p. telling] to count, as to *tell* beads; to narrate, as to *tell* a story; to inform; to command, as I *told* him to leave; to find out, recognize, decide; to state with emphasis, as I *tell* you I did; to give an account, as he *told* of his war experiences; to have a perceptible effect, as the privation *told* on him.

teller (tel′ ẽr), n. one who narrates; a bank clerk who receives, pays out and counts the money banked.

telling (tel′ ing), adj. effective, striking.

telltale (tel′ tāl), n. a tattler, one who reveals secrets or maliciously reports the wrongdoing of others. adj. revealing; tattling.

*tellurium (te lū′ ri um), n. a rare nonmetallic element related to sulphur and selenium, usually combined with metals.

temerity (tē mer′ i ti), n. rashness, boldness, foolhardiness.

temper (tem′ pẽr), n. disposition in a general way, as he has a good *temper;* the quality of being easily angered; an angry state, as you are in a *temper;* condition of a metal with regard to toughness, as steel has a stronger *temper* than iron. v.t. to give a mixture the correct degree of consistency; to harden metal; to moderate, as God *tempers* the wind to the shorn lamb.

*temperament (tem′ pẽr a ment), n. the mixture of qualities in one's nature; characteristic traits, as he has the artistic *temperament.*

temperance (tem′ pẽr ans), n. moderation, self-control and restraint from overindulgence of any kind.

temperate (tem′ pẽr it), adj. moderate, abstemious; mild, calm.

*temperature (tem′ pẽr a tūr), n. the degree of heat or cold as shown by the thermometer; the state of a body as regards heat; a high degree of bodily heat, as in fever, as he has a *temperature.*

*tempest (tem′ pest), n. a violent storm with high winds; tumult.

*tempestuous (tem pes′ tū us), adj. very stormy, violent, agitated, turbulent.

template (tem′ plit), n. a pattern or mold used by masons in laying out their work, by potters in shaping pottery and by sculptors for architectural detail; a stone or timber set over a doorway to distribute stresses; a wedge upon the keel of a ship while on the ways: also spelled *templet.*

temple (tem′ pl), n. a building in which to worship. n. the flat part on either side of the head above the cheekbones.

*temporal (tem′ pō ral), adj. pertaining to time, especially limited time; worldly, not eternal. adj. belonging to the temples, as the *temporal* artery.

temporary (tem′ pō rer i), adj. for the time being, not permanent.

temporize (tem′ pō rīz), v.i. to keep putting things off; to refuse to commit oneself; to follow expedient courses.

tempt (tempt), v.t. to lure, entice; to try to persuade to do something wrong; to invite indulgence, as that cake *tempts* me.

temptation (temp tā′ shun), n. that which lures or entices; the state of being prompted to do wrong things.

ten (ten), n. one more than nine; the symbol (10) representing this number.

*tenable (ten′ a bl), adj. capable of being held or defended, as either an army or a debater may be in a *tenable* position.

*tenacious (te nā′ shus), adj. holding strongly; adhesive; stubborn.

tenacity (tē nas′ i ti), n. the quality of holding firmly, refusing to let go; cohesiveness or adhesiveness.

tenancy (ten' an sl), *n.* [*pl.* tenancies] the state of occupying a rented house or building or using rented land; the period of such occupation or use.

tenant (ten' ant), *n.* one who rents and occupies a house; one who rents buildings or lands from the owner for a term of time.

tend (tend), *v.i. and v.t.* to have a leaning toward, as the court *tends* to leniency; to have an aptitude for, as he *tends* toward mechanical work; to move in a certain direction, as here the river *tends* west; to care for; to watch over; to keep in operation, as he *tends* the furnace.

tendency (ten' den sl), *n.* [*pl.* tendencies] inclination, drift or general trend, as an increasing national *tendency* to participate in deciding important political questions; natural bent, as a studious *tendency.*

tender (ten' dẽr), *n.* a ship carrying supplies for other ships; a car attached to a locomotive carrying fuel and water; a small boat used for communication between ship and shore. *n.* an offer, as I accept your *tender* of assistance; that which may be offered in payment of debt, as legal *tender. v.t.* to offer, as to *tender* advice, assistance or money. *adj.* readily cut or chewed, as *tender* meat; sensitive, as a *tender* skin; sympathetic, as a *tender* heart; gentle; youthful, as a boy of *tender* years.

tenderfoot (ten' dẽr foot), *n.* [*pl.* tenderfeet] one new to a place and unaccustomed to its ways, especially in a western mining camp or on a ranch; a Boy Scout of the lowest grade, second-class scout and first-class scout being the higher classes.

tenderloin (ten' dẽr loin), *n.* an especially juicy cut of beef.

tendon (ten' dun), *n.* the tough cord of fibrous tissue that connects the end of a muscle to the bone.

tendril (ten' dril), *n.* the slender, twining part of a climbing plant with which it grips a surface or support.

tenement (ten' ẽ ment), *n.* any house, building, shop or land rented by a tenant.

***tenet** (ten' et), *n.* a doctrine or belief held by a group of persons or an individual.

Syn. Position. The *tenet* is that to which we hold in our own minds; the *position* is our presentation of beliefs to others.

tenfold (ten' fōld), *adj.* 10 times as much. *adv.* 10 times as many; having 10 parts.

tennis (ten' is) *n.* a game played on a marked court by striking a ball across a net with rackets, also known as *lawn tennis;* the older game of *court tennis, squash* or rackets, in which the ball is struck against a court wall.

***tenon** (ten' un), *n.* end of a timber cut to fit into a mortise on another timber. *v.t.* to join timbers by means of mortise and tenon.

***tenor** (ten' ẽr), *n.* the general tendency or drift of anything, especially talk or writing; the highest male voice; one who has such a voice.

tenpins (ten' pinz), *n.* a game played with

ten wooden pins, usually set up in triangular formation, at the end of a bowling alley.

tense (tens), *n.* the change in form of a verb to indicate time of action. *adj.* drawn tightly; eagerly attentive; strained, as a *tense* situation.

tension (ten' shun), *n.* the act of stretching tight or state of being stretched tight; stress of a pulling force on a body; mental or nervous strain.

tent (tent), *n.* a shelter, usually of canvas, supported by poles and ropes.

tentacle (ten' ta kl), *n.* a part of certain invertebrate creatures with which they feel their way or seek food.

tentative (ten' ta tiv), *adj.* experimental, provisional, on trial, as a *tentative* offer or measure.

tenter (ten' tẽr), *n.* a frame for stretching cloth. *v.t.* to stretch on a frame, especially for drying without losing shape.

tenth (tenth), *n.* one of 10 equal parts. *adj.* next in order after the ninth.

tenuous (ten' ū us), *adj.* slender, thin; not dense; weak, unformed, as a *tenuous* idea.

***tenure** (ten' ūr), *n.* the conditions under which rented property is held; holding, as of lands or office; the period of such holding.

tepee (tē' pē), *n.* a tent shaped like a cone and used by the American Indians.

***tepid** (tep' id), *adj.* lukewarm, as *tepid* water.

***tercentenary** (tûr sen' tē ner i), *n.* [*pl.* tercentenaries] the 300th anniversary.

terebinth (ter' ē binth), *n.* a small tree of the Old World yielding a fine grade of turpentine.

***tergiversation** (tûr ji vẽr sā' shun), *n.* evasion, subterfuge; changeable conduct.

term (tûrm), *n.* a limit or boundary; a fixed period of time, as a school *term;* a word or expression naming something definitely. *v.t.* to designate, name, describe in a word, as I *term* his conduct disgraceful.

terms (tûrmz), *n.* the conditions of an agreement; an agreement, as they came to *terms.*

***termagant** (tûr' ma gant), *n.* a noisy, scolding woman.

terminal (tûr' mi nal), *n.* the end of a line, as a railroad *terminal,* an electric *terminal. adj.* relating to the end of something.

terminate (tûr' mi nāt), *v.i. and v.t.* to come to an end; to bring to an end.

termination (tûr mi nā' shun), *n.* the act of ending; place of ending.

terminology (tûr mi nol' ō ji), *n.* [*pl.* terminologies] the special words or forms of expression used in any particular science, industry or field of knowledge.

terminus (tûr' mi nus), *n.* [*pl.* terminuses] a limit or boundary; the end of a railroad, with a main station.

ternary (tûr' na ri), *adj.* coming in threes.

***terrace** (ter' is), *n.* a raised level space; a sloping surface of ground between two levels.

terra cotta (ter' a kot' a), a composition of fine clay and sand used in pottery.

terrestrial (te res' tri al), *adj.* pertaining to

the earth; living on land.

terret (ter' et), *n.* one of the two rings on a harness pad through which the reins pass.

***terrible** (ter' i bl), *adj.* exciting fear or awe, appalling, dreadful.

terrier (ter' i ēr), *n.* a breed of small dogs originally trained to hunt animals that burrow in the ground.

terrific (te rif´ ik), *adj.* fearful, dreadful, terrible, appalling, intense, awesome.

terrify (ter' i fi), *v.t.* [*p.t. and p.p.* terrified, *pr.p.* terrifying] to frighten or alarm exceedingly.

territory (ter' i tō ri), *n.* [*pl.* territories] the extent of land over which a government or ruler has control; a large tract of land.

terror (ter' ēr), *n.* extreme fear; one who or that which excites dread; a period of great fear, as the *Terror* in the French Revolution.

terrorism (ter´ ô riz´ ûm), *n.* violence which is committed for political purposes such as the release of prisoners.

terry (ter' i), *n.* a fabric, especially cotton, with uncut loops in the weave, used for towels and beach robes.

terse (tûrs), *adj.* concise, as *terse* speech; written simply, directly and with point, as a *terse* essay.

tertian (ter' shan), *adj.* recurring every third day, as a *tertian* fever.

***tertiary** (tur' shi er i), *adj.* third in order of occurrence or importance.

test (test), *n.* that by which the nature or quality of anything is tried; a trial that shows what one knows or can do, as a *test* in mathematics; analysis to show the elements of which a substance is composed; a substance employed to show the presence of an ingredient in a compound, as litmus is a *test* for acids. *v.t.* to put to the proof; to apply in order to determine whether right or wrong, as to *test* a theory by putting it in practice; to measure capacity or ability through experiment or examination.

testament (tes' ta ment), *n.* a will; a covenant; the old or new covenant of the Christian Bible, as the Old and New *Testaments*.

testate (tes' tāt), *adj.* having left a will, as he died *testate*.

testator (tes tā' tēr), *n.* one who makes and leaves a will.

testify (tes' ti fi), *v.i. and v.t.* [*p.t. and p.p.* testified, *pr.p.* testifying] to bear witness; to state as evidence; to serve as proof.

testimonial (tes ti mō' ni al), *n.* a formal token of esteem; a written and signed recommendation. *adj.* pertaining to the giving of evidence.

testimony (tes' ti mō ni), *n.* [*pl.* testimonies] presentation of evidence; things stated before a court as bearing upon a case under trial.

testy (tes' ti), *adj.* [*comp.* testier, *superl.* testiest] peevish, irritable.

***tetanus** (tet' a nus), *n.* an exceedingly painful and frequently fatal infectious disease with spasmodic tension of the muscles: called *lockjaw* when limited to the muscles of the lower jaw.

***tête-à-tête** (tāt a tāt), *n.* a private conversation between two persons; a kind of settee that is arranged in an S-curve so as to seat two persons face to face.

tether (teth' ēr), *n.* a rope confining an animal as a horse to a certain space; scope, range of resources, as he is at the end of his *tether*.

***tetragon** (tet' ra gon), *n.* a plane figure with four sides.

***tetrameter** (te tram' ē tēr), *n.* a line of verse consisting of four measures; verse written in such a meter.

***tetrarch** (tē' trärk), *n.* a Roman governor ruling a fourth part of a province; a subordinate ruler.

tetter (tet' ēr), *n.* any of various skin diseases marked by itching, as eczema, ringworm and herpes.

text (tekst), *n.* a topic or theme; a verse of the Bible from which a sermon is preached; the main body of print on a page, as distinguished from notes, pictures, and other added matter; a version of a book or story, as the *text* differs in the two editions.

textbook (tekst' book), *n.* a volume used in schools as a basis for instruction in a given subject.

***textile** (teks' til), *n.* a woven fabric; cotton, linen, jute, rayon or woolen cloth of any kind. *adj.* capable of being woven; formed by weaving; pertaining to weaving, as *textile* machinery.

***textual** (teks' tū al), *adj.* relating to a topic; found in or relating to the main body of a book or essay.

texture (teks' tūr), *n.* the quality given to woven cloth by the way the threads are set, as this piece of goods has a firm *texture;* the manner in which particles are combined or arranged in a substance, as the *texture* of a piece of wood or stone.

***than** (than), *conj.* compared with, as no sooner said *than* done, this is better *than* that; except, as no other *than* yourself.

thane (thān), *n.* an attendant of an Anglo-Saxon lord, ranking above a freeman, owning land and doing military service to his lord.

thank (thangk), *v.t.* to express gratitude to.

thankful (thangk' fool), *adj.* grateful, appreciative.

thankfulness (thangk' fool nes), *n.* gratitude, appreciation for kindness done or service rendered.

thankless (thangk' les), *adj.* ungrateful; unappreciative.

thanks (thangks), *n.* an expression of gratitude; owing to, as *thanks* to your support, we made good.

***thanksgiving** (thangks giv' ing), *n.* the expression of gratefulness: *Thanksgiving Day,* the day set aside each year for praising God for His mercies.

that (that), *demonstrative pron.* the person or thing mentioned or understood in a given situation, as *that* is the man, *that* is what I want. *relative pron.* [*pl.* those] the individual or object referred to, as the man *that* spoke. the book *that* is last on the shelf. *adj.* pointed out, as I want *that book*. *adv.* so; to such extent, as I cannot be ready *that* soon. *conj.* the fact, as I notice *that* he did not do it; I warn you *that* you may be late; for the purpose of, as eat *that* you may live; with the result, as so tired *that* I must sleep; because, as joy *that* he had won.

thatch (thach), *n.* a thick covering of reeds or straw on a stack or roof; anything compared to it, as a thick *thatch* of hair on one's head. *v.t.* to cover, as a roof, with straw or reeds.

thaumaturgy (thô' ma tûr ji), *n.* the act of performing pretended miracles, magic.

thaw (thô), *n.* the melting of ice and snow as the weather grows warmer. *v.i. and v.t.* to melt, to turn to water, as ice and snow on a warm day; to become more affable, unbend; to clear of ice by applying heat, as to *thaw* frozen water pipes.

theater, theatre (thē' a tēr), *n.* a public building where plays are performed; a place resembling a theater with stage and seats, as the operating *theater* in a hospital; a scene of great and spectacular action, as the *theater* of war; the drama.

theatrical (thē at' ri kal), *adj.* resembling the manner of actors, stagy; of or pertaining to the theater, as *theatrical* costumes.

theft (theft), *n.* the act of stealing, robbery; that which is stolen.

theism (thē' izm), *n.* belief in a personal God or gods.

their (thâr), *possessive adj.* of or belonging to them, as *their* home.

theirs (thârz), *possessive pron.* belonging to them, as the car is *theirs*.

theme (thēm), *n.* the subject of a discourse or essay; a short essay.

themselves (them selvz'), *pron.* an emphatic form of *they* and reflexive form of *them*, as they *themselves* chose the play so they had no one but *themselves* to blame; plural form of *himself, herself* and *itself*.

then (then), *n.* a certain time, as by *then* there was nothing left. *adj.* being at a given time, as the *then* governor. *adv.* at that time, as I was *then* away from home; next in order of time. *conj.* in that case; therefore, as *then* I must refuse.

theocracy (thē ok' ra si), *n.* [*pl.* theocracies] a government by churchmen or priests as the representatives of God, as early Israel was a *theocracy*.

theology (thē ol' ô ji), *n.* [*pl.* theologies] the study of the existence, nature and laws of God.

theorem (thē' ô rem), *n.* a proposition in geometry to be proved; a demonstrated proposition in mathematics.

theoretical (thē ô ret' i kal), *adj.* based upon a belief but not proved or put into practice.

theorize (thē' ô rīz), *v.i.* to speculate about things without testing the resultant beliefs in practice.

theory (thē' ô ri), *n.* [*pl.* theories] a belief not yet tested in practice; the general prin-

ciples on which a science is based and built up; a hypothesis; something assumed as a starting point for scientific investigation.

theosophy (thē os' ô fi), *n.* [*pl.* theosophies] any of various systems of philosophy or theology claiming to receive knowledge of God by special mystical revelation.

therapeutics (ther a pū' tiks), *n.* the art or science of curing disease; the science of remedies.

there (thâr), *adv.* in that place, not here, as I was *there* at the time; introducing a sentence or clause when the verb precedes the subject, as *there* was once a princess. *interj.* so, as *there*, you have broken it.

thereafter (thâr áf' tēr), *adv.* after that; consequently.

thereby (thâr bī'), *adv.* by that means; in connection with that.

therefor (thâr fôr'), *adv.* for it or for that.

therefore (thâr' fôr), *adv.* for that reason, as a result.

therein (thâr in'), *adv.* in or into that place, time or thing; in that respect.

thereof (thâr ov'), *adv.* of it or of that, as the tree and the fruit *thereof*.

thereupon (thâr u pon'), *adv.* upon that; therefore; thereafter.

therewith (thâr with'), with that.

thermal (thûr' mal), *adj.* pertaining to heat; having heat, warm.

thermometer (thēr mom' ē tēr), *n.* an instrument for measuring the degree of heat, commonly through a column of colored mercury expanding or contracting in a glass tube with a scale marked beside it.

thermostat (thûr' mō stat), *n.* an automatic apparatus for controlling the amount of heat given by a furnace or oven; a self-operating temperature regulator.

thesaurus (thē sô' rus), *n.* [*pl.* thesauri] a storehouse or treasury; a book with a treasure of information, especially as to words and their uses; a cyclopedia.

these (thēz), *pron. pl.* plural of *this*.

thesis (thē' sis), *n.* [*pl.* theses] a proposition to be maintained by the person who advances it; a long essay, especially by a candidate for a university degree.

thew (thū), *n.* a muscle, sinew.

thews (thūz), *n.* bodily strength, muscular power.

they (thā), *personal pron. pl.* of *he, she* or *it*.

thick (thik), *n.* the part measuring most from side to side or around, as the *thick* of one's leg; the densest part or scene of greatest activity, as the *thick* of night, the *thick* of the battle. *adj.* having the third dimension great in proportion to length and width; relatively deep from one surface to the other, as a *thick* plank; dense, as a *thick* liquid, a *thick* growth of weeds; dull-witted. *adv.* densely, as bread spread *thick* with jam.

thicken (thik' en), *v.t. and v.i.* to give more substance to, as to *thicken* soup; to grow more dense, as the clouds *thickened;* to become increasingly complicated, as the plot *thickens.*

thicket (thik' et), *n.* a dense growth of underbrush or small trees.

thickly (thik' li), *adv.* compactly, densely; in husky or guttural tones, as he spoke *thickly*.

thickset (thik set'), *adj.* having a short, solid body; stocky; closely planted.

thief (thēf), *n.* [*pl.* thieves] one who steals.

thieve (thēv), *v.i. and v.t.* to steal.

thievery (thēv' er i), *n.* [*pl.* thieveries] the practice of stealing.

thigh (thī), *n.* the upper part of the leg from knee to hip.

thill (thil), *n.* a wagon shaft; one of the two wooden pieces between which a horse is hitched to a wagon.

thimble (thim' bl), *n.* a metal cover to protect the end of a finger in sewing.

thin (thin), *adj.* having little thickness in proportion to length and breadth; slim, slender; lacking in substance, as a *thin* sheet of metal, *thin* soup; lightweight, filmy, as *thin* material; slight, as a *thin* excuse. *v.i. and v.t.* to become or make less thick; to make less dense, as to *thin* the paint.

thine (*th*īn), *pron.* possessive form of *thou.*

thing (thing), *n.* any individual object; any separate and distinct object of thought; a special condition or circumstance, as the *thing* did not happen again: *things,* wraps, as put on your *things;* possessions, baggage, circumstances, as *things* look more hopeful.

think (thingk), *v.t. and v.i.* [*p.t. and p.p.* thought, *pr.p.* thinking] to form a conception of, imagine; to form a judgment or estimate of, to believe as likely, as I *think* the weather will be fair; to study, analyze, meditate upon, as I *thought* the problem through; to concentrate the thoughts upon, as he *thinks* boats; to use judgment, reason, imagination as opposed to mere sense perception; to reflect, muse; to become aware of, remember, as suddenly I *thought* of my keys; to hold an opinion, as I *think* we will not have war; to intend, as I *thought* of going.

Syn. Cogitate, contemplate, muse, imagine, suppose, believe. To *think* is a general term referring to any mental effort; to *cogitate* usually implies a problem to be solved or a plan to be made; to *contemplate* is to consider or meditate upon, as to *contemplate* a change of residence; to *muse* is to reflect or ponder with absorption and sometimes to dream; to *imagine* is to picture to oneself; to *suppose* is to think probable; to *believe* is to accept as true.

third (thûrd), *n.* one of three equal parts; the one next after the second.

third (thûrd), *adj.* next after the second.

thirdly (thûrd' li), *adv.* in the third place.

Third World (thurd wurld), *n.* used with capital or small letters to mean the underdeveloped nations of the world such as in Asia or Africa.

***thirst** (thûrst), *n.* the sensation of need for water; desire to drink; strong desire for anything, as a *thirst* for learning.

thirsty (thûrs' ti), *adj.* [*comp.* thirstier, *superl.* thirstiest] having a feeling of dryness in mouth and throat; parched.

***thirteen** (thûr tēn') *n.* one more than 12; a symbol (13) denoting that number.

thirtieth (thûr' ti eth), *n.* one of 30 equal parts; one more than the 29th.

thirty (thûr' ti), *n.* one more than 29; a symbol (30) denoting that number.

this (this), *demonstrative pron.* that which is at hand or near in locality, time or thought, as *this* is the house; *this* is the year; *this* is the plan: plural is *these.*

this (this), *adj.* designating that which is at hand or near in time or space; indicating a special person or thing, as *this* book will give you the information you wish; a person or thing just indicated, as *this* man is the one whom I just mentioned.

thistle (this' l), *n.* a plant with prickly leaves and flower heads.

thither (thith' ẽr), *adv.* to that place, as we went *thither.*

thole (thōl), *n.* a pin set in the gunwale of a boat as a brace or fulcrum for an oar in rowing.

***thong** (thông), *n.* a thin leather strap or cord, a whiplash.

thoracic (thō ras' ik), *adj.* pertaining to the chest.

thorax (thō' raks), *n.* [*pl.* thoraxes or thoraces] the chest, the part of the body between the neck and the abdomen, enclosed by the ribs and containing the heart and lungs.

***thorn** (thôrn), *n.* a prickle or spine on a stem or branch; a shrub with spiny stems; a source of distress, as his actions are a *thorn* in my side.

thorny (thôr' ni), *adj.* [*comp.* thornier, *superl.* thorniest] having sharp spines on the stems or branches; full of hardships, distressing.

***thorough** (thûr' ō), *adj.* painstaking, complete, overlooking no detail.

thoroughbred (thûr' ō bred), *n.* an animal descended from the purest stock; a person of fine background with courage and aristocratic ways.

thoroughfare (thûr' ō fār), *n.* a passage open at both ends; a navigable channel; a waterway connecting two lakes; a main street or road.

though (thō), *adv.* however, nevertheless.

though (thō), *conj.* supposing that, notwithstanding.

thought (thôt), *n.* something held in the mind; the process of reasoning; meditation; study.

thoughtful (thôt' fool), *adj.* contemplative; solicitous for the welfare of others, considerate.

thoughtless (thôt' les), *adj.* heedless, inconsiderate.

***thousand** (thou' zand), *n.* one more than 999; a large number, as *thousands* will use this book.

***thousandth** (thou' zandth), *n.* one of 1,000 equal parts; the one after the 999th.

thraldom (thrôl' dum), *n.* a state of slavery, bondage.

thrall (thrôl), *n.* a slave or serf; bondage, as

in *thrall*.

*thrash (thrash), *v.i. and v.t.* to throw oneself about, as I *thrash* in my sleep; to beat; to thresh or flail, as grain; to argue, as we must *thrash* out this matter.

thrashing (thrash' ing), *n.* a beating.

*thread (thred), *n.* a very thin cord; a filament or fiber; the spiral ridge of a screw or bolt; anything likened to a string because it is continuous, as the *thread* of a discourse. *v.i. and v.t.* to make one's way windingly, as we must *thread* through the crowd; to put a filament through the eye of, as to *thread* a needle; to put on a string, as to *thread* beads.

threadbare (thred' bâr), *adj.* worn, having lost the nap, shabby; trite, hackneyed.

threat (thret), *n.* a menace; an expressed intention to injure.

threaten (thret' n), *v.i. and v.t.* to give evidence of impending evil or danger, as the skies *threatened;* to give notice of intended reprisal or injury to, as to *threaten* a person.

three (thrē), *n.* one more than two; a symbol (3) denoting that number.

*threnody (thren' ŏ di), *n.* [*pl.* threnodies] a dirge.

*thresh (thresh), *v.i. and v.t.* to beat grain with a flail or separate the grain from the chaff by means of machinery; to toss about; to 'thrash, as grain; to go over repeatedly, as to *thresh* out a matter under discussion.

*threshold (thresh' ōld), *n.* a doorsill, an entrance; a starting point, as we stand at the *threshold* of a great era.

thrice (thrIs), *adv.* three times; in a threefold manner.

thrift (thrift), *n.* frugality, economical management; strong growth, as of a plant.

thrifty (thrif' ti), *adj.* [*comp.* thriftier, *superl.* thriftiest] frugal, economical, careful in management.

thrill (thril), *n.* a wave of emotion, a tremor of feeling. *v.i. and v.t.* to tingle with sensation or feeling, as I *thrilled* at sight of the flag; to cause to feel a tremor of excitement or emotion, as the sight of the flag *thrilled* me.

thrive (thrIv), *v.i.* [*p.t.* throve or thrived, *p.p.* thriven or thrived, *pr.p.* thriving] to prosper, flourish, grow vigorously, as celery *thrives* in that sort of soil

*throat (thrōt), *n.* the esophagus; the passage for food through the neck; the front part of the neck, containing the tonsils, vocal cords, windpipe and gullet.

throaty (thrōt' i), *adj.* [*comp.* throatier, *superl.* throatiest] guttural.

throb (throb), *n.* a strong pulsation, a beat like that of the heart; a thrill.

throb (throb), *v.i.* to pulsate, beat like the heart; to thrill with emotion.

throe (thrō), *n.* a pang, a stab of pain, agony; great distress of mind.

throne (thrōn), *n.* a royal chair of state; kingly power.

*throng (thrŏng), *n.* a multitude, a dense crowd. *v.i. and v.t.* to gather in multitudes;

to crowd together, fill with people, as to *throng* the streets.

*throttle (throt' l), *n.* a lever operating a valve that closes the steam feed of an engine; the windpipe. *v.t.* to choke, as by squeezing the windpipe; to shut off power, as to *throttle* an engine.

*through (thrōō), *prep.* from end to end of, as *through* a tunnel; from one side to the other side of, as to stick a pin *through* cloth; by means of, as I succeeded *through* your help; over the whole extent of, as to read *through* a book; during, as *through* the week. *adj.* going all the way from one point to another without stop, as a *through* train. *adv.* from one end to the other, as he read the book *through;* from one side to the other, as come *through* at this gate.

throughout (thrōō out'), *prep.* in every part of, as *throughout* the argument. *adv.* in all respects, in every part, as the novel is interesting *throughout*.

throw (thrō), *n.* the act of hurling or flinging; the distance to which a thing is hurled or flung, as that was a long *throw*. *v.t.* [*p.t.* threw, *p.p.* thrown, *pr.p.* throwing] to hurl or fling; to put down, as in wrestling; to unseat, as the horse *threw* its rider.

throwback (thrō' bak), *n.* reversion to an earlier type in race or ancestry; introduction between scenes in a motion picture of scenes from an earlier time.

thrum (thrum), *n.* a monotonous humming, strumming or tapping. *v.i. and v.t.* to finger a stringed instrument without formal musical expression, to strum.

thrums (thrumz), *n. pl.* loose, coarse yarn waste.

*thrush (thrush), *n.* any of numerous small songbirds having a brown back and brown-spotted white breast, as the song *thrush*, hermit *thrush*, wood *thrush*.

thrust (thrust), *n.* a sudden forward movement, such as the plunge of a spear or a sharp advance movement of troops; a stress in a structure tending to force parts out of place, as the *thrust* of a beam.

thrust (thrust), *v.i. and v.t.* [*p.t. and p.p.* thrust, *pr.p.* thrusting] to push forward sharply; to jab or stab, pierce.

thud (thud), *n.* a dull sound caused by a blow upon or with a yielding substance, as the *thud* of practice on a punching bag, the *thud* of a body falling on the floor.

thug (thug), *n.* a cutthroat, a ruffian.

thumb (thum), *n.* the shortest and thickest digit of the human hand; the part of a glove or mitten that covers this digit.

thumb (thum), *v.t.* to handle awkwardly; to soil by handling; to turn rapidly with the thumb, as to *thumb* the pages of a book.

thump (thump), *n.* a heavy blow; a blow that makes a dull sound. *v.i. and v.t.* to throb heavily, as my heart *thumps;* to strike with a dull heavy blow; to make the sound of such a blow.

thunder (thun' dẽr), *n.* the resounding noise caused by the sudden air expansion that accompanies a flash of lightning; the boom of cannon. *v.i. and v.t.* to produce a roar or boom like that of the clouds when lightning flashes; to utter in a loud, imperative or threatening tone.

thunderstruck (thun' děr struk), *adj.* amazed, astounded.

thurible (thū' ri bl), *n.* a censer used at Mass.

thurifer (thū' ri fěr), *n.* a priest's attendant who carries the censer at Mass.

thus (thus), *adv.* in this or that manner, as do it *thus;* to this extent, so; consequently, hence.

*****thwack** (thwak), *n.* a blow with some flat instrument. *v.t.* to strike with something flat and heavy.

thwart (thwôrt), *n.* a seat in a boat extending from side to side. *v.t.* to oppose, run counter to, frustrate.

thy (*thi*), *adj.* [possessive singular of *thou*] belonging to thee, your.

*****thyme** (tim), *n.* a common aromatic herb used as seasoning.

thymus (thi' mus), *n.* a gland of the throat that disappears entirely or largely in adult human beings; the corresponding gland in lambs and calves, called neck- or throat-sweetbread when it is used for food.

thyself (*thi* self'), *pron.* [reflexive or emphatic form of *thy*] yourself.

tiara (tē är' a), *n.* the triple crown worn by the Pope; a coronet or crownlike head-dress.

tibia (tib' i a), *n.* the inner and larger of the two bones of the leg below the knee, the shinbone.

tic (tik), *n.* a twitching of the muscles, especially of the face.

tick (tik), *n.* a small, bloodsucking insect that gets on the skin of animals, as a sheep tick; any of numerous tiny blood-sucking spiders that get on the skin of man and other animals. *n.* the stout covering of a mattress or pillow. *n.* a light, repeated sound, like that of a running clock. *v.i. and v.t.* to make a light, repeated, regular sound, as a running watch or clock; to measure with light, repeated, regular sounds, as a clock *ticks* the hours.

ticker (tik' ěr), *n.* a device that prints news or stock-market quotations on a long strip of paper telegraphically.

ticket (tik' et), *n.* a card showing that the bearer is entitled to something, as admittance to a public performance; a political party's list of candidates, as this is the party *ticket;* a card or slip of paper containing a notice; a tag, a label.

ticket (tik' et), *v.t.* to attach a label to.

ticking (tik' ing), *n.* stout fabric used for making mattresses and pillows.

*****tickle** (tik' l), *v.t.* to touch lightly so as to produce a nervous reaction, usually laughter; to amuse in a light, pleasant way, as this letter *tickles* me.

ticklish (tik' lish), *adj.* sensitive to light touches; precarious, difficult, as this is a *ticklish* job.

*****tidal** (tid' al), *adj.* flowing and ebbing, as

tidal waters; affected by tides, as a *tidal* river.

tidbit (tid' bit), *n.* a choice morsel, a titbit.

tide (tid), *n.* the alternate rise and fall of the sea along a coast; the rise and fall of events; a period of time, a season, as Yule-*tide, noontide, eventide. v.t.* to cause to float with a high tide, as to *tide* a stranded vessel; to carry along in time of trouble as if on a *tide,* as this will *tide* you over.

tidewater (tid' wô těr), *n.* rivers into which the sea tides enter; the land as far back as the tides enter.

tidings (ti' dingz), *n. pl.* news.

tidy (ti' di), *adj.* [*comp.* tidier, *superl.* tidiest] neat, orderly, as a tidy room; moderately large, as a *tidy* inheritance.

tidy (ti' di), *n.* [*pl.* tidies] a light ornamental covering for the back or arms of a chair.

tidy (ti' di), *v.t.* [*p.t. and p.p.* tidied, *pr.p.* tidying] to make neat, set in order.

tie (ti), *n.* a knot or fastening; something to be knotted, as a neck*tie* or a shoelace; an even score in a contest, as the game was a *tie;* a timber laid crosswise to support a structure, as a railroad *tie;* a legal obligation; a bond as of affection, duty or interest. *v.i. and v.t.* to form a knot; to come to an equal score; to fasten with a knot; to attach, as friendship *ties* me to you; to restrict or limit.

tier (těr), *n.* one row in a series of rising banks or terraces, as a *tier* of seats in a stadium.

tiff (tif), *n.* a slight quarrel; a peevish burst of temper.

*****tiger** (ti' gěr), *n.* a large fierce flesh-eating animal of the cat family with striped sleek coat.

tight (tit), *adj.* taut, not loose; fastened, held or tied securely; close-fitting, as a *tight* shoe; so closely built as to be impervious to water, as a *tight* roof, a *tight* boat; hazardous, as a *tight* squeeze.

tigress (ti' gres), *n.* a female tiger.

tile (til), *n.* a thin piece of baked clay used as roofing; a hollow block of baked clay used in making inner walls; a short section of earthen pipe used in drainage.

tile (til), *v.t.* to cover, as a floor or roof, with blocks or slabs of baked clay.

till (til), *n.* a money drawer. *v.t.* to prepare land for the planting of seed, cultivate. *prep.* to the time of, as *till* next year. *conj.* to a certain time, as do not start work *till* I give you the order.

tillage (til' ij), *n.* cultivation of land; land under cultivation.

tiller (til' ěr), *n.* one who cultivates the land; a lever to turn the rudder of a vessel.

tilt (tilt), *n.* a slope or slant, an incline; a duel with lances; a thrust of a lance.

tilt (tilt), *v.i. and v.t.* to tip sidewise; to engage in a combat with lances; to slant by raising one end, as to *tilt* a board.

timber (tim' běr), *n.* wood suitable for building, either in the tree or dressed and cut; a heavy piece of wood, as a beam or joist.

*****timbre** (tim' běr), *n.* quality of musical

sound, tone color.

time (tīm), *n.* the measure of duration; an age or period of history; a moment or date fixed for an event, as it is *time* to go; a period characterized by some special quality or experience, as I am having a hard *time;* instance of repetition or multiplication, as I called you three *times*, 2 *times* 2 are 4; a system for identifying the moment, as solar *time* or standard *time;* the metrical arrangement of notes in music, rhythm, as three-four *time.*

time (tīm), *v.t.* to record the duration or speed of, as to *time* a race; to adapt or arrange to the moment, schedule, as to *time* a visit; to regulate, as a watch; to set the beat for, as to *time* an orchestra.

timeless (tīm' les), *adj.* eternal.

timely (tīm' li), *adj.* [*comp.* timelier, *superl.* timeliest] opportune.

timid (tim' id), *adj.* lacking courage, faint-hearted, fearful.

timorous (tim' ēr us), *adj.* fearful of danger; indicating fear, as a *timorous* voice.

timothy (tim' ō thi), *n.* a tall, valuable grass grown for hay.

timpano (tim' pa nō), *n.* [*pl.* timpani] a kettledrum; a percussion instrument in the orchestra: sometimes *tympano*, *tympani.*

tin (tin), *n.* a silver-white, soft metal easily rolled out and melted; a vessel or implement made of this metal or coated with it, especially a can to hold preserved foods. *v.t.* to put in cans to preserve, as food.

*tincture (tingk' tūr), *n.* a medicinal substance dissolved in alcohol; a tinge, a small amount. *v.t.* to impart a shade of color to, tinge; to flavor lightly.

tinder (tin' dēr), *n.* any material that will ignite from a spark, formerly used in starting fires with a spark struck by steel on flint.

tine (tīn), *n.* a spike, as of a pitchfork; a prong, as of a table fork or a deer's antler.

tin foil (tin foil), tin or an alloy of it rolled into very thin sheets and used for airtight wrapping and in electrical work.

tinge (tinj), *n.* a slight degree of some color or flavor imparted to a substance. *v.t.* to color lightly; to add a slight flavor to.

tingle (ting' gl), *n.* a prickly or tingling sensation. *v.i.* to feel a prickly or stinging sensation, as my ears *tingle.*

tinker (tingk' ēr), *n.* one who mends pots and pans. *v.i. and v.t.* to work as a pot and kettle mender; to work in a bungling way; to mend, especially botchily.

tinkle (ting' kl), *n.* a small, sharp ringing sound. *v.i.* to make or cause to make a small, sharp ringing sound.

tin plate (tin plāt), sheet iron coated with tin.

tinsel (tin' sel), *n.* thin glittering metallic threads; a fabric ornamented with such threads. *adj.* showy but having no value.

tint (tint), *n.* a tinge of color; a light shade of a color. *v.t.* to color lightly, tinge with color.

tiny (tī' ni), *adj.* [*comp.* tinier, *superl.* tiniest] very small.

tip (tip), *n.* a point or the end of anything; anything attached to the end of something, as the *tip* of an arrow. *n.* a small gift as a reward for personal service; secret information on something about to happen, advice supposed to be based on actual knowledge, as a *tip* on a race. *v.t.* to cause to lean or dip, tilt, as to *tip* a table, *tip* a hat. *v.t.* to reward for personal service, as to *tip* a waiter; to give secret information or a hint to, as to *tip* a friend on the market. *v.i. and v.t.* to form a point; to furnish with a point or cap, to cover the point of.

tippet (tip' et), *n.* a narrow cape or covering of cloth or fur for the neck and shoulders.

tipple (tip' l), *n.* liquor. *v.i.* to drink liquor frequently, a little at a time.

tipsy (tip' si), *adj.* [*comp.* tipsier, *superl.* tipsiest] slightly intoxicated, unsteady from the effects of liquor but not drunk.

tiptoe (tip' tō), *v.i.* to walk on the toes. *adv.* on the toes, expectantly; quietly, silently.

tiptop (tip' top), *adj.* extra good, best of its kind.

*tirade (tī' rād), *n.* a long, violent speech, especially one of a scolding nature.

tire (tīr), *n.* a band or hoop of metal or rubber for the rim of a wheel. *v.i. and v.t.* to grow weary; to make weary.

tiresome (tīr' sum), *adj.* wearisome, tedious.

*tissue (tish' ū), *n.* muscular or nerve fiber in a plant or animal body; any thin or delicate woven texture or fabric; a web or interwoven network, as his testimony was a *tissue* of falsehoods.

tit (tit), *n.* any of several small birds, as *titmouse. n.* tap or light blow, as tit for tat.

titanic (tī tan' ik), *adj.* huge, having enormous strength.

titbit (tit' bit), *n.* a choice morsel.

*tithe (tīth), *n.* the 10th part of anything; a tax of one-tenth, especially collected to support churches.

titillate (tit' i lāt), *v.t.* to tickle.

title (tī' tl), *n.* an appellation indicating dignity, rank or office; a rightful claim; the name of an article, a book, poem, picture or other work of art.

titmouse (tit' mous), *n.* a small songbird.

titter (tit' ēr), *n.* a giggle; a restrained laugh.

title (tit' l), *n.* a tiny bit.

tittle-tattle (tit' l tat' l), *n.* idle chatter, gossip.

titular (tit' ū lēr), *adj.* pertaining to a title; existing in name only, nominal.

to (tōō), *adv.* toward or into a certain direction or condition, as heave *to*, come *to*, push the door *to;* nearby, as close *to.*

to (tōō), *prep.* in the direction of or into, as *to* the north, I am going *to* the city; resulting in, as *to* my great joy, burned *to* ashes; in honor of, as drink *to* the king, sing *to* the Lord; in accord with, as *to* the best of my belief; for, as a key *to* the house; against, as hand *to* hand; as far as, as come *to* the corner, burned *to* the ground.

*toad (tōd), *n.* a froglike, tailless animal that feeds on insects, breeds in water, but lives mostly on land.

toadstool (tŏd' stōōl), *n.* an umbrella-shaped fungus usually a poisonous variety of mushroom, growing on decayed vegetable matter.

toady (tōd' ĭ), *n.* [*pl.* toadies] a flatterer, a sycophant, one who fawns upon the wealthy or influential. *v.i. and v.t.* [*p.t. and p.p.* toadied, *pr.p.* toadying] to flatter, fawn upon, seek favor.

*****toast** (tōst), *n.* sliced bread browned by dry heat; the person named when a health is drunk; a sentiment expressed and drunk to.

toast (tōst), *v.t.* to brown sliced bread by dry heat; to brown or heat by fire, as he *toasted* his shins as he stood before the hearth; to drink to the health of.

*****tobacco** (tō bak' ō), *n.* [*pl.* tobaccos] a plant native to America, the dried and cured leaves of which are used for smoking and chewing; the dried and cured leaf of this plant.

tobacconist (tō bak' ō nĭst), *n.* one who deals in cigars, cigarettes, pipe tobacco, chewing plugs and the like.

toboggan (tō bog' an), *n.* a long, flat sled without runners, with the front end curving upward and backward, used for coasting.

toboggan (tō bog' an), *v.i.* to coast down a hill on a runnerless sled; to make any swift descent that might be compared to such a slide, as he fairly *tobogganed* down from the heights of his earlier success.

tocsin (tok' sin), *n.* an alarm bell; any warning signal.

today (too dā'), *n.* the present day, time or era. *adv.* nowadays, as there is no slavery in the U. S. *today.*

toddle (tod' l), *v.i.* to move with short, uncertain steps like those of a child learning to walk.

toe (tō), *n.* one of the digits on the human foot; the forward part of a hoof; the part of an article of footgear covering the forward part of the foot.

toe (tō), *v.i. and v.t.* to hold the toes, as he *toes* in when he walks; to touch with one's toes, as to *toe* the mark.

tofu (tō ´ fōō), *n.* a custard like food, originally from Japan, made from soybeans.

tog (tog), *v.i. and v.t.* to dress, to put clothes on, as he was *togged* out in his best.

toga (tō' ga), *n.* [*pl.* togas] a loose outer garment worn by the citizens of ancient Rome; a symbol of dignity, as of a judge or senator.

*****together** (too geth' ẽr), *adv.* in company each with the other, as we were *together;* jointly, at the same time, as let us work *together;* into contact or collision, as to clap the hands *together,* two cars ran *together;* without intermission, as to read for hours *together.*

toggery (tog' ẽr ĭ), *n.* [*pl.* toggeries] clothing, articles of finery.

toggle (tog' l), *n.* a fastener used in place of a button and passing through a loop of cord instead of a buttonhole; an iron bolt or wooden pin with a groove around the middle to be passed through a ring or loop of rope as a temporary fastening.

togs (togz), *n. pl.* clothing.

*****toil** (toil), *n.* hard work; work that wearies the mind or body.

toil (toil), *v.i.* to work hard and with close application, as I am *toiling* on this lesson.

toilsome (toil' sum), *adj.* laborious, wearisome.

token (tō' ken), *n.* a symbol; indication, evidence, as a *token* of friendship; a keepsake; a piece of metal used in place of a coin, as for paying carfare on conveyances operated by those who sell the tokens.

*****tolerable** (tol' ẽr a bl), *adj.* endurable, supportable; permissible, acceptable, fairly good.

tolerance (tol' ẽr ans), *n.* liberality toward the opinions of others; patience with others.

tolerant (tol' ẽr ant), *adj.* forbearing; patient with the ideas or acts of others.

tolerate (tol' ẽr āt), *v.t.* to endure, permit, put up with; to refrain from opposing.

toleration (tol ẽr ā' shun), *n.* the act of permitting to go on without interference; acceptance of something not entirely approved.

*****toll** (tōl), *n.* a charge for the use of something, as a bridge or a telephone, maintained usually by private operators for use by the public. *n.* the sound of a bell rung with slow, regular strokes. *v.i. and v.t.* to ring slowly at regular intervals of time, as the bell *tolls,* the sexton *tolls* the bell.

tomahawk (tom' a hôk), *n.* a weapon of the North American Indians resembling a hatchet.

*****tomato** (tō mā' tō), *n.* [*pl.* tomatoes] a plant with a red-skinned, red-fleshed juicy fruit eaten raw as a vegetable or cooked in various ways.

tomb (tōōm), *n.* a grave or burial vault.

tomboy (tom' boi), *n.* a wild, romping girl.

tome (tōm), *n.* a large book; a bulky volume.

*****tomorrow** (too mor' ō), *n.* the day after this day, as *tomorrow* is the day set; the future. *adv.* on the next day after today, as I shall go *tomorrow;* in the future.

tom-tom (tom' tom), *n.* a primitive drum, originally made of a hollowed log; a drum used in Oriental countries.

*****ton** (tun), *n.* a measure of weight: *short ton,* 2,000 pounds; *long ton,* 2,240 pounds; *metric ton,* 2,204.6 pounds. *n.* a unit of measure applied to the internal capacity of ships and equal to 100 cubic feet; a unit of measure used to reckon the displacement of vessels and equal to 35 cubic feet.

*****tone** (tōn), *n.* a sound; the quality of a sound; the characteristics of sound, in respect of vibration, duration, volume and pitch; the characteristic quality of a voice, as to speak in strong *tones* or sweet *tones;* the character or quality of anything, as the *tone* of this essay is harsh, this painting is in soft *tones;* physical condition, as the patient's general *tone* is good.

tone (tōn), *v.i. and v.t.* to harmonize, as this color *tones* well with the general scheme of decoration; to bring to a required shade of sound or color; to bring into a certain condition, as he should *tone* up his condition, to *tone* down one's enthusiasm.

tone poem (tōn pō' ĕm), a musical composition expressing poetic images.

tong (tŏng), *n.* a Chinese secret society.

*****tongs** (tŏngz), *n. pl.* an implement with two pivoted arms, used to grasp, as ice *tongs*, sugar *tongs*.

*****tongue** (tung), *n.* the organ of taste and speech, located in the mouth; anything thought of as resembling this organ in shape or use, as the *tongue* of a buckle, the *tongue* of a bell, a *tongue*-and-groove board; a language.

tonic (ton' ik), *n.* a strengthening medicine.

tonic (ton' ik), *adj.* strengthening, bracing, as this air is *tonic*, your ideas have a *tonic* quality.

tonight (too nīt'), *n.* the present night, the night following today. *adv.* on or during this night or the night following today.

tonnage (tun' ij), *n.* weight measured by the ton; the carrying capacity of a ship calculated in units of 100 cubic feet; displacement of a ship, figured by the number of tons of water it pushes aside when not in motion; a tax on ships or shipping according to amount of displacement.

*****tonneau** (tun ō'), *n.* [*pl.* tonneaus or tonneaux] the rounded rear section of some automobiles.

tonsil (ton' sil), *n.* one of two small glands at the opening of the throat.

tonsillectomy (ton si lek' tō mi), *n.* [*pl.* tonsillectomies] removal of one or both of the small glands of the throat by a surgical operation.

*****tonsillitis** (ton si lī' tis), *n.* inflammation of the two small glands at the back of the mouth, a form of sore throat.

tonsorial (ton sō' ri al), *adj.* pertaining to barbers or their business.

*****tonsure** (ton' shĕr), *n.* the act of shaving the crown of the head; the bare crown of a shaved head, worn by monks and some priests.

too (tōō), *adv.* excessively, very, as *too* much, I shall be only *too* glad to do it; likewise, also, as let me come *too*.

tool (tōōl), *n.* an instrument for doing work, as a hand *tool*, machine *tools;* a person used as an instrument by another, as he is the *tool* of a gang of crooks.

tooling (tōōl' ing), *n.* work done with a hand implement, as decorative designs on a fine leather bookbinding.

toot (tōōt), *n.* a short note sounded with horn or whistle, as the *toot* of your car.

toot (tōōt), *v.i. and v.t.* to sound, as a horn or whistle, with short notes.

tooth (tōōth), *n.* [*pl.* teeth] one of the hard structures growing in the jaws to bite or grind food; any projection likened to such a structure, as the *teeth* of a saw, a *tooth* on a cog wheel. *v.t.* to supply with an edge having notches and projections in a regular series.

toothsome (tōōth' sum), *adj.* palatable, pleasant-tasting.

top (top), *n.* the highest point, summit, as the *top* of a mountain; the part of a plant above ground, as beet *tops;* a platform at the head of a mast; the highest position,

person or rank, as he stands at the *top* in his profession. *n.* toy with sharp point or peg on which it spins. *v.t.* to rise above others, as this peak *tops* the whole range; to cover the peak of, as the mountains are *topped* with snow; to cut off the part of a plant above ground or ends of rising stems; to excel, as this car *tops* them all.

topaz (tō' paz), *n.* a semiprecious, transparent, yellow stone, having a luster and sparkle like that of crystal.

top boot (top bōōt), a high leg covering or boot of old style, now worn by huntsmen and liveried servants.

top coat (top cōt), a light overcoat.

toper (tōp' ēr), *n.* a hard drinker, a drunkard.

*****topic** (top' ik), *n.* a subject of discourse, argument or conversation, as live *topics* of the day.

topmast (top' mȧst), *n.* the second mast upward from the deck of a ship.

*****topography** (tō pog' ra fi), *n.* [*pl.* topographies] the detailed description of the physical features of a region; the art of making maps showing the characteristic features of the land.

topple (top' l), *v.i. and v.t.* to totter and fall; to overturn.

topsy-turvy (top' si tûr' vi), *adv.* upside down, higgledy-piggledy, confused, in disorderly manner.

toque (tōk), *n.* a woman's hat, fitting close and having no brim; a knitted cap.

*****torch** (tôrch), *n.* a flaming light from burning wood, tallow or the like; a mass of inflammable material carried burning on a pole to light the way or kindle a fire; anything that enlightens, as the *torch* of research; a can filled with oil and having a wick, carried on the end of a pole; a flameblower used in burning off paint, melting metals or welding.

*****toreador** (tor' ē a dôr), *n.* a bullfighter, especially a mounted one.

*****torment** (tôr' ment), *n.* extreme pain, torture or anguish of body or mind.

    Syn. Torture. *Torture* is extreme *torment*. We may suffer *torment* from any of a great variety of indirect means; *torment* has come to mean often very little more than harassment; *torture* is the infliction or experiencing of exquisite physical or mental pain or agony.

torment (tôr ment'), *v.t.* to torture, cause agony to; to vex, tease.

*****tornado** (tôr nā' dō), *n.* [*pl.* tornadoes or tornados] a violent storm with a black, funnel-shaped whirling cloud and wind that follows a narrow path.

torpedo (tôr pē' dō), *n.* [*pl.* torpedoes] a toy of twisted paper containing gravel and a charge of powder to explode when thrown against a hard surface; a cap placed on a railroad track, exploded by the passing of a train and giving the signal to stop; a case or shell with high explosive charge; a large cigar-shaped self-propelling projectile discharged underwater and aimed to strike the hull of an enemy ship.

torpid (tôr' pĭd), *adj.* numb, inactive, sluggish, as a *torpid* liver.

torpor (tôr' pĕr), *n.* numbness, inactivity, sluggishness.

torrent (tor' ent), *n.* a violent, rapid stream; a violent downpour, as the rain came down in *torrents;* any violent outpouring, as a *torrent* of bad language.

torrid (tor' ĭd), *adj.* extremely hot, scorching, burning.

torso (tôr' sŏ), *n.* [*pl.* torsos] the human trunk; a statue of the human trunk.

tort (tôrt), *n.* any wrongful act except breach of contract for which a civil suit can be brought.

***tortoise** (tôr' tus), *n.* a turtle, especially one that lives on land or in fresh water.

***tortuous** (tor' tū us), *adj.* winding, twisting, crooked, devious.

torture (tôr' tūr), *n.* agony of mind or body, excruciating mental or physical pain. *v.t.* to cause to suffer greatly, cause agony to; to inflict great pain upon; to distort or twist, put to great strain, as to *torture* a Bible text to get new meanings.

***toss** (tôs), *n.* a short throw; an upward movement, as a *toss* of the head.

***toss** (tôs), *v.t. and v.i.* to throw with the hand; to lift with a quick motion, as to *toss* one's head; to move from side to side or be lifted up and down, as branches *toss* in a heavy wind, boats *toss* on rough water.

tot (tot), *n.* anything small and insignificant; a small child.

total (tō' tal), *n.* the whole sum or amount; the aggregate. *v.i. and v.t.* to form complete whole; to add up to, as the bill *totals* $5; to find the complete sum, as *total* the items of this account.

total (tō' tal), *adj.* complete, entire, as *total* cost, a *total* loss.

***totem** (tō' tem), *n.* an animal or other natural object considered as being related to or significant of a clan or tribe among primitive people; the image of this animal or object used as a symbol.

totter (tot' ĕr), *v.i.* to shake as if about to fall; to be unsteady.

***touch** (tuch), *n.* the sense by which we perceive through contact with things; the sensation produced through physical contact; a trace, as a *touch* of fever; style or manner, as this shows the *touch* of an expert; relationship or communication, as to be in *touch* with someone.

touch (tuch), *v.i. and v.t.* to come in contact, as two things *touch;* to make contact with, as this wire *touches* the beam; to perceive by feeling; to move the sensibilities of, as your news *touches* me deeply.

touching (tuch' ing), *adj.* pathetic, moving the emotions.

touchy (tuch' ĭ), *adj.* [*comp.* touchier, *superl.* touchiest] peevish; sensitive.

***tough** (tuf), *adj.* tenacious; hard to break or pull apart; hard-fibered; strong.

toughen (tuf' en), *v.i. and v.t.* to strengthen; to harden.

***toupee** (tōō pē'), *n.* a small or partial wig.

tour (toor), *n.* an excursion; a trip; a journey through many places.

***tour** (toor), *v.t. and v.i.* to go through, as to *tour* a state or country; to journey from place to place, as we *toured* all summer.

***tournament** (toor' na ment), *n.* a series of sport contests or games; a mock battle by knights in olden times.

***tourney** (toor' nĭ), *n.* a tournament.

***tousle** (tou' zl), *v.t.* to disarrange, put in disorder.

tousled (tou' zld), *adj.* disordered, disarranged, as *tousled* hair.

tow (tō), *n.* coarse fiber of flax, hemp or jute, distinguished from fine clean fiber: *tow-colored*, flaxen, yellow. *n.* a boat or number of boats pulled through the water by another vessel; a barge; the state or an instance of being towed, as to take in *tow. v.t.* to pull by means of a rope, as to *tow* a boat, *tow* a disabled car.

towage (tō' ĭj), *n.* the act of hauling a boat; the charge for such hauling.

***toward** (tō' ĕrd or tôrd) or **towards** (tō' ĕrds or tôrds), *prep.* in the direction of, as *toward* the north; contributing to, for, as here is a dollar *toward* your expenses; near to, as *toward* the end of day; regarding, as your attitude *toward* religion; near in time, as it happened *toward* noon.

***towel** (tou' el), *n.* a piece of cloth or paper for drying things by wiping, as a hand *towel*, a dish *towel*.

toweling (tou' el ing), *n.* material for making towels.

***tower** (tou' ĕr), *n.* a lofty structure rising above its surroundings, either a separate structure or part of a building, as the radio *tower. v.i.* to rise to great height, project above surrounding things, as mountains *tower* over a lake.

town (toun), *n.* a settlement larger than a village, smaller than a city.

township (toun' ship), *n.* a subdivision of a county; a land section of 36 square miles.

toxemia (toks ē' mĭ a), *n.* a morbid condition of the blood, the presence of poison in the blood; a form of blood poisoning.

toxic (tok' sĭk), *adj.* poisonous.

toxicology (tok sĭ kol' ŏ jĭ), *n.* the science that treats of poisons and their antidotes.

***toxin** (tok' sĭn), *n.* a poison produced in organic matter, as the tissues of plants or animals.

***toy** (toi), *n.* a plaything; a bauble; something of no real value.

toy (toi), *v.i.* to dally with, trifle.

***trace** (trās), *n.* a mark left by anything; a footprint; a barely perceptible quantity or amount, as a *trace* of poison in the cup.

trace (trās), *v.t.* to delineate, sketch; to copy by following the lines through a transparent sheet placed over an original drawing; to follow by means of tracks left by something that passed before; to hunt out evidence of, as to *trace* the development of a city.

***trachea** (trā' kē a), *n.* the windpipe.

track (trak); *n.* a mark left by something

passing; footprints showing the passage of a person or animal; any regular course; a double line of rails for trains; contact or knowledge, as to keep *track* of things or events.

track (trak), *v.t.* to leave marks on, as to *track* a floor; to trail, as to *track* a fugitive; to make footprints with, as to *track* mud on the carpet.

tract (trakt), *n.* a short treatise, especially on matters of religion or politics.

tractable (trak′ ta bl), *adj.* docile, easily managed.

traction (trak′ shun), *n.* the act of drawing over a surface; the friction of a body moving over a surface; the power to move over a surface and stick to it, as slippery mud kills the *traction* of car wheels.

tractor (trak′ tẽr), *n.* an automotive vehicle to furnish power to pull a plow, draw stumps, or the like.

trade (trād), *n.* commerce; exchange of goods; buying and selling for gain; a special craft or those engaged in it, as the building *trade*; a bargain or swap.

trademark (trād′ märk), *n.* a symbol registered with the Government to distinguish and protect a line of goods or some particular product.

trade price (trād prīs), the cost of goods to the retailer buying from a wholesaler.

trader (trād′ ẽr), *n.* one who engages in commerce.

trade union (trād ūn′ yun), *n.* an organized combination of workers engaged in the same craft, promoting their common interests.

trade wind (trād wind), a steady air current in the Torrid Zone, blowing strongly and steadily from the northeast on the north of the equator and from the southeast on the south of the equator.

tradition (tra dish′ un), *n.* the handing down of knowledge, beliefs and customs from one generation to another; a belief or custom so taught; anything handed down from the past and so strongly rooted as to be as inviolable as law.

traduce (tra dūs′), *v.t.* to slander; to make deliberate false statements about another person's acts or character.

traffic (traf′ ik), *n.* business or trade, commerce; transportation; movement of vehicles on street or highway, as *traffic* is very heavy. *v.i.* [*p.t.* and *p.p.* trafficked, *pr.p.* trafficking] to buy and sell; to do business in a commercial way, as he *traffics* in dry goods.

traffic manager (traf′ ik man′ ij ẽr), a superintendent in an industrial establishment or railway office who routes shipments, checks waybills or controls traffic.

*tragacanth (trag′ a kanth), *n.* a gum obtained from certain Asiatic and East European herbs and used in finishing textiles and in making medicines and mucilage.

*tragedy (traj′ e dē), *n.* [*pl.* tragedies] any human experience of disaster; a play presenting situations that show people undergoing and reacting to such experiences of failure and trial.

tragic (traj′ ik), *adj.* involving calamity, trial and suffering.

*trail (trāl), *n.* the track left by anything in motion; the track, as of marks on the ground or scent in the air, by which hounds and hunters follow fleeing game; a path or fixed route, as an Indian *trail*; a train, anything dragged behind, as the war brought depression in its *trail*.

trail (trāl), *v.i. and v.t.* to drag behind or be drawn along; to follow in a straggling line; to lag; to drag along behind; to pursue by following a track, as to *trail* game.

train (trān), *n.* a series, as a *train* of events, a *train* of arguments, a *train* of cars; the part of a gown or robe that trails; a line of gunpowder laid to a charge of explosive to set it off. *v.i. and v.t.* to prepare for a contest, make oneself fit for high exertion, as athletes *train*; to prepare, as a person or persons, for sports, as to *train* a ball club; to teach, as an animal to do tricks or obey orders; to direct, aim, as to *train* a gun on a mark; to keep company or fraternize, as he *trained* with a rough group.

training (trān′ ing), *n.* instruction, drill; the state of being instructed or drilled, as to be in *training*, his *training* is excellent.

train oil (trān oil), an illuminating and lubricating oil obtained from the blubber of the right whale or some other sea animal, used in soapmaking, preparing leather, tempering steel.

*trait (trāt), *n.* a distinguishing characteristic of character or mind.

traitor (trā′ tẽr), *n.* one guilty of treason; one who is false to a trust; one who betrays his country, a cause or an associate.

*trajectory (tra jek′ tō ri), *n.* [*pl.* trajectories] the curved path of a body hurled horizontally into space, as of a baseball or a bullet.

tram (tram), *n.* a coal car in a mine; a streetcar; a street railway.

*trammel (tram′ el), *n.* anything that impedes progress or action; anything that limit freedom; a fetter. *v.t.* to impede or hinder; to shackle.

tramp (tramp), *n.* a vagrant; one who wanders from place to place aimlessly. *v.i. and v.t.* to walk with heavy steps; to wander through on foot, as to *tramp* the hills; to tread upon heavily and repeatedly, trample, as to *tramp* the lawn.

trample (tram′ pl), *v.t.* to tread underfoot; to crush with the feet, as you boys have *trampled* the lawn.

tramway (tram′ wā), *n.* a pathway with light rails on which small cars may run.

*trance (tràns), *n.* a temporary cessation of consciousness; a hypnotic state; a deep sleep from which one cannot be aroused; a state of ecstatic dreaming.

*tranquil (trang′ kwil), *adj.* calm, quiet, undisturbed.

tranquilize (trang′ kwil iz), *v.t.* to calm and quiet; to free from disturbance.

*tranquility (tran kwil′ i ti), *n.* serenity; a

state of calm and peace.

*transact (trans akt'), *v.t.* to carry through, accomplish, as to *transact* business.

transaction (trans ak' shun), *n.* something accomplished; a business deal.

*transcend (tran send'), *v.i.* to rise above, surpass, exceed, as this *transcends* belief.

transcendent (tran sen' dent), *adj.* surpassing, superlative, extraordinary.

*transcendental (tran sen den' tal), *adj.* beyond the limits of human experience; outside the field of perception by the senses.

transcribe (tran skrib'), *v.t.* to copy; to write out from notes, as a stenographer *transcribes* a dictated letter.

transcript (tran' skript), *n.* a copy made directly from an original.

transcription (tran skrip' shun), *n.* a copy; the act of copying.

*transept (tran' sept), *n.* the part of a church at right angles to the chancel, making the short arms of a cross.

*transfer (trans' fûr), *n.* removal from one place to another; conveyance of property from one owner to another; a station where passengers change from one conveyance to another; a ticket entitling a passenger to finish his journey in another vehicle without further charge.

*transfer (trans fûr'), *v.i. and v.t.* to move from one place to another; to change to another vehicle; to convey to another, as property.

transfigure (trans fig' ūr), *v.t.* to change the outward form or appearance of.

Syn. Transform, transfigure, metamorphose. *Transform* is the general term and means to change completely both the inner nature and the outward form or appearance; *transfigure*, because of its Biblical connotation, implies a change that glorifies or exalts; *metamorphose* means to change into something entirely different, as a tadpole is *metamorphosed* into a frog, and Ulysses' men were *metamorphosed* into swine.

transfix (trans fiks'), *v.t.* to pierce through, as with a spear or with surprise or horror.

transform (trans fôrm'), *v.t.* to change the shape, appearance or character of.

transformation (trans fôr mā' shun), *n.* a complete change, as of appearance or personality.

transformer (trans fôr' mêr), *n.* an induction coil to raise or lower the strength of an electric current.

transfuse (trans fūz'), *v.t.* to pour from one vessel to another; to pump from one person's veins into those of another, as blood.

transfusion (trans fū' zhun), *n.* the transference of blood from one person into the veins of another; any injection into the blood, as of salt.

transgress (trans gres'), *v.i. and v.t.* to break or violate a law; to violate or sin against, as to transgress a law; to go beyond, as to *transgress* a boundary.

transgression (trans gresh' un), *n.* an offense against or violation of a law or moral rule; a sin.

transgressor (trans gres' ĕr), *n.* an offender; a sinner.

*transient (tran' shent), *n.* something that exists for a short time only; a temporary guest, especially at a hotel.

transient (tran' shent), *adj.* fleeting, brief, passing quickly, as *transient* beauty; not staying long, as *transient* guests.

transistor (tran zis´ ter), *n.* a simple computer pathway that carries, routes, magnifies, or stores electrical charges.

transit (tran' sit), *n.* passage through or over, as to permit *transit*, rapid *transit*; a surveyor's instrument to measure angles.

*transition (tran zish' un), *n.* passage from one place to another; a state of change from one state of being or development to another; the change effected or the period of time during which the change takes place; change from one key to another in a musical composition.

transitive (tran' si tiv), *n.* a verb taking an object. *adj.* requiring an object, either expressed or understood, as a *transitive* verb.

*translate (trans lāt'), *v.t.* to render from one language into another, as to *translate* a Latin text into English; to carry from one state to another, as Enoch was *translated*, that is, carried to heaven without dying; words are *translated* into action.

translation (trans lā' shun), *n.* the act of rendering from one language to another; a book, article or the like rendered from one language into another; the action of being carried from one state to another, as the *translation* of a poem into music, the *translation* of thought into words or action.

*translucent (trans lū' sent), *adj.* permitting light to pass through but not permitting objects to be distinguished, as frosted glass is *translucent*.

*transmigration (trans mī grā' shun), *n.* the passing of the soul from one body into another at the time of death.

transmissible (trans mis' i bl), *adj.* capable of being passed from one to another or through a body or substance, as electricity is *transmissible* through any conductor; permitted to be sent, as *transmissible* matter for the mails or telegraph.

*transmission (trans mish' un), *n.* the act of sending or transferring; the state of being transferred; that by which power is conveyed; passage of radio waves between sending and receiving stations.

*transmit (trans mit'), *v.t.* to send through or across, pass on, as to *transmit* a message; to conduct, as to *transmit* heat.

transmitter (trans mit' ĕr), *n.* the sending apparatus of a telegraph; the part of a telephone into which one speaks.

transmute (trans mūt'), *v.t.* to change from one form, nature or substance into another, as the alchemists of old sought to *transmute* baser metals into gold.

*transom (tran' sum), *n.* a small window above another window or above a door.

*transparency (trans pâr' en si), *n.* [pl. transparencies] the state of permitting passage of light so that objects can be discerned, as the *transparency* of clear glass; clear simplicity of character or of style in writing; a picture on glass, to be held in front of a light.

*__transparent__ (trans pâr' ent), *adj.* permitting the passage of light so that objects can be seen: opposite of *opaque;* absolutely clear, as a *transparent* style of writing.

transpire (tran spīr'), *v.i. and v.t.* to leak out, become known; to pass off as vapor; to happen, come to pass, occur; to exhale, as plants *transpire* moisture.

*__transplant__ (trans plănt'), *v.t.* to take up and plant in another place; to remove and re-establish in another place, as to *transplant* colonists.

*__transport__ (trans' pŏrt), *n.* conveyance, as the *transport* of goods overseas; any conveyance used in moving passengers or goods; a vessel used to carry troops and stores overseas in wartime; a state of rapture or great emotion.

*__transport__ (trans pŏrt'), *v.t.* to carry from one place to another, as this vessel *transports* freight; to move or carry away with violent emotion, as to be *transported* with joy; to remove or deport from a country, as to *transport* an undesirable alien.

transportation (trans pōr tă' shun), *n.* the act or business of moving passengers and goods; the means of conveyance used; banishment, especially of convicts to a penal colony.

transpose (trans pōz'), *v.t.* to change about, putting one in place of the other; to reverse; to move from one side of an algebraic equation to the other.

transposition (trans pō zĭsh' un), *n.* the act of interchanging; an accidental misplacing of letters in print.

transship (trans shĭp'), *v.t.* to transfer from one conveyance or line to another.

*__transubstantiation__ (tran sub stan shĭ ā' shun), *n.* the conversion of the bread and wine into the body and blood of Christ; the doctrine that supports belief in this change and holds that only the appearances of the bread and wine remain.

transverse (trans vûrs'), *adj.* lying crosswise, as a *transverse* beam; athwart.

trap (trap), *n.* a device closing suddenly with a spring to catch game or other animals; an ambush; a contrivance preventing escape indoors of foul air from a drain. *n.* any of various dark-colored igneous rocks. *v.t.* to take or catch in a snare; to catch by means of a trick, as to *trap* a burglar.

*__trapeze__ (tra pēz'), *n.* a swinging horizontal bar used in a gymnasium or a circus.

trapezium (tra pē' zĭ um), *n.* a four-sided plane figure of which no two sides are parallel.

*__trapezoid__ (trap' ē zoid), *n.* a plane figure with four sides, having only two sides parallel.

trappings (trap' ĭngz), *n. pl.* ornamental harness or decoration for a horse; any decorations.

trash (trash), *n.* refuse, waste or worthless matter, rubbish.

trashy (trash' ĭ), *adj.* [*comp.* trashier, *superl.* trashiest] worthless, useless; cheap and insubstantial, as writing.

travail (trav' ăl), *n.* labor with pain; the pains of childbirth.

travel (trav' el), *n.* the act of journeying; amount of traffic, as heavy *travel: travels,* journeys, trips; a literary record of one's journeyings. *v.i.* to journey, tour, go from place to place.

traveler (trav' el ēr), *n.* one who journeys; a salesman who goes from city to city.

*__traverse__ (trav' ērs), *n.* a crosspiece. *v.t.* to cross over or pass through; to go from one end to the other, as to *traverse* a state; to cross to and fro, to review, as to *traverse* a subject; to deny, as to *traverse* an indictment. *adj.* lying crosswise. athwart.

*__travesty__ (trav' es tĭ), *n.* [*pl.* travesties] a burlesque or parody; a fantastic resemblance. *v.t.* [*p.t. and p.p.* travestied, *pr.p.* travestying] to burlesque or parody; to treat a serious subject in such a way as to make it seem ridiculous.

*__trawl__ (trôl), *n.* a fish 'net shaped like a bag for dragging along the bottom; a long fishing line with many hooks. *v.i.* to fish with a dragged bait or net.

trawler (trôl' ēr), *n.* a fishing boat equipped for trawling.

tray (trā), *n.* a broad, flat, shallow vessel with raised edges to carry things on, as dishes when serving at table; a shallow box at the top of a trunk.

treacherous (trech' ēr us), *adj.* false to a trust; appearing trustworthy but actually faithless and ready to betray; untrustworthy, as *treacherous* footing.

*__treachery__ (trech' er ĭ), *n.* [*pl.* treacheries] perfidy; an act of betrayal.

*__treacle__ (trē' kl), *n.* the sirup drained from sugar in refining; molasses.

tread (tred), *n.* the horizontal part of a step in a flight of stairs; the part of a tire that comes in contact with the ground; manner of walking; sound of footsteps. *v.i. and v.t.* to step, walk; to put the foot down, as don't *tread* on the *wet* floor; to step on, as to *tread* grapes for wine.

treadle (tred' l), *n.* a foot lever operating a machine.

*__treason__ (trē' zn), *n.* betrayal of one's country; treachery.

*__treasure__ (trezh' ēr), *n.* accumulated wealth; riches; something highly valued. *v.t.* to value highly; to collect and keep.

treasurer (trezh' ēr ēr), *n.* an officer in a government, a business concern or a private organization having charge of the funds.

treasury (trezh' er ĭ), *n.* [*pl.* treasuries] a place where public or private moneys are kept; funds or money on hand, as the *treasury* is low.

treat (trēt), *n.* something given as refreshment or entertainment; a pleasant experience, as it was a *treat* to hear you play.

treat (trēt), *v.i. and v.t.* to negotiate, as he

treated with his competitor over the matter; to take in a certain way, as to *treat* a proposal with scorn; to subject to some process, as to *treat* wood with creosote; to deal with medically or surgically, as to *treat* sickness; to give refreshment or entertainment to, as he *treated* her to a show; to act toward, as he *treats* his mother well.

*treatise (trē tis), *n.* a written study of a subject.

treatment (trēt' ment), *n.* manner of dealing with, as old people deserve good *treatment*, this subject should have a different *treatment*, the doctor gave the right *treatment*.

treaty (trēt' i), *n.* [pl. treaties] a formal agreement between two or among several governments.

*treble (treb' l), *n.* the highest vocal or instrumental part; a high, thin sound. *v.i.* and *v.t.* to become or to make threefold; to multiply by 3. *adj.* high-pitched; the part above middle C on a piano or similar keyboard. *adj.* threefold.

trebly (treb' li), *adv.* in threefold manner, triply.

tree (trē), *n.* the largest kind of plant having a single trunk and spreading branches; anything thought of as resembling a trunk and branches, as a family *tree;* a shaped piece of wood or metal to fit within, as a shoe *tree*. *v.t.* to drive up into the branches, as to *tree* a coon.

trek (trek), *n.* a long journey, as a *trek* across the desert. *v.i.* to travel by wagon, migrate; to make a long, difficult journey.

*trellis (trel' is), *n.* a structure of latticework on which a vine is trained.

trelliswork (trel' is wûrk), *n.* a grating of light bars or wooden strips in a crisscross pattern; a lattice.

tremble (trem' bl), *n.* a quiver or shiver from fright, anxiety or excitement. *v.i.* to shake unintentionally, as with fear, cold, weakness, excitement or anxiety.

trembling (trem' bling), *n.* a condition of shaking with fear, excitement or weakness.
Syn. Tremor, trepidation. *Trembling* may be caused by physical or mental conditions; a *tremor* is a slight *trembling*, arising from fear or weakness; *trepidation* implies a state of great alarm or agitation.

tremendous (trē men' dus), *adj.* terrifying; causing astonishment by reason of great size or force, as a *tremendous* crash, a *tremendous*, black cloud.

*tremolo (trem' ō lō), *n.* [pl. tremolos] a vibrating sound, a trembling effect in a tone.

*tremor (trem' ẽr), *n.* a trembling; a shake of the earth; one of the successive shocks in an earthquake.

tremulous (trem' ū lus), *adj.* trembling, quivering; wavering.

*trench (trench), *n.* a long, narrow ditch; a long ditch with earth piled in front of it and a firing ledge along the side, for protection of troops in warfare.

trench (trench), *v.t.* to dig ditches in, as a method of drainage, as to *trench* a field.

*trenchant (tren' chant), *adj.* sharp, keen, cutting, as *trenchant* wit; forceful, penetrating, lucid.

trencher (tren' chẽr), *n.* a wooden plate used at table in the olden times.

trencherman (tren' chẽr man), *n.* an eater, as a poor *trencherman*.

trend (trend), *n.* a tendency, general direction, as that is the *trend* of public opinion today. *v.i.* to take a general course; to incline to a certain conclusion.

*trepan (trē pan'), *n.* a surgeon's cylinder-shaped saw for cutting a hole in the skull; also *trephine*. *v.t.* to operate on by cutting the bones of the skull.

*trephine (trē fīn'), *v.* to perforate the skull with a trepan or trephine.

trepidation (trep i dā' shun), *n.* involuntary trembling; a state of great fear.

*trespass (tres' pås), *n.* a deliberate breaking of the law; an invasion of the rights of another; a transgression, a sin. *v.i.* to commit any offense; to enter unlawfully upon the land of another.

tress (tres), *n.* a lock of hair.

*trestle (tres' l), *n.* a bar with spreading legs at each end to form a support, as a *trestle* for a platform; a framework of timbers or steel girders supporting railroad tracks above a ravine or over a river.

trestle board (tres l bōrd), a draftsman's designing board supported on wooden horses.

trestlework (tres' l wûrk), *n.* a system of connected frames supporting a heavy structure, as a viaduct, pier or scaffold.

triad (trī' ad), *n.* any group of three; a chord of three tones.

*triangle (trī' ang gl), *n.* a plane figure with three sides and three angles.

triangulate (trī ang' gū lāt), *v.t.* to divide into three-sided sections; to survey land by dividing in that way.

tribe (trīb), *n.* a community of primitive people under one chief; in ancient states, a division of the people into groups, as the *tribes* of Israel; any class or group, as the newspaper *tribe*.

tribulation (trib ū lā' shun), *n.* a severe affliction, great sorrow.

*tribunal (trī bū' nal), *n.* a magistrate's bench; a court of justice.

*tribune (trib' ūn), *n.* a magistrate of ancient Rome; a champion of the people's rights.

tribune (trib' ūn), *n.* a stand from which addresses were delivered in ancient Rome; a platform for public speaking.

*tributary (trib' ū ter i), *n.* [pl. tributaries] a river that flows into a larger one; a state that pays money to another for protection.

tributary (trib' ū ter i), *adj.* serving to enlarge or increase; subordinate, as a *tributary* state; pertaining to tribute payment.

*tribute (trib' ūt), *n.* money paid to a superior state by a subordinate and dependent one; acknowledgment of worth, as a *tribute* of praise.

trice (trīs), *n.* an instant,' as in a *trice*.

trice (trīs), *v.t.* to pull or lash with a small rope, as to *trice* up a sail.

trick (trik), *n.* a stratagem or artifice; a

puzzling deception, as the *tricks* of a magician; one man's turn, as a *trick* at the helm; a knack, as you haven't the *trick* of it; all the cards played in one round, as he won the *trick*.

trickery (trik' ẽr i), *n.* [*pl.* trickeries] deception, cheating, fraud, imposture.

trickle (trik' l), *v.i.* to drip, flow in a thin stream.

trickster (trik' stẽr), *n.* a cheat, a deceiver.

tricolor (trī' kul ẽr), *n.* a national flag of three hues, in about equal parts, as the French *tricolor*.

tricycle (trī' sik l), *n.* a vehicle with three wheels.

*****trident** (trī' dent), *n.* a fork or spear with three prongs, especially a fish spear; the emblem of Neptune or Poseidon, god of the sea.

*****triennial** (trī en' i al), *n.* the third anniversary; a plant that lives 3 years. *adj.* taking place every third year or lasting 3 years.

trifle (trī' fl), *n.* anything of little value or importance. *v.i.* to act or talk with levity; to spend time on small matters; to sport, jest, as to *trifle* with one's affections.

trigger (trig' ẽr), *n.* a means of releasing a catch or spring; a catch that is pulled with the finger and releases the hammer of a gun.

*****trigonometry** (trig ō nom' e trĭ), *n.* [*pl.* trigonometries] the science of measuring the sides and angles of triangles; a textbook on this subject.

trilateral (trī lat' ẽr al), *adj.* three-sided.

trill (tril), *n.* a quaver of the voice; a vibrating tone.

trillion (tril' yun), *n.* the number represented by 1 followed by 12 ciphers in the United States and France and by 1 with 18 ciphers in Great Britain.

*****trilogy** (tril' ō ji), *n.* a series of three, as dramas, musical compositions or novels, each complete in itself but all on the same general theme.

trim (trim), *v.t.* to make neat by cutting, as to *trim* a hedge, to make neat by smoothing, as to *trim* a board; to adorn, as to *trim* a hat; to adjust sails; to keep a ship well balanced by shifting cargo or ballast.

trim (trim), *adj.* neat, in good order.

trimmer (trim' ẽr), *n.* one who holds a middle position on any issue and refuses to take sides; one who trims any article of manufacture; one who keeps coal or cargo in safe position on shipboard.

trinket (tring' ket), *n.* a small article, as an ornament or jewel, usually of little value, a trifle.

*****trio** (trē' ō), *n.* [*pl.* trios] a set of three; a musical composition arranged for three musicians.

trip (trip), *n.* a stumble; a mistake; a journey.

*****tripartite** (trī pär' tīt), *adj.* divided into three sections.

*****tripe** (trip), *n.* a part of the stomach of a cud-chewing animal used as food.

*****triplane** (trī' plăn), *n.* an airplane with three main planes.

triple (trip' l), *v.i. and v.t.* to increase threefold; to multiply by 3. *adj.* consisting of three united things or three parts of one thing, as a *triple* play.

triplet (trip' let), *n.* one of three children born at one birth.

tripod (trī' pod), *n.* a three-legged stool or table; a three-legged stand used to support a surveying instrument or a camera.

*****trisect** (trī sekt'), *v.t.* to divide into three equal parts.

*****trisyllabic** (tris i lab' ik), *adj.* having three syllables.

trite (trīt), *adj.* worn-out, stale, repeated till commonplace, as a *trite* remark.

*****triturate** (trit' ū rāt), *v.t.* to rub or grind to powder.

*****triumph** (trī' umf), *n.* a great victory; celebration of a victory. *v.i.* to win a victory; to celebrate a victory.

triumphant (trī um' fant), *adj.* victorious and rejoicing.

triumvirate (trī um' vi răt), *n.* government by three people sharing authority equally; a group of three people, as a *triumvirate* of friends.

triune (trī' ūn), *adj.* consisting of three in one.

trivet (triv' et), *n.* a stand or support having three legs and so standing steady, as right as a *trivet;* a metal plate with ornamental design and feet, used to protect a table from hot dishes.

*****trivial** (triv' i al), *adj.* of little value, unimportant, insignificant.

*****troche** (trō' kē), *n.* a medicinal lozenge.

*****trochee** (trō' kē), *n.* a metrical foot of one long syllable and one short syllable or one accented and one unaccented.

*****troglodyte** (trog' lō dīt), *n.* an early caveman; anyone who lives in a cave.

*****troll** (trōl), *n.* a being supposed to live in mountain caves, pictured sometimes as a giant, sometimes as a mischievous dwarf.

*****troll** (trōl), *v.t. and v.i.* to fish for, as with hook and line from a moving boat, the bait dragging behind, near the surface of the water; to fish by drawing a hook and line through water behind moving boat. *v.t.* to sing in parts in succession, as in a round; to sing in a strong, hearty voice.

trolley (trol' i), *n.* a grooved metal wheel that rolls on a charged electric wire overhead, propelling a street car; a car propelled in this manner: also called a *trolley car*.

*****trombone** (trom' bōn), *n.* a brass wind instrument with a U-shaped slide.

troop (trōōp), *n.* a number of persons moving together; a cavalry company.

troop (trōōp), *v.i.* to move in numbers, as they all came *trooping* in.

*****trope** (trōp), *n.* a word or expression used in an unusual sense; a word used figuratively; a figure of speech; a turn of language.

*****trophy** (trō' fĭ), *n.* [*pl.* trophies] something taken from an enemy and kept as a memorial; a memorial of a victory; a prize won in an athletic competition.

tropic (trop′ ĭk), *n.* one of the two imaginary circles around the earth, one on each side of and parallel to the equator 23° 27′ distant from it and enclosing the Torrid Zone.

tropics (trop′ ĭks), *n.* the region between the Tropic of Cancer and the Tropic of Capricorn.

trot (trot), *n.* the gait of a horse when the fore and hind legs on opposite sides move at the same time; a jogging run.

trot (trot), *v.i. and v.t.* to run by lifting the front and hind legs on opposite sides at the same time; to jog; to cause to trot, as I am going to *trot* this horse a mile.

*troth** (trŏth), *n.* fidelity, truth, faithfulness, as to pledge, (or plight) one's troth.

*troubadour** (trōō′ ba door), *n.* one of a class of poets who sang their own songs in Provence in the 12th century.

trouble (trub′ l), *n.* worry, distress, grief, afflictions, such as loss of health, wealth or dear ones; effort, as to take the *trouble* to do something; pathological condition, as heart *trouble.*

Syn. Disturbance, molestation. *Trouble* may be permanent; *disturbance* and *molestation* are temporary and both refer to the peace that is destroyed. A *disturbance* ruffles us and throws us out of a tranquil state. A *molestation* affects either the body or the mind.

trouble (trub′ l), *v.t.* to distress; to cause to worry; to inconvenience.

Syn. Disturb, molest. We may be *troubled* by the want of a thing or by that which is unsuitable. We are *disturbed* and *molested* only by that which *troubles* actively.

*trough** (trŏf), *n.* a receptacle like an open-topped tub or tank to hold a liquid, as water for horses; a basin in which dough is kneaded; a gutter on a roof; any long narrow depression, as between waves of the sea.

trounce (trouns), *v.t.* to beat soundly.

troupe (trōōp), *n.* a company of actors.

*trousseau** (trōō sō′), *n.* [pl. trousseaux] a bride's outfit.

trout (trout), *n.* a fresh-water game fish; a number of varieties of fish resembling it, some living in salt water.

trow (trō), *v.i. and v.t.* to think, suppose.

trowel (trou′ el), *n.* a flat-surfaced tool used by masons and plasterers to spread and smooth mortar or plaster; a small scoop with a handle used in working in a garden.

troy weight (troi wāt), a system of measures based on a 12-ounce pound and used in weighing precious metals and gems.

*truant** (trōō′ ant), *n.* one who stays away from duty or business; a student who stays away from school without permission.

truant (trōō′ ant), *adj.* neglectful of duty; idle, lazy; not attending school.

truce (trōōs), *n.* an agreement to cease fighting for a certain time; a lull in a period of action, respite.

truck (truk), *n.* a stout vehicle to move heavy articles or goods; the structure with wheels

supporting one end of a railroad car; a hand-pushed or motor vehicle on which porters move things, such as trunks and hand luggage. *v.i. and v.t.* to move heavy loads as a business; to carry in stout wagons. *v.i.* to barter, peddle.

truckle (truk′ l), *n.* a small wheel.

truckle (truk′ l), *v.i. and v.t.* to move on rollers; to seek favor through flattery and obsequious service.

*truculent** (truk′ ū lent), *adj.* savage, aggressive, fierce.

trudge (truj), *n.* a long, weary walk.

trudge (truj), *v.i.* to walk ploddingly.

true (trōō), *adj.* conforming to fact; faithful, loyal, genuine.

true (trōō), *v.t.* to bring into correct line; to cause to fit exactly, as you should *true* that window frame.

*truffle** (truf′ l), *n.* a potato-shaped fungus that grows underground and is valued as a table delicacy.

truism (trōō′ izm), *n.* a self-evident truth, a platitude.

truly (trōō′ li), *adv.* in agreement with truth or fact, honestly.

trump (trump), *n.* a card of the suit outranking others for the time being: *trumps,* the ranking suit, as diamonds are *trumps.* *v.i. and v.t.* to play a card of the ranking suit; to take a trick with such a card.

trumpet (trum′ pet), *n.* a metal wind instrument with a single curved tube with a flaring end; the call of an elephant; a trumpet-shaped devise or instrument, as an ear *trumpet. v.i. and v.t.* to make clear, strong, sustained tones; to proclaim as if by the call of the trumpet.

*truncheon** (trun′ chun), *n.* a short staff or cudgel; the baton of a high military officer.

trundle (trun′ dl), *n.* a small broad wheel, like that of a caster: *trundle bed,* a bed with a low frame resting on casters, so that it can be rolled under a large bed. *v.i. and v.t.* to roll on casters; to cause to roll, as a child *trundles* a hoop.

trunk (trungk), *n.* the main stem of a tree; the body without the head and limbs, the torso; the long, flexible snout of the elephant; a stout case with compartments in which to pack a traveler's wardrobe and personal effects.

trunk line (trungk lin), the main stem of a railroad or electric wire system.

trunks (trungks), *n.* a short-legged garment that extends from the waist to the upper part of the thighs, worn by swimmers, athletes and others.

trunnion (trun′ yun), *n.* one of the two pivots that project from the opposite sides of a cannon and form a bearing on which it can be raised or lowered.

truss (trus), *n.* a support for a ruptured place in the body; a braced framework in the structure of a roof, bridge or airplane; a bundle of hay or straw.

truss (trus), *v.t.* to pack; to support with a bracing framework; to hold together with skewers or cord before roasting, as to *truss* a roast of beef, or a fowl.

trust (trust), *n.* confidence, faith; credit; a combination of corporations; an estate held for another. *v.i. and v.t.* to have faith, feel secure; to place confidence in; to sell to on credit.

trustee (trus tē'), *n.* a person to whom property is turned over to be managed for the benefit of others.

trusty (trus' ti), *n.* [*pl.* trusties] a convict who has been found worthy of confidence and receives special privileges. *adj.* [*comp.* trustier, *superl.* trustiest] justly deserving confidence; faithful.

truth (trōōth), *n.* agreement with reality; the eternal principle of right or the natural law of order; fidelity, constancy.

  Syn. Veracity. *Truth* belongs to the thing, *veracity* to the person. The *truth* of the story is admitted upon the *veracity* of the narrator.

try (trī), *v.i. and v.t.* to make an attempt or effort; to put to a test; to test by experiment; to argue and decide, as to *try* a case; to purify by melting, as to *try* out fat.

*tryst (trist), *n.* an arrangement to meet at a specified place and time; the place of meeting.

tsetse fly (tset' se fīl), *n.* a blood sucking insect of South Africa, dangerous as a carrier of sleeping sickness.

tub (tub), *n.* a small cask; a broad open-topped vessel of wood or metal to hold water, as a wash*tub*, a bath*tub*; the amount contained in a small cask, as a *tub* of butter; a broad, clumsy boat. *v.t. and v.i.* to wash or bathe in a tub.

tuba (tū' ba), *n.* a large, low-pitched, brass wind instrument, a saxhorn.

*tube (tūb), *n.* a long, hollow stem of glass, rubber or metal to conduct water or gas; a tubelike organ of the body, as the bronchial *tubes;* a pipe; the barrel of a gun or a telescope; a subway or tunnel; a cylindrical, collapsible container made of thin, flexible metal with a screw cap to hold a paste or cream.

tuber (tū' bĕr), *n.* a thick, round part of a root, as the potato.

*tuberculosis (tū bûr kū lō' sis), *n.* a disease caused by a bacillus, with formation of little rounded growths in the tissues, commonly called *consumption* when it affects the lungs.

*tuberose (tūb' rōz), *n.* a plant that produces a long spike with a tuft of leaves at the lower end and clusters of fragrant, white funnel-shaped flowers at the other.

tuck (tuk), *n.* a fold in a dress, stitched in for ornament or to make it fit. *v.t.* to fold under; to roll up, as a sleeve; to cover snugly; to put away for safekeeping, as to *tuck* something in a drawer.

tucker (tuk' ĕr), *n.* that which tucks; a part of a sewing machine. *n.* a covering of lace or fine muslin worn over shoulders and folded across breast by women of 17th-18th cent.

*tufa (tōō' fa), *n.* a porous Italian limestone; a light rock composed of volcanic dust.

*tuft (tuft), *n.* a knot or bunch, as a *tuft* of grass or hair.

tug (tug), *n.* a strong pull; a boat that tows other boats or ships; a rawhide trace in harness. *v.i. and v.t.* to pull hard; to tow, as another vessel.

tuition (tū ish' un), *n.* instruction; a charge for instruction.

tularemia (tōō la rē' mi a), *n.* a disease of rodents, especially rabbits, which may be communicated to human beings and causes a depressing fever that lasts several weeks.

*tulip (tū' lip), *n.* a bulbous-rooted plant of the lily family having single, cup-shaped flowers in many colors and combinations of colors.

tumble (tum' bl), *n.* a fall.

tumble (tum' bl), *v.i. and v.t.* to roll about; to fall awkwardly; to perform acrobatic stunts; to throw down; to muss, rumple.

tumbler (tum' blĕr), *n.* a drinking glass without a stem; an acrobat; a part of a lock.

*tumid (tū' mid), *adj.* swollen, distended, as *tumid* flesh; bombastic, pompous, as a *tumid* style of writing.

*tumor (tū' mĕr), *n.* a local swelling or abnormal growth in any part of the body.

*tumult (tū' mult), *n.* commotion made by a number of people, with uproar and disorderly movement; agitation, as my mind is in a *tumult.*

tumultuous (tū mul' tū us), *adj.* disorderly, agitated, turbulent, as *tumultuous* feelings, a *tumultuous* storm.

tun (tun), *n.* a large cask; a fermenting vat used in brewing; a measure of wine, 252 gallons.

*tune (tūn), *n.* a melody; proper pitch or key, as the piano is in *tune;* harmony, as in *tune* with the universe.

tune (tūn), *v.t. and v.i.* to adjust so as to produce the proper tones in music, as to *tune* a violin; to bring into harmonious relation, as his spirit is *tuned* with nature; to put into smooth running order, as to *tune* an engine; to make or break radio connections, as to *tune* in or out; to get in harmony, as the orchestra is *tuning* up.

tungsten (tung' sten), *n.* a hard, heavy, grayish-white metallic element used in hardening steel and in making electric-light filaments.

tunic (tū' nik), *n.* a loose, skirted blouse; a type of military coat.

tunnel (tun' el), *n.* an underground passageway cut through a hill or under a river.

tunnel (tun' el), *v.i. and v.t.* to make or dig a passageway through, as to *tunnel* a hill for a railroad.

turban (tûr' ban), *n.* an Oriental headdress; worn by men; a close-fitting, brimless hat worn by women.

turbid (tûr' bid), *adj.* clouded, muddy, disturbed, as a *turbid* stream; confused, as *turbid* thoughts.

*turbine (tûr' bin), *n.* a motor operated by water or steam directed against cups on the rim of a wheel.

turbot (tûr' bot), *n.* a flat fish or flounder.

turbulence (tûr′ bũ lens), *n.* disorder, agitation; a disturbed state of mind, with confused thoughts.

turbulent (tûr′ bũ lent), *adj.* agitated; disorderly; in great confusion, unsettled, as a *turbulent* mind.

*****tureen** (tũ rēn′), *n.* a deep, covered and usually footed vessel from which soup is served at the table.

turf (tûrf), *n.* closely sodded grass, as in a fine lawn; the matted mass of grass and roots covering the soil: *the turf,* horse racing and all connected with it.

turf (tûrf), *v.t.* to sod; to cover with turf; to produce a fine, close-growing lawn.

turgid (tûr′ jid), *adj.* distended, swollen, as a gland; inflated, pompous, as a *turgid* style of writing.

turkey (tûr′ ki), *n.* [*pl.* turkeys] a large bird related to the pheasant, valued as food.

turmeric (tûr′ mēr ik), *n.* the dried and powdered root of an East Indian plant used in making yellow dye and as seasoning and coloring for pickles or other food.

turmoil (tûr′ moil), *n.* confusion of motion, noise and excitement.

turn (tûrn), *n.* motion about a center, as a *turn* of a wheel; a bend or curve, as a *turn* in a road; a place in a series of acts, as it is my *turn* to go; manner of expression, as the *turn* of a sentence; tendency, as he has a mathematical *turn* of mind; an act affecting another, as you have done your good *turn* today; a purpose, as it has served its *turn;* a winding, as give that rope a *turn* around the post.

turn (tûrn), *v.i. and v.t.* to rotate or revolve; to bend aside or reverse; to sour, as the milk *turned;* to move in a circle, as to *turn* a crank; to fold back, as *turn* your sleeves up; to go around, as you must *turn* a corner; to cause to go, as *turn* the horse loose; to form symmetrically, as to *turn* on a lathe.

Syn. Bend, twist, distort, wring, wrest, wrench. We *turn* a thing by moving it; we *turn* the soil over in digging. To *bend* is to change the direction of; to *twist* is to bend many times; to *distort* is to *turn* or *bend* something out of its right line or course; to *wring* is to *twist* vigorously; to *wrest* or *wrench* from is to separate by means of twisting; thus a stick may be *wrested* out of one's hand, a door *wrenched* off its hinges.

turncoat (tûrn′ kōt), *n.* one who abandons his professed principles and goes over to the other side, a renegade, as a political *turn-coat.*

turnkey (tûrn′ kē), *n.* a jailer, a prison keeper.

turnover (tûrn′ ō vēr), *n.* a complete transaction of purchase, sale and replacement of stock in a store; the amount of such business done in a given period; the number of new workers hired in a given period, in proportion to the entire force: called *labor turnover;* a pie or tart made of a single crust folded to form a shell.

turnpike (tûrn′ pīk), *n.* a road with tollgates.

turnstile (tûrn′ stīl), *n.* formerly a post with a pivoting top consisting of four arms with sufficient space between to permit a person to pass through by turning it; a similar device at the entrance to a subway.

turntable (tûrn′ tā bl), *n.* a revolving platform for turning a wheeled conveyance, as a locomotive.

turpentine (tûr′ pen tīn), *n.* an oil distilled from the resin of several varieties of cone-bearing evergreens, especially the pine, and used largely in making paints and varnishes.

*****turpitude** (tûr′ pi tūd), *n.* gross depravity, vileness.

*****turquoise** (tûr′ koiz), *n.* a semiprecious stone of a bright blue or greenish blue color, found mostly in Persia; the color of this stone.

turret (tûr′ et), *n.* a small tower.

turtle (tûr′ tl), *n.* a tortoise; any of a number of species of reptile, some living on the land, some in fresh water and some in the sea, all having a hard shell in two sections, under and over the body, into which the animal draws its head and legs when threatened with harm.

turtledove (tûr′ tl duv), *n.* a bird of the pigeon family but slightly smaller than the common pigeon.

tusk (tusk), *n.* the long, projecting tooth on either side of the jaw of certain animals, as the walrus and elephant; any large tooth.

tussle (tus′ l), *n.* a scuffle, a struggle.

tussle (tus′ l), *v.i.* to scuffle, struggle.

*****tutelage** (tũ′ tē lij), *n.* guardianship; state of being a tutor or guardian or of having a tutor or guardian.

*****tutor** (tũ′ tēr), *n.* a teacher, especially one who gives a student private instruction.

tutor (tũ′ tēr), *v.t.* to instruct.

twain (twān), *n.* two: *in twain,* in two parts.

twang (twang), *n.* a sharp, vibrating sound, as that of a plucked wire; a nasal tone of voice. *v.t.* to pluck at a stringed instrument, unmusically.

tweak (twēk), *n.* a sudden twisting jerk. *v.t.* to pinch or pull with a sudden jerk or twist, as to *tweak* someone's nose.

tweed (twēd), *n.* a fabric, usually of wool, used extensively in making tailored suits and coats: *tweeds,* clothing made of tweed.

tweezers (twēz′ ērz), *n.* small pincers to grip tiny things, as in pulling out a hair.

twelfth (twelfth), *n.* one of 12 equal parts. *adj.* next in order after the 11th.

twelve (twelv), *n.* one more than 11; a symbol (12) representing that number.

twentieth (twen′ ti eth), *n.* one of 20 equal parts. *adj.* next in order after the 19th.

twenty (twen′ ti), *n.* one more than 19; a symbol (20) representing that number.

twice (twīs), *adv.* two times; doubly.

twiddle (twid′ l), *v.t.* to twirl lightly or idly, as to *twiddle* the thumbs.

twig (twig), *n.* a small shoot or branch.

twilight (twī′ līt), *n.* the time between sunset and darkness or just preceding the sunrise.

twill (twil), *n.* a fabric with the lines of the

weave formed to cross it diagonally, as in serge; the diagonal pattern in this cloth.

twin (twin), *n.* one of two born at a single birth; a person or thing closely resembling another. *adj.* matching exactly, duplicating.

twine (twin), *n.* stout cord of twisted strands; a tangle; the act of twisting around. *v.i. and v.t.* to twist or wind around something; to meander, as the woodbine *twines* around the fence; to form by twisting.

twinge (twinj), *n.* a sharp, shooting pain; a sharp misgiving, as a *twinge* of conscience.

twinge (twinj), *v.i. and v.t.* to have or cause a sudden, darting pain.

twinkle (twing' kl), *n.* a quick motion of the eye; a tremulous sparkle of light; a moment. *v.i.* to shine with a tremulous, sparkling light; to shine; sparkle, as the eyes *twinkle* in a moment of merriment.

*twirl (twûrl), *n.* a quick circular motion, a whirl, as he gave the baton a *twirl*.

twirl (twûrl), *v.t.* to cause to whirl, turn round and round, as to *twirl* a stick.

twist (twist), *n.* a quick turn or sharp bend, as a *twist* in a stream; anything made of tightly intertwined strands, as a *twist* of rope; a bias, prejudice or characteristic, as his books all have a political *twist*.

twist (twist) *v.i. and v.t.* to wind around and around, intertwine; to wrench violently.

twister (twis' tẽr), *n.* a tornado.

twit (twit), *v.t.* to taunt, annoy by reminding of a fault or error.

twitch (twich), *n.* a sudden jerk; involuntary tightening of a muscle. *v.t. and v.i.* to pull with a sudden jerk; to contract spasmodically, as my muscles *twitch*.

twitter (twit' ẽr), *n.* a succession of chirping sounds. *v.i. and v.t.* to chirp, as sparrows *twitter;* to be excited; to sing with chirpy notes, as to *twitter* a song.

two (tōō), *n.* one more than 1; a symbol (2) representing this number.

twofold (tōō' fōld), *adj.* double; consisting of two.

two-ply (tōō' plī), *adj.* consisting of two thicknesses; woven double.

*tympanum (tim' pa num), *n.* [*pl.* tympanums] the thin membrane separating the outer from the inner ear, the eardrum.

type (tīp), *n.* a unit representative of a class; the class represented; a character in wood or metal to print from; such pieces collectively or the print made from them.

type (tīp), *v.t.* to produce a copy of, prefigure; to write by means of a machine.

typewriter (tīp' rīt ẽr), *n.* a keyboard machine that may be operated to print characters on paper by striking an inked ribbon against it.

*typhoid (tī' foid), *n.* a fever caused generally by drinking water or milk containing germs of the disease.

*typhoon (tī fōōn´), *n.* a cyclonic storm occurring in the China Sea and Western Pacific.

*typhus (tī' fus), *n.* a fever caused by insanitary conditions and conveyed by body lice.

*typical (tip' i kal), *adj.* representative, symbolic, characteristic.

typify (tip' i fi), *v.t.* [*p.t. and p.p.* typified. *pr.p.* typifying] to represent, symbolize, stand as an example of.

typist (tīp' ist), *n.* one who operates a typewriter.

*typography (tī pog' ra fi), *n.* [*pl.* typographies] the art of printing; the character of print, as this book shows excellent *typography*, a school course in *typography*.

tyranny (tir´ a ni), *n.* [*pl.* tyrannies] despotism, misuse of power over others.

tyrant (tī' rant), *n.* a despot, an oppressor.

tyro (tī' rō), *n.* [*pl.* tyros] a beginner, a novice: often spelled *tiro*.

U

*ubiquitous (û bik' wi tus), *adj.* seeming to be everywhere at once.

*ubiquity (û bik' wi ti), *n.* omnipresence.

U-boat (ū' bōt), *n.* a German submarine or *Unterseebot*.

udder (ud' ẽr), *n.* a milk bag with two or more nipples, as the *udder* of a cow.

ugly (ug' li), *adj.* [*comp.* uglier, *superl.* ugliest] unpleasing to the eye; implying danger, as an *ugly* rumor; threatening to have serious results, as an *ugly* wound; bad-tempered.

*ukulele (ū ku lā' lē), *n.* a Hawaiian musical instrument like a guitar but much smaller.

ulcer (ul' sẽr), *n.* an open, festering sore; a corrupting influence in public affairs.

ulcerate (ul' sẽr āt), *v.i.* to form an open, discharging sore, as the tooth ulcerated.

ulna (ul' na), *n.* the larger of the two bones of the forearm.

ulster (ul' stẽr), *n.* a long, loose, heavy overcoat, first made in Belfast, Ulster.

ulterior (ul tēr' i ẽr), *adj.* more remote; hidden, kept secret, as he had *ulterior* motives.

*ultimate (ul' ti mit), *n.* the last or final step or result, the conclusion.

ultimate (ul' ti mit), *adj.* final, last, farthest; fundamental, as the *ultimate* truth.

*ultimatum (ul ti mã' tum), *n.* [*pl.* ultimatums or ultimata] a final statement or offer of terms, the last word.

ultimo (ul' ti mō), *adv.* in the last preceding month, in the month before this one.

ultra (ul' tra), *adj.* extreme, uncompromising, as he belongs to the *ultra* group.

ultramarine (ul tra ma rēn'), *n.* a blue pigment. *adj.* lying beyond the sea; having any of the shades of blue given by a certain pigment.

ululation (ūl ū lā' shun), *n.* a howling like that of a wolf.

ultraviolet rays (ul' tra vī' ō let rāz), invisible light beyond the violet of the spectrum, having faster and shorter vibrations than the eye can perceive.

umber (um' bēr), *n.* a brown pigment or its dark, yellowish-brown color.

umbilicus (um bil' i kus), *n.* [*pl.* umbilici] the navel.

*umbrage (um' brij), *n.* shade, shadows, obscurity; resentment, a sense of injury.

*umbrageous (um brā' jus), *adj.* shady.

*umbrella (um brel' a), *n.* a sliding, opening and closing frame of wire ribs covered with cloth or paper and carried overhead as a screen against sun, rain, snow.

umpire (um' pīr), *n.* a third party to whom a dispute is referred; an official who applies the rules and settles points in dispute in a sports contest or arbitration.

umpire (um' pīr), *v.t. and v.i.* to settle referred disputes; to act as an official in sports or games to settle disputes by the rules.

unabridged (un a brijd'), *adj.* not reduced in content, complete, as an *unabridged* dictionary.

unaccountable (un a koun' ta bl), *adj.* not responsible; inexplicable, as an *unaccountable* absence.

*unanimity (ū na nim' i ti), *n.* [*pl.* unanimities] agreement by all concerned.

*unanimous (ū nan' i mus), *adj.* agreeing in opinion or desire, with no dissenters.

unawares (un a wârz'), *adv.* unexpectedly, by surprise, as we came upon them *unawares.*

unbend (un bend'), *v.i. and v.t.* to relax, free from strain, release tension; to become more genial; to make straight, as to *unbend* wire.

unbelief (un bē lēf'), *n.* doubt; a withholding of acceptance of a statement or doctrine.

uncanny (un kan' i), *adj.* weird, mysterious, not explainable.

uncertain (un sûr' tin), *adj.* doubtful in one's mind; hesitant; unpredictable, as the outcome is *uncertain.*

uncle (ung' kl), *n.* the brother of one's father or mother; the husband of one's aunt.

unconcern (un kon sûrn'), *n.* indifference, lack of interest.

unconditional (un kon dish' un al), *adj.* absolute, without limitation; as my terms are *unconditional* surrender.

unconscionable (un kon' shun a bl), *adj.* out of all reason or expectation.

uncover (un kuv' ēr), *v.i. and v.t.* to remove the hat as a sign of respect; to make known, as to *uncover* the facts of a case, expose.

unction (ungk' shun), *n.* the act of anointing; ointment; anything that soothes; religious fervor; a sacrament administered to those about to die, as extreme *unction;* suavity, smoothness of manner; gush, pretended fervor.

unctuous (ungk' tū us), *adj.* soothing; smooth and oily; suave.

undaunted (un dôn' ted), *adj.* fearless, undismayed.

under (un' dēr), *adj.* lower, as the *under* dog; subordinate, as an *under* officer. *adv.* underneath; in or into a state of inferiority, as the business went *under* in the depression. *prep.* beneath, as *under* the stars, *under* water; accountable to, as *under* the jurisdiction of a higher court; subject to the conditions of, as *under* the terms of the agreement; less than, as *under* 21 years of age.

underbrush (un' dēr brush), *n.* a dense growth of small shrubs and trees; undergrowth.

undercurrent (un' dēr kûr ent), *n.* a circulation, as of air or water, beneath an upper, similar circulation; a thought or feeling that is observable but not definitely expressed, as an *undercurrent* of disapproval.

undergo (un dēr gō'), *v.t.* [*p.t.* underwent, *p.p.* undergone, *pr.p.* undergoing] to submit to, as to *undergo* an operation; to pass through, as an experience, as to *undergo* a great loss.

undergraduate (un dēr grad' ū āt), *n.* a college student who has not taken his first degree.

underground (un' dēr ground), *adj.* subterranean, as an *underground* tunnel; transmitted or conveyed by secret means.

underhand (un' dēr hand), *adj.* crafty, sly, secret. *adv.* in a sly, secret, mean manner; underhandedly.

underling (un' dēr ling), *n.* a person of inferior station, a subordinate.

undermine (un dēr min'), *v.t.* to weaken, to work against in secret, as to *undermine* a person.

underneath (un dēr nēth'), *adv.* beneath, on the lower side. *prep.* directly beneath; beneath the guise of, as *underneath* a pretense of gayety.

undershot (un' dēr shot), *adj.* turned by water flowing under, as an *undershot* water wheel; with the lower jaw projecting beyond the upper.

underslung (un dēr slung'), *adj.* built, as an automobile, so that the frame of the chassis is below the axles.

understand (un dēr stand'), *v.i. and v.t.* [*p.t. and p.p.* understood, *pr.p.* understanding] to perceive with the mind; to be informed upon, as he *understands* engines; to comprehend, as I cannot *understand* you; to know fully, realize, as you do not *understand* the reason; to be sympathetic.

understanding (un dēr stand' ing), *n.* the faculty of reasoning; discernment; knowledge; an agreement, as they came to an *understanding;* sympathy.

Syn. Intellect, intelligence. The *understanding* rests upon mental power to perceive and to form images in the mind. *Intellect* implies understanding of abstruse subjects; it is a matured state of the *understanding. Intelligence* may shine forth in the facial expression of a child, though his *intellect* is as yet almost completely undeveloped.

Ant. Dullness, stupidity, ignorance.

understudy (un' dẽr stud ĭ), *v.t.* to learn the part of, as an actor, in order to serve as substitute in case of necessity.

undertake (un dẽr tāk'), *v.t.* [*p.t.* undertook, *p.p.* undertaken, *pr.p.* undertaking] to assume charge; to attempt, promise to do if possible.

undertaker (un' dẽr tāk ẽr), *n.* one who prepares the dead for burial, provides the shroud and casket and oversees funeral arrangements; one who manages a business, an entrepreneur.

undertaking (un' dẽr tāk ĭng), *n.* an enterprise, business, project; a promise or guarantee.

undertone (un' dẽr tōn), *n.* a low tone of voice; a murmured utterance, as he said it in an *undertone;* subdued color, as an *undertone* of blue.

undertow (un' dẽr tō), *n.* a current beneath the water's surface that moves in an opposite direction to the current of the surface, especially the current at the seashore that drags against the force of the incoming waves, as the *undertow* is dangerous this morning.

underworld (un' dẽr wûrld), *n.* the dwelling place of the dead, Hades; the criminal classes.

underwrite (un dẽr rīt'), *v.t.* [*p.t.* underwrote, *p.p.* underwritten, *pr.p.* underwriting] to sign with one's name; to agree to buy all for which other buyers are not found, as to *underwrite* an issue of bonds; to insure.

undue (un dū'), *adj.* improper, excessive, more than is reasonable.

undulate (un' dū lāt), *v.i. and v.t.* to move or cause to move in waves or like waves.

unearthly (un ûrth' lĭ), *adj.* supernatural, weird.

uneasy (un ēz' ĭ), *adj.* ill at ease in mind or body; constrained.

unequal (un ē' kwal), *adj.* not equivalent, disproportionate, varying.

unequivocal (un ē kwĭv' ō kal), *adj.* clear and plain, unmistakable in meaning, definite.

unerring (un ûr' ĭng), *adj.* accurate, certain, infallible.

uneven (un ē' ven), *adj.* not smoothly level, rough-surfaced; not uniform; unfair in distribution.

*•unguent** (ung' gwent), *n.* an ointment; a salve for sores or burns.

unicorn (ū' nĭ kôrn), *n.* a fabulous creature like a horse but having a single horn projecting from its forehead.

uniform (ū' nĭ fôrm), *n.* an official or regulation costume. *adj.* not varying, each one like all the others, all alike in shape, character or manner; consistent and unchanging.

unify (ū' nĭ fī), *v.t.* [*p.t. and p.p.* unified, *pr.p.* unifying] to form into a unit, unite, join together.

unimpeachable (un ĭm pēch' a bl), *adj.* unquestionable, free from fault.

*•union** (ūn' yun), *n.* the act of joining together or state of being united; an organization of workers in one trade; a league of states; harmony.

unique (ū nēk'), *adj.* alone of its kind.

*•unison** (ū' nĭ sun), *n.* a state of concord or harmony; the same pitch for all, as voices in *unison.*

unit (ū' nĭt), *n.* a single person or thing considered as part of a group, as each student is a *unit* in a class; a group regarded as a part of a whole, as the class is a *unit* in the organization of a school; a standard quantity by which to measure, as the pound is a *unit* of weight.

unite (ū nīt'), *v.i. and v.t.* to join together; to combine.

unity (ū' nĭ tĭ), *n.* [*pl.* unities] the state of oneness, as national *unity;* concord; wholeness, as the *unity* of action in a play.

universal (ū nĭ vûr' sal), *adj.* all-pervading; relating to the whole world, general, common to all.

universe (ū' nĭ vûrs), *n.* the whole system of created things, including the world we know and any others that may exist.

university (ū nĭ vûr' sĭ tĭ), *n.* [*pl.* universities] an educational institution of highest rank, with various departments of instruction and professional schools in addition to the academic branches; a number of colleges under a single administration.

unkempt (un kempt'), *adj.* disheveled, untidy, rough in appearance.

unless (un les'), *conj.* if not, as I shall go *unless* you forbid; *unless* it snows, the game will be played.

Syn. Except. *Unless* is employed for the particular case. *Except* has reference to some general rule. I shall not do it *unless* he asks me. No one can enter *except* those who have tickets.

unlettered (un let' ẽrd), *adj.* ignorant, lacking education, illiterate.

unlike (un līk'), *adj.* dissimilar, having no resemblance.

unlimited (un lĭm' ĭ ted), *adj.* boundless, unrestricted in scope.

unnerve (un nûrv'), *v.t.* to deprive of courage, reduce to a state of helpless fear; to cause to lose control.

unprincipled (un prĭn' sĭ pld), *adj.* having no conscience, unscrupulous.

unqualified (un kwol' ĭ fīd), *adj.* without the qualifications necessary; without reservations, as *unqualified* approval.

unravel (un rav' el), *v.i. and v.t.* to become disentangled; to present a solution of, as to *unravel* a mystery; to separate the threads of, as to *unravel* a knitted garment.

unreasonable (un rē' zn a bl), *adj.* immoderate, asking too much, as an *unreasonable* request; absurd, irrational.

unregenerate (un rē jen' ẽr it), *adj.* not spiritually renewed; unreformed.

unremitting (un rē mit' ĭng), *adj.* persistent, never relaxing.

unruffled (un ruf' ld), *adj.* undisturbed, tranquil, as *unruffled* calm.

unruly (un rōōl' ĭ), *adj.* disregarding restraint

and defying authority, hard to manage or control.

unsearchable (un sûr' cha bl), *adj.* hidden, mysterious.

unseasonable (un sē' zn a bl), *adj.* coming at an unusual or inappropriate time of year, as *unseasonable* heat; untimely.

unseat (un sēt'), *v.t.* to throw, as a horse its rider; to remove from office, as a legislator.

unsightly (un sīt' li), *adj.* hideous, ugly, as an *unsightly* building.

unspeakable (un spēk' a bl), *adj.* unutterable; not to be expressed.

Syn. Ineffable, unutterable, inexpressible. Anything beyond the descriptive power of language is *unspeakable*, as the *unspeakable* glory of God; *ineffable* means unable to be adequately stated, as the *ineffable* sweetness of a person's look; that is *unutterable* or *inexpressible* which cannot be made wholly comprehensible to another.

Ant. Describable; communicable.

unstrung (un strung'), *adj.* having the strings loosened or broken; nervously upset.

until (un til'), *conj.* to the time, degree or place that, as he worked *until* he was exhausted. *prep.* to or up to. as she stayed *until* evening.

unto (un' tōō), *prep.* to.

untold (un tōld'), *adj.* not describable, uncounted, as *untold* wealth.

untoward (un tō' ērd), *adj.* willful, refractory; awkward; unfortunate.

untutored (un tū' tērd), *adj.* lacking in education; unsophisticated, naive.

unusual (un ū' zhoo al), *adj.* out of the ordinary, rare, strange.

unveil (un vāl'), *v.t.* to remove a covering from, as to *unveil* a statue or portrait.

unutterable (un ut' ēr a bl), *adj.* beyond the power of words to describe, inexpressible.

unwieldy (un wēld' i), *adj.* not easily managed, bulky, clumsy, as an *unwieldy* package.

unwitting (un wit' ing), *adj.* unaware, ignorant, unknowing, as she was the *unwitting* cause of the misunderstanding.

unworthy (un wûr' thi), *adj.* [*comp.* unworthier, *superl.* unworthiest] lacking merit or soundness; unsuitable, unbecoming.

Syn. Worthless. *Unworthy* is a term of less reproach than *worthless*. There are many *unworthy* members in a religious community, but every society that is conducted upon proper principles finds it necessary to exclude the *worthless*.

Ant. Worthy; deserving; useful.

unwrap (un rap'), *v.i. and v.t.* to unfold, open up; to open, to remove the covering from, as a package.

up (up), *adj.* moving or sloping in a direction thought of as tending higher, as an *up* grade. *adv.* on high; above the horizon; from a lower to a higher position: opposite of *down*, as a kite goes *up*; a successful man goes *up* in the world; someone who has been downstairs goes *up*; prices go *up* when they increase; we get *up* and stand *up*. *prep.*

toward the top or beginning, as *up* the hill, *up* the river.

upbraid (up brād'), *v.t.* to reproach, chide.

upbringing (up' bring ing), *n.* training, rearing.

upheaval (up hēv' al), *n.* the act or state of being raised or overturned, especially a raising of a part of the earth's crust; a violent turmoil.

uphill (up' hil), *adv.* toward a higher level; upward. *adj.* sloping in an upward direction; difficult, arduous, as he had an *uphill* fight to success.

uphold (up hōld'), *v.t.* [*p.t. and p.p.* upheld, *pr.p.* upholding] to support, maintain; to defend.

upholstery (up hōl' stēr i), *n.* [*pl.* upholsteries] the act of decorating a room with textile hangings and draperies, and particularly fitting furniture with springs, padded seats and coverings; materials used for stuffing and covering furniture and for curtains and drapery.

upkeep (up' kēp), *n.* the act or cost of keeping anything in working order, maintenance, as it is not the initial cost but the *upkeep* that counts.

upon (u pon'), *adv.* on; resting on the top or surface of, as it rests *upon* the shelf; depending on or springing from, as it rests *upon* such evidence; at the time of, as *upon* departure of the ship; so as to encounter, as we came *upon* a lovely scene.

upper (up' ēr), *n.* a top part, as the *upper* of a shoe. *adj.* higher in place, rank or dignity, as the *Upper* House of Congress, the *upper* levels of literature, the *upper* story of a house.

upper (up' er), *n.* slang for a drug that is a stimulant such as an amphetamine.

upright (up' rīt), *n.* something in a vertical position, as the *uprights* in a wall.

upright (up' rīt), *adj.* erect, vertical, as an *upright* piano; honest, just, square-dealing.

uprising (up riz' ing), *n.* rebellion, mutiny.

*uproar (up' rōr), *n.* noisy disturbance, bustle and clamor.

uproot (up rōōt'), *v.t.* to pluck up by the roots; to remove.

upset (up set'), *n.* the act of overturning or state of being overturned; a reversal of form, as that game was an *upset* for the champions. *v.t.* to overturn, overthrow; to disturb, put out of normal condition.

upshot (up' shot), *n.* the final result or outcome, conclusion.

upstart (up' stärt), *n.* a person who has a sudden success or rising in the world, a parvenu.

upstream (up' strēm), *adv.* toward the source of a stream; against the current.

upturn (up tûrn'), *v.t.* to turn over, as soil with a plow; to tilt upward, as *upturned* faces.

upward (up' wērd), *adv.* toward a higher place or level, in a rising direction.

uranium (ū rā' ni um), *n.* a heavy, white metallic element which is obtained from pitchblende and from which radium and helium are extracted.

*urban (ûr' ban), *adj.* pertaining to cities or towns.

*urbane (ûr băn'), *adj.* polite, refined, courteous.

urchin (ûr' chin), *n.* a pert or mischievous little fellow.

urge (ûrj), *n.* the act of trying to persuade; a strong desire or impulse. *v.t.* to try to persuade to do something, advise strongly; to push or drive, as to *urge* a horse onward, *urge* consideration of a matter.

urgent (ûr' jent), *adj.* calling for immediate consideration.

*urine (ū' rin), *n.* the fluid secreted by the kidneys, stored in and discharged from the bladder.

urn (ûrn), *n.* a rounded vessel of metal or pottery, usually having a base or pedestal; a closed metal receptacle with a faucet for making tea or coffee and keeping it hot.

*ursine (ûr' sin), *adj.* pertaining to a bear; like a bear.

usable (ūz' a bl), *adj.* suitable to be employed for a given purpose.

*usage (ūs' ij), *n.* treatment, as hard *usage;* habitual custom; manner of expressing, as good *usage* in language.

*use (ūs), *n.* application of anything to a particular end; custom or practice; occasion to employ, as I have *use* for that book; state of being in employment, as the car is in constant *use.*

*use (ūz), *v.t.* to employ; to practice constantly, as to *use* good judgment in business; to make familiar by constant association or practice, as I am *used* to hard work.

useful (ūs' fool), *adj.* serving a purpose, helpful in accomplishing an end.

useless (ūs' les), *adj.* not serving any purpose, not helpful.

usher (ush' ēr), *n.* a person who conducts others to their seats, as in a church or theater; a pupil who acts as teacher, an untrained instructor. *v.t.* to introduce or lead in, as bright days *usher* in spring; to conduct or escort.

*usual (ū' zhoo al), *adj.* customary, habitual, occurring in the regular course of things.

*usufruct (ū' zū frukt), *n.* the privilege of using the property of another and enjoying its profits without reducing its substance.

usurer (ū' zhoo rēr), *n.* one who lends money, especially at more than a legal rate of interest.

*usurp (ū zûrp'), *v.t.* to take and hold by force without legal right.

*usury (ū' zhoo ri), *n.* [*pl.* usuries] the practice of lending money at more than legal interest.

*utensil (ū ten' sil), *n.* an implement or vessel serving a practical purpose, as kitchen *utensils,* agricultural *utensils.*

utilitarianism (ū til i târ' i an izm), *n.* the belief that good and evil should be measured by the usefulness of actions in contributing to human happiness and welfare.

utility (ū til' i ti), *n.* [*pl.* utilities] usefulness; a corporation supplying public necessaries, as water, electricity and gas companies are public *utilities.*

utilize (ū' til iz), *v.t.* to make use of; to make profitable by using, as to *utilize* spare time.

utmost (ut' mōst), *n.* the extreme limit or extent, as to the *utmost* of one's ability.

utmost (ut' mōst), *adj.* greatest; farthest, as the *utmost* extent.

utter (ut' ēr), *v.t.* to speak, pronounce; to give out by sound, as to *utter* a sigh.

Syn. Express, enunciate, voice, deliver, issue. To *utter* and to *voice* imply giving expression to and both are applied rather generally; to *express* is to give voice to, either privately or publicly; to *enunciate* usually means to pronounce, as to *enunciate* each word clearly; to *deliver* is to give forth in words, often in forceful words, as to *deliver* an ultimatum; to *issue* usually implies official action, as to *issue* a proclamation, to *issue* a command.

utter (ut' ēr), *adj.* complete, absolute, entire.

utterance (ut' ēr ans), *n.* the act of speaking; that which is spoken.

uttermost (ut' ēr mōst), *n.* the farthest extent or highest degree. *adj.* farthest.

*uvula (ū' vū la), *n.* the fleshy, cone-shaped body attached to the soft palate.

*uxorious (uks ō' ri us), *adj.* fond of one's wife to the point of doting.

V

vacancy (vā' kan si), *n.* [*pl.* vacancies] the state of being empty or unoccupied; empty-mindedness; an office or position to be filled.

vacant (vā' kant), *adj.* empty, unoccupied; lacking intelligence, as a *vacant* look.

*vacate (vā' kāt), *v.i. and v.t.* to give up and leave, as a house, office or position of employment; to make empty, as to *vacate* a house; to set aside, nullify and make void, as to *vacate* a court order.

*vacation (vā kā' shun), *n.* the act of leaving without occupants, as the *vacation* of premises; a period of absence from work, for recreation.

*vaccinate (vak' si nāt), *v.t.* to inoculate with germs developing resistance and giving immunity from a disease, as smallpox.

*vaccine (vak sēn'), *n.* the substance taken from a cow with cowpox and the fluid used in inoculating the body against smallpox.

vacillate (vas' i lāt), *v.i.* to waver, be unsteady, move one way and then the other; to hesitate in making up one's mind.

vacuity (va kū' i ti), *n.* [*pl.* vacuities] emptiness; complete inactivity of the mind.

vacuous (vak' ū us), *adj.* empty; blank, as a *vacuous* expression; stupid.

vacuum (vak' u um), *n.* a space devoid of matter and air; an utter void.

vacuum bottle (vak' u um bot' l), a container in which liquids are kept at the temperature they had when poured in.

vacuum pump (vak' u um pump), a machine to raise water through a pipe by exhausting the air; a machine to remove air from an inclosed space.

vacuum tube (vak' u um tūb), a sealed glass used in radio to cause, detect or increase electrical movements or to rectify an alternating current: also *electron tube.*

*vagabond (vag' a bond), *n.* a wanderer, one who rambles about and does not work, a tramp. *adj.* roaming, idle and wandering.

*vagary (va gâr' i), *n.* [*pl.* vagaries] a whim, a fanciful turn of the mind, a wild notion.

vagrancy (vā' gran si), *n.* a state of wandering without a settled home.

*vagrant (vā' grant), *adj.* wandering from place to place; rambling, as thoughts; sometimes, especially in poetry, *vagrom.*

vague (vāg), *adj.* indefinite, not clear, hazy.

*vain (vān), *adj.* without value; without force, fruitless; conceited.

vainglorious (vān glō' ri us), *adj.* boastful over one's own accomplishments or achievements.

valance (val' ans), *n.* a short curtain hung at the top of a window or around the sides of a bed or other furniture.

*vale (vāl), *n.* a valley.

valedictorian (val ē dik tō' ri an), *n.* the member of a graduating class (usually highest in rank) who delivers the farewell address to classmates at commencement.

valedictory (val ē dik' tō ri), *n.* [*pl.* valedictories] a farewell speech; an address to a graduating class at commencement. *adj.* pertaining to a farewell.

valence (vā' lens), *n.* the degree of combining power of an atom, as chlorine has a *valence* of 1.

valentine (val' en tīn), *n.* a sweetheart chosen on St. Valentine's Day, February 14; a love message sent to a sweetheart on that day.

*valet (val' et), *n.* a manservant who personally attends a gentleman and takes care of his clothes.

*valetudinarian (val ē tū di når' i an), *n.* an invalid; one who spends too much time thinking about his health.

valiant (val' yant), *adj.* courageous, brave, fearless.

valid (val' id), *adj.* resting upon fact, sound, logical; having legal force.

*valise (va lēs'), *n.* a traveling bag, usually of leather or a substitute made in two equal parts on hinged frames that close lengthwise.

valley (val' i), *n.* [*pl.* valleys] a tract of lower land lying between two lines of hills or mountains; a low spot in a curve on a diagram or graph.

valor (val' ẽr), *n.* courage, bravery.

valorous (val' ẽr us), *adj.* brave.

valuable (val' ū a bl), *adj.* having real worth; possessing useful qualities.

*valuables (val' ū a blz), *n.* personal possessions, such as jewelry, art objects, silverware, mortgages, deeds, policies, wills, stocks and bonds, which one usually places in safe deposit.

value (val' ū), *n.* that which renders anything desirable or useful, worth; the exact use and meaning, as what is the *value* of this word; a market price; a fair price.

value (val' ū), *v.t.* to estimate the worth of; to esteem, regard highly.

Syn. Prize, esteem. To *value* is to set a price upon. It may be based upon intrinsic worth or upon special, personal considerations. An appraiser *values* goods in one way, the owner in another. To *prize* and to *esteem* are only mental actions. We *value* books for their market price; we *prize* them for their contents. In this sense *prize* is a stronger term than *value.*

valve (valv), *n.* a lid or cover opening in one direction and shutting in the other to open a conduit to passage of a liquid one way and prevent it from moving in the reverse direction; any device to regulate flow in a pipe, as of steam in radiators.

vamp (vamp), *n.* the leather piece forming the upper front part of a shoe. *v.t.* to put on an upper piece of leather; to patch.

vampire (vam' pīr), *n.* a fabled creature that sucks the blood of sleeping persons.

van (van), *n.* the leading units of an army or fleet; the persons who lead any movement; the place of leadership. *n.* a large, covered truck used to move furniture and household goods; a railway baggage car.

vanadium (va nā' di um), *n.* a metallic element used as an alloy to increase the resistance of steel to shock.

*vandal (van' dal), *n.* one who destroys ruthlessly; one who destroys beautiful things.

*vane (vān), *n.* a weathercock; a flat arm in a propeller or the wheel of a windmill; any flat piece attached to an axis so that it moves with the wind or with the passage of a fluid.

vanguard (van' gärd), *n.* the troops that march at the head of an army.

vanilla (va nil' a), *n.* a tropical American climbing plant of the orchid family; its pods or beans, from which a flavoring extract is made.

vanish (van' ish), *v.i.* to disappear; to be lost.

vanity (van' i ti), *n.* [*pl.* vanities] shallow pride, desire for admiration, conceit; a vanity bag.

*vanquish (vang' kwish), *v.t.* to conquer, subdue, defeat.

*vapid (vap' id), *adj.* stale, stupid, empty, as *vapid* talk.

*vapor (vā' pẽr), *n.* mist in the air; the gas into which a solid or liquid is transformed, steam, smoke; anything that vanishes like mist.

vaporize (vā' pẽr īz), *v.t. and v.i.* to convert or be converted into steam or gas.

vaporous (vā' pẽr us), *adj.* misty; unreal.

*variable (vâr' ı *a* bl), *n.* anything that is subject to change.

variable (vâr' ı *a* bl), *adj.* changing, unreliable.

variance (vâr' ı ans), *n.* the state of being subject to change; the extent of change; a disagreement or dispute.

variant (vâr' ı ant), *n.* something that differs in a particular respect from something else that it otherwise closely resembles; an alternative form or spelling, as theatre is a *variant* of theater. *adj.* differing in a particular respect from others that it closely resembles· alternative, as a *variant* spelling.

variation (vâr ı ā' shun), *n.* a difference between two things; a difference between two states of the same thing; the extent of change a thing undergoes or may undergo, as there has been little *variation* in the weather this week.

varicolored (vâr' ı kul ērd), *adj.* marked with different colors.

*varied (vâr' ıd), *adj.* consisting of different sorts, as you need a more *varied* diet.

*variegate (vâr' ı e gāt), *v.t.* to mark with different colors.

*variety (va rī' e tı), *n.* [*pl.* varieties] change from one thing to another; intermixture of different things, diversity; a group within a class, as a *variety* of apple.

*varioloid (vâr' ı ō loid), *n.* a mild form of smallpox, occurring in patients who previously have had smallpox or have been vaccinated.·

*variorum (vâr ı ō' rum), *adj.* indicating an edition of a text with comments by a number of critics and editors, as a *variorum* edition of *Hamlet.*

*various (vâr' ı us), *adj.* different; several.

varlet (vär' let), *n.* a menial; a rogue.

varnish (vär' nish), *n.* a thick, resinous liquid used to gloss wood or metal; polish of manners. *v.t.* to coat with varnish; to gloss over, palliate.

vary (vâr' ı), *v.i. and v.t.* [*p.t. and p.p.* varied, *pr.p.* varying] to undergo a change, differ; to alternate kinds; to mix different sorts, as you should *vary* your diet.

vascular (vas' kū lēr), *adj.* relating to the vessels and ducts of the body.

*vase (vās), *n.* a tall vessel of glass, pottery or similar ware, ornamental and used for such purposes as holding flowers.

*vaseline (vas' e lēn), *n.* petroleum jelly, used as an ointment and a lubricant, and other proprietary articles made from petroleum: a trade name.

vassal (vas' al), *n.* a tenant in the feudal system; a bondman or slave.

vassalage (vas' al ıj), *n.* services rendered to a feudal lord in payment for protection; bondage, slavery.

*vast (vàst), *adj.* of great extent; very great in quantity or amount, as a *vast* sum.

vat (vat), *n.* a large flat tub or tank used in some processes of manufacture, especially dyeing or tanning; a liquor for dyeing which colors material only after the material has been dipped in it and then exposed to the air.

*vaudeville (vōd' vil), *n.* an entertainment with a varied program of songs, dances, acrobatics, juggling and short dramatic sketches; a topical song.

*vault (vōlt), *n.* a leap over a fence or other barrier or bar with the help of the hands or a pole. *n.* a chamber with an arched roof, as a burial *vault;* a steel-walled room in which a bank keeps money and papers; the broad arch of the skies. *v.i. and v.t.* to leap over a high bar with the help of a pole; to leap, placing the hands on the barrier, as to *vault* a fence.

*vaunt (vônt), *n.* a boast or brag.

vaunt (vônt), *v.i. and v.t.* to boast or brag; to display proudly.

VDT, video display terminal.

vector (vek' tēr), *n.* a line studied with regard to direction as well as length; a quantity that can be represented by such a line, as velocity.

vedette (vē det'), *n.* a sentinel, usually mounted and occupying an advanced position nearer the enemy than the sentinels of his own force; a small naval vessel used for scouting.

veer (vēr), *v.i. and v.t.* to change direction, as the wind *veered* to the south; to turn the course of, as a ship going into a new tack; to change one's opinion or allegiance, as he *veers* toward the other party.

vegetable (vej' ē ta bl), *n.* a plant especially one grown for food; the edible parts of such plants as marketed and used at the table. *adj.* pertaining to plants; produced by plants, as *vegetable* food or fiber.

*vegetarian (vej ē târ' ı an), *n.* one who eats only vegetable foods, fruits and nuts, with no animal products except perhaps milk and eggs.

vegetate (vej' ē tāt), *v.i.* to grow as a plant; to live with no more activity than a vegetable, or with little physical or mental energy.

vegetation (vej ē tā' shun), *n.* plants collectively, plant life.

*vehement (vē' ē ment), *adj.* violent, as a *vehement* wind; ardent, earnest, as a *vehement* speech.

*vehicle (vē' ı kl), *n.* any kind of conveyance; that by which anything is carried or conveyed, as the radio is a great *vehicle* for news; magazines and newspapers are *vehicles* for advertising.

veil (vāl), *n.* a light fabric or net worn over the face; a piece of fabric hanging from the head over the shoulders, as worn by nuns; a curtain hiding something from sight, as a statue about to be revealed to the public; anything that conceals. *v.t.* to screen from sight, conceal, as to *veil* a meaning.

*vein (vān), *n.* one of the tubes in the body through which blood flows back to the heart; a branching rib of a leaf; a seam of rock bearing ore; a wandering line of another color in marble; a particular character or style of speaking or writing, as this essay has ℩ strong *vein* of humor.

*vein (vān), v.t. to form lines resembling veins, as to vein imitation marble.

vellum (vel' um), n. fine parchment made of calfskin, lambskin or kid leather, used for binding or as a writing or printing material.

*velocipede (vē los' ĭ pēd), n. a child's light vehicle with a large wheel in front and two smaller wheels behind, with a saddle and a handle bar to steer by, propelled by foot power; an early form of the bicycle.

velocity (vē los' ĭ tĭ), n. [pl. velocities] speed, rate of movement.

velours (ve loor'), n. a woven fabric with a pile like that of velvet.

velum (vē' lum), n. the soft palate.

velure (ve lūr'), n. a velvety material of linen, cotton, jute or silk, with a short pile; a velours; a silk pad used to brush and polish hats.

velvet (vel' vet), n. a closely woven silk, rayon or cotton fabric with a short, thick pile.

velveteen (vel ve tēn'), n. a cotton velvet.

*venal (vē' nal), adj. mercenary, willing to take a bribe.

*vendee (ven dē'), n. one to whom anything is sold.

vendetta (ven det' a), n. a blood feud.

vendor or vender (ven' dēr), n. a seller.

vendue (ven dū'), n. a public sale, an auction to the highest bidder.

veneer (ve nēr'), n. a thin layer of fine wood over a piece of ordinary wood used for cabinet work; pretense. v.t. to overlay with a thin layer of fine wood or other more valuable outer material, as to veneer pottery.

*venerable (ven' ēr a bl), adj. worthy of great respect; impressively old.

venerate (ven' ēr āt), v.t. to hold in highest respect, revere.

vengeance (ven' jans), n. injury done to retaliate for injury received: with a vengeance, furiously, in excessive amount or to an excessive degree.

vengeful (venj' fool), adj. vindictive.

*venial (vē' nĭ al), adj. excusable, capable of being forgiven.

*venison (ven' ĭ zn), n. deer meat.

venom (ven' um), n. the poison in certain snakes and spiders that is injected by their bites; malignity.

venous (vē' nus), adj. pertaining to veins.

vent (vent), n. a small opening for the escape of air or a liquid; an outlet; expression, as to give vent to one's feelings. v.t. to permit to escape through an opening; to air, as to vent opinions, anger, spite.

ventilate (ven' tĭ lāt), v.t. to cause air to circulate through; to expose for free public investigation and discussion; to air, as to ventilate a grievance.

ventral (ven' tral), adj. pertaining to or situated on or near the belly or abdomen.

ventricle (ven' tri kl), n. any small cavity in a body or in an organ of the body, particularly one of the two lower chambers of the heart.

*ventriloquism (ven tril' ŏ kwĭzm), n. the art of throwing the voice so that it seems to come from another person or place.

*venture (ven' tūr), n. an undertaking of dan-gerous or daring nature; an enterprise involving risk, as a business venture. v.i. and v.t. to dare, to risk; to expose to chance of loss; to present at risk of incurring criticism, as to venture an opinion.

venturesome (ven' tūr sum), adj. daring; dangerous.

*venue (ven' ū), n. the place where a court action or trial takes place, as the attorney asked for a change of venue.

*veracious (vē rā' shus), adj. truthful.

veracity (vē ras' ĭ tĭ), n. [pl. veracities] truthfulness.

veranda (ve ran' da), n. an outside porch, usually having a roof.

verb (vûrb), n. the part of speech that expresses being or action.

verbal (vûrb' al), adj. expressed in words.

*verbatim (vûr bā' tim), adv. word for word.

*verbiage (vûr' bi ij), n. a superabundance of words.

*verbose (vûr bōs'), adj. wordy.

verdant (vûr' dant), adj. green; inexperienced.

verdict (vûr' dikt), n. the finding by a jury; a judgment, as my verdict is that you are right.

*verdigris (vûr' di grēs), n. the blue-green pigment that is produced by the action of acetic acid or vinegar on copper; the blue-green deposit that forms on corroding copper and brass.

*verdure (vûr' dūr), n. the fresh greenness of vegetation.

verge (vûrj), n. a rod or staff carried before a bishop or dean as an emblem of his office; an edge or brink. v.i. to tend, to come near, as this verges on the absurd.

verger (vûr' gēr), n. one who carries a bishop's or dean's staff; the servant of a high church official; a sexton, one who cares for a church building.

verify (ver' ĭ fī), v.t. [p.t. and p.p. verified, pr.p. verifying] to prove to be true; to examine the truth of; to support by facts.

verily (ver' ĭ lĭ), adv. in truth.

*verisimilitude (ver ĭ si mil' ĭ tūd), n. appearance of truth; probability; realism.

veritable (ver' ĭ ta bl), adj. actual, genuine.

verity (ver' ĭ tĭ), n. [pl. verities] that which is true; agreement with fact.

*vermicelli (vûr mi sel' ĭ), n. a stiff paste or dough of white flour cut into long threads, smaller than spaghetti and not hollow like macaroni.

vermifuge (vûr' mi fūj), n. a medicine to remove worms from the intestines.

vermilion (vûr mil' yun), n. a brilliant red pigment or its color.

vermin (vûr' min), n. any small animal or insect pests, such as rats and mice, fleas, lice, bedbugs, cockroaches.

vernacular (vēr nak' ū lēr), n. the native tongue; native idiom; forms of speech peculiar to a locality or a business or profession, as the vernacular of printing.

vernacular (vēr nak' ū lēr), adj. pertaining to or characteristic of one's native country or its language; peculiar to a locality or group or class of people; belonging to those persons who use the native or local language, as Dante, who wrote in Latin, was also a *vernacular* poet.

vernal (vûr' nal), *adj.* pertaining to spring, springlike.

vernier (vûr' ni ẽr), *n.* a movable scale for precise measurements; a small auxiliary part used with a main device in order to attain sensitive adjustment in radio.

*versatile (vûr' sa til), *adj.* turning with ease from one thing to another, able to do many things well.

verse (vûrs), *n.* poetry; a single line in meter; a type of poetry, as blank *verse*, heroic *verse*; a stanza of a hymn; one of the numbered divisions of a chapter of the Bible.

versify (vûrs' i fī), *v.i.* and *v.t.* [*p.t.* and *p.p.* versified, *pr.p.* versifying] to compose in meter; to put into verse.

version (vûr' zhun), *n.* a translation from one language to another; one person's account of anything as compared with someone else's.

versus (vûr' sus), *prep.* against, as Princeton *versus* Yale: abbreviated *v.* or *vs.*, especially in naming the parties to a lawsuit.

*vertebra (vûr' tē bra), *n.* [*pl.* vertebrae or vertebras] a single bone of the spinal column.

vertex (vûr' teks), *n.* [*pl.* vertexes or vertices] the top, summit, highest point.

vertical (vûr' ti kal), *adj.* at right angles with the horizon, pointing straight up.

*vertigo (vûr' ti gō), *n.* [*pl.* vertigoes] giddiness, dizziness.

verve (vûrv), *n.* enthusiasm for creative work; energy, vigor, spirit; talent, creative ability.

very (ver' i), *adj.* real, actual, as the *very* truth; exactly the same, as the *very* one; mere, the *very* thought of it. *adv.* truly, extremely, as it is *very* hard work.

vesicle (ves' i kl), *n.* a small sac containing liquid; a water blister.

vespers (ves' pẽrz), *n.* evening prayer or evensong.

vessel (ves' l), *n.* a container to hold liquids; a ship; a tube or canal in the body holding fluids, as the blood *vessels*.

vest (vest), *n.* a body garment like a tight coat without sleeves, worn by men beneath a suit coat. *v.i.* and *v.t.* to rest or take effect, as title to property *vests* in someone, a *vested* interest; to clothe, as with authority or garments symbolizing it.

vestal (ves' tal), *n.* a virgin; a nun. *adj.* chaste.

vested (ves' ted), *adj.* fixed by law, in effect, already acquired, as a *vested* right.

*vestibule (ves' ti būl), *n.* a lobby between the inner and outer doors of a house; an enclosed porch at the door of a building; an enclosed entrance to a railroad car.

vestige (ves' tij), *n.* a mark left in passing, a trace or fragment of something long gone.

vestment (vest' ment), *n.* a garment, especially a robe in a church ceremony.

vestry (ves' tri), *n.* [*pl.* vestries] a room in a church where vestments are kept.

*vesture (ves' tūr), *n.* clothing, apparel.

veteran (vet' ẽr an), *n.* one grown old in serv-ice; one who has served in a war.

*veterinary (vet' ẽr i ner i), *n.* [*pl.* veterinaries] one who treats the diseases and injuries of animals.

veterinary (vet' ẽr i ner i), *adj.* pertaining to the art of healing the diseases of animals.

veto (vē' tō), *n.* [*pl.* vetoes] the right of a chief executive to refuse to approve an act of legislation submitted to him for signature.

veto (vē' tō), *v.t.* to refuse to sign, as a legislative bill; to forbid, with authority, as I must *veto* your proposal.

vex (veks), *v.t.* to irritate with small annoyances, provoke.

vexed (vekst), *adj.* much debated but not settled, as a *vexed* question.

viaduct (vī' a dukt), *n.* an arch-supported structure carrying a highway or railroad over a ravine, valley or low ground.

*vial (vī' al), *n.* a small glass bottle or vessel: sometimes *phial.*

viand (vī' and), *n.* an article of food, especially meat: *viands*, provisions.

vibrant (vī' brant), *adj.* pulsing, throbbing, resonant; lively, animated, vigorous, as a *vibrant* personality.

*vibrate (vī' brāt), *v.i.* and *v.t.* to move back and forth with even timing, oscillate; to waver, vacillate; to quiver; to cause to quiver; to cause to move back and forth.

vibration (vī brā' shun), *n.* oscillation; a quivering of the voice.

*vicar (vik' ẽr), *n.* one who is authorized to act in place of another, a deputy; a clergyman serving as deputy to one of higher rank.

*vicarious (vī kâr' i us), *adj.* delegated, as *vicarious* power; done or endured in place of another, as *vicarious* suffering.

vice (vīs), *n.* a bad habit; depravity; fault.

*vicegerent (vīs jēr' ent), *n.* one delegated to act for another; an officer with authority to act for another, a lieutenant.

vice-president (vīs' prez' i dent), *n.* an official ranking next below a president, acting for the president in his absence or disability and succeeding as president on the president's death.

viceregal (vīs rē' gal), *adj.* pertaining to a viceroy.

vice-regent (vīs rē' jent), *n.* an officer substituting for a regent.

*viceroy (vīs' roi), *n.* a governor of a colony or province, in the name and by the authority of the sovereign of the empire of which it is a part; a deputy of the sovereign.

*vice versa (vī' sē vûr' sa), the order being reversed, conversely, the other way round.

*vicinage (vis' in nij), *n.* neighborhood; state of being neighbors.

vicinity (vi sin' i ti), *n.* [*pl.* vicinities] nearness, neighborhood.

vicious (vish' us), *adj.* having bad habits, depraved; ugly, malicious.

*vicissitude (vi sis' i tūd), *n.* change in circumstances; any of the hazards of life.

victim (vik' tim), *n.* a human being sacrificed to a deity; a person hurt or killed by intention or in an accident; a sufferer from disease; a dupe.

victor (vĭk' tẽr), *n.* the winner in a battle or contest, a conqueror.

victorious (vĭk tō' rĭ us), *adj.* having conquered an enemy in battle; having won a contest; triumphant, successful in any struggle.

*victory (vĭk' tō rĭ), *n.* [*pl.* victories] the defeat of an enemy in battle or of an opponent in a contest.

*victual (vĭt' l), *v.t.* [*p.t. and p.p.* victualed, *pr.p.* victualing] to furnish with supplies of food; to stock with provisions, as to *victual* a ship.

*victuals (vĭt' lz), *n.* food, especially when ready to be eaten.

*vicuña (vĭ kōōn' ya), *n.* an animal resembling the llama, found in Mexico and the Andes, furnishing a fine, long reddish wool used in delicate and expensive fabrics; a fabric made from the wool of this animal or a wool-and-cotton imitation of it.

video (vĭd´ ē ō), *adj.* pertaining to television and in particular to the picture.

vie (vī), *v.i.* [*p.t. and p.p.* vied, *pr.p.* vying] to strive for superiority, rival, compete, as he is fit to *vie* with champions.

view (vū), *n.* the act of seeing, as I had a good *view* of the parade from my window; a landscape, as there is a beautiful *view* from the top of the hill; a mental survey; a belief or opinion, as according to my *view;* purpose, as with a *view* to increasing profits.

view (vū), *v.t.* to look upon, regard, see; to survey mentally; to form an opinion of.

viewpoint (vū' point), *n.* a position from which objects, principles or acts are considered and judged, as her *viewpoint* is always charitable.

*vigil (vĭj' ĭl), *n.* the act of staying awake during the normal time for sleeping in order to watch or wait for something; evening or nighttime devotions.

vigilant (vĭj' ĭ lant), *adj.* watchful, alert, cautious.

*vignette (vĭn yet'), *n.* a small design usually decorating the page preceding the title page; a drawing or an illustration that shades off at the edges without a sharp border; a short, graphic description, a word picture.

vigor (vĭg' ẽr), *n.* physical or mental strength and force; vital energy in a plant or animal.

vigorous (vĭg' ẽr us), *adj.* strong, energetic, robust, forceful, as a *vigorous* person, a *vigorous* style of writing.

*viking (vī' king), *n.* one of the Northmen who ranged the known seas in the 8th, 9th and 10th centuries terrorizing the coasts of Europe.

vile (vīl), *adj.* despicable, worthless, ignoble, evil.

vilify (vĭl' ĭ fī), *v.t.* [*p.t. and p.p.* vilified, *pr.p.* vilifying] to defame, slander, abuse.

villa (vĭl' a), *n.* a country seat, a fine suburban residence.

village (vĭl' ĭj), *n.* a small assemblage of houses and other buildings, larger than a hamlet but smaller than a town.

*villain (vĭl' ĭn), *n.* a scoundrel; the character in a play or novel who complicates the plot

with his evil designs and actions.

villous (vĭl' us), *adj.* covered with soft, fine hair, downy.

vindicate (vĭn' dĭ kāt), *v.t.* to defend successfully; to clear from suspicion of wrongdoing or dishonorable action; to justify.

vindication (vĭn dĭ kā' shun), *n.* justification against charges of wrongdoing or dishonorable acts.

vindictive (vĭn dĭk' tĭv), *adj.* revengeful, inclined to hold grudges.

vine (vīn), *n.* a climbing or trailing plant, as a grape*vine*, a sweet-potato *vine*.

vinegar (vĭn' ē gẽr), *n.* an acid obtained by the fermentation of cider, malt or wine and used in seasoning and pickling; a weak form of acetic acid.

vinegary (vĭn' ē gẽr ĭ), *adj.* thin and sour, as a *vinegary* speech.

vinery (vīn' ẽr ĭ), *n.* [*pl.* vineries] a place where grapes are grown indoors.

vineyard (vĭn' yẽrd), *n.* a plantation of grapevines.

*vinous (vī' nus), *adj.* pertaining to wine; like wine.

vintage (vĭn' tĭj), *n.* the year's output of a vineyard or of the vineyards of a given region.

*viol (vī' ul), *n.* a four-stringed musical instrument played with a bow.

*viola (vē ōl' a), *n.* a stringed instrument between the violin and violoncello in size, tuned a fifth lower than the violin.

violate (vī' ō lāt), *v.t.* to transgress; to ravish; to treat a sacred place with irreverence; to trespass upon.

violence (vī' ō lens), *n.* great force; fury and vehemence; unwarranted change of words or meaning in a text.

violent (vī' ō lent), *adj.* urged or driven by force, as a *violent* nature; marked by physical force, as a *violent* storm; vehement, as *violent* speech; unnatural, due to accident or attack, as a *violent* death.

Syn. Furious, boisterous, vehement, impetuous. A man may be *violent* in his opinions, measures, resentments; he is *furious* in his anger or has a *furious* temper; he is *vehement* in his affections or passions, in love, zeal, pursuit of an object. *Violent* persons wreak their passions upon another person or an object; *vehemence* is confined to the person himself. An *impetuous* nature is one of extreme *vehemence*. One is *boisterous* in manner and behavior, not in the mind.

Ant. Gentle, mild, calm.

violet (vī' ō let), *n.* a low-growing herb with dainty flowers, (often purple), some very fragrant and some odorless; the bluish blue-red color of the purple violet, one of the colors of the spectrum, at the end opposite to the color red.

violet rays (vī' ō let rāz), the shortest vibrations of light perceptible by the human eye; to be distinguished from ultraviolet rays, used in the treatment of disease.

*violin (vī ō lin'), *n.* a four-stringed musical instrument played with a bow and developed from the viola.

*violoncello (vē ō lon chel' ō), n. [pl. violoncellos] a large four-stringed musical instrument of the viol class, tuned an octave lower than the viola; often called cello.

*viper (vī' pēr), n. a venomous snake.

viperous (vī' pēr us), adj. treacherous, malignant.

*virago (vi rā' gō), n. [pl. viragoes] a bold, quarrelsome woman; a scold.

virgin (vûr' jin), n. a maiden: the Virgin, Mary, the mother of Jesus. adj. pure, untouched, as virgin soil, a virgin forest.

*virile (vir' il), adj. pertaining to mature manhood; manly, forceful, as a virile style of writing.

virtual (vûr' tū al), adj. in essence or effect though not in name, as he is the virtual head of this business.

*virtue (vûr' tū), n. inherent power or merit; moral excellence, chastity.

*virtuoso (vûr tū ō' sō), n. [pl. virtuosos or virtuosi] one with special knowledge of or skill in a fine art; a connoisseur of artistic things; one who has mastered the technique of an art.

*virulence (vir' ū lens), n. the quality of being poisonous or venomous; bitter enmity, rancor.

virulent (vir' ū lent), adj. poisonous; actively injurious to life or health; hostile.

virus (vī' rus), n. venom; a poison that is produced in the body by a disease; something that poisons the mind.

visa (vē' za), the official endorsement on a passport, indicating that it has been examined by governmental authorities so that the traveler may proceed.

*visage (viz' ij), n. the face or countenance.

*viscera (vis' ēr a), n. the internal organs, as heart, liver and intestines.

*viscid (vis' id), adj. thick and sticky.

*viscount (vī' kount), n. a nobleman next in rank below an earl, higher than a baron.

*viscous (vis' kus), adj. adhesive, sticky.

vise (vīs), n. a two-jawed instrument to hold things steady while being worked on.

visé (vē zā'), n. a visa.

visibility (viz i bil' i ti), n. the state of being perceptible to the eye; the range of vision for those in an airplane und · existing conditions of atmosphere and clouds.

visible (viz' i bl), adj. perceptible to the eye; in view.

*vision (vizh' un), n. the sense of sight; act of seeing; that which is seen; an apparition; understanding and insight, as he has great vision in matters of administration.

visionary (vizh' un er i), n. [pl. visionaries] a · dreamer; one who tends to accept fancied things as facts; one who is not a realist.

visionary (vizh' un er i), adj. existing only in the imagination; not realistic or practical.

visit (viz' it), n. the act of calling upon another; a short stay.

visit (viz' it), v.t. and v.i. to call on; to stay with as a guest; to send upon, as the sins of the fathers shall be visited upon the children; to be a guest.

visitation (viz.i tā' shun), n. an official inspection; a judgment.

visor (vī'zēr), n. the front piece of a helmet that protects the face; the projecting part of a cap that shades the eyes: sometimes spelled vizor.

vista (vis' ta), n. a view down a comparatively long and narrow channel of sight, as this avenue affords a lovely vista.

*visual (vizh' ū al), adj. pertaining to sight. n. a rough sketch for a layout or design.

visualize (vizh' ū al īz), v.t. to form a mental picture of; to make a rough sketch of, as he visualized the idea of the advertisement.

vital (vī' tal), adj. pertaining to life; essential, indispensable.

vitality (vī tal' i ti), n. living force; ability to sustain or retain life; vigor and endurance.

vitalize (vī' tal īz), v.t. to animate, give life to, increase the vigor of, as to vitalize an essay.

vitals (vī' talz), n. the organs of the body that are essential to life, as the heart, liver, lungs and brain are the vitals.

vitamin (vī ta .nin), n. a constituent of many foods, that strengthens the body tissues and prevents contraction of such diseases as pellagra and scurvy.

*vitiate (vish' i āt), v.t. to render faulty or defective; to impair the quality of; to corrupt, debase.

viticulture (vit' i kul tūr), n. the growing of grapes.

vitreous (vit' rē us), adj. consisting of or resembling glass.

vitrify (vit' ri fī), v.t. [p.t. and p.p. vitrified, pr.p. vitrifying] to convert into glass, glaze; to cause to become glass or to resemble glass.

*vitriol (vit' ri ul), n. sulphuric acid; anything sharp and burning, as sarcasm.

vitriolic (vit ri ol' ik), adj. pertaining to sulphuric acid; caustic, sharp and stinging, as a vitriolic speech.

*vituperate (vī tū' pēr āt), v.t. to berate, censure abusively.

*vivacious (vī vā' shus), adj. lively, gay, animated.

vivacity (vī vas' i ti), n. [pl. vivacities] liveliness, animation.

*viva voce (vī va vō' sē), by the living voice; oral; expressed orally, as a viva voce vote.

vivid (viv' id), adj. brilliant; forming lifelike images in the mind, realistic.

vivify (viv' i fī), v.t. [p.t. and p.p. vivified, pr.p. vivifying] to give life to, enliven, quicken, animate.

vivisect (viv' i sekt), v.t. to dissect the living body of.

vixen (vik' sn), n. a female fox; a quarrelsome, ill-natured woman.

viz. (viz), adv. namely, to wit. (An abbreviation of Latin videlicet, meaning namely; usually read "namely" but sometimes pronounced as it is spelled.)

*vocable (vō' ka bl), n. a word or term.

vocabulary (vō kab' ū ler i), n. [pl. vocabularies] a collection of words arranged alphabetically for reference and defined or explained; the special stock of words employed by an individual, in a business or by an author, as the *vocabulary* of finance, the *vocabulary* of Shakespeare.

vocal (vō′ kal), *adj.* pertaining to the voice, oral, spoken.

vocal cord (vō′ kal kôrd), either of two pairs of bands of fibrous tissue attached to the larynx and producing the human voice through vibration.

vocalize (vō′ kal īz), *v.t. and v.i.* to utter with the voice; to express in words or tones; to sing.

vocation (vō kā′ shun), *n.* calling, occupation.

*****vocative** (vok′ a tiv), *n.* a case of noun or pronoun indicating address; a noun naming a person or thing addressed.

vociferate (vō sif′ ēr āt), *v.i. and v.t.* to clamor, utter loudly, cry out noisily.

vociferous (vō sif′ ēr us), *adj.* noisy, clamorous.

*****vogue** (vōg), *n.* fashion, the prevailing style; popularity, as his books have a great *vogue*.

voice (vois), *n.* utterance; faculty of speech; sound made by air passing through the larynx and made audible through the vibrations of the vocal cords; opinion. *v.t.* to give expression to, express in speech, as he *voiced* his discontent strongly.

void (void), *n.* an empty space, a vacuum.

void (void), *v.t.* to make empty or vacant, eject; to make ineffective or invalid, annul.

void (void), *adj.* empty, vacant, unoccupied; without effect.

voile (voil), *n.* a thin fabric of cotton, silk or wool used as a material for women's dresses, especially light, summer dresses.

*****volatile** (vol ′ a til), *adj.* easily changed into gas; tending to turn into vapor; fickle, changeable, as a *volatile* personality.

*****volcano** (vol kā′ nō), *n.* [*pl.* volcanoes or volcanos] an aperture in the earth's surface from which molten lava and steam are ejected; a conical hill or mountain formed from the erupted matter.

vole (vōl), *n.* any of several small rodents, such as the field mouse and meadow mouse.

volition (vō lish′ un), *n.* the act or power of willing or exerting choice; that which is willed.

volley (vol′ i), *n.* the shooting of many missiles at once; a sudden burst of anything, as a *volley* of words; a ball in its flight without touching the ground, as a *volley* in tennis, cricket and other games.

*****volplane** (vol′ plān), *v.i.* to bring an airplane down by gliding with little or no engine power.

*****volt** (vōlt), *n.* the unit of electromotive force.

voltaic (vol tā′ ik), *adj.* pertaining to the production of electricity by chemical action or galvanism.

voltaic cell (vol tā′ ik sel), a device to produce electrical energy by chemical action.

voluble (vol′ ū bl), *adj.* fluent in speech, talkative.

volume (vol′ ūm), *n.* the amount of space occupied by an object, as measured in cubical units; mass or bulk; a large quantity, as a great *volume* of steam; a single book.

voluminous (vō lū′ mi nus), *adj.* occupying much space, bulky; filling many volumes.

*****voluntary** (vol′ un ter i), *n.* [*pl.* voluntaries] a musical prelude, especially an organ solo.

voluntary (vol′ un ter i), *adj.* acting from choice or free will, done of one's own accord, not compulsory.

volunteer (vol un tēr′), *n.* one engaged in a service, especially military or naval, by his own will; one who offers his services.

volunteer (vol un tēr′), *v.i. and v.t.* to enter the army or navy of one's own accord; to offer of one's own free will, as to *volunteer* one's services, to *volunteer* information.

voluptuary (vō lup′ tū er i), *n.* [*pl.* voluptuaries] one devoted to gratification of the senses.

voluptuous (vō lup′ tū us), *adj.* sensual; luxurious.

*****volute** (vō lūt′), *n.* a spiral ornament on an architectural detail, such as on the capital of a column.

vomit (vom′ it), *v.t. and v.i.* to throw up from the stomach through the mouth; to discharge, as a volcano *vomits* lava.

voodoo (vōō′ dōō), *n.* a system of magic practiced by the Negroes of Africa and Haiti.

*****voracious** (vō rā′ shus), *adj.* greedy, ravenous, insatiable.

vortex (vôr′ teks), *n.* [*pl.* vortexes or vortices] an eddy, whirlpool, the depression at the center of a body of whirling air or water, drawing things in and down.

votary (vō′ ta ri), *n.* [*pl.* votaries] a devotee; one who has concentrated upon some particular subject of interest, service or pursuit.

vote (vōt), *n.* an expression of choice or preference by ballot or some other method of suffrage; decision by a majority; the right to express political preference; the whole number of ballots cast in an election.

votive (vō′ tiv), *adj.* given, consecrated or promised by vow; done in fulfilment of a vow.

vouch (vouch), *v.i.* to attest, as to *vouch* for another's trustworthiness; to confirm, bear witness.

voucher (vouch′ ēr), *n.* a paper that bears witness, as to payment made, as the *vouchers* in a checkbook.

vouchsafe (vouch säf′), *v.t.* to condescend to grant, permit.

vow (vou), *n.* a solemn promise or pledge; a pledge of faithfulness.

vow (vou), *v.t. and v.i.* to promise solemnly; to make a solemn pledge.

vowel (vou′ el), *n.* an open sound of the voice with no shaping by or with the tongue, teeth or lips; a letter representing such a sound, as *a, e, i, o, u*.

*****voyage** (vol′ ij), *n.* a journey of considerable distance by water or by air.

vulcanize (vul′ kan īz), *v.t.* to change the properties of by combination with certain substances (notably sulphur) that give toughness, as to *vulcanize* rubber.

vulgar (vul′ gēr), *adj.* common, unrefined, coarse.

vulgarity (vul går' ĭ tĭ), *n.* [*pl.* vulgarities] coarseness of speech or manners.

vulnerable (vul' nẽr *a* bl), *adj.* capable of being wounded; open to attack.

*vulpine (vul' pĭn), *adj.* foxy, like a fóx, cunning.

vulture (vul' tũr), *n.* a large flesh-eating bird of prey related to the hawks and eagles.

W

*wad (wod), *n.* a small mass of soft material; a soft piece of material like cotton or wool used to stop an opening or give extra thickness to a garment; a plug of soft fiber to hold the charge of a muzzle-loading gun in place. *v.t.* to form into a compact mass, as to *wad* paper; to pack or close up with a mass of soft material, as to *wad* up a crack; to pad or line with soft substance, as a garment; to insert a plug or stopper into, as to *wad* a gun.

wadding (wod' ĭng), *n.* any soft stuff used for padding garments, in surgical dressings or to protect fragile articles in wrapping.

waddle (wod' l), *n.* a clumsy, rocking gait like that of a duck. *v.i.* to walk with a clumsy roll from side to side, as the duck *waddles*.

wade (wād), *v.i.* to walk through water, mud, snow or anything fluid or semifluid; to advance with difficulty, as to *wade* through a tiresome book.

wafer (wā' fẽr), *n.* a thin, dry biscuit; the thin cake of unleavened bread used in the communion service; a small disk of glued paper used in sealing papers; a disk of wax used to seal papers and attached by heating.

waffle (wof' l), *n.* a battercake cooked in a waffle iron over an open fire or electric heating apparatus.

waft (wȧft), *n.* the act of floating lightly or causing to float lightly; a light puff of wind; a passing odor or taste, a whiff.

*waft (wȧft), *v.i. and v.t.* to float through the air; to cause to float lightly.

wag (wag), *n.* a side-to-side motion, as the *wag* of a dog's tail; a to-and-fro motion, as the *wag* of head or finger. *n.* a practical joker; a witty person. *v.i. and v.t.* to move from side to side, as a dog's tail *wags;* to cause to move from side to side, as a dog *wags* its tail; to move up and down, as to *wag* one's head or one's finger, both signs of amusement or derision.

wage (wāj), *v.t.* to carry on or engage in, as war.

wager (wā' jẽr), *n.* a bet. *v.i. and v.t.* to bet; to put up, as stakes.

wages (wāj' ez), *n.* money paid for work, by the hour, day or week.

waggery (wag' ẽr ĭ), *n.* [*pl.* waggeries] mischievous merriment, jesting, good-humored teasing.

waggle (wag' gl), *v.t.* to cause to move back and forth. *n.* the swinging of a golf club back and forth over the ball before striking it.

wagon (wag' un), *n.* a four-wheeled vehicle for heavy work.

*waif (wāf), *n.* a stray person or thing; a lost child.

*wail (wāl), *n.* a cry of grief.

wail (wāl), *v.i.* to cry in grief; to make a mournful, long-drawn sound, as the wind *wails* around the house.

wailing (wāl' ĭng), *n.* lamentation.

wain (wān), *n.* a wagon, as in *Charles's Wain,* the British name for the Great Dipper.

*wainscot (wān' skut), *n.* a paneled wooden lining on walls, generally on the lower part. *v.t.* to line or face, as the lower part of a room wall, with wood in strips or panels.

waist (wāst), *n.* the narrowest part of the trunk of the body, below the ribs; the middle part of anything resembling a body, as the *waist* of a ship; the slender middle section of an hourglass. *n.* a garment that covers body from shoulders to belt line.

waistband (wāst' band), *n.* the edge of a garment, as skirt or trousers, encircling the body at the belt line.

*waistcoat (wes' kut), *n.* a short garment for men covering the trunk of the body, like a sleeveless coat, a vest.

*wait (wāt), *n.* the act of delaying or lingering; a stay in one place; time spent in expectation of something about to happen, as a long *wait* for a train; hiding, as to lie in *wait*. *n.* one of a band of musicians who play and sing music in the streets at Christmas time. *v.i.* and *v.t.* to linger in expectation of something; to continue in one place, as we *waited* for you all morning; to serve, as he *waited* on us very competently; to await, as *wait* orders.

waiter (wāt' ẽr), *n.* one who serves others at table; a serving tray.

*waive (wāv), *v.t.* to forgo, as to *waive* a right.

waiver (wāv' ẽr), *n.* a voluntary relinquishment, as a *waiver* of a legal right; the legal document stating this relinquishment.

wake (wāk), *n.* a trail left by some moving object, as the *wake* of a ship, in the *wake* of the storm, the *wake* of an invading army. *n.* a vigil; the watch over a dead body awaiting burial. *v.i. and v.t.* [*p.t.* waked or woke, *p.p.* waked, *pr.p.* waking] to be aroused from sleep; to emerge from slumber; to cause to stop sleeping, arouse, as you *woke* me too soon.

wakeful (wāk' fool), *adj.* unable to sleep; watchful, vigilant.

    Syn. Watchful, vigilant. To be *wakeful* is to be physically unable to sleep; to be *watchful* may mean to stay awake for a purpose or to be on the alert; to be *vigilant* is to be on guard against impending evil or danger.

Ant. Slumbrous, heedless.

wale (wāl), *n.* a mark left by the stroke of a lash; a rib in the weave of cloth; a timber fastened horizontally to a row of piles to hold them in position.

***walk** (wôk), *n.* the act of advancing by alternate steps without running; manner of moving afoot; a stroll; a place for moving afoot; the distance one goes afoot, as it was a long *walk;* gait; a way of living, as a different *walk* of life.

walk (wôk), *v.t. and v.i.* to traverse afoot, as to *walk* the floor; to cause to traverse afoot; to drive or ride at a slow pace, as I *walked* my horse; to proceed by steps at a pace slower than a run; to stroll.

walking beam (wôk' ing bēm), a horizontal, pivoted lever with connecting rods at the ends, transmitting the power of a steam engine from the piston rod to the wheel shaft.

walking delegate wôk' ing del' ē gāt), a labor union official who visits the different unions in his craft.

***wall** (wôl), *n.* a structure of stone, brick, wood or other material constituting the side of a building, enclosing a room or marking and protecting a boundary.

wall (wôl), *v.t.* to enclose, surround with vertical enclosing surfaces or structures, as to *wall* a garden; to fill, as a hole; to fortify.

wallet (wôl' et), *n.* a large pocketbook that holds money or papers flat; any pocketbook or leather kit.

wall-eyed (wôl' īd), *n.* having eyes that turn outward, to the sides; opposite of cross-eyed; having a white-irised, staring eye.

wallflower (wôl' flou ēr), *n.* a plant belonging to the mustard family, with fragrant flowers, yellow to red in color.

wallop (wol' up), *v.t.* to strike, beat.

wallow (wol' ō), *n.* the act of rolling, as in mud; a muddy place in which animals roll.

wallow (wol' ō), *v.i.* to roll or flounder about in mud, as a hog; to live in vice or filth.

***walnut** (wôl' nut), *n.* a nut-bearing tree, the English *walnut* or the American black *walnut;* the nut borne by this tree; its wood, used in making furniture.

***walrus** (wôl' rus), *n.* [*pl.* walruses or walrus] a large sea animal living in the Arctic Regions and valuable for its blubber, skin and tusks.

waltz (wôlts), *n.* a round dance in triple time; the music for such a dance.

waltz (wôlts), *v.i. and v.t.* to perform a round dance in triple time; to whirl.

***wampum** (wom' pum), *n.* beads made of shells and strung, used by the North American Indians as money and for ornament.

***wan** (won), *adj.* pale, sickly.

***wand** (wond), *n.* a long, slender rod; a magician's staff; a staff, symbol of authority; a musician's baton.

wander (won' dēr), *v.i. and v.t.* to ramble aimlessly, stroll; to be delirious, as his mind *wanders;* to roam through or over, traverse.

wane (wān), *n.* the decreasing phase of the moon; a decline in power or influence. *v.i.* to grow less, decline in power or impor-

tance.

***want** (wont), *n.* deficiency, need, penury, lack, scarcity.

want (wont), *v.i. and v.t.* to be in need; to be deficient in, as the stew *wants* salt; to lack, need, require.

Syn. Need, lack. To *want* is to be without that which contributes to comfort or is desired; to *need* is to be without that which is essential to existence or to our purposes; to *lack* is simply to be without, and the word carries no collateral idea. What we *want* would meet artificial desires, what we *need* would satisfy real requirements.

Ant. Have, hold, possess.

wanton (won' tun), *n.* a person of unrestrained behavior. *adj.* unrestrained, sportive, reckless.

***war** (wôr), *n.* an armed conflict between states or nations; any contest or strife, as a *war* of words.

war (wôr), *v.i.* [*p.t.* warred, *pr.p.* warring] to fight, carry on hostilities.

warble (wôr' bl), *n.* a soft, sweet flow of melodious sounds, as of a bird.

warble (wôr' bl), *v.i. and v.t.* to trill, as the bird *warbled;* to sing in a trilling manner, as to *warble* a tune.

ward (wôrd), *n.* protection; a person under protection; one committed to the care of another as guardian and protector; a hospital section with a number of patients in one large room; a section of a prison; a voting section in a town; a projection in a lock or on a key to prevent use of any but the proper key.

ward (wôrd), *v.t.* to guard, protect, care for, defend against danger; to avert, as to *ward* off a blow or an attack.

warden (wôr' dn), *n.* a guardian; trustee, as a church*warden;* head keeper, as a jail *warden.*

warder (wôr' dēr), *n.* a guard or keeper.

wardrobe (wôrd' rōb), *n.* a portable closet for clothes; an outfit of wearing apparel.

wardroom (wôrd' rōōm), *n.* the living quarters on a warship for commissioned officers of all ranks between ensign and captain.

ware (wâr), *n.* manufactured articles, pottery, as earthen*ware,* silver: *wares,* merchandise, goods.

warehouse (wâr' hous), *n.* a building for storing goods, for holding goods to be distributed locally or for holding imports until duties are paid.

warehouse (wâr' hous), *v.t.* to place in a building for storing or for local distribution.

warfare (wôr' fâr), *n.* the waging of armed conflict.

warily (wâr' i li), *adv.* in a cautious manner.

warm (wôrm), *adj.* having heat in a moderate degree; giving out mild heat; keeping heat in, as a *warm* blanket; having tones that suggest heat, as red, orange and yellow are *warm* colors; genial, cordial, as a *warm* welcome; fresh, as a *warm* scent.

warmth (wôrmth), *n.* moderate heat; earnestness, as he spoke with *warmth;* friendliness, as *warmth* of feeling.

warn (wôrn), *v.t.* to give notice of danger, caution; to advise, as I *warn* you not to go; to signal something that is coming, as the clock gave a warning sign that the hour was near; in zoology warning colorations or the ability to make warning sounds are provided for many venomous or otherwise offensive animals.

warp (wôrp), *n.* the act of twisting out of shape; state of being twisted out of shape; the threads that extend lengthwise in the loom and are crossed by the woof.

warp (wôrp), *v.i. and v.t.* to shrink and twist out of shape, as the board *warped;* to move, as a vessel, by pulling on a rope attached to some fixed point; to twist out of shape; to make biased, as her bitter experience *warped* her point of view.

warrant (wa·r´•, wawr´ ant), *v.t.* to give justification for; to authorize or sanction with assurance of safety; to guarantee to be as represented; to vouch for; to assure; to indemnify against loss; *n.* (*Law*) instrument which warrants or justifies act otherwise not permissible or legal; instrument giving power to arrest offender; authorization; guarantee; naval or military writ inferior to commission. -able *a.* -ably *adv.* -ableness *n.* -ed *a.* guaranteed. -er, -or *n.* -y *n.* security; guarantee. — **officer,** officer in Navy and Army intermediate between non-commissioned and commissioned officer.

warren (wor´ en), *n.* a place for breeding rabbits; any crowded area.

*warrior** (wor´ i ẽr), *n.* a soldier, a fighter.

wart (wôrt), *n.* a dry excrescence on the skin; a similar hard, dry lump on the stem of a plant.

wart hog (wôrt hog), *n.* a wild pig of South Africa, has upward curving tusks on both jaws and warty face.

*wary** (wâr´ i), *adj.* [*comp.* warier, *superl.* wariest] watchful, cautious; alert and circumspect.

was (wuz´), *pa.t.* of verb *to be.*

wash (wosh), *n.* the act of cleansing; a collection of clothes to be cleaned with soap and water, as the family *wash;* the dash of water against something, as the *wash* of the waves on the shore; the churned air or water behind the propellers of an airplane or surface ship; a lotion or liquid with which anything is cleansed or tinted; a thin coat of water color in painting.

wash (wosh), *v.t. and v.i.* to take the dirt out of by scrubbing in soapy water, as to *wash* clothes; to flow against, as the waves *wash* the shore; to carry off by the action of water, as the waves *washed* out the railroad tracks; to become cleansed with soap and water, as I *washed* in the lake; to cleanse clothes, as she *washes* on Mondays; to pass through the application of soap and water without injury, as that material will not *wash;* to come through any sort of test, as his explanation will not *wash;* to move with a lapping sound, as the waves *washed* against the side of the sailboat.

washboard (wosh´ bôrd), *n.* a ribbed or ridged

surface upon which to rub the dirt out of clothes in cleansing them with soap and water.

washer (wosh´ ẽr), *n.* a ring of metal, leather or rubber to give more tightness to a joint or prevent wear on wood by a nail or nut; a machine for cleansing clothes with soap and water, generally run by electricity.

washout (wosh´ out), *n.* a carrying away of earth by running water.

*wasp** (wosp), *n.* a winged insect with a poisonous sting.

*wassail** (wos´ l), *n.* an ancient toast or expression of good will given on a festive occasion; a spiced ale used on occasions of feasting and merrymaking.

waste (wāst), *n.* useless expenditure of time, effort or money; refuse matter; leftover parts in a process of manufacture; a mass of otherwise worthless remnants of textiles used to wipe grease off machinery; a vast, unproductive tract of land, as a desert *waste.*

wasteful (wāst´ fool), *adj.* spending or using with extravagance.

wastrel (wās´ trĕl), *n.* waster; profligate; spendthrift.

*watch** (woch), *n.* vigilance; a guard; a guard's spell of duty; one of the periods into which the day is divided on ships; a timepiece carried in a pocket.

watch (woch), *v.i. and v.t.* to keep guard; to observe carefully and closely; to guard, as I'll *watch* the house while you are gone.

watchful (woch´ fool), *adj.* vigilant, on guard.

watchword (woch´ wûrd), *n.* a password; a secret word used to identify friends.

*water** (wô´ tẽr), *n.* a transparent fluid without color or odor, composed of hydrogen and oxygen; the liquid used for cooking, washing, drinking; a sea, river, lake, pond; the fluid that falls from the clouds in the form of rain; the luster of a precious stone; the wavy shine of silk.

water (wô´ tẽr), *adj.* relating to the use, storage or distribution of water, as *water* bread, *water* tank, *water* main, *water* boy.

*water** (wô´ tẽr), *v.i. and v.t.* to run, as the wind makes my eyes *water;* to secrete saliva, as the mouth *waters;* to provide with a drink, as to *water* a horse; to sprinkle, as to *water* a lawn; to irrigate, as to *water* a farm; to add water to, as he *watered* the milk he sold.

water back (wô´ tĕr bak), a coil or chamber alongside the fire pot of a stove or furnace, in which water is heated.

water color (wô´ tĕr kul´ ẽr), a paint to which water is added before using; a picture in the delicate colors produced by such paint.

waterfall (wô´ tĕr fôl), a cascade of water, as over a dam; a cataract.

water gate (wô´ tĕr gāt), a valve to control the flow of water.

water line (wô´ tĕr līn), farthest reach of a stream, as this is the *water line* of the last flood; a mark on the side of a ship showing how deep she will lie when loaded.

watermark (wô´ tĕr märk), *n.* a mark that indicates the farthest extent of the rise of water; a marking on certain kinds of paper that becomes visible when the paper is held to the light.

watermelon (wô′ tẽr mel′ un), *n.* the fruit of a trailing plant of the gourd family, with tough rind and a sweet, juicy pulp.

water meter (wô′ tẽr mē′ tẽr), an instrument that measures the flow of water through pipes as used in a building.

water polo (wô′ tẽr pō′ lō), a game resembling basketball but played in a pool or tank by swimmers.

waterproof (wô′ tẽr prōōf), *n.* a garment made of material that sheds moisture.

watershed (wô′ tẽr shed), *n.* a ridge of land separating waters flowing into two river systems, a divide.

waterspout (wô′ tẽr spout), *n.* a moving column of water drawn up from the sea by a whirlwind; a pipe to carry off rain.

watertight (wô′ tẽr tīt), *adj.* made so compactly that water cannot enter or escape.

water wheel (wô′ tẽr hwēl), a mill wheel turned by the force of a passing or falling stream; there are various types, such as overshot, breast and undershot.

waterworks (wô′ tẽr wûrks), *n.* a pumping station; the system of public water supply, including reservoir, pumps, pipe line, dams and other adjuncts.

watt (wot), *n.* a unit of power, especially electrical.

wattage (wot′ ij), *n.* the amount of electrical power used, expressed in watts.

wattle (wot′ l), *n.* a twig; flexible rod; a framework made of such rods; the featherless, fleshy flap under the neck of some birds or reptiles.

wave (wāv), *n.* a moving mass of liquid on the surface of a larger mass; a wind-driven ridge or swell of water at sea, one of a series separated by troughs or lower levels; a long ridge on any surface, resembling a wave of the sea; a swelling state, as a *wave* of anger; a vibrating motion through the air, as light *waves*, heat *waves;* a to-and-fro motion, as a *wave* of the hand.

Syn. Billow, surge, breaker. The *waves* that swell more than ordinarily are termed *billows;* those that rise unusually high are called *surges;* those that break and dissolve in foam as they reach the shore are *breakers.*

waver (wā′ vẽr), *v.i.* to move to and fro; to vacillate, hesitate, unable to make up one's mind.

wax (waks), *n.* the material of which bees make their honeycomb or any material resembling it in being adhesive, plastic, easily melted by heat but not dissolving in water. *v.t.* to treat with wax, as the cobbler *waxes* his thread. *v.i.* to grow, increase in size or any other respect, as the moon *waxes* and wanes.

waxen (wak′ sen), *adj.* composed of or coated with wax; pale, as a *waxen* face.

way (wā), *n.* a road or passage; the route from one place to another; a manner of doing things, as this is the *way* to write; a

characteristic, as he is set in his *way;* progress, as to make one's *way* in the world; room, space to advance, distance, as a long *way;* regard, respect, as the project appeals to me in every *way.*

wayfarer (wā′ fâr ẽr), *n.* a traveler, especially one who travels on foot.

*****waylay** (wā lā′), *v.t.* [*p.t. and p.p.* waylaid, *pr.p.* waylaying] to lie in wait for; to beset by the road or in ambush.

wayward (wā′ wẽrd), *adj.* impatient of discipline, unruly, disobedient; vacillating.

we (wē), *personal pron.* plural of I.

weak (wēk), *adj.* lacking strength; deficient in moral courage; diluted, as a *weak* mixture; easily influenced, as *weak*-willed; below standard, as he is *weak* in mathematics; lacking distinctness, faint, as a *weak* cry.

Syn. Feeble, infirm. We may be *weak* in body or mind, but we are commonly *feeble* or *infirm* only in the body. We may be *weak* from disease or *weak* by nature. An old man is *feeble* from age; he may likewise be *infirm* in consequence of sickness.

Ant. Strong, vigorous, healthy.

wealth (welth), *n.* riches, affluence.

wealthy (wel′ thi), *adj.* [*comp.* wealthier, *superl.* wealthiest] rich, affluent.

*****wean** (wēn), *v.t.* to accustom, as a child, to take other food than the mother's milk; to divert from any object of interest.

wean (wēn), *n.* a child, a half-grown baby.

*****weapon** (wep′ un), *n.* any instrument of offense or defense.

*****wear** (wâr), *n.* damage caused by use, as my coat shows *wear;* garments of a certain kind or for a certain season, as men's *wear*, summer *wear.*

wear (wâr), *v.i. and v.t.* [*p.t.* wore, *p.p.* worn, *pr.p.* wearing] to endure use, as this material *wears* well; to impair or waste by time, usage, friction; to pass slowly, as the day *wore* on; to carry as covering for the body, as we all *wear* clothes; to make by friction, as heavy traffic *wears* ruts in soft roads; to show, as to *wear* a cheerful look.

wearisome (wēr′ i sum), *adj.* tiring, tedious.

*****weary** (wēr′ i), *adj.* [*comp.* wearier, *superl.* weariest] tired, worn out physically or mentally.

weasel (wē′ zl), *n.* a small flesh-eating animal with a long, thin body and short legs.

*****weather** (weth′ ẽr), *n.* the state of the atmosphere with respect to cold, heat, rainfall, drought and storms. *v.t.* to season by exposure to the air; to endure, as to *weather* a storm. *adj.* facing the wind, windward, as the *weather* side of a ship: opposite of *lee.*

weathercock (weth′ ẽr kok), *n.* a vane, often in the shape of a cock, attached to the top of a spire or pole where it is turned back and forth by the wind and so indicates the direction of the wind.

weather vane (weth′ ẽr vān), a thin strip of wood or metal that turns with the wind and shows which way it is blowing.

*****weave** (wēv), *n.* a textile or woven fabric, any particular pattern in fabrics.

weave (wēv), *v.i. and v.t.* [*p.t.* wove, *p.p.* woven, *pr.p.* weaving] to make cloth on a loom; to wind in and out; to interlace, as threads, as to *weave* a fabric; to compose with several threads of narrative, as to *weave* a lively story; to take a winding course, as he *wove* his way through the crowd; to move from side to side, as the boxer was *weaving* to avoid his opponent's blows.

web (web), *n.* a texture of threads or of threadlike materials; anything woven, as a spider's *web;* a tangle, as the *web* of life; the skin in the foot of a swimming bird and some animals; a large roll of newsprint.

web-footed (web foot' ed), *n.* having the toes joined by a membrane for swimming, as a duck.

wed (wed), *v.i. and v.t.* [*p.t. and p.p.* wedded or wed, *pr.p.* wedding] to marry.

wedding (wed' ing), *n.* a marriage ceremony.

wedge (wej), *n.* a piece of hardwood or metal, thick at one end and sharp-edged at the other, used in splitting logs, raising heavy objects; anything shaped like this instrument, as a *wedge* of pie; anything used to create an opening.

*wedge** (wej), *v.t.* to cleave, force, drive or fasten with a block of wood or iron, thick at one end and sharp-edged at the other end.

wedlock (wed' lok), *n.* matrimony.

wee (wē), *adj.* very small, tiny.

*weed** (wēd), *n.* a wild plant growing in cultivated land and injurious to the planted crops; any plant without beauty or usefulness; a garment or costume, as widow's *weeds. v.t.* to free a plot of land from wild and useless plants; to remove harmful or useless parts of, as to *weed* out a mailing list.

*week** (wēk), *n.* a period of 7 consecutive days.

weekday (wēk' dā), *n.* any day but Sunday.

week end (wēk end), the time from Friday night or Saturday noon to Monday morning, when business offices are closed.

weekly (wēk' li), *n.* [*pl.* weeklies] a publication put out every 7 days.

weekly (wēk' li), *adj.* pertaining to a 7-day period; happening once every 7 days.

weekly (wēk' li), *adv.* once in 7 days.

weep (wēp), *v.i.* [*p.t. and p.p.* wept, *pr.p.* weeping] to shed tears; to exude moisture, as the heavens *weep.*

weevil (wē' vil), *n.* any of several species of beetles that feed on dry grain or other products, as the boll *weevil* that destroys growing cotton.

weft (weft), *n.* the woof or threads carried across the warp or lengthwise threads on a loom.

weigh (wā), *v.i. and v.t.* to have heaviness; to be valid or important, as his word does not *weigh* with me; to measure the heaviness of; to ponder and estimate the value of, as to *weigh* the facts in a case; to bear heavily upon, as his financial burdens *weigh* him down.

weight (wāt), *n.* heaviness; the relative pull of gravity on different objects; pressure; a system of units to determine the heaviness of things, as troy *weight;* a heavy block of matter, as a *weight* for use on scales; something that rests heavily on the mind, as a *weight* of care or sorrow; power or importance, as his word has much *weight* with me, a man of considerable *weight* in the community.

Syn. Burden, load. A person may sink under the *weight* that rests upon him. A platform may break down from the *weight* imposed upon it. A person gives way under his *burden.* A cart breaks under its *load.*

Ant. Lightness.

weighty (wāt' i), *adj.* [*comp.* weightier, *superl.* weightiest] heavy, ponderous; momentous or important, as a *weighty* matter.

*weir** (wēr), *n.* a dam to raise the level of water in a stream; a barrier of interwoven twigs to catch fish.

welcome (wel' kum), *n.* a greeting, friendly reception of a guest or newcomer. *adj.* received with gladness or hospitality, as a *welcome* guest. *v.t.* to greet with kindness, receive hospitably, as we *welcome* you.

weld (weld), *n.* a union of metallic pieces by melting; the place at which such joining occurs. *v.t.* to unite, as pieces of metal, by heating the parts to be joined, so that they fuse; to effect a permanent and harmonious union.

welfare (wel' fâr), *n.* prosperity, happiness.

welfare work (wel' fâr wûrk), organized activity to better the living conditions of the poor.

welkin (wel' kin), *n.* the sky.

well (wel), *n.* a spring or fountain; a shaft sunk in the earth to reach a supply of underground liquid, as water or oil. *adj.* healthy; in satisfactory state, as all is *well. adv.* in a proper manner, suitably; favorably; justifiably; intimately; considerably or extensively, as we were *well* on our way when you called.

welt (welt), *n.* a narrow strip of leather around a shoe between the upper leather and the sole; any edge or border ornamented or reinforced, as a strip of cloth enclosing a cord and sewed over a seam; a swollen mark made on the skin by a blow.

welter (wel' tẽr), *n.* a state of disturbance and confusion; turmoil.

welter (wel' tẽr), *v.i.* to roll in mud, wallow; to rise and fall, toss violently, as waves.

welterweight (wel' tẽr wāt), *n.* a boxer or wrestler who weighs no more than 147 pounds.

wen (wen), *n.* a fleshy tumor, not malignant; a cyst or sac full of fatty skin secretions.

wench (wench), *n.* a girl; a female servant.

wend (wend), *v.i. and v.t.* to go, pass; to direct, as one's way or course.

west (west), *n.* one of the four cardinal points of the compass: opposite of *east;* the direction of the setting sun: *the West,* the states of the United States between the Mississippi and the Pacific Ocean; the well defined western part of any country or of the whole world, as East is East and *West* is *West*, and never the twain shall meet.

western (wes' tẽrn), *n.* a motion picture showing scenes and characters of a conventionalized ranch life.

western (wes' tẽrn), *adj.* pertaining to, situated in or coming from the direction opposite to the east.

westward (west' wẽrd), *adj.* situated or moving in a direction opposite to the east, as a *westward* course. *adv.* toward the west, as to go *westward.*

wet (wet), *n.* moisture, liquid, rainy weather, as do not go out in the *wet.* *v.t.* [*p.t. and p.p.* wet or wetted, *pr.p.* wetting] to moisten or soak with a liquid. *adj.* moistened or soaked with liquid; abounding with water or rain, as a *wet* day.

*****whack** (hwak), *n.* a smart, resounding blow.

whack (hwak), *v.t.* to strike with a smart, resounding blow.

*****whale** (hwāl), *n.* a large warm-blooded air-breathing sea mammal, some species of which yield oil and whalebone.

whaler (hwāl' ẽr), *n.* one whose occupation is whale fishing; a ship used for whale fishing.

wharf (hwôrf), *n.* [*pl.* wharves] a structure on the shore of a navigable body of water where ships load and unload passengers and cargo.

*****what** (hwot), *interrogative pron.* which thing or things, as *what* is the matter? In exclamations, what things, how much, as *what* he has undergone! *Relative pron.* that or those which. *adj.* which, as *what* town is this? how much, as of *what* use is that? any, all, whatever, as I will give you *what* little I have. *adv.* how, in what regard, as *what* will it profit a man? partly, in part, used with a preposition following, as *what* with the dust storms and *what* with the drought, the West was devastated; in exclamations, as *what* a beautiful day!

whatnot (hwot' not), *n.* an article of furniture to hold bric-a-brac and odds and ends.

wheat (hwēt), *n.* a cultivated grass, the most important of the cereal plants, with seeds rich in starch and gluten and milled to make flour.

*****wheedle** (hwēd' l), *v.i. and v.t.* to coax, cajole; to get by means of flattery and indirect urging.

*****wheel** (hwēl), *n.* a circular spoked frame or solid disk of wood or metal that turns on an axle and is used on conveyances for ease and rapidity of transportation or to transmit power in a system of machinery; the circular spoked frame by means of which a ship or an automobile is steered; anything resembling a wheel in formation and movement, especially a maneuver in which a line of troops or ships pivots on a given point.

wheel (hwēl), *v.i. and v.t.* to move or cause to move by means of rotating disks or circular spoked structures pivoting on an axle, as to *wheel* a barrow; to turn or cause to turn as if rotating, as troops; to turn or change, as the wind has *wheeled* about.

wheelbarrow (hwēl' bar ō), *n.* a light vehicle with two handles, two legs and one wheel

and used to carry small loads.

wheel horse (hwēl hôrs), the animal nearest the vehicle when driven in tandem; the person who does the heavy work in an organization, as he is the *wheel horse* in this office.

*****wheelwright** (hwēl' rīt), *n.* one who makes or repairs wheels and vehicles.

*****wheeze** (hwēz), *n.* a puffing and blowing as in labored breathing, a whistling in the breath. *v.i.* to breathe with a whistling sound, breathe hard and audibly; to make such a sound, as the old car *wheezed* on hills.

wheezy (hwēz' i), *adj.* [*comp.* wheezier, *superl.* wheeziest] breathing hard and with a whistling sound, as a *wheezy* horse.

whelm (hwelm), *v.t.* to flood, overpower, destroy.

*****whelp** (hwelp), *n.* one of the young of certain animals, as the dog, lion, wolf or fox; a cub. *v.i.* to bring forth young.

when (hwen), *adv.* at what time; as they knew *when* they had to sing; *when* are we going?

when (hwen), *conj.* at or after the time; on any occasion that, as *when* I go, I always take the bus; as soon as, as *when* the work is finished, you may go home; whereas.

whence (hwens), *adv.* from what place, source or origin, as whence comes the wind?

where (hwâr), *adv.* at which place; whither, as *where* is it? *where* are you going? the place *where* I was born.

whereas (hwâr az'), *adv.* considering that, it being the case that; when in fact, as he left, *whereas,* had he only waited, he would have been sent to London with the other delegates.

whereby (hwâr bī'), by which.

wherefore (hwâr' fôr), *adv.* for which or what reason, why.

whereof (hwâr ov'), *adv.* of whom, of which, as I know *whereof* I speak.

whereupon (hwâr u pon'), *adv.* as a result of which, after which, as *whereupon* he left abruptly.

wherever (hwâr ev' ẽr), *adv.* at, to or in whatever place, as I shall find it *wherever* it is.

whet (hwet), *n.* anything that sharpens the appetite; the act of sharpening. *v.t.* to sharpen by rubbing; to stimulate, as this exercise *whets* my appetite.

whether (hweth' ẽr), *conj.* in case that, in either case, if, as I do not care *whether* you go or stay; *whether* it is successful depends upon your effort; I go, *whether* or not.

whetstone (hwet' stōn), *n.* a slab on which edged tools are rubbed to sharpen them.

whey (hwā), *n.* the thin, watery part of milk after separation from the curd.

which (hwich), *pron.* what one of two or more, as *which* book do you want; that, as the truth, *which* is known by some, must be published; the thing that, as the book, *which* is much worn, has been returned.

whichever (hwich ev' ẽr), *pron.* any one or ones that, as take *whichever* you wish.

whichever (hwich ev' ẽr), *adj.* any, as *whichever* road you take will lead into heavy traffic.

whiff (hwĭf), *n.* a sudden breath of air or smoke, a puff, as a *whiff* of a pipe; a faint odor, as a *whiff* of springtime fragrance.

whiff (hwĭf), *v.t.* to puff lightly, as smoke; to move by puffing at or in some similar manner, as to *whiff* something away.

whiffletree (hwĭf' l trē), *n.* a swinging bar to which the traces are attached at the front of a wagon or carriage.

while (hwīl), *n.* a short space of time, as he only stayed a *while;* time needed for an action, as it would not be worth his *while* to travel so far. *conj.* as long as; during the time that, as stay here *while* I ask the way. *v.t.* to pass, as time; to spend, as to *while* away the hours.

whim (hwĭm), *n.* a capricious fancy, notion, unreasonable wish.

whimper (hwĭm' pẽr), *n.* a fretful, whining cry. *v.i.* to cry in a whining way; to make a complaining sound; to complain, be dissatisfied.

whimsical (hwĭm' zĭ kal), *adj.* fanciful; having a humorous quirk, quaint.

*whine** (hwīn), *n.* a plaintive tone, a sound of fretful complaining.

whine (hwīn), *v.i.* to cry plaintively, complain in a fretful manner.

*whinny** (hwĭn' ĭ), *n.* [*pl.* whinnies] a horse's call; a subdued neigh. *v.i.* [*p.t.* and *p.p.* whinnied, *pr.p.* whinnying] to neigh softly.

*whip** (hwĭp), *n.* a flexible rod or a stick with a lash attached at one end, with which to urge or discipline; a hoist with rope and pulley worked by a horse; one whose duty it is to maintain discipline in a party representation in a parliamentary or legislative body; a light dessert made of stewed fruit and whipped cream or whites of eggs beaten stiff, as prune *whip. v.i.* and *v.t.* to have the motion of a lash, as the awning *whipped* in the gale; to cast a fishing line with a lashing motion; to cast in all parts, as of a pool, as we *whipped* the stream for trout; to lash or beat; to beat to a froth, as to *whip* cream; to sew with an overcasting stitch, as to *whip* a seam; to snatch, as he *whipped* out his knife.

*whippoorwill** (hwĭp poor wĭl'), *n.* a night-flying North American bird, mottled brown and black, with a cry resembling its name.

whir (hwûr), *n.* a sound as of mixed buzzing and swishing caused by rapid motion, as the *whir* of a bird's wings, the *whir* of machinery. *v.i.* to move very fast, with a sound of buzzing and whizzing.

*whirl** (hwûrl), *n.* a rapid rotation, swift circular motion; something rotating fast, as a *whirl* of dust in the wind.

whirl (hwûrl), *v.i.* and *v.t.* to be moved fast with a circular motion, as the leaves *whirled* in the wind; to move fast with a circular motion, as the wind *whirls* fallen leaves.

whirligig (hwûr' lĭ gĭg), *n.* anything rotating rapidly; a child's toy that spins; a merry-go-round.

whirlpool (hwûrl' pool), *n.* an eddy or deep swirl of water with circular motion that draws down floating things within its scope.

whirlwind (hwûrl' wĭnd), *n.* a gale with circular motion about a central point, a tornado, cyclone.

*whisk** (hwĭsk), *n.* the act of brushing with short, quick strokes; a small brush made like a broom; a mechanical device that moves with short, quick strokes.

whisk (hwĭsk), *v.i.* and *v.t.* to move or be moved briskly, with swift action; to move or carry off nimbly, as he *whisked* away.

whiskers (hwĭs' kẽrz), *n. pl.* the hair on a man's cheeks; the bristly hairs at the corners of the mouth of a cat or other animal.

whisky (hwĭs' kĭ), *n.* [*pl.* whiskies] an intoxicant distilled from starchy grains, as barley, corn and rye.

whisper (hwĭs' pẽr), *n.* a subdued utterance or way of uttering; anything said under the breath; a rumor, as *whispers* may do much harm; a subdued rustling sound.

whisper (hwĭs' pẽr), *v.i.* and *v.t.* to speak without vibrating the vocal cords; to say under the breath; to circulate rumors.

*whist** (hwĭst), *n.* a card game for two pairs of partners.

whistle (hwĭs' l), *n.* a shrill sound produced by forcing air or steam through an opening in a tube or through the lips; an instrument especially made to produce such a sound.

whistle (hwĭs' l), *v.i.* and *v.t.* to make a shrill sound by forcing the breath through the pursed lips or by forcing air or steam through a shaped hole in a pipe or tube; to move swiftly with a shrill sound, as bullets *whistled* all around them; to express by a shrill sound through pursed lips, as to *whistle* a tune.

whit (hwĭt), *n.* the smallest particle.

*white** (hwĭt), *n.* absence of hue, the condition of reflecting all the rays of light and absorbing none; a Caucasian; the albumen of an egg; the uncolored part of an eyeball, the *white* of the eye; the bull's-eye of a target. *adj.* being without color; fair-skinned; clear and colorless, as a *white* wine; pure.

whitecap (hwĭt' kap), *n.* the fringe of foam that tops a breaking wave offshore.

white gold (hwĭt gōld), gold alloyed with other metals, usually nickel and zinc, to make it look like platinum.

white lead (hwĭt lĕd), lead carbonate, used as a pigment.

white plague (hwĭt plāg), tuberculosis, consumption.

whitewash (hwĭt' wosh), *n.* a mixture of lime and water used to whiten walls and fences.

whitewash (hwĭt' wosh), *v.t.* to cover with a coat of lime mixed with water; to cause to appear better than is the case, as to *whitewash* a person who is at fault.

*whither** (hwĭth' ẽr), *adv.* to what place; to what degree or end.

whittle (hwĭt' l), *v.i.* and *v.t.* to cut aimlessly with a knife; to cut down or shape with a knife, a bit at a stroke.

*whiz** (hwĭz), *n.* the humming sound made by an object in fast motion, as the ball passed my head with a *whiz. v.i.* to move fast and with humming or buzzing sound, as a ball *whizzed* past.

whiz-bang (hwiz' bang), *n.* a high-explosive shell.

who (hōō), *pron.* whatever person; the person that, as I will tell you *who* did it, Mrs. Jones *who* lives next door to us; which person, what person, as *who* is this?

whoever (hōō ev' ẽr), *pron.* every one that, as *whoever* knows must tell.

*****whole** (hōl), *n.* the entirety; a unity or total.

whole (hōl), *adj.* containing all parts, complete; sound in body; not defective; unbroken.

   Syn. Entire, complete, total, integral. *Whole* excludes subtraction; *entire* excludes division; *complete* excludes deficiency. A *whole* orange has had nothing taken from it; an *entire* melon has not been cut; a *complete* disaster has reached its full extent. *Total* is the opposite of partial; *integral* is applied to parts or numbers not broken.

   Ant. Partial, divided, incomplete.

wholehearted (hōl härt' ed), *adj.* complete, sincere, as *wholehearted* enthusiasm.

wholesale (hōl' sāl), *n.* the purchase of goods in large quantities for reselling, as bought at *wholesale*. *adj.* in large quantities, as we do a *wholesale* business.

wholesome (hōl' sum), *adj.* sound and healthful; good for the health of body, mind or morals, salubrious, salutary.

wholly (hōl' li), *adv.* completely, fully, as I am *wholly* in sympathy with your aims.

whoop (hōōp), *n.* a loud shout of triumph; the sound that accompanies a deep sonorous coughing.

*****whooping cough** (hōōp' ing kôf), *n.* an infectious disease, often of children, with spasms of coughing accompanied by long loud and resonant respiration.

*****whorl** (hwûrl), *n.* the spiral design in fingerprints; a circular arrangement of leaves or petals on one stem.

*****whortleberry** (hwûr' tl ber' i), ·*n.* [*pl.* whortleberries] a small shrub and its edible fruit; the huckleberry.

*****why** (hwī), *n.* reason or explanation, as that's the *why* of it. *adv.* for what cause or reason; for what purpose, as *why* did you do it? *interj.* an exclamation indicating surprise, impatience, hesitation, as *why*, he can't possibly know.

wick (wik), *n.* the cord in a candle or piece of absorbent fabric that draws up fuel for the flame of an oil lamp.

wicked (wik' ed), *adj.* evil in principle or practice, sinful, immoral.

   Syn. Iniquitous, nefarious. It is *wicked* to deprive another of his property or rights. It is *iniquitous* to do this by fraud and circumvention; and *nefarious* if it involves a breach of trust.

   Ant. Virtuous.

wicker (wik' ẽr), *n.* a flexible twig or rod of willow. *adj.* made of pliant rods, interwoven, as a *wicker* chair.

wickerwork (wik' ẽr wûrk), *n.* the interweaving of pliant rods; anything made by interweaving pliant rods, as this chair is *wickerwork*.

wicket (wik' et), *n.* a small gate; a minor entranceway through a large door; a small opening resembling a window, especially one having a grill, as in a ticket office; the three upright stumps with bails crossing at the top at which a bowler in cricket hurls the ball; a wire arch through which the ball is to be shot in croquet.

wide (wīd), *adj.* extended far from side to side; broad, vast, spacious; comprehensive in scope, as a man of *wide* interests.

wide (wīd), *adv.* broadly; all the way, as the gate is *wide* open.

widen (wīd' n), *v.i. and v.t.* to become or to make more broad; to expand sideways.

widow (wid' ō), *n.* a woman who survives her husband and remains unmarried.

widower (wid' ō ẽr), *n.* a man whose wife has died and who has not married again.

width (width), *n.* the measure from side to side, breadth.

wield (wēld), *v.t.* to use with the hands, as to wield a pickax; to exercise, as to *wield* influence.

wife (wīf), *n.* [*pl.* wives] a married woman.

wig (wig), *n.* false hair worn to conceal baldness, to complete a fancy dress costume or as part of official dress, as of a court judge in England.

wiggle (wig' gl), *v.i.* to wriggle; to move to and fro with a quick, jerky motion.

wigwag (wig' wag), *n.* a signal by the movement of flags or lights.

wigwag (wig' wag), *v.t.* to send, as a message, by waving lights or flags in a certain way.

*****wigwam** (wig' wom), *n.* an Indian hut.

wild (wīld), *n.* unsettled country, desert, wilderness, as the *wilds* of Arabia.

wild (wīld), *adj.* living in a state of nature, untamed, uncontrolled; not cultivated; fantastic; visionary, as a *wild* scheme; wide of the mark, as a *wild* shot.

wildcat (wīld' kat), *n.* an undomesticated animal of the feline species, such as the bobcat or lynx. *adj.* out of control, as a *wildcat* railroad locomotive; unsound, haphazard, risky, speculative, as a *wildcat* project.

wilderness (wil' dẽr nes), *n.* waste land, a tangled growth of plants; an uncultivated and uninhabited region.

*****wile** (wīl), *n.* a sly artifice, a trick.

wile (wīl), *v.t.* to beguile, wheedle.

will (wil), *n.* desire or power to control by mental force; determination; a document disposing of one's property at death; a testament.

will (wil), *v.t. and v.i.* to determine, decree, as the king *wills* war; to bequeath, as to *will* a fortune to an heir; to influence by mental power, as she *willed* that he should think of her; to choose, as you can if you *will*. As an auxiliary verb *will* is used with the infinitive of other verbs (without the *to*) to express the future tense, as he *will* sing at the next concert; to express willingness or determination, as he *will* do as you say, I *will* do it no matter what you say; to express probability, as the bridge *will* hold 6 tons; to express inevitability, as boys *will* be boys.

willing (wil' ing), *adj.* inclined to do or grant; done freely and with pleasure, as *willing* to help, a *willing* service.

*****wily** (wī' li), *adj.* [*comp.* wilier, *superl.* wiliest] sly, cunning, crafty.

wimble (wim' bl), *n.* a boring tool such as the gimlet or auger.

wimple (wim' pl), *n.* a kind of silk or linen head and neck covering formerly worn by women and now used by some orders of nuns.

win (win), *v.i. and v.t.* [*p.t. and p.p.* won, *pr.p.* winning] to acquire by effort or gain by superiority; to be successful, triumph; to be victorious in, as to *win* a game; to obtain, as to *win* consent.

wince (wins), *n.* the act of flinching, as from pain. *v.i.* to shrink, draw back, flinch, as he *winced* at the touch.

winch (winch), *n.* the crank of a wheel; the handle that turns a machine like the grindstone; a hoisting machine in which the work is done by winding a rope or chain about a turning axle.

wind (wind), *n.* a current of air; air in motion; scent, as to get *wind* of something; *winds*, musical instruments played by blowing the breath through a tube.

wind (wind), *v.t.* to blow, sound by blowing, as he *winded* the bugle; to make breathless, as he was *winded;* to rest so as to recover breath, as they *winded* their horses for an hour.

wind (wīnd), *v.i. and v.t.* to twist around; to get started, as the pitcher is *winding* up; to coil about or encircle, as the river *winds* through a valley, *wind* the rope around the post; to set the machinery in motion, as to *wind* a watch; to complete or finish, as they *wound* up the company.

windfall (wind' fôl), *n.* fruit blown down by the wind; unexpected good fortune.

wind gauge (wind gāj), an instrument to determine the direction and force of air in motion.

winding sheet (wīn' ding shēt), a cloth in which a body is enfolded for burial, a cerecloth.

windlass (wind' làs), *n.* a cylinder or roller by means of which weights are raised by the turning of a rope or chain.

*****windmill** (wind' mil), *n.* a mill operated by the rotation of a large wheel having oblique blades that are turned by the wind.

window (win' dō), *n.* an aperture in a wall to admit light, usually glazed or covered with paper.

window envelope (win' dō en' ve lōp), an envelope with a transparent section through which an address written on the paper inside is visible.

windpipe (wind' pīp), *n.* the trachea, the breathing tube.

windward (wind' wẽrd), *n.* the direction from which the wind blows: opposite of *leeward.*

windward (wind' wẽrd) *adj.* toward the wind,

as the *windward* side of a building.

windy (win' di), *adj.* [*comp.* windier, *superl.* windiest] breezy, exposed to the movement of the air; boastful, talkative.

wine (wīn), *n.* the fermented juice of the grape or of certain berries and leaves; a color like these beverages, usually a shade of red.

wing (wing), *n.* a broad, flat member by means of which a bird or insect flies; one of the main supporting surfaces of an airplane; a part of a building added to and projecting from the main structure; the side extension of a stage; anything else that resembles a bird's wing.

wing (wing), *v.i. and v.t.* to fly; to make fly, as to *wing* an arrow or a shaft of wit; to pass through or across by flying, as the geese *winged* their way South; to injure in the wing, to disable, as to *wing* a bird.

wing loading (wing lōd' ing), the weight carried by an airplane per unit of wing area.

wing rib (wing rib), one of the rigid parts of the supporting surface of an airplane.

wing skid (wing skid), a brace extending down from an airplane's wing, at the end, to keep the wing from touching the ground.

wing spar (wing spär), one of the long, rigid ribs of an airplane wing.

wink (wingk), *n.* a quick closing and reopening of the eyelid; a short time, as he had returned in a *wink.*

wink (wingk), *v.i.* to close and open the eyelid with quick motion; to hint or suggest.

winnow (win' ō), *v.i. and v.t.* to separate chaff from grain; to separate by blowing, as to *winnow* chaff from grain; to sift.

winsome (win' sum), *adj.* attractive, pretty, winning.

winter (win' tẽr), *n.* the cold season of the year. *v.i. and v.t.* to spend the cold months, as to *winter* in Florida; to keep through the cold weather, as the cattle were *wintered* in the barns.

wintergreen (win' tẽr grēn), *n.* a low-growing evergreen herb with red berries and pungent leaves from which oil of wintergreen is extracted.

wipe (wīp), *n.* the act of rubbing; a projecting part in machinery that raises another part and lets it fall by its own weight.

wipe (wīp), *v.t.* to dry or clean by rubbing, as with a cloth.

wire (wīr), *n.* a metallic thread of one diameter throughout its length.

wire (wīr), *v.i. and v.t.* to equip with metallic threads, as to *wire* a house for electricity; to send a telegram, as to *wire* a message.

wireless (wīr' les), *adj.* not using metalthread conveyors of electricity, as a *wireless* message.

wireless telegraphy (wīr' les tē leg' ra fi), direct telegraphic electric wave communication without the use of metal threads to carry the electric impulse; radio.

wireless telephony (wīr' les tē lef' ō ni), the sending of vocal messages by radio.

wirepulling (wīr' pool ing), *n.* secret influence

or intrigue, as in political maneuvering.

wiry (wir' ĭ), *adj.* [*comp.* wirier, *superl.* wiriest] like a metal thread; strong and flexible; lean and sinewy.

*****wisdom** (wiz' dum), *n.* sagacity, prudence, good judgment; great learning.

Syn. Prudence. *Wisdom* directs all matters, present or to come. *Prudence,* acting by foresight, directs what is to come. Rules of conduct are framed by *wisdom.* It is the part of *prudence* to apply these rules to the business of life.

Ant. Folly, recklessness, rashness.

wisdom tooth (wiz' dum tōōth), the third molar on each side in each jaw, usually cut between the ages of 17 and 22.

wise (wiz), *adj.* having the ability to form true judgments; discerning.

wiseacre (wiz' ă kẽr), *n.* a would-be wise person; a stupid person who thinks he knows it all.

wish (wisḥ, *n.* a strong or eager desire.

wish (wish), *v.i. and v.t.* to desire strongly; to long for.

wishbone (wish' bōn), *n.* the forked bone in front of the breastbone of a fowl; when broken and wished upon, the longer end supposedly bringing its holder good luck.

wisp (wisp), *n.* a handful or small bundle, as of hay or straw.

wistful (wist' fool), *adj.* longing, pensive, wishful.

wit (wit), *n.* knowledge, sagacity; talent, ingenuity; keen humor; a humorist.

*****witch** (wich), *n.* a woman supposed to be in contact with evil spirits and to possess supernatural powers; a sorceress. *v.t.* to fascinate, enchant, bewitch.

witchcraft (wich' kráft), *n.* the practice of sorcery or black magic.

witchery (wich' ẽr ĭ), *n.* [*pl.* witcheries] fascination; enchantment.

witch hazel (wich hã' zl), a shrub with small yellow flowers and a bark from which a soothing lotion is made.

*****with** (with), *prep.* beside, in the company of, close to, as I am *with* you; by, as fill it *with* water; in the manner or state of, as I shall do it *with* pleasure; because of, as to laugh *with* joy, suffer *with* hunger; in the care of, as leave him *with* me; by means of, as he was killed *with* a knife.

withdraw (with drô'), *v.i. and v.t.* to depart, retreat, as to *withdraw* from the town; to take back, retract, as I *withdraw* my statement; to remove, as to *withdraw* a child from a school.

*****withe** (with), *n.* a tough flexible twig, especially of willow, used for tying or binding.

wither (with' ẽr), *v.i. and v.t.* to shrivel and shrink, as this plant *withers* in the sun; to cause to fade and dry up, as the heat *withers* this plant.

*****withers** (with' ẽrz), *n. pl.* the highest part of a horse's back, between the shoulderblades.

within (with in'), *adv.* inside, as look *within;* in or into a house, indoors, as step *within.*

within (with in'), *prep.* inside, inside of, as *within* the charmed circle; not farther or

longer than, as *within* 6 feet, *within* a week.

without (with out'), *adv.* outside, outdoors; externally, as painted *without.*

without (with out'), *prep.* out of, at or on the outside: opposite of *within;* lacking, as *without* food, *without* fear.

witness (wit' nes), *n.* attestation of anything, testimony; one who has seen; one who gives evidence, as he had a reliable *witness.*

witness (wit' nes), *v.i. and v.t.* to give evidence of, to prove, as his failure *witnessed* his honesty; to see or behold, as the bystander *witnessed* the accident; to attest, be present to observe, as the servants *witnessed* the signing of the will.

witticism (wit' ĭ sizm), *n.* a joke; a keenly humorous remark.

wittingly (wit' ing li), *adv.* with knowledge, knowingly; intentionally.

witty (wit' ĭ), *adj.* [*comp.* wittier, *superl.* wittiest] smartly or cleverly facetious; having keen humor.

*****wizard** (wiz' ẽrd), *n.* one supposed to possess supernatural powers; a sorcerer.

wizened (wiz' nd), *adj.* dried up, shriveled, as a *wizened* old man, a *wizened* face.

*****wobble** (wob' l), *n.* an irregular swaying or rocking motion; a rolling or rocking from side to side unsteadily and irregulary.

wobble (wob' l), *v.i.* to move unsteadily, swaying from side to side; to vacillate; to lack steadiness and decision.

woe (wō), *n.* sorrow, grief, misery.

wok (wok), *n.* a Chinese cooking pan with handles and a rounded bottom set in a ring-like stand.

wolf (woolf), *n.* a fierce flesh-eating wild animal of the dog family.

wolf (woolf), *v.t.* to eat like a wild beast, as he *wolfed* his food.

wolverine or **wolverene** (wool vẽr ēn'), *n.* a flesh-eating animal of Canada and the northern United States, related to the weasels and martens.

*****woman** (woom' an), *n.* [*pl.* women] an adult female human being.

womb (wōōm), *n.* the organ in which the young of mammals grow and develop before birth, the uterus.

*****wonder** (wun' dẽr), *n.* astonishment; a marvel.

Syn. Miracle, marvel, prodigy, monster. *Wonders* are natural; *miracles* are supernatural. The whole creation is full of *wonders;* the Bible contains an account of the *miracles. Wonders* are real; *marvels* are often fictitious; *prodigies* are extravagant and often imaginary; *monsters* are violations of the laws of nature.

*****wonder** (wun' dẽr), *v.i. and v.t.* to be astonished at; to feel surprise and amazement; to have doubt about and a desire to know, as I *wonder* why he did not come.

wonderful (wun' dẽr fool), *adj.* strange, extraordinary, amazing, astounding, as radio communication is a *wonderful* achievement.

*****wont** (wunt), *n.* habit or custom, as it is her *wont* to rise early. *adj.* accustomed to, in the habit of, as he is *wont* to do good.

woo (wōō), *v.t.* to make love to, urge to

marry; to invite with importunity.

*wood (wood), *n.* the hard part of a tree or shrub under the bark; trunks and branches of trees cut into boards for use in building, timber, lumber; logs and branches cut for use in fires: *woods,* a forest, a thick growth of trees, as the *woods* were fresh and green.

woodcock (wood' kok), *n.* a wild fowl allied to the snipe.

wooden (wood' n), *adj.* made of wood; stiff, awkward, as *wooden* movements.

woodpecker (wood' pek ēr), *n.* a bird that drills into the trunks and branches of trees with its beak to discover and eat insects living under the bark.

woody (wood' i), *adj.* [*comp.* woodier, *superl.* woodiest] covered with forests; like wood; containing wood fiber, as a shrub is a *woody* plant.

woof (woof), *n.* the weft or threads that cross the warp in weaving; texture.

*wool (wool), *n.* the soft fine coat of the domestic sheep and certain kindred animals; cloth or clothing made from it; anything fleecy or resembling wool.

woolen (wool' en), *adj.* made of wool: as a noun, plural, *woolens,* goods or garments made of wool.

woolly (wool' i), *adj.* made of or resembling wool; bearing wool, as a *woolly* sheep.

*word (wûrd), *n.* a sound or combination of sounds used to express an idea or name a thing; a report, as we have had no *word* of it. *v.t.* to express in language, as to *word* a note politely.

wording (wûr'ding), *n.* phrasing, style or manner of using words in writing or speech, as the *wording* of a letter.

wordy (wûrd' i), *adj.* [*comp.* wordier, *superl.* wordiest] verbose, containing or using too many words.

*work (wûrk), *n.* physical or mental effort directed toward an end; labor; employment; something brought into being by man's toil and skill, as a *work* of art: *works,* the moving parts of a mechanism, as the *works* of a clock; buildings and machines for manufacture, as iron*works.*

Syn. Labor, toil, drudgery, task. *Work* is necessary for support if one does not have independent means. *Toil* and *labor* are hard, tedious forms of work. *Drudgery* is still more taxing. A *task* is a specific piece of work to be accomplished, self-imposed or assigned by another.

Ant. Play, pleasure, leisure, idleness.

work (wûrk), *v.i.* and *v.t.* to put forth physical or mental effort toward a set end; to labor, toil; to be employed, as he *works* in a mill; to be useful for a special purpose, as this is not the right thing, but it *works;* to reach a certain stage or condition step by step or bit by bit, as this screw has *worked* loose; to operate, as I do not know how to *work* this machine; to cause to move, as to *work* a beam into place; to cause to labor, as to *work* a team too hard.

workhouse (wûrk' hous), *n.* a public insti-

tution where petty offenders are confined and required to labor for their support.

workmanship (wûrk' man ship), *n.* art and skill in making, craftsmanship, as her *workmanship* is excellent.

world (wûrld), *n.* the earth and its inhabitants; the system of created things; the universe as we know it; any separate system or sphere of interest, as the *world* of art; a large amount, as a *world* of troubles.

worldling (wûrld' ling), *n.* one who is devoted to the pleasures and advantages of the earthly life.

worldly (wûrld' li), *adj.* [*comp.* worldlier, *superl.* worldliest] pertaining to earthly life; devoted to earthly things; not spiritual.

*worm (wûrm), *n.* a small creeping legless, usually hairless animal, as an angleworm; a rotating screw whose threads engage the teeth of a gear wheel in a machine.

worm (wûrm), *v.t.* to crawl; to make one's way by obsequious service; to relieve of parasites, as to *worm* a dog.

worm gear (wûrm gēr), a wheel with teeth that engage the threads of a rotating screw and work with it.

wormwood (wûrm' wood), *n.* a bitter plant used as a tonic and in making absinthe; anything bitter, as grief.

worrisome (wûr' i sum), *adj.* causing anxiety and distress.

worry (wûr' i), *n.* [*pl.* worries] anxiety; perplexity; mental distress and misgiving; anything that causes mental distress, as *worry* caused his mental breakdown.

worry (wûr' i), *v.i.* and *v.t.* to be fretful, perplexed, anxious; to cause mental distress to; to tease, as do not *worry* the dog.

worse (wûrs), *adj.* [*comp.* of *bad*] more bad, less well, as he is *worse* today.

worse (wûrs), *adv.* in a more unsatisfactory manner, as it works *worse* than it did before you repaired it.

*worship (wûr' ship), *n.* the act of paying reverence to God; adoration, as hero *worship;* a title of reverence, as his *worship,* the master of the lodge.

*worship (wûr' ship), *v.i.* and *v.t.* to perform religious service; to reverence, adore.

*worst (wûrst), *n.* the most evil state, as be prepared for the *worst. adj.* [*superl.* of *bad*] evil or inferior in the highest degree.

worst (wûrst), *adv.* to the extreme degree of badness or inferiority, as this is the *worst* built house I have ever seen.

*worsted (woos' ted), *n.* twisted thread spun of wool yarn.

*worth (wûrth), *n.* value; price; moral excellence, her *worth* to the community was recognized. *adj.* equal in value to, as this article is *worth* a dollar.

worthless (wûrth' les), *adj.* having no value, virtue or excellence; morally bad, as a *worthless* fellow.

*worthy (wûr' thi), *adj.* [*comp.* worthier, *superl.* worthiest] deserving, as *worthy* of close attention; estimable.

would (wood), *v.t.* wish, desire, as I *would*

that I could swim.

would (wood), *auxiliary v.* [past tense of *will*] is apt to or sure to, as that *would* hurt his feelings; was or were accustomed to, as the cat *would* purr by the hour, they *would* come every day: used in quoting a phrase originally containing *will*, as they said he *would* go for he *will* go.

*****wound** (woond), *n.* a hurt; an injury, especially one that breaks the skin. *v.t.* to hurt, injure, as to *wound* a man with a dagger; to hurt the feelings of, as your words *wound* me deeply.

wove (wōv), *pa.t.* of **weave. -n** *pa.p. of* **weave. — paper** *n.* paper with no marks of wire as in laid paper.

wow (wou´), *interj.* exclamation of astonishment; *n. (slang)* great success.

wrack or **rack** (rak), *n.* seaweed cast up on a beach; ruin, destruction, as *wrack* and ruin, the storm's *wrack* along the shore.

*****wraith** (rāth), *n.* the ghost of a person supposed to be seen just before or just after his death; any specter.

wrangle (rang´gl), *n.* an angry or a noisy dispute, a quarrel, as their *wrangle* disturbed the neighbors. *v.i.* to dispute noisily and angrily.

wrap (rap), *n.* a blanket; a garment that can be folded about one.

wrap (rap), *v.t.* to roll or fold around, as *wrap* this blanket around you, *wrap* yourself in this robe.

wrapper (rap´ẽr), *n.* a loose overgarment; a covering, as the *wrapper* of a book.

*****wrath** (rāth), *n.* great anger, rage; indignation, as the king's *wrath* made his attendants tremble.

wrathful (rāth´fool), *adj.* very angry, full of rage.

wreak (rēk), *v.t.* to give free course to, inflict, as to *wreak* one's wrath.

wreath (rēth), *n.* a garland or chaplet; anything curled or twisted into a circular form, as a wreath of roses.

wreathe (rēth), *v.t.* to intertwine and make in circular form; to give the form of a garland or chaplet to; to encircle, adorn, as a face *wreathed* in smiles.

wreck (rek), *n.* destruction by accident or storm, especially of a ship; shipwreck; destruction of a car or train in a collision or derailment; total failure or destruction of anything, as the *wreck* of a business, a life, a home.

wreckage (rek´ij), *n.* the remains of anything ruined.

wrecker (rek´ẽr), *n.* one who destroys, especially one who lures a ship to destruction so that he may steal part of its cargo; a person, train, car or vessel employed to salvage wrecks; one who or that which demolishes a building.

wren (ren), *n.* a family of small insectivorous birds of which there are many varieties in America and Europe.

wrench (rench), *n.* an implement with a vise, socket or opening adapted to turn or twist

mechanical parts; a violent turn or twist, a sprain, as his foot suffered a severe *wrench*. *v.t.* to twist; to distort, pervert, as you wrench my words out of their meaning.

wrest (rest), *v.t.* to take from by wrenching, turning or twisting with force or violence.

wrestle (res´l), *v.i.* to contend by grappling and striving to throw down another; to struggle with a difficulty, as I have *wrestled* 2 hours with this lesson.

wretch (rech), *n.* miserable creature; one sunk in vice or degradation; one profoundly unhappy. **-ed** (rech´ id), *a.* very miserable; very poor or mean; despicable.

wretched (rech´ed), *adj.* miserable, unhappy; worthless, as this is a *wretched* makeshift.

*****wriggle** (rig´l), *v.i.* to move or writhe to and fro, squirm, as the dog will *wriggle* under the fence.

wring (ring), *v.t.* to twist so as to expel moisture, as to *wring* washed clothes; to twist violently, as *wring* its neck; to force out by twisting and pressure, as to *wring* a secret from its possessor; to torture, as sorrow *wrings* one's heart.

wrinkle (ring´kl), *n.* a fold or crease.

wrinkle (ring´kl), *v.i. and v.t.* to form folds, as this material *wrinkles* easily; to cause to form folds and creases, as he *wrinkles* his nose unconsciously.

*****wrist** (rist), *n.* the joint uniting the hand to the arm.

writ (rit), *n.* a court order, as the *writ* was served promptly; anything written.

write (rit), *v.i. and v.t.* [*p.t.* wrote, *p.p.* written, *pr.p.* writing] to make intelligible symbols with a pointed instrument, as letters on paper with a pen or pencil; to express in words on paper, as to *write* a letter; to compose, as to *write* an essay.

writer (rīt´ẽr), *n.* an author; one who writes for publication as a livelihood.

writhe (rīth), *v.i.* to twist one's body about; to squirm as if in pain.

writing (rīt´ing), *n.* the act of making letters with a pen or pencil; that which is written; the literary art or profession: *writings,* literary works, as the *writings* of Poe.

*****wrong** (rông), *n.* that which is contrary to moral right, evil; injury, as you have done me a *wrong. adj.* not morally correct or justifiable; unjust; mistaken, as you are *wrong* in thinking such things; incorrect, as to get the *wrong* answer to problem. *v.t.* to hurt, injure, treat unjustly, as such an act will *wrong* your friend.

*****wroth** (rôth), *adj.* much exasperated, indignant.

wrought (rawt), *pa.t.* and *pa.p.* of **work.** *a* hammered into shape, as metal products. **—iron** *n.* purest form of commercial iron, fibrous, ductile, and malleable, prepared by puddling. **—up** *a.* excited; frenzied.

wry (rī), *adj.* [*comp.* wrier, *superl.* wriest] twisted, distorted, askew.

WW II, World War II.

X

xanthous (zan' thus), *adj.* pertaining to the yellow-skinned races, especially the Mongolian.

*xebec (zē' bek), *n.* a small, three-masted ship used in Mediterranean waters.

xenon (zē' non), *n.* a heavy, inactive gaseous element.

xeroderma (zē rō dûr' ma), *n.* a disease of the skin characterized by abnormal dryness.

xerophthalmia (zē rof thal' mi a), *n.* abnormal dryness of the eyeball.

Xerox (zir´ oks), *n.* the trade name for a particular copying process.

X ray (exs' rā), a Roentgen ray.

*xylograph (zī' lō gráf), *n.* an engraving on a block of wood or an impression made from it.

xylonite (zī' lon it), *n.* a manufactured material resembling ivory or celluloid: a trade name.

*xylophone (zī' lō fōn), *n.* a musical instrument consisting of hard wooden bars set on a frame, played with small mallets.

*xyster (zis' tēr), *n.* a surgeon's implement for scraping diseased bones.

Y

*yacht (yot), *n.* a light, fast boat for pleasure cruising or racing, propelled by the wind or motor power or both.

yak (yak), *n.* a Central Asiatic wild ox with long hair fringing its sides.

yam (yam), *n.* a tropical vine with edible, tuberous roots; a large kind of sweet potato.

yard (yärd), *n.* a unit of linear measure, 36 inches or 3 feet; a spar hung crosswise on a sailing ship's mast; an area about a dwelling or its outbuildings and commonly enclosed, as a front *yard;* an enclosed area in which some particular kind of work is done, as a brick*yard,* railroad *yards.*

yardstick (yärd' stik), *n.* a measuring stick 36 inches long; a means of measuring, a test or criterion, as the TVA will furnish a *yardstick* of public utility rates.

yarn (yärn), *n.* spun thread for weaving or knitting.

*yaw (yô), *n.* a momentary deviation from the straight course by a ship or an airplane.

yaw (yô), *v.i.* to deviate momentarily from the right course, as a ship or airplane.

*yawl (yôl), *n.* a boat with two masts, the smaller being aft of the rudder post, and fore-and-aft rigged.

*yawn (yôn), *n.* an involuntary opening of the jaws from drowsiness. *v.i.* to gape, to stand wide open, as a chasm; to open the jaws wide and inhale deeply from drowsiness, fatigue, boredom.

*yea (yā), *n.* an affirmative vote taken by rollcall. *adv.* yes; indeed; even, as a hundred, *yca,* a thousand.

yean (yēn), *v.i. and v.t.* to bring forth young, as sheep or goats.

*year (yēr), *n.* the period of 365¼ days during which the earth makes one complete revolution about the sun.

*yearling (yēr' ling), *n.* an animal that is a year old, especially a horse, sheep, cow or deer; one in his second year at West Point.

yearn (yûrn), *v.i.* to long for, desire greatly and incessantly, as the traveler *yearns* for home; to be filled with compassion.

*yeast (yēst), *n.* a minute-celled fungus that causes fermentation and is used in making bread dough or beer.

yell (yel), *n.* a sharp shout; a school or college cheer, as we heard the Harvard *yell.*

yell (yel), *v.t. and v.i.* to cry out or cheer loudly, as he *yelled* vengeance; to utter a sharp shout.

*yellow (yel' ō), *n.* a bright elementary color, between green and orange in the spectrum.

yellow daisy (yel' ō dā' zi), the black-eyed Susan of the fields.

yellow fever (yel' ō fē' vēr), an infectious disease in which the skin turns yellow.

yellowjacket (yel' ō jak' et), *n.* a hornet with a yellow-banded, black abdomen.

yelp (yelp), *v.i.* to utter a short, sharp cry, as a dog when hurt.

*yeoman (yō' man), *n.* [*pl.* yeomen] a small landowner in England; a petty officer who does clerical work in the United States Navy.

yes (yes), *adv.* the primary word of affirmation: opposite of *no.*

yesterday (yes' tēr dā), *n.* the day before this day; the day last past; a recent time, as it seems only *yesterday* that we were in school together, though years have passed.

*yesterday (yes' tēr dā), *adv.* on the day before this, as he came *yesterday.*

*yet (yet), *adv.* up until now, as it has not happened *yet;* up to the present, as I have it *yet;* in future time, as I shall do it *yet;* still, as that is more important *yet.*

*yew (yōō), *n.* a large evergreen tree with dark foliage; its fine-grained wood; an archer's bow made from this wood.

Y-gun (wī gun), *n.* a gun with two barrels on a Y-shaped frame used in the navy for dropping depth bombs to wreck enemy submarines.

*yield (yēld), *n.* the return on labor expended or money invested; that which is produced, as the *yield* of grain from wheat fields, or the mixture of oil and vinegar *yields* an emulsion. *v.i. and v.t.* to produce as a return on investment of labor or money; to submit, give up; to concede, as a point, in an argument.

yielding (yēld' ing), *adj.* inclined to give way under any kind of pressure, physical, mental, or moral; gentle, submissive.

yodel (yō' dl), *v.i.* [*p.t. and p.p.* yodeled, *pr.p.* yodeling] to sing in Swiss fashion with changes from chest tones to head tones.

yoke (yōk), *n.* a curved wooden bar with which a team of draft oxen is hitched together; a similar device fitting over the shoulders for carrying heavy loads; part of a dress fitting over the shoulders or hips to support the lower part of the garment; that which unites two, as the *yoke* of marriage; a symbol of slavery. *n.* yellow part of an egg: sometimes *yelk.*

yonder (yon' dẽr), *adj.* situated some distance away, as *yonder* lake; more distant, as the *yonder* side of the lake. *adv.* over there, as *yonder* lies the town.

yore (yōr), *n.* olden times; the days of long ago.

*you (yōō), *personal pron.* the second person, sing. and pl., signifying the person or persons addressed.

*young (yung), *n.* offspring; those, collectively, who are in early life. *adj.* in the early stages of life or growth; not old; fresh, healthy, clear and strong.

youngster (yung' stẽr), *n.* a young person; a lad.

*your (yoor), *possessive pron.* belonging to you, as *your* house.

*yours (yoorz), *possessive pron.* belonging to you, as here is my hat, where is *yours?*

*yourself (yoor self'), *pron.* [*pl.* yourselves] you personally: a more emphatic form than *you.*

*youth (yōōth), *n.* the period of life between childhood and maturity; a young man; young persons collectively, as the *youth* of America.

youthful (yōōth' fool), *adj.* pertaining to the young; having the qualities of youth; immature.

Syn. Juvenile, puerile. To be *youthful* or *juvenile* is, strictly, merely to stand at a certain period of life; to be *puerile* is to be literally boyish, no matter how old one may be. We are surprised and displeased at *puerile* words or acts by a grown man.

Ant. Mature, venerable, senile.

yucca (yuk' a), *n.* a plant with a clump of long, pointed leaves from which rises a tall spike of white flowers.

yucca moth (yuk' a mŏth), an insect that lays its eggs in the seed pods of the yucca, and the larvae of which eat the seeds of the plant.

yuletide (yōōl' tīd), *n.* the Christmas season.

yuppies (yŭp' pēs), *n.* young, upwardly mobile, professional group of people.

Z

*zeal (zēl), *n.* ardor, earnestness, fervor, as their *zeal* in party politics exceeded their patriotism.

*zealot (zel' ut), *n.* a zealous person, especially one who is overzealous; a fanatic.

zealotry (zel' ut ri), *n.* a state of excessive zeal, fanaticism.

zealous (zel' us), *adj.* characterized by zeal, ardent, earnest, fervent, as a *zealous* Christian.

*zebra (zē' bra), *n.* an African animal related to the horse and the ass and having a white or buff coat striped with black.

zebrawood (zē' bra wood), *n.* the hard, striped wood of a tropical tree and used in cabinetwork.

*zebu (zē' bū), *n.* a breed of cattle domesticated in India, China, East Africa and the East Indies.

zed (zed), *n.* the letter z, as everything from *a* to *zed.*

*zenana (ze nä' na), *n.* the part of a dwelling in India or Persia that is reserved for women, a harem.

*zenith (zē' nith), *n.* the highest point in the sky, directly overhead; the highest point in the orbit of a planet; the peak, acme, culmination of any activity or enterprise.

*zephyr (zef' ẽr), *n.* the west wind, named for the ancient Greek god, Zephyrus; any gentle breeze.

zero (zē' rō), *n.* nought; one less than one; the point from which a numerical scale starts, as on a thermometer.

zero hour (zē' rō our), the time set for starting a planned military movement; the moment of beginning any ordeal; any moment of crisis.

zest (zest), *n.* eagerness for and enjoyment of something; relish.

zigzag (zig' zag), *n.* a series of sharp turns in a line or course, as the *zigzag* of his path showed great uncertainty. *adv.* first this way, then that in a continuous course, as to run *zigzag. adj.* having sharp turns and angles, as a *zigzag* pattern. *v.i. and v.t.* to move or cause to move in a zigzag course, as the lightning *zigzags* across the heavens, the designer will *zigzag* the lines of the pattern.

*zinc (zingk), *n.* a bluish-white metallic element used in alloys for roofing, galvanizing, electrical work and the like.

*zincography (zing kog' ra fi), *n.* a process of printing or engraving zinc.

zinnia (zin' i a), *n.* a brilliantly colored flower

of the aster family.

zip (zip), *n.* speed, energy.

zipper (zip' ẽr), *n.* a sliding device used for fastening clothing, bags and the like.

*****zircite** (zûr' kit), *n.* a mineral found principally in Brazil and used for lining furnaces.

zircon (zûr' kon), *n.* a mineral, of which some varieties, reddish and transparent, are used as gems and called *hyacinth*.

zirconia (zẽr kõ' ni a), *n.* zirconium dioxide, useful because of its resistance to heat.

zirconium (zẽr kõ' ni um), *n.* a metallic element used as an alloy with other metals to increase their resistance to heat.

*****zither** (zith' ẽr), *n.* a musical instrument consisting of 36 to 40 strings stretched over a horizontal sounding box and played with a plectrum.

*****zodiac** (zõ' di ak), *n.* an imaginary strip in the sky on each side of the sun's path, including 12 major constellations and used by astrologers in predicting the future.

*****zodiacal** (zõ di' a kal), *adj.* relating to the zodiac.

zonation (zõ nã' shun), *n.* an arrangement in zones.

*****zone** (zõn), *n.* a girdle or belt; one of the five belts into which the earth's surface is divided, as the Arctic, Antarctic, North and South Temperate and Torrid *zones;* an area set off from surrounding regions by some distinct characteristic, as a business *zone,* the cotton *zone,* the Panama Canal *Zone;* one of the circular areas about a shipping

point on which parcel post charges are based; a section in a city in which building is restricted to certain types; a field or territory, as a *zone* of influence. *v.t.* to arrange in belts or sections.

zoo (zõõ), *n.* a building or enclosed space in which live animals are kept for exhibition; a zoological garden.

*****zoology** (zõ ol' õ ji), *n.* the science of animal life; animal life, as the *zoology* of the tropics.

*****zoom** (zõõm), *n.* a sudden upward turn at an angle sharper than an airplane's ordinary climbing power can master.

zoom (zõõm), *v.i.* to execute an upward turn of an airplane at a very sharp angle.

*****zwieback** (swi' bak), *n.* a kind of sweetened bread, first baked then sliced and toasted.

zygoma (zī gõ' ma), *n.* the bony structure that connects the bones of the face with those about the ear.

*****zyme** (zīm), *n.* a fermentation; the ferment that spreads certain disease germs in the body.

zymology (zī mol' õ ji), *n.* the scientific study of fermentation.

*****zymosis** (zī mõ' sis), *n.* the development and spread of bacteria through fermentation.

zymotic (zī mot' ik), *adj.* pertaining to the spread of disease germs through fermentation, as in smallpox.

*****zymurgy** (zī' mûr ji), *n.* scientific application of fermentation, as in making beer and wine.

PRESIDENTS OF THE UNITED STATES

Name (and party)	State of Birth	Born	Term	Died
George Washington (F)	Va.	1732	1789-97	1799
John Adams (F)	Mass.	1735	1797-1801	1826
Thomas Jefferson (D-R)	Va.	1743	1801-09	1826
James Madison (D-R)	Va.	1751	1809-17	1836
James Monroe (D-R)	Va.	1758	1817-25	1831
John Quincy Adams (D-R)	Mass.	1767	1825-29	1848
Andrew Jackson (D)	S.C.	1767	1829-37	1845
Martin Van Buren (D)	N.Y.	1782	1837-41	1862
William Henry Harrison (W)	Va.	1773	1841	1841
John Tyler (W)	Va.	1790	1841-45	1862
James Knox Polk (D)	N.C.	1795	1845-49	1849
Zachary Taylor (W)	Va.	1784	1849-50	1850
Millard Fillmore (W)	N.Y.	1800	1850-53	1874
Franklin Pierce (D)	N.H.	1804	1853-57	1869
James Buchanan (D)	Pa.	1791	1857-61	1868
Abraham Lincoln (R)	Ky.	1809	1861-65	1865
Andrew Johnson (R)	N.C.	1808	1865-69	1875
Ulysses Simpson Grant (R)	Ohio	1822	1869-77	1885
Rutherford Birchard Hayes (R)	Ohio	1822	1877-81	1893
James Abram Garfield (R)	Ohio	1831	1881	1881
Chester Alan Arthur (R)	Vt.	1830	1881-85	1886
Grover Cleveland (D)	N.J.	1837	1885-89	1908
Benjamin Harrison (R)	Ohio	1833	1889-93	1901
Grover Cleveland (D)	N.J.	1837	1893-97	1908
William McKinley (R)	Ohio	1843	1897-1901	1901
Theodore Roosevelt (R)	N.Y.	1858	1901-1909	1919
William Howard Taft (R)	Ohio	1857	1909-13	1930
Woodrow Wilson (D)	Va.	1856	1913-21	1924
Warren Gamaliel Harding (R)	Ohio	1865	1921-23	1923
Calvin Coolidge (R)	Vt.	1872	1923-29	1933
Herbert Clark Hoover (R)	Iowa	1874	1923-33	1964
Franklin Delano Roosevelt (D)	N.Y.	1882	1933-45	1945
Harry S. Truman (D)	Mo.	1884	1945-53	1972
Dwight David Eisenhower (R)	Tex.	1890	1953-61	1969
John F. Kennedy (D)	Mass.	1917	1961-63	1963
Lyndon B. Johnson (D)	Tex.	1908	1963-69	1973
Richard M. Nixon (R)	Calif.	1913	1969-74 (r)	
Gerald R. Ford (R)	Nebr.	1913	1974-77	
James Earl Carter, Jr. (D)	Ga.	1924	1977-81	
Ronald W. Reagan (R)	Ill.	1911	1981-89	
George Bush (R)	Mass.	1924	1989-	

VICE-PRESIDENTS OF THE UNITED STATES

Name (and party)	State of Birth	Born	Term	Died
John Adams (F)	Mass.	1735	1789-97	1826
Thomas Jefferson (D-R)	Va.	1743	1797-1801	1826
Thomas Jefferson (D-R)	Va.	1743	1801-09	1826
Aaron Burr (R)	N.J.	1756	1801-05	1836
George Clinton (R)	N.Y.	1739	1805-12	1812
Elbridge Gerry (R)	Mass.	1744	1813-14	1814
Daniel D. Tompkins (R)	N.Y.	1774	1817-25	1825
John U. Calhoun (R)	S.C.	1782	1825-32	1850
Martin Van Buren (D)	N.Y.	1782	1833-37	1862
Richard M. Johnson (D)	Ky.	1780	1837-41	1850
John Tyler (W)	Va.	1790	1841	1862
George M. Dallas (D)	Pa.	1792	1845-49	1864
Millard Fillmore (W)	N.Y.	1800	1849-50	1874
William R. King (D)	N.C.	1786	1853	1853
John C. Breckinridge (D)	Ky.	1821	1857-61	1875
Hannibal Hamlin (R)	Me.	1809	1861-65	1891
Andrew Johnson (R)	N.C.	1808	1865	1875
Schuyler Colfax (R)	N.Y.	1823	1869-73	1885
Henry Wilson (R)	N.H.	1812	1873-75	1875
William A. Wheeler (R)	N.Y.	1819	1877-81	1887
Chester A. Arthur (R)	Vt.	1830	1881	1886
Thomas A. Hendricks (D)	Ohio	1819	1885	1885
Levi P. Morton (R)	Vt.	1824	1889-93	1920
Adlai E. Stevenson (D)	Ky.	1835	1893-97	1914
Garrett A. Hobart (R)	N.J.	1844	1897-99	1899
Theodore Roosevelt (R)	N.Y.	1858	1901	1919
Charles W. Fairbanks (R)	Ohio	1852	1905-09	1918
James S. Sherman (R)	N.Y.	1855	1909-12	1912
Thomas R. Marshall (D)	Ind.	1854	1913-21	1925
Calvin Coolidge (R)	Vt.	1872	1921-23	1933
Charles G. Dawes (R)	Ohio	1865	1925-29	1951
Charles Curtis (R)	Kan.	1860	1929-33	1936
John N. Garner (D)	Tex.	1869	1933-41	1967
Henry A. Wallace (D)	Ia.	1888	1941-45	1965
Harry S. Truman (D)	Mo.	1884	1945	1972
Alben W. Barkley (D)	Ky.	1877	1949-53	1956
Richard M. Nixon (R)	Calif.	1913	1953-61	
Lyndon B. Johnson (D)	Tex.	1908	1961-63	1973
Hubert H. Humphrey (D)	S.D.	1911	1965-69	1978
Spiro T. Agnew (R)	Md.	1918	1969-73 (r)	
Gerald R. Ford (R)	Nebr.	1913	1973-1974	
Nelson A. Rockefeller (R)	Me.	1908	1974-77	1979
Walter F. Mondale (D)	Minn.	1928	1977-81	
George Bush (R)	Mass.	1924	1981-89	
Dan Quayle (R)	Ind.	1947	1989-	

F–Federalist; D–Democratic; R–Republican; W–Whig; (r)–resigned

CHIEF JUSTICES OF THE UNITED STATES SUPREME COURT

Name (and party)	State of Birth	Born	Term	Died
John Jay	N.Y.	1745	1789-95	1829
John Rutledge	S.C.	1739	1795-	1800
Oliver Ellsworth	Conn.	1745	1796-99	1807
John Marshall	Va.	1755	1801-35	1835
Roger B. Taney	Md.	1777	1836-64	1864
Salmon P. Chase	Ohio	1808	1864-73	1873
Morrison R. Waite	Ohio	1816	1874-88	1888
Melville W. Fuller	Ill.	1833	1888-1910	1910
Edward D. White	La.	1845	1910-21	1921
William H. Taft	Ohio	1857	1921-30	1930
Charles E. Hughes	N.Y.	1862	1930-41	1948
Harlan F. Stone	N.Y.	1872	1941-46	1946
Fred M. Vinson	Ky.	1890	1946-53	1953
Earl Warren	Calif.	1891	1953-70	1974
Warren E. Burger	Minn.	1907	1969-86	
William H. Rehnquist	Wisc.	1924	1986-	

DIMENSIONS OF CONTINENTS

Africa .... 11,500,000 Square Miles
Asia .... 17,000,000 Square Miles
Europe .... 3,750,000 Square Miles
North America .... 8,000,000 Square Miles
Oceania .... 4,000,000 Square Miles
Polar Regions .... 6,205,000 Square Miles
South America .... 6,800,000 Square Miles

The latest estimates of the earth's area place the fertile regions at 33,000,000 square miles, steppes at 19,000,000 miles; deserts at 5,000,000 square miles.

Asia, the largest continent, is about 6,000 miles from East to West, and over 5,300 miles from North to South. Africa is 5,000 miles from North to South. Europe is 2,400 miles from North to South, and 3,300 miles from East to West. South America is 4,600 miles from North to South and 3,200 miles from East to West. North America is 4,900 miles from North to South and over 4,000 miles from East to West.

LARGEST CITIES OF THE UNITED STATES

1980 and 1970 Census

Figures immediately following state are area and population

*Indicates capital

	1980	1970
ALABAMA		
51,279 Sq. Mi.-3,742,000		
Bessemer	31,294	33,231
Birmingham	280,413	297,364
Decatur	41,927	37,771
Dothan	46,868	36,080
Florence	36,825	33,535
Gadsden	48,693	52,864
Huntsville	142,238	136,102
Mobile	207,741	187,717
*Montgomery	158,724	129,375
Prichard	40,265	41,267
Tuscaloosa	69,263	61,933
ALASKA		
586,400 Sq. Mi.-403,000		
Anchorage	47,042	46,137
*Juneau	19,249	6,002
ARIZONA		
113,810 Sq. Mi.-2,354,000		
Glendale	78,188	35,771
Mesa	117,840	62,499
*Phoenix	681,355	580,275
Scottsdale	82,297	66,852
Tempe	99,194	63,030
Tucson	331,506	258,303
ARKANSAS		
52,525 Sq. Mi.-2,186,000		
Ft. Smith	68,432	61,549
Hot Springs	40,602	35,319
*Little Rock	151,756	128,880
N. Little Rock	62,823	59,014
Pine Bluff	55,857	55,597
CALIFORNIA		
155,652 Sq. Mi.-22,294,000		
Alameda	63,700	66,031
Alhambra	60,363	61,289
Anaheim	207,007	165,183
Arcadia	46,587	44,853
Bakersfield	86,800	67,955
Baldwin Park	50,538	47,634
Bellflower	50,510	52,166
Berkeley	103,134	113,165
Beverly Hills	25,867	32,952
Buena Park	63,391	63,656
Burbank	83,781	88,659
Carson	79,934	72,144
Chula Vista	81,192	64,474
Compton	74,193	75,312
Concord	98,974	84,785
Costa Mesa	79,191	72,412
Culver City	38,338	35,340
Daly City	73,838	62,636
Downey	85,158	87,765
El Cajon	69,741	58,063
El Monte	66,597	70,795
Escondido	59,273	36,013
Fairfield	54,605	42,561
Fremont	122,028	100,379
Fresno	199,273	162,326
Fullerton	100,844	84,974
Gardena	46,919	41,191
Garden Grove	122,749	121,504
Glendale	137,279	131,723
Hawthorne	56,101	53,161
Hayward	95,802	92,241
Hunt'ton B'h	167,897	115,557
Huntington Pk	38,546	32,885
Inglewood	94,148	88,781
La Habra	44,075	41,349
Lakewood	79,520	82,183
La Mesa	50,006	38,824
Livermore	49,688	35,520
Long Beach	339,629	346,975
L. Angeles	2,787,176	2,781,829
Lynwood	39,819	43,060
Manh'tan B'h	31,544	34,978
Modesto	97,538	60,348
Montebello	49,271	42,820
Monterey Pk.	51,125	48,680
Mt'n View	55,727	54,222
Napa	49,398	34,717
National City	46,936	38,858
Newport B'ch	67,113	48,805
Norwalk	83,262	91,217
Oakland	338,721	358,486
Oceanside	68,626	40,686
Ontario	72,534	64,160
Orange	86,359	76,296
Oxnard	115,692	70,128
Pacifica	37,242	36,756
Palo Alto	54,293	55,413
Paramount	31,026	34,329
Pasadena	106,208	111,826
Pico Rivera	50,549	53,980
Pomona	92,636	88,486
Redlands	36,566	36,558
Redondo B'ch	59,935	56,866

(California, continued)

	1980	1970
Redwood City	54,858	54,170
Richmond	74,217	78,016
Riverside	157,087	139,217
Rosemead	40,165	38,736
*Sacramento	274,488	257,860
Salinas	78,999	58,365
S Bernardino	103,982	106,676
San Bruno	37,894	35,889
San B'n'tura	83,012	57,089
San Diego	816,659	675,790
San Francisco	649,315	704,217
San Jose	592,773	436,965
San Leandro	67,829	68,385
San Mateo	79,150	78,606
San Rafael	45,153	38,493
Santa Ana	185,155	154,640
Santa Barbara	74,810	69,631
Santa Clara	84,217	85,504
Santa Monica	88,122	87,272
Santa Rosa	74,419	48,464
Seaside	33,067	35,659
Simi Valley	77,185	60,643
South Gate	60,171	56,397
S.Sh Fr'ncisco	49,142	46,669
Stockton	125,526	102,663
Sunnyvale	106,162	96,425
Thous. Oaks	82,109	34,425
Torrance	129,511	135,818
Vallejo	71,692	67,905
Walnut Creek	10,299	36,606
West Covina	79,256	67,783
Westminster	70,238	59,619
Whittier	69,039	67,009

COLORADO
103,658 Sq. Mi.-2,670,000

	1980	1970
Arvada	83,901	47,374
Aurora	141,548	74,425
Boulder	76,289	65,977
Col. Springs	206,939	124,856
*Denver	474,595	512,691
Englewood	42,529	33,850
Fort Collins	66,725	43,098
Greeley	50,472	39,167
Lakewood	126,469	93,403
Pueblo	101,504	96,746

CONNECTICUT
4,820 Sq. Mi.-3,096,951

	1980	1970
Bridgeport	142,459	155,359
Bristol	57,177	54,782
Danbury	59,303	50,469
E. Hartford	52,554	57,086
Enfield	42,709	46,682
Fairfield	54,699	55,484
Greenwich	58,667	59,404
Groton	40,995	33,805
Hamden	51,015	49,169
*Hartford	136,319	155,868
Manchester	49,802	47,940
Meriden	56,506	55,073
Middletown	39,030	36,653
Milford	49,103	50,434
New Britain	73,674	82,685
New Haven	125,787	133,543
Norwalk	76,730	78,577
Norwich	38,052	41,274
Stamford	101,636	107,907
Stratford	50,533	49,544
Wallingford	36,704	35,801
Waterbury	102,230	106,431
W. Hartford	61,342	67,379
West Haven	53,128	51,216

DELAWARE
1,965 Sq. Mi.-594,711

	1980	1970
*Dover	23,460	17,165
Wilmington	70,363	79,978

DISTRICT OF COLUMBIA
62 Sq. Mi.-635,185

	1980	1970
Washington	635,185	746,169

FLORIDA
54,861 Sq. Mi.-8,594,000

	1980	1970
Clearwater	77,598	50,787
Coral Gables	42,550	42,069
Daytona B'ch	48,880	44,206
Ft.Lauderdale	149,408	139,122
Gainesville	71,590	63,818
Hialeah	125,365	101,829
Hollywood	114,943	104,018
Jacksonville	592,787	513,439
Lakeland	50,368	41,146
Melbourne	42,307	39,885
Miami	347,862	331,553
Miami B'ch	88,466	85,209
N. Miami	42,407	34,899
Orlando	120,181	97,565
Pensacola	66,539	65,442
Pompano B'ch	52,629	38,137
St. Petersb'g	230,965	213,189
Sarasota	50,814	38,740
*Tallahassee	86,121	71,763
Tampa	264,325	274,359
W. Palm B'ch	59,125	56,865

GEORGIA
58,725 Sq. Mi.-5,084,000

	1980	1970
Albany	17,011	68,181
Athens	49,185	43,286
*Atlanta	405,437	487,553
Augusta	50,526	58,483
Columbus	163,837	152,123
East Point	34,855	39,399
Macon	121,122	118,764
Savannah	135,896	114,155

HAWAII
6,423 Sq. Mi.-897,000

	1980	1970
*Honolulu	722,689	319,784
Kailua	35,529	33,529

IDAHO
83,354 Sq. Mi.-878,000

	1980	1970
*Boise City	114,033	73,330
Idaho Falls	39,198	35,318
Pocatello	46,341	38,826

ILLINOIS
56,043 Sq. Mi.-11,243,000

	1980	1970
Alton	33,862	39,200
Arlington Hts.	71,277	62,578
Aurora	80,671	73,614
Belleville	45,081	41,123
Berwyn	46,561	52,274
Bloomington	41,632	39,393
Calumet City	38,938	36,553
Champaign	57,982	55,976
Chicago	3,049,479	3,322,855
Chicago Hts.	38,530	39,931
Cicero	58,873	66,695
Danville	40,763	42,090
Decatur	89,585	89,468
De Kalb	32,830	34,822
Des Plaines	56,317	59,288
E. St. Louis	51,399	68,026
Elgin	63,132	55,016
Elmhurst	44,249	46,325
Evanston	70,326	80,010
Galesburg	32,776	36,025
Granite City	38,699	36,086
Harvey	32,156	33,864
Joliet	72,372	78,623
Lombard	36,242	36,520
Moline	43,323	45,995
Mt. Prospect	52,955	35,286
N. Chicago	41,436	44,769
Oak Lawn	61,206	61,637
Oak Park	55,151	61,745
Park Ridge	40,387	41,243
Peoria	122,981	125,736
Quincy	41,226	44,904
Rockford	139,999	144,707
Rock Island	45,992	48,609
Skokie	60,406	68,404
*Springfield	86,159	89,816
Waukegan	63,948	64,665

INDIANA
36,045 Sq. Mi.-5,374,000

	1980	1970
Anderson	68,556	69,923
Bloomington	50,344	43,188
E. Chicago	39,656	46,470
Elkhart	48,267	42,455
Evansville	134,388	137,997
Fort Wayne	181,066	175,083
Gary	156,056	174,132
Hammond	93,440	107,108
*Indianapolis	704,045	742,613
Kokomo	52,153	43,359
Lafayette	49,561	44,668
Marion	39,710	40,043
Michigan Cty.	41,467	38,950
Mishawaka	39,517	3o,012
Muncie	81,076	68,066
New Albany	37,863	37,968
Richmond	43,440	43,800
South Bend	113,147	122,797
Terre Haute	63,817	69,247

IOWA
55,586 Sq. Mi.-2,896,000

	1980	1970
Ames	45,820	39,171
Cedar Rapids	107,071	109,111
Clinton	33,342	34,402
Council Bluffs	58,429	59,923
Davenport	101,478	97,614
*Des Moines	190,910	198,427
Dubuque	62,794	61,351
Iowa City	48,587	46,444
Sioux City	84,394	83,626
Waterloo	79,613	75,994

KANSAS
81,774 Sq. Mi.-2,348,000

	1980	1970
Hutchinson	41,831	36,294
Kansas City	164,250	166,682
Lawrence	50,780	45,143
Overland Pk.	82,917	77,332
Salina	38,798	37,095
*Topeka	122,100	123,043
Wichita	267,748	274,448

KENTUCKY
40,181 Sq. Mi.-3,489,000

	1980	1970
Bowling Gr'n	38,709	33,757
Covington	45,756	52,016
*Frankfort	24,831	20,054
Lexington	190,686	107,944
Louisville	317,503	356,982
Owensboro	50,612	49,751

LOUISIANA
45,409 Sq. Mi.-3,966,000

	1980	1970
Alexandria	49,816	41,557
*Baton Rouge	311,053	161,783
Bossier City	48,182	43,066
Lafayette	81,127	65,999
Lake Charles	79,276	76,522
Monroe	64,036	54,647
New Orleans	556,913	585,787
Shreveport	201,920	178,061

MAINE
29,895 Sq. Mi.-1,123,562

	1980	1970
*Augusta	21,712	22,104
Lewiston	40,534	41,817
Portland	61,530	64,304

MARYLAND
9,941 Sq. Mi.-4,143,000

	1980	1970
*Annapolis	31,426	28,042
Baltimore	791,857	895,222
Bowie	37,072	34,883
Hagerstown	36,957	35,154
Rockville	43,622	41,164

MASSACHUSETTS
8,039 Sq. Mi.-5,725,983

	1980	1970
Arlington	48,263	52,720
Beverly	37,038	38,073
*Boston	562,118	628,215
Braintree	36,243	35,373
Brockton	94,990	87,444
Brookline	54,675	58,090
Cambridge	95,351	98,942
Chicopee	55,048	66,416
Everett	37,121	42,216
Fall River	92,240	95,679
Fitchburg	39,332	42,906
Framingham	64,616	63,233
Haverhill	46,815	45,643
Holyoke	44,819	49,434
Lawrence	62,770	66,216
Lowell	92,160	92,929
Lynn	78,299	87,817
Malden	53,431	55,851
Medford	65,397	63,481
Melrose	29,926	32,881
Methuen	36,616	34,986
New Bedford	98,397	101,262
Newton	83,586	91,194
Peabody	45,664	47,650
Pittsfield	51,942	56,673
Quincy	83,907	88,171
Revere	42,256	42,634
Salem	38,302	39,971
Somerville	77,393	87,047
Springfield	152,212	162,078
Taunton	44,675	43,766
Waltham	58,298	61,108
Watertown	34,399	38,853
Weymouth	56,171	55,325
Woburn	36,533	37,307
Worcester	161,384	175,140

MICHIGAN
57,480 Sq. Mi.-9,189,000

	1980	1970
Allen Park	34,166	40,859
Ann Arbor	105,213	98,414
Battle Creek	41,328	37,914
Bay City	41,588	49,075
Birmingham	21,654	34,069
Dearborn	90,589	103,870
DearbornHts.	67,680	80,040
Detroit	1,257,879	1,492,914
East Detroit	38,309	45,814
East Lansing	50,164	47,393
Flint	159,576	193,571
Garden City	35,667	41,647
Grand Rapids	181,602	195,892
Highland Pk.	28,882	35,126
Inkster	35,245	38,264
Jackson	43,057	45,733
Kalamazoo	78,279	84,444
*Lansing	125,229	129,021
Lincoln Park	45,508	52,988
Livonia	104,660	109,746
Madison Hts.	35,211	38,560
Midland	37,290	34,691
Muskegon	40,518	44,377
Oak Park	31,561	36,700
Pontiac	76,501	84,951
Portage	36,974	33,155
Port Huron	33,901	35,530
Roseville	54,376	60,505
Royal Oak	70,795	84,081
Saginaw	77,529	90,603
St. Clair Shrs.	76,227	87,378
Southfield	75,492	68,844
Southgate	32,000	33,725
Sterling Hts.	108,998	58,843
Taylor	77,454	69,673
Troy	67,003	39,143
Warren	161,173	179,217
Westland	43,278	86,291
Wyandotte	33,961	40,832
Wyoming	59,589	56,196

MINNESOTA
80,858 Sq. Mi.-4,008,000

	1980	1970
Bloomington	78,624	81,761
Brooklyn Ctr.	30,969	34,717
Duluth	92,789	99,761
Edina	48,791	44,039
Minneapolis	353,992	431,977
Minnetonka	45,390	35,480
Richfield	40,465	47,215
Rochester	56,732	51,568
Roseville	39,331	34,472
St. Cloud	41,309	39,286
St. Louis Pk.	44,778	48,812
*St. Paul	263,147	308,686

MISSISSIPPI
46,362 Sq. Mi.-2,404,000

	1980	1970
Biloxi	43,927	47,814

	1980	1970
Greenville	40,444	38,834
Gulfport	44,666	39,415
Hattiesburg	41,397	37,461
*Jackson	190,791	150,332
Meridian	44,027	44,405

MISSOURI
68,727 Sq. Mi.–4,860,000

	1980	1970
Columbia	65,781	54,126
Florissant	70,387	67,102
Independence	112,544	110,790
*Jefferson Cty.	37,749	31,921
Joplin	41,061	38,424
Kansas City	456,907	495,405
Raytown	32,513	32,965
St. Joseph	72,748	71,996
St. Louis	508,496	607,718
Springfield	138,833	118,950
Univer'y Cty.	44,159	45,902

MONTANA
146,131 Sq. Mi.–783,674

	1980	1970
Billings	68,317	60,549
Great Falls	56,568	58,761
*Helena	23,818	22,557

NEBRASKA
76,808 Sq. Mi.–1,565,000

	1980	1970
*Lincoln	166,311	149,092
Omaha	368,347	327,789

NEVADA
109,821 Sq. Mi.–663,000

	1980	1970
*Carson Cty.	29,694	15,264
Las Vegas	164,275	124,161
N. Las Vegas	42,618	35,315
Reno	91,986	72,121

NEW HAMPSHIRE
9,031 Sq. Mi.–918,959

	1980	1970
*Concord	30,360	29,573
Manchester	90,757	87,342
Nashua	67,871	55,378

NEW JERSEY
7,514 Sq. Mi.–7,327,000

	1980	1970
Atlantic City	41,978	45,386
Bayonne	64,982	69,898
Belleville	36,428	39,226
Bloomfield	49,318	52,154
Camden	84,763	100,966
Clifton	74,427	81,865
East Orange	70,499	74,846
Elizabeth	105,384	111,414
Fair Lawn	34,951	36,765
Hackensack	37,207	35,234
Hoboken	42,378	45,559
Irvington	54,989	59,958
Jersey City	222,764	253,467
Kearney	35,716	37,262
Linden	37,761	41,059
Montclair	39,736	43,856
Newark	314,412	378,222
New Bruns'ck	41,713	41,909
Passaic	48,193	53,751
Paterson	145,426	142,819
Perth Amboy	35,244	38,564
Plainfield	45,368	46,344
*Trenton	94,772	102,211
Union City	55,360	56,662
Vineland	52,701	46,781
Westfield	30,324	33,606
West N.Y.	39,101	40,061
West Orange	41,053	43,222

NEW MEXICO
122,503 Sq. Mi.–1,212,000

	1980	1970
Albuquerque	295,150	242,411
Las Cruces	44,902	37,705
Roswell	39,698	32,794
*Santa Fe	46,162	39,107

NEW YORK
47,654 Sq. Mi.–17,748,000

	1980	1970
*Albany	115,781	113,857
Auburn	32,020	34,319
Binghamton	55,745	63,229
Buffalo	357,002	457,808
Elmira	35,363	39,873
Freeport	39,818	40,438
Hempstead	40,245	41,562
Jamestown	35,634	39,222
Mt. Vernon	76,534	72,302
New Rochelle	70,861	74,697
N.Y. City	7,134,542	7,798,757
Niagara Falls	71,344	84,752
N.Tonawanda	35,717	35,813
Rochester	241,539	293,695
Rome	46,314	47,926
Schenectady	71,676	77,134
Syracuse	174,899	192,529
Troy	58,209	62,007
Utica	78,718	90,802
Valley Stream	38,924	40,332
White Plains	47,196	49,573
Yonkers	190,240	204,789

NORTH CAROLINA
48,470 Sq. Mi.–5,577,000

	1980	1970
Asheville	58,551	55,444
Burlington	36,853	35,338
Charlotte	299,444	239,056
Durham	105,060	93,935
Fayetteville	59,476	51,696
Gastonia	48,844	46,742
Greensboro	163,493	140,672
High Point	68,339	60,519
*Raleigh	138,410	117,676
Rocky Mount	40,627	33,297
Wilmington	41,848	45,667
Winston-Salem	140,438	126,106

NORTH DAKOTA
70,183 Sq. Mi.–652,000

	1980	1970
*Bismarck	44,447	33,572
Fargo	61,281	52,697
Grand Forks	43,760	38,626

OHIO
40,740 Sq. Mi.–10,749,000

	1980	1970
Akron	239,229	273,266
Barberton	26,819	33,003
Canton	96,339	108,872
Cincinnati	399,072	448,492
Cleveland	594,529	738,956
Clwe. Hgts.	55,563	60,437
*Columbus	524,304	533,418
Cuyahoga Falls	44,293	49,463
Dayton	190,564	239,591
E. Cleveland	36,915	39,237
Elyria	57,039	53,359
Euclid	59,641	71,769
Findlay	37,570	35,591
Garfield Hts.	34,956	41,197
Hamilton	67,535	64,058
Kettering	61,223	72,928
Lakewood	61,921	69,778
Lima	50,602	53,373
Lorain	73,743	76,733
Mansfield	54,704	54,154
Maple Hts.	29,731	34,071
Marion	38,725	37,630
Mentor	41,903	36,680
Middletown	47,958	46,612
Newark	39,947	41,258
N. Olmsted	36,480	34,639
Parma	92,578	99,691
Shaker Hts.	31,225	36,143
Springfield	73,376	82,188
Toledo	351,686	379,104
Up. Arlington	37,101	38,367
Warren	55,456	64,269
Youngstown	115,429	139,903

OKLAHOMA
69,414 Sq. Mi.–2,880,000

	1980	1970
Enid	50,166	43,557
Lawton	85,073	69,069
Midwest Cty.	50,430	47,512
Muskogee	41,325	36,015
Norman	63,382	50,500
*Okla. City	372,690	363,225
Tulsa	328,684	328,219

OREGON
95,607 Sq. Mi.–2,444,000

	1980	1970
Corvallis	38,823	34,798
Eugene	102,591	77,284
Portland	364,735	375,161
*Salem	89,770	68,309

PENNSYLVANIA
44,832 Sq. Mi.–11,750,000

	1980	1970
Allentown	102,077	108,926
Altoona	68,043	62,385
Bethel Park	38,362	33,806
Bethlehem	72,550	72,320
Chester	44,113	56,197
Erie	122,152	125,941
*Harrisburg	55,027	65,828
Johnstown	35,417	42,065
Lancaster	56,996	57,693
Mc Keesport	31,902	37,655
New Castle	35,187	38,457
Norristown	34,626	38,310
Phila.	1,680,235	1,927,863
Pittsburgh	423,962	512,789
Reading	76,742	86,470
Scranton	89,890	102,294
State College	38,369	33,167
Wilkes-Barre	53,832	57,946
Williamsport	33,904	37,694
York	45,622	50,008

RHODE ISLAND
1,067 Sq. Mi.–945,761

	1980	1970
Cranston	72,034	73,633
E. Providence	50,906	47,615
Newport	29,266	33,866
Pawtucket	71,033	76,213
*Providence	156,421	176,920
Warwick	87,064	82,985
Woonsocket	45,876	46,465

SOUTH CAROLINA
30,495 Sq. Mi.–2,918,000

	1980	1970
Charleston	59,280	64,591
*Columbia	108,216	111,706
Greenville	55,407	61,242
Rock Hill	37,684	33,619
Spartanburg	46,279	43,536

SOUTH DAKOTA
76,868 Sq. Mi.–687,643

	1980	1970
*Pierre	11,966	9,732
Rapid City	46,340	43,815
Sioux Falls	80,747	72,557

TENNESSEE
41,687 Sq. Mi.–4,357,000

	1980	1970
Chattanooga	162,778	113,003
Jackson	47,532	39,262
Johnson City	39,763	32,959
Knoxville	185,236	169,766
Memphis	663,769	620,873
*Nashville	425,424	444,489

TEXAS
262,398 Sq. Mi.–13,014,000

	1980	1970
Abilene	96,573	88,433
Amarillo	143,665	123,973
Arlington	132,932	88,385
*Austin	319,194	246,904
Baytown	53,024	39,175
Beaumont	117,764	115,716
Brownsville	71,554	51,080
Corp. Christi	214,647	201,581
Dallas	847,420	836,121
Denton	43,571	38,864
El Paso	424,522	317,462
Fort Worth.	367,432	388,123
Galveston	59,402	60,714
Garland	131,263	80,659
Grand Prairie	62,885	52,404
Harlingen	41,897	34,005
Houston	1,572,981	1,213,064
Irving	105,101	97,457
Killeen	52,236	34,953
Laredo	81,383	63,491
Longview	56,231	44,357
Lubbock	168,127	146,379
Mc Allen	53,604	36,761
Mesquite	63,060	55,136
Midland	67,251	58,199
Odessa	90,366	76,109
Pasadena	104,385	89,291
Port Arthur	61,439	56,552
Richardson	67,518	47,596
San Angelo	68,626	63,928
San Antonio	798,195	650,188
Texas City	42,748	38,393
Tyler	66,741	56,301
Victoria	49,394	39,349
Waco	103,768	92,600
Wichita Falls	94,875	94,976

UTAH
82,184 Sq. Mi.–1,454,630

	1980	1970
Ogden	64,444	68,480
Provo	74,007	53,491
*SaltLakeCty	164,960	176,793

VERMONT
9,124 Sq. Mi.–511,297

	1980	1970
Burlington	37,135	38,266
*Montpelier	8,059	9,102

VIRGINIA
40,262 Sq. Mi.–5,148,000

	1980	1970
Alexandria	104,085	109,841
Charlot'sville	39,245	38,047
Chesapeake	113,965	89,918
Danville	45,832	46,029
Hampton	125,116	118,584
Lynchburg	64,466	53,134
Newpt. News	144,023	137,348
Norfolk	280,568	260,331
Petersburg	40,885	35,610
Portsmouth	108,297	109,827
*Richmond	219,429	248,074
Roanoke	98,074	90,955
Virginia B'ch	245,076	166,060

WASHINGTON
66,836 Sq. Mi.–3,774,000

	1980	1970
Bellevue	71,471	57,751
Bellingham	44,205	39,797
Everett	52,690	51,926
*Olympia	29,696	22,413
Seattle	485,487	524,263
Spokane	170,993	168,654
Tacoma	156,625	151,061
Vancouver	48,438	40,083
Yakima	53,820	45,060

WEST VIRGINIA
24,022 Sq. Mi.–1,860,000

	1980	1970
*Charleston	66,811	69,531
Huntington	68,261	72,970
Parkersburg	38,827	43,225
Wheeling	42,237	46,854

WISCONSIN
55,256 Sq. Mi.–4,679,000

	1980	1970
Appleton	61,017	56,673
Beloit	35,602	35,256
Eau Claire	49,336	41,892
Fond du Lac	36,506	35,330
Green Bay	91,347	87,239
Janesville	50,372	44,173
Kenosha	78,949	78,063
La Crosse	49,231	51,448
*Madison	170,382	170,073
Manitowoc	33,208	33,180
Milwaukee	633,220	709,537
Oshkosh	49,828	52,460
Racine	92,718	94,720
Sheboygan	48,815	47,957
Waukesha	50,252	39,645
Wauwatosa	51,173	58,668
West Allis	63,678	71,511

WYOMING
97,548 Sq. Mi.–468,909

	1980	1970
Casper	50,704	39,145
*Cheyenne	47,207	40,020